About This Book

How the Text is Organized

The study of Canadian federal income taxation is made more complex, particularly at the introductory level, not because of the lack of good interpretive materials to guide the student, but, in the authors' opinion, because of the lack of organization in the presentation of these materials for systematic study. While the *Income Tax Act* (the Act), the statute governing the federal taxation of income in Canada, is organized generally by source of income, interpretive material available to students at the introductory level is often organized by topics which may cover elements of several sources.

Since the authors of these materials feel that it is important to the understanding of the Act that the student generally studies the major provisions of the statute in sequence, the chapters of this book generally follow the organization of the Act. The purpose of these materials is to guide the student in the study at the introductory level of the major provisions of the Act and some of the related provisions in the *Excise Tax Act* (the ETA) pertaining to the Goods and Services Tax/Harmonized Sales Tax. A copy of the Act plus the Canada Revenue Agency's (CRA's) Interpretation Bulletins, Information Circulars, and Advance Tax Rulings are considered to be important materials for the course. The purpose is to organize the student's reference to interpretive material in the order of presentation in the Act. This book is designed to encourage students to refer to the Act, case law, and the CRA's publications. CRA publications are available at no charge on the CRA website: www.cra-arc.gc.ca.

The Importance of Problem Material

The commentary presented in this book highlights key areas of the Act. The textbook provides additional interpretation of particularly difficult provisions of the Act or elements of the common law or case law in the area. The basic concepts and principles underlying the rules of the legislation are emphasized throughout these materials. Most important for the study of income taxation, the textbook provides fact situations or example problems which demonstrate the application of the provisions of the Act to realistic situations. In fact, the primary teaching approach used in this commentary is the presentation of example problems and exercises with solutions. These solutions demonstrate various methods of approaching actual problems in income taxation. The solutions also provide explanatory and interpretive notes, which are an important component of these materials, often expanding a topic beyond the confines of the particular facts under discussion.

These materials are designed to present situations which will help students to focus their attention on the reading and understanding of a particular provision or set of provisions with the objective of developing more generalized skills to be used in the interpretation of the Act.

References

References are provided in the outer margin of the text beside the paragraphs to which they pertain. These references are to the following sources:

(1) ITA refers to the sections of the *Income Tax Act* to be discussed in the chapter;

(2) ITAR refers to the *Income Tax Application Rules, 1971*, which are found in the volume containing the Act immediately following the provisions of the Act;

(3) ITR refers to the Income Tax Regulations, which are also found in the volume containing the Act;

(4) ETA refers to sections of the *Excise Tax Act* in which provisions of the Goods and Services Tax (GST)/Harmonized Sales Tax (HST) can be found;

(5) IT, IC, TR, and ATR refer, respectively, to Interpretation Bulletins, Information Circulars, Tax Rulings, and Advance Tax Rulings — Second Series, and are available in a one-volume softcover edition published by CCH Canadian Limited;

(6) ITTN refers to Income Tax Technical News releases that are published by the CRA intermittently to provide current technical interpretation;

(7) *Folios* refers to *Income Tax Folios* which are being published by the CRA in chapters by topic to update and replace ITs and ITTNs.

(8) Cda-U.S. TT refers to the *Canada–United States Income Tax Convention (1980)*; and

(9) Doc refers to documents released by the federal government under *Access to Information* legislation and contained in the Tax Window Files of CCH Canadian's Tax Library.

An explanation of these references is provided in Chapter 1. References to sections of the Act are provided for exercises and assignment problems. It should also be understood that in the course of their use within the paragraph of the text, all references preceded by such specific terms as "section", "subsection", "paragraph", "subparagraph", etc., without any indication of the pertinent statute, refer to the provisions of the *Income Tax Act*. Similarly, the provisions of the Income Tax Regulations are preceded by the term "Regulation" without specifying the relevant legislation. In the margin, these references are preceded by "ITA" and "ITR", respectively.

References to the *Excise Tax Act* are usually confined to the GST/HST part of a chapter and are specifically indicated as being to that legislation. References in the margin are preceded by "ETA". An attempt has been made to integrate GST/HST with relevant transactions discussed under the *Income Tax Act* in the chapters where these transactions are discussed.

Acronyms

An alphabetical list of acronyms used in the book appears in the first section of the Study Guide, immediately following the Table of Contents. The list provides the meaning of the acronym and paragraph references where the term is used in this textbook.

Knowledge Reference List

A mapping of the Knowledge Reference List (KRL) to the book is provided in the next section of the Study Guide. Paragraph references and titles in the textbook are shown for each line of the KRL. Students who are interested in reviewing problems and questions on those topics can follow a paragraph listing in the KRL map to the Leaning Charts for each chapter in the Study Guide.

Review Questions

A set of review questions is provided at the end of each chapter. These short-answer questions attempt to review key points made in the text or points that are not integrated into the example problems, multiple choice questions, exercises, or assignment problems in the chapter. Discussion notes on the review questions are provided in the Study Guide.

Multiple Choice Questions

Since multiple choice questions are common in professional examinations, this textbook provides six or seven such questions covering the material in each chapter, starting with Chapter 2. Annotated solutions are provided in the Study Guide to enhance learning through self-study.

Exercises

Exercises have been provided at the end of each chapter. These usually consist of short problems to highlight particular areas of the chapter. They are designed to be fairly narrow in scope, to provide the student with an opportunity to apply the material in the chapter to a specific problem situation. Solutions to these exercises have been provided in the Study Guide.

Assignment Problems

Assignment problems are provided for each chapter of these materials. These problems are designed to have the student apply the material discussed in each chapter to an actual fact or problem situation. While these problems focus on the key elements of the chapter in much the same way that the solved example problems in the commentary do, the problems are not identical in their coverage or presentation. As a result, it will be necessary for the student to read the assignment problems very carefully in preparing a solution. Solutions to these problems are not available. However, similar additional problems with solutions are provided on the accompanying DVD, as discussed below.

Additional Problems with Solutions

Students often request additional problems with solutions that they can use on a self-study basis for preparation for tests and examinations. For this purpose, a comprehensive compilation of problems similar to the assignment problems in this book and multiple choice questions are provided on the DVD accompanying this book. There are many problems and solutions on the DVD, classified by coverage of chapters in this textbook. The problems, most of which have previously been used as examination questions, will provide students with an opportunity to deal with problems of a comprehensive nature. Since these supplemental problems may cover material from several chapters, as examination questions often do, they provide an excellent source for review in preparation for examinations.

Suggested Approach

The authors suggest the following approach to the use of these materials. First, the students should identify the issue they need to research in an assignment problem and then scan the headings of the particular chapter and look for the topics that relate to that issue. Once the relevant parts of the chapter are identified, they should read the commentary, including any referenced material such as sections of the Act or Regulations, Interpretation Bulletins, Folios, Information Circulars, and Advance Tax Rulings. Reviewing any example problems to see how the provisions work will also help develop understanding. The solutions provided for these problems will demonstrate the approach that can be taken for the type of example problem under consideration. The solutions can also be used as a check on the student's understanding as well as a means of providing further interpretation and explanation of the material covered. The exercises at the end of the chapter can be used in a similar manner. The additional problems with the solutions provided on the accompanying DVD can be used as a means of self-study and reinforcement. Once the parts of a chapter have been completed in this manner, the student should be sufficiently prepared to attempt the assignment problems relevant to a particular part or to the whole chapter. When reviewing material for examination or other purposes, the multiple choice questions at the end of each chapter and the problems on the accompanying DVD can be attempted. The solutions in the Study Guide and on the DVD can then be checked. Review might also focus on the approaches used to address the various types of problems presented.

Learning Goals

To be a successful tax adviser it is not enough to just know the technical material found in the Act and supporting materials. You need to understand the purpose behind the rules so you can explain to others why your tax plan does not violate either the provision as it is written or purpose behind the provision. You also need to be able to blend a number of complex provisions into a comprehensive plan to accomplish the goals of your client or employer. As shown in the learning model below, you need to know the technical provisions and understand them well enough to be able to craft a comprehensive plan. The end goal is the successful application of knowledge and understanding.

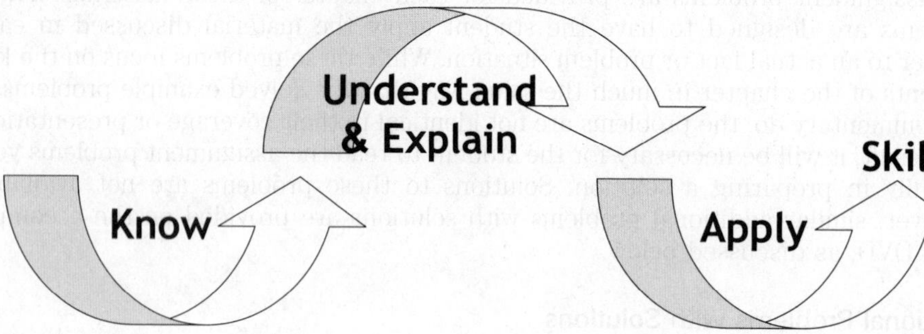

In each chapter of this book we will provide you with what you should Know, Understand & Explain, and Apply as a result of studying that chapter.

Materials at the introductory level on Canadian income tax legislation are not easy to study. A conscientious effort to do the work and, particularly, to do problems and apply what has been read is essential to a good understanding of this material. The authors have attempted to meet the challenge of presenting the material by setting out the work that must be done and by explaining, as best they can, the major provisions of the legislation. The challenge of learning the material is, of course, left to the student.

July 2013

Robert E. Beam

Stanley N. Laiken

James. J. Barnett

Acknowledgements

Many people have participated in the preparation of these materials. In particular, we are greatly indebted and most grateful for the contributions of two individuals. Lisa Feil and Shirley Lamarre, as the principal contributors on the previous CGA Taxation 1 course textbook, have used their knowledge and expertise to ensure that this textbook is a great element of the Taxation 1 course. Their help in reviewing these materials and suggesting improvements has been invaluable.

To create the first and subsequent editions of the book, a very considerable editorial effort was required by CCH editors. Paul Love and Carrie Shimkofsky have done outstanding work under tight deadlines to produce an integrated text of consistent high quality. For this edition, Kristen Charles-Vardon provided assistance to Paul with her editorial work on *Introduction to Federal Income Taxation in Canada*.

July 2013

Robert E. Beam

Stanley N. Laiken

James. J. Barnett

Note on Legislation

This edition of the book has been updated to include draft legislation up to and including that resulting from the March 21, 2013 federal Budget, some of which was included in the April 22, 2013 Notice of Ways and Means Motion and as Bill C-60, which received Royal Assent and became law on June 26, 2013. Also, referenced is Bill C-48, which received Royal Assent and became law on June 26, 2013.

Table of Contents

Chapter 1

Introduction

TOPICS DISCUSSED

LEARNING GOALS

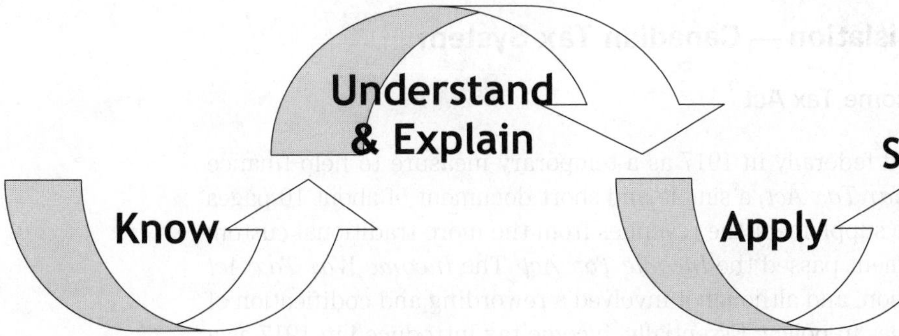

Know

By the end of this chapter you should know some of the history and policy principles of income tax in Canada and how the *Income Tax Act* and the *Excise Tax Act* (pertaining to the goods and services tax) are structured, interpreted, and administered.

Understand and Explain

You should understand and be able to explain how to find what you need in the Act and how to put together the calculation of income for tax purposes, taxable income, and federal income tax for individuals. In addition, you should be able to explain how to interpret tax legislation. Completing the Exercises (¶1,850) is a good way to deepen your understanding of the material.

Apply

You should be able to use your general knowledge and understanding of the calculation of income and the interpretation of tax laws to put together the calculation of income, taxable income, and federal income tax for individuals and to find the meaning of certain words and phrases in the *Income Tax Act*. Completing the Assignment Problems (¶1,875) is an excellent way to develop your ability to apply the material in increasingly complex situations.

OVERVIEW

This chapter covers the basic areas of income taxation in Canada. First, it provides a historical, legal, and theoretical policy perspective. Second, it introduces the *Income Tax Act* (ITA or the Act),[1] the legal statute governing income taxation in Canada, by providing an overview of the structure of this legislation. Third, it provides a general overview of the practice of taxation and the role of the professional accountant. Fourth, the materials introduce the concepts of income and taxable income. The last section presents an overview of the administration and enforcement of the legislation.

This chapter also introduces, on a conceptual basis, the goods and services tax (GST)/harmonized sales tax (HST). Subsequent chapters will discuss the related GST/HST implications of the topics described in those chapters. This chapter first gives an overview of the GST/HST system and, in particular, certain basic concepts such as taxable transactions, exempt transactions, and GST/HST refunds. It then describes the organization of the GST/HST in the context of its legislative authority, the *Excise Tax Act* (ETA),[2] and various interpretive sources.

[1] Unless otherwise stated, all statutory references are to the *Income Tax Act*, R.S.C. 1985, c. 1 (5th Supplement), as amended (referred to as "the Act").

[2] Unless otherwise stated, the *Excise Tax Act*, R.S.C. 1985, c. E-15, will be referred to as the "ETA".

¶1,000 BACKGROUND AND INTRODUCTION

¶1,001 History and Legislation — Canadian Tax System

¶1,010 Brief history of the Income Tax Act

Income tax was first imposed federally in 1917 as a temporary measure to help finance World War I under the *Income War Tax Act*, a simple and short document of about 10 pages in length. It generated revenue to supplement the revenues from the more traditional custom and excise taxes. In 1948, Parliament passed the *Income Tax Act*. The *Income War Tax Act* was merged into this new legislation, and although it involved a rewording and codification of the old law, there were few changes in policy. Essentially, income tax introduced in 1917 as a temporary measure persists today.

A major reform of federal income tax legislation began in 1962 with the setting up of the Royal Commission on Taxation under the chairmanship of the late Kenneth Carter. The Carter Commission presented its seven-volume report in 1967 recommending fundamental changes in tax legislation that would use a comprehensive tax base including capital gains, which were previously tax-free.

This report led to the issuing of the November 1969 White Paper on Tax Reform followed by the Budget address on June 18, 1971 and Bill C-259 to amend the *Income Tax Act*. This bill was given Royal Assent on December 23, 1971, and became effective January 1, 1972. Since then, every Budget address has presented a considerable number of amendments to the tax legislation to both "fine-tune" the existing legislation and introduce new fiscal policy.

Sixteen years later, on June 18, 1987, the government released a White Paper on Tax Reform which was to be implemented in two phases. Phase One, implemented in 1988, included changes to the personal and corporate income tax systems and interim changes to the existing federal sales tax. Phase Two replaced the existing federal sales tax with a broad-based multi-stage sales tax referred to as the goods and services tax (GST), effective January 1, 1991. In provinces which have agreed to harmonize their provincial sales tax (PST) with the GST, this tax has become the harmonized sales tax (HST).

The fact that income tax, introduced in 1917 as a temporary measure, is still in existence, albeit in a substantially modified form, is easily explained. In order to finance public expenditures and implement its economic and social policy, the government has had to collect revenues in various forms. Taxing the income of individuals and corporations has provided it with a reliable and increasing source of revenue.

Currently, based on 2013-2014 projections, income taxes comprise about 63% of total federal government revenues, with personal income taxes raising almost four times the amount of revenue as corporate income taxes. Sales and excise taxes, including the GST, represent about 17% of total federal government revenues. Exhibit 1-1 gives some indication of the relative importance of various taxes.

EXHIBIT 1-1
Government of Canada Budgetary Revenues
(2013-2014 Projection)

Revenue item	*Billions of dollars**	*Percentage*
Personal income tax	131.5	49.9
Corporate income taxes	34.6	13.1
Employment insurance contributions	21.9	8.3
Goods and services tax	29.9	11.3
Customs import duties	4.0	1.5
Other tax revenue	16.3	6.2
Non-tax revenue	25.6	9.7
Total budgetary revenues	263.8	100.0

* Source: Table 4.2.5, "Outlook for Budgetary Revenues", Chapter 4.2 "Fiscal Planning Framework", Budget 2013, Department of Finance Canada, March 21, 2013.

¶1,015 Constitutional basis for income taxation

The *British North America Act, 1867*, renamed the *Constitution Act, 1867* in the process of the repatriation of the Constitution, grants authority for all taxation in Canada, separating federal and provincial powers to impose income taxes. Subsection 91(3) of the *Constitution Act, 1867* provides the federal government with unlimited powers of taxation by permitting the "raising of money by any mode or system of taxation". On the other hand, subsection 92(2) of the same Act limits provincial powers to direct taxation of income earned in the province and of income of persons resident in the province. Even with a fairly liberal interpretation of the provincial powers of direct taxation, in order to meet increasing provincial requirements over the years, there has been a constant trading of tax points through federal–provincial taxation agreements. Nevertheless, intergovernmental problems of raising revenues through taxation persist.

¶1,020 Introduction to Income Tax Legislation

¶1,021 The federal budgetary process

There are special procedures for adopting fiscal legislation and several levels of government are involved in the passage of new or amended tax law. (See Figure 1-1.)

All proposals for change originate in the Department of Finance. A bill to amend the ITA cannot be tabled before a "Notice of Ways and Motion to Amend the *Income Tax Act*" has been presented to the House of Commons. The Minister of Finance will clear major proposals with the Prime Minister and Cabinet before presenting a *Notice of Ways and Means Motion to Amend the Income Tax Act* to the House of Commons. Once permission is granted in the House of Commons, a bill is introduced. Before the bill receives Royal Assent by the Governor General, it is reviewed and discussed in detail by the Standing Committee on Finance and Economic Affairs and a total of three readings take place in the House of Commons and the Senate. A discussion of this process follows.

Figure 1-1

Budgetary Process

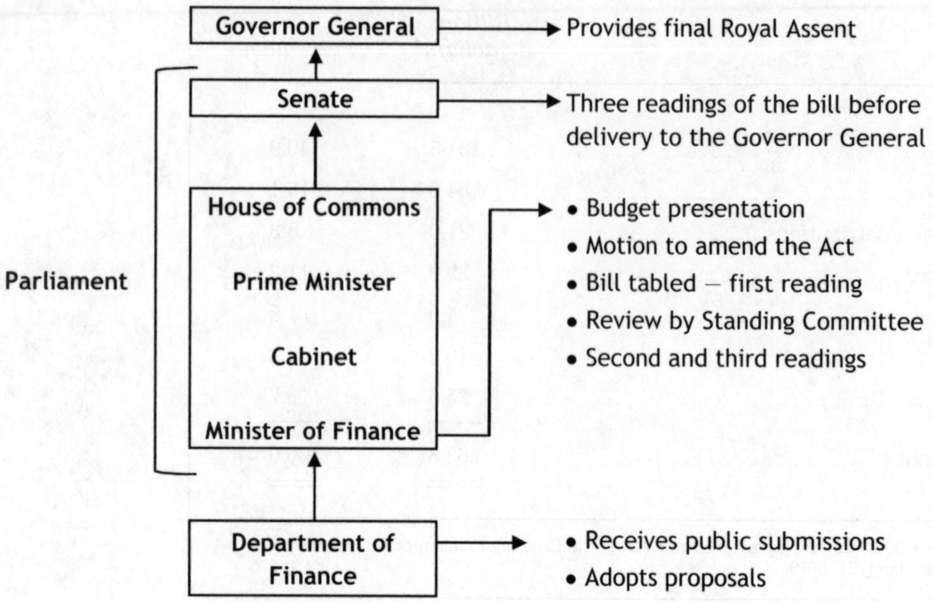

¶1,022 Public submissions for change or amendment

On an ongoing basis, and before initiating detailed work on the Budget, the Minister of Finance accepts and reviews "submissions for change" to the income tax system. The Minister also encourages submissions from politicians, economists, tax advisers, academics, and other interested parties, including taxpayers.

¶1,023 Adoption of specific proposals

The Minister considers and adopts specific proposals for the Budget. Secrecy is critical during this stage to prevent arbitrage in the marketplace. There is absolutely no public involvement at this point — no formal way to publicly debate the proposals considered. Tax professionals and economists criticize this approach because the Minister does not call upon them for professional advice or comments. To ensure that taxpayers do not have an unfair advantage in planning their transactions, the proposed legislation has an "effective date", generally the Budget date, not the date on which the bill is adopted. The department also introduces many proposed tax law changes in the form of Department of Finance News Releases. These are often released without prior announcement and generally take effect immediately upon release of the proposal. For example, changes to the tax benefits of charitable donations made under tax shelter arrangements were announced, and were effective that day. While often the intent of these releases is to counter tax avoidance schemes, they can, and often do, address relatively minor tax changes.

¶1,024 Federal Budget presentation to the House of Commons

The Minister of Finance presents the Budget, in substance, in the House and tables a "Notice of Ways and Means Motion to Amend the *Income Tax Act*". This Notice is then available to the public in readable format and includes a summary of the draft income tax changes to rules and regulations based on the first reading of the Budget. ITA: 222(1)

At this point, taxpayers may determine the effect of the proposed changes and may make submissions to the Department of Finance. However, the Act provides that the Governor in Council (the federal cabinet) may introduce regulations without the consent of Parliament. The Income Tax Regulations supplement the provisions of the Act and are specifically intended to provide direction, definitions, and requirements for specific tax rules. An example includes the regulations relating to the computation of capital cost allowance, which is the amortization or depreciation permitted for computing net income for tax purposes. Changes to the Income Tax Regulations do not result in a change in the *Income Tax Act* itself. ITA: 221(1) ITR: 1100

¶1,025 Passage of law

At a later date, the Minister moves for acceptance of the Notice of Ways and Means Motion and then the House of Commons passes a resolution to accept the bill to amend the *Income Tax Act*. The bill contains detailed measures to repeal, amend, or add to provisions of the Act. A second reading of the bill, clause by clause, and a third reading in the House of Commons, as well as a similar process of three readings in the Senate, take place prior to Royal Assent. The Notice of Ways and Means Motion to Amend the *Income Tax Act* must receive Royal Assent before the proposed changes become statute law. This process will often take several months — sometimes more than a year.

Not all Budget proposals become law immediately. For example, in 1984, the Minister of Finance proposed significant changes to registered retirement plans and other deferred pension plans with most of the legislation delayed until 1990. Delay in tax legislation can create uncertainties for taxpayers, particularly at the time of tax filing. Most proposed changes are retroactive to the date of announcement of the proposed rule.

Parliament passes the statutory laws of Canada, and the CRA enforces and administers the tax laws. The interpretation and the administrative practice of tax law is left to the CRA. Some of the tax rules are becoming more complex because many of the tax provisions are mathematical formulas in legal format. The Act also contains many phrases that reference other sections or subsections of the Act. For many years, the government did not release any interpretations or explanations with the draft legislation. This created significant confusion until 1982, when the Department of Finance began publishing Technical Notes (Explanatory Notes) with draft legislation. While these notes do not represent official or statutory interpretations, they are useful in helping to determine the underlying legislative intent and promoting understanding of the tax rule.

¶1,030 Tax Principles and Concepts

¶1,035 Classification of taxes

¶1,035.10 *Basis of the tax*

Taxes can be classified in a number of different ways. One such method is the basis of the tax, with the name of the tax reflecting to some extent the tax base or what is to be taxed.

Head tax: A tax on the existence of a particular type of taxpayer such as a tax of $X paid by all individuals over the age of 18.

Income tax: A tax on the income of the taxpayer and is exemplified by a tax on the income of individuals or corporations.

Wealth tax: A tax on capital gains or succession duties, or a tax on the accumulated capital of a taxpayer.

Commodity tax: A tax on the consumption of the commodity subject to tax as is the case of a provincial retail sales tax.

User tax: A toll for a bridge or road; a tax on the use of a facility or service.

Tariff: A tax or duty usually imposed on imported goods to increase the price of such goods relative to domestic goods.

Transfer tax: A tax on the value of property transferred from one owner to another, as is the case on the transfer of land under certain conditions.

Business transfer tax: A value-added tax, or a multi-stage sales tax, such as the goods and services tax, is a tax on the increase in value of a commodity created by the taxpayer in moving it from one stage of production or distribution to another.

¶1,035.20 *Incidence of the tax*

Another method of classifying taxes is by the incidence of the tax, which determines the taxpayer who ultimately bears the tax.

The incidence of a direct tax is likely to be on the initial payer of the tax. For example, the burden of the individual income tax is generally considered to be on the individual who pays the tax. On the other hand, the incidence of an indirect tax is usually not on the initial payer of the tax, but is on someone else. A sales tax imposed at the manufacturer's level is an example of such an indirect tax. While an income tax may be paid by a corporation, the incidence of the tax may be on customers, suppliers, employees, or shareholders of the corporation, depending on its economic ability to pass the tax on to the others.

¶1,035.30 *Nature of the tax*

Finally, taxes can be classified by the nature of the tax levy. A proportional or flat tax is levied at a constant percentage of the income of the payer of the tax. Under certain conditions, the corporate income tax can be considered as such a tax. A progressive tax is levied at an increasing percentage of the income of the payer, as is the case of the personal income tax. Similarly, a regressive tax is levied at a decreasing percentage of the income of the payer. A sales tax is considered to be a regressive tax to the extent that those with higher income may spend a lower proportion of that income on the item subject to the sales tax.

¶1,040 Desirable characteristics of an income tax

¶1,040.10 *Horizontal equity*

One of the most important principles of a tax system is that it be fair. An income tax should be equitable on two dimensions. It should be equitable horizontally so that persons at the same economic level are affected by the tax to the same degree in terms of the amount of tax irrespective of the form of income generated. A taxpayer who earns $100,000 in salary should pay the same amount of tax as one who earns $100,000 in investment income.

¶1,040.20 *Vertical equity*

An income tax should also be equitable vertically so that persons at a higher economic level pay a greater share of the tax based on their greater ability to pay than those at a lower economic level. This implies that persons with income levels of $100,000 should proportionally pay more tax than those who earn $25,000 because they have at their disposal more funds in excess of what is required to satisfy their personal needs.

¶1,040.30 *Neutrality*

An income tax should be neutral so that the tax does not affect economic decisions. Thus, for the tax system to be considered neutral, a decision based on the after-tax results of an economic opportunity should not be any different than it would have been in the absence of taxation. However, the Canadian tax system provides many incentives that affect business decisions and is far from neutral.

¶1,040.40 *Flexibility*

At the same time, the income tax system must be sufficiently flexible to permit its use as an instrument of economic policy to achieve specified economic objectives. Of course, what might be considered economically desirable may not be politically feasible. For example, the Carter Commission recommendation to achieve horizontal equity by taxing all sources of economic gain equally, because "a buck is a buck", was apparently rejected for political reasons.

¶1,040.50 *Certainty*

Certainty means that taxpayers know in advance the tax consequences of any transaction so that they may plan their affairs accordingly. The taxpayer must be in a position to understand and determine with some certainty the payer of the tax, the base of the tax, the amount of the tax, the deadline for payment of the tax, and the method of payment. There are many areas of uncertainty in the Canadian tax system, mostly due to the fact that all sources of income are not taxed in the same way. For example, employment income is subject to a less favourable tax treatment than business income; the distinction between an employee and a self-employed person is often difficult to make and creates uncertainty as to the tax treatment that applies in a particular situation. If the tax treatment of employment income and business income were the same, there would be less uncertainty. In order to mitigate the risk of uncertainty, the CRA provides taxpayers with the opportunity to apply for an advance tax ruling on transactions they propose to undertake. However, it is difficult to provide complete certainty when complex transactions are undertaken.

¶1,040.55 *Simplicity and compliance*

The Canadian tax system is based on self-assessment, which means that taxpayers are required to assess their income tax and file the appropriate income tax return on an annual basis. The CRA then assesses the return and has the power to investigate and make changes when inaccuracies or omissions are found. In order to ensure compliance by taxpayers and limit the number of investigations and reassessments, the tax system must be simple. Ideally, individuals with simple tax situations should not be compelled to seek professional advice to prepare their returns.

Naturally, a tax system is expected to have some degree of complexity, particularly with regard to business transactions. It should not, however, be so complex that only a limited number of tax professionals can understand how it works. This level of complexity seems to vary. In some areas there appears to be tax simplification, especially as it relates to an individual earning salary income. On the other hand, complexity seems to be the direction that the ITA is taking in some areas, such as the rules on forgiveness of debt and foreign investments. When taxpayers and government officials can no longer apply the provisions of the ITA without professional assistance, the degree of dissatisfaction towards the system increases and may incite tax avoidance and tax evasion.

As is the case with the certainty objective, it is difficult to provide simplicity when complex transactions are undertaken.

¶1,040.60 *Feasibility and efficiency*

Administration of the tax must be feasible and efficient. Thus, the total costs, including those to the taxpayer, of administering and collecting the tax should be as low as possible. The relative costs of administration and collection of the Canadian income tax are very low when compared with those of other countries.

¶1,040.70 *How does the Canadian income tax measure up?*

Familiarity with the specifics of the Canadian income tax legislation will facilitate an evaluation of its characteristics relative to these ideal characteristics.

At the outset of its report on tax simplification,[3] the House of Commons Standing Committee on Finance and Economic Affairs made the following general observations on the current Canadian tax system.

> In addition to raising revenue efficiently, the ideal tax system is equitable and simple, and it assists the promotion of economic growth. Unfortunately, the goals of the ideal tax system often conflict. Changes made to make the system more equitable or to increase economic growth may make the system less simple. In fact since the early 1970s the trade offs between equity and simplicity and between growth and simplicity have been quite one-sided: if one of the goals had to give, it was always simplicity. The result, of course, is a Tax Act that even

[3] This report was released on June 19, 1986.

experts find confusing and a tax form for the average taxpayer that is daunting in length and complexity.

Any tax system is defined by six characteristics:

1. who pays the tax,
2. the base to be taxed,
3. the rates to be applied to the base,
4. general exemptions,
5. general deductions, and
6. other selective measures [including how and when the tax is to be paid].

The nature of the six characteristics determines how much revenue is produced by the tax system, as well as the equity of the system and its ability to promote growth. It is the exemptions, deductions and other selective tax measures that make modern tax systems so complicated. There are in Canada, for example, over one hundred selective tax measures dealing with personal income tax. There are even more measures dealing with corporate tax.

The *Income Tax Act* includes the tax measures, and the tax forms must allow for them. Too often the tax system is changed — the changes rationalized in terms of improved equity or economic growth — with no attention to the possible increased complexity of the Tax Act and tax forms. The Act and forms are treated as matters that can take care of themselves — an attitude that provides no check on the ever-increasing complexity of the Tax Act and tax forms. The Committee believes that the analysis of the tax system must be realigned with attention devoted to simplifying both the Act and the forms.

¶1,045 Tax reform guidelines

Guidelines for comprehensive tax reform announced by the Minister of Finance in 1986 in a speech to the House of Commons are summarized below. These guidelines can be used as a basis for evaluating the legislation as it exists at any time.

Fairness: The tax system should ensure fair sharing of the tax burden among taxpayers. People in similar circumstances should receive the same tax treatment; all high-income individuals and corporations should pay their fair share of tax; and similar products should bear the same rate of sales tax.

Simplicity and Compliance: Tax compliance should be made easier by making the system simpler and more readily understood.

Balance: Tax reform would redress the too-heavy share of tax revenues raised through the personal income tax, by requiring more of profitable corporations and by broadening the sales tax base.

Stability: Stability and dependability of tax revenues are essential for government budgeting. Raising more total tax revenues is not an objective of tax reform, but it should increase the certainty of achieving the revenue goals that the government sets itself.

International Competitiveness: The tax system should reinforce the ability of Canadians to compete internationally.

Economic Growth: The tax system should encourage growth through lower tax rates on a broader tax base. Business opportunities, rather than tax planning, should be the driving force behind business decisions.

Canadian Priorities: The tax system should help meet national social and economic needs, including regional needs, in keeping with Canadian priorities and values.

Transitional Implementation: Changes should be implemented with appropriate transitional provisions, to avoid leaving Canadians in doubt about tax rules.

Consultation: The government will consult broadly before making its final legislative proposals for tax reform.

¶1,100 STRUCTURE OF THE INCOME TAX ACT AND INTERPRETATION

¶1,110 The Income Tax Act

An overview of the Act can best be obtained from an inspection of the Table of Contents to the Act. A detailed sectional list of the Act is provided at the beginning of the CCH edition of the Act. A Table of Concordance is provided in the current CCH edition of the Act to relate revised provisions in the current Act to the equivalent provisions in the former Act. For example, it provides a mapping of references to the Act in court cases which may have changed in the *Fifth Supplemental to the Revised Statutes of Canada, 1985*.

CCH editions of the Act also contain several other important pieces of Canadian tax legislation, such as the Income Tax Regulations which support the Act, and the U.K. and U.S. tax treaties with Canada. The Act is divided into over 40 Parts, most of which represent specific types of tax, other than income tax. Of course, the largest Part deals with income tax and, because of its size, requires further classification into Divisions and Subdivisions. Exhibit 1-2 illustrates this structure of the Act with selected categories of provisions.

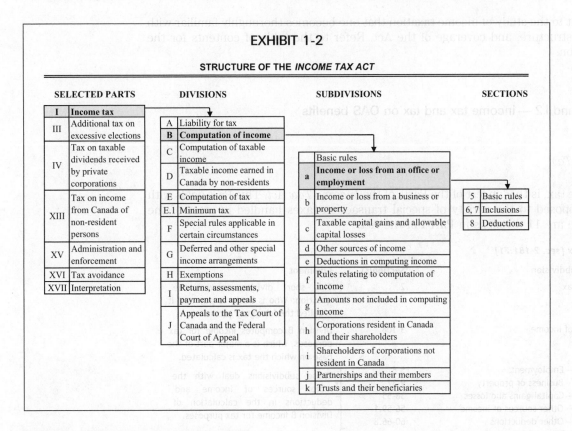

EXHIBIT 1-2

STRUCTURE OF THE *INCOME TAX ACT*

SELECTED PARTS

I	**Income tax**
III	Additional tax on excessive elections
IV	Tax on taxable dividends received by private corporations
XIII	Tax on income from Canada of non-resident persons
XV	Administration and enforcement
XVI	Tax avoidance
XVII	Interpretation

DIVISIONS

A	Liability for tax
B	**Computation of income**
C	Computation of taxable income
D	Taxable income earned in Canada by non-residents
E	Computation of tax
E.1	Minimum tax
F	Special rules applicable in certain circumstances
G	Deferred and other special income arrangements
H	Exemptions
I	Returns, assessments, payment and appeals
J	Appeals to the Tax Court of Canada and the Federal Court of Appeal

SUBDIVISIONS

	Basic rules
a	**Income or loss from an office or employment**
b	Income or loss from a business or property
c	Taxable capital gains and allowable capital losses
d	Other sources of income
e	Deductions in computing income
f	Rules relating to computation of income
g	Amounts not included in computing income
h	Corporations resident in Canada and their shareholders
i	Shareholders of corporations not resident in Canada
j	Partnerships and their members
k	Trusts and their beneficiaries

SECTIONS

5	Basic rules
6, 7	Inclusions
8	Deductions

¶1,115 How do I reference the Act?

For ease of reference, provisions are numbered, separating various elements of the provision. For example, consider the following reference:

6(1)(*b*)(i)(A)

The first number refers to the section of the Act and the second number refers to the subsection. Notice that section 6 subsection (1) is a fairly lengthy sentence covering several pages of text. The letter (*b*) refers to what is called a paragraph, and the lower case Roman numeral (i) refers to a subparagraph. The upper case letter (A) refers to a clause. If necessary, a subclause would be referred to with an upper case Roman numeral, and a sub-subclause would be referred to with an Arabic numeral. The above reference would be called "clause 6(1)(*b*)(i)(A)", stating the numerals and letters in order, in normal speech. From time to time an amendment is made to the Act and it is necessary to insert it between existing provisions without renumbering the whole Act. In such a case a reference such as section 6 subsection (2.1) will be entered between subsections 6(2) and 6(3). Some sections, like section 3, have no subsections. Hence, references skip directly to paragraphs as is the case in paragraph 3(*a*). As a short-form reference in this book, the following abbreviations may be used with a provision:

Sec. for section	Par. for paragraph
Ssec. for subsection	Spar. for subparagraph

¶1,120 Structure of the Income Tax Act

It is important to the study of income taxation that one becomes thoroughly familiar with the organization, structure, and coverage of the Act. Refer to the table of contents for the following discussion.

¶1,121 Parts I and I.2 — Income tax and tax on OAS benefits

Part I — Income Tax ITA: 2–180.2

Part I, income tax, is the longest of the Parts of the *Income Tax Act*. This Part deals with income tax, as opposed to the variety of special transaction taxes handled in most of the other Parts. There are 11 divisions in Part I of the Act.

Part I – Income Tax [sec. 2-181.71]

Division	Subdivision	Section(s)	Comment
A – Liability for Tax		2	This short division answers the question: Who is liable to pay tax? It is called the "charging" provision.
B – Computation of Income		3-108	Division B computes income for tax purposes, which is a major part of the base on which the tax is calculated.
	a – Employment	5-8	These subdivisions deal with the major sources of income and deductions in the calculation of Division B income for tax purposes.
	b – Business or property	9-37	
	c – Capital gains and losses	38-55	
	d – Other sources of income	56-59.1	
	e – Other deductions	60-66.8	
	f – Rules relating to the computation of income	67-80.5	These subdivisions provide rules that expand the rules set out in Subdivisions a to e, above. They do not provide for new sources of income or deductions.
	g – Amounts not included in income	81	
	h – Canadian corporations and their shareholders	82-89	
	i – Shareholders of corporations not resident in Canada	90-95	
	j – Partnerships and their members	96-103	
	k – Trusts and their beneficiaries	104-108	

C – Computation of Taxable Income	110-114.2	Division C contains deductions from Division B income (above) to arrive at taxable income that is the actual tax base.
D – Taxable Income Earned in Canada by Non-Residents	115-116	Division D contains special rules for non-residents.
E – Computation of Tax	117-127.41	Division E sets out the tax rates for individuals and corporations as well as a variety of tax credits.
a – Rules applicable to individuals	117-122.51	
a.1 – Child tax benefit	122.6-122.64	
a.2 – Working income tax benefit	122.7-122.71	
b – Rules for corporations	123-125.5	
c – Rules for all taxpayers	126-127.41	
E.1 – Minimum Tax	127.5-127.55	
F – Special Rules	128-143.4	These divisions deal with a variety of special situations and with procedural matters and appeals under the Act.
G – Deferred and Special Income Arrangements	144-148.1	
H – Exemptions	149-149.2	
I – Returns, Assessments, Payments and Appeals	150-168	
J – Appeals to the Courts	169-180	
Part 1.01 – Tax in Respect of Stock Option Benefit Deferral	180.01	
Part I.2 – Tax on Old Age Security Benefits	180.2	

¶1,122 Special transaction taxes

There are also special transaction taxes which are found in Parts II to XII.6 of the Act. This book will deal with several of these Parts as the need arises. ITA: 182–211.91

¶1,123 Non-residents

These parts of the Act are devoted to the taxation of non-residents: ITA: 212–219.3

Part XIII — Tax on Income from Canada of Non-Resident Persons ITA: 212–218.1

Part XIII.1 — Additional Tax on Authorized Foreign Banks ITA: 218.2

Part XIII.2 — Non-Resident investors in Canadian Mutual Funds ITA: 218.3

Part XIV — Additional Tax on Non-Resident Corporations [Branch Tax] ITA: 219–219.3

¶1,124 Administration and interpretation

The final parts of the Act deal with matters of administering the Act, outlining tax evasion and interpreting the Act: ITA: 220–262

Part XV — Administration and Enforcement ITA: 220–244

Part XVI — Tax Avoidance ITA: 245–246

Part XVI.I — Transfer Pricing ITA: 247

Part XVII — Interpretation ITA: 248–262

¶1,130 Related References

¶1,131 Historical footnotes

The history footnotes to each provision of the Act determine when the provision is applicable and what transitional rules, if any, apply in the implementation of new rules. The CCH edition provides, after each provision, a history of all changes subsequent to the enactment of the 5th Supplement in 1994. (A history of changes prior to 1994 can be found in a separate volume, "Former Income Tax Act, S.C. 1970-71-72, c. 63". In the electronic version, activate the "Former Act" link at the end of the provision and then activate the history link of that version of the ITA).

¶1,132 Related matters

After each provision there are often references to a wealth of information that may help you in your research.

- related sections;
- related regulations;
- related Interpretation Bulletins and Information Circulars divided into primary and secondary references;
- Advance Tax Rulings;
- authorized or "prescribed" forms;
- references to *Income Tax Technical News* issues;
- related Tax Window Files; and
- related landmark court decisions.

Some of the items listed are described below.

For example, refer to paragraph 20(1)(*q*), Employer's contributions to registered pension plan, in the Act. What other references are available that may help in your research on this particular tax provision?

You will find a wealth of information on items such as:

- Related sections: Subsection 146(5), Amount of RRSP premiums deductible, subsection 147(8), Amount of employer's contribution deductible
- Regulations: Part XXVII
- Interpretation Bulletins: Primary — IT-105 Administration costs of pensions plans
- Information Circulars: IC 72-13R8 Employees' pension plans
- Forms: T2 SCH 15

¶1,133 Draft legislation: Pending amendments

A federal Budget may introduce draft legislation to implement new tax policy initiatives. Alternatively, technical amendments may be made to correct anomalies in the law to either close down abuses or to rectify inequalities in the law. These amendments are placed in boxes under the heading "Pending Amendment" following the specific provision of the Act which they amend. The source and application date of the amendment is also shown.

¶1,134 Income Tax Application Rules

The next major component of the CCH edition of the *Income Tax Act* is the provisions of the *Income Tax Application Rules, 1971* (ITAR). These rules provide largely for the transition from the pre-1972 Act and its system of taxation to the current Act and its system of taxation including the introduction of the taxation of capital gains.

¶1,135 International tax conventions or treaties

The Act must be interpreted in light of International Tax Conventions which Canada has negotiated with many countries in order to reduce the impact of potential double taxation and tax avoidance. Both the Canada–United States Tax Convention (1980) and the Canada–U.K. Income Tax Convention (1978) are reproduced in the CCH edition of the Act. Over 80 others have been or are being negotiated. It is important to note that tax conventions override the provisions of the *Income Tax Act* and, hence, should be the first reference source when examining the tax implications of cross-border transactions.

¶1,136 Income Tax Regulations

The Income Tax Regulations ("Regulations") are set out to handle various specific situations and to carry on the general purposes and provisions of the Act. Unlike the Act itself, these regulations, which are part of the law, may be passed by Order-in-Council without ratification by Parliament. However, regulations must be written within the authority of a particular section of the Act and cannot be independent of the Act.

¶1,140 Other Interpretive Sources

Although not part of the Act itself, a number of sources have importance in the interpretation of the Act over the years of income taxation in Canada.

¶1,141 Judicial decisions (common law)

One of these interpretive sources is case law.

- Judicial decisions, which form the common law, on income tax matters may be appealed up to the Supreme Court of Canada (S.C.C.).
- The middle-level court hearing tax cases is the Federal Court of Appeal. Prior to 1990, income tax cases went to the Federal Court, which was divided into two divisions: the Federal Court–Trial Division (F.C.T.D.) and the Federal Court of Appeal (F.C.A.); cases would first go to the F.C.T.D., and then to the F.C.A. After 1990, only the F.C.A. was used for income tax cases, with the exception of some administrative matters pertaining to income tax, which were heard by the F.C.T.D. In 2003, the *Federal Courts Act*[4] was amended, creating two separate courts: the Federal Court of Appeal and the Federal Court (F.C.). The F.C.A. continues to hear income tax cases, while the F.C. hears administrative matters pertaining to income tax. Prior to 1972, this middle level of court was called the Exchequer Court (Ex. Ct.).
- The lowest level of court hearing tax cases is now called the Tax Court of Canada (T.C.C.). Prior to 1984, the lowest level was the Tax Review Board (T.R.B.), which was called the Tax Appeal Board (T.A.B.) prior to 1972.
- Court decisions, which are almost always based on particular sets of facts, interpret the application of the law to these facts. Most tax cases heard in Canada are published by CCH in the DOMINION TAX CASES. These cases are referred to using the name of the taxpayer, a reference such as 83 DTC 5041, and the court level, as follows: *Nowegijick v. The Queen*, 83 DTC 5041 (S.C.C.). The numeral 83 refers to the 1983 volume and the letters DTC refer to the DOMINION TAX CASES set. The numeral 5041 refers to the first page of the 1983 volume on which the case report begins. The CCH electronic version of the court cases also refers to the hard copy pages — just click on the page icon in the electronic text and a pop-up box will indicate the hard copy page.
- In 2009, the following note on referencing in the Dominion Tax Cases appeared:

> Beginning with cases reported in 2009, Dominion Tax Cases will no longer be cited by page number as has been the practice. The 2009 Tax Court cases will have cites in numerical order starting with 1001. Cases from other courts will be cited in numerical order beginning with 5001. For example, the cite for *Lewin v. The Queen* (T.C.C.) is 2009 DTC 1001 and *Gambino v. The Queen* (T.C.C.) is 2009 DTC 1002. Similarly, the cite for *Kossow v. The Queen* (F.C.A.) is 2009 DTC 5001 and *Kilbride v. The Queen* (F.C.A.) is 2009 DTC 5002. The numerical series will start again next year with the 2010 cases. Prior to 2009, the cites for Dominion Tax Cases had been based on the printed page number.
>
> Within a case, paragraphs are numbered, so references can be made to a specific paragraph, rather than to a page number.

While the courts' decisions represent the law, as interpreted for a specific set of facts, and may be useful as a guide in interpreting the law more generally, it must be remembered

[4] R.S., 1985, c. F-7.

that each set of facts differs from the previous cases in some degree and that a slight difference in the facts of a given case may materially affect the outcome.

Often a Canadian court will refer to a decision of a court outside Canada, such as a U.S. court or a court in a country with legislation and common law rooted in the British system. These decisions, at any level, made outside Canada are not binding on a Canadian court, but they may be referred to as persuasive, particularly, where principles of taxation or tax legislation are similar.

The part of a decided case that provides a binding precedent is referred to as the *ratio decidendi*, or reasons for judgment. Precedents established in previous cases create a foundation for applying principles of law (or for interpreting the law when a similar fact situation is presented to a court).

Often, a judicial decision will contain comments that are not necessary for the decision in the fact situation under consideration. These comments are known as *obiter dicta*, or comments made in passing. While these comments are not part of the precedent established by the case under consideration and, hence, not necessarily binding on other courts, they may provide insights to the interpretation of the law in different fact situations that might arise in subsequent cases.

¶1,142 Forms

Forms issued by the Canada Revenue Agency (CRA) and officially prescribed by the legislation may provide some insights to the interpretation of a provision in the legislation.

All of these forms can be obtained from the district taxation offices, the CRA's website (www.cra.gc.ca), or from commercial publishers either in print or electronic form.

¶1,143 CRA publications

The CRA releases some explanatory information on the official position in various taxation matters through a series of publications which are available on its website. The series of publications include:

Information Circulars (ICs): These deal mainly with administrative and procedural matters.

Interpretation Bulletins (ITs): These outline the CRA's interpretation of specific sections of the tax law.

Advance Tax Rulings (ATRs): These contain disguised summaries of certain advance income tax rulings given by the CRA and selected for publication. The last ruling published in the initial series was TR-101, dated December 9, 1980. Since many of the rulings in that initial series have become obsolete due to changes in the law, the CRA began with ATR-1, dated November 29, 1985, to reissue as part of a Second Series those former rulings that are still valid. The last published ATR was March 1996. The ATRs have been replaced by published technical interpretations discussed below.

Technical Interpretations: Through the *Access to Information Act* and advance income tax rulings, the CRA's responses to taxpayers' requests for technical interpretations on specific tax issues are published by commercial tax publishers. For example, CCH publishes in print form and electronically a summary, called WINDOW ON CANADIAN TAX, of the more significant interpretations. In addition, CCH publishes the full text of every one of these interpretations, referred to as TAX WINDOW FILES, but only in electronic form.

Information Booklets: In addition, the CRA publishes a number of non-technical information pamphlets for the general public and technical guides on specific topics, all of which are available at the district taxation offices, the CRA's website, or through the commercial tax services either in hard copy or electronic form.

Income Tax Technical News (ITTNs): The CRA issues this periodic newsletter, which provides timely commentary on recent tax issues and which can be found in the aforementioned sources, in particular, CCH's CANADIAN TAX REPORTER in print or electronic form.

Income Tax Folios: In August 2012, the CRA announced the introduction of a new technical publication to update interpretation bulletins, many of which are out of date. This publication will be organized by subject matter and subdivided into topic-specific chapters which will contain an updated version of one or more interpretation bulletins. Also incorporated will be material currently included in ITTNs. As updated versions of these publications are included in Income Tax Folios chapters, the ITs and ITTNs will be cancelled. This updating process is expected to take several years. In March 2013, the CRA released the first phase consisting of several folios on a variety of topics. The website can be found at: http://www.cra-arc.gc.ca/tx/tchncl/ncmtx/flndx-eng.html.

The above publications, representing what is known as "departmental practice", or "administrative practice", are not the law, although in the case of *Nowegijick v. The Queen*, Mr. Justice Dickson of the Supreme Court of Canada stated that "administrative policy and interpretation are not determinative, but are entitled to weight and can be an 'important factor' in case of doubt about the meaning of legislation". In the case of *The Queen v. Royal Trust Corporation of Canada*, it was noted that an Interpretation Bulletin interpreted a provision in a manner which Mr. Justice Urie of the Federal Court of Appeal concluded was correct.

83 DTC 5041 (S.C.C.)

83 DTC 5172 (F.C.A.)

¶1,144 Technical notes and explanations

Technical notes are issued by the Department of Finance to explain new legislation when it is introduced. These notes are provided for an understanding of amendments and not as an official interpretation of the provisions they describe. Although the impact of the technical notes on judicial decisions is not always known, they should at least establish the general or broad intention of Parliament in respect of a particular issue.

In these Technical Notes, the Department of Finance generally indicates that:

> These explanatory notes are provided to assist in an understanding of amendments to the *Income Tax Act*, the Income Tax Application Rules and related statutes. The notes are intended for information purposes only and should not be construed as an official interpretation of the provisions they describe.

¶1,145 Generally accepted accounting principles (GAAP)

Generally accepted accounting principles have been important guides in the interpretation of the Act where the statutory law was silent on a particular point. As a result of recent developments, Canada required public enterprises to adopt International Financial Reporting Standards (IFRS) by 2011. Due to these changes, references in this text to generally accepted accounting principles (GAAP) will include IFRS for public enterprises and Accounting Standards for Private Enterprises (ASPE) as appropriate.

¶1,150 Interpretation of Tax Legislation

It is important to be able to interpret the Act in order to advise clients of the tax consequences of their transactions and to deal with the CRA on assessments and rulings. Knowing the principles and rules used by the courts in their interpretation of the Act is important, since their interpretations are an essential part of the law.

¶1,151 Precision

The development of tax legislation over the years has included the acceptance of rules of interpretation or construction of the income tax law. First, every attempt is made to achieve precision in the language of tax legislation so that it is clearly understood, thereby providing the taxpayer with some degree of certainty about his or her tax liability. (To see how the drafters of the Act have succeeded in this respect, try to read subsection 256(3) as an example of such language!) To quote a famous British decision heard in 1891 on the question of the drafting of legislation:

> It is not enough to attain a degree of precision which a person reading in good faith can understand, but it is necessary to attain if possible to a degree of precision which a person

reading in bad faith cannot misunderstand (and) it is all the better if he cannot pretend to misunderstand it.[5]

It is important to read every word of a provision very carefully to determine the following components of a provision:

(a) to whom the provision applies, i.e., an individual, a corporation, a partnership or a trust and, if more than one, their relationship;

(b) the transactions to which the provision applies and the conditions that must exist for the provision to apply;

(c) the consequences of the provision, if it applies; and

(d) the time frame over which the provision applies, such as a particular year or a part of a year.

¶1,152 Plain and obvious meaning

It has long been held that the words used in a taxing statute must be given their plain and obvious meaning, unless there is a specific definition contained in the statute or unless another meaning is required in the context of the remainder of the Act. This has become known as the "Golden Rule" of interpretation or construction (from the verb "to construe"), and it was expressed by Lord Atkinson of the British House of Lords as follows:

> In the construction of statutes their words must be interpreted in their ordinary grammatical sense, unless there be something in the context, or in the object of the statute in which they occur, or in the circumstances with reference to which they are used, to show that they were used in a special sense different from their ordinary grammatical sense.[6]

In an elaboration of this principle, Lord Wensleydale stated:

> . . . the grammatical and ordinary sense of the word is to be adhered to, unless that would lead to some absurdity or some repugnance or inconsistency with the rest of the [statute], in which case the grammatical and ordinary sense of the words may be modified so as to avoid that absurdity and inconsistency but no farther.[7]

Again, this principle is intended to help increase the taxpayer's certainty of his or her position.

A word may have more than one ordinary meaning, depending on how it is used. For example, the word "rent" can be used as a noun in reference to an amount paid or received. The same word can be used as a verb by either the landlord or the tenant, i.e., to rent to or to rent from a person. In a similar landlord/tenant situation, the word "lease" can be used as a noun in reference to the contract between the two or as a verb in the same way that the verb "rent" can be used. Hence, it is important to determine the context in which the word is used and how it is used. The location in the Act or in a provision can affect the meaning to be used for a word or phrase.

The meaning of a provision cannot be extended by an interpretation which is not clear from the words used. Lord Cairns expanded on this point in an 1869 case by stating:

> . . . if the person sought to be taxed comes within the letter of the law he must be taxed, however great the hardship may appear to the judicial mind to be. On the other hand, if the Crown, seeking to recover the tax, cannot bring the subject within the letter of the law, the subject is free, however apparently within the spirit of the law the case might otherwise appear to be. In other words, if there be admissible in statute, what is called an equitable construction, certainly such a construction is not admissible in a taxing statute, where you can simply adhere to the words of the statute.[8]

This point is illustrated in the case of *Witthuhn v. M.N.R.*, in which a taxpayer was denied a deduction for certain medical expenses because the patient was confined to bed or a special type of rocking chair rather than "to a bed or wheelchair" as required at the time of the facts in the case and, in fact, until the provision was amended in 1986. 57 DTC 174 (T.A.B.)

[5] *In re Castioni* (1891), 1 Q.B. 149 at 167.

[6] *Victoria (City) v. Bishop of Vancouver Island* (1921), 2 A.C. 384 (P.C.) at 387.

[7] *Grey v. Pearson* (1857), 6 H.L.C. 61 at 106.

[8] *Partington v. Attorney General* (1869), L.R. 4 H.L. 100 at 122.

In more recent years, however, this approach appears to have been softened to some extent. For example, in the case of *Overdyck v. M.N.R.*, where the taxpayer used a leg brace to go to work and a chair with castor-like wheels while at work, the same wording was given a much more liberal interpretation on the basis that if the taxpayer had been left completely alone without external aid or assistance, he would have been in bed at all times as a result of paralysis in one leg. In fact, where courts have found wording to be unclear, they have interpreted the words in a manner that is fair in the situation under consideration. 83 DTC 307 (T.R.B.)

¶1,152.10 *Definitions in the Act*

Various provisions of the Act contain lists of defined words or phrases. Subsection 248(1) contains a long list of terms or phrases. The preamble (i.e., opening words) to that provision is very short, but it is very important. It states "in this Act" and means that the definition provided is to be used wherever the word or phrase is used in the Act. However, note that the definition of "private corporation" in subsection 248(1), for example, has the meaning assigned by subsection 89(1). Note, also, that the preamble to subsection 89(1) states, "in this subdivision", i.e., Subdivision h of Division B of Part I of the Act. This means that, generally, the definitions covered in subsection 89(1) apply when the words listed in subsection 89(1) are used in Subdivision h. However, in the case of a "private corporation", the definition is used wherever the term is used in the Act, as a result of its listing in subsection 248(1) and the cross-reference there.

Sometimes the definitions listed in a subsection are limited to the section of the Act in which the subsection appears. For example, the term "excluded consideration" is defined in subsection 74.4(1), which has the preamble "in this section", meaning that the definition applies only to the use of the term in subsection 74.4. The "in this section" preamble is important when the same term is defined differently in two different sections. For example, the term "earned income" is defined in subsection 63(3) for use in section 63 pertaining to the child care expense deduction. The same term is defined differently in subsection 146(1) for use in section 146 pertaining to registered retirement savings plans.

¶1,152.20 *Meaning and distinction in words commonly used in the Act*

Often a word or phrase will be defined using the word "means" or "includes". "Means" indicates that the definition of the word "given" is exhaustive or restrictive, at least, for the purposes of its use in the Act. In these cases, the definition stated applies only to the given word or phrase. For example, the definition of "balance-due day" in subsection 248(1) uses "means" to limit the meaning. Other definitions use the word "includes" to indicate that the definition is not exhaustive and that the ordinary meaning of the word or phrase can be used in addition to the included meanings. For example, the term "borrowed money" in subsection 248(1) uses the word "includes", leaving out many more common items that would ordinarily be referred to as borrowed money. Note that the definition of "office" in subsection 248(1) uses both "means" and "includes" in the same definition.

Provisions that require or allow someone to do something use the words "may" or "shall". The use of "may" makes the requirement permissive, while the use of "shall" makes the requirement obligatory. Note that in subsection 2(1) "an income tax *shall* be paid". However, specified amounts "may be deducted" by an employee under subsection 8(1).

Another important distinction in the use of words is between "and" and "or". For example, in paragraph 256(1)(*c*), there are three conditions and they are all joined by an "and". Thus, all three conditions must be met for the rule to apply. On the other hand, in paragraph 256(1)(*b*), there are two conditions stated and they are joined by an "or". Therefore, only one of the two conditions need be met for the rule to apply. In that case, the two conditions are mutually exclusive, so that only one can possibly apply in a given fact situation.

Noting the use of the word "except" can be very important in applying a rule. In paragraph 6(1)(*b*), the general rule is stated in about two lines and those words are followed by the word "except". The list of exceptions is long and very detailed and, as a result, the reader can easily forget the general rule.

The Act will often use the phrase "for greater certainty" to expand the application of a rule or definition to include something specific. This occurs, for example, in paragraph 256(1.2)(*b*).

It is common for the Act to use the word "deem". For example, subsection 250(1) deems an individual to be a full-year resident of Canada if certain specified conditions are met. If an individual fits one of the conditions, that person will be deemed to be a full-year resident, with the tax consequences of being a full-year resident, even if that individual would not otherwise be treated like a full-year resident because of physical absence for all or a part of the year.

The Act often uses the term "prescribed" in connection with the *Income Tax Regulations* or a form. For example, subparagraph 6(1)(*k*)(v) refers to an "amount prescribed". In the Regulation footnote to paragraph 6(1)(*k*), the reader is referred to Regulation 7305.1 for the prescribed amount. Another use of the word "prescribed" occurs in paragraph 8(6.1)(*a*) in reference to a form to be used by an employer to certify for deduction an eligible tool of a tradesperson. The prescribed form (T777) is found under the "Form" heading of the footnotes at the end of section 8.

¶1,153 Intention of Parliament

In interpreting or construing a taxing statute, inferences about the intention of Parliament are often made. As indicated previously, the Department of Finance now often publishes detailed explanatory notes to accompany draft legislation. These notes may be helpful in determining intention but are not binding on a court. No interpretation is allowed to defeat the plain intention of the legislation. The courts assume that what is stated in the Act is what was meant by Parliament.[9] Thus, a meaning that is consistent with the intention of Parliament is allowed to prevail.

¶1,154 Remission orders

Taxing statutes were to be interpreted strictly, according to early rules of interpretation. However, where doubt exists, the construction of the statute was to be resolved in favour of the taxpayer in the case of a charging provision and in favour of the Crown in the case of an exemption provision. In addition, if it was not possible for the Courts to render what they would consider to be an equitable decision in a particular case, relief for the taxpayer could be found under the *Financial Administration Act*. Subsection 17(1) of that Act provides for the remission of taxes and penalties when it is considered in the public interest.[10]

¶1,155 Contextual approach

The Supreme Court of Canada has suggested that the strict interpretation rule is still applicable where the plain meaning of the words is straightforward. Where the provision is vague and/or confusing, it is to be interpreted within its context in the Act on a basis consistent with the object of the Act and the intention of Parliament, which may reflect political, economic, social or technological objectives. This "object and spirit" test of interpretation was used in the case of *Stubart Investments Ltd. v. The Queen* by the Supreme Court of Canada and, at least to some extent, has been codified in the general anti-avoidance rule (GAAR) of the Act.[11] The Supreme Court has often quoted the authority on the interpretation of statutes, E.E. Driedger in *Construction of Statutes*,[12] as follows:

84 DTC 6305 (S.C.C.)

ITA: 245(4)

> Today, there is only one principle or approach, namely, the words of an Act are to be read in their entire context and in their grammatical and ordinary sense harmoniously with the scheme of the Act, the object of the Act, and the intention of Parliament.

In the case of *Corporation Notre-Dame de Bon-Secours v. Communauté Urbaine de Québec*, the Supreme Court of Canada again rejected the strict rule of interpretation in cases of doubt, as outlined above, and established the following rules of interpretation:

95 DTC 5017 (S.C.C.)

[9] This is illustrated by the case of *M.N.R. v. MacInnes*, 54 DTC 1031 (Ex. Ct.), on the meaning of "property substituted". The intention of Parliament as a means of interpretation was also raised in the case of *Duha Printers (Western) Ltd. v. The Queen*, 98 DTC 6334 (S.C.C.).

[10] For a case which refers a taxpayer to the *Financial Administration Act*, see *Bayraktaroglu v. M.N.R.*, 73 DTC 27 (T.R.B.).

[11] See *Antosko et al. v. The Queen*, 94 DTC 6314 (S.C.C.), and *Friesen v. The Queen*, 95 DTC 5551 (S.C.C.).

[12] E.E. Driedger, *Construction of Statutes*, 2nd ed. (Toronto: Butterworths, 1983), 87.

(a) tax legislation should be interpreted according to ordinary rules of statutory interpretation;

(b) a legislative provision should be given a strict or liberal interpretation depending on the purpose underlying it and that purpose must be identified in the light of the context of the statute, its objective and the legislative intent (i.e., the "teleological" approach);[13]

(c) the teleological approach will favour the taxpayer or the tax department depending solely on the legislative provision in question and not on predetermined presumptions;

(d) substance will prevail over form (see discussion below) where this is consistent with the wording and objective of the statute; and

(e) only a reasonable doubt, not resolved by ordinary rules of interpretation, will be settled by recourse to the residual presumption in favour of the taxpayer.

¶1,156 Form versus substance

The issue of form versus substance has long posed a problem in the application of the tax legislation to a taxpayer's situation. It was addressed in the often cited 1935 British case of the *Duke of Westminster*[14] in which a member of the House of Lords, Lord Tomlin, stated that:

> Every man is entitled if he can to order his affairs so that the tax attaching under the appropriate Acts is less than it would otherwise be. If he succeeds in ordering them so as to secure this result, then, however unappreciative the Commissioners of Inland Revenue or his fellow taxpayers may be of his ingenuity, he cannot be compelled to pay an increased tax. This so-called doctrine of "the substance" seems to me to be nothing more than an attempt to make a man pay notwithstanding that he has so ordered his affairs that the amount of tax sought from him is not legally claimable. . . .
>
> . . . There may be, of course, cases where documents are not *bona fide* nor intended to be acted upon but are only used as a cloak to conceal a different transaction. . . .

Thus, the form or legal effect of a transaction must prevail in attempting to determine the tax effects, unless the taxing statute requires that such form be disregarded in cases where form is inconsistent with the wording and objective of the Act, or unless the form is considered to be a "sham" which misrepresents the true form, based on the facts of the case.[15] Another British case[16] has described a "sham" as:

> . . . acts done or documents executed by the parties to the sham which were intended by them to give to third parties and to the Courts the appearance of creating between the parties legal rights and obligations different from the actual legal rights and obligations (if any) which the parties intended to create.
>
> . . . For acts and documents to be a sham, with whatever legal consequence falls from this, all the parties thereto must have a common intention that the acts or documents are not to create the legal rights and obligations which they give the appearance of creating. . . .

Furthermore, the Courts have even applied what has come to be known as a "repugnancy" or "smell" test in certain situations where substance was at considerable variance with the form of a transaction.

¶1,157 Exceptions override general

The Act contains a number of statements of general principle followed by an exception or series of exceptions to that rule. An exception or other specific provision of the legislation will override the general provision, but the former must be given a strict interpretation. This rule was followed in a Canadian case,[17] when the judge stated that:

---

[13] This approach was applied in the case of *Harvey C. Smith Drugs Limited v. The Queen*, 95 DTC 5026 (F.C.A.).

[14] [1936] A.C. 1 (H.L.), at pp. 19-20.

[15] This was confirmed by the Supreme Court of Canada in the case of *Stubart Investments Ltd. v. The Queen*, 84 DTC 6305.

[16] *Snook v. London and West Riding Investments Ltd.*, [1967] 1 All E.R. 518 at 528.

[17] *Dunkelman v. M.N.R.*, 59 DTC 1242 (Ex. Ct.), at 1244.

> . . . the subsection must, in my opinion, be regarded as an exception to the general rule, and while it must be given its full effect so far as it goes, it is to be strictly construed and not extended to anything beyond the scope of the natural meaning of the language used, regardless again of how much a particular case may seem to fall within its supposed spirit or intendment.

Thus, a taxpayer cannot obtain an exemption from tax unless the circumstances fall squarely within the wording of the provision.

¶1,158 Specific words followed by general

A principle that has been important in the interpretation of the Act over the years is the *ejusdem generis* rule for enumerations of similar items. According to this rule, when a series of specific words in a statute is followed by general words, the general words are confined to the same scope as the specific words. This rule could be involved in the interpretation of the words "other remuneration" as used in subsection 5(1) which states that ". . . a taxpayer's income for a taxation year from an office or employment is the salary, wages and other remuneration, including gratuities, received by him in the year". The scope of the meaning of the specific words "salary", "wages" and "gratuities" might be used to constrain the meaning of the words "other remuneration".

¶1,159 Precedents

Another principle deals with the role of court decisions as precedents often referred to as the concept of *stare decisis*. This principle establishes that decisions on similar facts are to be similar. The precedent value of a case is determined by the seniority of the court. A decision of a higher Canadian court is binding on a lower Canadian court in a subsequent decision. Exceptions to the rule are rare, but do occur where, for example, a lower court judge can show that a senior court judge's conclusions are based on incorrect reasons resulting in incorrect conclusions.[18] At a given level of court, consistency in decisions on similar facts is usually attempted. If a decided case is not to apply to a given situation, the facts of the decided case must be distinguished or differentiated sufficiently from the case under consideration to justify a different decision. In the case of *B.B. Fast & Sons Distributors Ltd. v. M.N.R.*, a member of the Tax Review Board, as it was then, invoked the "judicial comity rule" indicating that judgments of courts of equal or co-ordinate jurisdiction should be followed in the absence of strong reasons to the contrary. However, it has been recognized that too rigid adherence to precedent might lead to injustice in a particular case and also unduly restrict the proper development of the law.

82 DTC 1017 (T.R.B.)

¶1,160 Interpretation Act

Finally, the effects of the *Interpretation Act*, which deals with the interpretation of Canadian statutes, should be considered. In subsection 3(3), the *Interpretation Act* recognizes rules of construction such as those discussed to the extent that they are not inconsistent with a provision of this Act. In section 14, the *Interpretation Act* sets out some rules of construction of its own regarding the use of definitions and the interpretation of exceptions to rules. Section 27 deals with the interpretation of time limits specified in a statute. For example, if such a deadline falls on a holiday, the deadline is extended to the following day that is not a holiday. Section 32 provides that deviations from a prescribed form which do not affect the substance do not invalidate a form used. Gender is dealt with in subsection 33(1) which states that "words importing female persons include male persons and corporations and words importing male persons include female persons and corporations".

[18] *489599 B.C. Ltd. v. The Queen*, 2008 DTC 4107 (TCC).

¶1,180 AREAS OF PRACTICE AND THE ROLE OF THE PROFESSIONAL ACCOUNTANT

¶1,185 Why Study Taxation?

Taxation influences the economy and the amount that individuals earn, spend, and save.

More importantly, taxation affects the decisions that individuals and businesses make today for future transactions. Perhaps an individual plans to purchase a car, dispose of a cottage, move to a foreign location, or start a new business: a simple computation of taxes payable is often impossible.

Over the years, the Act has developed from a 10-page legal document to more than 3,000 pages of legislation, regulations, and definitions. Professional accountants require an in-depth understanding of tax law to process income tax returns and calculate taxes payable. Professionals involved in tax planning are necessary and important in financial planning for businesses, individuals, and estates. For businesses to be competitive in today's global economy, planning and decision making need to be timely and effective. Thus, those who study taxation and understand how the rules have evolved and how they affect taxpayers are better equipped to identify tax-related issues during operating, financing, and investment decision-making processes. Since taxation influences most decisions, such knowledge is necessary. Simplicity is a basic requirement of every tax system. However, deficits, taxpayer behaviour, and changing governments and demographics, as well as volatile economies, continue to result in new rules, amendments, and tax reforms.

¶1,190 The Practice of Taxation

In the field of taxation, there are essentially four extensive areas of practice.

¶1,191 Compliance

Compliance includes the preparation and review of personal and corporate tax returns, forms, and other documents with provincial and federal taxation authorities. The compliance area is essentially the responsibility of the accountant. In addition to tax accountants, tax lawyers will often be called upon for assistance in legal interpretation and the review of certain forms. In performing compliance tasks, it is necessary to understand the fundamental tax principles, the legislative intent underlying the income tax system, and the detailed rules in order to compute tax liability and complete the necessary forms, elections, and returns required by the Canada Revenue Agency ("CRA"). Accountants are best trained to perform these tasks because of their understanding of generally accepted accounting principles (GAAP) and the process of accounting for income and expenses.

¶1,192 Legal interpretation

Legal interpretation involves the interpretation of tax laws and the research of tax cases and court decisions. Lawyers are specifically trained to provide legal interpretation. Professional accountants who have completed a tax specialization program are also trained to interpret the law. This helps them to better advise their clients in the planning of future transactions, or in the event of an audit or reassessment by the CRA. Much of the work involved in the drafting of legal documents and contracts for business transactions requires extensive interpretation of tax jurisprudence. In general, all accountants should acquaint themselves with the legal interpretation of tax laws, and the principles underlying court decisions, to facilitate the evaluation of alternative tax treatments and acquire a better understanding of the tax system. This is crucial in effective tax planning for clients or employers. It is also necessary to know when to request legal assistance. Incorporation, corporate reorganizations, major business transactions, tax appeals, and tax litigation generally involve legal assistance together with the taxpayer's tax adviser. Some lawyers, accountants, and economists who focus their studies in this area also contribute to policy review, design, and implementation of tax laws.

¶1,193 Tax appeals and tax litigation

Tax appeals on reassessments and tax litigation require knowledge of compliance and the legal interpretation of tax laws. For this reason, both lawyers and accountants are often involved in the appeal process and the pre-court stage of tax litigation. Often the pre-court stage will involve lengthy calculations, valuations, and an assessment of generally accepted accounting principles. For a case to be successful, lawyers are necessary in appeals and tax litigation in order to comply with proper court procedures. In addition, lawyers trained in taxation are in a position to provide the extensive research necessary for legal interpretation.

¶1,194 Tax planning

Tax planning has often been referred to as the process of "tax minimization" in the planning of future events and transactions. This is a misnomer because of the many non-tax costs and economic complications that could arise with such a narrow focus. To achieve effective tax planning in the decision-making process, it is necessary to examine and integrate all business or investment factors. Tax planners should also consider how an individual investor's, shareholder's, or corporation's long-term profitability will be affected. Both lawyers and accountants participate in this function by assessing ambiguous tax rules and determining how a decision could be affected by the tax rule interpretation. It is management's role to integrate taxation with the entire management cycle and the corporation's pursuit of long-term domestic and global goals.

While some students may become tax professionals, many will enter into management, financial, or accounting positions. This book presents important concepts and provides the tools necessary for students to apply their knowledge to complex transactions and decisions — regardless of the students' chosen careers.

¶1,195 The Role of the Professional Accountant in Tax Matters

Professional accountants and others who are not qualified as lawyers very frequently play a major role in providing tax-related services to taxpayers. The basis of these services is, of course, tax law embodied in the legislation and jurisprudence discussed previously. It must be recognized that the practice of law by non-lawyers is an offence under certain provincial legislation which regulates that practice by lawyers. Often, there is a very fine and ill-defined line between an activity that constitutes the practice of law and services provided to clients by non-lawyers in the tax area. In addition to committing the foregoing offence, an adviser may be liable for the civil consequences of negligence in providing services for which the adviser is not qualified, such as drafting a will, incorporating a company, etc.

Often, the complementary nature of financial services and tax law makes the combination of the two by a single adviser most practical in providing service to clients. In these situations, the role of non-lawyers is generally recognized in most provinces and conflicts can be avoided if the non-lawyer is careful not to provide advice that can be construed as a legal opinion and not to prepare documents of a purely legal, non-tax nature arising from more general laws such as contract law and corporate law.

¶1,200 INTRODUCTION TO INCOME TAX AND TAXABLE INCOME

¶1,210 Approaches to Defining Income

There is no statutory definition of the word "income" in the Act. While section 3 might ITA: 3 be considered as such a definition, it really provides a set of rules for aggregating a taxpayer's income from various sources once these amounts have been identified as income either by a statutory provision of the Act or by judicial decisions. Since there is no statutory definition, it is customary to refer to prior judicial decisions which may define the term and which, in turn, may have referred to a standard dictionary to establish the ordinary meaning of the word. *The Concise Oxford Dictionary* defines "income" as "the money or other assets received, esp. periodically or in a year, from one's business, lands, work, investments, etc.". While income is usually thought of as a monetary receipt or currency, it may take the form of money's worth, that is, something of commercial value such as gold, shares, wheat, etc.

¶1,212 Income versus capital

Receipts can be classified as either income or capital. As long as taxation has existed in Canada, receipts of capital have received more favourable tax consequences than receipts of income. This situation continues to exist, since only half of capital gains are included in income.

The problem of determining whether a given receipt is one of capital or one of income has been the subject of countless court cases. In subsequent chapters, the major factors used by the courts in their determination will be examined, and a number of cases will be used to illustrate these factors. One factor is the nature of the asset which is determined from its use or intended use. The classic capital asset is one which produces income from holding it or using it. A common analogy used by the courts likens a capital asset to a tree which produces income during the period of ownership in the form of fruit. Sale of the tree results in a receipt of capital and capital gains treatment, whereas sale of the fruit results in a receipt of income.

This topic is covered in greater detail in Chapters 4 and 8, where we look at business income and capital gains, respectively.

¶1,215 The economist's perspective

Economist Adam Smith's concept of income was limited to the three sources of rent, profit and wages. Excluded from income would be capital gains, windfalls and gifts. Nevertheless, income was considered to be "net" income, that is, gross revenues less expenses incurred to produce revenues. This is a basic principle of the Canadian income tax system. In more recent years, the economist's concept of income has been broadened to include all net increases in economic power between two points in time. This would include gains of all kinds and imputed income such as the value of a tax professor's labour in preparing his or her own tax return. Obviously, there are considerable valuation and administrative problems in collecting taxes on such imputed income. However, the comprehensive tax base concept of the Carter Commission came close to this broader concept of income.

¶1,220 The role of generally accepted accounting principles

It will be seen in subsection 9(1) that income from a business is the "profit" therefrom and the computation of profit is not completely specified by provisions in the Act. Until the early 1990s, the courts have been inconsistent in their reference to generally accepted accounting principles (GAAP) as an authoritative source for interpretation of profit under the *Income Tax Act*. The Supreme Court decision in *Symes v. The Queen et al.* appears to have cleared the air by the following statement: 94 DTC 6001 (S.C.C.)

> . . . Any reference to G.A.A.P. connotes a degree of control by professional accountants which is inconsistent with a legal test for "profit" under s. 9(1). Further, whereas an accountant questioning the propriety of a deduction may be motivated by a desire to present an appropriately conservative picture of current profitability, the *Income Tax Act* is motivated by a different purpose: the raising of public revenues. For these reasons, it is more appropriate in considering the s. 9(1) business test to speak of "well accepted principles of business (or accounting) practice" or "well accepted principles of commercial trading".

Therefore, GAAP is still to be considered but should be put into the context of overall business practices and should not stand alone. In the case of *Canderel Limited v. Her Majesty the Queen*, the Supreme Court of Canada stated, as a principle, that 98 DTC 6100 (S.C.C.)

> well-accepted business principles, which include but are not limited to the formal codification found in G.A.A.P, are not rules of law but are interpretative aids. To the extent that they may influence the calculation of income, they will do so only in a case-by-case basis, depending on the facts of the taxpayer's financial situation.

It must be emphasized that the existence of specific statutory provisions, which are used in the computation of income for tax purposes, results in an income computation that will vary widely from income for financial accounting purposes. A major cause of this variance is the use of the capital cost allowance system for tax purposes based on a declining balance method of capital cost write-off in lieu of depreciation for financial accounting purposes often based on a straight-line method.

It has yet to be seen how IFRS will influence the courts and it may take many years before the influence of IFRS will be reflected in court decisions.

¶1,225 The doctrine of constructive receipt

The "constructive receipt" of income involves the inclusion of amounts which may not actually be received but are beneficially received or receivable. For example, there is a provision that deems the taxpayer to have received amounts withheld as tax by his or her employer. Although the taxpayer does not receive these amounts, they are included in his or her income subject to tax. The use of the accrual system is another example of the use of the concept of constructive receipt. While amounts in accounts receivable have not actually been received they result in amounts being included in income.

ITA: 153(3)

In applying the doctrine of constructive receipt, one of the key determinants is that the amounts must be beneficially received or receivable by the taxpayer so that his or her use of the amounts is free and unrestricted. The test was set out in the early Canadian case of *Kenneth B.S. Robertson Ltd. v. M.N.R.* in the form of the following questions:

2 DTC 655 (Ex. Ct.)

> Is his right to it (the amount) absolute and under no restriction, contractual or otherwise, as to its disposition, use or enjoyment? To put it another way, can an amount in a taxpayer's hands be regarded as an item of profit or gain from his business as long as he holds it subject to specific and unfulfilled conditions and his right to retain it and apply it to his own use has not yet accrued and may never accrue?

As an example of an amount that is not constructively or beneficially received, consider retail sales taxes collected by retailers and passed on to the provincial government. In this case, the retailer simply acts as a conduit or transmitter of the amount and, therefore, is not taxed on it.[19]

¶1,240 Computation of Income

¶1,245 Aggregation formula

For Canadian taxpayers, both income and capital receipts, resulting in income subject to tax, are aggregated by the rules of section 3 irrespective of geographic source. The computation of income for tax purposes is illustrated by Exhibit 1-3. We will return to these aggregation rules in a subsequent chapter after all of the sources of income have been considered so that the terminology used in the section is more meaningful. Until then, a cursory examination of the section will provide an overview of the coverage of subsequent chapters.

[19] For two Canadian cases which illustrate situations in which constructive receipt was at issue, see *Cliffe v. M.N.R.*, 57 DTC 305 (T.A.B.), dealing with unpaid salaries left in a corporation and *Green v. M.N.R.*, 50 DTC 320 (T.A.B.), dealing with unpaid interest left in a corporation. For an application of the concept of constructive receipt to a third-party payment in a marital breakdown situation, see the case of *The Queen v. Arsenault*, 96 DTC 6131 (F.C.A.), in which the "free and unrestricted use" test was at issue. For an example of a fact situation in which it was concluded that the test that an amount must have been received by someone for the benefit of the payee was not met, see *Markman v. M.N.R.*, 89 DTC 253 (T.C.C.).

EXHIBIT 1-3
Simplified Computation of Income Under Section 3
Division B

ITA Par.	*Type of income*	*ITA Subdivision*	*Chapter(s)*
3(*a*)	Worldwide income (positive amounts only after subtracting deductible expenses) from non-capital sources including:		
	• Office or employment	a	3
	• Business	b	4 and 5
	• Property	b	5 and 6
	• Other non-capital sources	d	9
Plus			
3(*b*)	Net taxable capital gains (not negative)*	c	7 and 8
Less			
3(*c*)	General deductions not attributable to any specific source	e	9
Less			
3(*d*)	Negative amounts or losses from non-capital sources including:		
	• Office or employment**	a	3
	• Business**	b	4 and 5
	• Property**	b	5 and 6
Equals			
3(*e*), (*f*)	Division B income or "income for tax purposes"		

* If allowable capital losses exceed taxable capital gains then this net capital loss is deductible in a carryover year (i.e., the previous three years or any future year) under Division C (see Chapter 10 for individuals and Chapter 11 for corporations).

** If the losses from an office, employment, business, and property exceed the income from other sources, then it will be necessary to calculate the non-capital loss that can be carried back to previous years or forward to future years under Division C (see Chapter 10 for individuals and Chapter 11 for corporations).

Note how section 3 represents the expression of a complex formula in words contained in one very long sentence. For example, paragraph 3(*a*) requires the taxpayer to "determine the total of all amounts" of income from all of the non-capital sources, e.g., employment income, business income and sundry receipts. In fact, this aggregate includes only positive amounts, i.e., an excess of inclusions over deductions, from these sources. However, it is only evident that these amounts must be positive when paragraph 3(*d*), referring to losses from the same non-capital sources, is read.

Paragraph 3(*b*) requires the taxpayer to "determine the amount, if any, by which the total of" two amounts exceeds a third amount which, itself, requires a sub-calculation. In the language of the Act, the use of the words "if any", when referring to the calculation of an excess, means that if the calculated amount is negative, the amount is set at nil. That is, if the calculated amount is negative, there is no excess of the sum required in subparagraph 3(*b*)(i) over the amount calculated in subparagraph 3(*b*)(ii). In interpreting a provision of this nature, it is often helpful to determine the underlying computational formula and to substitute numbers from a particular fact situation into the formula. This procedure will be demonstrated subsequently in an example problem.

¶1,250 Sourcing or tracing of income

A taxpayer must compute his or her income or loss from each source independently by allocating deductions in amounts that can be applied reasonably to each revenue source. For example, a taxpayer who is employed and also carries on a business must compute the income ITA: 4

from each of these sources separately. His employment expenses cannot be deducted from his business income. Similarly, in the allocation of business income among various provinces only the deductions that can be traced to or allowed by that particular jurisdiction can be deducted in arriving at income for tax purposes.

Generally, no provision under the Act should be interpreted as to require an amount to be included in or deducted from income more than once unless a provision is so worded to give a contrary intention.[19]

Although income is not defined in the Act, once it has been determined that there is income, then this income must be attached to a particular source. For example, income from employment found in Subdivision a of Division B gathers together all of the employment income inclusions as specifically determined in sections 5, 6, and 7 minus all of the permitted deductions found in section 8. This sourcing of income and deductions would be continued for:

Subdivision b — Business or Property Income

Subdivision c — Taxable Capital Gains and Allowable Capital Losses

Subdivision d — Other Income

Once the sourcing of income has been completed, then the ordering rules for Division B, which are found in section 3 of the Act, can be applied.

¶1,260 Determination of Income, Taxable Income, and Federal Income Tax for Individuals

The taxable income of a taxpayer is "income" for the year, plus or minus the additions and deductions permitted under Division C. Hence, this provision sets out the first ordering rule in the determination of taxable income. ITA: 2(2)

This is illustrated as follows:

Division B income or "income for tax purposes"

Less:

Division C deductions

Equals:

Taxable income

Once income for tax purposes (Division B income) has been determined, adjustments are made to this amount by the Division C additions and deductions according to the ordering rules (applicable to individuals) for this division (see Exhibit 1-4, which highlights some of these deductions). The result is taxable income which is the base for the application of tax rates to determine income tax. ITA: 111.1

Tax credits reduce the tax computed in Division E. An ordering rule for these tax credits is provided (see Exhibit 1-5). All of these tax credits are often referred to as non-refundable tax credits, because any excess of these credits over tax payable is not available for refund. Chapter 10 will provide a full discussion of Division C deductions and Division E non-refundable tax credits. ITA: 118.92

EXHIBIT 1-4

Ordering Rules Applicable to Individuals for Division C Section 111.1

Sec. 110	—Sundry deductions such as employee stock option and home relocation loan deductions
Sec. 110.2	—Lump-sum payments
Sec. 111	—Various loss carryovers arising from Division B calculations for another year such as non-capital losses and net capital losses
Sec. 110.6	—Capital gains deduction
Sec. 110.7	—Residing in prescribed zone

EXHIBIT 1-5

Ordering Rules Applicable to Individuals for Non-Refundable Tax Credits in Division E Section 118.92

Ssec. 118(1)	—Personal credits
Ssec. 118(2)	—Age credit
Sec. 118.7	—Employment Insurance premium and Canada Pension Plan contribution credits
Ssec. 118(3)	—Pension credit
Ssec. 118(10)	—Canada employment credit
Sec. 118.01	—Adoption expense tax credit
Sec. 118.02	—Transit pass tax credit
Sec. 118.03	—Child fitness tax credit
Sec. 118.031	—Child arts tax credit
Sec. 118.04	—Home renovation tax credit
Sec. 118.05	—First-time home buyer's tax credit
Sec. 118.06	—Volunteer firefighters tax credit
Sec. 118.3	—Mental or physical impairment credit
Sec. 118.61	—Unused tuition, textbook, and education credits
Sec. 118.5	—Tuition credit
Sec. 118.6	—Education and post-secondary textbook credits
Sec. 118.9	—Transfers to parent or grandparent
Sec. 118.8	—Transfer of unused credits to spouse
Sec. 118.2	—Medical expenses credit
Sec. 118.1	—Charitable gifts of individuals
Sec. 118.62	—Credit for interest on student loan
Sec. 121	—Dividend tax credit

Example Problem 1-1

The following list of income, losses, deductions, and tax credits has been determined correctly by a junior staff accountant prior to the preparation of the tax return for Ms. Beth Kelly.

Income (net)	
Employment	$60,000
Property (interest and dividends)	1,200
Taxable capital gains (net of allowable capital losses)	7,500
Pension income	5,000
Deductions and Losses	
Moving expenses	$600
Business loss	3,100
Carry forward Losses and Tax Credits	
Non-capital losses carried forward	$2,000
Net capital losses carried forward	6,000
Basic personal and spousal tax credits	3,311
Medical expenses tax credit	80
Charitable donations tax credit	202
Pension tax credit	300
Canada Pension Plan contributions tax credit	353
Employment Insurance premiums tax credit	134
Dividend tax credit	100
Canada employment credit	168

— *REQUIRED*

(A) From the structural outlines and exhibits on the preceding pages, determine the income, taxable income and basic federal tax net of non-refundable tax credits based upon the above correct information using the ordering rules in sections 3, 111.1, and 118.92. Assume federal tax before credits is $10,590 in 2013.

(B) Cross-reference each amount to the appropriate section of the Act. (Refer to Sectional List of the Act.)

— *SOLUTION*

Division B — Section 3

Par. 3(*a*) *Subdivision a*

Sec. 5, 6, 7, 8 Employment .... $ 60,000

	Subdivision b			
	Business income (net losses)		Nil	
	Property			
	Par. 12(1)(*c*), (*j*)	Interest and dividends	1,200	1,200
	Subdivision d			
	Ssec. 56(1)	Pension income		5,000
				$ 66,200
Par. 3(*b*)	*Subdivision c*			
	Sec. 38	Taxable capital gains net of allowable capital losses (not negative)		$ 7,500
				$ 73,700
Par. 3(*c*)	*Subdivision e*			
	Sec. 62	Moving expenses		(600)
				$ 73,100
Par. 3(*d*)	Sec. 9	Business loss		(3,100)
		Division B income		$ 70,000
Division C — Section 111.1				
	Par. 111(1)(*a*)	Non-capital losses carried over	$ (2,000)	
	Par. 111(1)(*b*)	Net capital losses carried over	(6,000)	(8,000)
Taxable income				$ 62,000
Division E — Section 118.92				
Federal tax before credits				$ 10,590
Less tax credits:				
Sec. 118		Personal tax credits	$ 3,311	
Sec. 118.7		CPP tax credit	353	
Sec. 118.7		EI premium tax credit	134	
Ssec. 118(3)		Pension tax credit	300	
Ssec. 118(10)		Canada employment credit	168	
Sec. 118.2		Medical expense credit	80	
Sec. 118.1		Donation tax credit	202	
Sec. 121		Dividend tax credit	100	(4,648)
Basic federal tax				$ 5,942

Several other non-refundable tax credits are available in Subdivision c of Division E, but these are deductible from basic federal tax as computed in the above example. These additional non-refundable tax credits include: foreign tax credits, political contribution tax credits and investment tax credits. ITA: 126, 127(3), 127(5)

The goods and services tax/harmonized sales tax (GST/HST) credit is a type of refundable tax credit available to individuals. This credit is actually paid separately in instalments to qualifying taxpayers. ITA: 122.5

¶1,300 GENERAL BACKGROUND ON ADMINISTRATION AND ENFORCEMENT OF THE ACT

The purpose of this section of the chapter is to provide a broad overview of how the tax legislation is administered and enforced. A discussion of the specific details of provisions dealing with these aspects of the law is deferred until Chapter 14 where it can be related more meaningfully to material covered in the intervening chapters.

¶1,310 Onus of Proof

In tax matters, it has been established by the Supreme Court of Canada in the case of *Johnston v. M.N.R.* that the taxpayer always has the burden of proving that an assessment is incorrect. Placing the burden of proof on the taxpayer is often referred to as a "reverse onus", because the usual burden of proof is on the Crown. In tax matters, the reverse onus is justified, since it is assumed that under our self-assessment system the taxpayer has all of the basic data under his or her own control.[20] This reverse onus may be challenged someday with a Supreme Court of Canada interpretation of the Charter of Rights and Freedoms. ITA: 163(3) [1948] 3 DTC 1182 (S.C.C.)

In the case of *M.N.R. v. Taylor*, it was established that the standard of proof in cases dealing with the Act need only be that of the "balance of probabilities" used in civil cases rather than the more rigorous standard of "beyond reasonable doubt" used in criminal proceedings. Where penalties are assessed, the burden of proof of the facts justifying the assessment of the penalties is transferred to the Minister. The standard of proof that the Minister must demonstrate is that of the "balance of probabilities". 61 DTC 1139 (Ex. Ct.)

¶1,320 Appeals

¶1,325 Initial steps

Prior to taking any formal steps in the appeal procedure, the taxpayer may consult with CRA officials responsible for his or her file in the appropriate Tax Services Office. Many differences can be resolved in this less formal manner. If, however, they cannot be resolved in this manner to the taxpayer's satisfaction, a notice of objection may be filed as the first formal step. There is no prescribed form at the present time. The notice of objection simply contains a statement of the facts and the reasons for objection. In the case of corporations or certain trusts, the notice of objection must be received by the CRA on or before the 90th day subsequent to the date of mailing of the notice of assessment. In the case of individuals or testamentary trusts, the deadline is the later of one year after the day the taxpayer is required to pay the balance of tax due for a year (i.e., April 30) and 90 days after the mailing of the notice of assessment for the year.

¶1,330 Tax Court of Canada

If the taxpayer is not satisfied with the CRA's decision on the Notice of Objection, he or she has 90 days, after the final decision rendered by the CRA on the Notice of Objection, to appeal to the Tax Court of Canada (T.C.C.) (formerly the Tax Appeal Board (T.A.B.) or the Tax Review Board (T.R.B.)). It is highly accessible, meeting in cities across Canada.

The Tax Court of Canada now has exclusive jurisdiction to hear appeals under the Act and certain other federal statutes. On appeal to the Tax Court, the taxpayer is given the option of an "informal procedure" or a "general procedure".

¶1,330.10 *Informal procedure*

The informal procedure may be elected when the amount of federal tax and penalties in issue for one taxation year is $12,000 or less or when the amount of the losses is $24,000 or less. [There is a proposal (not legislated at the time of writing) to increase these limits from $12,000/$24,000 to $25,000/$50,000.] The only requirement of the informal procedure is that the appeal is submitted in writing. Court rules of evidence are flexible and hence, the taxpayer can represent himself or herself or be represented by an agent (i.e., any individual) who may or may not be a lawyer. However, the taxpayer cannot appeal on questions of fact from a Tax Court decision reached through the informal procedure and the decision cannot be used as a precedent in subsequent cases. Judicial review of a judgment under the informal procedure lies with the Federal Court of Appeal (F.C.A.) on errors of law or erroneous findings of fact made in a perverse or capricious manner.

[20] This onus of proof was applied in the case of *Violi v. M.N.R.*, 80 DTC 1191 (T.R.B.).

¶1,330.20 *General procedure*

Where the general procedure is chosen in the Tax Court of Canada, the Court will be bound by strict rules of evidence. The taxpayer can only represent himself or herself or be represented by legal counsel.

¶1,335 Federal Court of Appeal

From the general procedure, either the taxpayer or the CRA can appeal the decision of the Tax Court to the Federal Court of Appeal and the Tax Court decision can be used as a precedent in other cases. This appeal must be made within 30 days from the date of the Tax Court decision.

¶1,340 Supreme Court of Canada

The ultimate court of appeal for tax cases in Canada is the Supreme Court of Canada (S.C.C.). According to subsections 31(2) and (3) of the *Federal Court Act*, an appeal can be made to the Supreme Court only if the Federal Court decides that the issue should be referred to the Supreme Court, or if the Supreme Court authorizes the appeal. At this level, questions of legal interpretation are raised rather than questions of fact alone. Not many cases on tax matters are given leave to appeal to the Supreme Court of Canada.

¶1,350 Administration and Enforcement

While the Department of Finance formulates tax policy, the CRA controls, regulates, manages and supervises the income tax system. Direct contact between the taxpayer and the CRA is generally made through one of the almost 30 Tax Services Offices. Trained assessors and special investigators who conduct desk audits of an individual's return or field audits of business returns are located in these offices.

The Head Office in Ottawa serves to maintain efficiency and uniformity of treatment across Canada, by supervising and directing the activities of the Tax Services Offices. In addition, a number of regional Taxation Centres are maintained to do routine operations and the initial processing of all individual income tax returns among other things.

¶1,360 Tax Evasion, Avoidance, and Planning

It is important to distinguish the terms "tax evasion", "tax avoidance" and "tax planning". Generally, tax evasion involves knowingly reporting tax that is less than the tax payable under the law with an attempt to deceive by omitting revenue, fraudulently claiming deductions (such as claiming personal expenses in calculating income), or failing to use all of the true facts of a situation. This is clearly illegal and can be prosecuted as such. Tax evasion IC 73-10R3
is enforced under both criminal law (the imposition of a fine and possibly imprisonment) and civil law (payment of the tax, applicable interest, and penalties imposed by the Act). An Information Circular provides a description of the consequences of tax evasion.

Tax avoidance is generally considered to arise in cases in which the taxpayer has legally circumvented the law resulting in the reduction or elimination of tax through a scheme or series of transactions which do not truly reflect the real facts. Although such tax avoidance is not illegal, the CRA will challenge it by various available means. Tax avoidance transactions do not have a *bona fide* business purpose and usually involve a misuse of the provisions of the Act read as a whole.

Finally, the CRA suggests that tax planning involves cases of tax reduction or elimination that are clearly provided for or not specifically prohibited in the law in a manner that is genuine and open within the framework of the law. For example, certain corporate reorganizations to shield business assets from liability are specifically allowed and can favourably reduce taxes payable. It is not only legal to undertake tax planning for clients, it is a proper and ethical use of the professional accountant's skills.

Despite these statements which attempt to distinguish the terms, there are undoubtedly judgments that must be made in distinguishing between cases of tax evasion and tax avoidance and between cases of tax avoidance and tax planning.

EXHIBIT 1-6
Legal and Illegal Methods of Reducing Tax

	Tax Planning	Tax Avoidance	Tax Evasion
Taxpayer goal	To favourably reduce taxes payable within the object and spirit of the law	Deliberate planning of events and transactions to circumvent the law and avoid paying taxes	To avoid taxes by failing to disclose complete and accurate information
Legality	Legal	Not illegal; Transactions can be ignored if successfully challenged	Illegal; Criminal offence; Civil wrongdoing
Penalty	None	Arrears and interest plus taxes owing and possible penalties owing	Fine, possible imprisonment, arrears, interest plus taxes, and civil penalties

The Act contains a general anti-avoidance rule (GAAR). In the words of the explanatory notes accompanying Bill C-139 which introduced the GAAR, issued on June 30, 1988, the rule is: ITA: 245

> intended to prevent abusive tax avoidance transactions or arrangements, but at the same time is not intended to interfere with legitimate commercial and family transactions. Consequently, the new rule seeks to distinguish between legitimate tax planning and abusive tax avoidance and to establish a reasonable balance between the protection of the tax base and the need for certainty for taxpayers in planning their affairs.[21]

¶1,400 INTRODUCTION TO THE GOODS AND SERVICES TAX (GST)/HARMONIZED SALES TAX (HST)

¶1,410 Overview and Basic Concepts

The GST was implemented on January 1, 1991, at a rate of 7%, to replace the federal sales tax system, which was riddled with inequities and inconsistent administrative practice, and which often led to distortions in business practices in the Canadian economy. The GST was intended to correct many of these deficiencies and to fulfill certain revenue objectives of the federal government.

The GST rate was reduced from 7% to 6%, effective July 1, 2006. The GST rate was then reduced to the current rate of 5%, effective January 1, 2008.

The HST was first implemented on April 1, 1997, in the provinces of Nova Scotia, New Brunswick, and Newfoundland and Labrador. In these provinces, the HST rate was originally 15% (8% provincial component and 7% federal GST component). Effective July 1, 2006, the HST rate was reduced from 15% to 14%, when the GST rate was reduced from 7% to 6%. Effective January 1, 2008, the HST rate was further reduced from 14% to 13%, when the GST rate was reduced from 6% to 5%. The HST is currently imposed at a rate of 13% (8% provincial component and 5% federal GST) in the latter two provinces. Nova Scotia increased its rate from 13% to 15%, effective July 1, 2010 (10% provincial component and 5% federal GST). In its April 2, 2012 provincial Budget, Nova Scotia announced that it will be reducing the provincial portion of the HST rate to 9%, effective July 1, 2014, and to 8%, effective July 1, 2015.

Effective July 1, 2010, Ontario and British Columbia adopted the HST. The HST rate in Ontario is 13%, consisting of an 8% provincial component and a 5% federal GST component, while the HST rate in British Columbia was 12%, consisting of a 7% provincial component and the 5% federal GST component.

[21] Reproduced in *Technical Notes to Bill C-139*, Special Report No. 851, Extra Edition, CCH Canadian Limited, June 30, 1988, p. 313.

The HST faced substantial opposition in British Columbia. The province held a referendum in the summer of 2011 to determine whether the HST would be abolished and the former 7% provincial sales tax reinstated. Following the referendum results, the British Columbia government announced on August 26, 2011 that it would exit the HST system and restore a provincial sales tax system. The target date was set for April 1, 2013. On February 17, 2012, British Columbia confirmed that it would make the transition as of April 1, 2013. On May 31, 2012, the *Provincial Sales Tax Act*, which reinstates a provincial sales tax in the province, received Royal Assent. As of April 1, 2013, HST ceased to apply in the province and supplies made in British Columbia became subject to the 5% GST and any applicable PST. Generally speaking, the transitional rules that were implemented reversed the transitional rules that applied at the time harmonization was introduced in British Columbia.

In its April 18, 2012 provincial Budget, Prince Edward Island announced plans to adopt the HST effective April 1, 2013, with a 9% provincial HST component. The province did in fact adopt the HST effective April 1, 2013.

The HST is administered by the CRA, as is the GST. Registrants account for GST/HST on a single form.

The intent of the discussion of GST/HST in this book is to give you a basic working knowledge of the rules. This book does not attempt to cover all the technical areas that are associated with the GST/HST. You are encouraged to do further research in this important area of taxation, which affects virtually every business organization in Canada. Unlike the former federal sales tax system, in which there were few accounting professionals who became actively involved in dealing with sales tax problems, the implementation of GST/HST has resulted in substantial work for tax and other accounting professionals. The adoption by additional provinces of the HST has resulted in additional work.

The GST/HST is a tax on the consumption of goods and services in Canada. The tax is collected by businesses (referred to as "registrants") who sell goods and provide services (collectively referred to as "supplies") in Canada. GST/HST is collected by registrants throughout the production and distribution chain. Any person who is engaged in a "commercial activity" is required to register and collect GST/HST. This includes persons who carry on business in Canada. "Business" is defined quite broadly in the legislation and does not require a profit motive. For example, charities and non-profit organizations are required to register if they engage in commercial activities, even if these entities are not subject to income tax.

The GST/HST is intended to be a tax on final consumption. Thus, while businesses are charged GST/HST on their purchases, they are entitled to a credit for this tax (referred to as an "input tax credit"). Input tax credits are available to the extent purchases are used in commercial activities. Businesses are required to remit to the government the difference between the amount of GST/HST collected or collectible and the amount of any input tax credit entitlement.

Supplies of goods and services are divided into three categories — taxable supplies, zero-rated supplies, and exempt supplies. "Taxable supplies" are subject to GST at the rate of 5%, or HST at the rate of 13% (in Ontario, New Brunswick, and Newfoundland and Labrador), 14% (Prince Edward Island), or 15% (in Nova Scotia), and the supplier is entitled to a full input tax credit, subject to certain temporary restrictions in Ontario and Prince Edward Island.[22] "Zero-rated supplies" are subject to tax at the rate of 0%, and the supplier may claim a full input tax credit on purchases used to provide these supplies. "Exempt supplies" do not attract GST/HST, and the supplier is not entitled to an input tax credit in respect of purchases used to provide these supplies.

The next two sections will expand on the concepts of "supply" and "input tax credits".

¶1,420 Supplies

The concept of "supply" is essential to an understanding of GST/HST. While in many cases the term will be synonymous with "sale", it has a much broader scope for GST/HST purposes.

---

[22] As noted above, British Columbia exited the HST on April 1, 2013, and transitional rules apply to certain transactions straddling that date. Nova Scotia has announced that it will be reducing the provincial portion of the HST rate to 9%, effective July 1, 2014, and to 8%, effective July 1, 2015; Prince Edward Island adopted the HST effective April 1, 2013, with a 9% provincial HST component.

The provision of a supply includes, among other things:

- sales or rentals of goods;
- rendering of services;
- leases, sales, or other transfers of real property;
- licensing of copyrights or patents; and
- barter and exchange transactions and gifts.

Once it is determined that there is a supply, a further determination must be made as to the type of supply. As discussed above, there are three types of supplies under the GST/HST: taxable, zero-rated, and exempt. A taxable supply is defined as a supply made in the course of a commercial activity, but does not include an exempt supply. Taxable supplies are subject to tax each time they are sold, with no exceptions. Most goods and services are taxable. However, zero-rated and exempt status is extended to a short list of goods and services for which the government has determined that GST/HST should not apply. Only limited relief from the tax is provided in the case of exempt supplies. Goods and services which are zero-rated are completely free of tax.

¶1,425 Zero-rated supplies

A short list of goods and services are subject to tax at the rate of 0%. These zero-rated supplies are still considered to be taxable supplies. Although this appears paradoxical, the distinction between taxable and exempt supplies is important. On taxable supplies, including zero-rated ones, the supplier is entitled to recoup the GST/HST paid on its inputs in the form of input tax credits, since input tax credits may be claimed on inputs used in commercial activities. Thus, even though GST/HST is not charged on the supply of zero-rated goods and services, the entitlement to input tax credits ensures that these supplies are effectively tax-free. The following are some examples of goods and services that are zero-rated:

- prescription drugs;
- medical devices;
- basic groceries; and
- exported goods and services.

¶1,430 Exempt supplies

Like suppliers of zero-rated supplies, suppliers of exempt goods and services are not required to collect GST/HST on these supplies. However, unlike zero-rated supplies, relief from GST/HST is not available on inputs used in the supply of exempt goods and services. The GST/HST paid by the supplier on purchases attributable to those exempt supplies is buried in the cost of the goods or services. For income tax purposes, however, the GST/HST paid on such inputs represents part of the cost of the inputs, and hence, is deductible.[23]

For example, when a bank purchases inputs to be used in the supply of financial services (which are exempt supplies), the bank is not entitled to recover the GST/HST incurred in respect of those inputs. Consequently, even though the bank does not charge GST/HST on the supply of those exempt financial services, the GST/HST incurred on the bank's purchases is buried in the cost of those financial services.[24] The bank will be able to deduct the GST/HST paid on these purchases for income tax purposes as part of the cost of the purchases.

[23] However, the May 2, 2006 federal Budget announced that interest and penalties incurred in respect of GST would no longer be deductible. These measures were implemented as of April 1, 2007.

[24] It is worth noting that because financial institutions are involved in a wide range of activities, some of which fall outside the definition of financial service and are thus taxable (and in respect of which input tax credits can be claimed), the rules relating to the supply of services by these institutions are quite complex. Uncertainties in terms of interpretation and application continue to arise.

The following are some examples of exempt goods and services:

- health care and child care services;
- educational services;
- most financial services; and
- sales of used residential housing and rentals of residential premises.

¶1,435 Point-of-Sale Rebates

Point-of-sale rebates are intended to provide consumers with targeted sales tax relief of the provincial portion of the HST (8% for Ontario, New Brunswick, and Newfoundland and Labrador; 9% for Prince Edward Island; and 10% for Nova Scotia[25]) on purchases of certain designated items. Generally, purchasers of these items automatically have their rebate paid or credited to them at the point of sale by the registrant supplier, and only pay the 5% federal GST component. If the rebate is not paid or credited at the time of sale, the purchaser may claim a rebate from the CRA within four years of the day the tax became payable. The rebates generally apply to designated items purchased from retailers located in the HST provinces, as well as to items imported into an HST province from outside of Canada and items brought into the HST province from a non-HST province.

The point-of-sale rebates are granted under the authority of provincial legislation, rather than under the *Excise Tax Act*, and the items eligible for rebate vary to some degree across the provinces.

Point-of-sale rebates of the provincial component of the HST are available in each of the HST provinces on purchases of printed books. This rebate is also available in respect of composite books, which are books packaged with read-only medium or a right to access a website, as well as audio recordings of books, and bound or unbound printed versions of scripture of any religion. A point-of-sale rebate of the provincial component of the HST paid on qualifying children's goods is available to consumers in Ontario, Prince Edward Island, and Nova Scotia (and formerly in British Columbia) only.[26] A point-of-sale rebate of the provincial component of the HST paid on qualifying feminine products is available to consumers in Ontario and Nova Scotia (and formerly in British Columbia) only. A rebate of the provincial component of the HST paid on qualifying residential energy purchases is available to consumers in Nova Scotia (and formerly in British Columbia) only. A rebate of the provincial component of the HST paid on qualifying heating oil is available to purchasers in Prince Edward Island.

In addition, point-of-sale rebates for the Ontario portion of the tax are available for print newspapers and qualifying prepared food and beverages sold for $4 or less. Since September 1, 2010, status Indians, Indian bands, and Indian band councils have been granted a point-of-sale rebate on the Ontario portion of the tax on qualifying off-reserve purchases of property and services.

Point-of-sale rebates for the British Columbia portion of the tax were available for consumer purchases of qualifying motor fuels. Point-of-sale rebates only applied in British Columbia where the provincial portion of the HST was paid. As noted above, British Columbia exited the HST on April 1, 2013.

¶1,440 Input Tax Credits

An integral part of the GST/HST system is the entitlement to claim input tax credits on business purchases. This relieves business inputs of GST/HST and thus avoids the pyramiding of tax. In order to qualify for an input tax credit (ITC), the goods and services must have been purchased for use in a commercial activity. As the GST/HST is designed to be a tax on consumption to be borne by the end user, there are certain restrictions on the claiming of

[25] As noted above, British Columbia exited the HST on April 1, 2013. Nova Scotia has announced that it will be reducing the provincial portion of the HST rate to 9%, effective July 1, 2014, and to 8%, effective July 1, 2015; Prince Edward Island adopted the HST effective April 1, 2013, with a 9% provincial HST component.

[26] In addition, currently a rebate for children's diapers applies only in Ontario and Nova Scotia, and a rebate for children's car and booster seats applies only in Ontario.

ITCs. These restrictions generally mirror the restrictions on claiming expenses under the *Income Tax Act*.

Input tax credits claimed by a registrant during a reporting period are subtracted from the tax collected on goods and services during the period to arrive at the net tax payable. Where input tax credits exceed tax payable, the registrant is entitled to a refund. An important concept related to ITCs is that purchases and sales need not be matched in order to claim an ITC. The credit can be claimed when the purchase is paid for or becomes due. Similarly, GST/HST paid on purchases of capital property need not be amortized over the life of the property (see Chapter 5).

Input tax credits are available where goods and services are purchased for use in a commercial activity. Conversely, if an input is not used at all in a commercial activity, no credit is allowed. A full credit is available where an input is used "exclusively" in a commercial activity. "Exclusively" is defined as "all or substantially all" and is interpreted by the CRA to mean 90% or more.

GST/HST registrants are entitled to claim input tax credits at the rate of 5% where only federal GST was paid or payable and the purchases are for use in a commercial activity. Registrants can recover 13% for the HST paid or payable on purchases made in the provinces of Ontario, New Brunswick, and Newfoundland and Labrador, 14% for the HST paid or payable on purchases made in the province of Prince Edward Island, and 15% for the HST paid or payable on purchases made in Nova Scotia, where those purchases are for use in a commercial activity,[27] subject to the temporary input tax restrictions in the provinces of Ontario and Prince Edward Island, discussed below in ¶1,445. The rate of recovery is not dependent on where the registrant is located.

There will be circumstances where a purchase is used in respect of a combination of taxable and exempt activities. In these cases, except where certain capital property is concerned, registrants will be required to apportion the ITC between the taxable (including zero-rated) and exempt activities. For example, consider the case of a hospital that purchases an industrial dishwasher for use in its kitchen. The dishwasher will be used to clean dishes from both patients and cafeteria patrons. Because meals provided to patients are exempt and cafeteria sales are taxable, the hospital will be required to apportion the ITC between the taxable and exempt activities.

The legislation does not prescribe allocation methods for use in apportioning ITCs. As long as the allocation is reasonable and is used consistently throughout the year, it will likely not be challenged.

Registrants will be required to maintain certain documentation to support ITCs. These requirements are discussed in Chapter 14.

¶1,445 Restricted Input Tax Credits

When they harmonized with the federal GST, the provinces of British Columbia and Ontario both implemented temporary input tax credit restrictions for large businesses similar to those that apply under the QST regime in Quebec. Large businesses generally include businesses with annual sales in excess of $10 million, and most financial institutions. Excluded from the application of these rules are farming businesses (businesses whose chief source of income is from farming activities, as defined in the *Income Tax Act*) and public service bodies (non-profit organizations, charities, municipalities, school authorities, public colleges and universities, and hospital authorities).

As originally enacted, during the first eight years of the application of the HST in Ontario and British Columbia, large businesses were required to recapture a portion of the 8% or 7% provincial component of their total input tax credits for HST paid or payable on specified property and services acquired, or brought into those provinces for use therein.

[27] As noted above, British Columbia exited the HST on April 1, 2013, and GST at the rate of 5% applies where tax is paid or payable after March 31, 2013. Nova Scotia has announced that it will be reducing the provincial portion of the HST rate to 9%, effective July 1, 2014, and to 8%, effective July 1, 2015; Prince Edward Island adopted the HST effective April 1, 2013, with a 9% provincial HST component.

These recapture requirements were to be phased out over the eight-year period. For the first five years, beginning on July 1, 2010, the rules required large businesses to recapture 100% of the provincial component of their British Columbia and Ontario HST input tax credits; the recapture rate was to be reduced by 25% over each of the following three years, and was to be completely phased out by July 1, 2018. This phase out still applies in Ontario. However, because British Columbia exited the HST on April 1, 2013, the recapture requirements apply in that province only where the provincial component of the HST was paid and thus will not apply for the entire duration of the eight-year period as originally planned.

The recapture requirements also apply in Prince Edward Island, which harmonized effective April 1, 2013. For the first five years that the HST is in effect in Prince Edward Island, the recapture rate is 100% of the provincial component of the HST. The recapture requirement will then be phased out by reducing the rate of recapture in equal increments over the remaining three years.

Specified property and services include items such as

- energy (except where purchased by farms or used to produce goods for sale);
- telecommunication services other than Internet access or toll-free numbers;
- road vehicles weighing less than 3,000 kilograms (and parts and certain services) and, in Ontario only, motive fuel to power those vehicles; and
- meals and entertainment.

¶1,450 Note on Organization of Legislation and Availability of Interpretive Sources

It is important in the study of the GST/HST to become familiar with the organization, structure and coverage of the *Excise Tax Act* (ETA). This knowledge is vital to the resolution of GST/HST problems.

The ETA is divided into 12 Parts, most of which represent specific types of tax, including the GST/HST, and 12 Schedules.[28] As in the *Income Tax Act*, for ease of reference, provisions are numbered, separating various elements of the provision. The history footnotes to each provision of the ETA are important to determine when the provision is applicable and what transitional rules, if any, apply.

As noted above, the ETA also contains 12 Schedules, which must be read in conjunction with the other provisions of the ETA. References to the provisions of the Schedules are read somewhat differently than references to the other provisions of the ETA. For example, consider the following reference:

V, VI, 20(*e*)(ii)

The first upper case Roman numeral refers to a Schedule and the second upper case Roman numeral refers to a Part. The number 20 refers to a section and the letter (*e*) refers to a paragraph. The lower case Roman numeral (ii) refers to a subparagraph. The above reference would be called Schedule V, Part VI, subparagraph 20(*e*)(ii).

In addition to the ETA, the GST/HST Regulations form part of the law and are set out to handle various specific situations and to carry on the general purposes and provisions of the ETA. Unlike the ETA, though, these regulations may be passed by Order-in-Council without ratification by Parliament. Forms issued by the CRA and officially prescribed by legislation may provide some insights to the interpretation of a provision in the legislation.

Additional sources also exist to provide assistance in interpreting the legislation. First, the CRA provides some explanatory information through a series of publications. These publications include GST/HST Memoranda, which are grouped under various topic headings and contain the CRA's interpretations of specific provisions of the ETA and outline its administrative practices. In addition, the CRA issues Technical Information Bulletins (TIBs) and Policy Statements, which are intended to provide current information on new policy or policy changes on a timely basis. Draft Policy Statements are also issued by the CRA, although

[28] The ETA also contains the legislation for the harmonized sales tax (HST).

these statements are subject to further review before being adopted as the CRA's policy. As well, various pamphlets, booklets and guides which provide general information, often targeted for specific groups of taxpayers, are issued from time to time. Based on the income tax jurisprudence referred to earlier in this chapter, publications of this nature, although not legally binding, may be considered by the courts. As taxpayers have been appealing decisions of the CRA through the court system, case law which provides an additional important source of interpretation for the GST/HST continues to evolve.

The Department of Finance issued explanatory notes to explain the GST/HST provisions when the legislation was first introduced as well as when amendments to the legislation have been introduced in the House of Commons. Finally, an authoritative book, article or tax service may also provide interpretive assistance.

The following discussion will focus on the structure of the ETA itself.

¶1,455 Excise Tax Act structure — Parts

Part I — Insurance Premiums Other Than Marine	ETA: 3–7
Part II — Air Transportation Tax	ETA: 8–21
Part II.1 — Telecommunication Programming Services Tax	ETA: 21.1–21.21
Part II.2 — Telecommunication Services Tax	ETA: 21.22–21.34
Part III — Excise Taxes on Cosmetics, Jewellery, Radios, etc.	ETA: 22–24
Part IV — Repealed	
Part V — Repealed	
Part V.1 — Repealed	
Part VI — Consumption or Sales Tax	ETA: 42–58
Part VII — General	ETA: 58.1–116
Part VIII — Transitional	ETA: 117–121.1
Part IX — Goods and Services Tax	ETA: 122–368

As can be seen from the titles of the various Parts set out above, the ETA imposes a number of taxes other than GST. This text will concentrate on the GST rules which are set out in Part IX of the ETA and will not examine the other taxes imposed under the ETA. The structure of Part IX of the ETA is set out below.

¶1,460 Structure of Part IX of the Excise Tax Act — GST/HST legislation

Division I — Interpretation ETA: 123–164.2

This Division contains a number of definitions and basic interpretive rules that are important to an overall understanding of the GST/HST.

Division II — Goods and Services Tax ETA: 165–211

Division II is the longest of the Divisions in Part IX. It contains rules which set out the rate of tax, the liability for tax, and the circumstances in which tax paid on inputs used in the supply of goods and services may be recovered. This Division contains the following four subdivisions:

Subdivision a — Imposition of Tax	ETA: 165–168
Subdivision b — Input Tax Credits	ETA: 169–170
Subdivision c — Special Cases	ETA: 171–194
Subdivision d — Capital Property	ETA: 195–211

Division III — Tax on Importation of Goods ETA: 212–216

As the title suggests, Division III sets out the rules relating to the liability for GST/HST on the importation of goods.

Division IV — Tax on Imported Taxable Supplies ETA: 217–220

This Division sets out rules for determining when GST/HST is payable in respect of imported services and intellectual property.

Division IV.1 — Tax on Property and Services Brought into a Participating Province ETA: 220.01–220.09

This Division sets out rules for the self-assessment of the provincial component of the harmonized sales tax (HST) in certain circumstances, where property or services are brought into a participating HST province.

Division V — Collection and Remittance of Division II Tax ETA: 221–251

Division V sets out the various requirements in respect of the collection and remittance of tax. The rules relating to the requirement to register are also contained in this Division. Division V contains the following five subdivisions:

Subdivision a — Collection ETA: 221–224.1

Subdivision b — Remittance of Tax ETA: 225–237

Subdivision c — Returns ETA: 238–239

Subdivision d — Registration ETA: 240–242

Subdivision e — Fiscal Periods and Reporting Periods ETA: 243–251

Division VI — Rebates ETA: 252–264

Division VI sets out the rules for claiming rebates of GST/HST paid on purchases in a variety of circumstances.

Division VII — Miscellaneous ETA: 265–274.2

Division VII sets out a number of miscellaneous provisions, including a general anti-avoidance provision. The three subdivisions in Division VII are as follows:

Subdivision a — Trustees, Receivers and Personal Representatives ETA: 265–270

Subdivision b — Amalgamations and Windings-up ETA: 271–272

Subdivision b.1 — Partnerships and Joint Ventures ETA: 272.1–273

Subdivision b.2 — Export Distribution Centres ETA: 273.1

Subdivision b.3 — Information Return for Financial Institutions ETA: 273.2

Subdivision c — Anti-Avoidance ETA: 274–274.2

Division VIII — Administration and Enforcement ETA: 275–335

Division VIII sets out various rules for administering the Act and enforcing its provisions. The seven subdivisions in Division VIII are as follows:

Subdivision a — Administration ETA: 275–277.1

Subdivision b — Returns, Penalties and Interest ETA: 278–285.1

Subdivision c — General ETA: 286–295

Subdivision d — Assessments, Objections and Appeals ETA: 296–312

Subdivision e — Collection ETA: 313–325

Subdivision f — Offences ETA: 326–332

Subdivision g — Evidence and Procedure ETA: 333–335

Division IX — Transitional Provisions ETA: 336–347

The GST came into effect on January 1, 1991. This Division contains a number of transitional rules intended to ensure an orderly transition from the federal sales tax system to the GST.

Division X — Transitional Provisions for HST Participating Provinces ETA: 348–363.2

The harmonized sales tax (HST) came into effect on April 1, 1997 in New Brunswick, Nova Scotia, and Newfoundland and Labrador. This Division contains transitional rules to deal with the implementation of the HST in those provinces. The four subdivisions of Division X are as follows:

Subdivision a — Interpretation	ETA: 348
Subdivision b — Application	ETA: 349
Subdivision c — Transition	ETA: 350–361
Subdivision d — Special Case	ETA: 362–363.2

Division XI — Tax Inclusive Pricing Repealed

¶1,465 Schedules to the Excise Tax Act

Schedule I	—[Rates of Excise Tax]
Schedule II	—Repealed
Schedule II.1	—Specific Tax Rates on Petroleum Products
Schedule III	—[Goods Exempt from FST]
Schedule III.1	—Goods Sold by Deemed Manufacturers or Producers
Schedule IV	—[Reduced Rate on Construction Materials]
Schedule V	—Exempt Supplies
Schedule VI	—Zero-Rated Supplies
Schedule VII	—Non-Taxable Importations
Schedule VIII	—Participating Provinces and Applicable Tax Rates
Schedule IX	—Supply in a Province
Schedule X	—Non-Taxable Property and Services for Purposes of Division IV.I of Part IX

Schedules V through VII relate to the GST/HST. Schedule V sets out those supplies that are exempt from GST/HST. Schedule VI sets out those supplies that are zero-rated, i.e., subject to tax at the rate of zero per cent. Schedule VII sets out a list of imported goods that are not subject to GST/HST.

¶1,850 EXERCISES

Exercise 1

ITA: 8, 15, 20, 38, 69, 81, 108, 150

For each of the following items, identify the appropriate provision of the Act which deals with the item listed. Be as specific as possible in citing the reference to the Act, i.e., Part, Division, Subdivision, Section, Subsection, etc. Use of the Sectional List at the beginning of CCH edition of CANADIAN INCOME TAX ACT and/or the Topical Index at the end of the book may be helpful. However, using the DVD included with this text may provide faster search results.

(A) Definition of "taxable capital gain".

(B) Deduction for certain annual professional membership dues paid by an employee.

(C) Taxability of payments received as income from property acquired as personal injury award.

(D) Deductibility of an expense based on its magnitude.

(E) Definition of a "parent" under the Act.

(F) Definition of an *"inter vivos"* trust.

(G) Deadline for filing of a tax return for a deceased person.

(H) Taxability of a benefit received from a corporation by a shareholder.

(I) Transaction price in a non-arm's length disposition of property.

(J) Deductibility of fees for investment advice.

Exercise 2

ITA: Divisions B and C

Mr. Malcolm Miller has provided you with a list of various sources of income, losses, deductions, and credits for the purpose of determining his basic federal tax.

Income (net):	
Business income	$10,000
Property income	3,000
Retiring allowance from a former employer	20,000
Employment income from new employer	60,000
Taxable capital gains (net of allowable capital losses)	20,000
Deduction and Losses:	
Rental property loss	4,000
Carry forward Losses and Tax Credits:	
Canada Pension Plan contributions tax credit	353
Non-capital losses from a previous year	4,000
Education and textbook tax credits transfer from son	80
Net capital losses from a previous year	5,000
Basic personal and spousal tax credits	3,311
Employment Insurance premiums tax credit	134
Tuition tax credit for night course on computer applications	68
Charitable gifts tax credit	550
Canada employment tax credit	168

— *REQUIRED*

(A) Determine the income, taxable income and basic federal tax based on the above correct information using the ordering rules in sections 3, 111.1, and 118.92. Assume that federal tax before credits is $19,464 in 2013.

(B) Cross-reference each amount to the appropriate section of the Act.

Exercise 3

ITA: 212(1)

Identify the following components of subsection 212(1):

(A) the person who is the subject of the provision,

(B) the activity, event, or condition that must be met for the provision to apply,

(C) the consequences of the activity or event to the person who is the subject of the provision, and

(D) the time frame for the application of the provision.

¶1,875 ASSIGNMENT PROBLEMS

Problem 1

Identify the provision of the Act which deals with each of the following items. Be as specific as possible in citing the reference to the Act (Part, Division, Subdivision, Section, Subsection, etc.). Use of the sectional list at the beginning of the CCH edition of the Act and/or the topical index at the end of the book may be helpful. However, using the DVD included with this text may provide faster search results.

(A) Definition of a "person".

(B) Tax credit for donation made by a Canadian resident individual to a Canadian university.

(C) Definition of "balance-due day".

(D) Taxability of group term life insurance premiums paid by an employer on behalf of an employee.

(E) Definition of "capital dividend".

(F) Computation of income tax instalments for individuals.

(G) Definition of a "qualified small business corporation share".

(H) Prescribed requirement to file an information return for a corporation paying a dividend.

(I) Definition of a "testamentary trust".

(J) The calculation of a benefit associated with an interest-free loan from an employer to an employee.

(K) Definition of a "disposition" of non-depreciable capital property.

(L) Limitation on deduction of RRSP administration fees.

(M) General limitation on the amount of deductible expenses.

(N) Deduction from taxable income for taxable dividends that were received by a Canadian corporation.

(O) Tax payable on excess contributions to an RRSP.

Problem 2

ITA: 245; Division B, C

Ms. Irene Vanburg had a tumultuous year in 2013. She broke her engagement early in the year and quit her job. She moved to a resort area to take a waitress job and to start up a fitness instruction business. She has had the following items correctly calculated and classified as either inclusions, deductions or tax credits for the purposes of determining her taxable income and federal tax.

Income (net):	
Employment Insurance benefits	$ 600
Employment income	32,600
Property income	775
Rental property income	975
Taxable capital gain (net of allowable capital losses)	100
Retiring allowance from previous employer	800
Deductions and Losses:	
Business loss	(275)
Deductions, Losses, and Tax Credits:	
Charitable gifts tax credit	26
Child care expenses	1,800
Canada Pension Plan contributions tax credits on employment earnings	216
Medical expenses tax credit	9
Moving expenses	1,700
Non-capital losses from previous year	600
Personal tax credit	1,656
Employment Insurance premiums tax credit	92
Canada employment credit	168

— *REQUIRED*

(A) Determine the income, taxable income and basic federal tax based on the above correct information using the ordering rules in sections 3, 111.1, and 118.92. Assume federal tax before credits is $4,721 in 2013.

(B) Cross-reference each amount to the appropriate section of the Act.

Problem 3

ITA: 2

Many words and terms used in the Act have very specific interpretations. Awareness of these interpretations is fundamental to understanding the scheme and application of the Act. These interpretations come from various sources. The primary source is statutory definition; that is, the term is explicitly defined in the Act. Common law principles also determine interpretations for terms. Many court cases have centred on the interpretation of specific words or phrases which were not explicitly defined in the statute. Once such terms are interpreted by the Courts, that interpretation becomes standard for that term. If a term is neither defined in the statute, nor the subject of a common law definition, the word or term must be assigned the meaning provided by everyday language. The definition is often that which can be found in a common dictionary.

Division A of Part I of the Act outlines who is liable for tax. This Division is a fundamental building block for the Act as it defines to whom the Act will apply. Therefore, it is essential that the terms used in this Division are clearly understood.

— *REQUIRED*

(A) Identify and define those words and terms found in section 2 of the Act, in the order of their use, which you believe require definition. Indicate the references in the Act to the source of the definition for those words or terms which you have so identified. If you use the DVD included with this text the words that are defined elsewhere in the Act are highlighted in red.

(B) Identify the following components of subsection 2(3):

(i) the person who is the subject of the provision,

(ii) the activity, event, or condition that must be met for the provision to apply,

(iii) the consequences of the activity or event to the person who is the subject of the provision, and

(iv) the time frame for the application of the provision.

Chapter 2

Liability for Tax

TOPICS DISCUSSED

LEARNING GOALS

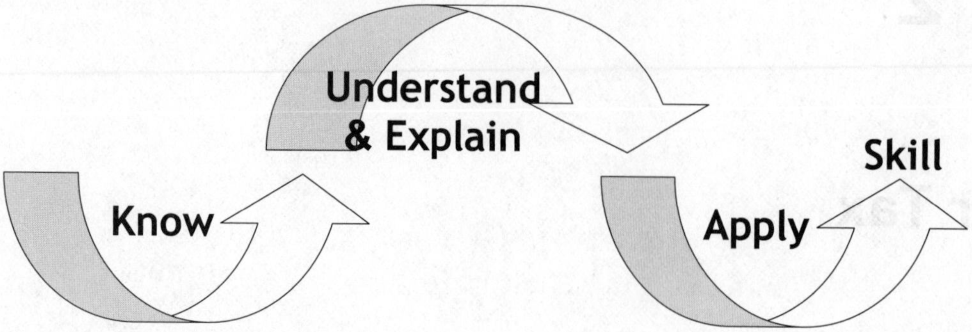

Know

By the end of this chapter you should know the basic provisions of the *Income Tax Act*, *Excise Tax Act*, and case law that relate to liability for tax and residency. Completing the Review Questions (¶2,800) and Multiple Choice Questions (¶2,825) is a good way to learn the technical provisions.

Understand and Explain

You should understand and be able to explain when an individual or a corporation is resident in Canada and whether they are liable for income tax or GST/HST. Completing the Exercises (¶2,850) is a good way to deepen your understanding of the material.

Apply

You should be able to use your knowledge and understanding of residency and liability for income tax in a practical fact situation to determine whether a person is or is not liable for income tax. Completing the Assignment Problems (¶2,875) and the Advisory Case (¶2,880) is an excellent way to develop your ability to apply the material in increasingly complex situations.

OVERVIEW

This chapter deals with liability for Canadian income tax and the goods and services tax/harmonized sales tax (GST/HST). The chapter addresses the question of who is liable to pay the tax. Whether it is to the taxpayer's advantage or disadvantage to be a resident/non-resident will depend upon the tax laws of each jurisdiction in which the taxpayer's income is earned, the interaction of these laws and any relevant tax treaty. Many non-tax factors may also impact the choice.

The following chart provides an overview of the provisions of the *Income Tax Act* covered by this chapter.

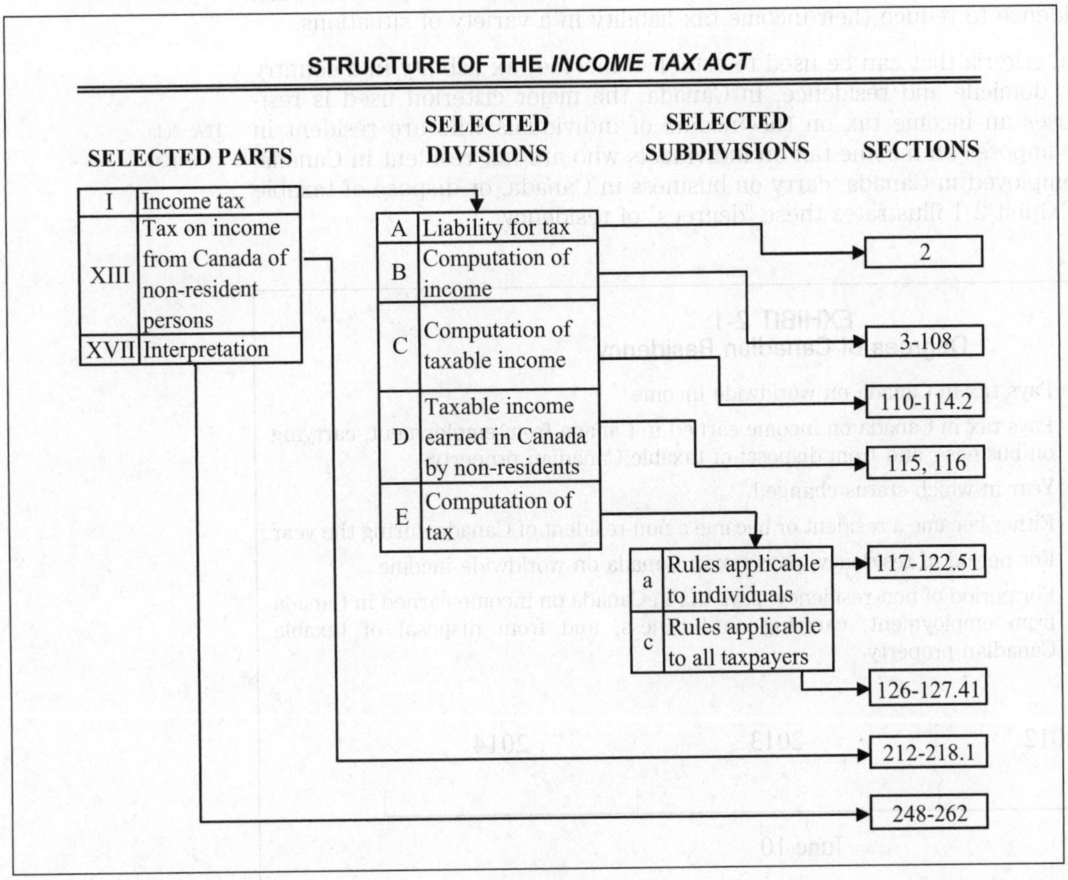

¶2,000 LIABILITY OF INDIVIDUALS FOR INCOME TAX

The major issue in this area is the residence of an individual. Residency has become more and more important in recent years as taxpayers with increased mobility attempt to establish residence or non-residence to reduce their income tax liability in a variety of situations.

There are several criteria that can be used to establish income tax liability in a country including citizenship, domicile and residence. In Canada, the major criterion used is residence. The Act imposes an income tax on the income of individuals who are resident in Canada. ITA: 2(1) The Act also imposes an income tax on individuals who are not resident in Canada, ITA: 2(3) but only if they are employed in Canada, carry on business in Canada, or dispose of taxable Canadian property. Exhibit 2-1 illustrates these "degrees" of residency.

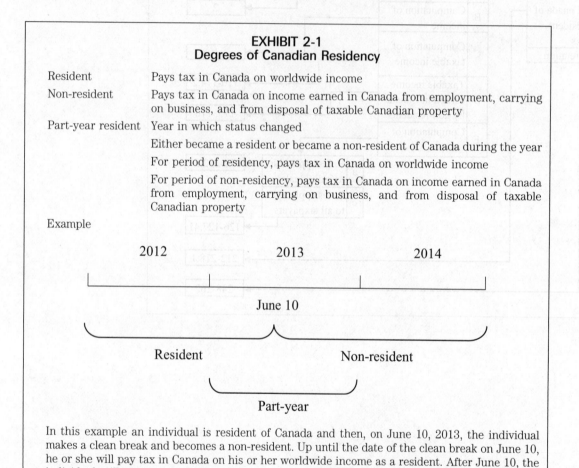

EXHIBIT 2-1
Degrees of Canadian Residency

Resident	Pays tax in Canada on worldwide income
Non-resident	Pays tax in Canada on income earned in Canada from employment, carrying on business, and from disposal of taxable Canadian property
Part-year resident	Year in which status changed
	Either became a resident or became a non-resident of Canada during the year
	For period of residency, pays tax in Canada on worldwide income
	For period of non-residency, pays tax in Canada on income earned in Canada from employment, carrying on business, and from disposal of taxable Canadian property

Example

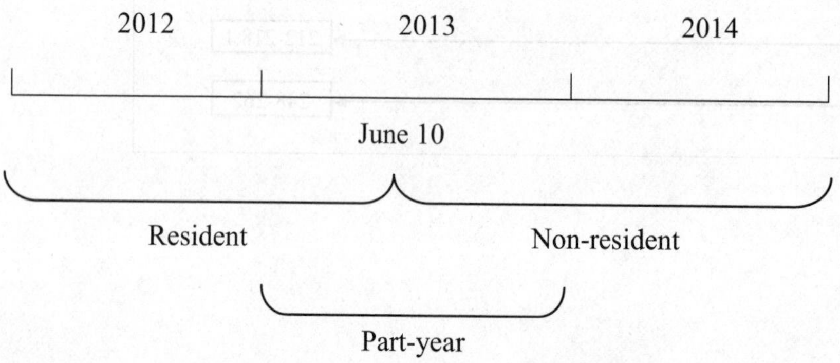

In this example an individual is resident of Canada and then, on June 10, 2013, the individual makes a clean break and becomes a non-resident. Up until the date of the clean break on June 10, he or she will pay tax in Canada on his or her worldwide income as a resident. After June 10, the individual will pay tax in Canada only as a non-resident. As a result, in 2013, he or she is considered a part-year resident, since he or she is a resident for only part of the year.

¶2,010 Liability of Individual Residents

The Act contains what is known as the charging provision for residents of Canada in ITA: 2(1) respect of income under Part I. The provision charges taxpayers with responsibility for paying the tax by the use of the words "an income tax shall be paid".

Read the following provision carefully and consider some of the key terms used in that subsection:

> An income tax shall be paid as required by this Act on the *taxable income* for each *taxation year* of every *person resident* in *Canada* at any time in the year.

As indicated in Chapter 1, the word "income" is not defined in the Act. The phrase "taxable income" is a technical phrase with a limited and special meaning and the phrase "taxation year" is defined. Note that the word "person" is defined to include both an individual and a corporation. The word "resident" is not fully defined in the Act and, as a result, is the subject of discussion in much of this chapter. However, a definition of "Canada" is provided for the purposes of the Act. The existence of a definition for a term or phrase used in a provision like section 2 can be found by checking the "Related Sections" footnotes to the section in the CCH edition of the Act, where defined words or phrases are listed in quotation marks.

ITA: 2(2), 249(1)
ITA: 248(1)
ITA: 255

Canadian residents are taxed on their worldwide income. Thus, taxable income of a resident of Canada is subject to Canadian income tax regardless of the country in which the income is earned or generated. To avoid potential double taxation, Canada has negotiated a number of international reciprocal tax agreements which will be discussed in more detail later in this chapter. A key principle followed by these agreements is that the country in which the income is earned has priority in taxing that income and the country of which the taxpayer is a resident allows all or some part of the foreign tax paid as a credit against the domestic tax.

¶2,020 Canadian Resident

¶2,030 Common law concept of Canadian resident

A Canadian resident is taxed on his or her worldwide income for the full year. It is possible for a person to be considered a Canadian resident by virtue of principles of the common law or case law which have evolved over the years. Residence is determined by the application of these general principles to the facts of each case.

Consider the following fact situation presented to a British court.[1] The taxpayer had lived in England throughout her lifetime. For the year in question she stored her furniture, travelled on the Continent with no permanent abode in any one place, stayed in England only a short time, maintained a bank account in England and held no salaried position anywhere. The court held that she was resident in England. The court considered the relationship between a person's life and the place in which the taxpayer spent, at least, part of his or her time. A person's ties to a country need not be manifested in a permanent home.

In another British case,[2] the following facts were presented. A British subject gave up a leased house in England. He lived on the Continent in an apartment. He made visits of four or five months to London to obtain medical advice, to visit relatives or the graves of his parents, and to take part in certain religious observances. Again, the court held that he was resident in England. An important fact in this case was that he returned to the proximity of relatives and friends. It should be noted that the courts have determined that an individual can be resident in more than one country and that an individual must be resident in at least one country at any moment in time.

A key statement describing the residence of an individual under common law principles was made in a 1921 British decision[3] which described residence as "a continuing state of relationship between a person and a place which arises from the durable concurrence of a number of circumstances". Thus, facts must be found to establish the continuing state of relationship, that is, ties to the country. The landmark Canadian case in this area is *Thomson v. M.N.R.*, and another often cited case is that of *Meldrum v. M.N.R.* Both cases involved individuals who stayed in Canada for short periods of time on a regular basis. The courts considered facts relevant to establishing the "continuing state of relationship".

2 DTC 812 (S.C.C.)
50 DTC 232 (T.A.B.)

In the *Thomson* case, the taxpayer lived in Canada until 1923, when he decided to establish his home outside of Canada. From 1925 to 1931, he lived mainly in the United

2 DTC 812 (S.C.C.)

[1] *Reid v. C.I.R.*, [1926] 10 T.C. 673.

[2] *Levene v. C.I.R.*, [1928] A.C. 217.

[3] *Weymys v. Weymys*, [1921] Sess. Cas. 30, at p. 40.

States, paying few visits to Canada. From 1932 to 1941, inclusive, the taxpayer spent the summers in Canada occupying a large home with a staff of servants at Riverside, New Brunswick. During this time, he did not file Canadian tax returns. In 1941, the Department of National Revenue (now the Canada Revenue Agency) requested that he file a return for 1940, which he refused to do. The Department then assessed him for income tax. An appeal to the Exchequer Court of Canada was dismissed and the taxpayer then appealed to the Supreme Court of Canada. There his appeal was dismissed on the basis that there was nothing of a casual or non-permanent character about his residence in New Brunswick, even though he lived there for slightly less than 183 days in each year. Hence, he was "ordinarily resident" in Canada and not a mere "sojourner".

In the *Meldrum* case, the individual, a sea-captain living in New York and sailing between ports in the United States and Canada, bought a property in Nova Scotia near his Canadian port-of-call. The house was furnished and occupied by his married daughter, but the captain and his wife stayed there during the captain's annual two weeks of vacation, and the two best rooms in the house were regarded as theirs whenever they might choose to visit. The Tax Appeal Board allowed the captain's appeal. They found that a degree of permanence and substance had to be present to create the status of "resident". Such elements were not present in sufficient degree in the appellant's case to make him resident or ordinarily resident. On the facts, the captain was more properly described as a visitor and not a resident.

50 DTC 232 (T.A.B.)

¶2,032 Deemed resident — Sojourning

A deemed resident is taxed on his or her worldwide income for a full year. While the Act does not define resident or residence, it does deem an individual to be a resident if one of the conditions of a deeming rule is met. It is important to note the use of the word "deemed" in provisions of the Act. The effect is to establish a set of conditions and treat a taxpayer or an action in a manner desired by the legislation. In this case, a deemed resident will be treated like a resident and taxed on worldwide income. Were it not for this deeming provision, the individual may not be considered to be a resident and, in fact, might be a non-resident. This provision states, among other conditions, that a person is deemed to be resident in Canada throughout the taxation year if he or she "sojourned" in Canada in the year for an aggregate of 183 days or more. The Canada Revenue Agency's (CRA's) practice is to count any part of a day as a "day" for this purpose. The word "sojourn" has the connotation of a temporary visit rather than a permanent stay. It should be noted, however, that spending less than 183 days in Canada does not necessarily make an individual non-resident, if he or she is not merely visiting, but has more substantial residential ties, as discussed below.

ITA: 250(1)

Consider the following fact situation as an example of deemed residence. Traci resides in southern California from November 1 to April 30 of each year, with the exception of 21 days during that period which are spent in the Canadian Rockies marketing new product lines. From May 1 to October 31 of each year, Traci travels extensively in and out of Canada, marketing her ski apparel. During this year, Traci spent a total of 190 days in Canada and 15 days in Europe. In this case, Traci could be deemed to be a resident of Canada, because she sojourned in Canada for an aggregate of 183 days or more. As a result, she would be liable for tax in Canada on her worldwide income for the whole year.

¶2,035 Administrative practice

Income Tax Folio S5-F1-C1: Determining an Individual's Residence Status categorizes the type of facts that can be used for an individual to establish residential ties for a "continuing state of relationship". Many of these facts would appear to have held some importance in previous court decisions. However, it must be remembered that statements on administrative practice in an Interpretation Bulletin represent the opinion of the CRA and not the law.

Income Tax Folio S5-F1-C1 — Determining an Individual's Residence Status

- Maintaining a dwelling, whether owned or leased, suitable for year-round occupancy and available for occupation, would establish an important residential tie. However, the dwelling need not be vacant at all times. If it is rented to a non-arm's length person or to an arm's length person on terms and conditions that are not arm's length, then it may be considered to be available for the taxpayer's use.

- A spouse or common-law partner and other members of the immediate family remaining in Canada when an individual leaves would be regarded by the CRA as an important residential tie. A separation due to the breakdown of a relationship would, of course, reduce the significance of this factor if the individual, in leaving, severs other residential ties.

- Maintaining personal property and social ties in Canada would indicate a "continuing state of relationship" through secondary residential ties. Personal property remaining in Canada might include furniture, clothing, cars, and recreational vehicles. Maintaining provincial or territorial hospitalization and medical insurance coverage and a seasonal residence might also be an indication of residential ties. Social ties such as recreational and religious organization memberships in Canada could be used in a similar way depending on the reasons for maintaining such ties. Economic ties such as employment with a Canadian employer, active investment in a Canadian business and Canadian bank accounts, retirement savings plans, credit cards and securities accounts, are also regarded as secondary residential ties. Other such ties include: Canadian landed immigrant status or appropriate work permits, a Canadian passport, a Canadian driver's license, Canadian vehicle registration and membership in Canadian unions or professional organizations. It should be emphasized that none of the ties in this third category taken singly would be enough to determine Canadian residence. However, one or more of these ties in combination with others, particularly in the first two bulleted categories above, would make a strong package of ties indicating such residence. In making a determination of residence, it becomes important to give each fact an appropriate weighting according to its importance in the situation.

In order to establish that an individual is not a Canadian resident, the severance of residential ties with Canada and the establishment of residential ties elsewhere is important, although an individual can be a resident of more than one country. An argument for continuing residential ties can be made, in particular, when the return could have been foreseen because of the existence of, perhaps, a contract of employment on return. No particular length of absence results in an individual becoming a non-resident. Occasional, but not regular, return visits for personal or business reasons would not likely jeopardize the severance of Canadian residence.

¶2,040 Part-Year Resident

¶2,045 Applicable law

At any particular point in time, an individual is either a resident of Canada, with the income tax consequences discussed above, or a non-resident, with possible income tax consequences to be discussed.

"Part-year residence" describes the position of an individual in the year he or she either became or ceased to be a Canadian resident. Part-year residence can occur when an individual, having had full residential ties, leaves Canada during a year. Similarly, when an individual who did not have such ties for a prior period, comes to Canada during a year and establishes full residential ties, he or she would be considered to be a part-year resident for that year. The year of exit or entry is the year of part-year residence status.

A part-year resident is taxed in Canada on his or her worldwide income earned during the part of the year in which he or she was resident in Canada. Deductions in the computation of taxable income are allocated, if applicable, to the period of part-year residence. A similar allocation of amounts deductible as non-refundable tax credits may be made. These provisions require that during some other part of the year the taxpayer was not resident in Canada. This means that an individual will be taxed in Canada on his or her worldwide income for the period in a year during which he or she was a resident. This period constitutes

ITA: 114

ITA: 118.91

the taxpayer's taxation year for the computation of income taxable in Canada during the year. Were it not for these rules, an individual might be regarded as a resident for the full year and taxable on worldwide income for the whole year. Thus, the part-year residence rules provide an exception to the more general residence rules.

¶2,050 Clean break or fresh start: The concept

To break residential ties or establish residence, facts must be found to show that the person made either a "clean break" from Canada during the year or a "fresh start" in Canada during the year. An example of a "clean break" might involve a person who has resided in Canada and leaves Canada with his or her family and all of their belongings in, say, August of the year, severing all ties and indicating an intention not to return. If such a "clean break" or severing of ties can be established by the facts, then the individual becomes a non-resident after the "clean break". The CRA will consider a "clean break" to have been made on the latest of the date on which:

Income Tax Folio S5-F1-C1 — Determining an Individual's Residence Status

(a) the individual leaves Canada,

(b) the individual's spouse or common-law partner and/or dependants leave Canada, or

(c) the individual becomes a resident of the country to which he or she is immigrating.

If the ties that have existed are not considered by the facts to have been severed, then the individual remains a Canadian resident.

An example of a "fresh start" might involve a non-resident person who moves to Canada to take up residence in, say, April of the year. In both cases, the person would be in Canada for more than 183 days, but his or her stay in the country for the period in question would not be temporary, as required by the rule to deem an individual to be a resident.[4]

ITA: 250(1)(*a*)

Consider the following fact situation as an example of the contrast between a resident with continuing ties and a resident who has severed ties and become a non-resident. On October 15 of this year, Jeremy began his new career managing a foreign manufacturing business in Thailand. He left Canada on October 10 and worked on a temporary basis for two months, while still maintaining his home, car, and other personal belongings in Canada. On December 20 of this year, Jeremy returned home for two weeks to visit his relatives during the holiday season. Jeremy kept his provincial health care insurance and transferred his club membership to non-resident status. In this case, Jeremy would be considered to be a resident of Canada for the entire taxation year. To become a non-resident next year, Jeremy should sever most of his residential ties with Canada and demonstrate that he does not have a continuing state of relationship, i.e., continuing significant ties, with Canada. This might require that he cancel his provincial health care insurance plan, sell (or rent on a long-term basis) his home and car, and sell or move other personal belongings.

¶2,055 Liability of Non-Residents

¶2,060 General determination of liability

Subject to the provisions of an international tax agreement, a non-resident individual, who

ITA: 2(3)

(1) was employed in Canada,

(2) carried on business in Canada, or

(3) disposed of taxable Canadian property

at any time in the year or a previous year, is liable to pay income tax.

The base for this tax is his or her taxable income earned only in Canada.

[4] The cases of *Schujahn v. M.N.R.*, 62 DTC 1225 (Ex. Ct.), and *Truchon v. M.N.R.*, 70 DTC 1277 (T.A.B.), may illustrate the differences between deemed full-time and part-year resident.

The addition of the phrase "or a previous year" means that income earned in Canada by a non-resident but not received until a later year will be taxed in that later year when the non-resident might not be employed or carrying on business in Canada. Thus, tax cannot be avoided by deferring salaries or business income until a year when no income is earned in Canada. ITA: 115

It should be emphasized that a person who is a non-resident for the entire year cannot be a part-year resident. To be a part-year resident, there must be a period in which the person was resident and a period in which the person was a non-resident. ITA: 114, 118.91

A non-resident who earns income in Canada, other than from sources listed above, may still be subject to withholding tax. For example, a non-resident earning interest or dividends in Canada will have a 25% tax withheld at source under Part XIII of the Act. This withholding tax rate can then be modified by an income tax treaty, if any, between Canada and the taxpayer's country of residence. ITA: 212(1)

¶2,065 The meaning of carrying on business in Canada

The phrase "carrying on business" is not specifically defined in the *Income Tax Act*. The courts have tended to interpret the phrase as implying a continuous business activity.[5] A "business", on the other hand, is not required to involve a continuous business activity by virtue of its definition, which includes an "adventure or concern in the nature of trade". An adventure in the nature of trade can be simply described as a scheme to make a profit in the same manner as a person who is in that line of business.[6] The definition of "extended meaning of carrying on business" describes activities which, if engaged in by a non-resident person, will result in the non-resident being deemed to have been carrying on business. ITA: 248(1) ITA: 253

Generally speaking, merely soliciting orders makes a non-resident person liable to be deemed to be carrying on business. Normally, the main determinant of carrying on business in a place is the location in which the contract in a transaction is made, not the location of the offering of an item for sale as envisaged by the definition of the term "carrying on business". It should be noted that the courts have also looked beyond the place where the contract was concluded to the place where the operations occur from which the profits arise in substance. This is indicated by where payment is made or where the work is done or delivery of the goods is made. These factors indicate the place of performance of the contract. Recognize, however, that the specific activities listed in the definition of "carrying on business" override the common law principle of place of performance. ITA: 253

A non-resident offering something for sale in Canada through an employee who is a salesperson is carrying on business in Canada. On the other hand, a non-resident selling to an independent contractor like a Canadian-based retailer or wholesaler who resells the item in Canada is not carrying on business in Canada. Hence, the distinction between an employee and an independent contractor is important and will be explained more fully in Chapter 3. The distinction must be made on the facts of each case. These facts must establish the degree of responsibility enjoyed by the person who is soliciting orders or offering goods for sale. The courts have considered the following factors in this distinction:

(a) whether the parties describe or refer to their relationship as one of an independent contractor and a supplier;

(b) whether the alleged independent contractor carries on business in the name of the supplier or in his or her own name; and

(c) whether the independent contractor acts for other suppliers.

The greater the independence from the supplier and the greater the degree of responsibility, the greater is the likelihood that the situation involves a non-resident supplier selling to

[5] See *Tara Explorations & Development Co. Ltd. v M.N.R.*, 72 DTC 6288 (S.C.C.), affirming 70 DTC 6370 (Ex. Ct.).

[6] See *M.N.R. v. Taylor*, 56 DTC 1125 (Ex. Ct.), and IT-459.

an independent contractor such that the supplier is not carrying on business in Canada and, is, therefore, not taxable in Canada on business income earned in Canada.

Note that the use of words like "carried on" or "carrying on", "solicited", and "offered" implies a continuity of activity over a period of time. The courts have indicated that an isolated transaction, even one that is described in the definition of "carrying on business", does not fit the concept of continuity over time. Hence, continuity of activity may, depending on the facts, be necessary to establish a "carrying on" of business, unless the isolated transaction in Canada is part of the normal international business activities of the non-resident. On the other hand, the CRA has expressed the view, in a memorandum obtained under Access to Information legislation, that the activity could be carried on in Canada for only a short duration and still be considered to be carrying on business. ITA: 2(3)(*b*), 253

¶2,070 International Tax Treaties and Individuals

Canada has negotiated many reciprocal tax treaties with other countries with the objective of preventing the incidence of double taxation or tax avoidance. These situations may result from the overlapping of tax provisions applicable to persons subject to tax in the two jurisdictions which are parties in the treaty. The treaty of greatest significance is probably the Canada–U.S. Tax Convention[7] because of the considerable interrelationship of the two countries. The major provisions are described very briefly below.

¶2,075 Services

The provision regarding employees in the Canada–U.S. Tax Convention is typical of many treaties that Canada has negotiated with other countries. The provision deals with the taxation of income from employment and exempts a resident of Canada from U.S. taxation on salaries, wages and other similar remuneration derived from an employment in the United States under certain conditions. The conditions are: Cda-U.S. TT: Art. XV

(a) that the remuneration does not exceed US$10,000, or

(b) that the employee is present in the United States for a period not exceeding an aggregate of 183 days in any 12-month period starting or ending in the year and the remuneration is not borne by an employer who is a resident of the United States or by a "permanent establishment" or a "fixed base" which the employer has in the United States.

Note, however, that as a resident of Canada, the individual would be taxable in Canada on worldwide income, including that earned in the United States and exempt from taxation in the United States.

Another provision deals with income from independent personal services, i.e., from self-employment. For example, an individual who is resident in Canada would only be taxed in the United States if the individual has or had a "permanent establishment", regularly available to him or her in the United States. The tax in the United States would be limited to that on income attributable to the permanent establishment in the United States. The provision is reciprocal in relation to residents of the United States performing personal services in Canada under the same conditions. Cda-U.S. TT: Art. VII

A Canadian individual earning self-employed income in the United States will be taxed in the United States if they have a permanent establishment in the United States or one of the following two conditions is met: Cda-U.S. TT: Art. VII Cda-U.S. TT: Art. V

(a) Those services are performed in the U.S. by an individual who is present in the U.S. for a period or periods aggregating 183 days or more in any twelve-month period, and, during that period or periods, more than 50 percent of the gross active business revenues of the enterprise consists of income derived from the services performed in the U.S. by that individual; or

[7] *Canada–United States Income Tax Convention (1980)*, S.C. 1984, c. 20.

(b) The services are provided in the U.S. for an aggregate of 183 days or more in any twelve-month period with respect to the same or connected project for customers who are either residents of the U.S. or who maintain a permanent establishment in the U.S. and the services are provided in respect of that permanent establishment.

¶2,080 Resident and "tie-breaker" rules

For the purposes of the Convention, the term "resident" is defined to mean: Cda-U.S. TT: Art. IV, par. 1

> any person that, under the laws of [one country], is liable to tax therein by reason of his domicile, residence, citizenship, place of management, place of incorporation or any other criterion of a similar nature. . . .

Paragraph 2 provides "tie-breaker" rules where an individual can be considered by paragraph 1 to be a resident of both countries. In this case, the individual's residence is determined as follows:

(a) he or she is deemed to be a resident of the country in which he or she has a permanent home available; if he or she has a permanent home available in both countries or in neither country, he or she is deemed to be a resident of the country with which his or her personal and economic relations are closer (i.e., centre of vital interests);

(b) if the country in which the individual has his or her centre of vital interests cannot be determined, the individual is deemed to be a resident of the country in which he or she has an habitual abode;

(c) if the individual has an habitual abode in both countries or in neither country, he or she is deemed to be a resident of the country of which he or she is a citizen; and

(d) if the individual is a citizen of both countries, or neither country, the "competent authorities" of the countries will settle the question by mutual agreement.

When these "tie-breaker rules" contained in a treaty apply and it is determined that an individual is a resident of another country, then the Act deems the individual to be a non-resident of Canada. ITA: 250(5)

The term "competent authority" is defined in Article III, paragraph 1(*g*) to mean the Minister of National Revenue in Canada and the Secretary of the Treasury in the United States, or their designates.

¶2,085 Permanent establishment

The term "permanent establishment" is defined in Article V to mean "a fixed place of business through which the business of a resident of a [country] is wholly or partly carried on". The term specifically includes a place of management, a branch, an office and a factory, among others. A person, other than an independent contractor, who has and habitually exercises an authority to conclude contracts in, say, Canada in the name of the resident of the U.S., is deemed to constitute a permanent establishment in Canada of the U.S. resident.

However, the term "permanent establishment" does *not* include a fixed place of business in one country used solely in one or more of the following activities of the resident of the other country: Cda-U.S. TT: Art. V, par. 6

(a) the use of facilities for the purpose of storage, display, or delivery of goods or merchandise belonging to the resident of the other country;

(b) the maintenance of a stock of goods or merchandise belonging to the resident of the other country for the purpose of storage, display, or delivery;

(c) the maintenance of a stock of goods or merchandise belonging to the resident of the other country for the purpose of processing by another person;

(d) the purchase of goods or merchandise, or the collection of information, for the resident of the other country; and

(e) advertising, the supply of information, scientific research, or similar activities which have a preparatory or auxiliary character for the resident of the other country.

¶2,090 Summary of the Residence Issue for an Individual

From the foregoing discussion, it can be concluded, generally, that an individual will be either a resident of Canada or a non-resident. A resident of Canada is taxable in Canada on worldwide income. A non-resident is taxable in Canada, generally, only on Canadian-source income. If, in a particular year, an individual leaves Canada and severs ties to Canada, after having been a resident, or enters Canada and establishes ties to Canada, after having been a non-resident, the individual will be a part-year resident for the part of that year while fully resident in Canada and a non-resident for the other part of the year. Hence, part-year residence is a transitional status. A part-year resident is taxable in Canada on worldwide income only for the part of the year while fully resident. An individual who is a non-resident of Canada can be deemed to be a resident of Canada. ITA: 250(1)

Exhibit 2-2 provides a series of steps you can take to help you address the issue of an individual's residency status.

EXHIBIT 2-2
Steps to Addressing Resident Issue

1 Gather all the facts leading up to, during, and after the move. Refer to Exhibit 2-3 for the facts needed.

2. Develop your best arguments for both resident and non-resident status. Be balanced in your analysis.

3. Analyze the strengths and weaknesses of your arguments.

4. Arrive at a conclusion of resident, non-resident, or deemed resident consistent with your analysis.

5. If there is a change in residency status, then determine the date on which that change most likely took place. In the year of change the individual will be a part-year resident, i.e., resident for part of the year and non-resident for part of the year.

6. If your conclusion is non-resident, then did the individual sojourn in Canada for 183 days or more while a non-resident?

7. If there is a change in residency status, then determine how the individual will pay tax:

   a. before the date on which his or her residency changed,

   b. after the date on which his or her residency changed, and

   c. for the year in which his or her residency changed.

Exhibit 2-3 may provide a helpful checklist of facts to evaluate a case in which there has been a change in the residence status of an individual. In essence, it elaborates on the common law principle of "a continuing state of relationship" by establishing the existence of either continuing ties to Canada or ties elsewhere. In a transitional year, when an individual leaves Canada, having been a resident, the ties to Canada may be severed (i.e., a "clean break" was made). Alternatively, when an individual moves into Canada, having been a non-resident, the ties to Canada may be established (i.e., a "fresh start" was made) and ties elsewhere may be severed. Note that resident status and non-resident status are mutually exclusive. An individual cannot be a resident of Canada and a non-resident at the same time. Therefore, the facts that support one status can usually be used to refute the other, although it is possible for an individual to be a resident of more than one country at the same time.

EXHIBIT 2-3
Checklist of Facts to Consider When Determining Residence Status of an Individual
(Based on Income Tax Folio S5-F1-C1)

Factor	*Resident*	*Non-resident*
Significant residential ties		
(a) dwelling place		
(b) spouse or common-law partner		
(c) dependants		
Secondary residential ties		
(a) personal property in Canada		
(b) social ties with Canada		
(c) economic ties with Canada		
(d) landed immigrant status or appropriate work permits		
(e) hospitalization and medical insurance coverage from Canada		
(f) driver's license from Canada		
(g) vehicle registration in Canada		
(h) seasonal dwelling place in Canada		
(i) Canadian passport		
(j) memberships in Canadian union or professional organization		
Other residential ties of limited importance		
(a) retention of Canadian mailing address		
(b) Canadian post office box		
(c) Canadian safety deposit box		
(d) personal stationery or business cards showing Canadian address		
(e) telephone listing in Canada		
(f) Canadian newspaper and magazine subscriptions		
Nature of absence from Canada		
(a) evidence of intention to permanently sever ties with Canada		
(b) regularity and length of visits to Canada		
(c) residence ties outside of Canada		

¶2,100 Comprehensive Consideration of the Residence of an Individual

¶2,105 Stages of involvement

In any of the areas of taxation that are not resolved by a provision of the Act, there are several stages at which the tax adviser may become involved.

Appeal: At the appeal stage, the facts of the case represent completed transactions which have been reported for income tax purposes and have been reassessed by the CRA. At this stage, the question is whether there is a sufficient basis to pursue the issue with the CRA further or to accept the reassessment as issued.

Filing: At the filing stage, the facts represent completed transactions, but the client has not yet filed the return which will report the transactions. Here, the issue is to determine the best way to report the transaction when filing the return, given a fixed set of facts.

Planning: At the planning stage, the facts of the situation have not been completed. The issue at this stage is how the fact situation will be regarded for taxation purposes and whether steps can be taken to achieve the desired outcome.

¶2,110 Consider both sides

At all stages, the type of analysis of the facts that should be done is essentially the same. If a framework of a test or a series of tests is available, as is the case in a residence situation, it should be applied to the facts to systematically evaluate the situation and enable the adviser to arrive at a logical conclusion. No matter how strongly the adviser may feel about a particular conclusion, it is important to consider both sides of the issue. A case for one particular side can be strengthened by considering the arguments for the opposing side and developing arguments against that opposing position. If this can be anticipated before actual discussions with the other side, fewer surprises will result. This concept was followed in the design of Exhibit 2-3.

¶2,115 Form of advice

While the method of analysis may be essentially the same at all stages of a tax situation, the form of the advice offered may differ, depending on the stage. At the reassessment stage, advice on whether there is a reasonably strong basis to pursue the client's position should be presented. At the initial compliance stage of filing the return, an indication of the alternatives and their tax consequences are needed to help the client decide on a filing position. The planning stage provides the greatest opportunity to help the client structure the situation to achieve the best tax result. At this stage, it is possible to modify the situation and its facts to achieve the desired outcome, because the originally planned facts have not been undertaken at this stage. However, even this stage requires a thorough evaluation of the situation and its potential tax consequences.

¶2,120 Application

The facts described in the following case situation could arise at any of the above three stages. The solution presented outlines a suggested method of systematic analysis based on the framework discussed and summarized in Exhibit 2-4.

EXHIBIT 2-4
Residency Tests
Framework for Analysis of Residence Fact Situation

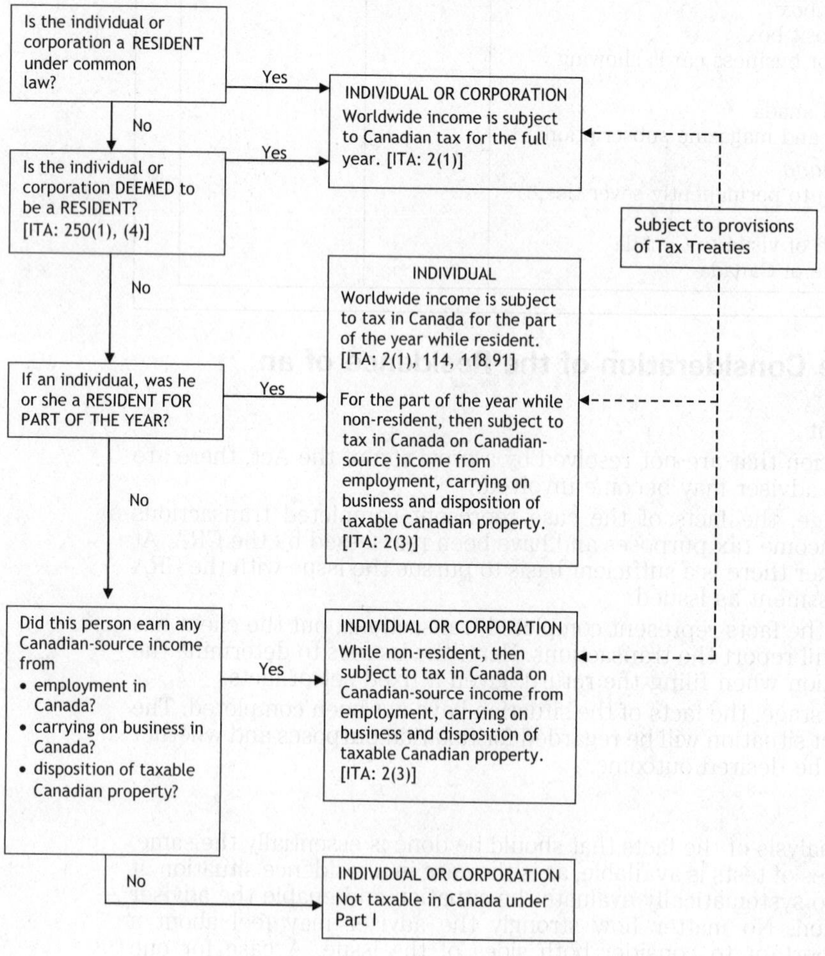

Example Problem 2-1

Eighteen years ago, Mr. Harv DeHaan, a U.S. citizen, moved to Vancouver with his parents. He went to high school in Vancouver and upon completion of his program he was employed in construction work in the Vancouver area. In time he became a construction supervisor. He married a Canadian five years ago. The couple subsequently purchased a home in Vancouver in which they lived and raised two children. He never became a Canadian citizen.

During the year in question, the state of the construction industry in Vancouver was such that he could not be employed on a regular basis although he did work on several jobs during the year. Effective August 1 of that year, he accepted an offer of employment with a construction company operating in the State of Washington and during the remainder of the year and the entire following year he worked on construction jobs in the State of Washington and in Alaska. He rented an apartment in Seattle, Washington, but maintained his home in Vancouver where his wife and children made their regular home. The household telephone listing in the Vancouver telephone directory was in his name.

He visited his family on such occasions as he was able to take time to go to Vancouver. The Vancouver address was the one to which he always returned when his duties permitted.

During the year in question, he worked a total of 800 hours on the new job, earning substantially more than US$10,000.

— REQUIRED

Prepare a memo for the tax person in your firm who will advise Mr. DeHaan on his income tax liability for the year in question. Evaluate in detail the alternatives in the residence issue as they relate to this fact situation for the year in question. Discuss each possible degree of residence and its tax consequences. State your conclusion on the case after considering the relevant international tax agreement and after appropriately weighing the significance of the facts in the case. You may wish to use the framework presented in Exhibit 2-2, as it applies to individuals.

— SOLUTION [See *Lawrence C. Gillis v. M.N.R.*, 69 DTC 488 (T.A.B.)]

(1) *Consideration of Canadian resident option* ITA: 2(1)

If the taxpayer is found to be a resident of Canada under the common law, he will be taxed in Canada on his worldwide income for the year. For this degree of residence to be found, "a continuing state of relationship between the person and a place" must be established. Citizenship is irrelevant to the question of residence. The facts of this case that could be used to establish the continuing relationship between the taxpayer and Canada include the following:

(a) he lived in Canada on a full-time basis for 18 years in which time he was educated in Canada, employed in Canada and married in Canada;

(b) he owned a house in Canada and the household telephone was listed in his name;

(c) his wife and children lived in Canada; and

(d) he visited his family whenever possible.

The fact that he rented an apartment in the United States does not make him not resident in Canada because an individual can have more than one residence.

(2) *Deemed resident option*

If the taxpayer is deemed to be resident, he will be taxed in Canada on worldwide income for the year. An individual is deemed to be resident in Canada if he or she sojourns in Canada for 183 days or more in a year. In this case, the taxpayer was in Canada more than 183 days during the year in question. However, he was not on a sojourn or temporary stay in Canada during the period of the year in question to August 1, given his previous ties to Canada. Therefore, the deeming rule is not applicable to deem him to be a resident. ITA: 2(1) ITA: 250(1)(*a*)

(3) *Part-year resident option*

The taxpayer can be found to be a part-year resident of Canada only in a year in which he has either become, or ceased to be, a resident of Canada. If there has been a clean break/fresh start, then he will be taxed in Canada on his worldwide income for the part of the year that he was resident in Canada. Personal credits taken in the computation of tax must be prorated. To establish this degree of residence, a "clean break" from Canada must have been made. In this case ITA: 2(1), 118.91

there was no "clean break" from Canada since the taxpayer maintained most of his ties with Canada. The only change was that his job took him away from Canada and he needed an apartment in the United States. This action is not indicative of a "clean break". Note that facts which support an argument for a "clean break" contradict an argument for "a continuing state of relationship" and *vice versa*. Therefore, it is only necessary to discuss these facts as supporting one degree of residence or the other.

(4) *Non-resident option*

The final possible degree of residence that could result in taxation in Canada in the year is that of the non-resident who is employed in Canada or carries on business in Canada. At this level of residence the taxpayer is taxed in Canada only on his employment or business income earned in Canada in the year or a previous year. In this case, employment in Canada must be established. During the first part of the year in question, the taxpayer was employed in Canada from time to time. ITA: 2(3)(*a*), 2(3)(*b*)

A possible exemption under the Canada–U.S. Tax Convention applicable in the year must be checked to establish an exemption from tax in either Canada or the U.S. To be exempt from tax in the United States, a resident of Canada must establish that he or she either was present in the United States for a total of less than 184 days and was employed by a Canadian business in the United States or earned less than US$10,000 there. In this case, the taxpayer was in the United States less than 184 days in the year in question, but he was not employed by a Canadian business and he did not earn less than US$10,000. To be exempt from tax in Canada, a resident of the United States must establish that he or she either was present in Canada for less than 184 days and was employed by a U.S. business or earned less than C$10,000. He was in Canada more than 183 days in the year, so he could not be exempt from Canadian tax.

It should be noted that under the Canada–U.S. Tax Convention, income from independent personal services, i.e., non-employment related services, earned by an individual who is resident in one country may be taxed in the other country if the individual has or had a "fixed base" regularly available to him or her in the other country. However, the income is subject to tax in the other country only to the extent that it is attributable to the fixed base in that country. The term "fixed base" is not defined.

(5) *Conclusion*

The facts of this case indicate that the taxpayer is most likely a resident of Canada. Deemed residence is not a possibility in this case, based on an evaluation of the facts. The evidence of a "clean break" is not very strong in the facts of this case. If a "clean break" is not established in the year the non-resident category is not possible in that year.

¶2,130 Non-Tax Factors Affecting Planning for the Residence of an Individual

Establishing that an individual is taxable as a full-time resident or a non-resident, or not taxable in Canada at all, is not the same as determining the best form of residency in a particular case. For example, being a resident of Canada, taxed on worldwide income, is not always worse than being a non-resident who is not taxable in Canada at all and, hence, taxed completely elsewhere. The best form of residency for an individual in a particular situation depends on many factors, some of which involve tax liability and some of which do not.

Newspaper and other articles frequently appear, presenting comparisons of the net tax burden of a particular individual taxed in Canada and in another jurisdiction. As a result of different income tax rates and allowable deductions in different jurisdictions, the net income tax differences can be considerable. The implication is often that the resident of Canada is better off or worse off on an after-tax basis in the other jurisdiction. These comparisons can be misleading, if they do not consider a number of non-tax factors that might have an impact on the situation. For example, differences in the cost of health care and how it is financed by an individual can offset differences in net tax. A Canadian Minister of Finance, commenting on relatively higher levels of taxation in Canada, was reported to have stated: "if taxes were the only reason [to leave Canada], the Cayman Islands would be the most populated area in the world".

While employment opportunities at the forefront of a particular field of interest or training and higher remuneration levels may be an attraction in a particular jurisdiction, quality-of-life factors should also be considered. For example, if there are differences in the cost of health care, they may result from differences in quality and in availability. On the other hand, differences in climatic conditions may solve certain health problems such as asthma or allergies. Differences in both the standard of living and the cost of living should be assessed. Cultural differences may require adjustments which may be made more difficult by geographic separation from family and social ties. Some countries may be less socially or politically stable, resulting in less personal safety and more crime. Economic differences, such as less availability of credit, may exist. Also, financial exchange risks may be encountered and exchange controls may make it difficult to remove capital from some jurisdictions.

¶2,200 LIABILITY OF CORPORATIONS FOR INCOME TAX

The liability of a corporation for income tax in Canada depends on whether it is a resident or a non-resident. The existence of a deeming rule to establish corporate residence, based on incorporation in Canada, means that contentious issues pertaining to corporate residence in Canada are limited. In recent years, there has been little litigation on the residence of corporations.

¶2,210 Charging Provision

Since the word "person" includes a corporation, the charging provision for corporations is the same as that for individuals. Also, since the taxation year of a corporation need not coincide with the calendar year and, in fact, need not be a full 12 months, there is no need for a concept of part-year residence pertaining to a corporation. When, at any time, a corporation is incorporated in Canada and commences operations, a taxation year begins. When a corporation terminates its incorporation in Canada, a taxation year ends. The appropriate rules pertaining to resident corporations are applied for those taxation years. ITA: 2, 249

¶2,220 Residence of Corporations

¶2,225 Deemed residence

Since a corporation is an artificial legal entity, it does not "reside" anywhere in the sense that an individual does. However, a corporation incorporated in Canada after April 26, 1965, is deemed to be resident in Canada throughout a taxation year. This deeming rule clearly settles the issue of corporate residence for corporations incorporated *in Canada* in recent years. A corporation incorporated in Canada before April 27, 1965 is deemed to be resident in Canada if it was resident by the common law principle discussed below or it carried on business in Canada during any taxation year ending after April 26, 1965.[8] A corporation that is not incorporated in Canada, may still be a Canadian resident under the common law principle that its central management and control are in Canada. ITA: 250(4)(*a*) ITA: 250(4)(*c*)

¶2,230 Common law concept of corporate residence

A 1906 British case,[9] which established the "central management and control rule", was based on the following facts. The company was incorporated in South Africa and had its head office there. The board of directors regularly met in London and the real control was exercised in London, although no business was carried on in the United Kingdom. The corporation was held to be resident in the United Kingdom because "a corporation resides where the real business is being carried on and the real business is carried on where the central management and control actually abide". Usually central management and control exists where the board of directors meets to make decisions on company policy.

---

[8] For the purposes of this chapter, paragraph 250(4)(*b*) can be ignored.

[9] *DeBeers Consolidated Mines Ltd. v. Howe*, [1906] A.C. 455.

In another British case,[10] the following facts were presented. The appellant company was a wholly owned subsidiary of an English company and so were three companies registered in Kenya. The appellant had made some payments to these companies which would be tax deductible only if the companies were resident in the United Kingdom for the year in question. In addition to being registered in Kenya, the companies carried on business entirely outside the United Kingdom and their articles of association expressly provided that their directors' meetings be held anywhere except in the United Kingdom. At a certain point in time, the situation of the companies had become so serious that it was unwise to allow them to be managed in Africa any longer and it was decided that management be taken over by the parent. From that time, any decision of importance that concerned the running of the companies was made in London by the directors of the parent.

The House of Lords of the United Kingdom held the following in this case:

> . . . on these facts the seat of the "central management and control" of the subsidiaries passed from Africa to the United Kingdom. This is a straightforward case of *de facto* control being actively exercised in the United Kingdom while the local directors stood aside from their directorial duties. . . .

This case has been used as an authority for the principle that central management and control and, therefore, residence of a company is not necessarily in the country where the board of directors meets even if they have *de jure* or legal control.

The case of *The King v. British Columbia Electric Railway Company Ltd.* established the principle that the place of incorporation of a company is not relevant by itself. Of course, deemed residence of a corporation requires incorporation in Canada. *Bedford Overseas Freighters Ltd. v. M.N.R.* illustrates the application of the "central management and control" rule to a Canadian fact situation. It should be noted that if a corporation is considered to be a resident in Canada at any time in the year, it is taxed on its worldwide income for the year as if it had been resident throughout the year. Thus, there is no concept of part-year residence for corporations.

2 DTC 824 (S.C.C.)

70 DTC 6072 (Ex. Ct.)

Consider the following fact situation as an example of the application of the common law concept of corporate residence. Offshore Co. was incorporated in Sri Lanka in 1984 and is 100% owned by a company incorporated in Canada. The Board of Directors meets and makes most decisions in Sri Lanka. Although one-third of the directors live in Canada, all operating decisions of Offshore Co. are made by the management team in Sri Lanka. Since central management and control does not appear to be exercised in Canada, in this case, the corporation could be considered to be a non-resident. Offshore would only be liable for tax in Canada on its Canadian-source income.

¶2,240 Liability of Non-Resident Corporations

To be considered a non-resident, a corporation cannot be incorporated in Canada after April 26, 1965, subject to certain specific exceptions. A non-resident corporation may be taxable in Canada on its Canadian-source income. While a corporation cannot be "employed", it is possible for a corporation that is not incorporated in Canada to carry on business in Canada and, hence, be taxable on its Canadian-source business income. The consideration of what constitutes a carrying on of business by a corporation in Canada is generally the same as that for an individual, as discussed previously. However, one perspective on carrying on business involving a corporation may not exist in the case of an individual. A corporation may be formed for a single business purpose which, if implemented in a single transaction, would involve no continuity of activity in the carrying on of business. In the case of *Placrefid Ltd. v. M.N.R.*, the court held that a single transaction in this type of corporate situation constituted a carrying on of business. The provisions of a tax treaty may eliminate the liability for tax in Canada of a non-resident corporation carrying on business in Canada.

ITA: 250(4)
ITA: 2(3)

92 DTC 6480 (F.C.T.D.)

[10] *Unit Construction Co. Ltd. v. Bullock*, [1959] 3 W.W.R. 1022.

¶2,250 International Tax Treaties and Corporations

Most of the major treaties carry a provision similar to that in Article VII of the Canada–U.S. Income Tax Convention in which a U.S. enterprise is not subject to taxation by Canada on its "business profits" unless the enterprise carries on business in Canada through a "permanent establishment" located in Canada. If it has such a permanent establishment, it is subject to tax in Canada only on the income attributable to the permanent establishment. As indicated above, the key determinants of a permanent establishment are a fixed place of business or a person who habitually exercises authority to contract for his or her principal. Note that an independent agent is not considered such a person. A list of activities that do not constitute a fixed place of business is provided in the discussion of international tax treaties and individuals, above.[11] The logic used by the Exchequer Court in the *Tara Explorations* case (cited in footnote 10) is particularly noteworthy in its comprehensiveness. A similar method of analysis of a residence question is used in the following example problems. It is also illustrated in Exhibit 2-2, which sets out a framework for the analysis of a fact situation on the residence issue in terms of levels or "degrees" of residence.

Cda-U.S. TT: Art. VII

Cda-U.S. TT: Art. V

Cda-U.S. TT: Art. V

The definition of the term "resident" quoted above from Article IV applies to a corporation as well as to an individual. Where that definition would determine that a corporation is a resident of both countries, then paragraph 3 of Article IV would deem the corporation to be resident in the country of its incorporation.

¶2,260 Comprehensive Consideration of the Residence of a Corporation

Example Problem 2-2

Niagara Corporation was incorporated in the State of New York on March 1, 1981. The head office of the corporation was established in Buffalo, New York, along with production and warehouse facilities. The directors of the company, the president, and the general manager were all U.S. citizens resident in Buffalo. Meetings necessary to maintain the corporate charter as well as major business meetings to discuss corporate strategy were held in Buffalo. The main corporation books and records were maintained at the company's head office.

One of the main reasons for locating the company facilities in Buffalo was to exploit the Canadian market for the company's product. As a result, immediately upon incorporation a sales office was set up in rented premises in Toronto from which orders for its product could be solicited from Canadian customers. A head salesperson was hired to manage the sales effort conducted through the Toronto office by himself and two subordinate salespersons. In addition, an office secretary reporting to the head salesperson was hired. All of these personnel were Canadian citizens resident in Canada.

The Toronto office was identified by the company name on the door. The office telephone was listed in the company's name. The salespersons solicited orders in the Canadian market, but they had to be approved in Buffalo by the head office there. Once authorized by head office, the merchandise was shipped from the warehouses there. However, the Toronto office invoiced its Canadian customers and payments were made to the Toronto office and deposited to a bank account in the company's name in Toronto. Expenses of operating the Toronto office including the salaries of all Toronto personnel and the commissions of the salespersons were paid from the Toronto bank account by cheques signed by the head salesperson in Toronto. Records of these receipts and disbursements were kept in a set of books at the Toronto office. At the end of each month, the Toronto office would remit to head office all but a nominal amount of the balance remaining in the bank account.

By the end of the last year, the Canadian market for its product was such that the expense of maintaining an office in downtown Toronto was not warranted. Effective January 1 of the current year, the head salesperson was instructed to carry out all of his duties from a room built to accommodate the work in the basement of his home. The two subordinate salespersons reported to him there. The home telephone with a listing in the head salesperson's name was used for the business. All salespersons carried business cards printed with the company name and the number

[11] The cases of *American Wheelabrator & Equipment Corporation v. M.N.R.*, 51 DTC 285 (T.A.B.), and *Tara Explorations and Development Company Limited v. M.N.R.*, 70 DTC 6370 (Ex. Ct.), consider the concept of a permanent establishment.

of this residence phone. It was felt that the services of the secretary were unnecessary at this location since the head salesperson's spouse could be paid to do the secretarial work on a part-time basis. A telephone answering service was hired to take messages when no one was home.

— *REQUIRED*

Prepare a memo for the tax person in your firm who will advise Niagara Corporation on the income tax consequences of these facts for the current year. Evaluate in detail the alternatives in the residence issue as they relate to this fact situation for the current year. Discuss each possible degree of residence and its tax consequences. State your conclusions on the case after considering the relevant international tax agreement and after appropriately weighing the significance of the facts in the case. You may wish to use the framework in Exhibit 2-1 for your analysis, as it applies to corporations.

— *SOLUTION* [See *American Wheelabrator & Equipment Corporation v. M.N.R.*, 51 DTC 285 (T.A.B.), and *Tara Explorations and Development Company Ltd. v. M.N.R.*, 70 DTC 6370 (Ex. Ct.)]

(1) *Canadian resident option*

Since the meaning of residence is not fully defined in the Act it is necessary to make a determination based on the specific facts of each case. A corporation can be found to be resident by common law principle. If this is the case, the corporation will be taxed in Canada on its worldwide income. The common law principle that must be in evidence by the facts is that "central management and control" are in Canada. In this case, the directors, president and general manager managed from head office in the United States. Corporate business and strategy meetings were held in the United States. Corporate books and records, with the exception of the Toronto records, were kept in the United States. The Toronto records are probably not sufficient to establish central management and control since they are subsidiary documents. Also, the management function undertaken by the head salesperson would probably not be major enough to indicate central management and control of the company. ITA: 2(1)

(2) *Deemed resident option*

A corporation can be deemed resident by meeting the conditions of subsection 250(4) and, as a result, it would be taxed in Canada on its worldwide income. To be deemed resident, the corporation must be incorporated in Canada. In this case, since the company was not incorporated in Canada, the date of incorporation is irrelevant and the questions raised in the deeming rule of residence (by common law principle) or of carrying on business in Canada need not be addressed. ITA: 2(1) ITA: 250(4)

(3) *Non-resident option*

Under the third degree of residence, the corporation can be considered a non-resident carrying on business in Canada. It can then be taxed in Canada on profits from its business in Canada. Carrying on business in Canada must be established by the facts of the case. Soliciting orders in Canada is enough to establish carrying on business in Canada. This raises the question as to whether the salesperson was an employee of the corporation or an independent contractor. If he is an employee, then the corporation could be considered to be carrying on a business in Canada. The following facts indicate that he is an employee rather than an independent contractor operating his own business in Canada: ITA: 2(3)(*b*), 253

(a) he carried on business in the name of the company;

(b) he acted only for the company and no one else;

(c) he had no stock of merchandise of his own; and

(d) the books and records kept in Canada were not those of an independent business, but were only enough to maintain an office in Canada.

The Canada–U.S. Tax Convention must be consulted to determine if the corporation can be exempted from tax in Canada on its profits from carrying on business in Canada. In order to be exempt, the corporation must establish that it is not operating from a "permanent establishment" in Canada. During the current year, the corporation did not have a fixed place of business in Canada. Other facts that can be used to show no permanent establishment in Canada include:

(a) the salesperson did not have authority to contract, because acceptance was given only in New York;

(b) there was no stock of merchandise in Canada (note that under Article V paragraph 6(*b*) of the Canada–U.S. Tax Convention, a fixed place of business used to maintain a stock of merchandise for the purpose of storage, display or delivery will not constitute a permanent establishment);

(c) the only office used was in the house which had no company identification; and

(d) the bank account and records were not sufficient to establish a permanent establishment in Canada.

(4) *Conclusion*

In conclusion, the corporation would not likely be taxable in Canada. The tax treaty would exempt the company from tax as a non-resident on its profits since they were not earned from a permanent establishment in Canada. Also, the facts do not warrant finding either full-time residence or deemed residence.

¶2,300 REGISTRATION REQUIREMENTS AND LIABILITY FOR THE GOODS AND SERVICES TAX AND HARMONIZED SALES TAX

¶2,310 Liability for GST/HST

This part of the chapter deals with liability for GST/HST and the requirements to register and charge GST/HST under the *Excise Tax Act* (ETA). While the legal liability for payment of GST/HST rests with the purchaser, the responsibility for collecting and remitting the tax generally lies with the supplier. These rules will also be examined in the context of the residency of the supplier, since the rules are somewhat different for resident and non-resident suppliers.

The charging provision requires that every recipient of a taxable supply made in Canada to pay to Her Majesty in right of Canada a tax of 5% (0% for zero-rated supplies) of the value of the consideration of the supply. As well, every recipient of a taxable supply made in a participating province (i.e., Ontario, New Brunswick, Newfoundland and Labrador, Nova Scotia, and Prince Edward Island[12]) is required to pay to Her Majesty in Right of Canada, in addition to the GST, tax in respect of the supply calculated at the tax rate for that province on the value of the consideration for the supply. The *recipient* of a supply is generally the person who enters into the agreement to acquire the property or service and is liable under that agreement to pay consideration for the supply. (Special rules apply where there is no agreement or no consideration is payable. A *taxable supply* is defined as a supply made in the course of a commercial activity. The term includes both supplies taxed at the general rate of 5% (or at the applicable HST rate) and those that are zero-rated. (A *zero-rated supply* is defined as a supply included in Schedule VI). Therefore, for a person to be subject to GST/HST, the supply must be (i) made in Canada, and (ii) made by another person who is engaged in a commercial activity. The definition of a commercial activity does not include activities engaged in by a business that involve the making of an exempt supply (which in turn is defined as a supply included in Schedule V. Rules have been introduced to determine when a supply is made in Canada and, hence, within the scope of GST/HST.

ETA: 165(1)–(2)

ETA: 123(1)

ETA: 123(1)

A relieving provision provides that if, at the time consideration is paid or becomes due for a supply, the supplier is a small supplier (who is not registered or required to be registered), no GST/HST is payable. However, this relieving provision does not apply to the sale of real property. Small suppliers are discussed in greater detail below.

ETA: 166

[12] As discussed at ¶1,400, British Columbia exited the HST on April 1, 2013, and GST at the rate of 5% applies where tax is paid or payable after March 31, 2013. Nova Scotia has announced that it will be reducing the provincial portion of the HST rate to 9%, effective July 1, 2014, and to 8%, effective July 1, 2015; Prince Edward Island adopted the HST effective April 1, 2013, with a 9% provincial HST component.

¶2,315 Supplies in Canada

Supplies are subject to GST/HST only if they are made in Canada. (It should be noted that imported goods and services are also subject to GST/HST in certain circumstances.) A sale of goods is deemed to be made in Canada if the goods are delivered or made available to the recipient in Canada. In the case of leased goods, the supply is deemed to be made in Canada if possession or use of the goods is given or made available to the recipient in Canada. In the case of a supply of real property or a service in relation to real property, the supply is deemed to be made in Canada if the real property is situated in Canada. In the case of a supply of any other service, if the service is to be performed in whole or in part in Canada, the supply of the service is deemed to be made in Canada. ETA: 142(1)

For supplies of intangible personal property, the determination of whether a supply is made in Canada can be more difficult. Intangible personal property is not defined in the ETA. However, the term "property" is defined to include "any property, whether real or personal, movable or immovable, tangible or intangible . . .". The main categories of property under the ETA are real property, tangible personal property (generally referred to as goods) and intangible personal property (movable and immovable property are terms used under civil law in the Province of Quebec). Intangible personal property includes a property that has no intrinsic or marketable value, but is merely evidence of value, and which is enforceable by law, such as contractual rights, stock certificates, intellectual property, etc. Intellectual property includes patents, trademarks, industrial designs, etc. The supply of intangible personal property is deemed to be made in Canada if the property may be used in whole or in part in Canada and the recipient is either a registrant for GST/HST purposes or a resident of Canada. If the intangible personal property is in respect of real property situated in Canada, or of goods ordinarily situated in Canada, or of a service to be performed in Canada, the supply is also deemed to be made in Canada. ETA: 123(1) ETA: 142(1)(*c*)(i) ETA: 142(1)(*c*)(ii)

¶2,317 Supplies in an HST province

Once it is determined that a supply is made in Canada, it must be determined whether the supply is made in an HST province to ensure the correct rate of GST/HST is charged, i.e., GST of 5% or the HST at the rate 13%, 14%, or 15%.[13] The sale of tangible personal property (or goods) takes place in the province in which the vendor delivers it or makes it available to the purchaser. When Ontario and British Columbia[14] implemented the HST on July 1, 2010, the Department of Finance introduced significant changes to the HST place of supply rules for intangible property and services — the rules respecting tangible personal property have not changed. Schedule IX of the ETA and the *New Harmonized Value-Added Tax System Regulations* set out the rules for the determination of the place of supply for the application of the HST in all participating provinces. In the past, it was only important to make a determination as to whether a supply was made in a participating province, because all participating provinces had the same provincial tax component. However, as provincial HST components are now different, determining the particular province a supply is made is essential.

When a taxable supply (other than a zero-rated supply) is made in Canada and is treated as being made in a harmonized province under the HST place of supply rules, the supplier must collect HST at the rate of 5% plus the rate of the provincial component of the HST for that province. Otherwise, the supplier must collect only 5% GST. The place of supply rules provided for in the Act and Regulations generally align the place of supply with the place of consumption for supplies of services and intangible personal property. This is intended to remove competitive disadvantages for businesses that sell from HST participating provinces.

[13] As discussed at ¶1,400, British Columbia exited the HST on April 1, 2013, and GST at the rate of 5% applies where tax is paid or payable after March 31, 2013. Nova Scotia has announced that it will be reducing the provincial portion of the HST rate to 9%, effective July 1, 2014, and to 8%, effective July 1, 2015; Prince Edward Island adopted the HST effective April 1, 2013, with a 9% provincial HST component.

[14] As discussed at ¶1,400, British Columbia exited the HST on April 1, 2013 and reinstated a provincial sales tax.

¶2,320 Supplies by non-residents

As a general rule, a supply of goods or services made in Canada by a non-resident is deemed to be made in Canada if: ETA: 143(1)

- the supply is made in the course of a business carried on in Canada;
- the non-resident is registered for GST/HST purposes at the time the supply is made; or
- the supply is in respect of a place of amusement, a seminar, an activity or an event, and the non-resident supplies admissions directly to consumers.

Unless any of the above situations apply, supplies by a non-resident are outside the scope of GST/HST.

Now that the rules for determining whether a particular supply is deemed to be made in Canada and in an HST province have been reviewed, the issue of whether GST/HST must be charged by the supplier will be examined. As a general rule, a supply made in Canada (and/or in an HST province) will only be subject to GST/HST if it is made by a registrant.

¶2,330 Registration Requirements for Residents

¶2,335 Test for registration

A person who is engaged in a commercial activity in Canada (discussed below) is required to register for GST/HST purposes. Persons registered or required to be registered under the legislation are referred to as *registrants*. The rights and obligations of registrants under the ETA are discussed in Chapter 14. It should be noted that as agents of the Crown, registrants are required to collect GST/HST as required under the ETA. ETA: 240(1) ETA: 123(1)

The definition of person for the purposes of GST/HST is broadly based to include an individual, partnership, corporation, trust or estate, or a body that is a society, union, club, association, commission, or other organization of any kind. Therefore, virtually any kind of organized unit or individual can be considered to be a person and, therefore, can be required to register. ETA: 123(1)

Unlike the *Income Tax Act*, the ETA treats partnerships as persons for purposes of the GST/HST. Therefore, the partnership is considered to be a person for registration purposes and is liable for GST/HST collected on taxable supplies, rather than the individual partners. Similarly, the partnership is eligible for an input tax credit for its purchases attributable to commercial activities.

¶2,340 Definition of commercial activity

Central to the determination of whether a person is required to register is the issue of whether the person is engaged in commercial activities. This topic will be discussed in greater detail in Chapter 4. However, for the purposes of the discussion of the registration requirements, it should be noted that a commercial activity is defined as: ETA: 123(1)

- a business that is carried on;
- an adventure or concern in the nature of trade; and
- the supply of real property.

Business is defined broadly to include a profession, calling, trade, manufacture, or undertaking of any kind whatever, regardless of whether the activity engaged in is for profit. This test is broader than the business test under the *Income Tax Act* in that there need not be a profit motive present for an activity to be considered a business for GST/HST purposes. The point to remember is that the GST/HST is a tax on consumption or value added, and not on income. Thus, many activities engaged in by non-profit organizations, charities and governments may constitute a business for GST/HST purposes. These entities engage in activities that add value to the economy in competition with profit-motivated businesses. For example, a non-profit organization will be considered to be engaged in a commercial activity for

GST/HST purposes if it supplies taxable goods or services for consideration. Therefore, subject to the exceptions discussed below in ¶2,345, any entity that engages in an activity of a commercial nature, regardless of whether the activity is engaged in primarily for profit, will be considered to be engaged in a commercial activity. Consequently, the entity will be required to register for GST/HST purposes.

An adventure or concern in the nature of trade, which is not defined but has the common law meaning discussed previously, also constitutes a commercial activity. This concept is discussed in Chapter 4. The supply of real property also constitutes a commercial activity unless the supply is exempt. Thus, most sales and leases of non-residential property constitute a commercial activity. Reference should be made to Chapter 7 for a discussion on supplies of real property.

¶2,345 Exclusions from commercial activity

The definition of commercial activity contains certain exclusions of which readers should be aware. First, activities that involve the making of exempt supplies do not constitute commercial activities. For example, the supply of medical services by a physician is exempt and, therefore, not a commercial activity. Consequently, physicians providing exempt medical services, only, are not able to register for GST/HST purposes and cannot claim input tax credits in respect of GST/HST paid on inputs. However, the GST/HST component of these expenses can be deducted for income tax purposes.

Second, commercial activity does not include any activity engaged in by an individual (or a partnership comprised of individuals) without a reasonable expectation of profit. Thus, hobbies and recreational pastimes of individuals would not be considered to be commercial activities and, hence, registration would not be required nor permitted. The phrase "reasonable expectation of profit" is discussed in Chapter 4.

¶2,350 Exceptions from the registration requirements

The registration requirements contain an exception for *small suppliers*. The rules for determining whether a person qualifies as a small supplier are set out in the ETA. Basically, this includes persons whose revenues from taxable supplies do not exceed $30,000[15] in the four preceding calendar quarters. This calculation is based on the supplier's total worldwide sales including any supply made outside Canada by its "associates". Small suppliers, who are not registered, are not required to collect GST/HST on taxable supplies. Persons who qualify as small suppliers and who are engaged in a commercial activity, however, may register on a voluntary basis. Registration would permit these persons to claim input tax credits and may be advantageous if taxable supplies are made to registrants. Since registrants are able to claim input tax credits on their purchases, they will likely prefer to deal with other registrants. Purchases from non-registrants may contain indirect GST/HST because non-registrants are unable to recover GST/HST paid on purchases through the input tax credit mechanism.

ETA: 148, 240(1)

In addition to the small supplier exception, a person whose only commercial activity is making supplies of real property by way of sale other than in the course of a business is not required to register. As noted above, supplies of real property are discussed in Chapter 7.

¶2,360 Registration and Collection Requirements for Non-Residents

The place of supply rules discussed earlier in this section must be read in conjunction with the registration requirements to determine when non-residents are required to register and collect GST/HST.

[15] $50,000 in the case of public service bodies, which include non-profit organizations, charities, municipalities, school authorities, hospital authorities, public colleges, and universities.

¶2,365 Meaning of non-resident

For purposes of the GST/HST, non-residents are defined as "not resident in Canada". In the absence of a definition of "resident", reference should be made to the dictionary meaning of the term and to the interpretation of the term under the *Income Tax Act*, as discussed earlier in this Chapter. The ETA does, however, contain deeming rules which provide that a corporation is deemed to be resident in Canada if it is incorporated in Canada, similar to the rules under the *Income Tax Act*. In addition, a corporation originally incorporated in a foreign jurisdiction that is continued (a special form of incorporation) in Canada and not elsewhere is deemed to be resident in Canada. ETA: 132

In the case of a partnership or unincorporated society, club, association, or organization, or a branch thereof, the entity is deemed to be resident in Canada if a majority of its members, having management and control, are resident in Canada at that time. A labour union is deemed to be resident in Canada if it carries on its activities in Canada and has a local union or branch in Canada at that time.

Where a non-resident person has a permanent establishment in Canada, the person is deemed to be resident in Canada in respect of the activities carried on through that particular establishment. For GST/HST purposes, a *permanent establishment* is defined as a fixed place of business, including a place of management, branch, office, factory, workshop, mine, oil or gas well, quarry, timberland, or other place of extraction of mineral resources through which supplies are made. It also includes a fixed place of business of another person (other than a broker, general commission agent, or other independent agent) making supplies on behalf of the person in the ordinary course of business. Because the definition of permanent establishment under the ETA is different from that generally found in Canada's income tax treaties, there may be situations where the existence of a permanent establishment is different for income tax and GST/HST purposes.

¶2,370 Mandatory registration

According to the registration requirements, non-resident persons, who do not *carry on any business in Canada*, are not required to register. Thus, while the test for residents is based on engaging in a commercial activity, the test for non-residents is based on the narrower concept of carrying on business. In basic terms, the difference for a non-resident is that registration is not required if the activities undertaken in Canada are not of a regular and continuous nature. Again, reference should be made to Chapter 4 for a discussion of the distinction between commercial activity and business. ETA: 240(1)

A non-resident who directly supplies admissions to a place of amusement, a seminar, an activity or an event, must register before making any such supplies in Canada. ETA: 240(2)

The legislation deems non-residents (as well as residents) who solicit orders for, or offer to supply, publications that are to be sent by mail or courier to recipients in Canada to be carrying on business in Canada, and requires these persons to be registered. ETA: 240(4)

The small supplier exemption, for suppliers with less than $30,000 in sales per year, is also available to non-residents, other than those who supply admissions as described above.

For individuals, an individual is deemed to be a resident of Canada at any time, if he or she meets certain conditions of the *Income Tax Act*. Thus, a deemed resident (other than a sojourner) for income tax purposes is also a resident for GST/HST purposes. ITA: 250(1)(*a*)–(*f*)

¶2,375 Voluntary registration

Voluntary registration is available to non-residents, provided certain requirements are met. The non-resident person must, in the ordinary course of carrying on business outside Canada, ETA: 240(3)

(a) regularly solicit orders for the supply of goods for delivery in Canada; or

(b) have entered into an agreement for the supply of:

- services to be performed in Canada, or
- intangibles to be used in Canada or that relate to real property in Canada, goods ordinarily situated in Canada or services performed in Canada.

Voluntary registration is also available to certain foreign banks and other corporations, as outlined in the legislation.

¶2,380 Imports

As the GST/HST is a tax on consumption in Canada, it also applies to imports. The ETA imposes GST/HST on the value of imported goods. The GST/HST is payable by the person who is liable under the *Customs Act* to pay duty on the imported goods. The value of the goods is based on the value for customs purposes plus duties and excise taxes (excluding GST/HST). No tax is payable on zero-rated goods, such as basic groceries and medical devices. ETA: 212 ETA: 215(1) ETA: 213

GST/HST is imposed on the recipient of imported taxable supplies. Imported taxable supplies are defined to include intangible personal property (e.g., intellectual property) and services that are supplied outside Canada to a Canadian resident for use in Canada. However, GST/HST is not imposed where the imported taxable supply is for use in Canada exclusively (90% or more) in a commercial activity. ETA: 217, 218

The duty-free limits that apply to Canadian individuals on non-commercial importations are as follows:

- For absences of less than 24 hours, there will continue to be no duty or tax exemptions, and volume and quantity limits on alcohol and tobacco products remain unchanged.
- For absences of 24 hours or more, the travellers' exemption increases from $50 to $200.
- For absences of 48 hours or more, the travellers' exemption increases to $800, replacing the previous exemptions of $400 and $750, which apply in respect of absences of 48 hours and 7 days, respectively.

¶2,800 REVIEW QUESTIONS

(1) Canadian citizens pay tax in Canada on their world income. Comment.

(2) If a non-resident vacations in Canada for 180 days during the year, then he or she will be considered a Canadian resident for the full year. Comment.

(3) If an individual sells his or her house and then leaves the country, the person will be considered to be a non-resident. Comment.

(4) Assume that an individual resided in Buffalo and carried on a proprietorship business in St. Catharines. How would he or she pay tax on the business income earned in Canada?

(5) An individual who moves to Canada on March 31 of the year will be considered resident in Canada throughout the year since he or she was resident here for more than 183 days. Comment.

(6) Since a corporation is an artificial legal entity, it does not "reside" anywhere in the sense that an individual does. Comment on how the residency of a corporation is determined.

(7) A company was incorporated in Canada on November 30, 1965, but has been carrying on business in Bermuda since that date and all of the officers and directors have always been resident there. Comment on the company's tax liability in Canada.

(8) A company was incorporated in Canada on November 30, 1964, but has been carrying on business in Bermuda since that date and all of the officers and directors have always been resident there. In the years from incorporation to 1971 the company actively solicited orders in Canada by telephone. It stopped this activity in Canada at the end of 1971. Comment on the company's tax liability to Canada.

(9) A Canadian executive is transferred to the U.S. with his company on a five-year contract. He and his family sell all their Canadian assets and move to the U.S. in December of the year. Due to the lower personal income tax rates in the U.S., he has the Canadian company defer the payment of the bonus of $100,000 that he earned in Canada in the year until the next year when he is resident in the U.S. Comment on whether the executive will be taxed in Canada on this bonus.

(10) If a U.S. corporation has an employee located in Canada who is selling goods on behalf of the employer, then would the U.S. company be taxable in Canada?

(11) If a U.S. corporation has an agent located in Canada who is selling goods on behalf of the U.S. company, then would the U.S. company be taxable in Canada?

(12) If a person is resident in Canada, can that same person also be resident in the U.S.?

(13) If a Canadian corporation is carrying on business in the U.S. through a permanent establishment in the U.S., will the Canadian company be considered resident in the U.S. and be subject to tax in the U.S. on the total corporate income?

(14) Mr. Smith is an independent consultant who provides his services wherever he can get the work. He has been asked by a U.S. company to go to the U.S. to consult with them. He thinks that he will have to spend 25 days travelling to their many locations in the U.S. over the next year and that he will earn $50,000 for his efforts. His lawyer has told him that he will be taxed in the U.S. on this business income. What do you think?

¶2,825 MULTIPLE CHOICE QUESTIONS

Question 1

X Ltd. is a corporation which has always been managed by the *same* Board of Directors. The Board of Directors has always met where the directors reside. Based on these facts, X Ltd. will NOT be resident in Canada for income tax purposes if X Ltd. was:

(A) incorporated in Canada in 1968 and its directors are all U.S. residents;

(B) incorporated in the U.S. in 1970 and its directors are all U.S. residents;

(C) incorporated in the U.S. in 1968 and its directors are all Canadian residents;

(D) incorporated in Canada in 1964 and its directors are all Canadian residents.

Question 2

Joe is legally separated from his wife and has two adult children who live with his wife and are not dependent on him for support. Joe is leaving Canada to take a job in Germany on June 30 of this year. He plans to stay in Germany indefinitely and has purchased a home there. Which one of the following things is the most important for Joe to do to help ensure that he is not a resident of Canada for Canadian income tax purposes after he leaves?

(A) Take his wife and children with him to Germany.

(B) Give up his Canadian citizenship.

(C) Sell his Canadian home or rent it under a long-term lease.

(D) Put all his household furniture and personal effects into storage in Canada.

Question 3

Mr. Ng is *not* a resident of Canada. In the year, he had worldwide income of $200,000, including $50,000 of employment income earned in Canada (from director's fees) and $10,000 of interest on Government of Canada bonds.

What amount of taxable income must Mr. Ng report on his Canadian personal income tax return for the year?

(A) $10,000

(B) $50,000

(C) $60,000

(D) $200,000

Question 4

Jay ceased to be a resident of Canada on April 30 of the year and moved to New Zealand on that date. During the first four months of the year, he earned $25,000 of employment income in Canada and $1,000 of interest income from his bank accounts in Canada. While living in New Zealand during the remainder of the year, he earned $30,000 (Cdn. $) of employment income in New Zealand and received $2,000 of interest income from his Canadian bank accounts.

What amount of taxable income must Jay report on his Canadian personal income tax return for the year?

(A) $58,000

(B) $56,000

(C) $26,000

(D) Nil

Question 5

In which of the following situations is the person considered a non-resident of Canada for Canadian income tax purposes in the year in question?

(A) James Hill, a 25-year-old engineer living in Ottawa, accepted a six-month transfer to an office in London, England for the period July 1 to December 31, of the year in question. He returned to Canada in the following year. James is not married and has always lived at his parents' house in Ottawa.

(B) Judy Gordon, a financial analyst, lives in a house she owns in London, England. She had lived in Toronto all her life, until she started a minimum three-year contract with CS Services Inc., which started in July of the year in question. Judy is single and terminated the lease on her apartment in Toronto before moving her belongings to England when her position started in July.

(C) ERT Limited was incorporated in Canada in 1987 and, until recently, its manufacturing plant was located in Ontario. In June of the year in question, it moved all of its operations, including the manufacturing plant, to Mexico.

(D) Doug Stewart, a member of the Canadian Armed Forces, has been stationed in Germany for the last 5 years, including the year in question. Doug was born in Canada and lived in Canada prior to moving to Germany.

Question 6

CART Ltd. is registered for HST purposes. The following is a summary of the transactions for CART Ltd. for the month of December:

Account	*Amount (Net of HST)*
Sales (Taxable at 13%)	$250,000
Exports	100,000
Purchase of supplies from a registrant	(30,000)
Salaries	(70,000)
Interest Expense	(20,000)
	$230,000

The HST that has to be remitted in respect of the above transaction is:

(A) $19,500

(B) $26,000

(C) $28,600

(D) $39,000

¶2,850 EXERCISES

Exercise 1

ITA: 2, 114, 115, 250(1)

Determine the form of residence, if any, for each of the following individuals.

(A) Alpha had lived all of his life in Vancouver until this year when he left with his family on August 27 to live in Los Angeles.

(B) Beta is a Canadian citizen who has lived in the United States with his family for the past nine years.

(C) Gamma lives in Niagara Falls, New York, but works Monday to Friday from 9:00 a.m. to 5:00 p.m. in an office in Niagara Falls, Ontario.

(D) Delta had lived all of his life in Dallas, Texas. He moved with his family to Calgary, Alberta, early this year to take a job with Dome Petroleum. He moved back to Dallas in the summer of this year. While in Canada he invested in the shares of a private corporation operating in Calgary. These shares were later sold during the year after he left Calgary.

(E) Epsilon was born in Philadelphia. He is now 10 years old and has never been to Canada but his mother has been consul in the Canadian Consulate there for the past 12 years.

(F) Mu is a German citizen who is married to a member of the Canadian forces stationed in Germany. She has been to Canada only for brief visits when her husband was on leave.

Exercise 2

ITA: 2, 114, 250; Income Tax Folio S5-F1-C1

This appeal concerns the appellant's place of residence in the taxation year 1964.

At the hearing on August 8, 1967 at Saint John, N.B., both counsel agreed on the following statement of facts:

(A) The appellant was about 58 years old in 1963.

(B) The appellant is and was at all material times an American citizen.

(C) The appellant is a sea captain and sails tankers around the world. His employer is the Cities Services Corporation of New York and the ships bear United States registry. He is paid in United States currency from New York and since 1956 he has been Master of the "S.S. Cities Services, Norfolk".

(D) Prior to 1962, the appellant and his wife had always lived in the United States. Until June 1962, they owned a house in Massachusetts.

(E) In September 1962, the appellant's wife and two of their children moved to Fredericton. At that time the two children were enrolled at Rothesay Collegiate School. In September 1963, a house was purchased at 146 Cambridge Crescent in Fredericton and was registered in joint tenancy in the names of the appellant and his wife.

(F) Prior to the purchase of the house in September 1963 the appellant's wife rented premises in Fredericton.

(G) The appellant filed a T1 Income Tax Return for his 1963 taxation year on which he stated, "the above taxpayer and his family are American citizens and are merely residents of Canada. He is a U.S. ship captain and is employed full-time by a U.S. company".

(H) The appellant paid $134.24 Canadian income tax for the 1963 taxation year after using his foreign tax credit.

(I) The routine into which the appellant and his wife have settled over the past years is as follows: The appellant receives his orders to sail from New York. He may be gone months at a time. He may dock at U.S. ports such as Galveston, Texas, or San Francisco.

(J) After the appellant's wife moved to Fredericton in 1963, the appellant retained two rooms in his sister's house at 48 Elm Street, Stoneham, Mass., U.S.A. The appellant gave his sister's number as his telephone number in the United States.

(K) At all material times, the appellant:

- worked for a U.S. company;
- was paid in U.S. currency;

- was a member of the First Baptist Church at Wakefield, Mass.;
- had two children living in the United States;
- had a bank account or accounts in the United States;
- had investments, including stocks and bonds, in the United States;
- had a pension plan with a U.S. company;
- intended and still intends to retire in Florida;
- banked his pay at the First National Bank in Malden, Mass. and enough to maintain his wife and children was sent to her. The rest stayed in the United States where he still retains a chequing account in Malden.

(L) The appellant, during 1964:

- had a joint bank account in Fredericton with his wife;
- had a family phone number in his wife's name;
- neither applied for nor received family allowance for his children;
- neither was employed nor carried on business in Canada;
- never belonged to a church or club in Fredericton;
- was never a member of a Canadian union;
- had no Canadian investments;
- owned a car jointly with his wife with a New Brunswick registry.

(M) The appellant's sole connections with Canada during 1964 were:

- his wife lived in Fredericton with one son;
- he visited Fredericton for a total of 166 days at the following times in the year:

January 3 to February 22	51 days
June 1 to August 7	68 days
November 14 to December 31	47 days
	166 days

(N) In June 1966 the house in Fredericton was sold and the appellant's wife moved back to the United States.

According to the appellant's wife's testimony, she moved in 1962 with their furniture from Massachusetts to the city of Fredericton, N.B., where she rented a house in her name to live nearer their two youngest sons, who were attending the Rothesay private boarding college in Saint John, N.B. Their two oldest children were married and another was attending the Springfield (Mass.) College. Upon moving, they sold their nine-room house in the United States.

On the advice of an American lawyer, the appellant and his wife tried to purchase a house in Canada within the year in order to avoid the American capital gains tax; unfortunately, they jointly bought one two months too late and had to pay the tax. As already mentioned, during the year 1964, her husband lived 166 days in Fredericton and spent the rest of the time at sea. While away, his pay cheques were sent directly from the New York office to the First National Bank in Malden, Mass., and his wife received monthly cheques of $600 for living expenditures in Canada. During his vacation, his pay cheques were deposited in a joint bank account in Fredericton. His trips usually lasted three to four months, and six months when bound for foreign ports. When he was unable to come home, his wife would visit him in New York or at his sister's home in Massachusetts. The appellant contended that, in 1964, he resided with his sister and could be reached there at any time, but did not enjoy the exclusive right to the use of rooms and furniture; during that period, his wife stayed there with him for three or four weeks.

— REQUIRED

Prepare an analysis of the residence issue. Evaluate in detail the alternatives in the residence issue as they relate to this fact situation for the year 1964. Discuss each possible degree of residence and its tax consequences. Weigh the relevance of the facts you consider and come to a conclusion on the case.

Exercise 3

ITA: 2, 250(4)

Determine the form of residence, if any, for each of the following corporations.

(A) Inch Incorporated was incorporated in 1982 in North Dakota. However, its directors are all residents of Saskatchewan where all meetings of the board of directors have been held since incorporation.

(B) Foot Limited was incorporated in Manitoba in 1972. However, it is managed in Japan where all directors' and shareholders' meetings have been held since incorporation.

(C) Yard Incorporated was incorporated in Ohio in 1967, but until five years ago all of the directors' meetings were held in Ontario and the president of the company was a resident of Ontario. However, five years ago the president moved to Ohio and from then on all directors' meetings have been held there.

(D) Mile Limited was incorporated in Nova Scotia in 1964 where all directors' meetings were held until 1971 when the directors moved to Boston where they met regularly.

Exercise 4

ITA: 2(3)

Samson Industries Inc. is a small American company located in Minneapolis, Minnesota. Samson sells various items by mail-order, mostly advertising trinkets such as pens, telephone diaries, post-it notes, and similar items, to Canadian businesses. Last year was the first year they did this and profits on its Canadian sales amounted to $76,000. The principals of Samson are worried about their liability for Canadian income tax and have come to you for advice. Advise Samson on their Canadian tax liability. Include an explanation of your rationale.

¶2,875 ASSIGNMENT PROBLEMS

Problem 1

ITA: 2, 114, 115, 250(1)

Identify the criteria you will use to determine residency for individuals and the steps you will use to apply them.

For each of the following individuals, apply your criteria and determine and explain their residency status for tax purposes. Where there is a change in resident status in a year, explain how the individual will be taxed in that year and the next.

(a) Anthony entered Canada on March 1, 2013, and worked as a domestic on a southern Saskatchewan ranch for the remainder of the year. On December 15, 2013, Anthony's wife moved to Canada with their three children and all of their belongings. They plan to stay permanently in Canada.

(b) Lubie is a U.S. citizen who has lived in Detroit her entire life. For the last 10 years she has been a full-time employee in Windsor, so she commutes across the border every day. She has also traded large volumes of shares and bonds in her own stock account at a broker in Windsor.

(c) Ephran, a computer programmer with Xion Corporation in Toronto, accepted a long-term transfer to Silicon Valley, California. He committed to stay for at least five years. On May 1, 2013, he flew to California and began work on the same day. Most of his belongings remained in Toronto until July 30, 2013. His common-law spouse waited until this day, when the house was sold, the bank accounts were closed, and her contract with the Toronto Public School Board was fulfilled.

(d) Julia, a citizen of the United States, moved with her parents in August 2012 to Edmonton, Alberta. From September 1, 2012 to April 30, 2013 she attended the University of Alberta after transferring credits from her U.S. university. Her parents moved to Edmonton as a result of a job transfer. On May 1, 2013 she accepted an employment position as a mountain bike guide in Colorado and resided there until August 30, 2013. Then, she returned to Edmonton to complete her commerce degree. On June 1, 2014, Julia began full-time employment with a public accounting firm in Edmonton.

(e) Helen Huang has lived in Florida for many years and is a U.S. citizen. All her children also live in Florida. While she enjoys Florida during the winter months, she prefers the relatively cooler weather in Toronto during the other months of the year. As a result, she owns a condo along Queen's Quay in downtown Toronto. Last year, she travelled back and forth between Florida and Toronto fairly often, and when she checked her calendar she found that she had stayed in Toronto on 205 nights. Her children would sometimes come up for short visits.

Problem 2

ITA: 2, 114, 250; Income Tax Folio S5-F1-C1

The client was born and raised in Canada. After obtaining his MBA in 1968, he began working as a consultant. In July 1976, the corporation of which he was a major shareholder entered into a contract with a Canadian Crown corporation to furnish consulting advice in Nigeria. Services were to commence July 15, 1976 and end January 14, 1978. A daily rate of fees was set, but total billings were not to exceed a specified maximum. The contract also provided for moving, travel and living expenses for the client and his dependants up to a specified maximum.

All fees and expenses were paid to the client's corporation in Toronto. He continued to be a shareholder, director and officer of the corporation and he remained very interested in its activities. The corporation paid the client and was instructed to deposit these payments in the client's Canadian bank account which he continued to maintain for this purpose and for the operation of the rental property that he owned. He felt that the Canadian bank account was necessary because of foreign exchange difficulties that he might otherwise encounter. He instructed the corporation not to withhold any income taxes on these payments because he intended to give up his Canadian residence status to establish an international consulting business abroad upon termination of the Nigerian contract.

Since the client had little time before leaving for Nigeria, he quickly rented the unit that he had been occupying in a duplex that he owned, on a month-to-month basis. He intended to sell the property when the market would provide him with a reasonable profit. He arranged to have his corporation manage the renting of this property for a fee which he paid to the corporation.

He stored his major furnishings and winter clothing in Canada. His smaller household and personal effects were shipped to Nigeria. He sold his car, cancelled his auto insurance and a gasoline company credit card and obtained an international driver's licence. He retained credit cards such as American

Express, Visa and MasterCard, as well as his RRSP accounts. Under the contract he was also required to maintain his provincial health insurance coverage.

When he left Canada for Nigeria, he was accompanied by his friend, Martha, who had been a part of his life for over a year before their departure. She had obtained leave from her university program of studies for the fall 1976 term. The couple took up residence in a hotel suite that was converted into an apartment at the Holiday Inn in Lagos, Nigeria. No conventional living quarters were available, because of the housing market. During his stay in Nigeria, the client obtained a Nigerian driver's licence and maintained two bank accounts and two cars. He joined sports, dining and social clubs in Lagos. He was provided with an office by the Nigerian government and he carried business cards which identified him as a consultant with that government. He promoted the consulting business of his Toronto corporation actively in Nigeria in the hope of establishing the business abroad, but he did not generate sufficient business to stay in Nigeria beyond the period of the existing contract. He did not seek to extend his visa or pay any form of tax on his income in Nigeria.

Martha returned to Canada for the winter 1977 term, and then returned to Nigeria for the summer of 1977, but returned again to Canada in September 1977 to begin a new program.

By December 1977 the client had billed the limit under the contract. He vacated his apartment, sold his cars, packed up his possessions, including some artwork, textiles and other souvenirs that he had acquired, and returned to Canada.

— REQUIRED

Prepare a memo for the tax person in your firm who will advise the client on the income tax consequences of these facts. Evaluate in detail the alternatives in the residence issue as they relate to this fact situation. Discuss each possible degree of residence and its tax consequences. State your conclusions on the case after weighing the significance of the facts considered.

Problem 3

ITA: 2, 114, 250; Income Tax Folio S5-F1-C1

The client is an electronic engineer. He was born in Erith, England, on the 7th day of July 1946. During the relevant times the client held a valid passport for the United Kingdom of Great Britain and Northern Ireland. The passport declares him a British subject with a residence in the United Kingdom with the right of abode therein. The passport was issued on September 26, 1978 for a 10-year period.

Prior to the client's second marriage in 1981, his parents maintained a bedroom for him in Kent, England.

In 1981, the client married Cathy, a Canadian citizen residing in Canada who had no income of her own and was wholly dependent on the client. She has always resided continuously in Canada.

In June of 1981, a house near Apsley, Ontario, was purchased by Cathy with money supplied by the client. In September of 1982, Cathy borrowed money by way of a mortgage. The client guaranteed the mortgage which has an affidavit attached dated September 13, 1982 where he swore that he was not then a non-resident of Canada. For a purchase of property in Ontario, he would otherwise have had to pay a 20% non-resident land transfer tax.

During the three-year period at issue in this case, 1981 to 1983, the client regularly returned to Canada when he was not working. Each time the client entered Canada, his passport was stamped by Immigration Canada with the majority of the entries setting out a date upon which he must leave Canada. The authorized period of stay varied from five days to 45 days. On some of the stamps the word "visitor" was written in by an immigration official. Throughout the three-year period, the client was employed full-time by a non-resident corporation and all work was performed outside Canada on an oil rig at sea. All income was deposited directly into a Canadian bank.

The client indicated that he was charged in Provincial Court for failure to file an income tax return for 1981 and was acquitted (likely on the basis that he was not required to file in Canada for that year).

During the three-year period, the client indicated or claimed that he:

(a) never filed a tax return or paid income tax anywhere;

(b) was not allowed to work in Canada;

(c) was given a fixed date to leave Canada on entry (i.e., not allowed to stay in Canada);

(d) could not join OHIP, pay EI, maintain an RRSP or join a pension plan;

(e) was out of the country more than 183 days per year;

(f) had no desire to work in Canada;

(g) had a residence in Britain in the home of his mother and father;

(h) held a mortgage in Britain on his first wife's house;

(i) could not live a normal life in Canada as he had to leave every 27 days; and

(j) had a bank account with the Royal Bank of Canada both in Canada and the Caribbean.

In 1984, the client purchased a car in Canada. In 1985, the client:

(a) obtained a Canadian driver's licence;

(b) obtained a Canadian visa; and

(c) became a landed immigrant in Canada.

— REQUIRED

Prepare a memo for the tax person in your firm who will advise the client on the income tax consequences of these facts. Evaluate in detail the alternatives in the residence issue as they relate to this fact situation for the period in question. Discuss each degree of residence and its tax consequences as it applies to this fact situation. Note that in this case, residence under the common law principle could only result from a "fresh start" at a point in time in the period in question. Therefore, part-year residence would depend on there being a period of non-residence prior to a "fresh start", if any.

State your conclusion on this case after appropriately weighing the significance of the facts considered. Your conclusion should indicate whether the client became a resident at any point in the period or remained a non-resident throughout the period. If you conclude that he became a resident, indicate the point in time when the "fresh start" was made.

Problem 4

ITA: 2, 114, 250; Income Tax Folio S5-F1-C1

The client is a mechanical engineer, born and educated in England. The client was married in England in 1962 and he and his wife, Dawn, had three sons born in 1964, 1966, and 1969. In 1967, the client and his wife and family moved to Canada where he immediately commenced employment with Imperial Oil in Sarnia, Ontario. With Imperial Oil and/or its parent corporation, Exxon Corporation, the client and his family moved to various locations throughout Canada until 1988. In 1988, while residing and working in Edmonton, Alberta, the client was offered the position as deputy manager of the Exxon refinery at Port Dickson in Malaysia. He accepted the position because it presented the opportunity to likely become manager of this same refinery within a three-year period.

At the time of his acceptance of the above position, the client and his wife were experiencing marriage difficulties. As a result of these difficulties, it was mutually agreed that the client would go to Malaysia on his own. His wife and youngest son remained in the family home in Edmonton. His older sons were living on their own by this time.

The client and his employer undertook the following steps in preparation for his move from Canada:

- his employer obtained a work permit for him in Malaysia;
- he sold his car;
- he cancelled his provincial health plan;
- his employer obtained private health insurance for him;
- he closed all of his existing bank accounts at Royal Bank;
- he opened a savings account at the Bank of Nova Scotia because this bank had a branch in Kuala Lumpur, the capital of Malaysia;
- he allowed his membership in the Edmonton Petroleum Club to lapse; and
- he allowed his participation in the Model Guided Plane Association to lapse.

The client moved to Malaysia in the last few days of September 1988. He stayed in a hotel in Malaysia for the first few weeks and then moved into a company-provided home. His employer charged him with a monthly rent of $1,000 for his use of this house. He took the following items with him from Canada to Malaysia:

- all of his clothes and personal effects; and

- an airplane kit for model guided planes and a radio control transmitter for his hobby of model guided planes.

Once in Malaysia, the client undertook to establish Port Dickson as his home. To this end, he:

- purchased a car;
- obtained a Malaysian driver's licence;
- joined the Port Dickson yacht club which was, in fact, a social/recreational club;
- joined the petroleum club at Kuala Lumpur;
- opened a chequing account at the Bank of Nova Scotia in Kuala Lumpur;
- opened a chequing account at the Standard Chartered Bank at Port Dickson;
- acquired two Malaysian credit cards;
- became a patient at a Port Dickson medical clinic and, as well, made regular visits to a dentist in Port Dickson; and
- joined the Port Dickson Golf Club in 1991.

In accordance with Exxon corporate policy, the client remained on the payroll and in the pension plan of the Canadian subsidiary. His monthly pay was deposited into his Edmonton bank account. There was no income tax withheld at source on the client's salary because the Canadian subsidiary knew that he was working full-time outside of Canada. The total cost of his salary and related benefits (including pension) were charged by the Canadian subsidiary to Exxon Corporation International.

The client made only two visits to Canada during the period from 1989 through 1994. He visited for 14 days in 1990 and 14 days again in 1992. On each of these visits, he stayed in the family home in Edmonton. During the same period, the client's spouse made eight visits to him in Malaysia. She made no visits after January 1992, but prior to that time, the length of her visits ranged from 19 days to 32 days. On each of these visits, she stayed with the client in his Malaysian home. The client and his wife remained married throughout the relevant period.

The client maintained the following Canadian investments while he was residing in Malaysia:

- his 50% interest in the family home in Edmonton;
- a 50% investment in a rental property which his wife purchased after his move to Malaysia, because she thought it would be a good investment;
- his RRSP;
- his company savings plan; and
- a few personal shares in Canadian public companies.

He did maintain his memberships in the Canadian Society of Mechanical Engineers and the Association of Professional Engineers and Geologists of Alberta.

The client became manager of the Port Dickson plant in 1991 and eventually retired from Exxon in the summer of 1995 under the terms of an early retirement package. Upon retirement from Exxon, the client returned to Edmonton to the family home. In late 1995 the client started seeking employment in Malaysia and in January 1996 he and his wife went to Malaysia hoping that he would find employment and they would both live there. His wife returned to Canada in February 1996 and he moved on to Thailand where he stayed through July 1997 (working for the 12-month period from August 1996 through July 1997). When the Thailand employment ended, the client returned to Canada. He and his wife then worked out a plan of separation.

— REQUIRED

Prepare a memo for the tax person in your firm who will advise the client on the income tax consequences of these facts. Evaluate in detail the alternatives in the residence issue as they relate to this fact situation for the period October 1, 1988 through the summer of 1995. Discuss each possible degree of residence and its tax consequences. State your conclusions on this case after weighing the relevance of the facts you have considered.

Problem 5

ITA: 2, 250(1)

For each of the following corporations, determine and explain the type of residency, for tax purposes for 2012.

(a) ABI, incorporated in Montreal, Quebec, in 1980, carries on a clothing manufacturing business in Hong Kong. All directors' meetings and staff meetings are held in Hawaii, United States, each year.

(b) Nickel Company, incorporated in the Bahamas in 1966, operates a mining business in Northern Ontario. All profits are paid out as dividends directly into a Swiss bank account. All books and records are maintained in the president's office in Ontario. The company directors all live in Toronto and meet monthly for their directors' meeting.

(c) Saffron Ltd. is a 40% subsidiary of a Canadian corporation located in Houston, Texas. The products manufactured by Saffron are sold directly to the Canadian market. No revenues are earned from U.S. sales.

Problem 6

ITA: 2, 250, 253

Far Eastern Airlines is a company incorporated in Korea in 1974. Its general manager and other active officers of the company are resident in Korea and have their offices there. The directors and corporate officers of the company live in Korea as well.

During the year in question, its sole business was operating an international airline which had no landing rights in Canada. However, in that year it had raised capital on the Canadian market for its international operations by selling an issue of its stock through an investment dealer in Vancouver. The vice-president–finance of the company, who believed the stock issue would sell better in Canada, travelled from the head office in Korea to Vancouver to instruct the investment dealer.

The stock issue was highly successful and the proceeds of the issue were accumulated in a bank account in Vancouver. During the several months in the year in question when these funds were being accumulated, the company became aware of an opportunity to purchase a vast quantity of aviation fuel at a very low price. A purchasing agent was dispatched from the head office in Korea to Canada to complete the purchase using some of the funds accumulated from the stock issue. The fuel was stored in Canada temporarily in rented facilities pending shipment to San Francisco, where it could be used by aircraft landing there. Subsequently, the company was unable to make suitable arrangements for shipment. The fuel was sold to a Canadian buyer at a considerable profit. All contracts involved in the purchase and sale transactions were drawn up by a Canadian lawyer under the direction of the purchasing agent who operated from a hotel room in Vancouver during the period of the transactions.

— *REQUIRED*

Prepare a memo for the tax person in your firm who will advise Far Eastern Airlines on the income tax consequences of these facts. Evaluate in detail the alternatives in the residence issue as they relate to this fact situation. Discuss each possible degree of residence and its tax consequences. State your conclusions on the case after considering the relevant international tax agreement and after appropriately weighing the significance of the facts considered.

Problem 7

ITA: 2, 250, 253

Wong Computer Games Inc. (WCG) was incorporated in the state of Illinois in the last decade. The founding shareholder, Mr. Andrew Wong, is an inventor of computer simulation models. His products include a wide variety of computer games as well as some programs which have industrial applications.

Mr. Wong is the controlling shareholder of WCG. His brother owns a minority interest, as does Walter Bends, a long-time associate of Mr. Wong, who often collaborates in the development of new products. All three shareholders are resident in Chicago. In addition to Mr. Wong, the WCG Board of Directors includes George Wolf, who represents the Chicago law firm, which advises WCG, and Tony Aster who represents First National Bank of Chicago, which provides most of the financing for WCG's operations. The Board meets approximately every six months to review financial results, discuss product development and decide on strategic initiatives. The meetings are usually held in the boardroom of George Wolf's law firm.

Two years ago, Mr. Wong achieved an industry breakthrough when he developed his latest game, SuperPilot. SuperPilot is a computer game in which the operator attempts to safely land a disabled airliner. SuperPilot provided special effects which were far beyond those available in any other commercially available product. Although other WCG products were only available in the U.S. market, Wong was convinced that SuperPilot would be a global success. To ensure the competitive advantage would be maintained, Wong Computer Games Inc. took the required legal steps to ensure copyright and patent protection of the program in a variety of countries, including Canada.

By last year, SuperPilot was doing very well in the U.S. market and WCG began to launch the product in other markets. Walter Bends was assigned responsibility for the Canadian market and took a short-term lease on a Toronto apartment in March of last year. WCG established a bank account with a Toronto branch of a Canadian bank. This account was to be used by Bends for promotional expenses and other incidentals. All other expenses, including Bends' salary, continued to be paid from Chicago.

Bends attended a number of Canadian trade shows, exhibiting the SuperPilot program. Prospective purchasers were provided with SuperPilot game cartridges as a promotional item. Bends was given the authority to sign supply contracts which would permit the purchaser a one-month supply of cartridges. At the end of the one month, if the distributor was still interested, a longer-term supply contract would be required. Bends was not permitted, however, to sign any of these long-term agreements without receiving prior approval from the WCG Board. All game cartridges, including promotional cartridges, were supplied from Chicago. If the product began to sell well in Canada, the WCG Board had discussed establishing a Canadian warehouse.

By January of this year, it became obvious that SuperPilot was not going to be a Canadian success. No distributors had requested a long-term supply contract and only one, Pete's Gaming Emporium, had agreed to stock the product for one month. At the end of the month, sales had been so slow that Pete's was not interested in continuing the relationship. Bends returned to Chicago, the bank account was closed, and WCG refocused its marketing efforts on the U.S. market.

— REQUIRED

Prepare a memo for the tax person in your firm who will advise WCG on the income tax consequences of these facts. Evaluate in detail the alternatives in the residence issue as they relate to this fact situation during last year and this year. Discuss each possible degree of residence and its tax consequences. State your conclusions on the case after appropriately weighing the significance of the facts considered.

Problem 8

ITA: 2, 250, 253

Capitol Life Insurance Company ("Capitol") was incorporated in the U.S.A. in the state of Colorado at the turn of the century. Its head office had always been in Denver, Colorado. Capitol was a subsidiary of Providence Capitol Corporation which in turn was a subsidiary of Gulf & Western Industries Inc. ("Gulf"). Gulf owned approximately 600 subsidiaries, 240 of which were in turn owned by Associates Corporation of North America ("Associates"). Six of these latter corporations were Canadian companies.

Capitol was in the business of writing individual and group life and health insurance policies. Capitol also wrote creditor's group life and health insurance policies for the 240 finance companies which were part of the Gulf group of companies. Under a creditor's group insurance policy, Capitol would pay to the finance company, upon the death or disability of the borrower, the outstanding amount of the loan in the case of death or the required instalment payments in the case of disability. The costs of the insurance were effectively passed on to the borrower, either as a separate charge or as a higher interest rate.

In the late 1960s, Capitol planned to expand into Canada and obtained licences in nearly every province and obtained federal registration under the *Foreign Insurance Companies Act* ("FICA"). The FICA registration required that Capitol name a chief agent in Canada and that he be given a power of attorney. Capitol was also required to make deposits with the insurance superintendent and maintain assets in Canada. Two bank accounts were opened in Canada. The planned expansion into Canada was cancelled. However, the licences and registration were maintained. This required that Canadian representatives and agents be retained as locations for the licensing authorities to serve legal notices. All reports to the licensing authorities and all inquiries of the licensing authorities were to be passed through the Canadian chief agent. The reports to the licensing authorities were prepared in Denver and all inquiries were passed on to Denver by the chief agent. The chief agent was required to maintain copies of records required by the superintendent of insurance. None of Capitol's representatives or agents ever solicited insurance or were expected or authorized to do any business.

The chief agent countersigned the cheques on Capitol's general bank account on the requirement of the insurance superintendent. He had no means to verify the legitimacy of the cheques; as all books and records were maintained in Denver where the cheques were prepared. The agent later deposited the premiums received in an effort to streamline the former procedure of having the premiums sent to

Denver and then sent back to Canada through the bank for deposit into the Canadian general account to meet licensing requirements. All investments were administered and managed in Denver.

Capitol did not have anyone in Canada who solicited insurance business, collected premiums, processed or paid claims, administered investments or countersigned any claim cheques. Capitol had five group insurance contracts under which the lives of Canadian residents were insured. These policies were all issued to affiliated companies without solicitation in Canada. Two of these policies were creditor's group insurance policies with Associates. They were each drafted in accordance with Denver law and signed in Denver by the president of Associates, who was a resident of Indiana. Associates was shown as the insured company and paid all premiums. On the insistence of the Canadian insurance authorities, the wording of the agreements was amended to reflect "a premium collection fee". The original agreement provided for a retroactive adjustment of premiums based upon past claim experience. Capitol and Associates continued to administer, interpret and apply the agreement in the same manner as the original agreement. Blank insurance certificates were also required to be issued so that they could be provided to borrowers whose loans were insured as a way of informing them of the terms of the coverage. The coverage took place independently of the issuance of a certificate to an individual. These certificates listed the Canadian head office of Capitol as being in Don Mills, Ontario, as required by the federal insurance superintendent. This office was never used as a head office. The federal insurance superintendent also required the issuance of a brochure for the information of the Canadian borrowers whose lives and health were insured.

The income that Capitol received from the Canadian insurance and investments represented a very small proportion of its total revenue. Canadian operations were not kept separately from U.S. operations, no Denver personnel were charged with Canadian operations, and there were no special Canadian claim forms or procedures. The only separation of Canadian business from U.S. operations to be found in the accounts of Capitol was to comply with the Canadian insurance authorities. All corporate meetings as well as all levels of management took place in the U.S.A.

— REQUIRED

Prepare a memo for the tax person in your firm who will advise Capitol on the income tax consequences of these facts. Evaluate in detail the alternatives in the residence issue as they relate to this fact situation. Discuss each possible degree of residence and its tax consequences. State your conclusions on this case after weighing the relevance of the facts you have considered.

[For more problems and solutions thereto, see the DVD accompanying this book.]

¶2,880 ADVISORY CASES

Case 1: Transfer to France

Sally has just come to you for advice on a possible job transfer to Paris, France. She is currently working for a large private corporation located in St. Catharines, Ontario. It is now April and the president of the company has asked Sally, who is the company's computer network expert, to move to Paris for at least two years. Her time there may extend beyond two years, but that will depend on the success of the project she will be working on.

Sally is married to Harry and they have two daughters, ages six and eight. The company wants Sally to be in Paris and working by May 15, so she will have to leave by May 10 to get there and settled in time. She is planning to rent a furnished apartment when she arrives. Her children are in school and won't be done until the end of June. Harry has his own career as a school teacher and is willing to take an unpaid leave of absence for two years, but he can't leave until the end of June or middle of July at the earliest.

Sally and Harry enjoy golf and have recently joined a fairly exclusive club in the St. Catharines area, after an eight-year waiting period and after paying a large initiation fee. They do not wish to give up this membership. Their home is located just outside the city on 20 acres and they are very reluctant to sell it, as they would not be able to replace it on their return.

Both Sally and Harry grew up in the St. Catharines area and their families still live there. Sally's parents and Harry's parents are retired.

Sally and Harry both want to move to Paris, and they have come to you for tax advice on whether they could be considered non-residents of Canada, or what, if anything, they could do to achieve this result.

Case 2: Move to Chile

The plaintiff, Jennifer Marken, is a 21-year-old Canadian citizen and has always lived and worked in Regina except for the last two years. During these two years, she obtained a position as an English teacher for a local school in Osorno, Chile. Originally, the two-year contract could have been extended into a permanent position at Jennifer's option. However, at the end of the two-year period Jennifer's brother became suddenly ill and she opted to return to Regina and complete her education degree.

She is scheduled to appear in court next week to claim that she was a non-resident of Canada during the two-year period and, therefore, should not be liable for Canadian tax. Both the CRA and Jennifer's counsel agree on the following facts:

- Jennifer is a Canadian citizen and all of her direct family resides in Saskatchewan.
- Jennifer's fiancé visited her five times during the two-year period and lived in Chile during his summer vacations. He plans to complete his accounting designation with a Canadian firm in Saskatchewan.
- All of Jennifer's income during the two-year period was paid by the Chilean school (January 2010–January 2012).
- Upon departing for Chile, Jennifer put all of her furniture in storage and leased her car to her younger sister on a month-to-month basis. Her household belongings were shipped to Chile.
- While in Chile, she maintained her provincial health care policy, her Canadian savings account and a Canadian American Express card. She cancelled her Canadian chequing account, and her Canadian Visa card.
- Before leaving, she cancelled all of her club memberships and abdicated her position as the honourary chair of the Beta Gamma Phi sorority.

- While in Chile she made no attempt to learn the Spanish language and did not join any Chilean organizations. She rented a one-bedroom apartment from another Canadian living in Osorno.
- Over the two-year period, Jennifer visited Canada each Christmas, at Easter, and for the marriage of her best friend. Her total number of days in Canada over the two-year period amounted to 50 days.

Jennifer's litigation counsel would like your advice on the income tax options for the two-year period during which Jennifer worked in Chile. Provide your perspective on the facts that support each place of residence and the tax consequences they entail. Weigh the relevance of the facts and conclude on the likely outcome in this situation.

Chapter 3

Employment Income

TOPICS DISCUSSED

LEARNING GOALS

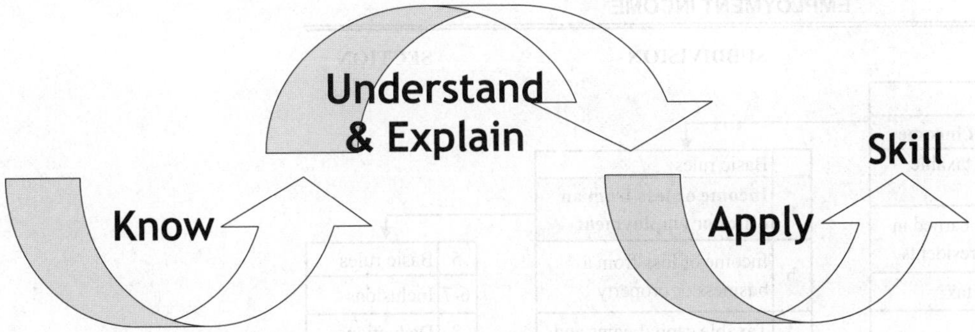

Know

By the end of this chapter you should know the basic provisions of the *Income Tax Act* that relate to employment income and expenses. You should be able to calculate employment income and distinguish between a self-employed independent contractor and an employee. Completing the Review Questions (¶3,800) and Multiple Choice Questions (¶3,825) is a good way to learn the technical provisions.

Understand and Explain

You should understand and be able to explain how employment income and expenses are calculated and why the provisions are designed the way they are. Completing the Exercises (¶3,850) is a good way to deepen your understanding of the material.

Apply

You should be able to apply your knowledge and understanding of employment income and expenses to real life situations. Completing the Assignment Problems (¶3,875) is an excellent way to develop your ability to apply the material in increasingly complex situations.

OVERVIEW

The first source of income mentioned in the Act is employment income. Net employment income, that is, employment inclusions minus employment deductions, is determined by the rules in subdivision a of Division B in Part I of the Act. This determination, although very basic, is important because it will be used in subsequent provisions to compute the limitations on the deductibility of certain items such as retirement plan contributions and child care expenses. The following list indicates the sections and basic content of this subdivision: ITA: 3(*a*)

Inclusions:

Sec. 5 — Salary, wages and gratuities received.

Sec. 6 — Other income inclusions arising from employment.

Sec. 7 — Stock option benefits.

Deductions:

Sec. 8 — Deductions allowed against employment income.

It is worth noting that the only expenses that can be deducted against employment income are those specifically set out in section 8. ITA: 8(2)

The following chart will help locate the major provisions discussed in this chapter.

PART I — DIVISION B, SUBDIVISION a

EMPLOYMENT INCOME

DIVISION

A	Liability for tax
B	**Computation of income**
C	Computation of taxable income
D	Taxable income earned in Canada by non-residents
E	Computation of tax
E.1	Minimum tax
F	Special rules applicable in certain circumstances
G	Deferred and other special income arrangements
H	Exemptions
I	Returns, assessments, payment and appeals
J	Appeals to the Tax Court of Canada and the Federal Court of Appeal

SUBDIVISION

	Basic rules
a	**Income or loss from an office or employment**
b	Income or loss from a business or property
c	Taxable capital gains and allowable capital losses
d	Other sources of income
e	Deductions in computing income
f	Rules relating to computation of income
g	Amounts not included in computing income
h	Corporations resident in Canada and their shareholders
i	Shareholders of corporations not resident in Canada
j	Partnerships and their members
k	Trusts and their beneficiaries

SECTION

5	Basic rules
6-7	Inclusions
8	Deductions

Examine carefully the contents of these sections, especially sections 6 and 8, which contain many specific inclusions and deductions from employment sources. Note that the T1 income tax return (an individual's tax return) does not actually show net employment income as a single number, since the return separates employment inclusions from employment deductions. While the net result is, of necessity, the same as that achieved by the Act, the T1 return approach does not show a net income from employment figure, although that number is very important for subsequent calculations.

This chapter will consider, first, whether a person is an employee or self-employed. Next, the major inclusions of employment income and the major deductions from employment income are considered. Since the system of rules that allows for deductions pertaining to the employment use of cars is extensive, these rules are considered in a separate part of this chapter. The deduction by an employee of expenditures which include GST/HST may provide the employee with a GST/HST rebate. The income tax implications of this rebate will be considered after the deductions for income tax purposes have been discussed.

¶3,000 BASIC RULES

¶3,010 Employed Versus Self-Employed or Independent Contractor

¶3,015 Overview

Sometimes it is difficult to determine if an individual is an independent contractor (i.e., self-employed) or an employee. In recent years, there has been a surge in new small businesses, together with more consultants and self-employed businesses. Many employers find it beneficial to hire short-term consultants, rather than long-term employees. Employer costs of EI, CPP, and benefit packages are reduced, and the employer does not need to commit to the contractor for a long term. For tax purposes the distinction between an employee and an independent contractor is important for the following reasons:

- The deductibility of expenses is considerably more restricted for employees. Self-employed individuals may be in a position to claim more deductions.
- Employers must remit income tax and EI and CPP payments to the CRA for employees only.

Non-tax implications for independent contractors include:

- they are ineligible for general EI benefits (special benefits, including maternity, parental, sickness, and compassionate care benefits are available), holidays, and employer-paid or other non-cash benefits;
- they have a potential liability issue for the services they perform;
- they cannot collect severance pay; and
- they lack job security, and thereby assume increased economic risk.

The issue of whether a person is an employee or self-employed (i.e., an independent contractor) often arises in connection with the deductibility of expenses. The issue is important because independent contractors are treated as businesses and are allowed to deduct all ITA: 67
reasonable expenses incurred for the purpose of gaining or producing income from business, ITA: 18(1)(*a*)
except capital outlays such as the cost of land and other fixed assets. Employees, on the other ITA: 18(1)(*b*)
hand, are strictly limited to those deductions specifically listed in section 8. Hence, for income ITA: 8(2)
tax purposes, self-employed status may be preferred by both the worker and the payer. In addition, the employee versus independent contractor issue is important in determining whether the employer is required to withhold income tax, Canada Pension Plan contributions or Employment Insurance premiums from amounts paid to the individual.

For labour law purposes, individuals usually prefer to be employees to gain protection for their severance, pension and injury compensation rights. While many individuals would prefer to be an employee for labour law purposes and self-employed for tax purposes, this option is not available.

There is no single test or factor that is decisive in determining whether an individual is an employee or an independent contractor. This principle was made clear by the Supreme Court in *671122 Ontario Ltd. v. Sagaz Industries Inc.*,[1] in which the Court considered all facts that reflected the relationship between the parties. In the case of *Wiebe Door Services* 87 DTC 5025 (F.C.A.)
Ltd. v. M.N.R. (a case dealing with Canada Pension Plan and Employment Insurance issues), the Federal Court of Appeal, a senior-level court, emphasized the need to examine the interaction of all of the facts in a situation and the following interrelated tests, which have evolved in the courts:

- economic reality or entrepreneur test;
- integration or organization test; and
- specific result test.

[1] [2001] 2 S.C.R. 983.

To analyze a fact situation effectively and efficiently, it often helps to apply a set of tests or factors, accepted by the courts, to the fact situation. Each of the tests, which determine the nature of the relationship rather than the nature of the services, must be understood. It is important to know how the tests work to distinguish between an individual who is considered to be employed and an individual who can be considered to be self-employed. Judgment must still be exercised to determine the importance of any test or factor to the particular fact situation being analyzed.

Exhibit 3-1 outlines the steps that should be taken in the analysis of this issue.

EXHIBIT 3-1
Steps to Addressing Employed Versus Self-Employed Issue

1. Gather all the facts relating to the person's position and activities.
2. Organize your thoughts around the following tests:
   a. Economic reality or entrepreneur test
      i. Control,
      ii. Ownership of tools, and
      iii. Chance of profit/risk of loss;
   b. Integration or organization test; and
   c. Specific result test.
3. Develop your best arguments for both employed and self-employed. Be balanced in your analysis.
4. Analyze the strengths and weaknesses of your arguments.
5. Arrive at a conclusion of employed or self-employed consistent with your analysis.
6. Assess the impact of your decision:
   a. Expenses deductible for tax purposes,
   b. Tax rates applicable to the income, and
   c. Non-tax factors such as employee and government benefits.

¶3,020 The economic reality or entrepreneur test

The *economic reality or entrepreneur test* examines several economic factors and draws from them an inference as to the nature of the relationship. In particular, three dimensions have been advanced involving (a) control, (b) ownership of the tools, and (c) chance of profit/risk of loss. In a civil law case,[2] the Supreme Court of Canada added another factor to consider: the degree of responsibility for investment and management held by the worker. However, in the application of the factor to the facts of the case, the Court suggested that responsibility for management was part of the control test. Responsibility for investment might be considered to be a broader concept of the ownership of tools test.

¶3,020.10 *Control*

The control subtest, listed as part of the economic reality or entrepreneur test above, determines whether the individual is directed by someone who is in a position to order or require not only what is to be done but how it is to be done. Where such control is exercised over the individual, an employer–employee relationship is implied. Hence, control is evidenced by the situation of an individual who is subject to a person who has the right to give orders and instructions to the individual regarding the manner in which to carry out the work.[3] In the view of the CRA, control "exists if the person for whom services are performed

[2] *671122 Ontario Ltd. v. Sagaz Industries Canada Inc.*, [2001] 2 SCR 983 (S.C.C.).

[3] This test was applied in the cases of *Di Francesco v. M.N.R.*, 64 DTC 106 (T.A.B.), and *Compton v. M.N.R.*, 65 DTC 578 (T.A.B.).

has the right to control the amount, the nature, and the management of the work to be done and the manner of doing it".[4]

Around the year 1900, the control test was regarded as a conclusive test. However, in our increasingly complex business environment, control is no longer appropriate as a conclusive test, but is just one of the four tests which must be examined together as part of the economic reality or entrepreneur test. The shortcomings of the control test reveal themselves in circumstances where it is difficult, because of the nature of the work, to exercise any control over the manner in which the work is performed. In particular, the courts have found the test to be too inflexible in determining the issue in respect of professionals and highly skilled tradespeople who are hired for their knowledge and expertise; that is, they do not need to be told how to do a job.

The control test was considered by the Federal Court of Appeal in the case of *The Royal Winnipeg Ballet v. M.N.R.* At issue was whether the dancers of the Royal Winnipeg Ballet (RWB) were employees or self-employed independent contractors. Justice Sharlow, in finding that the dancers were independent contractors, made the following statement, at paragraph 66 of the decision: 2006 DTC 6323 (F.C.A.)

> The control factor in this case, as in most cases, requires particular attention. It seems to me that while the degree of control exercised by the RWB over the work of the dancers is extensive, it is no more than is needed to stage a series of ballets over a well planned season of performances. If the RWB were to stage a ballet using guest artists in all principal roles, the RWB's control over the guest artists would be the same as if each role were performed by a dancer engaged for the season. If it is accepted (as it must be), that a guest artist may accept a role with the RWB without becoming its employee, then the element of control must be consistent with the guest artist being an independent contractor. Therefore, the elements of control in this case cannot reasonably be considered to be inconsistent with the parties' understanding that the dancers were independent contractors.

¶3,020.20 *Ownership of tools*

In cases where the taxpayer doing the work supplies neither funds nor equipment needed to do the work, takes no financial risks or managerial responsibility and has no liability, the courts have applied the economic reality test and held that the taxpayer is an employee. On the other hand, the major tool necessary for some work is the knowledge, expertise or skill of the person doing the work, as in the case of a professional consultant. In that case, the "ownership of the tools" subtest may not be conclusive.

¶3,020.30 *Chance of profit/risk of loss*

Where the taxpayer doing the work has a chance of making a profit, risks incurring a loss from bad debts, damages to assets or delivery delays, and must cover operating costs, there is evidence of an independent contractor or self-employed status.

¶3,025 Integration or organization test

The *integration or organization test* examines whether the individual doing the work is economically dependent on the organization. The more dependent the individual is on the organization, the more he or she will appear to be an employee. In the case of *Wiebe Door Services Ltd. v. M.N.R.*, the court held that the correct perspective was that of the individual in terms of how dependent the individual is on the organization. Consideration can be given, for example, to the proportion of the individual's income derived from the organization and the availability to the individual of benefits available to employees of the organization. In applying this test, it is important to determine whether services are performed as an individual in business on his or her own account. 87 DTC 5025 (F.C.A.)

[4] *Interpretation Bulletin* IT-525R, "Performing Artists" (Consolidated), May 16, 2001, paragraph 3.

¶3,030 Specific result test

The *specific result test* has also been used to distinguish an employee from an independent contractor. An employer–employee relationship usually contemplates the employee putting his or her personal services at the disposal of his or her employer during a given period of time without reference to a specified result and, generally, envisages the accomplishment of work on an ongoing basis. On the other hand, where a worker and payer agree that certain specified work will be done, possibly, with the use of assistants provided by the worker, it may be inferred that an independent contractor relationship exists. In the CRA's view, this test is satisfied where the facts suggest that "a person is engaged to achieve a defined objective and is given all the freedom to obtain the desired result".[5] The facts used in the application of the *integration or organization test* may, also, be useful in the specific result test since the tests appear to be closely related.[6]

¶3,032 Conclusion — No one test

The Supreme Court, in *671122 Ontario Ltd. v. Sagaz Industries Inc.*, made it clear, at paragraph 46, that no one test can be used to determine whether someone is an employee or is self-employed: 2001 SCC 59

> 46 In my opinion, there is no one conclusive test which can be universally applied to determine whether a person is an employee or an independent contractor. Lord Denning stated in *Stevenson Jordan* [(1952) 1 The Times L.R. 101 (C.A.)], *supra*, that it may be impossible to give a precise definition of the distinction (p. 111) and, similarly, Fleming observed that "no single test seems to yield an invariably clear and acceptable answer to the many variables of ever changing employment relations . . . " (p. 416). Further, I agree with MacGuigan J.A. in *Wiebe Door* [87 DTC 5025 (FCA)], at p. 563, citing *Atiyah* [Professor P.S. Atiyah, *Vicarious Liability in the Law of Torts*, London, Butterworths, 1967, p. 41], *supra*, at p. 38, that what must always occur is a search for the total relationship of the parties:
>
>> [I]t is exceedingly doubtful whether the search for a formula in the nature of a single test for identifying a contract of service any longer serves a useful purpose . . . The most that can profitably be done is to examine all the possible factors which have been referred to in these cases as bearing on the nature of the relationship between the parties concerned. Clearly not all of these factors will be relevant in all cases, or have the same weight in all cases. Equally clearly no magic formula can be propounded for determining which factors should, in any given case, be treated as the determining ones.

¶3,035 Other considerations

In the *Royal Winnipeg Ballet* case, the Federal Court of Appeal considered the relevance of the intention of the parties. Justice Sharlow, at paragraph 62, indicated that "a stipulation in a contract as to the legal nature of the relationship created by the contract cannot be determinative". However, she went on to state, at paragraph 64, ". . . it seems to me wrong in principle to set aside, as worthy of no weight, the uncontradicted evidence of the parties as to their common understanding of their legal relationship, even if that evidence cannot be conclusive". She concluded, at paragraph 67, ". . . this is a case where the common understanding of the parties as to the nature of their legal relationship is borne out by the contractual terms and the other relevant facts". As a result, the dancers were considered to be self-employed. 2006 DTC 6323 (F.C.A.)

The CRA does not have a specific Interpretation Bulletin dealing with the differences between employees and self-employed individuals. However, there is a brief description of the general principles involved in an Interpretation Bulletin, "Visual Artists and Writers". A more detailed application of the tests or factors used in the case of performing artists is provided in another Interpretation Bulletin, entitled "Performing Artists". IT-504R2, par. 2; IT-525R, par. 3–8

[5] IT-525R.

[6] The specific result test was adopted in the case of *Alexander v. M.N.R.*, 70 DTC 6006 (Ex. Ct.).

Example Problem 3-1

The taxpayer, a professional pathologist, was appointed Director of the Clinical Chemistry Laboratory of a hospital for a period of five years. He reported to the hospital's Director of Laboratories who advised the taxpayer what his work involved and decided the amount to be paid to the taxpayer. The hospital supplied all the necessary laboratory facilities and equipment. The laboratory conducted tests exclusively for the patients of the hospital, although some tests were referred out by the hospital to private laboratories.

The taxpayer's main responsibility was to ensure that the output and quality of the work done in the laboratory by 15 technologists who were employees of the hospital was acceptable. He did not have the authority to hire or fire any of the technologists who worked under him, but could, if necessary, request additional help from the hospital's administration. The taxpayer did not have to arrange for or pay his replacement if he was absent from the laboratory for vacations or other lengthy periods of time. Substitute pathologists were paid directly by the hospital.

The normal deductions from employees' salaries were made by the hospital in respect of the taxpayer's remuneration. The taxpayer also participated in the group insurance plan toward which the hospital made substantial contributions. The taxpayer also deducted expenses for professional dues, property taxes, business fees, liability insurance, books and journals, telephone, accounting fees, and travel and conventions.

— REQUIRED

Is the taxpayer in this case an employee or an independent contractor? In presenting your answer, discuss the tests that are applied by the courts in this type of situation and consider how the facts relate to these tests. What are the general tax consequences of your findings?

— SOLUTION

The following is based on the decision of the Chairman of the Tax Review Board in the case of *Hauser v. M.N.R.* 78 DTC 1532 (T.R.B.)

1. *The Economic Reality or Entrepreneur Test:* The control aspect of this test, which in certain circumstances is still applicable, has been found by the courts to be too inflexible in determining the issue, particularly in respect of professionals and highly trained, skilled tradespeople. In this instance, it is clear that the Director of Laboratories could not or would not interfere in the taxpayer's exercise of his professional skills. However, even though the usual strict controls of an employer over the employee's work are not found in this instance, it does not automatically rule out the possibility that an employer–employee relationship does in fact exist. The taxpayer as a staff member, therefore was under the hospital's control for the general assignment and reporting of his work and for the amount of remuneration that would be allocated to him. Although these factors would not be present if the appellant were in fact a private practitioner, the application of the control test is not, in the circumstances of this appeal, a wholly satisfactory or conclusive one.

The other aspects of the economic reality or entrepreneur test, however, are particularly revealing if we compare the economics of the taxpayer's professional activities in the hospital's chemistry laboratory with that of a private practitioner operating his own private laboratory. In the latter case, the private practitioner runs the risk of financing the equipment, supplying the help necessary to operate and administer his laboratory and he then has to ensure that he has sufficient clients to render his laboratory operation economically viable. The taxpayer, on the other hand, uses the equipment and supplies which are all furnished by the hospital. He neither hires nor fires any of the technologists who work under him but can, if necessary, request additional help from the hospital's administration and all the technologists and clerks working in the hospital's biochemistry laboratory are hired and paid directly by the hospital. The taxpayer does not seek out clients; the tests are made for patients of the hospital. The evidence is that in his absence from the laboratory the taxpayer is not obligated to arrange for or pay his replacement. Substitute pathologists are paid directly by the hospital. Note how, in this case, the "ownership of the tools" subtest pertaining to the knowledge, skills and expertise of the professional is not conclusive. These "tools" are provided by the professional, whether he acts in the capacity of an employee or of an independent contractor, in this type of situation.

On applying the Economic Reality Test to the facts, there is no valid evidence which might support the proposition that the taxpayer was under a contract for services of a self-employed individual. All the evidence tends to establish that, from an economic reality point of view, the taxpayer was under a contract of service and, therefore, an employee of the hospital.

2. *The Integration or Organization Test:* The taxpayer was appointed for a period of five years by the hospital under a contract of service. By this agreement, his knowledge and skills in pathology or in any other related field, in which the taxpayer may have been qualified, was employed in the hospital's general organization in the treatment of patients. The facts suggest an economic dependence on the organization. In such circumstances the courts have held that the taxpayer was an employee.

3. *The Specific Result Test:* This test distinguishes a contract for services of a self-employed individual from a contract of service of an employee. The taxpayer was appointed as Director of the Clinical Chemistry Laboratory of the hospital for a five-year period on a full-time basis. His income from the hospital, though paid periodically, was calculated on a yearly basis. It was the taxpayer's personal professional services which were at the disposition of the hospital and the taxpayer's work was done on a continuous day-to-day basis without there being any limited or specified amount of work that the taxpayer had, by contract, to accomplish. The taxpayer had to do the work personally and did not employ or pay substitute part-time pathologists to do his work in his absence. According to the Specific Result Test one can reasonably conclude that the taxpayer was an employee of the hospital. Note how closely related the conditions of this test are to those used in the Integration or Organization Test. In fact, the Specific Result Test might be regarded as a later stage in the evolution of the Integration or Organization Test.

As a result of applying all three tests to the facts of this case, there is nothing that supports the contention that the taxpayer was under a contract for services or was an independent contractor. All the evidence clearly indicates that the taxpayer was under a contract of service and was an employee.

The consequence of this finding is that the taxpayer's income would be taxed as employment income with the resultant restricted deductions. In this particular case, the taxpayer was allowed a deduction for professional dues, but denied deductions for property taxes, business fees, liability insurance, books and journals, telephone, accounting fees, and travel and conventions. In addition, the payer would be required to withhold from each payment the appropriate taxes at source.

¶3,037 Defining the Taxation Year

Employment income is reported on a calendar-year basis; there is no alternative. The taxation year of an individual always ends December 31. ITA: 249(1)(*b*)

Likewise, current legislation requires the self-employed to have a December 31 year end or to use a more complicated method of reporting business income.

An employee attempting to circumvent the mandatory calendar year reporting by incorporating his or her "business" and having a fiscal year end other than December 31 would find special rules are in place concerning the tax rate and deductions allowed this type of corporation. These special rules addressing the "incorporated employee" and the definition of "personal services business" effectively eliminate the incorporation advantage in this type of situation. ITA: 18(1)(*p*), 125(7)

¶3,040 Salary, Wages, and Other Remuneration Including Gratuities

"Salary" and "wages" are terms in common use, but "remuneration" has a somewhat more general meaning. Remuneration includes such items as bonuses, tips, honoraria, and commissions paid to employees. However, as discussed in Chapter 1, where specific words are followed by general words, the general words are confined to the same scope as the specific words. As a result, "remuneration" must be in the same scope as "salary" and "wages". ITA: 5

Numerous court cases have considered remuneration from employment as opposed to some other type of payment.[7] Two cases illustrate how payment by an employer for an expense incurred by the employee can be considered other remuneration or a benefit. In the case of *Pavel Bure v. The Queen*, the payment of the hockey player's agent's fee by the hockey club was included in the player's income. In the case of *Gernhart v. The Queen*, a tax equalization payment made by an employer to compensate for higher Canadian taxes was considered to be part of the employee's compensation. 2000 DTC 1507 (T.C.C.) 98 DTC 6026 (F.C.A.)

Notice that gratuities are specifically listed for inclusion. All amounts, received by an individual in his or her capacity as an employee both from his or her employer and from others by reason of his or her employment, must be included in income. Thus, in addition to any bonus or honorarium received from an employer, an individual must include any tips received from his or her employer's customers. However, if a payment is made to such an individual without reference to his or her employment and primarily as a personal gift, it is not income. This becomes a question of fact. The magnitude and frequency of payments are also factors.[8] ITA: 5

¶3,050 Amounts Received

The use of the word "received" in the Act means that the employee must report employment income on the cash basis. Thus, advancing or deferring a payment such as a bonus will affect the level of income of an individual for a given year. However, the voluntary deferment of an unconditional right to receive remuneration has not been accepted and, as a result, has been held to be taxable in the year it became receivable, as illustrated by the case of *Blenkarn v. M.N.R.* For example, an employee who was legally entitled to receive a bonus in December asks her employer to defer the payment until January. She would be deemed to have received the bonus in December under the principle of constructive receipt, as established in common-law court decisions. That principle would include an amount that is effectively received, or the receipt of which can be controlled by the recipient, if not actually received. In the case of *Markman v. M.N.R.*, the Court held that a retroactive pay increase over a number of taxation years is included in income in the year of receipt. ITA: 5 63 DTC 581 (T.A.B.) 89 DTC 253 (T.C.C.)

¶3,060 Volunteer Services Exemption

Only the taxable portion (over $1,000) paid to an emergency volunteer is included in income. The exemption from income is easier for municipalities to administer as they are not required to issue information slips (T4s) for what is usually a nominal amount. Payments that qualify are those received for the same or similar duties as: ITA: 81(4)

- volunteer firefighters [The June 6, 2011 federal Budget proposed a 15% non-refundable tax credit based on an amount of $3,000 for eligible volunteer firefighters. An individual who claims this credit will not be eligible to claim the $1,000 exemption.];
- volunteer ambulance technicians; and
- emergency service volunteers assisting in the search or rescue of individuals or in other emergency situations and disasters.

If the individual qualifies for the exemption, only expense allowance amounts/or payments that are more than $1,000 are included in employment income.

The exemption does not apply if the individual:

- was employed by the public authority for the same or similar duties (e.g., an individual already employed as a volunteer firefighter);
- received a salary for the emergency work in addition to the allowance.

[7] Court cases include: *Bell v. M.N.R.*, 62 DTC 1115 (Ex. Ct.), *Grant v. M.N.R.*, 67 DTC 249 (T.A.B.), and *Curran v. M.N.R.*, 59 DTC 1247 (S.C.C.), which will be considered again under subsection 6(3).

[8] For a case on this issue see *McLuhan v. M.N.R.*, 63 DTC 211 (T.A.B.).

¶3,100 SPECIFIC INCLUSIONS

Most benefits that must be included in income from employment are specified in section 6, with section 7 limited to the benefit from employer stock options. The major list of benefits is contained in subsection 6(1), with its many paragraphs listing different specific taxable benefits. Subsections 6(1.1) to (23) provide mostly amplification, exceptions, formulae or limits for benefits listed in subsection 6(1). Thus, when attempting to determine if a particular benefit is taxable, scanning the list of paragraph headings in subsection 6(1) should be the first step.

Note that before the rules of the paragraphs in subsection 6(1) are presented, there is a preamble which provides that amounts established to be taxable in the following paragraphs are to be "included in computing the income of a taxpayer for a taxation year as income from an office or employment". Also, each paragraph of subsection 6(1) is a continuation of the sentence commenced in the preamble. In essence, the single sentence which is subsection 6(1) covers several pages of the Act! This is a function of the particular drafting style chosen for the Act in which each subsection consists of only one sentence.

Exhibit 3-2 lists the benefits that are discussed in this chapter.

EXHIBIT 3-2
Taxable Benefits

	Discussed at ¶
Value of board and lodging	3,110
General rules	3,125
Statutory exceptions	3,125.20
Selected court decisions	3,125.30
Flexible benefit programs	3,125.40
Indirect benefits	3,125.50
Concepts and principles	3,125.60
Administrative practice	3,125.70
Housing loss and housing cost	3,130
Employee loans	3,135
Allowances	3,150
Director's or other fees	3,170
Employment insurance benefits	3,230
Payments by employer to employee	3,240
Restrictive covenant	3,250
Stock options	3,260

¶3,110 Value of Board and Lodging

Beyond establishing that board and lodging is a taxable benefit, as was the situation in the case of *Cockerill v. M.N.R.*, the inclusion of the value of board and lodging presents a valuation problem. In pars. 4 and 28 of the Interpretation Bulletin entitled "Employees' Fringe Benefits", the CRA indicates that board and lodging must be valued for tax purposes at the fair market value less any amount charged to the employee. However, if a "reasonable amount" is recovered from the employee, then board and subsidized meals are not subject to this rule. The CRA indicates that a "reasonable amount" is one which covers costs, including food preparation and service costs. Where a lesser amount is recovered, the difference between that amount and the above total costs will be a taxable benefit.

65 DTC 525 (T.A.B.)
IT-470R

As an exception to the benefit rule that requires the inclusion of the value of board and lodging, the Act excludes from the income of an employee, in carefully defined circumstances of employment at a special work site or remote location, the benefits he or she might otherwise be said to derive from board and lodging and transportation. The conditions that must be met for the exception to apply may be summarized as follows: ITA: 6(1)(*a*), 6(6)

(a) the special work site must be a distance away from the employee's ordinary residence such that he or she cannot reasonably be expected to travel daily, and the temporary nature of the duties or the remoteness of the work site must be such that it is not reasonable to establish and maintain a self-contained domestic establishment; and

(b) the board and lodging is necessary for not less than 36 hours and, if an allowance in respect of the board and lodging is paid by the employer, the allowance is not in excess of a reasonable amount.

Note that an employee's ordinary residence, referred to in part (a) above, is one in which he or she maintains a "self-contained domestic establishment" as his or her principal place of residence. ITA: 248(1)

This topic is covered in more detail in the CRA Interpretation Bulletin entitled "Employment at Special Work Sites or Remote Work Locations". IT-91R4

¶3,120 Other Fringe Benefits

¶3,125 General rules

¶3,125.10 *Concept of a benefit*

Paragraph 6(1)(*a*) itself begins with a preamble which states the general rule for including benefits that arise in the course of or by virtue of an office or employment. This preamble is very broadly worded, as emphasized by the Supreme Court of Canada in the case of *The Queen v. Savage*, so that it would seem to catch any possible benefit which arises from employment. The Court went on to quote from its decision in *Nowegijick v. The Queen*, where it stated that: ITA: 6(1)(*a*) 83 DTC 5409, at 5414 (S.C.C.) 83 DTC 5041 (S.C.C.)

> The words "in respect of" are . . . words of the widest possible scope. They impart such meaning as "in relation to", "with reference to" or "in connection with". The phrases "in respect of" is probably the widest of any expression intended to convey some connection between two related subject matters.

Paragraph 6(1)(*a*) includes benefits "enjoyed", as well as those benefits received, through an office or employment. A benefit enjoyed and, thereby, included in employment income by the employee-taxpayer, raises the whole question of valuation of the benefit.

The word "benefit", used on its own, is not defined in the Act. In the case of *The Queen v. Poynton*, Evans, J.A. stated, on the issue of determining whether a benefit is received or enjoyed: 72 DTC 6329, at 6355-6 (Ont. C.A.)

> . . . [a benefit] is a material acquisition which confers an *economic benefit on the taxpayer* [emphasis added] and does not constitute an exemption, e.g., loan or gift. . . .

This concept of a benefit was cited with approval by Justice Dickson in *The Queen v. Savage*. In the case of *A.G. v. Hoefele*, Linden, J.A. elaborated on that concept: 83 DTC 5409, at 5414 (S.C.C.) 95 DTC 5602, at 5604 (F.C.A.)

> According to the Supreme Court of Canada, then, to be taxable as a "benefit", a receipt must confer an economic benefit. In other words, a receipt must increase the recipient's net worth to be taxable. Conversely, a receipt which does not increase net worth is not a benefit and is not taxable.

¶3,125.20 *Statutory exceptions*

The general statement of the rule in paragraph 6(1)(*a*) is followed by specific statutory exceptions to the rule, outlined as follows:

(a) employer's contributions to:

(i) a registered pension plan or pooled registered pension plan,

(ii) a group sickness or accident insurance plan which includes all types of income protection plans,

(iii) private health services plan premiums and provincial health tax levies, but not provincial health plan premiums,

(iv) a supplementary unemployment benefit plan, including both public and private plans,

(v) a deferred profit sharing plan (which is similar to a registered pension plan except that only the employer contributes and the contribution is based on profits), or

(vi) a group term life insurance policy (but refer to subsection 6(4) for the income inclusion of the full employer-paid premium);

(b) benefits under a retirement compensation arrangement, an employee benefit plan or an employee trust, already included in income under other provisions;[9]

(c) benefits in respect of the use of an automobile (separate benefits for the availability of an employer-provided automobile, a standby charge and an automobile operating expense benefit are discussed later in the chapter);

(d) benefits from counselling services in respect of mental or physical health and re-employment or retirement of the employee;

(e) benefits under a salary deferral arrangement already included in income by reason of subsection 6(11); and

[(f) education assistance that is received by an individual other than the employee under a program, provided by the employer, that is designed to assist individuals further their education if (1) the employee deals with the employer at arm's length and (2) it is reasonable to conclude that the benefit is not a substitute for salary, wages, or other remuneration of the taxpayer (proposed in Bill C-48, which received Royal Assent and became law on June 26, 2013).]

Provincial employer health tax levies in part (a)(iii), above, are not taxable benefits (e.g., Ontario Employer Health Tax and similar plans in Manitoba, Nunavut, Quebec, and Newfoundland and Labrador), since the basis of this tax is the total payroll amount and the liability for this tax belongs to the employer and not the employee. However, premiums paid by employers for provincial health care services plans, where the employee is liable for the premium, are taxable because, as *public* health services plans (i.e., government operated plans), they do not fit the specific wording of the exception for *private* plans (i.e., private insurance plans).

Part (c), above, excludes the benefit in respect of the use of an automobile since there is a specific inclusion (discussed later in the chapter) of a standby charge for automobiles and for all operating costs paid by the employer for personal use of the automobile, such as gas, oil, maintenance, insurance, etc. ITA: 6(1)(*e*), 6(1)(*k*), 6(1)(*l*)

Any benefit related to parking for personal purposes is not considered to be a benefit in respect of the *use* of an automobile. As a result, any benefit related to personal parking will be included in employment income as a benefit. In the case of *Chow and Topechka v. The Queen*, the Court determined that free parking spaces were not a taxable benefit since the ITA: 6(1.1) 2001 DTC 164 (T.C.C.)

[9] Part (b), above, became an exclusion from paragraph 6(1)(*a*) with the introduction of the following specific income inclusion provisions which prevent employees from deferring the receipt of income to subsequent years:

- retirement compensation arrangements [pars. 56(1)(*x*) and (*z*)];
- employee benefit plans [par. 6(1)(*g*)]; and
- employee trusts [par. 6(1)(*h*)].

Employee benefit plan rules were introduced to prevent a timing difference between the employer's deduction and the employee's income inclusion for non-registered income deferral plans (i.e., non-government-approved pension plans). With the introduction of even further restrictions on deferred salary arrangements in 1986, these employee benefit plan rules have limited applicability. For example, they apply to "offside" retirement compensation arrangements (RCAs).

parking spaces were provided for the employer's advantage rather than the employee's advantage. This case rebuts the assumption that free parking spaces are automatically a taxable benefit.

¶3,125.30 *Selected court decisions*

For selected court decisions on fringe benefits that were included in income in respect of:

- holiday trips and prizes,[10] see *Philp et al. v. M.N.R.* and *Arsens v. M.N.R.*; 70 DTC 6237 (Ex. Ct.), 69 DTC 81 (T.A.B.)
- travelling expenses paid for an employee's spouse,[11] see *Hale v. M.N.R.*; and 68 DTC 5326 (Ex. Ct.)
- an economic benefit from a payment made by an employer, see *The Queen v. Huffman*. 90 DTC 6405 (F.C.A.)

¶3,125.40 *Flexible benefit programs*

An innovation in providing employee fringe benefits is a cafeteria program or flexible benefit program. These programs enable employees to select from a menu of available benefits some of which are taxable and some of which are not. In addition, some of these programs permit employees to select the quantum of the benefit within a certain defined range, e.g., group insurance plans. There is no specific provision within the Act that governs flexible benefit programs; instead each component of the flexible benefit program is governed by its own unique set of rules. However, in designing the program care must be taken to satisfy certain general conditions to ensure that there is no adverse tax consequences for all the benefits provided under the program. An Interpretation Bulletin, "Flexible employee benefit programs", discusses in great detail the various types of flexible benefit programs, overriding conditions, specific benefit provisions, and certain administrative interpretations. IT-529

¶3,125.50 *Indirect benefits*

Consider the following two independent situations.

1. An employee receives a cash reward from a supplier for reaching a record sales quota.

2. ABC Corporation's CEO owns a condominium in Hawaii where top executives and their spouses stay, from time to time, for personal leisure only. The CEO pays all upkeep and other incidental expenses of the condo.

Situation 1 — Reward from Supplier

The cash reward is received from a supplier rather than from the employer. However, the benefit was "received by virtue of employment". Paragraph 6(1)(*a*) is broad in its inclusion of benefits and does not specifically state that remuneration be from the employer. This statement has been interpreted several times in the courts with various results. A provision on "reimbursements and awards" was added to clarify that all awards should be included as a taxable benefit. The supplier will be able to deduct the cost of the reward since it was incurred as an incentive for salespersons to increase sales. In terms of taxable benefits, it should not matter who provided the reward, since the reward was received by virtue of employment. ITA: 6(1)(*j*)

Suppose the employee reward was an all-expense-paid trip for the salesperson and his or her spouse to the Annual Conference in San Francisco, where the salesperson would be involved in meetings and demonstrations for most of the trip. Since the employee would be learning about many of the new products and also meeting prospective customers, it is clear that the trip would be for employment purposes. However, it is unnecessary for the employee's spouse to be present and the value of the trip (airfare and meals) relating to the spouse will be considered a taxable benefit to the employee.

[10] In the case of *Romeril v. The Queen*, 99 DTC 221 (T.C.C.), where an employee attended a convention, it was held that the trip was not taken for pleasure, but was genuinely related to employment. Hence no benefit could be assessed.

[11] In the case of *Lowe v. The Queen*, 96 DTC 6226 (F.C.A.), an account executive for an insurance company was requested to accompany a group of prize-winning brokers on a trip to New Orleans. The company paid the costs of the executive and his spouse. It was established that the executive and his spouse had little personal time on the trip and no benefit could be assessed.

Situation 2 — Employee Use of a Resort Condominium

The condominium is owned and maintained by the CEO. The purpose of providing the condominium to employees is to reward senior employees with an annual trip. Over the past several years this has created longer-term employer–employee relationships and improved employee morale and effective team leadership. The company does not fund the trip and none of the expenses are deducted from the CEO's personal income. It is important to note that the CEO does not use any of the corporate funds to maintain the condominium.

Since the condominium is the personal-use property of the CEO, and the employer does not pay or contribute to the costs, the benefit provided to top executives would not be taxable. If, however, the corporation owned the condominium or reimbursed the CEO for maintenance costs, then a taxable benefit would be imputed to each employee who used the condominium. For example, if the employer owns a condominium in the Bahamas and it allows the employee to use it for two weeks while on vacation, the value of the benefit is not the cost of maintaining the condominium for the employer but the rent that the employee would have paid to an unrelated third party for the use of similar accommodation.

¶3,125.60 *Concepts and principles*

It would be economically unwise, and impossible from an administrative point of view, for the Act to formulate rules for every employee "fringe benefit". Some important concepts and principles that are useful in tax planning include:

- Fringe benefits that create inequity between taxpayers are generally considered a taxable benefit.
- Fringe benefits offered solely for personal enjoyment are taxable benefits.
- All-expense-paid trips taken for pleasure are taxable benefits.

It is also important to consider all the facts surrounding each situation. It may be worthwhile to review related court cases and precedents when determining whether or not a taxable benefit exists.

¶3,125.70 *Administrative practice*

As previously mentioned, Interpretation Bulletins reflect the CRA's position in interpreting a particular section of the Act. Often, the CRA uses an administratively practical interpretation of the law and, in certain cases, does not enforce the law strictly because it is simply not practical to do so.

The Interpretation Bulletin entitled "Employees' Fringe Benefits" clarifies the Agency's position on several important issues, some of which are summarized below. IT-470R

- The exclusion from employment income of fees, paid by an employer, for an employee's membership in a social club applies to those situations "where the membership was principally for the employer's advantage rather than the employee's". IT-470R, par. 34
- Personal-use benefits from frequent-flyer programs accumulated through employer-paid business trips are specifically included in employment income. However, subsequent to the publication of this Interpretation Bulletin, the CRA changed its administrative practice dealing with loyalty programs. These changes are discussed below. IT-470R, par. 14
- Financial counselling and tax return preparation provided directly or indirectly by an employer except for financial counselling in respect of re-employment or retirement are specifically included in employment income. IT-470R, par. 26
- The CRA's position in respect of business trips for spouses of employees indicates that there is no employment benefit to the employee if the spouse was, in fact, engaged *primarily* in the business activities on behalf of the employer as opposed to engaged primarily in personal activities. IT-470R, par. 15

This Interpretation Bulletin is an important reference for employment benefit planning. It contains a list of items which, if received or enjoyed by an employee, must be included in employment income and a second list of items which need not be included, despite the general wording of the preamble in paragraph 6(1)(*a*), if the CRA's conditions outlined in the Bulletin are met. Clearly, it may be worthwhile on an after-tax basis for an employee to trade taxable salary or fringe benefits for an equivalent amount of non-taxable benefits that are desired by the employee. IT-470R

In a change in assessing policy that is not yet reflected in this Interpretation Bulletin, the CRA assesses the taxable benefit based on certain guidelines: IT-470R ITA: 6(1)(*a*)

1. To mark special occasions, such as Christmas, Hanukkah, birthdays, or a marriage, employers can give their employees two non-cash gifts per year on a tax-free basis. In addition, to honour employment achievements, such as years of service or meeting safety standards, employers can give their employees two non-cash awards per year on a tax-free basis.
2. The total cost to the employer, including taxes, of the two gifts or the two awards cannot be over $500 per year.
3. Employers can deduct the total cost of the gifts or awards.
4. Employees do not have to declare the cost of the gifts or awards as part of their taxable income.
5. If the cost of a gift or an award is over the $500 limit, the employer must include the full fair-market value of the gift(s) or award(s) in the employee's income.
6. If an employer gives two or more gifts — or two or more awards — in a single year and their total cost is over the $500 limit, the employer may have to include the fair market value of one or more of the gifts or awards in the employee's income.
7. This inclusion is determined by the cost of each gift or award and, also, by the number of gifts or awards given in a single year.
8. The new policy does not apply to cash or near–cash gifts and awards such as gift certificates, gold nuggets, or other items that can easily be converted into cash. The value of a cash or near–cash gift or award is considered a taxable employment benefit.

In its publication, *Income Tax Technical News*, No. 40, dated June 11, 2009, the CRA announced changes to its policy on non-cash gifts and awards. The following was taken from this publication:

> The CRA's current gifts and awards policy was introduced in 2001 with an intention to remove the burden of determining the fair market value of small gifts and awards and recognize common business practices. It allowed for the non-taxation of up to two non-cash gifts costing the employer in total $500 or less, as well as the non-taxation of up to two non-cash awards costing the employer in total $500 or less. In addition, the condition that the employer could not deduct the costs as business expenses was also removed.
>
> The CRA has received submissions that the current policy has not significantly reduced administrative burden in cases where numerous immaterial items may be given to an employee in a year. Concerns also include employers introducing gift and award policies principally for the purpose of providing tax-free remuneration to employees. Additionally, numerous tax planning questions are received as to how to maximize the tax-free status by categorizing items in order to qualify for either the gift policy or award policy. Effective for 2010, to address these issues, the following changes and clarifications are being made to the CRA's gift and award policy:
>
> - Non-cash gifts and non-cash awards to an arm's length employee, regardless of number, will not be taxable to the extent that the total aggregate value of all non-cash gifts and awards to that employee is less than $500 annually. The total value in excess of $500 annually will be taxable.
> - In addition to the above, a separate non-cash long service/anniversary award may also qualify for non-taxable status to the extent its total value is $500 or less. The value in

excess of $500 will be taxable. In order to qualify, the anniversary award cannot be for less than five years of service or for five years since the last long service award had been provided to the employee. For the purposes of applying the $500 thresholds, the annual gifts and awards threshold and the long service/anniversary awards threshold are separate. In other words, a shortfall in value under one policy cannot be used to offset an excess value of the other.

- The employer gift and award policy will not apply to non-arm's length employees (e.g., relative of proprietor, shareholders of closely held corporations) or related persons of the non-arm's length employee.
- For clarification purposes, items of an immaterial or nominal value, such as coffee, tea, T-shirts with employer logos, mugs, plaques, trophies, etc., will not be considered a taxable benefit to employees. There is no defined monetary threshold that determines an immaterial amount. Factors that may be taken into account include the value, frequency, and administrative practicability of accounting for nominal benefits.

The CRA's administrative policies as to the qualifying nature of gifts and awards will remain unchanged. For example, performance-related rewards (e.g., sales targets) or cash and near cash awards (e.g., gift certificates) will continue to fall outside the administrative policy and will be required to be included in the taxable income of the employee.

The CRA has a policy[12] on home computers supplied by an employer. According to the guidelines, there is no taxable benefit, where providing the computer is primarily to the benefit of the employer. *Income Tax Technical News*, No. 13 (1999)

In addition to changes to its policy on non-cash gifts and awards, the CRA also announced other administrative policy changes, some of which are set out below. *Income Tax Technical News*, No. 40 (2009)

Administrative Policy Changes for Taxable Employment Benefits

In 2007, the Canada Revenue Agency (the "CRA") initiated a review of taxable benefits to employees and the related administrative costs to employers. During this review, the CRA has worked with other government and external stakeholders. Based on the findings, the CRA is announcing . . . changes to its administrative policies for taxable employment benefits in order to reduce a number of administrative difficulties and increase fairness.

Overtime Meals and Allowances Provided to Employees

The CRA's current administrative policy allows for a non-taxable status of certain overtime meals or reasonable allowances for overtime meals. This is the case if the employee worked three or more hours of overtime right after his or her scheduled hours of work; and the overtime was infrequent and occasional in nature (less than three times a week).

Concerns have been raised to indicate the economic benefit received by the employee are often minor, the meaning of a "reasonable allowance" is not always clear, employer policies often allow for meal allowances after two hours of overtime and the strict application of the limitation of "less than three times in a week" sometimes leads to certain inequitable results.

In order to address these issues, effective for the 2009 year, the CRA will consider no taxable benefit to arise if:

- the value of the meal or meal allowance is reasonable; a value of up to $17 will generally be considered reasonable,
- the employee works two or more hours of overtime right before or right after his or her scheduled hours of work, and
- the overtime is infrequent and occasional in nature. Less than three times a week will generally be considered infrequent or occasional.

This condition may also be met where the meal or allowance is provided three or more times per week on an occasional basis to meet workload demands such as major repairs or periodic financial reporting.

If overtime occurs on a frequent basis or becomes the norm, the CRA considers the overtime meal allowances to be a taxable benefit since they start taking on the characteristics of additional remuneration.

[12] The *Income Tax Technical News* series is another of the CRA's interpretive publications.

Municipality or Metropolitan Area

In some circumstances, employer-provided travel (including meal) allowances paid in respect of travel within the "municipality" or, if there is one, the "metropolitan area" can be excluded from income. Effective for 2009, the CRA will accept that these allowances paid for travel within the municipality or metropolitan area may be excluded from income if the allowance is paid primarily for the benefit of the employer. That is, an allowance may be excluded from income when its principal objective is to ensure that the employee's duties are undertaken in a more efficient manner during the course of a work shift, and where allowances paid are not indicative of an alternate form of remuneration.

Loyalty Programs

Many employees collect loyalty points (e.g., frequent flyer points) on their personal credit cards offered by third parties when travelling on employer reimbursed business trips or incurring other business related expenses. These points can be exchanged or redeemed for goods and services, including gift certificates.

The CRA has been of the view that where an employer does not control the points accumulated under such programs, it will be the responsibility of the employee to determine and include in income the fair market value of any benefits received or enjoyed. However, employees often face significant difficulties with respect to the valuation of these benefits as well as tracking and identifying the benefits attributable to points accumulated by way of employment versus personal use of the credit cards. Effective for 2009, the CRA will no longer require these employment benefits to be included in an employee's income, so long as:

- the points are not converted to cash,
- the plan or arrangement is not indicative of an alternate form of remuneration, or
- the plan or arrangement is not for tax avoidance purposes.

It should be noted that where an employer controls the points (e.g., a company credit card), the employer will continue to be required to report the fair market value of any benefits received by the employee on the employee's T4 slip when the points are redeemed.

Example — Personal Credit Card

Pauline's employer has allowed her to use her personal credit cards whenever possible to pay for business expenses, which the employer subsequently reimburses to Pauline. To maximize the points earned, Pauline used her personal credit cards to pay for various employer business costs, including travel expenses of other employees.

The CRA would not consider such an arrangement to qualify as a non-taxable amount under the administrative policy. The arrangement is indicative of having been made in order to provide a benefit to the employee as an alternate form of remuneration. In this case, Pauline must determine and include in income on her personal income tax return, the value of benefits received or enjoyed.

Example — Company credit card points as benefit to the employee

Jennifer's employer has a company credit card, under which loyalty points are earned. The employer is billed and pays the credit card charges. The employer allows Jennifer to redeem the points for her personal use. In such circumstances, the fair market value of the goods or services received by Jennifer will represent a taxable employment benefit. In this case, the employer must include and report the value of the benefit on the employee's T4 slip.

The Interpretation Bulletin on employee fringe benefits was last revised on October 12, 1999. Although it is still in force, these changes in CRA assessing policy suggest that the Interpretation Bulletin is becoming dated and may have to be revised again. Alternatively, the government might amend the Act on these issues. IT-470R

¶3,130 Housing loss and housing cost benefits

The Act addresses the income tax consequences of employer-provided compensation in respect of losses on a disposition of the employee's residence and other housing-related payments such as financing subsidies. ITA: 6(19)–(23)

Any amount paid in respect of a housing loss is included in income. However, this general rule is modified so that only one-half the amount in excess of $15,000 of an employer-paid amount is included in employment income for an *eligible housing loss*. For example, if an employee realizes a loss of $30,000 and his or her employer reimburses the employee for $20,000 of the loss, the employee's benefit would be computed as: 1/2 ($20,000 – $15,000) = $2,500. ITA: 6(1)(*a*), 6(19) ITA: 6(22)

- An eligible housing loss is the taxpayer's *housing loss* (see below) that is designated or chosen by the taxpayer as such and is in respect of an *eligible relocation* (see below) of the taxpayer or non-arm's length person. ITA: 6(22)
- In general terms, a housing loss is the cost of the residence to the taxpayer or a non-arm's length person minus the proceeds of disposition or fair market value depending on certain circumstances. ITA: 6(21)
- An "eligible relocation" is defined for purposes of these provisions and deductible moving expenses. This definition imposes a 40-kilometre minimum on the difference in the distance between the old residence and the new work location, and the distance between the new residence and the new work location. For example, if the distance between an employee's old residence and the new work location is 100 kilometres, and the distance between the new residence and the new work location is 20 kilometres, the difference in the two distances is 80 kilometres. The move between the two residences would qualify as an eligible relocation. This kilometre restriction is also referred to in Chapter 9, under the heading "Moving Expenses". ITA: 6(19), 6(23), 62, 248(1) "eligible relocation"

Finally, the Act contains a catch-all provision, "for greater certainty", that includes in the income of the employee all other employer-provided payments or any other type of assistance by anyone in respect of housing. ITA: 6(23)

¶3,135 Employee loans

¶3,135.10 *General system for inclusion and deduction*

Employment income includes an imputed interest benefit on an interest-free or low-interest loan made by an employer and received by an employee in his or her capacity as an employee. The benefit is defined as being the difference between the interest calculated at the prescribed interest rate, which may change for each quarter in the year during which the loan was outstanding, and the actual interest charged by the employer in respect of the calendar year and paid by the employee up to January 30 of the following year. Interest paid or *payable* in respect of the calendar year on behalf of the employee by the employer or related party is also included in the benefit calculation. Only the interest actually *paid* by the employee is deductible. Hence, interest not paid within the above time-frame does not reduce the benefit. ITA: 6(9) ITA: 80.4(1) ITR: 4300, 4301

A deeming rule states that this imputed interest benefit is, in turn, deemed to be interest paid. The effect of this deeming rule is to meet a condition in the provision which allows for a deduction of interest *paid* on funds borrowed to purchase a car for use in employment. By deeming the imputed interest benefit, which is included in employment income, to be interest *paid*, one of the conditions of the interest deduction provision is met. As a result, all or a part of the imputed interest benefit may be deductible. A similar effect is provided where funds are borrowed from an employer, for example, to purchase shares of a corporate employer. In this situation, one of the conditions, which provides for a deduction of interest paid on funds borrowed under specified circumstances, discussed in Chapter 6 at ¶6,260, would be met by this deeming rule. However, it must be emphasized that the interest is deductible only if the amount qualifies under all of the specific conditions of these provisions. ITA: 80.5 ITA: 8(1)(*j*) ITA: 20(1)(*c*)

¶3,135.20 *Specific rules for home purchase loans*

"Home purchase loans" and "home relocation loans" are defined terms in the Act. The benefit calculation for these loans is done for each quarter the loan is outstanding as the lesser of: ITA: 80.4(7), 248(1) ITA: 80.4(1), 80.4(4)

(a) the prescribed rate for the quarter while the loan was outstanding; and

(b) the prescribed rate in effect at the time the loan was made.

This is described as the quarter-by-quarter method.

Part (b) of this calculation is modified every fifth year, to use the prescribed rate on every fifth anniversary date, for home purchase loans. ITA: 80.4(6)

Note that where the Act uses the term "prescribed" as in prescribed rate, the "prescription" will usually appear in the Income Tax Regulations. Refer to the footnotes of the provision in which the term is used, under the "Regulation" heading, to locate the regulation that is applicable. Where a form is prescribed, the number of the form will usually be listed in the footnotes.

The Act contains a partial exemption for the imputed interest income inclusion, as described above, for basically the first $25,000 of a "home relocation loan". This type of loan results from any move of at least 40 kilometres by the taxpayer or his or her spouse to a new employment location in Canada. However, this exemption is deducted under Division C (deductions to arrive at taxable income) and is generally deductible during the first five years of the loan to the extent of the imputed interest net of qualified interest payments. This topic will be discussed in further detail in Chapter 10. ITA: 110(1)(*j*) ITA: 248(1) "home relocation loan"

Note that the CRA computes interest on a daily basis. Following normal commercial practice, the CRA calculates interest commencing with the first day that a debt is incurred and excluding the day on which the debt is repaid, unless a provision of the Act specifies another method of calculation.

Example Problem 3-2

On May 1 of this year, Mr. Roberts borrowed from his employer, Stanley Inc., $35,000 evidenced by a 3% promissory note with principal repayable in five equal instalments on the anniversary date and interest payable monthly. Mr. Roberts spent the $35,000 on the following acquisitions:

(a) $10,000 for a second-hand car which he needs to carry out his duties of employment (approximately 60% of the time);

(b) $5,000 for acquiring dividend-paying common shares in his brother's corporation; and

(c) $20,000 as a down payment on a new condominium which he moved into immediately.

Assume that the prescribed interest rates for this year are the following:

1st quarter	7%	3rd quarter	8%
2nd quarter......	6%	4th quarter	7%

— *REQUIRED*

Discuss the tax consequences of the above transactions, supporting them with all necessary computations. Ignore the effects of the leap year.

— *SOLUTION*

Income:

Mr. Roberts will have an imputed employment income inclusion for the accrued interest from May 1 to December 31[(1)] of this year under subsection 6(9) by virtue of subsection 80.4(1).

Car and shares portion of loan

2nd quarter: May 1 to June 30 (inclusive)

$$\frac{61}{365} \times 6\% \times \$15{,}000 = \ldots\ldots\ldots\ldots \quad \$\ 150$$

3rd quarter: July 1 to September 30 (inclusive)

$\frac{92}{365} \times 8\% \times \$15{,}000 =$	302	

4th quarter: October 1 to December 31 (inclusive)

$\frac{92}{365} \times 7\% \times \$15{,}000 =$	265	$717

Condominium portion of loan:[(2)]

May 1 to December 31 (inclusive)

$\frac{245}{365} \times 6\% \times \$20{,}000 =$	$ 805
Total	$1,522
Less: interest for the year paid on all loans	
$\frac{245}{365} \times 3\% \times (\$15{,}000 + \$20{,}000) =$	705
Imputed interest benefit inclusion	$ 817

Deductions:

Although deductions are really presented in subsequent chapters and the latter part of this chapter, a conceptual discussion of the deduction alternatives may be helpful in understanding the whole issue.

- Portion of loan used to acquire the car and shares ($15,000)

Under section 80.5, the imputed interest income in respect of both the shares and the car, in this case, is deemed to be paid and, hence, may be eligible for a deduction. However, both of these amounts must meet further tests in paragraphs 8(1)(*j*) and 20(1)(*c*), in order to qualify for a deduction.

- Portion of loan used to acquire condominium ($20,000)

There is no deduction available in connection with a home purchase loan except in Division C where the employee has moved, under certain defined conditions as described in Chapter 10.

— *NOTES TO SOLUTION*

(1) The days of interest were determined by counting the first day of the contractual arrangement.

(2) The condominium portion of the loan should qualify as a home purchase loan. Therefore, the imputed interest calculation would be based on the "lesser of" rule demonstrated above. Since the prescribed rate at the time the loan was made (6%) is less than the subsequent quarterly prescribed rates (8% and 7%), the 6% rate applies to all three quarters. The CRA's administrative practice is to apply these rules on a quarter-by-quarter basis, not on an annual basis. ITA: 80.4(4) [in combination with ssec. 80.4(1)], 80.4(7)

¶3,135.30 *Forgiveness of employee loans*

The Act determines the value of an employment benefit arising on the forgiveness of an employee loan. The effect of this provision is to include in employment income the amount of the employer loan or other indebtedness net of any payments made by the employee, i.e., the forgiven amount. This treatment is logical since the principal amount of the loan is not taxed when received. If a repayment with after-tax funds is not required because the loan was forgiven, the employee receives an economic benefit. ITA: 6(1)(*a*), 6(15)

¶3,150 Allowances

¶3,155 Overview

First, the differences between an allowance and a reimbursement must be identified. Typically, a reimbursement involves the payment by an employee of an expense of his or her employer and the recovery from the employer of the amount paid as substantiated by vouchers or receipts. Generally, a reimbursement is not a taxable benefit to the employee. On the other hand, an allowance is a fixed amount which is paid to an employee in excess of his or her salary without the requirement that the employee substantiate the amounts expended. An Interpretation Bulletin, "Vehicle, Travel and Sales Expenses of Employees", adopts these meanings for the terms "allowance" and "reimbursement", respectively. IT-522R, pars. 40, 50

Two precedent-setting judicial decisions on this issue are presented in *Ransom v. M.N.R.* and *Splane v. The Queen*. Both cases established a two-stage test for determining if a payment to an employee is employment income. First, a determination must be made as to whether the payment is an allowance or a reimbursement. If the payment is an allowance, then the rules in paragraph 6(1)(*b*) apply. If the payment is a reimbursement, then a further determination must be made as to whether the employee has received an "economic benefit". Normally, there is no benefit if the employee is in the same economic position as he or she was in prior to the employer-driven transaction which gave rise to payment. 67 DTC 5235 (Ex. Ct.), 92 DTC 6021 (F.C.A.)

Again, paragraph 6(1)(*b*) contains a preamble which establishes the general rule for the inclusion of allowances. The general rule is that all such allowances received must be included in the employee's income. However, there are many exceptions to this rule listed in the paragraph, some of which are discussed below. Any allowance received, that is not specifically excepted, is regarded as an allowance in respect of a personal or living expense. Since such an expense is not deductible, an amount received as an allowance for such an expense must be included in income.[13] ITA: 6(1)(*b*)

The nine exceptions are summarized as: ITA: 6(1)(*b*)

1. travel, personal, or living allowances fixed by an Act of Parliament or paid under the *Inquiries Act*;

2. travel and separation allowances received under regulation by a member of the Canadian Forces;

3. representation or special allowances received in a period of absence by a Canadian Forces member, servants of Canada or a province, those providing services under an international development assistance program, and Canadian Forces school staff;

4. representation or special allowances received by an agent-general of a province while in Ottawa;

5. reasonable travel expense allowances received in selling property or negotiating contracts for an employer;

6. reasonable allowances received by a Minister or clergy for transportation expenses;

7. reasonable allowances received by employees (other than one negotiating contracts or selling property) for travel away from the municipality or metropolitan area where they normally reported for work;

8. reasonable allowances received by employees (other than one negotiating contracts or selling property) for use of a motor vehicle in performing their employment duties;

9. allowances (not in excess of a reasonable amount) for an employee's child to attend and live at the closest school away from home at which the instruction language is an official Canadian language because there is no school using that language where the employee is required to live.

[13] For a case on the topic of personal or living expenses, see *Henry v. M.N.R.*, 72 DTC 6005 (S.C.C.).

Certain allowances, reimbursements, and other payments in respect of disabled persons for transportation to and from the workplace and for the services of an attendant to assist the employee to perform his or her employment duties are excluded from employment income. In order for these exemptions to apply the disabled person must be eligible for a disability tax credit which is discussed in some detail in Chapter 10. ITA: 6(1), 6(16) ITA: 118.3

¶3,160 Exception of allowance for travelling expenses of sales/negotiating persons

A common exception to the taxation of allowances deals with employees who sell property or negotiate contracts. Note the conditions that must be met for the allowance to be excluded: ITA: 6(1)(*b*)(v)

(a) the allowance must be reasonable;

(b) the allowance must be only for travelling expenses, including by implication motor vehicle expenses (this topic is covered separately, later in this chapter); and

(c) the recipient (hereinafter referred to as a "sales/negotiating person") must be involved in the selling of property or the negotiating of contracts for his or her employer.

The word "reasonable" is not defined in the Act and, therefore, must be applied to the particular facts of the situation. For example, a reasonable daily allowance for the travelling expense of the president of a large public corporation (a person who negotiates contracts) would be entirely different than a reasonable daily allowance for a salesperson for the same organization. 6(1)(*b*)(v)

In the case of *Hudema v. The Queen*, the taxpayer claimed that a car allowance was not reasonable because the allowance did not cover all of his expenses of operating the car. This was not sufficient evidence to prove that the allowance was not reasonable because the court was not convinced that the taxpayer was making a reasonable use of his vehicle. Since the taxpayer made very little personal use of the car, averaging about 15% per year over five years, he attributed most of the costs of operating his car to his work. The court indicated that the taxpayer did not establish that it was sensible to make such little personal use of the car that he used for work. The court further indicated that the employer's allowance should only be expected to pay for such reasonable use of his car as his work required. To be reasonable, the allowance should cover virtually all the costs of his car, both capital and operating. The court suggested that the taxpayer should have provided evidence of the number of hours per week for which he had to use the car for work. 94 DTC 6287 (F.C.T.D.)

In the case of *Lemire v. The Queen*, the judge suggested the type of evidence necessary to determine whether an allowance, to cover reasonable expenses of owning and maintaining a car, was inadequate. The judge indicated, at 1773, that: 94 DTC 1772 (T.C.C.)

> . . . I not only must have evidence as to how the allowance was calculated by the employer, but the intent of the employer when setting the allowance. I must also have the complete history of the vehicle such as the expenses over the years an allowance was received. Just looking at the one year, in light of the evidence before me, is not sufficient. An allowance cannot be reasonable for three years and unreasonable the fourth year. Obviously an Appellant has to demonstrate that his vehicle's expenses are reasonable for an employee in his employment.
>
> An employee earning an annual wage of $40,000 with an investment income of several hundred thousand dollars a year may choose to own and drive a $100,000 car. Obviously a normal reasonable mileage allowance would never cover the depreciation of an automobile this expensive. Even though the expense and depreciation for that car would be reasonable, it would not be reasonable for the employer or the taxpayers of Canada to subsidize this hypothetical employee.

Where a sales/negotiating person receives an allowance for the use of a motor vehicle, there are further conditions that must be satisfied in order to exclude such an allowance. These conditions and their effects will be considered separately, later in ¶3,410. ITA: 6(1)(*b*)(x) or 6(1)(*b*)(xi)

¶3,165 Exception of allowance for travelling expenses of other employees

Another common income exception concerns an allowance for travelling expenses of other employees and has the following conditions: ITA: 6(1)(*b*)(vii)

(a) the employee (hereinafter referred to as "ordinary employee") does not sell property or negotiate contracts;

(b) the allowance must be reasonable in the circumstances;

(c) the allowance must be for travelling expenses, but not for the use of a motor vehicle (which is discussed separately, later in the chapter); and

(d) the recipient must travel away from the municipality and metropolitan area of the employer's establishment at which the employee ordinarily worked.

Note the difference between the conditions for sales/negotiating persons and ordinary employees. First, the travelling expenses include motor vehicle expenses for sales/negotiating persons but exclude them for ordinary employees, since these are covered separately. Second, the ordinary employee has a geographical limitation placed on the travelling expenses. As will be seen in the discussion later in the chapter, there is no geographical limitation placed on an allowance for the use of a motor vehicle for sales/negotiating employees. ITA: 6(1)(*b*)(v) ITA: 6(1)(*b*)(vii) ITA: 6(1)(*b*)(vii.1) ITA: 6(1)(*b*)(vii.1)

¶3,170 Director's or Other Fees

A corporate director holds an "office", as defined in the Act. As a result, fees received by a director are received by virtue of an office and, hence, must be included as employment income. The effect of including such fees in employment income is to limit the deductions to those allowed against employment income. ITA: 6(1)(*c*), 248(1)

¶3,220 Benefit from Employer-Paid GST/HST

Where an employee receives a taxable benefit from his or her employer, the employer is liable for and must remit the relevant GST/HST. The employee in turn is deemed to receive a taxable benefit which generally includes the employer-paid GST/HST. This employment income inclusion of GST/HST places the employee in the same economic position as if he or she acquired the goods or services on the open market. In essence, the Act includes an employer-paid GST/HST in employment income. ITA: 6(1)(*a*), 6(1)(*e*)

Note that the inclusion of the full GST/HST paid by the employer in providing the benefit ignores any reimbursement by the employee for the taxable benefit/taxable supply. This is logical if the objective is to place the employee in the same position as if he or she acquired the supply on the open market and, therefore, would pay GST/HST on the full amount rather than a partial net payment.

The general rule is that any benefit included in income under either the general benefits inclusion rule or the standby charge is subject to the GST/HST. However, two significant exceptions are: ITA: 6(1)(*a*), 6(1)(*e*)

(a) zero-rated supplies found in Schedule VI of the ETA (e.g., gift food baskets); and

(b) exempt supplies found in Schedule V of the ETA (e.g., daycare services, low-rent and rent-free housing, low-interest and interest-free loans, premiums for government health services and tuition fees for exempt education services).

The practical application of including GST/HST paid by the employer in income is fairly limited. The most common applications would be:

(a) personal use of an employer's automobile by way of the standby charge; and ITA: 6(1)(*e*), 6(2)

(b) other payments by the employer which would be considered taxable benefits such as automobile operating and parking costs for personal purposes, travelling expenses relating to vacations, spouse's non-business-related travelling costs, and gifts valued in ITA: 6(1)(*a*) excess of $500 annually on which the employer would have paid GST/HST in providing the item to the employee.

Exhibit 3-3 lists some common taxable benefits and their GST/HST treatment.

EXHIBIT 3-3
Common Taxable Benefits and GST/HST Treatment

Taxable benefits	*GST/HST included*	*GST/HST excluded*
Automobile — Standby charge	√	
Employee counselling services	√	
Group term life insurance		√
Gift: in cash		√
not in cash	√	
Holiday trips	√	
Housing, board, and lodging	(depends on the accommodation)	
Subsidized meals	√	
Interest-free and low-interest loans		√
Provincial hospitalization and medical insurance plans		√
Stock options		√
Recreational facilities	√	
Moving expenses allowance	√	

¶3,230 Employment Insurance Benefits

Section 6 excepts the inclusion in employment income of premiums paid by an employer on behalf of an employee to a group sickness or accident insurance plan. However, amounts received as a result of a disability claim by an employee in respect of a sickness or accident, disability or income maintenance plan, if the employer has made any contribution, must be taken into employment income. Hence, such plans become tainted if the employer pays all or any portion of the premium. ITA: 6(1)(*a*) ITA: 6(1)(*f*)

In terms of employee benefit planning, there is a basic trade-off in the tax treatment of these plans. On the one hand, all employees can receive a relatively small tax-free benefit by having the employer pay the premium. However, those relatively few employees who become disabled and receive insurance payments will be taxed on those payments. On the other hand, all employees can incur a relatively small cost by paying the premium. In this case, the relatively few employees who become disabled and receive insurance payments will receive those payments tax free.

Where an employee has paid any amount of the premiums, these amounts are deductible from the disability benefits received in arriving at the benefit. ITA: 6(1)(*f*)

Non-group plans are treated in exactly the opposite manner. The premiums paid by the employer are treated as employment income. However, payments received in respect of these plans are not considered as income. IT-428, par. 20

Summary

	Sickness or Accident Insurance Plan			
	Group		**Non-group**	
	Premium	**Disability Benefit**	**Premium**	**Disability Benefit**
Employer pays all or part of premium	Not included in income	Included in income	Included in income	Not included in income
Employee pays all of premium	Not deducted from income	Not included in income	Not deducted from income	Not included in income

Example Problem 3-3

Mr. Beta is insured under a group plan which pays $3,000 per month while disabled. The premium is $25 per month, of which the employer pays one-half and has been so paying on Mr. Beta's behalf starting January 1, 1990. The employee's share of the premium is waived during the period of the disability. Mr. Beta was struck by a truck and was off work from January 1, 2012 to June 30, 2013.

— *REQUIRED*

How much must be included in Mr. Beta's income in respect of the disability payments received for the years in question?

— *SOLUTION*

2012

Total cumulative benefits received in 2012 (i.e., before end of 2012 and after 2011) (12 × \$3,000)	\$36,000
Less: total contributions made by employee before end of 2012 (½ × \$25 × 12 × 22[(1)])	3,300
Amount to be included in income	\$32,700

2013

Total benefits received in 2013 (i.e., before end of 2013 and after 2012) (6 × \$3,000)	\$18,000
Less: total contributions made by employee in 2013 (i.e., before end of 2013 and after 2012) (½ × \$25 × 6[(2)])	75
Amount to be included in income	\$17,925

— *NOTES TO SOLUTION*

[(1)] 1990 to 2011, inclusive (2012 is not counted because employee's share of the premium was not paid during disability).

[(2)] While no premium was paid by the employee during the six months of his disability, the premium was paid during the remaining six months in the year.

¶3,240 Payments by Employer to Employee

A few payments received may be regarded as a capital receipt, not subject to tax. However, most payments, such as a signing bonus, might be considered as "other remuneration" or as part of "other benefits of any kind whatever". The payment could also be considered consideration for entering into a contract of employment. This provision basically expands employment income to include payments which are received either immediately before or after the actual employment period and which arise from the employment contract. Each of these provisions must be read very carefully to determine the conditions, if any, necessary for the provision to apply.[14] The following example problem illustrates the need for a careful interpretation.

ITA: 5
ITA: 6(1)(*a*)
ITA: 6(3)

Example Problem 3-4

The appellant, a geologist highly regarded in his field, had been employed by General Oil Limited for many years. Had he continued until retirement, he would have been entitled to a substantial pension which would be lost if he left General Oil voluntarily.

Mr. Green was a substantial shareholder and chief executive of Prairie Oil Limited which held a large number of shares of Clean Oil Limited. Under an agreement made in the year, Mr. Green paid the appellant \$250,000 in consideration of the loss of pension rights, chances for advancement, and opportunities for re-employment in the oil industry. On the same day, the appellant entered into another agreement with Prairie Oil to act as its general manager at a salary of \$25,000 per year, subject to the condition that he would serve as manager of another company if the director so decided.

Pursuant to this consideration, the appellant became the president and manager of Clean Oil at a salary of \$25,000 per year with no superannuation benefits.

— *REQUIRED*

Resolve the foregoing fact situation with reference to paragraph 3(*a*), section 5, and subsection 6(3) of the current *Income Tax Act*.

[14] The case of *No. 261 v. M.N.R.*, 55 DTC 285 (T.A.B.), was heard to decide the meaning of the phrase "immediately after" used in paragraph 6(3)(*b*). Cases that resulted in payments which were considered taxable include *Butters v. M.N.R.*, 52 DTC 37 (T.A.B.), *Moss v. M.N.R.*, 63 DTC 1359 (Ex. Ct.), and *The Queen v. Blanchard*, 95 DTC 5479 (F.C.A.). Cases that resulted in payments which were considered not taxable include *Wilson v. M.N.R.*, 60 DTC 115 (T.A.B.), and *Segall v. M.N.R.*, 86 DTC 6486 (F.C.T.D.). Cases in which receipts were considered not to be taxable by subsection 6(3) include: *Ballard v. M.N.R.*, 87 DTC 157 (T.C.C.), and *The Queen v. Albino*, 94 DTC 6071 (F.C.T.D.).

— *SOLUTION* [see *Robert B. Curran v. M.N.R.*, 59 DTC 1247 (S.C.C.).]

The payment of $250,000 can be considered either as a non-taxable capital receipt or as income from employment. It can be argued that the payment was compensation for substantial benefits foregone, including the loss or relinquishment of a source of income which can be regarded as a capital asset. At least that part of the payment for the loss of pension rights, if such a part can be determined, could be regarded as a non-taxable capital receipt. It has been held that a lump sum paid to commute a pension is a capital payment which is substituted for a series of periodic sums in the nature of income. However, the payment did not come from General Oil to commute the pension.

On the other hand, the payment of $250,000 could be regarded as being made for personal services to be rendered by the appellant to the new employer. The mere fact that the agreement characterizes the $250,000 as a capital payment in consideration of the loss of pension rights, chances for advancement and opportunities for re-employment in the oil industry cannot change the true character of the payment as employment income. Mr. Green was seeking to acquire the skilled services of the appellant as a manager. The consideration was paid so that these services would be made available; therefore, it is income of the appellant within the meaning of paragraph 3(*a*).

Since the payment was not made by the appellant's employer as required by paragraph 6(3)(*b*), it is not *deemed*, for the purpose of section 5, to be remuneration for the appellant's services rendered during the period of employment. Although the payment is not deemed to be employment income, the more general paragraph 3(*a*) can be applied in determining income from employment from a source inside or outside Canada.

The Supreme Court of Canada held that this payment was income from employment under paragraph 3(*a*).

¶3,250 Restrictive Covenants

A proposed amendment provides that an employee may be required to include in employment income an amount that is receivable at the end of the year in respect of a covenant as to what the employee is, or is not, to do. Normally, only amounts received are included in employment income. This provision deems an amount that is receivable to be received. This provision is part of a comprehensive package of amendments related to payments received for covenants provided by individuals. For a full discussion on the treatment of payments received for restrictive covenants please refer to Chapter 9. ITA: 6(3.1) [Proposed]

¶3,260 Stock Options

¶3,265 General

Employee stock options are an incentive that may be offered to employees as part of their compensation package. Under these options, the employee has the right to purchase shares of the corporation at an option price, often the corporation's current value per share, agreed to at the time the option is granted. This form of compensation attempts to align the employee's interests with those of the shareholders. If the value of the company's stock rises, holders of options experience a direct financial benefit since they will be able to purchase the shares at a price lower than current market value. This gives employees an incentive to behave in ways that will increase the company's stock price. At some point in the future, the employee may elect to exercise the option and purchase the shares at the option price. Then the employee can decide to either sell the shares or hold them for future price appreciation.

Two income tax issues arise, at this stage, from an employee's perspective:

- The nature of the income inclusion: is it employment income or capital gain, or both?
- The timing of the inclusion.

The total amount of income that must be accounted for is equal to the difference between the proceeds of disposition on the sale of the shares and the original price paid for the shares. In general, employment income is the difference between the value of the shares at the time the option is exercised and the price paid for the shares. The capital gain or loss is then the difference between the proceeds of disposition on the sale of the shares and the value at the time the shares are exercised.

Conceptually it would be as follows:

Fair market value at exercise
Less: Price paid for the shares (exercise price)
= Employment income

then

Proceeds of disposition on sale to third party
Less: Fair market value at exercise
= Capital gain or capital loss

There are many rules that modify the amount and timing of this income. These will be covered in this chapter for employment income, in Chapter 7 for capital gains and losses, and in Chapter 10 for the Division C deduction available.

Exercising a stock option will result in employment income if the price paid under the option is less than the fair market value of the shares at the time of their purchase. However, the timing of the inclusion and the ultimate effect on taxable income will depend upon a number of factors:

- the type of corporation issuing the option;
- whether the employee and the corporation are dealing at arm's length;
- the relationship of option price to the fair market value of the shares when the option is granted; and
- the relationship of the option price to the value of the shares at the time they are purchased under the option.

The stock option benefit included in employment income must be received as a result of employment from a "qualifying person" that is a corporation or a mutual fund trust. Hence, rights or warrants provided by virtue of shareholdings alone would be excluded from this provision. ITA: 7(5) ITA: 7(7)

¶3,268 Stock options — Withholding tax

ITA: 153(1.01)

Starting in 2011, tax is required to be withheld at source on a stock option benefit, as if it were a bonus. However, this withholding requirement does not apply to:

- the portion of the benefit that is deductible under Division C; or
- benefits arising from rights granted before 2011 under an agreement that was entered into in writing before 4 p.m. EST March 4, 2010, and that included a written condition prohibiting the taxpayer from disposing of the securities acquired under the agreement for a period of time after exercise.

Prior to this amendment there was no requirement to withhold tax on stock options, which often caused difficulty for both the taxpayer and the CRA when it came time to pay and collect the tax liability. This requirement puts the onus on the employer to withhold the tax from the employee's salary and remit it.

¶3,270 Rules applicable for all types of corporations

An employment income inclusion is deemed, for employees of *all* corporations on the exercising of a stock option to be equal to the difference between the fair market value at the date the option is exercised and the option price. However, there is a partial offsetting deduction, in Division C, equal to one-half of the income inclusion, if the option price is equal to or greater than the fair market value of the share at the time the option was granted. In addition, there are certain limitations on the type of shares to be issued and the relationship of the parties before and after the transaction, all of which are discussed in Chapter 10. ITA: 7(1) ITA: 110(1)(*d*)

¶3,273 Stock option cash outs

Where an employee has been granted a stock option, he or she may have the right to sell that option back to his or her employer in exchange for cash. If this is done, then the employee will recognize employment income equal to the amount received and the employer will receive a tax deduction for the same amount. To prevent the possibility of both a Division C deduction for the employee and an income deduction for the employer, the tax deduction is limited. Please refer to Chapter 10 for more details on the Division C deduction.

¶3,275 Rules applicable to Canadian-controlled private corporations

An exception to the general rules described above is provided for stock options granted by Canadian-controlled private corporations (CCPC). There is still an employment income inclusion, equal to the excess of the fair market value at the date the option is exercised and the option price. However, the inclusion of that benefit occurs at the time that the shares are disposed of, thereby deferring the inclusion of the benefit. ITA: 7(1.1) ITA: 125(7)

Furthermore, there will be a Division C deduction, equal to one-half of the inclusion, if the shares have not been sold or exchanged before the second anniversary date of the day of acquisition. For the purpose of determining the length of the holding period of the shares, shares are deemed to have been disposed of in the order in which they were acquired (i.e., first in, first out). The excess of the actual selling price over the fair market value at the date the option is exercised will result in a capital gain at the appropriate inclusion rate, as discussed in Chapter 7. Note that stock options issued by CCPCs can qualify for a deduction under paragraph 110(1)(*d*) (referred to above) or under paragraph 110(1)(*d*.1), but not both, even if both sets of conditions are met. ITA: 110(1)(*d*.1) ITA: 7(1.3)

¶3,280 Rules applicable to public corporations — Deferral [Repealed]

There used to be another exception to the general rule that the stock option benefit must be included in income in the year of exercise. For public-company securities, the inclusion of the benefit could have been deferred to the earlier of the year in which the shares acquired under the option were disposed of and the year in which the individual died or became a non-resident. Now this deferral only applies to options exercised before 4 p.m. EST, March 4, 2010. ITA: 7(8)–(16)

¶3,285 Valuation of shares

There is usually little difficulty in establishing the value of shares which are traded regularly as would be the case with shares in a public company. However, establishing the value of shares where there is no listing or open market is more difficult. In recent years, comprehensive methods of determining the value of such shares have been used. The CRA's approach to valuations of this nature is contained in an Information Circular. IC 89-3

¶3,287 Risk factors

Over the years, stock options have proven to be a fairly successful compensation scheme for many executives and other employees. There are, however, risk factors common to all equity investments. Public share prices fluctuate constantly depending on industry trends, interest and exchange rates, government policies, and various other global factors. Exercising stock options and simultaneously disposing of the shares minimizes the risk of a taxable benefit in employment income and an economic loss on the disposition of the shares. This is possible if an employee exercises the option to acquire shares at a time when the market price is high and subsequently disposes of the shares when the market price is down. Consider the following example, which shows what happens if the shares either increase or decrease in value after they are acquired.

Employee benefit:	Increase	Decrease
FMV at exercise date	$10,000	$ 10,000
minus exercise price (cost)	(7,500)	(7,500)
Taxable benefit	$ 2,500	$ 2,500
Disposition:		
Proceeds	$12,000	$ 8,000
Adjusted cost base = FMV at exercise date	(10,000)	(10,000)
Capital gain (loss)	$ 2,000	($ 2,000)
Taxable capital gain (allowable capital loss)	$ 1,000	($ 1,000)

If the shares continue to increase in value after the option is exercised, then the economic benefit, before tax, is $4,500 ($12,000 – $7,500). Of that, $2,500 will be taxed as employment income and $1,000 will be taxed as a taxable capital gain.

If the shares decrease in value after the option is exercised, then the economic benefit, before tax, is $500 ($8,000 – $7,500). Of that, $2,500 will be taxed as employment income and $1,000 will be an allowable capital loss that can only be deducted against taxable capital gains. If the employee does not have any taxable capital gains in the year, then they may, in fact, lose money after tax since their tax on the $2,500 of employment income may exceed the economic gain of $500.

Please refer to ¶3,288, below, for special provision that have been made to deal with some of these situations.

This simplified example highlights that the nature of the income can have a significant impact on the economic benefit that results from the series of transactions resulting from the exercise of a stock option.

¶3,288 Employment income and capital loss — 2010 to 2015

To deal with the issue of employees exercising stock options, recognizing the employment income, and then realizing a capital loss on the eventual sale, the government instituted a measure to address this issue, but only in the years 2010 to 2015.

Once an employee exercises a stock option, any gain or loss from the exercise price is treated as a capital gain or loss. However, where the employee has exercised his or her option before March 4, 2010 and elected to defer the recognition of the employment income, the employee may be faced with a future difficulty if the shares decline in value. In this situation, when the employee disposes of the shares, he or she has to report the deferred employment income, has a capital loss he or she cannot claim, and may not have enough cash to pay the tax.

To deal with this, the federal Budget of March 4, 2010 resulted in the enactment of legislation to:

(1) repeal the tax-deferral election; and

(2) ensure that tax on the value of the employment benefit is required to be remitted to the government by the employer.

The repeal of the election applies to stock options exercised after 4:00 p.m. EST on March 4, 2010.

For those taxpayers who elected under the previous rules to defer the tax on stock options, there are special transitional rules to ensure that the tax liability on the deferred stock option benefit does not exceed the proceeds of disposition of the optioned securities, taking into account the tax relief resulting from the use of the capital losses on the optioned securities against capital gains from other sources.

In a year when a taxpayer is required to include a deferred stock option benefit in income, he or she may elect to pay a special tax for the year equal to the proceeds of disposition from the sale of the optioned securities. Where this election is made: ITA: 180.01

(1) The taxpayer can claim a deduction equal to the amount of the stock option benefit that was deferred.

(2) An amount equal to half of the lesser of:

(a) the stock option benefit, and

(b) the capital loss on the optioned securities

will be included in the taxpayer's income as a capital gain. This gain may be offset by the allowable capital loss on the optioned securities. ITA: 40(3.21)

Only stock option benefits for which an election has been made to defer the stock option benefit will qualify for this elective treatment.

Individuals who disposed of their optioned shares before 2010 have until April 30, 2011 to make this election. Individuals who have not yet disposed of their shares have until 2015 to do so to qualify for this election.

Example

Jessica exercised a stock option before March 4, 2010 and paid $70 per share to acquire her shares. The FMV at grant date was $40 per share. At the exercise date, the FMV was $100. She elected to defer the employment income of $30 per share until she disposed of the shares. When she disposed of the shares, she received $50 for each one, resulting in a capital loss of $20 per share and an allowable capital loss of $10 per share.

Special tax equal to proceeds	$ 50
Deferred stock option benefit	$ 30
Offsetting deduction	$(30)
Taxable capital gain (below)	$ 10
Allowable capital loss realized	$(10)

Taxable capital gain equal to half the lesser of:

1. the stock option benefit	$30
2. the capital loss realized	$20

50% × $20 = $10

¶3,290 Summary

The following diagram summarizes the rules for income inclusions for stock options.

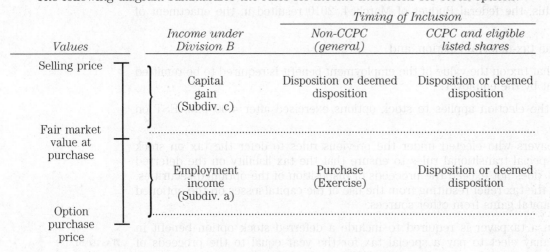

Values	*Income under Division B*	*Timing of Inclusion* *Non-CCPC (general)*	*CCPC and eligible listed shares*
Selling price			
	Capital gain (Subdiv. c)	Disposition or deemed disposition	Disposition or deemed disposition
Fair market value at purchase			
	Employment income (Subdiv. a)	Purchase (Exercise)	Disposition or deemed disposition
Option purchase price			

Example Problem 3-5

Mr. Dietrich, who is employed by Public Co. Ltd., was granted an option in year one to purchase up to 5,000 common shares at $10 after completion of his fifth year of employment. The fair market value of the common shares at the time of granting the right was $12. He does not have any other shares.

During Mr. Dietrich's seventh year of employment he decided to exercise part of his right and purchased 1,000 shares with a fair market value of $15 as at that date. Assume the exercise date was May 15, 2013.

Three years later, Mr. Dietrich sold the shares at $25 per share.

— *REQUIRED*

(A) Discuss the tax implications of each of the above transactions.

(B) How would your answer differ if the option price was $13 instead of $10?

(C) How would your answer to (A) differ if Mr. Dietrich was employed by a Canadian-controlled private corporation?

— *SOLUTION*

(A) *When option is granted:* There is no tax effect when Mr. Dietrich is granted the right to purchase shares through the stock option plan.

When option is exercised: Mr. Dietrich must take into employment income the difference between the fair market value and the option price: ITA: 7(1)

1,000 shares × ($15 – $10) = $5,000.

The adjusted cost base of the shares, used in the calculation of a capital gain or loss on the disposition of the shares, will be set at the fair market value of the shares at the time of exercising the options (i.e., $15 per share). This amount is equal to the amount paid for the shares with after-tax funds (i.e., $10 per share) plus the amount included in the employee's income and subjected to tax (i.e., $5). Hence, the total adjusted cost base can be considered to be the total tax-paid cost in the shares.

There will be no deduction of one-half, since the option price ($10) is less than the fair market value ($12) at the date the option was granted. As a result, one of the conditions necessary to defer the inclusion of the benefit to the year of disposition or deemed disposition is not met. ITA: 110(1)(*d*)

Note that there has been no disposition at this point; he will have to find the funds to pay the tax from other sources.

When shares are sold: Mr. Dietrich will have a capital gain in the year of disposal calculated on the difference between the proceeds of disposition ($25) and the fair market value as at the date the option was exercised ($15) which is his cost base.(1)

1,000 shares × ($25 – $15) = $10,000.

The taxable capital gain is ½ of $10,000 and is included in Subdivision c of Division B.

The results can be demonstrated as follows:

Proceeds of Disposition	$25	Capital gain of $10 per share
FMV at Exercise date	$15	
FMV at Grant date	$12	Employment income of $5 per share No Division C deduction is available
Option price	$10	

The fair market value at the grant date is only used to determine whether the Division C deduction is available. ITA: 110(1)(*d*)

(B) In this part of the question, the option price was changed to $13, which means that he will be eligible for the Division C deduction. However, since he exercised his option after March 4, 2010, he is no longer eligible to elect to defer the employment benefit. ITA: 110(1)(*d*)

When option is granted: There is no tax effect in the year the option is granted.

When option is exercised: He will have to take the stock option benefit into income. This will be calculated as follows:

1,000 shares × ($15 – $13) = $2,000

He will also be entitled to the one-half deduction, since the exercise price was greater than the fair market value at the date the option was granted. It is calculated as follows: ITA: 110(1)(*d*)

$$\tfrac{1}{2} \times \$2{,}000 = (\$1{,}000)$$

This one-half deduction, effectively, reduces the income inclusion for eligible stock options to the inclusion rate for capital gains.

When the shares are sold: He will report the following in the year of disposal:

Capital gain: 1,000 shares × ($25 – $15) = $10,000

The results can be demonstrated as follows:

Proceeds of Disposition	$25	Capital gain of $10 per share
FMV at Exercise date	$15	
Option price	$13	Employment income of $2 per share Division C deduction of $1 per share
FMV at Grant date	$12	

The fair market value at the grant date is only used to determine whether the Division C deduction is available. ITA: 110(1)(*d*)

(C) *CCPC* — If Mr. Dietrich had been employed by a Canadian-controlled private corporation (CCPC), with which he dealt at arm's length, then he would not have to include any amount in employment income upon exercising his right in the seventh year. Upon disposing of the shares in the tenth year, however, he would have employment income equal to the difference between the fair market value at the time he acquired the shares ($15) and his cost ($10): ITA: 7(1.1)

1,000 shares × ($15 – $10) = $5,000.

At the same time, he will also have a capital gain of $10,000:

1,000 shares × ($25 – $15(1)) = $10,000.

He would be eligible for a deduction of one-half of the employment income inclusion of $5,000, since he had retained the shares for more than two years. ITA: 110(1)(*d.1*)

Summary of solution	**Part A**	**Part B**	**Part C**
	Public Corporation Option Price < FMV at Grant and Exercise Dates	**Public Corporation Option Price > FMV at Grant**	**Canadian-Controlled Private Corporation**
Year 1: (Option granted)	No tax effects in the year the option is granted.	No tax effects in the year the option is granted.	No tax effects in the year the option is granted.
Year 7: (Option exercised)	Recognize employment income benefit.	Since the option was exercised after March 4, 2010, the election to defer the recognition of the employment benefit is not available. Therefore, recognize employment income benefit and deduct one-half of the benefit in Division C.	No tax effects until the shares are sold.
Year 10: (Shares sold)	Recognize capital gain only.	Recognize capital gain only.	Recognize employment income benefit, Division C deduction and capital gain.

Both stock option rules required an employment inclusion of $5,000; the difference was the timing of the inclusion. Where the stock option was offered by a Canadian-controlled private corporation, then the employment inclusion is at the time of disposition of the shares. For stock options from all other corporate employers, the employment inclusion is at the date the option is exercised (if after March 4, 2010). ITA: 7(1), 7(1.1)

The Division C deductions were designed to give the same net effect as a capital gain, at the appropriate net inclusion rate, without permitting these amounts to qualify for the capital gains deduction. Both of these deductions will be discussed in further detail in Chapter 10. ITA: 110(1)(*d*) or 110(1)(*d*.1)

— *NOTE TO SOLUTION*

(1) His cost is determined as the exercise price ($10) plus an addition to his cost base of the amount per share ($5) included in employment income under section 7. Both of these amounts represent tax-paid dollars which, by their inclusion in the cost base, will not be taxed further on disposition.

¶3,300 DEDUCTIONS FROM EMPLOYMENT INCOME

Subsection 8(1) lists all of the deductions that may be claimed in computing income from an office or employment. The Act specifically limits deductions from employment income to those specified in section 8. To qualify for these deductions, the provisions must be strictly adhered to. Note that the preamble to subsection 8(1) restricts these deductions to expenses which relate in some manner to the earning of employment income. ITA: 8(2)

At this point, it should also be noted that the Act imposes a general limitation on the deductibility of expenses. To be deductible, the amount of the expenditure must be "reasonable in the circumstances". What is reasonable in the circumstances depends on the particular facts of a situation and may be determined by reference to a standard, such as an industry average or a previously accepted historical average, among others. Another general limitation denies the deduction of an expense incurred to commit an offence under specified sections of the *Criminal Code*. ITA: 67 ITA: 67.5(1)

Selected Deductions From Employment Income Allowed Under Section 8

ITA		*Discussed at ¶*
8(1)(*b*)	Legal expenses of employee	3,352
8(1)(*c*)	Clergy residence	3,354
8(1)(*d*)	Teachers' exchange fund contribution	3,356
8(1)(*f*)	Sales expenses	3,310
8(1)(*g*)	Transport employee's expenses	3,360
8(1)(*h*)	Travel expenses	3,320
8(1)(*h*.1)	Motor vehicle expenses	3,320
8(1)(*i*)	Dues and other expenses of performing duties	3,342
8(1)(*j*)	Motor vehicles and aircraft costs	3,400
8(1)(*l*.1)	CPP contributions and EI premiums	3,362
8(1)(*m*)	Employee's registered pension plan contributions	3,380
8(1)(*m*.2)	Employee RCA contributions	3,364
8(1)(*n*)	Salary reimbursement	3,366
8(1)(*o*)	Forfeited amounts	3,368
8(1)(*p*)	Musical instrument costs	3,370
8(1)(*q*)	Artists' employment expenses	3,372

8(1)(*s*)	Deduction — tradesperson's tools	3,374
8(2)	General limitation	3,300
8(4)	Meals	3,335
8(6.1)	Eligible tool of tradesperson	3,374
8(7)	Cost of tool	3,374
8(13)	Workspace in the home	3,345

¶3,310 Sales/Negotiating Person's Expenses

There are many individuals who earn their living selling goods or services in return for commission income. These individuals often have to spend money on travel, meals, and promotional material in order to earn this income. The income tax issues revolve around the deductibility of the expenses that they incur to earn this commission income.

Expenses incurred for the purpose of earning income from employment for employees who sell property or negotiate contracts may also be deductible. The nature or type of the expenses is not restricted, unlike for other employees, except for expenses of a capital nature.[15] Of course, these expenditures are subject to the general restrictions, just discussed, and a number of specific restrictions and/or exceptions. For example, expenditures in respect of the use of a yacht, camp, lodge, golf course, and membership fees in private clubs are not deductible.

ITA: 8(1)(*f*)

ITA: 8(1)(*f*)(v)

ITA: 8(1)(*f*)(vi), 18(1)(*l*)

Also not deductible are payments to reimburse the employer for the personal use of an employer provided automobile, since these payments reduce the previously-included benefit.

ITA: 8(1)(*f*)(vii)

ITA: 6(1)(*e*)

The amount of expenses that can be deducted is limited to the amount of the employee's commission income or other amounts, that are fixed by reference to the volume of sales or contracts negotiated. The expenses claimed must be substantiated by vouchers or other records.

Note the conditions in the provision that must be met for the expenses to be deductible.

- The employee must be required to pay his or her own expenses as stipulated in the contract of employment.[16] ITA: 8(1)(*f*)(i)
- The employee must be ordinarily required to carry on the duties of employment away from the employer's place of business.[17] ITA: 8(1)(*f*)(ii)
- The remuneration must be dependent on volume of sales or contracts.[18] ITA: 8(1)(*f*)(iii)
- A non-taxable travel allowance cannot be received. Note, a travel allowance does not include an automobile allowance. ITA: 8(1)(*f*)(iv)

[15] In the case of *Gifford v. The Queen*, 2004 DTC 6120 (S.C.C.), the issues were:

(i) whether the payment made by an employee to a former employee for a client list was a deductible current expense under paragraph 8(1)(*f*) or a non-deductible capital outlay under subparagraph 8(1)(*f*)(v), and

(ii) whether interest on funds borrowed to buy the list was also deductible under paragraph 8(1)(*f*) or non-deductible under subparagraph 8(1)(*f*)(v).

Both payments were held to be "on account of capital" and, hence, were prevented by subparagraph 8(1)(*f*)(v) from being deducted.

[16] See two Federal Court of Appeal cases: *The Queen v. Moore*, 90 DTC 6200 (F.C.A.), and *The Queen v. Betz*, 90 DTC 6201 (F.C.A.). In these decisions, the Court expanded the concept of a contractual obligation to include unwritten conditions which would result in an unfavourable performance assessment.

[17] *Healy v. The Queen*, 78 DTC 6239 (F.C.A.).

[18] *Neville v. M.N.R.*, 88 DTC 1546 (T.C.C.). A payment that was made as a percent of an employer's gross profit was held not to be an amount based on volume of sales in *Griesbach v. M.N.R.*, 91 DTC 142 (T.C.C.).

If the travel allowance is not reasonable, then the sales/negotiating person must include the allowance in income. An unreasonable allowance is one that is less than a reasonable amount, greater than a reasonable amount, or deemed not to be reasonable. He or she may then deduct the expenses, since the employee would not be in receipt of an *excluded* allowance in such circumstances. ITA: 6(1)(*b*)(v) ITA: 8(1)(*f*)

The relationship between car allowances and car expenses for sales/negotiating persons and other employees is discussed later in the chapter. Other expenses for sales/negotiating persons will be discussed in more detail in Chapter 4, where comparisons with self-employed salespersons are made.

¶3,320 Any Employee's Travelling Expenses Other Than Motor Vehicle Expenses

¶3,325 Overview

The travelling expenses of employees who are not involved in the selling of property or negotiating of contracts are deductible under one of two provisions:

paragraph 8(1)(*h*) — Travelling expenses other than motor vehicle expenses

paragraph 8(1)(*h*.1) — Motor vehicle expenses (discussed later in this chapter)

Two separate provisions are used for reasons which will become apparent after the conditions for these deductions are explored.

Deductible travelling expenses are not restricted as to type of employee or employer. However, three specific conditions must be met to obtain the deduction for an expenditure. Many case situations, discussed below, involve an attempt to deduct expenses for travel between an employee's home and his or her place of work. These are not deductible travelling expenses, but personal or living expenses, unless the travel expenses are incurred between home and work sites away from the employee's usual place of work.[19] The reasonableness of the expenditures and the need for adequate record-keeping to substantiate the deduction were at issue in other court decisions.[20] ITA: 8(1)(*h*)

¶3,330 Conditions

The first condition imposed is that the employee must ordinarily be required to carry out his or her duties away from his or her employer's place of business. The CRA's interpretation of the word "ordinarily", in this paragraph only, is habitually or customarily. However, there should be some degree of regularity in the required travelling.[21] ITA: 8(1)(*h*)(i) IT-522R, par. 32

The second condition requires that the payment of the travelling expenses by the employee must be part of his or her contract. The contract can be either in a written or oral form, but the latter may be harder to prove in a court of law. There have been several court cases involving this issue.[22] ITA: 8(1)(*h*)(ii)

The third condition is that the employee cannot be in receipt of a tax-exempt allowance for travelling expenses, which exclude the allowance if it is reasonable. Therefore, employees who have received an allowance that is greater or less than a reasonable amount can include the allowance in income and can deduct the related expenses, because they would not be in receipt of an excluded (reasonable) allowance in such circumstances. Whether an allowance is reasonable depends upon *all* the facts in a particular circumstance. ITA: 6(1)(*b*)(v)–(vii), 8(1)(*h*)(iii)

[19] The following cases resulted in a decision for personal or living expenses: *Martyn v. M.N.R.*, 62 DTC 341 (T.A.B.); *Luks v. M.N.R.*, 58 DTC 1194 (Ex. Ct.); *Wilkinson v. M.N.R.*, 66 DTC 344 (T.A.B.); and *Carson v. M.N.R.*, 66 DTC 424 (T.A.B.). On the other hand, in *The Queen v. Merten*, 90 DTC 6600 (F.C.T.D.), the taxpayer was allowed to deduct expenses to travel to work sites away from his usual place of work.

[20] *No. 589 v. M.N.R.*, 59 DTC 41 (T.A.B.), *Niessen v. M.N.R.*, 60 DTC 489 (T.A.B.), and *Winter v. M.N.R.*, 88 DTC 1143 (T.C.C.).

[21] The interpretation of the word "ordinarily" was at issue in the cases of *Krieger v. M.N.R.*, 79 DTC 269 (T.R.B.), *The Queen v. Patterson*, 82 DTC 6326 (F.C.T.D.), and *Imray v. The Queen*, 98 DTC 6580 (F.C.T.D.).

[22] *The Queen v. Cival*, 83 DTC 5168 (F.C.A.); *Rozen v. The Queen*, 85 DTC 5611 (F.C.T.D.); and *Hoedel v. The Queen*, 86 DTC 6535 (F.C.A.).

Note that the receipt of an excluded allowance for employment use of a motor vehicle precludes the deduction of motor vehicle expenses, but does not preclude the deduction of more general travelling expenses. This is likely the reason for the existence of the two separate deduction provisions. The receipt of an excluded (reasonable) allowance for one type of travelling expense does not preclude the deduction of the other type of travelling expense. ITA: 6(1)(*b*)(vii.1), 8(1)(*h*), 8(1)(*h*.1)

Employees who make deductions under paragraph 8(1)(*f*), (*h*), or (*h*.1) and subparagraph 8(1)(*i*)(ii) or (iii) (office rent and supplies which are discussed in the next section) must file a prescribed form (T2200) signed by their employers certifying that the conditions set out in these provisions were met in the year. However, it appears that the CRA has simplified the administration of the application of some of the conditions in these provisions. For example, an Interpretation Bulletin indicates that, as long as the form T2200 is completed properly by the employer, then the requirement that there must be a contractual arrangement stipulating that the employee must pay for the travelling expenses will be met. Also this Interpretation Bulletin indicates in paragraph 58 that form T2200 should be kept with the taxpayer's records for examination on request. Thus, the form is not required to be filed with the tax return. ITA: 8(10) IT-522R, par. 33

¶3,335 Limitations

The deduction under paragraphs 8(1)(*f*) and (*h*) of the cost of meals consumed while travelling for an employer is restricted. These costs are deductible only where the meal is consumed when the taxpayer is away, for 12 hours or more, from the municipality or metropolitan area where he or she usually reports for work.[23] ITA: 8(4)

The deduction for the cost of meals consumed and entertainment is limited to 50% of the lesser of the amount paid or payable and a reasonable amount. There are a number of exceptions to these restrictions for meal expenses, as described in some detail in an Interpretation Bulletin entitled "Food, Beverages and Entertainment Expenses": ITA: 67.1 IT-518R

- moving expenses (see Chapter 9); ITA: 62
- childcare expenses (see Chapter 9); ITA: 63
- medical expenses which qualify for non-refundable credit (see Chapter 10); ITA: 118.2
- the specific products and services of taxpayers who are in the business of providing meals and entertainment;
- meals provided where the primary purpose is for fund-raising for a registered charity;
- reasonable reimbursements to the employer;
- exempted amounts for a special work site; ITA: 6(6)(*a*)(ii)
- the cost of meals and entertainment at special and remote work sites, subject to some additional restrictions; and ITA: 6(6)(*a*)(i), 67.1(2)(*e*)
- meals and entertainment, at up to six special events generally available to all employees at the particular place of business.

¶3,340 Receipts by part-time employees for travelling expenses

Personal travelling expenses are not deductible under the normal rules. However, where an individual receives an allowance for or a reimbursement of travelling expenses in respect of the individual's part-time employment, the receipts are treated as income unless exempt from tax by Subdivision g — "Amounts Not Included in Income". There are several tests which must be met in order to have these travelling expenses qualify for this provision: ITA: 81(3.1)

(a) the part-time employee must have other employment or business income;

[23] See the case of *Krieger v. M.N.R.*, 79 DTC 269 (T.R.B.).

(b) the amount received cannot exceed a reasonable amount and the travelling expenses must be in respect of travelling only to and from the part-time employment, not travelling expenses incurred *during* the part-time employment; and

(c) the part-time employment location must be at least 80 kilometres away from both the employee's ordinary place of residence and his or her principal place of business or employment.

Condition (a), above, is waived for individuals who are employed part-time as professors or teachers by designated educational institutions. The purpose of this exception is to facilitate the recruiting of part-time instructors by universities and other educational institutions outside major metropolitan areas.

ITA: 81(3.1)(*a*)(ii)

ITA: 118.6(1)

¶3,342 Dues and Other Expenses[24]

Also deductible are:

ITA: 8(1)(*i*)

- annual professional membership dues paid to maintain standing in a profession recognized by statute;
- office rent paid or salary paid to an assistant;
- the cost of supplies paid; and
- annual union membership dues paid.

In order for an amount to be deductible, either it must be paid by the employee or, if the employer paid the amount, it must be included in the employee's income as a taxable benefit. [Proposed amendment, Bill C-48, which received Royal Assent and became law on June 26, 2013.]

There are a number of restrictions that are placed on these expenses:

ITA: 8(1)(*i*)

(a) First, a limitation is placed on dues which prohibits the deduction of amounts that are not directly attributable to the ordinary operating expenses of the organization which is levying the dues.

ITA: 8(5)

(b) Second, there are the employment contract requirements placed on the amounts deductible for office rent or salary to an assistant and for the cost of supplies.

ITA: 8(1)(*i*)(ii)–(iii)

(c) Finally, remember that the preamble to section 8 restricts deductions to those that are wholly applicable to that source. Hence, a professional accountant who teaches English literature in the secondary school system cannot deduct his or her accounting association dues, but can deduct his or her teaching association dues.

ITA: 8(1)(*i*)(i), 8(1)(*i*)(iv)

As long as form T2200 is completed properly by the employer, it appears that the contractual requirement will be met through this certification procedure. The employer is required to certify by signing form T2200 that the employee was required to maintain an office away from the employer's place of business. Furthermore, an Interpretation Bulletin administratively requires that the deductibility of these expenses, except union dues and professional fees, requires a contract of employment (written or "tacitly understood"), certified by the employer signing form T2200, to permit the deduction of office rent, supplies, or salaries paid by the employee to an assistant or substitute.

ITA: 8(1)(*i*)(ii) (rent and salary paid to an assistant) and 8(1)(*i*)(iii) (supplies)

IT-352R2, par. 13

[24] The cases of *Daley v. M.N.R.*, 50 DTC 877 (Ex. Ct.), and *Montgomery et. al. v. M.N.R.*, 99 DTC 5186 (F.C.A.), deal with professional membership dues; the caseof *The Queen v. Thompson*, 89 DTC 5439 (F.C.T.D.), deals with the controversial topic of imputed office rent expense; the case of *Felton v. M.N.R.*, 89 DTC 233 (T.C.C.), deals with deductibility of home office expenses generally; the cases of *Luks v. M.N.R.*, 58 DTC 1194 (Ex. Ct.), and *Thibault v. M.N.R.*, 86 DTC 1538 (T.C.C.), deal with the meaning of "supplies". The case of *Sword v. M.N.R.*, 90 DTC 1798 (T.C.C.), deals with the deductibility of telephone expenses.

¶3,345 Workspace in Home

There are restrictions on the deductibility of expenses related to workspace in the home for employees. This provision parallels the rules for self-employed individuals as discussed in an Interpretation Bulletin. The provision only applies to individuals who are entitled to deductions for sales expenses or for rent or supplies related to a workspace in a home. The effect of the provision is twofold. A deduction is then only permitted if the workspace is: ITA: 8(13) ITA: 18(12) IT-514 ITA: 8(1)(*f*), 8(1)(*i*)

(a) the place where the individual *principally* (more than 50% of the time) performs the employment duties; or IT-352R2, par. 2

(b) (i) used *exclusively* for the purpose of earning employment income during the period, and

(ii) used on a regular and continuous basis for meeting customers or other persons in the ordinary course of performing the employment duties.

As long as more than 50% of the employment duties are performed in the home workspace, then test (a), above, has been met and test (b) above can be ignored. Where test (a) is not met, then the exclusive condition in test (b)(i), above, must be met. The word "exclusively" is not defined in the Act. *Merriam-Webster Online*[25] defines "exclusive", used in this context, as "single, sole . . . whole, undivided", which is a much more onerous test.

Once one of the conditions in (a) or (b), above, has been met in the year of the expenditure, then the workspace deduction is restricted to employment-source income. However, there is an indefinite carryforward provision as long as the employee can meet either test (a) or (b), above, in the future year of deduction. IT-352R2, par. 3

Supplies related to a workspace in the home include expenses paid for the maintenance of the home such as the cost of fuel, electricity, light bulbs, cleaning materials and minor repairs. For an individual earning commission income, property taxes and insurance paid on a home owned by the individual are deductible. All of these expenses must be allocated between the workspace and the personal space of the home on a reasonable basis such as floor space. IT-352R2, par. 5 ITA: 8(1)(*f*)

Note that no provision in section 8 allows the deduction of interest on funds borrowed in any manner for the purchase of a home for any use by the employee.

Exhibit 3-4 lists some common home office expenses and their treatment by employees earning commission income, or the like, and other employees.

EXHIBIT 3-4
Home Office Expenses

Expenses	*Commission employees*	*Other employees*
Rent	√	√
Repairs and maintenance	√	√
Supplies	√	√
Telephone (long-distance charges)	√	√
Utilities	√	√
Home insurance	√	X
Property taxes	√	X
Mortgage interest	X	X

[25] *Merriam-Webster Online*, 2009 <http://www.merriam-webster.com/dictionary/exclusive>.

¶3,350 Other Expenses

¶3,352 Legal expenses

Certain legal expenses incurred by employees are deductible. The expenses are limited to those incurred to collect or establish a right to remuneration owed to the employee by an employer or former employer. [There is a proposal (Bill C-48, which received Royal Assent and became law on June 26, 2013) to extend this deduction to amounts not owed to the employee directly by the employer, if the amounts, when received, would be taxable as employment income. For example, legal fees incurred by an employee to collect insurance benefits under a sickness or accident insurance policy provided through an employer would be deductible.] ITA: 8(1)(*b*)

¶3,354 Clergy's residence

A member of the clergy who is in charge of or ministers to a congregation, or is engaged exclusively in the full-time administrative duties of a religious order or denomination, is entitled to deduct an amount in respect of his or her living accommodation. ITA: 8(1)(*c*); Form T2200, T1223; IT-141R

The amount of the deduction depends upon whether the living accommodation the individual occupies is (a) supplied by virtue of employment, (b) rented by the individual, or (c) owned by the individual.

Where the living accommodation is supplied by virtue of employment, the amount of the deduction is equal to the value of the benefit derived from the supply of the living accommodation (the housing allowance), to the extent that the value is already included in income (section 6). The maximum deduction is the income from employment as a clergy person.

The deduction for rent or rental value is limited to the lesser of the following two amounts:

- the greater of 1,000 × the number of months employed as a member of the clergy (to a maximum of 10) and ⅓ of remuneration; and
- the fair rental value,

less any amount deducted in computing employment or business income for the residence in connection with another employment or business.

In total, the deduction cannot exceed the clergy's total remuneration from the office or employment.

In addition, employees claiming the clergy residence deduction must complete a form, "Clergy Residence Deduction", signed by their employers, certifying to the effect that the employees meet the requirements concerning their status and function as clergy. The forms do not have to be filed with the clergy's income tax return, but must be kept in case the CRA wishes to see it at a later date. Form T1223

¶3,356 Teacher's exchange fund

A provision allows a deduction for amounts paid, to a maximum of $250, by a teacher to a fund established by the Canadian Education Association for Commonwealth Teachers in Canada, under an exchange arrangement. ITA: 8(1)(*d*)

¶3,358 Railway employees

A deduction for meals (restricted by subsection 67.1(1) to 50% of the actual cost, or a cost that would be reasonable in the circumstances) and lodging incurred by a railway company employee (a) travelling away from the taxpayer's ordinary place of residence as a relieving telegrapher or station agent or on maintenance and repair work, or (b) travelling away from the municipality or metropolitan area of the taxpayer's home terminal where the taxpayer maintained a self-contained domestic establishment in which the taxpayer resided ITA: 8(1)(*e*); Form TL2 and actually supported a spouse or common-law partner or a person dependent on the taxpayer for support and connected with the taxpayer by blood relationship, marriage, or common-law partnership or adoption, where the taxpayer could not reasonably be expected to return to his or her residence daily.

¶3,360 Transport employees

A deduction for meals (limited to 50% of the actual cost, or a cost that would be reasonable in the circumstances) and lodging may be available for expenses incurred by a person who is employed by a firm whose principal business is passenger, goods, or passenger and goods transport, and whose duties require regular travel away from the municipality and metropolitan area where the employer's establishment was located, and to which the employee reported for work. The CRA publishes an annual dollar amount, currently $17 per meal, or $51 per day, that it is prepared to accept without receipts. ITA: 8(1)(*g*), 67.1(1); Form TL2

The deductible portion for food and beverages consumed by certain long-haul truck drivers is 80% after 2010. Certain eligibility conditions apply.

¶3,362 CPP and EI premiums payable in respect of an assistant

A salary paid by an employee to an assistant or substitute may be deductible if required by the contract of employment of the payer. Such payments may also require the payment of Canada Pension Plan or Employment Insurance premiums that are the responsibility of an employer. Amounts payable by an employee as premiums for CPP and EI in respect of an assistant are deductible. ITA: 8(1)(*i*)(ii); ITA: 8(1)(*l*.1)

¶3,364 Retirement compensation arrangements

Any contributions required to be made to a retirement compensation arrangement are deductible. ITA: 8(1)(*m*.2)

¶3,366 Salary reimbursements

Where an employee received salary/wages and reimbursed the employer because the employee did not perform the duties of the office/employment, that reimbursement is deductible by the employee. The same applies for any disability insurance amounts reimbursed to the employer. ITA: 8(1)(*n*), (*n*.1)

¶3,368 Forfeitures

Where amounts have previously been included in income under a salary deferral arrangement or a deferred profit sharing plan, and those amounts are subsequently forfeited, the forfeited amount is deductible. ITA: 8(1)(*o*), (*o*.1)

¶3,370 Musical instrument costs

Where the taxpayer is employed as a musician and is required to provide his or her own musical instrument, a deduction (not exceeding income) can be claimed for maintenance, insurance, and rental of the instrument. Additionally, capital cost allowance can be claimed on the instrument. Capital cost allowance is covered in detail at Chapter 5. ITA: 8(1)(*p*)

¶3,372 Artist's expenses

Where the taxpayer has employment income from an artistic activity (acting, singing, or dancing; creating works of art or dramatic, literary, or musical works), he or she may deduct expenses incurred in earning that income. The maximum deduction is limited to the lesser of $1,000 and 20% of their artistic activity income. This deduction is reduced by any expenses claimed under paragraphs 8(1)(*p*) (musical instrument costs) and 8(1)(*j*) (motor vehicle and aircraft costs). ITA: 8(1)(*q*)

¶3,374 Tradesperson's tool expenses

A deduction is allowed from employment income earned as a tradesperson in a taxation year to a maximum of $500 for eligible new tools. This deduction is computed as the excess, if any, of the total cost to the individual of one or more eligible tools over $1,065 to a maximum excess of $500. An "eligible tool" is defined to be a tool (including ancillary equipment) that: ITA: 8(1)(s) ITA: 8(6.1)

- was new and, hence, not used for any purpose whatsoever before it is acquired by the individual;
- is certified by the individual's employer in prescribed form to be required as a condition of, and for use in, the individual's employment as a tradesperson in the year; and
- is, unless the device or equipment can be used only for the purpose of measuring, locating, or calculating, not an electronic communication device or electronic data processing equipment.

The cost of the tools used for computing tax depreciation (i.e., capital cost allowance) or for capital gains purposes is reduced by the amount of this deduction. ITA: 8(7)

¶3,380 Registered Pension Plans

¶3,385 Overview

There are two different types of registered pension plans (RPPs): defined benefit and money purchase (defined contribution). Defined benefit plans guarantee a predetermined amount of retirement income based on a flat amount per year of service or a percentage of the employee's earnings over a defined period. The defined benefit RPPs are funded by actuarially-determined contributions by the employee and/or employer. Money purchase RPPs provide whatever pension income that the contributed funds in the plan can purchase through the acquisition of an annuity. No predetermined amount of pension income is guaranteed under a money purchase plan. Benefits will depend upon the actual contributions, the investment return of the plan and annuity rates at the date of purchase.

The major objective of pension reform, which became effective for years after 1990, was to eliminate the discrepancies among the various tax-assisted retirement plans by imposing a comprehensive single limit of 18% of employee earnings for all employee and/or employer contributions to registered pension plans (defined benefit and defined contribution), registered retirement savings plans (RRSPs) and deferred profit sharing plans (DPSPs).

Total annual comprehensive dollar limits for money purchase RPPs for employer and/or employee contributions are set at the following amounts:

2010	2011	2012	2013	2014
$22,450	$22,970	$23,820	$24,270	indexed

The maximum amount is indexed with the increase in the average wage for the year. The indexed amount for 2013 is $24,270. Contribution limits for RRSPs, which are discussed in detail in Chapter 9, will reflect benefits accruing under defined benefit RPPs and contributions to money purchase RPPs and DPSPs.

Defined benefit plans also have contribution limits for employees and employers; however, the limits that are imposed are set in terms of the maximum pension which can be received on retirement. Contributions to fund the pension are then actuarially determined. Generally speaking, the maximum defined benefit is calculated as 2% of the employee's income, usually an average of the highest income level for three to seven years, times the number of years of service.

Paragraph 8(1)(*m*) provides the statutory authority for an employment deduction in respect of registered pension plans, but only as determined by subsection 147.2(4), which is found under Division G, "Deferred and Other Special Income Arrangements".

A defined benefit RPP must meet the conditions described above and others in order to be "registered". Meeting the conditions implies that the contributions made by an employee, in whatever amount acceptable under the registration conditions, are deductible by the employee. On the other hand, deductible contributions to a money purchase RPP are restricted annually by the comprehensive dollar limit discussed above. ITA: 8(1)(*m*)

¶3,400 AUTOMOBILE BENEFITS, CAR ALLOWANCES, AND CAR EXPENSES

This part of the chapter discusses specific provisions pertaining to cars. Provisions pertaining to capital cost allowance restrictions on cars owned by either employees or employers will be discussed in Chapter 5.

To begin, we must understand the terminology. Several definitions in respect of cars are briefly *summarized* below: ITA: 248(1)

(a) Motor vehicle — an automotive vehicle (undefined) designed to be used on highways and streets but not trolley buses or vehicles on rails.

(b) Automobile — a motor vehicle designed to carry up to nine individuals plus baggage, including vans, certain pick-up trucks and station wagons but excluding ambulances, taxis, hearses, vehicle inventory and clearly marked fire department, police [or Emergency Medical Services (EMS)] vehicles.

(c) Passenger vehicle — an automobile acquired or leased after June 17, 1987.

It is important to determine which of the above definitions is being referred to. For example, paragraph 6(1)(*b*) on allowances refers to a motor vehicle, subsection 6(2) on the standby charge refers to an automobile, and section 67.2 on the limitation of deductions (discussed below) refers to a passenger vehicle.

¶3,402 Taxable Benefits for Automobiles Provided by Employer

Where an automobile is provided by an employer to an employee, the employee receives the benefit of not having to invest tens of thousands of his or her own dollars to purchase an automobile for use that would include both personal and employment. As a result, the *Income Tax Act* specifies how the quantity of the benefit will be calculated. These rules consider two primary benefits:

(1) the benefit that the employee receives from having the use of a capital asset, being the company-owned automobile — the standby charge, and ITA: 6(1)(*e*), 6(2)

(2) the automobile operating costs, if any, that are paid by the employer — operating benefit. ITA: 6(1)(*k*)

For purposes of these benefit calculations the definition used is "automobile", which is described above.

¶3,403 Calculation of the standby charge benefit from the use of the car itself

A standby charge represents a benefit conferred upon an employee through the availability of a company-owned or leased car for any use, whether for employment or personal. Since the employee, who has a company car made available for his or her use, does not have to spend tax-paid dollars on either purchasing or leasing a car, the government reasoned that this benefit should be taxed somehow, on the principle of equity.[26] The concept is not unreasonable. Since availability rather than actual use of the company car is the basis for this calculation, some unsuspecting employee could have an income inclusion of the rather high minimum standby charge.

[26] The term "made available" was at issue in *The Queen v. Adams*, 98 DTC 6266 (F.C.A.).

The Act provides a computational formula to establish a reasonable standby charge as: ITA: 6(1)(*a*), 6(2)

$$\frac{A}{B} \times [2\% \times (C \times D) + \tfrac{2}{3}(E - F)]$$

where A * is the lesser of:

(a) total personal-use kilometres driven during the available time period, and

(b) the value determined for B (as defined below) during the days the automobile is available;

B** is $1{,}667 \text{ km} \times \left(\frac{\text{total available days}}{30}\right)$;

C*** is the full original cost of an employer-owned vehicle, including HST;

D** is $\frac{\text{the total available days when the employer owned the automobile}}{30}$

E is the lease payments, including HST, made by the employer;

F is the portion of the lease payments which pertains to insurance for loss or damages and any liability in using the automobile.

* Note that amount A, above, is deemed to be equal to amount B unless:

(i) the taxpayer is required by the employer to use the automobile in respect of his or her duties of employment, and

(ii) the automobile is used primarily (more than 50%) in his or her duties of employment.

** Rounded according to the rule in the definition (i.e., to the nearest whole number, unless the fractional part is .5, in which case round the fraction down).

*** The capital cost limitations in paragraph 13(7)(*g*) and Regulation 7307, as subsequently described, do not apply.

A separate A/B ratio must be applied to each automobile available for use by an employee in a year. Thus, if an employee had both an employer-owned automobile and an employer-leased automobile available in a year, the formula would be applied with two different A/B ratios as: ITA: 6(2)

Employer-owned + Employer-leased

$$\frac{A}{B} \times [2\% \times (C \times D)] + \frac{A}{B} \times [\tfrac{2}{3}(E - F)]$$

¶3,404 Determining the operating cost benefit

As previously mentioned, the Act specifically excludes a benefit in relation to the use of an employer-provided automobile. However, operating expenses for personal use, which are paid by an employer and not reimbursed by the employee, do give rise to a taxable benefit to the employee. Automobile operating expenses include gasoline, insurance, and maintenance costs, but not parking costs. Any benefit related to personal parking is included in income separately unless the advantage from it accrues primarily to the employer, rather than the employee. ITA: 6(1)(*a*)(iii) ITA: 6(1)(*k*) ITA: 6(1)(*a*)

There are two options for computing the operating cost benefit. If the conditions for both are met, then the better option for the employee can be chosen.

¶3,404.10 *Kilometre method*

The default method (called the "kilometre method") computes the operating cost benefit to an employee whose employer pays for operating costs including those for the personal use of an employer-provided automobile. The kilometre method is required for employees who do not use their automobile primarily (more than 50%) for employment or for employees who choose not to elect the 50% calculation method, where the use is primarily for employment. ITA: 6(1)(*k*)(v), 6(1)(*k*)(iv)

The kilometre method alternative computes the amount of the operating cost benefit by reference to the number of kilometres driven for personal purposes at 27 cents per personal-use kilometre in 2013. The 27 cents amount is reviewed periodically. The amount computed by this method is reduced by any reimbursement paid within 45 days after the end of the year by the employee to the employer in respect of these operating costs. The inclusion based on 27 cents per kilometre is considered to include a GST/HST component, and no further income inclusion is required.

¶3,404.20 *Election where use is primarily (more than 50%) employment*

If an employee notifies his or her employer in writing before the end of the particular taxation year, he or she may compute his or her operating-cost employment income inclusion as 50% of the standby charge minus any reimbursement to the employer made by the employee within 45 days after the end of the year. However, this option is only available in situations where the vehicle is used *primarily* (more than 50%) in the performance of employment duties. The resultant income inclusion is considered to include an HST component and no additional income inclusion is required. ITA: 6(1)(*k*)(iv) IT-63R5, par. 6(d)

¶3,405 Summary of employer-provided automobile benefits

The illustration below provides a graphical summary of benefits derived from an employer providing an automobile and/or paying for operating costs.

Figure 3-1
Automobile Benefits

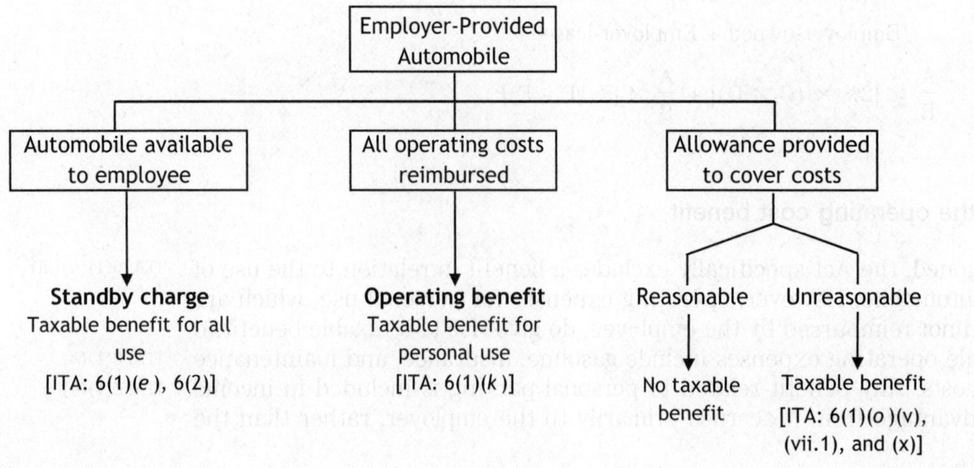

¶3,406 Application of the rules

The following examples will demonstrate how the standby charge and operating cost benefit rules should be applied. ITA: 6(1)(*e*), 6(1)(*k*), 6(2)

Example Problem 3-6

Automobile owned by employer

Original cost of automobile, including HST	$26,000
Operating costs for the year paid by employer, including HST	$ 3,000*
Employment-use kilometres	10,000
Total kilometres for year	30,000
Number of months available	12
Reimbursement to employer for personal use (to cover operating costs and standby charge) at 10¢ per kilometre	$ 2,000

* Includes insurance of $600, but excludes parking.

— *REQUIRED*

Compute the standby charge and operating benefit for the use of the automobile.

— *SOLUTION*

Standby charge ITA: 6(1)(*e*), 6(2)

$\frac{20{,}004 \text{ km}^{(1)}}{20{,}004 \text{ km}} \times [2\% \times (\$26{,}000 \times 12)] =$	$6,240	
Operating benefit (20,000 km × $0.27)[2]	5,400	$11,640
Less: amount reimbursed		2,000
Total car benefits		$9,640

ITA: 6(1)(*k*)(v)

— *NOTES TO SOLUTION*

(1) The employee does not qualify for the standby charge reduction, since the car is not used more than 50% in the performance of employment duties. Therefore, in this situation, the value of A in the formula (i.e., 20,004 kilometres) is deemed to be equal to the value of B in the formula (i.e., 1,667 × 12 rounded).

(2) The operating benefit election method is also not available, since the car is not used more than 50% in the performance of employment duties. Since this is an employer-provided automobile, the per kilometre method must be used. ITA: 6(1)(*k*)(v)

Example Problem 3-7

Automobile owned by employer — The facts are the same as Example Problem 1, except that the employment-use kilometres are 24,000.

— *REQUIRED*

Compute the standby charge and operating benefit for the use of the automobile.

— *SOLUTION*

Standby charge ITA: 6(1)(*e*), 6(2)

$\frac{6,000 \text{ km}^{(1)}}{20,004 \text{ km}}$ × [2% × ($26,000 × 12)] = ... $1,872

Operating benefit[(2)]	936	$2,808	ITA: 6(1)(*k*)(v)
Less: amount reimbursed (6,000 km × 10¢)		600	
Total car benefit		$2,208	

— *NOTES TO SOLUTION*

(1) Lesser of (a) 6,000 kilometres and (b) 1,667 kilometres × 12 months. In this situation the employee qualifies for the standby charge reduction since the car is used primarily (i.e., more than 50%) in the performance of employment duties.

(2) The operating benefit election method is available to the employee, since the car is used more than 50%. This method would result in a lower income inclusion ($936 (i.e., 50% of $1,872) versus $1,620 (i.e., 6,000 kilometres × $0.27)). ITA: 6(1)(*k*)(iv)

Example Problem 3-8

Automobile leased by employer

Lease cost including $500 of insurance and HST	$ 5,000
Operating costs for the year paid directly by the employer (includes HST, but excludes parking)	$ 3,000
Employment-use kilometres	4,000
Total kilometres for the year	16,000
Number of months available	12
Reimbursement to employer for personal use (to cover operating costs and standby charge) at 5¢ per kilometre	$ 600

— *REQUIRED*

Compute the standby charge and operating benefit for the use of the automobile.

— *SOLUTION*

Standby charge ITA: 6(1)(*e*), 6(2)

$\frac{20,004 \text{ km}^{(1)}}{20,004 \text{ km}}$ × ⅔ ($5,000 – $500) $3,000

Operating benefit (12,000 km × $0.27)	3,240	$6,240	ITA: 6(1)(*k*)(v)
Less: amount reimbursed		600	
Total car benefits		$5,640	

— *NOTE TO SOLUTION*

(1) In this situation, the employee does not qualify for the standby charge reduction or the operating benefit alternative, because he or she did not use the car more than 50% in the performance of the employment duties.

Example Problem 3-9

Automobile leased by employer — The facts are the same as Example Problem 3 except that the employment-use kilometres are 12,000.

— *REQUIRED*

Compute the standby charge and operating benefit for the use of the automobile.

— *SOLUTION*

Standby charge			ITA: 6(1)(*e*), 6(2)
$\frac{4{,}000 \text{ km}^{(1)}}{20{,}004 \text{ km}} \times 2/3$ (\$5,000 – \$500)	\$ 600		
Operating benefit(2)	300	\$ 900	ITA: 6(1)(*k*)(v)
Less: amount reimbursed (4,000 km × 5¢)		200	
Total car benefits		\$ 700	

— *NOTES TO SOLUTION*

(1) The employee qualifies for the standby charge reduction, since he or she used the car more than 50% (i.e., 75%) in the performance of his or her duties.

(2) The employee does qualify for the operating benefit alternative method of computing the operating cost benefits, since the car was used more than 50% in the performance of his or her duties. In this situation, the election would give a lower gross income inclusion of \$300 (i.e., 50% of \$600) versus \$1,080 (4,000 kilometres × \$0.27). ITA: 6(1)(*k*)(iv)

¶3,408 Employee-Owned Automobile Operating Expense Benefit

An automobile operating expense benefit arises when an employer provides the automobile and pays for some or all of the operating costs, including costs related to the personal use of the automobile. However, a separate rule applies in cases where the automobile is provided by the employee and where an employer pays for automobile operating costs, including costs for personal use of the automobile. For example, an employee may use his or her own automobile for employment purposes, but the employer pays, through a business credit card, for all operating costs of the automobile, including costs of driving to and from work which are personal costs. ITA: 6(1)(*k*) ITA: 6(1)(*l*)

The value of any benefit received by an employee for automobile operating expenses attributable to personal use must be included in income. To arrive at the value of this benefit, the total costs paid by the employer should be prorated by the ratio of personal-use kilometres to total kilometres driven by the employee. Amounts paid by the employee to the employer can be deducted from the benefit. Of course, this method requires record-keeping of employment and personal kilometres in a log, but there is no simpler, alternative method allowed for an employee-provided automobile. Note that the value of this benefit is determined using GST-included operating expenses. ITA: 6(1)(*l*)

Note the heading for paragraph 6(1)(*l*) is the single word "*idem*", which is a Latin word meaning "the same". Therefore, the heading for paragraph 6(1)(*l*) is considered to be the same as that for paragraph 6(1)(*k*) which is "automobile operating expense benefit".

¶3,409 Vehicles Other Than Automobiles

The standby charge and operating benefits discussed in the preceding pages apply only to *automobiles*. An "automobile" is defined in the Act as a "motor vehicle . . . designed or adapted primarily to carry individuals on highways and streets and that has a seating capacity for not more than the driver and 8 passengers". The definition then provides for some exceptions. ITA: 6(1)(*a*), 248(1); IT-63R5

Where an employee is provided with one of these "excepted" vehicles, or some other vehicle, this does not mean there is no taxable benefit associated with that employer-provided vehicle. The value of the benefit is taxable. While any reasonable approach to determining the benefit is acceptable, the Act indicates that it should reflect what an arm's length cost for substitute/similar transportation would be. In some circumstances, a per-kilometre rate would be acceptable. ITA: 6(1)(*a*)

¶3,410 Motor Vehicle Allowances Received from Employers

¶3,415 Overview

As previously discussed, all allowances received by employees are included in income with specified exceptions. Two of these exceptions were explained previously: ITA: 6(1)(*b*)

- *all* reasonable allowances pertaining to salespersons and persons who negotiate contracts, and ITA: 6(1)(*b*)(v)
- reasonable motor vehicle allowances for all other employees. ITA: 6(1)(*b*)(vii)

Note that the motor vehicle allowance rules are separate for "ordinary" employees, but included with all allowances for sales/negotiating persons. The reason for the distinction is that ordinary employee allowances for travelling, other than for motor vehicle expenses, have a territorial restriction and are limited to travel away from the municipality and metropolitan area of the employer's establishment. However, the other allowance rules mentioned above, as discussed next, do not have this territorial restriction. ITA: 6(1)(*b*)(vii), 6(1)(*b*)(vii.1)

The following table shows the applicable provisions.

Exceptions to Employment Income Inclusion of Travelling Allowances in Paragraph 6(1)(*b*)

	Sales/Negotiating Persons	***Other Persons***
Travel allowance other than for motor vehicles	Spar. 6(1)(*b*)(v)	Spar. 6(1)(*b*)(vii)
Allowance for motor vehicles	Spar. 6(1)(*b*)(v)	Spar. 6(1)(*b*)(vii.1)

¶3,420 Allowances for motor vehicles — Other persons

The Act sets out the initial conditions for exempting motor vehicle allowances for employees, other than those who are salespersons or who negotiate contracts. The conditions for exemption are: ITA: 6(1)(*b*)(vii.1)

(a) the allowances must be reasonable in the circumstances (therefore, motor vehicle allowances which are not reasonable, i.e., less than a reasonable amount, greater than a reasonable amount, or deemed not to be reasonable (as discussed below), must be included in income); and

(b) the allowances must be in respect of travelling in the performance of the duties of an office or employment.

An Interpretation Bulletin, "Vehicle and other travelling expenses — Employees", makes some important administrative comments on the application of this provision. First, where an employee receives a set periodic amount (i.e., monthly, weekly, etc.) the amount will be considered to be an excluded advance (prepaid reimbursement) rather than a potentially excludable allowance where: IT-522R, par. 44

(a) there is a beginning-of-the-year agreement between the employee and employer that the employee will receive a stated amount per kilometre for business-related travelling;

(b) there is a year-end accounting for any difference between the advances and the actual business-related kilometres; and

(c) the amounts above are reasonable.

The CRA will, as a general rule, consider the kilometre allowances permitted by regulation as deductions for *employers* as reasonable allowances. These amounts (for 2013), generally, are 54¢ on the first 5,000 kilometres and 48¢ on the remaining kilometres. (See Chapter 4 for further comments on these amounts.) However, at the same time, the CRA acknowledges that reasonableness of an allowance is normally decided based on the particular fact situation. IT-522R, par. 43; ITR: 7306

¶3,425 Allowance deemed not to be reasonable

Two additional subparagraphs and the preamble thereto modify and restrict the exclusion from income of certain motor vehicle allowances. The preamble deems the allowance received "not to be a reasonable allowance" where:

- the motor vehicle allowance is not based solely on kilometres in respect of use for the employer's business, or ITA: 6(1)(*b*)(x)

- both an allowance and a reimbursement, in whole or in part for expenses in respect of that use, are received. Excepted is the reimbursement of expenses for supplementary business insurance, toll and ferry charges. ITA: 6(1)(*b*)(xi)

Whether an allowance is excluded from employment income based on the reasonableness test is critical in determining the deductibility of expenses by the employee. As has been discussed previously in this chapter, if a reasonable allowance is excluded from employment income, then the related expenses cannot be deducted.

An allowance is deemed to be unreasonable and, therefore, included in income, if it is received for the use of a motor vehicle and is not based solely on the number of kilometres driven for employment purposes. ITA: 6(1)(*b*)(x)

The CRA has indicated that, if the employer pays an employee both a flat-rate allowance and a per-kilometre allowance for the same use of the automobile, the whole amount is deemed to be one allowance that is taxable, since it is not based solely on the number of kilometres driven. If an employee received a flat monthly rate for fixed expenses plus a reasonable per-kilometre rate, then the CRA considers the two allowances to be for the same use and combines them as one allowance which is not based solely on kilometres driven. They have indicated that the two allowances can be separated, if the employer pays a reasonable per-kilometre rate for travel outside the employment area and a flat monthly rate for travel inside the employment area. In this case, the two amounts are not for the same use and the per-kilometre allowance, in this case, would not be taxable, but the flat-rate allowance would be.

¶3,430 Expenses

¶3,435 Overview

The deductibility of motor vehicle expenses is treated separately from general travelling expenses for ordinary employees. Motor vehicle expenses for salespersons and negotiating persons (persons who negotiate contracts and who have commission income or income based on volume of sales) still remain deductible. Exhibit 3-5 summarizes and compares all employee deductions under paragraphs 8(1)(*f*), (*h*), and (*h*.1). ITA: 8(1)(*h*), 8(1)(*h*.1) ITA: 8(1)(*f*)

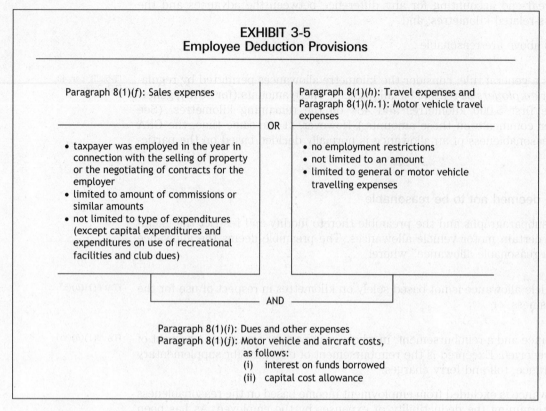

EXHIBIT 3-5
Employee Deduction Provisions

Paragraph 8(1)(*f*): Sales expenses	OR	Paragraph 8(1)(*h*): Travel expenses and Paragraph 8(1)(*h*.1): Motor vehicle travel expenses
• taxpayer was employed in the year in connection with the selling of property or the negotiating of contracts for the employer • limited to amount of commissions or similar amounts • not limited to type of expenditures (except capital expenditures and expenditures on use of recreational facilities and club dues)		• no employment restrictions • not limited to an amount • limited to general or motor vehicle travelling expenses

AND

Paragraph 8(1)(*i*): Dues and other expenses
Paragraph 8(1)(*j*): Motor vehicle and aircraft costs, as follows:
(i) interest on funds borrowed
(ii) capital cost allowance

Where travel expenses, alone, exceed the amount of commissions or similar income, it is advantageous to use the deduction under paragraphs 8(1)(*h*) and (*h*.1), instead of paragraph 8(1)(*f*). Where a deduction is possible for an amount either under paragraph 8(1)(*f*) or paragraph 8(1)(*i*), it is better to deduct under paragraph 8(1)(*i*), which is not limited by commissions or similar income, to preserve deduction room under paragraph 8(1)(*f*).

¶3,440 Motor vehicle and aircraft — Interest and CCA

The deduction of certain expenses that are capital in nature, namely interest on loans and the depreciation for tax purposes (i.e., capital cost allowance) in respect of motor vehicles and aircraft, is specifically allowed. A deduction is only available where an employee may deduct expenditures under paragraph 8(1)(*f*), (*h*), or (*h*.1). Hence, it is critical to establish that the employee was not in receipt of a tax-exempt allowance that would preclude a deduction of expenses under these three provisions. In the case of a sales/negotiating person, only a deduction under paragraph 8(1)(*f*) is limited to the amount of commission income. The interest and CCA deduction is not restricted to the amount of commission income or similar amounts received. These deductions are further restricted as explained below. ITA: 8(1)(*j*)

Capital cost allowance will be discussed in some detail in Chapter 5. However, at this stage, all that has to be understood is that accounting depreciation and capital cost allowance (CCA) are quite similar. The major exception is that in respect of depreciable capital properties that are motor vehicles and aircraft the maximum deduction *must* be based on the declining balance method (30% for motor vehicles and 40% for aircraft) and that in the year of acquisition the rates are one-half of the normal rate.

Note that in the case of an aircraft, the use thereof must be *required* for employment purposes. However, a motor vehicle need only be *used* for employment purposes to qualify for a deduction. In addition, the deduction in respect of an aircraft is limited to the amount that is reasonable in the circumstances in relation to the availability of other modes of transportation. ITA: 8(9)

For example, if a car costing $25,000 is purchased to be used for employment purposes, the maximum CCA claim in the year of acquisition will be $25,000 × 30% × ½ = $3,750. In the second year, the maximum CCA claim will be 30% × ($25,000 – $3,750) = $6,375.

¶3,445 Imputed interest deemed paid

There is an employment income inclusion for a benefit obtained through a low-interest loan to an employee. These benefits are computed, as previously discussed in this chapter. This interest income inclusion in employment income, in respect of interest on funds borrowed to purchase a motor vehicle or aircraft, is *deemed* to be interest *paid*. Hence, this deemed interest payment is eligible for a deduction along with interest actually paid. This rule allows for the deduction of "any interest paid", which would include amounts "deemed to be interest paid". This amount, however, must be prorated for employment kilometres driven or hours flown to arrive at the allowable deduction. ITA: 6(9) ITA: 80.4(1), 80.4(3)–(7) ITA: 80.5 ITA: 8(1)(*j*) ITA: 8(1)(*j*)(i)

For example, if an employee receives an interest-free loan of $25,000 from her employer to purchase an automobile, she will have an imputed interest benefit to be included in her employment income of $25,000 × the prescribed interest rate of, say, 4%. This would be $1,000 of employment income. This imputed interest benefit will be deemed to have been paid by her as interest expense and, therefore, eligible for deduction, subject to the limitations below, as an automobile expense.

¶3,450 Interest on money borrowed for passenger vehicle

The Act limits the amount deductible in respect of interest on funds borrowed or debt incurred on the acquisition of a passenger vehicle to the lesser of: ITA: 67.2

(a) the actual amount payable (or paid); and IT-522R, par. 28

(b) $300 for each 30-day period that the automobile loan or debt was outstanding in the year. ITR: 7307(2)

Note that there is no rounding of the number of periods to a number of full months as there is in the standby charge rules. The resulting lesser amount is further prorated by the portion of employment use to the total use based on kilometres driven.

¶3,455 Capital cost for passenger vehicle

The Act and Regulations place limits on the capital cost of a passenger vehicle. The limits are set out as follows: ITA: 13(7)(*g*); ITR: 7307(1)

Acquisition date	*Maximum capital cost*	*Reference*
After 2000	$30,000 plus HST on the $30,000	Par. 13(7)(*g*) Reg. 7307(1)

Where the passenger vehicle is acquired from a person with whom the purchaser does not deal at arm's length (usually a related person), the capital cost is deemed to be the least of: ITA: 13(7)(*h*), 251

(a) the fair market value;

(b) the undepreciated capital cost of the seller; and

(c) the dollar maximum found in the above summary.

¶3,460 Limitation re cost of leased passenger vehicle

Passenger vehicle leasing costs are limited in a manner equivalent to the $30,000 capital cost restriction as described above. The following formula calculates the deductible portion of the leasing cost. ITA: 67.3 ITR: 7307

Lesser of:

(a) $\left[\frac{A \times B}{30}\right] - C - D - E$

(b) $\left[\frac{F \times G}{.85H}\right] - D - E$

where A is a dollar monthly maximum, as prescribed and reflected in the notes below;*

B is the aggregate of the number of days the vehicle was leased for all years to the end of the present year;

C is the aggregate of the lease costs deducted in all preceding years;

D is imputed interest, at the prescribed rate, on refundable amounts (e.g., deposits) over $1,000;

E is total reimbursements receivable in respect of the lease in the year;

F is the total lease charges payable (including HST) for the year;

G is the dollar maximum capital cost prescribed;**

H is the greater of:

(a) a dollar maximum prescribed amount,*** and

(b) the manufacturer's list price.

* *Date of lease contract*	*Maximum monthly deduction*	*Reference*
After 2000	$800 plus HST on the $800	Sec. 67.3 Reg. 7307(3)

** The rules are similar to the capital cost limitations described above. See Reg. 7307(1)(*b*)(iii).

*** Regulation 7307(4) calculates the appropriate number for years after 1997 by multiplying the capital cost maximum amount (see above) by $^{100}/_{85}$, i.e., $^{100}/_{85}$ × [$30,000 × (1 + .13)] = $39,882, assuming an HST rate of 13%.

Note that there is no rounding of the 30-day periods in part (a), above, as in the rule pertaining to the standby charge. ITA: 6(2)

Part (a) of the above formula provides a dollar limit, $800 (prescribed for years after 2000) plus HST per month. Recognize, however, that a lease could be devised for almost any car, no matter how expensive, so that the monthly lease payments do not exceed that limit. To discourage this strategy, the further limit in part (b) of the formula was necessary. That part allows a fraction of the total lease charges as a maximum deduction. The fraction is based on the $30,000 maximum capital cost for capital cost allowance purposes for years after 2000, relative to 85% of the manufacturer's list price of the car. The higher the list price in the denominator of the fraction, the lower the value of the fraction and the lower the amount of lease payments that can be deducted.

Leasing a car involves paying for both the capital cost of the car consumed during the leasing period and an interest cost for spreading the payments over time. Therefore, the limit on the deduction of lease payments must provide for a limit equivalent to the limit on capital cost allowance and the limit on interest for a purchased car.

¶3,470 Application of Rules

The following examples will demonstrate the rules for car allowances and expenses.

Example Problem 3-10

Mr. Alex Otto acquired an automobile on July 1, 2013, to be used in connection with his duties of employment. Alex is required by contract to use his own car and to pay directly all the expenses. Alex does not have any commission income. The following information, some of which is estimated, relates to the newly acquired car:

Cost of car (including HST)	$37,290
Total kilometres driven in the ownership period	25,000
Total kilometres in respect of his employer's business	15,000
Capital cost allowance rate (½ × 30%)	15%
Interest paid on bank loan in respect of the car	$ 1,950
Gas and oil	1,800
Maintenance	300
Insurance	1,400
Licences	100

Alex lives in a province which has an HST rate of 13%.

— REQUIRED

Determine the amount deductible in the taxation year in respect of the car expenditures in the following situations, on the assumption that the above expenses were reasonable and ignoring the effects of the leap year: ITA: 8(1)(*h*.1)

(A) no kilometre allowance was received;

(B) a reasonable allowance of 38¢ per kilometre in respect of employment driving was received;

(C) an unreasonable allowance of 5¢ per kilometre in respect of employment driving was received;

(D) a reasonable allowance of 25¢ per kilometre in respect of employment driving plus a yearly allowance of $2,000 was received;

(E) an unreasonable allowance of $1 per kilometre in respect of employment driving was received.

— SOLUTION

Potentially deductible expenses (before prorating for employment use):

Capital cost allowance limit: ITA: 13(7)(*g*)

(½ × 30%) × ($30,000 × 1.13)	$5,085
Interest expense — lesser of:	
(a) $1,950 (actual)	
(b) $300 × $\frac{184}{30}$ = $1,840	1,840
Gas and oil	1,800
Maintenance	300
Insurance	1,400
Licences	100
	$10,525

Portion relating to employment use:

$$\frac{15{,}000 \text{ km}}{25{,}000 \text{ km}} \times \$10{,}525 = \underline{\underline{\$6{,}315}}$$

Alternative Fact Situations:

(A) All of the $6,315 automobile expenses would be deductible, since all the conditions of these provisions have been met as follows: ITA: 8(1)(*h*.1), 8(1)(*j*)

(1) the automobile is used in connection with his employment duties;

(2) there is a contractual obligation to use his own car and to pay directly all of the automobile expenses;

(3) a reasonable allowance had not been received; and

(4) he was not eligible for a deduction as a sales/negotiating person in respect of the automobile expenses. ITA: 8(1)(*f*)

(B) None of the $6,315 would be deductible, since subparagraph 6(1)(*b*)(vii.1) exempts reasonable allowances. ITA: 8(1)(*h*.1)(iii)

(C) Since the 5¢ per kilometre allowance is not a reasonable amount, Mr. Otto must include the allowance in income and would be permitted the $6,315 deduction. ITA: 8(1)(*h*.1), 8(1)(*j*)

(D) Although the combined package of the two allowances may be reasonable in the circumstances, the Act deems the two allowances not to be a reasonable amount and, hence, taxable, since one of the motor vehicle allowances received was not based solely on kilometres. Since these allowances are taxable, the $6,315 would be deductible. ITA: 6(1)(*b*)(x), ITA: 6(1)(*b*)(vii.1)

(E) An unreasonable allowance of $1 per kilometre would be taxable, since the amount is in excess of a reasonable amount. Hence, the restricted expenses of $6,315 would be deductible. ITA: 6(1)(*b*)(vii.1)

Example Problem 3-11

Mr. Jonathan is required by his contract of employment to use his own car in the performance of his employment duties and to pay for all expenses. Mr. Jonathan leased a BMW from Expensive Cars Unlimited. The following facts relate to the leased car:

Lease period	Jan. 1, 2013 to Dec. 31, 2014
Lease cost per month including HST	$ 800
Manufacturer's list price, excluding HST	$50,000

Mr. Jonathan was not reimbursed for any portion of the lease cost. Mr. Jonathan lives in a province which has an HST rate of 13%.

— *REQUIRED*

Determine the allowable lease cost which qualifies for a deduction under section 67.3 in 2013 before prorating for employment use. Ignore the effects of the leap year.

— *SOLUTION*

Lesser of:

$$\text{(a)} \quad \frac{(1.13 \times \$800) \times 365}{30} = \underline{\underline{\$10{,}999}}$$

(b) $\dfrac{(\$800 \times 12) \times (\$30{,}000 \times 1.13)}{85\% \text{ of the greater of (i) } \$39{,}882^{(1)} \text{ and (ii) } \$50{,}000} = \$7{,}657$

Deduction of the lesser amount: $7,657

— *NOTE TO SOLUTION*

(1) $\dfrac{100}{85} \times (\$30{,}000 \times 1.13) = \$39{,}882$

Example Problem 3-12

Ms. Elana is required by her contract of employment to use her own car in the performance of her employment duties and to pay for all expenses. Ms. Elana leased a Mercedes from Sky's-The-Limit Leasing. The following facts relate to the leased Mercedes:

Lease period	Oct. 1, 2011 to Sept. 30, 2014
Lease cost per month, including HST	$ 1,600
Manufacturer's list price, excluding HST	$60,000
Total kilometres	30,000
Total employment kilometres	20,000
Gas and oil	$ 1,500
Maintenance	700
Insurance	2,000
Licences	100

— *REQUIRED*

Determine the amount deductible in respect of the car for the year 2013 on the assumption that a total of $13,893 of leasing costs had been deducted *prior to* 2013. Assume an HST rate of 14%. Ignore the effects of the leap year.

— *SOLUTION*

Gas and oil		$ 1,500
Maintenance		700
Insurance		2,000
Licences		100

Leasing costs — lesser of:

(a) $\dfrac{(1.14 \times \$800) \times 822 \text{ days}^{(1)}}{30} - \$13{,}893 = \$11{,}096$

(b) $\dfrac{(12 \times \$1{,}600) \times (\$30{,}000 \times 1.14)}{85\% \text{ of the greater of (i) } \$40{,}235^{(2)} \text{ and (ii) } \$60{,}000} = \$12{,}875$

Lesser amount: 11,096

Total: $15,396

Portion relating to employment use:

$$\frac{20{,}000 \text{ km}}{30{,}000 \text{ km}} \times \$15{,}396 = \underline{\underline{\$10{,}264}}$$

— *NOTES TO SOLUTION*

(1) 92 days in 2011 + 365 days in 2012 + 365 days in 2013

(2) $(\$30{,}000 \times 1.14) \times \frac{100}{85} = \$40{,}235$

¶3,500 GST/HST REBATE ON EMPLOYEE DEDUCTIONS

Employees, who are able to deduct GST/HST-paid employment expenses, can obtain a refund of the GST/HST component of these expenses in a similar manner to their employers who are registrants. Although the employee refund mechanism is quite different from the input tax credit system, the effect of this refund is quite similar.

As a general rule, employees do not have GST/HST registration numbers and, hence, are not eligible for input tax credits. However, employees, who have deductible expenses for income tax purposes, may have paid GST/HST on some of those expenses and should be eligible for some sort of refund mechanism. Therefore, in order to refund employees of registrants, other than financial institutions, who have paid GST/HST on non-reimbursed expenses, a GST/HST "rebate" system, as opposed to a GST/HST "input tax credit" system, has been established. The following description is based on a provision of the *Excise Tax Act* (ETA). ETA: 253(1)

The GST/HST rebate system is based on amounts which are deductible from employment income. These deductible amounts will include the GST/HST component. In the calendar year following the year in which the deduction is made, the employee is eligible to file a rebate application in prescribed form. The employee has four years from the end of the taxation year, in which the expense was claimed for income tax purposes, to apply for the rebate. The amount of GST/HST rebate that is received is then required to be included in income in the year that it is received. This employment inclusion has the effect of offsetting the GST/HST component of the expense deducted in a preceding year. The reason for this effect is that a rebate received in respect of an expense that has been deducted lowers the net cost and, hence, should lower the net deduction. ITA: 6(8)(*c*)

The goods and services tax rebate is not considered to be a reimbursement received by the taxpayer. As a result, the employee is allowed to deduct, in the year of payment, GST/HST along with the expenses to which it attaches. In view of the required inclusion of the rebate, the rule in subsection 8(11) is needed to allow the deduction of GST/HST which is ultimately offset by the inclusion. ITA: 8(11) ITA: 6(8)

The employee GST/HST rebate is calculated as 13/113, 14/114, or 15/115 (assuming a provincial rate of 8%, 9%, or 10%, respectively[27]) times the amounts deducted for income tax purposes. An employee is not entitled to a GST/HST rebate for expenses in respect of which the employee has received an allowance unless the employer certifies that it did not consider the allowance to be a reasonable allowance and therefore must be included in income. If the allowance was considered to be a reasonable allowance by the employer, it would have claimed the input tax credit under a provision of the ETA. The certification precludes recovery of the GST/HST by both the employer and the employee. ETA: 174

[27] As discussed at ¶1,400, British Columbia exited the HST on April 1, 2013, and GST at the rate of 5% applies where tax is paid or payable after March 31, 2013. Nova Scotia has announced that it will be reducing the provincial portion of the HST rate to 9%, effective July 1, 2014, and to 8%, effective July 1, 2015; Prince Edward Island adopted the HST effective April 1, 2013, with a 9% provincial HST component.

In the year in which the employee actually receives the rebate, there is an offsetting adjustment under the *Income Tax Act* for the GST/HST component, if any, of the deductible expenses. The Act includes in employment income the GST/HST component of the deductible employment expenses, other than capital cost allowance, for the preceding year. The GST/HST component of the capital cost allowance, which is buried in the cost of the asset, is deemed to be government assistance and, thereby, reduces the capital cost of the respective automobile, aircraft, or musical instrument. ITA: 6(8)(*c*) ITA: 6(8)(*d*) ITA: 13(7.1)

Example Problem 3-13

Ms. Gina Tang, an employee of Treeline Ltd., which is a registrant for GST/HST purposes, has supplied you with the following information concerning her employment income for 2013.

Ms. Tang uses her own car in the performance of her employment duties away from her employer's place of business and is required by her employment contract to pay for her travel expenses. She is not reimbursed for any of her travel expenses, but she does receive a kilometre allowance. Her employer will certify that it did not consider the allowance to be reasonable at the time it was paid. The example is based on the assumption that her automobile was purchased in early 2013 and was subject to HST at the rate of 13%.

The following information pertains to Ms. Tang's 2013 employment income as correctly prepared by her accountant. The amount of the expenses indicated reflects all pertinent income tax restrictions (e.g., the limit on capital cost of the automobile, 50% for meals and a proration of employment kilometres to total kilometres). The deductible expenses, where appropriate, include HST, as indicated below.

Employment income		
Inclusions:		
Salary[(1)]	$85,000	
Car allowance[(1)]	3,000	
Premiums paid by Treeline Ltd. for non-group disability insurance[(2)]	400	
Imputed interest on a car loan[(2)]	2,160	$ 90,560
Deductions:		
Travel expenses:		
Transportation, including HST of $390	$ 3,390	
Accommodation, including HST of $520	4,520	
Meals, including HST of $325	2,825	(10,735)
Automobile expenses:		
Operating costs, including HST of $195	$ 1,695	
Interest[(2)]	3,120	
Insurance and licence[(2)]	800	
Capital cost allowance[(3)]	2,000	(7,615)
Professional fees, including HST of $85[(4)]		(735)
Employment income		$ 71,475

— *NOTES*

[(1)] Salary and car allowance are not subject to GST/HST since the definition of property in the ETA excludes money. ETA: 123(1)

[(2)] Insurance, licence and interest are exempt supplies. ETA: Schedule V

(3) Capital cost allowance is not subject to GST/HST. However, there is a GST/HST component in the capital cost allowance claimed.

(4) Membership fees in professional organizations of which an employee must be a member to maintain a professional status recognized by statute, are exempt supplies. However, an election is available to these organizations under this provision to deem these fees to be taxable supplies. This election would normally be made where the majority of the members can obtain a refund under either the input tax credit system or rebate system. In addition, the professional organization will also be able to claim an input tax credit on its acquisition of taxable supplies. ETA: Schedule V, Part VI, par. 18

— REQUIRED

(A) Calculate the amount of GST/HST rebate which Ms. Tang is entitled to receive in 2014.

(B) Indicate the income tax consequences of the GST/HST rebate.

— SOLUTION

(A) Ms. Tang can apply for a GST/HST rebate in 2014 based on her deductible expenses in 2013. This would normally be done on the filing of her 2013 income tax return. The amount of the rebate would be calculated as: ETA: 253(1)

13/113 of the sum of:

(a) Deductible expenses, including HST	
Transportation	$ 3,390
Accommodation	4,520
Meals	2,825
Automobile operating expenses	1,695
Professional fees	735
	$13,165
(b) Capital cost allowance	2,000
	$15,165
(c) Less: any expenses for which a reasonable allowance was received	Nil
	$15,165
13/113 thereof	$ 1,745

(B) On the assumption that Ms. Tang receives the GST/HST rebate in 2014 she would make the following income tax adjustments in 2014:

Par. 6(8)(*c*) employment income inclusion

$$\frac{\$13,165}{\$15,165} \times \$1,745 = \$1,515$$

Par. 6(8)(*d*) capital cost reduction

$$\frac{\$2,000}{\$15,165} \times \$1,745 = \$230$$

¶3,600 APPLICATION OF RULES UNDER SUBDIVISION "A"

The following illustration is a comprehensive example of how "employment income" is determined under Subdivision a of Division B. The solution is cross-referenced to the appropriate section in the Act. Read carefully these cross-references and the supporting notes ITA: 5, 6, 7, 8 which highlight the key points in each related paragraph. However, note that the assignment problems may contain additional points not covered in this illustration.

Example Problem 3-14

Ms. Elliott, who lives and works in Ontario, is employed as an internal auditor by MCS Ltd., a public corporation, for the calendar year 2013. She provides you with the following information concerning her receipts, taxable benefits, and expenditures:

Gross salary		$ 50,000
Income taxes withheld	$15,900	
CPP contributions	2,302	
EI contributions (max. amount)	891	
RPP contributions (money purchase)	3,000	
United Way donation	100	
Reimbursement paid to employer for use of company car and its operating costs	300	(22,493)
Net salary		$ 27,507

MCS Ltd. pays the following amounts on behalf of Ms. Elliott:

(A) Premiums for the following medical plans:

(i) Drug plan — Sun Life	$ 275
(ii) Extended health care — Liberty Mutual	350

The company paid a provincial employer health tax (not a premium).

(B) MCS Ltd. provides Ms. Elliott with a car to be used in connection with the duties of her employment. Ms. Elliott uses the car 80% for employment and 20% for pleasure based on total kilometres for 2013 of 25,000.

The company paid the following automobile expenses:

(i) Operating costs (including HST)	$3,200
(ii) Lease costs (including HST)	4,500

(C) Ms. Elliott, who must travel regularly away from her employer's place of business, receives a monthly allowance of $400 to cover her accommodation and meals while travelling. She is, however, required by her contract to pay for these expenses directly. Her actual expenses were $3,000, including HST, for meals and $4,000, including HST, for accommodation, all of which were reasonable in the circumstances.

Ms. Elliott also supplies you with the following selected expenditures:

(i) Registered retirement savings plan contributions	$1,500
(ii) Legal fees paid in collecting back pay from a former employer (including HST)	200
(iii) Professional accounting dues (including HST)	300

— *REQUIRED*

(A) Calculate Ms. Elliott's employment income for tax purposes for 2013 (as determined by Subdivision a of Division B of the Act).

(B) Compute the HST rebate that should be claimed and the income tax consequences of the rebate to be received in 2014.

— *SOLUTION*

(A) Employment income:

Reference				
Ssec. 5(1)	Salary[1]			$50,000
Par. 6(1)(*e*)	Standby charge[2]	$ 750		
Par. 6(1)(*k*)	Operating cost — car[3]	375	$1,125	
	Less: payments to company		300	825
Spar. 6(1)(*b*)(vii)	Travel allowance[4]			4,800
				$55,625
	Less:			
Par. 8(1)(*b*)	Legal fees[5]		$ 200	
Par. 8(1)(*h*)	Travel expenses[6]		5,500	
Par. 8(1)(*i*)	Professional dues[7]		300	
Par. 8(1)(*m*)	RPP contributions[8]		3,000	(9,000)
	Employment income — Subdivision a[9]			$46,625

(B) HST rebate income tax consequences:

(a) Rebate

13/113 of the sum of:

(i) Deductible expenses, including HST:	
Legal fees	$ 200
Travel expenses	5,500
Professional dues	300
	$ 6,000
(ii) Capital cost allowance	Nil
	$ 6,000
(iii) Less any expenses for which a reasonable allowance was received	Nil
	$ 6,000
13/113 thereof	$ 690

(b) Income tax consequences

The HST rebate of $690 must be included in employment income in the year of receipt. Since no capital cost allowance was deducted, there will be no capital cost reduction component of the rebate. ITA: 6(8)(*c*)

— *NOTES TO SOLUTION*

(1) The Act refers to remuneration *received* in the calendar year only, but this does not mean that the net salary is the amount included in employment income. The Act deems that taxes withheld have been received at the time remuneration etc. was paid. ITA: 5 ITA: 153(3)

(2) The standby charge will be computed as:

$$\frac{5{,}000 \text{ km}}{20{,}004 \text{ km}} \times (\tfrac{2}{3} \times \$4{,}500) = \$750$$

Ms. Elliott is entitled to the standby charge reduction, since she uses the car for business more than 50% of the total kilometres.

(3) Ms. Elliott qualifies for the election method of determining a benefit derived from employer-paid automobile operating costs, since her employment-use is in excess of 50% of the total use. The operating costs under this election method would result in a reduced income inclusion of $375 [20% × 25,000 kilometres × $0.27 = $1,350 under the kilometre alternative *versus* (50% × $750) = $375]. ITA: 6(1)(*k*)(iv)–(v)

(4) Allowances are dealt with in paragraph 6(1)(*b*), which includes all allowances in income with 10 specific exceptions. One such exception, which is applicable in this situation, applies to most employees, but not salespersons or persons who negotiate contracts, since there is a special provision for them. There are two specific conditions which must be met in order for the allowance not to be taxable. The first condition is that the allowance must be a reasonable amount. The second condition is that the employee must be travelling outside the metropolitan area where his or her employer is located. ITA: 6(1)(*b*)(vii)

On the assumption that Ms. Elliott's travelling expenses were reasonable in the circumstances, the monthly allowance of $400 ($4,800 annually) was not a reasonable amount since the actual expenses were $7,000. Therefore, the allowance is a taxable allowance and she can claim her actual travel expenses. ITA: 8(1)(*h*)

(5) Legal fees are deductible only if they are paid ITA: 8(1)(*b*)

- in the year
- to collect, or establish a right to, an amount that, if received, would be included in the employee's employment income.

(6) Ms. Elliott can deduct her travelling expenses because she meets all the conditions of the relevant provision. First, she must travel regularly away from her employer's place of business. Second, she is required by contract to pay for these expenses. Finally, she is not in receipt of an exempt allowance since the allowance which she receives is less than a reasonable amount and, as a result, has been included in income. ITA: 8(1)(*h*) ITA: 6(1)(*b*)(vii)

The deductible expenses are composed of:

Accommodation	$4,000
Meals and entertainment expenses (50% × $3,000)	1,500
	$5,500

Note how the determination of the reasonableness of the allowance was based on the full expenditures which were considered reasonable. The result was that the allowance was not reasonable and, hence, it was included in employment income. However, the meals expenditures were only 50% deductible.

(7) Professional dues are deductible only if the dues are for a profession recognized by statute and if the dues relate to the employment income as per the preamble to section 8.

[8] Registered pension plan: an employee is permitted to deduct, for tax purposes, his or her contributions to a money purchase registered pension plan to a maximum of $23,820 in 2012, but this amount is the maximum amount for the combined employee-employer contributions.

[9] Items excluded from computation:

(a) Employers' contributions to a private health plan, such as the drug and extended health care plans and provincial health service tax levies, are not taxable benefits. ITA: 6(1)(*a*)

(b) The Act includes all benefits received or enjoyed through employment with certain specific exemptions which do not include public medical plan premiums paid by an employer. However, in Ontario, as in several other provinces, provincial medical plan premiums have been replaced by a health services tax based on total payroll; hence, there is no taxable benefit for individual employees. ITA: 6(1)(*a*)

(c) Registered retirement savings plan contributions are deducted under Subdivision e, not Subdivision a.

(d) Income tax is not deductible. ITA: 8(2)

(e) United Way, a charitable donation, is not deductible under Division B. (A charitable donation made by an individual is eligible for a non-refundable tax credit under Division E.)

(f) CPP contributions and EI premiums are not deductible under Division B, but are eligible for non-refundable tax credits under Division E.

¶3,800 REVIEW QUESTIONS

(1) The best way to calculate employment income is to follow the format used on the personal tax return. Comment on the accuracy of this statement.

(2) It does not matter whether an individual is employed or self-employed since he or she can claim the same expenses under either category as long as the expense was incurred to earn income. Comment on the accuracy of this statement.

(3) If an individual fails any one of the tests which are used to determine employed versus self-employed status then the individual is employed. Comment.

(4) When determining whether a person is employed or self-employed, one of the subtests used in the economic reality or entrepreneur test is the "control test". What does this test involve?

(5) When determining whether a person is employed or self-employed, one of the tests used is the "integration or organization test". What does this test involve?

(6) When determining whether a person is employed or self-employed, one of the tests used is the "specific result test". What does this test involve?

(7) If a bonus cheque is received by an employee, Ms. Davis, on December 15 of this year and she chooses not to cash her cheque until January 5 of next year, then she will be able to defer the tax on the bonus until the next year since individuals are taxed on the cash basis. Comment.

(8) If a bonus is payable to an employee, Mr. Lee, on December 15 of this year and he decides that he wants to be taxed on the income in the following year instead of this year, then he can ask his employer to defer the payment of this bonus until next year and accomplish his goal. Comment.

(9) Employees are taxed on income from their employer to the extent that it is a gross payment before withholding tax or a taxable benefit. The employer can deduct, as an expense, the full amount of the gross payments before withholding tax and taxable benefits that are reported on the employee's T4. Comment.

(10) To maximize the after-tax income from a disability insurance policy to a disabled employee, the employer should not pay *any* of the premium for the coverage. Comment.

(11) On June 2 of this year, Opco loaned $10,000 to an employee and did not charge interest. The employee repaid the loan on June 30 of the same year. How many days are included for purposes of determining the deemed interest benefit?

(12) Explain the differences between a reimbursement and an allowance.

(13) Opco bought a new car for its owner-manager that cost the company $40,000 plus $5,200 for HST. How much is the standby charge for this car for a full year assuming it is driven 40% for business purposes?

(14) What are the five conditions that must be met before a sales/negotiating person can deduct expenses?

(15) What are the four conditions that must be met by an employee, who is not a sales/negotiating person, in order to allow him or her to deduct travelling expenses other than car expenses?

(16) Mr. Wang is a part-time lecturer at the University of Waterloo. He lives in a location in Toronto which is 105 kilometres away from the university. The rest of the time he has a tax consulting practice which he operates out of his home. The university pays him $0.40 per kilometre to travel to and from the university. He is issued a T4 at the end of the year for his teaching income on the basis that he is a part-time employee. How is the travel allowance of $0.40 per kilometre treated for tax purposes?

(17) Guidelines for the deductibility of expenses related to work space in the home for employees are included in subsection 8(13). Under paragraph (*a*) of this provision the expenses are allowed if one of two conditions are met. In these conditions, the words "principally" and "exclusively" are used. What do these words mean for tax purposes?

(18) Ms. Smith has come to you to ask your tax advice. She has just had a large bonus paid to her on December 31 and wants to defer some of it until next year. She is arguing that since the CRA's portion was not sent to the Receiver General until January 15 she should be able to defer that portion until the next year on the basis that it was not received until January 15 when it was sent to the CRA. What do you think?

¶3,825 MULTIPLE CHOICE QUESTIONS

Question 1

In 2013, Bob's employer provided him with an employer-owned automobile costing $34,500 (including HST) for 12 months. His kilometres for personal use were 15,000 out of a total of 20,000 kilometres. Operating costs paid by his employer during 2013 were $3,600 (including HST). Which one of the following statements is TRUE for 2013?

(A) Bob's minimum standby charge is $8,280.

(B) Bob's minimum operating cost benefit is $2,700.

(C) Bob's minimum operating cost benefit is $3,900.

(D) Bob can elect to use ½ of his standby charge as his operating cost benefit.

Question 2

In 2013, Mary earned a $50,000 annual salary as a computer repair person and received a car allowance of $3,500. The car allowance was paid to her monthly and was not based on the number of kilometres that she drove. Her employment-related expenses (all reasonable) were:

Automobile expenses (gas, parking, CCA)	$3,000
Entertainment	2,000

What is Mary's minimum employment income for 2013?

(A) $53,500

(B) $50,500

(C) $49,500

(D) $49,000

Question 3

Susanne Denholm is employed as a provincial payroll tax auditor and is required by contract to maintain an office in her home. Susanne works at home most of the time and has been provided with a laptop computer and a fireproof audit bag for her files. She has not been provided with any reimbursement or allowance in connection with her home office, which occupies 10% of the square footage of her home. She incurred the following costs to maintain her home in 2013:

Telephone (general line)	$ 600*
House insurance	2,000
Property taxes	4,000
Heat, hydro & maintenance	5,000
Mortgage interest	24,000

* Susanne estimates that she used her telephone 50% for employment purposes during the year.

What is the maximum amount that Susanne can claim for the costs she has incurred in respect of her home office?

(A) $500

(B) $1,100

(C) $1,400

(D) $3,800

Question 4

On April 1, 2010, E Ltd. made a loan of $100,000 to Mr. Walker, a new employee of the corporation, to assist him in purchasing a residence when he moved from Quebec to commence employment in British Columbia. The loan bears interest at 2%, which is to be paid monthly. The principal of the loan is to be repaid in full on April 1, 2020. The prescribed interest rate on April 1, 2010 was 4%. Assuming that the prescribed interest rate throughout 2013 was 3% and the interest owing on the loan is paid each month, which one of the following amounts represents the increase in Mr. Walker's employment income in 2013 due to the loan.

(A) $1,000

(B) $2,000

(C) $3,000

(D) $4,000

Question 5

Tanya, an employee of a Canadian public company, received an option to purchase 1,000 common shares of her employer at $30 per share in April 2012, when the shares were worth $19 per share. In December 2012, when the fair market value was $40 per share, she exercised her options. In January 2013, she sold all the shares for $48 per share. Tanya wants to know what employee benefit she will have to report on her tax return. She wants to pay the lowest amount of taxes possible.

(A) $5,000

(B) $18,000

(C) $14,000

(D) $10,000

Question 6

Tim began employment as a commissioned salesman in July of this year and received a base salary of $60,000 and $5,000 in commissions based on sales for the year. During the year, Tim worked away from the office negotiating sales contracts. Tim is required to pay his own travelling expenses and his employer has signed a T2200 form certifying that requirement and certifying that no reimbursements are paid for any expenses Tim incurs to earn commissions. Tim incurred the following work-related costs from July through December of this year and all expenses are reasonable:

Meals and entertainment for potential customers	$14,000
Automobile costs (90% of the following amounts were for employment purposes based on kilometres driven):	
Fuel	4,000
Insurance	750
Repairs	2,250
Leasing costs for a car costing $20,000 ($500 per month)	3,000

What is the maximum deduction Tim may claim for employment expenses for the year?

(A) $5,000

(B) $9,000

(C) $14,000

(D) $16,000

¶3,850 EXERCISES

Exercise 1

Isaac v. M.N.R., 70 DTC 1285 (T.A.B.)

The appellant is a qualified registered nurse, is entitled to use the traditional letters "R.N." after her name and, in answering the questions contained in her 1966 income tax return, described herself as a "private duty" nurse both in the space provided for employed persons and in the space provided for persons in business or practising a profession. Thus, in trying to answer all the official questions on her return, the appellant indicated, on the one hand, that she was employed "as a private duty nurse" by the Canadian Forces Hospital at Halifax and, on the other hand, that she was in business of practising her profession "as a private duty nurse" in connection with the same hospital. The basic issue to be decided in this appeal is, briefly, what was the taxpayer's correct status vis-à-vis the Canadian Forces Hospital, Halifax in her 1966 taxation year.

The appellant launched the present appeal by Notice of Appeal dated March 7, 1968 in which she alleged (in effect) as follows: that in the relevant 1966 taxation year she was employed by the Canadian Forces Hospital, Halifax, on a day-to-day basis terminable on 24 hours' notice; that the usual so-called fringe benefits made available to and enjoyed by the regular full-time army nursing sisters such as holidays, sick pay, retirement plan, and so on, were not made available to her as a private duty nurse; that the regional surgeon's office in Halifax classified her as a "self-employed R.N."; that in her 1965 return she claimed and was permitted to deduct from her income expenses of a similar type to those disallowed in the 1966 taxation year now under appeal; and that several of her fellow private duty nurses employed at the Canadian Forces Base, Halifax, were employed on the same basis as she was and had claimed expenses of a similar type to those disallowed in this appeal (i.e., the type of expenses one would associate with a private duty nurse). The Minister stated that, in making the assessment now in dispute, he had acted upon the following assumptions of fact — that the appellant is a registered nurse and was employed by the Department of National Defence at the Canadian Forces Hospital and Base, Halifax, during the 1966 taxation year, that in the course of carrying out her engagement as a general duty nurse the appellant was subject to supervision and discipline by the hospital authorities, and that of the expenses allegedly incurred by the appellant only the amount of $25 claimed as "R.N. fees" and the amount of $42.41 being her contribution to the Canada Pension Plan were permitted under the Act.

The appellant testified, in effect, as follows: that she is a registered nurse; that in the relevant 1966 taxation year she was living in Halifax and was employed at the Canadian Forces Hospital (Stadacona Hospital), "not as a staff nurse but more or less as a private duty nurse, though my times were made up ahead of time" (the correct interpretation to be placed on the word "employed" in this appeal appears to be the key to the solution); that private duty nurses are allowed to claim as deductions from income certain expenses such as laundry, uniforms including caps, white shoes and stockings, travelling expenses (in this matter that item amounted to $76.40 made up of 191 days at 40¢ per day) and so on; that the only difference between herself and a private duty nurse is that the hospital deducted her Canada Pension Plan contributions from the per diem amounts payable to her; that she acted as a private duty nurse at Stadacona Hospital in the years 1964, 1965, 1966, 1967 and until April 1968 when she moved from Halifax to Charlottetown and became associated with the Charlottetown Hospital as a relief nurse; that she is presently working under exactly the same conditions under which she carried on at the Canadian Forces Hospital, Halifax, i.e., "If I don't work, I don't get paid, I have no benefits or holidays. I get private duty wages (these amounted to $15 per day in Halifax and now amount to $20 per day). My time is made up. If they get full-time nurses they can let me go"; that she and other private duty nurses were hired by Stadacona Hospital (on a day-to-day basis) to fill in while the hospital "didn't have enough service nurses"; and that in the year 1967 the said hospital "did get a large supply of military nurses in and we were all cut down" (i.e., a number of private duty nurses were simply laid off which was easy to do because they were working on a day-to-day basis). The Hospital supplied all equipment and supplies used by the appellant. The Hospital hired and fired all nursing assistants and other support staff who assisted the appellant in the performance of her duties. The appellant could request the Hospital to hire additional support staff but she personally did not hire them.

During her cross-examination, the appellant also testified, in effect, as follows: that her time sheet in the Canadian Forces Hospital, Halifax, was made out a week in advance; that the said hospital's authority to hire civilian nurses to meet its requirements was only valid while there was a shortage of military nurses; that, as they became available, the civilian nurses were replaced; that the hospital asserted its right to dismiss civilian nurses on 24 hours' notice — "we were told that when we went there to work"; that she, herself, was not replaced by a military nurse in the 1966 taxation year, now under appeal, but later her shifts were cut down and she was eventually replaced in 1968; that she was, of course, obliged to follow hospital regulations with regard to the administration of drugs, medications, and so on, as she would be in any recognized hospital; that, when she was working at the Canadian

Forces Hospital, Halifax, she was told which patients to look after; and that she did not sign any form of contract with the above hospital when she started to work there.

— REQUIRED

Is the appellant in this case employed or self-employed? In presenting your answer, discuss the tests that are applied by the courts in this type of situation and consider how the facts relate to these tests.

Exercise 2

ITA: 248(1); *Wiebe Door Services Ltd. v. M.N.R.*, 87 DTC 5025 (F.C.A.)

Due to the poor economy, Davies Ltd., an architectural firm, has instituted a freeze in hiring. However, the company wants to engage the services of a specific architect, Anne Capwell, to manage the completion of a specific project over a two-year period. Following negotiations between the parties, a consulting contract was signed. Ms. Capwell will be paid $4,000 per month to work at least 14 days per month (i.e., between three and four days per week) for a two-year period. The agreement stipulates that Davies Ltd. will provide Ms. Capwell with an office and pay for underground parking at Davies Ltd. Ms. Capwell has other architectural work and she estimates that she derives approximately 30% of her consulting income from other sources.

— REQUIRED

Express your opinion as to whether Ms. Capwell is considered an employee or an independent contractor.

Exercise 3

ITA: 6(1)(*a*); IT-470R

William Winter works for an extremely generous employer, Benjamin's Ltd., which paid the following amounts on behalf of William:

(a) Registered pension plan contributions (defined benefit)	$1,000
(b) Provincial employer health tax	600
(c) Extended health care premiums — Sun Life	250
(d) Drug plan premiums — Mutual of Omaha	150
(e) Tuition fee for a basket weaving course offered by a local high school	75
(f) Non-cash Christmas gift which the company did expense for tax purposes	65
(g) Subsidized lunches at company cafeteria:	
Fair market value	640
Actual cost	420
Amount paid by William	200
(h) Membership fees in Exclusive Private Club	800
(i) Financial counselling — ABC Investment Counselling Ltd.	1,000

— REQUIRED

Comment on whether these amounts are taxable.

Exercise 4

ITA: 6, 8

Subdivision a — Income or loss from an office or employment, outlines the basic rules, inclusions and deductions when computing net income from employment.

— REQUIRED

Explain when legal expenses are deductible in computing income from employment. Identify your references and outline any related sections, other resources and other relevant information.

Exercise 5

ITA: 6(1)(*a*); IT-470R

Melanie Hughes, a division supervisor for Eli's Ltd., a large department store chain, receives a 35% discount on all merchandise purchased through Eli's Ltd. This discount is available to all executives above assistant department heads. Melanie calculated that the discount saved her $6,000 this year.

— *REQUIRED*

Discuss whether there is a benefit.

Exercise 6

ITA: 6(1)(*a*); IT-470R

John Scott, an employee of Kelly Ltd., lives in Burlington and commutes by GO Train to Toronto where Kelly Ltd. is located. John, who is bored by reading, decides to move to Toronto, about 50 kilometres closer to his work, in order to cut down his travelling time. Kelly Ltd. reimburses him for the following amounts:

Moving van costs	$2,500
Reimbursement of actual loss suffered in selling the house	5,000
	$7,500

— *REQUIRED*

Discuss whether there is a benefit.

Exercise 7

ITA: 6(1)(*a*), 6(1)(*f*)

Tanya Sims, who is chairperson of her union's negotiating team, has approached you concerning the management's offer in connection with fringe benefits. The company proposes to pay one-half of the premiums of the following plans:

(a) group term life insurance;

(b) extended health care — a private plan;

(c) dental care — a private plan;

(d) an accident and sickness income protection plan — a private group plan covering up to 50% of the wages.

All of these plans have premiums which are approximately the same. The company at present does not contribute to any of these plans.

— *REQUIRED*

Discuss the tax implications of the company's proposal.

Exercise 8

ITA: 6(9), 8(1)(*j*), 80.4, 80.5

Leonard Lewis, an employee of BGE Ltd., received the following loans on January 1 of this year from his employer:

6% ..... $15,000 loan to purchase a car to be used primarily for employment purposes,

4% ..... $100,000 loan to purchase a home, and

7% ..... $10,000 loan to consolidate his other debts.

Leonard does not receive a mileage allowance and is specifically required by his contract to pay his car expenses. According to Leonard's travel log, he used the car for employment purposes, for 27,000 kilometres out of a total of 45,000 kilometres.

Assume that the prescribed rates for this year were:

1st Quarter — 7%	3rd Quarter — 8%
2nd Quarter — 6%	4th Quarter — 7%

Leonard paid the interest on these loans on January 15 of the following year.

— *REQUIRED*

Compute the interest benefit and any deduction for interest. Ignore the effects of the leap year.

Exercise 9

ITA: 7; IT-113R4

Katrina Knorr was granted, in year one, an option to purchase 50,000 common shares at $1 per share from her employer, Michael Ltd., a Canadian-controlled private corporation. The shares had an estimated fair market value at this date of $1.50. However, according to the agreement, Katrina could not exercise her option until her fourth employment year. Katrina did exercise her entire option in year five; the fair market value of the shares at that time was $3. Katrina sold all the shares in year six, at $6 per share.

— *REQUIRED*

Discuss the tax implications of the above transactions.

Exercise 10

ITA: 6(1)(*e*), 6(1)(*k*), 6(2)

Ms. Singh has full use of an employer-owned Mustang GTS purchased for her use in mid-December of last year. It is now January. The original cost to the employer of this classic is $20,000, including HST. Other details of the car for the coming year are as follows:

Capital cost allowance to be claimed by employer	$4,792
Operating costs for the year paid by the employer, including HST and insurance ($600)	$3,500
Personal-use kilometres	12,000
Number of months available	12
Reimbursement to employer for personal use at 15 cents per kilometre	$1,800

— *REQUIRED*

Compute the taxable standby charge and operating cost benefits, if the business-use kilometres are:

(a) 10,000

(b) 20,000

Exercise 11

ITA: 8(1)(*f*), 8(1)(*i*), 8(4)

Reille travels extensively with Biotech Corporation to market new pharmaceuticals throughout Canada. He is paid a base salary of $2,200 per month plus a 2% commission on gross sales. Reille was required to incur the following expenses to earn $24,000 in commission income:

Hotel and airfare	$18,000
Out of town meals	4,000
Entertainment meals	2,500
Professional dues	250
Notebook computer	3,900
Total	$28,650

— *REQUIRED*

Compute employment expenses deductible under section 8 of the Act.

Exercise 12

ITA: 8(1)(*i*), 8(13); IT-352R2

Calvin Cheng, who is employed and lives in Calgary, takes a considerable amount of office work home and, therefore, has built and furnished an office in his fully paid home. On this year's tax return, he claimed the following expenses in respect of his office which represents approximately 1/8 of the home.

Estimated rental value for office space	$1,000
Maintenance — 1/8	250
Taxes — 1/8	200
Insurance — 1/8	80
	$1,530

— *REQUIRED*

Discuss whether Calvin's course of action was correct.

Exercise 13

ITA: 8(4), 67.1(1)

The deduction for meals under paragraph 8(1)(*f*) — (sales expenses), is restricted to those incurred while entertaining a client or a customer or a prospective client or customer.

— *REQUIRED*

Determine the condition(s) under which personal meals consumed by an employee while travelling on business are allowable. Are there any restrictions if a deduction is allowed?

Exercise 14

ITA: 6(1)(*b*), 13(7)(*g*), 67.2; IT-522R

Ms. Irvine, who is employed by Susan's Super Ltd., travels extensively across Canada in her role as an internal auditor. According to the terms of her contract, she receives an accommodation allowance of $10,000 per year.

The contract states that she must use her own automobile and pay for all travelling expenses. Ms. Irvine acquired a new car, on January 5, 2013, for $32,000 plus HST at 13%. Her kilometres for business purposes were 15,000 out of a total of 21,000 kilometres.

During the year, Ms. Irvine paid the following amounts, all of which are reasonable in the circumstances and which are supported by receipts:

(a) accommodation, including meals of $4,500 (including HST)		$12,000
(b) total car expenses:	gas (including HST)	1,500
	maintenance (including HST)	500
	insurance	1,200
	licences	90
	interest on bank loan	4,000

Ms. Irvine calculated her capital cost allowance to be:

$$(1/2 \times 30\% \times \$32,000) = \$4,800$$

Ms. Irvine also filed the prescribed form (T2200) which her employer had signed. Assume that the employment use of the car is reasonable in the circumstances.

— *REQUIRED*

Discuss the tax consequences of the allowance and related expenses plus the deductibility of the car expenses. Ignore the effects of the leap year.

Exercise 15

ITA: 6(8); ETA: 253(1)

Based on the facts and solution for Exercise 14 determine the potential HST rebate and income tax consequences upon receipt of this amount.

¶3,875 ASSIGNMENT PROBLEMS

Problem 1

ITA: 248(1); *Wiebe Door Services Ltd. v. M.N.R.*, 87 DTC 5025 (F.C.A.)

Chow Installation and Repair Ltd. ("Chow") is in the business of installing and repairing overhead doors. Chow maintained a list of qualified installers and repair-persons and would contact them as work became available. Chow informed these workers that they would be considered to be running their own business, so no withholding of income tax, EI or CPP was made. Workers were paid by the job and worked mostly on their own. If the person contacted refused the assignment, Chow would call the next person on the list. The person who agreed to the job would go directly to the job site; he or she was not required to report to Chow's work place, except to pick up a door or parts.

Chow supplied the doors and the parts used in the repair or installation. Each worker maintained his or her own truck and tools. Chow, however, owned specialized racks made for transporting the doors and a special drill which could be used on cement. These items were available to any worker who required them.

Chow guaranteed all work for one year. Under the terms of the agreement between Chow and the workers, if a guarantee had to be honoured, the worker would be responsible to fix any defects. If any parts were required to correct the defect, the worker would have to pay for them.

— *REQUIRED*

Determine whether the workers should be considered employees of Chow or independent contractors. Evaluate this fact situation in detail before arriving at your conclusion. In presenting your answer, discuss the tests that are applied by the courts in this type of situation and consider how the facts relate to these tests.

Problem 2

ITA: 5, 6(1)(*a*), 6(1)(*b*), 80.4; IT-470R

Miriam, the sole tax adviser of a financial planning firm, is contemplating an offer to become Director of Taxation of Neil Manufacturing Limited (NML) of Dundas, Ontario. The offered compensation package would include the following:

- a salary of $132,000 per year, payable monthly;
- a one-time flat allowance of $25,000, payable on acceptance of the position, to help move her and her family to Dundas;
- a company contribution of 6% of her salary to a defined benefit registered pension plan;
- company payment of the premiums for extended health coverage and a dental plan provided by Star Insurance;
- company payment, valued at $900, for the preparation of her tax return by the company's accountants;
- company payment, valued at $2,500, for her membership in the Dundas Valley Golf and Curling Club;
- a company loan of $200,000 to help finance the purchase of a new home in Dundas. The loan will bear interest at 3.5% per year payable monthly and will be made on May 1, 2013, the closing date on the purchase of the home.

— *REQUIRED*

Miriam does not deal with many employment-related tax issues and recognizes the need for a corroborating opinion on the tax consequences of this compensation package. She has asked you for your opinion. Comment on the income tax consequences for employment income of each item in the compensation package. Assume that the prescribed rate of interest for employee loans is 7% in the first quarter of the year, 6% in the second quarter, 4% in the third quarter and 7% in the fourth quarter. Ignore the effects of the leap year.

Problem 3

ITA: 5, 6(1)(*a*), 6(1)(*b*), 80.4; IT-470R

Erin is an employee of TD-ROM, Inc., a public company. In 2013, her compensation package was as follows:

Gross salary	$59,000
Less: Payroll deductions	
Employee contribution to a registered pension plan	(3,000)
Charitable donations — United Way	(55)
Canadian Pension Plan contributions	(2,356)
Employment Insurance contributions	(891)
Net pay received	$52,698
Non-cash perks	
Employer contribution to a registered pension plan	$ 3,500
Private dental plan valued at	$ 800
Mandatory employer-paid provincial health tax	$ 450
Reimbursement of moving expenses for relocating from Edmonton	$ 900
Club membership (for company promotion)	$ 1,800
Supplier's prize for outstanding employee sales — Hawaii golf trip valued at	$ 6,000
Bonus declared but not paid	$ 2,000
Hard hat and safety glasses	$ 450

The company states that club memberships should be used for business promotion.

TD-ROM also offered Erin a stock option to purchase 1,000 corporate shares at $12 a share. On June 4, 2013, she exercised the option. As of December 31, 2013, Erin had not disposed of the shares.

February 1, 2006, Fair market value — Grant date	$11
June 4, 2013, Fair market value — Exercise date	$19
December 31, 2013, Fair market value	$16

— *REQUIRED*

Compute Erin's income from employment for income tax purposes.

Problem 4

ITA: 5, 6, 7

Three senior executives are renewing their employment contracts with Global Consulting Ltd., a public corporation. The corporation has provided each of them with the following alternative compensation plans for 2014 in addition to the $145,000 base salary each receives:

(a) A cash raise of $5,000 in 2014.

(b) A bonus of $5,500 payable in 2015.

(c) Use of the company condominium in Hawaii for two weeks, valued at $3,000.

(d) A stock option arrangement to purchase 1,000 shares of Global Consulting, a public company, this month (December 2013). Today's fair market value of the shares is $5, and the option price would be $3.50 per share. Management anticipates the share price in December 2014 will be $6.50.

Assume a marginal tax rate of 45%.

— REQUIRED

Discuss the various alternatives and provide a recommendation to the senior executives.

Problem 5

ITA: 6, 110(1)(*d*)

Craig Hunt is the general manager of the local professional hockey team, the Vancouver Golden Seals Ltd. (a Canadian public corporation). Assume that today's date is November 15, 2013. Craig has obtained approval from the owner of the hockey club to offer a contract to a 27-year-old free agent player who is available to the highest bidder. In addition to an offer of a $300,000 signing bonus and a $750,000 annual salary, Craig is authorized to offer the following two items as additional compensation:

(a) an interest-free employee loan of $100,000 that will eventually be forgiven by the hockey club; and

(b) a stock option to buy 100,000 common shares of Vancouver Golden Seals Ltd. Assume that on the grant date, the fair market value of the common shares is $10 per share, and that the exercise price will be $10 per share.

— REQUIRED

(a) Craig has asked you to assume the player will exercise all shares when the FMV is $15.00 per share and then sell the shares immediately on the open market. Outline the income tax consequences with respect to the stock option and explain how this will affect the player's net income for tax purposes.

(b) From the player's perspective, what, if any, are the consequences of the signing bonus and the proposed employee loan that will be forgiven in the final contract year?

(c) Assume instead that the loan will not be forgiven. Calculate the deemed interest benefit of the loan for the 2013 and 2014 taxation years. Assume the prescribed rate of interest on the loan is 6%. Ignore the effects of the leap year.

Problem 6

ITA: 6(1)(*a*), 6(1)(*e*), 6(1)(*e*.1), 6(1)(*k*), 6(2), 6(2.2)

Your best friend, Mitch, was at a sales conference recently. During one of the breaks, he entered into a conversation with one of the other attendees, Darly, regarding the perks provided by their respective employers. In both cases, the employer provides a car. However, Darly commented on the significant tax advantage available to her since her employer leased the car instead of buying the car. Mitch was able to obtain all of the information from Darly regarding her car.

Mitch has come to you for some "free" tax advice. He has asked you to compare the tax position he is in currently with the employer-owned car to the position that Darly is in with the leased car.

Mitch

Capital cost of the car including HST	$38,772
Capital cost allowance claimed by the employer	6,375
Operating costs paid by the employer (including HST)	4,250
Kilometres (as calculated from Mitch's log):	
Employment	8,000
Personal	10,000
Amount reimbursed to the company for the personal use at 14 cents per kilometre	$ 1,400

Darly

Lease cost including $1,650 of insurance and HST	$12,450
Operating costs paid by the employer (including HST)	2,975
Kilometres (as calculated from Darly's log):	
Employment	23,000
Personal	9,000
Amount reimbursed to the company for the personal use at 9 cents per kilometre	$ 810

— REQUIRED

Calculate the minimum car benefit which would be included in employment income for 2013 for Mitch and Darly.

Problem 7

ITA: 8(1)(*h*.1)

Crowchild Pipelines Corporation has offered Bing Lee a base salary of $65,000. Bing must choose one of the following compensation packages for the use of his personal automobile.

(a) To receive a reasonable car allowance of $6,000 per year to compensate for the operating expenses and the depreciation of his Jeep, used to drive to remote work sites. The allowance is based on the kilometres to and from the remote location, multiplied by the number of workdays.

(b) To submit receipts for all of his operating expenses for full reimbursement. Bing estimates that his total operating expenses are $4,000 annually. However, this amount does not cover the wear and tear on his car. Bing will use his car approximately 65% of the time for employment and he will be able to claim capital cost allowance (tax depreciation) equal to $3,000.

— REQUIRED

Should Bing be indifferent to the choice between these two compensation packages? Explain. Assume a tax rate of 45%.

Problem 8

ITA: 5, 6(3)

Chrisa had been an employee of David Hardware, a hardware product distributor, for 15 years. Chrisa sold the David hardware products directly to hardware stores. She was a salesperson and she was paid 100% by commission. Chrisa was personally responsible for all of her business expenses. Expenses, for example, for office supplies, stamps, telephone, parking, entertainment, promotion and samples, were supported by receipts and she deducted them.

During the years that Chrisa was employed by David, she sold products and developed the hardware market in her geographic area. One of the ways in which she developed the market was by "renting" floor space in various stores to display the David products. However, no receipts were received from the various stores, because in many ways the money was considered a "tip" by the managers of the hardware stores. Chrisa did not deduct these expenses. Through this process, Chrisa had significantly increased David's sales in her sales region and she had developed a loyal following in the hardware business.

At the time of Chrisa's departure from David, David paid $15,000 to Chrisa. The conditions of the agreement surrounding the $15,000 payment were as follows:

- David was "buying back" Chrisa's sales territory;
- Chrisa agreed not to enter a similar business to that of David's business, in David's distribution area, for a period of three years; and
- David and Chrisa agreed that the $15,000 would constitute a reimbursement of capital invested by Chrisa (i.e., the amounts she had paid to the stores for the rental of floor space for David products).

— *REQUIRED*

Discuss the income tax implications for Chrisa of the receipt of the $15,000.

Problem 9

ITA: 5, 6(1), 7, 8(1)

The following information relates to Leonard, a middle-management accountant, not engaged in negotiating contracts, of a public corporation, Peter Productions Ltd. which is located in Ontario.

(A) Salary — gross		$ 80,000
Payroll deductions:		
Income taxes	$23,500	
Registered pension plan (money purchase; see (B) below)	5,500	
Canada Pension Plan contributions	2,356	
Employment Insurance contributions	891	
Charitable donations	350	
Employee's portion of benefit plans (see (B), below)	800	(33,397)
		$ 46,603

(B) The company paid the following additional matching amounts on behalf of Leonard (an equal amount was withheld from salary as the employee's contribution, as shown in (A) above):

Registered pension plan	$5,500
Dental plan — Sun Life Co.	175
Group income protection — Royal Insurance Co.	225
Extended health care — Liberty Mutual	150
Group term life insurance — General Insurance Co.	250

The group term life coverage for Leonard was $300,000.

(C) Selected additional information concerning Leonard's receipts, disbursements, and other benefits:

(i) Trip to Europe from one of Peter Productions Ltd.'s clients in appreciation of Leonard's services (including HST)	$ 6,000
(ii) Periodic payments received from Royal Insurance under the group income protection plan during a three-month illness. This plan had been in existence since 2001 and Leonard's share of the premium since that date was $2,300	12,000
(iii) Peter Productions Ltd. paid Leonard's annual membership fee in a golf club	2,100

(iv) Early in 2013, Leonard was granted an option to purchase 1,000 of the company's shares for $2 per share. At that time the shares were trading on the market at $3 per share. Later in the year, Leonard exercised the option and acquired 1,000 shares when they were trading at $4.50 per share. In December 2013, he needed cash, so he sold the 1,000 shares for $5 each.

(v) Leonard paid the following amounts during the year:

Annual membership fee of a professional accounting body (including HST)	800
Registered retirement savings plan	3,500
Legal fees in appealing an income tax assessment (including HST)	1,900

— *REQUIRED*

(A) Calculate the employment income of Leonard for 2013 in accordance with Subdivision a of Division B.

(B) Indicate why you omitted any of the above amounts.

(C) Compute the HST rebate that should be claimed and the income tax consequences of the rebate to be received in 2014.

Problem 10

ITA: 5(1), 6(4), 8(1)(*f*), 8(1)(*j*); IT-470R

On September 1, Maria Battelio, a Calgary resident, commenced work as an investment dealer with Top Investments Corporation. Prior to September, Maria was a fourth-year commerce student at the University of Edmonton. Maria's contract of employment required that she use her own car and incur the necessary expenses to earn commission income. Maria purchased her car on September 1 for $21,000. Top Investments Corporation lent her the $21,000 for the car and she agreed to repay them $7,000 annually, without interest, on December 31 of each year. Assume that Maria's deductible capital cost allowance (net of personal use) on her automobile is $2,000.

Total distance travelled from September 1 to December 31	
Total kilometres driven	12,500
Personal kilometres driven	5,000
Maria received the following net pay in the year:	
Gross salary	$ 4,000
Commissions	18,000
Christmas bonus	300
Employment Insurance contributions	(419)
Canadian Pension Plan contributions	(931)
Charitable donations	(280)
Income tax withheld at source	(4,200)
Net pay	$16,470

To earn commission income, Maria incurred the following:	
Meals and entertainment	$ 2,300
Client promotion materials	1,500
Gasoline and operating expenses	1,600
Total	$ 5,400

Top Investment paid for the airfare and accommodation for Maria and her spouse to attend a conference in New York. The trip cost $800 for each person attending the conference. The company also pays premiums of $400 per employee for group life insurance with coverage of $100,000. Assume a 7% prescribed rate of interest on the employee loan.

— *REQUIRED*

Compute Maria's net income from employment. Ignore the effects of the leap year.

Problem 11

ITA: 5(1), 6(1)(*a*), 7(1), 8(1)(*f*), 8(1)(*i*)

Susanna Sculley, a marketing representative with MBI Technology Inc. (a public company), provided the following information relating to her current year's personal income tax return. Susanna's cumulative pay at year end revealed the following:

Gross pay	
Base salary	$32,000
Gross commissions	23,500
Daycare subsidy program	1,200

Deductions from gross pay		
	Employment Insurance contributions	(891)
	Canadian Pension Plan contributions	(2,356)
	Union dues	(280)
	Income tax paid	(19,800)
Net pay		$33,373
Expenses to earn commission income		
	Meals and entertainment	2,300
	Hotel and travel incidentals	1,780
	Airfare	1,800
Total		$ 5,880

MBI also granted Susanna a stock option, which she exercised in April of the current year. The following information relates to the stock option:

Number of shares for options exercised	1,000
Fair market value — grant date	$1.50
Option price	$1.80
Fair market value — exercise date	$2.50

Susanna's employer did not reimburse her, or provide her with an allowance for the expenses incurred to earn commission income. However, MBI did expect her to take clients out for lunch and travel when necessary.

— REQUIRED

Compute Susanna's net income from employment for the current year.

Problem 12

ITA: 5, 6, 7, 8

Sylvanna Chapelle, a national sales manager at Merche Tools Ltd. in Peterborough, Ontario, presented the following information for the current taxation year.

1) Gross salary	$48,000
Bonus based on sales	40,000
Less payroll deductions:	
Employee contribution to a Registered Pension Plan	(4,000)
Charitable donations — Heart Foundation	(150)
Canada Pension Plan contributions	(2,356)
Employment Insurance contributions	(891)
Net salary	$80,603

According to Sylvanna's contract of employment, she must travel to Vancouver, Edmonton, Calgary, and Regina to oversee operations in western Canada. Sylvanna must pay for travelling and promotional expenses. The company does not provide her with a travelling allowance. Instead, Sylvanna receives a bonus based on a percentage of western Canada sales. Syvanna's travelling expenses were as follows:

2) Meals while travelling out of town (45 days)	$ 1,500
Accommodation	5,200
Airfare	7,800
Taxi	500

3) Client promotion costs:

Company logo shirts and golf balls	700
Client meals and entertainment	2,200
Holiday gifts for prospective clients	3,500
Annual golf membership	1,800

4) Sylvanna's employment contract also required her to travel to the Oshawa manufacturing plant and four other warehouse outlets in Southern Ontario. The corporation provided her with a new four-door van last year. The cost of the van, including HST of 13%, was $36,000. The company also paid $2,400 for 100% of the operating cost. Sylvanna used the vehicle for the full calendar year for both employment and weekend pleasure. Personal kilometres driven totalled 9,900 and total kilometres driven is 18,000.

5) Merche Tools also paid out the following amounts:

Tax return preparation for Sylvanna	$ 350
Life insurance premium	150

— REQUIRED

Compute Sylvanna's net income from employment for income tax purposes for the current year.

Problem 13

ITA: 5, 6; IT-470R

Anita Lee, Vice-President of Gary Inc., has asked for your assistance concerning the tax implications of certain amounts and benefits she received from her employer during 2013.

Salary, gross		$ 90,000
Payroll deductions:		
Income taxes	$36,000	
Canada Pension Plan premiums	2,356	
Employment Insurance premiums	891	
Group accident disability insurance premiums	110	(39,357)
Net pay		$ 50,643

Additional Information

(1) In November 2013, Anita was in a skiing accident and was unable to work for four weeks. During this period she received disability payments totalling $1,600 from Paris Life Insurance Ltd. Half of the disability insurance premiums were paid by Gary Inc. and half by Anita (see payroll deduction above). Anita has paid a total of $350 in disability insurance premiums since she commenced employment at Gary Inc. in 2010.

(2) In 2013, Gary Inc. paid $424 (including HST) for the preparation of Anita's 2012 income tax return and $530 (including HST) for Anita to see a financial planning consultant regarding retirement planning.

(3) Anita is taking courses towards her M.B.A. degree on a part-time basis during the evening. She is taking the courses on her initiative and for her own benefit. During 2013, Gary Inc. paid for the tuition for these M.B.A. courses which amounted to $1,000. Gary Inc. also paid $400 in tuition for Anita to

attend a two-day computer workshop on company time to learn about the new software system that the company had just installed.

(4) Director's fees of $2,000 were received by Anita from Clint's Hi-Tech Ltd., a company owned by Anita's spouse.

(5) Christmas gift of $200 cash was received and was expensed by Gary Inc.

(6) Anita received an employee loan of $8,000 on January 15, 2013, at 3% interest to purchase a notebook computer for personal use. The interest was payable on each anniversary date of the loan, and Anita paid the interest owing on the loan on the due date in 2014. Assume that the prescribed interest rates applicable to employee loans for 2013 are: first quarter, 7%; second quarter, 6%; third quarter, 8%; fourth quarter, 7%.

(7) For 12 months, Gary Inc. paid Anita a monthly gas allowance of $250 regardless of the number of kilometres she drove. In addition, she was provided with a company-owned automobile costing $38,500 (including HST) at the beginning of January. Anita's kilometres for personal use were 16,000 out of a total of 25,000 kilometres. Operating costs paid (excluding gas) by Gary Inc. during 2013 amounted to $2,920, including insurance of $600 and HST.

(8) Anita and her spouse Clint were provided with Gary Inc.'s condo in the Bahamas for a one-week holiday during the winter. Excluding HST considerations, such accommodation during this peak period would have cost them $500 as opposed to the $100 actually paid by Anita.

(9) Anita used her frequent-flyer points accumulated as a result of her business trips (which had been paid by Gary Inc.) for her holiday in the Bahamas. She saved $800, plus $104 of HST, by using the frequent-flyer points.

(10) Anita bought merchandise from Gary Inc. during the year and saved $180 (excluding HST of $23) using its 30% employee discount, which is available to all employees. Gary Inc.'s mark-up is 100%.

— REQUIRED

(A) Calculate Anita Lee's employment income inclusions for 2013 in accordance with the Act and the CRA's administrative position. Ignore the effects of the leap year.

(B) Explain why you omitted any of the above amounts from your answer in part (A).

(C) If the facts were changed so that Anita had not been provided with a company-owned automobile and instead used her own car for employment purposes, how would this affect the computation of Anita's employment income in accordance with the Act? Assume that Gary Inc. continues to pay for Anita's car operating costs.

Problem 14

ITA: 5, 6, 7, 8, 67.1, 67.2, 67.3; IT-352R2

Robby Beamon has recently been appointed vice-president of sales and marketing for Lori's Unpublished Books Limited, a public company. Robby has come to you for advice regarding the tax implications of his new position. During your meeting you were able to determine the following information:

(A) Remuneration for the year:

Salary — gross		$84,800
Less: Canada Pension Plan contributions	$2,356	
Employment Insurance contributions	891	
Disability insurance premiums	600	3,847
		$80,953
Bonus based on company sales		24,000

Allowances for the year (paid monthly):	
meals, accommodation and air travel	13,000
car	6,300
entertainment	2,000
Moving allowance	15,000

Robby has also been granted an option to acquire 7,500 previously unissued fully paid shares of Lori's Unpublished Books Limited at $11.50 per share. The fair market value at the time of the grant was $15. One of the conditions was that he must exercise one-third of the option immediately upon it being granted. He did so in May and acquired 2,500 shares.

(B) Robby has summarized the following expenses related to his employment:

Gas and oil — automobile	$ 3,900
Painting (office only)	100
Licences — automobile	100
Meals (consumed while travelling away for more than 12 hours)	7,000
House insurance	800
Accommodation (while travelling on company business)	10,000
Interest expense — car loan	3,600
General maintenance (house)	300
Car insurance	1,900
Hydro	700
Air travel	4,200
Car maintenance	1,000
Supplies	700
Fuel (house)	1,200
Property taxes	4,500
Mortgage interest	24,000
Salary (to wife, including payroll taxes and employer contributions)	15,000

(C) Lori's Unpublished Books Limited requires Robby to provide an automobile in order to carry out his duties of employment. Robby is responsible for his travelling expenses. On March 17, 2013, he acquired a new car for $46,000, including HST at 15%, financing part of the acquisition through a bank loan arranged for the same date. The capital cost allowance rate in the first year is effectively 15%. He estimates that he will drive 38,000 kilometres in the course of his employment. He expects his total kilometres to the end of the year to be 45,000. The car and the employment use are reasonable for his position and his work requirements.

(D) Robby's contract also requires that he maintain an office in his home, since no other office is provided. He is responsible for all costs related to the operation of the office. He does not receive an allowance or reimbursement related to any of these costs. Robby has estimated that the office occupies approximately 15% of his home. This estimate is based on square footage. Robby estimates that if he had to rent a comparable amount of space he would have to pay $850 per month plus utilities.

— REQUIRED

(A) Calculate Robby's employment income for 2013, assuming that all expenses are reasonable in the circumstances and will be documented. Ignore consideration of the HST rebate.

(B) If the facts in part (A) were changed as follows, what would be the deductible expenses for 2013? ITA: 8(1)

(i) Lease entered into on March 17, 2013.

(ii) Monthly lease payments are $1,100 including HST at 15%.

(iii) Employment use accounts for 38,000 kilometres out of a total of 45,000 kilometres for 2013.

(iv) Manufacturer's list price is $46,000 excluding HST.

(C) How would your conclusions in parts (A) and (B) change if Robby was an internal auditor and, therefore, did not receive a bonus based on sales?

Problem 15

ITA: 5, 6, 7, 8, 67.2, 67.3; IT-470R

Anita Flare is a skilled tool and die worker. She has been working for Car Parts Inc., a large manufacturer of parts for the automobile industry for over 10 years. Car Parts Inc. is a Canadian-controlled private corporation. Anita has become their "Jane on the Spot" as far as diagnosing and quickly retooling machinery that breaks down or needs to be updated to run a short order. Anita is single and she rents a home in north Toronto. Because Anita is required to travel for 75% of the year, Car Parts Inc. actually pays the $1,200 monthly rent on Anita's home in Toronto. Anita reimburses the company for 25% of this amount ($300 per month) through payroll deduction as set out below.

The head office of Car Parts Inc. is located in north Toronto. The company, however, has plants that are located throughout Ontario and Quebec, wherever there are large automobile manufacturing operations to be supplied with parts. When a plant requires emergency retooling or repair Anita is sent out to that location to supervise and organize the work. As stated above, this involves about 75% of Anita's total employment hours for any given year. She stays at a particular location for a period of days or weeks depending on the nature of the job involved. She is never at a site for less than 36 hours. For the balance of the year, Anita works at the head office in the research department.

Anita's final 2013 pay stub showed the following totals for the year.

Gross salary		$115,000
Payroll deductions:		
Income tax withheld	$44,200	
Canada Pension Plan contributions	2,356	
Employment Insurance premiums paid	891	
Contributions to company group RRSP	1,750	
RPP contributions on account of current service	5,000	
Union dues to Canadian Union of Automobile Workers (HST exempt)	800	
Group accident income protection insurance premiums (matched by company)	240	
Monthly rent reimbursement (as described above)	3,600	

In discussion with Anita you determined that the company also provides the following fringe benefits.

Payment of board and lodging costs at special work sites as required — at cost to company	$18,000
Bonus based on company profits for the year above budgeted targets	12,500
Provision of safety boots and company uniform consisting of five shirts and five matching pairs of pants; the shirt is embroidered with her name on the front pocket and has the company name on the back	450
Registered pension plan contributions to defined benefit plan	6,750
Monthly allowance of $150 to cover personal phone calls, laundry costs and other incidentals while travelling. (She estimates that she spends $100 per month.)	1,800
Fitness club membership dues to a club with locations across Ontario (including HST); Anita feels that it is important to her productivity to remain in top physical shape as her work can be physically demanding	805

Anita was injured on the job early in the year and received total payments of $11,500 out of the company group income protection plan for 2 months while she was recuperating. She had not previously received any payments under this plan and has paid total premiums of $2,880 into the plan since she began employment 12 years ago (this includes all of the year 2013 premiums paid through December 2013).

Due to her extensive travel, Anita's employer requires her to have an automobile for employment purposes. Anita has provided you with the following details of her automobile expenses.

	Owned car[1]	Leased car
Leasing costs[2]	n/a	$3,680
Gasoline and oil (including HST)	$2,880	1,440
Insurance	1,333	667
Maintenance (including HST)	400	240
Licence	90	30
CCA	1,207	n/a

NOTES:

[1] She owned an automobile until August 31, 2013, at which time she disposed of that vehicle and began leasing a new one. Assume that there are no tax consequences to Anita of the disposition of the automobile other than the fact that she can claim CCA in 2013 on this vehicle, as set out above, since it was a luxury vehicle.

Anita received an automobile loan to purchase the owned automobile. She received the loan on April 1, 2008, for $40,000, but has been making principal repayments annually on April 1 each year. She made the last principal repayment of $8,000 on April 1, 2013. There was no interest payable on the loan. Assume that the prescribed interest rate for employee loans was 6% for all of 2013.

During 2013, Anita drove the owned car a total of 40,000 kilometres, of which 35,000 kilometres were employment related.

[2] Anita leased the car as of September 1, 2013, at a cost of $920 a month that includes HST. The lease is for a three-year period that will expire August 31, 2016. At the time that she leased the car, the manufacturer's list price on the vehicle was $55,000 excluding all taxes.

During 2013, Anita drove the leased car a total of 20,000 kilometres, of which 18,000 kilometres were employment related.

— REQUIRED

(A) Determine Anita Flare's income from employment under Subdivision a of Division B of the Act for 2013, and cross-reference your answer to the appropriate section of the Act and/or Interpretation Bulletin. Round your answer to the nearest dollar. Ignore the effects of the leap year.

(B) Indicate why you did not include any of the above amounts in your answer with the appropriate cross-reference.

(C) Compute the HST rebate that should be claimed and the income tax consequences of the rebate to be received in 2014.

Problem 16

ITA: Subdiv. a of Div. B, 67.1, 67.3; IT-470R

Mr. Ned Newell is employed by Snoopy-Snacks Ltd. (a Canadian-controlled private corporation). As of February 15, 2013, Ned was promoted to vice-president sales due to his hard work negotiating puppy snack contracts on behalf of the company. This promotion required Ned to relocate from the Toronto office of Snoopy-Snacks Ltd. to its Victoria, British Columbia office.

Ned has provided you with the following information regarding his 2013 income and expenses. He requests your assistance in determining his 2013 employment income for tax purposes.

Payroll details:		
Gross salary		$125,000
Less:		
Income taxes	$45,000	
Canada Pension Plan contributions	2,356	
Employment Insurance contributions	891	
Registered pension plan contributions: defined benefit	6,750	
Group income protection premiums paid	120	
Group term life insurance premiums paid	180	55,297
		$ 69,703

Employer-paid amounts and fringe benefits paid by Snoopy-Snacks Ltd.:	
Dental plan premiums — paid to Star Insurance Company	$ 245
Group term life insurance premiums	90
B.C. provincial health care premiums	640
Group income protection premiums	400
Monthly allowance to cover travel and automobile expenses (based on a flat monthly amount of $400 for travel and $400 for auto)	9,600
Travelling expenses for Ned and his wife to Bermuda for a sales conference. Ned's time was spent attending the conference but his wife was on vacation the entire time. No HST was payable on the trip since it was outside of Canada. One-half of the expenses related to Ned and one-half to his wife.	2,800
A birthday gift (a watch) received while in Ontario (including HST). Snoopy-Snacks Ltd. deducted the cost of this gift as a business expense.	150
Outside financial counselling fees (including HST). The counselling firm indicated that 80% of its fees relate to counselling for future retirement while the remaining 20% of its fees relate to tax preparation.	2,568

Other Information:

1. Snoopy-Snacks Ltd. provided Ned with some assistance that relates to his move from Toronto to Victoria. The details of that assistance are set out below.

a) Ned purchased a new home in Victoria just prior to his move. However, he could not take possession of that home until April 30, 2013. Snoopy-Snacks Ltd. paid Ned's rent for a Victoria apartment for the months of February through April 2013. The rent paid was $1,200 per month.

b) Ned and Snoopy-Snacks Ltd. agreed that he would receive reimbursement from Snoopy-Snacks Ltd. for one-half of the loss realized by him on the sale of his Toronto home. Ned received $16,500 as a result of this agreement.

c) Ned received an allowance of $15,000 to cover his moving expenses.

In addition to the above, Ned's employer agreed to reimburse him an amount equal to one-quarter of his annual mortgage interest payment for the first five years of his mortgage on his new Victoria home. This was intended to compensate for higher real estate prices in Victoria. For 2013, Ned received $2,000 under the terms of this agreement.

2. Snoopy-Snacks Ltd. maintains an employee stock purchase plan for certain of its employees. Ned became eligible for this plan after his promotion. During 2013, he was granted an option to purchase 1,000 shares in Snoopy-Snacks Ltd. at an exercise price of $15 per share. At the time this option was

granted the fair market value of the shares was $20 per share. On September 15, 2013, Ned exercised the option to purchase 600 of the above shares. The fair market value of the shares was $25 at that time.

3. Ned had unlimited use of the company's private swimming pool. All management level employees are permitted to utilize this pool. The local private swimming pool charges annual fees of $1,800 per year before HST.

4. Ned had the following expenditures during 2013.

Automobile operating expenditures:	
Lease payments for 12 months ($850 a month including HST of 12%) (lease commenced July 1, 2012 for a period of three years; deducted lease costs for 2012 were $4,585)	$10,200
Gasoline and oil	1,300
Insurance	1,050
Maintenance	180
Licence	120
Travelling expenditures:	
Meals (consumed while out of metropolitan area for greater than 12 hours)	7,200
Accommodation	12,000

During 2013, Ned travelled a total of 36,000 kilometres, of which 22,500 kilometres were employment-related. The manufacturer's list price on his automobile was $33,000 before HST.

— *REQUIRED*

(A) Determine Ned's employment income for tax purposes for 2013, and cross-reference your answer to the appropriate sections of the Act and/or Interpretation Bulletins.

(B) Indicate why you did not include any of the above amounts in your answer with the appropriate cross-reference.

(C) Compute the potential GST rebate in 2014 and the income tax consequences upon receipt of the HST rebate. Assume an HST rate of 12% for this purpose. ITA: 6(8)

[For more problems and solutions thereto, see the DVD accompanying this book.]

¶3,880 ADVISORY CASES

Case 1: Sandra Rae

Sandra Rae has worked in the investment business in Calgary for 12 years and is a salaried plus commissioned employee. Recently, however, Sandra has wished for more independence in her career. The alternative of starting her own mutual fund company is neither feasible nor cost effective. A recent offer from a new investment corporation has drawn her attention.

Sandra decided to enter into a contract arrangement with Global Investments Inc. According to the agreement, a license costing $10,000 would give her the right to use the Global name on her letterheads, business cards, and any promotional materials. Sandra could also participate in selling any Global Investment product. The arrangement is peculiar. According to the agreement, Sandra is required to execute a minimum of $750,000 in sales each year before her contract can be renewed for another year. Although Global Investments has an office in Calgary, the agreement stipulates that Sandra use her own office, supplies, computer, printer, fax, telephone, and automobile. The agreement also stipulates that Sandra not work for any other investment firm, nor act as her own agent. Although Sandra will execute transactions, closing a sale requires the signature of the client, herself and a vice-president of Global Investments. Upon the close of a sale, Sandra submits an invoice to Global Investments earning her a management fee equal to 4% of gross sales.

Sandra converted her guest bedroom into a full-time and sole-purpose home office. She will not be reimbursed for any expenses incurred for setup, travelling or office expenses. She is also required to carry professional liability insurance. On the other hand, Global Investments will provide the expertise, research, promotion, and ordering materials. Last week, Global Investments placed an announcement in the newspaper introducing five new sales associates, including Sandra.

How does this new venture affect her computation of net income?

Case 2: Betina Harty

Betina Harty, a well-known Vancouver artist, signed a contract with the University of Calgary to beautify the campus. Betina spent all of the year in completing the beautification. During that time, she enhanced the campus with her own artwork and pieces bought at local auctions.

The University restricted Betina's choice of art to Canadian artists. As well, the University controlled the colour schemes and the types of art selected (e.g., paintings, sculptures, or murals) for the various locations on campus. However, within these requirements, Betina was permitted to exercise artistic discretion over the actual pieces chosen. This gave her a great degree of latitude over the beautification of the campus.

She could produce the art herself, purchase another artist's work and focus on any theme she desired. Betina worked at her own studio and used her own tools for her own productions. If the University did not like the art she produced or bought, she was not reimbursed costs and had to sell the art on the open market. Over the year, Betina channelled all of her energy into the University's beautification and did not produce art for any outside clients.

How should Betina's income from this contract be treated?

Case 3: Sherry Cane

The taxpayer, Sherry Cane, is an unmarried research analyst and senior executive for TSE Consultants in Toronto. In January 2011, TSE entered into a contract with the Iraq government, for $390,000, requiring that Ms. Cane be in Iraq from March 2011 to October 2012 to examine the long-term energy issues facing OPEC countries. TSE terminated

Ms. Cane's employment and engaged her as an independent subcontractor to perform this task.

Sherry gave up her office downtown, terminated her condominium lease, moved out, and stored her furniture and personal effects at her mother's house. Further, she shipped her clothing and books to Iraq. She retained her Canadian bank account so TSE could deposit the monthly contract income of $12,000 directly into her Canadian bank account. They did not withhold any income taxes. Similarly, in Iraq, no taxes were payable, and the government provided Ms. Cane with suitable living quarters, meals, and a part-time domestic for house-keeping. Since she intended to visit her boyfriend, Shawn, and family in Canada, she retained her Visa card and Ontario Health Care. Ms. Cane wanted to retain non-residency status for obvious reasons.

While in Iraq, Ms. Cane carried her business card with the TSE logo and promoted herself as a TSE representative. Shawn, an English professor from Queen's University, spent one six-month term on sabbatical at the University of Iraq. The letters mailed to the Canadian company from Iraq, however, indicated that she wanted to come home. She also noted that the cultural differences and political uncertainties were extreme. Ms. Cane returned home on October 17, 2012, married Shawn and purchased a lovely home in Waterloo, Ontario, with her savings.

It is now October 29, 2013, and Sherry Cane is sitting in your office as you read the following Notice of Reassessment from the CRA:

> We have completed our review of your personal returns of income for the taxation years 2011 and 2012. Based on our findings, you are a resident of Canada for tax purposes. Thus, we have adjusted your computation of net income to include the receipts of income from TSE, plus a portion of the personal benefits received during your temporary stay in Iraq.

Determine whether a Notice of Objection should be filed.

Case 4: Claire Jordan

Claire Jordan, a registered dental hygienist, would like to file a Notice of Objection with the CRA for taxation years 2010 and 2011. The CRA has reassessed Claire as a resident in Canada for 2010 and as an employee for 2010 and 2011. Claire describes herself as an independent self-employed dental hygienist. For the past two years, Claire was employed by the Canadian Forces Dental Unit to work on a day-to-day basis. Generally, the Mobile Dental Unit contracts for her, in advance, depending on the regional demand for dental cleaning and examinations.

In 2010, Claire contracted with the Canadian Forces Mobile Dental Unit to temporarily work at a Canadian Forces base in Saudi Arabia. The terms of the contract specified that she would work on a day-to-day basis depending on the demand for dental services over the next two years. Economically, the contract was very worthwhile because her room and board were provided by the government and her pay each day was $340. Despite the risk of no work, the pay she received was earned tax-free because she considered herself as a non-resident during her absence. Prior to leaving Canada, Claire sold her condominium and car and stored her furniture at her parents' home. She also cancelled her membership at the YWCA in New Brunswick and put her engagement on hold for an indefinite period. Her plan was to stay away for the full two years, assuming that all went as planned. Unfortunately, after 12 months, the Mobile Dental Unit ceased operations and Claire was scheduled to return to Canada. The Department of Finance had severely reduced the budget for National Defence. Claire was happy to return home on January 1, 2011. She married three months after her return and resumed her work with the Mobile Dental Unit in Moncton, New Brunswick.

Claire's compensation package with the mobile dental unit differs from other employees of the Canadian Forces. Other employees are assistants and support staff who are paid on a monthly basis with fringe benefits. Claire does not receive any benefits or holidays. In Canada she is paid on a day-to-day basis ($280 per day with no deductions for EI, CPP, or tax). All dental clinics are headed by a dentist who is professionally responsible for overseeing the work of both contract and salaried dental hygienists and dental assistants. The Canadian Dental Association does not permit dental hygienists to administer anaesthetic or work without supervision. The clinic provides all of Claire's tools, supplies, and support staff. If a workday is not more than 60% booked, patients are rescheduled to another day and Claire does not work. It is not unusual for the contract dental hygienists to be temporarily laid off. This does create problems because the contract specifies that Claire must be available to work at least four days per week (so she cannot work elsewhere). This has not bothered Claire because she has claimed all of her laundry, uniforms, shoes, stockings, and travelling expenses as a deduction against her self-employed business earnings. Travelling expenses are justifiable because the mobile unit moves to various remote locations outside of Moncton.

Advise Claire on the filing of a Notice of Objection in respect of 2010. How would you treat the various expenses incurred by Claire Jordan in each of the taxation years?

Chapter 4

Income from Business: General Concepts and Rules

TOPICS DISCUSSED

LEARNING GOALS

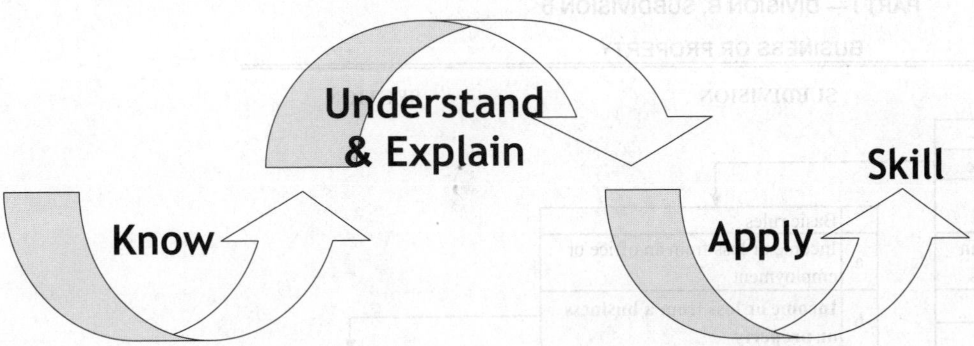

Know

By the end of this chapter you should know the basic provisions of the *Income Tax Act* that relate to the calculation of business income and expenses, and some of the GST/HST implications for business activity. You should be able to start with accounting income and make the necessary adjustments to arrive at business income for tax purposes. Completing the Review Questions (¶4,800) and Multiple Choice Questions (¶4,825) is a good way to learn the technical provisions.

Understand and Explain

You should understand and be able to explain what business income and expenses are, when to recognize them, and why they are treated the way they are for tax purposes. Completing the Exercises (¶4,850) is a good way to deepen your understanding of the material.

Apply

You should be able to use your knowledge and understanding of business income and expenses to identify and resolve practical problems. Completing the Assignment Problems (¶4,875) and Advisory Case (¶4,880) is an excellent way to develop your ability to apply the material in increasingly complex situations.

OVERVIEW

The focus of this chapter is on Subdivision b of Division B, Part I of the Act. In particular, the provisions dealing with income from business (both inclusions and deductions) will be covered. The final section of the chapter presents the impact of GST/HST legislation on the business activity discussed in the earlier sections of the chapter. The following chart will help to locate in the Act the key provisions discussed in this chapter.

PART I — DIVISION B, SUBDIVISION b

BUSINESS OR PROPERTY

DIVISION

A	Liability for tax
B	**Computation of income**
C	Computation of taxable income
D	Taxable income earned in Canada by non-residents
E	Computation of tax
E.1	Minimum tax
F	Special rules applicable in certain circumstances
G	Deferred and other special income arrangements
H	Exemptions
I	Returns, assessments, payment and appeals
J	Appeals to the Tax Court of Canada and the Federal Court of Appeal

SUBDIVISION

	Basic rules
a	Income or loss from an office or employment
b	**Income or loss from a business or property**
c	Taxable capital gains and allowable capital losses
d	Other sources of income
e	Deductions in computing income
f	Rules relating to computation of income
g	Amounts not included in computing income
h	Corporations resident in Canada and their shareholders
i	Shareholders of corporations not resident in Canada
j	Partnerships and their members
k	Trusts and their beneficiaries

SECTION

9-11	Basic rules
12-17	Inclusions
18-21	Deductions
22-25	Ceasing to carry on business
26-37	Special cases

Income from a business for tax purposes is added to total income in the first paragraph of section 3, while losses from a business are deducted in a different paragraph of section 3. Recall that the taxpayer is required to determine income from each source and to include income from employment, business and property. "Source" is defined as "something that comes into existence . . .".[1] For tax purposes, "source" generally refers to the cause giving rise to the activity and each business must be recognized as a "distinct source" of income, separate from employment income, income from property, and taxable capital gains. ITA: 3(*a*), 3(*d*)

Further, section 4 provides the general rule for determining a taxpayer's income or loss from a particular source. The general rule requires that only deductions applicable to a specific source may be claimed against income from that source. Taxpayers who carry on a business in more than one place should also apportion business income by territorial place. The Act provides little guidance, yet apportionment by geographic location becomes significant when operations are scattered internationally and among provinces. Should revenues and expenses be based on reasonable allocations or should expenses be allocated based on revenues of specific jurisdictions? Regulations provide some guidance for income earned from a business in a province by corporations and individuals, respectively. It is important to recognize that in defining income from a business, many interpretative ambiguities distinguish business income from other sources of income. ITA: 4(1) ITA: 4(1)(*b*) ITR: 400, 2603

Subdivision b of Division B of Part I of the Act contains the primary rules for the computation of income from business. Most of what will be covered will be found in sections 9 through 21. Some of the more important provisions are as follows:

[1] *Webster's New World Dictionary*, 3rd edition.

Inclusions

Sec. 9 — A taxpayer's income (loss) for a taxation year from a business is their profit (loss) from that business for the year

Sec. 10 — Rules related to inventory

Sec. 12 — Income inclusions

Sec. 13 — Rules related to capital cost allowance

Sec. 14 — Rules related to eligible capital property

Deductions

Sec. 18 — Limitations on the deductibility of expenses

Sec. 19 — Limitation on advertising expenses

Sec. 20 — Deductions permitted

The interaction between section 18 and section 20 is interesting. For example, paragraph 18(1)(*b*) does not allow any deduction that is on account of capital, including amortization. However, paragraph 20(1)(*a*) allows a deduction for capital cost allowance and paragraph 20(1)(*l*) allows a deduction for doubtful debts. Both of these items are capital in nature. So, just because you find a provision in section 18 that would disallow a particular expense, don't give up. Look in section 20 to see if there is another provision that will allow the expense in question.

¶4,000 BASIC RULES

¶4,010 The Concept of Business Income

¶4,015 Income from a business

The word "business" is very broadly defined the Act, although the definition specifically excludes an office or employment. Income from a business for a taxation year is the "profit" therefrom for the year. While the word "profit" is not defined in the Act, Subdivision b contains numerous specific rules regarding amounts to be included in income and amounts which may or may not be deducted for income tax purposes. Furthermore, it must be understood that the word "income" when used in the Act means income after the deduction of expenses currently incurred to produce it.

ITA: 248(1)

ITA: 9(1)

¶4,015.10 *What is profit?*

Profit is the portrayal of income, according to common law, on "sound commercial principles", which may include generally accepted accounting principles (GAAP), unless a particular provision of the Act or principle of common law requires otherwise. This issue was explored by the Supreme Court of Canada in the case of *Canderel Limited v. The Queen*, and the Court provided the following framework for analysis.

98 DTC 6100 (S.C.C.)

(1) The determination of profit is a question of law.

(2) The profit of a business for a taxation year is to be determined by setting against the revenues from the business for that year the expenses incurred in earning that income.[2]

(3) In seeking to determine profit, the goal is to obtain an accurate picture of the taxpayer's profit for the given year.

(4) In calculating profit, the taxpayer is free to use any method which is not inconsistent with:

(a) the provisions of the *Income Tax Act*;

(b) established case law principles or "rules of law"; and

(c) well-accepted business principles.

(5) Well-accepted business principles, which include but are not limited to the formal codification found in GAAP, are not rules of law but interpretive aids. To the extent that they may influence the calculation of income, they will do so only on a case-by-case basis, depending upon the facts of the taxpayer's financial situation.

(6) On reassessment, once the taxpayer has shown that he has provided an accurate picture of income for the year, which is consistent with the Act, the case law, and well-accepted business principles, the onus shifts to the Minister to show either that the figure provided does *not* represent an accurate picture, or that another method of computation would provide a *more* accurate picture.

¶4,015.20 *The role of GAAP*

Canada required that, by 2011, public enterprises adopt International Financial Reporting Standards (IFRS) and private companies adopt Accounting Standards for Private Enterprise (ASPE). As a result, the term "generally accepted accounting principles" (GAAP) will be used to refer to both IFRS and ASPE, as appropriate.

Specific provisions of the Act can create considerable differences between income for tax purposes and income for accounting purposes. One of the major causes of such differences results from the write-off of capital expenditures over a period of years. However, tax treatment in certain areas of the Act, including the valuation of inventory and the deductibility of prepaid expenses, has moved closer to generally accepted accounting principles.

GAAP are often considered to reflect ordinary commercial principles, the legal concept, held by the courts to be a key determinant of profits. Nevertheless, it should be noted that the

[2] *M.N.R. v. Irwin*, 64 DTC 5227 (S.C.C.); *Associated Investors of Canada Ltd. v. M.N.R.*, [No. 2], 67 DTC 5096 (Ex. Ct.).

word "profit" is not required by the legislation to be interpreted in conformity with GAAP, even where the Act is silent on the treatment of a particular transaction.

While the Canada Revenue Agency (CRA) has often taken the position that profit computed under GAAP most accurately reflects income in these situations, the courts have, on occasion, rejected conformity between income for accounting and tax purposes, particularly in cases where GAAP were at variance with the court's legal concept of ordinary commercial trading and business principles and practices or with a legal concept of income.[3] The case of *The Queen v. Metropolitan Properties Co. Ltd.*, on the measurement of business profit, clearly indicates "the desirability of applying generally accepted commercial and business practice as reflected in the generally accepted accounting principles". Thus, according to the reasoning of the court in the *Metropolitan* case, in the absence of a specific provision, a legal principle, or recognized commercial practice to deal with the tax treatment of a particular transaction, GAAP are applied to meet the objectives of the income tax system. 85 DTC 5128 (F.C.T.D.)

On the other hand, in the case of *Symes v. The Queen*, the Supreme Court of Canada expressed the view that to rely on GAAP for a determination of profit would suggest a degree of control by professional accountants that was inconsistent with a legal test for profit. The Supreme Court suggested the use of "well accepted principles of business (or accounting) practice" or "well accepted principles of commercial trading", but did not suggest how to determine these principles or how to differentiate them from GAAP. Again, in the absence of a specific provision of the Act or a clearly stated legal principle, reliance on GAAP may provide a reasonable guideline. 94 DTC 6001 (S.C.C.)

Where GAAP envisage more than one method of determining income, the courts have adopted the "truer picture" approach, choosing the method that provides the truer picture of income as in the case of *West Kootenay Power and Light Co. Ltd. v. The Queen*. In this case, considerable emphasis was placed on the matching of expenses to the income that was generated by the expenditure.[4] 92 DTC 6023 (F.C.A.)

¶4,020 Business Income Versus Capital Receipt[5]

¶4,021 Overview

The argument over whether a particular receipt is income in nature or capital in nature has given rise to thousands of court cases over the years. This is primarily due to the taxation treatment of these two items; income receipts are fully taxed and capital receipts are only partially taxed as capital gains. Historically, the inclusion rate for capital gains has ranged from 0% to 75%, with the current inclusion rate being 50%.

The courts have at times applied the analogy of a fruit-bearing tree to cases in which the determination of a capital or income transaction was at issue, in order to focus on how an asset has been used. An investment or capital asset is likened to the tree which produces or can be expected to produce income in the form of fruit. Just as the sale of the tree would be regarded as a capital transaction, the sale of an investment that can produce a form of income from business or property can be regarded as a capital transaction. However, the analogy breaks down under the facts of certain cases.

Exhibit 4-1 outlines the steps that should be taken to analyze the issue.

---

[3] There have been many cases in this area, including *M.N.R. v. Publishers Guild of Canada Limited*, 57 DTC 1017 (Ex. Ct.).

[4] For further discussion of the role of GAAP in interpreting profit for tax purposes, see Joanne E. Magee, "The Profit GAAP", *CA Magazine*, April 1995, pp. 32–35.

[5] For a more detailed discussion of this topic, see Robert E. Beam and Stanley N. Laiken, "Adventure or Concern in theNature of Trade: The Key to Taxpayer Intention", (1996) vol. 44, no. 3 *Canadian Tax Journal*, pp. 888–913.

EXHIBIT 4-1
Steps to Addressing Income Versus Capital Gain Issue

1. Gather all the facts leading up to, during and after the transaction.
2. Develop your best arguments for both income treatment and capital gain treatment. Be balanced in your analysis. Consider the "badges of trade" in Exhibit 4-2.
3. Analyze the strengths and weaknesses of your arguments.
4. Arrive at a conclusion of income or capital gain consistent with your analysis.
5. Determine how the transaction will be taxed if the taxpayer is:
   (a) An individual, or
   (b) A corporation.

¶4,022 Objective of the analysis

At the time of a court hearing, the courts can view in perspective the taxpayer's whole course of conduct for the period before, during and after the transaction in question. To help make the distinction between an income and a capital transaction, the courts attempt to assess the intention of the taxpayer in the transaction. The courts attempt to answer the question: did the taxpayer deliberately seek a profit of an income rather than a capital gain nature? An attempt is made to substantiate this by facts which establish the taxpayer's general course of conduct.

Secondary intention is established by looking at whether the taxpayer has built into a transaction, at the time of purchase, a profitable alternative in the event that the primary intention is frustrated. For example, if land is acquired for development, but appropriate zoning changes are not approved or other extraneous circumstances frustrate the original intention and subsequently the land is sold at a profit, that profit may be considered to be the result of the alternative business intention and may be regarded as business income.[6]

The concept of secondary intention was clarified in the case of *Racine et al. v. M.N.R.* as follows: 65 DTC 5098 (Ex. Ct.)

> To give a transaction which involves the acquisition of capital the double character of also being at the same time an adventure in the nature of trade, the purchaser must have in his mind, at *the moment of the purchase*, the possibility of reselling *as an operating motivation* for the acquisition; that is to say that he must have had in mind that upon a certain type of circumstances arising he had hopes of being able to resell it at a profit instead of using the thing purchased for purposes of capital. (Italics added.)

In the case of *Armstrong v. The Queen*, the Court stated further "that circumstances which force the sale of property or make such a sale attractive do not have the effect of *retroactively converting* a property held to produce income and as a capital property into something of a trading nature". (Italics added.) 85 DTC 5396 (F.C.T.D.)

¶4,023 Observable behavioural factors or "badges of trade"

While the courts have indicated that taxpayer intention is the objective in a determination of whether a transaction results in a receipt of business income or capital, it should be recognized that intention is a state of mind. Intention must be inferred from an observation of a taxpayer's behaviour or a taxpayer's whole course of conduct. The observable behaviour of a taxpayer may be classified by a set of behavioural factors which may point to the existence of "an adventure or concern in the nature of trade" from which an intention to enter a profit-making scheme can be inferred. The courts have developed a set of indicators, often referred

[6] Two good examples of this situation are given by the cases of *Regal Heights Ltd. v. M.N.R.*, 60 DTC 1270 (S.C.C.), and *Fraser v. M.N.R.*, 64 DTC 5224 (S.C.C.).

to as "badges of trade" to determine whether an adventure or concern in the nature of trade was present in a transaction and, hence, whether business income resulted.

To determine whether a gain on the disposition of property is business income from an adventure or concern in the nature of trade or a capital gain, it is useful to apply an analytical framework to a fact situation. The objective of applying such a framework is to systematically evaluate the facts to determine whether a transaction or series of transactions bear the "badges of trade". A list of behavioural factors or badges of trade that can be used as a reference might be comprised of the following.

(i) *Relation of the transaction to the taxpayer's business:* A transaction may be regarded as an income transaction if it is very similar to one in which the taxpayer would be involved in his or her normal business or profession. If a taxpayer undertakes a transaction in association with others, then the relationship of the transaction to the normal business or profession of these associates can be considered. This factor is helpful in determining whether a taxpayer had a secondary intention to make a profit on the sale of an asset. If a taxpayer has special knowledge or expertise or had direct access to these, it might be inferred that in a particular transaction a profitable "escape hatch" was known at the time of the purchase.

(ii) *Activity or organization normally associated with trade:* The nature of the activity surrounding a transaction or the level of organization of the transaction may be such that the transaction can be considered "an adventure in the nature of trade" or a transaction which is very similar to one which would be undertaken by a business person normally engaged in such transactions. Two classic cases of this involved British taxpayers one of whom purchased a carload of toilet paper and resold it at a profit[7] and the other of whom purchased a carload of whisky and sold it at a profit[8]. Transacting in such commodities by the carload is an indication of an intention to trade which would result in the gains being assessed as business income. To apply this factor, it is necessary to determine how the transaction in question was organized. If a transaction was handled in the same way as a normal business transaction was handled, in terms of quantities of a commodity purchased, method of promotion and sale, etc., there may be evidence of an adventure in the nature of trade. The Interpretation Bulletin entitled "Adventure or concern in the nature of trade" deals with the concept in more detail, in particular, under the heading "Taxpayer's Conduct". IT-459, par. 5–8

(iii) *Nature of the assets involved:* The courts distinguish between fixed assets, which if sold result in a capital transaction, and "circulating" or working capital assets, which if sold result in an income transaction. Hence, the particular use of an asset by a given taxpayer may determine its nature for that taxpayer. Some assets, by their nature, can only be regarded as inventory. For example, whisky or toilet paper cannot produce income in such forms as interest, dividends, rents, etc. Income from these commodities can only be earned when they are sold, as inventory, for a price higher than their cost. The Interpretation Bulletin entitled "Adventure or concern in the nature of trade" deals with this factor under the heading "Nature of the Property". IT-459, par. 9–11

(iv) *Number and frequency of transactions by the same taxpayer in a given period of time:* A relatively large number of transactions in a given period of time may indicate that the taxpayer is involved in a business activity which will result in income transactions. Hence, extensive involvement in a particular type of transaction may be indicative of business activity. It should be emphasized, however, that an isolated transaction may still be considered an "adventure in the nature of trade", that is, of a business nature.

(v) *Length of the period of ownership of the asset:* The length of the holding period for an asset may be used to determine whether the asset is being treated as inventory or as a capital asset. The shorter the period of ownership, the more likely is the gain to be regarded as business income from an adventure in the nature of trade.

(vi) *Supplemental work on or in connection with the property disposed of in the transaction:* Work done on a property to enhance its value or to make it more marketable may indicate an adventure in the nature of trade resulting in business income on the disposition. Intensive advertising and promotion of the property for sale would be a similar indicator.

(vii) *Circumstances that caused the disposition:* An unsolicited offer that results in the sale or a sale motivated by an unforeseen need for funds may argue against the existence of an

[7] *Rutledge v. C.I.R.*, [1929] 14 T.C. 490.

[8] *C.I.R. v. Fraser*, [1942] 24 T.C. 498.

adventure in the nature of trade, because of the evidence of the lack of a plan to turn a profit on a sale.

(viii) *Corporate objects or partnership agreement:* Articles of incorporation may suggest that the corporation was engaged in a business which it had been created to carry on. Some judicial decisions, in the past, have held that a transaction, although unrelated to the taxpayer's usual business, fell within the objects of a corporation as represented by its charter and, as a result, was a transaction of a business nature. This can occur when the objects of a corporation are set out in a very broad manner in its charter to provide for future flexibility. On the other hand, in the case of *Sutton Lumber & Trading Company Ltd. v. M.N.R.*, the Supreme Court of Canada ignored a corporation's objects on the basis that what is relevant is not what a corporation can do under its objects, but what, in fact, it did do. Furthermore, it should be noted that, although some provincial corporation legislation provides for corporations having objects, the *Canada Business Corporations Act* and the Ontario *Business Corporations Act* do not provide for stated corporate objects. Thus, the relevance of this factor may be diminished. It should be noted that the stated objectives of a partnership organization, as outlined in a partnership agreement or other document, might be regarded in the same way.

53 DTC 1158 (S.C.C.)

This is not an exhaustive list of behavioural factors that can be observed. The factors used to determine whether a receipt is one of income or capital may depend on the type of property involved. For example, on the sale of real estate, the CRA has developed a list of about 12 factors which the courts have considered and lists them in the Interpretation Bulletin entitled "Profit, capital gains and losses from the sale of real estate".

IT-218R, par. 3

Factors or badges of trade pertaining specifically to real estate transactions not already indicated in the foregoing list include:

(a) feasibility of the taxpayer's stated intention;

(b) geographical location and zoned use of the real estate;

(c) extent to which stated intention was carried out by the taxpayer;

(d) evidence of a change in stated intention after the purchase (care must be taken to establish the intention at the time of purchase because it has been regarded as more important by the courts);

(e) the extent to which borrowed money was used to finance the acquisition and the terms of the financing; and

(f) factors that motivated the sale.

The Interpretation Bulletin entitled "Transactions in securities" lists some of the factors or badges of trade that are used in distinguishing between a receipt of income and a receipt of capital on the disposition of securities. Some of the factors listed in paragraph 11 of the bulletin and not listed among the factors already discussed include:

IT-479R, par. 11

(a) knowledge of or experience in securities markets;

(b) time spent studying the securities markets and investigating potential purchases;

(c) financing primarily by margin or other forms of debt; and

(d) advertising or otherwise making it known that the taxpayer is willing to purchase securities.

¶4,024 Summary

Exhibit 4-2 diagrams the analytical framework developed. Note how an assessment of the existence of badges of trade from the facts is used to infer intention of the taxpayer at the time of the purchase of the property in question. Evidence of the existence of significant badges of trade suggests an intention to engage in a profit-making scheme or an adventure in the nature of trade. The lack of that evidence may suggest an investment intention.

EXHIBIT 4-2

Analytical Framework for Capital Versus Income Issue

Evidence of Adventure Based on Behavioural Factors or "Badges of Trade"

- relationship of transaction to taxpayer's business;
- activity or organization associated with trade;
- nature of asset;
- number and frequency of transactions in a given period of time;
- length of period of ownership of asset;
- supplemental work on or in connection with property;
- circumstances that caused disposition;
- if transaction completed by organization, stated objectives of organization as outlined in articles of association or partnership agreement;
- other factors.

↓ inference ↓

Intention of the Taxpayer

Primary:

Did the taxpayer intend to use the asset like an item of inventory or like a capital asset?

Secondary:

If the primary intention to use the asset like a capital asset was frustrated, did the taxpayer have, *at the time of the purchase*, a motivating intention to sell the property at a profit?

↓ determination ↓

Issue for Determination

Is the gain (or loss) from the disposition of property a capital gain (or loss) or business income (or loss)?

Source: Reproduced with the permission of the Canadian Tax Foundation from Robert E. Beam and Stanley N. Laiken, "Adventure or Concern in the Nature of Trade: Badges of Trade as the Key Indicator of Taxpayer Intention", (1996) vol. 44, no. 3 *Canadian Tax Journal*, pp. 888–913.

Example Problem 4-1

The taxpayer was the president and general manager of a Canadian company involved in the fabrication of various products of non-ferrous metals, including lead. The company purchased all its lead requirements from a Canadian supplier which was the only producer of lead in Canada. However, the Canadian supplier held the company to a quota and, as a result, the company lost considerable business.

In these circumstances, the Canadian company requested the permission of its U.S. parent to import foreign lead. This meant buying it for future delivery in about three months. The risk of importing lead for future delivery was contrary to the business policy set for the Canadian company by the U.S. parent. However, the taxpayer was granted permission to purchase the lead himself and sell it to the Canadian company, assuming personally whatever risk was involved in the transaction.

The taxpayer made arrangements for the purchase of 1,500 tons of the foreign lead and for its sale to the Canadian company, on its arrival, at the market price of lead on the date of its arrival. He did not, himself, have to put up any money for the purchase of the lead. On the transaction, the taxpayer made a substantial profit.

— REQUIRED

Determine whether the profit made by the taxpayer was a capital gain or income from business or property.

— SOLUTION

[See *M.N.R. v. James A. Taylor*, 56 DTC 1125 (Ex. Ct.).] 56 DTC 1125 (Ex. Ct.)

The taxpayer purchased the lead with the intention of selling it to the Canadian company. His purpose was to alleviate the short supply of lead to which the Canadian company had been held by its Canadian supplier and, hence, to enable the Canadian company to meet the demand for its products. Since the taxpayer, as president and general manager of the Canadian company, was an employee, he was not carrying on a business of his own. Hence, the transaction in question was not related to a business that he was carrying on personally, as might be the case of a commodity dealer.

If the transaction can be considered "an adventure in the nature of trade", then the profit resulting from the transaction would be income from business. An 1896 British case[9] provided the following definition of "trade":

> . . . Trade in its largest sense is the business of selling, with a view to profit, goods which the trader has either manufactured or himself purchased.

A 1904 British case[10] set out a test for determining whether the gain from a transaction was capital or income as follows:

> . . . Is the sum of gain that has been made a mere enhancement of value by realising a security, or is it a gain made in an operation of business in carrying out a scheme for profit-making?

The element of speculation may determine that a transaction is characteristic of what a trader would do. It can be said that the transaction has the "badges of trade". Thus, if the transaction is of the same kind and is carried on in the same way as a transaction of an ordinary trader or dealer in the same kind of property, it may be called an adventure in the nature of trade.

The nature and quantity of the subject matter of the transaction may be such as to exclude the possibility that its sale was the realization of an investment of a capital nature. This would lead to the conclusion that the taxpayer's purchase and sale of 1,500 tons of lead was an adventure in the nature of trade. He could not do anything with the lead except sell it. In fact, he dealt with the lead in the same manner as any dealer in imported lead would have done.

The fact that this was an isolated transaction cannot preclude it from being an adventure in the nature of trade. The word "adventure" implies a single or isolated transaction. Furthermore, it is not essential to a transaction being an adventure in the nature of trade that an organization be set up to carry it into effect. Finally, the fact that a transaction is totally different in nature from any of the other activities of the taxpayer and that he has never entered into a transaction of the kind before or since does not, by itself, preclude it from being an adventure in the nature of trade.

The Exchequer Court of Canada, the predecessor of the Federal Court of Canada, concluded in this case that the taxpayer's transaction was an adventure in the nature of trade and, hence, the profit was taxable as income from business.

---

[9] *Grainger and Son v. Gough* (1896), 3 R.T.C. 462.

[10] *Californian Copper Syndicate Ltd. v. Harris*, [1904] 5 T.C. 159.

¶4,025 Damages as a Receipt of Income or Capital

¶4,026 Non-performance of business contracts

Damages received for non-performance of business contracts are usually intended to place the recipient in the same position as he or she would have been had the contract been performed. Since the performance of a business contract usually results in income, damages for non-performance are generally regarded as income.[11]

¶4,027 Cancellation of agency agreements

While the cancellation of an agency agreement has been held to be income, if such an agreement is of sufficient importance to constitute part of the company's total business structure, the compensation paid on the termination of such a contract may be capital. This was the situation in a U.K. decision.[12] In that case an English company entered into an agreement with a competing Dutch company to co-operate in the manufacture and sale of margarine and to share in the resulting profits and losses. The agreement was to last for about 30 years, but it had to be terminated earlier and the Dutch company paid the English company a large sum of money to terminate the agreement. The British House of Lords held that the rights of the English company under the agreement constituted a capital asset and the sum paid for its cancellation was a capital receipt. For a Canadian case in this area see *Parsons-Steiner Limited v. M.N.R.*, which dealt with the cancellation of an agency agreement of 22 years standing accounting for 80% of the appellant's business. In *Pepsi-Cola Canada Ltd. v. The Queen*, a payment made on the termination of a bottling and distributorship agreement was held to be for goodwill and, hence, a capital receipt. On the other hand, compensation for cancelling a contract entered into in the course of the appellant's regular business was held to be taxable as income in *The Great Lakes Paper Company, Limited v. M.N.R.*

62 DTC 1148 (Ex. Ct.)

79 DTC 5388 (F.C.A.)

61 DTC 564 (T.A.B.)

¶4,028 Loss of property

Damages for loss of property may be regarded as a receipt of capital if the property involved was fixed capital and a receipt of income if the property was working capital such as inventory.[13]

¶4,030 Other Receipts or Benefits

¶4,031 Profits from an illegal business

A taxpayer may be carrying on a business of an illegal nature and yet be taxable on the profits. This principle was established in a 1932 U.K. case[14] in which the following statement was made:

> . . . The revenue [authorities], representing the state, are merely looking at an accomplished fact. It is not condoning it, or taking part in it. It merely finds profit made from what appears to be a trade, and the revenue laws say that profits made from a trade are to be taxed.

---

[11] The cases of *Sutherland v. M.N.R.*, 60 DTC 13 (T.A.B.), on compensation for losses in construction delays and *Hill v. M.N.R.*, 60 DTC 362 (T.A.B.), on compensation for lease cancellation illustrate this result.

[12] *Van den Berghs, Ltd. v. Clark*, [1935] A.C. 431.

[13] The cases of *Gagnon v. M.N.R.*, 53 DTC 273 (T.A.B.), and *Federal Farms Limited v. M.N.R.*, 59 DTC 1050 (Ex. Ct.), deal with such damages. Whether property was lost or profits were foregone was at issue in *Donald Hart Limited v. M.N.R.*, 59 DTC 1134 (Ex. Ct.), and whether a capital source of income or the income itself was lost was at issue in *Dr. Georges Garneau v. M.N.R.*, 68 DTC 132 (T.A.B.).

[14] *Mann v. Nash*, [1932] 1 K.B. 752.

This was re-established in the Canadian case of *No. 275 v. M.N.R.* Having established this principle, the question of deductions arises in terms of substantiating expenses incurred to produce the profits from an illegal business. This was the situation in *M.N.R. v. Eldridge* involving the operator of a call-girl organization who attempted to claim certain cash expenditures. Substantiated, non-capital expenditures incurred to produce income from an illegal business are normally deductible, under conditions discussed later in this chapter. However, the deduction of specified illegal payments is prohibited. Hence, illegal payments under specified sections of the *Criminal Code* made to government officials in Canada, officials engaged in the administration of justice in Canada, persons under a duty as agents or employees and persons responsible for collecting fares or admission fees are not deductible where the payments are made to induce, or attempt to induce, the recipient to breach his or her duty and the payment is made for doing anything that is an offence under the specified sections of the *Criminal Code*. Refer to the Interpretation Bulletin entitled "Gains from theft, defalcation or embezzlement" for the CRA's position in this area.

55 DTC 439 (T.A.B.)

64 DTC 5338 (Ex. Ct.)

ITA: 67.5

IT-256R

¶4,032 Profits from betting, gambling, and windfalls

The proceeds of private betting or gambling for mere pleasure have generally been regarded as not taxable as long as the activity is not organized and of a business nature. This will be the case even if the bets, perhaps even made with borrowed funds, are high and the gains substantial. However, someone like a bookmaker will be taxable on his or her profits because he or she will be regarded as carrying on a business. The existence of a system for the minimization or management of risk may indicate a professional gambler. In this case, the winnings would be taxable and, conceivably, the losses would be deductible.[15]

A non-taxable windfall can be distinguished from income if the recipient has no expectation of receiving the payment.[16] Perhaps a more widely recognized form of windfall is a lottery winning, which is not taxable.

¶4,033 Subsidies

The question of whether a government or any other subsidy is capital or income will depend on the purpose of the subsidy. An income receipt may result from a subsidy to:

- supplement the taxpayer's income or enable him or her to operate at a profit; or
- ensure a reasonable return to the taxpayer on capital invested.

On the other hand, a capital receipt may result from a subsidy to:

- reimburse or assist the taxpayer in respect of a capital outlay; or
- encourage an activity in the public interest such as the prevention of unemployment.

The case of *Saint John Drydock & Shipbuilding Co. Ltd. v. M.N.R.* is a leading Canadian decision on the question of whether a subsidy should be regarded as a receipt of income or capital. The general principles followed by the CRA in making this distinction are set out in the Interpretation Bulletin entitled "Government Assistance — General Comments".

2 DTC 663 (Ex. Ct.)

IT-273R2

¶4,034 Forgiveness of debt rules

When a taxpayer incurs a debt obligation, the principal amount that is borrowed is not considered to be income. Hence, there is no deduction on the repayment of this debt. Therefore, repayments of principal are made with after-tax funds. As well, when a debt is settled or forgiven by the creditor for less than its principal amount, there should be no tax consequences. However, where interest was paid or payable on the debt amount and was or could be deducted from a source of income, then the debtor has received a tax benefit from the interest expense write-offs. The debt forgiveness rules apply to commercial obligations

[15] See the case of *Belawski v. M.N.R.*, 54 DTC 457 (T.A.B.), in this area.

[16] As an example of such an amount see *J.E. Cranswick v. The Queen*, 80 DTC 6057 (F.C.T.D.).

which are debt obligations incurred for the purpose of earning income from a business or property. Personal debt would normally be excluded from these rules.

The Act contains complex rules that reduce certain tax-loss carryovers or tax accounts by the amount of debt forgiven, generally where interest charged on the debt was deductible to the debtor. ITA: 80

The following is a summary of the tax values that are reduced where a taxpayer has had some debt forgiven. The forgiven amount of the debt reduces tax values in this sequence or order. ITA: 80(3)–(12)

1. Non-capital losses
2. Net capital losses
3. Depreciable property
4. Cumulative eligible capital
5. Non-depreciable capital property

To the extent there is still some forgiven debt that has not been applied the balance will be treated as follows:

1. Capital gain, or
2. 50% will be included in income (100% if a partnership).

The effect of this is to increase income either now or in the future.

Where the debt was incurred in a business activity, the income inclusion is considered to be income from the business. The effect of this provision is to fully offset the benefit of not having to repay all or part of a debt with after-tax funds. The specific rules on debt forgiveness are beyond the scope of this text. ITA: 80(13) ITA: 80

¶4,035 Business Income Versus Property Income

Individuals and corporations may hold property for a variety of reasons. For example, Joan, an individual, may purchase land to build a personal residence, whereas another taxpayer, Zed Rent Co., may purchase an adjacent piece of land with the intention of earning rental income. Realtor Co. may purchase the parcel of land down the road as a piece of inventory for speculation.

When a taxpayer purchases and holds property to earn income, the income is reported as either:

- income or loss from a business; or
- income or loss from property.

Alternatively, when a taxpayer disposes of property, the proceeds minus the cost will result in either:

- a capital gain or loss; or
- income or loss from a business or from a property.

Therefore, two separate types of transactions exist:

- the income or loss produced during the ownership of property; and
- the income or loss produced from the disposition of property.

In determining the type of income produced, it is necessary to consider all the surrounding facts, together with the legislation.

In determining whether the source is property or business income, it is necessary to establish whether the taxpayer has purchased property or inventory. "Property" is defined as ITA: 248(1) "property of any kind whatever, whether real or personal or corporeal or incorporeal" and specifically includes:

- a right of any kind, a share or a chose[17] in action;
- unless a contrary intention is evident, money;[18]
- a timber resource property; and
- work in progress of a business that is a profession.

¶4,036 General classification of income/loss from using/holding property

Over a taxation period, income or losses generally arise from holding or using property. Whether this income is income from property or income from a business, is not always easily determined. The basic test is whether the income earned is active or passive income. If the income requires little or no activity by the taxpayer (or his or her employees), the income is usually considered passive and is income from property. Examples would include dividends on shares, interest on bank savings, and similar investments such as bonds, royalties, and rental income. It does not result from the same degree of time and effort as does business income, which may be described as active income. The passive *versus* active test has proven to not always be easy to apply or administer as there is always the question of the "degree" of required activity. Consequently, the Act contains specific directives for many cases.

¶4,037 Determination by corporations

Corporations, like individuals, are affected by the distinction between business income and income from property. Where a corporation has a business, the principal purpose of which is to earn income from property (defined as interest, dividends, rents, and royalties, but excluding leasing income from other than real property), that income is considered inactive (hence, income from property) unless the corporation employs more than five full-time employees. The subjective test of activity has been replaced by the objective test of the number of full-time employees. It is also possible for a corporation to earn income from property as well as business income. The difference between business income and other income is very important for corporations, as it affects the rate of tax used. This will be reviewed in Chapters 11 and 12. ITA: 125(7)

Investment income earned by a corporation is generally considered income from property. However, the Act excludes income from property that is "incident to or pertains to an active business carried on by [the corporation], or that is used or held principally for the purpose of gaining or producing income from an active business". Examples of active business income are, interest charged on accounts receivable, interest on monies held in short-term investments, and rents received from renting an (otherwise) unused portion of a manufacturer's premises. Where any short-term investment becomes more or less permanent — that is, it is never depleted in the course of carrying on the business — the interest earned is income from property. ITA: 129(4)

¶4,038 Determination by partnership

Where a person is a limited partner or a person not actively engaged in the partnership business on a regular, continuous, or substantial basis, his or her partnership income is deemed to be income from property and not income from a business. While the latter portion of this provision relies on the activity test, it at least provides some guidance on the degree of required activity. ITA: 96(1.8)

[17] "Chose" is defined in Webster's dictionary as, "a thing, or a piece of personal property".

[18] "Money" is perhaps an arbitrary word choice; however, the intent is to indicate that property includes gold, silver, copper, nickel, coins, and any paper notes, such as bank notes and cheques, and extends to property, possessions, and wealth. Although inflationary and deflationary gains are not recognized, the disposition of foreign currency can lead to foreign exchange gains and losses.

¶4,039 Reasons for distinction between business and property income

Although the Act groups income from a business with income from property, the distinction between the two sources is still important for the following reasons. ITA: 9

- Property income earned by an individual is considered a return on equity, or passive income, and, except for rental income, is excluded from the earned income calculation in the determination of the maximum RRSP contribution limit, whereas self-employed business income is included in the earned income calculation.[19]
- The definition of "earned income" for eligibility for a deduction for child care expenses includes business income but excludes all income from property.
- Property income derived from rental properties is subject to separate rules. For example, capital cost allowance claimed against rental income may not create or increase a loss from rental properties.
- Business income earned by a corporation has special rules, such as the small business deduction for active business income, and the manufacturing and processing deduction for profits derived from manufacturing. Alternatively, corporations holding properties and investments are taxed at a much higher rate.
- The income attribution rules (discussed in Chapter 8) generally apply only to the non-arm's length transfer of property income and not to the transfer of business income.
- Non-resident taxpayers are taxed on income from a business carried on in Canada, while income from property is subject to withholding tax under a different part of the Act.

¶4,040 Inventory Valuation

¶4,045 Basis of valuation

¶4,045.10 *Market or lower of cost or market*

The Act permits the valuation of each item in an inventory at the lower of cost or market. ITA: 10(1) A degree of variation is permitted by an income tax regulation which allows all of the items in ITR: 1801 the inventory to be valued at fair market value. This regulation might be used, where the fair ITA: 10(1) market value of all items is lower than the valuation provided by the lower of cost or market for each item, to maximize cost of goods sold, and, thereby, minimize tax. However, there could be situations where the higher value would be desirable, for example, to reduce a loss that might expire. Again, the choice permitted between the Act and the regulation could be ITA: 10(1); ITR: 1801 used to provide the higher valuation as necessary, but the effect may be minimal, given the choices permitted. Furthermore, as will be seen from a subsequent discussion, the choice may be permanent, such that the long-term effects of the alternate choice should be considered. ITA: 10(2.1)

¶4,045.20 *Specific identification*

Where the cost of items in an inventory can be identified, it is the actual laid down cost that must be used. This would include invoice cost plus duties, freight and insurance. In the case of goods in process and finished goods in the inventory of a manufacturing concern, cost will also include the cost of direct labour and in some cases the applicable share of overhead expenses. According to an Interpretation Bulletin, the cost of manufactured goods must IT-473R include overhead allocated on a direct costing or absorption costing basis. The Act requires ITA: 10(1.1) the inclusion in cost any non-deductible interest and property taxes on vacant land held as inventory of a business.

[19] Subsection 146(1) defines "earned income" for the purpose of computing the maximum RRSP contribution limit. It is important to note that earned income carries a different definition for the purpose of computing earned income for the child care deduction.

¶4,045.30 *First in, first out*

Where individual items cannot be identified for costing, a convention or assumption, usually "first in, first out" (FIFO), must be applied for the purpose of determining cost of inventory on hand.

The use of "last in, first out" (LIFO) as an assumption about cost has long been fought by the CRA as illustrated by the case of *M.N.R. v. Anaconda American Brass Ltd.* In that case it was held by the Judicial Committee of the Privy Council of the House of Lords of the United Kingdom (to which decisions of the Supreme Court of Canada could be appealed until the mid-1950s), first, that an assumption of any kind in determining inventory value could only be made to the extent that the facts about actual cost were not ascertainable. Furthermore, in the particular case of Anaconda, the LIFO assumption disregarded the actual flow of inventory through the business. This disregard of facts in relation to the flow of goods also made the use of the LIFO assumption objectionable in the case of *Wickett and Craig Ltd. v. M.N.R.* As a result, LIFO is only acceptable if it reflects the physical flow of inventory, otherwise it is prohibited. In addition, LIFO is not acceptable under IFRS and Canadian GAAP.

55 DTC 1220 (Privy Council)

78 DTC 1382 (T.R.B.)

¶4,045.40 *Meaning of "cost" and "market"*

For the meaning of the word "market" in the valuation of inventory, refer to the CICA (Canadian Institute of Chartered Accountants) *Handbook*. Market price may be interpreted to mean:

(a) the current purchase price prevailing for the quantities of goods normally purchased by the taxpayer (useful for raw materials);

(b) realization value, i.e., the selling price which the goods on hand will realize, after deducting the direct cost of making the sale (useful for finished goods); or

(c) replacement value, i.e., the cost of reproducing the article into its present state of completion (useful for semi-finished goods where it is usually not possible to obtain a purchase price and it is not possible to sell the article).

The meaning of the terms "cost" and "market" are further considered in the Interpretation Bulletin entitled "Inventory Valuation". IT-473R

It is interesting to note that the Act specifies that replacement cost must be used for the fair market value of certain property that is advertising or packaging material, parts, supplies or other property of this nature which is considered to be inventory. Note, also, that work in progress of a business that is a profession is considered to be inventory with a fair market value equal to the amount that can reasonably be expected to become receivable after the end of the year. However, for greater certainty, these types of property are considered to be inventory and, hence, subject to the Act's valuation rules for inventory.

ITA: 10(4)(*b*)

ITA: 10(1), 10(4)(*a*), 10(5)

The Act requires that the value attributed to the opening inventory be the same as that attributed to the closing inventory of the year before. This ensures that no profits escape tax by a break in the continuity of the inventory figures between the end of one year and the beginning of the next. ITA: 10(2)

A taxpayer must value inventory at the end of a year using the same method as that used at the end of the preceding year. A taxpayer is permitted to change the valuation method used for inventory of a business where permission is obtained from the CRA. The result is to restrict the flexibility in the choice of inventory valuation method from one year to another. However, there may be some flexibility within a particular inventory valuation method. For example, a business that is required to value its inventory at the lower of cost or market at the end of a year because that method was used at the end of the preceding year, may still have a choice in determining cost for the purposes of this valuation method. This provision appears to codify accounting principles requiring that the opening and closing inventories of a given year be valued on the same basis.

ITA: 10(2.1)

ITA: 10(2.1)

The CRA can correct the value of opening inventory where it has not been valued as required by the Act. As a result, corrected opening inventory may differ from closing ITA: 10(1), 10(3)

inventory of the preceding year, thereby forcing the effects of the change on the income of the year of the correction only.

Example Problem 4-2

Sam Brown builds houses in various parts of the city. At the end of his fiscal year he has four homes left in his inventory. Sam's records show the following information on each house:

	Actual total cost	*Cost to rebuild house*	*Market list price*
1. Happy Valley Road	$40,000	$50,000	$75,000
2. Thruway Drive	25,000	20,000	18,000
3. Creekside Place	40,000	45,000	42,000
4. Briar Lane	25,000	22,000	24,000

From past experience Sam knows that he can sell each house for its market list price less 10% for commissions and bargaining.

— REQUIRED

Using the valuation alternatives available to him, determine the value of Sam's closing inventory. Indicate the basis for each valuation and select the one more advantageous to him, assuming he wants to minimize income for tax purposes. (Assume that the method of valuing inventory could change with permission.) ITA: 10(2.1)

— SOLUTION

In this case, since the houses are finished, net realizable value would be the appropriate indicator of market value. This would be calculated from the information given by reducing market list price by the 10% direct cost of making the sale. The following would form the basis of the decision:

House	*Cost*	*Market*		*Lower on each unit*
1	$40,000	$ 67,500	(90% of $75,000)	$ 40,000
2	25,000	16,200	(90% of $18,000)	16,200
3	40,000	37,800	(90% of $42,000)	37,800
4	25,000	21,600	(90% of $24,000)	21,600
		$143,100		$115,600

Using the rules in the Act, the inventory could be valued at $115,600 which is the lower of cost or market for each item. The Regulations would permit the use of the market value of all items ($143,100). In this case, if the business is profitable, the more advantageous valuation would be based on the lower of cost or market for each item because it would provide the lower valuation, thereby increasing cost of goods sold and decreasing income subject to tax. On the other hand, if the business is in a loss position for the year, some of the losses can be absorbed by choosing the regulation alternative of market value to decrease cost of goods sold, thereby increasing the gross margin available to offset losses for the year. The choice is limited by the provision of the Act that requires that the method chosen for ending inventory in the current year must be the same as the method used for closing inventory at the end of the previous year unless ministerial permission for a change is granted. ITA: 10(1) ITR: 1801 ITR: 1801 ITA: 10(2.1)

¶4,050 Adjustment for amortization allocation to inventory: Absorption accounting

To the extent that the cost of closing inventory for financial accounting purposes *includes an allocation* by the use of absorption costing of amortization, obsolescence or depletion write-offs, such an allocation must be added to income for the year. This rule requires the full add-back of amortization in the reconciliation of income for tax purposes with income for financial accounting purposes. The add-back is required despite the fact that any amortization included in the cost of closing inventory is not charged as an expense in the year, because the value of closing inventory reduces the cost of goods sold. Since the same allocation for accounting purposes will be included in the cost of opening inventory of the next year, a deduction of the amount of the allocation added in the current year for tax purposes is made in the subsequent year. These adjustments are unnecessary if the taxpayer has used the direct costing method and, as a result, has not included in the cost of inventory for financial accounting purposes an allowance in respect of amortization, obsolescence or depletion.

ITA: 12(1)(*r*)

ITA: 20(1)(*ii*)

Example Problem 4-3

Absolute Co. recorded total amortization of $5,000 in Year 1 (first year of operations), of which $1,000 is included as part of the cost of its ending inventory. In Year 2 the amounts were $10,250 and $1,250. For tax purposes Absolute Co. claimed capital cost allowance of $12,000 in each year.

Net income per financial statements, using absorption costing, was computed as follows:

	Year 1	Year 2
Gross revenue	$170,000	$340,000
Opening inventory	$ 0	$ 20,000
Cost of goods manufactured	100,000	205,000
Closing inventory	(20,000)	(25,000)
Cost of goods sold	$ 80,000	$200,000
General and administration	$ 40,000	$ 50,000
Net income per financial statements	$ 50,000	$ 90,000

— *REQUIRED*

Compute net income for tax purposes for Years 1 and 2.

— *SOLUTION*

Year 1	**Absorption costing**	**Amortization expense**	**Direct costing(1)**
Gross revenue	$170,000		$170,000
Opening inventory	$ 0		$ 0
Cost of goods manufactured	100,000	$ 5,000	95,000
Closing inventory	(20,000)	(1,000)	(19,000)
Cost of goods sold	$ 80,000	$ 4,000	$ 76,000
General and administration	$ 40,000		$ 45,000(2)
Net income per financial statements	$ 50,000		$ 49,000
Add back:			
Amortization expense (net)	4,000		5,000
Paragraph 12(1)(*r*) amortization	1,000		0

Deduct:			
Capital cost allowance	(12,000)		(12,000)
Net income for tax purposes	$ 43,000		$ 42,000
Year 2			
Gross revenue	$340,000		$340,000
Opening inventory	$ 20,000	$ 1,000	$ 19,000
Cost of goods manufactured	205,000	10,250	194,750
Closing inventory	(25,000)	(1,250)	(23,750)
Cost of goods sold	$200,000	$10,000	$190,000
General and administration	$ 50,000		$ 60,250
Net income per financial statements	$ 90,000		$ 89,750
Add back:			
Amortization expense	10,000		10,250
Paragraph 12(1)(*r*) amortization	1,250		0
Deduct:			
Paragraph 20(1)(*ii*) inventory adjustment	(1,000)		0
Capital cost allowance	(12,000)		(12,000)
Net income for tax purposes	$ 88,250		$ 88,000

— *NOTES TO SOLUTION*

(1) Direct costing is provided for comparative purposes only. Note how the adjustments to net income for tax purposes for absorption costing amortization result in a higher net income amount in comparison with direct costing.

(2) Under direct costing, general and administration expenses include amortization of $5,000 in Year 1 and $10,250 in Year 2.

¶4,060 Sole Proprietorship

Individuals who report business income, including professional income, generally must report that income on a calendar year basis, according to the definition of "fiscal period". This requirement applies to a sole proprietorship and a professional corporation, which is any corporation that carries on the professional practice of an accountant, dentist, lawyer, medical doctor, veterinarian, or chiropractor. The requirement, also, applies to partnerships in which at least one member is an individual, a professional corporation or another affected partnership. ITA: 249.1(1) ITA: 248(1)

However, there is a provision for an alternative fiscal period for a business carried on by an individual. A change in the end of a fiscal period can only be made with ministerial concurrence. An off-calendar fiscal year-end for an unincorporated business is possible, if an individual files an election in prescribed form by the date on which the individual must file a tax return for the year. The election can be revoked in a future period, in which case the calendar-year fiscal period must be used. ITA: 249.1(4) ITA: 249.1(7) ITA: 249.1(6)

To prevent a deferral in the reporting of income on an off-calendar fiscal period, additional rules for the reporting of business income must be followed. A formula is provided that effectively computes income from an unincorporated business with an off-calendar year-end on a calendar year basis by the use of an estimating procedure. ITA: 249.1(4) ITA: 34.1

The system applies to, for example, a January 31 business year-end as follows. First, the taxpayer includes income from the unincorporated business for the fiscal period ended, say,

January 31, 2013. To this amount, the taxpayer must add an estimate of business income for the "stub period" from February 1, 2013 to December 31, 2013. The estimate is based on a proration of $^{11}/_{12}$ or 11 months of income in the fiscal period ended January 31, 2013. From the sum, the taxpayer can subtract the stub period addition made in the 2012 tax return. However, the alternative method recognizes that there are valid non-tax business reasons for using an off-calendar year-end and allows such a year-end to be maintained.

The following illustrates this adjustment for a January 31 year end:

Income for the year ended January 31, 2013	$120,000
Add: estimate of income for the period February 1, 2013 to December 31, 2013 = $^{11}/_{12}$ × income for the 12 months ended January 31, 2013	110,000
Deduct: last year's estimate	(105,000)
Income for tax purposes for 2013	$125,000

When an off-calendar year-end reflects less than 12 months of business operations, due to the commencement of business, the stub-period income addition is adjusted so that an appropriate amount not exceeding 12 months of income is reported in a calendar-year period. ITA: 34.1(1), 34.1(2)

¶4,070 Conversion of Accounting Income to Net Business Income for Tax Purposes

In this systematic conversion to net income for tax purposes, accounting net income is adjusted for non-taxable income, taxable income not included in accounting income, non-deductible expenses deducted for accounting purposes, and expenditures deductible for tax purposes but not for accounting purposes. Corporations use Schedule 1, *Net Income (Loss) for Income Tax Purposes*, attached to the corporate tax return. Self-employed individuals attach a similar schedule to their personal tax return.

All taxpayers follow the same general rules in aggregating net income. The computation of net income from a business is only one source of income included in income for tax purposes.

The Act contains broad provisions governing the conversion of accounting income from a specific source to income for tax purposes. Most of the differences between accounting income and income for tax purposes from a business are dealt with in subdivision b, sections 9 to 37.

- Section 9, Starting point is profit from the business.
- Section 10, Inventory valuation.
- Section 11, Proprietorships.
- Sections 12 to 17, Income inclusions, i.e., all amounts receivable.
- Sections 18, 19, 19.1, Non-deductible expenses.
- Section 20, Deductions specifically permitted.
- Sections 22 to 25, Rules that apply if the business ceases to exist.
- Sections 26 to 37, Special situations that may apply.

The four principal sections relating to the determination of business income are sections 9, 12, 18, and 20. The other sections of subdivision b refine the principal rules and should not be ignored. There is an important relationship between those four sections of the Act when determining business income. These sections form the pillars on which the entire structure for the taxation of business income stands.

Each section will be reviewed in more detail later, but the following is a brief summary:

- Section 9 sets out the basic rules of general application for determining the taxpayer's income from a business.
- Section 12 states when income should be taxed, according to the amounts, received or receivable, that have not been included in the profit established under section 9. However, even if certain amounts are to be included in income under section 12, some reserves may be allowed under section 20 to reduce the business income. For example, a business deducts $4,000 as a bad debt reserve in 2012. In 2013, the $4,000 bad debt reserve from 2012 must be included in income and the business would deduct a new bad debt reserve for 2013. ITA: 20(1)(*l*) ITA: 12(1)(*d*)
- Section 18 includes the general rule that no deduction of an outlay or expense may be claimed against income unless it was made or incurred by the taxpayer for the purpose of gaining or producing income from a particular business or property. Section 18 itemizes certain deductions that are disallowed in computing a taxpayer's income from business. It is one of the key sections to refer to in order to establish if an amount is deductible or not, or included or not when computing business income.
- Section 20 is another key section that contains deductions that are specifically permitted by the statute in computing income from business or property. As a general rule, section 20 deals with deductions of certain items that were either included in income in compliance with section 12 or did not qualify as deductions because of the section 18 limitations. For example, paragraph 18(1)(*b*) disallows a deduction on account of capital, while paragraph 20(1)(*a*) allows the deduction for capital cost allowance for part of the capital cost of a property in accordance with income tax regulations. This is an example of how a specific provision, such as paragraph 20(1)(*a*), overrides a general limiting provision, such as paragraph 18(1)(*b*). While section 20 also sets out rules for the deductibility of certain other items such as interest expense, finance charges, and various other items, section 18 specifically prohibits the deduction of certain outlays in the computation of net income from business or property.
- Section 67 needs particular attention, being a general limitation provision regarding expenses. To restrict taxpayers from deducting unreasonable expenses, section 67 was added to ensure that all expenses deducted are reasonable in the circumstances. This section essentially gives the CRA the right to reduce a deductible expense to a reasonable amount. Items that are deductible for accounting purposes may not always be reasonable in the circumstances. For example, section 67.1 requires that 50% of meals and entertainment expense be added to accounting net income in the computation of net income for tax purposes.

Also, note the existence of other differences, such as the fact that consolidated and equity statements are not allowed for tax purposes. Consolidated financial statements represent multiple legal entities bound as a single economic unit. By reason of the definition of a "taxpayer", each legal entity is required to report separately for tax purposes. Because of these variances, it is necessary to reconcile the differences by adjusting net income for accounting purposes to net business income for tax purposes. The basic formula in arriving at business income for tax purposes may be simplified[20] as follows. ITA: 248(24)

Income from a business for tax purposes is equal to:

Starting Point:	Subsection 9(1)	"Profit", or accounting net income
plus	sections 12 to 17	Income inclusions not included in "profit"
plus	sections 18(1), 19	Disallowed expenses and reserves
plus	section 67	Unreasonable amounts
minus	subsection 20(1)	Expenses specifically allowed but not deducted in "profit"

[20] The objective in this basic formula is to show the underlying flow of the calculation. Many other sections may apply, depending on the taxable entity, type of business, type of transactions, legal reorganizations, etc., that require the inclusion of other sections of the Act.

plus	Capital losses — book losses on the disposal of capital property
minus	Capital gains — book gains on the disposal of capital property

Finishing Point: Income from a business for tax purposes

Capital gains and losses are not recognized as a source of business income; therefore, any gain or loss from the disposition of capital property is backed out of income from a business and accounted for separately. ITA: 3(*b*)

¶4,100 INCLUSIONS

¶4,105 Inclusions in Income for Tax Purposes

There can often be differences between the calculation of income for accounting purposes and for tax purposes. Many small corporations and self-employed individuals engaged in a business do not prepare financial statements using GAAP. This is often because the sole users of financial statements are owners, managers, and the CRA. If financial statements are not prepared in accordance with GAAP, there is the possibility that the cash basis of accounting, rather than the accrual method of accounting is being used. The Act resolves this possibility by requiring that any amount receivable by the taxpayer (including amounts receivable in future taxation years) for goods or services rendered in the course of business in the taxation year are to be included in income. ITA: 12–17 ITA: 12(1)(*b*)

However, the Act also allows the cash basis of accounting where that method is accepted under the Act. Farmers and fishers are permitted to use the cash basis, and professionals are allowed to exclude work-in-progress. ITA: 28(1) ITA: 34

In accordance with GAAP, many accrued estimates are necessary to satisfy the principles of matching and conservatism, estimates that may conflict with legislative intent. For example, an allowance for doubtful accounts is set up to ensure that the company has matched the potential bad debt expense with current revenues, and to ensure the accounts receivable balance is fairly stated. Generally, the Act does not accept accounting reserves. Instead, reserves are added back to income and the Act then may offer a limited and regulated deduction to offset this income inclusion. Although this may appear unusual and overly administrative, the purpose is to force taxpayers to calculate their reserves on a tax basis every year.

Another intent is to allow for an inclusion of certain items that are generally not recorded as revenue for tax purposes. For example, inducement payments such as amounts received by a tenant from a landlord for leasehold improvements would not be taxable unless a specific provision required it. ITA: 12(1)(*x*)

It is impossible to commit to memory all of the items required to be included in income and all the deductions disallowed by section 18 or allowed by section 20. Understanding the Act and the underlying intent will assist students and professionals in income tax research, analysis, and preparation. When computing net income from a business for tax purposes, section 12 is first reviewed for amounts to be added to GAAP net income, and expenses are checked against section 18 to ensure they pass the test of deductibility. Finally, section 20 is examined to see if any alternative reserves or limited deductions are available. In this chapter, the intent is to provide users with a logical understanding of the computation of net income and not all inclusions, deductions, or disallowed deductions will be covered in detail. If additional research is warranted, interpretation bulletins, information circulars, and case law should be considered.

The following table provides a brief summary of items that are usually included in the calculation of income from a business or property.

Calculation of Income from a Business or Property

ITA Reference	Description	Related Reference
12(1)(*a*)	Services to be rendered in future	20(1)(*m*), (*m*.2)
12(1)(*b*)	A/R for services rendered	20(1)(*n*), 68
12(1)(*d*), (*e*)	Reserves — bad debts and warranties	20(1)(*l*), (*m*), (*n*)
12(1)(*f*)	Insurance proceeds — depreciable property	
12(1)(*g*)	Payments based on production or use	
12(1)(*i*)	Bad debts recovered	
12(1)(*c*), (*j*), (*k*)	Interest, dividends	82(1), 84, 89
12(1)(*l*)	Partnership income	96 to 103
12(1)(*x*)	Inducement payments, reimbursements	20(1)(*hh*)

¶4,110 Amounts Received and Receivable

Amounts received for services to be rendered or goods to be delivered are included in income. This represents a divergence from accounting principles which would defer such amounts of income until the year in which they are earned. However, a reasonable reserve for unearned amounts included in income can be taken. The Act's system for reserves will be discussed later in this chapter. The Act would include amounts received such as prepaid rent, payments for the warranty of merchandise and container deposits. A deduction for refunds of amounts previously included in income under this paragraph is provided to offset the fact that a reserve would not be available for a refunded amount.

ITA: 12(1)(*a*)
ITA: 20(1)(*m*)
ITA: 12(1)(*a*)
ITA: 20(1)(*m*.2)

Amounts receivable in respect of services rendered or property sold during the year in the course of business are brought into income. A complementary reserve (limited to three years) is available at least for property sold to recognize the uncertainty of collecting these amounts. An amount will be deemed to have become receivable on the earlier of the day when the account was rendered and the day on which it would have been rendered had there been no undue delay.

ITA: 12(1)(*b*)
ITA: 20(1)(*n*), 20(8)

Amounts included because they are receivable must be legally receivable as a result of the taxpayer's having completed the performance of the service contracted for.[21] Holdbacks, common in the construction industry, are not legally receivable until the year in which the architect's or engineer's final certificate accepting and approving work done is issued. The Act provides that these rules are enacted "for greater certainty" and should not be interpreted to imply that any amount not referred to, such as amounts received and earned in the year, are not to be included in income from business.

ITA: 12(1)(*b*)
ITA: 12(2)

¶4,120 Inducement Payments or Reimbursements

All receipts in the nature of reimbursements or inducements in respect of the acquisition of an asset or the incurring of a deductible expense must be included in income from business or property unless this amount already has reduced the cost of the property or the amount of the expense. The types of receipts contemplated by this provision include inducements, grants, subsidies, reimbursements, etc., and amounts received indirectly from these sources, perhaps, through a not-for-profit entity. An example of such inducements would be receipts by a commercial tenant who was reimbursed by a landlord for part or all of the cost of making leasehold improvements. As an alternative, the recipient may elect to reduce the capital cost or the cost of the related property or the amount of the related expense. The provision brings the tax treatment of such receipts in line with generally accepted commercial principles. This area has been a source of contentious issues which were not fully resolved by the CRA's Interpretation Bulletin, "Premiums and other amounts with respect to leases". Note that this Interpretation Bulletin also deals with the position of the payer which is not specifically dealt with in the legislation.

ITA: 12(1)(*x*)
ITA: 13(7.4), 53(2.1)
IT-359R2

[21] The question of when expropriation proceeds are receivable was addressed in the case of *M.N.R. v. Lechter*, 66 DTC 5300 (S.C.C.).

Government subsidies, inducement payments to tenants, reimbursements, forgivable loans, or allowances received in a form of payment must be included in income of the taxpayer. There are exceptions, for example, if the subsidy or inducement is used to acquire capital property. A taxpayer can elect to offset an inducement payment against the capital cost of property acquired with the payment.[22] ITA: 12(1)(*x*) ITA: 12(2.2)

¶4,130 Restrictive Covenants

In 2003, the government proposed that payments received for a restrictive covenant must be included in income. To the extent that a taxpayer receives an amount for a restrictive covenant, the amount must be included in income except to the extent that a related person is required to take it into income. This proposal had not been legislated at the time of writing. For a full discussion on the treatment of payments received for restrictive covenants please refer to Chapter 9, under the heading "Restrictive Covenants". ITA: 12(1)(*x*)(v.1) ITA: 56.4(2)

¶4,140 Partnership Income

Partnerships, trusts, and corporations are considered separate legal entities. However, partnerships are *not* taxable entities within the income tax system in Canada. Partnerships do not file tax returns, though an annual information return must be filed. The intent of this regulation is to provide the CRA with information on the income of the partnership and the partners who share in the sources of income. In addition, each partner must include in his or her tax return the partner's share of partnership income. This requires the preparation of a statement of partnership income that includes an allocation of each partner's share of the income. The income allocated from the partnership to each partner remains the same source of income as it was at the partnership level. For example, income from property at the partnership level is reported as property income by the individual partner; income from business remains income from business; and taxable capital gains remain taxable capital gains. ITA: 96(1); ITR: 229 ITA: 12(1)(*l*)

¶4,150 Barter Transactions

When one taxpayer accepts property (goods or a right to services) in exchange for goods and/or services, a barter transaction exists. If you provide dental services in exchange for dance lessons, you would be entering into a barter transaction. In such a situation, sales revenue equal to the fair market value of the goods or services *provided* must be recognized in income for tax purposes. It is important to note that payment in kind (non-cash consideration) is not a "gift". A voluntary and gratuitous transfer of property without any expectation of reward or payment from one person to another is a non-taxable gift. This distinction is important because the barter transaction is a reciprocal exchange and is fully taxable. As with any other revenue-earning process, the cost of the goods or services provided in the exchange are deductible. When payment in kind is for personal use, an additional problem exists. For example, the exchange of legal services for a sprinkler system for a personal residence is complex. The law firm has earned revenues equal to the fair market value and a distribution in the form of salary, dividend or draw is made to the lawyer. ITA: 69(1); IT-490

¶4,200 DEDUCTIONS

¶4,205 Overview

¶4,206 Disallowed or restricted deductions

To proceed with the calculation of net income for tax purposes, it is necessary to determine which expenses are disallowed or restricted as a deduction for tax purposes. Section 18 is the principal section outlining the amounts that are *not deductible* in calculating net income from a business. Remember that the Act does not specifically list all of the

[22] The taxpayer must elect by the filing date of the taxation year applicable to the inducement payment.

deductible expenses and cannot be relied on to test the deductibility of an expense. In practice, if an expense is not specifically addressed in the Act, it is usually deductible for tax purposes if the expense is:

- deductible using generally accepted accounting principles;
- not a capital expenditure;
- incurred to earn income for tax purposes;
- not a personal expense or expenditure; and
- reasonable in the circumstances.

If the amount in question is material, taxpayers generally consult tax professionals to assist them in interpreting the law and the administrative treatment. It is often necessary to require professional assistance, particularly if case research and further interpretation of the statute are warranted. Difficulty arises with expenses that are deductible for accounting purposes but not for tax purposes.

¶4,206.10 *Deductible for accounting purposes but not for tax purposes*

Many deductions for accounting purposes, such as the writedown of property to fair market value and deductions for amortization, are disallowed for tax purposes. In particular, the Act disallows any deductions for capital expenditures. It is also possible that some expenses properly taken for accounting purposes do not fit into our income tax system at all. An area of concern is the treatment of future costs of environmental clean-up. Accounting standards require that when reasonably determinable, provisions should be made for future removal and site restoration costs. However, the *Income Tax Act* has not specifically addressed how estimated environmental clean-up costs should be treated.

ITA: 18(1)(*b*)

CICA: 3060.39

An expense taken for tax purposes must be for the purpose of gaining or producing income from the business or property, but the Act disallows a provision for reserves for a contingent liability. Several cases involving the deductibility of estimated future environmental clean-up costs have been tried in the courts. The courts have been reluctant to adopt the new generally accepted accounting principle in the calculation of taxable income, mainly because of the difficulty in estimating the amount of the future liability. In *The Queen v. Nomad Sand & Gravel Ltd.*, the judge cited a precedent decision by Viscount Simonds that "new theories of accountancy, though they may be accepted and put into practice by business men, do not finally determine a trading company's income for tax purposes".[23]

ITA: 18(1)(*a*)

ITA: 18(1)(*e*)

91 DTC 5032 (F.C.A.)

¶4,210 Deductibility of Expenditures

The first test of deductibility is actually contained in the words of subsection 9(1) which state that:

> ... subject to this Part, a taxpayer's *income* for a taxation year from a business or property is his *profit* therefrom for the year. (italics added)

As previously indicated, the courts have often relied on ordinary commercial practices (which may also embody GAAP) to provide the basis of profit, unless the Act specifically requires an alternate treatment. Hence, the deductibility of an expenditure under GAAP, subject to ordinary commercial practices, should be considered where the Act is silent on the treatment of the expenditure. The specific provisions of the Act that may require an alternate treatment are contained, generally, in sections 18, 19, 20, and 67.[24]

Sections 18 and 19, in essence, prohibit the deduction of specified expenditures through the use of the words "no deduction shall be made". However, the rules in sections 18 and 19 actually establish general principles or tests of deductibility under the Act. If an expenditure

[23] Robin J. MacKnight, "Square Pegs and Round Holes: Environmental Cost Under the Income Tax Act", *1990 Conference Report*, Canadian Tax Foundation, p. 10:5.

[24] This system of testing the deductibility of an expenditure was discussed in the case of *The Queen v. MerBan Capital Corporation Limited*, 89 DTC 5404 (F.C.A.).

is not prohibited by a rule in section 18 or 19, that is, if an expenditure passes the set of sequential tests in these provisions, the expenditure is deductible. If an expenditure fails one of the tests in section 18 or 19, then subsection 20(1) should be consulted for the existence of a specific exception which would allow the deduction of the expenditure. Some of the more common tests of deductibility pertaining to income from business are discussed here.

¶4,215 General test — To gain or produce income

To pass the general test of deductibility, an expense or outlay must: ITA: 18(1)(*a*)

(a) be made or incurred by the taxpayer for the purpose of gaining, producing or maintaining income; and

(b) be expected to generate income related to the taxpayer's business or property.

The meaning of "for the purpose of gaining or producing income" has been at issue in many cases. While the club dues at issue in *The Royal Trust Company v. M.N.R.* are now specifically not deductible, the case is important in demonstrating the relative remoteness between the expenditure and its purpose to produce income. That is, while the items listed, including club dues, are not deductible, the principle established in the *Royal Trust* case may still hold for items not specifically prohibited by that paragraph or others.[25] 57 DTC 1055 (Ex. Ct.) ITA: 18(1)(*l*) ITA: 18(1)(*l*)

Generally, all that need be demonstrated is that the expenditure was expected to generate income, although no income may have been generated. This was the issue in *Booth v. M.N.R.* involving a poet and painter who claimed certain expenses as deductions. Also, *The Queen v. Lalande and Watelle* (affirmed by the Federal Court of Appeal) dealt with the deduction by doctors of legal fees and payments under loan guarantees in situations which could increase their clientele. In the case of *Speck v. M.N.R.*, the Tax Court of Canada held that a full-time teacher, who incurred losses for three years followed by small profits for two years when he started a part-time business involving the restoration of automobiles, had reasonable expectations of turning a profit and these expectations had been met within the expected five years. 79 DTC 595 (T.R.B.) 84 DTC 6159 (F.C.T.D.), aff'd 89 DTC 5178 (F.C.A.) 88 DTC 1518 (T.C.C.)

¶4,220 Expenditure of a capital nature

An expenditure may pass the test of having been made for the purpose of gaining, producing, or maintaining income, but may still be prohibited as a deduction of an outlay of a capital nature. A capital expenditure has been described in a United Kingdom case[26] by the following statement: ITA: 18(1)(*b*)

> . . . when an expenditure is made, not only once and for all, but with a view to bringing into existence an asset or advantage for the enduring benefit of a trade, . . . there is very good reason (in the absence of special circumstances leading to an opposite conclusion) for treating such an expenditure as properly attributable not to revenue but to capital.

¶4,222 Personal and living expenses

One would presume that paragraph 18(1)(*a*) and section 67 would automatically disallow personal and living expenses because they were not incurred to earn income. However, paragraph 18(1)(*h*) confirms that personal or living expenses, other than travel away from home in the course of carrying on business, are not deductible. Subsection 248(1) defines "personal and living expenses" as an expense incurred for: ITA: 18(1)(*h*); IT-487

- properties that are for the benefit of the taxpayer or a person connected by blood relationship, marriage, common-law partnership, or adoption, and that are not maintained in connection with a business carried on with a reasonable expectation of profit;

[25] Other cases include: *Premium Iron Ores v. M.N.R.*, 66 DTC 5280 (S.C.C.), on legal fees to prepare a U.S. tax appeal; *M.N.R. v. Algoma Central Railways*, 68 DTC 5096 (S.C.C.), on the cost of a geological survey; *Canada Starch Co. Ltd. v. M.N.R.*, 68 DTC 5320 (Ex. Ct.), on the cost of protecting a trademark; and *Bowater Power Co. Ltd. v. M.N.R.*, 71 DTC 5469 (F.C.T.D.), on engineering studies.

[26] *British Insulated and Helsby Cables Ltd. v. Atherton* [1926], A.C. 205.

- premiums for life insurance, annuities, and similar contracts; and
- expenses for property maintained for the beneficiary of an estate or trust.

This definition is not exhaustive, so it includes anything that has the ordinary meaning of this expression. For example, a taxpayer who carries on a business may incur travelling expenses to go to Europe to meet clients. If reasonable, these expenses are deductible (subject to the restrictions in subsection 67.1(1) for any meals and entertainment). But if the business trip is extended to provide a vacation, these additional expenses will be considered personal outlays and will be denied by paragraph 18(1)(*h*). The most common personal and living expenses dealt with in court cases are automobile, home office, and entertainment expenses.

¶4,225 Other Prohibited Deductions

¶4,226 Reserves

The deduction of a reserve, a contingent liability or a sinking fund is prohibited, except as permitted by the Act. Allowable reserves will be discussed later in this chapter. ITA: 18(1)(*e*) ITA: 20(1)

A contingent liability is one where the existence of the liability depends on an event occurring that may or may not happen, sometimes referred to as a condition precedent. This type of liability only becomes deductible in the year that it becomes an unconditional liability. For example, a product defect is found, so the manufacturer records a liability and expense to recognize that customers may make claims in the future to fix the defect. This liability is contingent on a customer coming forward with an actual claim. Until that event happens and the liability becomes measurable, there is no deduction. In summary, potential liabilities that depend on future events happening to establish them as real liabilities are not deductible until that future event occurs.

A variation of the contingent liability is a liability that is unconditional or "real" today, but that has the possibility of being reduced or eliminated in the future by a subsequent condition. This liability is deductible now, with the possibility of a future event reducing the liability. This possibility has led to the potential for abuse, as evidenced by the case of *Collins v. The Queen*, where the Court allowed the taxpayer to deduct interest expenses as they accrued, even though the taxpayer had a right to reduce the amount payable in respect of the interest expenses. As a result, draft legislation was released on March 16, 2011 that would apply to an otherwise unconditional expenditure in respect of which there is a contingent amount. This anti-avoidance provision would apply where it is reasonable to conclude that the taxpayer will exercise their right to trigger an event that would reduce the liability. The result will be that an otherwise unconditional liability will become a conditional liability and not be deductible. 2010 DTC 5028 (FCA) ITA: 143.4

¶4,227 Payments on discounted bonds

When bonds are issued at a discount, usually because the contractual interest rate is lower than the market interest rate, the cost of the discount is incurred on the repayment of the debt at its face value. A deduction is not permitted for the amount paid or payable in respect of the discount except as specifically permitted. This prohibition exists to discourage the issue of debt at a relatively large discount which might provide the holder of the debt with more advantageous capital gains treatment. ITA: 18(1)(*f*) ITA: 20(1)(*f*)

¶4,228 Use of recreational facilities and club dues

Note the prohibition on the deduction of club and other recreational facilities dues, no matter how important they may be to the revenue-producing process. In addition, this provision denies the deduction of expenses incurred for the *use or maintenance* of a yacht, a camp, a lodge or a golf course, unless these facilities are provided to the general public as in the course of the taxpayer's business.[27] Note, also, that the prohibition applies only to expenditures incurred in respect of a yacht, camp, lodge or golf course. Similar expenditures incurred in respect of a restaurant or hotel would not be prohibited. In its decision, the Supreme Court upheld the intention of Parliament to discriminate in this way, based on the very specific words used in the provision. However, the CRA indicated that it had reconsidered its interpretation of the word "facility" in relation to a golf course. The CRA will consider that "facility" as used in that subparagraph should be interpreted in connection with the words "golf course" as to only include recreational amenities provided by a golf club. Accordingly, a "facility" will not include the dining room, banquet halls, conference rooms, beverage rooms or lounges of a golf club and thus the deduction of the cost of meals and beverages incurred at a golf club will not be denied. As a result, the tax treatment of meals and beverages at a golf club will parallel that of meals and beverages consumed at a restaurant.[28]

ITA: 18(1)(*l*)

ITA: 18(1)(*l*)

ITA: 18(1)(*l*)(i)

¶4,229 Political contributions

There is a specific prohibition against the deduction of political contributions. A limited tax credit is provided.

ITA: 18(1)(*n*), 127(3)

¶4,230 Automobile expenses

The deduction of an allowance paid or payable to an employee for the employment use of an automobile is limited. However, there is no deduction limit if the amount of the allowance must be included in the employee's income. The *Income Tax Regulations* (ITR) prescribe the deductible limit. For 2013, the present rates are 54 cents per kilometre for the first 5,000 kilometres driven and 48 cents per kilometre thereafter, with a four cent per kilometre premium for driving in the Yukon Territory, Northwest Territories, or Nunavut.

ITA: 18(1)(*r*)

ITR: 7306

¶4,231 Payments under the Act

Any amount paid or payable under the Act is not deductible. This provision would prohibit, for greater certainty, the deduction of federal income taxes, interest and penalties, all of which are imposed under the Act. However, a deduction for interest paid on tax refund that a taxpayer is required to repay because the refund was excessive is allowed.

ITA: 18(1)(*t*)

ITA: 20(1)(*ll*)

¶4,232 Prepaid expenses

In a move to bring the treatment of certain prepaid expenses for tax purposes in line with the treatment for accounting purposes, the deduction of such expenses in the year of outlay is prohibited. These expenses are deductible only in the taxation year to which the expenses relate. Expenditures treated in this manner are the following: payments for services to be rendered after the end of the year; payments of interest, taxes, rent or royalties in respect of a period after the end of the year and payments for insurance in respect of a period after the end of the year.

ITA: 18(9)

[27] In the case of *Sie-Mac Pipeline Contractors Ltd. v. The Queen*, 93 DTC 5158 (S.C.C.), the Supreme Court of Canada held that to use a lodge does not require that it be owned or rented or exclusively controlled.

[28] "Entertainment at golf clubs", TAX WINDOWS FILES, Document No. 9803677, February 17, 1998.

¶4,233 Expenses of investing in sheltered plans

While interest and certain financing expenses are usually deductible under several provisions in section 20, section 18 prohibits the deduction of these expenses in respect of indebtedness incurred for the purposes listed therein. Note that the items listed pertain to deductible investments in sheltered retirement plans in which income is not taxed as long as it remains in the plan. Also, the deduction of administration fees and investment counselling fees pertaining to certain plans, as discussed in Chapter 9, are prohibited. ITA: 18(11) ITA: 18(1)(*u*)

¶4,234 Workspace in home

The deduction of the costs of maintaining a workspace in an individual's home (i.e., "a self-contained domestic establishment in which the individual resides"), are prohibited unless the office meets one of the following two tests: ITA: 18(12)

(a) the workspace is the individual's principal place of business; or

(b) it is used on a regular and continuous basis for meeting clients, customers or patients of the individual in earning income from business.

In the case of these exceptions, the costs are deductible only to the extent of income from the business. Thus, these home office expenses cannot be used to create a loss from the business, although a carryforward is available for excess expenses. This carryforward may be indefinite, according to an Interpretation Bulletin, "Work space in home expenses", as long as one of the two tests stated above is met. For the CRA's interpretation of the term "principal place of business" and "regular and continuous basis", see the Interpretation Bulletin. The case of *Jenkins et. al. v. The Queen* addressed the meaning of "principle place of business" for a fisher. The Court concluded that the principal place of business is where the "business elements" of the business are engaged in, such as "telephoning customers and suppliers, filling in invoices, doing payroll, maintaining books and records, contacting authorities for licences, preparing tax returns, chasing down receivables, handling complaints, creating business plans, preparing financial statements, talking to accountants and lawyers, etc." The courts stated that "the actual harvesting of fish is the core of a fishing business, but it is not where the business side of fishing occurs." IT-514, par. 5 2005 DTC 384 (T.C.C.)

¶4,235 Deductibility of provincial capital and payroll taxes

The federal Budget of February 26, 1991, proposed to limit the deduction of provincial capital and payroll taxes. Payroll taxes would include any provincial tax imposed on a taxpayer and set by reference to the salary, wages or other remuneration paid by the taxpayer, except pension and worker's compensation contributions. Provincial health levies are an example of a provincial payroll tax. Capital taxes would include any tax imposed by a province and set by reference to a taxpayer's equity, liabilities or assets, but would exclude real property taxes. This proposal has not yet been legislated. ITA: 18

Until a solution to the problems of the deductibility of these taxes is implemented, they are fully deductible. A temporary financial incentive was enacted, by an amendment to the *Federal–Provincial Fiscal Arrangements Act*, for provinces to eliminate their general capital taxes and capital taxes on financial institutions, or to change existing capital taxes on financial institutions to minimum taxes. Most provinces have eliminated their capital taxes.

¶4,236 Limitation on accrued expenses

In normal circumstances a deductible expenditure incurred by one taxpayer is matched, within a reasonable period of time, by the income receipt in the hands of the creditor. However, the Act has provisions to thwart contrived situations between persons not dealing at arm's length or between employers and employees where the debtor uses the accrual method of accounting and the creditor is on the cash method and where actual payment is unduly deferred. ITA: 78

Related persons are deemed not to deal at arm's length with each other. Chapter 6 deals with related individuals and Chapter 12 deals with related corporations and individuals. For the time being, assume that the normal interpretation of "related" applies. In addition, the provision indicates that it is question of fact whether persons not related to each other were, at a particular time, dealing with each other at arm's length. The Interpretation Bulletin entitled "Meaning of Arm's Length" lists the following criteria that could be used in determining whether a transaction has occurred at arm's length: ITA: 251(1) IT-419R2, par. 23–26

- a common mind directs the bargaining for both parties to the transaction;
- the parties to the transaction were acting in concert without separate interests; and
- one party in fact controls the other party.

In order for an expense (e.g., accrued wages) that remains unpaid at the end of the taxation year to be deductible for tax purposes, it must constitute a genuine liability of the taxpayer. For a genuine liability to exist there must be an enforceable claim by the creditor (e.g., the employee) with a reasonable expectation that the debt in fact will be paid. Where there is not a genuine liability, the amount will be treated as contingent liability or reserve and will be denied.[29] IT-109R2, par. 15(e) ITA: 18(1)(*e*)

(i) *Unpaid amounts*

Unpaid amounts, in non-arm's length circumstances, are subject to specific rules. Such an unpaid amount must be paid within two years of the end of the taxation year in which it was declared payable or accrued. If an amount remains unpaid after that two-year period, it must be brought back into income on the first day of the third taxation year following that in which the payable was declared. Thus, an unpaid amount declared payable in 2011 must be paid by the end of the 2013 taxation year or be included in income at the beginning of the 2014 taxation year. ITA: 78(1)

The two parties can file an election by the date on which the corporation is required to file its tax return for the 2013 taxation year (i.e., by June 30, 2014) that the amount be deemed to have been paid on the first day of the 2013 taxation year and to have been loaned, net of appropriate withholding tax, back to the corporation. Then, the corporation would be liable to remit the amount deemed to have been withheld, by departmental practice, on or before July 15, 2014 in this case, and a repayment of the loan would have no further tax consequences. An Interpretation Bulletin provides further explanation of this provision and a more complete discussion of the interplay of these provisions is contained in Chapter 13, under the heading "Accrued bonuses and other amounts". ITA: 78(1)(*b*) IT-109R2

(ii) *Unpaid remuneration and other amounts*

In the case of items of remuneration, the Act requires that salaries, wages, or other remuneration (other than specified exceptions) must be paid within 179 days of the end of the taxation year in which the expense was incurred. If an amount is unpaid after that day, it will be deemed not to have been incurred as an expense and, therefore, will not be deductible until the year in which it is actually paid. However, by administrative practice, the CRA indicates in the Interpretation Bulletin entitled "Unpaid amounts" that a payment made on the 180th day is considered to have been made within the time limit and the rule that denies the accrual will not apply. Other remuneration includes unfunded obligations in respect of pension benefits and retiring allowances. The election for deemed repayment, as described above, is not available for unpaid remuneration. An amount of accrued remuneration must be legally paid. ITA: 78(4) IT-109R2, par. 10 ITA: 78(4) ITA: 78(1)

[29] The question of whether an amount was deductible at all as a real liability or not deductible as a contingent liability was at issue in *The Queen v. V&R Enterprises Limited*, 79 DTC 5399 (F.C.T.D.), and *Toronto Heel Limited v. M.N.R.*, 80 DTC 1250 (T.R.B.).

¶4,237 Reasonable Expectation of Profit

The deduction of personal or living expenses, as defined, in part, as expenses not in connection with a business carried on for profit or with a reasonable expectation of profit (REOP), is prohibited. Travel between home and work is one of the expenditures prohibited as personal or living expenses. In this regard, note the difference in treatment between the case of *Mildred Cohen v. M.N.R.*, involving a physically challenged employee who, as a person deriving income from employment, cannot deduct the expenses of travel between home and work, no matter what the hardship may be, and, by contrast, *Cumming v. M.N.R.*, involving a self-employed doctor with an office in his home. Since his base of operations was his home, expenses of travel from that base to the hospital where he rendered services were deductible. The provision would also prohibit the deductibility of interest on funds borrowed to purchase personal items such as cars and houses.

ITA: 18(1)(*h*)

ITA: 248(1)

52 DTC 356 (T.A.B.)

67 DTC 5312 (Ex. Ct.)

To be deductible, an expenditure must not only be made or incurred by the taxpayer for the purpose of gaining or producing income, but, as a result of another test and the definition of "personal or living expense", it must be made with "a reasonable expectation of profit". What constitutes a reasonable expectation of profit is dependent on the facts of each particular case. For a long period of time, the CRA, sometimes supported by the Canadian courts, attempted to expand the application of this reasonable expectation of profit, or REOP, test to deny the deduction of losses from business or property sources. Where there was a personal expenditure element to the fact situation, as in the case of a hobby or a partially rented personal residential property, the case for a reasonable expectation of profit was more difficult to make. On the other hand, where the expenditure involved no personal benefit element, that is, it was of a purely commercial nature, the Federal Court of Appeal had suggested in the case of *Tonn et al. v. The Queen*, and confirmed in the case of *Attorney General of Canada v. Mastri et al.*, that the case against a reasonable expectation of profit test is more difficult to make. In the case of *Stewart v. The Queen*, the Supreme Court of Canada clarified and limited the application of the REOP test. The Court indicated that the REOP test has no application where there is no personal benefit element to a transaction. Where there is a personal benefit element, the test is only one of a number of factors that can be used to assess the commercial nature of an activity, thereby, undertaken in the pursuit of profit.[30]

ITA: 18(1)(*h*), 248(1)

96 DTC 6001 (F.C.A.)

97 DTC 5420 (F.C.A.)

2002 DTC 6969 (S.C.C.)

Exhibit 4-3 provides a checklist for planning purposes to provide evidence of a reasonable expectation of profit, where there is a personal benefit in an activity. The checklist may help to assess the commercial nature of an activity and the businesslike behaviour of the taxpayer in that activity. The factors were derived largely from two U.S. studies of jurisprudence on a similar issue in U.S. tax law. Since the factors are based on U.S. jurisprudence, they have no direct precedent value in Canada. However, they are of more general applicability and may provide a basis or a framework for developing arguments for the existence, or lack thereof, of a predominant intention to make a profit from an activity in a Canadian fact situation.

[30] For a more complete discussion of the *Stewart* case and the jurisprudence that led to that decision, see Rayna F. Laiken and Stanley N. Laiken, "Working with the Source Test, the Supreme Court's Replacement for the Reasonable Expectation of Profit Test", (2002) vol. 50, no. 3, *Canadian Tax Journal*, pp. 1147-1177.

EXHIBIT 4-3
Checklist of General Factors Used to Determine the Existence of a Reasonable Expectation of Profit or of Operating in a Businesslike Manner

(1) Manner in which activity is operated:
- (a) activity held out to community as a business
- (b) activity operated in a businesslike manner
- (c) activity operated in manner similar to comparable profitable businesses
- (d) unsuccessful methods discontinued and new ones adopted
- (e) formal books and records maintained
- (f) separate bank account maintained
- (g) record-keeping system provides for the determination of segment profits and relevant costs
- (h) detailed non-financial records maintained
- (i) operating methods changed to improve profitability
- (j) level of advertising or promotion undertaken
- (k) development plan formulated, followed and adjusted
- (l) scale of operations sufficient to be profitable

(2) Elements of personal pleasure or recreation:
- (a) taxpayer obtains personal pleasure from the activity
- (b) facilities are utilitarian
- (c) conduct of activity involves social or recreational functions (apart from the activity itself)
- (d) long-time interest in activity as a hobby
- (e) operating methods constrained by personal motives
- (f) personal use separately accounted for

(3) Expertise of the taxpayer or his or her advisers:
- (a) prior experience in the activity
- (b) profit potential determined prior to entry
- (c) pre-entry advice (or prior preparation) sought and followed
- (d) post-entry advice sought and followed
- (e) taxpayer belongs to business-related associations
- (f) new or superior techniques developed

(4) History of income and loss:
- (a) average ratio of receipts to disbursements
- (b) percentage of years where receipts less than 5% of disbursements
- (c) average magnitude of losses
- (d) trend of losses declining
- (e) number of years activity was operated
- (f) losses due to circumstances beyond taxpayer's control
- (g) percentage of years with profits
- (h) reasonable start-up period
- (i) trend of gross revenues

(5) Time and effort expended:
- (a) competent and well-informed manager employed
- (b) competent labour employed
- (c) average time spent on activity by taxpayer
- (d) taxpayer withdrew from another business to devote most of his/her time to the activity
- (e) taxpayer did physical labour

(6) Financial status of taxpayer:
   (a) taxpayer's average income before activity loss
   (b) extent of tax savings from net losses
   (c) average ratio of activity losses to other income
   (d) taxpayer maintains an extravagant standard of living
   (e) majority of taxpayer's other income is from investments
   (f) extent of other net assets of taxpayer
   (g) amount of capital invested in the operation

(7) Amount of occasional profits:
   (a) ratio of average profit to average loss
   (b) amount of largest profit earned
   (c) ratio of net losses to net assets

(8) Sale or discontinuance of activity:
   (a) activity sold or discontinued because no chance for profit
   (b) activity sold or discontinued for any reason

(9) Success of taxpayer in other activities:
   (a) extent of experience in similar successful business
   (b) history of losses in a similar activity

(10) Expected appreciation of asset value:
   (a) taxpayer expected property to appreciate in value as the major source of investment return

Sources: Jane O. Burns and S. Michael Groomer, "An Analysis of Tax Court Decisions That Assess the Profit Motive of Farming-Oriented Operations," *The Journal of the American Taxation Association*, Fall 1983, pp. 23-39.

Jack Robison, "Tax Court Classification of Activities Not Engaged in for Profit: Some Empirical Evidence," *The Journal of the American Taxation Association*, Fall 1983, pp. 7-22.

¶4,238 Proposed amendments related to REOP

On October 31, 2003, the Department of Finance released draft proposals on interest deductibility which also included legislation related to REOP.

The proposal provides that a taxpayer can deduct a loss from a source that is a business or property only if, in that year, it is reasonable to expect that the taxpayer will realize a cumulative profit from the business or property. Then, a new provision makes it clear that profit, in this context, does not include capital gains or capital losses. ITA: 3.1(1) ITA: 3.1(2)

While these changes seem straightforward, consider what would happen if a new business began to have financial difficulty and realized losses in excess of previous income. If they determined that they were going to have to close the business, then this proposed rule would deny any losses from that time forward. These future losses from expenditures such as wages, lease payments, severance and other recurring expenses, were previously deductible.

Since their release, there has been significant discussion between tax professionals and the Department on the implications of their proposals. The report of the Joint Committee on Taxation of the Canadian Bar Association and the Canadian Institute of Chartered Accountants states that:

> . . . we are of the view that the Draft Proposals would introduce a fundamental change to the *Income Tax Act* which goes well beyond the case law and administrative practice prior to recent court decisions. We are concerned that the proposals could be used to disallow losses resulting from wholly-legitimate business expenses the deductibility of which would not have been an issue under prior case law or administrative practice. They would create significant issues with respect to the treatment of investments in securities.

In the March 23, 2004 federal Budget the following statement was made:

> Assurances were given by the Minister of Finance, Finance officials and the CRA that these releases were not intended to adversely affect the past assessing practices regarding the

deductibility of interest on equity investments. The Budget materials acknowledge that significant issues have been raised with them that warrant further consideration.

The Budget Plan 2005, published by the Department of Finance to accompany the February 23, 2005 federal Budget, contained the following statement at page 410:

> Many commentators expressed concerns with the proposals' structure, in particular, that the proposals' codification of the "reasonable expectation of profit" test might inadvertently limit the deductibility of a wide variety of ordinary commercial expenses. The Department of Finance has sought to respond by developing a more modest legislative initiative that would respond to those concerns while still achieving the Government's objectives. The Department will, at an early opportunity, release that alternative proposal for comment. This will be combined with a Canada Revenue Agency publication that addresses, in the context of the alternative proposal, certain administrative questions relating to deductibility.

At the current time, this matter does not seem to be a priority for the Department of Finance.

¶4,239 Limitations on Deductible Expenditures

Items listed in subsection 18(1) are prohibited from being deducted because of the nature of the expenditure. Another section places a limitation on the amount of an outlay or expense that may be deducted. To be deductible, the amount must be "reasonable in the circumstances." This would suggest a comparison of the amount of an expenditure with the amount of similar expenditures made in similar situations by other taxpayers. The question of a reasonable salary paid to the wife of an owner-manager of a corporation for full-time work as the secretary-treasurer was at issue in *Mulder Bros. Sand & Gravel Ltd. v. M.N.R.* The payment of large bonuses to the wife of the major shareholder of a corporation was at issue in *Doug Burns Excavation Contracting Limited v. M.N.R.* In the case of *Robinson v. M.N.R.*, the Tax Court of Canada indicated that the costs of operating a luxury vehicle for business purposes should be limited in their deduction to a reasonable charge.

ITA: 67

67 DTC 475 (T.A.B.)

83 DTC 528 (T.C.C.)

85 DTC 84 (T.C.C.)

Summary of Deductions
Specifically Not Deductible or Restricted

ITA Reference	Item Not Deductible or Restricted
18(1)(*a*)	Not deductible unless incurred to earn income from business or property
18(1)(*b*)	Capital expenditures including depreciation, obsolescence or depletion except as expressly permitted
18(1)(*c*)	Expense incurred to earn exempt income
18(1)(*e*)	Reserves and contingent liabilities
18(1)(*h*)	Personal or living expenses
18(1)(*l*)	Use of recreational facilities and club dues
18(1)(*n*)	Political contributions
18(1)(*p*)	Personal service business expenses
18(1)(*r*)	Automobile mileage rates
18(1)(*t*)	Interest and penalties under the *Income Tax Act* or interest under the *Excise Tax Act*
18(2)	Interest and property taxes on land
18(3.1)	Costs related to construction of building or ownership of land
18(9)	Prepaid expenses
18(12)	Workspace in the home limitations
18(13)	Superficial loss
67	Outlay or expense must be reasonable in the circumstances
67.1	Expenses for food and entertainment
67.2	Interest on loans to buy a passenger vehicle
67.3	Costs of leasing a passenger vehicle
67.5	Illegal payments
67.6	Fines and penalties

GST/HST is not deductible to a registrant where the GST/HST provides an input tax credit. The input tax credit, in effect, eliminates the GST/HST as a cost and, hence, GST/HST should not be deductible in these cases. ITA: 248(16)

A deduction is prohibited in respect of an expenditure incurred for the purpose of doing anything that is an offence under section 3 of the *Corruption of Foreign Public Officials Act* involving bribery of a foreign public official to obtain a business advantage or any of the following sections of the *Criminal Code*: ITA: 67.5(1)

- section 119 — bribery of judicial officers, etc.
- section 120 — bribery of officers
- section 121 — frauds on the government
- section 123 — municipal corruption
- section 124 — selling or purchasing office
- section 125 — influencing or negotiating appointments or dealing in offices
- section 393 — fraud in relation to fares, etc.
- section 426 — secret commissions

Deductions are, also, prohibited where the payment is made in a conspiracy to commit an offence under one of the above sections or a conspiracy in Canada to commit a similar offence under the law of another country.

Recent court cases have allowed the deductibility of fines and penalties incurred in the ordinary course of earning income unless the underlying action was so offensive that the fine or penalty could not reasonably be considered to have had an income-earning purpose. To bring certainty to this area of tax law, fines or penalties incurred are not deductible if they are imposed by law — whether by a government, government agency, regulator, court or other tribunal, or any other person with statutory authority to levy fines or penalties. This would include fines and penalties imposed under the laws of a foreign country. This would not include penalties or damages paid under private contracts. Part of this provision includes authority to exempt prescribed fines and penalties from its application, although there are no exemptions at this time. ITA: 67.6

¶4,240 Deductions Specifically Permitted

Usually, the general principles and rules (e.g., sections 18, 67, etc.) determining the deductibility of an outlay or expenditure are to be applied first. If a particular outlay or expenditure does not pass the tests of deductibility set out in section 18 or 19, then the lists in section 20 of exceptions to the general principles and rules should be consulted. The wording of subsection 20(1) recognizes that some of the deductions listed in the subsection may be prohibited by a general rule in subsection 18(1), and negates that effect by inserting the words "notwithstanding paragraphs 18(1)(*a*), (*b*) and (*h*), . . . there may be deducted . . .". The following are some of the more common deductions provided in section 20.

Summary of Deductions Specifically Permitted (Section 20)

ITA Reference	Deductions Specifically Allowed	Related References
20(1)(*a*)	Capital cost allowance	18(1)(*b*)
20(1)(*b*)	Cumulative eligible capital amount	18(1)(*b*)
20(1)(*c*), (*d*)	Interest	IT-533
20(1)(*e*)	Expenses of issuing shares or borrowing money	18(1)(*b*)
20(1)(*e*.2)	Premiums on life insurance used as collateral	18(1)(*c*)
20(1)(*f*)	Discount on debt obligations	18(1)(*f*)
20(1)(*l*)–(*p*)	Reserves	18(1)(*e*)

20(1)(*q*)	Employer's contribution to registered pension plan	147.2
20(1)(*y*)	Employer's contribution under a deferred profit sharing plan	147(8)
20(1)(*z*)	Cancellation of lease	18(1)(*q*)
20(1)(*aa*)	Landscaping of grounds	18(1)(*b*)
20(1)(*cc*)	Expenses of representation	18(1)(*b*)
20(1)(*dd*)	Investigation of site	18(1)(*b*)
20(1)(*ee*)	Utilities service connection	18(1)(*b*)
20(1)(*qq*), (*rr*)	Disability-related modifications and equipment	18(1)(*b*)
20(10)	Convention expenses	

¶4,241 Write-offs of capital expenditures

While section 18 prohibits the deduction of a capital nature, section 20 overrides this prohibition and permits the deduction of the capital cost of depreciable capital property and the cost of eligible capital property, respectively, through a system of annual write-offs to be discussed in Chapter 5. ITA: 18(1)(*b*) ITA: 20(1)(*a*), 20(1)(*b*)

¶4,242 Interest

Interest paid or payable on funds borrowed to finance the capital expenditures of a business would be considered as payment on account of capital and, therefore, would be prohibited from deduction. However, the Act specifically provides for the deduction of interest on funds borrowed to earn income, i.e., on the purchase of assets or on indebtedness arising from the acquisition of capital assets. Compound interest is deductible if the base interest is deductible. ITA: 18(1)(*b*), 20(1)(*c*) ITA: 20(1)(*c*), 20(1)(*d*)

On October 31, 2003 the Department of Finance released its Draft Proposals on Interest Deductibility. Along with proposed amendments related to REOP (discussed above) was a new Interpretation Bulletin, "Interest deductibility and related issues". This new bulletin is now a prime source for the CRA's administrative position on interest deductibility in that it replaces and cancels five other bulletins and provides commentary on all the key issues and some of the tax planning techniques used to ensure the deductibility of interest. IT-533

¶4,243 Expenses of issuing shares or borrowing money

The type of expenses contemplated by paragraph 20(1)(*e*) includes printing and advertising costs, filing fees, legal and accounting fees, registration and transfer fees and commissions or bonuses on the issue or sale of shares. Also deductible by this provision are similar expenses incurred in the course of becoming indebted on the purchase of capital property acquired to earn income. Similarly, refinancing costs such as rescheduling, restructuring or assumption of debt used for the purpose of earning business income are also deductible under this provision.

Not included in the deduction would be amounts paid or payable on account of the principal amount of the indebtedness. Since the deductible expenditures are still considered to be of a capital nature, the Act requires that the deduction be amortized equally over five years (prorated on a daily basis for short taxation years) to achieve a better matching of expenses and revenues. Any undeducted balance of borrowing costs are deductible for the year in which the debt is fully repaid (otherwise than as a part of a refinancing).[31] ITA: 20(1)(*e*)

Annual fees payable as a standby charge, guarantee fee, registrar fee, transfer agent fee, filing fee or any similar fee in respect of borrowing money, incurring indebtedness or rescheduling or restructuring a debt obligation are also deductible. ITA: 20(1)(*e.1*)

[31] Two cases heard under this provision are: *Enterprise Foundry Co. Ltd. v. M.N.R.*, 59 DTC 318 (T.A.B.), on a capital reorganization and *Dominion Electrohome Industries Ltd. v. M.N.R.*, 68 DTC 256 (T.A.B.), on a call premium.

¶4,244 Premiums on life insurance used as collateral

A limited deduction is allowed for life insurance premiums where the policy has been assigned as collateral for a loan. The lender must require the assignment of the policy as collateral for the loan. The principal business of the lender must be the lending of money or the purchase of debt obligations. The interest payable on the funds borrowed must be deductible. The deduction is limited to the portion of the premium that represents the net cost of pure insurance. ITA: 20(1)(*e*.2) ITA: 20(1)(*c*)

¶4,245 Discount on debt obligations

Subsection 18(1) contains several provisions that would deny the deduction of all or any part of a discount from the face value of a debt obligation like a bond, debenture, note, mortgage, etc. Since the discount would be considered to be of a capital nature, its deduction is prohibited. The amortization of the discount, for financial accounting purposes, over the life of the debt instrument would not be deductible for tax purposes, because the annual amortization would be considered to be in the nature of a prohibited reserve. In addition, the deduction of the *actual cash outlay* on redemption or open market purchase is specifically denied, except to the extent permitted by the Act. The latter provision permits a full deduction of the discount (an actual cash outlay on redemption or maturity) at the earlier of redemption or maturity if: ITA: 18(1)(*b*) ITA: 18(1)(*e*) ITA: 20(1)(*f*)

(i) the debt security is issued at not less than 97% of face value; *and*

(ii) the yield to maturity is not more than 4/3 of the nominal or coupon interest rate.

If one, or both, of these conditions is not met, then only 1/2 of the discount is deductible, again at the earlier of redemption or maturity. The 1/2 fraction is intended to reflect the allowable or deductible portion of a capital loss.

This rule discourages the issue of debt securities at a large discount by agreeing to pay a low rate of interest relative to the market. The concern is that only the lower than normal interest rate would be taxable to the debtholder at full rates and the gain from the discounted issue price to the par value would be a fractionally taxed capital gain to the debtholder. On the other hand, an acceptable discount of 3% is sufficient to account for normal market fluctuations in interest rates between the time of setting the rate and the time of issue of the debt.

¶4,246 The system for reserves under the Act

The deduction of a reserve is prohibited except for those reserves that are specifically permitted in Part I of the Act. A number of cases have been heard in this area on the question of distinguishing between a reserve that would be prohibited and an amount that represents a real and subsisting liability resulting in a deductible expense.[32] ITA: 18(1)(*e*)

The reserves that may be deducted include: ITA: 20(1)

- reserve for doubtful debts; ITA: 20(1)(*l*)
- reserve for goods not delivered and services not rendered or deposits on returnable containers (other than bottles), but limited by another rule; ITA: 20(1)(*m*), 20(6)
- manufacturer's warranty reserve for amounts paid or payable to an insurer to insure liability under warranty agreement; and ITA: 20(1)(*m*.1)
- reserve for an amount not due until a later year under an instalment sales contract limited by another rule. ITA: 20(1)(*n*), 20(8)

A reasonable reserve can be claimed for an amount not due until a later year where products or services are provided to a customer but some or all of the payment is not "due" until after the year end of the business. Generally, some of the payment must be due at a time that is two years later than the time of the sale. However, a reserve cannot be claimed in a ITA: 20(1)(*n*), 20(8)

[32] These cases include: *No. 297 v. M.N.R.*, 55 DTC 611 (T.A.B.), on employee bonuses; *Canada Packers Ltd. v. M.N.R.*, 68 DTC 682 (T.A.B.), on an income normalization reserve; *Time Motors Limited v. M.N.R.*, 69 DTC 5149 (S.C.C.), on credit notes; and *Acadia Overseas Freighters Halifax Ltd. v. M.N.R.*, 62 DTC 84 (T.A.B.), on contributions to a mutual insurance fund.

year if the sale occurred more than 36 months before the end of the year. Thus, a reserve can be deducted for no more than three years, including the year of sale.

Any reserve taken in a given year under one of these provisions must be brought back into income in the following year under one of the following provisions in subsection 12(1):

- reserve for doubtful debts; and ITA: 12(1)(*d*)
- reserve in respect of certain goods and services, deposits or manufacturer's warranty reserve. ITA: 12(1)(*e*)

In that following year, a new reserve can be taken based on the taxpayer's circumstances at that time. The inclusion of last year's reserve in income and the deduction of a new reserve this year forces the taxpayer to re-evaluate the circumstances and to establish a new reserve which can be substantiated by these circumstances.

The Interpretation Bulletin entitled "Bad debts and reserves for doubtful debts" describes the method suggested by the CRA for determining an appropriate reserve for doubtful debts. A deduction for bad or doubtful debts can only be taken to the extent that the amount has already been taken into income. IT-442R, par. 24

Where a debt has been established by the taxpayer to have become a bad debt, rather than merely a debt of doubtful collectibility, the amount of the bad debt can be written off as an expense. A bad debt written off in this way need not be included in income in the following year. However, if and when a bad debt is recovered, then the amount of recovery is added to income in the year of receipt. It is a question of fact whether a debt has become a bad debt and, hence, uncollectible, rather than simply of doubtful collectibility. ITA: 20(1)(*p*) ITA: 12(1)(*i*)

Example Problem 4-4

The Greyduck Bus Lines Limited issues books of junior student tickets containing 20 transportation passes for $20 per book. The following information relates to books sold and tickets used:

	Year 1	*Year 2*	*Year 3*
Number of books sold	2,000	2,500	4,000
Number of tickets used:			
from Year 1 sales	25,000	11,000	expired
from Year 2 sales		31,250	13,750
from Year 3 sales			50,000

— *REQUIRED*

Compute the effect of these transactions on the net income from business of this company, assuming 10% of the tickets sold in a year are expected to expire at the beginning of the second year from the end of the year of sale.

— *SOLUTION*

		Applicable provisions
Year 1		
Include amount received in income ($20 × 2,000)	$40,000	par. 12(1)(*a*)
Less: reserve for services not provided(1)	11,000	par. 20(1)(*m*)
Income	$29,000	
Year 2		
Include amount received in income ($20 × 2,500)	$50,000	par. 12(1)(*a*)
Add: reserve from previous year	11,000	par. 12(1)(*e*)
	$61,000	
Less: reserve for services not provided(2)	13,750	par. 20(1)(*m*)
Income	$47,250	

Year 3

Include amount received in income ($20 × 4,000)	$80,000	par. 12(1)(*a*)
Add: reserve from previous year	13,750	par. 12(1)(*e*)
	$93,750	
Less: reserve for services not provided[3]	22,000	par. 20(1)(*m*)
Income	$71,750	

— *NOTES TO SOLUTION*

[1] The reserve is limited to a reasonable amount based on services that it is reasonably expected will have to be provided. In this case, no service will have to be provided for 10% of all tickets sold in the year. Of the 40,000 tickets (20 tickets × 2,000 books) sold in Year 1, 25,000 have been used and 4,000 will expire (10% of 40,000) leaving 11,000 for which service will have to be provided. At $1 per ticket ($20 ÷ 20) a reasonable reserve would be $11,000 ($1 × 11,000). Note that subsection 20(6) limits this reserve to the amount included in income for transportation not provided before the end of the year. In this case transportation has not been provided on 15,000 tickets (40,000 – 25,000) providing a limit at $1 per ticket of $15,000.

[2] Using the above process, service will have to be provided for 13,750 tickets since 5,000 (10% of 50,000) will expire and 31,250 have been used. Thus, a reasonable reserve at $1 per ticket is $13,750. The limit on this reserve would be on 18,750 tickets (50,000 – 31,250) at $1 per ticket or $18,750. ITA: 20(6)

[3] Service will have to be provided for 22,000 tickets since 8,000 (10% of 80,000) will expire and 50,000 have been used. The reserve at $1 per ticket would be $22,000 and the subsection 20(6) limit on that reserve would be on 30,000 tickets (80,000 – 50,000) at $1 per ticket or $30,000.

Example Problem 4-5

On July 1, 2010, Delta Company sold some inventory with a value of $100,000 and a cost of $40,000. A cash down payment of $10,000 was made and the balance was payable in four annual instalments of $20,000 and a final payment of $10,000. The purchaser is at arm's length.

— *REQUIRED*

How much of an inventory sales reserve can the company take in each year covered by the instalment sale? Use a December 31 year-end. ITA: 20(1)(*n*)

— *SOLUTION*

The Act limits the inventory sales reserve available to a three-year period. A reserve is not deductible for a year-end that is more than 36 months after the sale. ITA: 20(1)(*n*), 20(8)(*b*)

Calculation of reserve:

		Accounts receivable	*Profit content*
July 1, 2010	— sale price of article	$100,000	$60,000
	— cash down payment	10,000	6,000
Dec. 31, 2010	— balance receivable	$ 90,000	
	— reserve allowable[1]		$54,000
2011	— instalment due	20,000	12,000
Dec. 31, 2011	— balance receivable	$ 70,000	
	— reserve allowable[1]		$42,000
2012	— instalment due	20,000	12,000
Dec. 31, 2012	— balance receivable	$ 50,000	
	— reserve allowable[1]		$30,000
2013	— instalment due	20,000	12,000
Dec. 31, 2013	— balance receivable	$ 30,000	$18,000
	— reserve allowable (more than 36 months after sale)		Nil

Income effect:

			Net reported income
2010	— Profit on sale [par. 12(1)(*b*)]	$ 60,000	
	— Reserve [par. 20(1)(*n*)]	(54,000)	$ 6,000
2011	— Previous year reserve [par. 12(1)(*e*)]	$ 54,000	
	— Reserve [par. 20(1)(*n*)]	(42,000)	12,000
2012	— Previous year reserve [par. 12(1)(*e*)]	$ 42,000	
	— Reserve [par. 20(1)(*n*)]	(30,000)	12,000
2013	— Previous year reserve [par. 12(1)(*e*)]	$ 30,000	
	— Reserve [par. 20(1)(*n*) and ssec. 20(8)]	—	30,000
	Total income reported over four years		$60,000

— *NOTE TO SOLUTION*

(1) $\text{Reserve} = \dfrac{\text{gross profit}}{\text{gross selling price}} \times \text{amount receivable}$

¶4,247 Employer's contribution to registered pension plan

The deduction of employer contributions to a registered pension plan (RPP) is permitted. Deductible contributions may be made by the employer either in the year to which the deduction is to apply or within 120 days after the end of that taxation year. Contributions made in the 120-day period which are in excess of the deduction limit for the preceding year may be deductible in the year in which they are made if the deduction limit for the year is not exceeded. ITA: 20(1)(*q*), 147.2

Two types of RPP are envisaged.

- A defined benefit plan promises a defined retirement benefit which is specified by a formula. In the case of a defined benefit RPP, all contributions are deductible if they are determined by an actuary to be necessary to fund the benefits for which the RPP was registered to provide.
- A money purchase or defined contribution plan specifies a contribution requirement with the retirement benefit dependent on the funds accumulated in the plan at the time of retirement.

In the case of a money purchase RPP, the total of employer and employee contributions are limited to: ITA: 147.1(8)

the lesser of:

(i) 18% of the employee's compensation defined to be employment income inclusions under sections 5 and 6 for the particular year; and ITA: 147.1(1)

(ii) a specified dollar limit, defined as the money purchase limit. ITA: 147.1(1)

The limits for money purchase RPPs are as follows:

- for 2010 .... $22,450
- for 2011 .... $22,970
- for 2012 .... $23,820
- for 2013 .... $24,270
- for 2014 .... indexed

A violation of the limits set for either type of plan can lead to the revocation of the RPP registration status. If this occurs, all amounts in the plan become taxable, having lost their sheltered status.

¶4,248 Employer's contribution under a deferred profit sharing plan

Employer contributions to a deferred profit sharing plan (DPSP) are deductible within limits. An employer may deduct an amount which is paid in the year or within 120 days after the end of the year to a trustee to the extent that the amount was paid in accordance with the terms of the plan and was not deducted by the employer in a previous year. ITA: 20(1)(*y*) ITA: 147(8)

A formula is provided to determine the amount of an employer's contribution to a DPSP that is deductible. Generally, where there is no RPP, the employer's contribution limit in respect of an employee for a year is the lesser of: ITA: 147(5.1) ITA: 147(5.1)(*a*)

(a) one-half of the money purchase dollar limit for the year, as discussed above; and

(b) 18% of the employee's compensation (as defined) for the year. ITA: 147.1(1)

Therefore, to be deductible in a year, contributions should not exceed the lesser amount computed.

Where an employer participates in both a DPSP and an RPP for the benefit of an employee, the employer's total contribution to both plans is limited. It is rare for an employer to provide both a DPSP and an RPP together. ITA: 147(5.1)(*c*)

¶4,249 Cancellation of lease

Where the owner of a property is required to pay an amount to a lessee for the cancellation of the lease, the costs of cancelling the lease are treated as a type of prepaid expense, as long as the property continues to be owned by the lessor or by a non-arm's length person. As a result, the costs may be deducted over what would have been the remaining term of the lease, including renewal periods, to a maximum of 40 years. The unamortized balance of these costs (½ of the unamortized balance, in the case of capital property) is deductible if the property is sold. An amount that does not meet the conditions of these two paragraphs is not deductible. ITA: 20(1)(*z*) ITA: 20(1)(*z*.1) ITA: 18(1)(*q*)

¶4,250 Landscaping of grounds

A deduction of an amount paid in the year for landscaping of grounds around a building that is used to produce income from business is allowed. Were it not for this provision the expenditure would be considered to be of a capital nature. ITA: 20(1)(*aa*)

¶4,251 Expenses of representation

The expenses of representation for the purpose of obtaining a licence, permit, franchise or trademark related to the business of a taxpayer are deductible. Given the capital nature of the assets acquired, these expenditures would otherwise be prohibited. Note that the representations must be made to a government body or agency to be deductible. ITA: 18(1)(*b*), 20(1)(*cc*)

Instead of deducting the full amount allowed, a taxpayer may elect to deduct one-tenth of the full amount in the year of expenditure and the nine immediately following taxation years. The Regulations set out the documents that must be filed to implement the election. ITA: 20(1)(*cc*) ITA: 20(9) ITR: 4100

¶4,252 Investigation of site

The deduction of an amount paid in the year for investigating the suitability of a site for a building or other structure planned for use in the taxpayer's *existing* business is permitted. ITA: 20(1)(*dd*)

¶4,253 Utilities service connection

An amount paid in the year to an arm's length person to make connections for the supply of electricity, gas, telephone service, water or sewers, is deductible. Without this provision no deduction would be permitted, since the expenditure is of a capital nature. Furthermore, no capital cost allowance would be permitted, because the taxpayer normally does not own the service connections. ITA: 20(1)(*ee*)

¶4,254 Disability-related modifications and equipment

A deduction, in the payment year, of the full cost of prescribed renovations or alterations to a building used primarily in a business is allowed. The expenditures must be made to enable individuals who have a mobility impairment to gain access to the building or be mobile within it. The building need not be owned by the taxpayer making the expenditure. ITA: 20(1)(*qq*)

The deduction, in the payment year, of the cost of any prescribed disability-specific device or equipment which assists individuals with a sight, hearing, or mobility impairment is allowed. The type of expenditure envisaged includes installation of elevator car position indicators, visible fire alarm indicators, telephone devices, listening devices for group meetings and disability-specific computer software and hardware. ITA: 20(1)(*rr*)

If it were not for these provisions, the expenditures could be considered of a capital nature and could not be expensed. Clearly, the rules provide an incentive to implement social policy.

¶4,255 Convention expenses

Attendance at a convention may be considered to give rise to expenditures of a capital nature, perhaps, in the form of increased knowledge. However, the Act permits the deduction from a taxpayer's business income of amounts paid in attending up to two conventions per year. Attendance at the convention must be in connection with the business. The location of the convention must be within the territorial scope of the organization holding the convention. Note that an internal business meeting, such as a sales conference within a business, is not considered to be a convention. ITA: 20(10)

¶4,256 Application of the Rules for Deduction

To determine the deductibility of an outlay or expenditure after considering the general principles and rules in section 18, the list of deductions under section 20 should be scanned. This can be done quickly by reference to the table of contents for the Act. In addition, commentary under these sections contained in the "Canadian Tax Library" of CCH TAX lists court case decisions for a wide variety of expenditures. This list is based on court decisions made on the question of the deductibility of many types of expenditure for tax purposes. However, it should be noted that because the commentary list is based largely on case law, the deductibility of any particular type of expenditure is heavily dependent on the specific facts of the case and the specific law in force at the time of the case. Care should be taken to determine the facts that resulted in a particular decision and the wording of the Act at the time of the case, since some court decisions may be at variance with current law.

Example Problem 4-6

You are the auditor for Corporate Welfare Limited and you have been given an income statement prepared for financial accounting purposes showing a loss for its fiscal year ended December 31, 2013 of $112,000. Your audit uncovers the following:

(a) appraisal expense contains cost of determining asset values for insurance purposes		$ 4,000
(b) wages expense contains amounts (matched by employees) relating to money purchase (defined contribution) registered pension plan contributions, made during the first 120 days of 2014 but allocated by the accountant to 2013, in respect of current services on behalf of the following executives (employment compensation for the year shown in brackets):		
President (Mr. C.S. Bloom, 100% owner; $200,000)	$ 15,600	
Vice-President ($95,000)	6,000	
Accountant ($80,000)	5,000	
Plant Supervisor ($65,000)	4,000	30,600

(c) cost of landscaping written off		10,000
(d) legal expenses for		
(i) defence of a suit, brought by a customer, for failure to deliver merchandise on time	$ 2,500	
(ii) articles of amendment to revise company's articles of incorporation	3,500	
(iii) cost of disputing income tax	4,000	10,000
(e) revenues included a dividend received from a Canadian subsidiary		80,000
(f) interest expense included amortization of bond discount on bonds maturing in 2014		12,000
(g) opening inventories were valued on the FIFO basis at $184,750 while closing inventories were valued on the LIFO basis rather than the FIFO basis which would have exceeded the LIFO valuation by		36,950
(h) miscellaneous expense contained donations for the year to		
(i) duly registered charities	$ 4,000	
(ii) the Conlibdem political party (a registered party)	7,000	11,000
(i) insurance expense contained whole life insurance premium paid on the life of Mr. C.S. Bloom (proceeds payable to the company; not group life)		10,000
(j) salaries expense contained a dividend payable to Mr. Bloom		8,000
(k) bad debts expense including $4,000 in respect of a loan to a shareholder of a supplier totalled		10,000
(l) extraordinary maintenance arising from conversion of premises including replacement of heating and air-conditioning systems, plumbing, electrical wiring and concrete foundations in respect of a building was written off to repairs and maintenance in the amount of		150,000
(m) salaries expense included a bonus paid to Mr. Bloom		15,000
(n) interest expense included interest in respect of the acquisition of 90% of the shares of another Canadian corporation		115,000
(o) convention expenses over three days of Mr. Bloom and his family ($2,000 thereof represents costs relating to Mrs. Bloom and their two children, who attended for social purposes only; $500 of the remaining amount relates to the cost of meals consumed by Mr. Bloom)		5,000
(p) administration expense contains an embezzlement loss caused by a minor employee of the company		10,000
(q) (i) management bonuses included in wages expense but not paid in 2013		50,000
(ii) bonuses accrued at the end of 2013 which were not, and will not be, paid in 2014		35,000
(r) property taxes paid in 2013 include an amount paid for the company's fishing lodge		1,000
(s) the company as a lessor agreed to pay and expensed $15,000 on June 30, 2013 to cancel a lease that could have been in force until December 31, 2019 with renewal periods, but in 2013 actually paid only		10,000
(t) the company paid damages for failing to deliver goods on time under an action for breach of contract brought by one of its suppliers and the amount was expensed in the financial accounts		12,000
(u) cost of constructing a cement ramp to facilitate wheelchair access to the company's premises, capitalized by the accountant		6,000

— REQUIRED

Compute the company's income or loss from business or property for tax purposes, but do not compute tax deductions in respect of depreciable capital or eligible capital property. Indicate the applicable sections of the Act or brief reasons to substantiate your answer. Indicate in a separate list the applicable section of the Act or brief reasons for not considering an item in your computations. Make sure all items are accounted for. Ignore the effects of the leap year.

— *SOLUTION*

			Applicable sections
Loss for financial accounting purposes		$(112,000)	sec. 9
Add items not deductible for tax purposes:			
Excess allocations to 2013 of RPP contributions[(1)]	$ 6,930		par. 20(1)(*q*)
Legal expenses for articles revision[(2)]	3,500		par. 18(1)(*b*)
Amortization of bond discount[(3)]	12,000		par. 18(1)(*b*)
Excess of FIFO over LIFO[(4)]	36,950		ssec. 10(1)
Donations[(5)]	11,000		par. 18(1)(*a*)
Life insurance premium[(6)]	10,000		par. 18(1)(*a*)
Dividend payable[(7)]	8,000		
Bad debt re: loan to shareholder of supplier[(8)]	4,000		par. 20(1)(*p*)
Extraordinary maintenance[(9)]	150,000		par. 18(1)(*b*)
Convention expenses[(10)]	2,250		par. 18(1)(*h*)
Bonuses accrued and not paid[(11)]	35,000		ssec. 78(4)
Property tax on fishing lodge[(12)]	1,000		par. 18(1)(*l*)
Non-deductible prepaid lease cancellation amount[(13)]	13,837	$ 294,467	par. 20(1)(*z*)
		$ 182,467	
Deduct items deductible for tax purposes:			
Wheelchair access ramp		$ 6,000	par. 20(1)(*qq*)
Income from business or property for tax purposes[(14)]		$ 176,467	

— *NOTES TO SOLUTION*

[(1)] In this case, involving a money purchase RPP, assuming the employee contributions are matched by the employer corporation and that the employee's contributions are fully deductible, the corporation will have a non-deductible contribution in respect of 2013 computed as follows:

	Pres.	*V.P.*	*Acct.*	*Super.*
Least of:				
(a) Employer plus employee RPP contributions	*$31,200*	*$12,000*	*$10,000*	*$ 8,000*
(b) Money purchase dollar limit for 2013	*$24,270*	*$24,270*	*$24,270*	*$24,270*
(c) 18% of compensation	*$36,000*	*$17,100*	*$14,400*	*$11,700*
Least amount	*$24,270*	*$12,000*	*$10,000*	*$ 8,000*
Less: employer and employee contributions	*31,200*	*12,000*	*10,000*	*8,000*
Employer's non-deductible contributions for 2013	*$ 6,930*	*Nil*	*Nil*	*Nil*

Total amount to be added back: $6,930

Since the $6,930 non-deductible amount was contributed in the first 120 days of 2014, it can be a part of the deductible contribution for 2014 without danger of a revocation of the registration status of the RPP, as long as contributions in 2014 do not exceed deduction limits for 2014.

[(2)] Expenditures on articles of incorporation or articles of amendment are regarded as eligible capital property and are written off over time for tax purposes. This topic will be covered in Chapter 5.

[(3)] The Act specifically prohibits the amortization of an amount that is capital in nature. The Act prohibits all reserves, except as expressly provided for in the Act. The Act specifically denies the deduction of an actual cash outlay on redemption or open market purchases except to the extent permitted.

ITA: 18(1)(*b*), 18(1)(*e*), 18(1)(*f*), 20(1)(*f*)

(4) Departmental practice has disallowed the use of LIFO as an assumption in the costing of inventory when actual cost cannot be identified. This practice is based on the decision in *M.N.R. v. Anaconda American Brass Ltd.*, which established the principle that the facts of inventory flow cannot be disregarded in using an assumption about inventory cost. The same disregard of the facts and substitution of assumptions in relation to the flow of goods made the use of the LIFO method of valuation objectionable in *Wickett and Craig Ltd. v. M.N.R.* 55 DTC 1220 (J.C.P.C.) 78 DTC 1382 (T.R.B.)

(5) Donations are not deductible in the computation of income if they were not incurred to earn income. However, charitable donations of a corporation are deductible in Division C dealing with the computation of taxable income, and political contributions are eligible for a tax credit in Division E dealing with the computation of tax. ITA: 110.1, 127(3)

(6) Life insurance premiums paid on the lives of officers, employees or shareholders where the policies are payable to the company do not produce income. Hence, the premiums are not deductible unless the policy is required to obtain financing, such as a bank loan. The Act limits the amount of a deductible premium to the net cost of pure insurance, determined by reference to standard mortality assumptions. ITA: 20(1)(*e.2*)

(7) Dividends are not paid to produce income; they are a distribution of income after it has been earned.

(8) The Act requires that an amount be previously included in income if it is to be written off as a bad debt. On this loan, which was not a trade account receivable, no amount would have been included in sales and, hence, in income. However, a further adjustment may be allowed under section 50 which will be discussed in Chapter 8, under the heading "Debts Established to be Bad Debts". ITA: 20(1)(*p*)

(9) An expenditure which prolongs the life of an asset is regarded as capital in nature, but an expenditure which restores an asset to its original condition is regarded as an expenditure of an income nature. In this case, the expenditure, as described, appears to be of a capital nature. ITA: 18(1)(*b*)

(10) Personal or living expenses are specifically prohibited as a deduction, except, for example, an item such as convention expenses specifically allowed. The Act provides that the deductible cost of meals while attending a convention is 50% of the actual cost, on the assumption that the cost is reasonable. Where the fees for a convention do not specify the cost of meals or entertainment included in those fees, the Act will deem the cost to be $50 per day and that amount will be subject to the 50% limitation. In this case, since the cost is specified, 50% of $500, or $250, is not deductible and must be added in the reconciliation. ITA: 18(1)(*h*), 20(10) ITA: 67.1(1) ITA: 67.1(3)

(11) The bonuses accrued at the end of 2013 are not deductible in 2013, since they were not paid within the time limit. The $35,000 would, therefore, have been added back to 2013 income. These bonuses can only be deducted when they are actually paid. ITA: 78(4)

(12) The Act arbitrarily disallows certain listed expenditures including one made for the maintenance of a lodge. ITA: 18(1)(*l*)

(13) The costs of cancelling a lease are treated as a prepaid expense, as long as the property continues to be owned by the lessor or a person with whom he or she does not deal at arm's length. As such it may be deducted over the remaining term of the cancelled lease, including renewal periods, subject to a maximum limit of 40 years. In this case, the number of days in the remainder of the lease is 184 in 2013 and 6 years of 365 days per year (ignoring leap years) for a total of 2,374 days. Thus, the deduction for 2013 is given by 184/2,374 × $15,000 or $1,163. Therefore, the non-deductible amount of the $15,000 payment is $13,837 (i.e., $15,000 – $1,163). Another rule provides a deduction of the unamortized balance if the property is sold. ITA: 20(1)(*z*) ITA: 20(1)(*z.1*)

(14) Other items:

(a) The cost of an appraisal made for the purpose of maintaining adequate insurance coverage is regarded as a normal business expense and is deductible.

(b) The Act allows a deduction for an employer contribution to a registered pension plan of the amount calculated in another provision. The amounts calculated in respect of all employees shown other than the President are deductible, as shown in Note (1). ITA: 20(1)(*q*), 147.2(1)

(c) The deduction of landscaping costs is allowed, even though they might otherwise be considered of a capital nature. ITA: 20(1)(*aa*)

(d) (i) The cost of defending a suit brought by a customer is regarded as a business expense if it pertains to trading transactions.

(ii) The cost of disputing an income tax case has been held in the case of *Premium Iron Ores Ltd. v. M.N.R.* to be a business expense. The legal expenses of $4,000 could also be deducted, in which case they should be added back in the computation of income from business. 66 DTC 5280 (S.C.C.) ITA: 60(*o*)

(e) A dividend received is to be included in income from property. ITA: 12(1)(*j*)

(f) Bad debt expenses are deductible as long as the account has previously resulted in an inclusion in income. In the normal course of setting up an account receivable a credit would be made to sales, thereby including the amount in income. The treatment of a bad debt expense for tax purposes is identical to the treatment of the expense for financial accounting purposes. In fact, the tax treatment of both the reserve and the expense parallels the accounting treatment. The previous year's reserve is reversed by including it in current income and a new reserve is set up for the current year by taking a deduction. A debt established to be bad is written off and a recovery of such a debt previously written off is included in income. ITA: 12(1)(*d*), 12(1)(*i*), 20(1)(*l*), 20(1)(*p*)

(g) A bonus expense is a deductible business expense to the extent that it meets the test of being "reasonable in the circumstances." The $50,000 bonus expensed in 2013 is deductible in 2013 as long as it is paid on or before June 28, 2014. ITA: 18(1)(*a*), 67

(h) The deduction of interest on funds borrowed to buy shares is permitted since dividend income will be earned. ITA: 20(1)(*c*)

(i) The deduction of Mr. Bloom's convention expenses is permitted (except for part of the cost of meals which is limited), as long as the conditions of that provision are met. ITA: 20(10), 67.1, 67.3

(j) Losses in cash or misappropriation of merchandise sustained by the criminal action of employees or officers will be allowed as deductions from income as being incidental to carrying on of business. However, such a loss attributable to a partner or senior officer is not usually regarded as a normal business risk and is not deductible. In the case of *Cassidy's Limited v. M.N.R.*, the Tax Court of Canada disagreed specifically with the statement in an Interpretation Bulletin in which the CRA stated that, because a theft was committed by a senior employee, the losses resulting from the theft are not deductible by the employer. The Court held that "the amounts lost due to the defalcation were non-capital losses, the deductions of which are deductible in computing profit in accordance with ordinary commercial principles and are not prohibited by the Act" and, hence, allowed the deduction. IT-185R; 89 DTC 686 (T.C.C.); IT-185R, par. 2(b)

(k) Damages for failure to deliver goods are regarded as normal business expenses.

¶4,257 Sales/Negotiating Person's Expenses Revisited

One of the topics dealt with in the preceding chapter on employment income was the deductibility of the expenses of sales/negotiating persons (i.e., individuals employed in connection with the selling of property or negotiating of contracts). Unlike other employees, sales/negotiating persons can deduct expenses incurred to produce employment income. However, these allowable expenses are limited to the amount of commission income or other similar amounts, fixed by reference to the volume of sales made or the contracts negotiated, received in the year. It is interesting to compare the limited deductions for expenses available to a sales/negotiating person who is an employee with the broader deductions available to a person performing similar functions as an independent business person. ITA: 8(1)(*f*), 8(1)(*j*)

Comparison of Deductions

	Ordinary Employee*	Salesperson/Negotiator		Proprietor
	[s. 8(1)(*h*), (*h*.1), (*i*), (*j*)]	[s. 8(1)(*f*)]	[s. 8(1)(*i*), (*j*)]	
Home Office:				
Utilities	√		√	√
Mortgage interest				√
House insurance		√		√
Property taxes		√		√
Maintenance and repairs	√		√	√
Office supplies	√		√	√
CCA on computer				√
Automobile expenses:				
Operating	√	√		√
CCA	√		√	√
Interest on loan	√		√	√
Convention (excl. meals)				√
Promotional expenses		√		√
Limit on expenses	None	Commission Income	None	None

* Required to travel for employer, but no sales commission earned.

¶4,258 Automobiles

ITA: 248(1)

The following are some of the common deductions related to automobiles:

- Interest on money borrowed for passenger vehicles; ITA: 67.2
- Deductible lease payment restriction; ITA: 67.3
- CCA restriction on passenger vehicles; ITA: 13(7)(*g*), 13(7)(*h*)
- Limit on which CCA may be claimed ($30,000 plus GST/HST for 2013); ITR: 7307(*b*)
- Definition of passenger vehicles. ITA: 248(1)

¶4,260 Automobile allowances

As discussed previously in this chapter, the Act and the ITR limit the deduction by an employer of allowances paid to employees for the use of an automobile in the course of employment or business to a prescribed amount per kilometre, except where the allowance is required to be included in the employee's income under paragraph 6(1)(*b*). ITA: 18(1)(*r*); ITR: 7306

¶4,265 Office in the home

Also, as previously discussed, the deductibility of the costs relating to a place of business in the residence of a self-employed individual is restricted. A prorated portion of these "home office" expenses, such as rent, capital cost allowance, property taxes, and mortgage interest or operating costs, including heating, electricity, insurance or maintenance may be deducted only if the space is either: ITA: 18(12)

- the individual's principal place of business; or
- used exclusively by the individual on a regular and continuous basis for meeting clients, customers or patients.

The deduction for home office expenses is further restricted to the income for the year from the business for which the office is used. However, any excess of deduction disallowed in a year may be treated as home office expenses incurred in a following year, according to the Interpretation Bulletin entitled "Work space in home expenses". A parallel provision to restrict the deduction of home office expenses by an employee was presented in Chapter 3. IT-514, par. 5 ITA: 8(13)

¶4,270 Meals and entertainment

The amount of a deduction by all taxpayers for food, beverage, and entertainment is restricted to the lesser of 50% of the amount paid or payable or a reasonable amount. This limitation applies to all business meals, including food and beverage, as well as to the cost of meals while travelling or attending a seminar, conference, convention or similar function. The restriction also applies to tickets to an entertainment or sporting event, gratuities and cover charges, room rentals to provide entertainment and the cost of private boxes at sports facilities. The limitation applies to the taxpayer incurring the costs in the case where a reimbursement is made. The following are exclusions from the 50% limitation: ITA: 67.1

(a) the cost to a restaurant, airline or hotel of providing meals to customers in the ordinary course of business;

(b) meals or entertainment expenses relating to an event intended primarily to benefit a registered charity;

(c) the cost of meals or entertainment that is included as a taxable benefit to the employee or where the employer is reimbursed for the cost; and

(d) the cost of meals and recreation provided by an employer for the general benefit of all employees at a particular place of business in respect of occasional events not exceeding six events per year.

IT-518R

The Interpretation Bulletin entitled "Food, Beverages and Entertainment Expenses" presents the CRA's interpretation of this provision.

Example Problem 4-7

Ms. Jo Schmaltz is a salesperson who earned a total of $25,000 in 2013, including $4,000 in commissions. She was required to travel in her job and she was required to pay her own expenses, all of which were reasonable in the circumstances and consisted of the following:

(a) entertainment of clients including golf club membership dues of $500 (incurred in equal monthly amounts)		$3,700
(b) home office expenses (allocated by floor space of office portion of home):		
mortgage interest	$ 450	
municipal taxes	400	
capital cost allowance	300	
utilities	1,000	
maintenance and repairs	850	3,000
This is the only office space available for her work.		
(c) capital cost allowance on car used 75% for business		3,570
(d) car operating expenses		3,100
(e) convention dues (excluding meals and entertainment)		1,000
(f) travellers' association (a trade union) dues		300
(g) meals while travelling		900

— *REQUIRED*

(A) Compute Jo's minimum employment income for 2013.

(B) Compute Jo's minimum business income, assuming she is an independent business person with $25,000 in sales rather than an employee.

— *SOLUTION*

			Applicable provisions
(A) Employment income			
Salary and commissions		$25,000	sec. 5
Deductions:			
Entertainment(1) (50% of $3,200)	$ 1,600		par. 8(1)(*f*) par. 18(1)(*l*) ssec. 67.1(1)
Home office:(2) municipal taxes	400		par. 8(1)(*f*)
Car operating expenses (75% of $3,100)	2,325		par. 8(1)(*f*)
Meal expenses (50% of $900)	450		ssec. 67.1(1)
Total	$ 4,775		
Deductions not in excess of commission(3)		$(4,000)	par. 8(1)(*f*)
		$21,000	
Less: association dues(4)	$ 300		par. 8(1)(*i*)
CCA on car (75% of $3,570)	2,678		par. 8(1)(*j*)
Utilities	1,000		par. 8(1)(*i*)
Maintenance and repairs	850	(4,828)	par. 8(1)(*i*)
Employment income(5), (6)		$16,172	

(B) Business income

Sales		$25,000	sec. 9
Deductions:			
Entertainment[7] (50% of $3,200)	$ 1,600		par. 18(1)(*a*)
CCA on car (75% of $3,570)	2,678		par. 20(1)(*a*)
Car operating expenses (75% of $3,100)	2,325		par. 18(1)(*a*)
Convention expenses	1,000		ssec. 20(10)
Meals (50% of $900)	450		par. 18(1)(*a*)
Association dues	300	(8,353)	par. 18(1)(*a*)
Income from business[8] (before home office expense)		$16,647	par. 18(1)(*a*) par. 20(1)(*a*)
Less: home office expense[9]		(3,000)	par. 20(1)(*c*)
Income from business		$13,647	

Note that the difference between employment income of $16,172 and business income of $13,647 is $2,525. This amount consists of the following expenses that are not deductible from employment income but are deductible from business income:

Interest and CCA on home office ($450 + $300)	$ 750
Non-deductible excess of employment expenses over commissions	775
Convention expenses	1,000
Total	$2,525

— *NOTES TO SOLUTION*

(1) To be deductible as a salesperson's expenses, an expenditure must be made to earn employment income. However, the relevant provision specifically denies deductions which fall under paragraph 18(1)(*l*), which lists an outlay for the use of a golf course. ITA: 8(1)(*f*) ITA: 8(1)(*f*)(vi)

(2) Outlays on account of capital are not deductible except for interest and capital cost allowance on a car used in the course of employment. The interest is on account of the home mortgage and the capital cost allowance is not for a car. Municipal taxes and home insurance are deductible, as confirmed by the decision of the Tax Court of Canada in *Felton v. M.N.R.* In that case, the taxpayer sought to deduct mortgage interest, property taxes, insurance premiums and the cost of utilities for his home as rent. The court held that rent involves only a payment arising out of a landlord and tenant relationship, such that the expenses incurred for an owner-occupied home could not be considered as rent. However, the court did recognize the CRA's assessing practices in respect of maintenance costs and utilities. The Federal Court–Trial Division concurred with the *Felton* decision in *The Queen v. Thompson*. ITA: 8(1)(*f*)(v), 8(1)(*j*) IT-352R2, par. 6 89 DTC 233 (T.C.C.) ITA: 8(1)(*i*)(ii) 89 DTC 5439 (F.C.T.D.)

The Act sets out two tests, one of which must be met, if any amount of home office expense is to be deductible. One requires that the workspace be the place where the individual principally performs the duties of the office or employment. The alternative test requires that both of the following conditions be met: ITA: 8(13) ITA: 8(13)(*a*)(i) ITA: 8(13)(*a*)(ii)

(a) the workspace is used exclusively for employment during the period in respect of which the deduction relates, and

(b) the workspace is used on a regular and continuous basis for meeting customers or other persons in the ordinary course of employment.

If one of the two tests is met, the deductible expenses are limited to the employee's employment income for the year. Therefore, workspace deduction cannot create a loss from employment. However, the provision allows for what amounts to an indefinite carryforward. In this case, where all expenses are limited to the amount of commission income, the limitation on home office expenses will have no effect. ITA: 8(13)(*a*)(i), 8(13)(*a*)(ii) ITA: 8(13)(*c*)

(3) Note that the salesperson's expense deduction requires that expenses, to be deductible, cannot exceed the commission. ITA: 8(1)(*f*)

(4) Paragraph 8(1)(*f*) does not restrict the deductions under paragraph 8(1)(*i*) or 8(1)(*j*) (i.e., interest and capital cost allowance on car, utilities and maintenance) to commission income.

(5) Convention expenses may not be deducted from employment income since they are not listed in subsection 8(1). ITA: 8(2)

(6) Due to the limitation placed on deductible expenses, i.e., expenses cannot exceed commission income, an alternative set of provisions may be preferable. In this case, the employee could make use of the deductions covering travelling expenses and motor vehicle expenses, rather than the salesperson's deduction. Although these rules do not provide for the deduction of entertainment expenses, there is no commission income limitation on the amount of meal expenses deductible (except for the 50% limitation on the cost of meals) or on car operating expenses deductible. Thus, the meal expenses and car operating expenses of $2,775 (i.e., $2,325 + $450) would be deductible as travel and car expenses, and office maintenance and utilities expenses of $1,850 would be deductible; the traveller's association dues would be deductible and capital cost allowance on the car would be deductible. This would result in employment income of $17,397 computed as follows:

ITA: 8(1)(*f*)
ITA: 8(1)(*h*), 8(1)(*h*.1)
ITA: 8(1)(*h*)
ITA: 8(1)(*h*.1)
ITA: 8(1)(*i*)(iii); IT-352R2, par. 6
ITA: 8(1)(*i*)(iv), 8(1)(*j*)(ii)

Salary and commissions		$ 25,000	sec. 5
Deductions:			
Car operating expenses (75% of $3,100)	$2,325		par. 8(1)(*h*.1)
Meal expenses (50% of $900)	450		par. 8(1)(*h*)
Association dues	300		par. 8(1)(*i*)
CCA on car (75% of $3,570)	2,678	(5,753)	par. 8(1)(*j*)
Employment income (before home office expense)		$ 19,247	
Less: home office expense		(1,850)	par. 8(1)(*i*), ssec. 8(13)
Employment income		$ 17,397	

Therefore, in this particular case, using the paragraphs 8(1)(*h*) and (*h*.1) alternative is not better.

(7) Golf club membership dues are not deductible because of the prohibition. ITA: 18(1)(*l*)

(8) The issue of employment versus self-employment was considered in the previous chapter.

The courts have applied the following three tests as discussed in the previous chapter:

(a) the economic reality or entrepreneur test, i.e., control, ownership of the tools, chance of profit and risk of loss;

(b) integration or organization test, i.e., whether the worker is economically dependent on the organization; and

(c) the specific result test, i.e., a contract envisaging the accomplishment of a specific job or task.

(9) All of the home office expenses, including the interest and capital cost allowance, are deductible to the extent incurred to earn income, if the conditions are met. However, she may not want to claim the capital cost allowance because of the principal residence rules which will be discussed in the chapters on capital gains taxation. The deduction of expenses pertaining to work space in a home are allowed where it is either the individual's principal place of business or used exclusively on a regular and continuous basis for meeting clients, customers or patients of the individual. Deductible expenses cannot exceed the individual's income from business before the deduction of these expenses. However, excess expenses of this nature may be carried forward. As a result of this restriction, home office expenses should be separated from other deductible expenses and deducted last, as shown.

ITA: 18(12)
ITA: 18(12)
ITA: 18(12); IT-514

¶4,275 Summary of Business Income Adjustments

The following chart summarizes some of the various adjustments to accounting income needed to arrive at income for tax purposes.

Add		Deduct	
Income received but not earned	12(1)(*a*)	Reserve in respect of future goods and services	20(1)(*m*)
Amounts receivable	12(1)(*b*)	Doubtful debts	20(1)(*l*)
		Bad debts	20(1)(*p*)
Expenses not incurred to earn income	18(1)(*a*)		
Capital outlay or loss	18(1)(*a*)	CCA/CECA	20(1)(*a*), (*b*)
		Interest	20(1)(*c*)
		Expenses of financing	20(1)(*e*)
		Terminal loss	20(16)
		Bad debts	20(1)(*p*)
		Landscaping	20(1)(*aa*)
		Investment counsel	20(1)(*bb*)
		Investigation of site	20(1)(*dd*)
		Utility service connection	20(1)(*ee*)
		Disability related modifications to buildings, equipment	20(1)(*qq*), (*rr*)
Incurred to earn exempt income	18(1)(*c*)	Premiums on life insurance used as collateral	20(1)(*e*.2)
Reserves, contingent liabilities, etc.	18(1)(*e*)	Doubtful debts	20(1)(*l*)
		Reserve in respect of future goods and services	20(1)(*m*)
		Reserve for unpaid amounts	20(1)(*n*)
Payment on discounted bonds	18(1)(*f*)	Discount on certain obligations	20(1)(*f*)
Personal or living expenses	18(1)(*h*)	Limit on food and entertainment	67.1
		Limit on interest and lease costs for a passenger vehicle	67.2–67.4
		Capital cost of luxury automobile	13(7)(*g*)
		Convention expenses	20(10)
Use of recreational facilities and club dues	18(1)(*l*)		
Political contributions	18(1)(*n*)		
Limitation re personal service business expenses	18(1)(*p*)		
Limitation re cancellation of lease	18(1)(*q*)	Cancellation of lease	20(1)(*z*)
Limit on certain interest and property tax	18(2)		
Costs related to construction of building or ownership of land	18(3.1)		
Prepaid expenses	18(9)		
Unreasonable expenses	67		
Illegal payments, fines, and penalties	67.5, 67.6		

¶4,280 Ceasing to Carry On Business

¶4,285 Sale of accounts receivable

In order to deduct a reserve for doubtful debts or to write off a bad debt, an amount in respect of the debt must have been included previously in income. This would not be the case, if accounts judged to be doubtful or bad were purchased from someone else. To alleviate the problems that this may cause where a person ITA: 20(1)(*l*), 20(1)(*p*)

- has sold all or substantially all of the property used in a business
- to a purchaser who will continue the business,

the Act provides for a joint election by the vendor and purchaser which permits the purchaser to take the reserve or write-off in respect of accounts receivable. ITA: 22

To illustrate this election, assume that accounts receivable having a face value of $14,000 with an existing reserve of $3,000 are sold for their assessed fair market value of $10,000. The following represents the procedure that must be followed jointly by the buyer and seller to allow the buyer future reserves and write-offs on the accounts purchased: ITA: 22

SELLER

Accounts receivable (Dr.)	*Accounts receivable* (Cr.)	*Reserve* (Dr.)	*Reserve* (Cr.)
$14,000			$3,000
	$10,000(1)		
	4,000(3)	(2) $3,000	
NIL			NIL

BUYER

Accounts receivable (Dr.)	*Accounts receivable* (Cr.)	*Reserve* (Dr.)	*Reserve* (Cr.)
(1) $14,000			NIL

Seller:

(1) Cash	$10,000	
Accounts receivable		$10,000
(2) Reserve	3,000	
Income		3,000
(3) Business loss	4,000	
Accounts receivable		4,000

Buyer:

(1) Accounts receivable	$14,000	
Cash		$10,000
Income		4,000

NOTE: Buyer could then set up an appropriate reserve for doubtful debts and could write off any of these debts should they prove bad.

Note that the loss to the seller under the election is a business loss. If the election were not made, the loss of $4,000 would be a capital loss, only ½ allowable as a deduction and only deductible against taxable capital gains of $2,000.

¶4,290 Sale of inventory

Where a taxpayer disposes of a business or part of a business, any inventory sold is deemed to have been sold in the course of carrying on the business. Thus, the proceeds of the sale result in income for the seller and become the cost of the inventory to the buyer. The purpose of this provision is to ensure that a lump-sum sale of inventory on the sale of a business is treated in exactly the same way as the usual sale of inventory in the normal course of carrying on business. ITA: 23

¶4,300 Professional Business

Amounts receivable in respect of services that have been billed are required to be included in income from the business of a professional. Work in progress at the end of a year, representing unbilled services of a business that is a profession, is considered to be inventory. ITA: 10(5)(*a*)

An election is available to a taxpayer whose business is the professional practice of an accountant, dentist, lawyer, medical doctor, veterinarian or chiropractor. The election allows the taxpayer to exclude from business income any amount in respect of work in progress at the end of the year. Where the election is made, it must be used in all subsequent taxation years unless the election is revoked with the permission of the CRA. The CRA's interpretation of these rules is contained in the Interpretation Bulletin entitled "Election by professionals to exclude work in progress from income". ITA: 34(*a*), 34(*b*) IT-457R

¶4,310 Scientific Research and Experimental Development

¶4,315 Meaning of scientific research and experimental development

"Scientific research and experimental development" (SR&ED) is defined to mean the "systematic investigation or search carried out in a field of science or technology by means of experiment or analysis ... ", including basic research, applied research and experimental development. Activities which result in deductible expenditures in support of the three types of research include engineering or design, operations research, mathematical analysis or computer programming, data collection, testing and psychological research. However, activities which do not result in a deductible expenditure include market research or sales promotion, quality control or routine testing, social sciences or humanities research, natural resource exploration, commercial development of material, products or processes, style changes or routine data collection. The CRA has issued an Information Circular and an Interpretation Bulletin that offer some guidelines in the area.[33]

ITA: 248(1)

IT-151R5

The term "scientific research and experimental development" recognizes that the bulk of industrial scientific research is concentrated on the experimental development of new products or processes rather than pure or applied research. The inclusion of the words "experimental development" confirms that research does not include projects involving only routine engineering or routine development.

¶4,320 General deduction of expenditures

Generally, research and development expenditures, including most capital expenditures (made before 2014), made in a year are fully deductible. However, any allowable expenditures that are not deducted in a year are placed in a pool and may be deducted in any future year in which the taxpayer carries on business in Canada.

As shown in Figure 4-1 below, this "pool" is made up of both current and capital SR&ED expenditures, less any investment tax credit (ITC) deducted from tax that is related to these expenditures. Each year, the company can determine how much, if any, of this pool is deducted from income for tax purposes. This is especially useful for companies that have heavy research expenditures and little income, since it allows them to defer the expense into a future period when there is income to deduct it against.

ITA: 37(1)

Figure 4-1
SR&ED Pool

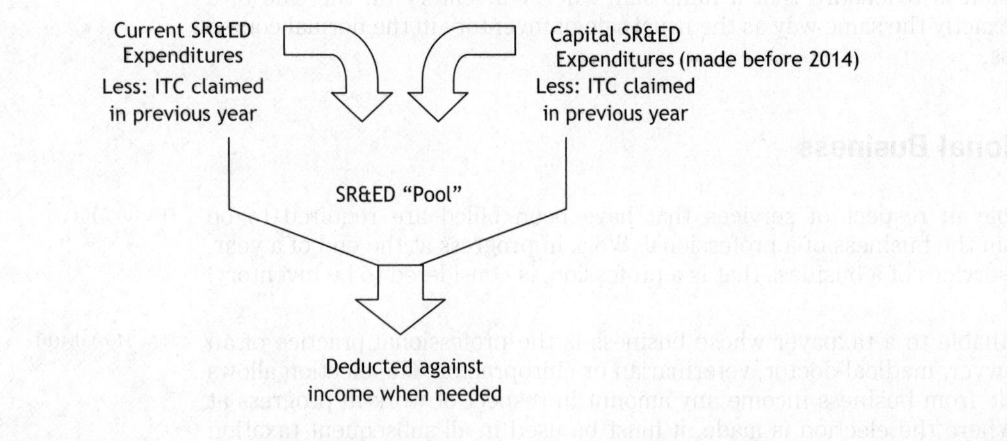

[33] The Tax Court of Canada had occasion to consider the definition of the term in the case of *Sass Manufacturing Limited v. M.N.R.*, 88 DTC 1363.

Certain scientific research and experimental development expenditures made in the year can be deducted from income of a business carried on in Canada. The following is a list of expenditures of a current nature: ITA: 37(1)(*a*)

(a) for scientific research and experimental development related to the business and directly undertaken by or on behalf of the taxpayer;

(b) to an approved association that undertakes scientific research and experimental development related to the class of business of the taxpayer;

(c) to an approved university, college, research institute or other similar institution to be used for scientific research and experimental development related to the class of business of the taxpayer;

(d) for scientific research and experimental development in Canada to non-profit corporations resident in Canada;

(e) to a corporation resident in Canada for scientific research and experimental development in Canada related to the business of the taxpayer; or

(f) to an approved organization that makes payments to an association, institution or corporation described in (b) to (d), above, for use in scientific research and experimental development related to the class of business of the taxpayer, and where the taxpayer may exploit the results of such research and development.

Expenditures on scientific research and experimental development of a capital nature (other than land or other non-depreciable property) can also be deducted, if made before 2014. ITA: 37(1)(*b*)

The zone in which deductible SR&ED expenditures can be incurred extends to the area that is up to 200 nautical miles from the low-water line along the coasts of Canada, as recognized in the *Oceans Act*. This is known as the exclusive economic zone (EEZ) and includes the airspace above and the subsoil or seabed below that zone. ITA: 37(1.3)

Expenditures must be related to a business carried on by the person making the expenditure. As indicated, SR&ED expenditures are added to a pool of such costs. They are eligible for a 100% deduction in the year incurred or may be carried forward indefinitely. ITA: 37(1)(*a*), 37(1)(*b*)

As a further incentive to invest in SR&ED activity, the Act provides for an investment tax credit (ITC, discussed in subsequent chapters) which is a direct reduction of the taxpayer's tax liability. The investment tax credit is calculated as a specified percentage of the SR&ED expenditures made. Since an investment tax credit in respect of SR&ED lowers the cost of the research and development activity, the amount of the investment tax credit reduces the amount of the pool available for deduction in the year following the year of the investment tax credit claim. If there is no balance in the pool in that year, because all amounts were previously deducted and no new expenditures were made in the current year, then the investment tax credit is included in income. A reduction of the balance in the pool reduces the future deduction and has the same effect as the income inclusion. The effect of this adjustment for the investment tax credit is to permit a deduction of the net cost of the expenditure after the partial recovery of cost through the investment tax credit. This effect can be illustrated with the following two options: ITA: 37(1)(*e*) ITA: 127(9) ITA: 12(1)(*v*)

	Fully deducted	*Pooled*
Expenditure in year 1	$ 1,000	$1,000
Deducted in year 1	(1,000)	Nil
Available for future deduction	Nil	$1,000

	Fully deducted	Pooled
ITC @ 35% of $1,000 claimed in year 1:		
Income inclusion in year 2	$ 350	
Reduction of pool in year 2		(350)
Available for future deduction		$ 650
Net deduction:		
Deduction in year 1 net of inclusion in year 2 (i.e., net deduction over 2 years)	$ 650	
Available for future deduction		$ 650
Net cost:		
Initial expenditure	$ 1,000	$1,000
ITC claimed in year 1	(350)	(350)
Tax saving at, say 20%:		
year 1 — $1,000 × .20	(200)	
later years — $1,000 × .20		(200)
Tax cost: year 2 ($350 × .20)	70	70
Net cost	$ 520	$ 520

Only certain expenditures of a current nature made for scientific research and experimental development carried on outside Canada may be deducted and only in the year that they are incurred. They are not pooled. ITA: 37(2)

Expenditures on buildings are excluded from the 100% write-off. This includes the capital cost of a building or rent and lease expense incurred in respect of a building. However, expenditures on structures such as a wind tunnel or an experimental wind or hydro energy prototype are not affected and, hence, are eligible for the 100% write-off. ITA: 37(8)(*d*)

However, capital expenditures incurred in 2014 and subsequent years will be removed from the base of eligible expenditures and will no longer be either deductible or pooled.

Expenditures eligible for the SR&ED deduction must be all or substantially all attributable to the prosecution or to the provision of premises, facilities or equipment for the prosecution of such research and development. The Regulations amplify the definition of expenditures that are directly attributable to the prosecution of and to the provision of premises, facilities and equipment for the prosecution of SR&ED in Canada. ITA: 37(8)(*a*) ITR: 2900(2), 2900(3)

Current expenditures that are "directly attributable" to scientific research also qualify. This allows for the prorating of the direct costs of personnel who, while not solely involved with research, do directly perform scientific research part of the time, support scientific research personnel or directly supervise researchers. In the case of capital expenditures, minor or incidental use of equipment for non-research purposes is possible under the "all or substantially all" requirement.

¶4,325 Election method to determine deduction

An election is available as an alternative method for determining which expenditures incurred in Canada will qualify as SR&ED, to be included in the pool. This alternative method, which must be elected in prescribed form each year, is generally simpler for the taxpayer. If the election is used, the Act specifically lists six types of expenditures which will be considered to be for SR&ED carried on in Canada and, therefore, will be included in the taxpayer's SR&ED pool under subsection 37(1). The alternative method is described in more detail in Chapters 11 and 12. ITA: 37(8)(*a*)(ii)(B)

This elective method for determining SR&ED expenditures does not account for general overhead expenditures, even if they are directly attributable to the prosecution or the provision of premises for the prosecution of SR&ED in Canada. Such overhead expenditures are treated, under the elective method, as ordinary expenses which are, generally, deductible in the year incurred or eligible for capital cost allowance. However, general overhead expenses are recognized in the method of calculating the investment tax credit discussed in Chapter 12.

¶4,400 THE GST/HST IMPACT ON BUSINESS ACTIVITY

¶4,410 Commercial Activity

As noted in Chapter 2, the issue of whether a person is engaged in a commercial activity is central to the determination of whether the person is required to register and collect GST/HST. Commercial activity means any business that is carried on, an adventure or concern in the nature of trade, or the making of a supply of real property. The meaning of the first two phrases is discussed below, while supplies of real property will be reviewed, in part, in Chapters 5 and 6. As discussed in more detail below in ¶4,425, exempt activities and activities without a reasonable expectation of profit, engaged in by individuals, personal trusts, or partnerships consisting solely of individuals, are excluded from the definition. ETA: 123(1)

¶4,415 Carrying on business

To some extent, the concept of carrying on business under the *Income Tax Act* has been adopted for GST/HST purposes. Generally, if an entity is carrying on business for income tax purposes, it is also considered to be carrying on business for GST/HST purposes. However, some entities not considered to be carrying on business for income tax purposes may still be considered to be carrying on business for GST/HST purposes, as the comparable provisions under the ETA are generally broader in scope than those under the *Income Tax Act*.

The term "business" is defined to include a profession, calling, trade, manufacture or undertaking of any kind whatever. However, unlike the definition of carrying on business in the *Income Tax Act*, it is generally not necessary to establish that the business has a reasonable expectation of profit. Therefore, an entity engaged in activities with continuous, repetitious effort is generally considered to be a business for GST/HST purposes, whether the activity or undertaking is engaged in for profit. The definition specifically excludes an office or employment. ETA: 123(1)

Because of the absence of the profit test, a number of organizations established on a not-for-profit basis are considered to be carrying on business for GST/HST purposes and, thus, to be engaged in commercial activities. For example, where a hospital operates a parking lot, this is considered to be a commercial activity and the hospital is required to collect GST/HST on that supply. Therefore, even if an activity is considered ancillary to achieving a not-for-profit purpose for income tax purposes, and, therefore, outside the definition of carrying on business for purposes of the *Income Tax Act*, it is still considered to be a business for purposes of the GST/HST.

Another distinction from the *Income Tax Act* is the inclusion of leasing activities in the definition of business. Any activity that is engaged in on a regular and continuous basis that involves the supply of property by way of lease, licence or similar arrangement, is considered to be a business. Thus, rents received from the rental of an automobile, for example, are regarded as being earned from a business for GST/HST purposes, regardless of the effort required by the owner of the automobile to earn the rental income. This can be contrasted with the treatment under the *Income Tax Act*, where the activity may not be considered to be a business, but rather, may be regarded as income from property. This distinction for income tax purposes will be discussed in Chapter 6. ETA: 123(1)

¶4,420 Adventure or concern in the nature of trade

As noted earlier in this chapter, the definition of business for income tax purposes includes an adventure or concern in the nature of trade. In contrast, this latter phrase is referred to separately in the definition of commercial activity under the ETA. In any event, as the phrase is not defined in the ETA, its meaning under the *Income Tax Act* should offer some insight into its meaning for GST/HST purposes. In this regard, the *Taylor* case referred to earlier in this chapter should be reviewed.

¶4,425 Exclusions from the definition of commercial activity

There are two key activities which are specifically excluded from the definition of commercial activity. As a result, supplies made in the course of these activities will not be considered to be taxable supplies. The supplier of these goods and services is not required to collect GST/HST on these supplies and, in turn, is not entitled to claim input tax credits. They include: ETA: 123(1)

- that part of a business or adventure or concern in the nature of trade that involves the making of an exempt supply; or
- a business engaged in by an individual, a personal trust, or a partnership consisting solely of individuals without a reasonable expectation of profit.

Exempt supplies include, for example, health care services, educational services, and legal aid services. While the making of exempt supplies is excluded from the definition of a commercial activity, the making of zero-rated supplies is not excluded. Thus, any person who sells zero-rated groceries or exports goods in the course of a business or an adventure or concern in the nature of trade, is considered to be engaged in a commercial activity and is entitled to claim input tax credits in respect of GST/HST paid on purchases. Zero-rated supplies are set out in another schedule of the ETA. If a supply is not considered to be made in the course of a commercial activity because it falls within one of these exclusions, or if the supply is not made in the course of a business or an adventure or concern in the nature of trade or is not a supply of real property, the supply will not be a taxable supply and no GST/HST will apply. Although no input tax credit may be claimed for GST/HST paid in respect of these supplies, this GST/HST is deductible for income tax purposes. ETA: Schedule V; ETA: Schedule VI

¶4,430 Value for tax

GST/HST is imposed on the value of consideration for a supply. Consideration is the price paid for property or services and is, generally, expressed in monetary terms. ETA: 165(1)

Goods or services are often sold on terms that allow for a discount for prompt payment, or for a penalty in the case of a late payment. The value on which GST/HST is imposed is not affected by the discount or penalty. In either case, GST/HST applies to the amount of consideration shown on the invoice (i.e., the full sale price). If, however, the invoice is for an amount that is net of a cash discount, GST/HST applies on the net amount. ETA: 161

¶4,435 When GST/HST is payable

GST/HST is generally payable by a recipient of a taxable supply at the time the consideration for the supply is paid to the supplier or the time the consideration becomes due, whichever is earlier. Where partial payments are made in respect of a supply, GST/HST must be paid on each payment. GST/HST generally becomes due when it is invoiced. Specifically, the consideration becomes due on the earliest of: ETA: 152(1), 168(1), 168(2)

(a) the day on which the invoice for the amount is issued;

(b) the date on the invoice;

(c) the day on which the invoice would have been issued, if not for an undue delay; and

(d) the day on which the amount becomes due under an agreement in writing.

Where property is supplied by way of lease, licence, or similar agreement, the consideration is deemed to become due on the day the recipient is required to pay the consideration under the agreement. ETA: 152(2)

Notwithstanding the general rule, a number of special cases are dealt with in other subsections. For example, where the supply involves goods, liability occurs on the earlier of the date determined under the general rule and the end of the month following the month in which ownership or possession of the goods is transferred to the purchaser. In the case of a deposit, GST/HST is not payable on the deposit until the time the supplier applies the deposit against the consideration for the supply. ETA: 168(1), 168(3), 168(9)

¶4,440 Automobile operating cost benefits paid by employer

Recall from Chapter 3 that an employer provides a taxable benefit when the employee's operating costs for an employer-provided automobile are paid by the employer. The value of the benefit is determined by one of two methods. The employee may use a per kilometre method or elect to value the benefit as 50% of the standby charge in respect of the employer-provided car. Likewise, where the employee uses his or her own car but the operating costs are paid by the employer, an operating cost benefit is required to be determined under the *Income Tax Act*. In either case, the registrant employer is required to remit GST equal to a prescribed percentage of 3%[34] of the benefit, however computed. The prescribed percentage is less than 5% to recognize that the benefit includes exempt supplies such as insurance and licence fees. ITA: 6(1)(*k*), 6(1)(*l*); ETA: l. 173(1)(*d*)(vi)(A)

¶4,450 Input Tax Credits

¶4,455 General rules

Input tax credits are available to registrants for GST/HST paid on goods and services that are purchased for use in a commercial activity. For persons other than financial institutions, the general rule is that if the use of the input is exclusively in a "commercial activity", which is defined in the ETA to mean "all or substantially all" (and which is interpreted to mean 90% or more), a full credit may be claimed. Conversely, if a business input will not be used at all in respect of a commercial activity, no credit will be allowed. Under this latter rule, if the extent of use in a commercial activity is less than 10%, no credit may be claimed. For example, if an input is to be used 90% or more in the course of making an exempt supply, no credit may be claimed. It is important to note that the test for eligibility is the intended use of the input at the time of purchase. Apart from the change-of-use rules for capital real property discussed in Chapter 8, a registrant is not required to adjust the input tax credit for subsequent changes of use. Registrants are entitled to claim the credit in the reporting period in which the GST/HST is paid or, if earlier, when it becomes payable. ETA: 169(1) ETA: 123(1)

There are circumstances where a purchase will be used in respect of a combination of taxable and exempt supplies. In these cases, except for certain capital goods which are discussed in Chapter 5, registrants are required to apportion the input tax credit between the taxable and exempt activity. For example, if use in a commercial activity represents 70% of the total use, a credit equal to 70% of the GST/HST paid or payable may be claimed. ETA: 169(1)

For apportionment purposes, inputs acquired for use in a business or other activity (referred to as an "endeavour" in the *Excise Tax Act*) are considered to be for use in commercial activities and thus to qualify for input tax credits only to the extent that they are for use in making taxable supplies (including zero-rated supplies) for consideration (which in this context does not include nominal consideration). On the other hand, to the extent inputs are for use in making exempt supplies for consideration, they are treated as being for use in non-commercial activities (and thus not eligible for input tax credits). Inputs that are not for use in making supplies of any kind are also regarded as being for use in non-commercial activities. ETA: 141.01

[34] The prescribed percentage varies where HST applies.

The legislation does not prescribe allocation methods to be used in apportioning input tax credits. Provided the allocation basis is fair and reasonable and is used on a consistent basis throughout the fiscal year, the allocation will likely not be challenged by the CRA. The documentation requirements that are necessary to support input tax credit claims are discussed in Chapter 14.

The general rules discussed above do not apply to capital property, which for GST/HST purposes is divided into capital personal property and capital real property. As discussed in greater detail in Chapter 5, when determining the amount of an input tax credit for capital personal property, the "primary use" test generally applies. While this term is not defined in the Act, it is generally interpreted by the CRA to mean more than 50%. Therefore, if more than 50% of the use of the property is intended for use in a commercial activity, a full input tax credit is available, while no credit may be claimed if this test is not satisfied. A full credit may also be claimed where property acquired for use primarily in non-commercial activities begins to be used primarily in commercial activities. Where a full input tax credit has been claimed and commercial use declines to 50% or less, the input tax credit must be repaid. Special rules apply to capital personal property that is a passenger vehicle or aircraft, as discussed at ¶4,460.60.

Special rules also apply to capital real property, as discussed in greater detail in Chapter 8. Proportional input tax credits are available for purchases of capital real property, even where the property is not used primarily in a commercial activity. However, input tax credits are not available if the property is acquired primarily for the personal use and enjoyment of the registrant. Change-of-use rules apply where there is a significant shift in the proportion of non-commercial and commercial usage.

¶4,460 Restrictions

Certain purchases made by a registrant have a personal consumption element or are for goods and services that are available to employees. As a result, there are certain circumstances where input tax credits are not allowed, in full or in part. In many circumstances, the GST/HST restrictions parallel the restrictions contained in the *Income Tax Act* in respect of business deductions.[35] The more significant restrictions include:

¶4,460.10 *Club memberships*

Input tax credits are not allowed in respect of membership fees or dues in any club whose main purpose is to provide dining, recreational or sporting facilities. Common examples of these clubs include business persons' clubs, golf clubs and fitness clubs. However, if meal and entertainment expenses are incurred at the club in respect of a commercial activity, input tax credits are allowed, subject to the recapture rule discussed below. ETA: 170(1)(*a*)

¶4,460.20 *Home office expenses*

Input tax credits are not allowed in respect of expenses incurred by an individual in respect of a home office where the office is neither the individual's principal place of business nor a place that is both used exclusively for the purpose of earning income from a business and used on a regular and continuous basis for meeting clients, customers or patients. This provision is consistent with the *Income Tax Act*, which denies a deduction in such circumstances. ETA: 170(1)(*a.1*) ITA: 18(12)

¶4,460.30 *Personal or living expenses*

No input tax credit is allowed where a property or service is purchased exclusively for the personal consumption, use or enjoyment of an officer, employee or related individual. ETA: 170(1)(*b*), 170(1)(*c*)

[35] Note that, in addition to these restrictions, the provinces of Prince Edward Island and Ontario have both implemented temporary input tax credit restrictions for large businesses similar to those that apply under the QST regime in Quebec; these temporary restrictions are discussed in Chapter 1.

As discussed at ¶1,400, British Columbia exited the HST on April 1, 2013, and GST at the rate of 5% applies where tax is paid or payable after March 31, 2013. The temporary input tax credit restrictions that were implemented in that province apply only where the provincial component of the HST was paid.

This restriction was referred to in Chapter 3, in the context of employee benefits. An exception to this rule is provided where a registrant acquires property or service exclusively for an employee's personal use; but the input tax credit will be disallowed, unless the property is re-supplied for fair market value consideration to the employee in the reporting period. In these circumstances, as GST/HST will be collected on the resale, an input tax credit is allowed. An additional exception where an input tax credit is allowed is where the property or service would not be a taxable benefit for purposes of the *Income Tax Act*.

For leases in respect of property rented to individuals, no input tax credit is allowed where the property is primarily for personal consumption, use or enjoyment. However, similar to the rule discussed above, an input tax credit is allowed where the property is supplied to the individual and GST/HST is collected on the fair rental value.

¶4,460.40 *Reasonableness*

Another concept is borrowed from the *Income Tax Act*, namely, that of reasonableness. ETA: 170(2)
In claiming an input tax credit, the nature or cost of the property or services purchased by the registrant must be reasonable in the circumstances, having regard to the nature of the commercial activities of the registrant. In addition, the amount of the input tax credit must be calculated on consideration that is reasonable in the circumstances.

¶4,460.50 *Automobile allowances*

Where an employer has paid an automobile allowance to an employee for travel in ETA: 174
respect of the employer's business and the employee is not required to include the allowance in income because the allowance is a reasonable one, the employer is permitted to claim an ITC on that amount.

¶4,460.60 *Passenger vehicles and aircraft*

Although passenger vehicles and aircraft used in a registrant's commercial activities are considered to be capital personal property, special rules apply for ITC purposes. Passenger vehicles and aircraft owned by registrants other than individuals and partnerships are subject to one set of rules, while more detailed rules apply to passenger vehicles or aircraft for use in commercial activities of a registrant who is an individual or a partnership. These are discussed in Chapter 5.

¶4,470 Adjustments to Net Tax

The legislation sets out a series of adjustments in computing the net tax to be remitted by a registrant for a particular period. The most common of these adjustments are discussed below.

¶4,475 Excess charges

Where a supplier has charged an amount of GST/HST in excess of what is collectible ETA: 232(1), 232(3)
under the legislation, the supplier may adjust the amount of GST/HST charged if it has not already been collected. If the excess has already been collected, it may be refunded or credited to the customer, provided a credit note is issued to the customer (or a debit note is issued by the recipient of the supply). The supplier is permitted to deduct the excess amount refunded or credited in determining his or her net tax for the reporting period in which the credit or debit note is issued. Conversely, the recipient, if a registrant, is required to add that amount to his or her net tax for that period, or a preceding period, to the extent it was deducted in determining his or her net tax. The refund or credit must be made within two years after the day the GST/HST was charged or collected.

¶4,480 Price reductions

Where a registrant reduces the price in respect of a supply for which GST/HST has been ETA: 232(2), 232(3)
charged but not collected, the registrant may adjust the amount of GST/HST charged. If the

GST/HST has already been collected, a refund or credit may be given to the customer, provided a credit note (or debit note) is issued, as described above. The refund or credit must be made within four years of the time the price was reduced.

This rule does not apply where the rules which are discussed earlier in this chapter apply, in respect of cash discounts for prompt payment. The adjustments outlined above may not be made for cash discounts. Registrants are required to collect GST/HST on the full invoice price, regardless of whether a cash discount is subsequently granted for prompt payment. Similarly, registrants who purchase goods that are subject to a cash discount for prompt payment are entitled to claim an input tax credit based on the full invoice price. ETA: 161, 232(4)

¶4,485 Bad debts

Relief is provided for bad debts. Where GST/HST is remitted but not collected on a debt that is subsequently written off, a registrant is permitted to deduct an amount equal to the tax payable in respect of the supply multiplied by the ratio of the total amount equal to $^5/_{105}$ (or the appropriate factor, depending on the applicable rate of HST in the province) of the bad debt written off to the total amount payable for the supply. To be eligible for this relief, the bad debt must be in respect of a supply made to an arm's length party, and the relief must be claimed in the reporting period in which the debt is written off or within four years after the due date of the return for that period. If a bad debt is subsequently recovered after the deduction is made, the ETA requires that the registrant add back to net tax an amount equal to the amount of the bad debt recovered multiplied by the ratio of the tax payable in respect of the supply to the total amount paid or payable on the supply (including GST/HST and/or applicable provincial taxes). ETA: 231(1), 231(3)

¶4,490 Lease of passenger vehicles

Where a registrant leases a passenger vehicle, to the extent the lease costs exceed the maximum amount deductible under section 67.3 of the *Income Tax Act*, a portion of the input tax credit will be recaptured. This restriction parallels the restriction that limits the maximum input tax credit that can be claimed in respect of the purchase of a passenger vehicle, which is discussed in Chapter 5. The recapture is provided by way of an adjustment to the net tax determination for the appropriate reporting period. For annual filers, the appropriate reporting period is the taxation year. For quarterly and monthly filers, it is the reporting period that begins immediately after the taxation year. ETA: 235(1), 235(2)

¶4,495 Food, beverages, and entertainment expenses

Section 236 of the ETA contains the rules for food, beverages and entertainment expenses that are subject to section 67.1 of the *Income Tax Act*. Input tax credits for GST/HST paid expenses are allowed in full in the reporting period in which they are incurred. However, at the end of the registrant's fiscal year, there will be a recapture of 50% of the total input tax credits in respect of these expenses. The amount recaptured will be included in the registrant's GST return for the first reporting period in the next fiscal year. ETA: 236(1.1)

As noted in Chapter 1, the provinces of British Columbia and Ontario both implemented temporary input tax credit restrictions for large businesses in respect of acquisitions of specified property and services when they harmonized effective July 1, 2010. These temporary restrictions, which were to be phased out over the initial eight-year period of HST in these two provinces, apply to (among other things) the provincial component of the HST in respect of food, beverages, and entertainment that are subject to the 50% input tax credit recapture under the *Excise Tax Act* (i.e., that are subject to section 67.1 of the *Income Tax Act*). As discussed at ¶1,400, British Columbia exited the HST on April 1, 2013, and GST at the rate of 5% applies where tax is paid or payable after March 31, 2013. The temporary input tax credit restrictions in British Columbia apply only where the provincial component of the HST was paid. When Prince Edward Island adopted the HST effective April 1, 2013, it also implemented these temporary input tax credit restrictions for large businesses, which will be phased out over the initial eight-year period of HST in the province.

¶4,500 Application of the Rules

Example Problem 4-8

Reconsider the facts of Example Problem 4-6 in ¶4,256, which involves Corporate Welfare Limited.

— *REQUIRED*

Outline the proper GST/HST treatment by the corporation of the items presented.

— *SOLUTION*

(1) General

Since the corporation is carrying on business, it is engaged in a commercial activity. Therefore, the corporation is required to register and collect GST/HST on its supplies, i.e., sales of goods or services, which are "taxable supplies." As a registrant, the corporation is entitled to a full input tax credit (ITC) in respect of GST/HST paid or payable on goods and services that it purchases exclusively for use in its commercial activity. If GST/HST collected or collectible on its sales exceeds its ITCs, the corporation must remit the difference. On the other hand, if ITCs exceed GST/HST collected or collectible, a refund of the excess is available. ETA: 123(1), 169(1)

(2) Items Listed

(a) The appraisal expenses incurred for insurance appraisal purposes are for the provision of an exempt supply of a financial service which does not give rise to an ITC since no GST/HST was payable. ETA: Schedule V, Part VII

(b) Employer contributions to a registered pension plan involve a payment for an exempt supply on which GST/HST is not charged. As a result, no ITC is available. ETA: 123(1)

(c) Landscaping costs involve a payment for taxable supplies of goods or services resulting in the availability of an ITC.

(d) Payments for legal services give rise to an ITC since the services are taxable supplies.

(e) Dividends received involve an exempt supply of a financial service on which no GST/HST is collected. ETA: Schedule V, Part VII

(f) The payment of interest is a financial service which is an exempt supply.

(g) The purchase of inventory involves a taxable supply on which GST/HST is paid. Hence, an ITC is available.

(h) No GST/HST is charged on a donation which involves a transfer of money. As a result, no ITC is available. ETA: 123(1), 164

(i) Insurance premiums are for an exempt supply of a financial service and no ITC is available since no GST/HST was paid.

(j) The payment of a dividend is an exempt supply of a financial service. No ITC is available.

(k) A loan is a financial instrument which is an exempt supply, on which no GST/HST is charged. Hence, the write-off of this bad debt has no GST/HST effect.

(l) Improvements that are not normal repairs or maintenance are considered to be capital outlays. However, as will be discussed in Chapter 5, there is no amortization of the GST/HST paid on capital outlays. The GST/HST paid provides an ITC at the time of payment.

(m) Amounts paid to employees as remuneration are not supplies, since these amounts are excluded from the definition of services. As a result, remuneration is not subject to GST/HST. ETA: 123(1)

(n) Interest paid involves an exempt supply of a financial service.

(o) Initially, an ITC is available on the full amount of GST/HST paid in respect of meals and entertainment. However, 50% of the ITC in respect of such expenditures is recaptured in the first reporting period of the next fiscal year. As well, temporary input tax credit restrictions may apply in Ontario and Prince Edward Island. ETA: 236

(p) Embezzlement losses involve a transfer of money for which there are no GST/HST implications.

(q) Bonuses are employment remuneration excluded from the definition of service and, hence, are not subject to GST/HST.

(r) Property tax involves an exempt supply on which no GST/HST is charged.

(s) A lease cancellation fee paid by a lessor is subject to GST/HST. The payer is deemed to have paid GST/HST equal to 5/105 (or the appropriate factor, depending on the applicable rate of HST in the province) of the payment and, hence, an ITC is available.

(t) The payer of damages is deemed to have paid or the recipient deemed to have received GST/HST equal to 5/105 (or the appropriate factor, depending on the applicable rate of HST in the province) of the damages. As a result, the corporation is entitled to an ITC. ETA: 182

(u) Construction and repair costs involve a payment for taxable supplies for goods or services resulting in the availability of an ITC.

¶4,800 REVIEW QUESTIONS

(1) Mr. Fritz is a commissioned real estate client of yours. He has just bought and sold a piece of land in a "quick flip" transaction. What kind of income might this be to him: employment, business, property or capital gain?

(2) Does the Act require that the "profit" from a business be calculated in accordance with generally accepted accounting principles?

(3) Opco Ltd. is in the business of manufacturing equipment under contract for other manufacturers. One of its customers failed to live up to its contract and would not take delivery of or pay for its order. Opco took the customer to court and was awarded the amount of $100,000 as damages. Can this amount be treated as a non-taxable capital receipt by Opco?

(4) Aco Ltd. and Xco Ltd. entered into an agreement to manufacture a new product for the next 20 years. This represented 80% of Aco's business. After five years it was decided that the two parties could not work together so Xco paid Aco $500,000 to terminate the agreement. Is the receipt of this amount by Aco considered to be business income?

(5) Donald Corleone owns an illegal gambling house. He has made significant "profits" on this activity, but has not reported the income since he believes it is not taxable. Is he correct?

(6) Opco Ltd. took advantage of a program offered by the government and hired two employees whose wages were partially offset by a government subsidy. The owner felt that since he was really just getting some of his tax dollars back through this subsidy, the amount received would not be taxable. What do you think?

(7) As long as an expenditure was made for the purpose of earning income from a business or property then it is deductible. Is this statement true? Comment. ITA: 18

(8) One of your clients is having some short-term cash flow problems and cannot pay his year-end tax liability. He decides that he will defer his payment to the Receiver General instead of trying to get another short-term bank loan. He reasons that in either case the interest will be deductible. Comment.

(9) Subsection 18(1) lists those items that are prohibited from being deducted because of the nature of the expenditure. If an expense passes those tests, will it be deductible?

(10) A client had to replace the roof on its factory at a cost of $100,000. The client deducted the cost of the roof on the basis that it was simply replacing the previous roof with a new one of the same quality. Is the cost deductible?

(11) Is the portion of the airline ticket that represents the meal subject to the 50% limitation on meal expenses?

(12) Will a company that offers a warranty with its product be able to deduct a reserve? ITA: 20(1)(*m.1*)

(13) Under certain circumstances, can capital expenditures be written off in the year?

¶4,825 MULTIPLE CHOICE QUESTIONS

Question 1

Which one of the following items is NOT deductible in computing the income of a corporation under Division B of the Act?

(A) Amounts paid for landscaping business premises.

(B) Interest on money borrowed to finance the purchase of a factory for use in its business.

(C) The premium on a $100,000 term life insurance policy on an employee if the beneficiary of the policy is the employee's family.

(D) Interest and penalties on late income tax payments.

Question 2

Which one of the following amounts is DEDUCTIBLE in computing the income of a corporation under Division B of the Act?

(A) $11,000 of accrued legal fees for a pending law suit. The accrual is an estimate because no work has been done to date by the lawyers.

(B) $4,000 of donations to registered charities made for no business reason.

(C) $15,000 spent on three social events in the taxation year for all employees at a particular location.

(D) $1,500 for golf club membership dues for employees.

Question 3

Which one of the following amounts is DEDUCTIBLE in computing income of a corporation under Division B of the Act?

(A) $5,000 of donations to federal political parties.

(B) $44,000 in accrued bonuses unpaid 7 months after year-end. The amounts were legal liabilities at year-end.

(C) A $10,000 increase in the financial accounting reserve for warranty expenses.

(D) The $2,000 cost of tickets for meals and entertainment at a gala fund-raising event for a registered charity.

Question 4

XYZ Ltd.'s current financial statement shows a deduction for $20,000 of legal and accounting expenses. This amount consists of the following items:

- $5,000 of legal expenses related to the purchase of an investment in shares;
- $5,000 of legal expenses incurred to dispute a tax assessment;
- $5,000 of legal expenses related to the issuance of debt; and
- $5,000 of accounting fees related to the preparation of a prospectus regarding the issuance of shares.

What amount is deductible under Division B of the Act?

(A) $7,000

(B) $8,000

(C) $15,000

(D) $5,000

Question 5

Ten years ago, Sam, a real estate agent, purchased a piece of land for $50,000. His intention at that time was to build a rental building on the land and use it to earn rental income, which he did four years ago. In the current year, he sold the land and building for $100,000 and $80,000 respectively after receiving an unsolicited offer.

Based on the facts, which one of the following statements is true?

(A) The CRA may argue that the gain on the sale of the land is a capital gain, because Sam is a real estate agent.

(B) The CRA may argue that the gain on the sale of the land is business income, because of the 10-year holding period of the land.

(C) The CRA may argue that the gain on the sale of the land is business income because of the unsolicited offer for sale.

(D) The gain on the sale of the land will likely be treated as a capital gain for income tax purposes.

Question 6

Which of the following amounts is DEDUCTIBLE in computing the income of a corporation under Division B of the Act?

(A) $13,000 of legal fees to defend a lawsuit brought by a customer.

(B) Accounting loss on the sale of a capital property.

(C) The principal amount of a mortgage on a company's warehouse.

(D) The personal and living expenses of the shareholder who works very hard in the business and is not paid a salary.

¶4,850 EXERCISES

Exercise 1

ITA: 9, 11, 18, 20

Each of the following employee perks were provided to a senior executive of IPL Engineering Services:

Value of university tuition fees for the employee's child (age 21)	$ 2,800
Out-of-town meals for a three-day management seminar	150
Entertainment meals for clients (reimbursement)	1,500
Professional dues to Civil Engineering Society	250
Notebook computer provided for employment use	3,500
Membership to Centre Health Club (client promotion)	1,400
Interest-free loan for the purchase of company stock	40,000
Premiums paid for group term life insurance	150
Reimbursement for engineering systems software	2,000

Assumptions:

(a) Prescribed rate of interest throughout the year is 6%.

(b) The senior executive takes the notebook computer home to complete IPL assignments and memos. Personal use is minimal.

— *REQUIRED*

For each of the above, *discuss and quantify* the income tax implications to the employer and to the employee.

Exercise 2

ITA: 9; IT-218R

The taxpayer corporation, Singh Enterprises Ltd., purchased a property consisting of some eight separate residential apartment buildings. When purchased, the property was ready for profit-producing operation and immediate arrangements were made for such operations.

The principal shareholder of the corporation, Sam Singh, was an individual with a long history of trading in real estate in many different countries. He fully expected that the property would increase in value in the future.

About 11 months after the purchase of the property, circumstances dictated a change in the investments of the corporation and the property was sold for a substantial profit.

— *REQUIRED*

Determine whether the profit realized by the sale of the property was income from a business or a capital gain.

Exercise 3

ITA: 9, 11, 18, 20

Samuel, an employee of the Fish Company, needs a vehicle to complete his employment duties. Samuel generally drives approximately 10,000 kilometres for personal reasons. His manager estimates that Samuel will need to drive 7,000 kilometres to complete employment duties. Samuel estimates that his total operating expenses will be $2,500. The corporation offered Samuel three alternatives:

(a) Twelve months use of a leased vehicle plus a reimbursement for 100% of the total operating expense. The leased vehicle costs the corporation $400 per month (including HST).

(b) The same vehicle can be purchased for a total cost (including 13% HST) of $22,000 and Samuel would be reimbursed for the total operating expense.

(c) Samuel provides his own vehicle and is reimbursed 54 cents for each of the first 5,000 kilometres and 48 cents for the balance of employment kilometres.

— REQUIRED

Assess the tax impacts for each alternative for both the employee and the employer for the current tax year.

Exercise 4

ITA: 9

Cars Limited had a franchise for the distribution in Saskatchewan of Belchfire automobiles made in Argentina. The business had grown rapidly in its 10 years of existence. However, soon after the expansion of its facilities, Argentina Motor Industries terminated the distribution agreement and voluntarily agreed to pay Cars Limited $225,000.

— REQUIRED

What are the tax implications to Cars Limited?

Exercise 5

Alta Management Corporation purchased three parcels of land in July of this year at an estate auction. Immediately after, the purchase plans were in place for the development of the properties into community shopping plazas. As a result of an unsolicited offer, two parcels of land were resold for an immediate and substantial gain. The third parcel of land sat vacant for three months while the corporation waited for the development and building permits from City Hall. The city would not approve the project because of several complaints from local residents. Consequently, the property was listed for sale with a realtor, Charles Roonie. Charles is also the major shareholder of Alta Management Corporation. The sale took place, with a substantial profit, six months after the purchase of the land.

Presently, the corporation holds two other pieces of undeveloped land, which it intends to develop if the economy improves. It also manages several apartment blocks and one shopping centre. The corporation often sells property when it becomes unfeasible to develop. For this reason the company always ensures that any real estate purchased has good resale value.

— REQUIRED

What type of income was earned from the disposition of each real estate property? Provide reasons for your answer, and consider all factors that the courts may consider in substantiating the intent of the taxpayer.

Exercise 6

ITA: 10

Holey Mufflers Limited operates a fast-service repair shop. At the end of its fiscal year its inventory records showed the following:

Item	*Number*	*Actual cost*	*FIFO cost*	*Replacement cost*	*Net realization value*
Mufflers	64	$17.50	$16.25	$18.40	$15.50
Tailpipes	157	4.75	4.25	5.00	4.50
Exhaust systems	39	16.25	16.30	17.00	15.50
Shock absorbers	256	19.45	18.85	20.50	19.75
Brackets	932	1.40	1.35	1.50	1.30
Clamps	1,746	.65	.70	.75	.80

— REQUIRED

What values could be used for the total inventory for tax purposes? (Assume that the method of valuing inventory could change with permission.) ITA: 10(2.1)

Exercise 7

ITA: 18(1)(*a*), 18(1)(*b*), 18(1)(*c*), 18(1)(*e*), 18(1)(*h*), 67, 248(1)

The Act restricts the deduction of certain expenses incurred. In general, the following limitations determine the deductibility of expenses from a business:

(a) Income earning purpose test

(b) Capital test

(c) Exempt income test

(d) Reserve test

(e) Personal expense test

(f) Reasonableness test

— *REQUIRED*

Cite the appropriate references for the above tests in specific provisions of the Act, including up to three related sections, ITs (primary), or ICs from the footnotes to those provisions in the Act.

Exercise 8

ITA: 18(1)(*l*)

Advice Limited, a consulting firm in Calgary, owns a small lodge in the Banff area. The lodge is used throughout the year for the purposes of entertaining clients.

— *REQUIRED*

(A) Comment on the deductibility of maintenance costs in respect of the lodge.

(B) Reconsider the deductibility of these costs if the property is rented during the week to the public and used to entertain clients only on the weekends.

Exercise 9

ITA: 18(12)

Amina and Karim are married and work together as self-employed management consultants. They both work full-time on various projects in a 500-square-foot office located in their home. The total square footage of their home (bedrooms, kitchen, living room, and dining room) is 2,000 square feet. Amina teaches one evening course at the university each week. She earned $70,000 in consulting income and Karim earned $65,000. Other expenses, as listed below, were also incurred:

Expenses:	
Supplies and materials	$ 1,800
Computer and software lease	2,300
Total	$ 4,100
Total home overhead costs incurred during the year:	
Mortgage interest	$16,000
Utilities, water, and electricity	2,400
Property taxes	2,200
House cleaning	2,400
Home insurance	600
Total	$23,600

— *REQUIRED*

Advise Amina and Karim on the deductibility of their home office expenses.

Exercise 10

ITA: 17, 20(1)

Mr. M. Black is the controller with responsibility for tax compliance of International Widget Manufacturing Limited based in Calgary. He has called to ask your advice, as the company's accountant, on various matters pertaining to the company's 2013 tax return. He has asked you the following questions.

(A) On March 1, 2014, the company paid $234,000 for the benefit of 30 employees to a defined benefit registered pension plan. Of the $234,000 paid, $129,000 represents an adjustment required as a result of an actuarial valuation; the remainder was based on a current service contribution equal to 6% of each employee's wages for 2013. What is the total amount that can be deducted for tax purposes in 2013?

(B) The company paid $15,000 representation costs to obtain a special licence from the State of Montana to sell its widgets in the state. This amount was written off in the financial accounts but added back and amortized over a 20-year period in calculating income for tax purposes. How should this item be treated?

(C) The amount of $1,500 spent to connect gas lines on conversion from oil to gas in the Toronto plant was added to the cost of the building for financial accounting purposes and depreciated with the building. How should the amount be treated for tax purposes?

(D) The president's wife is employed full-time as his secretary and paid $7,000 per month. Is this amount deductible and if not, how much is deductible?

— *REQUIRED*

Provide brief answers to the questions posed by the controller.

Exercise 11

ITA: 20(1)(*f*)

In August 2008, Steel Blind Manufacturing Co. Ltd., a venetian blind manufacturer, issued a series of bonds at $891.90 per $1,000 par value. The issue matured in August 2013 and was redeemed at that time at par value. It bears a coupon rate of 9% to yield 12% to maturity.

— *REQUIRED*

How much of the bond discount can be deducted and in what year can it be deducted?

Exercise 12

ITA: 9–12, 18–20

The following information concerning the financial statements of Incredible Incubators Incorporated for its fiscal year ended September 30, 2013 has been presented to you in order to prepare tax returns.

(a) Net income after tax per financial statements	$150,000
(b) Provision for income taxes — current	25,000
— future	130,000
(c) Amortization expense	40,000
(d) Inventory — on LIFO* basis: opening	125,000
closing	145,000
— on FIFO basis: opening	140,000
closing	155,000
(e) Interest on income taxes paid after due date	2,500
(f) Bond interest expense (including annual discount amortization of $7,500 re bonds issued this year)	39,500
(g) Landscaping costs re factory premises — debited to land account	12,000

* LIFO is used by the company for financial statement purposes, even though it is not in accordance with GAAP.

— *REQUIRED*

Using the foregoing information, compute income for tax purposes for Incredible Incubators for their fiscal year ended September 30, 2013. [Ignore capital cost allowance in respect of depreciable capital property.]

Exercise 13

ITA: 9, 12(1)(*e*)(ii), 20(1)(*n*), 20(8)(*b*)

Quickturn Land Limited bought for cash 25 acres of land at a cost of $107,500 during the year. About two months later the land was sold to a developer for $250,000 consisting of a $110,000 down payment in cash and a note without interest due in one year for the balance. A real estate commission of $12,500 was paid. The company often engages in this type of transaction.

— *REQUIRED*

Compute the minimum net income for the company in the year of sale and the next year in respect of this transaction.

Exercise 14

ITA: 22

Mr. Flint has arranged to sell substantially all of the assets of his proprietorship business, including accounts receivable valued at $36,000, to Mr. Small who will continue the proprietorship business. At the end of last year, Mr. Flint had deducted a reserve for doubtful debts of $6,500. The face value of the accounts being sold is $45,000.

— *REQUIRED*

What are the tax implications to both Mr. Flint and Mr. Small of using section 22 on the sale of accounts receivable?

Exercise 15

ETA: 123(1), 169(1), Schedule V, Part VII

Reconsider the facts of Exercise 12.

— *REQUIRED*

Outline the proper HST treatment by the corporation of the items presented.

¶4,875 ASSIGNMENT PROBLEMS

Problem 1

ITA: 9; IT-218R

A piece of land was purchased by Yacov Corporation Ltd. for the purpose of constructing a high-rise residential building. Plans were made for the development of the property, surveys were made and the land was stripped and excavated in preparation for construction. Subsequent to this work on the land, it was determined that the location was not suitable for the intended purpose, due to heavy truck traffic in the area. As a result, the property was listed for sale with the realtor who acted in the original purchase. The sale at a substantial profit took place approximately six months from the purchase.

The corporation had been newly formed when the above land was purchased. At about the same time, another piece of land was purchased and was developed into a commercial/industrial plaza which the corporation continues to own as a rental property. The principal shareholder of the corporation, Jake Yacov, owns and operates an electrical contracting business.

The Articles of Incorporation of the corporation contain the following statement of objects:

> . . . to purchase, lease, acquire, hold, manage, develop, operate, pledge and mortgage, either absolutely as owner or by way of collateral security or otherwise, alone or jointly with others and either as principal or agent, property, real or personal, and assets generally of any and every kind of description.

No mention is made of the purchase and sale of land as a business activity.

— REQUIRED

Write a memo for the Yacov Corporation Ltd.'s file evaluating the issue of whether the sale of the land should be treated as a receipt of income or capital gain for tax purposes. Arrive at a conclusion consistent with your analysis of the facts, but indicate the basis for any areas of potential opposition to your conclusion.

Problem 2

ITA: 6(1)(*a*)

The following are independent situations.

(a) Dan, a construction contractor, entered into a verbal agreement with his friend, Mike, last year. Dan agreed to oversee a small renovation to Mike's house in exchange for Mike's painting services.

(b) Yoko's company won a $100,000 lawsuit against a competitor for patent infringement.

(c) Isaac Corporation, a local observatory, hired Cornell for the summer. For each hour that Cornell worked, Isaac received $5 an hour from the government as part of a student employment grant. Cornell's total compensation is $10 per hour.

(d) Jessy works part-time as the residential manager in an apartment block. In exchange for the management and cleaning services she offers, she receives free rent in a two bedroom apartment. Jessy uses her own supplies and equipment. One bedroom is used as an office for carrying out her duties and meeting existing and potential tenants.

— REQUIRED

Comment on the income tax consequences for each situation.

Problem 3

ITA: 18(1)(*a*), 18(1)(*h*), 248(1)

The taxpayer, in 1959, purchased 200 acres of property in the Calabogie area of Lanark, as a holiday property for himself and his family. In 1961 it became their principal residence. He worked in Ottawa, both at that time and in the subsequent years; initially he commuted between the Lanark property and his Ottawa job on a daily basis. In the early 1970s he began living in Ottawa during the week and commuting home to the property only on weekends. When the property was first purchased, there was an old brick house on it which was not suitable as a residence for the family. A new house (referred to in the evidence as the D.V.A. house) was built; the family moved into it. It is clear that the family's lifestyle was such as to enjoy the rural location.

In 1974 the taxpayer decided to turn part of the property into a campground; 8 serviced campsites and approximately 12 unserviced sites were created for this purpose. There was as well room for at least 10 other unserviced campsites more or less immediately available and potential for expansion to a much larger number (e.g., 100). Outhouses were built; a trout pond constructed; and the requisite service roads installed. The tax treatment of the expenses incurred with respect to this construction is not part of the dispute in this case.

After these initiatives had been taken, sometime towards the end of 1975 or the beginning of 1976, the taxpayer sought the advice of a consultant with the Ontario Ministry of Tourism, a Mr. Bingham. The advice sought was with respect to the possibility of developing the campground and obtaining a business loan for this purpose. The taxpayer had applied in early 1975 for a loan and was turned down in September of that year.

The taxpayer's consultations with Mr. Bingham in the later half of 1975 and beginning of 1976 led to suggestions for the development of the campsite through the construction of additional facilities: additional serviced sites; proper toilets; laundry facilities; a store on the property; a swimming pool; an activities building which might be used by the campers in bad weather. The taxpayer's accountant, Mr. McCoy, in early 1976 prepared projections as to the proposed profitability of the venture if the proposed development took place. These projections showed losses in the first year (1976-77) but a profit thereafter. The projections were based on information given to Mr. McCoy by the taxpayer and they envisaged the obtaining of a $280,000 loan. The taxpayer applied to the Eastern Ontario Development Corporation, in 1979, for a loan ($45,000, not $280,000). Mr. Bingham was asked to evaluate the loan application from the Department of Tourism's point of view. He was asked to consider: whether the taxpayer had the management capability to effect and operate the proposed development; whether there would be any negative effects on competitors in the area if the development took place; whether the taxpayer's marketing plans looked reasonable. Mr. Bingham's evaluation did not involve any financial analysis of the application. Mr. Bingham recommended that the loan application go forward for the next step, evaluation by the Eastern Ontario Development Corporation. The taxpayer was unable to obtain the loan, because the Eastern Ontario Development Corporation's funds are new money for new projects.

The taxpayer purchased a "pre-fab" house for $40,000 which was constructed across the road from the D.V.A. house. The family moved into that house in January of 1980. The taxpayer contends that he had decided to proceed with the plans for the development of the campsite by turning the D.V.A. house into the general activities building envisaged in the projected development. He states that he planned to add laundry facilities, toilets, etc., thereto. During 1980, the taxpayer rented the D.V.A. house to his daughter for $100 per month. This was not sufficient to cover the mortgage costs of the property. In May 1980 the taxpayer had a massive heart attack. He was incapacitated until at least September of that year. The taxpayer continued to charge the mortgage expenses of the property as a business expense.

The profit and loss record of the taxpayer's business never showed a profit from the first year of its operation, in 1975 to 1985. The taxpayer has consistently reported losses for the years 1977 to 1983 as follows:

1977	$ 7,985.54
1978	$ 8,676.84
1979	$ 8,383.37
1980	$14,491.57
1981	$24,414.44
1982	$14,350.77
1983	$14,508.35

The gross income for the campground itself for the years 1977 to 1980 was:

1977	$ 86
1978	$134
1979	$258
1980	$520

After 1980, the campground income was reported in a combined fashion with that received from the cottage and farmhouse property; therefore, it cannot be separately identified. The evidence is sketchy with respect to the renting of the cottage, the farmhouse and the D.V.A. house. That which exists does not show a vigorous and concerted effort to run a business. The D.V.A. house, as well as being rented to the taxpayer's daughter for $100 per month in 1980, was rented during a few of the winter months in 1981-82 to some loggers and for approximately six months in 1984 to some miners who were prospecting in the area.

Camp Coupland was listed in a Government of Ontario camping brochure published for the 1981 season and the taxpayer had had some calling cards made with Camp Coupland, the address, a map and rates listed thereon. No expenses for advertising of the Camp were included in his 1975–1985 tax returns.

— *REQUIRED*

Determine whether expenses incurred by the taxpayer during the 1980 and 1981 taxation years are business expenses that are deductible for tax purposes.

Problem 4

ITA: 12(1), 18(1), 20(1); IT-442R

TalkTech Inc. is a manufacturer and wholesaler of cellular communication products. TalkTech Inc's customers are retailers who promote TalkTech Inc.'s products to the general public. TalkTech Inc. has an October 31 year-end. You are conducting a review of TalkTech Inc's year-end accounting records for its 2013 fiscal year and have been provided with the following information.

TalkTech Inc. has the following recorded reserves:

Account	*Opening*	*Additions*	*Subtractions*	*Closing*
Warranty reserve	$35,000	$10,000	$17,500	$27,500
Allowance for doubtful accounts	32,000	7,500	5,000	34,500

TalkTech Inc. provides a one-year warranty on most of its products. The warranty is for defects in workmanship or component parts. This warranty is provided as part of the purchase price of TalkTech Inc.'s products. TalkTech Inc. honours its own warranties. The 2013 addition of $10,000 represents a standard percentage of sales made in the 2013 fiscal period. The 2013 subtraction of $17,500 represents an amount actually paid to honour warranties.

The addition of $7,500 to the allowance for doubtful accounts is a result of the application of TalkTech Inc.'s annual year-end aging analysis. In conversation with the controller of TalkTech Inc. you determine that this $7,500 increase in the allowance for doubtful accounts was computed by applying the company's historical collection percentages to the aged accounts receivable balances. Also, during its 2013 fiscal period, TalkTech Inc. wrote off $5,000 (the subtraction noted above) of amounts previously expensed and included in the opening allowance for doubtful accounts. TalkTech Inc. also ended up collecting $1,500 of previously written-off bad debts.

In an attempt to attract a particular retail customer, TalkTech Inc. provided this new customer with an incentive to make a large initial purchase of its products. On April 1, 2013, TalkTech Inc. sold $300,000 worth of cellular phones to CellBlock Limited. TalkTech agreed to the following payment terms in an attempt to entice CellBlock Limited to make the purchase:

- $100,000 due and payable May 1, 2013; and
- $50,000 due and payable January 1 each year starting January 1, 2014 through January 1, 2017.

The cost of the good sold under this contract was $180,000. The delivery date for the cellular phones sold under this contract was May 1, 2013.

One of TalkTech's customers, Phones'N'Things, was experiencing financial trouble. As a result, TalkTech Inc. had agreed to make shipments only if payments were received well in advance of the anticipated shipping dates. Under the terms of this agreement, TalkTech Inc. received $40,000 from Phones'N'Things on September 30, 2013. This payment was an advance payment for a shipment of new technology cellular phones which TalkTech Inc. expected to be shipping to customers commencing February 1, 2014. In the event that TalkTech Inc. was unable to honour its contract with Phones'N'Things, a full refund of the $40,000 was payable.

— *REQUIRED*

(A) Prepare a schedule showing the effect of the above information on income for tax purposes of TalkTech Inc. for the year ended October 31, 2013. From this comparison, determine any adjustments that would be necessary to reconcile accounting income and income for tax purposes for the year.

(B) What would be the tax consequences if the $5,000 subtraction in the allowance for doubtful accounts in 2012 included an account receivable of $800 which was written off only because it has been outstanding for more than 180 days. In fact, it has been outstanding for one year and is part of the opening allowance of $32,000. This $800 could still be collected and there has been no serious attempt to collect it. In fact, the remainder of that customer's account is current and further sales have been made to that customer.

Problem 5

ITA: 9, 18, 20

Leo is self-employed in the T-shirt distribution business. The following is Leo's income statement, for the calendar year ending December 31.

Statement of Income
For the year ended December 31

Gross revenue		$60,000
Cost of goods sold		(10,000)
Gross profit		50,000
Expenses:		
Accounting and legal	$2,000	
Advertising	800	
Golf dues	3,000	
Reasonable estimated bad debt expense	2,000	
Business, taxes, and licenses	1,000	
Amortization expense	8,000	
Cycle Safety Program	1,200	
Interest	7,800	
Meals and entertainment	4,000	
Rent and lease	2,200	
Office rent	1,000	
Salaries and wages — staff	6,000	(39,000)
Net income per financial statements		$11,000

Notes:

(a) Legal fees include $500 of accrued fees for a pending lawsuit against Leo for the sale of distasteful T-shirts.

(b) Accounting fees include the purchase of a $1,200 computerized cash register.

(c) Interest expense includes $3,000 paid to the CRA for late instalment interest.

(d) The Cycle Safety Program cost was for Leo, who is an active environmentalist and rides his bicycle to work every day.

(e) Included in the cost of goods sold is $3,200 incurred for the purchase of shelving and lighting.

(f) Due to the nature of the transaction, the sale of Disney rights were not included in the financial statements. Leo actively trades rights for T-shirt logos. Net proceeds from the sale of the Disney rights were $15,000, and the cost of the logo rights was $6,800.

— REQUIRED

Compute Leo's income from a business for tax purposes, before CCA, for the calendar year ending December 31.

Problem 6

ITA: 12(1)(*b*), 18(1)(*a*), 18(1)(*f*), 18(1)(*l*), 67.1(1)

Source Renovations Ltd. specializes in home renovations and interior design in the Montreal area. Most of the construction and finish carpentry work is subcontracted to self-employed contractors. The following information relates to the corporation's net income for the year ended July 31.

Sales revenue	$4,100,000
Direct contracting expenses	3,750,000
Gross profit	$ 350,000

General and administrative expenses:		
Salary to Ginny (president)	$ 110,000	
Salary to spouse (accounting)	50,000	
Meals and entertainment (Note a)	12,200	
Advertising expenses (Note b)	4,900	
Travelling expense (Note c)	19,500	
Interest and bank charges (Note d)	18,000	
Amortization (Note e)	8,000	
Office expenses	6,000	
Total expenses	$ 228,600	
Other:		
Gain on sale of real estate (Note f)	$ 55,000	
Rental income	9,600	
Sale of design contracts (Note g)	19,000	
Interest income on operating cash	1,200	
Net income	$ 206,200	

Ginny informed you that there was one unrecorded receivable of $14,500 for a renovation project completed on July 30.

Notes:

(a) Meals and entertainment includes:

Club dues	$ 1,800
Promotional meals and season hockey tickets	10,400
Total	$12,200

(b) Advertising expenses include:

Charitable donations	$2,200
Community promotion	650
Local advertising and mail outs	2,050
Total	$4,900

(c) Travelling expense includes both air travel and travel reimbursement to employees for business travel. The company's policy is to reimburse employees 54 cents per kilometre for the business use of their automobiles. The employees drove less than 5,000 kilometres.

(d) Interest and bank charges include:

Interest expense — operations	$ 9,400
Penalty interest for late filing prior year's corporate tax	8,100
Bank charges	500
Total	$18,000

(e) The company uses the straight-line method of amortization. The maximum capital cost allowance that may be claimed is $8,900.

(f) During the year, the company purchased two homes. After Ginny redecorated, the corporation sold the homes for a profit. The corporation has sold six homes in the last two years using the same strategy.

(g) The sale of design contracts resulted from Ginny's desire to downscale her involvement in commercial design. The gain on sale is net of all costs and expenses.

(h) The salary to Ginny's spouse is considered reasonable because he spends most of his working day administering her business.

— *REQUIRED*

Calculate Source Renovation Ltd.'s income from a business for tax purposes.

Problem 7

ITA: 18, 19, 20, 67.1(1), 78(4)

Duncan Ltd. is a Canadian-controlled private corporation owned by Mr. William Duncan. Mr. Duncan purchased all shares of Duncan Ltd. on July 1 of the prior year for $500,000 in an arm's length transaction. Duncan Ltd. manufactures fabrics and will continue with its June 30 year end. The following is Duncan Ltd.'s income statement for the period of July 1 to June 30 of the current year.

Duncan Ltd.
Statement of Income
For the period July 1 to June 30

Gross revenue		$6,000,000
Cost of goods sold		(4,000,000)
Gross profit		2,000,000
Expenses:		
Accounting and legal	$ 60,000	
Advertising	100,000	
Personal expense of Mr. Duncan	30,000	
Bad debts	20,000	
Business taxes and licenses	10,000	
Amortization	80,000	
Interest	90,000	
Meals and entertainment	40,000	
Rent and lease	220,000	
Office	10,000	
Salaries and wages	600,000	(1,260,000)
Net income per financial statements		$ 740,000

Notes:

(a) Legal fees include $15,000 of estimated fees for a threatened lawsuit against the company.

(b) Accounting fees include a $10,000 cost to reorganize the share capital of the company. This amount is not deductible because it is a cumulative eligible expenditure. However, a deductible claim for cumulative eligible capital of $525 is permitted.

(c) Advertising expenses include a $10,000 payment to a television station in the United States for commercials promoting the company's products to the Vancouver market.

(d) Interest expense includes $5,000 of interest paid to the CRA for late instalments.

(e) Capital cost allowance deductible under paragraph 20(1)(*a*) is $14,210.

(f) On July 31 in the current fiscal year, Duncan Ltd. paid $30,000 to an agent for services to raise financing. The amount is included in the advertising expense.

(g) An $80,000 bonus is included in salary and wages. The amount will be paid on January 15, next year.

(h) Included in the cost of goods sold is $50,000 incurred for the purpose of earning exempt income.

(i) On January 1 of the current year, Duncan Ltd. paid $100,000 to one of its tenants to cancel a rental lease agreement because Duncan Ltd. required the space for its own business operations. The amount has been included in the rent expense figure. The lease of property commenced on January 1 and had five years remaining at that time.

— *REQUIRED*

Compute Duncan Ltd.'s income from a business for tax purposes for the year ended June 30.

Problem 8

ITA: 9, 12(1), 18(1)

A senior tax partner in your office has requested that you meet with Mr. Jehangir Dauwalla, a new client, to assist in preparing his personal income tax return. During your initial client meeting, you obtained the following information about Mr. Dauwalla's new business, which he started on June 1. The proprietorship provides hot air balloon rides and weekend leisure trips. His accounting is prepared on the cash basis.

Up and Away
Cash Flow Statement from Proprietorship
June 1 to December 31

Cash receipts (Note a)		$27,220
Cash disbursements:		
Advertising (Note b)	$ 2,200	
Charitable donations	380	
Equipment rental	3,450	
Liability insurance	2,860	
Licences (Note c)	680	
Salary paid to Jehangir	14,750	
Supplies	3,870	
Telephone — Long distance	610	(28,800)
Cash outflow		($1,580)

Notes:

(a) Payments received from customers in January for all December flights and outstanding accounts receivable total $4,650 and are not included above.

(b) Advertising includes $462 of meals and entertainment expenses relating to promoting business with clients.

(c) Licences expense includes $460 for golf memberships for Jehangir and his spouse. He has met several potential new customers through the club and feels that this cost should be deductible. The remaining amount was for business licensing.

(d) In September, Jehangir won a new car through a minor hockey association ticket raffle. The prize had an estimated fair market value of $12,500.

— *REQUIRED*

Compute Jehangir's income from a business for tax purposes.

Problem 9

ITA: 18(1)(*a*), 18(1)(*b*), 18(1)(*l*), 18(1)(*n*), 67.1

Marty started a self-employed bakery business in a North Bay warehouse on March 1, and he has selected a fiscal year end of December 31. His business includes the baking and delivery of muffins and bagels to various coffee shops throughout the city.

Ma Bagels
Statement of Income
For the period March 1 to December 31

Gross revenue		$340,000
Cost of goods sold		(190,000)
Gross profit		150,000
Expenses:		
Accounting amortization (Note a)	$4,000	
Repairs and maintenance	2,800	
Annual tennis club dues	2,500	

Uncollectible bad debts (Note b)	4,200	
Political donations	1,000	
Charitable donations	8,000	
Hotel and travel	7,800	
Meals and entertainment (Note c)	3,400	
Building rent	12,000	
Salary to spouse (Note d)	40,000	(85,700)
Net income		$ 64,300

Notes:

(a) On March 1, Marty purchased a large gas oven, a computerized blender, and a used van for his business. Marty only used the van for deliveries. Assume the deductible CCA on this equipment is $2,400.

(b) Uncollectible bad debts are from Jo Jo's coffee shop. The owner has declared bankruptcy and the business closed on September 15.

(c) Meals and entertainment expenses were incurred in the attempt to gain new business with several coffee shops.

(d) Diane, Marty's spouse, worked full-time for Marty overseeing hiring, orders and delivery of all goods.

— *REQUIRED*

Compute Marty's income from a business for tax purposes for the calendar year ending December 31.

Problem 10

ITA: 9, 18, 20(1)(*l*)

Traci works evenings and weekends as a computer consultant. Weekdays she is employed full-time as a network administrator with Jimac Distributors Ltd., a Canadian-controlled private corporation. Traci has an office organized for her consulting business in her four-room condominium where she takes care of paperwork as well as the assembly and repair of computers. This room is the smallest in the condominium taking up only 50 m^2 of the 400 m^2 total space. The following information was provided by Traci.

Receipts for condo fees	$1,800
Mortgage interest	5,250
Receipts for utilities (light, heat, water)	800
Telephone bills	600
Deductible CCA on computer equipment used for diagnostic purposes	1,500

The telephone is used personally and for business. Long distance bills for business total $250. All consulting revenues are deposited into her personal account but she keeps a record in her consulting journal. All payments for supplies are paid out of her personal bank account. She provided you with the following information from her cheque book.

Money received for consulting services	$35,000
Cheques issued:	
CompWorld for parts	18,000
Computer Association	50
Savoir Faire cocktail party for clients	300
Future Shop for a television and DVD player	200
Straw Warehouse for living room furniture	5,500
Computer World magazine subscription	80

Notes:

(a) By looking at Traci's last year's tax return, you notice she claimed a reserve of $500 for amounts not collected. This year, $1,200 is outstanding on doubtful customers' accounts. Traci's records indicate that she was unable to collect $300 for two jobs completed last year.

(b) At the beginning of the year, Traci had $1,500 worth of parts. At the end of the year, she held an inventory of SIMMS that had dropped drastically in price; while the original cost was $2,000, the replacement cost is only $1,200.

(c) Traci often travels to a customer's place of business to provide training, installation, and Home Page design services. Traci uses her own car and charges the customer an extra $50 (included in consulting services) for the on-site service. Assume that Traci's capital cost allowance is $600. Traci kept track of her receipts and the kilometres she drove during the calendar year.

Total kilometres driven	15,000
Kilometres for business	4,500
Gas and oil	$ 1,500
Repairs (tires and muffler)	$ 350

— REQUIRED

Calculate Traci's income from business for tax purposes.

Problem 11

ITA: 18, 19, 20(1), 147.2(1)

You have been assigned to the audit team for B.B. JAMS Ltd., one of your significant clients. Below is the income statement prepared by the company's accountant for the December 31, 2013 year end.

B.B. JAMS LIMITED
INCOME STATEMENT

FOR THE YEAR ENDED DECEMBER 31, 2013

Sales	$147,840,000
Cost of sales (Note (1))	(119,859,000)
Gross profit	$ 27,981,000
General and administrative expenses (Notes (2)–(7))	(12,374,000)
Selling expenses (Note (8))	(9,311,000)
Income from operations	$ 6,296,000
Other income (Notes (9)–(10))	16,000
Net income before income taxes	$ 6,312,000
Provision for income taxes	(2,528,000)
Net income	$ 3,784,000

Notes:

Through various discussions with the accountant, you have been able to determine that the following information has been recorded in the financial statements:

(1) JAMS had a number of items of inventory that did not sell well in the current year. For accounting purposes, the accountant has recorded a reserve for inventory obsolescence. The reserve was calculated based on the carrying value of any inventory item that had not had a sale in the last 180 days. The reserve at year-end was $1,285,000.

(2) JAMS provides insurance for employees and paid the following amounts to Nat Insurance Company during the year:

$2,000,000 insurance policy on the life of the president included in insurance expense ($300 per month)	$ 3,600
$1,000,000 insurance policy on the life of the vice-president — marketing included in insurance expense	2,000
Group term life insurance for employees included in salaries and benefits ($37,000 × 12 months)	444,000
Total	$449,600

JAMS is the beneficiary of the policies on the president and vice-president. On June 1, 2013, JAMS renegotiated its bank debt, and due to the ever increasing responsibilities of the president, the bank required the insurance policy on the life of the president as part of the collateral for the loan. The premiums on the policy are equal to the net cost of pure insurance for the policy.

(3) An analysis of the professional fees for 2013 revealed the following expenses:

Legal and accounting fees related to the issuance of shares	$29,300
Legal fees related to amending the articles of incorporation	2,300
Costs incurred regarding the renegotiating of the bank loans	46,100
Costs incurred to defend the company against a wrongful dismissal charge	59,600
Costs related to the structuring of an agreement for the purchase of equipment from a foreign company	38,700
Appraisal costs to determine value of the equipment for the bank	5,100

(4) During the year, there were substantial repairs completed to the outside of the building. After the repairs some of the landscaping had to be redone. The total costs were $139,000. Of this, $23,500 relates to the landscaping costs. The entire $139,000 was included in general and administrative expenses.

(5) A review of the other expense accounts included in general and administrative expenses showed the following:

Amortization	$4,560,000
Interest on late payment of municipal taxes	900
Severance payments to four managers*	245,000
Loss from theft by accounting clerk	4,500
Donations to various registered charities	57,000

* All of the amounts were paid in the year.

(6) The salaries and benefits account shows contributions for certain employees to the company's registered pension plan. The contributions were not actually made until March 31, 2014. The pension plan is a defined contribution (money purchase) plan. The company matches the employees' contributions on a dollar for dollar basis.

	Registered pension plan	*Employment compensation*
President	$13,250	$250,000
Vice-president	10,250	150,000
Accountant	5,400	70,000

(7) In early November 2013, JAMS announced an early retirement package that was made available to employees over the age of 60. In order to provide employees with the time required to assess the offer, the deadline for accepting the package has been set at February 15, 2014. While no formal replies were received as of December 31, 2013, the personnel manager anticipates a high acceptance rate. She expects that the costs associated with the packages will be $672,000. This cost has been accrued in the 2013 financial statements.

(8) The following information was taken from the various selling expense accounts:

Cost of sponsoring presentations at a local theatre company	$15,000
Hockey game tickets given to customers	8,000
Meals and entertainment costs of salespeople	109,500
Staff Christmas party and summer barbecue	43,800
Cost of sponsoring local little league teams	5,000
Memberships for salespeople at local golf courses	12,700

(9) The other income includes a loss on the sale of various fixed assets of $35,900.

(10) During the year, the company had cash on hand for a short period of time due to the timing of certain contract payments. The funds earned interest income of $10,400 while they were held.

Other Information:

(11) The accountant has calculated that JAMS is entitled to claim capital cost allowance and CECA of $5,835,000 in 2013. You have confirmed that this calculation is correct.

(12) In reviewing the income tax assessments, you noted that JAMS had been charged interest of $4,900 on the late payment of instalments. You discussed this with the accountant and determined that the interest was recorded in the income tax expense account.

— REQUIRED

Based on the information that you have obtained, calculate the income from business for tax purposes for JAMS for December 31, 2013. Show all calculations whether or not they seem relevant to the final answer. Comment on all items omitted from the calculation.

Problem 12

ITA: Subdivisions a and b

Coco Hardy is an apprentice with Sepp, a design house in Toronto. In her spare time, during some evenings and on weekends, she operates a sewing service for clothing manufacturers. She has set aside a spare room in her apartment where she keeps her equipment and materials and performs her services. This room occupies approximately 20% of her apartment. She sews for many of the same companies that deal with her employer, Sepp. The demands of her employment with Sepp will continue to prohibit her from expanding her sewing services. Consequently, she has not advertised for additional sewing work. Her sewing billings average approximately $600 per month.

She and the manufacturers mutually agree upon what type of sewing is to be done in order to meet the manufacturers' production deadlines. Her hourly rates are determined by the type of sewing required for a particular manufacturer. At the end of each month, she will issue a bill to the manufacturers bearing her name, home address, and home telephone number. Her clients pay her the gross amount on the invoice which does not include HST.

Ms. Hardy has incurred some direct sewing expenses and has allocated some of her other costs to her sewing services in respect of the past year as follows:

Direct expenses:		
Sewing supplies		$ 2,890
Meals and entertainment for manufacturers		500
Sewing machine repairs		425
Long distance telephone calls to manufacturers		710
Delivery of finished product		1,500
Total direct expenses		$ 6,025
Allocated costs:		
Rent ($1,000 per month)	$12,000	
Utilities	2,100	
Insurance	400	
	$14,500	
Allocation to sewing room	× 20%	$ 2,900

Capital cost allowance:			
Sewing room furniture	$ 450		
Sewing machine	325		
Automobile for deliveries	1,200	$ 1,975	
Total allocated costs		$ 4,875	
Total		$10,900	

— *REQUIRED*

(A) Discuss the issues involved in determining whether Ms. Hardy is earning employment income or business income from her sewing service and then reach a conclusion based on the facts.

(B) Compute both income from employment and business, and comment on whether the listed expenses and allocated costs are deductible for income tax purposes under each alternative.

Problem 13

ITA: 8(1)(*f*), 8(1)(*h*), 8(1)(*h*.1), 8(1)(*i*), 8(1)(*j*), 8(3), 18–20

Mr. Peter Rajagopal, who is a salesman in Regina, Saskatchewan, has incurred the following expenses in connection with his employment in 2013. He was not reimbursed and did not receive an allowance in respect of any of these expenses. Peter has a form T2200, signed by his employer, attesting to all of these expenses.

(1) Peter uses one room in his home exclusively as a home office. He uses his home office most days and evenings to do paperwork and make phone calls and his home office computer is connected to his employer's computer system by modem. He visits his office at his employer's premises approximately once a week and spends the remainder of the time on the road, making sales calls throughout Western Canada.

(2) The following expenses relate to Peter's home office which occupies 10% of the square footage of his house:

Utilities	$ 3,100
Mortgage interest	12,000
House insurance	1,150
Municipal taxes	3,050
Maintenance and repairs	2,700
Total	$22,000
10% thereof	$2,200
Capital cost allowance on computer equipment	1,035
Rental of photocopier	1,200
Office supplies	750
Cellular phone charges (used for employment-related calls only)	700
Long distance calls related to business	1,000

(3) Peter also has the following promotional expenses:

Meals (with clients in Regina, Peter's meals)	$2,000
Client's meals	$2,100
Theatre tickets	1,200
Promotional gifts	1,300
Country club membership	3,200

(4) Peter paid the following automobile expenses:

Gas and oil	$2,000
Insurance	1,100
Licence	90
Repairs	800
Parking (employment related)	320

Peter purchased the car that he uses for employment purposes on August 1, 2012 for $50,000 plus $2,500 GST and $2,500 PST. Peter did not claim CCA on the car in 2012; therefore, the capital cost allowance rate for the car is 30% in 2013. The car was driven a total of 40,000 kilometres in 2013; 32,000 of the kilometres driven related to Peter's employment use.

(5) Peter also incurred the following travel expenses (while away at least 12 hours):

Airfare	$ 4,520
Meals and accommodation (including $2,400 for meals)	4,960
Registration fees for convention in Vancouver to increase product knowledge	800
Out-of-town entertainment	3,200

(6) Interest on bank loan:

— to buy the computer equipment for the home office in (1) above	$ 320
— to buy the car in (4) above	800

(7) Peter's remuneration from employment is as follows:

Salary	$40,000
Bonus based on company sales	17,000

— REQUIRED

Compute the total deductible amount of expense under each of the following sets of assumptions:

(A) Peter chooses to use the following deductions as an employee:

(i) paragraphs 8(1)(*h*), (*h*.1), (*i*), and (*j*), or

(ii) paragraphs 8(1)(*f*), (*i*), and (*j*).

(B) Peter's situation is changed to that of an independent sole proprietor.

Assume that all the amounts given are accurate, supported by receipts and reasonable in the circumstances. Present your answer in tabular form for ease of comparison of alternatives. Saskatchewan has GST of 5% and PST of 5%.

Problem 14

ITA: 12(1)(*a*)(ii), 18(1)(*a*), 18(1)(*b*), 18(1)(*h*), 18(1)(*l*), 20(1)(*b*)

On February 1, 2013, Wynn, a recent commerce graduate, began a self-employed, unincorporated coffee business, Chino's & Beano's Unlimited. Wynn would like assistance preparing his 2013 tax return. He has prepared a brief, unaudited statement of income.

Chino's & Beano's Unlimited
Statement of Income
For the year ended December 31, 2013

Sales revenue		$95,000
Less: Provision for returns	$1,200	
Cost of goods sold	22,000	23,200
Gross profit		$71,800
Expenses:		
Travel — meals	$1,500	
Travel — accommodation	2,000	
Travel — total operating expenses — car	2,350	
Sales manager's convention	600	
Salaries paid to staff	30,000	
Health club dues	2,200	
Child care and housekeeping expenses (nanny — single parent)	12,000	
Home office expenses (Note e)	1,400	
Telephone bills	350	
Office supplies	1,700	
Entertainment — drinks and meals	1,800	

Private dental plan — for staff members	2,400	
Restaurant structural renovation costs	21,200	
Straight-line amortization	3,800	
Total expenses		83,300
Net loss before tax		($11,500)

Wynn also supplied the following additional information:

(a) Wynn used his personal automobile for all his business travel. The $2,350 represents his total expenses for the 12-month period. His travel log included business mileage of 14,400 kilometres; the total number of kilometres driven during the 12-month period totalled 18,000 kilometres.

(b) Wynn would like to deduct all of his nanny expenses against his income since the expenses were incurred to earn income.

(c) There are no unrecorded revenues. However, Wynn feels that $380 of his accounts receivable balance is uncollectible because the customers recently declared bankruptcy. Wynn did not provide for this bad debt expense in his financial statements.

(d) The structural renovation of the coffee shop included new walls, flooring, an office for Wynn, and a kitchen.

(e) To ease the burden of being a single parent, Wynn set up a home office. Wynn uses the office to complete his administrative work in the evenings. The home office expenses relate to a proportion of heat, light and power.

— REQUIRED

Ignoring CCA, compute Wynn's net income from a business for tax purposes.

Problem 15

ITA: 37; ITR: 2900(2), 2900(3), 2903

Joe's Widget Manufacturers Inc. (JWMI) is an established manufacturing company with a growing research and development (R&D) department. JWMI is a Canadian-controlled private corporation with no associated companies. The research part of the business is new and the company's accountant has no experience dealing with the tax implications of the expenditures in this area. He has correctly computed the company's net income for tax purposes before specific R&D related adjustments as $615,000 and would like your input on the impact of the transactions described below.

For the year ended December 31, 2013, the following R&D related expenditures were made.

Description	*Amount*
Purchase of lab machinery and lab equipment	$450,000
Purchase of a new building to house laboratory	120,000
Salaries of lab staff	100,000
Operating costs directly related to the lab	40,000

For financial accounting purposes, the salaries and operating costs, net of the investment tax credit below, have been expensed. The lab machinery, equipment and building are used 100% for R&D activities. The lab machinery and equipment have been capitalized for accounting purposes and are being amortized over an eight-year period (net of available investment tax credits as set out below). Thus, amortization expense of $36,562 was recorded for accounting purposes on the lab machinery and equipment. Amortization expense of $4,800 was recorded on the building. Capital cost allowance for the building will be $2,400.

The company is eligible for investment tax credits at a rate of 35% and has correctly determined that they are eligible for investment tax credits at this rate on all of the above expenditures with the exception of the building. No investment tax credit is allowable on the purchase price of the building. For accounting purposes, the company's accountant has netted the investment tax credits against the related expenditures as follows.

Expenditure	*Gross amount*	*ITC*	*Amount recorded for accounting purposes*
Lab machinery and equipment . . .	$450,000	$157,500	$292,500
Building	120,000	0	120,000
Salaries of lab staff	100,000	35,000	65,000
Operating costs of lab	40,000	14,000	26,000

— *REQUIRED*

Based on the above information, explain to JWMI's accountant the adjustments necessary in computing income for tax purposes for the years ended December 31, 2013 and 2014.

Problem 16

ITA: 9–12, 18–20, 37, 67.1, 78, 147

The *unaudited* income statement for Lomas & Sons Limited for its year ended December 31, 2013 shows the following:

Sales		$ 795,000
Cost of sales	$350,000	
General and administrative expenses	225,000	
Research and development expenditures	76,700	(651,700)
Operating income		$ 143,300
Other income		20,000
Net income before taxes		$ 163,300
Provision for income taxes:		
— current	$ 27,000	
— future	25,000	(52,000)
Net income after income taxes		$ 111,300

The information in the following notes has already been reflected in the above income statement.

(1) Payment made by company on April 1, 2014, to a defined contribution (money purchase) registered pension plan for the president of the company in respect of current employment service, allocated to 2013 expenses by the company's accountant; in addition, the president had $7,500 withheld from his compensation of $74,000 for the RPP	$ 7,000
(2) Increase in warranty reserve on company's product (net of expense incurred; based on self-insurance warranty program)	16,000
(3) Amortization expense recorded in the financial statements	30,000
(4) Landscaping costs re: factory premises	2,500
(5) Interest on bank loan obtained for the purpose of purchasing common shares in Advanco Ltd., a dividend-paying Canadian corporation	6,300
(6) Legal costs of arranging an agreement among shareholders	8,500
(7) Legal and accounting fees related to issue of shares	12,700
(8) Interest on municipal real estate taxes paid late in error	1,000
(9) Golf club membership fees	2,200
(10) Donation to United Way	3,000
(11) Meals and entertainment for clients	4,000
(12) Appraisal fees to determine selling price of fixed assets	6,200
(13) Premium on term insurance on life of president with the corporation as beneficiary; policy was not required to be assigned as collateral for corporate borrowing from the bank	2,800
(14) Management bonuses ($20,000 of the bonuses expensed in 2013, and shown as "Bonus Payable" on the Balance Sheet as at December 31, 2013 has not been paid at the time of filing the corporate tax return on June 30, 2014)	40,000

(15) Amortization of bond discount on bonds issued in 2008	3,400
(16) The company has capitalized and will amortize over five years $90,000 of costs incurred in 2013 related to the purchase of machinery to be used for qualifying research and development. The resultant amortization of the net cost after the investment tax credit was $11,700 and is included in the income statement deduction for research and development expenditures. As well, the company incurred current research and development expenditures of $100,000. These current expenditures will qualify the company for an investment tax credit of $35,000. The $35,000 has been deducted from the expenditure on SR&ED, as shown in the income statement.	
(17) Interest and penalties on income tax assessments, expensed for accounting purposes	1,250
(18) Items included in the financial accounting statements in arriving at the net profit:	
Amount paid by an insurance company on its business interruption insurance to compensate for loss of profits when company was closed down for a month during the year because of a fire	26,800
Dividends received	1,700
Volume rebates and discounts on purchases	16,000

— *REQUIRED*

Based on the foregoing information, compute the income from business or property for tax purposes, ignoring tax deductions in respect of depreciable capital or eligible capital property for Lomas and Sons Limited in respect of its 2013 fiscal year. In addition, comment on all items not included in your derivation of income from business or property.

Problem 17

ETA: 123(1), 161, 164, 169(1), 170(1)(*a*), 232, 236, Sched. V, Part VII

Reconsider the facts of Problem 16.

— *REQUIRED*

(A) Outline the general HST requirements applicable in this corporate situation.

(B) Indicate which of the items listed in the additional information notes represent costs incurred for:

1. taxable supplies, eligible for an ITC, and
2. exempt supplies, not eligible for an ITC.

(C) Comment on the appropriate HST treatment of the other items listed in the additional information notes and on the income statement.

Problem 18

ITA: 5(1), 6(1)(*a*), (*b*), (*c*), (*e*), (*g*), (*k*), 6(2), 7(1), 7(8), 6(9), 80.4(1), 110(1)(*d*); IT-470R

Valerie Borg is a vice-president of Program Management with an equipment leasing company in Calgary. Recently, Valerie was approached by a large public company, Key Equipment Finance Limited ("Key"), which is based in Toronto, about the possibility of joining their firm. Valerie has always been looking for opportunities for career advancement and Toronto is an ideal city for relocation.

Valerie is in the process of negotiating her compensation package. She has just received a letter outlining a proposed package from Key. The package looks very attractive, but she would like to know the tax impact on various items outlined in the letter. Valerie is also interested in knowing the tax implications of the compensation package to her future employer. She believes that if she knows the cost to the employer, she will be in a better position to negotiate.

1. An annual salary of $150,000 and bonus, tied to the company's financial performance. Calculation of the bonus is based on the firm's December year-end results, with payment to occur on June 30.
2. Key offers to loan Valerie $200,000, interest-free, to help finance a new house. In addition, Key will reimburse all of her moving costs.
3. Key will pay the premium for Valerie to join its group term life insurance plan. Key will pay the premiums for a private health plan, a dental plan, and a drug plan. The company's insurance company is Green Shield.

4. Valerie is required to travel to Europe on a regular basis. Company policy permits a spouse to accompany its executives for these trips. Valerie's husband, Matt, is a freelance writer working from home. He is very excited about going to Europe with Valerie. The main purpose of the trips will be for Valerie to oversee the company's global operations. Her husband will spend his time visiting local museums. Key will pay a portion of the travelling expenses related to Matt.

5. Key will provide a BMW to Valerie. Valerie expects to drive the car 30% for business and 70% for her personal use. Valerie will receive a company credit card to be used to pay for gas and maintenance of the car. Key will pay a monthly lease of $850, including HST. Valerie will drive the car approximately 20,000 kilometers per year.

6. Key recently installed a fitness club in its building. All employees are encouraged to use the club free of charge. The club also offers free personal training. The equivalent value for similar facilities at a private club would be $1,100 per year, including applicable taxes.

7. Key pays for counselling services related to the physical health of its employees. Valerie will be covered by this service.

8. Valerie will participate in Key's deferred profit sharing plan. The maximum contribution will be made to this plan only when the company's earnings from operations for the year increase by more than 5% over the prior year's earnings from operations.

9. Key owns a yacht and it is made available to all of its executives. This offer is extended to Valerie. She can have it free for one week each year.

— *REQUIRED*

(A) Discuss with Valerie the tax implications of the compensation package to both herself and Key.

(B) Discuss tax-related issues to be considered when designing an employee compensation package.

[For more problems and solutions thereto, see the DVD accompanying this book.]

¶4,880 ADVISORY CASES

Case 1: Nine Iron Ltd.

Ryan Holeman, the president of Nine Iron Ltd., has come to your office seeking a second opinion. Nine Iron Ltd. carries on a mini golf and retail business in southern Manitoba. The CRA has reassessed Nine Iron Ltd. for the following transactions that occurred during last year:

(a) Eighteen months earlier, the company purchased two acres of land just outside of Winnipeg with the intention of possibly developing a second retail outlet. Ryan did not have firm plans when he purchased the land. At the time, he thought he could either develop the property into a mini golf and retail outlet or build a gas station with an overnight park for recreation vehicles. Unfortunately, a significant lender backed down and the company was forced to sell the land. Luckily, as Ryan had speculated, the land was sold for a profit of $90,000. The new owner plans to develop an overnight park for recreation vehicles.

(b) Nine Iron Ltd. immediately purchased a smaller plot of land within walking distance. The company is planning to build a second mini golf and retail outlet location next year. During the year, the company expensed interest and property taxes of $26,000 relating to the vacant land. The company also expensed $7,000 in architect's fees, and legal and surveying costs for the development of the amusement park. The CRA reassessed Nine Iron Ltd. for $26,000 plus $3,500 in interest charges, claiming that Nine Iron Ltd. purchased the first plot of land with the intention of trading for profit. The CRA is also disallowing the expenses incurred on the second plot.

Advise Ryan on the income tax issues that Nine Iron Ltd. must address with respect to the above transactions.

Case 2: Greater Prospects Ltd.

Samara, the president of Eden Prospects Ltd., has come to your office for a second opinion. Eden Prospects is a national marketing firm specializing in the development and implementation of marketing plans for partners in practices of law, accounting, medicine and dentistry. Samara is on the premises daily, carrying out her duties as president and a senior adviser to clients. The CRA recently reassessed Eden Prospect's 2012 taxation year and is requesting that an additional $140,000 in taxes and $28,000 in interest and penalty charges be paid immediately for the following transactions.

(a) In December 2012, the company declared a bonus of $280,000 to Samara and several senior vice-presidents. The amount was paid in September 2013.

(b) In 2012, the corporation provided three senior executives with an interest-free loan of $240,000 for the purchase of shares of Eden Prospects Ltd. The company borrowed the funds from the bank and incurred $20,000 in interest charges. The executives began repayment in 2014. No amount was shown by Eden Prospects as a taxable benefit for these employees.

(c) The corporation pays Samara a nominal salary to act as president. Samara provides her senior advisory services to Eden Prospects through a proprietorship, Sole Trust. Every month, Samara prepares an invoice on behalf of the proprietorship for services rendered to Eden Prospects. Prospects is Sole Trust's only client. The CRA imposed a large penalty on Eden Prospects for not treating Samara as an employee and remitting Canada Pension Plan, Employment Insurance and withholding taxes.

(d) In 2012, the corporation rented a fishing lodge to carry out group think sessions with three of their most senior clients. The purpose of the sessions was to provide a comfortable setting for the company's largest clients to share marketing ideas. The sessions also helped Eden Prospects to become closer to their clients — especially while fishing and golfing. The corporation was denied a deduction for the rent of the lodge, although it was allowed 50% of the meals, entertainment and green fees.

Advise Samara by preparing a memo on the various income tax issues that both Samara and Eden Prospects must address with respect to the above transactions.

Case 3: London City Electronics Inc.

London City Electronics Inc. has been a client of yours since it started in business five years ago. Isabelle Joy, the founder, has been very successful with her main product, which is a valve that measures and controls the flow of liquids. It is now the middle of March and you have just started your review engagement field work for the company's December year end when Isabelle asks you to come into her office to talk to her.

The first thing you do is congratulate her on the good year she had last year. Her sales, gross profit, and net income are all up substantially over the previous year. You are surprised when she starts to complain about the poor results so far this year. She indicates that her customers are just now starting to stretch their payments because they are facing increased competition from imports. In fact, one of her customers has given London City Electronics some of its products in exchange for the amount it owed.

To compound this problem, Isabelle has had some quality control problems in her manufacturing process and she has been receiving a large number of warranty claims. Sometimes she is able to repair the valve before there is significant cost to the customer, but in some cases the customer has had financial losses as a result of the faulty valve.

Isabelle would like your advice on the tax implications of her situation.

Case 4: Kitchener Medical Inc.

Joe McMillan and Bill McDonald were finally able to hold the grand opening for their medical supply import business. It had been an expensive party, but both Joe and Bill felt that their suppliers, customers, and new employees had appreciated it.

It seemed like a long time ago that they got the idea and started to develop their plans. In fact, the idea had been introduced to them 12 months ago during a trip they took to California to look for business opportunities. Once they returned, they began to do their own research. They had one of the local universities do some market research for them to see whether their idea was viable. The research supported their idea of importing medical supplies from a large U.S. supplier to compete against other importers for the Canadian market.

Six months ago, the U.S. supplier put them in touch with their local importer, Beam Inc., whose owner wanted to retire. Since that time, they have been busy negotiating with Mr. Beam and the supplier, finding their own leased warehouse space (Beam Inc.'s space was too small), visiting customers, setting up the office and modern control systems and assessing the employees of Beam Inc. Even before the opening, they had spent $25,000 of their own money on expenses such as:

- their initial travel costs to California (July, last year);
- market research (September, last year);
- negotiating the operating line of credit (May, this year);
- leasehold improvements, equipment (May, this year);
- travel and entertainment expenses (January to June, this year); and
- legal and accounting costs for the incorporation (June, this year).

But now it is all coming together. Joe is going to provide the initial capital, including the personal guarantee to the supplier and the bank, and Bill is going to manage the business. They have bought the inventory, customer lists, accounts receivable, and equipment from Beam Inc. Their initial lease is for five years with two, five-year renewal options.

Advise Joe and Bill on the tax implications of the issues raised by this situation. Assume that they incorporated a company in June, but they have not used it in any way yet, and that it is now July when they are asking for your advice.

Chapter 5

Depreciable Property and Eligible Capital Property

TOPICS DISCUSSED

LEARNING GOALS

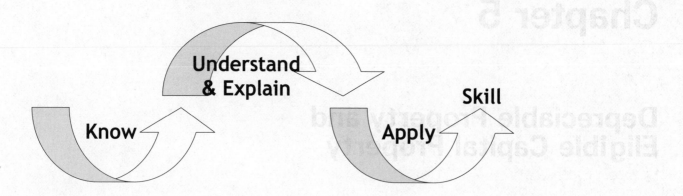

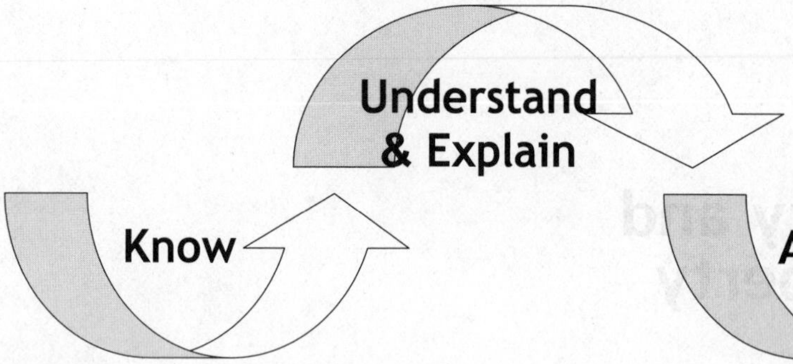

Know

By the end of this chapter you should know the basic provisions of the *Income Tax Act*, and the *Excise Tax Act*, pertaining to the GST/HST, that relate to depreciable and eligible capital property. Completing the Review Questions (¶5,800) and Multiple Choice Questions (¶5,825) is a good way to learn the technical provisions.

Understand and Explain

You should understand and be able to explain how to calculate capital cost allowance and cumulative eligible capital amount, which is the tax equivalent of amortization for capital and intangible property. Completing the Exercises (¶5,850) is a good way to deepen your understanding of the material.

Apply

You should be able to use your knowledge and understanding of depreciable and eligible capital property to advise taxpayers on the tax implications of the purchase of these assets. Completing the Assignment Problems (¶5,875) is an excellent way to develop your ability to apply the material in increasingly complex situations.

OVERVIEW

The system in the Act for amortizing the capital cost of depreciable property and intangibles is fairly straightforward in its concept. Depreciable property write-offs are not encumbered by many of the complicated rules and computations necessary for the financial accounting. However, economic policy incentives to invest in depreciable property are reflected in the rates and methods of write-off of cost.

Although the rules pertaining to depreciable property and eligible capital property (intangibles) have many similarities, the differences require separate discussion in the two major sections of this chapter. The third major section of the chapter discusses the input tax credit system under the GST/HST pertaining to capital property.

The following chart shows that the above rules related to deductions for depreciable and eligible capital property are found in Subdivision b (income or loss from a business or property) of Division B of the Act and in the Regulations.

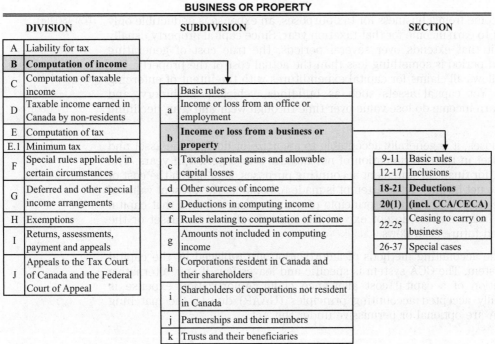

PART I — DIVISION B, SUBDIVISION b

BUSINESS OR PROPERTY

DIVISION

A	Liability for tax
B	**Computation of income**
C	Computation of taxable income
D	Taxable income earned in Canada by non-residents
E	Computation of tax
E.1	Minimum tax
F	Special rules applicable in certain circumstances
G	Deferred and other special income arrangements
H	Exemptions
I	Returns, assessments, payment and appeals
J	Appeals to the Tax Court of Canada and the Federal Court of Appeal

SUBDIVISION

	Basic rules
a	Income or loss from an office or employment
b	**Income or loss from a business or property**
c	Taxable capital gains and allowable capital losses
d	Other sources of income
e	Deductions in computing income
f	Rules relating to computation of income
g	Amounts not included in computing income
h	Corporations resident in Canada and their shareholders
i	Shareholders of corporations not resident in Canada
j	Partnerships and their members
k	Trusts and their beneficiaries

SECTION

9-11	Basic rules
12-17	Inclusions
18-21	**Deductions**
20(1)	**(incl. CCA/CECA)**
22-25	Ceasing to carry on business
26-37	Special cases

The major rules related to these deductions are found in the following parts of the Act:

Depreciable capital property

Inclusions and Special Rules		*Deductions*	
Ssec. 13(1)	Recaptured CCA	Par. 18(1)(*b*)	No deduction for amortization
Ssec. 13(2)	Luxury automobiles	Par. 20(1)(*a*)	Deduction for capital cost allowance
Ssec. 13(4)	Replacement property	Ssec. 20(16)	Terminal loss
Ssec. 13(7)	Special rules	Reg. 1100	CCA rules
		Reg. 1100(2)	Half-year rule
Ssec. 13(21)	Definitions	Reg. 7307(1)	CCA limits on automobiles
Ssec. 13(21.1)	Loss on certain transfers within affiliated groups	Reg. Sch. II–VI	Classes of property
Ssec. 13(26)	Available for use		

Eligible capital property

Inclusions and Special Rules		*Deductions*	
Ssec. 14(1)	Recaptured CECA	Par. 18(1)(*b*)	No deduction for amortization
Ssec. 14(3)	Acquisition of eligible capital property	Par. 20(1)(*b*)	Deduction for cumulative eligible capital amount
Ssec. 14(5)	Definitions		
Ssec. 14(6)	Replacement property		
Ssec. 14(12)	Loss on certain transfers within affiliated groups		

¶5,000 THE CAPITAL COST ALLOWANCE SYSTEM

¶5,005 Basic Rules

¶5,006 Introduction

In computing net income from a business for tax purposes, an expense is deductible only to the extent it is laid out to earn income for that taxation year. Since capital property usually provides a future benefit that extends over several periods, the true cost of generating revenues for one taxation period is something less than the actual cost of the property. For this reason, the Act disallows all claims for capital expenditures with the intent of enforcing the matching principle. Yet capital assets such as buildings, vehicles, machinery, and intangibles acquired to earn income do lose value over time through wear and tear, declining utility, and obsolescence. ITA: 18(1)(*a*) 18(1)(*b*)

For accounting purposes, it is generally acceptable to amortize or deplete the asset and reflect the cost of the asset in the determination of net income over a period of years. The objective of amortization, for financial statement accounting purposes, is to match the cost of producing the revenues to net income. Little attempt is made to compute the present value of the asset for the balance sheet, although the principle of conservatism requires that capital assets presented on the balance sheet do not exceed the market value of the asset or the present value of estimated future cash flows.

For tax purposes, the accounting methods of amortization are replaced by the capital cost allowance (CCA) system. The CCA system is specific and leaves few, if any, alternative choices in the computation of a capital cost allowance claim. Amortization expense is mandatory under generally accepted accounting principles (GAAP) due to the matching principle. CCA and CECA are optional or permissive under the Act.

¶5,007 Types of capital property

In Canada, capital property is separated into three general categories:

- Non-depreciable capital property
- Depreciable property
- Eligible capital property

Non-depreciable capital property is not defined in the Act; it includes receivables and other capital property such as land, investments, personal-use property, and listed personal property. Since this property, except for some personal-use property, is not used up or worn out over time in the production of income, non-depreciable capital property is not eligible for capital cost allowance.

Eligible capital property generally includes intangibles such as goodwill, patents, unlimited life franchises and incorporation costs. When an eligible capital expenditure (ECE), that is, the cost, is incurred, 75% of the cost is included in a single common pool referred to as cumulative eligible capital (CEC) and is subject to a rate of tax depreciation of 7%. The deduction is referred to as cumulative eligible capital amount or CECA. This will be discussed later in this chapter. ITA: 14(5)

Depreciable property is defined as property acquired by the taxpayer where CCA has been allowed or will be allowed. Since depreciable property is also treated as capital property, a capital gain may arise. Conversely, a capital loss can never arise on the disposition of depreciable property. The Act permits a deduction from net income to reflect the wear and tear of depreciable property based on the capital cost allowance system. For the most part, the CCA system is based on the declining balance method. A significant feature of the CCA system is the grouping of assets into one of prescribed classes. By prescribing a specific method and specific rates to each prescribed class (depending on the type of the depreciable asset), alternative methods and the range of possible results are minimized. This reduces tax-motivated transactions and enhances neutrality. ITA: 13(21) ITA: 54 ITA: 39(1)(*b*) ITA: 20(1)(*a*)

¶5,008 CCA and neutrality

The CCA system is not tax neutral because the allowance claimed on a depreciable asset affects the after-tax cash flow received on the asset. Tax-neutral amortization would not permit the tax law to govern or influence investment decisions. However, the CCA system was designed and implemented not only to narrow the choices of amortization methods to taxpayers but also to provide the government with a means of implementing fiscal policy. Although policy makers do consider the economic life and utility received from an asset, many of the rates and class categories were determined with fiscal policy objectives and budgetary requirements in mind. For example, in 1981 the government implemented a separate class (Class 29) for manufacturing equipment in order to encourage investment in the manufacturing and processing industry. This class essentially permitted corporations to depreciate the machinery over three years. In 1988, as a result of tax reform, the allowable CCA for these types of assets was reduced (with a transitional phase-in) to 25% (Class 39) and then later increased to 30% (Class 43). The 2007 federal Budget reintroduced the Class 29 formula for a temporary period and the 2008 federal Budget accelerated the rate for Class 43 for an adjustment period. This was done to encourage investment in the manufacturing and processing sector regardless of the equipment's expected or actual useful life. Modified capital cost allowance rules for computer equipment and, for certain manufacturing equipment, provide a rate that more accurately reflects the technological obsolescence of such equipment.

¶5,009 CCA and tax planning

From a tax planning perspective, every capital investment decision should include consideration of the capital cost allowance system. Depending on the profitability of the taxpayer and the availability of losses claimed, a corporation has a certain amount of discretion as to the amount of CCA deducted. This is especially relevant when a corporation has loss carryforward amounts with a high probability of expiration. The opportunity to claim capital cost allowance is never lost, as long as the asset is in a tax pool. Suppose, for instance, that a corporation decided not to claim CCA in a taxation period because of current year losses, in addition to loss carryforward amounts from prior years. This does not mean that the corporation may claim double CCA in the following taxation year; however, it does mean that the asset balance is available for depreciation in a future year. Each year, the taxpayer may claim any amount of CCA from zero to the maximum allowable claim, regardless of how much CCA was claimed in a prior year.

Management can quantify the net present value of the tax savings that will result from claiming declining-balance capital cost allowance and so determine the net-of-tax cost of an asset by applying a relatively simple formula:

$$\frac{\text{Cost} \times \text{Tax rate} \times \text{CCA rate}}{\text{Rate of return} + \text{CCA rate}}$$

Where the asset is subject to the half-year rule (explained later in this chapter), the answer provided by the above formula is adjusted by another formula:

$$\frac{1 + \dfrac{\text{Rate of return}}{2}}{1 + \text{Rate of return}}$$

Example Problem 5-1

ABC Canada Limited is considering a new piece of equipment that costs $100,000. It is a Class 10 asset (30% CCA rate) and would be subject to the half-year rule. ABC's corporate tax rate is 35% and the company expects at least a 12% return on the investment in the asset.

— REQUIRED

What is the cost of the asset after considering the net present value of the tax reductions associated with the capital cost allowance allowed in measuring income for tax purposes?

— SOLUTION

Cost of asset	$ 100,000
Less income tax recovery from CCA:	
$\frac{\$100{,}000 \times .35 \times .30}{.12 + .30} \times \left[\frac{1 + .12/2}{1 + .12} \right]$	= $ 23,661
After tax cost of asset	$ 76,339

¶5,012 Eligibility for capital cost allowance

¶5,012.10 *Depreciable property— Important exclusions*

The Act is not very helpful in determining what is "depreciable property" since the definition refers to property in respect of which a taxpayer is entitled to claim a deduction under paragraph 20(1)(*a*). Therefore, property must fit into one of the prescribed classes of CCA or Schedule II to be depreciable. However, even if a property fits in a prescribed class, it may not be depreciable property if it is excluded under a regulation. The following items are the most important exclusions:

ITR: 1100
ITR: 1102(1), (2), (3)

- property, the cost of which is deductible in computing income;
- property that is described in inventory;
- property not acquired for the purpose of gaining or producing income;
- property that is a yacht, camp, lodge, golf course, or facility for which expenses are not deductible by reason of paragraph 18(1)(*l*);
- land; and
- property situated outside Canada that is owned by non-residents.

¶5,012.20 *Employees*

Employees are generally prohibited from claiming capital cost allowance. Very limited exceptions to this rule are provided for motor vehicle and aircraft costs, and for musical instruments. To qualify for these capital cost allowance claims, the employee must use the automobile, aircraft, or instrument to perform his/her employment duties.

ITA: 8(2)
ITA: 8(1)(*j*), (*p*)

These restrictions on CCA pose problems when an employee must use his or her own computer or home office equipment. Employees are only allowed CCA on the three types of assets noted above. Where applicable, the employee and employer should recognize other alternatives, such as a leasing arrangement, where a deduction may be available under paragraph 8(1)(*f*), or an independent contractor arrangement, where technically feasible under tax law.

¶5,012.30 *Businesses*

As a general rule, businesses may deduct CCA for capital assets used in the income-earning process. The Act allows a deduction for such part of the capital cost, as prescribed by the Regulations of the Act.

ITA: 20(1)(*a*)

Certain intangible assets are not eligible for CCA, but rather are entitled to be amortized under the Act. The assets are grouped in a pool known as the cumulative eligible capital property pool, and a 7% declining-balance rate of amortization is authorized. These assets, and this pool, will be discussed separately in this chapter. ITA: 20(1)(*b*) ITA: 14

¶5,015 Classes of assets for tangible capital property

¶5,015.10 *Common classes*

An important feature of the capital cost allowance system is the grouping of depreciable property into prescribed classes which are established by the Regulations (Part XI and Schedule II, primarily). When a taxpayer has a number of properties within a particular class, the properties of that class are treated as one unit for the purposes of capital cost allowances. Classes for some of the more common assets are contained in the following list: ITA: 13(21)

Class 1 (4%)	— Most buildings or other structures, including component parts such as electrical wiring and fixtures, plumbing, heating and central air conditioning, acquired after 1987;
Class 1-MB (10%)	— New (not resale) manufacturing buildings (MB) used at least 90% (measured by square footage) for manufacturing and processing purposes, acquired on or after March 19, 2007; each building added to this class is put in its own separate class; ITR: 1100(1)(*a*.1)
Class 1-NRB (6%)	— Non-residential buildings (NRB), acquired on or after March 19, 2007; each building added to this class is put in its own separate class; ITR: 1100(1)(*a*.2)
Class 8 (20%)	— Miscellaneous tangible capital property, such as furniture, fixtures, and outdoor advertising signs, and machinery or equipment, such as photocopiers, refrigeration equipment, telephones, and tools costing $500 or more, not included in another class (i.e., general default class for tangible capital property);
Class 10 (30%)	— Automotive equipment, such as automobiles (except taxis and those used in a daily rental business), vans, trucks, tractors, wagons, and trailers;
Class 10.1 (30%)	— A passenger vehicle with a cost in excess of the prescribed limit (i.e., $30,000 if acquired after 2000); each vehicle added to this class is put in its own separate class; ITA: 13(7)(*g*)
Class 12 (100%)	— Tools, instruments, and kitchen utensils costing less than $500; linen, uniforms, dies, jigs, or moulds; rental video cassettes; computer application software;
Class 13	— Leasehold interest;
Class 14	— Patent,[1] franchise, concession or licence for a limited period;
Class 17 (8%)	— Roads, parking lots, sidewalks, airplane runways, storage areas, or similar surface construction;
Class 29 (50%)	— Property that is machinery and equipment used in manufacturing or processing, acquired after March 18, 2007 and before 2016 [proposed in the March 21, 2013 federal Budget]. (The CCA rate in the year of acquisition is 50%, on a straight-line basis, but the half-year rule applies.) For acquisitions after 2016, this property will be included in Class 43, with its 30% declining balance rate;
Class 43 (30%)	— Manufacturing and processing machinery and equipment acquired after 2016;
Class 44 (25%)[1]	— Patents and rights to use patented information acquired for a limited or unlimited period;
Class 50 (55%)	— General purpose electronic data processing equipment and systems software for the equipment that would otherwise qualify for Class 45 acquired after March 18, 2007.

[1] Regulation 1103(2h) provides that taxpayers may elect not to use Class 44 for such patents, in which case the property will be classified in Class 14.

A convenient alphabetical list of many depreciable assets can be found in an "Alphabetical List of Assets" in the preface materials and in the Topical Index to the CCH edition of the *Income Tax Act*, under the heading "capital cost allowance". However, the latter listing contains only property specifically itemized in the class descriptions. Hence, property referred to in more general terms in the class description may not appear in the list.

¶5,015.20 *Basic rules of the system*

The basic rules of the capital cost allowance system are illustrated in Exhibit 5-1 and can be stated for many classes quite simply as follows:

(a) whenever an asset of a particular class is purchased, the full purchase cost (capital cost) is added to the balance known as undepreciated capital cost (UCC) of the class of assets; ITA: 13(21)

(b) whenever an asset of a particular class is sold, the full proceeds of disposition, not in excess of original cost (i.e., the lesser of proceeds and capital cost (LOCP)), is subtracted from the balance in the class of assets (proceeds in excess of capital cost may give rise to a capital gain); and ITA: 13(21)

(c) at the end of the taxation year,

(i) if the balance in the class of assets (i.e., UCC) is positive and there are still assets in that class,

(A) subtract from the balance in the account ½ of the excess, if any, of purchases minus disposals made in the year (i.e., ½ × (a – b), above), ITR: 1100(2)

(B) deduct up to the maximum capital cost allowance (CCA) at the prescribed rate for the class on the positive balance, and ITA: 20(1)(*a*)

(C) add back the ½ of the net amount subtracted in (A), above;

(ii) if the balance in the class of assets is negative, take the negative balance into income as recaptured capital cost allowance and set the balance in the class at zero; and ITA: 13(1)

(iii) if the balance in the class of assets is positive, but all of the assets in the class have been disposed of such that there are no more assets physically in the class, take the positive balance, known as a terminal loss, as a deduction from income and set the balance in the class at zero. ITA: 20(16)

EXHIBIT 5-1
Basic Rules of the Capital Cost Allowance System Applied to a Prescribed Class of Assets

Undepreciated capital cost of the class at the beginning of the year		$ xxx
Add: purchases during the year		xxx
		$ xxx
Deduct: dispositions during the year at the lesser of (LOCP):		
(a) capital cost	$ xxx	
(b) proceeds of disposition	$ xxx	(xxx)
Undepreciated capital cost before adjustment		$ xxx
Deduct: ½ net amount*		(xxx)
Undepreciated capital cost before CCA		$ xxx
Deduct: capital cost allowance in the class for the year		(xxx)
Add: ½ net amount*		xxx
Undepreciated capital cost of the class at the beginning of the following year		$ xxx

* Purchases during the year	$ xxx
Deduct: lesser of capital cost and proceeds of disposition above	(xxx)
Net amount (positive amounts only)	$ xxx

¶5,015.25 *Recapture and terminal loss*

The role of the recapture and terminal loss concepts in the capital cost allowance system is to provide for a deduction for tax purposes of the full decline in value of assets over the period of their use. Thus, capital cost allowance will be recaptured when proceeds of disposition exceed undepreciated capital cost, i.e., when assets in a class have been overdepreciated relative to their disposal value as in the following case where there has been no decline in value of the assets:

Capital cost	$10,000	
		→ Previously claimed as CCA
Proceeds	8,000	Recapture of CCA claimed
		→ reflecting disposition value in excess of UCC
Undepreciated capital cost	7,000	

Similarly, a terminal loss provides for a deduction when proceeds of disposition are less than undepreciated capital cost and there are no assets remaining in the class, i.e., when assets in a class have been underdepreciated relative to their disposal value as in the following case where the decline in value of the assets exceeds the amount of capital cost allowance previously taken:

Capital cost	$10,000	
Undepreciated capital cost	7,000	→ Terminal loss reflecting additional decline in value over $3,000 of CCA previously claimed
Proceeds	5,000	

These rules are depicted graphically below.

Dispositions of Depreciable Property

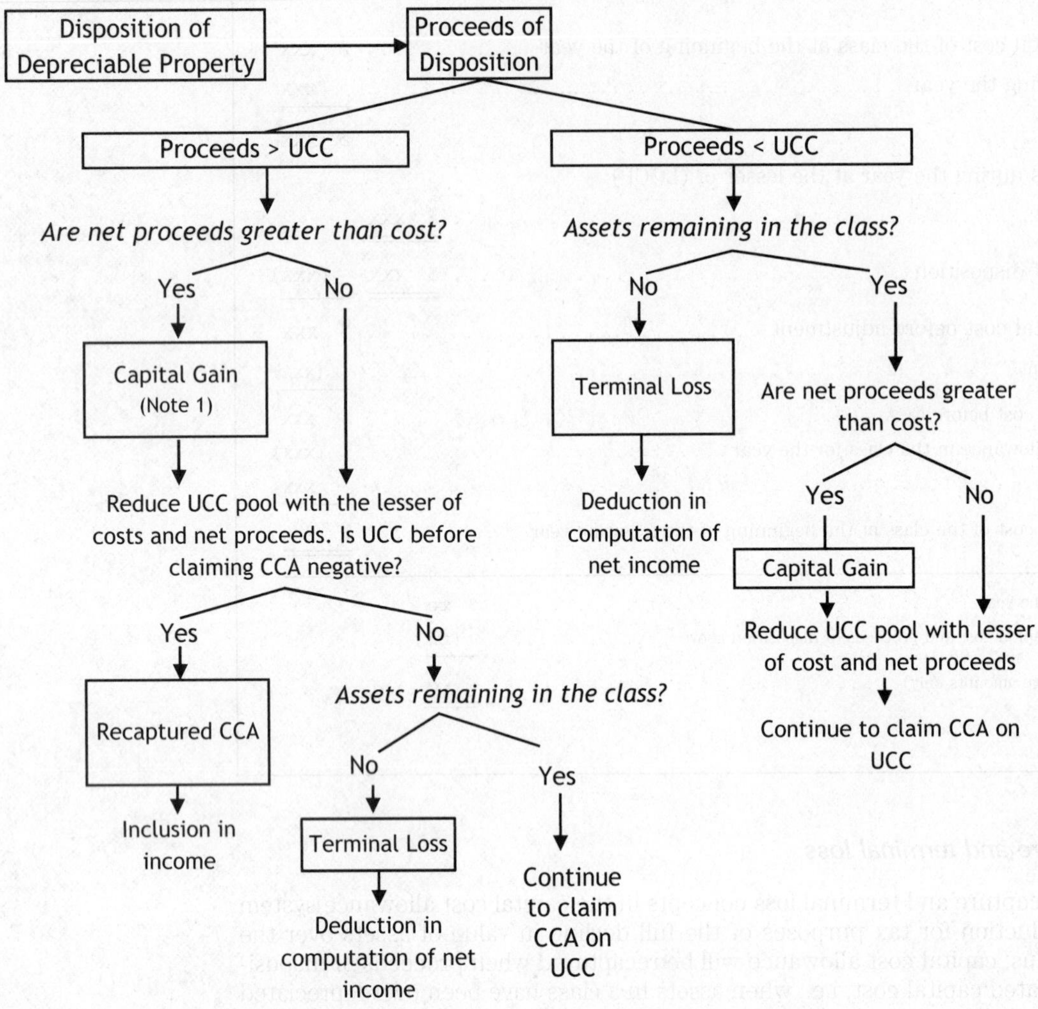

Note 1: The capital gain (net proceeds minus cost) arises only when proceeds exceed the capital cost of the property. The UCC is reduced by the lesser of cost and net proceeds.

Note that the central definition is that of undepreciated capital cost. The capital letters in brackets shown after each item below coincide with the letters in the algebraic formula in the definition. Some of the less mainstream items have been omitted. The definition can be paraphrased, in part, as: ITA: 13(21)

the sum of:

(a) the capital cost of depreciable property (A),

(b) all amounts previously included in income as recapture (B), and

(c) all amounts of grants and other assistance deemed to be capital cost that were repaid (C), ITA: 13(7.1) less the sum of:

(a) total depreciation previously allowed (E), ITA: 20(1)(*a*), 20(16)

(b) for dispositions the lesser of (i) proceeds of disposition net of expenses of disposition and (ii) capital cost (F),

(c) all amounts of investment tax credit claimed (I), and ITA: 127(5) or 127(6)

(d) grants and other assistance received or receivable (J). ITA: 13(7.1)(*f*)

Example Problems 5-2 and 5-3 are designed to show what happens when assets are disposed of, either with or without assets remaining in the class after the disposition.

Example Problem 5-2

In each case, the asset disposed of is the only asset in the class.

	(A)	(B)	(C)
Original cost	$10,000	$10,000	$10,000
Undepreciated capital cost	$ 5,000	$ 5,000	$ 5,000
Proceeds of disposition	$12,000	$ 7,000	$ 2,000

— *REQUIRED*

What are the tax consequences if the asset is sold for its fair market value in each of these situations?

— *SOLUTION*

(A) Since it is sold for more than its cost, there will be a capital gain of $2,000. Then the lower of cost or proceeds ($10,000) will be credited to the class, resulting in a negative balance of $5,000. This will result in the recapture of the previous CCA claims of $5,000.

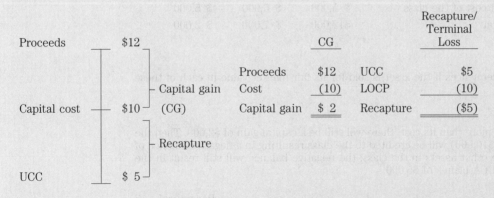

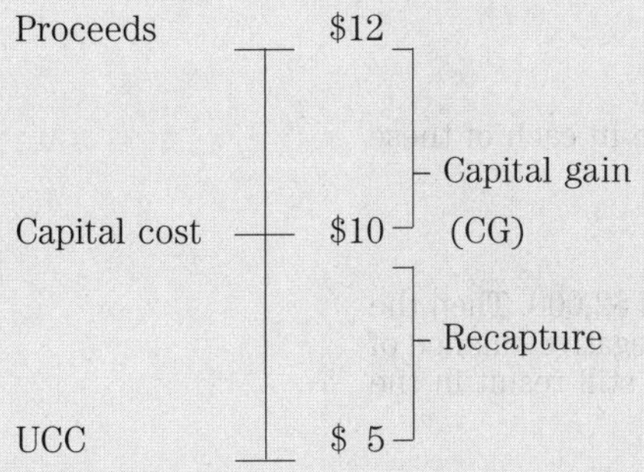

		CG		Recapture/ Terminal Loss
Proceeds		$12	UCC	$5
Cost		(10)	LOCP	(10)
Capital gain		$ 2	Recapture	($5)

(B) In this case, proceeds are between the UCC and original cost. Although proceeds are less than original cost, there is no capital loss since any reduction in value is taken care of through the CCA system. The lower of cost or proceeds ($7,000) will be credited to the class, resulting in a negative balance of $2,000. This will result in the recapture of the previous CCA claims of $2,000.

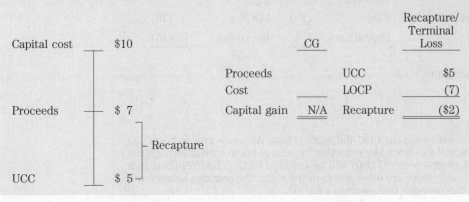

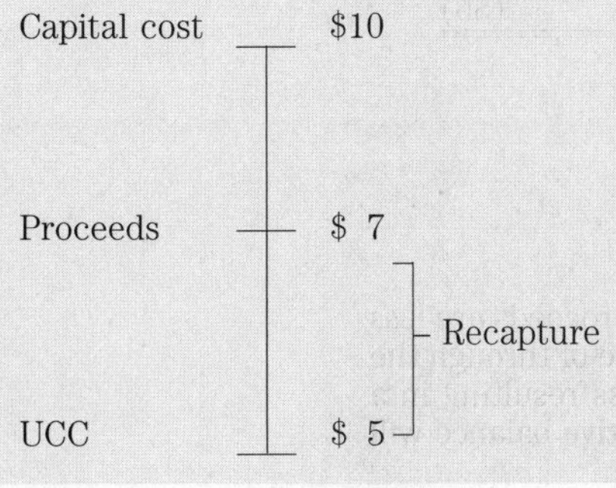

	CG		Recapture/ Terminal Loss
Proceeds		UCC	$5
Cost		LOCP	(7)
Capital gain	N/A	Recapture	($2)

(C) In this case, proceeds are lower than the UCC. Again, there is no capital loss, since any reduction in value is taken care of through the CCA system. The lower of cost or proceeds ($2,000) will be credited to the class, resulting in a positive balance of $3,000 with no assets left in the class. This will result in a terminal loss of $3,000, since not enough CCA was claimed to reflect the true decline in economic value of the asset.

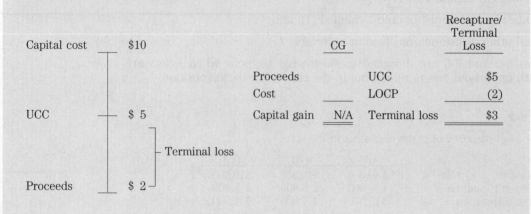

Capital cost	$10	
UCC	$ 5	
		Terminal loss
Proceeds	$ 2	

	CG		Recapture/ Terminal Loss
Proceeds		UCC	$5
Cost		LOCP	(2)
Capital gain	N/A	Terminal loss	$3

Example Problem 5-3

This problem uses the same facts as above, but in this case, assume that there are other assets in the class after the disposition.

	(A)	(B)	(C)
Original cost	$10,000	$10,000	$10,000
Undepreciated capital cost of the class	$ 5,000	$ 5,000	$ 5,000
Proceeds of disposition	$12,000	$ 7,000	$ 2,000

— *REQUIRED*

What are the tax consequences if the asset is sold for its fair market value in each of these situations?

— *SOLUTION*

(A) Since it is sold for more than its cost, there will still be a capital gain of $2,000. Then the lower of cost or proceeds ($10,000) will be credited to the class resulting in a negative balance of $5,000. Although there are other assets in the class, the negative balance will still result in the recapture of the previous CCA claims of $5,000.

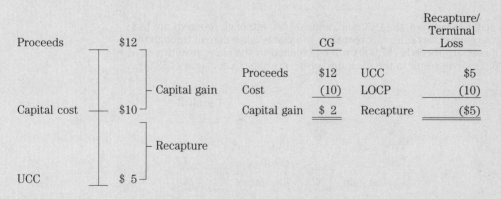

Proceeds	$12	
		Capital gain
Capital cost	$10	
		Recapture
UCC	$ 5	

	CG		Recapture/ Terminal Loss
Proceeds	$12	UCC	$5
Cost	(10)	LOCP	(10)
Capital gain	$ 2	Recapture	($5)

(B) In this case, proceeds are between the UCC and original cost. Although proceeds are less than original cost, there is no capital loss since any reduction in value is taken care of through the CCA system. The lower of cost or proceeds ($7,000) will be credited to the class resulting in a negative balance of $2,000. Although there are other assets in the class, the negative balance will still result in the recapture of the previous CCA claims of $2,000.

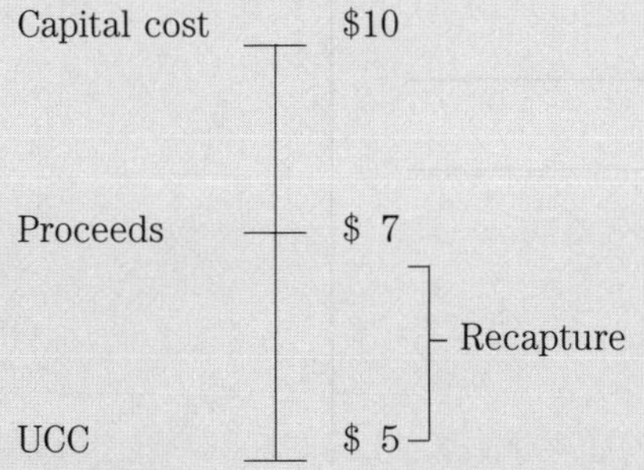

	CG		Recapture/ Terminal Loss
Proceeds		UCC	$5
Cost		LOCP	(7)
Capital gain	N/A	Recapture	($2)

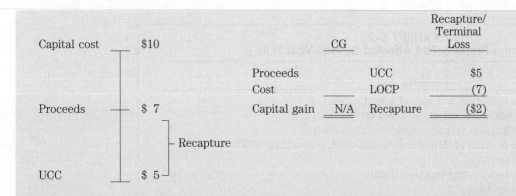

(C) In this case, proceeds are lower than the UCC. Again, there is no capital loss, since any reduction in value is taken care of through the CCA system. The lower of cost or proceeds ($2,000) will be credited to the class, resulting in a positive balance of $3,000, but with assets still left in the class. This will not result in a terminal loss; instead CCA will be claimed on the remaining balance of $3,000, since there are remaining assets in the class.

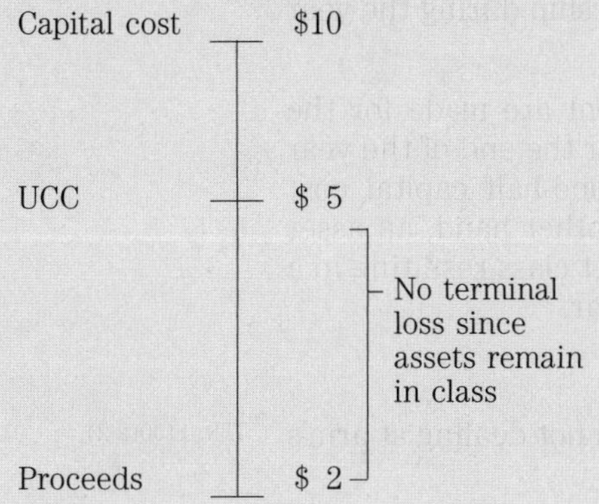

	CG		Recapture/ Terminal Loss
Proceeds		UCC	$5
Cost		LOCP	(2)
Capital gain	N/A	UCC before CCA	$3

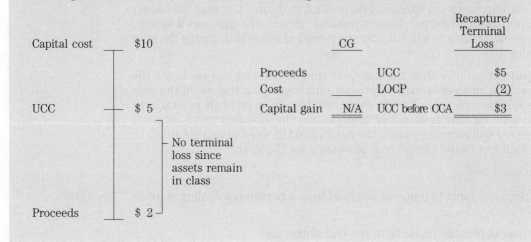

¶5,015.30 *The half-year rule*

The half-year rule, illustrated above, as set out in the Regulations under the heading "Property Acquired in the Year", applies to all classes *except* the following: ITR: 1100(2)

(a) property described in the Regulations pertaining to certified vessels; ITR: 1100(1)(*v*)

(b) Class 12 paragraphs (*a*) to (*c*), (*e*) to (*i*), (*k*), (*l*), and (*p*) to (*s*) in Schedule II; and

(c) Classes 13, 14, 15, 23, 24, 27, 29, and 34 in Schedule II.

However, despite these exceptions, an adjustment similar in effect to the half-year rule is provided for some classes as follows:

(a) property described as certified vessels in the Regulations; ITR: 1100(1)(*v*)(iv)

(b) property of Class 13 in Schedule II (leasehold improvements); and ITR: 1100(1)(*b*)

(c) property of Classes 24, 27, 29, and 34 (some accelerated write-off classes) in Schedule II. ITR: 1100(1)(*t*), 1100(1)(*ta*)

Thus, it would appear that the only property for which some form of adjustment to reflect the half-year rule is *not* made is the following:

(a) property in Class 12 paragraphs (*a*) to (*c*), (*e*) to (*i*), (*k*), (*l*), (*p*) to (*s*); and

(b) property in Classes 14, 15, and 23.

Exhibit 5-2 lists some common capital property not affected in some manner by the half-year rule. Some of these classes will be discussed further in this chapter. ITR: 1100(2)

EXHIBIT 5-2
Common Property Not Affected by Half-Year Rule

Class	*Paragraph*	*Property*
12	(*a*) . . .	a book that is a part of a lending library
	(*b*) . . .	chinaware, cutlery or other tableware
	(*c*) . . .	a kitchen utensil costing less than $500
	(*e*) . . .	a medical or dental instrument costing less than $500
	(*g*) . . .	linen
	(*h*) . . .	a tool costing less than $500
	(*i*) . . .	a uniform
	(*k*) . . .	rental apparel or costume, including accessories
14		a patent, franchise, concession or licence for a limited period

The half-year rule adjustment was implemented to correct the fact that assets purchased at the end of a taxation year would, otherwise, provide a balance in a class that would be eligible for the maximum capital cost allowance in the year. By effectively reducing the capital cost allowance on purchases (in excess of dispositions) during the year, whenever they are made, the advantage of a late purchase is reduced. Hence, the Act uses a simple, arbitrary adjustment as an alternative to adjusting for the period of ownership during the year of acquisition or disposition.

Notice that no adjustments other than the half-year rule adjustment are made for the length of time in the year that an asset is owned. An asset purchased near the end of the year will normally increase the balance in the asset class resulting in a one-half capital cost allowance claim for the year for that asset net of dispositions. On the other hand, an asset sold near the end of the year will normally reduce the balance in the asset class resulting in a decrease in the amount subject to the capital cost allowance for the year.

Non-Arm's Length Transactions

The half-year rule does not apply to property acquired from a person not dealing at arm's length with the acquirer if: ITR: 1100(2.2)

(1) the property was depreciable property of the transferor; and

(2) the property was owned continuously by the transferor from a day that was at least 365 days before the end of the taxation year of the acquirer in which the property was acquired by him or her to the date of acquisition.

This exception is very important when corporate reorganizations are undertaken among related corporations, since it allows the transfer of property between such corporations without the impediment of the half-year rule, except for property that was acquired less than 365 days before the end of the taxation year of the acquiring corporation.

Example Problem 5-4

Ferguson, a professional landscaper, operates an unincorporated yard maintenance business. He has been in business for five years. At the end of the prior year, the UCC in Class 10, containing two mowing tractors, was $3,000. This year, Ferguson purchased two more mowing tractors for a total cost of $6,800.

— REQUIRED

Calculate the maximum CCA claim this year and next year.

— SOLUTION

UCC at the beginning of this year	$ 3,000
Add: purchases during the year	6,800

	$ 9,800
Deduct: dispositions (LOCP)	Nil
UCC before adjustment	$ 9,800
Deduct: ½ (additions – disposals) = ½ ($6,800 – nil)	(3,400)
UCC before CCA	$ 6,400
Deduct CCA @ 30% for Class 10	(1,920)
Add: ½ net amount	3,400
UCC at the beginning of the following year	$ 7,880
Purchases net of dispositions @ LOCP in the year	Nil
UCC before CCA	$ 7,880
Deduct CCA @ 30%	(2,364)
UCC at the beginning of the following year	$ 5,516

¶5,015.40 *Available-for-use rule*

Taxpayers may not start claiming capital cost allowance until the property has become "available for use" by the taxpayer. Very generally, the property is available for use when it is delivered and capable of performing the function for which it was acquired. A building is available for use at the earlier of: ITA: 13(26) ITA: 13(27)–(32) ITA: 13(28)

(a) when all or substantially all of the building is first used for its intended purpose, and

(b) the second taxation year after the year of acquisition.

These rules must be consulted for their application to a specific asset under the particular conditions of the asset's purchase.

Since an asset is eligible for a capital cost allowance claim in the year in which it becomes available for use, the half-year rule applies to the asset in that year, in most cases. ITR: 1100(2)

A similar rule pertaining to capital expenditures in respect of scientific research and experimental development applies. ITA: 37(1.2)

¶5,015.45 *Cost of depreciable property with trade-in*

The capital cost of a new depreciable property that is added to a class cannot exceed the cash paid plus the fair market value of the old property traded in. For example, if a new depreciable property is purchased for $18,000 in cash plus a trade-in with a fair market value of $7,000, the capital cost of the new asset cannot exceed $25,000. Establishing the upper limit on the value of the trade-in at its fair market value is of particular importance in computing investment tax credits, as discussed in subsequent chapters. Using an inflated value for the trade-in would increase capital cost eligible for the investment tax credit. ITA: 13(33)

¶5,015.50 *CCA as a permissive deduction*

The rate of capital cost allowance applied to each class is specified as a maximum rate. The taxpayer may, therefore, claim any amount of capital cost allowance up to a maximum of the amount given by the capital cost allowance rate multiplied by the balance in the class at the end of the taxation year. Under certain conditions, it may be advantageous for the taxpayer to take less than the maximum amount of capital cost allowance allowed. Only the amount actually taken is deducted from the balance in the class of assets. The remaining balance is carried forward and is available for future capital cost allowance claims. In IC 84-1, the Canada Revenue Agency (CRA) indicates some conditions under which it will accept a request from a taxpayer to reassess a return for a previous year to adjust a permissive deduction such as capital cost allowance. IC: 84-1

¶5,020 Taxation year less than 12 months

The statement has been made previously that there is no need to prorate capital cost allowance (other than through the half-year rule adjustment) for the period in a taxation year ITR: 1100(3) that an asset was owned by the taxpayer. This applies to full 12-month taxation years. However, in the first or last years of the operation of a business or in a year in which there has been a change in fiscal year, it is possible to have a taxation year of less than a full 12 months. In this case, capital cost allowance must be prorated by the proportion that the number of days in the taxation year is of 365. Hence, the proration pertains only to a short taxation year. It is completely independent of the half-year rule adjustment which must be made, where applicable, irrespective of the length of the taxation year.

A common exception to this short-year proration rule is Class 14, which includes limited-life patents, franchises, licences, etc. However, as will be seen later in this chapter, there is a proration of capital cost allowance for assets in Class 14 based on the number of days the asset is owned in a taxation year. Therefore, the effect is quite similar to the short-year proration rule. ITR: 1100(3)

Note that an employee does not have to prorate the capital cost allowance on his or her automobile in the first year of use of an existing car for employment purposes, although the half-year rule applies to the purchase of a new automobile. Also, where depreciable capital property is used by an individual to produce income from a source that is property (e.g., rental income), rather than business, the full calendar year is considered to be the taxation year of the individual and, therefore, no prorating is necessary. IT-522R, par. 24

Example Problem 5-5

Nadia began her unincorporated advertising business on March 1 of this year; her year end is December 31. In this year, her first year of business, she purchased furniture (Class 8) for $3,000 and a computer and systems software (Class 50) for $4,200.

— REQUIRED

Calculate the maximum CCA that Nadia can claim in her first year of business.

— SOLUTION

	Class 8	**Class 50**
	20%	**55%**
UCC at the beginning of this year	Nil	Nil
Add: purchases during the year	$ 3,000	$ 4,200
	$ 3,000	$ 4,200
Deduct: dispositions (LOCP)	Nil	Nil
UCC before adjustment	$ 3,000	$ 4,200
Deduct: ½ (additions – disposals)	(1,500)	(2,100)
UCC before CCA	$ 1,500	$ 2,100
Deduct CCA × 306/365 days in year	(252)	(968)
Add: ½ net amount	1,500	2,100
UCC at the beginning of the following year	$ 2,748	$ 3,232

¶5,025 Ownership of property

Generally, in order to be eligible for capital cost allowance on depreciable property, the taxpayer must have either title to the asset or all the incidents of title such as possession, use and risk. An exception is Class 13 leasehold improvements that are made by the tenant but the owner of the building has title to the improvements.

In some circumstances, a taxpayer does not always have ownership or a leasehold interest (Class 13) in a capital asset for which he or she has incurred a cost. In this situation the cost incurred does not give rise to a claim for capital cost allowance. Capital cost allowance may not be claimed for such an expenditure. This was the situation in *Saskatoon Community Broadcasting Co. Ltd. v. M.N.R.*, in which the appellant constructed at its cost a new broadcasting gondola in an arena and was given the sole right to use the new gondola, but the facility was the property of the arena company. In this case, the construction costs were held to be a non-deductible capital outlay and the broadcasting company could not take capital cost allowance because it did not own the property and it did not have a leasehold interest in the facility. Under the tax legislation in force since 1972, this type of expenditure would be considered an eligible capital expenditure. This concept will be discussed later in this chapter.

IT-128R, par. 3
58 DTC 491 (T.A.B.)
IT-143R2

¶5,030 Disposition of property

A disposition of property is defined to *include* "any transaction or event entitling a taxpayer to proceeds of disposition of the property". The use of the word "include" in the definition does not necessarily limit the meaning of disposition of property to a situation where there are proceeds of disposition. Thus, the CRA gives examples of events that it considers to be dispositions without any actual proceeds, including cases of property that is stolen, destroyed, confiscated or expropriated without any compensation or property that is lost or abandoned without expectation of recovery. Furthermore, in the case of *The Queen v. Compagnie Immobilière BCN Limitée*, the Supreme Court of Canada indicated that a claim for capital cost allowance could not be made in lieu of a terminal loss deduction when a building no longer existed. Thus, capital cost allowance can only be claimed when property in a class continues to exist. This follows from the operation of the system in which no claim can be made for capital cost allowance on an asset in the year of its disposition.

ITA: 248(1)
ITA: 13(21)
IT-460, par. 3
79 DTC 5068 (S.C.C.)

¶5,035 Automobiles used in employment or business

¶5,035.10 *Class 10.1 automobiles*

Recall that employees who use their own automobiles to earn employment income and who are entitled to a deduction:

- for sales/negotiating person's expenses, ITA: 8(1)(*f*)
- for travel expenses (other than motor vehicle expenses), or ITA: 8(1)(*h*)
- for motor vehicle expenses ITA: 8(1)(*h*.1)

are entitled to deduct capital cost allowance on the automobiles. ITA: 8(1)(*j*)

Where an automobile is used to earn income from business, capital cost allowance is also deductible. In either case, the capital cost used as the basis for capital cost allowance is limited to $30,000 plus federal sales tax (i.e., GST) and provincial sales tax (PST) or harmonized sales tax (HST) (for acquisitions after 2000) for all taxpayers, whether employed or self-employed and whether incorporated or unincorporated. In the case of a registrant, since the input tax credit resulting from a purchase is used immediately to offset the HST paid, there is no effective HST cost to add to capital cost and, therefore, HST is excluded.

ITR: 7307(1)(*b*)
ITA: 13(7)(*g*), 13(7)(*h*)
ITA: 248(16)

Furthermore, the rules relating to recapture of capital cost allowance and terminal losses do not apply to automobiles having a cost in excess of the prescribed limit. For this reason, each automobile, having a cost in excess of $30,000 plus HST, must be placed in a separate Class 10.1 and not pooled.

ITA: 13(2), 20(16.1)
ITR: 1101(1af)

Since the terminal loss rules do not apply to automobiles in Class 10.1, a special capital cost allowance calculation applies in the year of disposition. In the year of disposition of the automobile, one-half of the capital cost allowance that would have been allowed in respect of the automobile, had it not been disposed of, may be deducted. To qualify for this special "half-year rule", the taxpayer must have disposed of an automobile that was included in Class 10.1 and was owned by him or her at the end of the preceding year.

ITR: 1100(2.5)

¶5,035.20 *Class 10 automobiles*

For automobiles that are not included in Class 10.1, but are in Class 10 because they cost less than the prescribed limit, the amount of capital cost allowance claimed is subject to recapture, if the automobile was owned by an employee. A terminal loss on the disposition of the automobile is not allowed as a deduction from employment income. The only deduction in respect of the capital cost of an automobile allowed as an employment income deduction which allows such part of the capital cost "as is allowed by regulation". A terminal loss is not allowed by regulation. Since a terminal loss is not specifically allowed as a deduction from employment income, the Act would prohibit its deduction. ITA: 13(1), 13(11) ITA: 8(1)(*j*)(ii) ITA: 8(1), 8(2)

When an automobile costs less than the prescribed limit and is owned by a taxpayer other than an employee, the usual rules for deducting capital cost allowance, subject to the half-year rule, including recapture, or deducting a terminal loss apply. Hence, these usual rules would apply to an automobile used in a business by and owned by, for example, a proprietor, a partner or a corporation.

¶5,040 Comparison of capital cost allowance and accounting amortization — Main differences

Although capital cost allowance for tangible capital assets is the tax equivalent of amortization there are a number of important differences which give rise to the need for future income tax accounting. While financial accounting uses useful life as the basis of the write-off of a capital expenditure, the tax system might be based on useful life, legal life (as in the case of leasehold improvements or patents) or fiscal policy. While accounting amortization must adhere to the principles of consistency, the tax system allows for a deduction of any amount up to the maximum permitted for each class. For accounting purposes, differences between book value and proceeds of disposition are considered gains or losses on the sale of an asset. However, the tax system provides for the write-off of the actual decline in value of assets during their holding period. The system requires the inclusion in income of recapture of capital cost allowance where the capital cost allowance deductions have resulted in an undepreciated capital cost that is less than the proceeds of disposition, and the recognition of a terminal loss where capital cost allowance deductions did not fully reflect the decreased value of the asset pool. Under appropriate circumstances, the sale of an asset may also result in a capital gain. However, there can never, under any circumstances, be a capital loss on depreciable capital property. All declines in value are handled through the capital cost allowance deduction and the final adjustment through either recapture or a terminal loss.

¶5,045 Separate class rule for electronic office equipment

Taxpayers may elect to place one or more specified properties that would ordinarily be classified in Class 8 or Class 10 in a separate class. The specified properties are: ITR: 1101(5p)

(a) general purpose electronic data processing equipment and systems software, normally included in paragraph (*f*) of Class 10;

(b) computer software, presumably systems software for electronic process control or monitor equipment and electronic communications control equipment, normally classified in Class 8 (i.e., not classified in Class 10 or Class 12);

(c) a photocopier, normally included in Class 8; and

(d) electronic communications equipment, such as a facsimile transmission device or telephone equipment, normally included in Class 8.

Property placed in separate classes in this manner must have a capital cost of at least $1,000.

The election allows one or more such properties to be placed in a separate Class 8 or Class 10. The advantage of the separate class would be the availability of a terminal loss deduction when all of the assets in such a class are sold for less than the UCC of that class. If assets of this nature decline in value more rapidly than the CCA rates of 20% for Class 8 and

30% for Class 10 imply, perhaps due to technological obsolescence, then a terminal loss on disposition is likely if these assets are separated from other Class 8 or Class 10 assets.

A special transfer rule allows the transfer of Class 8 and Class 10 assets of a separate class back to their main Class 8 or Class 10 after four taxation years. Hence, if the assets in a separate class have not been disposed of after the four-year period from the end of the taxation year of their acquisition, the potential terminal loss deduction in the separate class will not be available. ITR: 1103(2g)

The separate class election is extended to manufacturing and processing property included in Class 43 costing more than $1,000. The election must be filed with the income tax return for the taxation year in which the property is acquired. After five years, any remaining UCC in each separate class must be transferred into the general Class 43 UCC pool. ITR: 1101(55) ITR: 1101(59) ITR: 1103(29)

¶5,045.10 *Computer equipment acquired on or after March 19, 2007*

General purpose electronic data processing equipment and related systems software acquired on or after March 19, 2007 are added to Class 50, which has a CCA rate of 55% declining balance. Again, a separate class election is not available for computer equipment added to Class 50.

¶5,054 Example of CCA over time

Example Problem 5-6

Portable Tools Rental Limited incorporated and commenced business on April 1, 2008 and has a December 31 year-end. The company rents portable tools for short terms and the following are its transactions:

		Portable Tools Class 10: 30%
2008	100 tools purchased at various times during the year for $950 each	$ 95,000
2009	20 tools purchased in June for $1,000 each	20,000
2011	30 2008 tools (well-maintained) sold in November for $1,000 each	30,000
2013	50 2008 tools sold in February for $700 each	35,000

— REQUIRED

Prepare a schedule showing the effects of these transactions on Class 10 and on the income of the company for the period of years indicated. (Ignore the leap year effects.)

— SOLUTION

		Portable Tools Class 10: 30%
2008	Additions: 100 tools purchased for $950 each	$ 95,000
	UCC at the end of 2008 before adjustment	$ 95,000
	Less: ½ of net amount during the year	(47,500)
	UCC before CCA	$ 47,500
	CCA claimed @ 30%; prorated, because of short first year, for 275 days ($47,500 × .3 × 275/365)	(10,736)
	Add: ½ of net amount during the year	47,500
	UCC at the beginning of 2009	$ 84,264
2009	Additions: 20 tools purchased for $1,000 each	20,000
	UCC at the end of 2009 before adjustment	$104,264
	Less: ½ of net amount during the year	(10,000)
	UCC before CCA	$ 94,264
	CCA claimed @ 30% ($94,264 × .3)	(28,279)
	Add: ½ of net amount during the year	10,000
	UCC at the beginning of 2010	$ 75,985

2010	No additions or dispositions	
	CCA claimed @ 30% ($75,985 × .3)	(22,796)
	UCC at the beginning of 2011	$ 53,189
2011	Disposals: 30 tools sold for $1,000 each (cost: $950 each; $1,500 total capital gain)	(28,500)
	UCC before CCA	$ 24,689
	CCA claimed @ 30% ($24,689 × .3)	(7,407)
	UCC at the beginning of 2012	$ 17,282
2012	No additions or dispositions	
	CCA claimed @ 30% ($17,282 × .3)	(5,185)
	UCC at the beginning of 2013	$ 12,097
2013	Disposals: 50 tools sold for $700 each (cost: $950 each; no capital loss on depreciable property)	(35,000)
	UCC at the end of 2013	$(22,903)
	Recapture of CCA taken into income	22,903
	UCC at the beginning of 2014	Nil

— NOTE TO SOLUTION

Had all 90 of the remaining tools in the class been sold for less than $12,097 in 2013, there would have been a positive balance in the class at the end of the taxation year. This would have been written off as a terminal loss under subsection 20(16) against income and the balance in the account would have been set at nil to carry forward.

¶5,056 Transfers to another class — Avoiding recapture

The government will often make classification changes to effect a change in the percentage rate of CCA allowed. For example, at one time, frame buildings were a Class 6 asset and 10% CCA was allowed. Then these were reclassified in Class 3 (the class for brick buildings) and only 5% CCA was allowed. Later, both brick and frame buildings became included in Class 1, which has a 4% CCA rate. However, only newly acquired buildings were put in the reclassified prescribed class. Buildings that were already in Class 3 or 6 stayed in that class. ITR: 1103(2d)

Suppose that a business is replacing a building that has been depreciated through Class 3. In this circumstance, it is possible that the business could end up with a recapture of CCA if the disposition proceeds were greater than the UCC. Normally the capital cost of the new building would eliminate any negative UCC, but here the new building goes to Class 1, not Class 3. In this situation, the Act provides relief. The UCC of the old property in the existing Class 3 may be transferred to the newly acquired Class 1 immediately before the disposition. This will allow a recapture of CCA in the old Class 3 to be wholly or partially avoided. ITR: 1103(2d)

Such a transfer satisfies the principle of fairness, as the taxpayer has no control over the class categorization of assets. The taxpayer should not bear taxes simply because the government has revised the applicable class.

¶5,057 Interest expense

Most profitable businesses are looking to minimize their income for tax purposes and so generally prefer to deduct interest expense as it is incurred. However, other taxpayers may not need deductions, such as where their income is minimal and/or they have losses being carried forward. Non-capital loss carryforwards expire if not used within 20 years. These taxpayers might prefer to defer some deductions. ITA: 20(1)(*c*)

The Act allows taxpayers to elect to capitalize certain interest expense rather than claim it as a deduction when incurred. Only interest incurred in respect to the acquisition of depreciable property is eligible for this election. By making the election, the interest is added to the capital cost of the acquired depreciable property instead of being claimed as a current-year deduction. The interest-inclusive capital cost is the amount on which CCA is then claimed. A taxpayer may make this election if there is insufficient taxable income to use the interest deduction. Such an election provides a useful way of deferring the deduction to future years as capital cost allowance. If in a taxation year, the taxpayer ceases to add the borrowing costs to the capital cost of the depreciable property, the election will not be available for this depreciable property in subsequent years. A similar election exists for interest incurred in connection with many natural resource exploration and development properties. ITA: 21(1) ITA: 21(2)

Where a taxpayer is involved in construction, renovation, or alterations of buildings, interest, and other expenditures are capitalized until the building is completed or "all or substantially all"[2] of the property is used for its intended purpose. Any interest captured by this provision is ineligible for the above discussed election. ITA: 18(3.1)

¶5,058 Capital cost reduction for cost assistance

When a grant, subsidy, forgivable loan, deduction from tax, investment allowance or other assistance is received on the acquisition of property, the amount of such assistance received reduces the capital cost of depreciable property, so that CCA is claimed only on the net cost of the asset. ITA: 13(7.1)

Investment tax credits (ITCs) are a form of subsidy from the government. As ITCs reduce the capital cost of depreciable property. Since investment tax credits are difficult to compute until tax payable is determined, the credit reduces the UCC in the year following the taxation year in which it is claimed. As well, any GST input tax credit received during the year will reduce the UCC amount before CCA is determined.

¶5,059 Inducement payments

The capital cost of a depreciable capital property may also be reduced when a taxpayer receives an inducement payment, in respect of the cost of the property, that would otherwise be taxable. To be entitled to a capital cost reduction instead of being subject to an inclusion in income, the taxpayer must make an election to this effect no later than the date on which he/she is required to file an income tax return for the taxation year during which the taxpayer received the inducement payment, or for the subsequent year if the property was acquired during that subsequent year. ITA: 12(1)(*x*) ITA: 13(7.4)

The amount chosen as a capital cost reduction cannot exceed the least of the following amounts:

- the amount received as an inducement payment;
- the capital cost of the property; or
- zero, if the property was disposed of before the year during which the reduction could be sought.

¶5,060 Exceptions to the Declining Balance Method

¶5,065 Leasehold improvements

Not all classes of assets use a declining balance method of computing capital cost allowance. Special treatment is accorded to a leasehold interest. The capital cost allowance that may be claimed for a leasehold interest (Class 13) after the first year of ownership is the lesser of: ITR: 1100(1)(*b*), Sch. III

(a) ⅕ of the capital cost of the leasehold interest; and

(b) the capital cost of the leasehold interest divided by the number of 12-month periods from the beginning of the taxation year in which the cost was incurred to the end of

[2] "Substantially all" is interpreted by the CRA administratively to mean greater than 90%.

> the term of the lease plus the first renewal term (i.e., the number of months in the remainder of the lease term plus one renewal option divided by 12). The divisor is not to exceed a total of 40 such 12-month periods.

The first year write-off would be ½ of the above amount to provide the equivalent of the half-year rule.

For example, if a $16,000 leasehold improvement is made on a rented building on which the taxpayer has a lease for five years with two successive options to renew of three years and two years, the capital cost allowance for a year other than the first year would be calculated as follows:

Lesser of: (a) ⅕ of the capital cost (⅕ × $16,000) $3,200

(b) capital cost divided by the number of 12-month periods from the beginning of the taxation year in which the cost was incurred to the end of the term of the lease plus first renewal term not to exceed 40 years

$\frac{\$16,000}{5 + 3}$ $2,000

Thus, $1,000 capital cost allowance would be taken in the first year, $2,000 in each of the next seven years and the remaining $1,000 in the ninth year.

If an option to renew, in the denominator of the fraction in (b), is not exercised, then there may be a terminal loss at the end of the lease, if there are no other leasehold interests being amortized on other leases. One Class 13 exists for all of a taxpayer's leasehold interests on all leased properties used in a source of income.

¶5,070 Class 14 limited-life intangibles

Straight-line capital cost allowance is also used for items in Class 14 which generally includes limited-life intangibles such as patents, franchises, concessions or licences. For this class, the capital cost of each property in the class is divided by the remaining legal life, as at the acquisition date, of the property to obtain the amount of capital cost allowance for the year. (Note that the legal life of a patent registered after 1989 is 20 years. If the patent was registered before 1990, its legal life is 17 years.) An Interpretation Bulletin indicates the CRA's view that the capital cost should be prorated over the number of days in the remaining life of the Class 14 asset. Note that this is one of the classes not affected by the half-year rule. IT-477, par. 4

A taxpayer must classify property that is a patent or a right to use patented information for a limited or unlimited period in Class 44 with a 25% declining balance rate. However, a taxpayer can elect that such property not be included in Class 44. Under this election, patents for a limited period would be classified in Class 14. This election might be used when the patent is purchased late in its legal life, such that the straight-line capital cost allowance of Class 14 would exceed the 25% declining balance capital cost allowance of Class 44. ITR: 1103(2h)

¶5,075 Manufacturing and processing machinery and equipment

For property used in manufacturing or processing acquired after March 19, 2007 and before 2014, the asset is added to Class 29 where the CCA rate is 50%, on a straight-line basis. [The March 21, 2013 federal Budget proposes to extend the time period to acquire this equipment from "before 2014" to "before 2016".] The half-year rule applies.

For example, if an eligible piece of equipment costing $100,000 is purchased in 2012 and another costing $100,000 is purchased in 2014, then CCA can be claimed as follows:

		Class 29 50% SL
2012	Opening balance	$ —
	Addition	100,000
	Half-year rule adjustment	(50,000)
		50,000
	CCA @ 50% SL	(25,000)
	Half-year rule adjustment	50,000

	Closing balance	75,000
2013	Opening balance	75,000
	CCA @ 50% SL	(50,000)
	Closing balance	25,000
2014	Opening balance	25,000
	Addition	100,000
	Half-year rule adjustment	(50,000)
		75,000
	CCA @ 50% SL + $25,000	(50,000)
	Half-year adjustment	50,000
	Closing balance	75,000
2015	Opening balance	75,000
	CCA SL	(50,000)
	Closing balance	25,000

¶5,080 Insurance Proceeds Expended on Damaged Depreciable Property

Any part of insurance proceeds payable for damaged depreciable property that has been expended on repairing the damage within the year or within a reasonable time after the damage must be included in income. The amount included will be offset by the amount that will be deducted as an expense of repairing the property so that there will be no net effect on the taxpayer's income. If any part of the insurance proceeds is not expended in this manner, the unused portion will be treated as proceeds of disposition of depreciable property and will, thus, be treated according to the basic rules for proceeds.

ITA: 12(1)(*f*)

ITA: 13(21) "proceeds of disposition" (*f*)

¶5,090 Involuntary and Voluntary Dispositions

¶5,095 Involuntary dispositions

(Consideration of this segment of the chapter can be deferred, without a loss of continuity, until the material under the heading "Exchanges of Property" is considered in Chapter 8 where the capital gain component of the problem is discussed.)

ITA: 44

Ordinarily any insurance recovery for stolen, lost or destroyed (but not merely damaged) depreciable property or any expropriation proceeds would be considered as "proceeds of disposition" by paragraphs (*b*), (*c*), and (*d*) of the definition of that term. A potential recapture might be offset against the cost of property of the same class acquired later in the year. However, a replacement outlay might not be made in the same year for major assets which take some time to replace even if the taxpayer immediately begins to plan the reconstruction or replacement.[3]

ITA: 13(21)

ITA: 13(1)

The taxpayer may elect in the year of replacement of property stolen, lost, destroyed or expropriated to offset any recapture caused by proceeds for the loss as long as replacement is made by the later of either 24 months after the initial taxation year or by the end of the second taxation year following the year in which proceeds are considered receivable. Proceeds are deemed to have become receivable at the earliest of:

ITA: 13(4)

(a) the day the taxpayer has agreed to the full amount of the compensation;

(b) the day the compensation is finally determined by a court or tribunal;

(c) the day that is two years from the day of loss, destruction or taking where a claim or suit has not been taken before the courts;

(d) the day the taxpayer dies or ceases to be a resident of Canada; and

(e) the day immediately before the winding-up of a corporation (other than a Canadian subsidiary owned 90% or more) where the taxpayer is a corporation.

[3] For an example, see the case of *Korenowsky v. M.N.R.*, 64 DTC 235 (T.A.B.).

Basically, replacement property is property acquired for the "same or similar use" as the original property and used for gaining or producing income from the "same or similar business" by the taxpayer or related persons. Note that replacement property need not be of the same class of depreciable property as the original property. The CRA's interpretation of the term "same or similar use" and of the term "same or similar business" are set out in an Interpretation Bulletin. ITA: 44(5) IT-259R4, par. 16–21

¶5,100 Voluntary dispositions

(Consideration of this segment of the chapter can be deferred, without a loss of continuity, until the material under the heading "Exchanges of Property" is considered in Chapter 8 where the capital gain component of the problem is discussed.) ITA: 44

The same rules permitting an offset of recapture caused by proceeds of disposition apply on certain voluntary dispositions of depreciable "former business property". However, in this case, replacement must be made by the later of either 12 months after the initial taxation year or by the end of the first taxation year following the year of disposition. The term "former business property" is defined to mean real property (i.e., land and buildings) or an interest therein (i.e., a leasehold interest) that is capital property used primarily for the purpose of earning business income. These rules pertaining to a former business property might be used in a business relocation to avoid recapture on the disposition of buildings. ITA: 248(1)

Normally, a building is the only depreciable property eligible for the replacement property rules for voluntary dispositions. However, a limited-period franchise, concession or license will also be eligible. The replacement property rules are extended where the transferor and transferee jointly elect to have these rules apply. ITA: 13(4.2), 13(4.3)

Example Problem 5-7

Wally's is a department store operating in the area. Its operations are carried on in a building which is owned by the company. The capital cost of the building to Wally's in September 2009 was $400,000. The company has been taking capital cost allowance on the structure on the basis that it is a Class 1 asset with a capital cost allowance rate of 4%. In May 2011, a fire virtually destroyed the building. The only asset which was recovered was an F.A.D. computer, and it was substantially damaged. The computer had been purchased by Wally's in December 2010 at a cost of $75,000 and as a Class 50 asset it had been depreciated at a rate of 55% since 2010.

In August 2011, under an insurance policy with the Risk-Averters Insurance Company, Wally's received $385,000 for the destruction of the building and $25,000 for the damage to the computer. Wally's had the computer repaired to its original condition in 2011 at a cost of $23,000. In 2013, a new building was constructed for $465,000.

— REQUIRED

Trace the effects of these events on the balance of the undepreciated capital cost accounts for each asset from 2009 through to the beginning balance for 2014 in the building account and for 2013 in the computer account. As you trace the effects, indicate all deductions from and inclusions in income from the business for the years indicated. Assume that the appropriate election is made. ITA: 13(4)

— SOLUTION

(A) Building — Class 1: 4%

2009	Additions: purchase of building	$400,000
	UCC at the end of 2009	$400,000
	CCA claimed @ 4% (($400,000 — ½ × $400,000) × .04)	(8,000)
	UCC at the beginning of 2010	$392,000
2010	No additions or disposals	
	CCA claimed @ 4% ($392,000 × .04)	(15,680)
	UCC at the beginning of 2011	$376,320
2011	Disposals: insurance proceeds	(385,000)
	UCC at the end of 2011	$ (8,680)
	Recaptured CCA taken into income	8,680

ITA: 13(21) "proceeds of disposition" (*c*)

	UCC at the beginning of 2012		Nil	
2012	No additions or disposals			
	UCC at the beginning of 2013		Nil	
2013	File an amended return for 2011 as follows:			ITA: 13(4)
	UCC at beginning of 2011		$376,320	ITA: 13(4)(*c*)
	Reduction of UCC:(1)			
	— normal deduction is lesser of:			
	(i) proceeds	$ 385,000 →	$385,000	
	(ii) capital cost	$ 400,000		
	— reduced by lesser of:			ITA: 13(4)(*c*)
	(i) excess, if any, of $385,000 (as determined above) over UCC of $376,320 at the beginning of 2011 (i.e., recapture)	$ 8,680 →	(8,680)	
	(ii) cost of replacement property	$ 465,000		
			(376,320)	
	UCC at the end of 2011		Nil	
	Recaptured CCA		Nil	
	UCC at the beginning of 2012		Nil	

Building — Separate Class 1-NRB: 6%

2013	Additions: purchase of new building(2)	$465,000	
	Deemed proceeds of disposition (equal to reduction calculated above)	(8,680)	ITA: 13(4)(*d*)
	UCC at the end of 2013	$456,320	
	CCA @ 6% (($456,320 – ½ × $456,320) × .06)	(13,690)	
	UCC at beginning of 2014	$442,630	

(B) Computer — Class 50: 55%

2010	Additions: computer	$ 75,000
	UCC at the end of 2010	$ 75,000
	CCA claimed @ 55% (($75,000 — ½ × $75,000) × .55)	(20,625)
	UCC at the beginning of 2011	$ 54,375
2011(3)	Disposals: proceeds of disposition in the amount of unexpended insurance proceeds	(2,000)
	UCC at the end of 2011	$ 52,375
	CCA claimed @ 55% ($52,375 × .55)	(28,806)
	UCC at the beginning of 2012	$ 23,569
2012	No additions or disposals	
	CCA claimed @ 55% ($23,569 × .55)	(12,963)
	UCC at the beginning of 2013	$ 10,606

— *NOTES TO SOLUTION*

(1) To generalize the proceeds reduction rule, it would appear that as long as the cost of the replacement property exceeds the recapture that would otherwise result on the disposition (i.e., the $8,680, above), there will be no actual recaptured capital cost allowance on the disposition. In effect, part of the proceeds of disposition of the former property is transferred from the year in which the disposition occurred to the year in which the replacement property is acquired. This avoids recapture in the year of disposition and reduces the undepreciated capital cost of whichever class of property the replacement property falls into. ITA: 13(4)(*c*)

(2) The rules allow for a replacement with an asset of another class. The old building was in Class 1; the new building is in a separate Class 1-NRB and still qualifies as replacement property for the rollover. ITA: 13(4)

(3) In 2011, income would be increased by expended proceeds of insurance of $25,000, but this amount would be offset by the deduction of repair expense of $23,000. Thus, the net effect on income is nil which is as it should be. The other $2,000 received is a capital receipt which reduces undepreciated capital cost. ITA: 12(1)(f)

¶5,110 Change in Use and Part Disposition Rules

Rules are set out for the determination of capital cost and proceeds of disposition in the following five situations: ITA: 13(7)

- Change from income-producing to other purpose;
- Change from non-income-producing to income-producing purpose;
- Property acquired for multiple purposes;
- Change in proportion of use for producing income and other purposes; and
- Non-arm's length transfer of depreciable property.

¶5,115 Change from income-producing to other purpose

In this case, property is acquired for producing income, but its use is changed to another purpose. Consider the situation where a taxpayer had a house which he or she rented and later lived in himself or herself. At the time of the change in use, the taxpayer is deemed to have disposed of a depreciable asset at its fair market value. This deemed disposition may result in either recapture or a terminal loss. The deemed reacquisition at fair market value establishes the cost of the asset for personal use. The problem of determining fair market value without a transaction gives rise to cases such as that of *Tripp v. M.N.R.*, in which the value of a house relative to the value of the land on which it was situated was at issue. ITA: 13(7)(a); 63 DTC 313 (T.A.B.)

¶5,120 Change from non-income-producing to income-producing purpose

In this situation, property is acquired for a non-income producing purpose, but its use is later changed to producing income. Consider the case if the first situation were reversed. At the time of the change in use, the taxpayer is deemed to acquire a depreciable asset at its fair market value where that value is less than its cost, representing a decline in value. But where the fair market value of the asset is greater than its cost, representing an increase in value, the capital cost of the asset will, generally,[4] be limited to the lesser of: ITA: 13(7)(b)

(i) the fair market value of the property at the time of the change in use			xxx
(ii) the total of			
(A) cost at the time of the change in use		xxx	
(B) the fair market value of the property at the time of the change in use	xxx		
less: cost at the time of change in use	xxx		
excess, if any	xxx		
½ of excess		xxx	xxx

As a result of this latter rule, the capital cost of the asset for the purposes of computing capital cost allowance is limited to the sum of two components. That sum consists of the actual cost of the asset before the change in use plus the amount, if any, of taxable capital gain resulting from the deemed disposition on the change in use. Therefore, there can be no step-up in the capital cost to fair market value, because the step-up in capital cost is limited to ½ of the gain from actual cost up to fair market value.[5]

[4] The actual formula in paragraph 13(7)(b) provides for an adjustment in respect of the capital gains deduction. Such a deduction is only available for qualified farm property which might be subject to a change in use. As a result, the adjustment will not be common.

[5] For a more detailed discussion of paragraphs 13(7)(b), (d) and (e), see Robert E. Beam and Stanley N. Laiken, "Changes in Use and Non-Arm's Length Transfer of Depreciable Property", *Canadian Tax Journal*, Vol. 35, No. 2, March-April 1987, p. 453.

The capital cost of the asset after the change in use and the application of the limited step-up will reflect an amount that has been fully tax paid by the owner. Since the taxpayer will pay tax on only ½ of the capital gain, only ½ of the gain may be added to the original cost. The rationale for this limitation is that the stepped-up capital cost will provide the base for future CCA which is fully deductible from business or property income. A taxpayer should only expect to fully deduct a cost that was fully tax paid.

The half-year rule to reduce first-year capital cost allowance would appear to apply because the conditions which provide exceptions to this rule for property of a class in Schedule II are not met. In particular, the condition that the property, subject to the change in use to income-producing purposes, would not have been *depreciable* property at the time of the change in use if its previous use was non-income-producing is not met. It makes some sense to impose the half-year rule at the change in use to income-producing purposes, because the half-year rule would usually not have been applied on acquisition for the previous non-income-producing purpose. Note that a change in use from income-producing purpose to non-income-producing purpose should not be affected by the half-year rule, because the property would not be depreciable property if its purpose is not income-producing. ITR: 1100(2.2) ITR: 1100(2.2)(*f*)

¶5,125 Property acquired for multiple purposes

In this case, property is acquired both for producing income and for another purpose. For example, consider the situation where a taxpayer buys a duplex and lives in one half, renting the other half. At the time of the purchase, ½ of the cost of the building is allocated to depreciable assets of the taxpayer. On the sale of the property, ½ of the proceeds is regarded as proceeds of the depreciable asset by the same paragraph. ITA: 13(7)(*c*)

¶5,135 Non-arm's length transfer of depreciable property

These rules are discussed in more detail in Chapter 8, under the heading "Consideration in Non-Arm's Length Transfers". They apply where depreciable property is transferred between persons not dealing at arm's length, which is also discussed in Chapter 6, under the heading "Related persons". These rules prevent the realization of benefits from a transfer motivated by the fact that the increase in value over cost is taxable to the transferor as a capital gain (i.e., ½ taxable), but would be fully depreciable from fair market value at the time of the transfer to the transferee if it were not for these rules. The adjustment to the capital cost of property transferred to the non-arm's length transferee is similar to the calculation presented for a change in use of property, where only cost plus the taxable capital gain to the transferor can be depreciated by the transferee. ITA: 13(7)(*e*) ITA: 251 ITA: 13(7)(*e*) ITA: 13(7)(*b*)

¶5,150 Franchises and Similar Property

It should be noted that Class 14 includes certain property that is a patent, franchise concession or licence for a limited period. The cost of such property is expensed under the capital cost allowance system by taking straight-line capital cost allowance over the remaining legal life of the property as indicated earlier. Note in particular that this property must have a limited life. The amounts that can be considered as the capital cost of a patent were at issue in *Weinberger v. M.N.R.* The Court held that not only the amount paid to have the invention patented but also the costs to produce and perfect the invention to the point where the patent can be obtained are considered to be the capital cost of the patent. 64 DTC 5060 (Ex. Ct.)

If the cost of a patent is added to Class 14, because the taxpayer has elected that the property not be included in Class 44, it will be eligible for capital cost allowance on a straight-line basis over its remaining legal life (17 years if registered before 1990 and 20 years if registered after 1989), as discussed previously. However, the CRA suggests that expenditures incurred in making any representation for the purpose of obtaining a franchise or a patent (among others) to a government or public body relating to a business of the taxpayer would be deductible immediately. In lieu of an immediate deduction, the taxpayer may elect in prescribed manner to deduct one-tenth of the amount otherwise eligible for deduction in each of the 10 consecutive years beginning with the year in which the expenditure is made. Thus, three possibilities for dealing with expenses of representation, in this situation, may be available: ITR: 1103(2h) IT-99R5, par. 11 ITA: 20(1)(*cc*) ITA: 20(9)

(a) an immediate deduction of the cost; ITA: 20(1)(*cc*)

(b) a deduction of the cost over a 10-year period; and ITA: 20(9))

(c) capitalization of the cost in the appropriate CCA class (14 or 44) or in the eligible capital property pool (see below).

Any amount deducted immediately or over 10 years is subject to recapture. ITA: 13(12)

Certain property, such as franchises, may have an indefinite life in contrast to a limited life (Class 14). If this is the case, the property is likely an eligible capital property subject to amortization through the cumulative eligible capital account which will be discussed in the next section of this chapter. It will be seen that eligible capital property excludes intangible property that is depreciable property. A franchise of any kind may be considered as intangible property, but because a franchise for a limited period is listed in Class 14 it is depreciable property and, therefore, cannot be eligible capital property.

¶5,200 ELIGIBLE CAPITAL PROPERTY

¶5,210 Basic Rules

Under the pre-1972 Act, certain items of intangible property were known as "nothings" because they were capital in nature, and, hence, not deductible as a business expense, but not tangible assets and, hence, not depreciable. Such "nothings" included the cost of purchased goodwill,[7] the cost of a franchise for an indefinite life and incorporation costs among others. When these assets were sold, proceeds were treated by the vendor as a capital receipt with no tax consequences and by the purchaser as a non-deductible, non-depreciable expenditure.

Under the present Act, most of these items, and others discussed in the Interpretation Bulletin entitled "Meaning of Eligible Capital Expenditure", are defined as "eligible capital expenditures". This definition includes capital outlays that are not otherwise specifically allowed or disallowed as deductions under the Act and made after 1971 for the purpose of earning income (other than exempt income) from business. (See the Interpretation Bulletin entitled "Separate Businesses" for an indication of the concept of a "business".) Note that the definition of "eligible capital expenditures" specifically excludes certain expenditures. Also, note that expenditures made prior to 1972 are not now deductible. IT-143R3 ITA: 14(5) IT-206R

In general, three-quarters of each eligible capital expenditure is added to the "cumulative eligible capital" (CEC) account. ITA: 14(5)

The change to a ½ capital gains inclusion rate for dispositions after October 17, 2000 does not affect the ¾ fraction used to calculate additions to the CEC account or disposals of eligible capital property (ECP). Instead, a special ⅔ adjustment is applied when calculating the income inclusion for a negative balance in the CEC pool for taxation years ended after October 17, 2000. The ⅔ adjustment converts a ¾ amount in the CEC pool to a ½ amount (i.e., $2/3 \times 3/4 = 1/2$).

[7] The meaning of "goodwill" was considered in *Losey v. M.N.R.*, 57 DTC 1098 (Ex. Ct.).

The Act makes an adjustment to the amount added to the cumulative eligible capital account on a non-arm's length purchase. The adjustment is similar in effect to the adjustment on the purchase of depreciable property. The usual addition of 3/4 of the purchase purchaser's cost must be reduced by 1/2 of the non-arm's length seller's business income inclusion from the gain on the sale of eligible capital property (item A in the definition of "cumulative eligible capital"). ITA: 14(3) ITA: 13(7)(*e*) ITA: 14(1)(*b*) ITA: 14(5)

The balance in the CEC account is amortized on a declining balance basis using a maximum rate of 7%. The amount of annual amortization is referred to as the "cumulative eligible capital amount" (CECA). The Interpretation Bulletin entitled "Transactions Involving Eligible Capital Property" discusses the effects of transactions involving eligible capital property on the balance in the CEC account and provides an extended numerical example in Schedule B. ITA: 20(1)(*b*) IT-123R6

¶5,220 Comparison to the Capital Cost Allowance System

The system for taking deductions on eligible capital expenditures is very similar to that for depreciable capital property. The major differences, based on the rules in effect after the adjustment time, are:

(a) there is only one account or pool that is used to record purchases and dispositions of eligible capital expenditures (ECE) for a particular business. This account is called the "cumulative eligible capital" (CEC) account, as indicated above, and is amortized on a declining balance basis to a maximum of 7% of the balance in the account. (The definition of the cumulative eligible capital account appears somewhat more complex because it accumulates all adjustments to the account since 1971. Note that the ECE definition parallels directly the definition of undepreciated capital cost); IT-206R ITA: 20(1)(*b*) ITA: 14(5) ITA: 14(5) ITA: 13(21)

(b) expenditures made prior to 1972 are completely ignored (but dispositions of property whenever purchased are considered);

(c) only 3/4 of eligible capital expenditures (ECE) (which is equivalent to capital cost in the capital cost allowance system) and 3/4 of proceeds called an "eligible capital amount" (ECA) affect the account;[8] and

(d) there is no half-year rule.

Similar to the capital cost allowance system, it is the balance of cumulative eligible capital (CEC) which is equivalent to undepreciated capital cost at the end of the taxation year or on termination of the business that is important. At that time:

(a) if the balance of CEC is positive and the business is to continue, take amortization as a deduction at a maximum of 7% of the balance of CEC and subtract that amount from the balance to be carried forward to the next year;

(b) if the balance of CEC is negative, for any taxation year ending after October 17, 2000, take into business income:

(i) the lesser of:

(A) the negative balance, and

(B) all cumulative eligible capital amounts claimed in prior years

less

deductions previously recaptured in prior year business income inclusions

PLUS

(ii) 2/3 of the negative CEC balance less (i), above (i.e., 2/3 of the excess, if any, of (A) minus (B), above).

[8] The eligible capital amount (ECA) is determined in item E of the definition of "cumulative eligible capital" in subsection 14(5) and referred to in subsection 14(1).

The business income is effectively a recapture of previous deductions plus ½ of the absolute gain on the disposal. The ⅔ adjustment factor effectively converts from a ¾ rate to a ½ [⅔ × ¾ = ½].

(c) if the balance of cumulative eligible capital is positive, but the business has been terminated, take the positive balance as a deduction which is the equivalent of a terminal loss from income; ITA: 24

(d) the provision related to non-arm's length transactions operates in much the same way as for capital cost allowance purposes. The ECP system restricts the eligible capital expenditure of a non-arm's length purchaser of eligible capital property where the vendor has claimed a capital gains deduction[9] in respect of the disposition of the eligible capital property; and ITA: 14(3) ITA: 13(7)(e) ITA: 110.6

(e) replacement property rules defer recognition of recaptured cumulative eligible capital amounts on the disposition of eligible capital property where the property is replaced within one year of the end of the year of disposition, in the same manner as the CCA system. ITA: 14(6), 14(7) ITA: 13(4)

¶5,230 Illustration of the Rules

¶5,235 Common aspects

The more common aspects of these rules are illustrated in Exhibit 5-3.

EXHIBIT 5-3
Cumulative Eligible Capital Account
[Sec. 14]

Facts

Assume a corporation commencing business purchases a store in year one and pays $5,000 for goodwill. In year one and in year two the full 7% deduction is claimed. In year three the store is sold and $6,500 is received for goodwill.

In year three, assume that the corporation purchases another store and pays $4,450 for goodwill. In year three the full 7% deduction is claimed. In year four, the corporation ceases to carry on the business and sells the business to a person other than a corporation controlled by it. No part of the proceeds can be attributed to goodwill.

Application of Rules and Definitions

Year	*Ssec. 14(5) Cumulative eligible capital item A*	*Ssec. 14(5) Cumulative eligible capital item E*	*Par. 20(1)(b) Cumulative eligible capital amount 7% deduction*	*Ssec. 14(5) Cumulative eligible capital*
1 Purchase	¾ × $5,000 = $3,750			$ 3,750
1 CECA			$263 (7% × $3,750)	$ 3,487
2 CECA			$244 (7% × $3,487)	$ 3,243
3 Disposal		(¾ × $6,500 = $4,875)		($1,632)*
3 Purchase	¾ × $4,450 = $3,338			$ 1,706

[9] Available to an individual who has disposed of qualified farm property, such as a farm marketing quota.

[Exhibit 5-3 — continued]

3 CECA	$119 (7% × $1,706)	$ 1,587	
4 Business Closed	$1,587 (sec. 24)	Nil	

* $263 + $244 + ¾ ($6,500 – $5,000) = $1,632 (equal to the negative balance for post-adjustment time purchases). If the goodwill of $4,450 is not purchased in Year 3, then there would be a business income inclusion as follows:

a) the lesser of:
i) $1,632
and
ii) $263 + $244 = $507
lesser amount $507
PLUS
b) ⅔ × ($1,632 – $507) 750
$1,257

The $1,257 can also be calculated by adding the recaptured CECA of $507 to ½ of the gain ($6,500 – $5,000).

¶5,240 Non-arm's length transactions

The following examples illustrate the effects of a non-arm's length transaction in eligible capital property, assuming a sale for $100,000.

If the seller has no balance in the cumulative eligible capital account, the following would occur:

(a) sale of eligible capital property:

cumulative eligible capital balance		Nil
disposal: ¾ of $100,000		$ (75,000)
balance		(75,000)
inclusion in income — lesser of:		
• (i) negative balance above	$75,000	
(ii) amortization previously deducted	Nil	
lesser amount	Nil	
• plus ⅔ ($75,000 – Nil)	$50,000	50,000
untaxed amount		25,000
balance		Nil

Note that the $50,000 inclusion in income is one-half of the economic gain on the disposition of the property, i.e., $50,000 = ½ ($100,000 proceeds – Nil cost).

(b) purchase of eligible capital property by non-arm's length person:

purchase: ¾ × $100,000	$75,000
less adjustment: ½ of seller's gain inclusion (½ × $50,000)	(25,000)
cumulative eligible capital balance	$50,000

Note how the non-arm's length purchaser will be allowed to amortize only $50,000, which is the amount of the seller's gain that was subject to tax.

If the seller has a balance in the cumulative eligible capital account of, say, $20,000 and the seller has claimed amortization, previously, of $13,000 on property with a full cost of $44,000, the following would occur:

(a) sale of eligible capital property:

cumulative eligible capital balance			$20,000
disposal: ¾ of $100,000			(75,000)
balance			(55,000)
inclusion in income – lesser of:			
• (i) negative balance above	$55,000		
(ii) amortization previously deducted	$13,000		
lesser amount		$13,000	
• plus ⅔ ($55,000 – $13,000)		28,000	41,000
untaxed amount			14,000
balance			Nil

Note that the $41,000 inclusion in income is one-half of the seller's economic gain on the disposition of the property (i.e., $28,000 = ½ ($100,000 proceeds – $44,000 cost)) plus the "recapture" of amortization previously deducted (i.e., $13,000).

(b) purchase of eligible capital property by non-arm's length person:

purchase: ¾ × $100,000	$75,000
less adjustment: ½ of seller's gain inclusion (½ × $28,000)	(14,000)
cumulative eligible capital balance	$61,000

Note how the non-arm's length purchaser will be allowed to amortize only $61,000, which is equal to the seller's:

(i) cumulative eligible capital balance before the disposition	$20,000
(ii) "recapture" of previously deducted amortization	13,000
(iii) ½ of the economic gain of $56,000 (i.e., $100,000 – $44,000)	28,000
total	$61,000

The $20,000 represents a tax-paid cost that the seller had a right to recover through amortization and the other two amounts were subject to tax and, hence, became tax-paid. The total tax-paid cost of $61,000 can be recovered through amortization deducted by the purchaser in the future.

¶5,250 Election Re: Capital Gain

Although the capital gains inclusion rate of ½ is reflected in the income amount on the disposal of CEC, the additions and reductions to the cumulative eligible capital pool are still done at a rate of ¾. There may be instances where a taxpayer would prefer to recognize an economic gain on eligible capital property as a capital gain rather than as a reduction to the available cumulative eligible capital pool. An example of such an instance would be if the taxpayer has available capital losses, either currently or carried over from another taxation year. ITA: 14(1)

An election is available that allows a taxpayer to treat a gain on the disposition of eligible capital property as a capital gain. The following conditions are necessary to take advantage of this provision. ITA: 14(1.01)

(i) The property disposed must be eligible capital property of a business, but not goodwill.

(ii) The cost of the property to the taxpayer must be determinable.

(iii) The proceeds of disposition of the property must exceed the cost.

(iv) The taxpayer's exempt gains balance in respect of the business must be nil.

(v) The taxpayer must elect in the taxpayer's return of income for the year. ITA: 14(1.01)

If the above conditions are met, then the proceeds of disposition of the property are deemed to be equal to the cost of that property. Then, the taxpayer is deemed to dispose of a capital property with proceeds equal to the actual proceeds and an adjusted cost base equal to the cost of the eligible capital property. If the property disposed is an eligible capital property that is a qualified farm property, then the capital property deemed to be disposed is deemed to be a qualified farm property. ITA: 110.6(1)

Example Problem 5-9

Ms. Chalupshka has operated an accounting practice with a December 31 year end since 2010. She paid $16,000 for a client list when she started the practice in 2010. On August 27, 2013, she sold the practice, including her client list which was allocated $28,000 of the proceeds. The balance in the CEC account on January 1, 2013 was $8,976.

— *REQUIRED*

Compute Ms. Chalupshka's business income from the sale of the client list in 2013.

— *SOLUTION*

Election Made

	CEC a/c
Cumulative eligible capital, January 1, 2013	$ 8,976
2013 Disposal: deemed proceeds = cost of client list (3/4 × $16,000)	(12,000)
Cumulative eligible capital, December 31, 2013	$ (3,024)
Inclusion in business income	3,024(1)
Cumulative eligible capital on cessation of business	Nil

ITA: 14(1.01)

Deemed disposal of capital property	
Deemed proceeds	$ 28,000
Deemed ACB	(16,000)
Capital gain	$ 12,000
Taxable capital gain (1/2)	$ 6,000
Income inclusion	
Business income	$ 3,024
Taxable capital gain	6,000
Total	$ 9,024

No Election Made

	CEC a/c
Cumulative eligible capital, January 1, 2013	$ 8,976
2013 Disposal: deemed proceeds = 3/4 × $28,000	(21,000)
Cumulative eligible capital, December 31, 2013	(12,024)
Inclusion in business income	9,024(2)
Non-taxed 1/2 of "gain" (1/3 × 3/4 × ($28,000 – $16,000))	3,000
Cumulative eligible capital on cessation of business	Nil

— *NOTE TO SOLUTION*

(1) The business income inclusion is computed as follows:

(a) lesser of:		
(i) Negative balance	$ 3,024	
(ii) Total CECA claimed [(3/4 × $16,000) – $8,976]	$ 3,024	
lesser amount		$3,024
(b) 2/3 ($3,024 – $3,024)		nil
Inclusion in business income		$3,024

(2) The business income inclusion is computed as follows:

(a) lesser of:		
(i) Negative balance	$12,024	
(ii) Total CECA claimed	$ 3,024	
lesser amount		$3,024
(b) 2/3 × ($12,024 – $3,024) = 1/2 of economic gain ($28,000 – $16,000)		6,000
Inclusion in business income		$9,024

¶5,300 CAPITAL PERSONAL PROPERTY AND THE INPUT TAX CREDIT SYSTEM UNDER GST/HST

¶5,310 Basic Rules

An integral part of the GST/HST system is the ability to claim input tax credits (ITCs) on business inputs and thus avoid the cascading or compounding of tax through the production and distribution chain. In order to qualify for an ITC, the property or service must have been purchased for use in a *commercial activity*. In determining the net remittance for a reporting period, the total ITC for the period is deducted from the tax collected or collectible for that period. Where the total ITC for the period exceeds the tax collected or collectible, the registrant will be entitled to a refund.

An important feature of the ITC mechanism is that purchases and sales need not be matched in order to claim an ITC. The credit can be claimed for the period in which the tax is paid or becomes payable. Similarly, for purchases of capital property, there is no requirement for amortization. Under the general input tax credit rules, a registrant may claim an ITC for the tax paid on the purchase of property or a service which was acquired for use in commercial activities. However, special rules have been developed for capital property, due to the fact that the useful life of capital property generally often extends for several years and the use of the property may change over that period. Under the *Excise Tax Act* (ETA), capital property is divided into two main groups — capital personal property and capital real property, and different rules apply to each group.

For GST/HST purposes, capital property is defined to include any property that is capital property for income tax purposes, other than property included in Class 12 (for example, small tools or utensils costing less than $200, video tape, computer software, etc.) or Class 14 (for example, patents, franchises, concessions or licences for a limited period, etc.) of the capital cost allowance classes. This definition for GST/HST purposes applies regardless of whether the registrant is a taxpayer under the *Income Tax Act*. ETA: 123(1)

Separate rules apply to passenger vehicles and aircraft that are acquired by an individual or a partnership, and certain input tax credit restrictions apply to all passenger vehicles. These topics are discussed below.

The rules for capital real property are discussed in Chapter 8.

¶5,320 Passenger Vehicles and Aircraft

Restrictions on claiming ITCs apply to passenger vehicles owned by all registrants, with special additional rules applying to passenger vehicles owned by registrants that are individuals or partnerships. Many of these rules are based on the rules for passenger vehicles under the *Income Tax Act*. For example, the definition of passenger vehicle under the ETA has the meaning assigned under the *Income Tax Act*. As well, temporary input tax credit restrictions ITA: 248(1) of the Ontario and Prince Edward Island provincial component of the HST apply to large businesses (those making taxable supplies greater than $10 million) and financial institutions in respect of certain vehicles. As British Columbia exited the HST on April 1, 2013, the temporary input tax credit restrictions that also applied in that province only apply where the 7% provincial component of the HST was paid.

¶5,325 Passenger vehicles owned by registrants other than individuals and partnerships

Following the rules for deductibility under the *Income Tax Act*, the ETA refers to ETA: 201 specific paragraphs of the *Income Tax Act*. As a result, no input tax credit may be claimed on ITA: 13(7)(*g*), 13(7)(*h*) the portion of the cost of a vehicle that exceeds $30,000 excluding GST/HST and/or provincial sales tax. Similarly, an input tax credit may not be claimed in respect of an improvement to ETA: 202(1) the extent the accumulated cost of the vehicle, including the improvement, exceeds $30,000.

As with other capital personal property (i.e., capital property other than capital real property), a full input tax credit may be claimed for the first $30,000 of the cost of passenger vehicles where the primary-use test is met. If the use in a commercial activity is 50% or less, no input tax credit may be claimed.

On the actual disposition of a passenger vehicle, the sale is subject to GST/HST only where the vehicle was used primarily in a commercial activity prior to that time. In addition, a ETA: 203(1) registrant may be entitled to claim an input tax credit on all or a portion of the cost of the vehicle that exceeded the prescribed threshold, i.e., $30,000, which was previously denied.

As discussed in Chapter 1, when they adopted the HST, the provinces of British Columbia and Ontario have both implemented temporary input tax credit restrictions for large businesses, which generally include businesses with annual sales in excess of $10 million, and most financial institutions. As originally enacted, during the first eight years of the application of the HST in these two provinces, large businesses were required to recapture a portion of the 8% (Ontario) or 7% (British Columbia) provincial component of their total input tax credits for HST paid or payable on specified property and services acquired or brought into those provinces for use therein. These recapture requirements were to be phased out over the eight-year period. As British Columbia exited the HST on April 1, 2013, the temporary input tax credit restrictions only apply where the 7% provincial component of the HST has been paid. As a consequence, these restrictions will not apply for the entire duration of the eight-year period as originally planned. When Prince Edward Island adopted the HST effective April 1, 2013, it also implemented these temporary input tax credit restrictions for large businesses, which will be phased out over the initial eight-year period of HST in the province.

Subject to these temporary input tax credit restrictions are road vehicles that weigh less than 3,000 kilograms and are required to be licensed for use on public highways, including most cars, minivans, and pickup trucks, but not trailers and semi-trailers. Also included are parts and services relating to these road vehicles that are purchased, or brought into the province, within the first 12 months following the date of acquisition of the vehicle, except for parts and services acquired in the course of routine maintenance of the vehicle.

¶5,330 Passenger vehicles and aircraft owned by registrants who are individuals or partnerships

Registrants who are individuals (e.g., sole proprietorships) or partnerships are entitled to claim a full input tax credit in respect of the acquisition of a passenger vehicle only if the vehicle is used exclusively (i.e., 90% or more) in a commercial activity. Similarly, a full input tax credit may be claimed in respect of any improvement only if the vehicle was used exclusively in a commercial activity since its acquisition and will continue to be so used immediately after the improvement. As with other registrants, no input tax credit may be claimed on the portion of the cost of a vehicle (or improvements thereto) that exceeds $30,000, exclusive of provincial sales tax and GST/HST. ETA: 202(2) ETA: 202(3)

If the vehicle or aircraft is used less than exclusively in a commercial activity, a full input tax credit may not be claimed in respect of the acquisition or improvement. However, the individual or partnership is entitled to claim an input tax credit equal to $5/105$ (or the applicable HST factor, depending on the particular province) of the capital cost allowance claimed for income tax purposes, to the extent the vehicle or aircraft is used in a commercial activity. For example, if an individual purchases a car in Ontario for $16,000 (including GST/HST) for use 60% in a commercial activity, the individual would be able to claim an input tax credit equal to $166 (i.e., $1/2 \times 30\%$ of $16,000 $\times 60\% \times 13/113$) in the first year. An input tax credit may also be claimed in subsequent years based on capital cost allowance claims. ETA: 202(4)

On the actual disposition of a passenger vehicle or aircraft, GST/HST applies only if the vehicle or aircraft was used exclusively in a commercial activity since its acquisition. ETA: 203(3)

Where an individual or partnership sells a passenger vehicle that immediately before that time was used exclusively in a commercial activity the following applies. The individual or partnership is entitled to claim an input tax credit in the same manner as other registrants (as discussed above) on all or a portion of the cost on acquisition and any improvements, that exceeded $30,000 and that was previously denied. ETA: 203(1)

¶5,800 REVIEW QUESTIONS

(1) In the year of acquisition only one-half of the capital cost of an asset is added to the CCA class. Comment.

(2) If an asset is sold for less than the UCC balance in the class then there will be a terminal loss. Comment.

(3) The "cost amount" of depreciable property is the original cost of the asset. Comment.

(4) The "capital cost" of depreciable property is the original cost of the asset before any CCA is claimed. Comment.

(5) The half-year rule applies to all property acquired in all CCA classes. Comment.

(6) The half-year rule is designed to take into account the period of ownership during the year and the fact that not all assets are purchased at the beginning of the year. Comment.

(7) CCA can be claimed in the year that title and the incidence of ownership are acquired by the taxpayer. Comment.

(8) Once a CCA claim has been made a taxpayer cannot go back and change the amount of the prior year's claim. Comment.

(9) When the fiscal period of a business is less than 365 days then the CCA must be prorated for the number of days in the fiscal year. Comment.

(10) Once an asset has been disposed of, then no CCA can be claimed on that asset. Comment.

(11) A client just bought a new piece of equipment that cost her $50,000. Because of the nature of the asset she has received a government grant of $15,000 to help pay for it. She thinks she can only depreciate $35,000. Comment.

(12) It has just cost a client $20,000 in legal fees to obtain a patent on some new equipment. Given his profitability, he is unhappy that he can only depreciate these costs as a Class 14 asset over the 20-year life of the patent but his controller says that he does not have any choice. Comment.

(13) Mrs. Smith has just incorporated her company to carry on a retail business. As part of the start-up costs she has paid $800 to have the company incorporated and $10,000 to obtain the indefinite-life franchise that she wanted. Each of these expenditures are eligible capital expenditures and since they are different they each go into their own CEC pool. Comment.

(14) Mr. Fin has just come to tell you that he has decided to wind up his business and retire. He is in the process of selling all of his assets but he cannot find one buyer who will continue the business and pay him something for goodwill. He is disappointed since he has a balance of $15,000 in his CEC account that cannot be used. Comment.

¶5,825 MULTIPLE CHOICE QUESTIONS

Question 1

X Ltd. purchased a $50,000 passenger vehicle in 2013. What is the maximum amount that X Ltd. may claim as capital cost allowance for the vehicle in 2013, ignoring harmonized sales tax?

(A) $7,500

(B) $9,000

(C) $4,500

(D) $4,050

Question 2

R Ltd. owns a restaurant business which it carries on in rented premises. R Ltd. redecorated and renovated in 2013 and made $80,000 of leasehold improvements. The lease expires on December 31, 2018 (five years) and has two successive renewal options of three years each. Assuming that R Ltd. has a December 31 year-end, what is the maximum CCA that R Ltd. can claim in 2013 in respect of these improvements?

(A) $5,000

(B) $8,000

(C) $10,000

(D) $16,000

Question 3

In the year, ABC Ltd. purchased goodwill relating to a business for $100,000. Assuming ABC Limited has no other depreciable or eligible capital property, what is the maximum write-off that ABC Ltd. can claim for this goodwill in the year?

(A) $2,500

(B) $3,500

(C) $7,000

(D) $5,250

Question 4

On January 1, 2011, ABC Ltd. signed a five-year lease for retail space for a store. The lease expires on December 31, 2015, and has two successive renewal options for three years each, In 2013, ABC Ltd. made $60,000 of leasehold improvements to this space. Assuming that ABC Ltd. has a December 31 year end, what is the maximum capital cost allowance claim that ABC Ltd. can make in 2013 in respect of these improvements?

(A) $3,750

(B) $5,000

(C) $6,000

(D) $7,500

Question 5

During the year, Swiss Restaurants purchased the following assets for its restaurant and catering business:

Moulds for fancy chocolate items ($300 each)	$ 1,200
An accounting program (computer software)	600
Linens for tables in the restaurants	400
Cutlery, dishes, and kitchen utensils costing less than $500 each	15,000

What is the maximum CCA claim for these assets?

(A) $8,600

(B) $16,300

(C) $16,900

(D) $17,200

Question 6

The new controller of a pharmaceutical company has asked you how the legal costs to obtain a 20-year patent on a new drug are treated for tax purposes. Which one of the following options is not available?

(A) include in Class 14

(B) include in Class 44

(C) deduct in the year incurred

(D) treat as an eligible capital expenditure

¶5,850 EXERCISES

Exercise 1

ITA: 14(5), 20(1)(*a*); ITR: 1100

Businesses in two plazas operating on either side of a very busy city street decided to pool their promotional efforts. They also decided to build an overpass so that customers could avoid crossing the street when shopping at the plazas. The overpass was constructed at a cost of $150,000 after appropriate arrangements were made with the city because the footings to the overpass had to be placed on city property. These arrangements did not include a leasehold interest in the city property.

— *REQUIRED*

In what class of assets can the overpass be placed for capital cost allowance?

Exercise 2

ITA: 13(7); ITR: 7307(1)

Harrison Chen, an insurance salesperson, acquired a luxury antique sports car in 2013 for a capital cost of $42,000. The car will be used 40% of the time in performing his duties of employment.

— *REQUIRED*

Compute Harrison's estimated CCA in his first and second year of owning the car (ignore HST).

Exercise 3

ITA: 20(16.1), 21(1); ITR: 1100(2.5), 1100(6)

Scott is a commission salesman who has been claiming capital cost allowance on his automobile under paragraph 8(1)(*j*). The automobile was purchased for $38,000 (including 8% PST and 5% GST) in October 2011. The undepreciated capital cost of his automobile at January 1, 2013, was $18,475. In 2013, he sold the automobile for $12,000. Scott does 75% of his driving for employment purposes out of 16,000 kilometres of total driving.

— *REQUIRED*

(A) What are the tax consequences in 2013 to Scott on the sale of the old car?

(B) What are the tax consequences in 2013 if Scott buys a new car in October 2013 for $36,000 including HST (13%)? His net commission income after deducting cash expenses for 2013 is $3,000.

Exercise 4

ITA: 20(1)(*a*); ITR: 1100; Sched. II, III

The following balances were found in the various classes of depreciable assets on the books of Wasting Assets Ltd., as at January 1, 2013:

Class 1 (see (1) below)	$120,000
Class 8	75,000
Class 10 (truck for transportation of goods)	40,000
Class 13 (see (2) below)	42,000
Class 14 (see (3) below)	54,400

Additional information and transactions during 2013:

(1) The Class 1 undepreciated capital cost represents two buildings costing $100,000 each. One building was sold for $150,000 during 2013.

(2) The Class 13 balance relates to a long-term lease on a warehouse for 30 years with an option to renew for a further 20 years. The original cost of the leasehold improvements in 1997, when the lease was entered into, was $50,000.

(3) Class 14 consists of a patent for 20 years costing $68,000 on January 1, 2009. (Ignore the effects of the leap years in the period.)

(4) Purchases during the year:

Manufacturing equipment	$50,000
Office equipment	10,000

— REQUIRED

Prepare a schedule showing the maximum capital cost allowance deductions for tax purposes in 2013.

Exercise 5

ITA: 13

Liam O'Neille acquired an apartment building a few years ago for $240,000. The cost of the entire property was allocated as follows:

Land	$80,000
Building	$160,000

The UCC of the building as of the beginning of this year was $144,500, and the net rental income for last year was $4,800. Liam turned 65 years old this year and decided to begin his retirement by selling his apartment building. He received $280,000, $100,000 of which was allocated to the land and $180,000 to the building.

— REQUIRED

Calculate the maximum capital cost allowance that may be claimed in the current year, and compute the undepreciated capital cost, recapture, or terminal loss.

Exercise 6

ITA: 20(1)

The following are independent situations:

(a) Gimcrack Inc. purchases its sole asset, costing $100,000, on February 15. The company has a February 28 year-end. The asset purchased is a Class 8 asset.

— REQUIRED

Calculate the capital cost allowance that may be claimed in the taxation year under the following independent scenarios.

(i) Fiscal period is 365 days.

(ii) Fiscal period is 90 days.

(b) RSI Ltd. sells computers and has a December 31 year end. RSI Ltd. leased a warehouse this year for ten years with a renewal option of two years and a second renewal option of three years. Leasehold improvements of $25,000 were made to the warehouse during the year. RSI has no other leasehold improvement assets.

— REQUIRED

Calculate the maximum amount of CCA that may be claimed in this, the first taxation year.

(c) Constabulary Ltd. acquired franchise rights for the amount of $25,000 to operate a doughnut and coffee shop. The franchise is valid for a period of 15 years commencing March 1. Constabulary Ltd.'s year end is July 31.

— REQUIRED

What CCA or other deduction is Constabulary Ltd. allowed this year?

Exercise 7

ITA: 13(4)

(If consideration of the topics of involuntary and voluntary dispositions has been deferred to Chapter 8, this exercise should also be deferred.)

Windswept Storage Ltd. had a brick warehouse that was completely destroyed by a tornado early in its 2012 fiscal year ended December 31. The building had cost $300,000 and its Class 3 undepreciated capital cost at the time of its destruction was $221,000. Agreement was reached on the insurance claim later in 2012 when the company received only $295,000. A new brick building was fully constructed by August 2013 for $400,000.

— *REQUIRED*

Trace the effects of these events on the balance of the undepreciated capital cost from 2012 through to the beginning balance for 2014, assuming that the proper election is made. ITA: 13(4)

Exercise 8

ITA: 20(1)

Mr. E. Presley has been operating an automobile repair business since 2000. The fiscal period of the corporation ends on September 30. The business owns the following assets:

(a) A frame building used as a garage was acquired in 2003. The capital cost of the building in 2003 was $250,000. The UCC of this Class 1 asset was $208,985 as of the last year end. During the current year, renovations were made to the garage in the amount of $20,000.

(b) A warehouse adjacent to the frame building was leased. The lease has a term of five years with five options for renewal of five years each. The lease period commences April 15. The cost of leasehold improvements was $70,000.

(c) Computer equipment was acquired on April 15, 2010. The UCC at October 1, 2012 is $40,000. The equipment was used to perform analysis for repairs.

(d) Two trucks were acquired in a previous fiscal period. The UCC as of the last year end for these Class 10 assets was $25,000. One of the trucks was sold this year for gross proceeds of $10,000. The capital cost of the truck was $15,000. Selling costs incurred to sell the truck were $1,000.

(e) The rights to a licence to sell special racing car parts was purchased for $30,000. The licence is valid for a period of 15 years commencing June 1 this year.

— *REQUIRED*

Compute CCA for Mr. Presley's automobile repair business for the taxation year ended September 30, 2013. Ignore the leap year effects.

Exercise 9

ITA: 13(7)(*d*)

Steven purchased a car in 2011 for $14,600. His business use of the car during 250 days each year based on mileage of 16,000 kilometres in total and the fair market values of the car in each of the years to the present were as follows:

	Business use	*Fair market value*
2011	85%	$14,600
2012	80%	12,200
2013	90%	9,800

— *REQUIRED*

Compute the maximum capital cost allowance that can be claimed.

Exercise 10

ITA: 14(1), 20(1)(*b*)

Ms. Glutton sold her unincorporated grocery business in 2013 and received $45,000 for goodwill. The business had a December 31 year-end.

— *REQUIRED*

If the grocery store had been purchased on January 2, 2000 with a payment of $10,800 for goodwill at that time, compute the effect of the 2013 sale on Ms. Glutton's income. Assume that maximum deductions for amortization have been made in previous years, except in the years 2002 to 2011 inclusive when no amount was claimed since the business only had losses. ITA: 20(1)(*b*)

Exercise 11

ITA: 14(1), 20(1)(*b*)

Buylo Ltd., which has been in the same business, except as noted below, since 2005, made the following purchases and sales throughout the period 2005 to 2013.

Jan. 1, 2005	Purchased goodwill at $40,000.
June 1, 2007	Purchased a government licence with an indefinite life for $50,000.
Mar. 1, 2009	Purchased a trademark for $20,000.
Nov. 1, 2010	Purchased goodwill for $50,000.
Sept. 7, 2011	Sold 2005 goodwill for $100,000.
Aug. 3, 2013	Sold all of the remaining assets of the business to a competitor for $500,000 of which $150,000 could be attributed to the licence and $200,000 to the trademark.

— REQUIRED

Calculate the income for the 2011 and 2013 taxation years, assuming the company always took the maximum tax amortization deductions each year for its fiscal years ending December 31. Calculate the amount of cumulative eligible capital as at January 1, 2014. ITA: 14(1), 20(1)(*b*)

¶5,875 ASSIGNMENT PROBLEMS

Problem 1

ITA: 13, 20(16)

Silvia Fields is the self-employed operator of a VIP delivery service. Three years ago, Silvia purchased her only asset, a van, for a cost of $24,000. The van has been used 100% for business deliveries since it was purchased. The UCC balance in Class 10 at the beginning of this year is $14,280. On March 1, Silvia sold the van for $10,300 and leased a new van for $400 a month.

— *REQUIRED*

Compute the income tax implications of the disposition of the van.

Problem 2

ITA: 13(1), 13(2), 20(1)(a), 20(16.1); ITR: 1100(1), 1100(2.5), 1101(5p), 1103(2h), 7307(1)(b); Sch. II, III

On March 1, 2012, Jennifer Lobo began operating as a sole proprietorship and purchased the licence to manufacture the computer software version of the latest trivia game, "Tax is a Microcosm of Life on DVD". She acquired the following assets:

Manufacturing equipment	$20,000
Tools (each costing under $500)	16,000
Dies and moulds	8,000
Computer equipment and systems software	12,000
Photocopier	6,000
Office furnishings	15,000
Customer lists (expected to be used indefinitely)	4,000
Delivery van	28,000
TV commercial video tape	22,000
Chairs and tables (for the employee eating area)	2,500
Cutlery and dishes (for the employee eating area)	2,000
Table linens (for the employee eating area)	1,200
Automobile (for use by sales personnel visiting clients)	38,000
Licence to manufacture, based on patented information, "Tax is a Microcosm of Life on DVD" for three years ending February 28, 2015	30,000
Made improvements on the building that she leased on March 1, 2012; the lease was for three years with two successive options to renew of three years and four years	9,000

During 2013, she made the following additional purchases and disposals:

Bought a new brick building and land in May to be used 95% for manufacturing; an appraisal indicated that the building represented 45% of the total cost of the property	$200,000
Sold the photocopier	(4,000)
Sold the automobile	(23,000)
Sold the TV commercial video tape	(18,000)
Sold some of the tools (costing less than $500 each)	(5,000)

— *REQUIRED*

Prepare a schedule to show the maximum capital cost allowance for the fiscal years ended December 31, 2012 and December 31, 2013, ignoring HST considerations. Where choices are available, state the reasons for your decision. Ignore the effects, if any, of a leap year.

Problem 3

ITA: 13(7)

On January 20, 2012, a personal residence which originally cost $280,000 was converted into a rental property. At this time the property had a fair market value of $320,000. On June 1, 2014, the property was sold for fair market value of $305,000.

— *REQUIRED*

If the building is the only asset in Class 1, which has a 4% capital cost allowance rate, how much capital cost allowance may be deducted for the years 2012 through 2014, inclusive? [Note that where an individual has income from property, the taxation year for that income is the full calendar year, i.e., there cannot be a short taxation year for that income.]

Problem 4

ITA: 14, 20(1)(*b*)

Sharp is a musician who paid $500 in 2003 for an indefinite-life licence to perform in the subway walkway areas. In 2008, Sharp decided to try a different approach to developing a following. He purchased the name of a popular local band that stopped performing earlier that year. The cost of the name was $16,128 and the appropriate amount was included in the January 1, 2009 balance below. In 2009, he purchased an indefinite-life licence from the city for $5,000 which allowed him to perform on a street corner on Saturday afternoons. In 2010, Sharp found that he wanted to spend more time in the studio, so he sold the street corner licence for $6,000. In 2013, Sharp decided to break up his band and pursue a career as an accountant. He sold the band name for $20,000.

Sharp has not yet filed his tax return for 2013. The year-end of the business is December 31. The following information is available with respect to the cumulative eligible capital account:

(a) the balance in the cumulative eligible capital account, on January 1, 2009, was $11,492, and

(b) the total cumulative eligible capital amount claimed prior to 2009 was $979.

— *REQUIRED*

Prepare a schedule calculating the balance of the cumulative eligible capital account on January 1, 2014, and calculating the impact on income for 2013.

Problem 5

ITA: 14, 20(1)(*b*), 20(1)(*cc*); IT-206R

Con-Glo Corporation has been involved in various food services businesses since its incorporation in 2000. Con-Glo has a December 31 year-end. You have been asked by the controller to examine the transactions involving various intangible assets due to an impending sale of the business. The controller wants to ensure that he understands the implications on the sale. You have been provided with the following information.

Shortly after the business was incorporated, Con-Glo purchased its first family restaurant. The purchase price included $43,000 for goodwill. After operating this business for a number of years and ensuring that it was profitable, another restaurant was purchased in 2006. The purchase again included goodwill in the amount of $68,000. The second restaurant had more of a roadhouse atmosphere. The business had obtained an unlimited life liquor licence. The value of the licence at the time of the purchase was $21,133, and this amount was allocated to the licence in the purchase agreement.

Con-Glo operated the two restaurants until 2008 when it purchased a fast food franchise. The franchise was for an undefined number of years and cost $103,000.

The fast food restaurant, while successful, was too much of a drain on the time of the owners of Con-Glo and was sold in 2010. The value of the franchise agreement was determined to be $110,000.

In 2011, it was determined that the original family restaurant would be more successful if it obtained a liquor licence. In order to obtain the licence a presentation had to be made to the liquor licensing board. Con-Glo paid $29,000 in legal fees related to the presentation to the board.

In 2012, the second restaurant was sold. Con-Glo received $80,000 for the goodwill and $60,000 for the liquor licence.

Due to health problems of the owner's wife, Con-Glo is also considering a sale of the balance of their restaurants in 2013. The selling price will include $250,000 for goodwill.

— *REQUIRED*

Prepare a schedule calculating the balance of the cumulative eligible capital account as of January 1, 2014, and determine the impact of the above transactions on income for 2006 through 2013. Assume that the opening balance on January 1, 2006, was $20,865, the 2000 to 2005 CECA deductions were a total of $11,385, and that the company took the maximum tax write-offs that it was entitled to in each of the years 2006 to 2011. (Hint: consider paragraph 20(1)(*cc*).) Assume also that Con-Glo was deemed to be in the same business in respect of its restaurant and fast food business as per IT-206R.

Problem 6

ITA: 20(1), 20(16)

The following are independent situations.

(a) Janice Martin was an employee of XYZ Ltd. She was required to use her car in her employment duties and at the end of last year the UCC of her car (Class 10) was $3,500. She left XYZ during this year and began working for Executive Search Service, where she was not required to use her car. Janice sold her car this year for $3,200.

(b) Ramesh acquired a rental building on September 1 this year at a cost of $75,000. His net rental income for the four months is $2,000. He wants to claim the maximum CCA.

(c) In 2003, William acquired two rental buildings at a cost of $60,000 each. He has sold one for $90,000. The UCC of each building was $45,000. Ignore any capital gain.

(d) Colin bought a piece of land that he is renting to a farmer for pasturing his cows. The land cost $35,000 and Colin received $1,500 in rent. Is Colin restricted on the CCA he is allowed?

(e) Randi sold her rental property last year for $100,000. The allocation was $75,000 for the building and $25,000 for the land. Her legal fees for selling the property were $2,000. What are her proceeds of disposition for the building?

— *REQUIRED*

Identify the CCA, amortization, or other amount in each of the above situations.

Problem 7

ITA: 13, 14, 20(1)(*a*), 20(1)(*b*); ITR: 1100; Sched. II, III

Jon's Auto Parts Ltd., which manufactures small equipment, was incorporated in 1986 and had the following balances in its records concerning its capital assets as at January 1, 2013.

	Depreciation		*CCA*	
Type of asset	*Straight-line*	*Book value*	*Class*	*UCC*
Land	Nil	$102,000		Nil
Building	40 years	272,000	3	$153,000
Equipment	5 years	163,000	8	39,000
Rolling stock — trucks, etc. (for transportation of goods)	3 years	306,000	10	170,000
Leasehold improvements (see note (1), below)	life of lease	113,000	13	165,000
Licences	5 years	70,000	14	87,393

Additional Information

(1) The Class 13 assets consist of:

— Improvements to a leased warehouse costing $100,000 in 2012. The remaining length of the lease in 2012 was six years with two successive options of four years.

— Improvements to a leased office space for head office downtown, costing $81,600 in 2011. The remaining length of the lease was five years with an option to renew for an additional one year.

(2) The licences were purchased to start on April 22, 2011, at a cost of $110,500 and had a life of five years.

(3) During 2013, the company had the following capital transactions:

Additions:

— Purchased, in June, a new concrete manufacturing building costing $1,625,000, including $325,000 for land.

— Additional expenditures re the building:

Paved parking lot for employees	$ 97,000
Erected a steel fence around an outside storage area	65,000

— Further renovations to leased office space, costing 51,000

— Purchased equipment:

Office equipment	$ 47,000
Manufacturing equipment	255,000
Radio communication equipment	60,000

— Purchased a distributing licence on March 1, 2013, for five years from a foreign manufacturing company of a related product line, cost: $240,000.
— Paid $34,500 in legal fees in reorganizing the capital structure.

Disposals:

	Cost	*Book value*	*Proceeds*
Equipment — office	$ 16,250	$ 4,225	$ 1,950
Brick building in Cl. 3 (excluding land)	390,000	272,000	568,000

— *REQUIRED*

Prepare a schedule for tax purposes to reflect the above transactions and calculate the maximum write-off for tax purposes. (Ignore the effects of the replacement property rules in subsection 13(4) and the effects of leap years.)

Problem 8

ITA: 13, 14, 18–20; ITR: 1100; Sched. II, III

The controller of Choleva Products Limited has provided you with the following draft income statement as well as some notes that she made during the preparation of this statement.

Choleva Products Limited
STATEMENT OF INCOME
For the year ended December 31, 2013

Sales		$ 8,300,000
Cost of goods sold (Note (1))		(6,800,000)
Gross profit		$ 1,500,000
Commission income		70,000
		$ 1,570,000
Administrative and marketing expenses (Note (2))	$500,000	
Amortization (Note (3))	80,000	
Interest on long-term debt (Note (4))	70,000	
Interest on bank indebtedness	120,000	(770,000)
		$ 800,000
Gain on disposal of property, plant and equipment (Note (3))		40,000
Net income before income taxes		$ 840,000
Provision for income taxes		(400,000)
Net income after income taxes		$ 440,000

Notes Prepared by Controller:

(1) The cost of goods sold expense includes the following amounts:

(a) A $9,000 loss from a theft by a warehouse employee;

(b) A $15,000 reserve for future decline in the value of inventory because of new products expected to be introduced by the competitor. There was no such reserve in 2012.

(2) Administration and marketing expenses include:

(a) An $11,000 increase in the reserve for warranty expenses;

(b) $4,000 of donations to registered charities;

(c) $1,500 for golf club membership dues for the Vice-President of Sales and $2,000 for meals and entertainment expenses at the golf club. The Vice-President of Sales uses the club to generate sales;

(d) $85,000 in accrued bonuses, including $62,000 paid to employees on May 31, 2014, and $23,000 paid to employees on June 30, 2014;

(e) A $15,000 year-end party for all employees;

(f) $8,000 of financing fees incurred in connection with the mortgage of the corporation's new plant, including legal fees of $6,000 and an appraisal fee of $2,000;

(g) $5,000 of legal fees in connection with the purchase of shares of another company; and

(h) $300 for an upgrade of word processing software.

(3) The fixed asset section of the controller's working papers indicate the following:

(a) The undepreciated capital cost balances at December 31, 2012 were as follows:

Class 3	$200,000
Class 8	60,000
Class 10	80,000
Class 13	37,500
CEC	5,000

(b) Gain on disposal of property of plant and equipment consists of the profit on the sale of the corporation's only Class 3 asset (proceeds: $180,000; original cost in 1987: $300,000). The land on which the building was situated was also sold for its fair market value which was equal to its cost in 1987.

(c) During 2013, the corporation made the following purchases:

- A new office building was purchased in October for $700,000. The cost of the related land was $400,000. It cost $20,000 to pave part of the land for use as a parking lot and $30,000 to erect fencing;
- New office furniture was purchased for $25,000. This purchase replaced office furniture which was sold for its $4,000 net book value (original cost: $10,000);
- An unlimited life franchise was purchased for $100,000;
- A 10-year licence to use patented information (expiring June 30, 2023) was purchased on July 1 for $20,000; and
- Improvements on its leased head office premises which were rented in 2011 for four years with two successive options to renew for five years and five years. Improvements had originally been made in 2011 in the amount of $45,000. Additional improvements were made in 2013 at a cost of $28,000.

(d) During the year, the corporation sold some small tools (each costing less than $500) for their net book value of $500.

(4) Interest on long-term debt includes:

(a) Bond discount amortization in the amount of $2,000;

(b) $18,000 of interest on bonds issued to buy shares in another company; and

(c) $50,000 of interest on the mortgage on the new plant.

— *REQUIRED*

Calculate the corporation's minimum income from business or property for the year ended December 31, 2013, under the provisions of the Act. Assume all expenses are reasonable in the circumstances. Support your treatment of each item listed above with a reason or a section reference. Ignore the effects of leap years.

Problem 9

ITR: 1100(2)

Both cutlery and word processing software are included in Class 12.

— *REQUIRED*

Determine, by specific reference to the *Income Tax Regulations*, whether the half-year rule applies to these two Class 12 items.

Problem 10

ITA: 13(4)

(If consideration of the topics of involuntary and voluntary dispositions has been deferred to Chapter 8, this problem should also be deferred.)

Elaine Barblaik owns an apartment building which she holds for rental income. In November 2012, Elaine settled with municipal authorities on expropriation proceeds for the property including the building. The agreed expropriation proceeds for the building and the separate sale proceeds for the appliances and fixtures are indicated in the following data:

	Expropriated building Cl. 3	*Sold appliances & fixtures*
Cost	$406,000	$26,000
UCC January 1, 2012	188,500	7,250
Proceeds	362,500	2,600

Since negotiations had been prolonged, Elaine was able to anticipate the approximate date of settlement and, as a result, she was able to replace in 2013 the assets expropriated.

Replacement cost for the building and the cost of new appliances and fixtures were as follows:

Building	$1,276,000
Appliances and fixtures	46,400

— *REQUIRED*

Trace the effects of these events on the undepreciated capital cost for both assets through to the opening balance on January 1, 2014 assuming no further additions are made to either class of assets.

[For more problems and solutions thereto, see the DVD accompanying this book.]

¶5,880 ADVISORY CASES

Case 1: RBL Proprietorship

RBL Proprietorship was heavily damaged during a recent street riot. The mobs broke in, set fire to the store, and physically assaulted the owner, Larry. Fortunately the business was insured, and the owner received the following amounts without delay:

Personal injury damage award	$ 50,000
Insurance receipts — business interruption	80,000
Insurance receipts for delivery truck destroyed	30,000
Insurance receipts for leaseholds destroyed by fire	15,000
	$175,000

The undepreciated capital cost in Class 10 is $15,000 and in Class 13, $10,000. The original cost of the truck was $35,000 and the original cost of the leaseholds was $20,000.

Larry does not understand why the damages are not treated as an expense for tax purposes. RBL plans to replace the truck immediately. The damage to the leaseholds, however, presents a challenge because the cost to repair the damage far exceeds the insurance compensation. RBL is considering relocating its business to a safer location. The company will then be able to change its image to suit a new clientele. The architect estimates that the leasehold improvements could be completed in 12 months. The total cost for the move would be as follows:

Moving costs	$ 12,000
Business interruption	48,000
Leasehold improvements	60,000
Lease cancellation penalty	4,400
Total	$124,400

Larry would like your advice on the tax implications of his plans.

Case 2: Dundas Printing Inc.

Dundas Printing Inc. has been in business for the past 20 years. It has only been in the past three years that Bill Peach has taken over the operations from his father (who founded the company and is now retired). As a result of his new-found management freedom and changes in the marketplace, Bill has decided to expand his operations.

One of the printing presses he needed to buy would have been too expensive if he had bought it new, so he found a used press at half the price. The drawback is that it will take some time to get the press into production, since it needs some repairs to put it into workable condition. However, Bill feels that this is still a good buy since it will meet his needs for the next five years, by which time new technology will probably make it obsolete and he will be forced to buy a new machine.

Before his retirement, Bill's father drove a car that the company had purchased for his use at a cost of $45,000. The car was given to Bill for his use on his father's retirement. Bill has now decided that he is going to trade in this car for a car that he always wanted — a sports car that is going to cost $65,000 less the trade-in value of $25,000 for the old car. Bill promises to take you for a ride when it is delivered.

In order to increase his market share, Bill bought all of the assets of one of his competitors. This not only gave him access to some important customers, it also allowed him to acquire some specialized equipment and skilled operators. The vendor had wanted to sell Bill the shares of his company, but Bill had convinced the vendor to sell him the assets, instead, including goodwill of $40,000.

Bill would like your advice on the tax implications of his plans.

Case 3: Kingston Carpets Inc.

Kingston Carpets Inc. ("Kingston") has been operating a retail carpet business out of the same location for the past 18 years. It has been very successful in gaining business from the local developers, who use Kingston almost exclusively to provide their flooring. In addition, Kingston is used extensively by the area insurance adjusters for carpet replaced due to fire and other damages. This business did not come to Kingston overnight. The owners, Andy and Sue Greene, have always spent much of their time promoting their business to these markets.

Both Andy and Sue are avid golfers. They each belong to a different golf club, in order to be members at the clubs where most of their customers play. They find that golf is an activity that has paid off, since they have conducted a significant amount of business through their contacts at the golf clubs. They will often use these clubs for lunch and dinner meetings with customers, as well as for the company's seasonal holiday party.

Last year, the company bought a building across the street from its original retail store. The previous owner had been leasing out the building and had not spent much money on repairs over the last five years. As a result, while Kingston paid a relatively low price for the property, it has had to spend a considerable amount on repairs over the past year. Prior to this purchase, Kingston had been leasing its space.

To maintain their image of success, Sue and Andy both drive expensive cars and often entertain customers at their cottage or on their boat. This approach seems to work, and their customers are always asking when the next outing will be.

Besides treating their customers well, Sue and Andy also treat their employees well. All employees belong to the group benefit plan that provides extended health care, dental, life insurance, and disability coverage. Because of the low coverage from the company's group life and disability insurance, Andy and Sue have had the company take out individual policies on both of them. The beneficiary on the life insurance policies is the company, and on the disability policies the beneficiaries are Andy and Sue.

One of their valued employees was recently divorced and during the divorce her family home was sold. In order to keep her concentrating on business, Andy and Sue had the company loan her enough to buy a house. The loan was secured by the house and no interest was charged. At that time, the company did not have enough cash to make this loan so it had to borrow the funds at prime plus ½%.

In addition to all of this, Andy and Sue have been actively involved in a number of charitable and political activities and have made donations to both. Even these activities have turned into business opportunities. Last year, they gave a donation to a local charity and shortly thereafter they received an order for the new carpet that was to go in the charity's offices.

Advise Sue and Andy on the tax implications of their situation and that of Kingston Carpets.

Chapter 6

Income from Property

TOPICS DISCUSSED

LEARNING GOALS

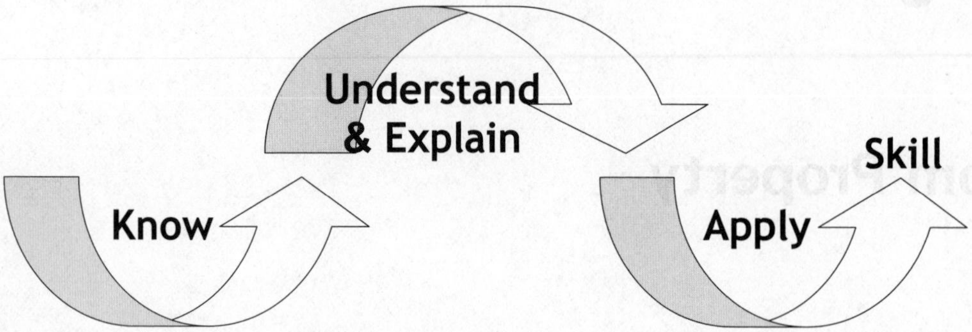

Know

By the end of this chapter you should know the basic provisions of the *Income Tax Act* (the Act) that relate to property income and the income attribution rules that are uniquely applicable to property income. It is important to know the distinction between property income and business income, since they are two separate sources of income on which different income tax rules may apply. You should also know a little about how the GST affects some property income issues. Completing the Review Questions (¶6,800) and Multiple Choice Questions (¶6,825) is a good way to learn the technical provisions.

Understand and Explain

You should understand and be able to explain the tax treatment of specific types of property income and expenses, including the basic questions of who will pay the tax, and when and how much tax will be paid. You should also understand some basic tax planning strategies that can be utilized in real life to maximize the after-tax return on investment. Completing the Exercises (¶6,850) is a good way to deepen your understanding of the material.

Apply

You should be able to apply your knowledge and understanding of property income to real life situations. Completing the Assignment Problems (¶6,875) is an excellent way to develop your ability to identify tax issues and to apply the material in increasingly complex situations.

OVERVIEW

Income for tax purposes (Division B income) is calculated by determining income from each source separately. We have already dealt with two sources of income before this chapter: employment income and business income. Both business income and property income are determined by Subdivision b of Division B in Part I of the Act. Although most of the rules dealing with these two sources of income are similar, it is important to notice that there are significant differences. Since some sources of income are treated more generously than the others for tax purposes, such as partial inclusion in income (even exemptions from income) for tax purposes, generous deductions, or lower tax rates, taxpayers will naturally try to characterize their income to a source which will give better tax treatments. Various anti-avoidance rules are introduced to prevent abusive planning. ITA: 3

The characterization of property income and business income is a question of fact. In general, investors earn income from property with a relatively passive approach. For example, when an individual invests in bonds, he or she can earn interest income without doing much work. This gives rise to property income. On the other hand, if an individual actively trades bonds in the capital market, the interest income may be classified as business income. In general, business income requires more activities in a process that combines time, effort, and capital investment.

Note that income or loss from property does not include capital gains or capital losses. This exclusion is important when considering the deductibility of an expenditure that depends on producing income from property.[1] ITA: 9(3)

The GST/HST implication of several of the topics introduced in the discussion of the Act are presented in this chapter.

The following chart provides an overview of the location of most of these provisions.

PART I — DIVISION B

SUBDIVISION b: BUSINESS OR PROPERTY

SUBDIVISION f: RULES RELATING TO COMPUTATION OF INCOME

DIVISION

A	Liability for tax
B	**Computation of income**
C	Computation of taxable income
D	Taxable income earned in Canada by non-residents
E	Computation of tax
E.1	Minimum tax
F	Special rules applicable in certain circumstances
G	Deferred and other special income arrangements
H	Exemptions
I	Returns, assessments, payment and appeals
J	Appeals to the Tax Court of Canada and the Federal Court of Appeal

SUBDIVISION

	Basic rules
a	Income or loss from an office or employment
b	**Income or loss from a business or property**
c	Taxable capital gains and allowable capital losses
d	Other sources of income
e	Deductions in computing income
f	**Rules relating to computation of income**
g	Amounts not included in computing income
h	Corporations resident in Canada and their shareholders
i	Shareholders of corporations not resident in Canada
j	Partnerships and their members
k	Trusts and their beneficiaries

SECTION

9-11	Basic rules
12-17	Inclusions
18-21	Deductions
22-25	Ceasing to carry on business
26-37	Special cases

67	General limitation re expenses
67.1	Meals and entertainment
67.2-67.4	Passenger vehicle
67.5	Illegal payments
67.6	Non-deductibility of fines and penalties
68	Allocation of amounts in consideration for disposition of property
69	Inadequate consideration
70-72	Death
73-75.1	**Attribution**
76	Security in satisfaction of
76.1	Non-resident and debt
78	Unpaid amounts
79-79.1	Foreclosure
80-80.04	Settlement of debt
80.1	Expropriation re foreign property
80.2	Reimbursement by taxpayer
80.3	Drought-induced sale of breeding livestock
80.4-80.5	**Deemed interest**

[1] The case of *The Queen v. Young*, 89 DTC 5234 (F.C.A.), illustrates this issue of deductibility.

Subdivision b of Division B of Part I of the Act contains the primary rules for the computation of income from property. Like the rules for business income discussed in Chapter 4, most of what will be covered will be found in sections 9 through 21.

Some of the more important provisions are as follows:

Inclusions

Sec. 9 Income (loss) for a taxation year from a property is the profit (loss) from that property for the year

Sec. 12 Income inclusions

Sec. 13 Rules related to capital cost allowance

Sec. 15 Rules for shareholder benefits (discussed in Chapter 13)

Deductions

Sec. 18 Limitations on the deductibility of expenses

Sec. 20 Deductions permitted

In addition, Subdivision f of Division B also provides some rules that are relevant to the computation of property income. For example, the attribution rules determine who is to report the property income received by a particular person. As well, there is a deemed interest benefit to be reported by an individual who received a loan by virtue of their shareholding (discussed in Chapter 13).

ITA: 74.1–74.5

ITA: 15, 80.4

¶6,000 INCLUSIONS

¶6,005 Specific Inclusions of Property Income

Section 12 requires the inclusion of the following returns on investments in the calculation of income from a property: ITA: 12(1)

- interest income from savings, deposits, loans, bonds, and debentures;
- dividends from shares; and
- income based on the production or use of property.

The Act identifies specific property income inclusions to ensure that individuals recognize all sources of property income. Although taxpayers receive information slips (T3s, T5s, T600s) from the investee for some property income, other property income, such as rental income, is reported in an income statement format.

¶6,010 Interest Income

¶6,015 The meaning of interest

The term "interest" is not defined in the Act. The Supreme Court of Canada has defined interest to be "the return or consideration or compensation for the use or retention by one person of a sum of money, belonging to, in a colloquial sense, or owed to, another." This definition has been adopted by the Canada Revenue Agency (CRA). It is unclear in many situations whether an amount paid or payable is in the nature of interest or, as in the case of a discount on a bond, is something else. Partly in order to clarify the issue and to forestall taxpayers from converting amounts from interest to capital, provisions have been legislated in the Act and the Regulations deeming amounts to be interest and requiring them to be brought into income at specified intervals. IT-396R, par. 12

¶6,020 Method of reporting income

In effect, the primary method for computing interest on a "debt obligation" is the annual accrual method. The Act requires the use this method for corporations, partnerships, certain trusts, and individuals. The term "debt obligation" is not defined in the Act, although the term is used in the definition of an "investment contract". The CRA indicates that "the term 'debt obligation' is considered to include, for example, bank accounts, term deposits, guaranteed investment certificates, Canada Savings Bonds, mortgages, corporate bonds and loans". Thus, the annual accrual method would appear to be required for most common sources of interest income. However, when interest is received, it must be included in income to the extent that the interest has not been included previously by the accrual method. As a result, it is not possible to defer the recognition of, for example, compounding interest by using the cash method to report that interest only when it is received. Therefore, there may be a disadvantage to a compounding-interest debt security, because interest must be accrued and reported annually such that tax is levied in a year when no payment of interest is actually received. ITA: 12(3) ITA: 12(11)(*a*) ITA: 12(4) IT-396R, par. 19 ITA: 12(1)(*c*)

¶6,025 Accrual rules for individuals

The Act requires that individuals holding an interest in an investment contract include in income, on every anniversary of that contract, any interest accrued to that day, to the extent that it has not previously been included in income. An "investment contract" is defined as any debt obligation other than a salary deferral arrangement, various types of income-based debt, certain government-sponsored debt for small businesses, or prescribed contracts (of which there are none at the present). "Anniversary day" is defined as the day that is one year after the day before the date of issue and every successive one year interval, unless the contract is disposed of before such a day. So, if any investment is issued on March 30, 2013, the anniversary day will be March 29, 2014 and subsequent years. ITA: 12(4), 12(11)(*b*) ITA: 12(11)(*a*)

Example Problem 6-1

Kelly purchased a $1,000 face value bond on January 2, 2013, for $1,000. The bond was issued on the same date, January 2, 2013. Interest is payable at 8% compounded semi-annually on uncashed coupons on each of June 30 and December 31 at the investor's option.

— *REQUIRED*

(A) If Kelly does not exercise her option to receive interest, when would she first have to include an amount in income?

(B) What would be the result if she exercised her option on December 31 for interest payable on both June 30 and December 31, 2013? Ignore the effects of the leap year.

— *SOLUTION*

(A) The first "anniversary day" would be January 1, 2014, which is the day that is one year after the day before (January 1, 2013) the date of issue (January 2, 2013). As a result, $81.61 would be required to be included in income in 2014. The inclusion was computed as follows: ITA: 12(4), 12(11)

timeline	Jan. 2, 2013 purchase bond	June 30, 2013 interest received	Dec. 31, 2013 interest received	Jan. 1, 2014 "anniversary date"

2013	$1,000.00 × .08 × $^{180}/_{365}$ =	$39.45
	$1,039.45 × .08 × $^{184}/_{365}$ =	41.92
		$81.37
2014	$1,081.37 × .08 × $^{1}/_{365}$ =	.24
	Total accrual to January 1, 2014	$81.61

(B) The $81.37, received on December 31, 2013, would be included in income to the extent it had not previously been included in income. Thus, $0.22 (i.e., $1,000 × 0.08 × $^{1}/_{365}$) would be included in income in 2014. Interest is included to the extent that it was not otherwise included in computing the taxpayer's income for the taxation year or any previous taxation year. ITA: 12(1)(*c*) ITA: 12(4)

¶6,030 Other interest income provisions

Interest and principal may be blended by making a loan at a discount but redeemable at par, or made at par but repayable at a premium. The question is whether the discount or premium is interest income or capital gain. A number of factors must be considered. These factors include the amount determined by the terms of the loan agreement and the price at which the property is sold.

There is not necessarily an interest component in all payments of this nature. A taxpayer need not charge interest in such a transaction. If the property is sold at fair market value, no interest component in the payments will be assumed. On the other hand, an interest inclusion provision will apply to the sale of property if the contractual price, in total, exceeds the fair market value of the property.[2] ITA: 16(1)

[2] This was the situation in the case of *Groulx v. M.N.R.*, 67 DTC 5284 (S.C.C.).

Interest on a scholarship trust fund is not taxable to a parent or grandparent who establishes the fund under the registered education savings plan (RESP) legislation.[3] This provision, which is discussed in more detail in Chapter 9, shelters the accumulated interest such that no tax is paid on it until it is paid out for the benefit of the child. At that time, if it arises, the interest is considered to be the income of the recipient child. ITA: 146.1

¶6,032 Purchasing a corporate bond at a discount

¶6,032.10 *The Investor's Position*

A corporate debenture may be purchased today, at a discount, for $790, but will be repayable at its face value of $1,000. The debenture pays annual interest of 7% or $70 per year. Is interest income equal to the amount received ($70); should it include the discount of $210 on the purchase of the bond; or should it be the effective interest rate?

From an economic perspective, the discount is set by the marketplace to compensate for an investor's desire for a higher rate of interest. The investor may want compensation for the increased inherent risk of the investment, or the prevailing market rate of interest may be higher than the stated interest rate on the bond. In theory, the discount that compensates for the higher market rate of interest should be considered interest income for tax purposes.

The Act requires that, if a payment can be regarded in part as interest and in part as capital, the interest portion should be included in income to the extent the amount is paid or payable. According to the CRA, a blended payment exists when the content of income and capital is not ascertainable. In this situation, it is very difficult to assess which part is interest. When an interest-bearing bond is purchased at a price that reflects the fair market value, the CRA accepts the view that subsection 16(1) would not apply and any discount or premium represents a capital portion. ITA: 16(1)(*a*), (*b*) IT-265R3 [archived]

¶6,032.20 *The Issuer's Position*

The legislation deals with potentially abusive situations. For example, a corporation could issue a bond at a deep discount to raise the effective interest rate on the bond and, hence, increase the amount of deductible interest to the corporation. The Act addresses this situation by defining and providing separate rules for a "deep" discount *versus* a "shallow" discount. A deep discount exists when (1) the obligation is issued at a discount greater than 3% or (2) the yield rate on the debt obligation exceeds the nominal rate by more than one-third. In either of these two cases, only 50% of the discount can be deducted as if it were interest expense. ITA: 20(1)(*f*)

Example Problem 6-2

A taxable corporation issues a bond with a face value of $1,000 and an annual coupon rate of 7% at a price of $970. The bond matures in five years.

Nominal rate of interest 7%

Effective rate of interest 7.75%

— *REQUIRED*

How much of the discount can be deducted and when can it be deducted?

[3] Interest on scholarship trust funds has had an interesting history. The CRA, initially, took the position in an Interpretation Bulletin that such interest credited to a taxpayer's account with the trust would be considered annual interest income of the contributing taxpayer. However, in some of these trusts the interest cannot be withdrawn, but is used to provide scholarships for the taxpayer's children if they qualify under the terms of the trust. If the children do not qualify, the interest is used to provide scholarships for other people's children and the original capital contributed is returned. This position was appealed by the taxpayer in the case of *The Queen v. Quinn*, 73 DTC 5215 (F.C.T.D.). The Court held that no taxpayer should be required to pay tax on money he had not received beneficially or had not the right to receive and might never, in fact, receive. This situation illustrates the fact that a departmental position, even if it is published as an Interpretation Bulletin, can be successfully challenged by the taxpayer, notwithstanding the weight that might be given to such administrative policy and interpretation by the courts as reiterated by the Federal Court of Appeal in *The Queen v. Royal Trust Corporation of Canada*, 83 DTC 5172, at 5177.

— *SOLUTION*

Since the yield is not greater than ⅘ of the nominal rate and the original discount did not exceed 3%, this is considered a shallow discount. The entire discount is deductible by the issuing corporation on payment at maturity or when paid, if earlier. It would have taken failure of only one of the two tests to invoke the 50% deduction rule.

Example Problem 6-3

Another taxable corporation issues a bond with a face value of $1,000 and a coupon rate of 5% at a price of $920. The bond matures in five years.

Nominal rate of interest 5%

Effective rate of interest 6.95%

— *REQUIRED*

How much of the discount can be deducted and when can it be deducted?

— *SOLUTION*

Since the yield is greater than ⅘ of the nominal rate and the discount exceeded 3%, this is considered a deep discount. Only 50% of the discount can be deducted by the issuing corporation on payment at maturity or when paid, if earlier. Again, only one of the two tests need have been failed to invoke this result.

¶6,033 Treasury bills

Treasury bills are always purchased at a discount. At maturity, the investor receives the face value of the treasury bill. The amount of the discount represents, in substance, a payment for interest; hence, the discount is included in income to the extent the amount was received or became receivable. ITA: 12(1)(*c*) ITA: 16(1)

Example Problem 6-4

On December 1, Henri Ltd. (December 31 year end) purchased $9,886 worth of 90-day T-bills. The treasury bills mature at $10,000 on March 1.

— *REQUIRED*

Determine the amount that must be included in Henri Ltd.'s income in the year of the purchase and the year of maturity. Ignore any effects of the leap year.

— *SOLUTION*

As long as the T-bills are not cashed in early, the difference between the price paid and the maturity value of the T-bill represents interest income. Since the Act requires that interest of a corporation be accrued at year-end, interest is computed using the treasury bill rate and prorating the interest based on days outstanding. ITA: 12(3)

Year 1 interest income ($10,000 – $9,886) × 31/90 = $39.27

Year 2 interest income ($10,000 – $9,886) × 59/90 = $74.73

¶6,034 Zero coupon bonds

Zero coupon bonds, or strip bonds sold without coupons, are long-term bonds with interest paid as part of the redemption proceeds at the date of maturity. For tax purposes, the Regulations, dealing with prescribed debt obligations, indicate that the difference between the cost of the bond and the maturity value represents the present value of the accumulated interest income. ITR: 7000

Example Problem 6-5

Assume that a strip bond is purchased today for $1,500 and will mature at $10,000 in 20 years. In other words, the taxpayer receives $8,500 in compound interest, but the amount is not receivable until year 20.

— *REQUIRED*

How much interest income should be recognized in Year 1 and Year 2?

— *SOLUTION*

For tax purposes, the Regulations require that the accrued interest portion be calculated and recognized in each taxation year. The annual accrued interest should be based on the investment's yields to maturity. Note that the yield (i) is the same each year. However, since the compound interest portion is added to the bond amount, more accrued interest is earned each year. ITR: 7000(1)(*a*)

Computation of yield: $1,500	$= \$10{,}000/(1 + i)^{20}$
i	= YTM
YTM	= 9.95%
Interest in Year 1	= $1,500 × 9.95%
	= $149.25
Interest in Year 2	= ($1,500 + 149.25) × 9.95%
	= $164.10

This type of investment works well in a self-directed RRSP or in a deferred-income fund, because the accrued interest is not taxed until the funds are ultimately withdrawn. In contrast, if the strip bonds are held outside a deferred-income fund, tax is payable each year on the calculated accrued interest. This could create a cash-flow burden because no annual interest is received to offset the taxes owing on the accrued interest.

Other situations are addressed in the Regulations, such as debt instruments with rates of interest changing depending on some future event (such as early disposition). The legislative intent of this regulation is to remove taxpayer bias towards certain investments and discourage tax-motivated purchases and dispositions of investments. The law is fairly strict and requires that interest be accrued based on the maximum interest potentially payable. ITR: 7000

¶6,035 Timing and recognition of interest income

The Act uses the words "received" or "receivable", and that appears to indicate that the taxpayer has a choice between using at least two bases of accounting for interest income — the cash basis and the receivable basis. However, consideration must be given to accrual rules which modify the requirements. ITA: 12(1)(*c*) ITA: 12(3), 12(4)

Under the cash method, interest is recognized as income only when actually received. Under the receivable method, interest is income only when the amount has become legally due and payment is enforceable. For example, assume a bond had an interest payment scheduled for December 15 but the payment was delayed and not paid/received until January. Under the cash method, the interest would be income in January, whereas under the receivable method it would be income at December 15. The Act requires that the chosen method be consistently followed. ITA: 12(1)(*c*)

The Act requires that corporations, partnerships and certain trusts use the accrual method of accounting for interest income (excluding interest on some types of debt). The two other bases are not available to these taxpayers. Therefore, in the example of the late December 15 payment, a corporation with a December 31 or later year end would have to include this in their income at that time plus any interest accrued from December 16 to December 31. ITA: 12(1)(*c*)

While individuals are allowed the cash or receivable basis, this option is tempered by the Act, which imposes a modified or annual accrual basis on these taxpayers. An individual must bring into income any interest accrued to each annual anniversary date of the investment contract. Investment contracts include any debt obligation except certain deferred compensation arrangements, an employee benefit plan, an income bond, a tax-free savings account (TFSA), and other specifically noted instruments. ITA: 12(4) ITA: 12(11)

The current rules are summarized as follows:

Summary
Interest income reporting

1. Corporations, partnerships, and trusts ITA: 12(3)
   - Accrual method of accounting.
2. Individuals ITA: 12(4), 12(11)
   - Annual accrual based on the anniversary date[4] of an investment contract.

Remember that the accrual rules applicable to an individual do not apply if the interest was received prior to the anniversary date, since the interest must then be reported under the general rule. Thus, these rules do not apply with respect to investment contracts of a duration of less than one year and investment contracts that provide for the payment of interest at intervals of one year or less. The interest on these investment contracts must be reported in the year the interest is received or receivable. ITA: 12(1)(*c*)

Example Problem 6-6

Claudette purchased a $10,000, 7%, five-year GIC (guaranteed income certificate) from her bank on February 2, 2011. All the interest will be paid to her at the end of the five years.

— REQUIRED

How much interest must Claudette include in each of 2011, 2012, and 2013?

— SOLUTION

Claudette will not report any interest income from this GIC in 2011. This is because:

- no amount has been received;
- no amount is receivable;
- she is not subject to the accrual method as she is not a corporation, partnership, or trust; and
- the anniversary date did not fall in 2011.

For the 2012 taxation year, Claudette must report the interest that has accrued to the February 1, 2012 anniversary date. That would be $10,000 × 7% = $700.

In the 2013 taxation year, Claudette will report the interest accrued to the second anniversary date of February 1, 2013. That would be $10,700 × 7% = $749. As the above example shows, some deferral is available to individual taxpayers where the interest is paid on an annual or greater period, if the timing of the investment acquisition is early in the year.

[4] The anniversary date of the contract is the day that is one year after the day immediately preceding the date of issue of the contract. For example, for a contract acquired on April 15, 2012, the anniversary date will be April 14, 2013. The individual will have to include in his or her 2013 income the interest accrued from April 15, 2012 to April 14, 2013.

¶6,036 Purchasing an accrued interest bond

Most corporate and other bonds and debentures (excluding Canada Savings Bonds (CSBs)) are traded securities, just like shares, and can be acquired/sold through an investment dealer. When these are traded at a date other than the specified interest date, interest will have accrued on the bond. The seller will receive the accrued interest as part of the selling price, and conversely, the buyer has paid for this accrued interest as part of the purchase price. The buyer can deduct this accrued interest as an expense in the year against the interest income. This happens because the bond issuer pays all the interest on the next due date to the then holder of the bond. ITA: 20(14)

When a debt obligation is transferred on a date other than the date of payment of interest, the Act stipulates how the interest income is to be divided between the transferor and transferee: ITA: 20(14)

- Transferor must include interest accrued up to the date of the transfer. The amount included in income is excluded from the proceeds of the debt obligation.
- Transferee must include interest from the date of the transfer.

Example Problem 6-7

Softco Ltd. has an outstanding bond issue with a face value of $10,000 on which it pays interest at 7%. The interest is payable semi-annually, on June 15 and December 15. On October 15, Randy sold his Softco Ltd. bonds on the open market and they were acquired by Saleem.

— *REQUIRED*

Compute the income that each of Randy and Saleem must report in the year from the bond.

— *SOLUTION*

Saleem would pay, and Randy would receive, the following amount (rounded) for the bonds.

Face value of bond	$10,000	
Interest from June 16 to October 15	233	(122 days of 183 days × $350)
	$10,233	

In filing their respective personal income tax returns for the year, Saleem and Randy would report the interest as follows:

	Randy		Saleem
	Dec.–June		June–Dec.
T5 slip received from Softco Ltd. for interest received from Softco	$350		$350
Add (subtract) interest received/paid on sale/acquisition of the bond	233	June–Oct.	(233)
Interest income from Softco Ltd. bond	$583		$117

Net result is that Randy receives interest income from December to October, and Saleem receives income from October to December.

¶6,040 Payments Based on Production or Use

¶6,045 Concept of the provision

Any amount received, usually on the sale of income-producing property, that is dependent on the use of or production from the property is taxed as income. Despite the clarity of the provision, it has been the subject of many appeals because ordinary instalment payments of principal which are not taxed as income may not be substantially different from payments based on production or use which are taxed as property income.[5] Also, the distinction between a receipt of income or a receipt of capital has some bearing in this area. Payments that may be expressed as instalments of the sale price of property, but are actually payments depending on the use of or production from that property are taxed, although they may appear to be capital in nature. In certain circumstances, therefore, payments that would otherwise be considered capital and given capital gains treatment are brought into income and fully taxed. Furthermore, property is broadly defined as including not only real and personal property, but also intangible property such as patents, franchises and rights of all kinds.

ITA: 12(1)(*g*)

ITA: 248(1)

When selling a property, the buyer and the seller can determine the sales price in various ways. For example, the price can be a lump-sum amount of money payable upon closing of the agreement, or, in the case of an instalment sale, the sales price can be payable over a period of time. Alternatively, the price may be determined by reference to a formula which is dependent on the use of, or production from, the property. The example problem below gives more description of such a transaction and its tax treatments.

The Act provides that any amount received based on production or use of property disposed must be included as property income. The purpose of this rule is to prevent taxpayers from characterizing property income as capital gains (a topic discussed in Chapters 7 and 8), which will attract lower tax rate through partial inclusion of income for tax purposes.

ITA: 12(1)(*g*)

Example Problem 6-8

The appellant, a farmer, entered into an agreement with the Department of Highways of Alberta under which she granted the Department the right to enter upon her land for the purpose of taking clay for use in the construction of a highway. Employees of the Department removed the crop growing on the land designated in the agreement, removed the topsoil from the area, removed the quantity of clay subsoil required for highway construction, replaced the topsoil and levelled off the area. Pursuant to the agreement, the appellant received compensation of $2,271 in full settlement of "general damages, loss of crop, cost of restoring areas and reduction of yields." The Minister added the $2,271 to the appellant's declared income. The appellant objected.

ITA: 9(1), 12(1)(*g*)

— *REQUIRED*

Decide this case on the basis of whether the receipt of $2,271 can be considered business or property income under either or both of the sections cited by the Minister.

— *SOLUTION* [see *Randle v. M.N.R.*, 65 DTC 507 (T.A.B.).]

Consider first whether the receipt was one of business or property income. At best the situation involved an adventure in the nature of trade which is part of the definition of the word business, thereby making the receipt part of business income. The receipt was not like normal income from property in the nature of dividends, interest, rents or royalties and there is little to connect the payment to business activity. There was no intention either of a primary or secondary nature to make a profit from a business operation in this situation. The receipt was more like a reimbursement for a capital item. The relation of the transaction to farming is fairly remote

ITA: 9(1)

ITA: 248(1)

[5] Cases under this provision can be classified by the type of property sold. Oil and gas rights were an issue in the case of *Ross v. M.N.R.*, 50 DTC 775 (Ex. Ct.). Timber was the subject of the cases of *Mouat v. M.N.R.*, 58 DTC 694 (T.A.B.), *Hoffman v. M.N.R.*, 65 DTC 617 (T.A.B.), and *The Queen v. Mel-Bar Ranches Ltd.*, 89 DTC 5189 (F.C.T.D.). Gravel and rock were sold in the cases of *Pallet v. M.N.R.*, 59 DTC 230 (T.A.B.), and *M.N.R. v. Lamon*, 63 DTC 1039 (Ex. Ct.). The rights to books and manuals were at issue in *Gingras v. M.N.R.*, 63 DTC 1142 (Ex. Ct.), and *LaRue v. M.N.R.*, 67 DTC 553 (T.A.B.), and the sale of equipment was considered in *R. C. Huffman Construction Co. Ltd. v. M.N.R.*, 65 DTC 597 (T.A.B.). A payment for the use of patents was considered in *Porta-Test Systems Ltd. v. The Queen*, 80 DTC 6046 (F.C.T.D.). Finally, the sale of a franchise was the subject of *M.N.R. v. Waintown Gas and Oil Co. Ltd.*, 52 DTC 1138 (S.C.C.). The exception for sales of agricultural land in paragraph 12(1)(*g*) does not apply to mineral and oil rights on the land. This was the situation in the case of *Ade v. M.N.R.*, 67 DTC 23 (T.A.B.).

except for the compensation for current crops. The nature of the asset involved is more like fixed capital in land than working capital in inventory except, again, for the current crop. Furthermore, it is unlikely that this was a frequent transaction, indicating a non-business income receipt. Finally, damages for loss of earnings capacity, as this seemed to be, are not income, but are generally regarded as a capital receipt which will be taxed more favourably with partial income inclusion.

Next, consider whether the payment was dependent on production or use. No relation between the amount received and the amount of clay taken is indicated. There was no continuing activity in the sale of clay which might indicate more clearly a payment dependent on production or use. Finally, the agreement indicated that the appellant did not sell the clay or the land, but received money in compensation for damages sustained. ITA: 12(1)(*g*)

It might be concluded, therefore, that most of the money was compensation for the loss of a portion of a capital asset and for restoring it to its former state of production. However, the amount paid for the current crop in the designated area as part of the appellant's inventory should be included in income.

¶6,050 Dividends from Corporations Resident in Canada

¶6,052 Overview

Profitable corporations may deal with cash profits in a variety of ways. They may either pay out such profits or choose to reinvest the cash in the operations of the corporation. When the corporation distributes after-tax profits to a shareholder, either in cash or in kind, the shareholder is said to have received a dividend. A dividend-in-kind is one paid by something other than cash. The term dividend is defined in the Act, but not in great detail. However, both the CRA and the courts have agreed that any distribution of income that is divided *pro rata* among shareholders may properly be described as a dividend, unless the corporation can show that it is another type of payment. ITA: 12(1)(*j*), (*k*) ITA: 248(1)

Taxpayers are required to include dividends from both resident corporations and non-resident corporations in income. Both of those provisions qualify the meaning of a dividend by referring to the amounts determined at subdivision h and subdivision i of the Act and include both cash and dividends in kind. ITA: 12(1)(*j*), (*k*)

The Act requires that all taxable dividends received from corporations resident in Canada be included in the calculation of income. A "taxable dividend" is defined as one *other than* a tax-free capital dividend or a qualifying dividend on tax-deferred preferred shares. ITA: 82(1), 89(1)

The Act also requires that all dividends received from non-resident corporations be included in the calculation of income. ITA: 90(1)

In summary, all dividends are income. Dividends (other than capital or qualifying dividends) from resident corporations are labelled "taxable dividends", whereas those from non-resident corporations are just labelled "dividends". There are special rules, outlined in this chapter, as to how taxable dividends are included in income. This is why the distinction between a taxable dividend and what we can call an ordinary dividend, is important. *Taxable* dividend should not be interpreted to mean "as opposed to a non-taxable dividend".

Further, there are a number of provisions in the Act that address and include in income the withdrawal of money or realization of other benefits by shareholders from corporations. These amounts are often characterized as deemed dividends. The Act will direct whether the deemed dividend is a taxable dividend. ITA: 84

Although most dividends are usually paid in the form of cash, corporations can (and sometimes do) pay a non-cash dividend or a dividend-in-kind. The cash equivalent (fair market value) of the asset received is the amount of the dividend for tax purposes. Consequently, a dividend-in-kind is no different from a cash dividend.

However, where the dividend is a stock dividend, special rules apply. These are discussed further in this chapter.

¶6,052.10 *Dividends included in income*

How a dividend is taxed as income to the recipient depends on whether the recipient is an individual (including a partner and a trust) or a corporation, whether the dividend is from a resident or a non-resident corporation, whether it is a stock dividend, and whether it is an income amount that is just being deemed a dividend. Each of the possibilities will be looked at separately.

Figure 6-1 illustrates how the type of payer corporation and the relationship to the recipient will affect the tax treatment of a taxable dividend.

Figure 6-1

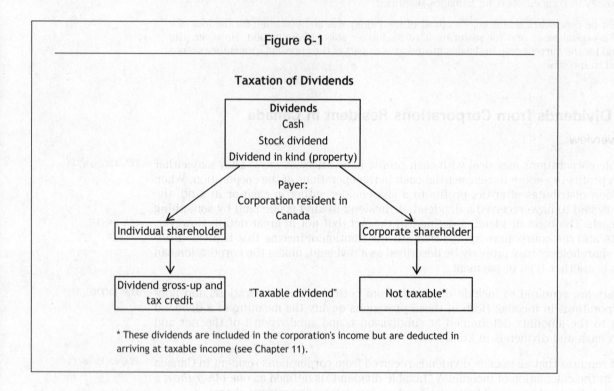

Taxation of Dividends

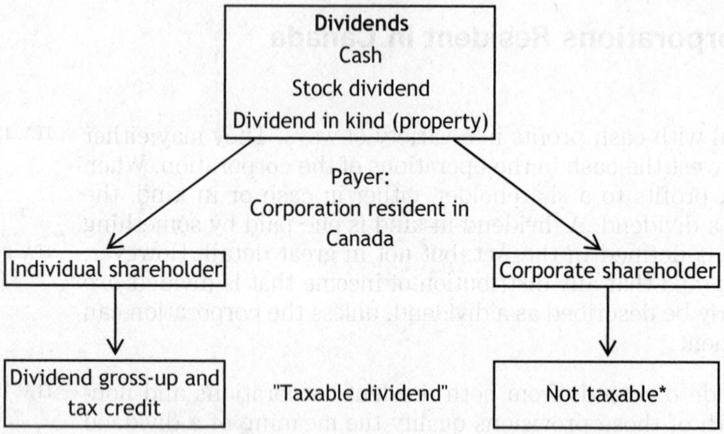

* These dividends are included in the corporation's income but are deducted in arriving at taxable income (see Chapter 11).

¶6,055 The issue

In Chapter 2, we discussed the question of who is liable for tax in Canada. We learned that an individual is liable for tax and so is a corporation. Therefore, generally, most corporate income is taxed twice: first at the corporate level as income and then in the hands of shareholders, as dividends. Without any adjustments in the tax rules, taxpayers would be penalized by double taxation, if they earn the same amount of income through corporations as opposed to earning income directly.

The Act contains a number of special rules designed to provide relief from double taxation of income earned through a corporation. In the following section, we will discuss one of the mechanisms introduced in the Canadian tax system to address the double taxation problem.

¶6,060 Overview of the Canadian dividend taxation system

There are different ways to mitigate the double taxation problem. The basic objective is that the same total amount of tax should be paid if a corporation earns an amount (then pays dividends to the shareholders from its after-tax earnings), or if the individual earns that same amount personally. The following is the tool used in the Act to achieve this objective in theory:

- the individual shareholder must include in income the full pre-tax income earned by the corporation by grossing up the amount of the dividend received and calculating tax on that base, and
- the individual should receive a dividend tax credit for all the income tax paid by the corporation.

¶6,060.10 *Difference between an income reduction and a tax credit*

You will see more examples of income reductions and tax credits in Chapters 9 and 10. In general, a tax credit reduces the tax otherwise payable and is a dollar-for-dollar reduction of a tax liability. The dividend tax credit that we will discuss in this section is a tax credit that will reduce the taxpayer's tax otherwise payable. On the other hand, an income reduction reduces taxable income. The tax savings from the income reduction is dependant on the person's marginal tax rate.

¶6,060.20 *The dividend gross-up and dividend tax credit system*

The Act uses two calculations of the gross-up and the dividend tax credit. The calculation used depends on the type of corporation that issued the dividends and the type of income from which the dividends are issued. Note that different types of corporations (e.g., public versus private) with different types of income (e.g., active business income versus investment income) will be taxed at different tax rates.

(i) Dividends from the active business income of a Canadian-controlled private corporation (CCPC) that is taxed at the low corporate rate or from the investment income of a CCPC (as discussed in Chapter 12)

[In the March 21, 2013 federal Budget it was proposed that the dividend gross-up and dividend tax credit be changed for dividends from:

1. The active business income of a Canadian-controlled private corporation (CCPC) that is taxed at the low corporate rate, and
2. Investment income of a CCPC.

This proposed change would affect any dividends paid after 2013.

The following table shows the current and the proposed systems:

	Current (2013)	Proposed (2014)
Cash dividend	$10,000	$10,000
Dividend gross-up		
Current — 25%	2,500	
Proposed — 18%		1,800
Grossed-up dividend	$12,500	$11,800
Dividend tax credit (federal)		
Current — 2/3 of gross-up	$ 1,667	
Proposed — 13/18 of gross-up		$ 1,300

These proposed 2014 gross-up and tax credit factors will be used, where appropriate, in the examples and problems.]

In this situation, the dividends received plus an 18% gross-up will be included in the individual's income. Thus, the individual shareholder's income would include the grossed-up dividend. Recall from the earlier discussion that the gross-up, when added to the actual dividends received, is to place the individual shareholder in approximately the same income position that the corporation was in before it paid corporate tax on its income. ITA: 82(1) ITA: 12(1)(j)

This dividend income (118% of the amount received) will be subject to tax in full at the individual's tax rate which is dependent on his or her income level. We will outline more about the progressive tax rate system in Chapter 10, ¶10,110. As discussed above, to mitigate the problem of double taxation, the Act allows for a dividend tax credit which will reduce the tax on dividends paid to the individual.

The federal dividend tax credit can be calculated in one of the following three ways (same amount but different calculations): ITA: 121

- 13% of the dividends paid

or

- $^{13}/_{18} \times 18\%$ (gross-up) = 13% of dividends paid,

or

- 11.02% × 118% (grossed-up dividend) = 13% of dividends paid.

Each province offers dividend tax credits which will reduce an individual's provincial tax payable. The federal tax credit together with the provincial dividend tax credit is intended to approximate the tax paid by the corporation on the individual shareholder's behalf. Note that the calculation may not work out to the exact amount of corporate tax paid. We will discuss this issue of imperfections in more detail in Chapter 12.

(ii) Eligible Dividends — Dividends from a public corporation resident in Canada taxed at the general corporate rate and a CCPC resident in Canada distributed from business income taxed at the general corporate rate (not the low corporate tax rate)

In this situation, the gross-up rate will be 38% (in 2012 and subsequent years) and the dividend tax credit can be calculated in one of the following three ways (same amount but different calculations): ITA: 121

- 20.7% of the dividends paid,

or

- $^{6}/_{11} \times 38\%$ (gross-up) = 20.7% of the dividends paid,

or

- 15% (rounded) × 138% (grossed-up dividends) = 20.7% of the dividends paid.

As a result of the reduction in the federal corporate income tax rates, the dividend gross-up and federal tax credit have been adjusted to coincide with the corporate tax rate reduction. ITA: 82(1); 121

	Gross-up	Dividend Tax Credit
2009	45%	11/18
2010	44%	10/17
2011	41%	13/23
After 2011	38%	6/11

¶6,060.30 *Conditions*

Note that the dividend gross-up and tax credit procedure applies where:

- individual shareholders receive the dividend (corporate shareholders are discussed in Chapter 11); and
- dividends are received from Canadian resident corporations (dividends received by individuals from non-resident corporations are fully taxed).

¶6,060.40 *Illustration*

As an example of the effect of the dividend treatment for individuals, consider two individuals, one paying federal tax at a marginal rate of 15% and the other paying federal tax at the top marginal rate of 29%. Assume that both individuals live in a province with a tax on income rate of 10% and 17%, respectively. Also assume that the combined federal and provincial dividend tax credit is equal to the gross-up. Each shareholder receives a dividend of $1,000 from:

(a) the active business income of a CCPC taxed at the low corporate rate, and

(b) the income of a public corporation resident in Canada.

The following computations would be made:

(a) Dividends from the active business income of a CCPC taxed at the low corporate rate

		2014	
Taxpayer's marginal tax rate (federal and provincial combined)		25%	46%
Dividend	(A)	$ 1,000	$ 1,000
Add: gross-up of 18% of dividend		180	180
Grossed-up dividend subject to tax		$ 1,180	$ 1,180
Tax on grossed-up dividend at marginal tax rate		$ 295	$ 543
Less: federal and provincial dividend tax credit (equal to the gross-up)		(180)	(180)
Net tax payable	(B)	$ 115	$ 363
After-tax dividend [(A) – (B)]		$ 885	$ 637

(b) Dividends from the income of a public corporation resident in Canada

		2014	
Taxpayer's marginal tax rate (federal and provincial combined)		25%	46%
Dividend	(A)	$ 1,000	$ 1,000
Add: gross-up of 38% of dividend		380	380
Grossed-up dividend subject to tax		$ 1,380	$ 1,380
Tax on grossed-up dividend at marginal tax rate		$ 345	$ 635
Less: federal and provincial dividend tax credit (equal to the gross-up)		(380)*	(380)
Net tax payable	(B)	Nil**	$ 255
After-tax dividend [(A) – (B)]		$ 1,000	$ 745

* The dividend tax credit is not affected by the individual's marginal tax rate because it represents the income tax paid by the corporation at its tax rate.

** The excess dividend tax credit of $35 ($345 – $380) is available to deduct from federal tax on other income.

Example Problem 6-9

Ian Plant faces a 12% provincial tax on income and a federal tax rate of 22% at the margin. On an investment of $5,000 in the shares of a Canadian-resident public corporation, he receives $362.50 of taxable dividends for a yield of 7.25%. He is considering the alternative of investing his funds in a bond paying 9%. Assume that the combined federal and provincial dividend tax credit is equal to the gross-up.

— REQUIRED

Compute the after-tax return in 2014 from the alternative investments to compare their desirability.

— SOLUTION

(A) Dividend

Dividend	$362.50
Add: gross-up of 38% of dividend	137.75
Grossed-up dividend subject to tax	$500.25
Tax on grossed-up dividend @ 34% (i.e., 22% + 12%)	$170.09
Less: dividend tax credit (federal and provincial)	(137.75)
Net tax payable	$ 32.34
After-tax dividend ($362.50 – $32.34)	$330.16

(B) Interest

Interest income (9% of $5,000)	$450.00
Tax payable @ 34%	$153.00
After-tax interest ($450.00 – $153.00)	$297.00

— NOTE TO SOLUTION

Although the pre-tax dividend yield of 7.25% is lower than the pre-tax interest yield of 9%, the after-tax return from the dividend of $330.16 or 6.60% of the investment is greater than the after-tax return from the interest of $297 or 5.94% of the $5,000 invested. Furthermore, it should be remembered that there may be a greater potential for a return from capital gains on the shares compared to the bond. This would influence the decision when the after-tax dividend yield is lower than the after-tax interest yield. Note that investment in shares will normally be riskier than investment in bonds.

¶6,065 Dividends Received from Non-Resident Corporations

Dividends received by individuals from non-resident corporations are still taxable but the dividend gross-up rules do not apply as they are not Canadian-sourced. This is justifiable because the government has no reason to try to integrate a foreign tax system or to provide an incentive for individuals to invest in non-resident corporations. ITA: 12(1)(*k*), 90(1)

The foreign dividend income may have had income tax withheld at the source as it was paid to a non-resident of the country of origin. The taxable amount of the dividend is not reduced by this tax. The taxpayer may be entitled to a foreign tax credit with respect to those taxes. Foreign tax credits are discussed in Chapter 10.

¶6,070 Income Attribution

¶6,075 The reason for attribution rules

Under the Canadian income tax system, an individual is a taxpayer who is liable for tax on his or her taxable income. An individual's taxable income is subject to a progressive tax structure. Under such a structure, if an individual earns more income, his or her tax rate increases. For example, if Mom earns $100,000, she will pay more tax than if Mom and Dad each earn $50,000. Thus, the high-income taxpayer will have an incentive to reduce tax by splitting income with family members who earn less income and pay tax at a lower rate. For example, if the high-income taxpayer, Ms. Abigail, has some bonds which earn interest income, Ms. Abigail pays tax on the interest income earned on the bonds at the top marginal tax rate. Ms. Abigail can transfer the bonds to her 5-year-old daughter who has no other source of income. Her daughter will not have to pay tax on the interest income (due to personal tax credits) or will pay tax at a much lower rate.

In order to protect the integrity of the progressive tax system, the Act has introduced various attribution rules to prevent certain forms of income splitting among the immediate family members. ITA: 74.1–74.5, 56(4.1)–(5)

"Income attribution" is a process of allocating income earned on the property that was transferred to a non-arm's length individual back to the original owner. In the case discussed earlier, although the 5-year-old daughter owns the bonds after the transfer, for tax purposes, the interest income earned on the bonds will be attributed back to Ms. Abigail and taxed in her hands.

The word "transfer" has been used frequently throughout the various attribution rules. It includes a sale, whether or not the proceeds are at fair market value. Financing the sale by a loan does not change the concept of a transfer in this context. Gifting is also a form of transfer.

¶6,080 Definition of related persons

The attribution rules apply to certain non-arm's length individuals. The Act deems related persons not to deal at arm's length with each other. Exhibit 6-1 attempts to present schematically all of the provisions defining related individuals, as well as the CRA's interpretations. Related individuals are diagrammed in relation to a taxpayer (i.e., "you"). On the horizontal axis, do not attempt to make the individuals at the extreme outer limits (i.e., the second bullet) related to each other. They are only related to "you" in respect of this chart. Note that where the word "spouse" is used, it is intended to include the concept of a common-law partner, including a same-sex partner. ITA: 251(1)(*a*) ITA: 251, 252; IT-419R2

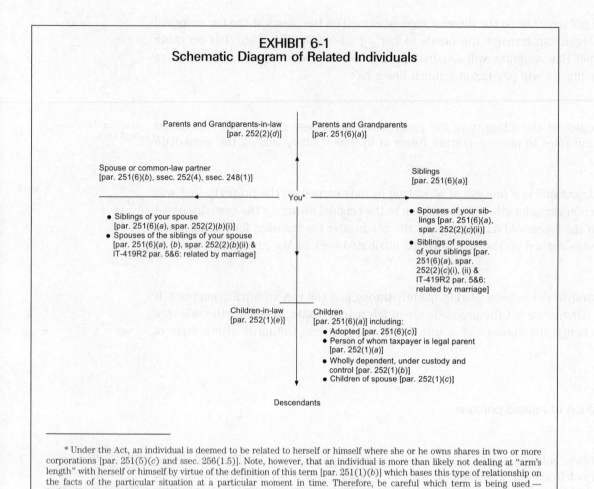

EXHIBIT 6-1
Schematic Diagram of Related Individuals

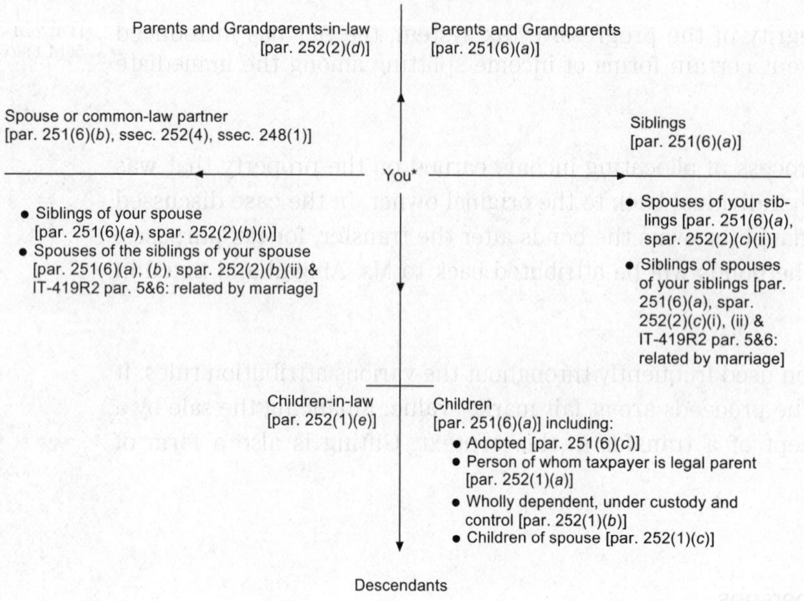

* Under the Act, an individual is deemed to be related to herself or himself where she or he owns shares in two or more corporations [par. 251(5)(*c*) and ssec. 256(1.5)]. Note, however, that an individual is more than likely not dealing at "arm's length" with herself or himself by virtue of the definition of this term [par. 251(1)(*b*)] which bases this type of relationship on the facts of the particular situation at a particular moment in time. Therefore, be careful which term is being used — "related" or "arm's length."

¶6,085 Transactions subject to income attribution

¶6,085.10 *An individual transfers or loans property to a spouse or common-law partner or to a person who becomes his or her spouse or common-law partner*

Income or loss incurred on the transferred property as well as capital gains and losses from the final sale (as discussed in Chapter 8) of the property to a third party may be subject to attribution. The attribution rules apply when an individual transfers or loans property to a spouse or common-law partner including a person who becomes his or her spouse or common-law partner. ITA: 74.1(1)

"Common-law partner" is defined as a person who cohabits at that time in a conjugal relationship with the taxpayer and either ITA: 248(1)

(a) has so cohabited with the taxpayer for a continuous period of at least one year, or

(b) would be the parent of a child of whom the taxpayer is a parent.

Where "at any time" the taxpayer and the person have cohabited in a conjugal relationship, they are "currently" deemed to be cohabiting in a conjugal relationship unless they were not cohabiting at the particular time for a period of at least 90 days because of a breakdown of their conjugal relationship. This definition covers both common-law spouses and same-sex partners.

¶6,085.20 *An individual transfers or loans property to a minor (i.e., under the age of 18) who is a non-arm's length person or a niece or nephew*

Attribution of income or loss from property will occur on a transfer or loan to a minor (i.e., under the age of 18) who is a non-arm's length person or a niece or nephew. Attribution continues until that person attains the age of 18. Both subsections pertain to direct or *indirect* transfers or loans to or *for the benefit of* the person. Thus, a transfer or loan to a trust in which the spouse or common-law partner or minor is a beneficiary will result in attribution. Attribution means that the income or loss earned by the spouse or common-law partner or minor is considered to be the income or loss of the transferor during his or her lifetime as long as he or she is resident in Canada. ITA: 74.1(2), 74.3, 251, 252 IT-419R2

¶6,090 Avoiding income attributions

An exception to the application of these attribution rules is provided by the legislation. This provision requires a number of very specific conditions to be fulfilled before the taxpayer will be exempted from the attribution rules. ITA: 74.5

1. Fair Market Value Transfer

If the fair market value of the property transferred does not exceed the fair market value of the consideration received in return, that is, if the property is sold for its fair market value, then these attribution rules will not apply. Therefore, all gifts of income-earning property are subject to the attribution rules as are transfers for consideration which is less than the fair market value of the property transferred.

2. Interest Charged

If the transferor takes back a debt, then interest that is at least equal to the lesser of the prescribed rate or an arm's length rate (to be referred to here as a "commercial" rate) must be charged. In addition, the interest must be paid within 30 days of the end of each and every year in which the debt was outstanding, or attribution will occur. If funds are loaned directly, then interest at a commercial rate, as determined above, must be charged and paid on the loan, or attribution will occur. ITA: 74.5

Note that where a transfer or loan takes place at fair market value, the benefits of income splitting are reduced or eliminated. Where one person buys an income-producing property for, say, cash, the purchaser acquires the income-producing property and may claim the income, but the seller receives the cash which might be invested in other income-producing property. The fair market value consideration will help to avoid attribution of income from property and, often more importantly, capital gains on a transfer to a spouse or a common-law partner. Avoiding the attribution of capital gains may provide a significant benefit. Similarly, a loan at a commercial rate creates income to the lender, thereby reducing or eliminating any splitting advantage on income from property, but places the borrower in a position to earn a capital gain that will not be attributed to the lender.

3. Spousal Election

An additional restriction is placed on all spousal transfers of property. Normally, accrued capital gains and recaptured CCA on depreciable capital property and other capital property is automatically deferred on the transfer of such property to a spouse or a common-law partner. However, to avoid attribution, the deferral must be waived by the transferor spouse. Hence, a disposition will occur at the fair market value, triggering a capital gain or loss and any recaptured CCA. However, if the property is qualified small business corporation shares or qualified farm property, the capital gains deduction could be used to offset all or part of the income inclusion. ITA: 73(1)

For example, consider the case of Spouse A, whose income is taxed in the top bracket and who owns a property worth $50,000 that produces $5,000 of income. If that property is sold for cash to Spouse B who has no other source of income and Spouse A elects to transfer the property at its fair market value, Spouse B will have the $5,000 of income from property. However, Spouse A will have the $50,000 in cash proceeds on the sale of the property. If that $50,000 is reinvested in Spouse A's hands, the income will attract tax at the top rate and the ITA: 73(1) benefits of income splitting would be negated, unless the original property generated a large capital gain on its ultimate disposition by Spouse B. At that time, the capital gain would not be subject to attribution because the original transfer of the property took place for fair market value consideration.

4. Marital Breakdown

There is an exception to the attribution rules which applies where spouses live separate and apart by reason of a breakdown of their marriage. Any income or loss that relates to the period of separation is excepted from attribution. ITA: 74.5(3)

Summary
Avoiding Income Attribution on Transferred Property

Subsection 74.5(1)

1. Fair market value consideration must be received by the vendor.
2. If part of the consideration is debt, then interest must be charged at the prescribed rate and always paid by January 30th.
3. If it is a transfer to a spouse or common-law partner, then they must elect out of the spousal rollover in subsection 73(1).

Subsection 74.5(3)

4. If the spouses or common-law partners are living separate and apart by reason of the breakdown of their relationship. (This exception applies to property income, but not capital gains, unless an election has been made.)

Example Problem 6-10

- Mr. A is taxed in the top bracket (highest personal tax rate) and he owns a bond which is worth $50,000. Mr. A paid $50,000 for the bond. It earns $5,000 of interest income (one type of property income).
- Mrs. A (Mr. A's spouse) has no income.
- Mr. A gave the bond to Mrs. A.

— REQUIRED

(a) What are the tax consequences to Mr. and Mrs. A?

(b) What are the tax consequences to Mr. and Mrs. A, if Mr. A sells the bond to Mrs. A at its fair market value of $50,000 for cash and they jointly elect out of the automatic rollover?

(c) What are the tax consequences to Mr. and Mrs. A, if Mr. A makes a loan of $50,000 to Mrs. A instead of giving the bond to her or taking cash from her. Mr. A charges Mrs. A interest on the loan at a rate which is lower than the prescribed interest rate?

— SOLUTION

(a) The tax consequences are as follows: when Mr. A gives the bond to Mrs. A, there will be no gain or loss (fair market value equals cost). After the bond has been given to Mrs. A, the $5,000 annual interest income will be subject to the attribution rule, since the transfer of the bond was not at fair market value when it was given to Mrs. A. Note that all gifts of income-earning property are subject to the attribution rules as well as any transfers of property not at fair market value. The $5,000 interest income will be included in Mr. A's income instead of Mrs. A's income. If Mrs. A sells the bond to a third party, any gains or losses from selling the bond will also be attributed back to Mr. A (as discussed in Chapter 8). ITA: 73(1) ITA: 74.1(1), 74.5(1) ITA: 74.2

(b) The tax consequences will change. The attribution rule will not apply to the $5,000 of interest income because Mrs. A paid fair market value for the bond and they elected out of the rollover. The $5,000 interest income will be included in Mrs. A's income. ITA: 73(1) ITA: 74.5(1)

(c) The tax consequences are that the $5,000 annual interest income will be included in Mr. A's income and taxed at his marginal tax rate.

If Mr. A charges interest at the lesser of the prescribed rate or an arm's length commercial rate, the $5,000 annual property income will be included in Mrs. A's income. The interest charged by Mr. A must be paid by Mrs. A within 30 days of the end of each year in which the loan is outstanding. The attribution rule will not apply, due to the fair market value consideration paid by Mrs. A in this situation. However, Mrs. A will be able to deduct the interest she pays from her interest income on the bond, leaving little, if any, income to be taxed at her lower rate. ITA: 74.5(2)

Example Problem 6-11

- Ms. A is taxed in the top bracket and she owns a bond worth $50,000. The original cost to Ms. A is $50,000. The bond produces $5,000 of interest income.
- Junior is Ms. A's son. He is 15 years old and he has no income.
- Ms. A gives the property to Junior.

— *REQUIRED*

(a) What are the tax consequences to Ms. A and Junior?

(b) What are the tax consequences to Ms. A and Junior, if Ms. A sells the property to Junior and takes back a loan?

— *SOLUTION*

(a) The tax consequences are similar to the ones between Ms. A and her spouse. However, when Junior sells the property to a third party, the capital gains or losses will not be subject to the attribution rules (as discussed in Chapter 8). Junior will include the capital gains or losses in his income.

(b) The attribution rule will apply unless the loan is for the $50,000 fair market value and Ms. A charges interest at the lesser of the prescribed rate or an arm's length commercial rate. Junior must pay interest to Ms. A within 30 days of the end of each year in which the loan is outstanding. Junior will be able to deduct the interest paid, minimizing the income-splitting benefit.

¶6,095 Anti-avoidance rules relating to attribution

A number of anti-avoidance rules are contained in these attribution provisions.

1. Repayment of Existing Indebtedness

One rule prevents a person from taking out a commercial loan to purchase an income-producing property and then borrowing money interest-free from his or her spouse to repay the commercial debt. If this is done, then any property income or capital gains or losses from the income-producing property will be attributed to the spouse who made the interest-free loan.

2. Back-to-Back Loans

An anti-avoidance rule is provided to prevent circumventing the attribution rules by the use of "back-to-back" loans and transfers. The rule envisages a situation where property is deposited with a financial institution paying no interest with an agreement that the same amount as that deposited be loaned to the depositor's spouse at a nominal rate of interest, say, 2%. In this case, the use of the intermediary would be disregarded. The attribution rules will apply to include, in the income of the original transferor, the income earned by the property owned by the ultimate transferee. Of course, if such a back-to-back loan is made at a commercial rate or a back-to-back transfer is made for fair market value consideration, then no attribution will take place. ITA: 74.5(6)

3. Loan Guarantees

The avoidance of the attribution rules by the use of loan guarantees is prevented. For example, instead of Spouse A lending income-producing property to Spouse B, Spouse A could guarantee a loan made by another person or a financial institution to Spouse B who would use the proceeds of the loan to buy income-producing property. Unless a commercial rate of interest is charged and paid on the loan to Spouse B, Spouse A will have to include the income from the property. ITA: 74.5(7)

4. Artificial Transactions

A general anti-avoidance rule is provided to prevent "artificial transactions" which would benefit from the application of the attribution rules. In the past, taxpayers have devised transactions or a series of transactions known as "reverse attribution plans" to have income attributed to a low-income taxpayer. Therefore, if one of the main reasons for a loan or transfer is to reduce the amount of tax that would be paid, the attribution rules discussed will not apply in cases where such reverse attribution is attempted. Another example of such artificial attribution is given in a CRA Interpretation Bulletin. ITA: 74.5(11) IT-511R, par. 26

5. Compensation

Two Interpretation Bulletins indicate that an individual can remunerate a spouse or a related minor for services provided in a business carried on by the payer as long as certain conditions in the Act are met. These conditions require that the amount paid must be deductible in determining the payer's business income (according to the general rules of deductibility discussed in Chapter 4) and included in the recipient's income. Payments under the child tax benefits program, as discussed in ¶10,460, are excepted from the income attribution rule applicable on transfers or loans to minors. As a result, the income attribution rules do not apply to income arising from child tax benefits transferred or loaned to the child. IT-510, par. 18; IT-511R, par. 25 ITA: 74.5(12)(*b*) ITA: 74.1(2)

6. Corporation

Finally, anti-avoidance rules generally prevent income splitting through the use of a corporation. This provision is discussed at greater length in Chapter 13. ITA: 74.4

¶6,100 More types of income subject to attribution

Note that the income attribution rules apply only to the transfer of property that results in income or loss from property rather than income or loss from business. This distinction was at issue in the case of *Lackie v. The Queen*, in which the taxpayer transferred a farm to his wife from which she sold gravel at an agreed price per ton. The amounts received were taxable as income. The CRA argued that this income was from property transferred by the taxpayer to his spouse and, therefore, was subject to the attribution rules and taxable as income in the hands of the taxpayer. On the other hand, the taxpayer contended that attribution was improper because the income was from business rather than property. The court held that the income was from property because the taxpayer's wife did not sell gravel as a business but granted a licence to work a gravel pit on her land. It was clear to the court that the amounts received were dependent on the use of property. 79 DTC 5309 (F.C.A.) ITA: 12(1)(*g*)

¶6,102 "Second-generation" income from property

The term "property" is defined in the Act. It includes substituted property, but does not include income earned on attributed income, often referred to as "second-generation" income. For example, if a $10,000 bond, bearing interest at 10% annually, is given to a spouse, the $1,000 of interest income received by the recipient of the bond is attributed to the transferor spouse. If the $1,000 is reinvested by the recipient spouse at, say, 10%, the $100 of interest earned on the reinvested interest is not attributed to the transferor spouse. The $100 is income earned on income, i.e., the $1,000, that has been attributed. Hence, the $100 is referred to as second-generation income. ITA: 248(1), 248(5)

¶6,105 Loans or transfers to non-arm's length individuals who are 18 years of age or older

The attribution rules do not apply to loans or transfers to non-arm's length persons who are 18 years of age or older. However, anti-avoidance rules prevent the avoidance of tax on *loans* between non-arm's length individuals. Income from property resulting from a low-interest or a no-interest loan by an individual to another non-arm's length individual will be attributed back to the lender. The key condition for the attribution rule to apply is that one of the main reasons for the loan is to reduce or avoid tax on income from the property or substituted property. Therefore, loans between non-arm's length individuals, both of whom are taxed at the same rate, would appear not to be caught by these provisions. Similarly, if the loaned funds are spent on non-income-producing property (e.g., personal-use property, living expenses, etc.), then the "one of the main reasons" test would not be met. Note that the attribution rules apply only to loans, but not to sales or gifts. ITA: 74.1–74.5 ITA: 56(4.1)–(4.3) ITA: 74.1 ITA: 56(4.1) ITA: 56(4.1)

Loans that bear a commercial or arm's length rate of interest are exempt from the attribution rule. The interest must, in fact, be paid within 30 days of the end of the year in respect of which it was charged for the exemption to apply. Refinancing a loan subject to the above attribution rule with another loan will not circumvent the attribution rule. ITA: 56(4.1), 56(4.2), 56(4.3)

¶6,110 Summary of income attribution rules

Exhibit 6-2 attempts to summarize the major rules pertaining to the attribution of income from property.

EXHIBIT 6-2
Attribution of Income* from Property**
Conceptual Summary

	Transaction		
Recipient	*Transfer by gift*	*Transfer by sale*	*Transaction involving loan*
*Spouse or common-law partner*** [ssec. 74.1(1)]*	• *Income or loss from property attributed to transferor*	• *If no fair market value considera-tion received: Income or loss from property attributed to transferor* • *If fair market value considera-tion received:**** No attribution*	• *If no interest at a commercial rate paid: Income or loss from property attributed to transferor* • *If interest at a com-mercial rate paid:**** No attribution*
Minors who are not at arm's length [secs. 251 and 252] or who are nieces and nephews [ssec. 74.1(2)]	• *Income or loss from property attributed to transferor*	• *Same as for trans-fer by gift (depen-dent on whether fair market value consideration received)*	• *Same as for transfer by gift (dependent on whether fair market value consideration received)*
Other non-arm's length individuals not subject to section 74.1 [ssec. 56(4.1)]	• *No attribution*	• *No attribution*	• *Income only from property attributed to transferor, if one of the main reasons for the loan was to reduce or avoid tax and mar-ket rate of interest not paid*

* Excluding second-generation income.

** Including substituted property as defined in subsection 248(5). Income from business is not attributed in any of these transactions. Attribution of capital gains or losses is discussed in Chapter 7.

*** Attribution of capital gains and losses on transfers or loans to a spouse is discussed in Chapter 7.

**** To avoid attribution, the taxpayer must elect to waive the deferral of accrued income under subsection 73(1) (discussed in ¶6,090 and ¶7,435.30) and must transfer for fair market value consideration. Where a loan is involved, interest at a commercial rate must be paid within 30 days of the end of every year in which the loan is outstanding.

¶6,115 Tax on split income earned by persons under 18 years of age (the "Kiddie Tax")

¶6,115.10 *Overview*

Note that the income attribution rules, discussed above, do not apply to income from a business, such as a proprietorship or a partnership, transferred to a minor. As will be seen in a subsequent chapter, the corporate attribution rules do not apply to dividends from certain private corporations that carry on an active business in Canada. To address this exclusion from attribution rules, a specific anti-avoidance rule has been introduced. In general, the "kiddie tax" rules apply to dividends from a private Canadian or foreign corporation. The tax rate on these dividends is the top marginal tax rate of an individual, and the amount of tax payable is net of the dividend tax credit and the foreign tax credit. This tax eliminates the incentive to income split through distributions of dividends from private corporations to minor children. ITA: 120.4

¶6,115.20 *Split income*

The special tax on split income applies to the following types of income that are earned by persons under 18 years of age: ITA: 120.4

- taxable dividends and taxable capital gains derived from shares that are not listed on a designated Canadian or foreign stock exchange (i.e., essentially, shares of a private corporation) and that are received directly or indirectly through a trust or partnership;
- shareholder benefits included in the minor's income under section 15;
- partnership or trust income, including taxable capital gains, derived from the provision of goods and services to a business that is carried on by

  (i) a person related to the minor,

  (ii) a corporation which has a "specified shareholder" who is related to the minor, or ITA: 248(1)

  (iii) a professional corporation which has a shareholder who is related to the minor.

As indicated above, the tax on split income extends to taxable capital gains that are included in the income of a minor and are from a disposition of shares to a non-arm's length person if taxable dividends on such shares would have been subject to the tax on split income. An amount equal to two times these taxable capital gains will be deemed to be dividends and subject to "kiddie tax" at the top marginal rate. Since capital gains are considered to accrue from reinvested retained earnings, it would otherwise be possible to avoid the tax on split income in a non-arm's length situation by retaining income rather than paying it out as a dividend. ITA: 120.4(4)

¶6,115.30 *Tax treatment of split income*

The split income is:

- subject to tax at the top marginal rate, including applicable surtax, instead of the graduated rates;
- not eligible for any deductions or credits, except for the dividend tax credit and foreign tax credits; and
- eligible for an offsetting deduction from taxable income equal to the specified income, so that this amount would not be taxed again normally under Part I of the Act.

Note that the tax on split income applies to the minor, at the top marginal tax rate, and not to the transferor of the property, on income that would not otherwise be subject to the attributions rules. ITA: 56(5), 74.5(13)

¶6,115.40 *Exceptions to tax on split income*

The special income splitting tax does not apply to:

- income from a corporation or a partnership paid to individuals over 18 years of age, i.e., not a "specified individual";
- taxable dividends from shares listed on a designated stock exchange, which may be subject to the attribution rules applicable to minors;
- reasonable remuneration to minors, which is not subject to the attribution rules;
- capital gains on the disposition of the shares of private Canadian or foreign corporation, which is not subject to the attribution rules;
- income from property inherited from a parent, which would not be subject to the attribution rules;
- minors who have no parent who is resident in Canada at any time in the year; or
- income from property inherited from someone other than a parent, if the minor is in full-time attendance at a post-secondary institution or is eligible for the disability tax credit.

Note, then, that the tax on split income replaces attribution of income that is split income.

Example Problem 6-12

Christine has heard that she can save some tax by having her children, ages 14 and 16, own shares in her company and then paying them dividends. Since her children only earn a small amount of income they will pay little, if any, tax and they can use the cash to finance their educations. She has been advised that she can exchange her common shares for preference shares and have her children purchase new common shares for a nominal price using their own cash thereby avoiding the attribution rules. Her company only earns active business income.

— REQUIRED

Advise Christine whether "kiddie tax" will apply.

— SOLUTION

The regular attribution rules will not apply, but "kiddie tax" will apply. The shares are private-company shares and dividends will be received by persons less than 18 years of age.

As a result, the dividends will be taxed at the top marginal tax rate and any income-splitting benefit will be lost.

¶6,120 What else can be income split?

In general, income splitting is still permissible under certain situations. For example, the spousal RRSP contribution is allowed. Also, the Act allows income splitting on pension income. We will discuss this topic more in later chapters. ITA: 56(1)(*a*.1)

¶6,200 DEDUCTIONS

¶6,210 Carrying Charges on Land

¶6,215 Limitation on deduction — Vacant land

Carrying charges, such as interest and property taxes, on vacant land are only deductible to the extent of the taxpayer's net income from the land. If the property is a capital property, the carrying charges that are not deducted will be added to the cost base of the land. An increased cost base of the land is only deductible when the land is sold, thereby, reducing the capital gain of the property. Capital gains are covered in Chapter 7. ITA: 18(2), 18(3); ITA: 53(1)(*h*)

These rules apply to property developers whose business is the sale or development of land, or to land that is held, but not used, in a business. This restriction discourages speculation in real estate (no intention to use the real estate for business purpose but to hold the piece of property for capital gains). Land which is used or held primarily for an income-producing purpose is exempted from the above limitation. In a special case where the land is vacant for part of the year and used for business for the remainder, the carrying charges would be deductible, as the Act does not specify a time period in the year. However, the costs during construction on the land would not be deductible. (See ¶6,220.) ITA: 18(2)(*d*) ITA: 18(2)

Corporations whose principal business is the leasing, rental or sale, and the development for lease, rental or sale of real property are permitted to deduct carrying charges on vacant land, in excess of net income before deducting carrying charges. The limit of this deduction is the corporation's "base level deduction". That limit is interest computed at the prescribed rate (as previously discussed in this Chapter in respect of shareholder loans) on a loan of $1 million outstanding throughout the year. ITA: 18(2), 18(3) ITA: 18(2)(*f*) ITA: 18(2.2)

Example Problem 6-13

In 2011, Mr. Walkovia acquired a vacant lot in a downtown area of the city, intending to build an office complex. By late 2013, he decided to abandon the project. The property was disposed of just before the end of the year. It was not considered to have been held for speculation because of the unforeseen problems encountered in the development.

While the property was owned by Mr. Walkovia, it had been used as a city parking lot with the following results:

	2011	*2012*	*2013*
Net income (loss) before interest and property taxes*	$11,000	$ 6,000	$ (3,000)
Interest and property taxes	9,500	10,000	10,500

* This amount is equal to gross revenue in excess of all other expenses

— *REQUIRED*

(A) Consider the effect of these data on the income of Mr. Walkovia for tax purposes.

(B) If the land had been owned by a corporation whose principal business was the development and sale of land, what would be the effects of these data? Assume a prescribed rate of interest of 8% throughout the period in question.

— *SOLUTION*

(A) Since the land, held for development in this case, is not excluded from the limitation, interest and property taxes will be deductible only to the extent of gross revenues in excess of all other expenses, i.e., net income before interest and property taxes. As a result, the following amount would be reported as income for the years indicated: ITA: 18(2)

	2011	*2012*	*2013*
Gross revenue less expenses other than interest and property taxes	$11,000	$ 6,000	$(3,000)
Less: Interest and property taxes	9,500	6,000	Nil
Income (loss) for the year	$ 1,500	Nil	$(3,000)
Non-deductible interest and property taxes added to adjusted cost base of land	Nil	$ 4,000	$10,500

(B) In this case, a loss created by the deduction of interest and property tax is permitted. However, the excess of interest and property tax that is deductible is limited to an amount of interest computed at the 8% prescribed rate, assumed in this case, on a notional principal amount of $1,000,000. The $80,000 limit in this case is referred to as the base level deduction. The following losses would be reported by a corporation: ITA: 18(2)(*f*)

	2011		2012		2013
Gross revenue less expenses other than interest and property taxes.		$ 11,000		$ 6,000	$ (3,000)
Less lesser of:					
(a) interest and property taxes	$ 9,500		$10,000		$10,500
(b) base level deduction	$80,000		$80,000		$80,000
lesser amount		(9,500)		(10,000)	(10,500)
Income (loss) for the year		$ 1,500		$(4,000)	$(13,500)

Note that the losses are of value to a corporation if it generates sufficient income from other sources to be shielded by the deduction of the losses. That is, the value of losses is inherent in the ability to shield income from tax.

¶6,220 "Soft Costs" Relating To Construction of Buildings or Ownership of Land

"Soft costs" include interest expenses, legal and accounting fees, mortgage fees, insurance, and property taxes. Soft costs incurred, during the period of construction, renovation, or alternation of a building, are not deductible as current expenses, and must be added to the cost of the building. Similarly, such costs in respect of the ownership of the land on which the building is under construction must also be capitalized.

Note that the restriction on the deduction of these expenses only applies to expenses incurred before completion of construction, renovation, or alternation of the building. The Act provides for the determination of the date on which the work is completed. ITA: 18(3.3) It is also worth noting that the Act specifies that capitalization is required for the costs "attributable" to, and not merely incurred in, the period of construction. ITA: 18(3.1) For example, a company must capitalize the interest on the bank loan it took out to construct a building for the time during which construction took place. If the company chose to prepay some of the interest before construction commenced, it still would not be able to deduct the interest in the current year.

Costs such as capital cost allowance on the building, the landscaping expenses, and disability-related modifications to buildings are exempted from the above rules. ITA: 18(3.1) The Act also permits a taxpayer to deduct soft costs incurred in the year up to the taxpayer's income earned on the building under construction, renovation, or alternation.

Issuance costs, such as accounting fees and underwriter fees, are one-time costs to acquire financing for the project of acquiring long term capital assets. While some portion of such costs is inevitably attributable to the period of construction, it is difficult to determine how much. Therefore, the general tax treatment is to amortize these costs over five years ITA: 20(1)(*e*) instead of through the CCA schedule of the underlying asset.

¶6,230 Rental Properties

¶6,235 Separate classes — Rental property costing over $50,000

In general, capital cost allowance (CCA) is computed on the balance at the end of the year in a pool or class of similar assets. Dispositions throughout the year reduce the balance in a class and may even cause the balance to be negative. However, such a negative balance, to the extent that it is offset by a purchase of more assets for the class during the year, will not result in recapture. Thus, the ability to offset a negative balance in a class of assets with purchases of similar assets during the year reduces or eliminates the need to pay tax on income from recapture of capital cost allowances.

Each rental property purchased that costs $50,000 or more must be placed in a separate CCA class. This will result in recapture when a building is sold for proceeds in excess of the undepreciated capital cost in the class (i.e., when the UCC balance becomes negative at the end of the taxation year). The purpose of the rule is to prevent taxpayers from avoiding recapture of CCA when selling a rental property by buying another rental property of the same class. If rental properties are allowed to be grouped together, a taxpayer can buy a new rental property by the end of the taxation year to offset a negative balance. The separate class rule intends to force recognition of recapture each time the pool has a negative balance, as a result of a sale.

¶6,240 Losses from rental property

The Act restricts the deduction of CCA on rental properties. CCA can only be deducted to the extent that it does not create or increase a net loss from all of a taxpayer's rental properties combined. By this rule, a taxpayer is prevented from using CCA on rental properties to create a loss or increase a loss from this type of asset to shelter other types of income from tax. For example, rental losses from CCA will not be available to shield income from employment or from business.

As an exception to this rule, losses created by capital cost allowances on rental property will not be deductible from non-rental income. However, rental property is narrowly defined to mean the rental building, thereby excluding furniture and fixtures from this treatment. As a result, the regulations dealing with leasing properties were added to prohibit the deduction of losses from non-rental income created by capital cost allowance on furniture and fixtures leased in a building except for corporations in the business of leasing property. Thus, a taxpayer cannot shelter other sources of income by offsetting a loss created by capital cost allowances on a rental building or leasing properties against those other sources of income, unless the taxpayer is a corporation or a partnership of corporations whose principal business was the property rental or leasing business.

ITR: 1100(11)–(14); IT-195R4

ITR: 1100(15)–(20)

Example Problem 6-14

Irene owns six rental buildings with the following information pertaining to each:

	Building 1	Building 2	Building 3	Building 4	Building 5	Building 6
Cost	$30,000	$132,000	$71,000	$49,000	$350,000	$47,000
UCC, January 1, 2013	22,000	90,000	49,000	40,000	238,000	38,000
Rental revenue in 2013	1,600	17,000	8,000	3,800	45,000	6,000
Cash expenses:						
Interest	Nil	$ 1,200	$1,700	Nil	$ 3,200	$1,400
Property taxes	$400	3,000	1,500	$ 800	8,000	1,200
Other expenses	800	11,000	7,500	1,600	29,000	5,800

Late in 2013, buildings 1 and 2 were sold for proceeds of $40,000 and $91,000 respectively. Building 5 was purchased in 1986. All other buildings were purchased after 1987.

— *REQUIRED*

Prepare a schedule showing the maximum capital cost allowance which may be claimed for tax purposes assuming she owns no other rental properties. Assume all buildings are of brick construction.

— *SOLUTION*

	Class 1: 4%			Class 3: 5%
	Under $50,000	Building 2	Building 3	Building 5
UCC, January 1, 2013	$100,000	$90,000	$49,000	$238,000
Dispositions during the year	30,000(1)	91,000	—	—
UCC, December 31, 2013	$ 70,000	$(1,000)	$49,000	$238,000
CCA for 2013 (max.: $4,300 below)	2,800(2)	—	1,500(2)	Nil(2)

Recapture	—	1,000	—	—
UCC, January 1, 2014	$ 67,200	Nil	$47,500	$238,000

Total rental revenue in 2013	$ 81,400
Add: recapture [ssecs. 13(1)–(3)]	1,000
Less: total cash expenses	(78,100)
Net before CCA	$ 4,300
CCA — Amount deductible re: limitation(2)	(4,300)
Loss on rental properties	Nil

— *NOTES TO SOLUTION*

(1) The balance is never reduced by more than the original cost on the disposition of an asset; capital gain of $10,000 (i.e., $40,000 – $30,000).

(2) CCA potentially available in 2013:

Buildings with cost under $50,000 (4% of $70,000)	$ 2,800
Building 3 (4% of $49,000)	1,960
Building 5 (5% of $238,000)	11,900
Total	$16,660

Where deducting the maximum allowable CCA is not possible, as in this case, or not desirable, it is usually advisable to take CCA in lower-rate classes first. This preserves a higher balance in the higher-rate classes for the future when it may be possible to deduct relatively higher amounts of CCA in the higher-rate classes.

¶6,250 Depreciation-Based or Similar Tax Shelters

Depreciation-based or similar tax shelters such as residential buildings, films, yachts, hotels, recreational vehicles and nursing homes have been available in the past. They have been used as a tool of fiscal policy to encourage investment in certain areas by providing a fast write-off. For example, a high CCA rate, or a large absolute dollar write-off of an amount invested will reduce the after-tax cash outflow of the initial investment. As extensive use of these shelters is perceived as abuse of the system by the Department of Finance, the ability to shelter other income with losses created by capital cost allowances has been either eliminated or reduced in effect. This was the case for residential buildings, films, yachts, hotels, nursing homes, recreational vehicles, computer software and other similar properties. The federal government imposed restrictive measures with the stated objective to "improve the fairness of the tax system and prevent abuses through aggressive tax shelter promotion." However, from time to time, other assets become the subject of depreciation-based tax shelters and, therefore, it is important to understand, conceptually, how they are used.

Consider the following typical example of a simple tax shelter, based on a hypothetical Class 10 asset. An investor could purchase a percentage of the asset through a partnership. The investor could be required to pay as little as 5% of the full investment in cash and he or she typically would sign an unconditional note for the balance which is usually payable in two to seven years. As long as the full investment amount is at risk by the investor, he or she could take Class 10 declining balance capital cost allowance of 30%, subject to the half-year rule, of the full amount of the investment in the year in which the investment was made. This principle was supported by the case of *Mandel v. The Queen*, and the Act codifies these "at risk" rules under specified conditions where a limited partnership is used. In the case of *Signum Communications Inc. v. The Queen*, based on facts which predated subsection 96(2.2), the Federal Court–Trial Division held that in the absence of a statutory at-risk rule, there was no reason to limit losses to the amount of capital invested in a partnership, despite the decision in the *Mandel* case.

78 DTC 6518 (F.C.A.)
ITA: 96(2.2)
88 DTC 6427 (F.C.T.D.)

Assets sold as tax shelters have been very high risk investments, with probably only a small chance that the investment would be profitable. The main advantage of an investment in a sheltered asset has been a tax deferral which was most valuable to those in the higher tax brackets. For example, an investor purchasing a $100,000 interest in an asset may have had to pay only $5,000 in the first year, but was entitled to a $15,000 tax deduction of capital cost allowance at the 30% rate for Class 10, subject to the half-year rule. However, the $95,000 balance will have to be paid, and the investor may be confronted by cash flow problems if he or she receives no income from the asset. These investments are also usually very illiquid.

It should be realized that *all* investments shelter the cost of the investment from taxation. For example, it will be demonstrated in the next two Chapters how the cost of an investment in stock is "written off" against the proceeds of disposition when the stock is sold. It can be shown that the advantage of the faster write-off of a tax shelter cannot provide a profit for an investment that does not return both its cost and its after-tax carrying charges. Thus, an investment decision should be made primarily on its value as an investment without regard to any accelerated tax write-off that may be available and should not be based solely on the advantage of an early or large write-off of the investment. There is little advantage to making a $100,000 investment that turns out to be almost worthless, in order to write off the $100,000 and save about $50,000 in taxes!

¶6,260 Interest Deduction

¶6,265 Proposed legislation

On October 31, 2003, the Department of Finance released, for public comment, draft proposals, regarding the deductibility of interest, which deal with the issue of reasonable expectation of profit. These proposals, along with an Interpretation Bulletin on interest deductibility and related issues, released on October 31, 2003 by the CRA, form the current government position on the deductibility of interest. However, actual legislation has not been passed at the time of writing (July 2012). IT-533

"Interest" is not a defined term in the Act. The determination of what is interest is a question of law. The definition of interest has been addressed in several court decisions, including *Shell Canada Limited v. The Queen* and *Miller v. The Queen*. As in *Miller*, interest for tax purposes is generally accepted to mean an amount that has met three criteria. These criteria are: 99 DTC 5669 (S.C.C.) 85 DTC 5354 (F.C.T.D.)

- the amount must be calculated on a day-to-day accrual basis,
- the amount must be calculated on a principal sum (or a right to a principal sum), and
- the amount must be compensation for the use of the principal sum (or the right to the principal sum).

In general, interest represents payment for the use of debt capital. The Act allows a taxpayer to deduct interest on money borrowed to earn income from business or property. ITA: 20(1)(c)

A taxpayer can deduct interest if it:

- is paid or payable in the year,
- arises from a legal obligation,
- is payable on borrowed money that is used for the purpose of earning income (other than exempt income) from a business or property, and
- is reasonable in amount.

Example Problem 6-15

A parent with two children is preparing a will. One child is active in the parent's business and the other is not. The parent is considering the following two options with respect to the business:

(a) leave the business to the child who will be active in the business on the condition that the child give the other child an amount equal to the 50% of the fair market value of the business on the parent's death, and

(b) leave 50% of the business to each of the two children on the condition that the child who will be active in the business buy the 50% left to the other child.

In either case, the active child will have to borrow the funds to pay the other child.

— REQUIRED

Advise the parent on the better alternative for the child who will be active in the business.

— SOLUTION

Based on the use of the borrowed funds, the interest incurred under the second alternative will be deductible, because the funds will be used to buy shares which will produce income. Interest incurred under the first alternative will not be deductible, because the use of the borrowed funds will not produce income.

There are some statutory limits on the deduction of interest. We have discussed some of them in Chapter 4. The followings are a few examples:

- the deduction of interest imposed under the Act is denied; ITA: 18(1)(*t*)
- the deduction of interest on funds borrowed to buy vacant land is limited; ITA: 18(2)
- interest that is part of "soft costs" must be capitalized; ITA: 18(3.1)
- the deduction of interest paid to certain non-residents is limited; and ITA: 18(4)–(8)
- the deduction for interest on borrowed fund to make a contribution to tax sheltered retirement savings fund, such as RRSPs, is denied. ITA: 18(11)

Note that the interest on interest is called compound interest. Compound interest is deductible if the original amount borrowed meets the test of interest deductibility. However, a compound interest is only deductible when it is paid and not when it is payable.

¶6,270 Loss of the source of income

From the above section, we know that the general principle of interest deductibility is that the borrowed money must be used for the purpose of earning income from a business or property. However, a problem can arise if an investment financed with debt declines in value and is sold at a loss. The investor reinvests the proceeds but does not pay off the loan. Should interest still be deductible when the source of income is lost?

Example Problem 6-16

A taxpayer borrows $10,000 to acquire an income-producing property. During the holding period of that property, the interest has been deducted from income for tax purposes. When the property declines in value to $6,000, the property is sold and the taxpayer invests the $6,000 of proceeds in another income-producing property. The original loan has not been repaid.

— REQUIRED

Determine whether the interest expense on the loan related to the $4,000 realized loss in value will be deductible.

— SOLUTION

If we use the general principle of interest deductibility, the interest on the remaining debt would no longer be deductible as it is not currently used for the purpose of earning income from a business or property. The Act addresses this issue. A rule applies to deem the $4,000 of borrowed money to continue to be used for the purpose of earning income from the property, as long as the original property was capital property (other than real estate or depreciable property). This allows the interest on the $4,000 to qualify for the deduction. ITA: 20.1

¶6,275 Capitalization of interest

At the taxpayer's election, the Act permits certain borrowing costs and interest to be treated as non-deductible expenses and added to the cost of depreciable property in respect of which the expenses were incurred. This election might be made, for example, if the deduction of such costs would create a loss that could not be absorbed in the loss carryover period which will be discussed in a later Chapter. The costs eligible for such deferment are amounts otherwise deductible as interest and other expenses of borrowing money. This is particularly advantageous if the interest is in respect of assets in fast write-off classes such as Class 12. ITA: 21; ITA: 20(1)(*c*), 20(1)(*d*), 20(1)(*e*)

¶6,290 Personal Loan Planning and Interest Deductibility

¶6,295 Deductibility of interest expenses

In general, as indicated above, expenditures made or incurred for the purpose of gaining or producing income from property are deductible from that income. The amounts of such expenditures must be reasonable in the circumstances. Under the current concept of interest deductibility, there need only be a reasonable expectation of earning income. The concept of income in this case is general, referring to gross income inclusions for tax purposes, not net income. No income need actually be earned in a year in order to deduct interest paid or payable in that year. In the case of preferred shares or fixed income securities producing interest held by an individual, the CRA will allow an interest expense deduction that is not restricted to the income from the investment. Interest at a reasonable rate on funds borrowed to buy common shares will be fully deductible irrespective of the dividend yield, which may even be zero, because of the reasonable expectation of an increase in the dividend rate on common shares. ITA: 20(1)(*c*); IT-533, par. 31

The deductibility of interest is determined by the use of the borrowed funds. Thus, interest paid on a mortgage, the proceeds of which are used to invest in certain securities, is deductible because the interest is paid in respect of funds used to produce income. On the other hand, interest on funds borrowed to purchase personal property is not deductible because it is not used to produce income. Also, interest on funds borrowed to invest in commodities as a capital investment was held by the Tax Court of Canada not to be deductible in *Hastings v. M.N.R.* The Court agreed with the Crown's position that the ordinary rules relating to expenses being deducted in the income-earning process do not apply to the capital gains sections of the Act. 88 DTC 1391 (T.C.C.)

Loan planning would suggest that the taxpayer borrow funds which will be used to produce income, thereby making the interest tax deductible. This permits the taxpayer to allocate his or her savings to purchases such as assets used for personal purposes including the family home or a car not used for business which do not produce income.

Great care must be taken in maintaining the connection between the interest paid and the use of the funds borrowed. In one case, a taxpayer received a loan from his employer and used the proceeds to finance the purchase of securities. He secured the loan with a mortgage on his house. In this situation, the interest on the loan was deductible. However, when the taxpayer was transferred and he sold his house, he had to pay off the loan from the proceeds of sale. He then purchased another house in his new work location and financed the purchase with a mortgage. He deducted mortgage interest on the new house against his investment income on the same basis as before, but the CRA disallowed that interest deduction. It was argued that the money was not used to produce income, but to acquire the new house. In this case, the taxpayer did not maintain the connection between the loan and the use of the funds. Had he not paid off the employer's loan but secured the loan with a new mortgage on the new home, he would have maintained that connection. IT-533, par. 9–14

This position, taken by the CRA, was confirmed in the case of *The Queen v. Bronfman Trust*, when the Supreme Court of Canada held that what was important was the use of the borrowed funds. In this case, the Supreme Court, in its examination, was not able to trace the funds borrowed directly to an income-earning source (eligible use source) and, hence, denied the deduction of the related interest. It would appear that in these cases, the decision in the *Bronfman Trust* case would stand. Therefore, in order for interest on borrowed funds to be deductible, the taxpayer must still trace the funds borrowed to an income-producing purpose. 87 DTC 5097 (S.C.C.); IT-533, par. 13

¶6,300 Commentary on two Supreme Court decisions on interest deductibility — Singleton and Ludco

¶6,300.10 *Singleton*

2001 DTC 5533 (S.C.C.)

(i) Facts

Singleton, involved a lawyer who had a capital account in his law firm with a balance of at least $300,000. Mr. Singleton's firm paid him his $300,000 capital and he used the funds to purchase a new house. On the same day, he borrowed $300,000 and contributed it to his firm as a capital contribution, where it was used by the firm as working capital in its business. The loan was secured on the house. Although the house was purchased in his wife's name, Mr. Singleton was legally obligated to make the mortgage payments, thereby fulfilling the requirement that the interest be paid pursuant to a "legal obligation".

(ii) Issue

The issue of *Singleton* is whether the borrowed money was used for the purpose of earning income from a business.

(iii) The Supreme Court of Canada Decision

The Supreme Court of Canada held that the interest payments were deductible under the *Income Tax Act*. The court concluded that, given the effect of the legal relationships, the taxpayer borrowed money and used that money to refinance the capital account in the law firm. This was a direct and eligible use of funds within the meaning of the provision which allows the deduction of interest on borrowed funds. ITA: 20(1)(*c*)

¶6,300.20 *Ludco*

2001 DTC 5505 (S.C.C.)

(i) Facts

In *Ludco*, the taxpayer used approximately $7.5 million of borrowed money to purchase shares in two offshore corporations in the Bahamas (known as a tax haven). During the period in which it held the shares, Ludco deducted approximately $6 million of interest and included $600,000 of dividends in its incomes. When the shares were disposed of, it reported a gain of $9,200,000. The Minister disallowed the deduction of the $6 million interest expense on the grounds that the shares were acquired to earn a capital gain (partially included in income for tax purposes as a different source) instead of for the purpose of earning income from property.

(ii) Issue

The issue in the *Ludco* case is whether the $7.5 million borrowed funds was used by the taxpayers for the purpose of earning income from property when the investment earned only $600,000 of dividend income.

(iii) The Supreme Court of Canada Decision

In its decision, the Supreme Court of Canada held that the word "income" in the provision of the Act which allows deduction of interest on borrowed funds meant gross and not net income. Therefore, the taxpayer only needs to have a reasonable expectation of earning some revenue to support his interest deduction. As a result, the interest was deductible in this case.

¶6,305 Tax planning

¶6,305.10 *Overview*

Tax is an important factor affecting investment decisions. The objective of this section is to provide a brief discussion that is useful for thinking about how taxes affect investment decisions.

When an investor has multiple investment opportunities, but limited funds, the rule of thumb is to compare the after-tax return on available funds. If the investor has to borrow to invest, the investment decision may depend on that financing. On the other hand, the interest deductibility depends on the type of investment undertaking. In general, if the funds are borrowed to acquire property that is used to generate property income, then interest paid on the loan is deducible for tax purposes. Interest on a loan used to buy a personal asset such as a home is, generally, not deductible. The following example illustrates the differences in after-tax returns on investments.

Example Problem 6-17

Ms. Prudent has always considered investing her savings to be a high priority. This year she has saved $5,000; however, she has just discovered that she will need to purchase a new car which will cost an additional $5,000 with her trade-in. She can borrow the funds for the car from the dealer at a very favourable rate of 5.9%, while funds borrowed from a stockbroker to invest in corporate shares will cost 7%. She is in a 25.5% (combined federal and provincial) tax bracket.

— *REQUIRED*

How could Ms. Prudent accomplish her goals at a minimum cost in this situation?

— *SOLUTION*

Ms. Prudent should buy the car with her accumulated savings of $5,000 and borrow $5,000 from the stockbroker for her investments. While the pre-tax cost of the investment loan will be higher than a car loan, the 7% will be deductible resulting in an after-tax cost of 5.2% (i.e., 7% (1-0.255)) compared with the 5.9% car loan which is not tax deductible. The result is a saving of 0.7% which, on a loan of $5,000, would amount to about $35 in the first year.

¶6,305.30 *Conclusion*

From the above analysis, we can see that the general strategy is that you should buy personal assets with your own funds (since interest is not deductible on borrowed funds used to purchase personal assets) and then use these assets as collateral to borrow to invest in assets that will earn property income (since interest is deductible in that situation).

If you already have a mortgage on the personal asset, and it can be prepaid without penalty, you should pay it down using your own cash. However, if the mortgage is not open for such payments in full or in part, it may be worthwhile setting aside savings for the purpose of paying down the mortgage when it is due for renewal. Paying down an old, low-interest mortgage may not be the best investment, but certainly paying down one at a higher interest rate is worth considering.

¶6,310 Carrying charges

Individual taxpayers may claim carrying charges as deductions against property income such as interest and dividends. The deductions available to individual taxpayers include: safety deposit box fees [for taxation years beginning before March 21, 2013, per the March 2013 federal Budget], management or safe custody fees, accounting fees, and any other carrying costs normally incurred to earn property income.

Brokerage fees incurred on the purchase and sale of securities are not deductible as a carrying charge. Commissions charged on the acquisitions of shares become part of the adjusted cost base and commissions charged on disposition reduce the capital gain or loss. These fees represent a capital charge and affect the capital gain or loss on eventual sale of the securities. ITA: 40

¶6,315 Investment counsel fees

Taxpayers can also deduct fees paid for the advisability of purchasing or selling a specific security or for the administration or management of shares or securities. These fees must be paid to advisers whose principal business is investment counselling and fund management and must be related to earning income outside of a tax-deferred account or registered retirement savings plan. ITA: 20(1)(*bb*); IT-124R6, IT-238R2

¶6,320 Legal and accounting fees

All legal and accounting fees are deductible to the extent that they are incurred for the purpose of gaining or producing business or property income. It is important to note that the purpose of the fees determines whether they are deductible. Generally, fees incurred for preparing financial records, minutes of shareholder meetings, making annual corporate findings, conducting appeals for taxes, and watching legislation that affects the taxpayer's business or property income are deductible. Specifically, the Act allows a deduction for fees paid for advice or assistance in preparing an objection or appeal to the CRA, Tax Court or other government office. Any costs awarded to taxpayers for amounts deducted under this provision must be included in income. Fees for preparation of income tax returns are also deductible if there is a source of property income. ITA: 20(1)(*cc*); IT-99R5 ITA: 60(*o*) ITA: 56(1)(*l*)

Fees incurred for the acquisition/sale of capital property are included as part of the cost of the property or reduce the sale proceeds.

¶6,325 Foreign non-business income tax

Investors with foreign investments are generally subject to withholding tax in the foreign jurisdiction. Taxpayers resident in Canada must pay tax on their worldwide income. To provide taxpayers with relief, a foreign tax credit is available. This credit is limited to 15% of the foreign income from property. However, the Act permits individuals to claim a deduction from property income equal to the foreign taxes paid in excess of 15%. A foreign tax credit is usually more advantageous than a deduction because the credit is applied directly against income taxes. ITA: 20(11), 20(12) ITA: 126 ITA: 20(11)

¶6,400 DIFFERENCES BETWEEN BUSINESS AND PROPERTY INCOME

At this point, it would be worthwhile to isolate the provisions which have been examined so far and identify which apply to either business or property income.

¶6,410 Applicable to Business Income Only

The following deductions apply only to business income:

- write-off of eligible capital property; ITA: 20(1)(*b*)
- reserves; ITA: 20(1)(*m*), 20(1)(*m*.1), 20(1)(*m*.2), 20(1)(*n*)
- certain specific expenses:
  - — expenses of representation, ITA: 20(1)(*cc*)
  - — site investigation, ITA: 20(1)(*dd*)
  - — utilities services connection; ITA: 20(1)(*ee*)
- convention expenses; and ITA: 20(10)
- short-year proration for capital cost allowance. ITR: 1100(3)

¶6,420 Applicable to Property Income Only

The following deductions apply only to property income:

- restriction on capital cost allowance for rental properties; ITR: 1100(15)
- attribution rules; ITA: 74.1
- foreign taxes on property income in excess of 15% deductible. ITA: 20(11)

¶6,500 GST/HST AND PROPERTY INCOME

¶6,510 Interest and Dividends

Interest and dividends are exempt from GST/HST. A number of provisions and definitions in the *Excise Tax Act* (ETA) must be reviewed to explain the basis for this exemption. First, financial services rendered to residents in Canada are exempt from GST/HST. A "financial service" is defined to include a broad range of transactions and services. For example, the payment or receipt of interest, dividends, or any other amount in respect of a "financial instrument" is included in the definition of financial service. A "financial instrument" is defined to include a debt security, an equity security, an insurance policy, etc. A "debt security" is defined in the same subsection to mean a right to be paid money and includes a deposit of money. An "equity security" is defined to mean a share of the capital stock of a corporation or any interest in or right to such a share. Consequently, payments of interest and dividends in respect of financial instruments are exempt from GST/HST. It is important to note that the definition of financial service contains several exclusions. For example, paragraph (*r*) of the definition excludes the provision of a professional service by an accountant, actuary, lawyer or notary in the course of a professional practice. Consequently, these services are subject to GST/HST in the normal manner.

ETA: Part VII of Sch. V
ETA: 123(1)
ETA: 123(1)

¶6,520 "Soft Costs"

GST/HST applies to sales and rentals of real property unless the supply is specifically exempt under Part I of Schedule V (such as sales of *used* residential housing and long-term residential rents). The GST/HST affects real estate developers and builders in the same manner that it affects other businesses that make taxable supplies. To the extent property and services are purchased for use in commercial activities, input tax credits in respect of the GST/HST paid on those purchases may be claimed. For example, when a builder incurs GST/HST in respect of legal and accounting fees during the period of construction, renovation or alteration of a building or in respect of the ownership of the related land, the tax may be recovered as an input tax credit.

Certain other soft costs incurred by builders are classified as exempt supplies under the ETA, and hence, not subject to GST/HST. These would include, for example, interest, insurance, and property taxes. As discussed above, interest is exempt as a financial service. Similarly, insurance premiums are exempt as financial services. Property taxes are exempt.

ETA: Part VII, Sch. V
ETA: sec. 21, Part VI, Sch. V

Since sales of *used* residential properties are exempt from GST/HST, special rules have been incorporated into the ETA to deal with "substantial renovations" of used residential properties. These rules are intended to ensure that persons in the business of renovating homes for resale are treated in the same manner as builders of new homes. The term "substantial renovation" is defined to mean:

ETA: 123(1)

> . . . the renovation or alteration of a building to such extent that all or substantially all of the building that existed immediately before the renovation or alteration was begun, other than the foundation, external walls, interior supporting walls, floors, roof and staircases, has been removed or replaced where, after completion of the renovation or alteration, the building is, or forms part of, a residential complex.

Since the sale of a substantially renovated home is treated as the sale of new residential property, GST/HST is charged on the sale and the builder is able to claim input tax credits on purchases of property and services. Consequently, any GST/HST paid on soft costs would be recoverable.

Where a residential property is renovated and the renovation is not considered to be substantial, the sale of the property is exempt as a sale of used residential property. However, the renovator is required to pay GST/HST on certain costs incurred in renovating the property. The GST/HST is calculated by reference to all costs of completing the renovation or alteration that would be included in determining the adjusted cost base of the property for income tax purposes, other than:

ETA: Part I, Sch. V
ETA: 192

- the costs of acquiring the property;
- interest and the cost of other financial services; and
- the cost of other purchases on which the renovator previously paid GST/HST.

¶6,800 REVIEW QUESTIONS

(1) Billy has come to you to tell you that he has found a great way of generating income of which only one-half is taxable as a capital gain. He buys a bond that pays interest annually and he holds it until just before the payment date and then he sells it, including the accrued interest, at a gain. Comment.

(2) One of your clients does not want to buy the compounding series Canada Savings Bonds any more since the new interest accrual rules cause the interest earned to be taxable annually rather than at maturity. Comment.

(3) Mr. Simpson owns an unincorporated business. In recognition of his wife's considerable contribution of her time and skills to the business he gives her a one-half share of the business income. Comment.

(4) Mr. Smith has just guaranteed a bank loan that his wife has taken out to buy shares in a corporation carrying on a business that she is starting. He is concerned about the attribution rules. Comment.

(5) Opco Inc. recently borrowed $300,000 to buy 30 acres of industrial land. The corporation has constructed a building, shipping and receiving areas and parking for employees on this property using up 20 acres. The remaining 10 acres is available for future needs. Is all of the interest on the $300,000 loan deductible?

(6) Rent Co. Ltd. is a corporation in the residential rental business. Because of some recent purchases, its financing costs are high and it is operating at a break-even before CCA this year. However, in the prior three years it made a profit. Can the corporation claim CCA to create a loss this year to carry back to the prior years, using the carryover rules in Division C, to offset income in those years?

(7) Ms. Campbell has just bought some gold as a protection against inflation. However, she did not have the cash to make the purchase so she borrowed from the bank to buy the gold. This is the first time that she has done this and she plans to hold the gold for some time. She is repaying the loan over three years. Will she be able to deduct all or some of her interest expense? Explain.

(8) You have been told of a court case where a taxpayer borrowed money initially to purchase a home, because some of the funds that he was to receive from Iran had not arrived when expected. When the funds at last arrived, interest rates had risen above that rate he was paying on his house mortgage. He then chose to invest his money at these higher interest rates instead of paying off the mortgage. He deducted the interest portion of his mortgage payments on his tax return. Comment.

(9) A client is in the process of selling his house and buying a bigger one. However, the real estate market has slowed down and in order to sell his existing house he is going to have to take back a mortgage for $100,000 at 8% for a five-year term. Since he does not have any extra cash, he is going to have to borrow that $100,000 from you in order to buy his new house. Is the interest going to be deductible on his mortgage? If not, how might he restructure the transaction to make it deductible?

(10) You have just interviewed a new client and have discovered that she borrowed to buy shares in a private corporation five years ago. The loan is still outstanding but the corporation has since gone bankrupt. Is the interest she is paying on the loan still deductible?

¶6,825 MULTIPLE CHOICE QUESTIONS

Question 1

Max is planning to invest in preferred shares of a friend's Canadian-controlled private corporation, which are paying a $12,000 dividend per year from income taxable at the low corporate rate. Assuming that Max is in the top federal tax bracket (29%) and that the provincial tax on income rate in his province is 17%, how much income tax will Max pay on this income in 2014? Also assume that the combined federal and provincial dividend tax credit is equal to the dividend gross-up.

(A) $1,946

(B) $4,354

(C) $6,514

(D) $5,520

Question 2

Wendy Jang owns three rental buildings. All of the buildings are in Class 1:

	Property		
	1	*2*	*3*
Original cost	$120,000	$ 80,000	$150,000
UCC at Jan. 1	100,000	75,000	150,000
Rental revenue for the year	58,000	22,000	20,000
Expenses for the year:			
Interest	20,000	10,000	8,000
Property taxes	13,000	6,000	11,000
Other	17,000	4,000	1,000

What is the maximum CCA that Wendy Jang can claim on the rental properties for the year?

(A) $13,000

(B) $10,000

(C) $7,000

(D) $6,500

Question 3

In the year, Mr. P made the following loans and gifts to family members to split income with his family members. Which one of the loans and/or gifts will result in income being attributed to Mr. P?

(A) A gift of $100,000 to his son, Peter, age 21. Peter invested the money in a term deposit and earned $3,000 of interest income.

(B) An interest-free loan of $100,000 to his mother-in-law, Mabel, age 81. Mabel invested the money in mutual funds and earned $12,000 of dividend income.

(C) An interest-free loan of $100,000 to his daughter, Daphne, age 28. Daphne bought a cottage and used it for personal use.

(D) A gift of $100,000 to his wife, Debbie. Debbie put the money in her non-interest bearing chequing account and paid all the family's household expenses from the account. She then used $100,000 of her own money to invest in the stock market and earned $10,000 of dividend income.

Question 4

Which of the following items is DEDUCTIBLE by Canadian taxpayers in the computation of income from business or property in Subdivision b of Division B of the Act?

(A) Commissions paid on the purchase of an investment in common shares.

(B) The premium paid on a $100,000 term life insurance policy on the taxpayer's life which is required as collateral for a $100,000 bank loan used to purchase a $100,000 investment in common shares.

(C) Interest expenses on a loan to invest in a registered retirement savings plan.

(D) Commissions paid on the sale of an investment in common shares.

Question 5

During the year, Mike received two cheques, one in the amount of C$20,000, the other in the amount of C$8,500. The $20,000 cheque was a dividend from business income taxed at the low corporate rate of a Canadian-controlled private corporation. The $8,500 cheque was a dividend from a foreign corporation, net of the $1,500 of foreign tax withheld by the foreign country from the dividend payment. Which of the following amounts must Mike include in his income in 2014 for Canadian income tax purposes in respect of these two dividend cheques?

(A) $20,000

(B) $28,500

(C) $30,000

(D) $33,600

Question 6

Ron Bordessa is 18 years of age. He inherited shares of Royal Roads Ltd., a private corporation, on his grandfather's death three years ago. Which of the following statements is true?

(A) Any dividend that Ron receives on these shares will be subject to the tax on split income.

(B) The tax on split income does not apply to any dividends on these shares because they were inherited.

(C) Any capital gains that Ron realizes on the disposition of these shares to an arm's length person, will be subject to the tax on split income.

(D) The tax on split income does not apply to any dividend on these shares because Ron has reached the age of 18.

¶6,850 EXERCISES

Exercise 1

ITA: 12(1)(*c*), 12(4), 12(11)

What would be the *first* year in which the taxpayer would have to include interest in income in each of the following cases and to which years would that interest relate?

(A) A corporation with a June 30 year-end buys a bond that pays interest semi-annually on March 31 and September 30 from its previous owner on January 1, 2013.

(B) An individual buys a compounding GIC on November 1, 2013.

(C) An individual buys a zero coupon bond, issued on January 1, 2013, in 2013.

(D) An individual buys a compound Canada Savings Bond issued November 1, 2013.

(E) On June 1, 2013, an individual buys a $1,000 bond paying $40 interest by cheque each May 31 and November 30. The bond was issued on December 1, 2012.

Exercise 2

ITA: 74.1, 74.5

(A) A husband wants his wife to have a $1,000 Canada Savings Bond that he owns paying interest at 7%. What are the consequences to the couple during the year if:

(i) he gives the bond to her without receiving any financial consideration from her in return?

(ii) he sells the bond to her for $1,000 plus accrued interest to the date of sale in return for cash?

(iii) he sells the bond to her for $1,000 plus accrued interest to the date of sale in return for a demand note which she signs payable to him without interest?

(iv) he cashes the bond lending the proceeds to her in return for a promissory note which she signs payable to him without interest but with a definite repayment period and she uses the funds from the loan to buy a similar bond?

(B) Would any of the above answers change for the current year if he undertook the same transactions with a trust set up in favour of a child aged 15 instead of his wife?

(C) Would any of the above answers change if he undertook the same transactions with a child aged 20?

Exercise 3

ITA: 18(2)

A downtown hotel bought a vacant lot adjacent to the hotel building. Comment on the deductibility of property taxes and interest paid on funds borrowed to buy the property if:

(i) the property is used as a parking lot for hotel guests;

(ii) the property was bought for potential gains on future sale but in the meantime it is being used as a public parking lot generating net revenues before the taxes and interest of 75% of the expenditures for taxes and interest;

(iii) the property was bought for future expansion of the hotel and in the meantime is being used under the same condition as in (ii) above.

Exercise 4

ITR: 1100

Mr. Provident is a salaried employee who invests in small residential rental properties. He bought Property 1 last year and at the beginning of this year the undepreciated capital cost balances for that property were as follows:

Class 1 — brick building	$148,000
Class 8 — furniture and fixtures	25,000

This year he bought Property 2 for $150,000 including land valued at $12,500. The net income before capital cost allowance for each property this year was:

Property 1	$ 9,270
Property 2	3,750

— *REQUIRED*

Compute the maximum capital cost allowance on these rental properties for the current year.

Exercise 5

ITA: 20(1)(*a*); ITR: 1100, 1101(1ac)

Ms. Alimeag owns two residential rental properties. One produced rental revenue of $13,500 and had allowable expenses (excluding capital cost allowance) of $11,250. The other had rental revenue of $22,500 and expenses of $18,750. Data on the two Class 1 buildings are as follows:

	Property A	*Property B*
Capital cost	$360,000	$600,000
UCC, January 1	$330,000	$480,000

During the year, Property A was sold for net proceeds of $336,000.

— *REQUIRED*

(A) What is the effect of the above information on the income of Ms. Alimeag for the year?

(B) Can an election be made under subsection 13(4) if Property A is replaced by the end of the next year?

Exercise 6

ITA: 20(1)(*c*)

Nadi borrowed $140,000 at an 8.5% annual interest rate from a local financial institution to finance the following investments.

	Cost
Common shares of a public corporation paying no dividends	$20,000
Gold bullion (treated as capital)	25,000
Corporate bond (yield is 9% *per annum*)	20,000
Preferred shares (7% annual dividend) purchased in RRSP	10,000
Common shares (5% annual dividend) in spouse's name	30,000
Paintings from well-known galleries	15,000
Guaranteed Investment Certificate paying interest at 9% *per annum*	20,000
Total cost	$140,000

— *REQUIRED*

Assuming that the investments were held for the full calendar year, determine the deductibility of interest expense for each investment.

Exercise 7

ITR: 1100(11), 1101(1ac)

Capital cost allowance, recapture, and terminal loss all form part of the net income calculation for rental properties. There are two special rules that apply only to rental properties that serve to limit the treatment of capital cost allowance.

One of the special rules stipulates that each rental property having a cost of $50,000 or more must be held in a separate capital cost allowance class.

— *REQUIRED*

Determine the second special rule.

¶6,875 ASSIGNMENT PROBLEMS

Problem 1

ITA: 12(1)(*g*); IT-462

The Country Pie is a highly recognized baker of quality pies in Beamsville, Ontario. The current proprietor, Rudolph Strudel, started the business about 20 years ago with an initial purchase of equipment of $150,000 and built up the name of the company by closely supervising the pie production process. Many have said that it is this attention and his recipes that have made the business a success. Rudolph has decided to sell his business and move to the coast to get away from the pressures of running a business. An offer has been made for the assets of The Country Pie by Big Food Corporation Ltd. ("BFC"). There was a meeting of the minds as to the value of the fixed assets of The Country Pie. However, there was considerable dispute as to the value of The Country Pie name in generating pie sales after a purchase by BFC. Consequently, it is proposed that the full proceeds be determined in part by future sales.

The BFC offer is for $50,000 cash; $60,000 to be paid on the basis of sales over the next three years with any balance of the $60,000 remaining at the end of the third year payable at that time; and 25% of gross sales in the next five years. As part of the agreement, Rudolph would provide consulting services to BFC as needed during the next three years.

— *REQUIRED*

Discuss the income tax implications to Rudolph of the proposal from BFC.

Problem 2

ITA: 12(1)(*c*), 12(1)(*j*), 74.1, 74.5, 82(1); IT-510, IT-511R

Mr. Wiser is contemplating investing in two different mutual funds. His investment options are set out below.

Amount	*Mutual Fund*	*Distribution*
$2,000	International Income Fund	Annual interest of 8.0%
$2,000	Canadian Dividend Fund	Annual dividend of 6.0%

Mr. Wiser contemplates holding both mutual funds for the same period of time — from purchase to December 31, 2017. Mr. Wiser is in the top federal income tax bracket (29%). Mr. Wiser's provincial tax on income rate is 17%. Assume that the combined federal and provincial dividend tax credit is equal to the dividend gross-up. Assume that the Canadian Dividend Fund receives and distributes dividends from Canadian-resident public corporations.

— *REQUIRED*

(A) Based on the above information, which mutual fund should Mr. Wiser prefer?

(B) Can Mr. Wiser achieve any advantage by purchasing the above mutual fund in the name of his 8-year-old daughter who has no other source of income?

(C) Mr. Wiser's spouse has no source of income. Can Mr. Wiser achieve any advantage by lending $200,000 to his spouse and having her purchase a rental property earning $16,000 per year? The $200,000 loan would be evidenced by a promissory note repayable in four equal annual instalments on each of December 31, 2013 to 2016 and bearing interest at the prescribed rate of 3%.

Problem 3

ITA: 18(2)–(3)

Furniture Focus Limited provides competitive prices to consumers by using a no-frills approach to displaying its product in large stores surrounded by ample parking. Furniture Focus Limited has excess land that is not currently used in its business. This vacant land is rented to the adjacent automobile dealer who stores new cars on it.

For the year ended December 31, 2013, Furniture Focus Limited had the following operating expenses:

Sales	$35,000,000
Cost of goods sold	(20,000,000)
Gross profit	$15,000,000
Selling expenses	(5,000,000)
General and administrative expenses	(2,000,000)

	$ 8,000,000
Other income	50,000
Net income	$ 8,050,000

The general and administrative expenses include $30,000 of interest and $5,000 of property taxes on the vacant land rented to the automobile dealer. There are no other expenses connected with this land. Other income includes $10,000 of rental income paid by the automobile dealer.

— REQUIRED

Determine the income tax consequences of the various payments related to the vacant land.

Problem 4

ITA: 20(1)(*a*); ITR: 1100(11), 1101(1ac); Sched. II

Sara Shimizu is the owner of two rental properties, 509 Brunswick Avenue and 356 Spadina Road. These properties were purchased six years ago for $525,000 and $600,000, respectively. In 2013, 509 Brunswick Avenue was sold for $550,000. A reasonable allocation of this amount is considered to be 75% to the building and 25% to the land. The following income and expenses were incurred in renting out the two properties in 2013:

Rental	$ 60,000
Interest on mortgage	(40,000)
Operating costs	(15,000)
Promotion costs for sale of property	(5,000)
Net income	0

There are no meal or entertainment expenses included in the $5,000 of sales promotion costs. At December 31, 2012, the undepreciated capital cost of 509 Brunswick Avenue was $383,500 and that of 356 Spadina Road was $400,000.

— REQUIRED

Determine the income from property for income tax purposes assuming Sara wishes to report the least amount possible for tax purposes in 2013.

Problem 5

ITA: 18, 20

It is early January 2013 and the president of BDC Distributing Limited, a client of your firm, called recently to discuss the tax implications regarding the construction of a new building. BDC has been growing rapidly and needs new warehouse space. They have been unable to locate any suitable space in the existing buildings in town and, therefore, have decided that their only option is to build their own building. They have identified the site and have estimated the costs of the project. These projected costs (and dates of completion) are as follows:

The land that has been identified will be purchased on February 15, 2013, for $405,000. There is no significant site preparation required so construction of the building can commence immediately. The cost of the building is estimated to be $1,348,000 plus the costs noted below. It is anticipated that BDC will be able to occupy the building on October 31, 2013.

BDC currently has an architect finalizing the drawings for the building. The architect fees, which will all be paid in 2013, will amount to $7,200. There will also be fees of $2,100 for an engineer to examine the drawings.

BDC has arranged for the financing required for the project. The project will be financed with a mortgage of $875,000 and $1,000,000 of preferred shares issued on January 15, 2013. Interest on the mortgage is payable semi-annually on July 15 and January 15 at a rate of 8% *per annum*. The preferred shares pay dividends of 5% *per annum*, payable semi-annually on July 15 and January 15. There will be a number of costs incurred in order to issue the debt and shares. These costs are legal and accounting fees of $18,450, commissions of $58,300 and registration fees of $1,800 for amending the articles of incorporation to allow the issuance of the preferred shares.

The balance of the costs related to the building are summarized below:

Building insurance from April 15, 2013 @ $450 per month	$ 3,825
Property taxes from February 15, 2013 @ $770 per month	8,085

Soil testing to determine location of footings for building	1,825
Relocation expenses	34,100
Utilities service connections estimated to be completed on May 20, 2013	3,800
Mortgage insurance premium from March 1, 2013 of $325 per month	3,250
Maintenance from October 31, 2013	2,500
Utilities from October 31, 2013	6,300
Landscaping	15,500

— *REQUIRED*

Advise the corporation of the impact of the proposed transactions on their December 31, 2013 income tax return. Ignore the effects of the leap year.

Problem 6

ETA: 123(1), Sch. V, Parts VI, VII

Reconsider the facts of Problem 5. Assume that HST was paid at 13%, where applicable, in addition to the amounts shown.

— *REQUIRED*

Calculate the HST consequences of the transactions presented.

Problem 7

ITA: 20(1)(*c*), 80.4(1)

Tim Markus, Vice President of Phone Lines, earned $92,000 in salary last year. In addition to his salary, he also received low-interest loans from his employer. Tim's interest rate on these loans is 3% and he owed $160,000 throughout last year. Tim used the loan to purchase a rental property (see Schedule 1). Assume a prescribed interest rate of 8% for the entire year. Five years ago, Tim invested in some common shares of a foreign corporation. He receives $18,000 in dividends (net of $2,000 withholding tax) annually from this corporation. Last year, he also received taxable eligible dividends of $30,000 from his investment in a Canadian public company which is resident in Canada. Tim also owns $100,000 worth of 10% bonds.

Schedule 1:

Rental revenue	$26,000
Maintenance expenses	5,500
Utilities on rental units	8,200
CCA — half-year rule	3,200

— *REQUIRED*

Compute Tim's income for tax purposes for last year.

Problem 8

ITA: Division B

Trent Zalinski recently retired as a football player with the Saskatchewan Roughriders. In the current year, he received his salary of $150,000 from the team and is eligible for a CFL pension in 15 years. He and his wife Mary have settled in Weyburn, Saskatchewan, where he runs a small sporting goods store as a proprietorship. He has provided you with the following additional information.

(a) His net income from the store for the fiscal year ended December 31 was $35,000. Next year he is hoping to double that. Mary works in the store about 35 hours a week and is paid $6 per hour. This is already included as an expense in determining the $35,000.

(b) Trent's other current-year receipts are: fees received from endorsement of a brand of football equipment, $30,000; eligible dividends from Canadian public corporations, $7,200; dividends from foreign public corporations, (net of $750 withholding tax) $6,750; interest from Canadian bank, $3,000.

(c) Trent also had the following expenses: cycling trip to Cypress Hills Provincial Park with family, $2,200; interest on bank loan to acquire public company shares, $4,050.

(d) In May of the previous year, Trent purchased a five-year GIC in Mary's name. The interest rate was 6%, and it was for $10,000. None of the interest is receivable until maturity in five years.

— *REQUIRED*

(a) Determine Trent's net income for tax purposes.

(b) Do you have any basic tax planning advice for Trent?

Problem 9

ITA: 12(1)(*j*), 74.1

The following are independent situations:

(a) Tony Lee gave $50,000 to his wife, Shannon, for the acquisition of shares of a Canadian company on the Toronto Stock Exchange. During the year, an eligible dividend of $5,000 cash was paid on the shares owned by Mrs. Lee.

(b) At the beginning of the year in which her daughter Carey turned 18 in December, Ellen gifted $25,000 directly to Carey. Carey invested the $25,000 in an income-bearing investment that paid her interest of $2,500 during the year. In addition to the $2,500, Carey also earned another $7,500 in interest income from monies received from her mother previously.

— *REQUIRED*

What are the tax consequences for the above situations?

Problem 10

ITA: Subdivision b

John Ingles has provided you with the following information related to his various investment holdings as of December 31, 2013.

Interest earned on joint bank account with his spouse (spouse contributes equally)	$ 2,000
Interest earned on his investment account (not joint) with his investment broker	800
Interest earned on 2012 personal income tax assessment	450
Interest on short-term investments:	
$20,000 term deposit taken out November 30, 2013 (interest at maturity in six months)	
Accrued interest from December 1 to December 31, 2013	85
$200,000 GIC purchased November 1, 2012 (interest payable at maturity on October 31, 2015)	
Accrued interest from November 1, 2012 to October 31, 2013	16,000
Accrued interest from January 1, 2013 to December 31, 2013	16,214
Government of Canada Treasury Bills purchased for $9,009 on January 3, 2013	
Amount received on maturity on December 31, 2013	10,000
Cash dividends received from investment in common shares of Canadian resident public corporations	24,000
Cash dividends received from common shares in US corporations (net of $3,000 of foreign withholding taxes; all in Canadian dollars)	17,000

Rental details from operation of two separate rental properties:

	Property 1	Property 2
Gross rental revenue	$ 30,000	$ 46,000
Utilities	5,000	8,000
Property taxes	2,400	3,500
Repairs	1,500	4,800
Mortgage interest	20,000	32,000
Opening UCC	$368,209	$520,225

Interest expenses paid during 2013:

Interest on bank line of credit used for investing in shares described above	$50,000
Interest on loan to acquire an automobile for his daughter for her 18th birthday	3,200
Interest on a parcel of vacant land (purchased in 2008, the land does not generate any income)	10,000

— REQUIRED

Prepare a calculation of John's property income. Comment on the income tax implications of items not included in your calculations.

Problem 11

ITA: 18(2), 20(1)(*c*), 74.1

Your client, Ashley, has come to you for some advice on computing her net income from property.

(a) In February, Ashley sold all her investments and paid off her personal residence mortgage. On March 1, she borrowed $90,000 to reacquire many of the same investments she previously held. Many of the common shares purchased do not carry dividend rights. Her spouse has insisted that 50% of the investments be placed in his name.

(b) On April 15, Ashley purchased a government bond that pays annual interest of 7%. When the bond was purchased, Ashley paid accrued interest of $262.50 to the previous owner of the bonds.

(c) On June 1, Ashley borrowed $450,000 to purchase the vacant land next to her apartment block. The land is used as a parking lot and she collected monthly revenues of $2,500. She plans improvements that will double her income from the lot. Ashley's only expenses were $45,500 for interest and property taxes.

— REQUIRED

Discuss the income tax implications of each item above.

Problem 12

ITA: 18(1), 20(1)(*c*); IT-533

Funds are borrowed by an individual from a financial institution at an 11% *per annum* interest rate to purchase the following unrelated investments:

(a) gold coins on which gains or losses will be treated as capital gains or losses;

(b) an RRSP portfolio of investments yielding 12.5% in interest;

(c) a five-year GIC paying interest at 8% *per annum*;

(d) common shares of a Canadian-resident public corporation paying no dividends;

(e) preferred shares of a Canadian-resident public corporation paying 7% dividends;

(f) preferred shares of a U.S. corporation paying 9% dividends;

(g) $100,000 of assets used in an unincorporated business which generated net income of $9,750 before drawings of $18,000 for the year;

(h) lottery tickets which yielded $75,000 in winnings which were reinvested in short-term securities yielding 13%; and

(i) common shares of a Canadian-resident public corporation paying dividends of 6%; later in the year the shares were sold at a small gain to repay a 14% second mortgage on a principal residence.

— REQUIRED

Determine the deductibility of the interest expense in each of the unrelated cases.

[For more problems and solutions thereto, see the DVD accompanying this book.]

Chapter 7

Capital Gains: Personal

TOPICS DISCUSSED

LEARNING GOALS

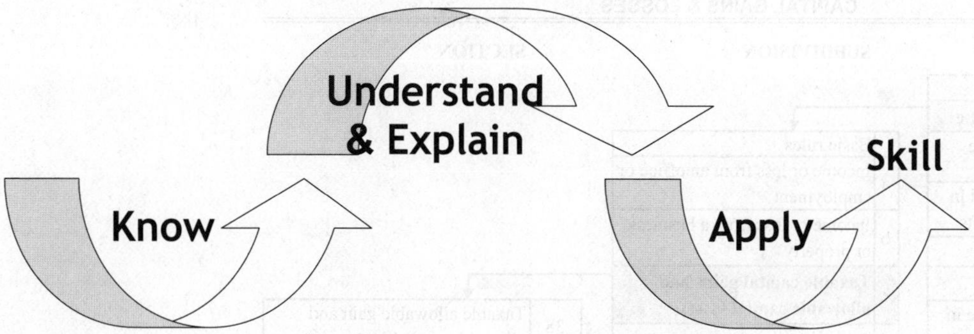

Know

By the end of this chapter you should know the basic provisions of the *Income Tax Act* that relate to capital gains and losses. The focus of the chapter is on provisions that would primarily affect individuals. Completing the Review Questions (¶7,800) and Multiple Choice Questions (¶7,825) is a good way to learn the technical provisions.

Understand and Explain

You should understand and be able to explain

- how to calculate proceeds of disposition and the adjusted cost base to determine the capital gain or loss;
- how capital gains and losses are taxed;
- the special rules for principal residences, personal-use property, and listed personal property;
- the special case of an allowable business investment loss; and
- how capital gains and losses fit into the calculation of income for tax purposes.

Completing the Exercises (¶7,850) is a good way to deepen your understanding of the material in this chapter.

Apply

You should be able to apply your knowledge and understanding of the rules pertaining to capital gains and losses in a way that accomplishes a client's goals. Completing the Assignment Problems (¶7,875) is an excellent way to develop your ability to apply the material in increasingly complex situations.

OVERVIEW

Subdivision c of Division B of Part I of the Act contains the primary rules for the computation of taxable capital gains and allowable capital losses.

The following chart will help to locate these provisions in the Act.

PART I — DIVISION B, SUBDIVISION c

CAPITAL GAINS & LOSSES

DIVISION

A	Liability for tax
B	**Computation of income**
C	Computation of taxable income
D	Taxable income earned in Canada by non-residents
E	Computation of tax
E.1	Minimum tax
F	Special rules applicable in certain circumstances
G	Deferred and other special income arrangements
H	Exemptions
I	Returns, assessments, payment and appeals
J	Appeals to the Tax Court of Canada and the Federal Court of Appeal

SUBDIVISION

a	Basic rules
	Income or loss from an office or employment
b	Income or loss from a business or property
c	**Taxable capital gains and allowable capital losses**
d	Other sources of income
e	Deductions in computing income
f	Rules relating to computation of income
g	Amounts not included in computing income
h	Corporations resident in Canada and their shareholders
i	Shareholders of corporations not resident in Canada
j	Partnerships and their members
k	Trusts and their beneficiaries

SECTION

38	Taxable allowable gain and allowable capital loss
39	Capital gain and capital loss
39.1	Exempt capital gains balance in respect of flow-through entity
40	General rules
41	Listed personal property
42	Dispositions subject to warranty
43	Part disposition
43.1	Life estates in real property
44	Replacement property
44.1	Small business corporation share rollover
45	Change in use
46	Personal-use property
47	Identical property
48.1	SBC goes public
49	Options granted
49.1	No disposition where obligation satisfied
50	Loss on debt/shares
51	Convertible property
52	Cost of certain property
53	ACB adjustments
54	Definitions
54.1	Exception: principal residence
54.2	Shares and capital property
55	Deemed capital gain

Some of the more important provisions are as follows:

Sec. 39 Meaning of capital gain, capital loss and business investment loss
Sec. 40 General rules including principal residence exemption
Sec. 41 Listed personal property
Sec. 44.1 Capital gains deferral
Sec. 45 Change in use
Sec. 46 Personal-use property
Sec. 47 Identical properties
Sec. 49 Options
Sec. 51 Convertible property
Sec. 52 Cost
Sec. 53 Adjustments to cost base
Sec. 54 Definitions

In addition, Subdivision f of Division B provides some rules that are relevant to the inclusion of capital gains income. For example, the attribution rules determine whether the capital gains or losses received by a particular person should be attributed to someone else. Rules pertaining to the deemed disposition on death are also covered. ITA: 74.2, 74.3 ITA: 70

Also, in Division F, the rules dealing with the treatment of capital property when an individual ceases to be or becomes a resident of Canada will be reviewed. ITA: 128.1

¶7,000 OVERVIEW OF THE TAXATION OF CAPITAL GAINS

¶7,010 History

In 1962, the Royal Commission on Taxation, led by Mr. Kenneth Carter, recommended the full taxation of capital gains on the disposition of all property, gifts, and unrealized gains in support of a comprehensive tax base on the grounds that "a buck is a buck". Taxing capital gains like other sources of income puts all taxpayers in the same position (horizontal equity). Equally important is ensuring that vertical equity is present so that taxpayers who can afford to contribute, do so. Prior to the taxation of capital gains, it was common for taxpayers to arrange transactions to look like capital dispositions rather than income transactions. Even after implementing the taxation of capital gains, taxpayers still tried to convert income gains to capital gains to reduce taxes payable. Over the years, neutrality and equality have been difficult to achieve.

Prior to 1972, capital gains were not taxed under the Act. Canada was one of the few western nations which had never levied a tax on the disposition of capital property. With our government's concern for equity among taxpayers, a complete set of rules for the taxation of capital gains was introduced to the legislation. These rules have become an additional source of confusion for tax practitioners, the Canada Revenue Agency (CRA) and taxpayers. Slowly since 1972, the government has been revising the rules in this particular subdivision, although these revisions have introduced more complexity during this time.

One of the most significant changes is to the inclusion rate for capital gains. The inclusion rate is the percentage that is applied to the capital gain with the result being included in income as a taxable capital gain. Since tax on capital gains was introduced in 1972 this inclusion rate has changed four times as shown below:

Time Period	Inclusion Rate
1972 to 1987	50%
1988 and 1989	66⅔%
1990 to February 27, 2000	75%
February 28 to October 17, 2000	66⅔%
After October 17, 2000	50%

¶7,012 Capital Property

¶7,013 General considerations

A capital gain is the amount by which proceeds of disposition exceed the adjusted cost base and any disposition costs on the sale of capital property. Capital property is defined as: ITA: 54

- any depreciable property; and/or
- any other property that would result in a capital gain or loss upon disposition.

"Property" is defined as, "property of any kind . . . and . . . includes . . . a right . . ., a share or a chose in action". Generally, capital gains or losses result from the disposition of capital property such as shares, investments, real estate, art, a machine, a house, a cottage, or another personal property. Capital property is generally referred to as an asset that provides the owner with a long-term and enduring benefit. It is not uncommon, however, for these same types of property, such as shares or real estate, to be held as inventory and treated as an item sold to produce business income. Often, too, it is necessary to call upon the courts to determine whether the nature of transactions is on account of income rather than capital. ITA: 248(1)

The asset that generates income from year to year is quite different from the asset that is used for personal consumption or enjoyment. Paragraph 3(*b*) contains the income inclusion provision that requires "net taxable capital gains" to be included in the calculation of net income. Within the aggregating formula, net capital gains are distinguished from net listed personal property gains and allowable capital losses. The Act has different rules for different types of property and the rules governing the calculation of the taxable capital gain for these properties are prescribed in sections 38 to 55 of the Act.

¶7,014 Personal-use property (PUP)

Personal-use property is property owned by a taxpayer (including a corporation or trust) for the personal use or enjoyment of the taxpayer or for a person or beneficiary related to the taxpayer. Examples of personal-use property include an individual's furniture, sports equipment, personal residence, cars, and effects. The Act distinguishes these from other property because personal property is used for personal consumption rather than for generating income. Since personal-use property is consumed and wears out, capital losses may never be offset against any capital gains or other sources of revenues. However, these and all other gains from the disposition of property are included in income. Please refer to ¶7,210 for more details. ITA: 40(2)(*g*)(iii), 54 ITA: 3(*b*)

¶7,015 Listed personal property (LPP)

Listed personal property is a subset of personal-use property designed to segregate collectibles that generally do not depreciate. Unlike personal-use property, losses on LPP may be claimed, but only against gains on LPP. The other rules applicable to PUP also apply to LPP. Please refer to ¶7,220 for more details. ITA: 41, 54

¶7,016 Other capital property

Other property includes capital property, other than personal-use or listed personal property, acquired for the purpose of earning income. Included are business assets and capital investments such as buildings, rental properties, machinery, and financial instruments that are not inventory. Gains and losses on the disposition of inventory are on account of income rather than capital. Eligible capital property is not a capital property, as any gains are included as business income.

¶7,017 Schematic classification

Figure 7-1 categorizes capital property graphically.

Figure 7-1

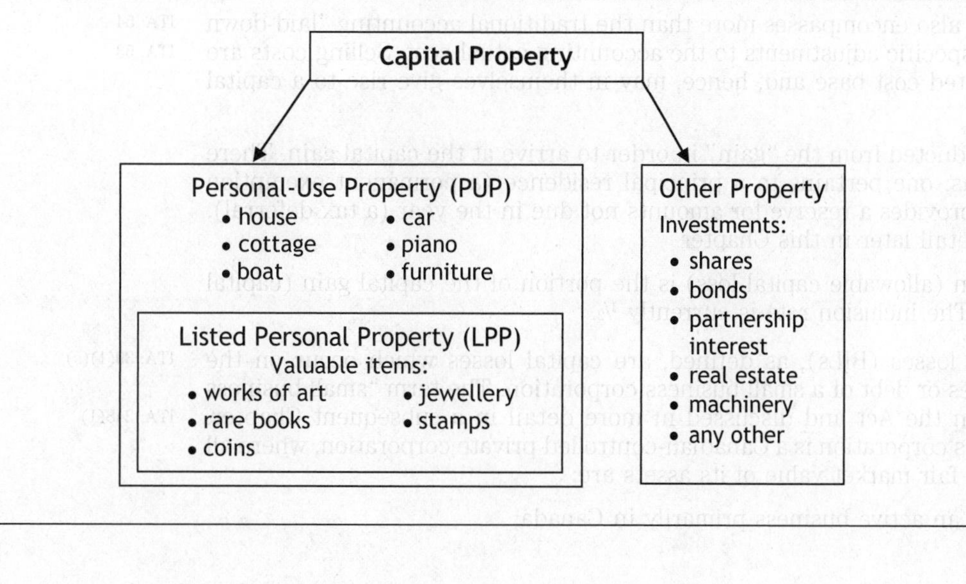

¶7,018 Restrictions

A capital loss cannot result from the disposition of depreciable capital property (any property eligible for CCA). Any decline in value of this property is addressed through the CCA system. When depreciable property is disposed of for proceeds less than the original cost, then the result will be either a terminal loss, a recapture, or a reduction of the UCC of the class. If proceeds of disposition exceed the capital cost of the depreciable property, a capital gain arises. Chapter 5 provides the tax treatment for disposing of depreciable property. ITA: 39(1)(*b*)(i)

¶7,020 Terminology

Before attempting to read the pertinent sections in Subdivision c, it is necessary to become acquainted with the basic terminology and abbreviations illustrated below.

Accounting terminology				*Income tax terminology*	
Selling price		$xx		Proceeds of disposition (P of D)	Sec. 54
Cost	$xx			Adjusted cost base (ACB)	Sec. 54
Selling costs	xx	(xx)		Expenses of disposition (SC)	Ssec. 40(1)
Profit (Loss)		$xx		Gain (Loss)	
		(xx)		Exemption or reserve, if any	Sec. 40
		$xx		Capital gain (CG) or Capital loss (CL)	Sec. 39
		$xx		Taxable capital gain (TCG) or Allowable capital loss (ACL)	Sec. 38

Capital gains treatment requires a disposition. The Act contains the definition of "disposition" of property. Generally, a disposition includes any transaction entitling a taxpayer to proceeds of disposition. This definition, then, specifies situations that are considered to be dispositions. In some cases, transfers of property, which do not give rise to actual proceeds, will be deemed to be dispositions for tax purposes. These will include deemed dispositions: ITA: 248(1)

- on the change in use of property; ITA: 45(1)
- on the death of a taxpayer; ITA: 70(5)
- by way of gift during the lifetime of a taxpayer; and ITA: 69(1)
- when a taxpayer ceases to be a resident of Canada. ITA: 128.1(1)

"Proceeds of disposition" is a much broader term than "selling price" because it includes deemed proceeds. ITA: 54

"Adjusted cost base" also encompasses more than the traditional accounting "laid-down cost". There are over 40 specific adjustments to the accounting actual cost. Selling costs are not included in the adjusted cost base and, hence, may in themselves give rise to a capital loss. ITA: 54 ITA: 53

"Exemptions" are deducted from the "gain" in order to arrive at the capital gain. There are two major exemptions: one pertains to a principal residence (a permanent exemption from tax) and the other provides a reserve for amounts not due in the year (a tax deferral). These are discussed in detail later in this Chapter.

A taxable capital gain (allowable capital loss) is the portion of the capital gain (capital loss) taken into income. The inclusion rate is currently ½.

Business investment losses (BILs), as defined, are capital losses which occur on the disposition of either shares or debt of a small business corporation. The term "small business corporation" is defined in the Act and discussed in more detail in a subsequent Chapter. Generally, a small business corporation is a Canadian-controlled private corporation, where all or substantially all of the fair market value of its assets are: ITA: 39(1)(*c*) ITA: 248(1)

(a) used to carry on an active business primarily in Canada;

(b) shares or debt of connected (as discussed in a subsequent Chapter) small business corporations; or

(c) a combination of (a) and (b).

While these BILs are still capital losses, only fractionally deductible, they are given special treatment as an incentive for investment. The fractional amount deductible, which uses the same inclusion rate as capital losses (i.e., ½ currently), is called an allowable business investment loss (ABIL). The use of ABILs will be discussed later in this chapter at ¶7,720.

Another way of looking at the terminology is to compare the description before (100%) and after (50%) the inclusion rate has been applied. For example,

100%	**50%**
Capital gain	Taxable capital gain
Capital loss	Allowable capital loss
Business investment loss	Allowable business investment loss
Capital gains exemption	Capital gains deduction

¶7,030 Capital Gains Deduction

From 1985 until February 22, 1994, there was a lifetime exemption for capital gains of $100,000 for individuals, other than trusts. This deduction was eliminated for taxable capital gains realized after February 22, 1994, but individuals were given an opportunity to elect to realize taxable capital gains accrued to February 22, 1994, which could be offset by the deduction in their 1994 tax return. The benefit of the election was to gain an increase in the adjusted cost base of the property on which the election was made or to create a notional account balance of elected gains. The increase in ACB reduces future capital gains exposed to tax. The notional account balance for eligible capital property or mutual funds can be used to reduce future gains on these properties. There continues to be a capital gains exemption of up to $750,000 [the March 21, 2013 federal Budget proposed to increase this limit to $800,000 in 2014 and then index it for future years] of capital gains on qualifying shares of a small business corporation and certain farming and fishing property. The application of these rules will be discussed in some detail in Chapter 13 which deals with planning for the corporate owner-manager. ITA: 110.6

¶7,040 Election re Disposition of Canadian Securities

A taxpayer can elect (on form T123) that the disposition of "Canadian securities" *only* will always be a capital receipt, despite the aforementioned common law guidelines. Until the introduction of these rules, the CRA had not consistently assessed taxpayers on trading transactions in which there was an obvious intention to make a quick profit rather than to hold the shares as an income-producing investment. The dilemma is resolved with this election. It should be noted, however, that once this election is made, it will remain in force forever unless the taxpayer, at the time of a disposition, is one of the prescribed taxpayers listed in the provision who are not permitted this election. One of the exclusions is a "dealer in securities" and, of course, it will be a matter of fact whether an individual will be considered to be a "dealer" because of his or her past and present trading activities. The general rules used by the CRA to determine whether securities transactions will be afforded capital or income treatment are outlined in an Interpretation Bulletin. ITA: 39(4)–(6) ITA: 39(5) IT-479R

The CRA's administrative position in respect of commodity transactions, including futures, is quite similar to the statutory provisions in respect of Canadian securities discussed above. The guidelines which must be adhered to are set out in the Interpretation Bulletin entitled "Commodity futures and certain commodities". IT-346R

¶7,100 GENERAL RULES

¶7,110 Computation of Capital Gains and Capital Losses

A gain on the disposition of property is determined as: ITA: 40(1)(*a*)(i), 54

(a) proceeds of disposition

minus

(b) the aggregate of:

(i) adjusted cost base, and

(ii) expenses of the disposition.

A loss is generally a negative amount resulting from the application of the above, that is, adjusted cost base and expenses of disposition minus proceeds of disposition. However, there can be no such loss on depreciable capital property, since the total decline in value should have been accounted for through the capital cost allowance system. ITA: 39(1)(*b*)(i)

¶7,115 Proceeds of disposition

In most cases, proceeds of disposition will be the value of the consideration received or receivable. Where a deemed disposition occurs, the proceeds usually will be deemed to be the fair market value of the property at the time of the disposition.

The definitions of terms for purposes of capital gains and losses are provided in a definition section within Subdivision c. The definition of "proceeds of disposition" found in this section provides some very specific inclusions and exclusions that go beyond our normal idea of proceeds. In addition, the following is a list of Interpretation Bulletins that give further guidance: ITA: 54

IT-185R	Losses from theft, defalcation or embezzlement
IT-220R2	Capital cost allowance — proceeds of disposition of depreciable property
IT-259R4	Exchanges of property
IT-460	Dispositions — absence of consideration

One of the components of the proceeds of disposition of shares, a partnership interest or business assets might be an agreement not to compete with the purchaser. This is known as a restrictive covenant. This topic is covered by a comprehensive package of provisions related to payments received by individuals for covenants. For a full discussion on the treatment of payments received for covenants, please refer to Chapter 9.

¶7,120 Adjusted cost base

Adjusted cost base starts with actual out-of-pocket cost or deemed cost on receipt of a gift or inheritance and is then modified. A provision establishes the cost base as amounts in respect of the value of the property which have been included in the taxpayer's income. For example, the cost of property received as a dividend in kind is the fair market value of the property received. Similarly, the cost of certain stock dividends is established as a defined amount depending upon the time frame in which the stock dividends were issued. ITA: 52; ITA: 52(2); ITA: 52(3)

Subsection 53(1) (additions) and subsection 53(2) (reductions) set out a number of adjustments such as:

- the employment income inclusion arising from the acquisition of share through a stock option is added to the cost of the share; and ITA: 7, 53(1)(*j*)
- the cost base of a bond is reduced by the amount of accrued interest paid for on the purchase of the bond and this accrued interest is deducted from interest earned during the holding period of the bond. ITA: 20(14), 53(2)(*l*)

A negative adjusted cost base could result at any time if the sum of the amounts deducted is greater than the cost of the property plus the sum of amounts added to it. With the exception of a partnership interest in a general (but not a limited) partnership, such a negative amount is deemed to be an immediate capital gain at the time that an adjustment causes the adjusted cost base to become negative. At the same time, the adjusted cost base is brought to zero and future adjustments are made from that zero base. ITA: 40(3) ITA: 53(1)(*a*)

There are also a number of adjustments in respect of shares of a corporation, many of which will be described in more detail in later chapters. But a conceptual understanding of these adjustments is necessary in determining the adjusted cost base of a particular class of shares.

- The cost base of shares is increased by deemed dividends that arise in transactions (with some exceptions) where the paid-up capital of the corporation is increased by more than the increase in the fair market value of the net assets of the corporation. (Paid-up capital of shares is generally (but not always) the stated or par value for accounting purposes.) ITA: 53(1)(*b*), 54(1)

- The cost base of shares received as consideration for any transfer of property to a corporation is increased by the amount of any capital loss denied by reason of a "stop-loss" rule applied on the transfer. ITA: 53(1)(*f.2*) ITA: 40(3.6)(*b*)

There are also some adjustments to cost where assets are transferred without any consideration.

- An asset transferred by way of gift is normally deemed to be disposed of by the transferor at fair market value and received by the transferee at the same value.
- If an asset is transferred from a corporation to its shareholder, then the corporation is deemed to have disposed of the asset at fair market value and the shareholder is deemed to have received the asset with a cost at the same value. In addition, the shareholder will have received a benefit that will be included in income.
- If an asset is won in a lottery, then it is deemed to be received with a cost base equal to fair market value.

¶7,125 Mutual funds and Dividend Reinvestment Plans

It is not unusual for mutual fund investors to reinvest the income received or allocated from their investment into acquiring more units of the fund. Similarly, many corporate shareholders participate in dividend reinvestment plans (DRIPs) where the dividends are used to acquire more shares in the company. In both instances, this reinvested income has to be added to the ACB of the mutual fund units or shares held by the taxpayer. If it is not added, the ACB will be understated and the result will be double taxation.

Example Problem 7-1

Martha sold all the units of some mutual funds that she owned for proceeds of $40,000. She had bought them for $20,000. This amount bought 1,185.319 units in the fund. She has never taken any money out of the fund; any income has been reinvested automatically. Over the years, her information slips have indicated the following:

	Dividend Received	Taxable Dividend	Federal Dividend Tax Credit	Taxable Capital Gain
2012	$ 2,000	$ 2,760	$415	$ 1,500
2011	1,000	1,380	207	300
	$ 3,000	$ 4,140	$622	$ 1,800

— *REQUIRED*

Determine Martha's capital gain or loss on the sale of her mutual fund units.

— *SOLUTION*

Proceeds		$40,000
Cost: Original cost	$20,000	
Dividend reinvestment	3,000	
CG reinvestment ($1,800 ÷ ½)	3,600	26,600
Capital gain		$13,400
Taxable capital gain (½)		$ 6,700

The income from the mutual fund was used to buy additional units of the fund. Since tax has been paid on this income, it is added to the cost base of the fund. In this case, since there have been no previous sales and all the units of the fund have been sold, we do not need to keep track of the number of units.

¶7,200 SPECIFIC PROVISIONS FOR THE TAXATION OF CAPITAL GAINS

¶7,210 Personal-Use Property

While gains on "personal-use property" (PUP), defined as property used primarily for personal use or enjoyment, are subject to tax, losses on such property may not be deducted. The loss on any particular item is considered to be a personal or living expense. Personal-use property will typically generate losses on disposal because such property often declines in value over time through use. ITA: 54 ITA: 40(2)(*g*)(iii)

For the purpose of calculating the capital gain or loss on any disposal of PUP, the taxpayer's cost is deemed to be the greater of the adjusted cost base of the property and $1,000. Similarly, the taxpayer's proceeds of disposition are deemed to be the greater of actual proceeds and $1,000. ITA: 46(1)

If a taxpayer disposes of any part of a personal-use property, for the purposes of computing the capital gain or loss on the disposal, the $1,000 minimum cost and the $1,000 minimum proceeds must be apportioned on the basis of the proportion of the PUP attributable to the part disposed of. These "part disposition" rules also apply to a disposition of part of a personal-use property that would ordinarily be disposed of as a set. Thus, several dispositions of pieces of the set would be considered to be parts of a single PUP disposition. If all of the pieces of a set are acquired by one person or by a group consisting of persons who are not dealing at arm's length, the taxpayer is deemed to have made a single disposition. ITA: 46(2) ITA: 46(3)

Example Problem 7-2

Consider the sale of the following personal-use properties:

	PUP #1	*PUP #2*
ACB	$ 800	$1,300
P of D	1,200	700

— *REQUIRED*

Compute the capital gain or capital loss in the two above situations.

— *SOLUTION*

	PUP #1		*PUP #2*
P of D	$1,200	Deemed P of D	$1,000
Deemed ACB	(1,000)	ACB	(1,300)
CG	$ 200	CL	Nil

Losses arising from debts, which are personal-use property and are uncollectible, will be recognized to the extent that the gain was previously recognized on the disposition of personal-use property in return for the debt. ITA: 50(2)

¶7,220 Listed Personal Property

"Listed personal property" (LPP) is a special subset of personal-use property. Hence, all of the personal-use property rules previously described also apply to listed personal property, except that capital losses arising on the disposition of LPP can be utilized, but only to the extent of LPP capital gains. In addition, there are carryover provisions so that unused LPP capital losses can be carried back three years and forward seven years but once again to be applied only against LPP gains. Unlike all other loss carryover provisions which are found in Division C, these carryovers are applied in Division B, using the capital loss amount rather than the allowable capital loss amount, i.e., 100% of the loss instead of ½. This result is achieved through a special term "net gain", which is defined as listed personal property capital gains minus: ITA: 54 ITA: 41(2)

(a) listed personal property capital losses in the year; and

(b) listed personal property capital losses arising from the seven preceding years or the three years immediately following.

As a result of the specification of the carryover amounts in this way, there need be no concern for differing capital gains inclusion rates in the carryover period for LPPs. Furthermore, these losses can be deducted at the option of the taxpayer, except that the earliest losses must be deducted before any losses of a subsequent year.

Examine carefully the very restrictive list of capital property, which qualifies for the listed personal property rules found in the definition of the term. The list is limited to a taxpayer's personal-use property that is a: ITA: 54

(a) print, etching, drawing, painting, sculpture, or other similar work of art,

(b) jewellery,

(c) rare folio, rare manuscript, or rare book,

(d) stamp, or

(e) coin.

If an item cannot be found in that list, it is not LPP and, therefore, capital losses cannot be applied against capital gains.

Example Problem 7-3

	Year 1	*Year 2*
Capital gain		
Other property	$1,000	—
Personal-use property (PUP)	200	—
Listed personal property (LPP gains)	100	$160
Capital losses		
Other property	200	300
PUP losses	120	1,200
LPP losses	160	—

—REQUIRED

Compute net taxable capital gains for taxation years 1 and 2. ITA: 3(*b*)

— *SOLUTION*

		Year 1		Year 2
Net taxable capital gain:				
Taxable capital gain				
Other property		$500		—
Personal-use property		100		—
Net listed personal property				
Listed personal property capital gain	$100		$160	
Listed personal property capital loss (Note a)	(100)		—	
Listed personal property carryforward	—		(60)	
Net × ½	0	0	100	$50
Total		600		50
Allowable capital loss				
Other property (Note b)		(100)		(50)
Net taxable capital gain		$500		$0

— *NOTES TO SOLUTION*

(a) Taxable net gains from LPP must be greater than or equal to zero. Losses from listed personal property are carried over in full amount as capital losses. Thus, $60 of the Year 1 LPP capital losses become net LPP capital losses and are available for carryforward to offset capital gains from listed personal property.

(b) The losses on personal-use property are not deductible. Allowable capital losses from other property are only deductible to the extent that net taxable capital gains are greater than or equal to zero. As a result, for Year 2, of the allowable capital losses of $150, $50 is applied to Year 2 and the $100 balance is available for carryforward indefinitely or may be carried back to Year 1 to reduce taxable income in either case.

¶7,230 Principal Residence Exemption

Generalizing that there are no capital gains subject to tax on principal residences may be inaccurate. In fact, there may be a gain but it can be exempted, wholly or partially, by designating the home as the taxpayer's principal residence for certain *specific* years. Note that the CRA states that a taxpayer may designate any residence as his or her principal residence as long as he or she ordinarily inhabits the home, even for a short period. This may be the case when the residence was disposed of early in the year or acquired late in the year. Also, a seasonal residence can be considered to be ordinarily inhabited.

Income Tax Folio S1-F3-C2 — Principal Residence

A "principal residence" defined as virtually any housing unit or right to such a unit owned by the taxpayer either by himself or herself or jointly and ordinarily inhabited by the taxpayer, the taxpayer's spouse or former spouse, or the taxpayer's child at any time in the year. To be a principal residence, the property must be designated as such in the year of disposal. The exemption applies not only to the building but also up to one-half hectare of subjacent and adjacent land. If all of the land exceeds one-half hectare, the additional land must be shown to be necessary to the taxpayer's use and enjoyment to be eligible for this exemption. There have been a number of court cases dealing with this issue of necessity to use and enjoyment.[1]

ITA: 54

[1] See *The Queen v. Yates*, 83 DTC 5158 (F.C.T.D.), affirmed by 86 DTC 6296 (F.C.A.), *Haber v. The Queen*, 83 DTC 5004 (F.C.T.D.), *Augart v. The Queen*, 93 DTC 5205 (F.C.A.), and *Carlile v. The Queen*, 95 DTC 5483 (F.C.A.).

A taxpayer owning more than one residence can designate only one of his or her residences for a given year as the principal residence for years after 1981. This is done at the time when an actual or deemed disposition is reported. Although the regulations require that a designation form (T2091) be filed with the tax return in the year of the disposition, the CRA does not require this form to be filed unless there is a taxable capital gain after applying the exempt portion according to the designation rules. Income Tax Folio S1-F3-C2 — Principal Residence

The exempt portion of a gain on the disposition or deemed disposition of a principal residence is calculated by the following *oversimplified* formula: ITA: 40(2)(*b*)

$$\frac{1 + \text{number of years designated}}{\text{number of years owned}} \times \text{gain}$$

In using this formula the following points should be noted:

(a) only one housing unit can be designated as a principal residence, after December 31, 1981, per family unit which is defined in the definition of "principal residence" to include spouses and their unmarried minor children; ITA: 54

(b) the years referred to in the numerator and denominator refer to those years after 1971;

(c) deemed dispositions and the resultant modification to the formula will be discussed in the next chapter;

(d) the taxpayer must be resident in Canada for tax purposes; and

(e) the actual formula contains a factor that reduces the gain by an amount based on an election made in 1994 to utilize the general capital gains deduction of $100,000 which was eliminated on February 22, 1994.

Since a family can only designate one housing unit as a principal residence for any particular year, the 1 + in the numerator of the fraction was intended to protect one housing unit in a situation where a family sells one house and buys another in the same year. In that situation, the family owns two houses in the year, but can only designate one as the principal residence for that year. In the following examples, the 1 + rule will be used in other situations involving the ownership of more than one housing unit by a family in a particular year.

Note that to be in the position to use the 1 + in the numerator, the taxpayer must be willing to designate the housing unit as a principal residence for at least one year. That is, the numerator can never be 1 + 0. The exemption formula containing the 1 + is not applicable at all if the taxpayer does not designate the housing unit as the principal residence for any year. Therefore, the minimum numerator will be 1 + 1.

Example Problem 7-4

Mr. Talbot is in the process of retiring and moving to another city. He decides to sell his two residences and provides you with the following information as at September 30, 2013, the date of sale.

Residence	*Date of purchase*	*Selling price*	*Cost*
City home	2004	$170,000	$100,000
Cottage	2009	90,000	40,000

— REQUIRED

Calculate the minimum total taxable capital gain on the disposition of the two residences.

— SOLUTION

In the five taxation years 2004–2008, Mr. Talbot owned only one residence — the city home. Therefore, there is no option in these years but to designate the city home as his principal residence.

The remaining problem is to find the allocation of the five "option" years 2009–2013 which will minimize the total capital gain on the two residences. To find this allocation, note two facts:

(1) Mr. Talbot can designate only one residence as his principal residence in any year.

(2) From the formula for the exempt portion of the capital gain, it can be seen that designating a particular residence as a principal residence for an additional year generally will decrease the capital gain on that residence by its gain per year of ownership.

Therefore, a first guess, as to the best allocation of the option years, is to use all of these years to designate, as a principal residence, the residence with the higher gain per year of ownership.

The city home has been owned during 10 years (2004–2013, inclusive) while the cottage has been owned during five years (2009–2013, inclusive). The gains per year are $7,000 for the city home and $10,000 for the cottage:

	City home		*Cottage*	
P of D	$170,000		$90,000	
ACB	(100,000)		(40,000)	
Gain	$ 70,000		$50,000	
Gain per year	$\frac{\$70,000}{10 \text{ years}}$	= $7,000	$\frac{\$50,000}{5 \text{ years}}$	= $10,000

Thus, a first guess would be to designate the cottage for all of the option years 2009–2013 (and to designate the city home for the no-option years 2004–2008). This produces a total capital gain on the two residences of $28,000, all of which is on the city home:

		City home		*Cottage*
Gain		$70,000		$ 50,000
Exemption	$\frac{1+5}{10} \times \$70,000 =$	(42,000)	$\frac{1+5}{5} \times \$50,000 =$	(50,000)*
Capital gain		$28,000		Nil

* The exemption cannot exceed the gain.

This first guess can be improved upon. Note that because of the "one plus" in the formula for the exempt portion of the capital gain, it is wasteful to designate the cottage for all of its years of ownership. The cottage would still have a zero capital gain if it was designated as a principal residence for four years instead of five years. This reduces the total capital gain to the minimum possible amount of $21,000:

		City home		*Cottage*
Gain		$70,000		$ 50,000
Exemption	$\frac{1+6}{10} \times \$70,000 =$	(49,000)	$\frac{1+4}{5} \times \$50,000 =$	(50,000)
Capital gain		$21,000		Nil
Taxable capital gain (½ × $21,000)		$10,500		Nil

Principal Residence Exemption
Steps to Follow

1. Calculate the capital gain per year for each principal residence.
2. Determine if any of the years of ownership have been allocated to previous principal residences.
3. Allocate the years available to each residence to optimize the exemption. More years are initially allocated to the residence with the highest gain per year. Change that allocation if you can increase the exemption.

¶7,240 Change in Use of a Principal Residence

¶7,245 Application of the change-in-use elections

ITA: 45(2), 45(3)

The change-in-use election can be used in connection with a principal residence where the initial change of use is from personal use to income-producing use. Paragraph (*d*) of the definition of a "principal residence" permits a taxpayer, who changes the use of his or her home, to choose to designate this home as his or her principal residence for up to four years, as long as he or she has elected not to have changed the use under subsection 45(2). You should note that the election and the designation as a principal residence are two separate and distinct acts. The CRA normally permits a taxpayer to file a retroactive election in connection with a principal residence *only*. A further consequence of the election is that the taxpayer cannot claim capital cost allowance against any income from that property.

ITA: 45(2)
ITA: 54
ITA: 45(2)
Income Tax Folio S1-F3-C2 — Principal Residence
ITR: 1102(1)(*c*)

The definition of a "principal residence", together with another rule, provides for a similar four-year maximum designation in situations where the property was converted from an initial income-producing purpose to personal use and is designated as a principal residence. This election must be made on the earlier of 90 days after a ministerial demand or the normal filing due date (see Chapter 14) for the year of the disposition of the property. Note that this provision is not applicable in respect of recapture and this election will be revoked if any capital cost allowance is claimed. The combination of the two change-in-use elections cannot exceed four years.

ITA: 45(3), 54
ITA: 45(4)
ITA: 45(2), 45(3)

The principal residence exemption formula must now be modified to take into account a possible change in use as follows:

ITA: 40(2)(*b*)

$$\frac{\text{1 + the number of years for which the property is designated after the later of December 31, 1971 and the date on which it was last acquired}}{\text{Number of years during which the property was owned after the later of December 31, 1971 and the date on which it was last acquired}} \times \text{gain realized}$$

"The date on which it was last acquired" can, if applicable, refer to a deemed reacquisition for personal use after a change in use.

Example Problem 7-5

Mr. Jacobs owned a home in Calgary which he purchased in 2002. During 2005, he decided to relocate because of business reasons and moved to Vancouver. He rented an apartment in Vancouver and rented out his Calgary home. In 2011, he returned to Calgary to live in his original home. He anticipates selling the Calgary home in 2013 and retiring. The following data relates to his home:

Calgary home:	Cost	2002	$140,000
	FMV	2005	200,000
	FMV	2011	320,000
	Proceeds	2013 (estimated)	415,000

— *REQUIRED*

(A) Compute the minimum capital gain, based on the above information. Assume Mr. Jacobs makes an election on a late-filed basis when he files his 2011 tax return.

ITA: 45(2); Income Tax Folio S1-F3-C2 — Principal Residence

(B) Re-do Part (A) on the assumption that Mr. Jacobs does not elect.

— *SOLUTION*

Part (A) — Election to be deemed not to have changed the use

ITA: 45(2)

When Mr. Jacobs moves out of the Calgary home and begins to rent it out, there is a deemed disposition on the change in use. However, if he makes an election, then the result is that there is no change in use and the property remains a personal-use property. In addition, paragraph (*d*) of the definition of a "principal residence" provides that it is possible for this property to be

ITA: 45(2)
ITA: 54

designated as his principal residence for up to four additional years even though he is not living there. This would allow him to designate the property as his principal residence for the years 2002–2005 and 2011–2013 based on the years he lived there and for the years 2006–2009 based on the four additional years. The only year missing is 2010 and it is protected with the "1+" rule.

	Calgary home
Gain	$ 275,000
Exempt portion	(275,000)[(1)]
Capital gain	Nil
Taxable capital gain	Nil

Since an election is made to deem there not to be a change in use of the Calgary home, then there is no need to determine UCC. ITA: 13(7), 45(2)

Part (B) — No election ITA: 45(2)

In 2005, when Mr. Jacobs moves out of his Calgary home and begins to rent it to earn income, there is a deemed disposition on the change in use. Since he has been living in the house since he bought it in 2001, he can claim the principal residence exemption on the gain that results from the deemed disposition. By designating the years 2002–2004 he can eliminate the full gain as shown below. ITA: 45(1)

	Calgary home
2005	
P of D, deemed	$ 200,000
ACB	(140,000)
Gain	$ 60,000
Exempt portion	(60,000)[(2)]
Capital gain	Nil

Since no election was made on the Calgary home, then the UCC in 2004 will be deemed to be $170,000 (cost of $140,000 plus the TCG equal to 50% of $60,000). (Refer to ¶5,135 for an explanation of this provision.) On the deemed disposition of the Calgary home in 2011, there will be recapture to the extent that any CCA was claimed on the home between 2005 and 2010. ITA: 13(7)(*e*)

In 2011, when he returns to Calgary and moves back into the house, there is another change in use and a resulting deemed disposition. In this case the principal residence exemption can be claimed for the years 2005 and 2011, since the house was his principal residence at some point during each of those years.

	Calgary home
P of D — actual	$ 320,000
ACB — deemed	(200,000)
Gain	$ 120,000
Exempt portion	(51,429)[(3)]
Capital gain	$ 68,571
Taxable capital gain (½)	$ 34,286

Finally, when the Calgary home is sold in 2013, there would be no capital gain as shown below.

	Calgary home
P of D — estimated	$ 415,000
ACB — deemed	(320,000)
Gain	$ 95,000
Exempt portion	(95,000)(4)
Capital gain	Nil

In summary, by making no elections, he will report a capital gain of $34,286 in 2011 along with any recaptured CCA that also has to be reported.

If he had made the election in 2011 when the house was changed from income-producing to personal-use property, then the capital gain could be deferred and would not have to be reported until the actual disposition in 2013. ITA: 45(3)

— *NOTES TO SOLUTION*

(1) $\frac{1 + 11}{12}$ × $275,000 = $275,000; 2002–2005 — owner-occupied
2006–2009 — paragraph (*d*) of the definition of "principal residence", maximum four years
2011–2013 — owner-occupied. ITA: 54

(2) $\frac{1 + 3}{4}$ × $60,000 = $60,000; 2002–2004.

(3) $\frac{1 + 2}{7}$ × $120,000 = $51,428; 2005, 2011 — owner-occupied.

(4) $\frac{1 + 2}{3}$ × $95,000 = $95,000; 2012-2013.

¶7,250 Income Tax Folio S1-F3-C2 — Principal residence

The Interpretation Bulletin is an excellent example of how administrative practice differs from the actual law. For example, the term "ordinarily inhabited" has been interpreted by the CRA, for purposes of this section only, to mean "a short period of time in the year". However the facts of each particular case must be considered. Therefore, a taxpayer who abuses the application of this CRA interpretation could conceivably be reassessed and potentially taken to court on this issue. Income Tax Folio S1-F3-C2 — Principal Residence

One should note the difference between partial changes in use where there are no structural changes and partial changes where there are structural changes. In cases where the change in use is "ancillary" or secondary to the main purpose of the residence, the CRA's view is that no change has taken place for the purpose of this section. Therefore, the taxpayer may still designate the residence as a principal residence as long as he or she does not claim any capital cost allowance. Where the change is more substantial, then this option does not exist. In this case, the residence will have more than one use and each must be treated differently for tax purposes. Income Tax Folio S1-F3-C2 — Principal Residence

¶7,255 Section 54.1 — Extended designation

This relieving provision was added to aid taxpayers and their spouses who are transferred by their employers to another location and keep their home in the original location. In such an event, paragraph (*b*) of the definition of a "principal residence" applies, without the four-year limitation, as long as the taxpayer complies with the specific conditions of this subsection. Since nothing is said to the contrary, the aforementioned interpretation of the word "ordinarily" should stand. ITA: 54

¶7,260 Principal Residence Exemption — Transfer between spouses

¶7,260.10 *Single-ownership situations*

This provision enables the transfer of a wholly owned principal residence from one spouse to another with complete or partial relief from the taxation of the capital gain depending upon the principal residence designation circumstances. This rule does not apply to the interspousal transfer of a home which was previously *jointly owned* (discussed later in this part of the chapter). The provision does apply where one spouse owns a residence solely and transfers this residence to the other spouse. ITA: 73(1), 70(6) ITA: 40(4)

A provision determines the period of ownership for the transferee spouse for purposes of the principal residence exempting formula. The result is that the transferee spouse is deemed to have owned the property since the time the transferor spouse originally acquired it. Thus, the recipient spouse will be able to designate the home as a principal residence for the same years that it would have qualified for the transferor spouse. ITA: 40(2)(*b*), 40(4)(*a*)

The years of designation by the transferee spouse for the period of ownership by the transferor spouse are those years which were actually designated by the transferor spouse, plus those years after the transfer for which the transferee spouse ordinarily resided in the transferred residence. This automatic interspousal rollover or deferral rule must be applicable (i.e., no election out of this rollover), so no gain would be recognized on the transfer. ITA: 40(4)(*b*) ITA: 73(1) ITA: 40(4)(*b*)(ii)

It is recommended that a designation form be completed by the transferor spouse, even if it is not filed, so that the recipient spouse can determine the appropriate designation on the ultimate disposition of the property. This would fully protect the capital gain on the residence, if it had been the only one owned by the family unit.

If the transfer to the recipient spouse takes place as a result of the death of the transferor spouse, the actual designation requirement by the transferor spouse is removed, but the residence must have been ordinarily inhabited by the transferor spouse for the years before death that the recipient spouse chooses to designate the home. ITA: 70(6) ITA: 40(4)(*b*)(i)

Where two residences are owned by one spouse, the transfer of one of the residences to the other only offers partial relief because of the limitation of one principal residence per family unit for years after 1981. In this situation, the transferee spouse will be deemed to have owned the property since the time the transferor spouse originally acquired the property. However, the years of designation will be limited to those years in which the transferor actually designates the transferred residence as his or her principal residence plus those years in which the transferee spouse "ordinarily inhabited" the transferred residence.[2] Therefore, one of the two properties will be left unsheltered at least, in part, by the designation rules in paragraph (*c*) of the definition of a "principal residence". A disposition by, or the death of the spouse who owns the two properties would trigger a taxable capital gain on the less-designated property minus an exemption based on the ever-present extra year of designation (one-plus rule) and the number of years owned. ITA: 54

Example Problem 7-6

Spouse A owns two residences:

	Residence 1	*Residence 2*
FMV	$100,000	$200,000
ACB	$ 50,000	$100,000
Year of acquisition	2001	2001

Both spouses have resided in both homes since 2002. In 2008, Spouse A transferred Residence 2 to Spouse B as a gift. Spouse B sold the transferred residence in 2013 for $300,000. Spouse A has not designated, at any time, Residence 2 as his principal residence.

[2] See the CRA Technical Interpretation Document No. 9502557, February 9, 1995.

— *REQUIRED*

(A) Compute the effect of the above transaction as if subsection 40(4) did not exist.

(B) Apply subsection 40(4) to the transaction.

(C) Apply subsection 40(4) to the transaction on the assumption that spouse A had previously designated Residence 2 for two years.

— *SOLUTION*

(A) As if subsection 40(4) did not exist

2008 — Transfer of residence to Spouse B (rollover automatically applies since the facts do not indicate that Spouse A elected not to have the rollover apply; refer to the discussion of the attribution rules later in this chapter for a more detailed explanation of this provision) ITA: 73

P of D (deemed)	$100,000	ITA: 73
ACB	(100,000)	
Gain	Nil	

Note that no principal residence designation was required to reduce the gain to nil.

2013 — Spouse B sells home

P of D		$300,000	
ACB (deemed)		(100,000)	ITA: 73
Gain		$200,000	
Exemption	$\frac{1 + 5 \text{ years designated by B}}{6 \text{ years owned by B}} \times \$200,000 =$	(200,000)	
Capital gain		Nil	

Years of designation: any five of 2008–2013

The gain of $200,000 was completely eliminated by Spouse B designating Residence 2 for five years under the principal residence rules, because:

- Spouse B owned the residence for six years (2008–2013, inclusive), and
- Spouse B ordinarily inhabited the residence for those years.

Hence, the entire gain is eliminated and Spouse A has saved the designation of years 2002–2007, plus one year of 2008–2013.

Note that there is no attribution since the capital gain is nil. However, depending upon the use of the $300,000 proceeds by Spouse B, there is potential attribution under the substituted property rule, discussed later in this chapter.

(B) With subsection 40(4)

2013 — Spouse B sells home

P of D		$ 300,000	
ACB (deemed)		(100,000)	ITA: 73
Gain		$ 200,000	
Exemption	$\frac{1 + 11^{(1)}}{12^{(2)}} \times \$200,000 =$	(200,000)	
Capital gain$^{(3)}$		Nil	

The application of subsection 40(4) results in the same nil capital gain, but has eliminated all the principal residence designation years for Spouse A for Residence 1, except for one year.

(C) The answer would be the same as Part (B). The years designated would be the two years designated by Spouse A, plus eight years by Spouse B for a total of 10 years, thereby, eliminating the entire gain.

— NOTES TO SOLUTION

(1) Spouse B can designate the transferred residence for the actual years or deemed years that he or she owned and ordinarily inhabited the residence (12 years) plus any other years for which Spouse A made a designation (in this case nil).

(2) The number of years owned includes the ownership years of Spouse A. ITA: 40(4)(*a*)

(3) The taxable capital gain, if any, will be attributed back to Spouse A, if realized during his or her lifetime.

Additional Notes:

- If this transfer had been as a consequence of Spouse A's death, the years of designation available would be expanded to include the potential designations available to Spouse A (or his or her legal representative). Hence, the entire gain would be exempt, but Residence 1 could not be designated for the years used to designate Residence 2.

- This example was designed to demonstrate how subsection 40(4) is applied and no tax planning was taken into account. Some of the factors which should be considered would be:
  - the relative size of the future gain on the two homes;
  - the tax rates of the respective spouses who own the homes; and
  - the potential application of the attribution rules to the ultimate non-exempt capital gains on the homes.

¶7,260.20 *Joint ownership situations*

Where two residences are each jointly owned by spouses, subsection 40(4) does not have any effect, since the definition of a "principal residence" governs years of joint ownership. Hence, each spouse enjoys an unrestricted right to designate either residence as his or her principal residence under the exemption formula. A transfer of ownership so that one residence is wholly owned by one spouse and the other residence is wholly owned by the other spouse will maximize the potential principal residence designation for years owned before 1982. Therefore, there will be no tax consequences, since both spouses have owned, although only partially, the residence for the entire period. The transferee spouse can designate the entire residence as his or her principal residence.

ITA: 54

ITA: 40(2)(*b*)

¶7,270 Capital Losses — General

Allowable capital losses can be deducted from taxable capital gains, and taxable net gains from listed personal property, to the extent needed to bring those gains to zero. Any excess losses, referred to as "net capital losses", can be carried back three years or forward indefinitely to reduce taxable capital gains in the applicable taxation years. Chapters 10 and 11 discuss the rules for applying net capital loss carryover amounts for individuals and corporations, respectively.

ITA: 111

¶7,280 Pooling of Identical Assets

There are many and varied methods of arriving at a cost base for identical assets for accounting purposes. However, for tax purposes, there is only one method, namely, the "*floating weighted average method*".

For stock transactions, the floating weighted average cost is calculated by dividing the aggregate of the costs of the identical properties by the number of such identical properties.

For bonds, debentures, notes, etc., the floating weighted average cost is calculated by dividing the aggregate of the cost of the identical properties by the quotient obtained when the principal amounts of all the identical properties are divided by the principal amount of the property disposed of. For example, assume that an individual purchased three $1,000 bonds of a corporation for $2,880. Later, a $500 bond of the same series of bonds of the corporation was purchased for $490. The weighted average cost of one of the $1,000 bonds is:

$$\frac{\$2,880 + \$490}{((3 \times \$1,000) + \$500)/\$1,000} = \$963$$

Similarly, the weighted average cost of the $500 bond is:

$$\frac{\$2,880 + \$490}{((3 \times \$1,000) + \$500)/\$500} = \$481 \text{ (or one-half the cost of a \$1,000 bond)}$$

Many investors purchase shares or units of mutual funds to hold outside of RRSP investments. Mutual funds allocate their income to their investors, such that the income is taxable to the investors and not to the mutual fund. As a result, investors must include in their income for tax purposes the amount of net investment income, such as interest and dividends, and net taxable capital gains paid or payable to them in the year. Often income so allocated to the investor is reinvested in additional units in the fund. Since reinvested income amounts would have been taxed in the hands of the investor, whether or not actually distributed, these amounts can be added to the adjusted cost base of the investor's units in the fund. However, the adjusted amount for capital gains would be the full capital gain rather than the taxable capital gain. For dividends, the adjusted amount would be the actual dividend, not the grossed-up dividend. After the reinvestment, the ACB of each unit owned in the mutual fund must be averaged by dividing the total ACB of all units in the mutual fund owned by the investor by the total number of units owned.

When an investor redeems or disposes of units in a mutual fund, a capital gain (or loss) is realized. The calculation of the capital gain (or loss) follows the normal formula of proceeds of disposition minus the sum of the investor's ACB and selling costs. This capital gain (or loss) is separate and distinct from the taxable capital gains allocated from the income of the fund which are made annually and taxed as paid or declared payable. Refer to Example Problem 7-1.

Example Problem 7-7

Consider the following transactions in the shares of Dachshund Airways Ltd:

Date	*Type of transaction*	*Number of shares*	*Cost per share (selling price)*	*Total cost (selling price)*
April 2001	Purchase	100	$1	$ 100
March 2003	Purchase	150	2	300
Aug. 2006	Sale	(200)	(3)	(600)
June 2009	Purchase	100	4	400
July 2011	Purchase	300	5	1,500
Oct. 2013	Sale	(250)	(6)	(1,500)

— *REQUIRED*

Compute the taxable capital gains, if any, on the 2006 and the 2013 sales.

— *SOLUTION*

August 2006 sale:	
P of D (200 shares @ $3)	$ 600
ACB (200 shares @ $1.60[(1)])	(320)
CG	$ 280
TCG (½ × $280)	$ 140
October 2013 sale:	
P of D (250 shares @ $6)	$1,500
ACB (250 shares @ $4.40[(2)])	(1,100)
CG	$ 400
TCG (½ × $400)	$ 200

There are 200 shares with a weighted average cost of $4.40 on hand after the 2013 sale.

— *NOTES TO SOLUTION*

(1)

100 shares @ $1 =	$100
150 shares @ $2 =	300
250	$400

$400 ÷ 250 = $1.60 per share

(2)

50 shares @ $1.60 =	$ 80
100 shares @ $4.00 =	400
300 shares @ $5.00 =	1,500
450	$1,980

$1,980 ÷ 450 = $4.40 per share

¶7,285 Identical properties exempt from cost-averaging rule

The Act requires that the cost of identical properties acquired by a taxpayer be averaged over all such properties. Generally, this results in each of the properties having the same adjusted cost base (ACB), thus, ensuring that the capital gain or loss on the disposition of any one of the properties can be determined without having to identify a particular property as the property that has been disposed of. ITA: 47(1)

Certain securities are exempt from the cost-averaging rule by deeming such securities not to be identical to any other securities acquired by the taxpayer for the purposes of this cost-averaging rule. The specific securities to which this exemption applies are as follows: ITA: 47(1), 47(3)

- Securities (i.e., shares of a corporation and units of a mutual fund trust) acquired under an employee option agreement for which a deferral is provided and securities acquired in exchange for such securities under specified circumstances. ITA: 7(1.1), 7(8) ITA: 7(1.1)

- Securities acquired under an employee option agreement where the securities are designated by the taxpayer and deemed by the Act to be the securities that are the subject of a disposition of identical securities occurring within 30 days after the acquisition. ITA: 7(1.31)

- Employer shares received by an employee as part of a lump-sum payment on withdrawing from a deferred profit sharing plan (DPSP), where the employee filed an election in respect of those shares. Such an election allows the taxpayer to defer taxation on the growth of the shares while they were held by the plan until such time as the employee disposes of the shares. ITA: 147(10.1)

The effect of a security being exempted from the cost-averaging rule is that the ACB of the security and, thus, the capital gain or loss on its disposition, is determined without regard to the ACB of any other securities owned by the taxpayer. In other words, each security to which the exemption applies has its own unique ACB. ITA: 47(1), 47(3)

It should be noted that it is possible to determine when each security which is exempted from the cost averaging rule is disposed of by the taxpayer. The Act deals with situations in which there is an acquisition of an employee option security and a disposition of an identical security within 30 days. Another provision of the Act deals with securities for which a deferral is provided (referred to as "deferral securities"). In general terms, the Act deems a taxpayer to dispose of deferral securities only after having disposed of non-deferral securities, and then to dispose of deferral securities in the order in which they were acquired. Since it is possible to determine exactly when a particular security is disposed of, the fact that the security has its own unique ACB is not problematic. ITA: 7(1.3), 7(1.31) ITA: 47(3) ITA: 7(1.31) ITA: 7(1.1) or 7(8) ITA: 147(10.1) ITA: 7(1.3) ITA: 47(3)

It should also be noted that, where an employee acquires a deferred security, the deferred employment benefit is added to the ACB of the security at the time it is acquired even though the benefit is not subject to taxation until the security is disposed of. ITA: 7(1.1), 7(8) ITA: 53(1)(*j*)

¶7,290 Disposition of Shares Acquired Under a Stock Option

¶7,295 Disposition of newly acquired securities

Under the stock option benefit rules, there is a special provision which applies when a taxpayer disposes of a security that is identical to other securities already owned by the taxpayer. The provision allows the taxpayer to designate the particular security that is being disposed of. In order for this subsection to apply, certain conditions, as set out in the technical notes to this subsection, must be met. ITA: 7(1.31)

- The particular security must have been acquired under an employee stock option agreement, as described in the Act. ITA: 7(1)
- The disposition must occur no later than 30 days after the taxpayer acquires the particular security.
- There must be no other acquisitions or dispositions of identical securities in the intervening period; that is, after the acquisition of the particular security and before the disposition in respect of which the designation is being made. It should be noted, however, that this does not preclude the taxpayer from acquiring other identical securities at the same time as the disposition in respect of which the designation is being made.
- The taxpayer must make the designation in the tax return that is filed for the year in which the disposition occurs. It is expected that the CRA will accept, as the form of designation, the calculation of the capital gain or loss in respect of the disposition on the basis that it is the particular security that is the subject of the disposition.
- The taxpayer must not have designated the particular security in connection with the disposition of any other security.

Example Problem 7-8

On May 1, 2011, Joseph acquires 750 shares of his corporate employer on the open market. On May 1, 2012, he acquires another 750 shares on the open market. On May 1, 2013, he acquires an additional 1,000 shares under employee stock options. Immediately thereafter, he sells 1,500 shares.

—REQUIRED

How should Joseph calculate his cost base on the disposition of his shares?

—SOLUTION

In his tax return for 2013, he can designate the 1,000 stock option shares as constituting part of the shares that were sold. The 1,500 shares being sold by Joseph are deemed to be comprised of the 1,000 stock option shares and 500 of the 1,500 shares that Joseph acquired on the open market. Alternatively, he can use the weighted average cost of all the shares. ITA: 7(1.3), 7(1.31)

It should be noted that the Act accommodates the practice of specific identification. The significance of specific identification is that it allows a taxpayer to deduct a portion of the employment benefit that the taxpayer is deemed to have received in respect of the taxpayer's acquisition of a qualifying employee option security, if the taxpayer disposes of the security by donating it to a qualifying charity within 30 days after its acquisition. ITA: 7(1.31) ITA: 110(1)(*d*.01) ITA: 7(1)

Also, securities to which this provision applies are deemed, for the purpose of the cost-averaging rule, not to be identical to any other securities owned by the taxpayer. Consequently, the ACB of each such security and, thus, the capital gain or loss on the disposition of the security, is determined without regard to the ACB of any other securities owned by the taxpayer. ITA: 47(3) ITA: 7(1) ITA: 47(1)

¶7,300 Adjusted cost base of shares acquired under a stock option

The Act provides for an addition to the ACB of a share acquired by a taxpayer under an employee option agreement. The amount that is added to the ACB is the amount of the employment benefit that the taxpayer (or a non-arm's length person) is deemed to have received in connection with the acquisition of the security. The amount is generally equal to the excess of the fair market value of the security at the time it is acquired over the amount paid to acquire the security under the option. The amount is added to the ACB in the year in which the benefit is deemed to have been received, which is generally the year in which the taxpayer acquires the security. However, in the case of an option granted by a Canadian-controlled private corporation (CCPC) to an arm's length person, a rule applies to defer recognition of the benefit to the year in which the taxpayer disposes of the security. ITA: 53(1)(*j*) ITA: 7(1) ITA: 7(1.1)

The employment benefit is included in the ACB of the security from the time of acquisition, even if recognition of the employment benefit is deferred, for tax purposes, until the taxpayer disposes of the security. ITA: 53(1)(*j*)

¶7,310 Cost of Certain Properties

¶7,315 General consideration

The cost of property is usually incurred by the acquisition of the property with after-tax funds. Thus, when a capital property is acquired for $100, the funds used in the purchase have usually been subjected to income tax. That is why, on the disposition of the property for, say, $150, the $100 of cost is not taxed; only the $50 of gain above cost is taxed. Thus, cost is recovered tax-free on a disposition, because it represents an amount on which tax was already paid.

Normally the cost of capital property or the capital cost of depreciable capital property is the laid-down cost for accounting purposes. However, a number of provisions deem the *cost* to be an amount other than laid-down cost. Where a taxpayer has acquired property and an amount in respect of the value of the property is included in the taxpayer's income, that amount is added to the cost of the property. For example, if a shareholder had a benefit in kind (i.e., in property) which was included in his or her income, then the income inclusion would be added to the cost of the property so received. Since the income inclusion in respect of the benefit would be taxed, the amount of the benefit can be considered as a tax-paid cost of the property, according to the concept of cost discussed above. There is one notable exception to this rule, namely, an employment income inclusion arising from a stock option benefit, which was discussed in the previous part of the Chapter. ITA: 52 ITA: 52(1) ITA: 15(1) ITA: 52(1) ITA: 7

¶7,320 Dividends in kind and lottery prizes

Sometimes a company will pay dividends in property other than cash; these are called dividends in kind. Since the shareholder will pay tax on the full fair market value of the property paid as a dividend, the cost to the shareholder of the property received will be the same fair market value. ITA: 52(2)

If a lottery prize is received, the cost of this prize to the winner is the fair market value of the prize. For example, if an individual wins a car as a lottery prize and the fair market value of the car is $35,000, then the cost to the individual is the same $35,000 even though the prize is not included in income. ITA: 40(2)(*f*); 52(4)

¶7,325 Stock dividends

A stock dividend is treated in the same manner as any other dividend for purposes of determining income. Its cost base, however, is deemed to be equal to its paid-up capital which is, generally, the stated capital[3] on the accounting balance sheet. ITA: 52(3)

[3] In some provinces, this amount may be the par value.

Example Problem 7-9

Mr. Arnett purchased 1,000 shares of Sure-Fire Limited, a public corporation, at $50 per share in 2008. Mr. Arnett received the following dividends subsequent to that time:

2009	A stock dividend of 10% which resulted in an increase in the paid-up capital of $10 for each share issued.
2010	A stock dividend of 10% which resulted in an increase in the paid-up capital of $10 for each share issued.
2011	Cash dividend of $5 per share.
2012	A stock dividend of 10% which resulted in an increase in the paid-up capital of $10 for each share issued.

— *REQUIRED*

Compute the taxable capital gain or allowable capital loss if Mr. Arnett sold 100 of the above shares in 2013 for $45 per share less brokerage of $100.

— *SOLUTION*

2013	P of D (100 shares @ $45)		$4,500
	ACB (100 shares @ $40.05[1])	$4,005	
	Selling cost	100	(4,030)
	Capital gain		$ 395
	Taxable capital gain (½ × $395)		$ 198

— *NOTE TO SOLUTION*

[1] 2008	1,000	shares — purchased @ $50 each	$50,000
2009	100	shares — stock dividend of 10% @ $10 each	1,000
	1,100		
2010	110	shares — stock dividend of 10% @ $10 each	1,100
	1,210		
2012	121	shares — stock dividend of 10% @ $10 each	1,210
	1,331		$53,310

$53,310 ÷ 1,331 = $40.05

¶7,330 Superficial Losses

A "superficial loss", as defined in the Act is usually, but not necessarily, associated with the trading of securities. A taxpayer might own securities with an accrued capital loss at the end of the year. The securities are sold to trigger the loss which is used to offset a capital gain previously realized in the year. Then the taxpayer repurchases the same or identical securities, almost immediately, because of their long-term potential. In this case, the taxpayer has converted a "paper" loss into a realized loss, but after the repurchase continues to own essentially the same securities. This is the essence of a superficial loss in which the taxpayer is denied the loss at the time of the disposition but is permitted to add the superficial loss to the adjusted cost base of the substituted property. This adjustment has the effect of delaying the triggering of the loss. There are three conditions necessary in order to establish a superficial loss: ITA: 54 ITA: 53(1)(*f*)

(a) the taxpayer or an "affiliated person", in essence, the taxpayer's spouse or a corporation controlled by either the taxpayer or the taxpayer's spouse, must dispose of the property; ITA: 251.1(1)

(b) the taxpayer or an affiliated person acquires or re-acquires the same or identical property during the period beginning 30 days before the disposition and ending 30 days after the disposition; and

(c) the taxpayer or an affiliated person, at the end of the period referred to in point (b) above, still owns at least some of the property.

Example Problem 7-10

Mr. Sung buys 1,000 shares of Norwood Ltd. at $10 per share on October 1, 2012. On December 15, 2012, Mr. Sung sells 1,000 shares at $5. On January 3, 2013, he buys 1,000 shares at $6. On November 15, 2013, he sells 1,000 shares at $10.

— *REQUIRED*

Compute the taxable capital gain or allowable capital loss on each of the above transactions.

— *SOLUTION*

Dec. 15, 2012	P of D (1,000 shares @ $5)	$ 5,000
	ACB (1,000 shares @ $10)	(10,000)
	Capital loss	Nil
	There is a superficial loss of $5,000, since he purchased the shares within the 30-day time limit and still owns the shares at the end of the period which is 30 days after December 15. In essence, the purchase on January 3, 2013 allows him to maintain his ownership position in the shares after the sale.	
Nov. 15, 2013	P of D (1,000 shares @ $10)	$10,000
	ACB (1,000 shares[(1)])	(11,000)
	Capital loss	(1,000)
	Since Mr. Sung has no shares on hand 30 days after the sale on November 15, 2013, there cannot be a superficial loss.	

— *NOTE TO SOLUTION*

(1) 1,000 shares @ $6 =	$ 6,000
Dec. 15 Sup. loss =	5,000
	$11,000

Example Problem 7-11

Ms. Tabuchi is considering selling all of her remaining shares of Open Mining Ltd., a public corporation. She is uncertain of the adjusted cost base of the shares. The following is the historical data concerning her holdings in Open Mining Ltd.

June 1, 2009	Purchased 500 shares @ $2 per share.
Jan. 15, 2010	Received a stock dividend of 10%. The paid-up capital of the corporation was credited with one dollar for each share issued.
July 1, 2011	Purchased additional 1,000 shares @ $5 per share.
April 15, 2012	Received a stock dividend of 10%. The paid-up capital of the corporation was credited with $6 for each additional share.
June 19, 2013	Purchased an additional 1,000 shares @ $9.
Aug. 1, 2013	Sold 500 shares @ $5 plus commission of $150.

— *REQUIRED*

Determine the adjusted cost base of Ms. Tabuchi's shares in Open Mining Ltd.

— SOLUTION

Adjusted cost base			
June 1, 2009	500 shares @ $2 — purchase		$ 1,000
Jan. 15, 2010	50 shares — 10% stock dividend @ $1		50
July 1, 2011	1,000 shares @ $5 — purchase		5,000
	1,550		
April 15, 2012	155 shares — 10% stock dividend @ $6		930
June 19, 2013	1,000 shares at $9		9,000
	2,705		$15,980
Aug. 1, 2013	(500) P of D 500 shares @ $5	$2,500	
	ACB (500 shares × $\frac{\$15,980}{2,705}$)	(2,954)	(2,954)
		$ (454)	
	SC	(150)	
	Capital loss	$ 604	
	2,205 shares @ $5.91		$13,026

¶7,340 Transfer of Property to an RRSP

The loss from the disposition of property to a trust governed by an RRSP to which taxpayers or their spouse are beneficiaries is deemed to be nil. ITA: 40(2)(*g*)(iv)

For example, when a taxpayer transfers shares of a public corporation that he or she holds personally to his or her self-administered RRSP, the value considered as proceeds of disposition of the shares is the FMV at the date of the transfer. If the taxpayer realizes a capital gain, it must be included in computing income. If the taxpayer incurs a capital loss, it is not deductible.

¶7,350 Options

There are two basic types of option: an option to buy property (known as a call option) and an option to sell property (known as a put option). As a general rule, when an option is granted, there is a disposition of a property with an adjusted cost base of nil by the grantor or issuer. The result is a capital gain to the grantor in the amount of the proceeds for the option. The grantee or holder of the option has acquired a capital property with an adjusted cost base equal to the amount paid for the option. If the option expires, the grantor's or issuer's tax position remains unchanged and the grantee has a capital loss in the year of expiration. ITA: 49(1)

There are two exceptions to the general rule noted above.

- When an option in respect of a principal residence is granted, there is no disposition. As a result, if an option on a principal residence expires, there would have been no inclusion for the grantor and, therefore, no tax effect. The grantee would be denied a loss on expiration, because the option on a principal residence would be regarded as a personal-use property. ITA: 49(1)(*a*), 40(2)(*g*)(iii), 54
- The other exception is for an option granted by a corporation to another person to buy securities to be issued by the corporation. In this case, the corporation has no disposition at the time the option is granted. However, if the option expires, the corporation is deemed to have disposed of a capital property with an adjusted cost base of nil. The proceeds are deemed to be equal to the amount, if any, received for granting the option. As a result, when this type of option expires, a capital gain is realized. ITA: 49(2)

¶7,352 Call option

If an option to acquire property (i.e., a call option) is exercised, then the granting of the option and its exercise are deemed not to be a disposition to the vendor. When the option is exercised, there is a disposition of the property underlying the option by the vendor and the purchaser acquires the optioned property. On the exercise of the option, the vendor of the optioned property must include the consideration received for the option in proceeds of disposition of the property sold in the year in which the option is exercised. The vendor, who was the grantor of the option, can file an amended return for the year in which the amount received for the option was included in income to remove the amount received for the option from income for that year. This amended return must be filed by the time the return for the year, in which the option was exercised, must be filed. The purchaser of the property must add the cost of the option held to the cost of the property acquired when the option was exercised. ITA: 49(3) ITA: 49(4)

For example, in Year 1, Jim pays $10,000 to Bill for an option to acquire his shares in Opco Inc. for $500,000. Bill will report the $10,000 as proceeds of disposition, but, since there isn't any cost base for the option, this will be a capital gain to Bill in Year 1. Jim owns the option with a cost base of $10,000. In Year 2, Jim exercises the option and pays Bill $500,000 for his shares of Opco Inc. Jim's cost base on these shares is $510,000, being the cost of the shares plus the cost of the option. Bill will have proceeds of disposition of $510,000 from the sale of his shares. He will then amend his return for Year 1 and take out the capital gain of $10,000 that he reported then.

	Jim	**Bill**
On grant	Pays $10,000	Receives $10,000
	Cost of option $10,000	Capital gain of $10,000
On exercise	Cost of $500,000	Proceeds of $500,000
	Plus cost of option = $510,000	Plus option proceeds = $510,000
		Amended Year 1 return

¶7,354 Put option

If an option to sell property (i.e., a put option) is exercised, the rules are similar to those for the exercise of a call option. Note, however, that the grantor of a put option is the purchaser of the property on exercise of the option and will have been paid an amount by the vendor of the underlying property. The granting of the option and its exercise are deemed not to be a disposition of property. The vendor of the optioned property, who paid for the right to "put" or sell the property to the purchaser of the optional property, must deduct the amount paid for the option from proceeds of disposition of the property sold. The purchaser of the optioned property must deduct the amount received for the put option from the cost of the property acquired. The grantor of the option (i.e., the purchaser of the property in this case) can file an amended return for the year in which the amount received for the option was included in income and to exclude the amount received for the option from income in the year of the grant. ITA: 49(3), 49(3.1) ITA: 49(4)

For example, in Year 1, Don pays $15,000 to Bruce for the right to sell 1,000 of Holdco Inc. shares to Bruce for $300,000 at any time in the next three years. In Year 1, Bruce will report the $15,000 as proceeds of disposition, but, since there isn't any cost base for the option, this will be a capital gain to Bruce in Year 1. Don owns the option with a cost base of $15,000. In Year 2, Don exercises the option and Bruce pays Don $300,000 for Don's shares of Holdco Inc. Don's proceeds of $300,000 can be reduced by the $15,000 cost of the option to reflect the actual proceeds on the sale. Bruce's cost base on these shares is $285,000, being the cost of the shares less the proceeds he received for the option. Bruce will then amend his return for Year 1 and take out the capital gain of $15,000 that he reported then. Thus, the proceeds of $15,000 can offset the cost of $300,000 to reflect the actual cost, after amending Bruce's Year 1 return.

	Don	**Bruce**
On grant	Pays $15,000	Receives $15,000
	Cost of option $15,000	Capital gain of $15,000
On exercise	Proceeds $300,000	Cost $300,000
	Less cost of option = $285,000	Less proceeds received = $285,000
		Amended Year 1 return

¶7,356 Summary

The basic rules for the taxation of options as capital property are summarized in Exhibit 7-1.

EXHIBIT 7-1
Basic Rules for Taxation of Options as Capital Property

	Option to buy property (Call)		**Option to sell property (Put)**	
Event	**Grantor (Seller)**	**Grantee (Buyer)**	**Grantor (Buyer)**	**Grantee (Seller)**
Option granted	• Amount received for option included as capital gain	• Amount paid for option is ACB of option	• Amount received for option included as capital gain	• Amount paid for option is ACB of option
Option exercised	• Amount received for option added to proceeds of underlying property sold	• Amount paid for option added to ACB of underlying property purchased	• Amount received for option deducted from cost of underlying property purchased	• Amount paid for option deducted from proceeds of underlying property sold
	• File amended return (if necessary) for year option granted to remove capital gain from income		• File amended return (if necessary) for year option granted to remove capital gain from income	
Option expired	• No change in tax position	• Amount paid for option realized as a capital loss	• No change in tax position	• Amount paid for option realized as a capital loss

Example Problem 7-12

Ms. Smart owned a capital property that had an adjusted cost base of $100,000. In 2011, she granted Mr. Li an option to buy the property from her by the end of 2013 at an option price of $160,000. Mr. Li paid $16,000 to Ms. Smart for the option.

— REQUIRED

(A) What are the income tax implications to Ms. Smart and Mr. Li in 2011?

(B) What are the income tax implications to Ms. Smart and Mr. Li in 2013 if:

(i) the call option expires?

(ii) the call option is exercised?

— SOLUTION

(A) In 2011, Ms. Smart has granted a call option with an adjusted cost base of nil and proceeds of disposition of $16,000. On this disposition, she must report a capital gain of

$16,000 in 2011. Mr. Li has acquired a capital property in the option with an adjusted cost base of $16,000.

(B)(i) If the option expires at the end of 2013 because Mr. Li chooses not to exercise it and acquire the capital property, then there are no further tax implications to Ms. Smart. She has already included the capital gain in 2011 on granting the option and she retains the capital property with an adjusted cost base of $100,000. In 2013, Mr. Li has a capital loss of $16,000, since the option held at that cost has become worthless on expiration. Of course, that capital loss can only be applied to a capital gain in the current year, 2013, the three preceding years, 2010, 2011, and 2012, or any year subsequent to 2013.

(ii) If the call option is exercised in 2013 and Mr. Li acquires the property for $160,000, then Ms. Smart can file an amended return for 2011 to remove the $16,000 capital gain from her income in that year. However, her proceeds of disposition on the sale in 2013 will amount to the $160,000 received as the agreed price under the option plus the $16,000 received for the option in 2011. Thus, she will report in 2013 a capital gain of $76,000 (i.e., $160,000 + $16,000 − $100,000). Mr. Li will have acquired the property which will have an adjusted cost base of $176,000 (i.e., $160,000 + $16,000).

¶7,360 Convertible Properties

Where a taxpayer acquires shares from a corporation on the conversion of a convertible security, referred to as a convertible property, the exchange is deemed not to have been a disposition of property. The cost to the taxpayer of the shares received is deemed to be the adjusted cost base to him or her of the convertible property immediately before the exchange. There is a further condition in this rollover provision that the taxpayer must not have received any consideration (such as cash) other than shares in exchange for his or her convertible property. ITA: 51

Consider, as an example, a convertible debenture acquired at face value of $100. The conversion privilege entitles the holder to five common shares. If the privilege is exercised, the taxpayer is deemed to have acquired the new shares at $20 each ($100/5). If the fair market value of the shares is $30 each, the taxpayer has effectively deferred recognition of a $50 per bond or a $10 per share capital gain.

¶7,370 Capital Gains Deferral

An individual is permitted to defer the recognition of a capital gain in respect of certain small business investments. To obtain the deferral, the proceeds from the sale of the small business investment must be used to acquire other small business investments. The deferred gain on the old investments will reduce the ACB of the new investments, which is similar to the treatment of replacement property discussed in Chapter 8. ITA: 44.1(2)

The following are some of the considerations:

- The individual can establish a permitted deferral less than the maximum amount available by designating a lesser amount of replacement shares.
- The permitted deferral is the amount of a capital gain from the disposition that can be deferred. It reduces the gain of the individual for the disposition.
- A "permitted deferral" of an individual is calculated using the formula

$(G/H) \times I$ where

G is the lesser of the individual's proceeds of disposition from the old small business investment and the cost to the individual of a replacement share;

H is the individual's proceeds of disposition from the old small business investment; and

I is the individual's capital gain from the old small business investment.

- A qualifying disposition of an individual is a disposition of common shares of the capital stock of a corporation owned by the individual where each such share was:
  - — an eligible small business corporation share of the individual,
  - — a common share of the capital stock of an active business corporation throughout the time it was owned by the individual, and
  - — owned by the individual throughout the 185-day period that ended immediately before the disposition.
- The active business of the corporation has to be carried on primarily in Canada at all times in the period that began when the individual last acquired the share and ended when the disposition occurred (the "ownership period"), if that period is less than 730 days. In any other case that active business has to be carried on primarily in Canada for at least 730 days during the ownership period. ITA: 44.1(9)
- The term "eligible small business corporation" is relevant for the purposes of the term "eligible small business corporation share". An eligible small business corporation, at a particular time, means a Canadian-controlled private corporation all or substantially all of the fair market value of the assets of which is, at that time, attributable to assets of the corporation that are
  - — assets used principally in an active business carried on primarily in Canada by the corporation or an eligible small business corporation related to it,
  - — shares of or debt issued by other eligible small business corporations related to the corporation, or
  - — a combination of those two types of assets.

An asset of the corporation that is a share or a debt issued by a related corporation is deemed to have a carrying value of nil.

An "eligible small business corporation share" of an individual is a common share issued by a corporation to the individual where:

- at the time the share is issued, the corporation was an "eligible small business corporation" (see above) and immediately before, and
- after that time the total carrying value of its assets and the assets of corporations related to it does not exceed $50 million.

Example Problem 7-13

Jennifer S. Lee disposes of shares of corporation A with an adjusted cost base of $3 million for proceeds of disposition of $4.5 million. Jennifer immediately purchases replacement shares in corporations B with a cost of $2.2 million and in corporation C with a cost of $2.3 million. All shares are eligible small business corporation shares.

— *REQUIRED*

Compute the capital gain, after the deferral, on the disposition of the shares of corporation A and the ACB of the replacement shares in corporations B and C.

— *SOLUTION*

Jennifer's capital gain without the deferral would be calculated as:

Capital gain otherwise determined:	
Proceeds	$4,500,000
ACB	3,000,000
Capital gain	$1,500,000
Permitted deferral:	
G/H × I = $4,500,000/$4,500,000 × $1,500,000 =	$1,500,000

G = lesser of:	
1. Proceeds of disposition =	$4,500,000
2. Cost of replacement shares =	$4,500,000
H = Proceeds of disposition =	$4,500,000
I = Capital gain =	$1,500,000

Jennifer's capital gain that will be reported is calculated as follows:

Capital gain otherwise determined	$1,500,000
Less: Permitted deferral	1,500,000
Capital gain	$ Nil

The ACB reduction is determined by the formula D × (E/F) found in the definition of the reduction, and is applied as follows:: ITA: 44.1(1)

Corporation B: $1,500,000 × ($2,200,000/$4,500,000) =	$ 733,333
Corporation C: $1,500,000 × ($2,300,000/$4,500,000) =	$ 766,667

Note that the sum of the ACB reductions is $1.5 million, which is equal to the total capital gain deferred.

The adjusted cost base of the replacement shares is, therefore:

Corporation B: $2,2000,000 – $733,333 =	$1,466,667
Corporation C: $2,300,000 – $766,667 =	$1,533,333

Note that the sum of these ACBs is $3 million, which is actual cost net of the permitted deferral.

¶7,380 Certain Shares Deemed to be Capital Property

Where a person disposes of all or substantially all of the assets used in an active business to a corporation, the shares received in consideration are capital property of that person. This provision allows a person to transfer business assets to a corporation in exchange for shares, then sell the shares and have the gain or loss treated as a capital gain or loss. It should be noted that the definition of "business" for purposes of this provision does not include an adventure or concern in the nature of trade. As a result, it must be an ongoing business that is transferred, not just a trading asset.

ITA: 248(1) "business"
ITA: 54.2

¶7,400 NON-ARM'S LENGTH TRANSFERS AND THE ATTRIBUTION RULES REVISITED

¶7,410 Non-Arm's Length Transfers

¶7,415 Who does not deal at arm's length?

The non-arm's length transfer rules are designed to prevent tax avoidance in certain transactions between persons not dealing at arm's length. The term "arm's length" is defined by providing that related persons are deemed not to deal with each other at arm's length. A taxpayer (or anyone not dealing at arm's length with the taxpayer) and an *inter vivos* or testamentary trust cannot deal at arm's length, if the taxpayer is an income or capital beneficiary of the trust.

ITA: 69(1)
ITA: 251(1)(*a*)
ITA: 251(1)(*b*)

It is a question of fact whether persons not related to each other are dealing with each other at arm's length. The CRA sets out in an Interpretation Bulletin the following criteria, which have generally been used by the courts to determine whether a transaction has occurred at arm's length: ITA: 251(1)(*c*) IT-419R2

- was there a common mind which directs the bargaining for both parties to a transaction?
- were the parties to a transaction acting in concert without separate interests?

and

- was there "*de facto*" control?

Refer to paragraphs 24 and 25 of the bulletin for more details on these points. These conditions may arise in dealings between business partners or close friends.[4]

Summary
Who Does Not Deal at Arm's Length?
Subsection 251(1)

1. Related persons.
2. A beneficiary, or anyone not dealing at arm's length with the beneficiary, and the *inter vivos* or testamentary trust.
3. It is a question of fact.

Related persons are further defined in terms of individuals and corporations. Related individuals are those connected by blood, marriage or adoption and these connections are further specified. A schematic diagram of related individuals under the Act was presented in Chapter 6 as Exhibit 6-1. Non-arm's length relationships between persons and corporations require control, either by one person or a group of related persons. Control in this situation means control of more than 50% of the voting shares. The concept of control is expanded in situations involving related groups and in the case of a person holding certain options. The subsection also indicates that a person is deemed to be related to himself or herself in cases where the person owns shares in two or more corporations. Remember that the word "person" is defined to include a corporation such that two corporations can be related. Furthermore, two corporations are related if they meet one of the six conditions set out in the Act. ITA: 251(2), 251(2)(*b*), 251(6); IT-419R2, par. 11 ITA: 251(5) ITA: 248(1) ITA: 251(2)(*c*)

¶7,420 Transactions with non-arm's length individuals

¶7,420.10 *Overview*

Normally, the market forces of demand and supply will place the value of a transaction at fair market value. However, non-arm's length transactions may not reflect a normal transaction driven by the market forces. For that reason, the Act deems related persons not to deal at arm's length with each other. In addition, it is a question of fact whether unrelated persons deal with each other at arm's length. ITA: 251(1)(*a*) ITA: 251(1)(*c*)

When a taxpayer enters into a transaction with a related party (non-arm's length person) or with an unrelated party in which the transaction is considered not to be at arm's length, special rules apply to prevent the elimination or reduction of tax by selling at a price other than the fair market value. ITA: 69

¶7,420.20 *Conceptual illustration*

Assume that Mr. A owns a property with a fair market value of $10,000 and that he originally paid $5,000 for that property. He decides to sell the property to his daughter, who is under 18, for $8,000. Note that this price is lower than the fair market value (FMV).

[4] In the case of *Grant et al. v. M.N.R.*, 87 DTC 16, the Tax Court of Canada describes in some detail the factors to be taken into account in determining whether unrelated persons are not dealing at arm's length.

Tax consequence to Mr. A:

	Sale at $8,000	Sale at $10,000
Deemed proceeds of sales (FMV)	$10,000	$10,000
Cost base (original payment)	(5,000)	(5,000)
Gain	$5,000	$5,000

If Mr. A's daughter sells the property immediately at $10,000 (FMV), she will have to recognize a gain of:

	Sale at $8,000	Sale at $10,000
Proceeds of sales	$10,000	$10,000
Cost base (amount she paid)	(8,000)	(10,000)
Gain	$2,000	Nil

Total gain from the transaction:

	Sale at $8,000	Sale at $10,000
Mr. A	$5,000	$5,000
Daughter	2,000	Nil
Total	$7,000	$5,000

If Mr. A sold the property to his daughter at fair market value, the total gain will be $5,000. Since the related party did not use fair market value as consideration, a total gain of $7,000 is subject to tax which means that the $2,000 gain is taxed twice. These special anti-avoidance rules in the Act penalize taxpayers who enter into transactions which are not at fair market value. ITA: 69

A penalty similar to the above also occurs when the selling price is higher than the fair market value.

¶7,420.30 *The technical rules*

Generally, in situations involving the non-arm's length transfer of anything, including both tangible and intangible property, the transferor is deemed to receive proceeds equal to its fair market value at the time of the transfer, if the actual transfer price is less than fair market value. This rule would include gifts for no proceeds. Note, however, that no downward adjustment is made to the actual price received if it is more than fair market value. On the other side, the transferee is deemed to have acquired property at a cost equal to its fair market value at the time of the transfer if he or she paid more than fair market value or if he or she received it as a gift, bequest or inheritance, but not if he or she paid less than fair market value. In the case of a payment of less than fair market value, no adjustment is made to the actual price paid. There are exceptions to these rules on the transfer of such property to a spouse under certain conditions.

As mentioned previously, non-arm's length transfers, for a price either greater than or less than fair market value, can involve a one-sided adjustment to the transfer price. This can be more easily seen in Exhibit 7-2. Where the amount is in excess of fair market value only the purchaser is deemed to have transacted at fair market value with the seller having received proceeds at the higher price. Thus, the seller may have income or a capital gain on the transaction and the purchaser may ultimately have to include a similar amount of income or capital gain on disposition. Where the amount is less than fair market value, but the transfer is not a gift, the seller is deemed to have received proceeds equal to fair market value while there is no adjustment made to the actual price paid by the purchaser. Again, the seller may have income or a capital gain on the transaction and the purchaser may ultimately have to include a similar amount of income or capital gain on disposition. In this case, a gift would be better since both the transferor and the transferee are deemed to have made the transfer at fair market value and no double-counting will result.

EXHIBIT 7-2
Consideration in Gifts and Non-Arm's Length Transfers

Non-arm's length transfer	*Seller or transferor*	*Purchaser or transferee*
Proceeds greater than fair market value	no adjustment to actual proceeds received	deemed acquisition at fair market value [par. 69(1)(*a*)]
Proceeds less than fair market value	deemed proceeds at fair market value [par. 69(1)(*b*)]	no adjustment to actual amount paid
Gift, bequest, or inheritance	deemed proceeds at fair market value [par. 69(1)(*b*)*]	deemed acquisition at fair market value [par. 69(1)(*c*)*]

* Note that these fair market value rules apply to gifts even at arm's length.

¶7,430 Attribution Rules

¶7,435 Capital gains on spousal transfers or loans

In Chapter 6, the attribution rules, relating to income from property only, were discussed for transfers and loans. Capital gains and losses are also similarly attributed back, but only to the transferor spouse or common-law partner for all transfers (i.e., gifts and sales) or for loans. Included in capital gains or losses attributed to a spouse or common-law partner are capital gains or losses on reinvested capital gains or losses or other previously attributed income from property. A careful reading of these attribution provisions and the concept of "substituted property" indicates that these gains or losses continue to be subject to attribution. Hence, there is no exemption from attribution for "second-generation" capital gains or losses, unlike the exemption for "second-generation" income from property. ITA: 74.2(1)

"Common-law partner" is defined as "a person who cohabits . . . in a conjugal relationship with the taxpayer . . . for a continuous period of at least one year". ITA: 248(1)

Capital gains and losses arising from transfers and loans to related and deemed related minors do not result in attribution to the transferor (except for *inter vivos* transfers of farming property which is tax-deferred by a rollover and beyond the scope of this text). A series of anti-avoidance provisions apply attribution to transactions such as: ITA: 75.1

- back-to-back loans and transfers to third parties, ITA: 74.5(6)
- repayment of loan through additional transfers and loans, ITA: 74.1(3)
- loan guarantees for all or part of the principal and/or interest, or ITA: 74.5(7)
- artificial transactions which use the attribution rules to the taxpayer's advantage. ITA: 74.5(11)

¶7,435.10 *Interspousal rollover*

The interspousal rollover rule has the effect of deferring any accrued gains on transfers between spouses or common-law partners. The deferral occurs because the transferor is automatically deemed to have transferred the property at proceeds exactly equal to his or her adjusted cost base immediately prior to the transfer. Note here that the transfer is an actual transaction which must be reported, even though the gain is nil. The transferee spouse, or common-law partner, will have an adjusted cost base exactly equal to the deemed proceeds of disposition at the time of transfer (the transferor spouse's, or common-law partner's, adjusted cost base). When the transferee spouse, or common-law partner, disposes of the property, the gain or loss will be attributed back to the transferor spouse, or common-law partner, as long as they are married or in a common-law relationship. ITA: 73

¶7,435.20 *Breakdown of relationship*

The provision which pertains to the attribution of capital gains, continues to apply to spouses, or common-law partners, living apart by reason of a breakdown of their marriage or common-law relationship. In this situation, however, when both spouses or common-law partners have jointly elected, capital gains attribution does not apply. The election must be filed with the tax return of the transferor spouse or common-law partner in any year ending after the separation occurs. Note that this provision is much harsher than the attribution relieving provision for income from property which does not require that an election be filed. ITA: 74.5(3)(*b*) ITA: 74.5(3)(*b*) IT-511R, par. 20 ITA: 74.5(3)(*a*)

¶7,435.30 *Elect out of interspousal rollover*

Alternatively, the transferor spouse or common-law partner can elect not to have interspousal rollover apply and the normal non-arm's length rules apply under section 69 as previously discussed. Hence, the property will be deemed to have been disposed of at the fair market value at the date of transfer. There would be no capital gains attribution on subsequent dispositions of transferred property, as long as consideration equal to the fair market value of the property transferred was received by the transferor and the taxpayer elected not to use the interspousal rollover. If the consideration included a loan, then the interest rate must be on a commercial basis (the lesser of the prescribed rate at the time the loan was made and the non-arm's length rate as determined by the marketplace) and the accrued interest must be actually paid no later than 30 days after each and every December 31 that the loan is outstanding. ITA: 73(1) ITA: 74.5(1)(*a*), 74.5(1)(*c*) ITA: 74.5(1)(*b*)

If the property is sold to a spouse or common-law partner at less than the fair market value and the taxpayer elects not to use the interspousal rollover, there would be a double penalty.

- First, the attribution rules would apply to both income and capital gains, since the fair market value of the property transferred and the consideration received are not equal. ITA: 74.5(1)(*a*)
- Second, the adjusted cost base of transferred property would be the actual price paid by the acquiring spouse and not the deemed proceeds of disposition of the transferor spouse since the adjustment to fair market value is one-sided. Hence, the avoided capital gain would be taxed twice. ITA: 69(1)(*c*)

If, however, the transfer had been a gift, then both the proceeds and the adjusted cost base would be bumped to the fair market value. Again, the attribution of future income and capital gain would not have been avoided, however, since no consideration was received. ITA: 69(1)(*b*)(ii), 69(1)(*c*)

¶7,440 Recapture

In order to prevent the avoidance of recapture on the transfer of depreciable property between spouses, the following additional rules apply. When the undepreciated capital cost is less than the capital cost to the transferor, then for purposes of capital cost allowance computations: ITA: 73(2)

(a) the capital cost to the transferee is deemed to be the capital cost to the transferor; and

(b) the difference between the capital cost and the deemed capital cost to the spouse will be treated as a capital cost allowance taken by the transferee.

¶7,445 Summary of provisions

Summary
Avoiding Income Attribution
on Transferred Property

Subsection 74.5(1) — Fair Market Value Transfer

1. Fair market value consideration must be received by the vendor.
2. If part of the consideration is debt then interest must be charged at the prescribed rate and always paid by January 30 of the following year.
3. If it is a transfer to a spouse or common-law partner, then they must elect out of the interspousal rollover.

Subsection 74.5(3) — Relationship Breakdown

4. The spouses or common-law partners are living separate and apart by reason of the breakdown of their relationship.

Exhibit 7-3 expands the exhibit on property income attribution rules introduced in Chapter 6 to include the application of the capital gains attribution rules discussed in this chapter. Exhibit 7-4 summarizes the rules pertaining to minors and other non-arm's length persons.

EXHIBIT 7-3
Transfers or Loans of Property to Spouse or Common-law Partner
Conceptual Summary

(A) Proceeds and Cost on Transfer

Transaction		*Transferor's proceeds*	*Transferee's cost*
(1) gift	• no election out of inter-spousal rollover*	Transferor's ACB/UCC	Transferor's ACB/UCC
	• elect not to have rollover	FMV [par. 69(1)(*b*)]	FMV [par. 69(1)(*c*)]
(2) sale	• no election out of inter-spousal rollover	Transferor's ACB/UCC	Transferor's ACB/UCC
	• elect not to have rollover	greater of: • actual proceeds • FMV [ssec. 69(1)]	Lesser of: • actual cost • FMV [ssec. 69(1)]

(B) Attribution of Income and Capital Gains

	Business income	*Property income***	*Capital gains****
On transferred or loaned property and substituted property****	n/a	Attributed [ssec. 74.1(1)]	Attributed [sec. 74.2]

However, neither property income nor capital gains are attributed if the following two conditions are met:

(1) fair market consideration is received,***** and

(2) the election out of the interspousal rollover is used.

* The interspousal rollover applies *automatically* on a transfer of property between spouses or common-law partners at the ACB of the property; that is, the transferor spouse or common-law partner is deemed to have received proceeds of disposition equal to ACB and the transferee spouse or common-law partner is deemed to have acquired the property at the same ACB. However, the provision contains an election that allows the spouses or common-law partners not to have the rollover apply, in which case the normal non-arm's length rules apply to the transaction which will be considered to have taken place at fair market value.

** Including losses but excluding second-generation income from property.

*** Including capital losses and including second-generation capital gains (losses) after December 31, 1987.

**** Substituted property is defined in subsection 248(5).

***** To avoid attribution, the taxpayer must elect to waive the deferral of accrued income afforded by the interspousal rollover and must transfer for fair market value consideration. Where a loan is involved, interest must be paid within 30 days of the end of every year in which the loan is outstanding.

EXHIBIT 7-4
Transfers or Loans of Property to Minors and Other Non-arm's Length Individuals
Conceptual Summary

(A) Proceeds and Cost on Transfer

	Transferor's proceeds	*Transferee's cost*
(1) gift	FMV [par. 69(1)(*b*)]	FMV [par. 69(1)(*c*)]
(2) sale	greater of: • actual proceeds • FMV [ssec. 69(1)]	Lesser of: • actual cost • FMV [ssec. 69(1)]

(B) Attribution of Income and Capital Gains

	Business income	*Property income**	*Capital gains*
Minors** who are not at arm's length (generally, related) or who are nieces and nephews • on transferred*** or loaned property and substituted property****	n/a	Attributed [ssec. 74.1(2)]	n/a
Other non-arm's length individuals not subject to section 74.1 • only on loaned property if one of the main reasons for the loan was to reduce or avoid tax	n/a	Attributed [ssec. 56(4.1)]	n/a

* Including losses but excluding second-generation income from property.

** An income-splitting tax applies at the top marginal tax rate on dividends or shareholder benefits received by minors from private corporations and certain income from a partnership or trust. (See Chapter 6 for a discussion of this provision.) Income that is subject to the income-splitting tax is not be subject to the attribution rules.

*** To avoid attribution the taxpayer must transfer for fair market value consideration. Where a loan is involved, interest must be paid within 30 days of the end of the year in which the loan is outstanding.

**** Substituted property is defined in subsection 248(5).

¶7,500 DEATH OF A TAXPAYER

¶7,510 Deemed Disposition on Death

Capital gains may be triggered upon the death of a taxpayer depending on the status of the beneficiaries and the type of assets transferred. Death is the final opportunity to tax unrealized gains that have accrued to the taxpayer. Generally, the taxpayer is deemed to have disposed of all his or her capital assets at their fair market value as at the date of his or her death. ITA: 70(5)(*a*)

In respect of non-depreciable capital assets transferred on death to a spouse, the basic rules are similar to those on transfer between living spouses. The deceased is deemed to have disposed of the assets at his or her adjusted cost base and the surviving spouse or common-law partner assumes that cost base. Hence, no capital gain or recapture will be triggered unless the estate so elects not to have the interspousal rollover on death apply, or until the surviving spouse or common-law partner disposes of the assets. ITA: 70(6), 73 ITA: 70(6.2) IT-305R4

Depreciable property received by a beneficiary, other than a spouse or common-law partner, is also deemed to be disposed of at fair market value at the date of death. Any resulting capital gain or recapture would be included on the deceased's final return. The beneficiary's deemed cost would be the fair market value of the property received. However, if the fair market value was less than the original cost, then the beneficiary's cost would be the deceased's cost and the excess of cost over fair market value would be deemed to have been taken as CCA. As a result, the beneficiary's UCC is the fair market value. Where a spouse or common-law partner is the beneficiary of depreciable property and where no election out of the rollover has been filed, the proceeds of disposition are deemed to be the undepreciated capital cost prorated on a capital cost basis. ITA: 70(5)(*a*) ITA: 70(6.2)

If a beneficiary inherits property from a deceased person who is not the beneficiary's spouse, then the beneficiary will have a cost base on this inherited property equal to the fair market value at the time of death. This will then be equal to the deemed proceeds to the deceased on his or her final return.

Chapter 14 discusses, in some detail, the various filing alternatives available upon death of a taxpayer.

¶7,600 LEAVING AND ENTERING CANADA

Tax rules for taxpayers who become or cease to be resident in Canada are provided by the Act. When a taxpayer ceases to be a resident of Canada, all of that person's capital property is deemed to have been disposed of at its fair market value. Such capital property would consist of shares, including shares of private corporations, bonds, real estate outside Canada, boats, recreational vehicles and automobiles, among others. Where the taxpayer is an individual, the following properties, generally, those that would be subject to Canadian tax in the hands of a non-resident, are exempted from the deemed disposition: ITA: 128.1 ITA: 128.1(4)

(a) Property that can be described, conceptually, as:

- Canadian property that is not very movable, such as real property or capital property used in a business carried on through a permanent establishment in Canada, or
- Canadian property that is not very liquid or marketable, such as employment-related stock options.

The taxpayer will continue to be liable for tax on the disposition of such property, but as a non-resident. However, the taxpayer may elect not to have this exemption apply so that capital gains (losses) are triggered to offset other capital losses (gains). ITA: 2(3)

(b) Property of a business carried on by the individual in Canada. Income from such property, including capital property, eligible capital property and property described in the inventory of the business, will be taxable as business income earned by a non-resident. ITA: 2(3)

(c) The right to receive certain payments such as pension payments and other retirement benefits, including rights under RRSPs, RPPs and DPSPs, or a right under a registered education savings plan on which the taxpayer will be liable for withholding tax.

A taxpayer is prevented from triggering only allowable capital losses while protecting potential taxable capital gains through the available elections previously described. In this situation, losses, except listed personal property losses, are restricted to the taxable capital gains actually triggered by the deemed disposition. ITA: 128.1(4)

The Act provides an exception in the case of a short-term resident of Canada. The tax on departure does not apply to capital property which an individual owned on last becoming a resident of Canada, if he or she resided in Canada for 60 months or less during the 10 years preceding his or her departure. Under these conditions, he or she will be exempt from the deemed disposition on any property, which he or she brought with him or her and took away again. Also exempt is property acquired by inheritance or bequest after the individual last became resident in Canada. However, the taxpayer will still be subject to the rules of this section on other property he or she acquired while he or she was resident in Canada. ITA: 128.1(4)

To set the cost of property for a person entering Canada such that the taxpayer is taxed only on gains subsequent to his or her entry, the Act provides that where a taxpayer becomes a Canadian resident, he or she is deemed to have acquired all of his or her property other than taxable Canadian property and inventory or eligible capital property of a business carried on in Canada at its fair market value at the time. ITA: 128.1(1)

¶7,700 COMPUTATIONAL RULES

¶7,710 Section 3 Revisited

In Chapter 1, Exhibit 1-3 showed a picture of how section 3 is organized. Now that several technical components have been examined, the carryover rules contained in section 3 will be highlighted.

Paragraph 3(*a*) includes the aggregate of all income from each non-capital source: property, business, office and employment, plus the other non-capital sources of income found in Subdivision d of Division B which is examined in Chapter 9. The amount determined for each source must be a positive amount (i.e., losses or an excess of deductions over inclusions from a particular source are not considered here).

Paragraph 3(*b*) deals with taxable capital gains and allowable capital losses, and is composed of the excess of:

(1) all taxable capital gains, excluding those from LPPs

plus

(2) listed personal property taxable net gains discussed previously ITA: 41(2)

minus

(3) allowable capital losses, except for

(i) LPP losses, and

(ii) allowable business investment losses (ABILs).

Paragraph 3(*c*) adds together paragraphs 3(*a*) and (*b*) and subtracts Subdivision e deductions such as moving expenses, alimony, RRSPs, etc. All of these topics will be covered in Chapter 9.

Paragraph 3(*d*) subtracts various types of losses from any excess amount calculated in paragraph 3(*c*). The losses deducted are from the following sources:

(1) office, employment, business and property (i.e., losses from non-capital sources), and

(2) ABILs.

Note the special treatment accorded to ABILs. Normally, allowable capital losses can only be claimed against taxable capital gains. However, ABILs have no such restriction and, hence, are deducted along with other losses from non-capital sources (e.g., losses from business and property). Deducting ABILs, effectively, against all sources of income, rather than only against net taxable capital gains may result in a more rapid deduction of ABILs, which is the intent of the ABIL investment incentive. As a capital loss, however, ABILs are still only ½ deductible. ITA: 3(*b*) ITA: 3(*d*)

¶7,720 Allowable Business Investment Losses

The definition of a "business investment loss" includes capital losses arising from the disposition of shares and debts of a small business corporation. ITA: 39(1)(*c*)

¶7,720.10 *Small Business Corporation (SBC)*

An SBC is generally defined to be a Canadian-controlled private corporation, where all or substantially all of the fair market value of the assets were, at that time, used principally in an active business carried on primarily in Canada. Assets would include the shares of SBCs which were connected to the holding corporation. (The concept of a "connected" corporation is discussed in Chapter 12.) For the purposes of a business investment loss only, an SBC which ceases to meet the conditions in the definition of an SBC will still be considered as an SBC if at any time in the 12 months preceding the disposition it met the conditions in the definition of an SBC. ITA: 248(1) ITA: 186(4) ITA: 39(1)(*c*)

¶7,720.20 *Terminology*

Since business investment losses (BILs) are really only a subset of capital losses, allowable business investment losses (ABILs) for a particular year are determined by the same inclusion rates as allowable capital losses as shown in ¶7,010.

100%	50%
Business Investment Loss	Allowable Business Investment Loss

¶7,720.30 *Disposition*

A business investment loss must arise from a disposition of shares or debt of a small business corporation where:

(1) The disposition of the shares or debt is to an arms length person,

(2) The debt has become a bad debt in the year, or

(3) For shares not actually disposed of, the company has become bankrupt during the year, is in the process of winding up or is insolvent, has no value, and has ceased to carry on business.

¶7,720.40 *Disallowed Portion*

A portion of a BIL, equal to an amount of capital gains that has previously benefited from a capital gains deduction, is disallowed. The capital gains deduction referred to is either a past claim for the general capital gains deduction that was eliminated or the continuing capital gains deduction for shares of a qualified small business corporation or qualified farm property. This disallowed portion reduces the BIL and resultant ABIL, for purposes of the deduction under paragraph 3(*d*). In effect, an individual cannot obtain a benefit of the capital gains deduction on capital gains that are not offset by capital losses in the form of BILs, at the same time as he or she obtains a benefit from ABILs which offset non-capital sources of income under paragraph 3(*d*). A fraction (see above chart) of the disallowed BIL reverts to an allowable capital loss for the year realized. This allowable capital loss will possibly offset taxable capital gains which will not be available for the capital gains deduction, as a result. ITA: 39(9)

The portion of a BIL that is disallowed is computed as the lesser of: ITA: 39(9)

(a) the BIL for the year (before deducting the disallowed portion)	$xxxx
(b) the cumulative capital gains deduction claimed in previous years × a factor (the factor is 2 for years prior to 1988, 3/2 for 1988 and 1989, 4/3 for 1990 to February 27, 2000, 3/2 for February 28, 2000 to October 17, 2000 and 2 after October 17, 2000 to adjust the capital gains deduction to a full capital gain amount which is parallel with the full BIL amount)	$xxxx
minus: the cumulative disallowed portion of BILs in preceding years	(xxxx)
	$xxxx

Note that part (a) above uses the full business investment loss (not the fractional allowable business investment loss). However, the capital gains *deduction* is a fractional amount. Therefore, to make parts (a) and (b) comparable, the capital gains deduction must be adjusted to convert the deduction to a full amount of gain that has been exempted. Hence, multiplying a 1999 capital gains deduction, for example, by 4/3 adjusts the 3/4 fractional amount to the required full amount (i.e., $4/3 \times 3/4 = 1$).

¶7,720.50 *Non-Capital Loss*

Any portion of the ABIL (i.e., an amount that has not been disallowed), which is not deducted under paragraph 3(*d*), is added to the non-capital losses for the year subject to the non-capital loss carryover rules, discussed in Chapter 10 for individuals and Chapter 11 for corporations. However, if the ABIL, which was treated as a non-capital loss, is not used by the end of the 20th carryforward year, it becomes a net capital loss, in essence, reverting to its original character as an allowable capital loss, restricted by the net capital loss carryover rules. ITA: 111(8) "non-capital loss"

Figure 7-2 attempts to map the treatment of BILs under the provisions described above.

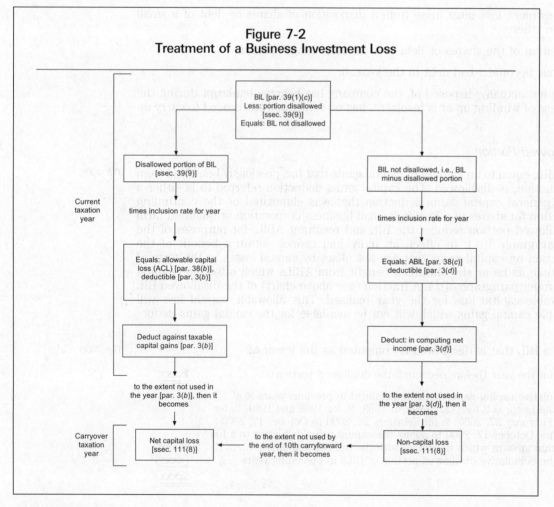

Figure 7-2
Treatment of a Business Investment Loss

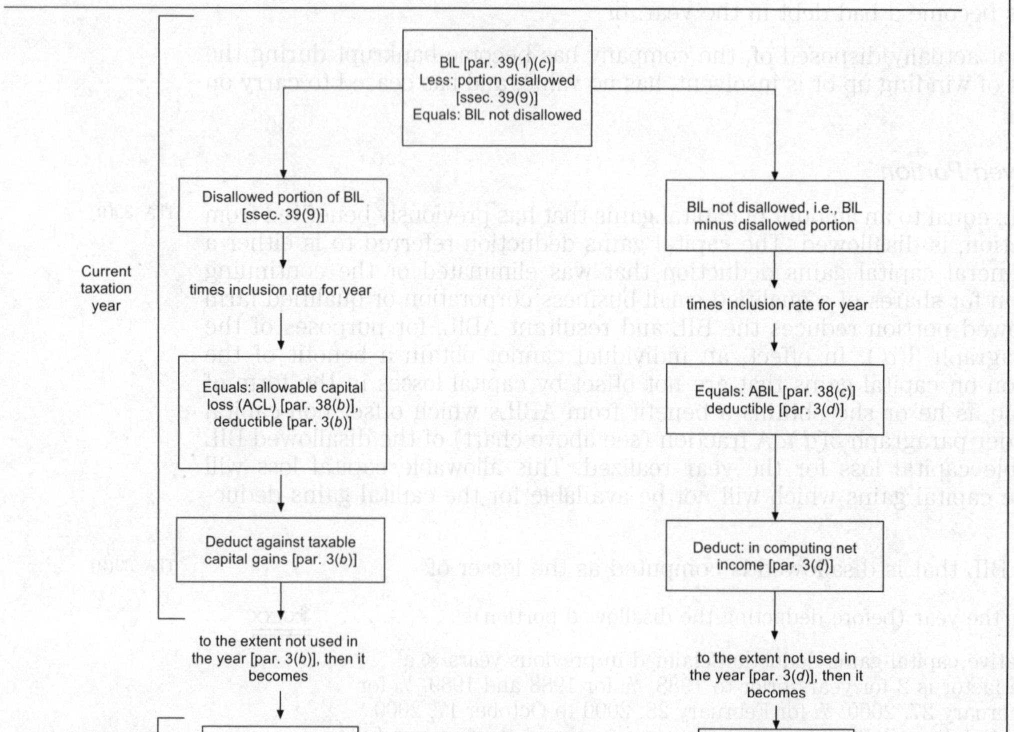

Example Problem 7-14

Andrew invested $5,000 in shares of Balance Corporation Ltd. The corporation is now bankrupt and the shares have a fair market value of nil.

— *REQUIRED*

(a) If Andrew has not claimed a capital gains deduction in previous years, what is Andrew's allowable business investment loss and what can it be deducted against in the year?

(b) If Andrew had claimed a capital gains deduction of $1,000 five years ago, what is Andrew's tax position with respect to the loss on the shares this year?

— *SOLUTION*

(a)	P of D	$ Nil
	ACB	(5,000)
	CL (Business investment loss)	$ (5,000)
	ABIL	$ (2,500)

Andrew can deduct the ABIL of $2,500 from any sources of income.

(b)	CL (above)	$ (5,000)	
	Less: disallowed BIL ($1,000 × 2)	2,000	remains a capital loss
	BIL	$ (3,000)	
	ABIL	$ (1,500)	
	ACL ($2,000 × ½)	$ (1,000)	

While the ABIL of $1,500 can be deducted by Andrew against any source of income, the allowable capital loss of $1,000 can only be deducted against a taxable capital gain.

Example Problem 7-15

	2011	2012	2013
Employment income	$10,000	$12,000	$15,000
Business income (loss)	(25,000)	6,000	10,000
Property income (loss)	3,000	(2,000)	1,000
Capital gains (capital losses)			
LPP	2,000	(5,000)	7,000
PUP	(4,000)	8,000	2,000
Other	10,000	(17,000)*	4,000

* Includes a business investment loss of $2,000.

— *REQUIRED*

Determine the income under Division B according to section 3, after filing any necessary amended returns for each of the years indicated above. (For the purposes of this type of problem, dealing with each item, line-by-line, across the years, will help keep track of carryovers more easily than dealing with income one year at a time.)

— *SOLUTION*

		2011	2012	2013
Par. 3(*a*)	— Sum of income from non-capital sources (non-negative):			
	Employment	$ 10,000	$12,000	$15,000
	Business (no losses)	—	6,000	10,000
	Property (no losses)	3,000	—	1,000
		$ 13,000	$18,000	$26,000

Par. 3(*b*) — Sum of net taxable capital gains (non-negative):			
LPP	Nil[1]	Nil	$ 2,000[2]
PUP	Nil[3]	$ 4,000[4]	1,000[5]
Other	$ 5,000[6]	(4,000)[7]	2,000[8]
	$ 5,000	Nil	$ 5,000
Sum of par. 3(*a*) and par. 3(*b*)	$ 18,000	$18,000	$31,000
Par. 3(*d*) — Sum of losses from non-capital sources:			
Business loss	(18,000)[9]	—	—
Property loss	—	(2,000)	—
ABIL	—	(1,000)[10]	—
Income under Division B	Nil	$15,000	$31,000

— *NOTES TO SOLUTION*

[1] The $2,000 listed personal property capital gain in 2011 was offset and removed by amending the 2011 return for the 2012 loss, carried back to 2011. Note how LPP losses are carried over in their full amount, not their fractional allowable amount. Therefore, no consideration need be given to changing capital gains inclusion rates, if applicable, in the carryover period for LPPs.

[2] There was still $3,000 of the listed personal property capital loss in 2012 to be applied against the listed personal property gain in 2013, of $7,000 (($7,000 – $3,000) × ½ = $2,000).

[3] No losses are allowed on the personal-use property assets.

[4] ½ × $8,000.

[5] ½ × $2,000.

[6] ½ × $10,000.

[7] Only $4,000 of the allowable capital loss of $7,500 [½ ($17,000 – $2,000)] was applied to reduce paragraph 3(*b*) amount to nil. The remaining $3,500 will be applied to another year but under Division C, not Division B.

[8] ½ × $4,000.

[9] Only $18,000 of the business loss of $25,000 was applied to bring the income under Division B to nil. The remainder ($7,000) may be carried back three years and forward seven, but these losses are deductible in the carryover year in Division C, not Division B.

[10] The *allowable* business investment loss is $1,000 (½ × $2,000).

¶7,800 REVIEW QUESTIONS

(1) A client invested in a rental property some years ago and paid $10,000 as a down payment and $150,000 was in the form of a mortgage. Recently, the vacancy rate has climbed and the value of the property has fallen. She thinks that she will just walk away from the property and let the mortgage company take over the property. What will her proceeds of disposition be?

(2) As a result of a reorganization in a company in which Mr. Smith is a shareholder, he has just had a return of some of the corporation's capital. As a result, the adjusted cost base of his shares has become negative. This does not bother him since he has been told that as long as he continues to own the shares he will not have to recognize this built-in capital gain. Comment.

(3) Mr. Chan has come to you with a problem. He owns the family cottage and his wife owns the house in town. Both housing units were purchased after 1981. They are thinking of selling both of these properties and moving to another province. He thought they could each claim the principal residence exemption to avoid any tax but someone has told him that they can only claim one of the residences. In general terms can you explain the rules to him?

(4) Ms. Starra bought a cottage property on a lake that has since become polluted. As a result, the value of the property has declined and she has sold it, since no one wants to go there anymore. She realized a loss on the sale and wants to claim the loss on her personal return. Can she do it?

(5) What is the "$1,000 rule" as it relates to personal-use property? Does the same rule apply to listed personal property?

(6) Mr. Davids has come to you to have his personal tax return done. He sold some shares of a public corporation that he has owned for some years and wants help in minimizing his tax on the transaction. One point that is confusing him is the stock dividend that he received this year. He does not know how to treat the dividend for tax purposes. Please help him.

(7) Under Divisions B and C, what happens when the capital losses exceed the capital gains in any one year?

(8) If you were to win a Mazda MX5 in a lottery, what would the cost base be to you given that you might want to sell it to buy a car more fitting (boring) for an accountant?

(9) Ms. Dempster has had her company buy her a car and register it in her name. The CRA discovered this and has assessed her with a shareholder benefit for $35,000, the value of the car. Ms. Dempster is going to have to sell the car to pay the tax liability. What will her cost base be on the car? ITA: 15(1)

(10) On July 1 of this year, John Smith died leaving his wife and four children in financial difficulty. In order to earn extra income Mrs. Smith painted the basement, put carpet down, and then rented it to students. Comment on the tax issues.

(11) On July 1 nine years ago, Ms. Marr was transferred with her family to Victoria from Toronto by her employer, a large public company. She was sure that the value of her Toronto house would go up significantly so she kept it and rented a house in Victoria. It was this year that the same employer moved Ms. Marr and her family back to Toronto, at which time they moved back into their house. However, they found that the neighbourhood had changed significantly so they decided to sell the house and buy in another location. Discuss how much of the principal residence exemption she can claim on the sale of the Toronto home.

(12) Last year Ms. Milne inherited $5 million from her uncle's estate and is now appalled by the amount of tax that she has to pay on her interest income. She has always liked the Cayman Islands and has decided to move there permanently in order to avoid Canadian tax. Her only assets are $5 million of term deposits but she has heard that there is a lot of tax to pay on leaving the country. What do you think?

(13) Mr. Shiloh was transferred to Canada by his employer four years ago and is now being transferred back to the U.S. At the time he entered Canada he held shares in his U.S. employer which are listed on the TSX Stock Exchange. He still owns all these shares and is unhappy about all the tax he is going to have to pay on the deemed disposition. Advise him. ITA: 128.1(4)

(14) Ms. Green has been told that a good way to create a capital gain is to buy shares on the stock market and then sell someone an option to buy the shares at a price slightly higher than the current market price. Her understanding is that the proceeds on the sale of the option is a capital gain. What advice can you give her?

(15) Mr. Oats is a farmer who is fortunate enough to have farm land close to the city. Because of the prime location he has been approached to sell the land, but he is reluctant to do so since he wants to farm for the next five years. However, he is willing to sell someone an option to buy the land in five years at what he thinks is a generous price. He is to receive $50,000 for granting this option. He thinks he can defer the gain on granting the option until the year of sale by reducing the ACB of his land by $50,000. What do you think?

(16) Mr. Rollins bought a convertible debenture two years ago for $10,000 and is now in the process of converting it into common shares of the company. The debenture is convertible into 1,000 common shares. At the time of the conversion the common shares are worth $20 each. What are the tax effects of the disposition of the debenture and the acquisition of the shares?

(17) Mrs. Gleba owns 20 acres of land that have an appraised value of $100,000. She is considering selling the land to a friend for $50,000 in order to have the friend living closer to her. The two individuals are not related. What tax issues would you discuss with her?

(18) Scott was 25 years old when his father Bill gave him shares in Bell Canada as a gift. Bill had paid $1,000 for them 10 years ago and they were worth $5,000 at the time of the gift. Scott has come to you to find out how much tax he will have to pay. Discuss the tax implications to Scott and Bill of the gift.

¶7,825 MULTIPLE CHOICE QUESTIONS

Question 1

During the year, Mina sold the following personal assets, all of which she had acquired after 1971:

	Cost	*Proceeds*
Automobile	$20,000	$18,000
Boat	600	1,500
Painting	600	1,300
Jewellery	1,400	200

Her capital gain for the year from these dispositions is:

(A) $900

(B) $800

(C) $500

(D) $400

Question 2

Amanda sold her cottage for $130,000 in May 2013. The cottage cost her $50,000 in 2006 and qualifies as a principal residence. The only other principal residence that Amanda has owned during her lifetime was her Toronto home, which she owned from 2004 to 2012. Even though she sold it for $200,000 more than it cost, she did not report the gain on her 2012 tax return because it was her principal residence. What is the minimum taxable capital gain that Amanda must report on her 2013 tax return in respect of the sale of the cottage?

(A) $80,000

(B) $25,000

(C) $30,000

(D) $50,000

Question 3

Gary Chin purchased his first and only principal residence in 1996 for $350,000. The residence was in Toronto, and when he was transferred to Windsor because of a promotion to managing partner in 2007, he rented the residence. The residence was worth $550,000 in 2007 and he elected to be deemed not to have changed the use of the residence. Gary rented an apartment in Windsor with the expectation of moving back into his Toronto residence on retirement. On January 1, 2013, Gary received an unsolicited offer of $850,000 for the Toronto residence and sold it. Which of the following is a true statement? ITA: 45(2)

(A) There is no taxable capital gain to report in 2007 or 2013 in respect of the principal residence.

(B) There is no capital gain to report in 2007 in respect of the principal residence. The taxable capital gain is $13,889 in 2013 in respect of the principal residence.

(C) The taxable capital gain is $100,000 in 2007 and $150,000 in 2013 in respect of the principal residence.

(D) The taxable capital gain is $250,000 in 2013 in respect of the principal residence.

Question 4

A Canadian resident individual received a stock dividend from a public corporation of one share. The dividend is a taxable dividend. The stock dividend resulted in an increase in the paid-up capital of $4 for each share issued but the fair market value of each share is $10. Which of the following statements is correct about the stock dividend received?

(A) The cost of the stock is deemed to be $4 and the individual's net income increases by $4.

(B) The cost of the stock is deemed to be $4 and the individual's net income increases by $5.52.

(C) The cost of the stock is deemed to be $10 and the individual's net income increases by $10.

(D) The cost of the stock is deemed to be $10 and the individual's net income is deemed to be $13.80.

Question 5

Donna Jailal has provided you with the following information in connection with her income tax return for the year:

Capital Gains:

Shares	$1,600
Personal-use property	700
Listed personal property	500

Capital Losses:

Shares	$ 820
Personal-use property	1,000
Listed personal property	140

Listed personal property losses from the previous year	100

What is the minimum net taxable capital gain that she must report as Division B income for the year?

(A) $370

(B) $740

(C) $870

(D) $920

Question 6

On December 31 of this year, Ms. Y gave her 6-year-old child some common shares of a public corporation with an adjusted cost base of $900,000 and a fair market value of $1,000,000. Which one of the following statements is TRUE?

(A) The attribution rule will apply to attribute to Ms. Y any future dividends received by her child on the shares. This attribution will continue until the year in which the child becomes 18 years old.

(B) The attribution rule will apply to attribute to Ms. Y any future dividends received by her child on the shares as well as any capital gains or losses if her child sells the shares. This attribution will continue until the year in which the child turns 18 years of age.

(C) Ms. Y will report no gain or loss on the transfer of property this year because it is a gift.

(D) Ms. Y will report a $100,000 taxable capital gain on the gift this year.

Question 7

Ms. Y sells a stock (adjusted cost base $900,000) to her husband for $800,000 cash (the fair market value of the stock) and elects out of the interspousal rollover. Which one of the following statements is TRUE? ITA: 73(1)

(A) Ms. Y will report an allowable capital loss of $50,000 which she can only deduct against taxable capital gains.

(B) Ms. Y does not have a capital loss because transfers to a spouse are made for proceeds equal to adjusted cost base.

(C) Ms. Y does not have a capital loss because of the superficial loss rules.

(D) The attribution rule will apply to attribute to Ms. Y any future dividends received by her husband on the shares as well as any capital gains or losses if her husband sells the shares.

Question 8

Mike purchased 100 shares of Pubco (a taxable Canadian corporation and public company) in 2010 for $3.11 per share plus $39 in commissions. In 2011, Mike purchased another 100 shares of Pubco for $4 per share plus a brokerage commission of $50. On March 1, 2013, when the shares were worth $6 per share, Mike gifted half the Pubco shares to his 8-year-old son and half to his wife (no special elections were filed). What is the amount of the taxable capital gain that Mike must report in 2013?

(A) $100

(B) $122

(C) $200

(D) $400

Question 9

Mr. Smith died on June 30 of this year and left his entire estate to his son, Mark. His executor has provided you with a list of assets and their fair market value at the date of death.

List of Assets	*Cost*	*Fair Market Value*
Toronto home (sole principal residence since 1993)	$300,000	$840,000
Rental property in London, Ontario		
— Land	50,000	100,000
— Building (UCC: $2,000)	25,000	35,000
Mutual fund units	12,000	60,000
Shares of a public companies	90,000	100,000

What is the amount that must be included in Mr. Smith's Division B income for the year of death?

(A) $59,000

(B) $70,500

(C) $82,000

(D) $352,000

Question 10

Mr. T ceased to be a resident of Canada on September 1, 2013. At that date, he owned the following assets:

	Year acquired	*Cost*	*Fair market value Sept. 1, 2012*
Rental real estate in Canada	1998	$50,000	$100,000
Registered retirement savings plan	2006	60,000	80,000
Painting	2009	6,000	10,000
Shares of a public corporation (listed) resident in Canada (owns less than 1%)	2010	10,000	40,000

Which one of the following amounts represents Mr. T's minimum taxable capital gain on the above assets for 2013?

(A) $15,000

(B) $17,000

(C) $27,000

(D) $42,000

¶7,850 EXERCISES

Exercise 1

ITA: 40(2)(*b*), 54

Ms. Amin has come to you for advice on the tax consequences of the disposition of the following two residences in 2013:

Residence	*Date of purchase*	*Cost*	*Selling price*
Regi2a home	2002	$400,000	$517,500
Cottage	2007	250,000	375,000

— *REQUIRED*

Compute the minimum amount of taxable capital gains.

Exercise 2

ITA: 40(2)(*b*)

Peter Patel has only two residences which he wishes to dispose of in 2013. The following facts relate to those residences:

	Date purchased	*Cost*	*Real estate commission*	*Estimated selling price*
City home	1998	$180,000	$12,000	$247,000
Cottage	2003	90,000	6,000	164,000

— *REQUIRED*

Determine how Peter must designate residences in order to achieve the minimum capital gain.

Exercise 3

ITA: 40(2)(*b*), 45, 54, 54.1

Howard Bauer, who presently lives in Vancouver, is considering moving to Montreal. Although Howard intends to purchase a home in Montreal, he does not want to sell his fully-paid Vancouver home in case he decides to return some time in the future. Howard would rent his Vancouver home which cost him $50,000 in 1999 and now has a fair market value of $350,000.

— *REQUIRED*

Discuss the tax implications concerning Howard's Vancouver home if:

(A) Howard is self-employed; or

(B) Howard is employed.

Exercise 4

ITA: 41, 54

Karl Kim disposed of the following assets in 2013, all of which were bought subsequent to 1971:

	Sale price	*Cost*	*Selling cost*
Painting	$2,000	$ 300	$100
Antique clock	1,200	250	20
Outboard motor	750	500	15
Gold coin	600	1,000	10

— *REQUIRED*

Determine Karl's net taxable capital gain for the year.

Exercise 5

ITA: 41, 46

Mr. Adam Lamb sold the following assets in 2013, all of which were purchased within the last 10 years:

	Cost	*Proceeds*
Oil painting	$2,500	$ 500
Canoe	700	500

Rare coin	1,300	500
Bible produced in 1635	800	5,000
Antique car	15,000	10,000
Antique chair	300	1,200
Antique table	1,500	2,000

Mr. Adam Lamb has an unclaimed capital loss on listed personal property of $1,200 arising in 2010.

— REQUIRED

What is the amount of Mr. Adam Lamb's net taxable capital gain for 2012?

Exercise 6

ITA: 53(1)(*f*), 54

Ivan Bedard purchased the following shares of Solid Investments Ltd.:

March 1, 2012	100 shares @ $30 including brokerage
June 1, 2013	150 shares @ $35 including brokerage
January 10, 2014	200 shares @ $26 including brokerage

On December 15, 2013, Ivan sold 200 shares @ $25 less brokerage of $75.

— REQUIRED

(A) Determine Ivan's taxable capital gain or allowable capital loss on his December 15, 2013 disposition.

(B) Compute the adjusted cost base of the shares on hand on January 10, 2014.

Exercise 7

ITA: 47(1)

Regan San Juan participated in the following stock transactions to December 31, 2013:

Date	Description	Share price	Number of shares	Broker fees
Jan. 1/07	Hi Growth Co. — purchased	$3.00	1,000	$70
Jun. 5/08	Hi Growth Co. — purchased	2.80	3,000	90
Aug. 5/08	Hi Growth Co. — purchased	3.80	1,500	70
Dec. 3/09	Hi Growth Co. — purchased	5.10	1,000	120
May 1/10	Hi Growth Co. — sold	7.50	3,000	420
Nov. 8/11	Hi Growth Co. — purchased	5.75	1,000	130
Jan. 9/12	Hi Growth Co. — sold	8.40	1,500	240
Jan. 10/07	Hi Risk Co. — purchased	0.25	20,000	200
Jan. 14/07	Hi Risk Co. — purchased	0.80	4,000	75
May 20/13	Hi Risk Co. — sold	0.30	24,000	150

— REQUIRED

(a) Compute Regan's adjusted cost base for the shares of Hi Growth Co. that he still holds at the end of 2013.

(b) Compute Regan's 2013 taxable capital gain or allowable capital loss.

Exercise 8

ITA: 3, 5, 6, 7, 8, 9

Fong currently earns $23,000 income from employment and $10,000 from operating a part-time coffee bar business. In 2004, Fong inherited an antique painting. At that time the heirloom was worth $9,000. Today, the painting is apparently worth $29,000.

— *REQUIRED*

What would Fong's income for tax purposes be if he sold the painting and realized a capital gain?

Exercise 9

ITA: 53(2)

Miriam Franklin decided to purchase shares in Strippit Limited, a public company, listed on the Canadian Venture Exchange. Miriam purchased 1,000 shares at $35 per share plus brokerage of $500 on December 10, 2004.

Miriam received the following dividends during the intervening years:

February 1, 2006	A stock dividend of 5% with a paid-up capital of $10 per share.
April 10, 2008........	A stock dividend of 10% with a paid-up capital of $10 per share.
August 1, 2010	A stock dividend of 20% with a paid-up capital of $10 per share.

— *REQUIRED*

Determine the adjusted cost base of Miriam's shares as at December 31, 2013.

Exercise 10

ITA: 53

Ivy Jackson invested $2,000 on April 1, 2012, in Growth Mutual Fund sold by a major financial institution. Her investment purchased 72.788 units of the fund. On December 31, 2012, the fund allocated $96.37 of capital gains to her account. As a result, the $96.37 was reinvested in the fund to purchase 3.774 units at the market value of $25.535 per unit.

On June 30, 2013, she sold 25 of her units for a total of $718.

— *REQUIRED*

Compute the effects of these events on income for tax purposes in 2012 and 2013.

Exercise 11

ITA: 49

Doctor Wright, a general practitioner, has decided to move into a larger office. On July 1, 2012, he paid $5,000 to Devalued Properties Ltd., a developer, for a one-year option to purchase a residential building which he would use for business. On February 1, 2013, Dr. Wright sold his option to another medical practitioner, Dr. Holmes, for $2,000. On May 1, 2013, Dr. Holmes exercised the option and paid $100,000 for the building.

— *REQUIRED*

Discuss the tax implications in the above situation for Doctors Wright and Holmes and for Devalued Properties Ltd.

Exercise 12

ITA: 251

Which of the following individuals are not at arm's length with Ms. Gamma:

(A) her brother's wife?

(B) her niece?

(C) her husband from whom she is legally separated?

(D) an unrelated person?

Exercise 13

James Meadows is not at arm's length with his son Hayden. James wants Hayden to have a painting that cost him $1,200 and now has a fair market value of $1,500. What are the consequences under the non-arm's length transfer rules to James and Hayden if: ITA: 69(1)

(A) he sells the painting to him for $2,000?

(B) he sells the painting to him for $1,200?

(C) he gives the painting to him without any financial consideration?

Exercise 14

ITA: 73, 74.1, 74.2, 74.5; IT-511R

Alice Verwey is considering the following courses of action in transferring assets to her spouse this year:

(A) gifting to her husband shares with a fair market value of $15,000 and an adjusted cost base of $12,000;

(B) selling to her husband shares with a fair market value of $15,000 and an adjusted cost base of $12,000 for cash of $15,000. An election out of the interspousal rollover was made; ITA: 73(1)

(C) selling to her husband shares with a fair market value of $15,000 and an adjusted cost base of $12,000 for a $15,000 non-interest bearing promissory note with a definite repayment period;

(D) gifting to her husband $15,000 such that he purchases the shares on the open market; and

(E) lending her husband $15,000 evidenced by a non-interest bearing promissory note with a definite repayment period such that he purchases the shares on the open market.

— REQUIRED

Discuss the tax implications arising from the above transactions and any subsequent disposition by the spouse.

Exercise 15

ITA: 128.1(4), 115

Mr. Emerson, a United States citizen, entered Canada on June 1, 2008, and became resident in Canada for tax purposes. Mr. Emerson had a capital asset A which he brought with him upon his entry to Canada. The cost of the asset was $2,000 and the fair market value was $5,000 at the time of entry. In 2009, Mr. Emerson purchased another capital property B for $10,000. Mr. Emerson is considering returning to the United States on a permanent basis in 2013. He estimates that the two properties will have fair market values of $12,000 for A and $20,000 for B.

— REQUIRED

Discuss the tax consequences of Mr. Emerson's pending departure from Canada.

Exercise 16

ITA: 3, 39, 41

Simon has the following sources of income and losses for tax purposes:

	2012	*2013*
Employment income	$25,000	$30,000
Property income	10,000	(4,000)
Business income — other	8,000	(9,000)
Capital gains (capital losses):		
— Listed personal property (Note 1)	4,000	(1,500)
— Personal-use property	8,000	(1,000)
— Shares — Canadian-controlled private corporation (Note 2)	(6,000)	(2,000)
— Public corporation	(12,000)	9,000

Additional Information

(1) Simon has a capital loss from listed personal property of $1,000 carried forward from 2009.

(2) These losses qualify as business investment losses. No capital gains deduction has ever been claimed.

— REQUIRED

Determine Simon's Division B income according to the ordering rules in section 3 for 2012 and 2013. (Deal with each item line-by-line across the years, rather than computing income one year at a time.)

¶7,875 ASSIGNMENT PROBLEMS

Problem 1

ITA: 40(2)(*b*), 54

Mr. Doug Hart, who lives in Ontario, is contemplating moving to Switzerland. He came to you to discuss the tax consequences of disposing of his residences, as indicated below, in April 2013. He is single and ordinarily inhabits each of the residences for several months each year. He has never used his principal residence exemption since purchasing these properties.

The following information relates to the proposed 2013 dispositions.

Residence	*Date of purchase*	*Cost*	*Selling price*
Toronto home	2006	$160,000	$240,000
Farm in Quebec	2008	100,000	148,000
Condominium in Florida	2011	150,000	186,000

— *REQUIRED*

Compute the minimum amount of taxable capital gains that Mr. Hart will have to report in 2013.

Problem 2

ITA: 40(2)(*b*), 45(2), 54

Ms. Andrews purchased a home in Waterloo in 2003 at a cost of $86,000. She lived in the home until January 29, 2006, at which time she moved to Vancouver and rented a home in Vancouver. At the time of the move, Ms. Andrew's Waterloo residence had risen in value to $230,000. Expecting that real estate prices would continue to rise, Ms. Andrews chose to retain ownership of her Waterloo home and rented it to a third party.

In June 2012, Ms. Andrews decided she missed living in Waterloo and chose to return. She returned to Waterloo where she took up residence in her Waterloo home. At the time, the Waterloo residence had a fair market value of $294,000. In March 2013, Ms. Andrews decided she was tired of living in the city. She sold her Waterloo home for $284,000 and moved to the countryside.

Prior to filing her 2013 personal tax return, Ms. Andrews has requested your advice in minimizing the capital gains she must report on the sale of her home.

— *REQUIRED*

Calculate the minimum capital gain for Ms. Andrews on the sale of her home under the following circumstances:

(A) assuming that Ms. Andrews elects to be deemed not to have changed the use, and — ITA: 45(2)

(B) assuming that the election is not made.

Problem 3

ITA: 47, 53

Sherman Schleuter likes to invest in the stock market for the long term. While some of his investments have been failures, some have been very successful. Generally, he has been very fortunate in buying certain stocks at a relatively low price and selling them at their peak. One such stock is Headed For the Sky Corporation, a public corporation. Sherman has provided the following trade information related to this investment:

Nov. 8, 2006	Purchased 1,000 shares at initial offering price of $5.
Apr. 15, 2007	Purchased 2,000 shares at price of $3.50.
June 6, 2008	Sold 500 shares at $2.75, incurred brokerage commission of $50.
July 2, 2008	Purchased 2,000 shares at $4.
Apr. 30, 2009	Received a stock dividend of 10% of shares held; stock dividend increased corporation's paid-up capital by $.50/share.
June 20, 2010	Two-for-one stock split.
Nov. 8, 2011	Purchased 2,000 shares at $6.
Jan. 12, 2012	Received a stock dividend of 10% of shares held; stock dividend increased corporation's paid-up capital by $1/share.
Nov. 5, 2013	Sold 10,000 shares for $7.50/share, incurred brokerage commission of $650.

— *REQUIRED*

Calculate the taxable capital gain or allowable capital loss on the above transactions.

Problem 4

ITA: 52; 53

Ms. Plant decided to purchase shares in Schvantz Ltd., a public company. She purchased 800 shares at $25 per share plus brokerage of $690 on May 24, 1999.

The following additional transactions took place:

June 30, 2000	— Purchased 500 shares of Shtupp Metals Ltd., a public company, at $35 plus brokerage of $600.
Aug. 20, 2000	— Purchased 1,100 additional shares of Schvantz Ltd. at $30 plus brokerage of $940.
Aug. 27, 2002	— Sold 900 shares of Schvantz Ltd. at $24.50 per share plus brokerage fee of $760.
Sept. 20, 2002	— Purchased 600 additional shares of Schvantz Ltd. at $19.50 plus brokerage of $400.
Oct. 31, 2002	— Sold 200 shares of Shtupp Metals Ltd. at $32 per share plus brokerage fee of $220.
June 9, 2004	— Sold 250 shares of Schvantz Ltd. at $32 per share plus brokerage fee of $275.
May 24, 2006	— Received a 10% stock dividend from Shtupp Metals Ltd. (i.e., 30 shares) of which $20 per share issued was credited to paid-up capital.
June 30, 2008	— Sold 150 shares of Shtupp Metals Ltd. at $36.50 per share plus brokerage fee of $165.
Aug. 20, 2010	— Received 10% stock dividend from Schvantz Ltd. of which $20 per share issued was credited to paid-up capital.
Dec. 28, 2013	— Sold 350 shares of Schvantz Ltd. at $29 per share plus brokerage fee of $355, settlement date January 4, 2014.

— *REQUIRED*

Calculate the taxable capital gain or allowable capital loss for Ms. Plant from each of the above sales.

Problem 5

ITA: 7, 69, 73, 74.1, 74.2, 74.5, 56(4.1), 110(1)(*d*)

During 2012, Madame Martel exercised a stock option that she held in her employer (a CCPC). It is now November 2013. She is currently contemplating a number of scenarios in terms of the shares she received under the 2012 stock option exercise. She has asked you to explain the tax consequences of her actual and contemplated transactions.

The details of the stock option exercised during 2012 are as follows.

Number of shares purchased	*Exercise price*	*Fair market value of shares at exercise date*	*Fair market value of shares at grant date*
6,000	$20	$35	$20

The current fair market value of a share is $42.

Madame Martel is married and has two children (ages 21 and 15). She is expecting large dividends to be paid on the above shares in December 2013 and each December on an ongoing basis. She also expects that the shares will increase in value quite considerably over the near future. As a result, she is looking for a means of splitting income with her immediate family. She is proposing the following scenarios in terms of distributing these shares amongst her immediate family:

(1) gift the shares to her spouse and children (1/3 to her spouse and 1/3 to each child);

(2) sell the shares to her spouse and children (1/3 to her spouse and 1/3 to each child) for cash proceeds of $20 per share; or

(3) sell the shares to her spouse and children (1/3 to her spouse and 1/3 to each child) in exchange for a note payable of $42 per share.

The note payable described in (3), above, will be payable over five years with no interest. Since the note pays no interest and is repayable over future years, the estimated present value of the note is $25 per share.

— REQUIRED

Prepare a memorandum to Madame Martel explaining the income tax consequences of her completed and proposed transactions.

Problem 6

ITA: 13(7)(*e*)

On October 1, Roxanne acquired her brother's West Vancouver condominium rental property for $600,000 (ignore any land portion). Her brother has owned it for five years and had a capital gain of $250,000 on selling it to Roxanne. He will include 50% of that in his income. Roxanne believes she can earn net rental income of $9,000 annually, and 1/4 of that amount for the final quarter of this year.

— REQUIRED

Compute the maximum CCA that Roxanne may claim in this first taxation year.

Problem 7

ITA: Division B, Subdivisions a, b, c

Mr. Richmond, a new client, has invested in rental properties, principal residences and other capital property with inheritance monies and other liquid cash. He provides you with the following information with respect to his 2013 taxation year.

Mr. Richmond is employed by Wealth Inc., a Canadian-controlled private corporation, and received the following income and benefits:

(1) Salary (net)		$49,953
Payroll deduction:		
Income taxes	$15,100	
CPP	2,356	
EI	891	
Registered pension plan (defined benefit: current service)	3,700	22,047
		$72,000

(2) Mr. Richmond paid professional fees of $500 to the Professional Engineers of Ontario.

(3) Mr. Richmond, who is engaged in negotiating contracts for his employer, received for the entire year a monthly allowance for travelling and car expenses of $550 and $650, respectively.

In September of 2013, Mr. Richmond sold his car for $12,500 and purchased a new car costing $35,000, including HST of 13%. Mr. Richmond purchased his previous car in January 2010 for $32,000 plus HST. The UCC at January 1, 2013 was $14,200. CCA has been taken each year on a prorated basis to reflect the use for employment purposes. Mr. Richmond's kilometres for personal use were 6,250 out of a total kilometres of 25,000.

Mr. Richmond's employment contract requires him to use his own car and pay all of his expenses.

Travelling expenses:	
Meals	$ 3,500
Accommodation	4,500
Gas and oil	2,100
Insurance	800
Maintenance	500
Licence	130
	$11,530

(4) Mr. Richmond sold two lots of his stock options. He provides you with the following:

1st lot — 450 shares sold on March 15, 2013, for $26.50 per share. These shares were purchased in February 2006 for $8 at which time the shares were valued at $10.50.

2nd lot — 600 shares sold on December 5, 2013, for $25 per share. These shares were purchased on April 12, 2013, for $15 at which time the shares were valued at $21. The fair market value at the date of grant was $17.

(5) Mr. Richmond received an interest-free loan of $9,000 on March 12, 2013, to enable him to purchase shares of Wealth Inc. The loan was outstanding until the shares were sold on December 5, at which time the loan was repaid. Assume that the prescribed rate throughout the year was 7%.

In addition, during 2013, Mr. Richmond received the following income from various sources including certain capital dispositions.

(A) Mr. Richmond sold the following assets:

	Cost	*Proceeds*
Antique foot stool	$1,100	$ 900
Painting	950	1,500
Stamp collection	250	850

(B) During 2013, Mr. Richmond sold his two residences, in order to purchase a larger home in an expensive suburb. The following facts relate to these two residences:

	Date purchased	*Cost*	*Commission*	*Proceeds*
City home	2004	$95,000	$21,000	$350,000
Cottage	1999	15,500	12,000	200,000

(C) In addition to his residences, Mr. Richmond owns two rental properties. The following information pertains to these two properties:

	Wealthier St.	*Richmount St.*
Cost of land	$70,000	$100,000
Cost of building	$55,000	$ 80,000
UCC — January 1, 2013, Class 1	$39,000	$ 65,000
Rental revenue in 2013	$18,000	$ 7,600
Expenses:		
Taxes (property)	$ 2,100	$ 1,800
Other expenses	4,300	6,100
Mortgage interest	3,600	Nil
	$10,000	$ 7,900

The Richmount St. rental property was sold in November for proceeds of $250,000 less $9,000 of selling costs. Of the proceeds, $140,000 was for the land.

Mr. Richmond purchased the Wealthier St. rental property by placing a mortgage on his home. His monthly payments are $450 per month, of which $300 per month represents interest.

(D) Mr. Richmond gifted his wife $10,000 in June 2013 to allow her to invest in the stock market. Mrs. Richmond decided to be a cautious investor for the first while; as a result, she invested the $10,000 in Treasury Bills which earned $600 from June to December 2013.

(E) In addition, Mr. Richmond decided to provide his younger brother, who is 22, with a non-interest bearing loan of $5,000 to allow him to complete his Masters in Marine Biology. Mr. Richmond's brother paid his tuition fees with the funds.

(F) Mr. Richmond gifted $8,500 to each of his twin children, Dolly and Camp, aged 15. Both children placed their monies in high interest-bearing savings accounts each receiving interest of $1,050 in 2013.

(G) Mr. Richmond received dividends from the following investments:

Foreign Co. — a foreign corporation (net of $88 withholding tax)	$500
Wealth Inc. — a Canadian-controlled private corporation (from income taxed at the low corporate rate)	800

(H) Mr. Richmond owns two mutual funds, Dumark Mutual Fund and Paget Mutual Fund. He received a T3 slip from Dumark Mutual Fund indicating the following income amounts allocated to his account and reinvested in 2013:

Capital gains	$1,200
Actual amount of dividends	347
Taxable amount of dividends	500

Mr. Richmond had invested $20,000 in the Dumark Fund in 2012. This resulted in the purchase of 1,640.824 units of the fund. In 2012, income of $46.31 was allocated to his account and reinvested. The reinvestment resulted in the purchase of 3.845 units at the market value of $12.044 per unit. The 2013 income allocation resulted, on reinvestment of the $1,544.97, in the purchase of 119.358 units at the market value of $12.944 per unit. Late in 2013, after the income allocation, Mr. Richmond sold 1,000 units for a total of $12,881.

He also received a T5 slip from Paget Mutual Fund indicating that he had received a $280 capital gains dividend during 2013.

(I) Mr. Richmond sold a $100,000 Government of Canada bond for $115,327. This bond paid interest semi-annually at an interest rate which was much higher than current interest rates. The proceeds received of $115,327 included accrued interest of $5,327. Mr. Richmond had purchased the bonds on the open market for $98,000.

(J) In 2010, Mr. Richmond loaned $120,000 to his brother-in-law's company which was a small business corporation. The loan paid interest at commercial rates, but no interest was received in 2013 because the company went into receivership. As an unsecured creditor, Mr. Richmond received 10 cents on the dollar ($12,000) in 2013 in full payment of this loan.

(K) Mr. Richmond has a listed personal property loss, carried forward from 2007, of $500.

— REQUIRED

Determine Mr. Richmond's Division B income according to the ordering rules in section 3 for 2013. Assume that Mr. Richmond claimed $60,000 of his capital gains exemption in prior years. Ignore the effects of the leap year.

Problem 8

ITA: 13(7)(*e*), 70(5)(*a*), 70(5)(*b*), 70(5)(*c*), 70(6)(*d*), 70(6)(*e*); ITR: 1100(2)(*h*), 1102(14)(*d*)

On July 31, 2013, Mary McArthur passed away after a lengthy illness. Mary was survived by her husband and one adult child, Margaret. Both her husband and daughter are residents of Canada. Information related to Mary's assets as at July 31, 2013, is set out below.

Description	*Capital Cost/ACB*	*UCC*	*Fair market value*	*Beneficiary*
Rental property — Toronto, Ontario				
Land	$40,000	n/a	$ 100,000	Spouse
Building (Class 3)	55,000	$15,000	145,000	Spouse
Rental property — Stratford, Ontario				
Land	25,000	n/a	45,000	Daughter
Building (Class 1)	65,000	42,000	93,000	Daughter
CBV shares (see Note below)		n/a	1,000,000	Spouse
View Canada shares (see Note below)		n/a	150,000	Daughter

Note:

Mary inherited these shares from her father upon his death in 2011. Her father had an adjusted cost base of $250,000 in the CBV shares. The fair market value of the CBV shares on the date of his death was $500,000. Her father had an adjusted cost base of $150,000 in the View Canada shares. The fair market value of the View Canada shares on the date of his death was $180,000.

— REQUIRED

(A) Compute the minimum income and/or taxable capital gains to be reported by Mary McArthur for 2013 in respect of the above noted assets. Ignore any available elections.

(B) Determine the cost amounts of the above assets to the respective beneficiaries.

Problem 9

ITA: 3, 41

Dave Stieb reported the following information for tax purposes:

	2011	*2012*	*2013*
Business income	$ 60,000	$ 65,000	$70,000
Property income	2,000	3,000	(1,000)
Capital gains:*			
Listed personal property	5,000	(7,000)	3,000
Personal-use property	(2,000)	5,000	4,000
Other	(8,000)**	6,000	(16,000)

* Brackets indicate capital loss.

** Includes a $4,000 business investment loss.

— REQUIRED

Compute the income under Division B for each year *after* making the necessary amendments to the returns of other years. (Deal with each item line-by-line across the years, rather than computing income one year at a time.) Assume that no capital gains deduction was ever claimed.

Problem 10

ITA: 3, 41

In Billy's attempt to sever all business and personal ties with Canada before beginning long-term and permanent employment in Beijing, he sold all his personal assets and most of his investments.

Description	*Sale proceeds*	*Cost*	*Disposition costs*
Personal residence	$175,000	$125,000	$3,600
Household furniture	20,000	35,000	800
Skis, bicycle, and skates	750	1,200	0
Rights to season tickets	4,000	3,500	0
Paintings	2,400	1,900	120
Chevrolet	3,600	12,000	350
Fishing lodge	45,000	31,000	4,500
Business loan — private	0	8,000	0
ABC shares (public co.)	46,000	20,000	200

Additional Information:

- All years available for a principal residence designation were used to exempt the gain on the personal residence, leaving no years available to designate the fishing lodge.
- The business loan was made to a private company which is now in receivership.
- Billy has never claimed a capital gains exemption.

— REQUIRED

Assuming that Billy has employment income of $48,000, calculate his income for tax purposes.

[For more problems and solutions thereto, see the DVD accompanying this book.]

¶7,880 ADVISORY CASES

Case 1: Theresa Vert

Theresa Vert is considering emigration to the United States. She has approached you to estimate the income tax consequences on her holdings of taxable capital property. Her plan is to dispose of all the real estate holdings and retain her investments in stocks and bonds. Theresa and her husband currently live in a downtown townhouse which was purchased in 1991 for a cost of $130,000. The estimated value is now $320,000. Theresa also inherited a cottage in 1992 (estimated fair market value was $55,000). The value of the cottage is now approximately $270,000.

In 1988, Theresa purchased a rental property for $105,000 of which $25,000 was allocated to the land. There is no mortgage on the property. The land and the building have a fair market value of $150,000 and $100,000, respectively. Legal costs at the time of purchase totalled $3,000 and the estimated cost of disposal is $20,000. The UCC on the building is $30,000.

Theresa also has the following investments:

- Common shares of Canadian publicly traded companies. These shares were purchased on October 19, 1993, at a cost of $140,000 and have current value of $190,000.
- A $100,000 10-year Province of Alberta 12% bond, due in five years, with interest payable annually on June 30. The bond has a current value equal to $110,000.
- A Steinway grand piano purchased at an auction for $8,000. Theresa can sell this to her piano teacher for $10,000.

Advise Theresa on the various income tax consequences of emigrating and the tax treatment of her holdings.

Case 2: Belleville Furniture Inc.

Belleville Furniture Inc. ("Belleville") is a manufacturer of high-quality dining room furniture. This is the second generation of the Parker family that has owned the company, and the founder's son, Dave Parker, is having some problems since foreign imports are being brought into Ontario and sold at a price lower than Belleville's cost. Dave is certainly concerned about the short term, but feels that within the next eight to twelve months Belleville can adjust its sourcing of raw materials and the manufacturing process in order to reduce its costs to the point where its can be competitive, not only in the local market, but also in the Northeastern United States.

Dave's immediate problem is that when he asked the bank to increase Belleville's operating line of credit enough to cover Belleville's operational problems for the next eight to twelve months, the bank became concerned since its sole security for the operating loan is the inventory and the under 90-day accounts receivables. To maintain the existing line of credit, and to even consider the increase, the bank wants personal guarantees from both of Dave and his wife, Nancy, as well as a collateral mortgage on the company's building. As a result, Dave has you working on cash flow projections to support the loan, his lawyer is preparing the collateral mortgage, and an appraiser is preparing a valuation of the property. Dave feels that his chances of being approved are good.

Dave has agreed that he will sell the 20% interest that he personally owns in a company that operates a lumber mill that supplies Belleville. Dave bought the shares from the company on incorporation five years ago for $50,000 to help the arm's length supplier start the lumber mill. The other 75% of the company is owned by the supplier who has agreed to have his holding company buy the shares from Dave for $40,000 in cash. Dave had borrowed all the money for this investment through an interest-only demand loan with the bank. The bank has agreed to leave the full amount of the loan outstanding as long as Dave contributes the full $40,000 of proceeds into Belleville.

To prepare for its entry into the U.S. market, Belleville will set up a U.S. dollar bank account at its local bank for deposits from U.S. customers.

Dave would like your advice on the tax implications of his situation.

¶7,900 SUPPLEMENTAL NOTES

(This section can be omitted without losing the continuity of the Chapter. None of the review questions, multiple choice questions, exercises, or assignment problems utilizes this information.)

¶7,910 Cost of Assets Owned on December 31, 1971

Since the government did not want to tax capital gains which had accrued up to December 31, 1971, certain special transition rules, called the *Income Tax Application Rules, 1971* (ITAR), were developed to eliminate these gains from taxation under this subdivision when property purchased prior to 1972 was disposed of after 1971.

The median rule or tax-free zone method applies automatically to all taxpayers. The rule establishes the cost of non-depreciable capital property owned on December 31, 1971 for the beginning of the new system which taxes capital gains, as follows: ITAR: 26(3)

ACB = The middle figure of:

(a) Proceeds of disposition
(b) valuation-day value
(c) Cost

} if any two of these are equal they become the initial ACB

The valuation-day (V-day) value rule is an election which applies only to individuals. As an alternative to the median rule, this V-day rule establishes the cost of capital property owned on December 31, 1971, for the beginning of the new system, as follows: ITAR: 26(7)

ACB = V-day value

Two V-days were designated to establish cost at the beginning of the new system under this rule. December 22, 1971 was chosen for publicly traded securities and December 31, 1971 was chosen for all other capital property. ITAR: 24

It is presumed by law that a taxpayer will use the median rule unless he or she elects the V-day value rule. The CRA has taken the position that when the capital gain is the same under both methods, then the taxpayer has the right to defer making the election until there is a difference between the two methods. From then on the taxpayer must adhere to the method chosen for all property owned prior to 1972. ITAR: 26(7)

The following six cases illustrate the application of the median rule (alternatively referred to as the tax-free zone method) and the V-day rule. Note how the rule used establishes a base against which gains or losses under the new system of taxation of capital gains are measured. The objective is to prevent pre-1972 gains or losses from being taxable or allowable.

	Facts			*Capital gain*			
				Under median rule		*Under V-day rule*	
Case	*Actual cost*	*V-day value*	*P of D*	*Adjusted cost base*	*Capital gain (loss)*	*Adjusted cost base*	*Capital gain (loss)*
1	$2,000	$3,000	$5,000	$3,000	$2,000	$3,000	$2,000
2	5,000	3,000	2,000	3,000	(1,000)	3,000	(1,000)
3	3,000	2,000	5,000	3,000	2,000	2,000	3,000
4	3,000	5,000	2,000	3,000	(1,000)	5,000	(3,000)
5	2,000	5,000	3,000	3,000	Nil	5,000	(2,000)
6	5,000	2,000	3,000	3,000	Nil	2,000	1,000

Note how the adjusted cost base is established at the same value under both rules in Cases 1 and 2. Note, also, how in Case 1, the $1,000 (i.e., $3,000 – $2,000) gain that accrued before 1972 is not included in the capital gain. Similarly, in Case 2, the $2,000 (i.e., $3,000 – $5,000) of loss that accrued prior to 1972 is not considered part of the capital loss. Note that when the median rule is used and the proceeds of disposition amount is the middle number, there is no gain or loss. That is because proceeds fall in the "tax-free zone" between cost and V-day.

¶7,930 Principal Residence on Farmland

The gain on the disposition of land used in a farming business that included a principal residence may be computed in one of two ways. The gain on the housing unit plus up to one-half hectare of land may be reduced by an amount computed by the general formula. Alternatively, the farmer may elect to compute an exemption of $1,000 plus $1,000 for every year after the later of 1971 and the last acquisition date that the property was designated as a principal residence and during which he or she was resident in Canada. The CRA's interpretation of these provisions can be found in an Interpretation Bulletin.

ITA: 40(2)(*b*)

ITA: 40(2)(*c*)

Income Tax Folio S1-F3-C2 — Principal Residence

¶7,940 GST/HST Rules for Dispositions of Residential Property and Used Goods

The disposition of capital personal property for GST/HST purposes was discussed in Chapter 5 while the rules relating to dispositions and changes in use of capital real property will be discussed in Chapter 8. The sale of shares is an exempt supply under the GST/HST and, hence, there are no GST/HST consequences. This part of the Chapter will address the GST/HST rules relating to dispositions of used residential or personal-use property and dispositions of used goods.

¶7,945 Sales of used residential or personal-use real property

GST/HST applies to all sales of real property unless a specific exemption is provided. For example, sales of new residential housing are subject to GST/HST. Sales of used residential complexes, or interests therein, are exempt from GST/HST. Unlike the principal residence exemption under the *Income Tax Act*, the exemption for GST/HST purposes is not limited to a single property.

ETA: Sch. V, Part I, s. 2

The term "residential complex" is defined to include a detached house, semi-detached house, rowhouse unit, multi-unit residential condominium or apartment complex, together with any common areas and land that are reasonably necessary for the use and enjoyment of the residential unit. A residential complex does not include a hotel, a motel, an inn, a boarding or lodging house, or other similar property that provides all, or substantially all, accommodation for periods of less than 60 days. A building generally constitutes a residential complex only in respect of the part that includes residential units. Thus, if an apartment building contains one floor of commercial space and 10 floors of residential units, only the latter 10 floors will constitute a residential complex.

ETA: 123(1)

A residential complex includes a single family dwelling in which a business is carried on, provided the dwelling is used primarily (i.e., more than 50%) as a residence for individuals. If the "primarily test" (i.e., the more than 50% test) is not met, a supply of real property that includes a residential complex and other real property that is not part of the residential complex is deemed to be two separate supplies. Accordingly, the supply of the residential portion will be exempt if it qualifies as a used residential complex, and the other part of the property will be subject to the general rules. This rule will apply, for example, where an accountant uses a house primarily for his or her practice and not primarily as a residence.

ETA: 136(2)

Although the sale of the residential complex may be exempt, various fees related to the sale are subject to GST/HST. These include, for example, real estate commissions, legal fees, appraisal fees, survey fees, and home inspection fees. No GST/HST is payable in respect of exempt financial services, such as mortgage brokerage or mortgage insurance fees.

Sales of real property by an individual or a personal trust are exempted, other than:

ETA: Sch. V, Part I, s. 9

- real property that is capital property used primarily
  — in a business carried on by the individual or trust with a reasonable expectation of profit, or
  — if the individual or trust is a registrant
    - in making taxable supplies of the real property by way of lease, licence, or similar arrangement, or
    - in any combination of the uses described above;

- real property sold
  - — in the course of a business of the individual or trust, or
  - — where the individual or trust has filed an election with the Minister in prescribed form and manner and containing prescribed information, in the course of an adventure or concern in the nature of trade of the individual or trust;
- a parcel of land that was subdivided or severed by the individual, trust or settlor of the trust (subject to certain exemptions);
- certain deemed supplies;
- a residential complex or an interest in a residential complex; or
- where an individual or personal trust has bought taxable real property and pursuant to a joint election, subsequently sells it back to the vendor within one year, pursuant to a right or obligation under the original purchase and sale agreement between the parties.

A "personal trust" is defined as a testamentary trust, or an *inter vivos* trust that is a personal trust (within the meaning assigned by the *Income Tax Act*) all the beneficiaries (other than contingent beneficiaries) of which are individuals, and all the contingent beneficiaries of which, if any, are individuals, charities, or public institutions. ITA: 248(1)

Under this provision, most sales of country properties kept for personal use, non-commercial hobby farms and other non-business land are exempt from GST/HST. Sales of residential complexes are excluded from this exemption because they are covered in another provision, as discussed above. Where real property is sold in the course of an adventure or concern in the nature of trade, an election may be made to treat the sale as taxable. Such an election may be made, for example, by an individual or trust who acquires real property for resale purposes and not for personal use. If such an election is made, the individual or trust, if a registrant, would be entitled to recover any GST/HST paid on the acquisition of the property (for example, if it was not purchased from another individual who held the property as personal-use real property) and on any subsequent improvements. As discussed in Chapter 6, sales of substantially renovated used housing in the course of a business are treated as sales of new housing and, therefore, are subject to GST/HST.

The rules relating to exempt sales of real property by public sector bodies will not be discussed in this Chapter.

The conversion of a commercial property to a residential complex, and *vice versa*, will be discussed in Chapter 8.

¶7,950 Sales of used goods and acceptance of trade-ins

Under the general GST/HST rules, the sale by a registrant of a used good is subject to GST/HST. If a used good sold by a registrant is purchased by another registrant for use in a commercial activity, the normal input tax credit rules apply. The sale of a used good by a non-registrant is not subject to GST/HST.

Where a registrant accepts a used good (or a leasehold interest therein) as full or partial consideration for another good, the supplier has to collect GST/HST only on the net amount if the trade-in is for consumption, use or supply by the supplier in the course of commercial activities and the person trading in the property is not required to collect GST/HST (i.e., is not a registrant). For example, this rule would apply to an automobile dealer who accepts a trade-in from a consumer. The dealer would charge tax on the difference between the value of the new car and the value of the trade-in. ETA: 153(4)

There are certain exceptions to this rule. For example, it does not apply to any supply of a trade-in that is a zero-rated supply (e.g., a supply of zero-rated farming equipment), or to a supply made outside Canada (e.g., a trade-in delivered outside Canada to the supplier of the new good).

If the used good is traded in by a registrant, the purchase of the new good and the trade-in are treated as two separate transactions, both of which are subject to GST/HST.

¶7,980 Stock option benefit — Tax-deferred election repealed

The special election to defer the recognition of the stock option benefit for public company shares has been repealed effective March 4, 2010. As a result, this deferral is no longer available for individuals when future options are exercised.

¶7,985 Special relief for tax-deferred elections made prior to March 4, 2010

ITA: 180.01

Some taxpayers have taken advantage of the special election to defer the recognition of the stock option benefit only to find that the fair market value (FMV) of the underlying security is less than the tax they will have to pay when they recognize the stock option benefit. The March 4, 2010 federal Budget introduced some amendments and a new election for taxpayers to deal with these situations.

Only stock option benefits for which an election to defer taxation has been made will qualify for this special election. Also,

- individuals who disposed of their optioned securities before 2010 will have to make an election for this special treatment on or before their filing due date for the 2010 taxation year; and
- individuals who have not disposed of their optioned securities before 2010 must do so before 2015 in order to make this election.

Please refer to the table below, which illustrates this issue. In all cases, the basic information is the same. A stock option is exercised when the FMV is $1,000 and the price paid is $400. It is assumed that the taxpayer, Tony, elects to defer the recognition of the $600 stock option benefit and the $300 Division C deduction until the underlying shares are disposed of. The only variable is the selling price of the shares.

To see the issue, refer to Case 1, below. When Tony goes to sell the shares, the FMV has dropped to $50. Under the old rules, on the sale of the shares, he would have realized an allowable capital loss of $475, which can only be offset against taxable capital gains and therefore may have little value to Tony. In addition, he would have to pay tax of $138 on the stock option benefit, net of Division C deduction. As a result, Tony does not have enough cash from the sale to pay the tax owing.

The amendments would solve some of Tony's problem. He would have to pay a tax equal to the proceeds on the sale of the shares or $50. He would then be allowed to deduct an amount equal to the deferred stock option benefit of $600 to eliminate any income effect. Then, he will be able to claim an allowable capital loss ("ACL") equal to the original ACL less an amount to reflect the $600 deduction he claimed to offset the stock option benefit. In the end, he has enough cash to pay his immediate tax liability and the price he pays is a loss of some of his allowable capital loss.

In Case 2, we increased Tony's proceeds to equal his tax liability on the stock option benefit. In this case, Tony has enough from his proceeds to pay his tax so he would not need to make the election and would maintain his ACL carryover of $431.

Once the proceeds exceed the tax on the stock option benefit, there is a clear disadvantage to considering this election.

Facts					
	FMV at exercise	$ 1,000			
	Stock option benefit	$ 600			
	ACB of shares after exercise	$ 1,000			
	Price paid at exercise	$ 400			
			Case 1	**Case 2**	**Case 3**
	Proceeds		$ 50	$ 138	$ 200
Old	Stock option benefit		$ 600	$ 600	$ 600
	Div. C deduction		(300)	(300)	(300)
	Impact on taxable income		$ 300	$ 300	$ 300

	Tax @ 46%	A	$ 138	$ 138	$ 138	
	Proceeds		$ 50	$ 138	$ 200	
	ACB		(1,000)	(1,000)	(1,000)	
	Capital gain (loss)		$ (950)	$ (862)	$ (800)	
	ACL on optioned securities	C	$ (475)	$ (431)	$ (400)	
New	Tax = Proceeds	B	$ 50	$ 138	$ 200	ITA: 180.01(2)
	Stock option benefit		600	600	600	
	Offset		(600)	(600)	(600)	
	Impact on taxable income		Nil	Nil	Nil	
	TCG = ½ × lesser					
	Stock option benefit		$ 600	$ 600	$ 600	
	Capital loss		$ 950	$ 862	$ 800	
	TCG = ½ lesser (above)		300	300	300	ITA: 180.01(2)
	ACL on optioned securities		(475)	(431)	(400)	
	Net ACL	D	$ (175)	$ (131)	$ (100)	
Tax advantage (disadvantage)		A-B	$ 88	Nil	$ (62)	
ACL advantage (disadvantage)		C-D	$ (300)	$ (300)	$ (300)	

Chapter 8

Capital Gains: Business Related

TOPICS DISCUSSED

LEARNING GOALS

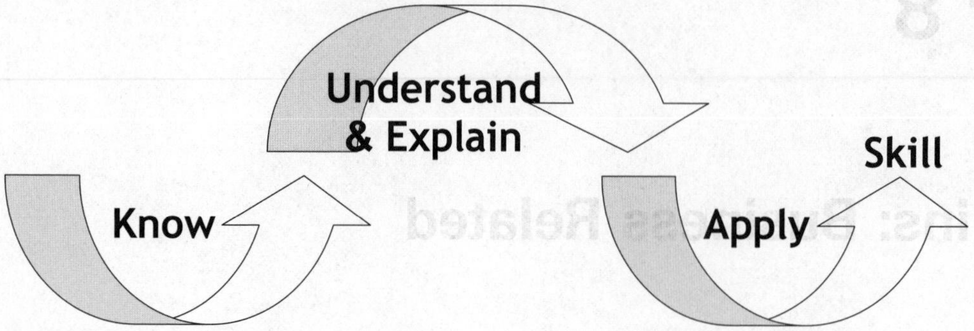

Know

By the end of this chapter you should know some provisions of the *Income Tax Act* that relate to capital gains and losses realized by business. Completing the Review Questions (¶8,800) and Multiple Choice Questions (¶8,825) is a good way to learn the technical provisions.

Understand and Explain

You should understand and be able to explain

- the difference between an income and a capital receipt;
- some of the points related to capital gains as they may arise in a business;
- bad debts on capital property.

Completing the Exercises (¶8,850) is a good way to deepen your understanding of the material.

Apply

You should be able to apply your knowledge and understanding of the rules pertaining to capital gains and losses in a way that accomplishes a client's goals. Completing the Assignment Problems (¶8,875) is an excellent way to develop your ability to apply the material in increasingly complex situations.

OVERVIEW

This chapter will focus on the taxation of capital gains as they may arise in a business context.

As mentioned in Chapter 7, Subdivision c of Division B of Part I of the Act contains the primary rules for the computation of taxable capital gains and allowable capital losses. Some of the more important provisions were reviewed at the beginning of the last chapter.

The following chart will help to locate in the Act the major provisions dealt with in this chapter.

PART I — DIVISION B, SUBDIVISION c

CAPITAL GAINS & LOSSES

DIVISION

A	Liability for tax
B	**Computation of income**
C	Computation of taxable income
D	Taxable income earned in Canada by non-residents
E	Computation of tax
E.1	Minimum tax
F	Special rules applicable in certain circumstances
G	Deferred and other special income arrangements
H	Exemptions
I	Returns, assessments, payment and appeals
J	Appeals to the Tax Court of Canada and the Federal Court of Appeal

SUBDIVISION

	Basic rules
a	Income or loss from an office or employment
b	Income or loss from a business or property
c	**Taxable capital gains and allowable capital losses**
d	Other sources of income
e	Deductions in computing income
f	Rules relating to computation of income
g	Amounts not included in computing income
h	Corporations resident in Canada and their shareholders
i	Shareholders of corporations not resident in Canada
j	Partnerships and their members
k	Trusts and their beneficiaries

SECTION

38	Taxable allowable gain and allowable capital loss
39	Capital gain and capital loss
39.1	Exempt capital gains balance in respect of flow-through entity
40	General rules
41	Listed personal property
42	Dispositions subject to warranty
43	Part disposition
43.1	Life estates in real property
44	Replacement property
44.1	Small business corporation share rollover
45	Change in use
46	Personal-use property
47	Identical property
48.1	SBC goes public
49	Options granted
49.1	No disposition where obligation satisfied
50	Loss on debt/shares
51	Convertible property
52	Cost of certain property
53	ACB adjustments
54	Definitions
54.1	Exception: principal residence
54.2	Shares and capital property
55	Deemed capital gain

¶8,000 OVERVIEW OF CAPITAL GAINS IN A BUSINESS CONTEXT

¶8,010 Avoidance

Prior to tax reform in 1987, there was a very broad anti-avoidance provision in respect of capital gains in Subdivision c. Many tax advisers were of the opinion that the provision was too wide in scope and could not be enforced. The provision was replaced by the general anti-avoidance rule (GAAR), which will be described in some detail in Chapter 13. However, there are a number of aspects concerning the GAAR to be aware of even at this stage. ITA: 245(2)

(1) According to the CRA and the courts, the GAAR is a provision of last resort and all other avenues (i.e., specific statutory anti-avoidance provisions) must be exhausted before the GAAR will be applied.

(2) The CRA has prepared an extensive Information Circular on the GAAR, including numerous examples as to when the GAAR would or would not apply in the opinion of the Department. IC 88-2; ITA: 245

(3) The GAAR will not apply to a transaction(s) which is primarily motivated by a non-tax purpose, e.g., estate planning.

Specific anti-avoidance provisions exist to prevent a corporation from converting a capital gain into a dividend which would normally avoid income tax when the parties involved are corporations. ITA: 55(2)

¶8,020 Capital Receipt Versus Income Receipt Revisited

The Act does not define a capital gain. The provisions merely set out the technical computations to be made once it has been determined whether a transaction is an income receipt or a capital receipt. Hence, taxpayers and their advisers must turn to the guidelines which have been laid down by the courts through past judicial decisions. Even then, there is no clear-cut set of rules which will apply in all situations. The result has been one of the most confusing and controversial areas of taxation giving rise to thousands of court cases since the advent of federal income taxation in Canada.

A set of behavioural factors, which were introduced in Chapter 4, were developed by the courts to help in determining whether the transaction may fall into the capital category or the income category. However, each situation must be judged in relation to facts surrounding the particular transaction and in many cases may warrant professional advice. In determining the facts, the taxpayer's whole course of conduct before, during and after the transaction in question should be reviewed.

¶8,025 Primary intention

The objective of most decisions is to determine the intention of the taxpayer. First, there may be an indicator in the taxpayer's behaviour of *primary intention*, that is, did the taxpayer intend to make a business or trading profit on the transaction? If the answer to this question, as determined by observing the facts of the taxpayer's behaviour, is affirmative, then the transaction is likely income.

¶8,030 Secondary intention

The courts may, also, examine the evidence of the taxpayer's behaviour to establish whether the taxpayer had any *secondary intention*, especially in respect of, but not limited to, real estate transactions. Secondary intention may be thought of as an alternative or secondary objective in the mind of the taxpayer at the time of the purchase which motivated the purchase and which would come into operation later if the primary objective is thwarted. For example, a developer purchases a piece of property for an apartment complex which he or she plans to operate as an investment property by collecting rent. However, zoning bylaws cannot be altered to accommodate the proposed project and the developer subsequently sells the property at a profit. The courts would likely view this as an income transaction by way of the taxpayer's secondary intention, on the assumption that the taxpayer, as a developer, would know at the time of purchase that he or she could remove himself or herself from the situation at a profit when the primary objective could not be achieved.[1]

¶8,035 Badges of trade or behavioural factors

The factors, often referred to as "badges of trade", used to establish intention to engage in an adventure or concern in the nature of trade and previously discussed in Chapter 4, include but are not limited to:

(a) the relationship of the transaction to the taxpayer's business;[2]

(b) the nature of the activity or organization associated with trade (recall the British cases of the large quantities of toilet paper and whiskey referred to in Chapter 4 and refer to the CRA's Interpretation Bulletin entitled "Adventure or concern in the nature of trade", also discussed in Chapter 4); IT-459

(c) the nature of the assets involved in the transaction;[3]

(d) the number and frequency of transactions within a given period of time;

(e) the length of the period of ownership of the asset;

(f) any supplemental work on or in connection with the property; and

(g) if the transaction was completed by an organization, the stated objectives of the organization, as outlined in articles of association or incorporation or a partnership agreement.[4]

The more complete description of these factors presented in Chapter 4 should be reviewed. Reference should also be made to an Interpretation Bulletin where the CRA lists about 12 factors pertaining to real estate transactions. Where a disposition of securities is at issue, the CRA lists some relevant factors to consider in its Interpretation Bulletin entitled "Transactions in securities". IT-218R, par. 3; IT-479R, par. 11

¶8,100 VARIOUS CAPITAL GAINS PROVISIONS IN A BUSINESS CONTEXT

¶8,110 Reserves

It is not uncommon for a taxpayer to receive proceeds of disposition for a property over a period of years. The most usual example is where the seller provides the purchaser with a first or second mortgage. When a taxpayer does not receive the full proceeds in the year of disposition, the Act allows a taxpayer to defer a portion of the gain realized by claiming a reasonable reserve on the gain calculated by formula for amounts not due until a later date. ITA: 40(1)(*a*) From a policy point of view, in accordance with the realization basis of capital gains taxation (that is, consistent with the definition of "disposition" in the Act), taxpayers should not pay tax on taxable capital gains until they collect the proceeds and they have the cash to pay the tax. However, the tax on taxable capital gains should not be postponed unduly, so limits should be imposed. If no limits were imposed, taxpayers could plan transactions to defer the ITA: 40(1.1) taxation of the gains over a very long period, if not indefinitely. For example, a parent could sell property to a child with payment in 25 years. If no limit was imposed, the gain would be taxable in 25 years. Regardless of the term of agreed repayment, the maximum deferral time

[1] The cases of *Rosenblatt v. M.N.R.*, 55 DTC 1205 (Ex. Ct.), *Stekl v. M.N.R.*, 59 DTC 1262 (Ex. Ct.), and *Regina Shoppers Mall Ltd. v. The Queen*, 89 DTC 5482 (F.C.A.), illustrate the focus on intention by the courts.

[2] This factor is illustrated by the cases of *Atlantic Sugar Refineries v. M.N.R.*, 49 DTC 602 (S.C.C.), and *Gairdner Securities v. M.N.R.*, 54 DTC 1015 (S.C.C.).

[3] This factor is illustrated by the case of *Great West Exploration Ltd. v. M.N.R.*, 57 DTC 444 (T.A.B.).

[4] This factor is illustrated by the cases of *Sutton Lumber & Trading Co. Ltd. v. M.N.R.*, 53 DTC 1158 (S.C.C.), *Laverne Asmussen Ltd. v. M.N.R.*, 61 DTC 440 (T.A.B.), and *Western Leaseholds v. M.N.R.*, 59 DTC 1316 (S.C.C.).

allowed by the reserve is five years. The reserve is extended to 10 years for certain property disposed of to a child of small business corporation shares or farm or fishing property.

A capital gains reserve for dispositions, where all or part of the proceeds are payable after the end of the year, is the lesser of a reasonable amount and an amount that brings 20% of the gain into income in the year of disposition and each of the immediately following four years. As a result, the usual maximum period over which the gain can be spread for inclusion in income is five years, including the year of disposition. A reasonable reserve is not defined in the Act. The CRA has taken the position that a reasonable reserve is based on prorated uncollected proceeds times the gain. The following examples are based on the CRA's interpretation of a reasonable reserve. The formula for the reserve is:

IT-236R4 (archived and no longer in force), par. 4
ITA: 40(1)(*a*)(iii)

Lesser of (a) $\frac{\text{proceeds not yet due}}{\text{total proceeds}} \times \text{gain} =$ reasonable reserve (i.e., the fraction of the gain represented by the portion of total proceeds not due at the end of the year)

(b) ($\frac{1}{5}$ of gain) × (4 – number of preceding taxation years ending after disposition)

The CRA's interpretation of the applicability of the reserve provision has indicated that the reserve is based on amounts that are payable to the taxpayer after the end of the year. Where a demand note is accepted on a disposition, eligibility for a reserve can be perfected by adding a condition that the note be payable, say, 10 days after demand. A demand made at the end of the year does not require payment until 10 days later with this condition.

IT-236R4, par. 2 [archived and no longer in force]

Consistent with the general scheme of the Act for the deduction of reserves, in the year following the deduction of a reserve, the preceding year's reserve will be taken into income, and a new reserve will be deducted in accordance with the above rules.

ITA: 40(1)(*a*)(ii)

Example Problem 8-1

Ms. Gamma sold a capital property for $200,000 on December 31, 2013. Of that price, $180,000 was not due until December 2014. The adjusted cost base of the property was $130,000 and the selling costs were $20,000.

— *REQUIRED*

Determine the taxable capital gain for 2013 and 2014 using the capital gains reserve provision.

ITA: 40(1)(*a*)

— *SOLUTION*

		2013
Proceeds of disposition		$200,000
Adjusted cost base	$130,000	
Expenses of disposition	20,000	(150,000)
Gain		$ 50,000
Less reserve — lesser of:		
(a) $\frac{\$180,000}{\$200,000} \times \$50,000 =$	$ 45,000	(40,000)
(b) ($\frac{1}{5}$ × $50,000) × (4 – 0) =	$ 40,000	
Capital gain		$ 10,000
Taxable capital gain ($\frac{1}{2}$ of capital gain)		$ 5,000

			2014
Inclusion in income of 2013 reserve			$ 40,000
Less 2014 reserve — lesser of:			
(a) $\frac{\text{Nil}}{\$200{,}000} \times \$50{,}000 =$	Nil	}	Nil
(b) ($\frac{1}{5}$ × $50,000) × (4 − 1) =	$ 30,000		
Capital gain			$ 40,000
Taxable capital gain (½ of capital gain)			$ 20,000

Note that the $50,000 of original capital gain is included in income over the two years in which proceeds were collected. The reserve simply allows the original gain to be spread over a maximum of 5 or 10 years, or the period of collection if that period is shorter.

Since a reserve is a permissive or optional deduction, it may not always be wise to take the reserve. For example, if the gain was triggered in a year in which the taxpayer's income and tax rate were lower than other years, deferral of the gain through a reserve would be pointless. However, a time-value of money advantage may be gained by a deferral to a future year, even if income will be taxed at a higher rate in that year. Similarly where the taxpayer wishes to use up the capital gains exemption for qualified small business corporation shares or qualified farm property immediately, the reserve should not be claimed.

The effect of this reserve system is to spread the capital gain realized on a disposition over a maximum of five years, including the year of the disposition. However, if the period of collection of the proceeds is less than five years, the system will spread the capital gain over the period of collection.

The reserve is only used to defer capital gains. There is no reserve against recaptured depreciation. Also, the reserve cannot be claimed by a non-resident, or where the purchaser is a controlled or controlling corporation if the purchaser is a partnership where the vendor is a majority interest partner, or in the year of death. ITA: 40(2) ITA: 72

¶8,130 Adjusted Cost Base and Capital Cost

The "adjusted cost base" of most capital property, as defined, is usually its cost plus or minus legislated adjustments. Cost is not defined for taxation purposes. The usual starting point is *cost* for accounting purposes which comprises laid-down cost, including the invoice cost, relevant sales, excise, and customs taxes, insurance, freight and, perhaps, some start-up costs. Where the person is a GST/HST registrant and is eligible for an input tax credit, the GST/HST should be excluded from adjusted cost base, because the GST/HST is not a cost if it is recovered by an input tax credit. ITA: 54 ITA: 53

There is an important exception to the above general rules in respect of depreciable property. In order to preserve the integrity of the capital cost allowance system, the adjusted cost base of depreciable property cannot be allowed to fluctuate as a result of the previously-mentioned adjustments. Hence, the "adjusted cost base" of depreciable property is defined to be its capital cost, which in turn takes us back to *cost* for accounting purposes without adjustments. ITA: 52 or 53 ITA: 54

Subsection 53(1) (additions) and subsection 53(2) (reductions) set out a number of adjustments some of which we have already examined.

- The cost base of land is increased by interest and property taxes denied. ITA: 18(2), 53(1)(*h*)
- Reasonable costs of surveying or valuing property in respect of its acquisition or disposition which are denied are added to the cost of the property. ITA: 18(1)(*b*), 53(1)(*n*)
- The cost of property is reduced by government assistance for capital property. ITA: 53(2)(*k*)

¶8,135 Non-arm's length transfer of depreciable property

If a depreciable property is transferred in a non-arm's length transaction, then this has implications for the operation of the capital cost allowance system. Deeming proceeds of disposition and cost of acquisition to be the fair market value will affect potential recapture of capital cost allowance on disposition and the base on which capital cost allowance is computed on acquisition.

If this type of transaction takes place, then there are special rules to determine what the undepreciated capital cost (UCC) of the property is to the acquirer. The results depend on whether an election is made under the interspousal rollover not to have the automatic rollover apply and whether there is an accrued gain on the property at the time of transfer. ITA: 13(7)(*e*) ITA: 73(1)

If no election is made on the interspousal transfer, then the property will automatically roll over at UCC. If an election is made, then the property will be disposed of at fair market value and the UCC of the property to the acquirer will be deemed to be equal to: ITA: 73(1) ITA: 13(7)(*e*)

the cost of the property to the transferor immediately before the transfer

plus:

the taxable capital gain realized on the transfer.

The addition of only the taxable capital gain restricts the UCC of the property to the transferee to the amount on which the transferor has paid tax.

¶8,140 Foreign Exchange Gains and Losses

Taxpayers must first determine whether the foreign exchange gain or loss arose from an income or a capital receipt, using the common law rules discussed in ¶4,020 and ¶8,020. For income receipts, the full gain or loss will be included in arriving at business or property income under Subdivision b. For capital receipts, the net capital gain or loss is determined in the normal manner. However, for individuals the net capital gain or loss is reduced by a maximum of $200. ITA: 39(2)

Example Problem 8-2

Mr. Coates made the following capital transactions which resulted in currency gains and losses during the following years:

	2011	*2012*	*2013*
Total currency gains	$800	$180	$250
Total currency losses	300	40	400

— *REQUIRED*

Compute the capital gains (losses) on foreign currency for each of the years shown.

— *SOLUTION*

	2011	*2012*	*2013*
Net capital gain (loss)	$500	$140	$(150)
Exempt portion of excess	200	140	(150)
Capital gain (loss)	$300	Nil	Nil

It should be noted that a currency gain or loss must be distinct and separate from another transaction that may have given rise to the currency transaction. For example, the sale of an article must be computed in Canadian dollars valued at the time of the sale in order to arrive at a gain or loss on that disposition. A subsequent conversion of foreign funds received would give rise to the currency gain or loss.

¶8,150 Debts Established To Be Bad Debts

Where a debt taken back from the purchaser of a capital property is established to have become a bad debt, the seller can elect to have disposed of the debt and to have reacquired it immediately at a cost equal to nil. The deemed disposition results in a capital loss to offset any part of the gain on disposition of the property represented in the debt. The deemed reacquisition at a nil cost may result in a further capital gain if any part of the debt is ultimately collected. ITA: 50(1)

A deemed disposition of the shares of an insolvent corporation occurs to realize the capital loss if: ITA: 50(1)(*b*)(iii)

- neither the corporation nor a corporation controlled by it carries on business in the year;
- the fair market value of the shares is nil;
- it is reasonable to expect that the corporation will be dissolved or wound up and will not start to carry on business; and
- the taxpayer elects to have this provision apply.

There will be another deemed disposition for proceeds of disposition equal to the ACB of the shares before the subsection 50(1) deemed disposition if: ITA: 50(1.1)

- the taxpayer elects a deemed disposition; and ITA: 50(1)(*b*)(iii)
- within 24 months of the disposition the corporation or a corporation controlled by it carries on business and the taxpayer or a non-arm's length person owns the shares.

This deemed disposition will result in a capital gain equal to the capital loss realized by the election. The shares are deemed to be reacquired at the adjusted cost base immediately before the disposition. ITA: 50(1)(*b*)(iii) ITA: 50(1.1)

Note that there is no provision for an "allowance for doubtful debts" in computing capital gains. At best, a reserve is provided for the uncollected gain portion of the proceeds, payable after the end of the year. This, of course, does not help the taxpayer when the amount of the debt is payable in the year but not collectible, because the debt has become bad. Also, the treatment of a bad debt resulting from the disposition of personal-use property is different. In that case, the Act allows a capital loss, only to the extent of the capital gains on the original disposition. ITA: 50(2)

When a business has accounts receivable from the sale of goods or services and some of those accounts become doubtful, then an allowance for doubtful accounts can be claimed as a deduction against business income (see ¶4,110). However, if these accounts receivable are sold to a third party, then any loss on the sale (the difference between the face amount of the receivables and the proceeds) is treated as a capital loss. If the purchaser also buys all of the other assets of the business and continues to carry on the business (see ¶4,285), then an election can be made to allow the loss to be claimed as a business loss. ITA: 22

¶8,160 Part Disposition

If a taxpayer makes a partial disposition of a capital property, he or she must allocate a reasonable portion of the total adjusted cost base of the capital property to the proceeds of partial disposition to determine the capital gain or loss. The portion of this cost allocated to the part sold should be in the ratio of the value of the part sold to the total value of the capital property. A valuation problem is very likely to arise, particularly if the value of the part sold is not, in fact, proportional to total value. This might be the case, for example, where a taxpayer owns land with lake frontage and the half of the property fronting on the lake is sold leaving the other half without such lake access. ITA: 43

¶8,170 Replacement Property

¶8,175 The basic deferral

This particular provision permits the deferral of some or all of the capital gain on property which is disposed of and which is subsequently replaced. There are two basic types of disposition which qualify for this deferral (often referred to in practice as a "rollover"):

(a) an involuntary disposition of property which has been lost, stolen, destroyed or taken by order of statutory authority (e.g., expropriation, bankruptcy); and

(b) a voluntary dispositions of real property referred to as "former business property" that usually occur on the relocation of a business.

The deferral for a voluntary disposition is limited to former business property. "Former business property" as used in this provision is defined as real or immovable property which has a common law definition of "land and buildings" and limited period franchises, concessions, or licences on which an election has been made [proposed in former Bill C-10]. ITA: 44(1)(*b*), 248(1) ITA: 13(4.2)

This topic has been partly covered in Chapter 5 in connection with the deferral of recapture realized on depreciable property. That material should be reviewed as preparation for the following discussion of the deferral of a capital gain in these situations. An election to defer either recapture or a capital gain is, also, deemed to be an election to defer the other. ITA: 13(4), 44(4) ITA: 13(4), 44(1)

In the year of the disposition, a taxpayer may choose to either:

(a) recognize the usual capital gain (i.e., P of D minus ACB and selling costs), or

(b) elect to report the capital gain as the lesser of:

(i) the actual capital gain in (a) above, and

(ii) the excess, if any, of proceeds for the old property over the cost of replacement (i.e., the amount of the proceeds not spent on the new property).

To qualify for this election, the property must be replaced:

(a) in the case of a voluntary disposition, by the later of the end of the first taxation year after the year of disposition and 12 months after the end of the year of disposition, or

(b) in the case of an involuntary disposition, by the later of the end of the second taxation year after the year of disposition and 24 months after the end of the year of disposition.

The disposition of the old property is deemed to have occurred only when the proceeds are "receivable". In the case of involuntary dispositions, the rules for determining when proceeds are receivable can be summarized (for situations excluding the death of a taxpayer or the winding-up of a corporation) as the earliest of: ITA: 44(2)

(a) the day the taxpayer has agreed to the full amount of the compensation;

(b) the day the compensation is finally determined by a court or tribunal; and

(c) the day that is two years from the day of loss, destruction or taking where a claim or suit has not been taken before the courts.

The election does not apply immediately where the taxpayer does not purchase the replacement property in the same year the proceeds of disposition become receivable. In the year in which proceeds of disposition become receivable, the disposition is handled in the normal manner by reporting the gain. If the replacement property is acquired within the allowed time, an amended return would be filed for the year in which the proceeds became receivable to implement the rollover.

The adjusted cost base for the replacement property under the election above will be reduced by the deferred capital gain. This is the essence of a rollover or deferral which, in this case, is accomplished by the reduction of the adjusted cost base of the new property. By ITA: 44(1)(*f*) reducing the adjusted cost base, a future capital gain (or reduced capital loss) in the amount of the deferred gain will arise on the ultimate disposition of the new property.

Replacement property is defined as property acquired for the same or a similar use as the original property and for gaining or producing income from the same or a similar business. The CRA's current interpretation of "same or similar use" and "same or similar business" is contained in an Interpretation Bulletin. ITA: 44(5) IT-259R4, par. 16-17, 18-21

Net capital gains reserves may arise from exchanges of property situations. For example, proceeds may become receivable in a year, but they are not due until a subsequent year, such that a capital gains reserve is available. When the reserve is included in income in the year after the reserve is deducted, the included reserve would normally qualify for this election.

Example Problem 8-3

Quick Growth Stores Ltd. has decided to change the present location of its retail store, now in a suburban area, to the Yonge Street strip in downtown Toronto. The following facts relate to the disposition of the original property in March 2012.

	Land	*Cl.3 Building*	*Cl.8 Equipment*
Cost	$30,000	$50,000	$5,000
UCC	—	30,000	1,500
Proceeds	70,000	100,000	500

Quick Growth Stores Ltd. purchased its Yonge Street property in August 2013 for the following amounts:

Land	$100,000
Building — brick	150,000
Equipment	20,000

The company wishes to elect to defer both the capital gain and the recapture. ITA: 13(4), 44(1)

— *REQUIRED*

Indicate the tax consequences if Quick Growth Stores Ltd. elects, assuming that its fiscal year-end is December 31.

— *SOLUTION*

This situation involves the voluntary disposition of a former business property in respect of the land and building. As a result, the taxpayer corporation must replace the land and building within the later of one taxation year or 12 months from the end of the December 31, 2012 taxation year (i.e., the taxation year of the disposition), in order to obtain the benefits of the rollover. It is often helpful to use a time line to graph the qualifying period of replacement as follows:

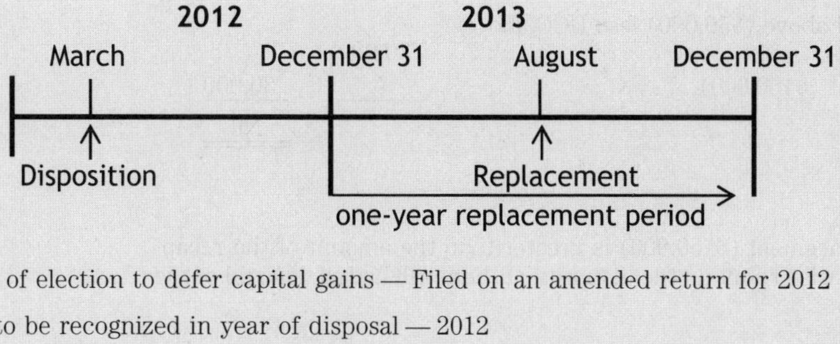

(A) Effect of election to defer capital gains — Filed on an amended return for 2012 ITA: 44

Gain to be recognized in year of disposal — 2012 ITA: 44(1)(*e*)

		Land	Building
(i) Capital gain, computed as:			
Lesser of: (I)	P of D	$ 70,000	$100,000
	ACB	(30,000)	(50,000)
	Capital gain	$ 40,000	$ 50,000

(II)	P of D	$ 70,000	$100,000
	Replacement cost	(100,000)	(150,000)
	Excess, if any	Nil	Nil

The lesser of the actual capital gain and the proceeds not spent on the replacement property is nil in both cases. Therefore, the full amount of the gain can be deferred by reducing the adjusted cost base of the replacement land and building.

Adjusted cost base of replacement land is
$100,000 – $40,000 = $60,000 ITA: 44(1)(*f*)
Adjusted cost base of replacement building is
$150,000 – $50,000 = $100,000 ITA: 44(1)(*f*)

(ii) Equipment — Nil

Equipment does not qualify as "former business property". In any case there is a loss which is not allowed as a capital loss. ITA: 39(1)(*b*)(i)

Comments:

(1) In the above situation, the entire capital gain is deferred through the reduction of the adjusted cost base of the replacement property, since the amount actually spent on the replacement property was greater than the proceeds of disposition for the old property. The intent of the provision is to allow a deferral of all or some part of the actual capital gain and, hence, the tax on that gain, where the proceeds have been spent to acquire a new property. Conceptually, if the proceeds have been spent in this manner, there would be no funds from the disposition of the old property to pay the taxes, so the taxes are deferred. Note how the reduction in the adjusted cost base of the replacement property implements the deferral. Consider the replacement land which was acquired at a cost of $100,000. Its cost base is $60,000 after the adjustment for the deferred gain. If that land were sold immediately for its indicated value of $100,000 (it was just purchased for that amount), a capital gain of $40,000 (i.e., $100,000 – $60,000) would be realized. That capital gain is exactly the gain on the old land that was deferred.

(2) Since the replacement property was acquired after the filing of the 2012 corporate tax returns (June 30, 2013), the resultant capital gain and any recapture must be reported in the year of disposition. A request for an amended return must be made in the year of acquisition. Acceptable security may be provided in lieu of the payment of outstanding taxes. IT-259R4, par. 3

(B) Effect of election to defer recapture, re building — Filed on an amended return for 2012.

2012		*Cl. 3: 5%*	
UCC immediately before disposal		$30,000	
Less: deemed disposal reducing UCC			ITA: 13(4)(*c*)
— normal deduction: lesser of:			
(i) cost ($50,000)			
(ii) P of D ($100,000)	$50,000		
— reduced by the lesser of:			
(i) amount determined above ($50,000) less UCC above ($30,000)	(20,000)		
(ii) cost of replacement ($150,000)		30,000	
UCC, December 31, 2012		Nil	

Comment:

As long as the cost of replacement ($150,000) is greater than the amount of the recapture ($20,000) that would otherwise result on the disposition, there will be full deferral of the recapture.

2013		*Cl. 1-NRB:* 6%*	
Add: Capital cost of replacement property			ITA: 13(4)(*d*)
Cost of replacement	$150,000		
Less: reduction for deferred gain	50,000		ITA: 44(1)(*f*)
Deemed capital cost	$100,000		

2013		*Cl. 1-NRB:* 6%*
Less: reduction for deferred recapture	20,000	$80,000
UCC, December 31, 2013		$80,000
CCA, 2013 (6% of ½ × $80,000)		2,400
UCC, January 1, 2014		$77,600

ITA: 13(4)(*d*)

* Separate Class 1 for non-residential buildings.

Comment:

Normally, when depreciable property of a class is sold and replaced with property of the same class in the year of disposition, all or some part of the potential recapture on the disposition is offset by the purchase before the end of the year. For example, if the new building had been purchased for $100,000 in 2012 and if it could have been added to the *same* class as the old building, the following UCC balance would have resulted:

UCC immediately before disposal		$ 30,000
Less lesser of:		
(i) cost of building disposed of	$ 50,000	
(ii) proceeds of disposition	$100,000	
lesser amount		(50,000)
Add: capital cost of replacement building		100,000
UCC, December 31, 2012		$ 80,000

Note that this is the same amount as the UCC balance at December 31, 2013 after the rollover is implemented. ITA: 13(4)

In deferring the recapture, the election provides two additional benefits: ITA: 13(4)

(i) it allows for a replacement to take place in a subsequent year, and

(ii) it allows for a replacement with a property in a different class.

Example Problem 8-4

Reconsider the facts in Example Problem 8-3. In this example, Quick Growth Stores Ltd. purchased less expensive land in 2013.

Land	$ 45,000
Building — brick (same as Example Problem 8-3)	150,000
Equipment (same as Example Problem 8-3)	20,000

— *REQUIRED*

Indicate the tax consequences for the land only, if Quick Growth Stores Ltd. elects under section 44 (assuming that its fiscal year-end is December 31).

— *SOLUTION*

The gain on the land to be recognized in year of disposal (2012) is now $25,000, computed as:

Lesser of: (A) P of D	$70,000
ACB	(30,000)
CG	$40,000

(B) P of D	$70,000
Replacement cost	(45,000)
Excess, if any	$25,000

Adjusted cost base in 2013 of replacement property is:

Replacement cost	$ 45,000
Deferred gain [$40,000 – $25,000]	(15,000)
ACB of replacement property	$ 30,000

ITA: 44(1)(*f*)

¶8,180 Election for additional deferral

This particular election permits the proceeds on the dispositions of former business property (land and buildings) to be reallocated between the two components so that less capital gain or recapture would be triggered. This election appears to recognize the fact that when a property consisting of land and building is sold, it is usually sold for proceeds which represent the fair market value of the total property. In this situation, the land and building are not priced separately. Therefore, the original allocation of proceeds between land and building may have been fairly arbitrary. ITA: 44(6)

Example Problem 8-5

Reconsider the facts in Example Problems 8-3 and 8-4, above.

— *REQUIRED*

Indicate tax consequences of electing an additional deferral in respect of the building, based on the facts in Example Problem 8-3, and the land, based on the facts in Example Problem 8-4. ITA: 44(6)

— *SOLUTION*

Re-examining the facts of Example Problem 8-4, above, it would be possible to elect to transfer $25,000 of the land proceeds to the building proceeds, thereby eliminating the capital gain. Note that the trade-off is a reduced capital cost of the building and, hence, a lower capital cost allowance base. Therefore, the cost of deferring tax on $25,000 of capital gain now is less capital cost allowance over the holding period of the building in the future.

(A) Effect of election ITA: 44(6)

Gain to be recognized in year of disposal (2012) ITA: 44(1)(*e*)

			Land	Building
(i) Capital gain, computed as:				
Lesser of:	(I)	Actual P of D	$ 70,000	$100,000
		Election	(25,000)	25,000
		Deemed P of D	$ 45,000	$125,000
		ACB	(30,000)	(50,000)
		CG	$ 15,000	$ 75,000
	(II)	Deemed P of D above	$ 45,000	$125,000
		Replacement cost	(45,000)	(150,000)
		Excess, if any	Nil	Nil

ITA: 44(6)

Adjusted cost base of replacement land is:

$45,000 – ($15,000 – Nil) = $30,000 ITA: 44(1)(f)

Adjusted cost base of replacement building is:

$150,000 – ($75,000 – Nil) = $75,000 ITA: 44(1)(f)

Comment:

Note that the key to a reallocation of proceeds that will successfully defer more of the capital gain is a replacement cost of one of the assets (i.e., either land or building) that is sufficiently in excess of original proceeds of disposition to allow for an increase in proceeds on that asset without triggering a gain. In this case, the replacement cost of the building, at $150,000, exceeds the original proceeds of the old building of $100,000. Therefore, up to $50,000 can be added to the proceeds and still leave the excess of proceeds over replacement cost of nil. In this case, only $25,000 needs to be removed from the proceeds of the land to allow all of the gain to be deferred.

(B) Effect of election to defer recapture on building — Filed on an amended return for 2012.

2012

		Cl.3: 5%	
UCC immediately before disposal		$30,000	
Less: deemed disposal reducing UCC			ITA: 13(4)(c)
— normal deduction: lesser of:			
(i) cost ($50,000)			
(ii) P of D ($100,000)[1]	$ 50,000		
— reduced by the lesser of:			ITA: 13(4)(c)
(i) amount determined above ($50,000) less UCC above ($30,000)	20,000		
(ii) cost of replacement ($150,000)		30,000	
UCC after disposal		Nil	

2013

			Cl. 1-NRB: 6%	
Add:	Capital cost of replacement property			ITA: 13(4)(d)
	Cost of replacement	$150,000		
	Less: reduction for deferred gain	75,000		ITA: 44(1)(f)
	Deemed capital cost	$ 75,000		
	Less: reduction for deferred recapture	20,000	$55,000	ITA: 13(4)(d)
UCC,	December 31, 2013		$55,000	
CCA,	2013 (6% of ½ × $55,000)		1,650	
UCC,	January 1, 2014		$53,350	

Comment:

The results of using the election for additional deferral can be compared with the original application of the deferral as follows: ITA: 44(6)

	Without election	*With election*	*Difference*
Capital gains recognized:			
land	$ 25,000	Nil	$25,000
building	Nil	Nil	Nil
ACB of replacement property:			
land	30,000	$30,000	Nil

building	100,000	75,000	25,000
UCC (before CCA) of replacement building	80,000	55,000	25,000

The above shows that no capital gain on the land has to be recognized as a result of the election. This is reflected in the adjusted cost base of the building which is $25,000 lower. This lower ACB will potentially result in a higher capital gain on the ultimate disposition of the building, if it is sold for a capital gain. Also, the UCC of the building is $25,000 lower, resulting in less annual CCA. To evaluate the trade-off the following should be compared: ITA: 44(6)

(i) the tax that would be paid now on a capital gain of $25,000 or a taxable capital gain of $12,500 (i.e., ½ × $25,000), and

(ii) the present value of the CCA tax shield[(2)] from $25,000 of capital cost in Class NRB.

— *NOTES TO SOLUTION*

(1) Note that the deemed proceeds arising from the election are not applicable for the purpose of a deferral of recapture, since the election is only applicable to Subdivision c which deals with taxable capital gains and allowable capital losses. ITA: 44(6) ITA: 13, 44(6)

(2) The present value of the CCA tax shield, including the effect of the half-year rule, can be computed from the following:

$$PV = \frac{C \times R \times T}{R + I} \times \frac{1 + I/2}{1 + I}$$

where PV = present value of the CCA tax shield,
C = capital cost of the asset,
R = rate of CCA for the class,
I = after-tax discount rate,
T = tax rate.

Summary
Replacement Property

Deferral of Capital Gain

Key Question: Did you spend at least the proceeds on the replacement property?

If you spend at least the proceeds from the sale of the former property to buy the replacement property, then the full amount of the gain will be deferred. The deferral is built into the reduction of the cost base of the replacement property.

If you sell both land and building then this concept applies to the combined proceeds and the combined replacement cost.

Deferral of Recapture

Key Question: Did you spend at least the amount of the recapture on the replacement property?

If you spend at least an amount equal to the potential recapture from the sale of the former property to buy the replacement property, then the full amount of the recapture will be deferred. The deferral is built into the reduction of the undepreciated capital cost of the replacement property.

¶8,190 Proceeds on Disposition of Building

An interesting situation arose in the case of *The Queen v. Malloney's Studio Limited*, in which the taxpayer agreed to sell land clear of buildings and, therefore, had to demolish an existing building before disposing of the land. The Minister allocated part of the proceeds of disposition for the property to the demolished building resulting in recapture. The taxpayer argued that all of the price related to the land. The Supreme Court of Canada held that the price related only to the land because the building was not part of the sale. No part of the price was for property "damaged, destroyed, taken or injuriously affected" because the purchase did not cause the damage as envisaged by the definition of "proceeds of disposition". Since none of the proceeds for the property had to be allocated to the building, the 78 DTC 6278 (S.C.C.) ITA: 13(21) taxpayer could deduct a terminal loss on the building, since it was the only building in its class, and, at the same time, all of the proceeds created a capital gain which was only fractionally taxable.

Perhaps as a reaction to the result of the above case, a provision was added to the Act to provide rules to allocate proceeds of disposition between land and buildings on their sale. Where a building is sold for proceeds that are less than its proportionate share of the undepreciated capital cost of its class, this provision will apply. In the situation where the land is sold in the same taxation year as the building, the amount which is treated as proceeds of disposition of the building may be greater than the fair market value of the building, thereby reducing or eliminating the potential terminal loss. At the same time, the capital gain on the sale of the land will be reduced by the amount of the terminal loss eliminated on the building. Thus, the potential terminal loss on the building will be used to offset the gain on the land. The result is to convert what might have been a terminal loss fully deductible into a reduction of a capital gain, in essence, one-half deductible. ITA: 13(21.1)

Where the land is not disposed of in the same year, one-half of the apparent terminal loss on the building will be deductible, resulting in what is, in effect, an allowable capital loss on the sale of the building instead of an ordinary loss. However, the deductible amount of the loss will technically be considered a business loss.

It is easiest to see and understand the concept of the provision if the building that is disposed is the only building in its class, as is the case in the following example problem. However, it should be realized that the provision applies, even if there is no actual terminal loss in the class because there is at least one other building in the class.

Example Problem 8-6

Trudeau Limited owned a real property which it sold during the current taxation year for a total of $200,000. The land had a fair market value of $150,000 and an adjusted cost base of $100,000. The building had a fair market value of $50,000. It was the only building in the class which had an undepreciated capital cost of $75,000 and a capital cost of $90,000.

— *REQUIRED*

(A) Determine the tax consequences of the sale of the building in this transaction.

(B) If the purchaser wanted to buy only the building for $50,000 and remove it at his or her own expense to another location, what would be the tax consequences of the sale of the building?

— *SOLUTION*

(A) If proceeds of disposition of the building are considered to be equal to its fair market value of $50,000 which is less than the undepreciated capital cost of the class and the capital cost, the proceeds of disposition of the building will be deemed to be the following: ITA: 13(21.1)(*a*)

P of D of building = lesser of:

(i)	(I) FMV of land and building		$200,000
	minus		
	(II) lesser of:		
	— ACB of land	$100,000	100,000
	— FMV of land	$150,000	
			$100,000
(ii)	greater of:		
	(I) FMV of building	$50,000	
	(II) lesser of capital cost and UCC of building	$75,000	$75,000

= $75,000

Since proceeds of disposition are deemed to be equal to the undepreciated capital cost of the class, there is no terminal loss and no recapture. Note that proceeds of disposition of the land will be deemed to be:

(i) P of D of land and building	$200,000	
minus		
(ii) deemed P of D of building (above)	75,000	$125,000

This will result in a capital gain of $25,000 on the land (i.e., $125,000 – $100,000).

If it were not for the rule being illustrated, there would have been a capital gain on the land of $50,000 (i.e., $150,000 – $100,000) and a terminal loss on the building of $25,000 (i.e., $50,000 – $75,000). The effect of the rule can be seen from the following comparison: ITA: 13(21.1)(*a*)

Income effect	*Without par. 13(21.1)(a)*	*With par. 13(21.1)(a)*
Taxable capital gain on land:		
½ × $50,000	$ 25,000	
½ × $25,000		$12,500
Terminal loss on building	(25,000)	(Nil)
Effect on net income	Nil	$12,500

The rule has converted the terminal loss on the building, which is normally fully deductible, into an amount that is, in effect, only ½ deductible by reducing the gain on the land (which is only ½ taxable). Note that this conversion of a terminal loss only occurs if there is a capital gain on the land. ITA: 13(21.1)(*a*)

(B) In this case, proceeds of disposition of the building will be deemed to be the following: ITA: 13(21.1)(*b*)

P of D of building =	(i) P of D of building (without ssec. 13(21.1))		$ 50,000
	plus		
	(ii) greater of:		
	(I) UCC of building (Class 3)	$75,000	
	(II) FMV of building	$50,000	
		$75,000	
	minus P of D of building in (i) above	$50,000	
	excess × ½	$25,000 × ½	$ 12,500
			$ 62,500
UCC of class			75,000
Terminal loss			$(12,500)

Note how the decline in value of $25,000 from undepreciated capital cost to fair market value of the building has been rendered, essentially one-half deductible in this situation. This effect parallels that illustrated in part (A) above.

Summary

Disposal of Land and Building

Ssec. 13(21.1)

Key Question: Was there a capital gain on the land and a terminal loss on the building?

If so, an amount equal to the terminal loss (but not greater than the capital gain) will reduce the proceeds on the land and increase the proceeds on the building. This will reduce the capital gain and the terminal loss will be eliminated.

¶8,200 Disposition of Depreciable Property

A capital gain will arise on the disposition of depreciable property if the proceeds of disposition exceed the total of the adjusted cost base of the property, plus the disposal costs. Recall that capital losses may never be claimed in respect of depreciable property and that the undepreciated capital cost is irrelevant in the determination of a capital gain. As such property depreciates over time, any decline in value is deemed to be normal depreciation and is therefore not considered to be a capital loss. Furthermore, if this type of property is sold for less than its capital cost, the rules on capital cost allowance will apply to recognize a terminal loss, recapture of capital cost allowance, or to reduce the UCC of the class in which the property was included. To claim a capital loss would, in fact, be double counting the decline in value.

The following diagrams may help to show the different possible outcomes on the disposition of depreciable property, where there is only one asset in the class. Remember, you cannot have a capital loss on depreciable property. If proceeds are less than capital cost, then the result is determined through the CCA system. To determine whether there is recapture or terminal loss, the lower of cost or proceeds (LOCP) is credited to the CCA class in which the asset was found.

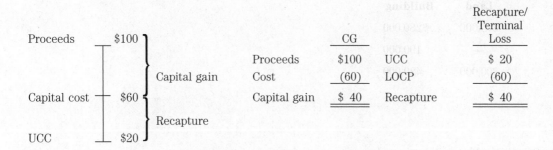

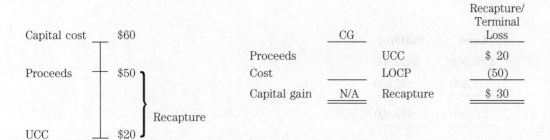

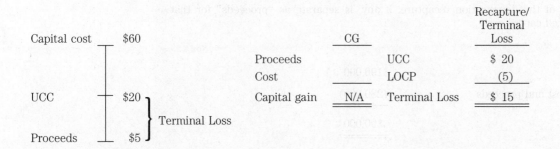

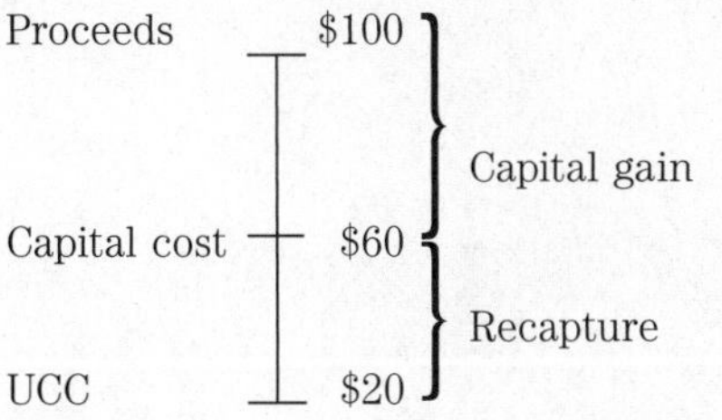

	CG		Recapture/ Terminal Loss
Proceeds	$100	UCC	$ 20
Cost	(60)	LOCP	(60)
Capital gain	$ 40	Recapture	$ 40

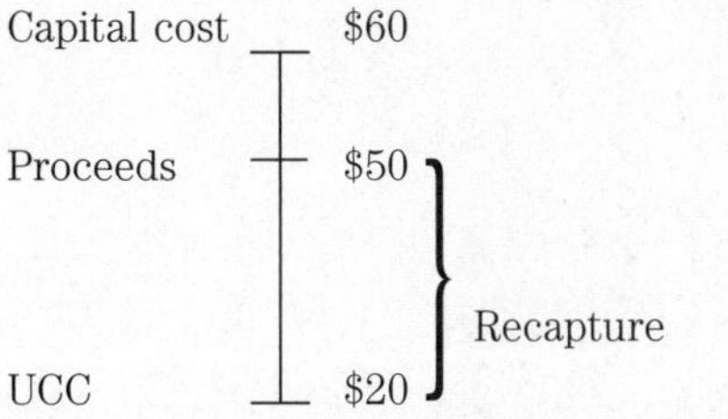

	CG		Recapture/ Terminal Loss
Proceeds		UCC	$ 20
Cost		LOCP	(50)
Capital gain	N/A	Recapture	$ 30

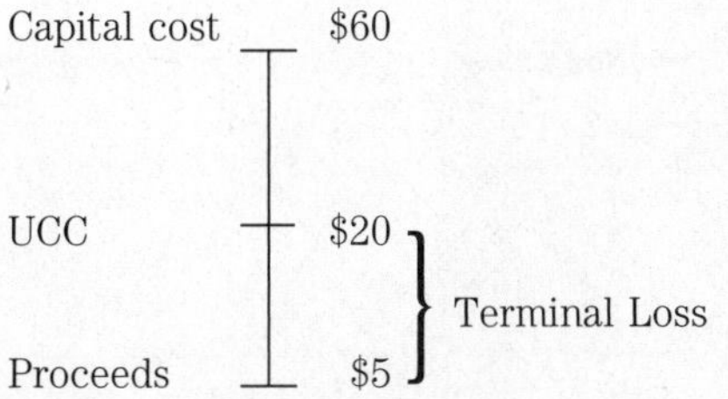

	CG		Recapture/ Terminal Loss
Proceeds		UCC	$ 20
Cost		LOCP	(5)
Capital gain	N/A	Terminal Loss	$ 15

Note: The difference between proceeds and UCC always needs to be accounted for.

If there is more than one asset in the class, then there are two options.

(1) If proceeds are greater than the adjusted cost base of the asset, then there is a capital gain and the lower of cost or proceeds is credited to the CCA class. If the CCA class then becomes negative, there is recapture. If there is a positive balance, then CCA continues to be claimed.

(2) If proceeds are less than the adjusted cost base, then the lower of cost or proceeds is credited to the CCA class. If the CCA class then becomes negative, there is recapture. If there is a positive balance, then CCA continues to be claimed.

Example Problem 8-7

Lanice J. Corporation disposed of its building in Victoria, B.C. The facts relating to the disposition were as follows:

	Land	**Building**
Adjusted cost base	$75,000	$280,000
UCC	—	190,000
Proceeds	200,000	420,000

— *REQUIRED*

Compute the corporation's taxable capital gain and recapture.

— *SOLUTION*

	Land	**Building**
Proceeds	$200,000	$420,000
Adjusted cost base	75,000	280,000
Capital gain	125,000	140,000
Taxable capital gain (50%)	$62,500	$70,000

The calculation of the depreciation recapture, if any, is separate as "proceeds" for that purpose cannot exceed capital cost.

UCC	$190,000
Lesser of capital cost and proceeds	(280,000)
Recaptured CCA	$90,000

¶8,210 Election on Change in Use

When a taxpayer changes the use of property, he or she is deemed to have sold that property at the fair market value and to have reacquired the same property immediately thereafter at the fair market value which becomes his or her new adjusted cost base. Where property has a dual use, its cost must be apportioned between the uses on a percentage basis and that basis will be used on the disposition of the property. If the percentage for a particular use is changed either up or down, there will be a proportionate deemed disposition and reacquisition at the fair market value at that time.[5] Note that these rules are similar in concept to the rules pertaining to depreciable property with respect to changes of use and the capital cost allowance system. ITA: 45(1)(*a*), 45(1)(*b*), 45(1)(*c*) ITA: 13(7)

The CRA indicates that a change in use does not include a transfer of property from one income-producing use to another such use by the same taxpayer. As examples, the CRA suggests that the change-in-use rules do not apply when real estate used to produce income from a business or property is converted to inventory, because holding the property as inventory is still an income-producing use. Similarly, the rules do not apply where inventory is converted to capital property which is used to produce income from a business or property. The Interpretation Bulletin provides numerical examples of how to handle these conversions to separate income gains from capital gains by the use of a "notional disposition". It is only on an actual disposition that income gains alone may be realized in these situations. IT-218R, par. 11 IT-218R, par. 15

For personal-use property *only*, a taxpayer may elect to defer the capital gain until such time as he or she:

- decides to dispose of the asset;
- is deemed to dispose of the asset; or
- decides to rescind the election.

This election applies only when the property was used originally for personal use and remains in force until one of the above conditions occurs. For example, a taxpayer may have a yacht which is used for personal use. Later, the taxpayer decides to rent out the yacht. He or she may elect to defer the potential gain on the change in use. This election will remain in force even when he or she changes its use back to personal use unless, of course, he or she rescinds the election. However, this election is not available in a situation where the property was first used to produce income and then is changed to personal use. ITA: 45(2)

Example Problem 8-8

A taxpayer purchased a yacht in 2005 at a cost of $24,000. In 2008, the taxpayer changed the use and rented the yacht for the next two years. The fair market value at the time the property became an income-producing asset was $30,000. During 2010, he converted the yacht back to exclusive personal use. The fair market value at this time was $33,000. In 2013, the taxpayer sold the yacht for $60,000.

— *REQUIRED*

Compare the taxable capital gain arising with and without the election to be deemed not to have changed the use. ITA: 45(2)

[5] The case of *Woods v. M.N.R.*, 78 DTC 1576 (T.R.B.), illustrates the application of subsection 45(1) and the consequences of a deemed disposition.

— *SOLUTION*

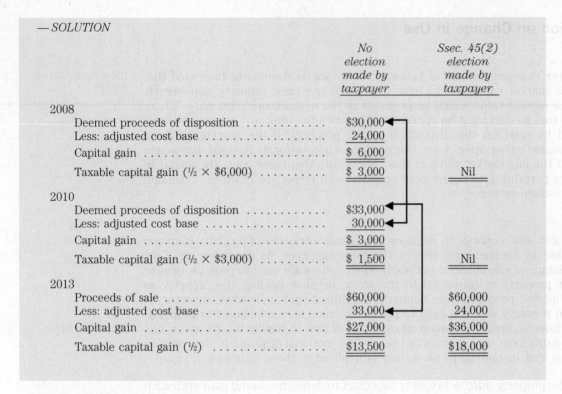

	No election made by taxpayer	*Ssec. 45(2) election made by taxpayer*
2008		
Deemed proceeds of disposition	$30,000	
Less: adjusted cost base	24,000	
Capital gain	$ 6,000	
Taxable capital gain (½ × $6,000)	$ 3,000	Nil
2010		
Deemed proceeds of disposition	$33,000	
Less: adjusted cost base	30,000	
Capital gain	$ 3,000	
Taxable capital gain (½ × $3,000)	$ 1,500	Nil
2013		
Proceeds of sale	$60,000	$60,000
Less: adjusted cost base	33,000	24,000
Capital gain	$27,000	$36,000
Taxable capital gain (½)	$13,500	$18,000

Notes to Example Problem

Theoretically, there should be no difference in the total taxable capital gain between the two options available, only a timing difference in the payment of the tax. Where the inclusion rate is constant, the election would normally be the preferred treatment, since the change in use has not generated any cash. Hence, there are a number of other factors to be considered: ITA: 45(2)

(a) Does the taxpayer have any capital losses which he or she may wish to trigger?

(b) Will the taxpayer move to a higher tax bracket in the future?

(c) Conversely, does the taxpayer anticipate a decrease in income at some time in the future?

If the facts in the example problem had been reversed and the taxpayer had acquired the yacht for rental purposes and subsequently converted the yacht to personal use, this election would not be available. However, if the property was a rental building which was converted to personal use and was designated as a principal residence in a subsequent disposition, a rollover or deferral would be provided. ITA: 45(3)

If an election is made not to have a change in use, then there will be no need to determine the UCC of the yacht, since it is deemed to still be personal-use property. If an election is not made, then a UCC must be determined and these rules, as explained in Chapter 5, will result in a UCC in 2008 of $27,000 (cost of $24,000 plus the TCG at 50% of $6,000). On the deemed disposition in 2010, there may be recapture to the extent that any CCA was claimed on the yacht. ITA: 45(2) ITA: 13(7)

¶8,300 INCOME RECONCILIATION REVISITED

One of the major adjustments to accounting income in its conversion to income for tax purposes is the exclusion of book gains and losses on the disposition of capital property and the inclusion of taxable capital gains and allowable capital losses.

Example Problem 8-9

Capital Hill Ltd. has disposed of the following capital assets during 2013:

	Proceeds of disposition	*Cost*	*Book value*	*Undepreciated capital cost*
Securities	$ 500	$ 5,000	n/a	n/a
Land	52,500	30,000	n/a	n/a
Building*	76,250	20,000	$ 3,000	$4,500
Equipment**	500	10,000	1,000	1,500

* Ignore section 44 considerations.

** Only asset in class.

— *REQUIRED*

Indicate the adjustments to be made in the reconciliation of accounting income to income for tax purposes.

— *SOLUTION*

Reference	ADDITIONS	
Sec. 3	Securities — book loss: ($500 – $5,000)	$ 4,500
Sec. 38	Land — taxable capital gain: ($52,500 – $30,000) × ½	11,250
Sec. 38	Building — taxable capital gain: ($76,250 – $20,000) × ½	28,125
Sec. 13	Building — recapture: ($4,500 – $20,000)	15,500
Sec. 3	Equipment — book loss: ($500 – $1,000)	500
		$ 59,875

Reference	DEDUCTIONS	
Sec. 38	Securities — allowable capital loss: ($500 – $5,000) × ½	$ 2,250*
Sec. 3	Land — book gain: ($52,500 – $30,000)	22,500
Sec. 3	Building — book gain: ($76,250 – $3,000)	73,250
Par. 39(1)(*b*)	Equipment — capital loss	Nil
Ssec. 20(16)	— terminal loss ($1,500 – $500)	1,000
		$ 99,000

* Can only be deducted to the extent that there are taxable capital gains.

¶8,800 REVIEW QUESTIONS

(1) Tom, Dick, and Harry formed a partnership in order to invest in a tract of land just outside a large urban area. Five years later, the partnership sold the property making a large profit. According to the partnership agreement, profits from this venture were to be split equally. Discuss whether this is an income or a capital receipt.

(2) Rachel is a real estate salesperson who invests her spare cash in "good land buys" which she occasionally finds. This year Rachel sold one of these properties and realized a large profit. Is this an income or a capital receipt?

(3) Winston White, an accountant, uses his spare time and cash to trade in low-cost mining shares listed on a Canadian stock exchange. Winston made a large profit this year on his stock market transactions. Is this profit income or capital gain?

(4) Diana purchased some land to erect a shopping centre which she intended to sell. However, zoning bylaws could not be changed and Diana sold the property at a large profit. Is this profit income or a capital gain?

(5) Doug spends his Saturday afternoons at the race track. This year Doug was extremely fortunate and his net winnings were $15,000. How will these winnings be taxed?

(6) Mrs. Garland has been going south for many years and usually keeps some U.S. currency handy in case she needs it. This year, because of some unusual fluctuations in the Canadian dollar, she realized an exchange loss on her U.S. dollar transactions of $2,500. How will this be taxed?

(7) Mr. Cole bought six acres of lake-front property 15 years ago for $24,000. This year, he sold the three acres that are not on the lake to a neighbour who wanted the woodlot. His proceeds on the three acres sold are $30,000. Discuss what the cost base of the three acres sold would be.

(8) Mr. Bosma had 20 acres of his farm expropriated by the city for industrial land in 2012. Because he disputed their value, the proceeds were not finally decided until 2013. How soon does he have to replace the land in order to defer the tax on the capital gain realized on the sale of the land?

(9) Opco Ltd. had a large piece of equipment destroyed by fire with the insurance proceeds being paid and the machine replaced in the same year. Can the replacement property rules be applied?

(10) Mrs. Smith owns 100% of Holdco Inc., which in turn owns 100% of Opco Inc. Holdco owns the building which is used by Opco in its active business and rents it to Opco under a five-year lease. Mrs. Smith wants to sell the building and buy a bigger one for the same purpose, but she has been told that the building is considered to be a rental property and, therefore, does not qualify for the replacement property rules since it is not a "former business property". She has asked for your comments. ITA: 248(1)

(11) Mr. Carr bought and operated a parking lot for the past 10 years. He has now decided that it is time to do something different. However, instead of selling the parking lot he wants to rezone the property and develop and sell condominium apartments. On July 1 of last year, he applied for rezoning and on December 1 of last year, he received the zoning change and a building permit. By October 31 of this year, he had completed construction and sold the units. What kind of income would he have to report and when?

(12) Last year Ms. Chung sold some land that was capital property and realized a capital gain of $150,000. As part of the proceeds she took back a note for $100,000 at 12% which unfortunately was unsecured. This year she realized that the note will become a bad debt, but since she has not disposed of the note she does not think that it can be used for tax purposes. What is your advice to her? What would be the result if the land that was sold was personal-use property?

¶8,825 MULTIPLE CHOICE QUESTIONS

Question 1

On April 1, 2013, X Ltd., with a December 31 year-end, sold a parcel of land, a capital property with an adjusted cost base of $100,000, for $600,000. The $600,000 proceeds were payable in the form of a mortgage, with principal payments of $90,000 due every six months, starting on October 1, 2013. What is the minimum taxable capital gain that X Ltd. must report in 2013?

(A) $100,000

(B) $50,000

(C) $75,000

(D) $37,500

Question 2

Mega Ltd., which has a May 31 year-end, had its land and building expropriated on June 30, 2013, and received $1 million of compensation from the government for the expropriation. Which one of the following is the deadline for Mega Ltd. to replace the property with another property costing at least $1 million in order to defer the entire recapture and capital gain on the disposition of the expropriated property?

(A) On or before May 31, 2015.

(B) On or before June 30, 2015.

(C) On or before December 31, 2015.

(D) On or before May 31, 2016.

Question 3

Steve is the proprietor of a sporting goods retail business. By chance, he discovered on the Internet a used motor boat for sale for $4,000 — a bargain price. He purchased the motor boat and immediately sold it for a profit of $3,000. He did not use the boat. Which of the following best describes the tax treatment of this transaction?

(a) The motor boat purchase is an investment, and the sale results in a taxable capital gain.

(b) The motor boat purchase is an investment, and the sale results in property income.

(c) The motor boat purchase is an adventure or concern in the nature of trade, and the sale results in business income.

(d) The motor boat purchase is an adventure or concern in the nature of trade, and the sale results in a taxable capital gain.

Question 4

Frames Inc. had a warehouse where it stored its inventory of picture frames, but a fire destroyed the Class 1 building in September 2012. The original cost of the building was $800,000 and the UCC value at the time was $540,000. The insurance company decided the building was a write-off and paid Frames Inc. $850,000 for the building in October 2013. Frames Inc. paid $950,000 to construct a new building by November 2013. What is the UCC of the building before CCA to Frames Inc. for its taxation year ended December 31, 2013, assuming they wish to minimize tax?

(a) $640,000

(b) $690,000

(c) $950,000

(d) $900,000

Question 5

Gloria owned a non-residential building, purchased in 1997, the original cost of which was $400,000, plus $150,000 for the cost of land. The UCC value of the building was $360,000, and the land and building were sold for $750,000 in 2013. The split the taxpayer used between land and building was $300,000 for building and $450,000 for land. Assuming that Gloria wishes to minimize her taxes, what are the tax implications regarding the sale?

(a) A capital gain of $300,000 and a terminal loss of $60,000.

(b) A capital gain of $240,000 and a terminal loss of nil.

(c) A capital gain of $150,000 and a terminal loss of $60,000.

(d) A capital gain of $120,000 and a terminal loss of nil.

¶8,850 EXERCISES

Exercise 1

ITA: 39(2)

When he was vacationing in Florida this year, Joe Raymer sold, for US$10,000, an asset used in his proprietorship business in Ottawa, which he purchased four years ago for C$4,000. Joe was paid in U.S. dollars. At the time of the sale, US$1 bought C$0.99. When Joe returned, he converted the U.S. currency to Canadian dollars and received C$10,200.

— REQUIRED

Compute the taxable capital gain or allowable capital loss, if any, arising on the above transactions.

Exercise 2

ITA: 13(4), 44

Tax Processing Ltd.'s computer was completely destroyed in a fire in 2011. The insurance company has been disputing the claim. In the meantime, the company is renting computer time until the claim is settled. The following facts relate to the destroyed computer:

Capital cost	$50,000
UCC immediately before the fire — Class 10	17,150

During 2013, the insurance company paid $60,000 in respect of the claim. The company continued to rent computer time for another 24 months, after which it purchased a new-generation computer for $70,000.

— REQUIRED

Indicate the tax consequences for Tax Processing Ltd. for the above years.

Exercise 3

ITA: 20(1)(*l*), 20(1)(*p*), 22, 38, 39, 50

Reconsider Exercise 14 of Chapter 4 and explain the tax implications if Mr. Flint and Mr. Small do not use the section 22 election on the sale of the accounts receivable.

Exercise 4

ITA: 13(21.1)

Sienna Research Inc. has one last building to dispose of in its liquidation process. Higher Peaks Ltd. has agreed to purchase the building for $1.28 million. The president of Sienna would like to maximize the after-tax profits of the disposition by creating a terminal loss on the building. He bragged about how the terminal loss on the building would nicely reduce the capital gain on the land. He drafted a sales contract allocating the total proceeds as follows:

Land	$ 895,000
Building	385,000
Total	$1,280,000

The capital cost of the land and building was as follows:

Land	$345,000
Building	520,000
Total	$865,000

The UCC of the building (last asset in Class 3) is $438,700.

— REQUIRED

The president would like you to confirm the tax implications of this disposition.

Exercise 5

ITA: 40(1)(*a*)

Mary Jane inherited a parcel of land from her father in 1991 when she inherited his proprietorship business assets. She sold the land in 2013 for $200,000. Her father paid $30,000 for the land and the value in 1991 was $60,000. The purchaser paid $50,000 cash, with the remaining $150,000 plus interest due in 2015. Mary Jane has calculated her capital gain as $140,000.

— REQUIRED

Determine if Mary Jane's calculation of her capital gain is correct. Indicate if she has any other alternatives for reporting the gain. Your answer should be supported with appropriate references to the Act.

¶8,875 ASSIGNMENT PROBLEMS

Problem 1

Schillaci v. M.N.R., 92 DTC 1648 (T.C.C.)

Jean-Luc, the taxpayer in this case, was experienced in retail real estate, having originally been employed by a fast-food chain of restaurants. His duties were to locate, acquire and open restaurants on behalf of his employer. He acquired extensive knowledge in packaging sites for retail operations.

Two years ago, Jean-Luc began to work as an employee for Jorge, a successful builder of homes and condominiums, real estate developer for investment of rental apartments and retail plazas, and trust company owner. Jean-Luc was employed on a salary and bonus basis. At the time, Jean-Luc was also a licensed real estate broker and owned a brokerage firm.

Jean-Luc's first project for Jorge involved developing a retail complex in Toronto. He was instrumental in obtaining two anchor tenants as well as two others. This was a successful venture.

His second venture involved a strip plaza in London, Ontario. By the time Jean-Luc and Jorge were prepared to purchase the property, most of the pre-development work had been completed and two nationally recognized restaurant chains had signed letters of intent and/or offers to lease. These two tenants represented 60% of the rentable area of the plaza. With those tenants in place, other tenants were prepared to rent because of the traffic which would be generated by the presence of the two popular fast-food restaurants. As a result, financing the project would not be a problem.

All of the leases which were negotiated were of the "net-net" type — the landlord being responsible only for its financing costs. The tenants were responsible for all other costs and expenses involved with the plaza, in addition to their own businesses.

A partnership of Jorge (74%), Jean-Luc (24%), and Shloimie (2%), the long-time accountant for Jorge, was established to own the plaza. Neither Jean-Luc nor Shloimie paid for his respective interest in the partnership. Jean-Luc considered this to be a long-term project that would provide income for his children's future. Jorge and Shloimie regarded the project as an opportunity to acquire and own an income-producing property with very little investment, since most of the funds were provided by debt financing.

City planning and zoning for the plaza was approved and most of the financing was in place. Last year, about a year after the purchase by the partnership, the building was completed to the point where the tenants took possession. Shortly thereafter, the tenants completed their respective areas and were in operation and paying rent. Temporary financing was in place and permanent financing was being negotiated pending a drop in interest rates at the time.

This year, Jorge began to have financial difficulties and his assets were liquidated by his creditors. Since his creditors did not have security on the plaza project, Jorge was in a position to sell that asset in an orderly manner. Although Jorge controlled the partnership, he received Jean-Luc's consent to sell the property. Jean-Luc's share of the gain on the sale was about $157,000.

Jean-Luc filed his tax return for this year showing the gain as a capital gain.

— REQUIRED

A CRA assessor has just called to indicate that she is considering a reassessment of the income in question as income from a business, an adventure in the nature of trade, or from a profit-making undertaking or concern.

As Jean-Luc's tax adviser, evaluate the fact situation and recommend a course of action.

Problem 2

ITA: 20(1)(n), 20(8), 40; IT-152R3

Len Jamal bought a parcel of land in 1993. It was his intention that he would relocate his proprietorship business to the land some day. However, the city continued to delay issuing permits to landowners in the area and eventually Len purchased another property. He held onto the land for a number of years but has now decided that he needs the cash and will sell the property. The details related to his purchase of the land are set out below.

Purchase Price: $4,000; Purchase Date: May 21, 1993

Len has received an offer from an acquaintance to purchase the land. The payment terms are set out below and are considered to represent fair market value.

Purchase Price: $160,000; Purchase Date: October 1, 2013

Payment terms: $40,000 down payment on purchase date; $20,000 payable on January 1 each year for the period January 1, 2014 through January 1, 2019 inclusive. Interest: Interest is payable at 6% annually on the unpaid balance.

Len is uncertain as to whether the disposition is on account of capital or income.

— REQUIRED

Compare the income tax consequences to Len of this sale if the sale is on account of capital and, alternatively, if it is on account of income. Do not calculate the interest income. Ignore the consequences and calculation of the interest income.

Problem 3

ITA: 13(4), 44

During its year ended December 31, 2013, Power Boat Corporation Ltd. sold its retailing facilities in Kingston. As the sale occurred in December, business activity was at a low. New facilities were purchased in February 2014 in Parry Sound on the shores of Georgian Bay. The corporation sold its Kingston land and building for $300,000 and $200,000, respectively. This land and building had a cost in 1997 of $50,000 and $100,000, respectively. At the end of 2012, the building had an undepreciated capital cost of $55,000 for income tax purposes. In Parry Sound, the corporation purchased land and building for $75,000 and $350,000, respectively.

— REQUIRED

(A) Prepare two calculations of the income tax consequences of the above move, one without an election for additional deferral and one with this election. ITA: 44(6)

(B) If the property disposed of by the corporation in 2013 had been an apartment building held for rental purposes and producing income from property:

(i) what would the tax consequences of a sale of the property have been after a replacement of the property with another apartment complex in 2014?

(ii) what would the tax consequences on an expropriation have been after a replacement of the property with another apartment complex in 2014?

Problem 4

ITA: 13(4), 44

On March 1, 2013, Raymond Fan, a sole proprietor, sold his garden supply store in downtown Toronto to a competitor because of declining sales caused by competition from large suburban hardware and grocery stores. The following information relates to the sale of the business:

	Proceeds	*Cost*	*UCC/CEC Jan. 1, 2013*
Accounts receivable	$ 6,000	$10,000	—
Land	120,000	65,000	—
Building — Class 1	170,000	62,000	$28,000
Equipment — Class 8	3,000	1,200	300
— Class 10	4,000	12,000	800
Inventory	5,200	7,000	—
Goodwill	52,000	—	—

Raymond's business year-end coincided with the calendar year. Raymond has been in the same business since 1995. As of December 31, 2012, there was a balance in the allowance for doubtful accounts for tax purposes of $1,300.

Subsequent to the sale of the business, Raymond worked for his brother, Kevin, who owned a shoe store. However, Raymond became bored and when a garden supply store on a busy highway north of Toronto came on the market in late November 2014, he immediately bought it. The following information relates to his purchase of assets of the new business:

Land	$105,000
Building	220,000
Equipment — Class 8	9,000
— Class 10	11,000
Goodwill	Nil

— *REQUIRED*

(A) Compute the minimum amount Raymond must include on his 2013 tax return in respect of the sale of the business, before any election is made to defer capital gains and recapture. ITA: 13(4), 44

(B) Show the effect on Raymond's 2013 (amended) and 2014 tax returns if he elects to defer capital gains and recapture after purchasing the new business, but does not elect for additional deferral. ITA: 13(4), 44 ITA: 44(6)

(C) Discuss whether Raymond should have elected for additional deferral.

(D) If the above situation had been an involuntary disposition instead of a voluntary disposition, how would your answer under part (B) differ?

Problem 5

ITA: 13(21.1)

Pidgeon Dock Ltd. (PD) sold a property in its year ended January 31, 2013. The details are as follows:

	Proceeds	Cost	UCC
Building	$300,000	$400,000	$350,000
Land	$175,000	$100,000	N/A

The building was the last remaining asset in Class 3. PD prepared its corporate tax return based on the proceeds of disposition shown above. The CRA is now auditing PD.

— *REQUIRED*

Identify and calculate any adjustment the CRA will make to PD's 2013 income tax return.

Problem 6

ITA: 13(21.1)

Johnny Wong had purchased a dilapidated apartment block, The Empress, 20 years ago for $220,000. At the time, the purchase price had been allocated $80,000 to the land and $140,000 to the building. The Empress is the only building Johnny owns and is considered a Class 3 asset for CCA purposes. To date, Johnny has claimed CCA of $37,000.

High Towers has acquired all the lots in the same block as Johnny's building, except for The Empress. Johnny realized that as the last hold-out he was in an enviable negotiating position with High Towers. High Towers was desperate to gain ownership of The Empress and tear it down. After receiving ever-escalating offers, Johnny agreed to accept High Towers' offer of $1,000,000.

— *REQUIRED*

Advise Johnny regarding the allocation of the purchase price between the land and building.

Problem 7

ITA: Subdivisions b and c; ETA: 123(1), 169(1), 170(1)(*a*), 174, 231, 236

PITA Co. Ltd. is a nutritional consulting firm that advises manufacturers and distributors on consumers' dietary needs and preferences. For its year ended December 31, 2013, it reported net income before taxes of $900,000 for financial statement purposes. This amount included a gain on the disposition of land held as capital property of $50,000 and of a building (not the only one in the class) of $95,000. The corporation also realized an accounting loss of $20,000 on securities and of $10,000 on a trademark. These assets were acquired for the following amounts:

land	$120,000 in 2002
building	100,000 in 2002 (UCC of the class is $125,000)
securities	50,000 in 2011
trademark	80,000 in 2010

The proceeds of disposition of these assets were as follows:

land	$150,000
building	120,000
securities	30,000
trademark	70,000

The corporation has reported accounting amortization of $80,000 and wishes to claim the maximum available capital cost allowance of $100,000. During 2013, the corporation also made payments in respect of interest on unpaid income taxes ($1,500), charitable donations ($10,000), and an annual employee dinner-dance in December 2013 ($14,000). During 2013, the corporation established that an unsecured $5,000 note receivable in respect of the sale (as capital property) of a parcel of land in the prior year had become a bad debt. This was not reflected in the financial statements.

— REQUIRED

(A) Prepare a reconciliation between net income for financial statement purposes and net income for income tax purposes for the year ended December 31, 2013. Support your reconciliation with references to the *Income Tax Act*.

(B) Discuss in general terms the treatment of these items by the corporation for purposes of the HST.

[For more problems and solutions thereto, see the DVD accompanying this book.]

¶8,880 ADVISORY CASES

Case 1: Sudbury Processing Inc.

Sudbury Processing Inc. has had some tough times. In December 2012, just before its December 31st year end, there was a fire in its processing plant which destroyed the building and most of the contents. Tom Haskett, the owner, had to move fast to get back in operation before he lost customers to the competition.

Tom owns all the shares of Sud Holdings Inc. ("Holdings"). Holdings owns all the shares of Sudbury Processing Inc. ("Processing"), which is the operating company. Holdings also owns the land, building, and equipment used by Processing (the ones destroyed by fire).

In order to get back into business, Tom had Processing lease a new building until he could make arrangements for a new permanent home. He had some delay in making any new arrangements, because he and the insurance company had a difference of opinion on the replacement value of the building and equipment that were destroyed. They eventually agreed in March 2013, and Holdings received the cheque shortly thereafter for the building, equipment, and some repairs. However, the delay meant Tom had to make alternate arrangements for acquiring new equipment, so Processing entered into an equipment lease with an option to buy it at the end of the five-year term. Luckily, Processing had business interruption insurance, which paid it $10,000 per month for four months until it was up and running again.

In July 2013, Tom made the final decision on a new factory. He decided not to build at the old location. Instead, that land is being sold and new property is being bought with the intention of constructing a new building in the next couple of years. On the sale of the existing land, the purchaser wants a warranty that there are no environmental problems as a result of the fire. Holdings and the purchaser agreed that if there were any problems, then Holdings would pay $20,000 of the purchase price back. Rather than purchase the new parcel of land at this time, Tom has had Holdings buy an option to acquire the land at any time in the next two years for an agreed-upon price.

Advise Tom on the tax implications of Sudbury's situation.

Case 2: Mac Tosh

Mac Tosh is 66 years old and was a self-employed apple farmer in Kelowna for 19 years. Since his children did not want to take over his farming business, he sold the farm (which qualifies for the lifetime capital gains deduction) to a real estate developer for $450,000. The developer sold the crop in late August, cleared the land and began the development of a 50-unit condominium complex.

Mac Tosh paid $10,000 for the land in 1978 and planted 500 apple trees with a cost base of $2,000. He was saddened by the attitude of the developer, as the farm had been his pride and joy. Since Mac never used insecticides or fertilizers, he could earn a premium on the sale of the "organic" apples. Mac had the land appraised at $400,000 by two independent appraisers. The appraisal values were supported by the price of a piece of raw land which had recently sold in a nearby community. To compensate Mac Tosh for all his hard work over the years as well as for the current crop, the developer agreed to pay an additional $50,000 over the appraised land value. Mac Tosh's annual revenues from his apple harvest were approximately $15,000. Mac was pleased with this additional offer because it was very similar to the offer he received the previous year for his entire farm and crop from a neighbouring farmer. Mac has not had any other dispositions of capital property, and has no other sources of earned income.

Just last week, Mac received a letter from the CRA requesting further details on the sale of his farm. He was requested to submit appraisals and a statement regarding the reason behind his tax treatment of the disposition. Mac reported the entire disposition as a capital gain and offset the gain by utilizing the necessary capital gains deduction. Mac did not have any cumulative net investment losses.

Mac can't understand why the CRA wants this information. He thought that he had considered all income tax implications of the disposition of the farm. He even read a professional tax planning book. How should Mac have reported the transaction?

Chapter 9

Other Sources of Income and Deductions in Computing Income

TOPICS DISCUSSED

LEARNING GOALS

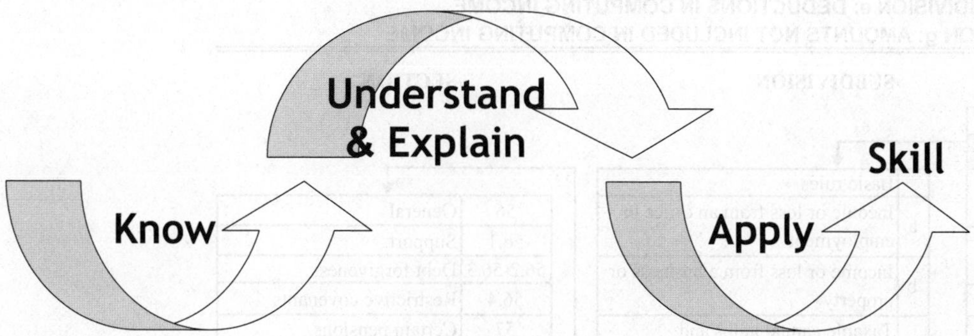

Know

By the end of this chapter you should know the basic provisions of the *Income Tax Act* that relate to other income and other deductions. Completing the Review Questions (¶9,800) and Multiple Choice Questions (¶9,825) is a good way to learn the technical provisions.

Understand and Explain

You should understand and be able to explain:

- The nature of income such as pensions, retiring allowances, support payments, and scholarships and bursaries.
- The nature of other deductions such as RRSPs, moving expenses, child care expenses, and the disability support deduction.

Completing the Exercises (¶9,850) is a good way to deepen your understanding of the material.

Apply

You should be able to apply your knowledge and understanding of these forms of income and deductions in a way that accomplishes a client's goals. Completing the Assignment Problems (¶9,875) is an excellent way to develop your ability to apply the material in increasingly complex situations.

OVERVIEW

This chapter will highlight the following:

Division B — Computation of Income

Subdivision d — Other sources of income

Subdivision e — Deduction in computing income

Subdivision g — Amounts not included in income

Division G — Deferred and Other Special Income Arrangements

Part XI.01 — Taxes in Respect of TFSAs

The sectional list for these subdivisions of the Act, located at the front of the CCH edition of the CANADIAN INCOME TAX ACT WITH REGULATIONS, should be used to find quickly specific inclusions and deductions in doing the problem material in this and subsequent chapters.

PART I — DIVISION B

SUBDIVISION d: OTHER SOURCES OF INCOME
SUBDIVISION e: DEDUCTIONS IN COMPUTING INCOME
SUBDIVISION g: AMOUNTS NOT INCLUDED IN COMPUTING INCOME

DIVISION

A	Liability for tax
B	**Computation of income**
C	Computation of taxable income
D	Taxable income earned in Canada by non-residents
E	Computation of tax
E.1	Minimum tax
F	Special rules applicable in certain circumstances
G	**Deferred and other special income**
H	Exemptions
I	Returns, assessments, payment and appeals
J	Appeals to the Tax Court of Canada and the Federal Court of Appeal

SUBDIVISION

	Basic rules
a	Income or loss from an office or employment
b	Income or loss from a business or property
c	Taxable capital gains and allowable capital losses
d	**Other sources of income**
e	**Deductions in computing income**
f	Rules relating to computation of income
g	**Amounts not included in computing income**
h	Corporations resident in Canada and their shareholders
i	Shareholders of corporations not resident in Canada
j	Partnerships and their members
k	Trusts and their beneficiaries

SECTION

56	General
56.1	Support
56.2-56.3	Debt forgiveness
56.4	Restrictive covenants
57	Certain pensions
58	Government annuities
59-59.1	Resource property

60-60.03	Other deductions
60.1	Support
60.2	Refund of AVCs
61-61.1	IAACs
61.2-61.4	Debt forgiveness
62	Moving expenses
63	Child care expenses
64	Attendant care
64.1	Individual absent from Canada
65-66.8	Resource property

81	Amounts not included in income

144	Employees profit sharing plans
145	Registered supplementary unemployment benefit plans
146	RRSP
146.01	Home Buyers' Plan
146.02	Lifelong Learning Plan
146.1	RESP
146.2	TFSA
146.3	RRIF
146.4	RDSP
147	DPSP
147.1-147.4	RPP
148	Life insurance policies
148.1	Eligible funeral arrangements

149	Miscellaneous exemptions
149.1	Charities

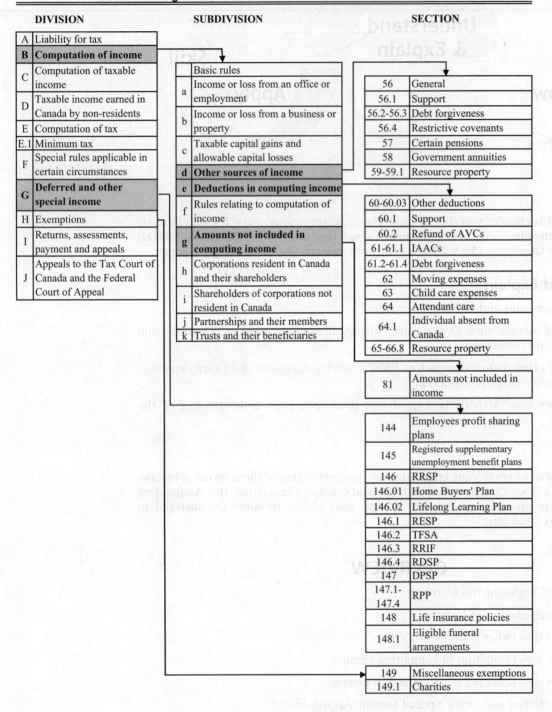

¶9,000 OTHER SOURCES OF INCOME

Section 56 presents a list of miscellaneous types of income from a non-capital source, other than employment in Subdivision a and business or property in Subdivision b. Section 56.1 extends the rules pertaining to marital breakdown situations. Sections 57 to 59.1, which will not be discussed in this text, deal with certain pension plans, government annuities and resource properties in more detail.

Summary of Other Sources of Income

ITA Reference	Other Sources of Income
56(1)(*a*)(i)–(iv)	Benefits in the nature of pensions
56(1)(*a*)(ii)	Retiring allowances and other payments on termination of employment
56(1)(*b*)	Support receipts and payments
56(1)(*d*)	Annuity payments
56(1)(*h*), (*i*), (*q*), (*t*)	Amounts received from deferred income plans
56(1)(*n*)	Education assistance payments
56(1)(*l*)	Legal costs awarded by a court
56(1)(*u*)	Social assistance payments
56(1)(*v*)	Workers' Compensation
56(2)	Indirect payments
56(6)	Child care benefit
56.4 [Proposed]	Restrictive covenants

¶9,010 Benefits in the Nature of Pensions

This provision includes in income superannuation or pension benefits including those received under the *Old Age Security Act* and the Canada Pension Plan. An Interpretation Bulletin discusses the inclusion of these benefits. "Retiring allowances" are included, as discussed further below. "Death benefits" are also defined very precisely for the purposes of the Act and are included. Note the exemption of a maximum of $10,000 of death benefit contained in the definition of the term. Any benefits received under the *Employment Insurance Act* are taxable.

ITA: 56(1)(*a*)(i)–(iv), 248(1) "retiring allowances"; IT-499R

248(1) "death benefits"

¶9,015 Income splitting — Canada Pension Plan

Spouses or common-law partners, who meet certain conditions, can split equally their Canada Pension Plan income. The term "spouse or common-law partner" is defined as two persons, regardless of sex, who cohabit in a conjugal relationship and have done so for a continuous period of at least 12 months. The amount which can be shared is 50% of the combined CPP benefits received but prorated by the length of the time the individuals have been living together in relation to the contributory period. This income sharing arrangement would be most useful where the individuals have different tax rates and amounts of income. Where one individual was a contributor and the other individual was not, then the non-contributor must be at least 60 years of age at the time of this election. Applications are available from the Income Security Programs Department of Human Resources Development Canada.

ITA: 248(1) "common-law partner"

¶9,020 Income splitting — Pension income

Since 2007, targeted assistance is provided to pensioners and seniors by allowing an individual resident in Canada to allocate to the individual's resident spouse or common-law partner up to one-half of the individual's pension income (eligible pension income) that qualifies for the pension income tax credit.

ITA: 118(3)

For individuals aged 65 years and over, eligible pension income includes annuity payments under a registered pension plan, a registered retirement savings plan, or a deferred profit sharing plan or payments out of a registered retirement income fund. For individuals less than 65 years of age, eligible pension income includes annuity payments under a registered pension plan and certain other payments received as a result of the death of the individual's spouse or common-law partner. ITA: 60.03(1), 118(7)

Since this will reduce one person's income, and probably cause another to pay tax, there is a requirement that both parties agree to the splitting of the income. ITA: 60.03(2)

¶9,030 Retiring Allowances and Other Payments on Termination of Employment

In the absence of any express terms as to termination in a contract of employment, which is covered in Chapter 3, the general principle is that all other payments on the termination of employment are taxable as a retiring allowance. The provision excepts amounts out of an employee benefit plan, a retirement compensation arrangement, or a salary deferral arrangement. All three of these are plans specifically defined and are not particularly common. ITA: 6(3), 56(1)(*a*)(ii), 248(1) "employee benefit plan", "retirement compensation arrangement", "salary deferral arrangement"

The definition of a retiring allowance excludes pension income and death benefits, but specifically includes payments in respect of: ITA: 248(1) "retiring allowance"

(a) retirement from an office or employment in recognition of long service; or

(b) loss of office including court-awarded damages received by the taxpayer, or as a bequest, by a dependant or relation of the taxpayer or his or her legal representative.

For information on transferring some or all of a retiring allowance to an RRSP, please refer to ¶9,430.

¶9,040 Support Receipts and Payments

¶9,045 Overview

The spousal support income inclusions and deductions are mirror images of each other. The recipient of spousal support has an inclusion, while the payer has a deduction. On the other hand, the recipient of child support has no inclusion, while the payer has no deduction, which is also a mirror image. The following discussion is applicable to both the receipts and payments. ITA: 56(1)(*b*), 60(*b*)

In the case of *Thibaudeau v. The Queen*, the Federal Court of Appeal ruled that a separated custodial parent did not have to include child support payments as part of her income. However, the Court did not rule on the deductibility of the husband's payments in this case. The Court's decision was based on a finding of instances of discrimination against separated custodial parents in the Act. As an example of such discrimination, the court indicated that a non-separated custodial parent is not required to include support payments from a spouse in income. (Of course, the payer spouse does not get a deduction in that case.) If this situation had been allowed to stand, such support payments, deductible to the payer but not includable by the recipient, would escape tax altogether. 94 DTC 6230 (F.C.A.)

In the decision of the Supreme Court of Canada on the appeal of the case of *The Queen v. Thibaudeau*, the Court ruled that the custodial parent was required to include the child support payments in her income. The majority opinion concluded that the fact that the tax saving resulting from the inclusion/deduction system does not benefit both parents equally does not infringe the equality rights protected by the *Canadian Charter of Rights and Freedoms*. 95 DTC 5273 (S.C.C.)

As a result of the *Thibaudeau* case, the inclusion–deduction system related to child support only was changed, as discussed below. These changes are applied to agreements or orders made or changed after April 30, 1997.

¶9,050 Spousal support

¶9,050.10 *Conditions*

The CRA is very strict on its interpretation of support receipts and deductions. All aspects of these rules must be adhered to. Support amounts, except amounts that relate to child support, are deductible if the following five tests are met: ITA: 56(1)(*b*), 56.1(4), 60(*b*)

- the payments are made as allowances on a periodic basis, as discussed below;
- the payments are made for the maintenance of the recipient;
- the recipient has discretionary use of the amounts;
- the payments are made to a spouse or common-law partner or former spouse or common-law partner who is living apart from the payer because of the breakdown of their marriage or common-law partnership, or paid by a natural parent of a child of the recipient; and
- the payments are made pursuant to an order of a competent tribunal or a written agreement.

¶9,050.20 *Definitions*

A spouse or common-law partner is described as an individual of either sex who cohabited with the recipient in a conjugal relationship or is the parent of the child of the recipient. ITA: 248(1) "common-law partner"

The definition of an allowance for purposes of the above paragraphs is embodied in the definition of the term "support amount". The provision does not completely define an allowance, but does limit an allowance to an amount over which the recipient has discretion as to how the funds will be spent. ITA: 56.1(4) "support amount"

In the case of *Gagnon v. The Queen*, the Supreme Court of Canada considered the meaning of allowance. Three conditions must be met for an amount to be regarded as an allowance in the Court's view: 86 DTC 6179 (S.C.C.)

- the amount must be limited and predetermined;
- the amount must be paid to enable the recipient to pay a certain type of expense; and
- the recipient must be able to spend the payment in any way he or she wants.

The Court elaborated on the last condition. As long as the recipient benefits from the amount, it is not relevant that he or she has to account for it or that he or she cannot apply it to certain types of expense at his or her complete discretion.

As noted previously, all of these provisions require that the payments be made on a periodic basis. The Federal Court of Appeal decision in *The Queen v. McKimmon* listed some of the criteria which should be used in determining whether a payment is made on a periodic basis and whether in fact the payment is a deductible allowance or an instalment of a lump or capital sum which is not deductible. 90 DTC 6088 (F.C.A.)

¶9,050.30 *Payments to third parties*

Certain payments to third parties made under an order or agreement or any variation of either are deductible as spousal support payments by the payer and deemed received and, hence, included by the person who benefits from the payment. Payments envisaged include medical bills, mortgage payments or tuition fees. ITA: 56.1, 60.1

Third-party payments, whether or not they are made on a periodic basis, will be deemed to be an allowance for the discretionary use of the recipient and, hence, deducted by the payer and included by the person who benefits, if they meet the following criteria: ITA: 56.1(2), 60.1(2)

- the payments are made in the year or preceding year under an order of a competent tribunal or written agreement;

- the expense was incurred for the maintenance of a spouse or common-law partner or former spouse or common-law partner; and
- the court order or written agreement alludes specifically to subsections 56.1(2) and 60.1(2).

Note that the use of this provision requires the agreement of both parties. If they do not agree to include the effects of these provisions in their documentation, the third-party amounts will not be deemed to be an allowance. These payments exclude the acquisition of tangible property, unless it involves an expenditure on medical expenses or educational expenses. The acquisition, improvement or maintenance of a self-contained domestic establishment, as defined, also qualify as payments that are deemed to be an allowance. Note that interest and principal payments are limited to 20% of the original principal amount of the debt. ITA: 248(1) "self-contained domestic establishment"

Amounts that are received/paid in respect of support before a court order or written agreement is made, are considered to have been received/paid under the order or agreement. However, the subsequent order or agreement must be made before the end of the year following the receipt/payment. In addition, the subsequent order or agreement must provide for the prior support to be deemed to have been received/paid under the order or agreement. ITA: 56.1(3)

¶9,055 Child support

Amounts paid in respect of support or maintenance of a child are not deductible by the payer and are not included in the income of the recipient. Any amount not identified in the agreement or order as being solely for the support of the recipient spouse or former spouse will be considered to be an amount payable for child support.

For this purpose, the term "child support amount" is defined. These rules apply to new written agreements or court orders made or to existing written agreements or court orders changed after April 30, 1997. ITA: 56.1(4) "child support amount"

¶9,060 Legal fees in connection with support payments

Under current common law, it appears that legal fees incurred to enforce pre-existing rights to support payments are deductible,[1] and the CRA agrees.[2] Subsequently, the CRA announced[3] that legal costs incurred to obtain spousal support under the *Divorce Act*, or under the applicable provincial legislation, in a separation agreement are considered to have been incurred to enforce a pre-existing right to support. This position is based on the case of *Gallien v. The Queen*. The CRA further indicated that it now accepts that legal costs of seeking to obtain an increase in support or to make child support non-taxable are also deductible. IT-99R5, par. 18; IT-99R5, par. 17; 2000 DTC 2514 (T.C.C.)

¶9,070 Annuity Payments

The concept of an "annuity" follows this definition: "an investment of money entitling [the] investor to [a] series of equal annual sums".[4] This enhances the definition found in the Act. The full amount of an annuity payment is included in income unless it is required to be included under another provision of the Act or unless it is subject to income accrual rules. If the full amount of the annuity payment is included in income, then the capital portion of the annuity, if any, is deducted (see ¶9,310). ITA: 12.2(1), 248(1); ITA: 56(1)(*d*), 60(*a*)

The full amount of an annuity payment that resulted from certain registered retirement savings plan contributions that were deductible by the taxpayer is included in income. ITA: 56(1)(*d.2*)

---

[1] See the *McColl* case, (T.C.C.) 2000 DTC 2148, which cites for support the cases of *Burgess*, (F.C.T.D.) 81 DTC 5192, *Evans*, (S.C.C.) 60 DTC 1047, and *Wakeman* (T.C.C. — Informal Procedure) 96 DTC 3220.

[2] Paragraph 18 of IT-99R5 also refers to the *Sembinelli* case (F.C.A.), 94 DTC 6636.

[3] *Income Tax Technical News*, No. 24, October 10, 2002.

[4] The *Concise Oxford Dictionary*.

¶9,080 Amounts Received from Deferred Income Plans

¶9,085 Inclusion provisions

The following paragraphs take into income amounts received by the taxpayer through the deferred income plans indicated:

Paragraph 56(1)(*h*)	Registered retirement savings plan (RRSP)
Paragraph 56(1)(*h*.1)	Home buyer's plan (HBP)
Paragraph 56(1)(*h*.2)	Lifelong learning plan (LLP)
Paragraph 56(1)(*i*)	Deferred profit sharing plan (DPSP)
Paragraph 56(1)(*q*)	Registered education savings plan (RESP)
Paragraph 56(1)(*q*.1)	Registered disability savings plan (RDSP)
Paragraph 56(1)(*t*)	Registered retirement income fund (RRIF)

The detailed rules governing these plans are found in Division G "Deferred and Other Special Income Arrangements". RESPs, RRSPs, HBPs, LLPs, DPSPs, and RRIFs will be discussed in more detail later in this chapter.

¶9,090 Registered education savings plan (RESP)

¶9,090.10 *Concept and limits*

RESPs, as defined, allow individuals to contribute, without an annual limit, to a plan to fund post-secondary education of a qualified beneficiary. The lifetime contribution limit in respect of a beneficiary is $50,000 over a maximum of 31 years. The maximum number of years is 35 for a single beneficiary RESP under which the beneficiary is an individual who is entitled to a disability tax credit. Contributions are not deductible when contributed to the plan and, hence, they are not taxable when the plan allows their withdrawal. Neither the trust holding the property of a plan nor the contributor or subscriber is taxable on the income earned by that property, so the investment income of the plan is sheltered.

ITA: 146.1(1)
ITA: 204.9(1)
ITA: 146.1(5), 146.1(6)

The following summarizes the time limits for a RESP.

ITA: 146.1 "specified plan" (*b*), (*c*), 146.1(2)(*h*)(i), (ii), 146.1(2)(*i*)(i), (ii)

Time Limit	**Type of Plan**	**Limit**
Years of contribution	Regular	31 years
	Disabled	35 years
Termination	Regular	35 years
	Disabled	40 years
Lifetime contribution limit		$50,000

The accumulated investment income is taxable to a beneficiary as he or she receives the funds to pay for education expenses while enrolled as a full-time student in a post-secondary educational institution, called "educational assistance payments". Educational assistance payments can be made in connection with occupational skills programs at educational institutions certified by the Minister of Human Resources and Skills Development.

ITA: 56(1)(*q*), 146.1(1)

Eligibility for education assistance payments from an RESP is extended to part-time studies. Students 16 years of age or older may receive up to $2,500 of education assistance payments for each 13-week semester of part-time study. A greater amount may be approved by the Minister of Human Resources and Social development on a case-by-case basis.

A family plan RESP can be established for a number of beneficiaries related by blood or adoption. The income from such an RESP can be paid to any one or more of the beneficiaries who pursue higher education. However, the RESP cannot allow an individual to become a beneficiary after he or she turns 21.

¶9,090.20 *Canada Education Savings Grant (CESG)*

Basic CESG

To increase the attractiveness of saving for education through an RESP, the government provides a CESG of 20% of the first $2,500 of annual contributions to an RESP for the benefit of children up to age 18.[5] This amounts to a maximum grant of $500 per year per child. The CESG is paid directly to the RESP. The maximum CESG that can be *paid* to an RESP in respect of a particular beneficiary is $7,200. In the case of a family plan RESP involving more than one beneficiary, the maximum CESG that can be *received* by a particular beneficiary as educational assistance payments is $7,200. CESG contribution room of $2,500 per year is accumulated for each child under 18 years old. Thus, where less than a $2,500 contribution is made in a year, the 20% grant will be paid in a subsequent year when RESP contributions are made. If a child does not pursue higher education to qualify for educational assistance payments, the CESG must be repaid to the government by the RESP.

Additional CESG

The CESG matching rate for contributions made to an RESP by low and middle-income families is determined as follows. Where a child is the beneficiary of the RESP and under the age of 18 throughout the year, the first $500 contributed in the year will attract:

- a 20% CESG matching rate, if the qualifying net income of the child's family is $43,561 or less; or
- a 10% CESG matching rate if the qualifying net income of the child's family is between $43,561 and $87,123.

All income levels are for 2013 and will change annually.

There is no carryforward of the enhanced rate to future years and the income thresholds are indexed to inflation.

Family net income in 2013	up to $43,561	between $43,561 and $87,123
CESG	20% on first $500	10% on first $500

¶9,090.30 *Canada Learning Bond (CLB)*

In addition, a CLB provides a source of education savings for children of low-income families. Each child born after December 31, 2004 is eligible for an initial CLB of $500 and subsequent annual CLB's of $100 in each year up to and including the year the child turns 15, provided that the child's family is entitled to the National Child Benefit (NCB) supplement in the year (Chapter 10). The total amount of the CLB payments cannot exceed $2,000 per child and can be transferred to an RESP at any time before the child reaches 18. While no separate application is required, eligibility is linked to entitlement for the National Child Benefit supplement. The CLB is payable into an RESP of which the child is a beneficiary.

¶9,090.40 *Distribution from an RESP*

An RESP is permitted to distribute any part of its accumulated income to the subscriber, under certain conditions, as follows:

- the subscriber is alive;
- each beneficiary of the RESP is either:

  (i) over 21 years of age and not eligible to receive educational assistance payments, or

  (ii) has died;

  and

[5] Part III.1 of the *Department of Human Resources Development Act*.

- the RESP has been in existence for at least 10 years. ITA: 146.1(2)(*d*.1)

These distributions are included in the subscriber's income. The Minister may waive the "over 21 years of age" and the "at least 10 years" restrictions where a beneficiary under an RESP is mentally impaired. The distributions may be rolled over to the subscriber's (or his or her spouse's) RRSP, to the extent that the subscriber has contribution room. The limit on this rollover is $50,000. A 20% tax is imposed on the amount of the RESP distribution received in excess of the limited amount transferred to RRSPs. ITA: 146.1(2.2), 204.94

¶9,095 Registered disability savings plan (RDSP)

To help parents and others save for the long-term financial security of a child with a severe disability, the Act provides for a registered disability savings plan (RDSP) with a Canada Disability Savings Grant (CDSG) program and Canada Disability Savings Bond (CDSB) program. The RDSP will be based generally on the existing RESP design. ITA: 146.4

¶9,095.10 *Eligibility*

Generally, any person eligible for the disability tax credit (DTC) and resident in Canada, or the parent or other legal representative of such a person, is eligible to establish an RDSP. The DTC-eligible individual is the plan beneficiary.

The plan termination is required only if the beneficiary's condition has factually improved to the extent that he or she no longer qualifies for the DTC. This deals with the concern that someone may qualify for the DTC but not claim it. ITA: 146.4(*p*)(ii), 146.4(12)(*d*)

¶9,095.20 *Tax treatment*

Contributions to an RDSP are not deductible, but the investment income accrues tax-free. Contributions are not included in income when paid out, but the investment income is included in the beneficiary's income when it is paid out.

¶9,095.30 *Contributions*

Contributions to an RDSP are limited to a lifetime maximum of $200,000 in respect of the beneficiary, with no annual limit. There is no restriction on who can contribute to the plan. Contributions are permitted until the end of the year in which the beneficiary attains 59 years of age.

Effective July 1, 2011, for deaths occurring after March 3, 2010, the existing registered retirement savings plan (RRSP) rollover rules are extended to allow a rollover of a deceased individual's RRSP proceeds to the RDSP of the child or grandchild who was financially dependent on the deceased individual and who has an impairment in physical or mental functions. These rules also apply to registered retirement income fund (RRIF) proceeds and to certain lump-sum amounts paid from registered pension plans (RPPs). ITA: 60.011 [proposed]

In recognition of the fact that families of children with disabilities may not be able to contribute regularly to their plans, a 10-year carryforward of CDSG and CDSB entitlements is available starting in 2011.

¶9,095.40 *Canada Disability Savings Grant (CDSG)*

To provide additional direct government assistance to help ensure the future financial security of a child with a severe disability, RDSP contributions made in the year qualify for CDSGs at matching rates of 100%, 200%, or 300%, depending on family net income and the amount contributed.

Family net income in 2013	up to $87,123	over $87,123
CDSG	300% on first $500 200% on next $1,000	100% on first $1,000

The family net income threshold will be indexed to inflation.

There is an annual limit of $3,500 and a lifetime limit of $70,000 on CDSGs paid in respect of an RDSP beneficiary. An RDSP is eligible to receive CDSGs until the end of the year in which the beneficiary attains 49 years of age.

¶9,095.50 *Canada Disability Savings Bond (CDSB)*

To ensure that RDSPs help promote the future financial security of children with a severe disability in lower-income families, CDSBs of up to $1,000 are paid annually to the RDSPs of low and modest-income beneficiaries and families. CDSBs are not contingent on contributions to an RDSP.

The maximum $1,000 CDSB is paid to an RDSP where family net income does not exceed $25,356. The CDSB is phased out gradually for those with family net income between $25,356 and $43,561.

There is a lifetime limit of $20,000 on CDSBs paid in respect of an RDSP beneficiary. An RDSP is eligible to receive CDSBs until the end of the year in which the beneficiary turns 49 years of age.

¶9,095.60 *Payments*

Payments from an RDSP are required to commence by the end of the year in which the beneficiary attains 60 years of age. Payments are subject to a maximum annual limit determined by reference to the life expectancy of the beneficiary and the fair market value of the property in the plan. The beneficiary or their legal representative is permitted to encroach on the capital and income of the plan.

¶9,095.70 *Death or cessation of disability*

Where the beneficiary of an RDSP either ceases to be eligible for the DTC or dies, the funds in the RDSP are required to be paid to the beneficiary or pass to his or her estate. That amount is included in the beneficiary's income

¶9,100 Education Assistance Payments

These provisions include in income:

(a) scholarships, fellowships, bursaries or prizes for achievement in a field of endeavour of the taxpayer in excess of the taxpayer's scholarship exemption for a taxation year, and project grants, received by artists, net of the related, contractual project expenses; and ITA: 56(1)(*n*), 56(3)(*c*)

(b) research grants in excess of expenses which are unreimbursed, non-personal or living expenses, except for *bona fide* travelling expenses, incurred in carrying on the research. ITA: 56(1)(*o*)

There is a full exemption for scholarships, fellowships, and bursaries received by a taxpayer in connection with the taxpayer's enrolment in a program in respect of which the taxpayer may claim the education tax credit, that is, a designated educational institution. For the 2010 and subsequent years, a program at a post-secondary school level will only include a program leading to a college or CEGEP diploma or a bachelor, masters, or doctoral degree. Post-doctoral fellowships will be taxable. ITA: 56(3)(*a*) ITA: 56(3)(*b*)

The full exemption of scholarships and bursaries is also available to those received for elementary and secondary school programs.

There are certain restrictions on the amounts which qualify as scholarships, bursaries, prizes, etc. Amounts received from a registered education savings plan, amounts received in the course of a business and amounts received in respect of employment are excluded. Note that the grant portion of provincial or federal education assistance payments is considered to be income under this paragraph. Certain prescribed prizes are excluded from income com- ITA: 56(1)(*n*) ITR: 7700 pletely. Generally, these prizes may be described as recognition by the general public for meritorious achievement in the arts, sciences or public service; thus these amounts do not represent a payment in respect of a contract of service.

If the scholarship, fellowship, or bursary amount is approved for a part-time program, the scholarship exemption is normally limited to the amount of tuition paid for the program plus the costs of program-related materials.

¶9,110 Other Inclusions

Included in income are amounts received as legal costs awarded by a court on an appeal from an assessment of any tax, interest or penalties, as well as any reimbursement of costs received as a result of decisions under the *Employment Insurance Act* or *Canada Pension Plan*. These receipts are included if the expenses incurred are deducted or deductible. (See ¶9,450.) ITA: 56(1)(*l*) ITA: 60(*o*)

A taxpayer must include amounts received as an award or reimbursement of legal expenses paid to collect or establish a right to a retiring allowance or benefits under a pension plan. The legal fees paid are deductible. (See ¶9,455.) A similar system is in place with respect to legal fees paid to collect or establish a right to salary or wages and other amounts that would be included in employment income. Reimbursements and awards of such costs are included in employment income and expenses are deductible from employment income. Excluded are legal expenses relating to a division or settlement of property arising from a marriage or other conjugal relationship. These legal fees are generally not deductible. ITA: 56(1)(*l*.1) ITA: 60(0.1) ITA: 6(1)(*j*) ITA: 8(1)(*b*)

Social assistance payments are included in income and, if the recipient is married, the amount received must be included by the spouse with the higher income. Finally, Workers' Compensation is included. ITA: 56(1)(*u*), 56(1)(*v*)

¶9,120 Indirect Payments

¶9,125 Overview

These anti-avoidance provisions invoke the principle of constructive or effective receipt by imputing to the taxpayer:

- income diverted at his or her direction to someone else either for the taxpayer's benefit or to satisfy the desire of the taxpayer to benefit the other person;[6] ITA: 56(2)
- any rights to income transferred by the taxpayer, while resident in Canada, to someone with whom he or she was not dealing at arm's length; and ITA: 56(4)
- income earned on non-arm's length loans which do not yield a commercial rate of interest (see Chapter 6). ITA: 56(4.1), 56(4.2), 56(4.3)

¶9,130 Conditions

The provision pertaining to indirect payments specifies the following four conditions: ITA: 56(2)

- there must be a payment or transfer of property to a person other than the taxpayer;
- the payment or transfer must be made pursuant to the direction or with the concurrence of the taxpayer;
- the payment or transfer must be for the benefit of the taxpayer, or a benefit that the taxpayer desired to confer on the other person; and
- the payment or transfer would have been included in the taxpayer's income if it had been made to the taxpayer.

[6] For a more detailed analysis of this provision, see Robert E. Beam and Stanley N. Laiken, "Recent Developments on Subsection 56(2): Indirect Payments", Personal Tax Planning Feature (1995), vol. 43, no. 2, *Canadian Tax Journal*, pp. 447–469.

If all of these conditions are met, the payment or transfer is included in the taxpayer's income to the extent that it would be if the payment or transfer had been made directly to the taxpayer.

The CRA has attacked certain family income splitting schemes by applying these indirect payments provisions. In the case of *Champ v. The Queen*, part of the dividends payable on shares owned by the taxpayer's wife was included in the taxpayer's income. It was found that the taxpayer had directed the payment of dividends on his wife's shares without the payment of dividends on his shares which were essentially the same. On the other hand, in the case of *The Queen v. McClurg*, subsection 56(2) was held not to be applicable in facts very similar to *Champ* but where there were contractual restrictions upon the payment of dividends. The case of *The Queen v. Neuman*, involved facts that were slightly different from those in the *McClurg* case. The decision to apply subsection 56(2) in the *Neuman* case was based on the power of the taxpayer to ratify the dividends paid to his wife and the distinction with the *McClurg* case on the wife's lack of contribution to the corporation.

83 DTC 5029 (F.C.T.D.)

91 DTC 5001 (S.C.C.)

96 DTC 6464 (F.C.A.)

In its decision on the case of *Neuman v. The Queen*, the Supreme Court of Canada held that subsection 56(2) does not apply to the dividend income received by Neuman's wife. This decision established that there is no requirement for the shareholder to make a business contribution to the corporation in order to earn the dividend. Dividends are paid to shareholders simply as a return on their investment in the corporation, not as compensation for work done for the corporation. This conclusion clarifies the uncertainty left by the *McClurg* case on the issue.

98 DTC 6297 (S.C.C.)

¶9,135 Child Care Benefit

Under the *Universal Child Care Benefit Act*, a payment of $100 per month is made at the beginning of each month to all families with a child under the age of six. The amount paid is not dependent on family income — it is universal.

ITA: 56(6)

Universal Child Care Benefit (UCCB) payments are taxable. Where the parents are married or in a common-law relationship, the payments must be included in the income of the parent with the lower income. If they have equal incomes, the payments must be included in the income of the parent who received the payments.

¶9,140 Restrictive Covenants [Proposed]

¶9,145 Inclusion

The proposed provisions on restrictive covenants set out rules with respect to amounts that are received or receivable after October 7, 2003 in respect of a restrictive covenant.

ITA: 56.4

The term "restrictive covenant" is defined to mean an arrangement, an undertaking or a waiver of a right or advantage that affects, in any way, the acquisition or provision of property or services by the taxpayer or someone not dealing at arm's length with the taxpayer.

ITA: 56.4(1)

The starting point is to include in income the total of all amounts received or receivable by the taxpayer, or non-arm's length person, in respect of a restrictive covenant.

ITA: 56.4(2)

A deduction is provided for a bad debt if the amount was previously included in income as a payment for a restrictive covenant. Section 68 addresses the allocation of amounts between restrictive covenants and the other property being disposed of.

ITA: 56.4, 60(*f*)

¶9,150 Exceptions

Generally, amounts received for restrictive covenants are included in income. The exceptions are for those amounts that are included in income somewhere else. The following are the three items that are not taxed as restrictive covenants because they are taxed elsewhere.

ITA: 56.4(2), 56.4(3)

¶9,150.10 *Employment income*

The restrictive covenant inclusion rule will not apply if the amount is included in employment income or will be included when received. This might be the case where an employee leaves and is paid an amount not to work for a competitor. In this case there may not be any shares or assets sold that might cause part of the payments to be allocated in a different way. While employment income is normally taxed on the received basis, if the employee agreed to the covenant more than 36 months before the end of the taxation year, then the payments for the restrictive covenant may be included in employment income even though it is not actually received. ITA: 56.4(2) ITA: 6(3.1)

¶9,150.20 *Eligible capital property*

The restrictive covenant inclusion rule will not apply to an amount if the payment received is required by the description of item E in the definition of "cumulative eligible capital", which requires that ¾ of the payment be credited to the CEC pool. The purchaser and the taxpayer must jointly elect for this exception to apply. This might apply, for example, where a partnership sells its business and the restrictive covenant proceeds are included in with the proceeds for the goodwill. ITA: 56.4(2) ITA: 14(5)

¶9,150.30 *Proceeds of disposition*

The restrictive covenant inclusion rule will not apply to the extent that the amount is added to the proceeds of disposition of an "eligible interest". An "eligible interest" is capital property that is a partnership interest or a share of a corporation where the partnership or the corporation is carrying on a business. This might occur where the share or the partnership interest is disposed of and the shareholder or partner enters into a restrictive covenant. For this to be the case, the following conditions must be met: ITA: 56.4(2)

- the amount must directly relate to the taxpayer's disposition of an "eligible interest"; ITA: 56.4(1)
- the disposition of the "eligible interest" must be to the purchaser of the restrictive covenant;
- the amount received or receivable must be consideration for an undertaking not to compete with the purchaser;
- the amount cannot exceed the amount determined by a formula;
- the amount is included in the proceeds of disposition of the "eligible interest"; and
- the taxpayer and the purchaser of the restrictive covenant have elected to apply this exception.

¶9,155 Schematic of the system for restrictive covenants

Figure 9-1 illustrates how section 56.4 fits into the taxation of restrictive covenant payments:

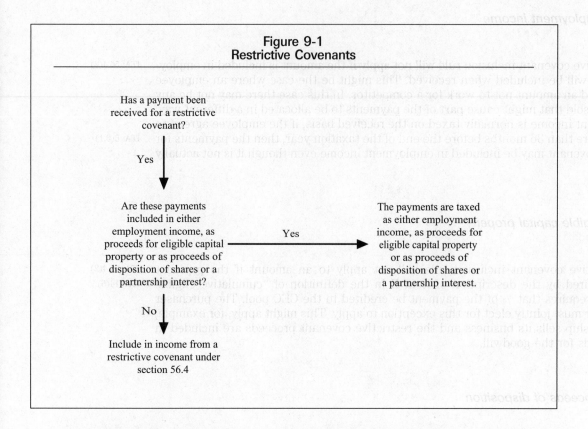

Figure 9-1
Restrictive Covenants

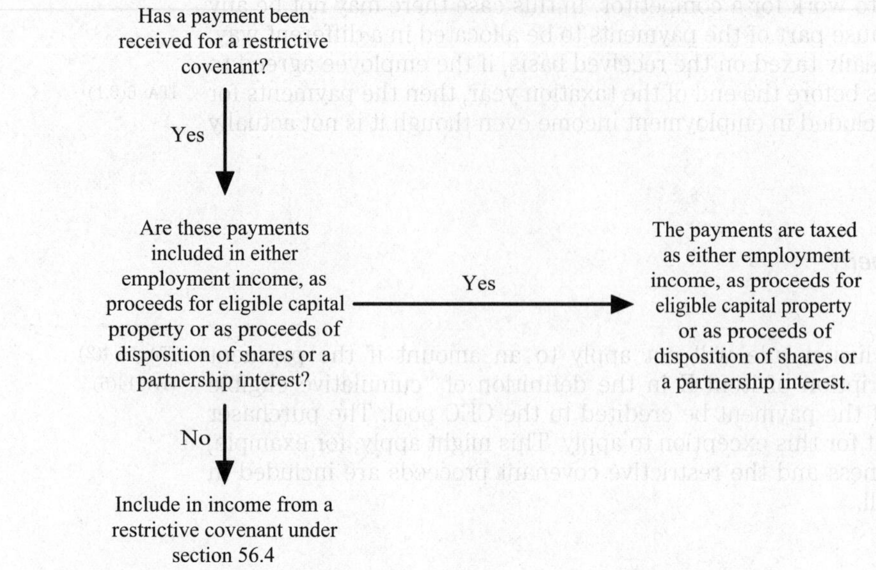
Has a payment been received for a restrictive covenant?
Yes
Are these payments included in either employment income, as proceeds for eligible capital property or as proceeds of disposition of shares or a partnership interest?
Yes
The payments are taxed as either employment income, as proceeds for eligible capital property or as proceeds of disposition of shares or a partnership interest.
No
Include in income from a restrictive covenant under section 56.4

¶9,200 AMOUNTS NOT INCLUDED IN COMPUTING INCOME AND EXEMPT ENTITIES

The Act lists a number of specific types of income that would ordinarily have to be included in income subject to tax, but are excluded from the computation of income. Note the very limited scope of these exclusions each of which meets a specific problem area. ITA: 81

¶9,210 Specific Examples

The more common components of this section are summarized below:

- amounts exempted by other federal statutes or foreign tax agreements; ITA: 81(1)(*a*)
- certain pension or other payments related to war services; ITA: 81(1)(*d*)
- war service pensions of a country which has reciprocal arrangements with Canada; ITA: 81(1)(*e*)
- compensation by the Federal Republic of Germany, for war victims; ITA: 81(1)(*g*)
- income and capital gains from personal injury award property for individuals under 21 years of age; ITA: 81(1)(*g*.1), 81(1)(*g*.2)
- social assistance payments based on a needs test; ITA: 81(1)(*h*)
- payments out of a profit sharing plan; ITA: 81(1)(*k*)
- expense allowances of elected municipal officers and members of provincial legislature; and ITA: 81(2), 81(3)
- allowance for or reimbursement of part-time employment travel expenses. (See Chapter 3 for a detailed discussion of this provision.) ITA: 81(3.1)

¶9,220 Tax-Free Savings Account (TFSA)

The tax-free savings account (TFSA) allows Canadian resident individuals, 18 years of age and older, to earn investment income, including interest, dividends, and capital gains, on a tax-free basis. Contributions to the TFSA are not deductible, but the income in the account is not taxed while in the account or upon withdrawal. ITA: 146.2

The following are the contribution limits for a TFSA: ITA: 207.01

	Annual	*Cumulative*
2009	$5,000	$ 5,000
2010	5,000	10,000
2011	5,000	15,000
2012	5,000	20,000
2013	5,500	25,500
2014 and on	indexed (rounded to the nearest $500)	

Unused contribution room can be carried forward indefinitely. Withdrawals from the account add to the contribution room to allow individuals who access their TFSA savings the ability to recontribute an equivalent amount in the future. However, a recontribution made earlier than January 1st of the year following the year of withdrawal may give rise to an excess contribution. For example, assume Javid had no contribution room from previous years and that he made his $5,500 contribution for 2013 in January. If he withdrew his contribution in July and then recontributed it in October, he would have made an $11,000 contribution in 2013 when he is only allowed $5,500, thus, giving rise to an overcontribution of $5,500. Excess contributions are subject to a tax of 1% per month. ITA: 207.02

A TFSA is generally permitted to hold the same investments as an RRSP. However, it is not able to hold investments in any entities with which the holder does not deal at arm's length.

Interest on money borrowed to invest in a TFSA is not deductible since the income is not taxable. ITA: 18(11)

The attribution rules do not apply to income earned in a TFSA which allows individuals to take advantage of contributions from their spouse or common-law partner. ITA: 74.5(12)

Upon the death of the taxpayer, the TFSA generally loses its tax-exempt status. However, if the beneficiary is a surviving spouse, then the TFSA can be transferred to the surviving spouse and retain its tax-free status. Alternatively, the assets of the deceased's plan can be transferred to the surviving spouse's TFSA. Special rules also deal with marital breakdowns. ITA: 207.01(2)

¶9,230 Exempt Entities

The following are some of the entities that are not taxable under Part I of the Act: ITA: 149(1), (5)

- municipal authorities;
- Crown corporations, commissions, or associations;
- an agricultural organization, board of trade, or chamber of commerce;
- registered charities;
- non-profit corporations for scientific research and experimental development;
- labour organizations;
- non-profit clubs, societies, or associations that are not charities but are organized and operated for purposes such as social welfare, civic improvement, or recreation;
- pension trusts and corporations;

- trusts under a registered retirement savings plan or a deferred profit sharing plan;
- registered education savings plans; and
- registered retirement income funds.

Note that these entities involve government and not-for-profit organizations, which should not have income to be taxed, and retirement savings plans (and similar plans), which are designed to shelter income from tax.

¶9,300 DEDUCTIONS IN COMPUTING INCOME

Subdivision e deals with deductions which are permitted by law but which are not attributed to a particular source of income like employment, business, property, or capital gains. This concept of a source is important because most deductions under Division B must be for expenditures incurred in order to earn specific types of income. However, this set of deductions, although deductible from certain types of income, applies to items which do not necessarily earn income themselves, such as tuition fees, alimony, etc. ITA: 4(2)

These deductions include:

- The capital element of annuity payments;
- Registered retirement savings plan (RRSP) contributions;
- Overpayments included in income;
- Fees related to objections and appeals;
- Legal fees to establish a right;
- OAS clawbacks;
- Moving expenses;
- Child care expenses; and
- Disability support deductions.

¶9,310 Capital Element of Annuity

All annuity payments received are included in income. Certain annuities are purchased out of tax-paid dollars and, hence, the capital portion of the annuity payment, representing this purchase price, is removed under this paragraph. The method of computing the capital element of a contractual annuity is set out in the Regulations. In essence, the capital element is given by the ratio: ITA: 56(1)(*d*), 56(1)(*d.2*) ITR: 300

$$\frac{\text{the capital outlay to buy the annuity}}{\text{the total payments to be received or expected to be received under the contract}}$$

This ratio would be multiplied by the annual annuity payment.

The following annuity payments do not qualify for this deduction:

(a) a superannuation or pension benefit;

(b) a payment under a registered retirement savings plan or registered retirement income fund; or

(c) a payment resulting from a deferred profit sharing plan.

These types of annuities are excluded because they are paid out of income which has not been subjected to tax; that is, the cost of these annuities has been allowed as a deduction in computing income.

¶9,320 Registered Savings Plans

¶9,325 Objectives of pension reform of 1990

The objectives of pension reform were:

- to provide equal access to tax assistance regardless of the type of plan with which an individual funds his or her retirement;
- to provide flexibility in the pension system; and
- to tighten up the system to close both actual and perceived loopholes.

These objectives have been accomplished through the integration of limits for various types of pension plans with the limits for RRSPs.

In order to provide the same amount of tax assistance to an individual for retirement savings, regardless of whether the retirement is funded through a registered pension plan (RPP), a deferred profit sharing plan (DPSP) or an RRSP, under pension reform a comprehensive annual limit for tax-assisted retirement savings — 18% of earned income up to a maximum phased-in dollar limit. The fairly generous contribution limits give individuals an incentive to provide for their retirement years.

¶9,330 Types of tax-assisted retirement plans

There are several basic types of pension plans, and the pension legislation attempts to equalize the tax assistance provided to an individual whether he or she earns retirement income through a defined benefit registered pension plan (DBP), a money purchase registered pension plan (MPP), a DPSP, or an RRSP.

¶9,330.10 *Defined benefit registered pension plans*

Under a DBP, *the benefit that is to be paid* to each employee *is defined* usually in regard to a certain percentage of an employee's earnings in the last few years of employment, regardless of the cost to the employer or the earnings experience of the plan. The benefit that is tax-assisted is limited to a maximum. The employer contributions are deductible, provided that they are certified by an actuary to be necessary to fund the accruing benefits of the plan as registered with the CRA. The employee contributions are deductible, subject to a maximum.

The maximum tax-assisted benefit that may be provided to an individual under a defined benefit registered pension plan is 2% per year of the individual's average best three years of remuneration times the number of years of pensionable service, with a phased-in dollar limit. For example, if an individual has pre-retirement earnings of $134,833 in 2013, it would provide for a maximum tax-assisted pension of $94,383, or 70% of the individual's pre-retirement earnings. Assuming that the individual has 35 years of pensionable service, $134,833 × 2% = $2,697 per year, which buys a pension of $94,383, if expended annually over an effective period of 35 years.

The following table summarizes the scheduled increases.

Year	*Money Purchase Limit*	*Maximum Pension Per year of Service*	*Maximum Pension (35 yrs)*	*Employment Income Needed*
2012	$23,820	$2,647	$92,633	$132,333
2013	$24,270	$2,697	$94,383	$134,833
2014	indexed	indexed	indexed	indexed

¶9,330.20 *Money purchase registered pension plans*

Under an MPP, which is sometimes called a defined contribution plan, *the contribution*, that is required by the employer and the employee, *is defined* rather than the benefit. The retirement benefit for the individual is acquired through the purchase of an annuity on the open market with the contributions made to the plan plus the earnings generated from those contributions while they are held in the plan. The tax-assisted contributions of both employees and employers are limited to a maximum each year as indicated in the above table in ¶9,330.10.

¶9,330.30 *Deferred profit sharing plans*

Under this type of arrangement, only an employer may contribute a limited amount to a plan for the employee, which is based on the performance or the profits of the business. The funds must vest irrevocably in the employee after two years of employment, and the plan may invest in equity shares of the employer if they qualify.

¶9,330.40 *Registered retirement savings plans*

Basically, an RRSP is a tax shelter provided under the Act to give an individual an incentive to save money for his or her retirement years. Within certain limits, the individual can claim tax deductions for contributions to his or her own RRSP, or a spousal RRSP. Since income can accumulate in the plan on a pre-tax basis, RRSPs can play an important part in an individual's overall retirement and tax planning.

If funds are withdrawn from an RRSP prior to maturity, the proceeds are subject to tax when received, as shown in Figure 9-2. If an RRSP is held until maturity, the accumulated RRSP funds may be received as a lump sum, in which case the funds are included in the individual's income and taxed at his or her marginal rate in the year received. Alternatively, the funds may be used to purchase a retirement annuity or may be transferred to a registered retirement income fund (RRIF). Both of these options would defer the receipt of the funds and, consequently, would defer tax on these funds until received in the form of retirement income. Tax savings will be realized if the funds are received and taxed in years when the individual's marginal tax rate is lower than in his or her pre-retirement years. The effect of the deferral of tax on income accumulating within the shelter can even offset the effect of a higher marginal tax rate on retirement income, making the RRSP shelter very attractive to most investors.

Figure 9-2
Taxation of RRSP Withdrawals

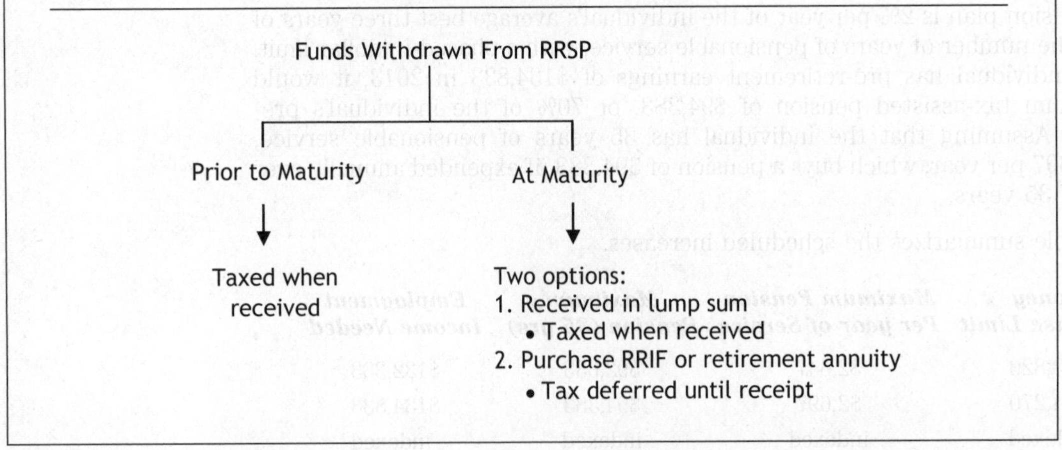

Technically, an RRSP is a contract, accepted for registration by the Minister of National Revenue, between an individual (the annuitant) and an entity that is authorized to carry on the business of selling such contracts (the carrier). RRSPs are available from banks, trust companies, life insurance companies, credit unions, caisses populaires, mutual funds and stockbrokerage firms.

¶9,335 Types of RRSPs

In general, the RRSPs available may be categorized into two types, both of which are of a money purchase nature:

- financial institution plans; and
- self-administered plans.

¶9,335.20 *Financial institution plans*

Financial institutions, such as insurance companies, banks, trust companies or credit unions, sponsor plans which are invested in savings deposits, term deposits and guaranteed investment certificates (GICs). They also offer plans which are invested in mutual funds or pooled fund trusts. These funds may be invested in mortgages, bonds, equities, money market instruments or a combination thereof. Some specialized funds are invested in high-risk investments providing venture capital. Others are invested in specific segments of the economy. Although one can select the type of fund for one's RRSP, the underlying investments are selected by the fund manager. Typically, investment management charges are levied against the underlying investment funds rather than the RRSP. However, sales or redemption charges may be applied against the RRSP on purchases or sales of units in the fund.

¶9,335.30 *Self-administered plans*

A self-administered RRSP can be set up with most financial institutions or a stock broker. A trustee will hold and administer the RRSP investments, but the individual can select investments or, if desired, an investment adviser can do it.

A self-administered RRSP can be invested in a wide variety of qualified investments, including publicly traded debt and equity securities, as well as publicly traded warrants or rights to acquire qualified investments. It can also be invested in certain mutual funds, mortgages, Canada Savings Bonds, treasury bills, and strip coupon bonds and certificates.

Often, administration fees are paid by a taxpayer in respect of a self-administered RRSP ITA: 18(1)(*u*) (or RRIF, as discussed subsequently). Investment counselling fees may, also, be paid in respect of property in these retirement shelters. However, no amount is deductible by a taxpayer in respect of payments made for services pertaining to these sheltered plans.

¶9,340 Integration of limits

In order to provide the same amount of tax assistance to an individual for retirement savings, regardless of whether it is funded through an RPP, a DPSP, an RRSP or a combination thereof, a comprehensive annual limit for tax-assisted retirement savings is being phased in.

This comprehensive annual limit is determined using certain key assumptions with respect to retirement savings.

First, the maximum amount of tax-assisted retirement savings that the government is willing to fund through tax assistance for each individual is $94,383 in 2013. That amount was derived as a multiple of the average wage. Second, it is assumed actuarially that $9 of contributions buys $1 of annual pension income.

Under a DBP, an individual generally must have a combined pension contribution of $2,697 year over the equivalent of 35 years to pay out the 2013 maximum pension of $94,383, and so at the maximum it will be possible to make combined employer/employee contributions equal to the lesser of 18% of the individual's compensation from the employer for the year, or $24,270 (= $2,697 × 9) per year.

Under an MPP, tax-assisted contributions at the maximum may equal the lesser of 18% (9 × 2%) of earnings or $24,270 per year (total contributions made by the employer and employee) and should result in an accumulation of funds in the plan of up to $94,383 of 2013 pension income, generally, after the equivalent of 35 years. The cap of $24,270 for 2013 limits the amount of pensionable earnings that may receive tax assistance to $134,833 (18% of $134,833 is $24,270).

Under a DPSP, the maximum contribution limit is the lesser of 18% of earnings and 50% of $24,270 for 2013, since only the employer may make contributions. This lower limit will leave more contribution room for the individual to make a deductible RRSP contribution.

To integrate the tax assistance provided to individuals who fund their retirement savings with a combination of RRSPs, pension plans and deferred profit sharing plans, the RRSP contribution limit is 18% of earned income for the *prior* year to a 2013 maximum of $24,270, plus or minus any adjustments for benefits provided to the individual under an RPP or a DPSP in the *prior* year. Since the RRSP contribution for 2013 will be based on earned income for 2012, this means that the dollar limit used will be for 2012, as well.

¶9,345 Contribution limits for RRSPs

Using these assumptions, a system has been put in place to determine an individual's RRSP deduction limit and RRSP dollar limit. These limits are defined in subsection 146(1) and are described in Exhibit 9-1.

Employers are to report the pension adjustment (PA) (a measure of the pension benefits an employee is entitled to under an RPP and/or a DPSP) on an employee's T4 slip on or before February 28 of the year following the year in which the benefits accrued. From February to August of that year, the CRA will use the PA reported by the employer plus the prior year's earned income as calculated from the individual's personal tax return to create a pension account for each individual. The CRA will then provide an RRSP contribution limit statement with the taxpayer's Notice of Assessment for the tax return filed. For example, the Notice of Assessment for a taxpayer's 2012 tax return filed by April 30, 2013 will contain a calculation of the RRSP contribution limit for 2013.

An individual may contribute to an RRSP at any time up to and including 60 days after the year-end, or, for example, until March 1, 2014 in order to claim an RRSP deduction on his or her 2013 tax return. The CRA will check the deduction against its pension file to determine if the RRSP contribution is deductible. ITA: 146(5)

An added advantage of the system is that if an individual is not able to contribute the maximum amount to an RRSP, he or she is allowed to "carry forward" any unused deduction limit. There is no time restriction on the carryforward of an individual's unused RRSP deduction room. This feature is discussed in more detail subsequently.

If funds are borrowed to make contributions to an RRSP (or an RPP or DPSP), interest on the borrowed funds is not deductible. The reason for this denial of an interest deduction is probably that the income from the investments in the sheltered retirement plans is not taxed as long as it remains in the plan. ITA: 18(11)

The annual deduction limits and earned income requirements for 2012 to 2015 are outlined in Exhibit 9-1.

EXHIBIT 9-1
2012–2015 Annual RRSP Deduction and Dollar Limits
[ssec. 146(1)]

If the individual is:	*The annual contribution limit for 2012–2015 is:*
• a member of an RPP or a DPSP,	(A) the individual's unused RRSP deduction room carried forward from the previous year *plus* (B) the lesser of: (i) the RRSP dollar limit (below) and (ii) 18% of earned income for the prior year *minus* (C) the pension adjustment for the prior year reported to the CRA by the individual's employer and any past service pension adjustment reported by his or her employer during that particular year.
• a self-employed individual or an individual not described above,	(A) the individual's unused RRSP deduction room carried forward from the previous year *plus* (B) the lesser of: (i) the RRSP dollar limit (below) and (ii) 18% of earned income for the prior year.

RRSP Dollar Limits

	2012	2013	2014	2015
RRSP				
RRSP Dollar Limit	$ 22,970	$ 23,820	$ 24,270	indexed
Earned income needed @ 18%	$127,611	$132,333	$134,833	indexed

¶9,350 Definition of earned income for RRSPs

If an individual was a resident of Canada throughout the year, earned income, as defined, will include the individual's income for a period in the year throughout which the individual was a resident in Canada from: ITA: 146(1)

- an office or employment, generally including all taxable benefits, less all employment-related deductions, but not including any deduction for RPP contributions, employee contributions to a retirement compensation arrangement (RCA) or a clergyman's residence;
- a business carried on by the individual either alone, or as a partner actively engaged in the business;
- property, when derived from the rental of real property or from royalties in respect of a work or invention of which the individual was the author or inventor;
- support payments included in computing the individual's income;

- an amount included in income from supplementary unemployment benefit plans, net research grants, and support receipts in computing the individual's income; and
- the amount of disability pension received after 1990 by an individual under the Canada or Quebec Pension Plan;

less the total of the individual's loss or deduction for a period in the year throughout which the individual was resident in Canada from:

- a business carried on by the individual either alone, or as a partner actively engaged in the business;
- property, where the loss is sustained from the rental of real property; and
- support payments deductible in computing the individual's income.

For the purposes of determining the earned income of such an individual, the income or loss of the individual for any period in a taxation year is the individual's income or loss computed as though that period were the whole taxation year.

Note that earned income does not include superannuation or pension benefits (including CPP/QPP and OAS benefits), retiring allowances, Employment Insurance benefits, death benefits, amounts received from an RRSP or taxable benefits from a DPSP or a revoked plan. It also does not include investment income, taxable capital gains, or scholarships and bursaries.

Also note that it is the earned income of the preceding year which is relevant for purposes of calculating the maximum deductible RRSP contribution.

¶9,355 Calculation of the pension adjustment (PA)

Since a pension adjustment is reported to the individual by his or her employer on a T4 slip, in most cases it will not be necessary for the individual to calculate his or her PA. To do some advance tax planning for an individual, it may be necessary to get a rough idea of what the individual's PA will be for future years. Conceptually, the PA represents the value of tax-assisted or sheltered benefits accruing to the taxpayer in a year. Hence, it reflects the amount of the dollar limit that has been used by employer and employee contributions to an RPP and/or DPSP, leaving the balance of the dollar limit available for a deductible RRSP contribution.

For example, if an individual's earned income is $72,000 and PA is $11,960, that individual's RRSP contribution would be limited to:

18% of earned income (18% of $72,000)	$12,960
Less: PA	11,960
Net limit for RRSP	$ 1,000

The following provides a non-technical indication of how the PA is determined.

(1) *PA for DBP:* The PA for a DBP is based on a formula which reflects the actuarial assumptions made about contributions providing pension income. The objective of the formula is to quantify the contribution room used by contributions to an RPP. The formula is beyond the scope of this text.

(2) *PA for MPP:* The PA for an MPP is equal to the total of the employer's and the employee's contributions in the year.

(3) *PA for DPSP:* The PA for a DPSP is equal to the employer's contributions in the year.

¶9,360 RRSP contribution room carried forward

An advantage of the system is that if an individual is not able to contribute the maximum amount, he or she is allowed to "carry forward" the unused deduction limit. There is no time restriction on this carryforward. The "unused RRSP deduction room" is defined in subsection 146(1). For example, if an individual's maximum annual RRSP contribution limit in 2008 is $10,000, but he or she made a contribution of only $7,000, he or she will be permitted to make an additional deductible RRSP contribution of $3,000 at any time in the future. However, even if he or she makes up the contribution in, for example, 2013, remember that he or she will lose the tax sheltering on the income that would have been earned on the $3,000 from 2008 until 2013, and on any future income earned on this amount for the balance of his or her career. Therefore, it is important to contribute the maximum to an RRSP as soon as possible.

RRSP Contribution Room for the Current Year = Sum of:

1. Unused RRSP room from prior years,

plus

2. Lesser of:

   a. RRSP dollar limit for current year, and

   b. 18% of earned income for prior year

   Less: Pension adjustment for prior year.

¶9,365 Excess contribution

¶9,365.10 *Penalties for excess contributions*

The penalty provisions for RRSP overcontributions are fairly severe. There is a 1% per month penalty until the "excess" for the year is removed from the plan. ITA: 204.1(2.1)

In determining whether there is an excess, the individual includes all amounts contributed by the individual to the plan (other than specified transfers) and all gifts made to the plan, other than gifts made by the individual's spouse. Overcontributions of premiums in the 60-day grace period after the end of the year usually are not considered to be part of the "excess", since the individual can claim them in the year or in the following year.

In order to avoid the 1% per month penalty, the excess amount may be withdrawn from the plan, but it will be included in the individual's income in the year of receipt. This income can be reduced by an offsetting deduction if it is withdrawn in the year in which the excess was contributed or in the following year. The withdrawal of contributions on a tax-free basis is allowed only where the taxpayer is not deliberately making excess contributions. ITA: 146(8) ITA: 146(8.2)

If the excess is not withdrawn in those particular years, but is instead left in the plan, then the individual will include in income this excess contribution when it is eventually withdrawn and yet there will have been no offsetting deduction in any year, resulting in double taxation. It is, therefore, not advisable to leave an excess contribution in an RRSP, as benefits of tax-free compounding in the plan are unlikely to offset the combination of the 1% per month penalty and the double taxation on withdrawal.

¶9,365.20 *Additional contribution*

There is a threshold amount for an excess contribution, which has been set at a cumulative amount of $2,000. This means that at any point in time[7] an individual may contribute up to $2,000 in excess of his or her deductible contribution limit without incurring a penalty. The purpose of this excess allowance is to provide a margin of error for inadvertent excess contributions and for the operation of group RRSP arrangements. In a family context, both spouses or common-law partners may contribute an additional $2,000, so that in total $4,000 may be sheltered without penalty. Children who did not attain the age of 18 in the previous year may not make this additional contribution. Individuals who contribute to both their own RRSP and a spousal RRSP may not make an additional contribution of more than $2,000 in total. ITA: 204.2(1.1)

[7] After February 26, 1995.

Even though the individual will not be able to deduct the excess $2,000 contribution for tax purposes as would be the case if it was a regular RRSP contribution, a sum of money could be accumulated using the benefits of tax-free compounding. If, however, the individual makes a maximum deductible contribution every year, when the excess is eventually withdrawn the individual may be subject to double tax, as the funds were not deductible when the contribution was made, but they are taxable when the individual withdraws them. This double tax may be avoided, since the rules provide for an indefinite carryforward of undeducted contributions. If the individual simply reduces the contribution that he or she would otherwise make in a later year (prior to the withdrawal) and claims the additional $2,000 contribution as a deduction under the carryforward provisions, no double tax will result, because all contributions will have been fully deducted.

Even if the individual was not certain that he or she would use the carryforward rules to eliminate double taxation, it may still be advantageous to make additional contribution. Assuming a 10% rate of return and a 50% personal tax rate, if the individual leaves the $2,000 in the RRSP for 15 years or longer, the benefits of tax-free compounding will outweigh the cost of the taxes that must be paid when the funds are withdrawn.

All or part of an individual's additional $2,000 contribution can be made by the individual to a spousal RRSP, but care must be taken so that the spousal attribution rules (see below) and the regular attribution rules do not apply. ITA: 74.5(12)

¶9,370 Contributions of property

In addition to cash contributions, an individual may be able to contribute certain types of property, such as shares, units of a mutual fund, or Canada Savings Bonds, to an RRSP. The individual will generally need to have a self-administered RRSP if he or she wishes to make a non-cash contribution. If an individual contributes property, he or she is entitled to a deduction equal to the fair market value of the property at the time of the contribution, but keep in mind that the individual is still subject to the normal contribution limits and that the Act restricts the type of property that may be held in an RRSP.

The individual will be considered to have sold the property at its fair market value at the date of contribution. Although any resulting capital gain is subject to tax in the individual's hands, the individual cannot claim any capital loss that arises from a disposition to a plan under which the individual is a beneficiary or from a disposition to a spousal RRSP. (See ¶9,380.) ITA: 40(2)(*g*)(iv)(A), (B)

¶9,375 Application

Example Problem 9-1

Mr. Clark reported the following income for tax purposes in 2012:

Employment income — Subdivision a	$81,000
Dividend received from taxable Canadian corporation (grossed up)	1,200
Rental loss	(2,500)
Total	$79,700

Included in the employment income computation was a deduction for a current contribution to a registered pension plan of $3,200. His employer reported a PA on his T4 for 2012 of $10,000. Mr. Clark made $5,000 of tax-deductible support payments to his former spouse in 2012.

— *REQUIRED*

Calculate the maximum RRSP contribution that Mr. Clark can deduct as an annual contribution in 2013, as determined under the definition of "RRSP deduction limit", and advise Mr. Clark as to when he can make his contribution. Is there any other advice that you might want to give Mr. Clark in 2013 regarding his contributions?

— *SOLUTION*

Mr. Clark's earned income for 2012 is calculated as follows: ITA: 146(1)

Employment income — Subdivision a	$81,000
Add back RPP contribution	3,200
Deduct: Support payment made	(5,000)
Rental loss	(2,500)
Total earned income for 2012	$76,700

In respect of 2013, Mr. Clark is able to deduct the following:

Lesser of:

(a) 18% of 2012 earned income of $76,700 = $13,806, and

(b) the dollar limit for 2013 of $23,820

less the PA for 2012 of $10,000 reported by his employer in respect of the year.

Mr. Clark is able to contribute $3,806 (i.e., $13,806 – $10,000) to his RRSP in respect of 2013. The contribution may be made at any time in 2013 and within the first 60 days of 2014, which is by March 1, 2014. However, Mr. Clark will probably have to wait until the end of February 2013 to make an early 2013 contribution, since he will not know his PA for 2012 until he receives his T4. If Mr. Clark was really cautious, he might want to wait until he receives his Notice of Assessment for his 2012 tax return in which the CRA will issue him a 2013 RRSP contribution limit statement. However, he will have lost the benefit of tax-free compounding on his contribution from March until he receives his Notice of Assessment and makes his contribution. You should inform him that if he has the information at hand respecting the pension benefits that he accrued in the year, you could assist him by calculating his PA and he could make his contribution on the first day of January 2013.

You should also advise Mr. Clark that because of the way the penalties for an overcontribution work, he may make a one-time additional contribution of up to $2,000 in 2013 and the funds may be left to accumulate tax-free in his RRSP. Although this contribution is not tax-deductible, a sum of money can be built up over the life of his RRSP. This will be preferable to Mr. Clark investing in debt instruments or stocks outside of his RRSP, since the income will not be taxed. In order to avoid tax when Mr. Clark withdraws the $2,000 from his plan, he may be able to use the carryforward rules to his advantage by making a contribution that is $2,000 less than his allowable contribution in a year just prior to the withdrawal of the $2,000 from the plan. Then, he will have room to deduct the $2,000. Even if Mr. Clark is not able to use the carryforward rules to eliminate the tax when he withdraws the funds from the plan, if Mr. Clark is able to leave the additional $2,000 in the plan for a period of about 15 years, assuming that his rate of return on the funds was 10%, he would still be better off making the additional contribution.

¶9,380 Contributions to spousal (or common-law partner) RRSP

A "spousal (or common-law partner) plan", which is a defined term, is a plan under which an individual makes contributions to an RRSP but his or her spouse (or common-law partner) is the annuitant. An individual's contributions to both his or her plan and a spousal (or common-law partner) RRSP are restricted in total to the individual's own contribution limit. Therefore, a contribution made by an individual to a spousal (or common-law partner) RRSP does not affect the spouse's or common-law partner's personal RRSP contribution limit for the year. ITA: 146(1), 146(5.1)

A spousal RRSP could be set up for a common-law partner. Two individuals of either sex are considered to be common-law partners of each other when they are cohabiting in a conjugal relationship and either (a) they have so cohabited throughout the preceding 12 months, or (b) they are parents of the same child. ITA: 248(1) "common-law partner"

A spousal (or common-law partner) RRSP can be used to achieve income splitting on retirement. Tax savings will be realized if the retirement income from the RRSP will be taxed at lower marginal tax rates in the spouse's or partner's hands. For example, assuming an ITA: 74.5(12)(*a*) individual intends to retire in 20 years and his or her RRSP earns a 10% annual rate of return, the individual could contribute $5,000 to a spousal (or common-law partner) RRSP for the next three years. At retirement, this would give the individual's spouse or partner a 15-year annuity of about $12,000 per year. If the spouse or partner will pay tax on this income at a marginal tax rate of about 26%, compared to about 46% in the individual's hands, the individual will realize annual tax savings of about $2,400 on this retirement income. To the extent that the contributions to a spousal (or common-law partner) RRSP exceed the individual's deductible limit, the income on withdrawal will be attributed back to the individual and will be subject to tax in his or her hands, because the non-deductible contribution would not meet the exception to the attribution rules.

Provided an individual has earned income, contributions can be made to a spousal (or common-law partner) RRSP until the end of the year in which the spouse attains 71 years of age. These deductible contributions can be made even if the contributor is over 71.

There are other factors that an individual should consider when deciding whether to contribute to a spousal (or common-law partner) RRSP. The individual should be aware that amounts contributed to a spousal plan become the property of his or her spouse. This should be considered in view of any provincial laws governing the division of assets in the event of a marital breakdown.

¶9,385 Attribution on spousal (or common-law partner) RRSPs

An individual may contribute to a spousal (or common-law partner) RRSP to gain some benefit from income splitting. However, special rules apply to curtail such income splitting if the RRSP is used for short-term income splitting.

Attribution applies to include in the contributing individual's income all premiums paid to any spousal (or common-law partner) RRSP in a three-year period, even if the premiums are not deducted or deductible in the three years. As a consequence, attribution will apply on withdrawal of the funds by the spouse if: ITA: 146(8.3)

- the individual paid a premium to *any* spousal (or common-law partner) plan in the current year or the preceding two years; and
- the premium is required to be included in computing the income of the individual's spouse or common-law partner. ITA: 146(8)

If such withdrawals are included in the spouse's or partner's income, the amount withdrawn, up to the amount of the premiums paid by the individual in the three-year period, will also be included in the individual's income. In order to eliminate double counting, if the income is attributed to the individual who made the contribution, an offsetting deduction is allowed to the spouse or common-law partner. ITA: 146(8.6)

Similar rules apply where the individual's spouse or common-law partner receives an amount in excess of the minimum amount from a RRIF and the RRIF received property from an RRSP to which the individual paid a premium in the three-year period. The amount received by the individual's spouse or common-law partner in excess of the minimum amount will be included in the individual's income rather than the spouse's or partner's. ITA: 146.3(5.1)

Example Problem 9-2

Christine and her spouse, Eric, have been setting money aside each year for retirement. A number of years ago, they decided that once they had children Christine would continue to work and Eric would stay home with the children. As a result, for the past five years Christine has been contributing $5,000 per year to a spousal RRSP owned by Eric. Early in 2013, Christine made her annual $5,000 contribution for 2013. However, in September Christine and Eric found they had a significant need for cash, so they withdrew $20,000 from the spousal RRSP set up for Eric.

— *REQUIRED*

How much of the $20,000 withdrawal should be reported by Eric and how much by Christine?

— *SOLUTION*

Christine must report the amount she contributed in the year and the preceding two years, i.e., $15,000.

Eric must report the remainder — $5,000.

¶9,390 Withdrawals before retirement

An RRSP may generally be terminated at any time prior to maturity (generally retirement) and the proceeds distributed to the individual. However, the gross amount received must be included in his or her income. Of course, the benefit of a tax-free accumulation of funds will be lost. An individual may make partial withdrawals from an RRSP without terminating the plan.

The trustee of the RRSP must withhold tax from the amount withdrawn by the individual. The tax withheld may be claimed as a credit on the individual's income tax return as income taxes paid in the year. The withholding tax rate is based on the amount withdrawn — 10% of the amount if it is $5,000 or less; 20% of the amount if it is between $5,000 and $15,000; and 30% of the amount if it exceeds $15,000, except in Quebec. ITR: 103(4), 103(6)

Tax withheld at source from RRSP withdrawals may be minimized by making sure that each withdrawal is for $5,000 or less. Any tax liability related to the withdrawal in excess of the amount withheld must be paid when the individual files his or her tax return for the year.

¶9,395 Home Buyers' Plan (HBP)

Under the HBP, individuals may withdraw up to an aggregate of $25,000 from any of their RRSPs to buy an owner-occupied home without having to pay tax on the withdrawal. Form T1036 must be used to report the withdrawal and to get the exclusion from income. These withdrawals must be repaid in annual instalments over a maximum period of 15 years. The repayment period begins in the second calendar year following the calendar year in which the withdrawal is made. However, the individual may elect to have a repayment made in the first 60 days of a year treated as having been made in the preceding year. Hence, if $25,000 is withdrawn in 2012, the minimum annual repayment of $1,667 (i.e., $25,000/15) must be made on or before March 1, 2015, being 60 days after 2014 which is the second calendar year after the 2012 year of withdrawal. ITA: 146.01

Figure 9-3 illustrates the timing.

Figure 9-3
HBP Payment Timing

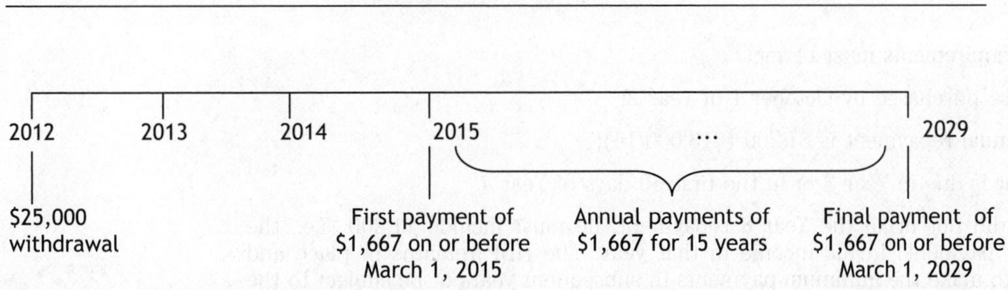

A qualifying home must generally be acquired before October 1 of the calendar year following the year of the withdrawal. Under specified conditions, this acquisition deadline can be extended. Only a first-time home buyer may make use of this plan. An individual will be considered to be a first-time home buyer, if neither the individual nor the individual's spouse or common-law partner owned a home and lived in it as the "principal place of residence" in any of the five calendar years beginning before the time of withdrawal. An individual is excepted from this five-year requirement on the termination of the marriage or common-law relationship.

An individual is allowed to participate in an HBP more than once in his or her lifetime. However, the individual must have repaid all amounts previously withdrawn under the HBP before the beginning of the year in which he or she participates in a new HBP.

The first-time home buyer condition need not be met, also, under specific circumstances. The conditions are that:

(a) the individual is entitled to claim the disability tax credit; and

ITA: 118.3(1) (as discussed in Chapter 10)

(b) the HBP withdrawal by the disabled individual or a related individual is to enable the disabled individual to acquire and live in a dwelling that is more accessible by the individual or that is better suited for the personal needs and care of the individual.

Ordinary contributions made to an RRSP within 90 days before a withdrawal will not be allowed as a deduction, except to the extent that the RRSP balance after the withdrawal is more than the amount of the contribution. Hence, an amount that is both contributed and withdrawn within the 90-day period will not be deductible as an RRSP contribution.

Any amount scheduled for repayment, but not repaid in the appropriate year will be included in the individual's income for the year. For example, if the minimum annual repayment is $1,667 and the individual only repays $1,000, the $667 will be included in income and subjected to tax. On the other hand, an individual may repay more than the minimum scheduled repayment for a year. In this case, there will be less to repay over the remainder of the 15-year period and the minimum annual repayments can, but need not, be reduced for subsequent years.

Example Problem 9-3

Graham plans to purchase his first home and withdraw $18,000 from his RRSP this year (Year 1). He properly completed the application for the Home Buyers' Plan (HBP) at the financial institution where his RRSP is on deposit.

— *REQUIRED*

(a) What are the minimum requirements that Graham must meet?

(b) Assume that Graham made all of his minimum payments for the first seven years of his plan. What are the income tax consequences if Graham does not make any payment in the eighth year?

— *SOLUTION*

(a) The following requirements must be met:

- The home must be purchased by October 1 of Year 2;
- The minimum annual repayment is $1,200 ($18,000/15);
- The first payment is due in Year 3 or in the first 60 days of Year 4.

(b) Since Graham did not make the Year 8 repayment, he must include $1,200 (i.e., the amount of the required payment) in his income in that year. The HBP remains in place and Graham must continue to make the minimum payments in subsequent years or be subject to the income inclusion of an amount that is not repaid.

¶9,400 Tax-free RRSP withdrawals for lifelong learning plan (LLP)

Individuals are allowed to make tax-free withdrawals from their RRSPs for lifelong learning. The objective is to give taxpayers greater access to funds for retraining. Similar to the HBP, individuals must repay the amount they withdraw over a fixed period of time.

ITA: 146.02

A maximum of $10,000 per year can be withdrawn from an RRSP by an individual who is enrolled at a designated educational institution in full-time training or higher education requiring not less than 10 hours per week on courses or work in the program for at least three consecutive months during the year. Students with disabilities qualify if engaged in part-time studies. Further withdrawals can be made for a period of up to four years, but total withdrawals cannot exceed $20,000. Also, contributions made within 90 days of a withdrawal are not eligible for tax-free withdrawal. ITA: 118.6(1)

Amounts withdrawn are repayable in 10 equal annual instalments. The first repayment must be made at the earlier of:

(a) the year following the last year that the student was enrolled on a full-time basis, that is, where the student is not entitled to annual full-time education tax credits for at least three months in two consecutive years; or

(b) 60 days following the fifth year after the first withdrawal.

Repayments simply replenish, without interest, amounts withdrawn from the RRSP. Hence, these repayments are not deductible. If an amount is not repaid on time, it is included in the individual's income in that year.

Individuals may participate in this withdrawal program any number of times during their lifetime. However, no new withdrawals are permitted until all repayments from a previously started program have been made. Of course, while the funds are not in the RRSP, they are not earning sheltered income and there is no opportunity to replenish that income.

¶9,405 Retirement options

¶9,405.10 *Overview*

Although an RRSP must mature by the end of the year in which the individual reaches the age of 71, the individual does not have to wait until then to obtain retirement income from the RRSP. An RRSP can be matured at any time before the end of the year in which an individual reaches the age of 71. As an alternative, the individual can make withdrawals from the plan. This allows an individual the flexibility to take an early retirement should he or she so desire.

At maturity, the accumulated funds may be withdrawn from an RRSP. Tax must be paid at the individual's marginal tax rate on these funds. As an alternative, he or she may purchase one or a combination of available maturity options. These options provide an individual with retirement income in varying amounts over different periods of time. Tax is deferred until he or she actually receives retirement income.

Retirement options which are currently available are:

Fixed-term annuities	• provide benefits up to age 90, or if the spouse or common-law spouse is younger than the individual, and he or she so elects, until the spouse or common-law partner reaches age 90
	• may provide fixed or fluctuating income
Life annuities	• provide benefits during the individual's life, or during the lives of the individual and his or her spouse or common-law partner
	• may have a guaranteed pay-out option
	• may provide fixed or fluctuating income
Registered retirement income funds . . .	• are essentially a continuation of an RRSP
	• provide the individual with retirement income from the investment of the funds accumulated in a matured RRSP for the individual's life

Under federal and provincial pension legislation, the proceeds of locked-in RRSPs that arise on the transfer of a lump-sum payment of vested benefits from an RPP must be used to purchase a life annuity or RRIF at retirement.

¶9,405.20 *Considerations when choosing an option*

A number of factors should be considered when deciding which option or combination of options to choose upon maturity of an RRSP:

- the rate of return;
- current and future income needs;
- the tax that would be payable currently if an annuity or RRIF were not purchased to defer tax;
- the income stream that would result from a particular annuity or RRIF;
- the present age of the individual and that of his or her spouse or common-law partner;
- the extent to which the individual wants to personally manage his or her retirement income; and
- the size of the estate the individual wishes to leave to his or her beneficiaries.

¶9,405.30 *Fixed-term and life annuities*

With a fixed-term annuity, all of the funds accumulated in an RRSP will be paid out over the term of the annuity. The monthly retirement income the individual receives will vary, depending on the interest rate the issuer anticipates earning on the funds. However, with a life annuity, the retirement income will also depend on the sex and age of the individual and the options he or she chooses to attach to the annuity. Retirement income is highest for a straight life annuity (i.e., payments cease upon death, even if this occurs shortly after purchasing the annuity). Retirement income is lower if a guaranteed pay-out or guaranteed term option is added. These options guarantee that a certain amount of funds will be paid out, or that funds will be paid for a specified number of years, regardless of when the individual dies.

When an annuity is purchased, the retirement income will be determined for the term of the annuity. Once the annuity is in place, no further involvement with regard to investment decisions is required on the individual's part. In addition, no adjustments in income occur if interest rates subsequently rise or fall.

¶9,410 Registered retirement income fund (RRIF)

Generally the following rules apply. ITA: 146.3

- A RRIF may be established at any time before the end of the year in which the individual reaches the age of 71. Early retirement can therefore be accommodated by a RRIF.
- It is possible to have more than one RRIF at a time. As a result, several different RRIFs can be set up in order to diversify a RRIF portfolio.
- Although a minimum amount must be withdrawn each year, an individual may withdraw any amount in excess of this minimum.

The fact that an individual is able to withdraw any amount in excess of the minimum allows him or her to match cash needs in any given year. The minimum rate of withdrawal from an RRIF is based on a complicated formula. The following table provides the factors that would be applied to the principal remaining to determine an estimate of the withdrawal for a particular year. As you can see, once the individual reaches age 94, the factor remains at 20% until all the money is withdrawn or the individual dies. ITR: 7308(3) IC 78-18R6

Age	Withdrawal Factor	Age	Withdrawal Factor
71	0.0738	83	0.0958
72	0.0748	84	0.0993
73	0.0759	85	0.1033
74	0.0771	86	0.1079
75	0.0785	87	0.1133
76	0.0799	88	0.1196
77	0.0815	89	0.1271
78	0.0833	90	0.1362
79	0.0853	91	0.1473
80	0.0875	92	0.1612
81	0.0899	93	0.1792
82	0.0927	94	0.2

Amounts withdrawn from a RRIF in excess of the minimum amount, however, will be subject to withholding tax at the same rates that are applicable to RRSP lump-sum withdrawals.

If an individual so elects at the commencement of the RRIF and his or her spouse or common-law partner is younger, the individual may have the minimum payment out of the RRIF based on the age of the spouse or common-law partner. This election does not automatically make the spouse or common-law partner the annuitant under the RRIF after the individual's death.

Generally, RRIF funds may be invested in the same types of investments as RRSPs. The RRIF may be self-administered. That is, an individual may personally determine, along with the trustees of the RRIF, what investments are made by it. As with an RRSP, a RRIF is not taxed on its earnings. Thus, income accumulates on a tax-free basis in the RRIF.

When choosing which investments to hold in a RRIF, an individual should consider the same factors that he or she would have considered in choosing investments for an RRSP. Liquidity is a particularly important factor when choosing investments to be held in a RRIF, since a portion of the funds must be withdrawn each year to provide retirement income.

¶9,415 Treatment of RRSPs and RRIFs on death

¶9,415.10 *Spouse or common-law partner as beneficiary*

If the individual has a RRIF at the time of death, his or her spouse or common-law partner may continue to receive the income from the RRIF (become the annuitant under the RRIF) or receive a lump sum under the RRIF (become the beneficiary under the RRIF), provided that the individual specified that this was his or her intention, either in the RRIF contract or under the terms of his or her will.

If the spouse or common-law partner becomes the annuitant under the RRIF, payments may continue to be made to the spouse or partner, or to the estate for the benefit of the spouse or partner. If the spouse or partner becomes the beneficiary under the RRIF, the lump sum may be paid directly to him or her, or to an estate for the benefit of the spouse or partner. In the situation where the spouse or partner does not become the annuitant or the beneficiary under the RRIF, the RRIF must be collapsed and the value of the RRIF must be paid to any other named beneficiary or the individual's estate.

Amounts paid to a spouse or common-law partner as a named beneficiary from an RRSP (whether lump-sum or otherwise), or as an annuitant or beneficiary under a RRIF, will be taxable to the spouse or partner when received. Amounts paid from an RRSP to the individual's estate for the benefit of his or her spouse or partner will also be taxable to that spouse or partner, provided that the spouse or partner and the legal representatives of the estate file a joint tax election to this effect. If this election is not filed, the fair market value of all of the property of the RRSP fund at the time of his or her death will be included in the deceased's income for the year of death. If the individual intends to have his or her spouse or partner as beneficiary, it will generally be preferable for the individual to name the spouse or partner as beneficiary under the RRSP, rather than to file the election after death, in order to minimize probate fees. The election is made by filing T2019 (RRSP refunds of premiums designation — Spouse).

In the CRA's view, a similar election may not be available where an amount out of a RRIF is paid to an individual's estate for the benefit of his or her spouse or common-law partner. If the individual intends to have his or her spouse or partner as an annuitant or a beneficiary under the RRIF, the individual should name the spouse or partner as an annuitant or as a beneficiary under the contract or under the terms of the will, so that the RRIF amounts will not be included in the individual's income for the year of death.

Where amounts received out of an unmatured RRSP are taxed in the spouse's or partner's hands, he or she may defer tax on all or any portion of the amount by making either a direct or indirect transfer of the funds to an RRSP (if the spouse or partner is under the age of 71, a RRIF, or by purchasing a fixed-term or life annuity within 60 days after the taxation year of receipt. ITA: 60(*l*)

As a result of the financial meltdown in late 2008, an amendment provided that if the value of an individual's RRSP or RRIF is taken into income at death and that value declines prior to the distribution from the plan, then the "loss" can be deducted on the individual's final return to offset the income that was originally reported. ITA: 146.3(6.3)

¶9,415.20 *Financially dependent child or grandchild as beneficiary*

Where the spouse or common-law partner is not the beneficiary, or the beneficiary or annuitant in the case of a RRIF, the proceeds from a RRIF, an unmatured RRSP or the commuted value of an RRSP annuity must be included in the individual's income for the year of death. An exception occurs in certain circumstances where the beneficiary is a financially dependent child or grandchild even if the deceased individual had a surviving spouse or partner when he or she died, if the proceeds are considered to be a "refund of premiums" as defined. ITA: 146(1)

A child or grandchild is not considered financially dependent if his or her income for the year preceding the year in which the annuitant died exceeded the basic personal credit amount ($10,822 in 2012) for that preceding year. This amount is increased by $7,546 to $18,368 if that child or grandchild is infirm. These are the values that apply for a death in 2013. ITA: 146(1.1)

In these circumstances, it is possible to have, or to elect to have such proceeds taxed in the hands of the child or grandchild. In the case where a dependent child or grandchild is mentally or physically infirm, tax may be deferred on such proceeds if either a direct or indirect transfer is made by the child or grandchild, or his or her representative, to an RRSP (if under the age of 71), a RRIF or an annuity within 60 days after the taxation year of receipt. ITA: 146(8.1), 146.3(6.1); ITA: 60(*l*), 60.011

In the case where the child or grandchild is not physically or mentally infirm, tax may be deferred on such proceeds if they are used to acquire an annuity with a term not exceeding 18 minus the age of the child or grandchild at the time the annuity is acquired. The annuity must be acquired in the year the proceeds are included in the child or grandchild's income. In these cases, it will generally be preferable for the individual to name the child or grandchild as the beneficiary under the terms of the will.

¶9,415.30 *Other beneficiaries*

If the individual names a person other than his or her spouse or common-law partner (or, in limited circumstances, a child or grandchild) as a beneficiary under the RRSP or as beneficiary or annuitant under the RRIF, the estate will be faced with paying any tax liability resulting from the individual's death, even though it may not have sufficient funds to do so because the proceeds have been paid to the named beneficiary.

¶9,415.35 *Transfer to an RDSP*

The RRSP rollover rules allow a rollover of a deceased individual's RRSP proceeds to the RDSP of a financially dependent infirm child or grandchild. The amount of RRSP proceeds rolled over into an RDSP will not be permitted to exceed the beneficiary's available RDSP contribution room and will reduce the beneficiary's RDSP contribution room and will not attract Canada Disability Savings Grants. The lifetime contribution limit for RDSPs is $200,000. ITA: 60.011 [proposed]

¶9,415.40 *Contributions for year of death*

If, at the time of death, the individual has not made an RRSP contribution for the year of death, his or her legal representative may make a spousal or common-law partner RRSP contribution under the normal rules. Such a contribution will be deductible in the year of death, provided the contribution is made within 60 days of the end of the year of death. ITA: 146(5.1)

The essential features of tax-assisted plans are summarized in Exhibit 9-2.

Exhibit 9-2
Summary of Tax-Assisted Plans

Plan	Purpose	Contributions Deductible	Contribution Limit	Taxation of Withdrawals
RRSP	Tax shelter to encourage individuals to save for retirement	Yes	Annually, lesser of: (i) RRSP dollar limit of $23,820 for 2013 (ii) 18% of earned income for prior year Less: pension adjustment Plus: unused contribution room from prior years	Prior to maturity: 1. Taxed as received 2. **Home Buyer's Plan (HBP)** — up to $25,000 withdrawn tax-free if repaid in annual instalments over 15 years 3. **Lifelong learning plan (LLP)** up to $10,000 per year withdrawn tax-free for higher education if repaid in annual instalments over 10 years At maturity: 1. Taxed as received 2. Purchase **RRIF or retirement annuity** so taxed deferred until receipt
RPP:				
DBP	Benefit to each employee is defined	Yes	$24,270 for 2013	Taxed as received
MPP	Contribution required by employer and employee is defined	Yes	$24,270 for 2013	Taxed as received
DPSP	Employer contributes to plan for employee based on performance of company	Yes — to employer	Annually, lesser of: (i) 18% of earnings and (ii) 50% of $24,270 for 2013	Taxed as received
TFSA	Earn investment income on a tax-fee basis	No	$5,000 annually	Not taxable
RESP	Fund post-secondary education for qualified beneficiary	No	$50,000 lifetime limit	Accumulated investment income taxable to beneficiary as funds received
RDSP	Save for the long-term financial security of a child with a severe disability	No	$200,000 lifetime limit	Accumulated investment income taxable to beneficiary as funds received

¶9,420 Transfers of Retirement Income and Sheltered Amounts

In general, lump-sum amounts of retirement income can be transferred on a tax-free basis, but only where the amounts are transferred directly from one plan to another. When ITA: 147.3

amounts are transferred directly, they generally are not included in income and consequently it is not necessary to claim an offsetting deduction.

The rollover of periodic pension income out of an RPP, DPSP, Old Age Security (OAS) and Canada Pension/Quebec Pension Plan (CPP/QPP) is generally prohibited. Restrictions are also placed on the amounts that may be transferred from defined benefit RPPs to money purchase RPPs and RRSPs. The result is to restrict the opportunity for individuals to obtain further tax deferral on receipts of periodic pension income.

¶9,425 Direct transfer

Lump-sum RPP and DPSP amounts are transferable on a tax-free basis, but *only through a direct transfer* for:

- lump-sum amounts out of RPPs (other than lump-sum amounts that relate to an actuarial surplus) to another RPP or to an RRSP under which the individual is an annuitant; ITA: 147.3
- lump-sum amounts of DPSPs to an RPP, an RRSP or to certain DPSPs; and ITA: 147(19), 147(20)
- property from an unmatured RRSP to an RPP, to another RRSP or to a RRIF. ITA: 146(16)

When such direct transfers are made, the amount transferred is not included in income, and does not give rise to a deduction. If, however, the individual receives the funds personally, the amount will be included in his or her income for tax purposes in the year it is received and the individual will not be able to contribute the funds (i.e., transfer them indirectly) to his or her RRSP to avoid the income inclusion.

Unlimited lump-sum transfers may be made directly from one MPP to another, from an MPP to a DBP, from a DBP to another DBP, but transfers from a DBP to an MPP or RRSP are limited to prescribed amounts.

¶9,430 Retiring allowances

A retiring allowance is defined to be an amount received (other than a superannuation or pension benefit, an amount received as a consequence of the death of an employee or employment benefits derived from certain specified counselling services): ITA: 6(1)(*a*)(iv), 248(1) "retiring allowance"

(a) upon or after retirement of an individual from an office or employment in recognition of his or her long service, or

(b) in respect of a loss of an office or employment of an individual, whether or not received as, on account or in lieu of payment of damages or pursuant to an order or judgment of a competent tribunal

by the individual or, after his or her death, by a dependant or relation of the individual or by the legal representative of the individual.

A retiring allowance is generally included in income in the year it is received. It includes payments received on retirement; it also includes payments received on loss of employment. So a payment that arose as a result of a lawsuit filed by a terminated employee will also be included in income as a retiring allowance.

¶9,430.10 *Rollover*

A retiring allowance may be transferred tax-free to an RRSP or RPP within the following limits: ITA: 60(*j*.1)

- $2,000 for each year or part thereof during which the individual was employed by the employer or related employer with respect to service before 1996;

plus

- $1,500 for each year or part year of service counted for the $2,000 limit prior to 1989 for which the employer RPP and DPSP contribution did not vest at the time of retirement.

It should be noted that, as time goes by, there are fewer and fewer people who can take advantage of this rollover, since, to benefit from the rollover of a retiring allowance, you would need to have worked for your current employer at least since before 1996, if not since before 1989.

The $1,500 limit is technically computed as the number of pre-1989 years or part years of employment in excess of the equivalent number of pre-1989 years in respect of which employer contributions had vested. The use of the term "equivalent number of years" allows for a fractional number of years to be used, when, to use the example presented in explanatory notes, an employee has worked seven pre-89 years and 60% of the employer's contributions have vested. In that case, the non-vested years would be counted as 2.8 years (i.e., 7 years – 60% of 7 years) and, hence, at $1,500 per non-vested years, $4,200 (i.e., 2.8 × $1,500) could be deducted on a transfer of a retiring allowance.

The amount that may be deducted may not exceed the total of the amounts paid by the individual in the year or in the 60 days after the end of the year as a contribution to an RPP. Excluded from that limit are amounts deductible: (1) for employee contributions to an RPP, and (2) as a premium to an RRSP under which he or she is the annuitant, other than the portion that has been designated as a transfer of a refund of premiums to a spouse or child as a consequence of death or for certain direct transfers of amounts out of a RRIF or an RRSP. ITA: 8(1)(*m*) ITA: 60(*l*)

The following is a *simplified* formula for the deductible amount of a retiring allowance transferred to an RRSP. The deductible transfer cannot exceed the least of:

(a) the sum of:	
(i) $2,000 × the number of pre-'96 years during which the individual was employed (as described above)	xxx
(ii) $1,500 × the equivalent number of non-vested pre-89 years (as described above)	xxx
	xxx
(b)* total RRSP premium contributions	xxx
(c) the amount of the retiring allowance	xxx

* Item (b), in the actual legislation, consists of total RRSP contributions and non-deductible RPP contributions made by the employee. However, it would be unusual for an employee to have made a non-deductible RPP contribution under the current legislation (unless past service contributions were made) and, as a result, that part of the rule has been omitted for simplicity.

The limit in part (b), above, reflects the fact that an individual cannot deduct more than the amount actually transferred or contributed into a sheltered plan.

Example Problem 9-4

Consider the following facts:

Retiring allowance received by Lee Zhang in 2013	$30,000
Earned income in 2012	66,000
PA reported by employer in 2012	10,880
Number of pre-'96 years during which he was employed since November of 1984	12
Percentage of vesting for pre-1989 years of service	60%

— *REQUIRED*

Determine the amount that Lee is able to deduct if he transfers the maximum he can to his RRSP. ITA: 60(*j*.1)

— *SOLUTION*

Lee is only able to contribute $27,000 to his RRSP without overcontributing to the plan in 2013, determined as: ITA: 60(*j*.1)

Sum of $2,000 × 12[(1)] =	$24,000
$1,500 × 2[(2)] =	3,000
Total	$27,000

Lee may deduct a $27,000 transfer in respect of his $30,000 retiring allowance to an RRSP, plus his annual contribution for 2013.

— *NOTES TO SOLUTION*

(1) Since the legislation only refers to years, not full years, it is reasonable to assume part years would qualify.

(2) In the five pre-1989 years (i.e., 1984 to 1988, inclusive) during which the taxpayer was employed, 60% of the employer's contributions vested. Therefore, the equivalent non-vested years would be counted as two years (i.e., five years – 60% of five years) and, hence, an additional $1,500 may be deducted in respect of each of those two equivalent non-vested years.

¶9,440 Overpayments and Other Deductions

¶9,445 Overpayments included in income

The Act permits the deduction of certain overpayments of receipts which have already been included in income, but to which the taxpayer was not entitled, and, hence, must repay (e.g., pension benefits, unemployment insurance and education assistance payments). ITA: 60(*n*), 60(*q*), 60(*v*.1)

¶9,450 Objections and appeals

Also, deductible are amounts paid in the year in respect of fees or expenses incurred in an objection or appeal under the Act and other specified legislation. The expenditures that are deductible could include accounting fees incurred in the preparation of an objection or appeal as well as legal costs. ITA: 60(*o*)

¶9,455 Legal fees to establish a right

Legal expenses paid by the taxpayer to collect or establish a right to a retiring allowance or pension benefits are deductible. The deduction of legal expenses is limited to the amount of retiring allowance or pension benefits at issue, net of any transfers of a retiring allowance to an RRSP or RPP. Excess legal expenses can be carried forward seven years to be deducted against related retiring allowance or pension benefits in those years. ITA: 60(*o*.1) ITA: 60(*j*.1)

¶9,460 OAS clawback

A deduction is permitted for the amount of Old Age Security (OAS) benefits that a taxpayer must repay under the clawback provision of the Act. Where an individual's income under Division B, before deducting the clawback, exceeds $70,954 in 2013, all or some part of the Old Age Security benefits are taxed back. The amount of repayment is computed as: ITA: 60(*w*), 180.2

The lesser of:		
(a) OAS benefits		$xxx
(b) income under Division B without par. 60(*w*) deduction	$ xxx	
Less:	70,954	
Excess, if any	$ xxx	
15% of excess, if any		$xxx

OAS benefits are currently about $6,500 per year. Therefore, a Division B income of $80,000 (before the clawback deduction) would result in a clawback of $1,357 (i.e., 15% of ($80,000 − $70,954)). Since $1,357 of the benefits must be repaid as a special tax, the clawback is allowed as a deduction. In essence, the deduction equates net income effects with cash effects as follows:

ITA: 60(*w*)

ITA: Part I.2, 180.2

	Income effect	*Cash effect*	
Receipt	$ 6,550	$ 6,550	ITA: 56(1)(*a*)
Clawback	(1,357)	(1,357) (Part I.2 tax)	ITA: 60(*w*)
Net effect	$ 5,193	$ 5,193	

¶9,470 Moving Expenses

¶9,475 Deductible expenditures

Taxpayers are permitted to deduct the moving expenses in respect of an eligible relocation under certain prescribed limitations imposed by the Act.

ITA: 62(3), 248(1) "moving expenses"

These deductible expenses include:

(a) reasonable travelling costs in moving the family members to the new residence;

(b) transporting or storing household effects;

(c) the cost of meals and accommodation near the old residence or an acquired new residence for a period not exceeding 15 days;

(d) lease cancellation costs in respect of the old residence;

(e) selling costs of the old residence;

(f) the cost of legal services, transfer taxes or registration taxes, but not goods and services tax, in respect of the new residence but only where the old residence is being sold;

(g) mortgage interest, property taxes, insurance premiums and costs associated with maintaining heat and power, to a maximum of $5,000, payable in respect of a vacant "old residence" for a period during which reasonable efforts are being made to sell the "old residence"; and

(h) the cost of revising legal documents to reflect the taxpayer's new address, replacing driving licences and automobile permits and obtaining utility connections and disconnections.

Note that selling costs of the old residence may be deducted as moving costs or as selling costs for capital gains purposes.

¶9,480 Flat-rate deductions by administrative practice

By administrative CRA practice, taxpayers may choose a simplified method to calculate certain travel expenses for moving. Instead of substantiating actual expenses by receipts, the taxpayer may use various pre-established flat rates. Individuals may claim a flat rate of $17 a meal, to a maximum of $51 per day, per person, without receipts. An individual may determine the deduction for vehicle expenses by multiplying the number of kilometres driven by the flat rate in the following list for the province or territory from which travel begins:

Province or Territory	*2012 Cents/km**
Alberta	50.0
British Columbia	49.5
Manitoba	47.0
New Brunswick	49.0
Newfoundland and Labrador	52.0
Northwest Territories	58.0
Nova Scotia	50.5
Nunavut	58.0
Ontario	55.0
Prince Edward Island	49.5
Quebec	57.0
Saskatchewan	45.0
Yukon	61.5

* www.cra.gc.ca/travelcosts — 2013 rates will be available on the CRA website in 2014.

Vehicle expenses covered by the flat rate include operating and ownership expenses as follows:

- operating expenses: fuel, oil, tires, licence fees, insurance, maintenance, and repairs; and
- ownership expenses: depreciation, provincial tax and finance charges.

¶9,485 Eligible relocation

There are two distinct categories of taxpayers contained in the definition of "eligible relocation": ITA: 248(1) "eligible relocation"

(a) taxpayers who move to carry on business or be employed in Canada may deduct their moving expenses from that business or employment income; or

(b) students who move to attend a post-secondary institution on a full-time basis either in or out of Canada may deduct their moving expenses from student income. ITA: 62(2)

There are a number of specific limitations imposed upon the above two groups of taxpayers. The following are the most important:

(a) the taxpayer must move 40 kilometres (measured by the shortest normal route available to the travelling public)[8] closer (as discussed in Chapter 3, under the heading "Housing loss and housing cost benefits") to his or her work location or post-secondary institution;

(b) moving expenses, which exceed the income from the work location in the year of move, can be deducted, in any following year, against income from that new work location; and ITA: 248(28)

(c) the taxpayer cannot be reimbursed by or be in receipt of an allowance from his or her employer for the moving expenses he or she is claiming, unless the reimbursement or allowance is included in income.

[8] The case of *Giannakopoulos v. The Queen*, 95 DTC 5477 (F.C.A.), appears to have established this method of measurement of the 40 kilometres.

There has been some debate about how soon a move needs to take place after the change in employment location. In recent court cases, it has been determined that there is no requirement that the work location be a new one at the time of the move and that there is no time period by which the taxpayer must move after a change in his or her work location. *Beaudoin v. The Queen*, 2005 DTC 282; *Wunderlich v. The Queen*, 2012 DTC 1040; *Dierckens v. The Queen*, 2011 DTC 1136

The income limitation on moving expenses may not be clear in its application to the situation of an individual who fits both categories of taxpayer recognized in paragraph (a) of the definition of "eligible relocation". For example, a full-time student who moves to a university over 40 kilometres away may have both income from a research grant and part-time employment income from outside of the educational institution in the new location. The provision limits the *aggregate* of moving expenses, ITA: 62(1)(*c*), 248(1) "eligible relocation" ITA: 62(1)(*c*)

(a) in the case of an employee or self-employed individual, to income from employment or business in the new location, *and*

(b) in the case of a full-time student, to income from a research grant.

The use of the word "and" between cases (a) and (b), above, may allow a deduction of moving expenses from the sum of both categories of income in the case of the student, as presented. The relevant Interpretation Bulletin does not address the issue directly, but deals with the two cases separately, without commenting on a situation involving a combination of the two categories of income for a student. The authorized form T1-M and the accompanying information are not entirely clear either. Note that, with the full exemption for scholarship income, the exclusion from a student's income of scholarships means that they provide no base for a moving expense deduction. IT-178R3, par. 2(d), 10(e)

Also it appears that the actual move does not have to be accomplished in the same year as the change in the work location.[9]

Example Problem 9-5

In October of last year, Kenzo moved from his rented Vancouver townhouse to his new home in Halifax to commence a sales position with a life insurance company. After training and client development time, his earnings from this new position were $3,000 for the year, but they were expected to increase as he developed his client base. As a result of his move, Kenzo incurred the following expenses:

Lease cancellation payments on his Vancouver townhouse	$1,000
Commissions and legal fees to acquire a new home	6,000
Moving van	3,800
Flight and five days' accommodation in Halifax	2,400
Shipping his car	850

— *REQUIRED*

What are the income tax consequences of the move for Kenzo?

— *SOLUTION*

- Subject to the new work location income test, Kenzo can claim all of the moving costs, except for the $6,000 pertaining to the acquisition of his Halifax home. Those costs do not qualify, since he did not own (and, hence, sell) his Vancouver townhouse.
- While Kenzo can only claim $3,000 in moving expenses for last year, the excess can be carried forward to the next year.

[9] See *Beyette v. M.N.R.*, 89 DTC 701 (T.C.C.), for a decision on this issue.

¶9,490 Child Care Expenses

¶9,495 Eligibility

Child care expenses are permitted to be deducted in the same year that the taxpayer incurs these expenses in the process of earning income. Note that these provisions restrict the deduction to the parent or supporting individual with the lower income, except during a period where that individual is:

- a student in full-time or part-time attendance at a designated educational institution or a secondary school in Canada; ITA: 63(2)(*b*) (clause (i)(A) of factor C)
- infirm and incapable of caring for children for at least two weeks; ITA: 63(2)(*b*) (clause (i)(B) of factor C)
- confined to prison for at least two weeks; or ITA: 63(2)(*b*) (clause (i)(C) of factor C)
- living apart from the higher-income taxpayer throughout a period of at least 90 days commencing in the year due to a marital or common-law relationship breakdown. ITA: 63(2)(*b*) (clause (i)(D) of factor C)

Income for this purpose is determined to be the income before the child care expense deduction and the deduction for the clawback of certain social assistance payments like OAS. Where the incomes of two taxpayers are equal, the individuals must agree to treat the income of one of them as higher. ITA: 63(2), 63(2.1) ITA: 60(*w*)

The case of *Fiset v. M.N.R.*, challenged successfully the above interpretation. In this particular situation, the Tax Court of Canada determined that since one spouse had no income and since nil is not an amount (of income), the provision could not be applied. However, section 3 was amended subsequently so that no income is zero amount, not nil. Therefore, a taxpayer with no income will have a zero "amount". 88 DTC 1226 (T.C.C.)

Another interesting judicial development involving child care expenses is the case of *Symes v. The Queen et al.* In this case, the self-employed taxpayer claimed the expenses as a business expense rather than a child care expense. The CRA had denied the expenses as personal living expenses. The taxpayer also argued that there was a violation of rights under subsection 15(1) of the *Canadian Charter of Rights and Freedoms*. The Supreme Court of Canada held that the language of the child care expense deduction provision specifically encompasses the purpose for which the taxpayer had incurred her nanny expenses. As a result, the business expense deduction provisions could not be interpreted to permit her a child care business expense deduction. Furthermore, the taxpayer failed to show that women disproportionately pay child care expenses, to prove that the child care expense deduction provision violates subsection 15(1) of the Charter. The taxpayer's evidence showed only that women disproportionately bear the responsibility for caring for children in society. ITA: 18(1)(*h*) 94 DTC 6001 (S.C.C.) ITA: 9(1), 18(1)(*a*), 63 ITA: 18(1)(*h*) ITA: 62 ITA: 9, 18(1)(*a*), 18(1)(*h*)

¶9,500 Limitations

There are several additional restrictions which should be noted:

- an eligible child includes a child who turned 16 years of age during the year, since he or she was "during the year" under 16 years of age; ITA: 63(3)
- the payments cannot be made to certain individuals listed under paragraph (*b*) of the definition of "child care expense", including persons under 18 years of age who are related to the taxpayer by blood, marriage or adoption and a person claimed as a dependant; ITA: 63(3), 118, 251(6)
- the maximum amounts deductible while a child is at a boarding school or camp are: ITA: 63(3)
  - for each child who has a severe and prolonged mental or physical impairment — $250 (i.e., 1/40 of $10,000) per week,
  - for each child who is under the age of seven at the end of the year — $175 (i.e., 1/40 of $7,000) per week,
  - for any other eligible child — $100 (i.e., 1/40 of $4,000) per week; ITA: 63(2.3), (3)

- earned income, which is one of the limiting factors in determining the child care deduction, is defined very specifically (note the difference between this definition and the "earned income" definition for a registered retirement savings plan). This definition of earned income reflects the original purpose of the child care expense deduction provision which was to encourage individuals who had to care for young children to enter the workforce as employees, to carry on a business, to carry on research under a grant, or attend an educational institution to upgrade work skills and knowledge; and ITA: 63(3), 248(1) "salary or wages" ITA: 146(1)
- expenses must be substantiated by receipts bearing the social insurance number of the person performing the service. ITA: 63(1)

The following chart provides a comparison of what is included in "earned income" for purposes of the RRSP deduction and child care expenses.

	RRSP	**Child Care Expenses**
Earned income definition	Individual's income from:	Individual's income from:
	• an office or employment, generally including all taxable benefits, less all employment-related deductions, but not including any deduction for RPP contributions, employee contributions to RCA or a clergyman's residence;	• all salaries, wages, and other remuneration and taxable benefits received from office or employment;
	• a business carried on by individual either alone, or as a partner actively engaged in the business;	• a business carried on by individual either alone, or as partner actively engaged in business;
	• property, when derived from rental of real property or from royalties in respect of a work or invention of which the individual was the author or inventor;	
	• support payments included in individual's income;	
	• an amount included in income from supplementary unemployment benefit plans, net research grants, and support receipts; and	• an amount included in income from supplementary unemployment benefit plans and net research grants; and
	• disability pension received after 1990 under CPP or QPP.	• disability pension received under CPP or QPP.

¶9,505 Deduction calculation

The following formulae reflect the maximum child care deduction.

The Lower-Income Spouse ITA: 63(1)

The deduction is restricted to the least of:

(i) generally an amount paid in the year by the taxpayer or supporting person;[10] ITA: 63(1)(*a*), 63(2)(*b*)(vi)

(ii) $4,000 for each eligible child seven years of age or older, $7,000 for each eligible child under age seven at the end of the year and $10,000 for each child who has a severe and prolonged mental or physical impairment; and ITA: 63(3) "annual child care expense amount"

(iii) ⅔ of the earned income of the taxpayer as defined ITA: 63(2.3)(*e*), 63(3)

minus the amount deducted by the higher-income spouse below. ITA: 63(1)(*f*)

[10] A "supporting person" is defined in subsection 63(3). However, where the taxpayer is the higher-income spouse, the payments made by a supporting person and deductible by the taxpayer are restricted to those payments made by a person living separate and apart from the taxpayer for a period of at least 90 days due to marital or common-law relationship breakdown.

The Higher-Income Spouse ITA: 63(2)(*b*)

The higher-income spouse is restricted to a deduction of the lesser of:

(1) the least of (i)[11], (ii) and (iii) described above and computed using the earned income of the higher-income supporting person; and

(2) the sum of:

(A) $250 (i.e., 1/40 of $10,000) times the number of children who have a severe and prolonged mental or physical impairment,

(B) $175 (i.e., 1/40 of $7,000) times the number of children under seven years of age at the end of the year, and

(C) $100 (i.e., 1/40 of $4,000) times the number of other eligible children,

times the number of weeks the lower-income spouse was a student, was incapable of caring for the children because of mental or physical infirmity, was in prison, or was living separate because of a breakdown of the marriage or common-law partnership. ITA: 63(2)(*b*)

For the lower-income spouse to be considered a student, he or she must be a full-time student; that is, one who is enrolled in a program of not less than three consecutive weeks duration that requires not less than 10 hours per week on courses or work. The dollar limit on the deduction that may be claimed by the working spouse when the other spouse is a part-time student, described in subparagraph (ii) of the definition of factor C, is, also, $175 (i.e., 1/40 of $7,000) per child under age 7 and $100 (i.e., 1/40 of $4,000) per child age 7 to 16. However in the case of a part-time student, the limit is computed for each month or part-month of studies during which child care expenses are incurred. Months are counted where the part-time student is enrolled at an educational institution in Canada in an eligible program lasting at least three consecutive weeks and involving a minimum of 12 hours spent on courses each month. ITA: 63(2)(*b*)

¶9,510 Encouragement for parent to attend school

The legislation provides a child care expense deduction to single parents in full-time or part-time attendance at either a designated educational institution or a secondary school in Canada and to two-parent families when both parents are in full-time attendance in school at the same time. Full-time attendance is defined, for that purpose, as enrolment in a program of at least three consecutive weeks duration that requires the individual to spend at least 10 hours per week on courses or work in the program. Part-time attendance is defined as enrolment in a program of at least three consecutive weeks duration that requires the individual to spend not less than 12 hours per month on courses in the program. The limits of the deduction are the amounts paid in respect of child care to a maximum of $250 (i.e., 1/40 × $10,000) per week of attendance per child who has a severe and prolonged mental or physical infirmity, $175 (i.e., 1/40 of $7,000) per week of attendance per child under 7 at the end of the year and $100 (i.e., 1/40 of $4,000) per week of attendance per child over age 6 and under age 16 at any time during the year. The income limit for this deduction is based on all amounts included in computing the individual's Division B income for the year, not just earned income. ITA: 63(2.2), 63(2.3) ITA: 63(2.2)(*a*)(i) ITA: 63(2.2)(*a*)(ii) ITA: 63(2.3)(*b*)

¶9,515 Application

Example Problem 9-6

Evan and Mary are married. The cost of child care expenses for three eligible children (ages 4, 5, and 9) was $175 per week for 52 weeks.

Evan's earned income	$45,000
Mary's earned income	12,000

[11] Paragraph 63(1)(*c*) excludes, from the deductible amount paid, amounts used in computing a child care deduction of another individual.

Mary was determined to be physically infirm by a qualified medical practitioner and she was confined to bed for a period of 10 weeks.

— *REQUIRED*

Compute the child care expense deduction under section 63 for 2013.

— *SOLUTION*

Since the lower-income spouse (Mary) is infirm and incapable of caring for children for at least two weeks in the year, it is possible for the higher-income spouse (Evan) to claim a deduction for part of the child care expenses as demonstrated below.

Evan's child care deduction is the lesser of:

(a) the least of:			
(i) an amount paid in the year ($175 × 52)		$ 9,100	
(ii) $7,000 × 2 children =	$14,000		
$4,000 × 1 child = . . .	4,000	$18,000	. . . . $9,100
(iii) ⅔ × $45,000 = ...		$30,000	
(b) the sum of:			
(i) $175 × 2 children = ...	$350		
(ii) $100 × 1 child = ...	100	$450 × 10 weeks =	$4,500
Lesser amount: $4,500			

Mary's child care deduction is the least of:

(i) ($175 × 52 weeks) = ...	$ 9,100	
(ii) ($7,000 × 2 children) + ($4,000 × 1 child) = ...	$18,000	$8,000
(iii) (⅔ × $12,000) = ...	$ 8,000	
minus the amount deducted by Spouse A		4,500
		$3,500

Therefore, the sum of both spouses' claim ($4,500 + $3,500) is limited, in this case, to the $8,000 amount which is ⅔ of the lower-income spouse's earned income. The computational format used above is similar to that found in form T778. The format simplifies the effect on the calculation, which might otherwise require that the amount used in part (a)(i) of Evan's deduction calculation be determined as the minimum amount after all other parts of the calculation, so that only the $4,500 amount actually deductible by Evan is shown in part (a)(i). This follows from a possible strict interpretation of the rule, which would not permit Mary to deduct an amount that is "included in computing the amount deductible" by Evan, in this case. Technically, the full $9,100 used in part (a)(i) of Evan's calculation was included in computing the amount deductible by Mary. The simplified calculation used in the example problem, above, arrives at the correct distribution between Evan and Mary and is apparently acceptable, as evidenced by the computational format used in the authorized form, T778.

ITA: 63(1)(*c*)

ITA: 63(1)(*c*)

¶9,520 Disability Support Deduction

Disability support expenses incurred to enable a taxpayer to work or to attend a secondary school or a designated educational institution are fully deductible from the disabled person's income. The deduction is subject to a dollar deduction limit. The following services or equipment, among others, used by disabled persons qualify for the deduction: sign-language interpretation services, real-time captioning services, teletypewriters, optical scanners and electronic speech synthesizers.

ITA: 64

In addition, the refundable medical expense supplement (RMES) provided in the calculation of an individual's tax includes 25% of the total of the allowable expenses claimed under the non-refundable medical expense tax credit and the new disability supports deduction. For details on this supplement, please refer to Chapter 10. ITA: 122.51

An individual, who has a specified impairment in physical or mental function, such as speech, hearing, eyesight or learning or who has a severe and prolonged mental or physical impairment and who qualifies for the impairment credit, may deduct expenses paid to an unrelated attendant, who is at least 18 years of age, to enable the individual to work as an employee, carry on a business, carry on research, or attend a designated educational institution or a secondary school at which the individual is enrolled in an educational program. The deduction for disability support is limited to the lesser of: ITA: 118.3 ITA: 64

(a) the amount paid in the year to the attendant, net of any reimbursement; and

(b) the sum of:

(i) the total of:

(A) employment income inclusions or the taxable portion, if any, of scholarships and bursaries or net research grants, or

(B) income from business, and

(ii) where the taxpayer is a student, the least of:

(A) $15,000,

(B) $375 times the number of weeks in the year during which the individual attends the institution or school, and

(C) the amount by which the individual's total income exceeds the individual's income, that is income aggregated in (b)(i), above.

Example Problem 9-7

Donalda was employed in the year for six months and attended school the other six months (i.e., 26 weeks). She requires the full-time care of an attendant. Her income for the year consisted of employment income inclusions of $12,000 and interest income of $2,000.

— REQUIRED

What is the maximum that Donalda can claim for the attendant care deduction?

— SOLUTION

To obtain the maximum deduction, the amount paid to the attendant cannot exceed:

The sum of:

(a) The total of:

Employment income inclusions	$ 12,000	
Income from business	Nil	$ 12,000

(b) The least of:

Dollar amount	$ 15,000
$375 × weeks of school attendance ($375 × 26)	$ 9,750

Total income	$ 14,000		
Less: income in (a), above	12,000	$ 2,000	2,000
Total deduction			$ 14,000

¶9,530 Expenses of Residents Absent from Canada

The Act extends the deductibility of child care expenses and disability support expenses ITA: 63, 64, 64.1, 250(1) to an individual who is absent from, but still resident in, Canada. Such an individual, who is physically absent from Canada throughout all or some part of a taxation year, would otherwise be precluded from these deductions for expenditures made outside of Canada by the wording contained in the child care and disability support deduction provisions. This provision in ITA: 63, 64 section 64.1, to extend deductibility, is an apparent reaction to the strict interpretation of the ITA: 63, 63 child care expense and disability support deduction provisions taken by the courts in cases involving members of the Canadian Armed Forces. The provision appears to be directed to individuals who are physically absent from Canada for most of a year, but are deemed to be resident. However, the wording of the provision would also appear to apply to individuals who are considered to be resident by the common law principle of continuing ties to Canada.

¶9,800 REVIEW QUESTIONS

(1) Ms. Tang had been working for the same employer for the past 10 years and was tired of her job. She decided to quit and travel to Australia for a year. On leaving, her employer paid her a lump-sum amount of $15,000, since Ms. Tang had been a good employee of theirs and they were hoping she might come back to work for them when she returned to Canada. Ms. Tang had no intention of working for them again but was grateful for the payment. Comment on how this payment should be taxed.

(2) Mr. Everett has worked for the provincial government for the past 35 years and was now eligible for early retirement. As part of his retirement package he is entitled to a lump-sum payment for unused sick days in the amount of $20,000 and unused vacation days of $25,000. On retirement, he is going to receive a cheque for $45,000 as payment for the above amounts. How will this amount be taxed?

(3) Charles and Dee Bowan have decided to end their 12-year marriage. As part of their written separation agreement, they agree that Charles will pay Dee $3,000 per month for her personal support and maintenance, including $1,200 per month for the mortgage on the house that Dee will be living in. The original principal amount of the mortgage is $120,000. What limitations, if any, will Charles encounter when deciding the deductibility of the payments related to the mortgage?

(4) Mark and Ann have agreed to a separation agreement that requires Ann to pay $2,000 per month to Mark as an allowance for his maintenance. Initially, this payment will consist of $1,500 paid to Mark directly and $500 paid to the financial institution that holds the mortgage on his condominium. Mark may change this arrangement at any time to have the full $2,000 paid to him directly. Comment on the deductibility of these payments.

(5) Sam Sider reached an agreement with his employer to pay for his education and living expenses while he returned to university. The agreement was that, if he returned to work for his employer when he graduated, there would be no repayment of the amounts he received. If he did not return to work for his employer, the payments he received would have to be repaid in full. How would this be treated for tax purposes?

(6) Mrs. Smith, a 75-year-old widow, has applied for and received the Old Age Security Supplement. This payment is based on the fact that her income is below a certain threshold amount. She has asked you to tell her how this is treated for tax purposes.

(7) Mr. Singh, a consultant, did some work for ACME Corporation with the agreed-upon fee being $15,000. When the time came for the billing to be done, Mr. Singh sent an invoice to ACME with instructions that the cheque be made payable to his wife. What would your comments be to Mr. Singh and his wife on this arrangement?

(8) How do you determine how much of the employer's contributions to a defined benefit pension plan are deductible?

(9) What is the maximum tax-assisted benefit that may be provided to an individual under a defined benefit plan?

(10) What is the major difference between a defined benefit pension plan and a money purchase pension plan?

(11) One of the RRSP contribution limits is 18% of the prior year's earned income. How was this limit determined?

(12) In 2013, one of the RRSP contribution limits is $23,820. How was this limit determined?

(13) Joe is confused. He is trying to understand the pension rules and he cannot understand why the limit on a money purchase pension plan is based on 18% of this year's income while the limit for an RRSP is based on last year's income. Explain this difference to him.

(14) It has been said that if an individual makes a $2,000 overcontribution (i.e., under the penalty limit) to an RRSP, and as long as the money is left in the RRSP for 15 years or longer at a 10% return and a 46% personal tax rate, then the benefits of compounding will outweigh the cost of the taxes that might be paid when the funds are withdrawn, even if the $2,000 is never deductible. Can you show how this calculation was arrived at? If the rate of return was only 8%, how long would the funds have to be left in the RRSP?

(15) Jennifer wanted to withdraw $20,000 from her RRSP in January in order to buy a new car. She had spent a long time accumulating this amount, but felt that it was more important to buy a car now than accumulate for retirement later. How can she minimize the tax that is withheld on the $20,000 taken out of the plan?

(16) Mr. McDonald, a widower, has died and now his executor has come in to administer the will. His only assets on his death were an RRSP worth $150,000 and his house and other personal assets worth $150,000. Both of his children were grown up so he thought that his was a simple estate. He left the RRSPs to his daughter, Kim, and the residue to his son, Jim. Is there likely to be any conflict between the beneficiaries?

(17) Joan had worked for the same employer for 20 pre-'96 years. Two years ago she was fired. She took legal action against her former employer on the basis that it was wrongful dismissal. This year she won her case and was awarded $40,000. She then paid her legal fees of $8,000 and contributed $35,000 to her RRSP as a retiring allowance. She is glad the case has been settled since she has not worked since her dismissal. What would you show on her personal tax return for the year based on this information? ITA: 60(*j*.1)

¶9,825 MULTIPLE CHOICE QUESTIONS

Question 1

Max retired in 2013 and received a $100,000 retiring allowance. Max worked for his employer from April 1975 to January 2013. He never belonged to a registered pension plan or a deferred profit sharing plan during any of those years. What is the maximum amount of retiring allowance that Max can shelter from tax by transferring it to his RRSP?

(A) $42,000

(B) $63,000

(C) $66,500

(D) $99,000

Question 2

Ms. Assad wants to know the maximum RRSP contribution she can make in 2013 or in the first 60 days of 2014 that will be fully deductible on her 2013 tax return. The following information was taken from Ms. Assad's 2012 tax return:

Income from employment	$44,000
RPP contributions	1,000
Moving expenses	300
Support received	3,600
Pension income	6,000
Real estate rental income	1,400
Interest income	

The pension adjustment reported by Ms. Assad's employer for 2012 was $4,000. Ms. Assad also has a $1,000 unused RRSP deduction limit room which has carried forward from 2012.

What is the maximum RRSP contribution that Ms. Assad can make in 2013 or in the first 60 days of 2014 and deduct fully on her 2013 tax return?

(A) $4,920

(B) $5,000

(C) $6,000

(D) $17,000

Question 3

Meg and James Rashev were both employed full-time during the year. The Rashevs have four children: Joanne (age 17), Susie (age 14), and Sarah and Kelly (4-year-old twins). The Rashevs employed a nanny to look after their children and paid her $15,000 for the year. In addition, during July, Susie went to overnight camp for two weeks at a cost of $250 per week. The Rashevs' family income is summarized below:

	Meg	*James*
Salary & taxable benefits	$ 46,000	
Employment expenses [sec. 8]	(2,800)	
Business income:		
Revenues		$ 50,000
Expenses deductible for tax purposes		(32,000)
Interest income	800	1,500

Which one of the following represents the maximum child care deduction that can be claimed by the Rashevs in the year?

(A) James can claim a deduction of $12,000.

(B) Meg can claim a deduction of $13,000.

(C) James can claim a deduction of $18,000.

(D) James can claim a deduction of $15,200.

Question 4

Ms. Chiu moved from Toronto to Vancouver to start a new job. She earned $40,000 from her Toronto job and $50,000 from her Vancouver job in the year of the move. Ms. Chiu incurred the following costs of moving all of which can be substantiated by receipts:

Moving van to transport household effects	$ 5,000
Travelling costs — self, spouse and two children	3,000
Legal fees — Vancouver house	900
Legal fees — Toronto house	1,100
Loss on sale of Toronto house	25,000
Hotel costs while waiting for Vancouver house — $100 per day for 30 days	3,000
House hunting trip (prior to Vancouver move)	800

Travelling costs consist of three meals a day for four persons over five full days, gas and other car costs, and hotel for five nights at $100 per night. The distance moved between Toronto and Vancouver was 4,430 kilometres.

Which one of the following amounts represents the maximum amount that Ms. Chiu can deduct as moving expenses on her personal income tax return for the year of the move?

(A) $9,500

(B) $12,457

(C) $13,957

(D) $13,800

Question 5

Sahar's income for tax purposes for 2012 and 2013 is as follows:

	2012	*2013*
Salary	$100,000	$110,000
Taxable benefits under sections 6 and 7	8,000	8,000
Travel expenses under section 8	(3,000)	(2,000)
Registered pension plan contributions under s. 8	(4,200)	(4,200)
Business losses	(1,000)	(1,200)
Rental income (net of expenses and CCA)	3,200	3,600
Spousal support paid	(12,600)	(12,000)
Net income under Division B	$ 90,400	$102,200

Which of the following statements is correct?

(A) The earned income that should be used to calculate her child care expense deduction for 2013 is $110,000.

(B) The earned income that should be used to calculate her RRSP deduction for 2013 is $106,400.

(C) The earned income that should be used to calculate her child care expense deduction for 2013 is $102,200.

(D) The earned income that should be used to calculate her RRSP deduction for 2013 is $94,600.

Question 6

Natalie Doak moved 1,000 kilometres from Winnipeg, on March 1, 2013, to a new job and earned $40,000 in her new work location. Her employer reimbursed the costs of selling her old residence and purchasing her new residence. She did not receive any allowance or reimbursement in respect of the following expenses, all of which she paid in 2013:

Moving van	$ 2,600
Travelling costs to move Natalie and family (four persons in all)	900
Cost of cleaning house in new work location	100
Cost of painting and installing new carpets and windows	10,000
Cost of maintaining vacant former residence for three months until it was sold (mortgage interest and property taxes of $3,000 per month)	9,000
Cost of changing address on legal documents	100
House hunting trips for new residence	3,000
	$25,700

Travelling costs consist of three meals a day for four persons over three full days, gas and other car costs, and hotel for two nights at $100 per night.

What amount can Natalie claim for moving expenses in 2013?

(A) $25,700

(B) $15,982

(C) $12,600

(D) $8,982

¶9,850 EXERCISES

Exercise 1

ITA: 56(1)(*b*), 56.1, 60(*b*), 60.1

Uriah and Ursalla Underhill decided to terminate their marriage of 10 years. On June 1 Uriah moved out. From the period of June 1 to October 31, Uriah paid Ursalla $900 per month, made up of $200 for the support of herself and $700 for their two children. On November 1, 2012, Uriah and Ursalla signed a written separation agreement which confirmed the $900 a month payment. In addition the agreement provided that Uriah would pay the monthly mortgage payment of $400 on the home which is in Ursalla's name and all medical expenses for the children. During November and December Uriah made the appropriate payments as per the written agreement and paid $100 of dental bills in respect of the children.

— *REQUIRED*

Discuss the tax implications of the above facts for both Uriah and Ursalla.

Exercise 2

ITA: 63(3), 146(1)

Subsection 248(1) is one of the key definition sections found in the *Income Tax Act*. Definitions are also found elsewhere in the Act.

— *REQUIRED*

Find the section in the Act that contains the definition for "earned income" used in the calculation of the RRSP contribution limits.

Exercise 3

ITA: 60(*i*), 146(1), 146(5)

Don Bickle contributed $5,000 to a spousal RRSP on February 15, 2014. Don's income for tax purposes for 2012 is as follows:

Salary	$70,000
Taxable benefits	1,200
	$71,200
Less: Registered pension plan contributions — defined contribution	(2,800)
Employment income — Subdivision a	$68,400
Rental loss	(5,000)
Dividend income from taxable Canadian corporations grossed up	800
Interest income — Canada Savings Bonds	400
Division B income	$64,600

Don's employer reported a PA of $6,084 in respect of 2012.

— *REQUIRED*

Determine the maximum amount Don can deduct on his 2013 tax return in respect of his 2014 contribution to his spouse's RRSP and the amount, if any, that he can deduct in respect of his own RRSP.

Exercise 4

ITA: Division B

A taxable investment of $15,000 in bonds yields 8% per year before tax. The same investment can be acquired in a self-directed RRSP (tax sheltered). Assume that the yield is reinvested each year at the same 8% before tax. Further assume that the investment is held for 10 years, at which time the RRSP will be cashed in and taxes paid at 45%.

— *REQUIRED*

Which investment approach provides the best cash return?

Exercise 5

ITA: 146(1)

Douglas has been contributing $3,000 annually to a spousal RRSP for his wife, Donna, in each of the last six years, but not this year. The RRSP has grown to $30,000 and Donna has withdrawn $10,000 of the RRSP this year. The withholding tax was $2,000.

— REQUIRED

Describe the full income tax aspects and consequences of this RRSP withdrawal.

Exercise 6

ITA: 60(*i*), 60(*j*.1)

Ivan Reimer received the following amounts for 2013, the year of his retirement:

Employment income (see (1), below)	$ 7,000
Pension income:	
Lump-sum RPP payment from a defined benefit plan	100,000
Superannuation payments (eight monthly pension payments of $3,000)	24,000
Old Age Security pension	6,550
Canada Pension Plan	12,100
Retiring allowance	50,000
Interest income	8,000
	$207,650

Additional Information

(1) Ivan resigned his position on April 1, 2013. The employment income for tax purposes above includes a $300 contribution to his employer's RPP.

(2) On April 1, 2013, Ivan had his employer transfer directly the lump-sum payment from the RPP to his RRSP. In addition, Ivan's employer transferred $20,000 of his retiring allowance directly to his RRSP.

(3) Ivan has been employed by the same employer for 12 pre-'96 years beginning in October 1984, and all of the employer pension contributions have vested.

(4) Ivan was 65 on October 31, 2012.

(5) Ivan's employer reported a PA for him of $700 in respect of 2012. Ivan's earned income for 2012 was $120,000.

— REQUIRED

Determine the tax consequences of the above transactions for 2013, supported by your computations.

Exercise 7

ITA: 62

Edwin Edwards was transferred from Vancouver to Montreal by his employer on October 1, 2013. The following expenses were incurred by Edwin:

Airfare for family	$ 1,300
Moving cost of furniture	1,000
Cost of disposing of Vancouver home	
— legal fees	500
— real estate commission	10,000
Cost of purchasing Montreal home	
— prepaid realty taxes	500
— legal fees	1,000
— Quebec transfer tax	300

Edwin's employment income for tax purposes earned in Montreal during 2013 was $7,000. Edwin's employer reimbursed Edwin for $5,000 of the moving expenses.

— REQUIRED

Calculate the amount that Edwin can deduct as moving expenses. ITA: 62

Exercise 8

ITA: 63

Charles Hughes was a university student in full-time attendance for 30 weeks and worked as a salesman for the balance of the year. His wife, Cathy, was also employed. The Hughes have four children: Sharon 17, Shawn 14, Sally 6 and Stephen 4. Child care expenses for the year amounted to $200 per week for 52 weeks. Charles' and Cathy's receipts and withholdings are summarized below:

	Charles	*Cathy*
Gross salary	$23,000	$47,000
Taxable fringe benefits	850	4,000
Interest income	200	—
Scholarship	3,600	—
Student loan	2,500	—

Deductions from Charles' and Cathy's employment income were:

	Charles	*Cathy*
Income taxes withheld	$ 3,800	$13,700
RPP contributions	2,000	3,700

— REQUIRED

Calculate the child care expenses deduction allowed to Charles and Cathy for 2013.

Exercise 9

ITA: 62(3)

Diane Weber is employed as Personnel Director of B. Ltd., an international corporation. Diane was living in Vancouver at the beginning of last year, but B. Ltd. moved her to Hamilton effective December 1. Diane rented a three-bedroom townhouse in Vancouver but purchased a two-bedroom house in Hamilton on December 20. Diane has supplied you with the following information concerning her moving costs:

Travelling	$3,000
Air transportation and moving	3,100
Temporary living expenses (hotel and meals) in Hamilton for 20 days	2,500
Storage	1,250
Lease cancellation fee paid to Vancouver landlord	1,200
Legal fees to purchase new home	3,600
Property taxes paid from December 21–31	400
Moving allowance paid by B. Ltd.	4,000
Diane's net employment income in Hamilton December 1–31	5,600

— REQUIRED

What is the deductible amount of moving expenses that Diane can claim in her personal income tax return for the year of the move?

¶9,875 ASSIGNMENT PROBLEMS

Problem 1

ITA: 146(1), 146.2

The following table provides information relating to three individuals who each plan to invest $4,500 per year, before tax, starting in 2013. Each individual's before-tax rate of return on a 10-year investment is 8%. Note that each has a different marginal tax rate today (Year 0). However, in 10 years, all are expected to have a marginal tax rate of 40%.

	Taxpayer A	Taxpayer B	Taxpayer C
Earned income	$65,000	$45,000	$25,000
Marginal tax rate (Year 0)	45%	40%	27%
Marginal tax rate (Year 10)	40%	40%	40%
Before-tax rate of return	8%	8%	8%

— *REQUIRED*

(A) Compute the future value of the investment for each taxpayer assuming:

(i) The individual does not contribute to an RRSP but invests the after-tax proceeds of the $4,500 earned income in a tax-free savings account (TFSA).

(ii) The individual contributes to a self-directed RRSP and withdraws the amount in Year 10.

(B) Should each individual contribute to an RRSP or to a TFSA?

Problem 2

ITA: 146(5)

Diana Capriati, a Canadian resident for income tax purposes, has the following income for 2011 and 2012:

	2011	*2012*
Income from employment		
Gross salary	$130,000	$135,000
Less contribution to employer's RPP	(1,500)	(3,000)
	128,500	132,000
Income from property		
Taxable dividends from a Canadian controlled private corporation	32,000	20,000
Gross-up	8,000	5,000
	40,000	25,000
Bank interest received	3,000	5,000
	43,000	30,000
Rental income — gross	25,000	30,000
Deductible rental expenses	(18,000)	(12,000)
	50,000	48,000
Other income		
Alimony payments received	10,000	10,000
Loss from business		
Share of loss from partnership	(30,000)	(20,000)
	$158,500	$170,000

— *REQUIRED*

Based upon the information provided, determine the maximum RRSP contribution that Diana can deduct in 2013. Assume that Diana put $10,000 into her self-administered RRSP on February 12, 2014. Further, assume that Diana was an active member of the partnership and that her pension adjustment for 2011 and 2012 was $4,000 and $7,000, respectively. She did not make an RRSP contribution for 2012.

Problem 3

ITA: 5, 6, 8, 18, 56(1)

Sibbald Kay, age 30, earned $48,000 last year as a dental hygienist for Hi Care Dental Associates. During the year, Sibbald also received director's fees of $600, and incurred the following expenses:

Uniforms purchased for employment purposes	$480
Parking expenses ($80/month)	$960
Hygienist association fees	$280

Sibbald also earned interest income of $3,200 from holding a $50,000 cash balance in T-bills and paid $1,200 in interest expense relating to a loan for an RRSP contribution. Sibbald has not repaid this loan because she believes that saving is more important. Sibbald also has 600 shares of Battery Inc. in her self-directed RRSP. During the year, she sold 400 shares at $20 for a capital gain of $6,000. She withdrew the proceeds of disposition and purchased living room furniture.

— *REQUIRED*

Compute Sibbald's income for tax purposes, and provide her with tax-planning opportunities for the upcoming years.

Problem 4

ITA: Subdivision b, 248(1)

Mariah Holt, a management consultant, provided you with the following statement for the year ended December 31.

Fees received (gross)	$145,000
Salaries and benefits expense	55,500
Liability insurance expense	5,000
Office expense	1,200
Office equipment	1,000
Automobile expenses	1,000
Interest expense (loan for business use)	10,500
Professional courses	1,400
Beginning undepreciated capital cost	
Automobile (Class 10.1)	20,000
Office equipment (Class 8)	30,500

For the year, Mariah drove her automobile 30,000 kilometres, of which 15,000 kilometres were driven for business purposes. Mariah and her sister purchased a commercial rental property on December 5. The cost of the property was as follows:

(1) land $950,000,

(2) building $500,000, and

(3) furnishings $3,000.

The rental income and expenses for the 26 days were as follows:

(1) rent $24,000,

(2) operating expenses $20,000, and

(3) interest expense $6,250.

Mariah, a single parent of two children aged three and five, paid $800 per month to a babysitter to care for the two children in her home. In January, Mariah had purchased her first home for $115,000, paid $2,400 for commissions and $1,900 to move 45 kilometres closer to her consulting office. She withdrew $20,000 from her RRSP under the Home Buyers' Plan.

— *REQUIRED*

(a) Calculate Mariah's net income for the taxation year.

(b) Identify any area of Mariah's income that may be controversial, particularly with the CRA.

Problem 5

ITA: 60(*i*), 60(*j*.1), 146(5), 146(5.1), 146(8.2), 146(8.3), 147.3(4), 147.3(9)

Mr. Rui retired from his job with Wise and Foresighted Consulting Ltd. on February 28, 2013. Mr. Rui expects his 2013 income for tax purposes to be as follows:

Employment income	$ 7,000
Pension income:	
Monthly superannuation (10 months of $3,450)	34,500
Old Age Security	6,550
Canadian Pension Plan	12,100
Farming income	20,000
Income from rental of apartment	10,800
Royalty income from books written by Mr. Rui	14,200
Interest income	12,000
Total income	$117,150

Additional Information

(1) Mr. Rui's 2013 employment income is net of an RPP contribution of $300. His PA for 2013 is expected to be $600.

(2) Mr. Rui will be 71 in February 2014. His wife is now 67.

(3) In 2013, Mrs. Rui withdrew $6,000 from her RRSP. Mr. Rui had made the following contributions to Mrs. Rui's RRSP: January 2013 — $2,000; April 2012 — $1,000; February 2011 — $1,000; December 2010 — $3,000. Mr. Rui did not deduct the January 2013 contribution in 2012.

(4) Mr. Rui's employer reported a PA for him of $7,000 in 2012. His earned income in 2012 was $66,000.

(5) Mr. Rui has unused RRSP deduction room from prior years of $5,000.

— *REQUIRED*

(A) Determine the tax implications of Mrs. Rui's $6,000 RRSP withdrawal.

(B) Determine Mr. Rui's maximum tax deductible RRSP contribution for 2013. What additional RRSP contribution should Mr. Rui make for 2013?

(C) What should Mr. Rui contribute to his RRSP for 2014?

(D) What additional planning steps would you advise Mr Rui to take in connection with his RRSP in 2014?

Problem 6

ITA: 5, 6, 8, 12, 20, 39, 40(2), 56, 60, 75, 146

Ms. Sui is an executive of a large public retail corporation, Clothes to You Ltd., situated in Dundas, Ontario. Ms. Sui is not married. However, she has two adopted children, ages 8 and 10, who reside with her.

Ms. Sui has provided you with the following information for 2013:

Clothes To You Ltd.:

Gross salary	$150,000
Commission income	30,000
Canada Pension Plan contributions	(2,356)
Employment Insurance premiums	(891)
Registered pension plan contributions (money purchase)	(6,000)
Income taxes deducted	(55,000)

(1) Clothes To You Ltd. provides Ms. Sui with an automobile. The annual lease cost of the car, including HST, is $18,400. Ms. Sui is reimbursed for her operating expenses when using the car for business. Clothes To You Ltd. also pays for any insurance, licence fees and repairs and maintenance related to the operation of the automobile. The operating expenses for the year totalled $6,200, including HST. She used the car 10,000 kilometres for pleasure and 30,000 kilometres for business. She is charged $200/month for the use of the car and operating costs.

(2) Ms. Sui received stock options in the year. She has the option to purchase 20,000 shares at $3.50/share. The value of the shares at the date of the issue of the option was $3.50/share. Ms. Sui has not yet exercised any of her options.

(3) Ms. Sui received a piece of artwork worth $750, including HST, from the company at Christmas time.

(4) Clothes To You Ltd. paid $1,300, including HST, for her membership in a fitness club. The corporation also paid Private Health Insurance premiums of $350.

Investment Receipts:

Interest income	$1,100
Dividends received from Canadian-resident public corporations	7,500
Dividends from U.S. corporation — net of 15% withholding tax (in Cdn. $)	680

Other Items:

(1) Annuity payments under contract from Profound Life Assurance Co. The capital portion of the annuity was $650 . . . $2,000

(2) Net proceeds on the sale of her house on March 15, 2013 — net of real estate commission of $12,000 . . . $188,000

The house cost $90,000 in 2000. She had previously sold her pre-1971 cottage in 2002, giving the cottage the maximum designation as a principal residence in order to have a nil taxable capital gain.

(3) At Christmas 2012, Ms. Sui gave each of her children a 6%, $2,000 five-year bond.

Expenditures/Losses:

(1) Investment counsellor's fees . . . $ 1,100

(2) Interest on bank loan to purchase shares . . . 850

(3) Registered retirement savings plan contribution . . . 14,000

Ms. Sui's earned income in 2012 was $170,000. The PA on her 2012 T4 was $7,000.

(4) Ms. Sui incurred meals and entertainment expenses . . . 8,300

(5) Rental loss (before CCA) . . . 3,500

(6) Ms. Sui invested in a limited partnership tax shelter in 2013. The loss per form T5013 is $3,200. She invested $5,000 in the partnership units in early 2013.

— REQUIRED

Calculate Ms. Sui's income under Division B for 2013, using the ordering rules in section 3.

Problem 7

ITA: 62; IT-178R3

Sue and George Shaker lived in Halifax, Nova Scotia, while George completed his combined law and MBA degree at Dalhousie University. The Shakers purchased a home in Halifax when they first moved to Nova Scotia. Due to contracting mononucleosis in his second year of the program, George completed his degree in December 2013 rather than in the spring of 2013.

George excelled in the program and had numerous job offers. He finally accepted a job with NorthAm Co. in Toronto. In order to convince George to accept the job, NorthAm Co. offered to pay the Shakers an amount equal to any loss that they incurred on the sale of their Halifax home and provide them with a $10,000 moving allowance.

Sue has been working for an insurance company in Halifax while George has been attending school. Sue intends to find work in Toronto, but will be unable to continue working for the same insurance company.

George accepted the job with NorthAm Co. in September 2013. During October 2013, George and Sue flew to Toronto to look for a home. They spent a week in Toronto and on the fifth day managed to find and purchase a home with the purchase contract closing on December 15, 2013. The remaining two days were spent arranging for painting and cleaning of the new home. Their expenditures on that trip were:

Two Air Canada tickets (return Halifax to Toronto)	$ 1,200
Motel room, 7 days @ $75 per day	525
Meals, 7 days @ $50 per day	350
Car rental	350

George and Sue managed to sell their Halifax home. That sale closed on December 15, 2013. The statement of account from the lawyer (dated January 15, 2014) revealed the following expenses:

Real estate commission	$7,000
Legal fees, old home	2,000
Legal fees, new home	2,500
Land transfer tax, new home	1,000

The house in Halifax was sold for $140,000. The Shakers had originally paid $160,000 for the house. NorthAm Co. provided a cheque for $27,000 in February 2014 to reimburse them for the loss and the real estate commission. (NorthAm Co. did not include the legal costs when calculating the loss eligible for reimbursement.)

Subsequent to finalizing the sale of their Halifax home and George's completion of his exams, Sue and George packed up their car and drove to Toronto. The trip took 7 days due to a leisurely pace and some bad weather delays, and since their home was not ready when they arrived, they stayed in a nearby motel for 11 days.

The cost of trip and stay in motel was as follows:

Meals, 18 days @ $100 (substantiated by receipts)	$1,800
Motel room, 18 days @ $80	1,440
Gasoline (2,000 kilometres driven)	250

In late December, the Shakers paid a moving bill consisting of $5,000 for the actual move and $250 for storage. George received the $10,000 allowance for moving expenses in December 2013. He commenced work for NorthAm Co. in January 2014 at a salary of $80,000 per year. Sue commenced work for Toronto Insurance Co. in September 2014 at a salary of $85,000 per year.

— *REQUIRED*

Calculate the allowable moving expenses for the Shakers for both 2013 and 2014. Discuss the tax treatment of the loss reimbursement. Assume that all expenditures made were reasonable and can be substantiated by receipts.

Problem 8

ITA: 63

Nina Diamond and Len Dirkfeld are married and have five children: Lindsay age 18, Trevor age 15, James age 7, Ben age 5, and Rebecca age 3. During 2013, they paid a nanny $250 per week for 50 weeks to look after their children while they worked. During July, they paid $3,000 ($1,500 each) for Trevor and James to go to an overnight summer camp for four weeks. In addition, they paid their child Lindsay $300 to babysit the other children at various times when they worked late.

Len is a doctor and has his own practice. Nina worked full-time as a computer consultant during the first eight months of the year. In September, she went back to university on a full-time basis for 13 weeks. On December 11, her courses were finished and she went back to work.

Nina and Len's incomes are summarized below:

	Nina	*Len*
Salary	$50,000	
Taxable benefits	3,000	
Employment expenses	(800)	
Employment income	$52,200	
Business income		$120,000
Interest income	2,000	3,000
Rental income		6,000
RRSP contribution	(5,000)	(10,000)
Net income under Division B	$49,200	$119,000

— REQUIRED

(A) Compute the maximum 2013 child care deductions for Nina and Len. Show all calculations.

(B) How would your answer to (A) change if Nina went back to university for 13 weeks on a part-time basis rather than a full-time basis. Assume Nina took a minimum of 12 hours of courses each month, but do not redo all the calculations.

Problem 9

ITA: 63

Ed Sigmond was transferred from England to Ottawa by Pharmadyne Supplies Inc. on April 1, to assume the permanent position as Vice President, Canadian operations. Ed was a permanent resident of England prior to the move. His earnings for the year are as follows:

Gross salary — January 1 to March 30	$ 12,000
Income tax paid in England	(3,200)
Gross salary — April 1 to December 31	$ 62,000
Income tax withheld	(21,000)
CPP/EI withheld	(2,100)
Donations to United Way withheld	(400)

Ed's spouse, Laura, arrived in Ottawa on July 15, with three children (all over six years of age). On August 1, she resumed her full-time studies at the University of Ottawa, where she was awarded a $500 scholarship. In England, she had attended the University of Cambridge from January 1 to April 30. In England, Laura paid $1,000 per month for a nanny for the children. In Canada, she took her children to the local daycare for $1,360 per month. The Sigmonds also incurred the following moving expenses:

Airfare/lodging — house hunting in Ottawa	$3,500
Airfare — family move	7,000
Moving van fees	3,200
Legal fees and land transfer taxes on acquiring the Ottawa home	5,500
Meals and hotel expenses (12 days prior to employment)	3,800

— REQUIRED

Ed is having some problems in calculating his and Laura's income for Canadian tax purposes, and has come to you for assistance. Compute Ed's net income for tax purposes.

Problem 10

ITA: 56(1)(*a*), 60(*b*), 60(*i*), 60(*j*.1), 60(*o*), 60.1, 62, 63, 146(1), 146(5), 146(8.2), 147.3

In early July 2013, Dr. Elaine Matthews separated from her husband of some years. She maintained full custody of the couple's only child, a seven-year-old girl. Since May 1, 1998, Dr. Matthews had been working as a public health consultant for the Oshawa region. Just prior to her separation she had chosen to take advantage of a severance package from the Oshawa region. She accepted a staff position at Joseph Brant Memorial Hospital in Burlington, Ontario and moved directly from Oshawa to Burlington on September 1, 2013. She sold the former family home in Oshawa on September 15, 2013. Her husband had rented an apartment in Oshawa in late July 2013.

Dr. Matthews has some experience preparing her own tax returns but she has been particularly busy in recent months. She started her 2013 return but quickly decided she simply did not have time to finish it. She requested your assistance in completing her return.

You met with Dr. Matthews to go over her tax information related to 2013 and determined that she had correctly calculated her income under Subdivisions a, b, and c of Division B to total $158,488. Included in this correct computation were the following items:

Salary (from former employer)	$ 96,000
Salary (from Joseph Brant Memorial Hospital)	60,000
Taxable benefits under section 6 of the *Income Tax Act*	1,743
Registered pension plan contributions (defined benefit plan)	(6,750)
Consulting income (reported as business income)	8,000
Interest income from investments	540
Taxable dividends from investments	1,250
Share of rental loss from childhood home inherited from her parents	(1,495)
Net taxable capital gains	4,800
Interest paid on investment loans	(2,400)
Loss from limited partnership investment (rental property)	(3,200)
	$158,488

She provided you with the following *additional details* relating to 2013:

Miscellaneous income	
Severance from former employer	$ 41,538
Transfer of RPP accrued from former employer	
Her former employer made a direct transfer of her accumulated RPP benefits (within prescribed limits) to her RRSP; her former employer had made vested contributions for the years 1998 through 2013	$210,000
Spousal support	
Under the terms of her separation agreement signed in September 2013, Dr. Matthews paid the following amounts for support of her husband:	
Support ($500 a month for September–December)	$ 2,000
Rent on his new Oshawa apartment ($750 a month for September–December)	3,000
Moving expenses from Oshawa to Burlington	
Gas for house-hunting trips (four trips made during late August 2012)	$ 40
Selling costs of former Oshawa home (owned 100% by her; sold September 15, 2013):	
Real estate commissions	$ 12,000
Legal fees	1,050
Costs of purchasing new Burlington home:	
Legal fees	$ 850
Land transfer tax	3,250
Costs of moving herself and her household effects:	
Moving van to transport belongings	$ 600
Gas to drive herself and her daughter (120 km driven)	15
Hotel (2 nights while new home was being painted and cleaned; 2 × $100)	200
Meals (same two days as above 2 × $55)	110
You have determined that the distance from her new home to Joseph Brant Hospital is 3.5 kilometres. The distance from Joseph Brant Hospital to her former home was 115 kilometres.	
Care of her daughter	
Part-time nanny employed January 1–August 31	$ 8,976

YMCA overnight summer camp for two weeks in July while nanny was on vacation ($200 a week)	400
Fall term (September–December) tuition fees for private school (excluding before and after school daycare)	4,000
Before and after school daycare for September–December (provided on premises of private school)	720
Fall term (September–December) transportation to private school	1,200
Registered retirement savings plan contributions	
Personal contributions through employment (March–December 2013)	10,000
Personal contributions through employment (January–February 2014)	4,000

Her 2012 earned income for RRSP purposes was $120,000; her employer had reported a pension adjustment on her 2012 T4 of $9,500; she had no unused RRSP contribution room at the start of 2013 and no undeducted balance of RRSP contributions

Legal fees paid	
Legal representation during separation proceedings to establish requirements to make support payments	$ 1,600
Appeal of her 2011 income tax assessment (which she won)	1,200

— REQUIRED

Complete the calculation of income under Division B. Show all calculations whether or not they are necessary to the final answer. Explain briefly any items not used in your calculations.

Problem 11

ITA: Division B

Ms. King had a busy year in 2013. During the year, she formally separated from her husband and retained custody of her five-year-old daughter, Kelly. She also decided that she needed a fresh start in another city, so she quit her job in Belleville, Ontario, and got a new job in Windsor. Ms. King and her daughter moved to Windsor, Ontario, in November 2013. She has asked you to help her estimate her 2013 personal income tax liability. In order to help you, she has prepared the following list of all the transactions which she thinks might be of interest to you.

(1) Her employment income from her employer in Belleville for the first 11 months of 2013 was $55,000. Her deductions at source included CPP/EI of $3,247 and income tax of $20,000.

Before she left the Belleville employer, a public company, she exercised a stock option that she had for 800 shares. When this option had originally been granted, the share price was $15. The exercise price of the option was $17. At the time she exercised the option, the market price was $25. She immediately sold these shares on the open market for $25.

(2) Her new employer in Windsor agreed to pay some of her moving expenses, but in order to simplify things, they were going to give her an allowance of $8,000. She was responsible, then, for her own expenses.

Her moving costs were as follows:

Moving company charges	$5,500
Gas for trip to Windsor at the time of the move (600 km driven)	50
Motel in Belleville for one night on the day of the move	75
Meals during the one-day move to Windsor	100
Lease cancellation charge in Belleville	200
	$5,925

She had made a trip to Windsor to look for an apartment for her and Kelly and she had incurred the following expenses:

Gas for trip to Windsor	$ 50
Motel costs in Windsor	150
Meals	75
	$275

(3) Her income from her new employer in Windsor during the month of December was $5,000.

(4) During the year she incurred the following expenses for the care of Kelly:

Food and clothing	$6,000
Babysitter costs while she was at work	3,000

(5) Ms. King incurred legal fees of $3,200 to establish her right, under the *Divorce Act*, to support payments in connection with the finalization of the separation agreement. She feels that this was well spent, since her lawyer was successful in getting her husband to pay child support to her for Kelly in the amount of $800 per month, starting in February 2013. So far, her husband has been making these payments on time.

She also had trouble with her 2011 tax return and had to pay her previous accountant $400 to deal with the CRA. It turns out that the CRA has correctly assessed her return.

(6) She is totally confused by the RRSP rules, so she wants you to tell her what the maximum amount is that she can contribute to her RRSP for 2013. She wants you to assume that she will make these payments within the time deadlines when you calculate her tax liability.

(7) Five years ago, Ms. King inherited some shares in a Canadian-resident public company, Facai Ltd., from her mother. She believed that the shares were capable of making money for her. She sold the shares in 2013, in order to put money into a mutual fund that a friend recommended. Her mother had paid $5,000 for these shares in 1986 and at the time of her mother's death, the shares were worth $60,000. Ms. King sold them for $180,000.

Ms. King received cash dividends from these shares during the year in the amount of $9,058.

(8) One of her good friends had been a battered wife, so Ms. King had donated $2,000 to the local registered charity which protects battered women.

(9) Ms. King gave you a copy of her 2012 tax return and it showed employment income of $55,000, child care expenses of $2,000 and taxable dividends of $10,000. She made the maximum RRSP contribution for 2012.

— *REQUIRED*

Calculate Ms. King's income under Division B for 2013. Explain why you omitted any amounts from your calculations. Show all calculations.

[For more problems and solutions thereto, see the DVD accompanying this book.]

¶9,880 ADVISORY CASES

Case 1: Myron and Jennifer

Myron Van Doulis, age 42, just left your office with his spouse, Jennifer Barnes. Over the past several years Myron, a former VP at TNS Communications, has been successfully promoted and now earns $220,000 annual salary. The couple worked assiduously for their social position; Myron encouraged his wife to learn bridge, tennis, and to work as a charitable member of the local community. Jennifer continues to pay her law society dues, hoping that someday she will return to her profession. Myron's treadmill was running at full-speed until last month when TNS was suddenly acquired by MIC International. Myron's life was in crisis when the president, accompanied by a security officer, guided him from his office with a $120,000 severance package. The presidents of TNS and MIC both agreed that Myron's work ethic and performance were less than marginal when compared with the performance of MIC's senior vice president.

While the couple's children (ages 8, 10, and 13) are in school, Jennifer has been secretly writing and working on the computer. Over the past five years, Jennifer has developed a few unique software packages for specialized legal services. Her software was tested and favourably accepted by a large international law firm. Jennifer now has a lucrative proposal from a leading software publishing company. Over the past month, Myron has had time to reflect, ponder, and examine his future needs.

Myron just finished reading the best-selling book, *Take Your Money and Run*. Given the ever-increasing debt load, Myron believes that the government will continue to raise his federal income tax rates. He also believes that the cost of health care and education will increase dramatically. The current market value of Myron's net assets are as follows:

Cash	$ 13,000
Treasury bills and bonds	120,000
Penny stocks (cost $95,000)	4,000
RRSP: Securities	149,000
House (cost $210,000)	240,000
Bank loan for trading	(140,000)
Net assets	$386,000

Myron's most immediate concern is his severance pay. He has a few options. His marginal tax rate this year will be 50% and, in 20 years, when he retires, he estimates a marginal tax rate of 40%.

(a) In the details of Myron's severance package, MIC is willing to pay an $80,000 retirement allowance. Assume for the purposes of this case that all of the $80,000 may be transferred directly to his RRSP (some of it being the eligible portion of the retiring allowance according to paragraph 60(*j*.1) of the Act and the rest being the ineligible portion that can be transferred due to Myron's unused RRSP room). Myron can invest the $80,000 in the Province of British Columbia strip bonds with an annual yield to maturity (YTM) of 10%. MIC has also agreed to pay a cash settlement of $40,000. Currently, the annual GIC rate is 8%.

(b) Alternatively, MIC is willing to provide Myron with 12,000 ITT shares, currently trading at $8, and a cash settlement of $40,000. The shares pay an annual 5% dividend; the company expects growth of about 4% per year. This assumes that the new vice president will improve the financial returns and reap greater rewards in the derivative marketplace.

Myron feels like escaping for a few years. He's thinking of selling his home and purchasing a yacht outfitted with communications technology. According to the book, *Take Your Money and Run*, he could sever all ties (for about two years), transfer his assets and severance to a tax haven, and incorporate offshore. The company could rent a home in Canada for the children while they complete their education. The technology on board would permit his wife to communicate with her publisher (although she insists that she would have to spend at least four months of the year in Canada, visiting the children). Further, Myron can continue his adventurous trading in the options and derivative markets. One last problem: the CRA has disallowed his business loss of $90,000 in last year's income tax return. His trading in the options market generated losses of $90,000, including commission expenses. The CRA has assessed the loss as a capital loss because, in the prior year, Myron had reported his $22,000 in profits from trading in the options market as a capital gain and not as business income.

Draft a report to Myron, detailing and quantifying where possible, the income tax position he faces. Include the financial quantification of the two retirement packages he has been offered. Assume the tax rate on dividends equals approximately 25%.

Case 2: Cam Renaz

Cam Renaz, a self-employed geologist, is a single parent with full custody of his two daughters, Sharee and Susanna (ages 13 and 15). During the past year, Cam retained the full-time services of a nanny to care for them while he worked. Unfortunately, this was a difficult year in Cam's field and his earnings were low. To assist in financing his living expenses, he withdrew $12,000 from his RRSP. He also settled with his wife and she paid him $20,000 as a lump sum in exchange for being relieved of any liability for future alimony payments. To save even more money, Cam prepared his own income tax return, instead of using his accountant's services.

Below is a summary of Cam's income tax information:

Consulting income, net of expenses	$28,000
Car purchased — used 40% for business use	(18,000)
Nanny's salary ($1000/month)	(12,000)
RRSP withdrawals (gross)	12,000
Canadian dividends — cash amount (from CCPCs whose active business income is eligible for the small business deduction)	1,500

When Cam filed his income tax return, he deducted the nanny expense from his consulting income, and wrote off 40% of the cost of the car as business expense. He did not report the RRSP withdrawals because 20% tax was withheld at source.

When Cam received his notice of assessment from the CRA, he was shocked to see that he owed substantially more income tax. The following comments were made in his notice of assessment:

- Child care expenses are not deductible as a self-employed business expense and have been disallowed.
- Cannot deduct price of car as a business expense, and the item has been disallowed.
- Your dividend income has been increased by $375.
- Our records indicate that you withdrew $12,000 from your RRSP and received $20,000 from your ex-spouse for alimony; these amounts have been added to your income.

Cam does not understand why the CRA is assessing him this way. He particularly recalls his accountant telling him that the nanny expenses would be tax deductible.

Compute Cam's net income, considering the legislation, common law and administrative practice, and the correct income tax treatment of each of the items creating problems in Cam's income tax return.

Chapter 10

Computation of Taxable Income and Taxes Payable for Individuals

TOPICS DISCUSSED

LEARNING GOALS

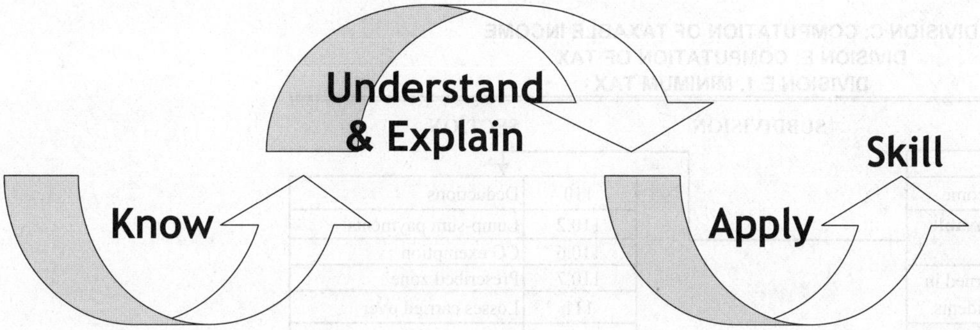

Know

By the end of this chapter you should know the basic provisions of the *Income Tax Act* that relate to the calculation of taxable income and taxes payable for individuals. Completing the Review Questions (¶10,800) and Multiple Choice Questions (¶10,825) is a good way to learn the technical provisions.

Understand and Explain

You should understand and be able to explain how taxable income is computed. With this base you should then understand and be able to explain how federal tax is calculated and how the many refundable and non-refundable tax credits are determined. Completing the Exercises (¶10,850) is a good way to deepen your understanding of the material.

Apply

You should be able to apply your knowledge and understanding of the determination of taxable income and tax liability in a way that accomplishes a client's goals. Completing the Assignment Problems (¶10,875) is an excellent way to develop your ability to apply the material in increasingly complex situations.

OVERVIEW

This chapter is divided into two major parts. The first major segment deals with a discussion of the provisions used to compute taxable income. The Act simply defines taxable ITA: 2(2)
income as income plus or minus amounts permitted under Division C. This chapter will cover a list of miscellaneous items in Division C which specifically pertain to individuals. The capital gains deduction will be introduced briefly in this chapter and discussed more fully in ITA: 110.6
Chapter 13. This chapter will deal with the carryover of losses incurred in another year from the perspective of an individual taxpayer.

The second major segment of this chapter discusses the computation of tax for individuals, including coverage of tax rates, tax credits and minimum tax. This discussion follows a long list of tax credits for such things as marital status, dependants, age, pension income, charitable donations, medical expenses and disability, among others, and for transfers of certain of these credits to another taxpayer. Many of the tax credits in Division E are dependent in some way on Division B income. Therefore, it is necessary first to calculate Division B income and, then, to determine if a Division E tax credit is deductible to the limit of tax on Division C taxable income. If the Division C deductions result in a negative taxable income, taxable income becomes zero.

The following chart will help locate the major provisions of the Act considered in this chapter.

PART I
DIVISION C: COMPUTATION OF TAXABLE INCOME
DIVISION E: COMPUTATION OF TAX
DIVISION E.1: MINIMUM TAX

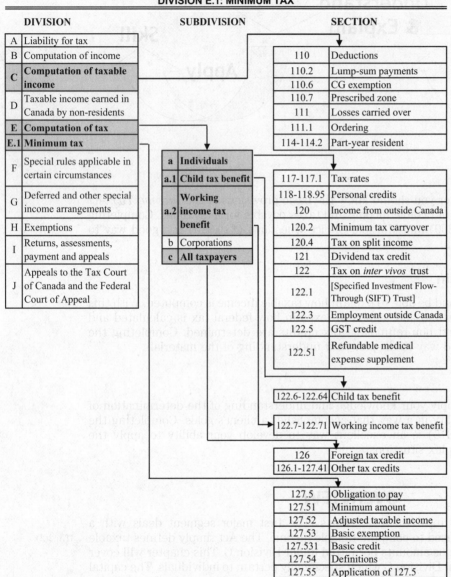

DIVISION

A	Liability for tax
B	Computation of income
C	**Computation of taxable income**
D	Taxable income earned in Canada by non-residents
E	**Computation of tax**
E.1	**Minimum tax**
F	Special rules applicable in certain circumstances
G	Deferred and other special income arrangements
H	Exemptions
I	Returns, assessments, payment and appeals
J	Appeals to the Tax Court of Canada and the Federal Court of Appeal

SUBDIVISION (Division E)

a	**Individuals**
a.1	**Child tax benefit**
a.2	**Working income tax benefit**
b	Corporations
c	**All taxpayers**

SECTION

Division C:

110	Deductions
110.2	Lump-sum payments
110.6	CG exemption
110.7	Prescribed zone
111	Losses carried over
111.1	Ordering
114-114.2	Part-year resident

Subdivision a:

117-117.1	Tax rates
118-118.95	Personal credits
120	Income from outside Canada
120.2	Minimum tax carryover
120.4	Tax on split income
121	Dividend tax credit
122	Tax on *inter vivos* trust
122.1	[Specified Investment Flow-Through (SIFT) Trust]
122.3	Employment outside Canada
122.5	GST credit
122.51	Refundable medical expense supplement

Subdivision a.1:

122.6-122.64	Child tax benefit

Subdivision a.2:

122.7-122.71	Working income tax benefit

Subdivision c:

126	Foreign tax credit
126.1-127.41	Other tax credits

Division E.1:

127.5	Obligation to pay
127.51	Minimum amount
127.52	Adjusted taxable income
127.53	Basic exemption
127.531	Basic credit
127.54	Definitions
127.55	Application of 127.5

¶10,000 COMPUTATION OF TAXABLE INCOME FOR AN INDIVIDUAL

¶10,005 Calculation of Taxable Income

"Taxable income" is defined in the Act as a taxpayer's net income for the year, plus or minus ITA: 2(2) the deductions permitted by Division C. While Part I, Division B, of the Act focuses on the computation of income for tax purposes, Division C contains the statutory rules for determining taxable income from net income for tax purposes. The following illustrates the three distinct steps in computing income tax liability. These steps apply to both corporations and individuals.

Three Distinct Computations

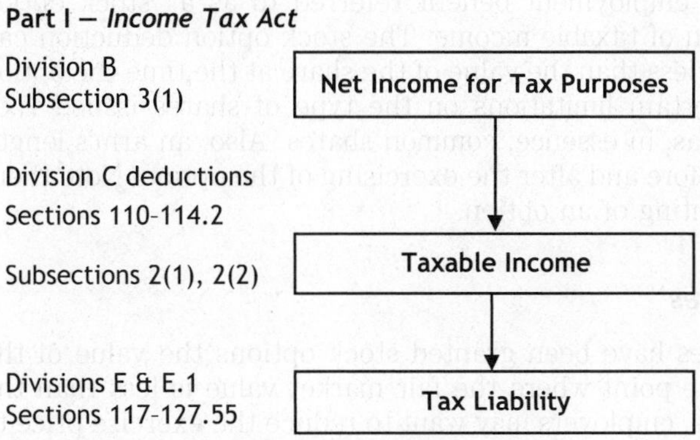

Division C includes a number of allowable deductions but only a few of these apply to individuals. Division C deductions applicable to individuals include those for:

Section 110 — employee stock options, charitable donations of employee stock option shares, shares received under a deferred profit sharing plan, home relocation loans, worker's compensation, social assistance, treaty and international organization exemptions, and vows of perpetual poverty.

Section 110.2 — deduction for lump-sum payments.

Section 110.6 — deduction for capital gains on farm property and shares of a qualified small business corporation.

Section 110.7 — deduction for northern residents.

Section 111 — deduction for carryover losses including non-capital losses, net capital losses, restricted farm losses, and farm losses.

As shown, the deductions permitted are quite specific and, hence, will not be available to ITA: 111.1 all taxpayers. Where an individual claims more than one deduction in the same taxation year, an ordering rule is provided.

¶10,010 Miscellaneous Division C Deductions

Summary of Miscellaneous Division C Deductions

ITA Reference	Division C Deductions
110(1)(*d*)	Employee stock option deduction
110(1)(*f*)	Social assistance receipts
110(1)(*j*)	Home relocation loan
111(1)(*a*)	Non-capital loss carryovers
111(1)(*b*)	Net capital loss carryovers
111(8)	Farm loss
110.6	Capital gains deduction

¶10,015 Employee stock options

¶10,015.10 *Granted by corporations other than Canadian-controlled private corporations*

Employees, who acquire shares from a corporation other than a Canadian-controlled private corporation (CCPC) under a stock option agreement, are required to include in their employment income a benefit. The benefit is computed as the amount by which the fair market value of the shares at the time the shares were acquired exceeds the price actually paid (i.e., the exercise price). The employment benefit is then added to the adjusted cost base of the shares, so that any resultant capital gain reflects the increase in value since the acquisition date. Also, the adjusted cost base reflects the sum of amounts that have been previously taxed, that is, amounts that have been tax-paid. ITA: 7(1) ITA: 53(1)(*j*)

There is a deduction of ½ of the employment benefit referred to as a "stock option deduction" available in the computation of taxable income. The stock option deduction can be claimed if the exercise price was not less than the value of the share at the time the option was granted. In addition, there are certain limitations on the type of shares issued (i.e., prescribed shares which are described as, in essence, common shares. Also, an arm's length relationship of the parties must exist before and after the exercising of the option. Note there are no tax consequences upon the granting of an option. ITA: 110(1)(*d*) ITR: 6204

¶10,015.20 *Decline in value of shares*

In some instances where employees have been granted stock options the value of the shares has subsequently declined to the point where the fair market value is less than the exercise price. As a result of this decline, employers may want to reduce the exercise price to the current fair market value. This, however, will disqualify the option for the Division C deduction, since the exercise price may be less than the fair market value at the time the option was granted. In recognition of this, employers are allowed to reduce the exercise price without jeopardizing the employee's Division C deduction, as long as the following conditions are met: ITA: 110(1)(*d*) ITA: 110(1.7), 110(1.8) ITA: 110(1)(*d*)

- the exercise price is reduced at a time when the fair market value of the securities is less than the old exercise price,
- the old exercise price was not less than the fair market value of the securities when the option was granted, and
- the new exercise price was not less than the fair market value of the securities at the time of the price reduction.

For example, assume that the original option was granted when the fair market value of the shares was $20 and the option had an exercise price of $22. This option would have qualified for the Division C deduction. If the share value drops to $10 and the company reduces the option price to $12 then this security will continue to qualify for the deduction. ITA: 110(1)(*d*)

¶10,015.35 *Special relief for tax-deferred elections*

In situations where a taxpayer has taken advantage of the special election to defer the recognition of the stock option benefit and then finds that the fair market value (FMV) of the underlying security has dropped to less than the tax they will have to pay on the stock option benefit, there is some relief.

¶10,015.40 *Granted by a Canadian-controlled private corporation*

Another exception to the requirement to include the benefit in the year of exercise of the option is provided for stock options granted by a CCPC. There is an employment inclusion of the same amount, but the income is deferred until the year the shares are disposed of. Furthermore, the stock option deduction can be claimed if the shares have not been sold or exchanged before the second anniversary date of the day of acquisition. ITA: 7(1.1), 110(1)(*d*.1)

Note that for stock options granted by a CCPC, there are two possibilities for a stock option deduction.

(1) The shares acquired under the option are held for the two-year period and, thus, qualify for the CCPC deduction, or ITA: 110(1)(*d*.1)

(2) the exercise price is not less than the value of the shares at the date the option was granted and, thus, qualify for the general deduction. ITA: 110(1)(*d*)

Only one of the two possibilities need apply.

¶10,015.50 *Summary of stock option rules*

Where the stock option deduction is claimed, effectively, only ½ of the difference between the exercise price and the value at the date of exercise is taxable, similar to a capital gain. While the net numerical result is a ½ inclusion, the net amount is not a taxable capital gain and, therefore, not eligible for the capital gains deduction on qualified small business corporation shares (QSBCS).

The schematic diagram on stock options introduced in Chapter 3 can be expanded now to include the effects of the stock option deduction.

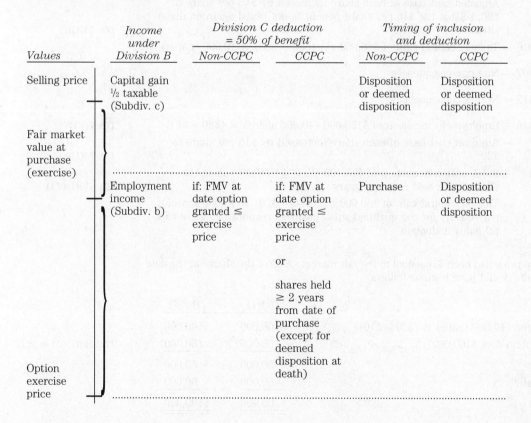

Values	*Income under Division B*	*Division C deduction = 50% of benefit* — *Non-CCPC*	*CCPC*	*Timing of inclusion and deduction* — *Non-CCPC*	*CCPC*
Selling price	Capital gain ½ taxable (Subdiv. c)			Disposition or deemed disposition	Disposition or deemed disposition
Fair market value at purchase (exercise)					
	Employment income (Subdiv. b)	if: FMV at date option granted $\leq$ exercise price	if: FMV at date option granted $\leq$ exercise price or shares held $\geq$ 2 years from date of purchase (except for deemed disposition at death)	Purchase	Disposition or deemed disposition
Option exercise price					

Note that the fair market value of the shares at the date that the option is granted is relevant only for the condition that allows the ½ stock option deduction.

Example Problem 10-1

Malenkov Mfg. Ltd. granted Ms. Yampolsky, its vice-president, an option to purchase 10,000 shares for $5 per share. On March 10, 2013, she acquired the 10,000 shares under the option. The following pertains to the shares:

	Date	FMV
Option granted	March 10, 2007	$10
Option exercised	March 10, 2013	20
Shares sold	March 10, 2016	30

— *REQUIRED*

(A) Determine the tax consequences on the above dates if Malenkov Mfg. Ltd. was:

(i) a public company, or

(ii) a CCPC.

(B) Redo Part (A) assuming the exercise price had been set at $10 per share.

— *SOLUTION*

(A) (i) March 10, 2007 — No tax consequences

March 10, 2013 — Employment income of $150,000 (10,000 shares × ($20 – $5)) ITA: 7(1)

— No stock option deduction, since the exercise price ($5) was less than the value on the grant date ($10) ITA: 7(9)(*b*), 110(1)(*d*)

— Adjusted cost base of each share increased by $15 per share to $20, so that the $15 per share benefit is not taxed again on disposition ITA: 53(1)(*j*)

March 10, 2016 — Taxable capital gain of $50,000 (½ ($30 – $20) × 10,000 shares)

(ii) March 10, 2007 — No tax consequences

March 10, 2013 — No tax consequences

March 10, 2016 — Employment inclusion of $150,000 (10,000 shares × ($20 – $5)) ITA: 7(1.1)

— Adjusted cost base of each share increased by $15 per share to $20 ITA: 53(1)(*j*)

— Stock option deduction of $75,000 (½ × $150,000), since the shares were held over two years ITA: 110(1)(*d.*1)

— Taxable capital gain of $50,000 (½ ($30 – $20) × 10,000 shares); may qualify for the qualified small business corporation share capital gains deduction

(B) If the exercise price had been $10, equal to the fair market value of the shares at the date of grant, the two results would have been as follows:

	(B)(i)	(B)(ii)	
Employment income (10,000 shares × ($20 – $10))	$100,000	$100,000	
Division C deduction (½ × $100,000)	(50,000)	(50,000)	ITA: 110(1)(*d*) or (*d.*1)
	$ 50,000	$ 50,000	
Taxable capital gain	50,000	50,000	
	$100,000	$100,000	

The primary difference between (A) and (B) is that the stock option deduction is available to the non-CCPC, since the exercise price is not less than the fair market value at the time the option was granted. Also, for the CCPC option, the benefit does not have to be reported until the year of disposal. ITA: 110(1)(*d*)

The effect of these provisions is to give a treatment equivalent to capital gains for stock option benefits accruing up to the date of acquisition and included in employment income, without providing eligibility for the QSBC share capital gains deduction where applicable.

¶10,020 Deduction for certain receipts

A number of refundable and non-refundable tax credits provided to an individual taxpayer are reduced by the individual's Division B income. Certain social assistance payments received by individuals are included in their Division B income and may affect these tax credits. However, there is no intention to tax these payments in the hands of the recipient. As a result, a deduction is provided in Division C, in the computation of taxable income, to offset the inclusion of the payments in Division B. The sources of income which qualify for this treatment are: ITA: 110(1)(*f*)

- the Guaranteed Income Supplement,
- social assistance payments,
- workers' compensation, and
- amounts that are exempt income by virtue of a tax treaty.

¶10,025 Home relocation loan

A special deduction is available to partially offset an imputed interest income inclusion in situations where an employee has obtained a "home relocation loan" as a result of an employment relocation. A home relocation loan is defined as, in essence, a loan used to acquire a home which is at least 40 kilometres closer to an employee's new work location than his or her old residence. The intention of this special deduction is that an employee could receive the equivalent of a $25,000 interest-free loan without including a deemed interest benefit in taxable income. The maximum deduction is the imputed interest benefit and the duration of the deduction is the lesser of five years or the life of the home relocation loan. A loan received by a taxpayer that is used to repay a home relocation loan is deemed to be the same loan as the home relocation loan and to have been made on the same day. The low-interest benefit can be computed on the principal amount of the loan outstanding in the year at a rate which is the lesser of: ITA: 80.4 ITA: 110(1)(*j*) ITA: 248(1) "home relocation" ITA: 80.4 ITA: 110(1.4) ITA: 80.4(4)

(a) the prescribed rate at the time the loan was made, and

(b) the changing prescribed rates during the year the loan was outstanding.

The deduction is computed as the least of three amounts: ITA: 110(1)(*j*)

(a) interest on the whole home relocation loan as computed using the "lesser of" rule *minus* interest paid during that year and 30 days thereafter (i.e., the net imputed interest benefit on the home relocation loan itself); ITA: 80.4(1)(*a*), 80.4(4)

(b) interest on a $25,000 home relocation loan using the "lesser of" rule, but restricted to a maximum of five years (i.e., interest at the appropriate prescribed rate computed on a principal amount of $25,000); and ITA: 80.4(1)(*a*), 80.4(4)

(c) total benefits from all low-interest or no-interest loans. ITA: 80.4

Example Problem 10-2

Ms. Kishke joined May Kostcha Ltd. on February 1, 2013 as chief corporate tax officer. On that date she received an interest-free loan of $100,000 to assist her in the financing of a new home, since she was moving from Kingston in eastern Ontario, to Dundas in southern Ontario, to take the position. In addition, she was given a loan of $20,000 bearing interest at 3% payable on December 31 of each year that the loan is outstanding. This loan was to assist her with other costs associated with her move. The interest was paid when due.

— REQUIRED

Determine the effects of these loans on Ms. Kishke's taxable income in 2013. Assume prescribed rates for 2013 as follows: 4% for the first quarter, 5% for the second quarter, 4% for the third and fourth quarters. Ignore any impact of the leap year.

— *SOLUTION*

The imputed interest benefit would be computed on these loans with the "lesser of" rule for a home relocation loan as follows. ITA: 80.4(1), 80.4(4)

Loan to purchase house: ITA: 80.4(1)(*a*), 80.4(4)

The "lesser of rule" can be applied in each quarter of the year during the year that the loan is outstanding. Since the 4% rate applicable in the first quarter of the loan is less than or equal to the prescribed rate in each of the other three quarters, the 4% rate will be applicable for all of the year, computed as follows:

4% of \$100,000 × 334/365 =		$3,660	
Loan for general purposes:			ITA: 80.4(1)(*a*)
4% of \$20,000 × 59/365 =	$ 129		
5% of \$20,000 × 91/365 =	249		
4% of \$20,000 × 92/365 =	202		
4% of \$20,000 × 92/365 =	202	782	
		$4,442	
Interest paid (3% of \$20,000 × 334/365)		(549)	ITA: 80.4(1)(*c*)
Benefit		$3,893	ITA: 80.4

Since the \$100,000 loan is a home relocation loan, the following deduction may be taken in the calculation of taxable income: ITA: 110(1)(*j*)

Least of:		
Benefit computed on \$100,000 home relocation loan net of reduction for interest paid (interest-free loan)	$3,660	ITA: 80.4, 110(1)(*j*)(i)
Interest computed on a \$25,000 loan 4% of \$25,000 × 334/365)	$ 915	ITA: 80.4(1)(*a*), 110(1)(*j*)(ii)
Total benefit net of interest paid for year	$3,893	ITA: 80.4, 110(1)(*j*)(iii)

Therefore, the Division C deduction would be \$915 in 2013. ITA: 110(1)(*j*)

It may be rare to see a case where the deduction is equal to the total benefit for the year. ITA: 80.4, 110(1)(*j*)

¶10,030 Loss Carryovers

¶10,032 Legislative intent and government policy

Income and losses are computed for a taxation year, which is a somewhat arbitrary period. Over a longer period, losses might be expected to offset income, with only the net income being taxable in that longer period. The availability of a carryover period for losses is intended to broaden the period within which losses can offset income. The statute provides for losses to be carried back against prior years' income or forward against future years' income. Taxpayers are thus provided some relief from the economic risk of an activity and are provided with encouragement to persevere. The necessity for limitations is, however, crucial. Limitations, together with the broad general rules that apply to the utilization or restriction of various types of losses, will be discussed in this chapter.

Commentary in previous chapters has alluded to the fact that losses which cannot be applied in the year in which they occur because of a restriction in Division B may be deducted in Division C by carrying the losses back three years through amended returns and/or applying the balance of the losses to future years, subject to any further restrictions as indicated below.

¶10,035 Non-capital loss carryovers

ITA: 111(1)(*a*)

A "non-capital loss" (non-CL) available for carryover is a defined term. For individuals, the definition can be summarized in computational form as follows: ITA: 111(8)

Aggregate of:				
Amounts computed as losses from non-capital sources:				ITA: 3(*d*)
Loss from an office or employment			$xxx	
Loss from business			xxx	
Loss from property			xxx	
Allowable business investment loss			xxx	
Amount deducted as capital gains deduction			xxx	ITA: 110.6
Amount deducted as net capital losses			xxx	ITA: 111(1)(*b*)
Amount deductible as:				
Stock options		$xxx		ITA: 110(1)(*d*), (*d*.1), (*d*.2), (*d*.3)
Social assistance and other payments		xxx		ITA: 110(1)(*f*)
Home relocation loan		xxx	xxx	ITA: 110(1)(*j*)
			$xxx	
Less: aggregate of net incomes:				ITA: 3(*c*)
Income from office or employment		$xxx		
Income from business		xxx		
Income from property		xxx		
Income from other sources		xxx		ITA: 56–59
Taxable capital gains (other than from listed personal property)	$xxx			
Taxable net capital gain from listed personal property	xxx			
	$xxx			
Less: allowable capital losses (other than from listed personal property and allowable business investment losses)	xxx	xxx*		
		$xxx		
Less: other deductions		xxx	xxx*	ITA: 60–66
			$xxx*	
Less: farm loss (included in loss from business above)			xxx	
Non-capital loss carryover			$xxx*	

* Cannot be negative [sec. 257].

Note that in order to become a carryover non-capital loss, a current year's loss from non-capital sources must, in essence, exceed income from all other sources in the current year. Non-capital losses may be carried over as follows, with the earliest losses being applied first:

	Carry back	*Carry forward*
For taxation years ending before March 23, 2004	3	7
For taxation years ending after March 23, 2004 and before 2006	3	10
For taxation years ending in 2006 and later	3	20

Note that the portion of an allowable business investment loss, which is discussed in some detail in Chapters 7 and 13, not used in the year of loss, becomes a non-capital loss and is available for carryover in the manner just described. However, if the ABIL that is embedded in the non-capital loss is not used up with a 10-year carryforward, then it reverts to its original nature and becomes a net capital loss available for indefinite carry forward, but only for deduction from net taxable capital gains.

¶10,040 Net capital loss carryovers

ITA: 111(1)(*b*)

A "net capital loss" (net CL) for a particular taxation year available for carryover to another year is defined to be the excess of allowable capital losses over taxable capital gains for that particular year plus allowable business investment losses not absorbed in the 10-year carryforward period as a non-capital loss, as discussed above. Net capital losses may be carried back three years and forward indefinitely. It is important to note that net capital losses for a particular year are calculated using the inclusion rate of that year. The following are the historical inclusion rates.

ITA: 111(8) "net capital loss"

Capital Gains Inclusion Rate:

Years	*Inclusion Rate*
1972–1987	½
1988, 1989	⅔
1990–February 27, 2000	¾
February 28, 2000–October 17, 2000	⅔
After October 17, 2000	½

Since net capital losses may arise in years with different capital gains inclusion rates to be deducted against other net taxable capital gains computed by other inclusion rates, it is necessary to convert net capital losses to the capital gains inclusion rate appropriate to the carryover year in which the net capital loss is deducted. Net capital losses realized in a year with a lower inclusion rate must be increased when carried forward to a year with a higher inclusion rate. Net capital losses realized in a year with a higher inclusion rate must be decreased when carried back to a year with a lower inclusion rate.

The amount of the net capital loss to be deducted in the year, taking into account any differences in the rates of inclusion, is computed using the following formula:

ITA: 111(1.1)

the lesser of:

(a) net taxable capital gains for the year; and

ITA: 3(*b*)

(b) the total of each amount for different years of net capital losses determined by the formula

$$A \times \frac{B}{C}$$

where A is the amount of the net capital loss arising from a particular "loss year" and claimed in Division C in the current year;

ITA: 111(1)(*b*)

B is the inclusion rate for the year in which the net capital loss is to be deducted; and

C is the inclusion rate for the year in which the loss was realized.

For example, a net capital loss of $9,000 realized in 1999 with its ¾ inclusion rate would be converted to $6,000 in 2013 with its ½ inclusion rate (i.e., $9,000 × ½/¾ = $6,000). Conceptually, the $9,000 net capital loss in 1999 resulted from a $12,000 capital loss (i.e., $9,000 × 4/3). The same $12,000 capital loss in 2013 would result in a net capital loss of $6,000 (i.e., $12,000 × ½).

Note that both the words "deducted" and "claimed" are used in reference to net capital losses. The word "claimed" appears to refer to net capital losses in their original, unadjusted amount as computed in the "loss year" at the inclusion rate for that year. The word "deducted" appears to refer to the net capital losses after they have been adjusted by the formula to the inclusion rate appropriate for the year in which they will offset taxable capital gains.

ITA: 111(1.1)

ITA: 111(1.1)(*b*)(iii)(A) to (B)

Example Problem 10-3

Larry Laplante had net capital losses of $10,000 in the taxation year ending December 31, 1987 and $2,000 in each of the taxation years ending December 31, 1989 and 1994. He had capital gains of $5,000 in 1998, $4,000 in 1999, and $3,000 in 2013. He has had no other capital gains or losses.

— *REQUIRED*

Determine the maximum amount to be deducted in the taxation years 1998, 1999, and 2013. ITA: 111(1)(*b*), 111(1.1)

— *SOLUTION*

	1998		1999		2013		
Net taxable capital gain:							ITA: 3(*b*)
Capital gains realized	$ 5,000		$ 4,000		$ 3,000		
Taxable capital gain	$ 3,750		$ 3,000		$ 1,500		
Adjusted deduction — Lesser of:							ITA: 111(1.1)(*a*)
(i) TCG above	$ 3,750		$ 3,000		$ 1,500		ITA: 3(*b*)
(ii) total of adjusted net capital losses of loss years (see carry-over below)	$19,250		$15,500		$ 8,333		
Lesser amount		$3,750		$ 3,000		$ 1,500	

Net capital loss carryovers:

Year loss incurred	*1987*	*1989*	*1994*	*Total*
Unadjusted net CL	$10,000	$2,000	$2,000	
Adjusted to 1998 inclusion rate at $^3/_4$	$15,000[(1)]	$2,250[(1)]	$2,000	$19,250
Utilized in 1998 (see above)	(3,750)	Nil	Nil	(3,750)
Available in 1999	$11,250	$2,250	$2,000	$15,500
Utilized in 1999 (see above)	(3,000)	Nil	Nil	(3,000)
Available in 2012	$ 8,250	$2,250	$2,000	$12,500
Adjusted to 2012 inclusion rate	$ 5,500[(2)]	$1,500[(2)]	$1,333[(2)]	$ 8,333
Utilized in 2012	(1,500)	Nil	Nil	(1,500)
Available in 2013	$ 4,000	$1,500	$1,333	$ 6,833

— *NOTE TO SOLUTION*

(1) The $10,000 of 1987 net capital loss is a fractional amount computed at a $^1/_2$ inclusion rate. This amount is adjusted to the 1998 inclusion rate of $^3/_4$ as follows:

$$\$10,000 \times {}^3/_4/{}^1/_2 = \$15,000$$

The $2,000 of 1989 net capital loss is a fractional amount computed at a $^2/_3$ inclusion rate. This amount is adjusted to the 1998 inclusion rate of $^3/_4$ as follows:

$$\$2,000 \times {}^3/_4/{}^2/_3 = \$2,250$$

The $2,000 of 1994 net capital loss is a fractional amount computed at a $^3/_4$ inclusion rate. Therefore, it need not be adjusted for use before February 28, 2000.

(2) The losses are adjusted from the $\frac{3}{4}$ inclusion rate (as adjusted above) to the $\frac{1}{2}$ inclusion rate as follows:

1987: $8,250 × $\frac{1}{2}/\frac{3}{4}$ = $5,500

1989: $2,250 × $\frac{1}{2}/\frac{3}{4}$ = $1,500

1994: $2,000 × $\frac{1}{2}/\frac{3}{4}$ = $1,333

These adjustment factors do nothing more than convert the fractional loss of a particular year into a full loss by dividing by $\frac{1}{2}$, $\frac{2}{3}$ or $\frac{3}{4}$ in the denominator (i.e., item C in the formula) and then computing the net capital loss at the inclusion rate for the year of the deduction by multiplying by $\frac{3}{4}$, $\frac{2}{3}$, or $\frac{1}{2}$ in the numerator (i.e., item B in the formula). Hence, $10,000 divided by $\frac{1}{2}$ is $20,000 which was the full capital loss in 1987 before the $\frac{1}{2}$ inclusion rate was applied. Then $20,000 multiplied by $\frac{3}{4}$ produces $15,000 which is the net capital loss stated in terms of a $\frac{3}{4}$ inclusion rate used before February 28, 2000.

Note that the losses carried forward from the "loss year" are those from the earliest loss year. This is illustrated in the net capital loss carryover calculation presented above. Note, also, how net capital losses deducted in a particular year, as modified by the adjustments for different inclusion rates, are limited to net taxable capital gains of that year. ITA: 111(3) ITA: 111(1)(*b*) ITA: 111(1.1)(*a*)

¶10,045 Farm loss

ITA: 111(1)(*c*)

When a taxpayer incurs an operating loss from carrying on a farm business, current-year losses generally are not treated any differently than losses are treated for any other type of business that result in a non-capital loss, unless the restricted farm-loss rules or hobby farm considerations apply. ITA: 111(8)

Where farming is not the taxpayer's chief source of income, the CRA will frequently attempt to apply the restricted farm-loss rules. These have been the source of considerable tax litigation over the years. The difficulty of the provision is in the wording "where a taxpayer's chief source of income for a taxation year is neither farming nor a combination of farming and some other source of income". ITA: 31

¶10,045.10 *Farming as a chief source of income*

In *Moldowan v. The Queen*, the Supreme Court defined the principal criteria for determining whether a taxpayer is carrying on a farm business as his/her chief source of income as: 77 DTC 5213 (S.C.C.)

- time devoted to the farming business;
- capital committed to the business; and
- the actual and potential profit as indicative of a reasonable expectation of profit.

According to the Supreme Court of Canada (S.C.C.), these criteria were considered among other relevant facts. For example, in this case, Mr. Moldowan devoted all his time in July and August to breeding horses and invested a significant amount of capital in the development of a racetrack and stables. The taxpayer also had other investments and was a full-time businessman. Justice Dickson, writing for the S.C.C., described Moldowan as carrying on one of many businesses and, in here the ownership and training of horses was held to be a sideline business. The S.C.C. pointed out that the *Income Tax Act* considers three classes of farmers:

- those for whom farming can be reasonably expected to provide their chief source of income;
- those for whom farming is carried on as a sideline business; and
- those who carry on farming as a hobby.

¶10,045.20 *Sideline farming business*

[The Supreme Court of Canada, in *The Queen v. Craig* (2012 SCC 43), found that the restricted farm loss rules did not apply and that farm losses could be fully deducted where a taxpayer places significant emphasis on both farming and non-farming sources of income. This finding overruled *Moldowan v. The Queen*. As a result, the March 21, 2013 federal Budget has proposed to restore the *Moldowan* interpretation that a taxpayer's other sources of income must be subordinate to farming in order for the farm losses to be fully deductible. In addition, the Budget proposes to increase the restricted farm loss limit to $17,500 ($2,500 + ½ of the next $30,000). Both of these changes are applicable to taxation years that end on or after March 21, 2013.]

Generally, individuals who carry on a sideline farming business will be subjected to the restricted farm-loss provisions. This category assumes (and it must be demonstrated when necessary) that there is a reasonable expectation of profit from the farming operation. The amount of farm losses that may be deducted from other sources of income during a taxation year is restricted. The amount of farm loss from a sideline farming business that may be deducted during the current year is the lesser of: ITA: 31(1)

- the actual loss; and
- $2,500, plus half of the next $12,500 [$30,000 proposed in the March 2013 federal Budget] of losses for a year (maximum $8,750 [$17,500 per Budget proposal]). Farm losses in excess of $8,750 [$17,500] become restricted farm losses and may not be utilized during the year. Restricted farm losses are deductible under paragraph 111(1)(*c*), in computing taxable income for the three preceding taxation years as a loss carryback, or in the following 20 taxation years as a loss carryforward. A restricted farm loss from other year(s) is only deductible in calculating taxable income to the extent of the lesser of net farming income in the year and income calculated under section 3. Unless there is farm income in the year, restricted farm losses will not be deductible in arriving at taxable income.

¶10,045.30 *Hobby farm losses*

A "hobby" farmer is a category of a farming operation that is considered by the CRA or the courts to have no reasonable expectation of profit. The reason for distinguishing a hobby farm from a farming business is to ensure that hobby farmers do not obtain deductions for expenses incurred for personal hobbies. The loss incurred is considered to be a personal or living expense, and hence, not deductible. This treatment is consistent with the treatment of any other hobby where there is no reasonable expectation of profit. ITA: 18(1)(*h*)

¶10,060 Capital Gains Deduction

¶10,061 Historical overview

Individuals can shelter up to $750,000 of capital gains on qualified small business corporation shares, qualified farm property, or qualified fishing property by claiming a capital gains deduction in the computation of taxable income.

[The March 21, 2013 federal Budget proposes to increase the capital gains exemption limit from $750,000 to $800,000 starting in 2014. In addition, the exemption will be indexed for 2015 and future taxation years.]

The capital gains deduction originated in 1985. The 1985 federal Budget introduced a lifetime cumulative deduction for net taxable capital gains (net TCGs) for individuals (other than trusts) resident in Canada. The announced purpose of this deduction was to provide an incentive for investment. Until the February 25, 1992 federal budget, the deduction was virtually unrestricted as to type of capital gains on a disposition. The February 25, 1992 federal budget imposed a restriction on the capital gains deduction resulting from the disposition, after February 1992, of most real property (i.e., land and buildings), described as non-qualifying real property. Since the whole thrust of the present Act is to tax a fraction of capital gains, the introduction of this provision created considerable complexity in the legislation, to accommodate this exception.

The capital gains deduction available on qualified small business corporation shares will be discussed in Chapter 13.

¶10,065 The qualified farm property CGD

The maximum CGD may be claimed as a deduction against any capital gains on qualified farm property (QFP). QFP is defined at subsection 110.6(1) as: ITA: 110.6(2)

- real property, used in a farming business in Canada by either the taxpayer (including beneficiaries under certain trusts), a spouse or common-law partner, a child or a parent, a corporation (which is a family farm corporation), or a partnership (which is a family farm partnership);
- share capital in a family farm corporation;
- an interest in a family farm partnership; and
- an eligible capital property used in a farming business in Canada.

There are definitions in the Act for each of these four types of QFPs, and also certain "time period" tests are imposed. These definitions and tests are far too extensive to elaborate on in this text.

¶10,066 The qualified fishing property CGD

The maximum lifetime capital gains exemption is extended to include capital gains realized on dispositions (occurring on or after May 2, 2006) of a fishing property, a share of the capital stock of a family fishing corporation, an interest in a family fishing partnership, or a qualified fishing property. The terms "share of the capital stock of a family fishing corporation" and "interest in a family fishing partnership" are defined in a manner similar to the family farming definitions. ITA: 110.6(1)

One half of gains realized on the disposition of eligible capital property that is qualified fishing property are eligible for the capital gains exemption.

¶10,070 Ordering of Division C Deductions

¶10,075 General ordering rules for Division C

Section 111.1 provides the following order of relevant deductions under Division C:

Sec. 110	Other deductions, such as employee stock option and home relocation loan deductions
Sec. 110.2	Lump-sum payments
Sec. 111	Loss carryovers, such as non- and net capital losses
Sec. 110.6	Capital gains deduction
Sec. 110.7	Residing in prescribed zone.

¶10,080 Ordering of section 111 loss carryovers

Loss carryovers can be applied in any order within section 111, subject to the general ordering rules for Division C, except that the oldest losses are always applied first. Therefore, careful consideration should be given as to which type of losses are used first. Generally speaking, the most restricted types of loss carryovers should be applied first. For example, since net capital losses can only be applied against net taxable capital gains, then net capital losses should be applied in years in which net taxable capital gains arise, unless it is expected that these gains will arise regularly in the future. Losses which have a carryback provision should be used immediately, if possible, so that taxes are refunded as soon as possible. ITA: 111.1, 111(3)(*b*)

Example Problem 10-4

The following information has been provided by your client, Karl Kraft:

	2011	*2012*	*2013*
Capital gains (CG)	—	$84,000	$44,000
Capital losses (CL) (excluding BIL)	$ 6,000	—	—
Business investment loss (BIL) before adjustment	18,000	—	30,000

ITA: 39(9)

Additional Information

(1) Karl had a $10,000 net capital loss which arose in 1998, and has not been deducted previously.

(2) Karl had no capital gains prior to 2011 and he did not claim any net capital losses in any preceding years.

(3) In 2013, Karl had a rental property loss of $1,000 and had no property income in 2011 or 2012.

— *REQUIRED*

(A) Determine Karl's income from the sources indicated for 2011 to 2013 according to the ordering rules in section 3.

(B) Determine Karl's taxable income from the sources indicated for 2011 to 2013 according to the ordering rules in Division C after amending the returns.

— *SOLUTION*

(A)	*2011*	*2012*	*2013*	
Income from non-capital sources (≥0)	Nil	Nil	Nil	ITA: 3(*a*)
Net taxable capital gains (≥0):				ITA: 3(*b*)
taxable capital gains	Nil	$ 42,000	$ 22,000	
allowable capital losses	$ (3,000)	—	—	
	Nil	$ 42,000	$ 22,000	
Sum of non-capital and capital sources	Nil	$ 42,000	$ 22,000	ITA: 3(*c*)
Losses from non-capital sources and ABILs:				ITA: 3(*d*)
rental property loss	—	—	(1,000)	
ABIL	$ (9,000)	—	(15,000)	
Division B income	0	$ 42,000	$ 6,000	ITA: 3(*e*)

(B)				
Division B income from (A)	0	$ 42,000	$ 6,000	
Less: net capital losses	Nil	(9,667)[1]	Nil	ITA: 111(1)(*b*)
non-capital losses (2011 ABIL carried forward to 2012)	Nil	(9,000)	Nil	ITA: 111(1)(*a*)
Taxable income (Division C)	Nil	$ 23,333	$ 6,000	

The foregoing solution illustrates how the various components fit into the full calculation of Division B income and taxable income.

— *NOTE TO SOLUTION*

[1] Loss continuity schedule	*1998*	*2011*	*Total*
Unadjusted net CL	$ 10,000	$ 3,000	
Adjusted to 2012 inclusion rate ($10,000 × ½ / ¾)	$ 6,667	$ 3,000	$ 9,667
Utilized in 2012	(6,667)	(3,000)	(9,667)
Available in 2013	Nil	Nil	Nil

Example Problem 10-5

Larry Hewitt provides you with the following income (losses) for tax purposes for the years 2011 to 2013:

	2011	*2012*	*2013*
Employment income	$25,000	$ 32,000	$40,000
Business income:	20,000	(36,000)	40,000
Property income from Canadian interest	3,000	4,000	5,000
Capital gains (capital losses):			

	2011	2012	2013
Listed personal property	6,000	(10,000)	12,000
Other	15,000	(14,000)	2,250

Larry also provides the following additional information:

(1) Loss carryovers:

Listed personal property loss arising in 2008	$ 2,000
Non-capital loss arising in 2009 from a business	35,000
Net capital loss arising in 1999	18,000

(2) Larry did not claim a capital gains deduction or net capital losses in the years 1985 to 2010.

— REQUIRED

Dealing with each item line-by-line across the years, rather than one year at a time:

(A) determine Larry's income for 2011 to 2013 according to the ordering rules in section 3, and

(B) determine Larry's taxable income for 2011 to 2013 according to the ordering rules in Division C after amending the returns.

— SOLUTION

(A)

	2011	2012	2013	
Income from non-capital sources (≥0):				ITA: 3(*a*)
Employment	$25,000	$ 32,000	$ 40,000	
Business income	20,000	Nil	40,000	
Property from Canadian interest	3,000	4,000	5,000	
	$48,000	$ 36,000	$ 85,000	
Net taxable capital gains (≥0):				ITA: 3(*b*)
Listed personal property[(1)]	Nil	Nil	$ 3,000	
Other	$ 7,500	(7,000)	1,125	
	$ 7,500	Nil	$ 4,125	
Sum of non-capital and capital sources	$55,500	$ 36,000	$ 89,125	ITA: 3(*c*)
Losses from non-capital sources		(36,000)		ITA: 3(*d*)
Income — Division B	$55,500	Nil	$ 89,125	ITA: 3(*e*)

(B)

	2011	2012	2013	
Income — Division B	$55,500		$ 89,125	
Net capital loss[(2)]	(7,500)		(4,125)	ITA: 111(1)(*b*)
Non-capital loss[(3)]	(35,000)		Nil	ITA: 111(1)(*a*)
Taxable income (Division C)	$13,000	Nil	$ 85,000	

— NOTES TO SOLUTION

[(1)] The listed personal property loss from 2008 is applied against the 2011 listed personal property gain of $6,000 leaving $4,000 which will be offset by the listed personal property capital loss of 2012 carried back. The remaining 2012 listed personal property capital loss of $6,000 will be carried forward and applied against the 2013 listed personal property capital gain of $12,000 leaving a net capital gain of $6,000 of which ½ will be taken into income. Note that listed personal property losses are carried over in their full capital loss amounts.

ITA: 111(1)(*b*), 111(1.1)(*a*), 111(8)

(2) (A) Net capital losses

	2011		2012	2013	
Lesser of:					
(i) net TCGs for the year	$ 7,500		N/A	$ 4,125	
(ii) total of adjusted net capital losses of loss years	$12,000		N/A	$11,500	
Lesser amount		$ 7,500			$ 4,125

(B) Net capital loss continuity schedule

	1999	2012	Total
Unadjusted net CL	$18,000	$7,000	
Adjusted to 2011 inclusion rate (÷ 3/4 × 1/2)	$12,000	N/A	$12,000
Utilized in 2011	(7,500)	N/A	(7,500)
Available in 2012	$ 4,500	—	$ 4,500
Realized in 2012	—	$7,000	7,000
Utilized in 2012	Nil	Nil	Nil
Available in 2013	$ 4,500	$7,000	$11,500
Utilized in 2013	(4,125)	Nil	(4,125)
Available in 2014	$ 375	$7,000	$ 7,375

(3) Non-capital loss continuity schedule

Non-capital loss — 2009		$35,000	
2011 application		(35,000)	
Balance of 2009 non-capital loss		Nil	
Non-capital loss — 2012			
Business loss	$36,000		
less: sum of income sources for the year	(36,000)	Nil	ITA: 3(*c*)
Balance		Nil	

Since individuals are eligible for non-refundable tax credits, it is advantageous to have at least $10,527 of taxable income in 2011. This amount increases to $10,822 in 2012 and $11,038 in 2013, as discussed later in this chapter.

¶10,090 Taxable Income of Non-Residents

In the discussion of residence in Chapter 2, it was established that a part-year resident of Canada is taxed on worldwide income for the part of the year that the individual is resident in Canada. The taxable income for the period of part-year residence of an individual is calculated under Division D. A non-resident individual is subject to Part I tax on income from employment in Canada, from carrying on business in Canada and from the disposition of taxable Canadian property. In addition, a non-resident is subject to Canadian withholding tax on Canadian-source income such as interest, dividends, alimony and pension receipts. ITA: 114 ITA: 115 ITA: 212

Consider the case of an individual who is an international business consultant who decided to move the base of operations of the business to another country and to continue to provide service to Canadian clients from that base. Assume the individual ceases to be a resident on May 15 of the year, but continues to carry on the unincorporated business of providing consulting services in Canada periodically after that date. This individual would be taxed in Canada on worldwide income for the period to May 15 and only on Canadian-source business income after that date for the rest of the year. If the individual remains a non- ITA: 114(*a*), 114(*b*) resident in the following year, then only Canadian-source business income would be taxed in that year.

Income for the period of part-year residence is computed in the normal manner, including the deduction of most amounts allowed in Division B. The Division C deductions reasonably applicable to the period of part-year residence are also deductible. The taxable income of a non-resident with Canadian-source income is computed under Division D. Certain Division C deductions may be claimed in respect of that income earned in Canada.

Non-residents are required to pay tax on their "taxable income earned in Canada" for the year. "Taxable income earned in Canada" is the income that would be determined under section 3 with some adjustments to confine the calculation to Canadian-sources of the non-resident. In particular, the term "taxable Canadian property" necessary for the determination of income from its disposition is defined. Then, Division C deductions as appropriate to the Canadian-source income may be claimed. These deductions include those in respect of stock options exercised, charitable donations, and loss carryovers reasonably applicable to Canadian-source income. The Canada Revenue Agency's (CRA) interpretation of these provisions is contained in their Interpretation Bulletin entitled "Non-residents — Income earned in Canada". See Appendix I for more information. ITA: 2(3), 110.1(1), 111; ITA: 2(3)(*c*); ITA: 115(1)(*b*); ITA: 115(1)(*d*)–(*f*); ITA: 110(1)(*d*), 110(1)(*d*.1); ITA: 110.1(1), 111; IT-420R3

¶10,100 COMPUTATION OF TAX FOR INDIVIDUALS

¶10,110 Basic Computation of Tax

Our federal tax system has progressive tax rates for individuals. This means that as a person's taxable income increases from one income bracket to another (refer to the brackets below), the rate of tax on the next dollar earned also increases. This follows the tax policy argument that those who can afford to should pay a higher proportion of their income in tax. In a flat rate system, everyone would pay the same rate of tax regardless of their income.

¶10,115 Tax rates

A provision sets out the rates of tax applicable to individuals. These amounts, which have been indexed for 2013, are presented in Exhibit 10-1. ITA: 117(2)

EXHIBIT 10-1
2013 Federal Income Tax Brackets

Taxable income	*Tax*	
$43,561 or less		15%
In excess of $43,561	$6,534*	+ 22% on next $43,562
In excess of $87,123	$16,118**	+ 26% on next $47,931
In excess of $135,054	$28,580***	+ 29% on remainder

* Computed as 15% of $43,561 = $6,534 (rounded)

** Computed as $6,534 + 22% of $43,562 = $16,118 (rounded)

*** Computed as $16,118 + 26% of $47,931 = $28,580 (rounded)

¶10,120 Annual indexing adjustment

The Act provides for the annual indexing of certain dollar amounts used in the calculation of tax or tax credits. ITA: 117.1

The indexing formula is based on the annual increase in the Consumer Price Index for the 12-month period ending September 30 of the year before the year in which the indexing is to apply.

¶10,125 Overview of tax credit and tax calculation system

Exhibit 10-2 summarizes the key items in the calculation of tax credits and income tax payable. The first line in Exhibit 10-2 results from applying the tax table in Exhibit 10-1 to the taxpayer's taxable income for the year. Total federal income tax is reduced by two basic types of credits, non-refundable and refundable, which are deducted at one of three different stages of the calculation.

EXHIBIT 10-2
Summary of Income Tax Calculation

Total federal income tax on taxable income		$xxx	ITA: 117(2), 117.1
Subtract: Total non-refundable tax credits (see Exhibit 10-3)	$xxx		
Federal dividend tax credit	xxx	xxx	ITA: 121
Basic federal tax		$xxx	
Subtract: Federal foreign tax credits		xxx	ITA: 126
Federal tax		$xxx	
Subtract: Federal political contributions tax credit	$xxx		ITA: 127(3)
Other federal tax credits	xxx	xxx	
Net federal tax		$xxx	
Add: Tax on Old Age Security benefits		xxx	ITA: 180.2
Total federal tax		$xxx	
Add: Provincial tax	$xxx		
Provincial surtax	xxx	xxx	
Total payable		$xxx	
Subtract: Total income tax deducted at source	$xxx		
Federal refundable tax credits (e.g., employee and partner GST/HST rebate)	xxx		
Tax paid by instalments	xxx		
Provincial refundable tax credits	xxx	xxx	
Balance payable or refundable		$xxx	

¶10,125.10 *Non-refundable tax credits*

Non-refundable tax credits like the marital status tax credit or the dividend tax credit are subtracted from federal tax. To the extent that these credits exceed federal tax, the excess is not refundable and, therefore, is of no value to the taxpayer. Some non-refundable tax credits are referred to as "above-the-line tax credits", because they are subtracted from federal tax to arrive at basic federal tax. Exhibit 10-3 lists these non-refundable tax credits. Some non-refundable tax credits like federal foreign tax credits and federal political contributions tax credits can be termed "below-the-line tax credits", because they are subtracted after the calculation of basic federal tax. These "below-the-line tax credits" are not magnified by the territorial or non-resident tax effects, discussed below.

EXHIBIT 10-3
Types of Non-Refundable Tax Credits

- Basic personal amount
- Spousal amount
- Equivalent-to-spouse amount
- Infirm dependent children (if ≥18 years and infirm)
- Child amount (child tax credit)
- Additional personal amounts
- Caregiver amount
- Age amount
- Canada employment amount
- Adoption expense amount
- Public transit tax credit
- Children's fitness amount
- Children's arts tax credit
- First-time home buyers' tax credit
- Volunteer firefighters tax credit
- Canada or Quebec Pension Plan contributions
- Employment Insurance premiums
- Pension income amount
- Mental or physical impairment amount (disability)
- Disability amount transferred from a dependant other than spouse
- Tuition, education, and textbook amounts
- Tuition, education, and textbook amounts transferred from a child
- Amounts transferred from spouse
- Medical expenses
- Charitable gifts (donations)
- First-time donor's super credit
- Interest paid on student loans
- Dividend tax credit

¶10,125.20 *Refundable tax credits*

Some tax credits are refundable and, hence, are subtracted last. To the extent that these tax credits, such as the federal credit for employment outside Canada or certain provincial tax credits, exceed total tax payable, the excess is refunded, along with excess tax withholdings from payroll or excess tax instalments on income not subject to withholdings. Other tax credits like the GST/HST credit and the child tax benefit involve a calculation of an amount that is deemed to be tax-paid and, hence, result in a "refund" of the deemed tax.

¶10,125.30 *Tax credit versus tax deduction*

It is important to understand the difference between a tax credit and a tax deduction. A tax deduction is really a misnomer as an expenditure, such as an RRSP contribution, reduces a taxpayer's income subject to tax at a particular marginal tax rate and does not reduce tax payable directly. Therefore, a deduction from income or taxable income saves the taxpayer an amount that increases with the taxpayer's level of income and, hence, tax rate. For some taxpayers, it may take $4 of deduction to save $1 in tax (i.e., at a 25% tax rate), while for other taxpayers, only $2 of deduction will save the $1 in tax (i.e., at a 50% tax rate). A tax credit is a direct reduction of the taxpayer's tax bill at a specified rate. A "below-the-line" credit of $1 results in a tax reduction of $1. An "above-the-line" credit of $1 results in a tax reduction of $1 plus the savings in non-resident tax, discussed below. The objective of the tax credit system is to provide all taxpayers with the same level of tax reduction regardless of their marginal tax rate.

¶10,130 Provincial and territorial tax

All of the provinces and territories use a "tax on income" (TONI) structure for computing provincial tax. In such a structure, provinces may adopt the federal calculation of taxable income or make adjustments to it. Provinces may use the federal brackets or change them. Provincial rates are specified for income in these brackets. Provinces specify their own non-refundable credit amounts. For provincial tax rates, tax brackets and tax credit amounts, see the preface material in a current edition of the CCH CANADIAN INCOME TAX ACT WITH REGULATIONS. For the purposes of this book, where provincial tax is calculated for individuals, the following table, using the federal brackets, will be used. In addition, the provincial rate for the non-refundable credits will be assumed to be 10% of the federal base. For example, the provincial basic personal amount will be 10% of $11,038 or $1,104.

Taxable income	*Tax*	
$43,561 or less		10%
In excess of $43,561	$4,356*	+ 12% on next $43,562
In excess of $87,123	$9,583**	+ 15% on next $47,931
In excess of $135,054	$16,773***	+ 17% on remainder

* Computed as 10% of $43,561 = $4,356 (rounded)

** Computed as $4,356 + 12% of $43,562 = $9,583 (rounded)

*** Computed as $9,583 + 15% of $47,931 = $16,773 (rounded)

¶10,135 Marginal tax rates

Marginal tax rates represent the amount of tax payable on the next dollar of income earned. Since not all income is taxed in the same way, a calculation of the marginal tax will depend on the type of income being earned and the amount of income already earned. For example, assume that someone already earns $150,000 and wants to know what the federal and provincial marginal tax rate would be on an additional $1,000 of interest, dividends, and capital gains. Since this person is already in the top bracket with income over $135,054, his or her marginal tax rate will be a 29% federal rate and a 17% provincial (notional) rate for a combined rate of 46%. However, the manner in which the types of income is taxed may result in a lower effective marginal tax rate, as follows:

		Interest	Dividends (38% Gross-Up)	Dividends (25% Gross-Up)	Dividends (18% Gross-Up)	Capital Gains
Income	A	$1,000	$1,000	$1,000	$1,000	$1,000
Gross-up			380	250	180	
Untaxed portion						(500)
Taxable		$1,000	$1,380	$1,250	$1,180	$ 500
Federal @ 29% . . .		$ 290	$ 400	$ 363	$ 342	$ 145
Federal DTC (6/11 / 2/3 / 13/18 × gross-up)			(207)	(167)	(130)	
		290	193	196	212	145
Provincial @ 17%		170	235	213	201	85
Provincial DTC (5/11 / 1/3 / 5/18 × gross-up)			(173)	(83)	(50)	
	B	$ 460	$ 255	$ 325	$ 363	$ 230
Effective marginal tax rate	B/A	46%	26%	33%	36%	23%

Interest income does not receive any special tax treatment, so it is fully taxed at the top marginal rate of 46%. Only 50% of capital gains are taxed, so the effective marginal tax rate on this type of income is 23%. Dividends receive special tax treatment to reflect the underlying tax paid at the corporate level so, generally speaking, dividends from public companies have a top effective marginal tax rate of 26% and dividends from active business income and investment income of a CCPC taxed at the low rate have a top marginal rate of 33% in 2013 and earlier and 36% in 2014 and later.

[The March 21, 2013 federal Budget announced that, starting in 2014, the gross-up and dividend tax credit on non-eligible Canadian dividends would change from a 25% to an 18% gross-up, and the federal dividend tax credit would change from 2/3 of the gross-up to 13/18 of the gross-up.]

¶10,140 Section 118 Tax Credits

The provision for personal tax credits begins by presenting the following general formula for computing non-refundable personal tax credits: ITA: 118(1)

$$A \times B$$

where A is the appropriate percentage for the year, defined to mean the lowest percentage rate of individual tax (i.e., 15% for 2013), ITA: 117(2), 248(1)

B is the aggregate of the following tax credit bases:

(a) married or common-law partnership status,

(b) wholly dependent person (i.e., equivalent-to-married status),

(b.1) child amount (i.e., child tax credit),

(c) single status,

(c.1) in-home care of relative (i.e., caregiver credit),

(d) infirm dependants, and

(e) additional amount (re dependant).

Therefore, the personal tax credits are computed as 15% of a dollar amount indexed for 2013. The personal tax credit for individuals, other than the taxpayer, are limited by the Division B income of the dependant. However, dependants are allowed to earn a certain amount of Division B income before the tax credit is reduced.

For the purposes of this chapter, the amount of Division B income of a dependant before the tax credit is reduced will be called the "threshold income".

¶10,145 Married or common-law partnership credit

ITA: 118(1)(*a*)

The tax credit base for married or common-law partner (referred to as spouses) status is computed as the sum of the following two amounts: ITA: 118(1)(*a*)

Basic personal tax credit base in 2013		$11,038
Spouse's tax credit base in 2013	$11,038[1]	
Less: spouse's Division B income in 2013	xxx	
Net amount (non-negative)		xxx
Total tax credit base		$ xxx
Tax credit (15% of total)		$ xxx

ITA: 257

The total tax credit is a maximum of $3,312 (i.e., 15% of $11,038 + 15% of $11,038, or $3,617 if eligible for the family caregiver amount of $2,040). This tax credit is available if an individual supports his or her spouse. Note, however, that the spouse's tax credit base is reduced by the Division B income of the dependent spouse for the whole year, even if the marriage occurred in the year.

On the other hand, if the individual was living apart from his or her spouse at the end of the year because of a marriage breakdown, only the spouse's income for the year, while married and not separated, is considered.

A common-law partner is treated like a spouse. The term "common-law partner" is defined as two persons, regardless of sex, who cohabit in a conjugal relationship and have done so for a continuous period of at least one year or who is the parent of a child of whom the taxpayer is also a parent. ITA: 248(1) "common-law partner"

Hence, the married status tax credit is allowed in a common-law relationship if the conditions in the extended meaning are met and the conditions in paragraph 118(1)(*a*) are met.

¶10,150 Equivalent-to-married status for wholly dependent person credit

ITA: 118(1)(*b*)

A tax credit base equal to the tax credit base for married status is provided in respect of a wholly dependent person where the taxpayer is not entitled to a married credit (i.e., an individual who is not married or living in a common-law relationship). This provision might apply to an individual who, at any time in the year, was single, divorced, separated, widowed and who supported a relative. The calculation of the credit is the same as that shown for the married credit, with the Division B income of the wholly dependent person reducing the credit. ITA: 118(1)(*b*) ITA: 118(1)(*a*)

A number of additional conditions must apply for the tax credit to be available.

- The dependent person must live, at some time in the year, in the same self-contained domestic establishment as the taxpayer claiming the tax credit. The dependant must be wholly dependent for support on that taxpayer and/or other persons. The taxpayer need not own the residence. A rental unit qualifies. ITA: 248(1) "self-contained domestic establishment" IT-513R, par. 11–22
- The dependant must be related to the taxpayer by blood, marriage or adoption. As a result, nieces, nephews, aunts, uncles and cousins would not qualify as a marital equivalent under this provision (unless they fit the definition of child which is very broad and should be examined). ITA: 251(6) ITA: 252(1)
- Unless the dependant is a child of the taxpayer, the dependant must be resident in Canada.[2]

[1] $13,078, if eligible for the family caregiver amount of $2,040 for a spouse or common-law partner who is dependent by reason of mental or physical infirmity.

[2] Refer to *Ruzicka v. The Queen*, 95 DTC 365 (T.C.C.), for a discussion of the rules related to non-residents.

- Unless the dependant is the parent or grandparent of the taxpayer, the dependant must be either under 18 years of age at any time in the year or dependent by reason of physical or mental infirmity. In the case of *The Queen v. Mercier*, the taxpayer argued that the age requirement for children discriminates against single parents with children 18 years of age or older who, in the opinion of the taxpayer, should qualify for the credit and, hence, violates the *Canadian Charter of Rights and Freedoms* (Charter). The Court held that the provision does not violate the equality guarantee of the Charter. 97 DTC 5081 (F.C.T.D.)

- Only one equivalent-to-married tax credit is available to a taxpayer. ITA: 118(1)(*b*), 118(4)(*a*)

- The dependant cannot be claimed under this tax credit if the dependant has been claimed under the married status credit by another taxpayer. ITA: 118(4)(*a*.1)

- Where two taxpayers are eligible for the equivalent-to-married tax credit in respect of the same person or the same domestic establishment, only one person is permitted the tax credit and only one equivalent-to-married tax credit can be claimed for a given domestic establishment. If the taxpayers cannot agree as to who should have the tax credit, then neither can have the tax credit. For example, Tom and Donna, who are both single, support their mother in the same domestic establishment. Either Tom or Donna can have the tax credit, but not both. If they cannot agree, then neither can have the tax credit. ITA: 118(1)(*b*) ITA: 118(4)(*b*)

- Where a taxpayer has claimed a dependant under this paragraph, neither the taxpayer nor any other taxpayer can claim that dependant for the 18 years of age or older and infirm credit or the caregiver credit. For example, if a married couple with one infirm child, 20 years of age, separates during the year and the spouse who supports the child claims the child under the equivalent-to-married credit, then that spouse cannot make an additional claim as a dependent child 18 years of age or older and infirm. The other spouse also cannot make a claim for that child even if he or she did, in fact, wholly support the child during part of the year. Where feasible, a choice should be made to maximize total tax credits of the taxpayer. ITA: 118(4)(*c*) ITA: 118(1)(*b*) ITA: 118(1)(*d*)

- Where an individual is required under the terms of a written agreement or court order to make payments in the year in respect of the support of a child, the individual is not entitled to claim any personal tax credit in respect of the child. ITA: 118(5)

It might be noted that the interpretation of the phrase "at any time in the year is an unmarried person" appears to have the effect of enabling a person who presently qualifies for an equivalent-to-married tax credit and marries during the year to still qualify for this tax credit in the year of marriage, but not subsequently. Of course, the person claiming a dependant would not be allowed a claim for marital status. ITA: 118(1)(*b*); IT-513R, par. 11–17 ITA: 118(1)(*b*) ITA: 118(1)(*a*)

¶10,155 Child amount (child tax credit)

ITA: 118(1)(*b*.1)

The child amount is a non-refundable child tax credit for parents based on an amount of $2,234[3] × 15% = $335 for each child under the age of 18 at the end of the year.

Where the child resides together with the child's parents throughout the year, either of those parents may claim the credit. In other cases, the credit is claimable in respect of a child by the parent who is eligible to claim the wholly dependent person credit for the year in respect of a child (or who would be eligible if that child were the parent's only child).

For the year of the birth, adoption or death of a child, the full amount of the credit is also claimable.

Any unused portion of the credit is transferable to the parent's spouse or common-law partner. ITA: 118.8

[3] $4,274, if eligible for the family caregiver amount of $2,040 for a child who, by reason of mental or physical infirmity, is likely to be, for a long and continuous period of indefinite duration, dependent for significantly more assistance in attending to the child's personal needs and care, when compared to children of the same age.

¶10,160 Single status — Basic personal tax credit

ITA: 118(1)(*c*)

The base of the basic personal tax credit is set at $11,038 in 2013 and, when multiplied by 15%, provides a tax credit of $1,656 (rounded) for 2013. ITA: 118(1)(*c*)

¶10,165 Caregiver credit for in-home care of relative

ITA: 118(1)(*c*.1)

Individuals are entitled to a credit of up to $674 (i.e., 15% of $4,490[4]) for residing with and providing in-home care for an adult relative. For this purpose, the relatives include the individual's child or grandchild or the individual's or spouse's common-law partner's parent, grandparent, brother, sister, aunt, uncle, nephew or niece. A parent or grandparent must either have attained the age of 65 years or be dependent because of physical or mental infirmity. All other dependent relatives must have attained the age of 18 and be dependent because of mental or physical infirmity.

The base amount of $4,490[5] is reduced by the dependant's income in excess of $15,334. The credit is not available if the dependant's income exceeds $19,824.

Where an individual is entitled to an equivalent-to-married credit for a dependent, no one can claim the caregiver credit or the credit for infirm dependants age 18 or older in respect of that dependant. ITA: 118(1)(*b*), 118(4)(*c*), 118(4)(*d*)

¶10,170 Infirm dependant credit

ITA: 118(1)(*d*)

A dependant is defined to include, for this purpose, a child, grandchild, parent, grandparent, brother, sister, uncle, aunt, niece or nephew of the taxpayer or the taxpayer's spouse or common-law partner. However, the dependants must have attained the age of 18 before the end of the year in order to qualify for the tax credit. Also, the individual must be dependent on the taxpayer because of mental or physical infirmity. ITA: 118(1)(*d*) ITA: 118(6)

The tax credit is computed for 2013 as:

Dependant's tax credit base (including family caregiver amount)		$6,530
Less: dependant's Division B income	$ xxx	
threshold amount	6,548	
Net amount (non-negative)		xxx
Net tax credit base (non-negative)		$ xxx
Dependant's tax credit (15% of net) (maximum of $980 — rounded)		$ xxx

The CRA indicates that mental or physical infirmity in respect of the dependent person should require the infirm person to be dependent during a considerable period of time and not just temporarily.[6] IT-513R, Appendix A

Note that the maximum amount of the dependant credit is the same as that of the caregiver credit if the taxpayer is eligible for the family caregiver addition, but the income threshold is much lower for the dependant credit. Thus, the dependant credit can be eliminated more quickly, making the caregiver credit more attractive, numerically. However, the caregiver credit has the more restrictive condition that the dependant must ordinarily reside in the same self-contained domestic establishment as the taxpayer claiming the credit.

The tax credit available for a dependent person must be shared by all individuals who are entitled to a tax credit in respect of the same dependant. Where these supporting individuals cannot agree on an allocation of the tax credit, the Minister may make the allocation. Furthermore, a taxpayer who is entitled to a deduction for support payments for a spouse is not entitled to claim a tax credit for the spouse. However, the CRA does permit a tax credit claim in the year of separation or divorce. Where an individual is required under the terms of a written agreement or court order to make payments in the year in respect of the support of a child, the individual is not entitled to claim any personal tax credit in respect of the child. This provision is necessary to parallel the non-deductibility of child support payments as ITA: 118(4)(*e*) ITA: 60(*b*) ITA: 118(5) IT-513R, par. 27 ITA: 118

[4] $6,530, if eligible for the family caregiver amount of $2,040 for a person who is dependent by reason of mental or physical infirmity.

[5] $6,530, if eligible for the family caregiver amount of $2,040. This additional $2,040 credit base is not reduced by income in excess of the income threshold for the base amount.

[6] A court case dealing with this issue is *The Queen v. Diaz*, 81 DTC 5112 (F.C.T.D.).

discussed in Chapter 9. The subsection ensures that, since the child support payments are not deductible, the supporting parent would not be able to claim this deduction.

¶10,173 Family caregiver tax credit ITA: 118(1)

The provisions listed below allow for an additional 15% non-refundable tax credit based on an amount of $2,040. This is an enhanced tax credit administered through the following dependency-related credits:

- spousal or common-law partner credit; ITA: 118(1)(*a*)
- child tax credit; ITA: 118(1)(*b*.1)
- eligible dependant credit; ITA: 118(1)(*b*)
- caregiver credit; and ITA: 118(1)(*c*.1)
- infirm dependant credit. ITA: 118(1)(*d*)

A child will be considered infirm only if they are likely to be — for a long, continuous, and indefinite time period — dependent on others for significantly more assistance than is generally the case for a person of the same age.

Only one family caregiver tax credit will be available for each infirm dependant.

¶10,175 Additional amount

Where a taxpayer is entitled to claim a dependant for the equivalent-to-married (ETM) credit, the dependant cannot be claimed under the caregiver credit or the credit for infirm dependants age 18 or older. ITA: 118(4)(*c*)

Where the caregiver credit or the credit for an infirm dependant age 18 or older would have been larger than the ETM credit, the difference can be claimed under this provision as an additional credit. The effect is to allow the equivalent of the caregiver credit for a person in respect of whom the ETM credit is claimed. ITA: 118(1)(*e*)

¶10,180 Age credit ITA: 118(2)

The non-refundable age tax credit is computed on a base of $6,854 for 2013. Since the appropriate percentage for the year is 15%, the tax credit for 2013 is $1,028 (rounded). It is available to an individual who has attained the age of 65 years before the end of the year. ITA: 118(2)

However, this age tax credit is reduced by 15% of the excess of the individual's Division B income over $34,562 and is, thus, completely eliminated when the net income exceeds $80,255.

For example, if an individual's Division B income is $80,255, the age tax credit would be computed as:

Age tax credit base			$6,854
Less: base reduction of lesser of:			
(a) Credit base		$6,854	
(b) Division B income	$80,255		
Less: threshold	34,562		
Excess, if any	$45,693 × .15 =	$6,854	
Lesser amount			6,854
Net base			Nil
Age tax credit: 15% of Nil			Nil

¶10,185 Pension income amount ITA: 118(3)

This non-refundable pension tax credit is determined as follows:

Age 65 and Older

The pension credit is equal to 15% of the lesser of:

1. $2,000, and

2. the "pension income".

Pension income includes, but is not limited to: ITA: 118(7)

(a) a payment in respect of a life annuity arising from a superannuation pension fund or plan;

(b) an annuity payment under a registered retirement savings plan or a payment under a registered retirement income fund;

(c) an annuity payment under a deferred profit sharing plan; and

(d) the income portion of other annuity payments.

Under Age 65

The pension credit is equal to 15% of the lesser of:

1. $2,000, and

2. the "qualified pension income".

The only difference is to change the definition of pension income to qualified pension income. Qualified pension income includes: ITA: 118(7)

(a) a payment in respect of a life annuity arising from a superannuation pension fund or plan; or

(b) certain annuities or payments received by the individual as a consequence of the death of the individual's spouse.

Certain amounts are not included in pension income or qualified pension income. These excluded amounts are: ITA: 118(8)

(a) the Old Age Pension or Supplement;

(b) the Canada Pension Plan (or provincial plan) pension;

(c) a death benefit; ITA: 248(1) "death benefit"

(d) the amount of any payment which is included in income and then deducted under another provision such as lump-sum payments from withdrawing from a pension fund, an RRSP or a DPSP, retiring allowances, or pension benefits or DPSP benefits transferred into a spousal RRSP; and

(e) a payment out of or under a salary deferral arrangement, a retirement compensation arrangement, an employee benefit plan, an employee trust or a prescribed provincial pension plan.

¶10,190 Canada employment credit

This non-refundable credit is computed as 15% times the lesser of: ITA: 118(10)

- The individual's employment income for the year, and
- $1,117.

¶10,195 Summary of personal tax credits

Exhibit 10-4 provides a summary of the numerical components of the most common personal tax credits. ITA: 118, 118.3

EXHIBIT 10-4
Section 118 Tax Credits (rounded)

	Maximum tax credit	*Tax credit base*	*Division B income threshold*
Par. 118(1)(*a*), (*b*), or (*b*.1):			
Basic personal	$1,656	$11,038	N/A
Spouse or equivalent	1,656*	11,038**	N/A
Child amount	335	2,234**	N/A
Par. 118(1)(*c*): Single person	1,656	11,038	N/A
Par. 118(1)(*c*.1): Caregiver	674*	4,490**	$15,334
Par. 118(1)(*d*): Infirm dependant	980	6,530	6,548
Ssec. 118(2): Age	1,028	6,854	34,562
Ssec. 118(3): Pension	300	2,000	N/A
Ssec. 118(10): Canada Employment Credit	168	1,117	N/A
Sec. 118.3: Disability amount (see ¶10,300)	1,155	7,697	N/A

* Add $306 (i.e., 15% of $2,040) if eligible for the family caregiver amount.

** Add $2,040 if eligible for the family caregiver amount.

EXHIBIT 10-5
Credits Available to be Claimed With Respect to Children of a Taxpayer

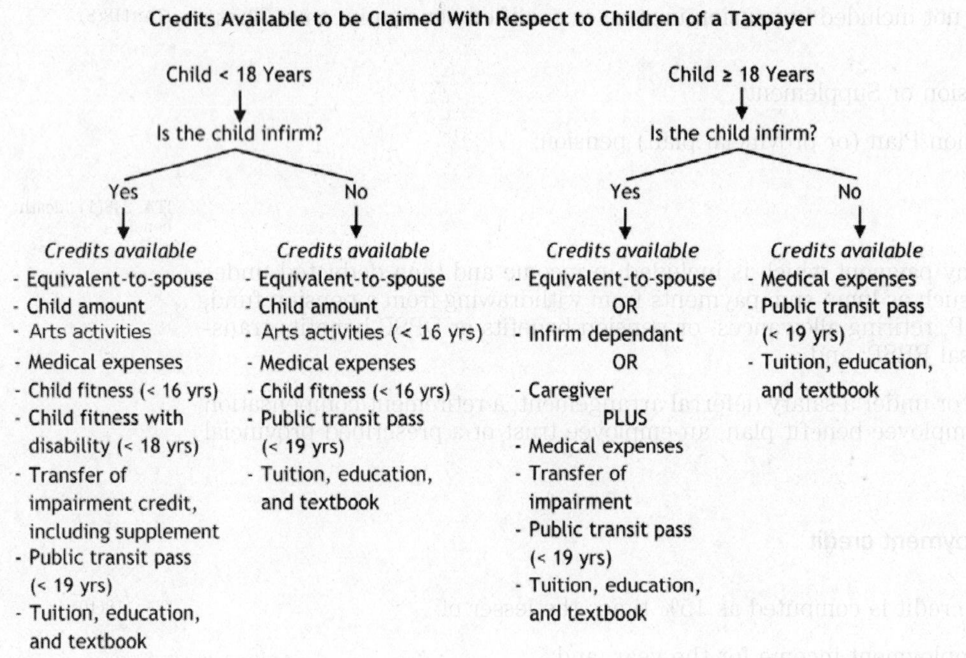

Notes:

1. A taxpayer may only claim the equivalent-to-spouse credit for one dependant in a year.
2. The equivalent-to-spouse credit can only be claimed by taxpayer for a dependant related by blood, marriage, or adoption.
3. If the equivalent-to-spouse credit is claimed for a dependant, the taxpayer may not claim the caregiver or infirm dependant credit for the same dependant.

4. The caregiver credit may be claimed by a taxpayer for more than one dependant in a year.
5. The infirm dependant credit may be claimed for more than one dependant.
6. A taxpayer cannot claim the impairment credit if a claim for the medical expense credit for a full-time attendant or care in a nursing home has been made in excess of $10,000.

For the purposes of this book, where provincial tax credits are calculated for individuals, a rate of 10% (equal to the lowest provincial rate used in this book) will be applied to the above federal tax credit base, net of any applicable reduction for income in excess of the federal Division B income threshold.

Example Problem 10-6

George, age 50, has the following dependants, each of whom has Division B income as indicated for 2013:

Dependant	*Age at year-end*	*Division B income*
Spouse	45	$3,500
Son (residing with George and his spouse)	14	2,725
Son (residing with George and his spouse)	16	2,800
Daughter (physically infirm, but not living at home)	18	5,000
Mother (residing with George and his spouse)	70	10,000

— *REQUIRED*

Determine the personal tax credits available under section 118 for each of George's dependants for 2013. All of the dependants live with George.

— *SOLUTION*

	Wife [118(1)(a)]	*Children × 2 (< 18) [118(1)(b.1)]*	*Daughter (18 and infirm) [118(1)(d)]*	*Mother (age 65) [118(1)(c.1)]*
Division B income	$ 3,500		$5,000	$10,000
Threshold income	N/A	N/A	(6,548)	(15,334)
Excess income	$ 3,500		$ 0	$ 0
Tax credit base	$11,038		$6,530	$ 4,490
Excess income	(3,500)		0	0
Net tax credit base	$ 7,538	$4,468	$6,530	$ 4,490
Tax credit @ 15% (rounded)	$ 1,131	$ 670	$ 980	$ 674

Note that neither of the sons provides a dependant tax credit. They are covered under the Child Tax Benefit system, discussed later in this chapter. ITA: 118(1)(*d*)

¶10,200 Adoption Expense Tax Credit

ITA: 118.01

The Act provides a non-refundable tax credit of up $1,750 (15% × $11,669) in the year in which an adoption is completed for eligible adoption expenses incurred during the adoption period.

Eligible adoption expenses include:

(i) fees paid to an adoption agency licensed by a provincial or territorial government,

(ii) court costs, legal and administrative expenses,

(iii) reasonable travel and living expenses of the child and the adoptive parents,

(iv) document translation fees,

(v) mandatory fees paid to a foreign institution, and

(vi) any other reasonable expenses required by a provincial or territorial government or an adoption agency licensed by a provincial or territorial government.

[The March 21, 2013 federal Budget proposes to extend the adoption period by beginning the period at the earlier of the time an application is made to register with a provincial ministry responsible for adoption or with a licensed adoption agency or the date an application is made to a Canadian court. This applies for adoptions finalized after 2012.]

The adoption period ends at the time of the adoption.

An eligible child is one who has not reached the age of 18 years at the time that the adoption is completed.

¶10,210 Public Transit Passes Credit

This non-refundable tax credit is based on the total of all amounts paid in the year in respect of eligible public transit passes. The amounts paid for passes for the use of the individual taxpayer, the individual's spouse or common-law partner, or a child of the individual, who has not reached the age of 19 before the end of the year. An eligible public transit pass is a public transit pass that is valid for a period of at least one month of public transit. Public transit includes transit by local bus, streetcar, subway, commuter train, commuter bus, and local ferry. Receipts for passes must be retained for verification purposes. ITA: 118.02

This credit accommodates:

- electronic payment cards for costs related to the use of public transit for at least 32 one-way trips during an uninterrupted period not exceeding 31 days, and
- weekly passes where an individual purchases at least four consecutive weekly passes.

¶10,220 Children's Fitness Credit

This non-refundable tax credit of up to $75 (15% × $500) is based on up to $500 of eligible fees paid in the year for enrolment of a child under the age of 16 at the beginning of the year in an eligible program of physical activity. The credit can be claimed by either parent. It must be supported by a tax receipt that contains sufficient information for the CRA to monitor compliance. ITA: 118.03

Eligible expenses include those for the operation and administration of the program, instructors, renting facilities, equipment used in common (e.g., team jerseys provided for the season), referees and judges, and incidental supplies (e.g., trophies). Expenses that are not eligible include the purchase or rental of equipment for exclusive personal use, travel, meals, and accommodation.

An eligible program of prescribed physical activity is defined as:

> An ongoing, supervised program, suitable for children, in which substantially all of the activities undertaken include a significant amount of physical activity that contribute to cardio-respiratory endurance, plus one or more of muscular strength, muscular endurance, flexibility and balance.

To recognize the particular challenges that children with disabilities face, the age limit for them to qualify is 18 years instead of 16 years. In addition, a separate $500 non-refundable tax credit for disabled children who spend a minimum of $100 on registration fees for eligible programs is provided. The extra $400 recognizes the extra costs that children with disabilities encounter when involved in programs such as these.

¶10,222 Children's Arts Tax Credit

This non-refundable credit of up to $75 (15% × $500) is based on up to $500 of eligible fees paid per child in the year. For a child under 16 years of age at the beginning of the year, the credit is available for an eligible program of artistic, cultural, recreational, or developmental activities. For a child under 18 years of age at the beginning of the year, who is eligible for the Disability Tax Credit, the 15% credit may be claimed on an additional $500 disability supplement amount when a minimum of $100 is paid for eligible expenses. ITA: 118.031

"Eligible expense" means an amount paid to a qualifying entity for the cost of the program, but does not include the cost of accommodation, travel, food, beverages, or the purchase or rental of equipment for personal use. Likewise, expenses eligible for the child care expense deduction or the Children's Fitness Tax Credit are ineligible for the Children's Arts Tax Credit.

A qualifying entity cannot include the spouse or common-law partner of a person claiming the credit for his or her child.

An eligible activity is a supervised activity, suitable for children, that:

- contributes to the development of creative skills or expertise in an artistic or cultural activity;
- provides a substantial focus on the wilderness or natural environment;
- helps develop and use particular intellectual skills;
- provides enrichment or tutoring in academic subjects; or
- helps develop interpersonal skills using structured interaction.

An eligible program must be ongoing and include a significant number of eligible activities. For example, either a weekly program that is a minimum of eight consecutive weeks or a children's camp that lasts a minimum of five consecutive days. Programs that are part of the school curriculum are not eligible.

Either parent may claim the credit or it can be shared as long as the total is not more than the maximum allowable amount.

¶10,225 First-Time Home Buyers' Credit and Disability Home Purchase Credit

This is a non-refundable credit of $750, i.e., 15% of $5,000 for the purchase of a qualifying home by a first-time home buyer. To be considered a first-time home buyer, neither the purchaser nor the purchaser's spouse or common-law partner can have lived or owned another home in the year of purchase, nor in any of the four preceding calendar years. The credit can be split between the spouses or common-law partners, but the total credit cannot exceed $750. ITA: 118.05

The credit may be claimed if a qualifying home is purchased for the benefit of an individual entitled to claim the disability credit to enable the disabled person to live a more accessible home or better suited home. In this case, the purchaser does not have to be a first-time home buyer.

A qualifying home can include a single-family house, a semi-detached house, a townhouse, a mobile home, and a condominium unit, among others. In addition, the following conditions must be met:

- The home is located in Canada.

- The home is registered in the name of the purchaser or the purchaser's common-law partner.
- The purchaser, the purchaser's common law partner, or a person eligible for the disability credit intends to inhabit the home as their principal residence within one year of the date of purchase.

¶10,227 Volunteer Firefighters Tax Credit

This credit enables eligible volunteer firefighters to claim a 15% non-refundable tax credit based on an amount of $3,000. However, individuals who claim this credit will not also be able to claim the exemption of up to $1,000 received for their volunteer firefighting activities. ITA: 118.06 ITA: 81(4)(b)

To be eligible, the person must perform a minimum of 200 hours of volunteer firefighting services for one or more fire departments. They will be ineligible if they also provide firefighting services which are not voluntary to that fire department.

Certification will be required from the fire department confirming the number of eligible volunteer firefighting hours.

¶10,230 Charitable Gifts Credit

ITA: 118.1

¶10,235 Basic rules

The non-refundable charitable donation tax credit is calculated by the following formula: ITA: 118.1(3)

$$(A \times B) + C\ (D - B)$$

where A is 15% (i.e., the appropriate percentage for the year);

B is the first $200 of total gifts; ITA: 118.1(1) "total gifts"

C is 29% (i.e., the highest federal marginal tax rate for the year); and

D is the individual's total gifts (if over $200) for the year.

In essence, the tax credit amounts to 15% of total gifts up to $200 and 29% for total gifts in excess of $200. For the purposes of this book, where provincial tax credits are calculated for individuals, a rate of 10% will be applied to total gifts up to $200 and 17% (equal to the highest provincial tax rate used in this book) for total gifts in excess of $200.

The definition of total gifts indicates the following four components:

(a) total charitable gifts, including gifts to:

- Canadian registered charities (including Canadian universities),
- registered Canadian amateur athletic associations,
- prescribed universities outside Canada,
- certain tax-free housing organizations in Canada,
- Canadian municipalities,
- the United Nations or its agencies, and
- charities outside Canada to which the Government of Canada has made a donation in the year or the preceding year;
- municipal and public bodies performing a function of government in Canada,
- housing corporations in Canada constituted exclusively to provide low-cost housing for the aged,
- universities outside Canada, the student body of which ordinarily includes students from Canada, and

- certain other charitable organizations outside Canada that have received a gift from Her Majesty in right of Canada.

(b) total Crown gifts;

(c) total cultural gifts; and

(d) total ecological gifts.

By administrative practice, donations made by either spouse or common-law partner can be combined in one claim. Thus, only one $200 threshold for the low credit rate need be applied.

¶10,240 Income limit and carryforward

If the eligible donations in a year exceed the maximum of 75% of Division B income, the excess amount should be carried forward and claimed first, before the current year gifts, in the next five years. Donations may only be carried forward five years subject to the 75% limitation in that year. The income limitation is found in the definition of "total gifts". This carryforward is permitted to the extent that the donations are not claimed in the current year, even though they may not exceed 75% of Division B income in the current year. The annual Division B income limitation of 75% of the donor's net income for the year is increased by 25% of: ITA: 118.1(1) ITA: 118.1(2.1) ITA: 118(1) "total gifts"

- recapture of CCA arising on a gift of depreciable capital property; and
- taxable capital gains arising on the donation of a capital property.

A limit of 100% of Division B net income applies for gifts:

- made in the year of death; or ITA: 118.1(4)
- of ecologically sensitive land. ITA: 118.1(1)

The 75% of Division B income limit should not be expected to apply in most cases. However, the limit would become an effective limit, if gifts are made in an unusual year of relatively low income or a loss year.

¶10,245 Total charitable gifts

Gifts made to certain types of organizations listed under the definition of "total charitable gifts" may be eligible for the tax credit to a maximum tax credit base of 75% of Division B income. Only the gifts to these specified organizations are eligible and they must be supported by proper receipts. ITA: 118.1(1) ITA: 118.1(2)

Where gifts of capital property and works of art, which are inventory to the donor, have a fair market value greater than adjusted cost base or cost amount, and the gift is not cultural property, the taxpayer may make a designation of a transfer price. The taxpayer can designate a transfer price between fair market value[7] and adjusted cost base or cost amount as proceeds of disposition and the value of the gift. Capital gains or income could, thus, be avoided by selecting the adjusted cost base or cost amount; but the value of the gift and the resultant tax credit under these paragraphs would be lower. ITA: 118.1(1) ITA: 118.1(6) ITA: 118.1(7)

If personal-use property is acquired as part of an arrangement under which the property is gifted to a charity, then the $1,000 rule will not apply. This rule is designed to prevent abuses connected with the donation of art and other personal-use property. ITA: 46

¶10,250 Gifts of publicly traded securities

The income inclusion rate for capital gains from gifts of publicly traded securities is reduced to zero for this purpose, instead of the usual 50%. Securities eligible for this treatment include shares listed on a designated stock exchange. ITA: 38(a.1); ITR: 3200, 3201

[7] An interesting court case on the issue of fair market valuation in this context is *Friedberg v. The Queen*, 89 DTC 5115 (F.C.T.D.), affirmed by the Federal Court of Appeal (92 DTC 6031).

Legislation eliminates tax on capital gains realized on the exchange of unlisted shares and partnership interests for publicly traded securities, if the publicly traded securities are then donated to a qualified donee within 30 days of the exchange (in which case, any further capital gain on the donation would also be nil). The unlisted securities must include, at the time they are issued, a condition allowing the holder to exchange them for publicly traded securities, and the publicly traded securities must be the only consideration received on the exchange. Special rules apply where the exchanged securities are partnership interests. ITA: 38(*a*.1), 38(*a*.2)

Flow-through shares have special features that allow resource expenses to flow from the corporate issuer to the shareholder. As a result, the adjusted cost base of these shares is nil. If these shares are then donated to a charity and no capital gain is recognized, then the shareholders who bought the share originally will have received a 100% deduction of flow-through expenses, and will be exempt from the capital gain and receive a tax credit for the value of the shares. This was viewed as too generous, so, for flow-through shares acquired pursuant to an agreement issued on or after March 22, 2011 and subsequently donated to a charity, the donor is deemed to have realized a capital gain. The effect is that the exemption from the capital gain on donations of publicly listed flow-through shares is only permitted to the extent that the capital gain realized on the donation exceeds the amount originally paid for the shares. ITA: 40(12)

¶10,255 Total cultural gifts

Where an artist makes a cultural gift that is a work of art created by the individual and that is property in the artist's inventory, the artist is deemed to have received proceeds of disposition equal to the cost to the artist of the work of art. A cultural gift is included in the definition of "total cultural gifts" and means objects that the Cultural Property Export Review Board has determined meets certain conditions. The result of this provision is that the artist is entitled to a credit based on the full fair market value of the art donated, but has no income to report as a result of the donation and its consequent disposition of the art from inventory. There is no net income limitation and there is a five-year carryforward. ITA: 118.1(7.1) ITA: 118.1(1)

¶10,260 Tickets to events

Where a charitable organization issues receipts for the price of tickets to fund-raising events involving an element of entertainment or other benefit for the donor, only the excess of the amount paid over the fair market value of the benefit received is allowed to be considered part of the charitable gift.

¶10,265 Total Crown gifts

Gifts made to the Government of Canada or to the government of a province are considered to be gifts made to Her Majesty and are defined as Crown gifts. There is a 75% of net income limitation to equal the limitation on other charitable gifts. Again, there is a five-year carryforward on these gifts. ITA: 118.1(1)

¶10,270 Total ecological gifts

A net income limitation of 100% applies to donations of certain ecologically sensitive land. This provision is meant to encourage the conservation and protection of Canada's environmental heritage and applies to qualified donations of land including qualified donations of covenants, servitudes and easements. As a further incentive, for ecological gifts, any capital gain realized on the donation (other than gifts to a private foundation) are subject to a zero capital gains inclusion rate. ITA: 38(*a*.2)

¶10,275 First-time donor's super credit

[To encourage charitable giving by new donors the March 21, 2013 federal Budget proposes to supplement the regular charitable donation tax credit with an additional 25% non-refundable credit for first-time donors on up to $1,000 of donations.

As a result, first-time donors will be entitled to a 40% federal credit for the first $200 of donations and 54% on the balance.

However, there are a number of conditions that have to be met to qualify for this super credit:

— It only applies to a maximum of $1,000 of donations;

— It only applies to cash donations;

— Neither the donor nor his or her spouse or common-law partner can have claimed the regular donation tax credit nor the first-time donor's super credit in any taxation year after 2007;

— A spouse or common-law partner can share the super credit;

— A spouse or common-law partner can only make one claim; and

— Only donations made on or after March 21, 2013 and before 2018 can be claimed.]

¶10,280 Medical Expense Credit

¶10,285 Calculation of the credit

Not all medical and health care costs are fully covered by a provincial health insurance plan or by a private health services plan. Expenses that must be borne by the taxpayer may qualify for the non-refundable medical expense credit. For example, certain cosmetic or elective procedures and a fraction of dental services may not be covered.

The medical expense tax credit is calculated as: ITA: 118.2(1)

$$A\,[(B - C) + D]$$

where

A is 15% (i.e., the appropriate percentage for the year)

B is medical expenses listed in the legislation for the individual, spouse or common-law partner and children not reaching 18 before the end of the year ITA: 118.2(2), 118.2(3)

C is the lesser of:

- $2,152 (indexed for 2013), and
- 3% of the individual's net income

D D applies only to dependants who are 18 and over and is calculated as E – F

where

E is the total of all medical expenses incurred by the taxpayer on behalf of any other dependant, and ITA: 118(6)

F is the lesser of:

- $2,152 (indexed for 2013), and
- 3% of the other dependant's net income

The C and F calculations in the formula show that a certain level of medical expenses must be paid by the individual before a credit can be earned. This level of expense that is borne by the individual, increases with net income until, at $71,733 ($2,152/0.03) of income or above, it remains the same.

In essence, the federal tax credit is 15% (10% used for provincial tax credit) of medical expenses in excess of the $2,152 for 2013 or 3% of the Division B income threshold. The medical expenses must be proven by filing receipts and must be paid within any 12-month period ending in the year unless the individual dies in the year. Where the individual dies in the year, the medical expenses must be paid by the claimant for the deceased person within any period of 24 months that includes the date of death.

¶10,290 Medical expenses

The legislation includes over 30 detailed paragraphs outlining the very technical rules and conditions defining medical expenses. A brief description of these paragraphs is provided below; however, a careful examination of these provisions and an Interpretation Bulletin must be made in order to determine the eligibility of each item.[8]

ITA: 118.2(2)

Income Tax Folio S5-F1-C2, S5-F1-C1, S5-F1-C3

(*a*) — general medical expenses (illness, hospitalization, etc.) paid to dentists, nurses and medical practitioners (a wider term than medical doctors for the taxpayer, his or her spouse and dependants of the individual. Hence, either spouse may qualify for a tax credit for the expenses of each other. For other dependants, the definition includes most individuals related to the taxpayer and dependent on the taxpayer for support.

ITA: 118(6), 118.4(2); Income Tax Folio S5-F1-C2, S5-F1-C1, S5-F1-C3

Expenses that are incurred for purely cosmetic procedures (including related services and travel) are not eligible to be claimed under the medical expense tax credit. Expenses aimed purely at enhancing appearance, such as liposuction, hair replacement, botulinum toxin injections, and teeth whitening, are not deductible. Those expenses such as surgery to improve a deformity arising from a congenital abnormality, personal injury, or disease will continue to be covered.

(*b*), (*b*.1), (*b*.2), (*c*), and (*d*) — full-time or part-time attendants or attendants for the care of an individual eligible for the impairment credit and/or full-time care in a nursing home, group home or otherwise. Each provision has its own unique conditions. The amount eligible for the credit in respect of attendant care for an individual eligible for the impairment credit is limited to $10,000 ($20,000 in the year of death).

ITA: 118.3

(*e*) — care and training for the mentally or physically handicapped, is not completely medical in nature.

(*f*), (*g*), and (*h*) — transportation of taxpayers to medical centres. Note that for travel expenses envisaged in paragraph (*h*), individuals may choose a detailed or simplified method to calculate certain travel expenses. The detailed method would use actual costs, substantiated by receipts. The simplified method applies to meals and vehicle expenses which can be based on flat rates. The flat rate for meals is $17 per meal to a maximum of $51 per day, per person. The flat rate for vehicle expenses is based on the province or territory in which the individual travels and varies by province or territory. (See Chapter 9, under moving expenses, for a detailed list of rates for vehicle expenses.)

(*i*), (*i*.1) — certain specific medical equipment or products.

(*j*) — expenses of eyeglasses, etc. for the taxpayer, his or her spouse or a dependant.

(*k*) — specialized equipment dealing with oxygen and of insulin and of other specified substances is allowable by virtue of this paragraph.

(*l*) — specific expenses related to the care of a trained dog who assists the blind or deaf and the cost of an animal trained to assist an individual who has a severe and prolonged physical impairment.

(*l*.1) — a reasonable cost for arranging a bone marrow transplant or organ transplant.

[8] For cases dealing with a variety of medical expense claims, see: *Demont v. The Queen*, 2002 DTC 3924 (T.C.C. — Informal Procedure), dealing with health care services and transportation expenses; *Weeks v. The Queen*, 2001 DTC 5035 (F.C.A.), dealing with the cost of devices, equipment or other chattels purchased for in-home care of a disabled person; *Pagnotto v. The Queen*, 2001 DTC 3797 (T.C.C. — Informal Procedure), dealing with medical services and drugs; *Donahue v. The Queen* (T.C.C. — Informal Procedure), dealing with medical services and devices; *Klywak v. The Queen* 2004 DTC 3143 (T.C.C. — Informal Procedure), dealing with medical devices; *Motkowski v. The Queen*, 2003 DTC 3968 (T.C.C. — Informal Procedure), dealing with home alterations; and *Seely v. The Queen*, 2002 DTC 4009, dealing with home alterations.

(*l*.2), (*l*.21) — expenses for modifying a home if an individual is confined to a wheelchair for a long period of time, lacks normal physical development, or has a severe and prolonged mobility impairment.

(*l*.3) — expenses for rehabilitative therapy to adjust for speech or hearing loss, including training in lip reading and sign language.

(*l*.4) — sign language interpretation or real-time captioning services, if the payment is made to a person who is in the business of providing such services, for an individual with a speech or hearing impairment.

(*l*.41) — note-taking services on behalf of an individual with a mental or physical impairment, if the payment is made to a person who is in the business of providing such services and the individual has been certified as requiring those services.

(*l*.42) — voice recognition software used by an individual with a physical impairment if the individual has been certified as requiring that software.

(*l*.43) — expenses for reading services used by an individual who is blind or who has a severe learning disability, if the need for the service is certified in writing by a medical practitioner and paid to persons engaged in the business of providing such services.

(*l*.44) — expenses for deaf-blind intervening services used by an individual who is both blind and profoundly deaf (if paid to persons engaged in the business of providing such services).

(*l*.5) — a maximum of $2,000 incurred to move an individual to housing that is more accessible or in which the individual is more mobile or functional.

(*l*.6) — reasonable expenses relating to alterations to a home driveway to facilitate access to a bus by an individual with a severe and prolonged mobility impairment.

(*l*.7) — the lesser of $5,000 and 20% of the cost of a van adapted within six months of its purchase for use by an individual using a wheelchair.

(*l*.8) — reasonable expenses incurred to train an individual to care for a relative having a mental or physical infirmity. The relative must be either a member of the taxpayer's household or dependent on the taxpayer for support.

(*l*.9) — expenses for remuneration for therapy provided to the patient because of the patient's severe and prolonged impairment.

(*l*.91) — expenses for remuneration for tutoring services that are rendered to, and are supplementary to the primary education of, the patient who has a learning disability or mental impairment.

(*m*) — this paragraph provides the statutory authority for a regulation which supplements the equipment listed in paragraphs (*i*) and (*k*), noted above, and may stipulate a dollar limit for claims in respect of a particular device or equipment. ITA: 5700

(*n*) — drugs and prescriptions, etc., as prescribed by a medical practitioner and administered by a pharmacist, are allowed by virtue of this paragraph.

(*o*) — certain diagnostic services such as X-rays, laboratory tests, etc.

(*p*) — the cost of dentures made in a province by an authorized person.

(*q*) — a premium for a private health services plan. To the extent that the premium has been deducted in computing the individuals business income, it is not deductible as a medical expense.

(*r*) — the incremental cost, to an individual who suffers from celiac disease,of acquiring gluten-free products if the individual has been certified as requiring a gluten-free diet.

(*s*), (*t*) — expenses for drugs or medical devices obtained under Health Canada's Special Access Programme.

(*u*) — expenses:

- for the purchase of medical marijuana or marijuana seeds, from Health Canada, for use by a patient who is authorized to possess marijuana for medical purposes under the *Marihuana Medical Access Regulations* (MMAR) or who holds an exemption for possession under section 56 of the *Controlled Drugs and Substances Act* (CDSA); and
- for the purchase of medical marijuana, for use by a patient who is authorized to possess marijuana for medical purposes under the MMAR or who holds an exemption for possession under section 56 of the CDSA, from an individual who possesses a designated-person production licence under the MMAR to cultivate or produce marijuana for medical purposes on behalf of that patient or who holds a designated person Exemption for cultivation or production under section 56 of the CDSA to cultivate or produce marijuana for medical purposes on behalf of that patient.

Example Problem 10-7

Mr. Moyer has income under Division B of $25,000 and $30,000 for 2012 and 2013, respectively. His wife and children have no income in these years. He incurs the following receipted medical expenses on behalf of himself, his wife, and three dependent children.

2012 — None prior to August			
	August	Dental bills for children	$ 325
	September	Hospital bill and drugs	200*
	November	Prescription drugs	65
	December	Prescription drugs	125
	Total medical expenses		$ 715 (B)
	Less the lesser of:		
	(a) $2,109		
	(b) 3% of Division B income (3% of $25,000)		750 (C)
	Net base for tax credit (B – C)		Nil
2013 —	January	Eyeglasses for himself and wife	$ 225
	February	Eyeglasses for three children	340
	March	Orthodontic work for children	1,500
	July	Chiropractor for Mr. Moyer	400*
	Total medical expenses		$2,465

* Excess over amount paid by a provincial medicare program.

— *REQUIRED*

Determine the maximum amount Mr. Moyer can claim as a medical expense tax credit in 2013. ITA: 118.2(1)

— *SOLUTION*

Since the only restriction on the 12-month period is that it must end in the particular taxation year, Mr. Moyer should choose the 12 months ending in July 2013.

The medical expense tax credit is computed by the following formula:

$$A\,((B - C) + D)$$

where A = .15

B = total medical expenses (as computed below)

C = lesser of:

(a) $2,152
(b) 3% of Division B income (as computed below)

D = nil in this case

2012 — August to December: total medical expenses	$ 715
2013 — January to July: total medical expenses	2,465
Total	$3,180 (B)
Less the lesser of:	
(a) $2,152	
(b) 3% of Division B income (3% of $30,000)	900 (C)
Net base for medical expense tax credit (B – C)	$2,280
Medical expense tax credit: A (B – C) = .15 × $2,280 = . . .	$ 342

Note that had Mr. Moyer's wife had some income that would attract tax in excess of her other tax credits, but less than her husband's, there may be a greater benefit to the family if she claimed the medical expense tax credit because the 3% threshold would be lower.

Note, also, that the CRA has indicated that prepaid medical expenses only qualify as valid medical expenses when they are made in the same 12-month period during which the medical services are rendered.[9]

¶10,295 Notch provision for dependants

As discussed above, a taxpayer may claim a medical expense tax credit for the medical expenses of the taxpayer, the taxpayer's spouse or a dependent individual. Where a person, other than the taxpayer's spouse, qualifies as a dependant (including a child who has reached the age of 18, grandchild or parent, grandparent, brother, sister, uncle, aunt, niece, or nephew, if resident in Canada), the taxpayer may include the medical expenses of that person when computing the medical expense tax credit. ITA: 118(6) ITA: 118.2(1)

Specifically, medical expense claims made on behalf of minor children are pooled in item B of the medical expense tax credit formula with those of the taxpayer and his or her spouse or common-law partner, subject to the taxpayer's minimum expense threshold (the lesser of 3% of net income and $2,152) without regard to the income of the minor child.

For medical expenses paid on behalf of other dependent relatives (e.g., child who has reached the age of 18, parent, grandparent, niece, nephew, etc.) taxpayers can claim qualifying medical expenses paid on behalf of such a dependant that exceed the lesser of 3% of the dependant's net income and $2,152. This reduction is embedded in item D of the medical expense tax credit formula.

Example Problem 10-8

Mr. Jones' father is a dependant. His father's Division B income is only $8,500 for 2013. During the year, Mr. Jones paid medical expenses of $1,000 on behalf of his father and $2,500 for himself. Mr. Jones' Division B income is $100,000 for 2013. ITA: 118(6)

— *REQUIRED*

Determine the maximum amount that Mr. Jones can claim as a medical expense tax credit in 2013. ITA: 118.2(1)

— *SOLUTION*

The medical expense tax credit is computed by the following formula

[9] See TAX WINDOWS FILES, Document No. 2005-13326117.

$$A\,[(B - C) + D]$$

If Mr. Jones claims his father's medical expenses:

A = .15

B = total medical expenses, i.e., $2,500 for taxpayer

C = lesser of $2,152 and 3% of $100,000, i.e., taxpayer's Division B income = $2,152

D for the dependent father is

E − F

where

E = the total of all medical expenses incurred by the taxpayer on behalf of the father, i.e., $1,000, and

F = lesser of:

- $2,152, and
- 3% of the father's net income, i.e., 3% of $8,500 = $255

15% × [($2,500 − $2,152) + ($1,000 − $255)] = $164

¶10,300 Credit for Mental or Physical Impairment (Disability Tax Credit)

¶10,305 Amount of and conditions for impairment credit

The Act provides the formula for calculating the non-refundable tax credit for an individual with a mental or physical impairment and the conditions for entitlement to the credit. The tax credit for 2013 is $1,155 (i.e., 15% of $7,697). This tax credit is available to taxpayers who have "one or more severe and prolonged impairments in physical or mental functions" that has been certified by a medical doctor. A health professional, other than a medical doctor, may be eligible to certify the impairment. An optometrist may certify the existence of an impairment of sight. An audiologist may certify an impairment of hearing. An occupational therapist may certify the existence of an impairment with respect to an individual's ability to walk or to feed or to dress himself or herself. A psychologist may certify to the existence of an impairment with respect to an individual's ability to perceive, think and remember. A speech-language pathologist may certify a severe and prolonged speech impairment. A physical therapist may certify a marked restriction in walking. Cumulative effects of multiple restrictions must usually be certified by a medical doctor. ITA: 118.3(1)

The impairment, or the cumulative effect of multiple restrictions, must have caused the individual to be markedly restricted all or almost all of the time in his or her basic activities of daily living. The impairment must have lasted or be expected to last for a continuous period of at least 12 months. Such impairment would include blindness, deafness and other listed impairments. It would also occur where, even with the use of appropriate devices, medication or therapy, the individual is generally unable (or requires an inordinate amount of time) to feed or to dress himself or herself or perform specified fundamental functions.[10] ITA: 118.4(1)

No claim can be made under this subsection if a claim has been made for a full-time attendant or care in a nursing home. However, a claim for expenses of an attendant costing up to $10,000 in computing the medical expense tax credit will not deny this impairment tax credit. ITA: 118.2(1) ITA: 118.2(2)(*b.1*)

A supplement amount of $4,490 for 2013 is available for each disabled child under the age of 18 years at the end of the year. The supplement amount is reduced by the excess of the total of child care and attendant care expenses, paid in the year and deducted in respect of the child, over $2,630 (for 2013).

[10] For cases on various impairments, see *The Queen v. Hamilton*, 2002 DTC 6836 (F.C.A.), dealing with celiac disease; *Johnston v. The Queen* (F.C.A.), 98 DTC 6169, dealing with arthritis; *Overdyk v. M.N.R.*, 83 DTC 307 (T.R.B.), dealing with partial paralysis; *Tanguay v. The Queen*, 97 DTC 3309 (T.C.C.), dealing with an individual who could not dress himself due to a hip problem; and *Radage v. The Queen*, 96 DTC 1615 (T.C.C. — Informal Procedure), dealing with intellectual limitations or perceiving, thinking and remembering.

¶10,310 Transfer of impairment credit

A transfer of this credit is available to a taxpayer, if the dependants themselves cannot use all or some part of this credit. The impaired dependant must use as much of the credit as necessary to reduce his or her federal income tax to zero, before the remainder can be transferred. The transfer of the unused part of the impairment credit is available to a taxpayer if: ITA: 118(1)(*c*.1), 118.3(2)

- the taxpayer claimed an equivalent-to-married credit for the dependant; ITA: 118(1)(*b*)
- the dependant was the taxpayer's child, grandchild, parent, grandparent (including in-laws), brother, sister, aunt, uncle, nephew or niece, and the taxpayer could have claimed an equivalent-to-married credit for that dependant if the taxpayer did not have a spouse or common-law partner and if the dependant did not have any income; ITA: 118(1)(*d*)
- the dependant was the taxpayer's child or grandchild and the taxpayer claimed them as a dependant or for the caregiver credit; ITA: 118(1)(*d*) ITA: 118(1)(*c*.1)
- the dependant was the taxpayer's child or grandchild and the taxpayer could have claimed them as a dependant or for the caregiver credit if they had no income; or ITA: 118(1)(*c*.1), 118(1)(*d*)
- the dependant was the taxpayer's parent or grandparent (including in-laws) and the taxpayer could have claimed them as a dependant of for the caregiver credit if they had no income.

The net result of these rules is that if a parent supports two or more disabled children, the parent is entitled to the transfer of the unused portion of the impairment tax credit of those children, even though only one child may be claimed as an equivalent-to-married tax credit.[11] The spousal transfer of this credit is discussed later. ITA: 118.8

The legislation deals with the allocation of the impairment tax credit where more than one individual is entitled to the credit for the same dependant. A definition of impairment is contained in the provision and applies not only to the disability credit, but also to the medical expenses credit. A definition of the term used to describe a medical practitioner is also contained in the provision and appears to codify the description in an Interpretation Bulletin. ITA: 118.3(3) ITA: 118.2, 118.3, 118.4 ITA: 118.4(2) Income Tax Folio S5-F1-C2, S5-F1-C1, S5-F1-C3

¶10,320 Tuition, Education, and Textbook Credits

¶10,325 Tuition tax credit

The federal tuition fee tax credit is equal to 15% (10% used for provincial tax credit) of eligible tuition fees paid in respect of that year. The Act provides for a tax credit in respect of tuition fees paid to an educational institution in Canada. The fees must be paid to a university, college or other educational institution in respect of courses at a post-secondary school level, or an institution certified by the Minister of Human Resources Development providing courses that furnish a person, who is at least 16 years of age at the end of the year, with skills for an occupation. The total of fees paid to a qualified institution in a year must exceed $100.[12] ITA: 118.5 ITA: 118.5(1)(*a*)

Tuition fees for full-time and part-time students include items such as library and laboratory charges. Also, eligible for the credit are mandatory ancillary fees, other than student association fees, required to be paid by all full-time and part-time students for courses at the post-secondary school level. Eligible fees include those charged for health services and athletics. In addition to student association fees, the following are excluded: charges for property to be acquired by students, services not ordinarily provided at post-secondary educational institutions in Canada and tax exempt financial assistance to students. Also, mandatory charges paid for the construction, renovation or maintenance of a building or facility, generally, do not qualify for the credit. A fee that would be eligible, but for the fact that it is not required from all students, may be claimed to a limit of $250.

---

[11] See *Blais v. M.N.R.*, 85 DTC 61 (T.C.C.).

[12] See *Dumas v. M.N.R.*, 79 DTC 726 (T.R.B.), which was decided when the threshold was $25.

The tax credit for tuition paid in the year to a university outside Canada is more restricted. The student must be in full-time attendance at a university in a course leading to a degree. The course must be of at least three consecutive weeks' duration. A tax credit for fees paid by a Canadian resident who commuted to an educational institution providing courses at the post-secondary level in the United States is allowed. Again, the amount of the fees paid in the year to a particular institution must exceed $100.

ITA: 118.5(1)(*b*)

ITA: 118.5(1)(*c*)

Examination fees paid to an educational institution, professional association, provincial ministry, or other institution for an examination required to obtain a professional status recognized by federal or provincial statute, or to be licensed or certified to practise a trade or profession in Canada, will be eligible for the tuition tax credit.

ITA: 118.5(1)(*d*)

¶10,330 Education credit

This federal credit is calculated by a formula which multiplies 15% (10% used for provincial tax credit) of $400 by the number of months in the year during which the individual was enrolled in a qualifying educational program as a full-time student at a designated educational institution. Part-time students at a qualifying post-secondary educational institution who are eligible for the disability tax credit or who, by reason of their certified mental or physical impairment, cannot be enrolled on a full-time basis are treated like full-time students. The enrolment must be proven by filing a certificate issued by the educational institution. Where the student is enrolled at an institution certified by the Minister of Human Resources Development, the purpose of the enrolment must be to obtain or improve skills for an occupation. The terms "designated educational institution" and "qualifying educational program" are defined.

ITA: 118.6(1), 118.6(2), 118.6(3)

Part-time students (other than students eligible for the impairment tax credit) may claim a federal credit of 15% (10% used for provincial tax credit) of $120 per month during which he or she was enrolled at a designated educational institution and specified educational program. The program must require the student to spend not less than 12 hours in the month on courses in the program.

Post-secondary students enrolled in distance education programs or correspondence courses may meet the full-time or part-time requirements if the courses meet the required standards.

Two Interpretation Bulletins discuss the detailed rules governing the education tax credit and tuition fee tax credit, respectively. These bulletins provide some very important interpretation of the technical terms relating to these credits and should be examined carefully. While the bulletins indicate a number of different situations that might qualify as "full-time attendance", it appears to be up to the educational institution to determine who is full-time and who is part-time. This is suggested in the bulletins by a statement to the effect that the determination must be made on the basis of the facts in each case. The only elaboration in the bulletins appears in a statement suggesting that a student who is in regular attendance in a qualifying educational program is considered to be enrolled as a full-time student.

Income Tax Folio S1-F2-C1 — Education and Textbook Tax Credits, S1-F2-C2 — Tuition Tax Credit

As noted under the tuition tax credit above, the minimum course duration requirement at foreign universities is three consecutive weeks.

¶10,335 Textbook credit

A non-refundable textbook tax credit is available in addition to the education tax credit. The credit base is:

ITA: 118.6(2.1)

- $65 for each month for which the student qualifies for the full-time education tax credit amount, and
- $20 for each month that the student qualifies for the part-time education tax credit amount.

As noted under the tuition tax credit above, the minimum course duration requirement at foreign universities is three consecutive weeks.

¶10,340 Carryforward

The unused portion of a student's tuition fee, education, and textbook tax credits can be claimed by the student in a subsequent taxation year. This allows an indefinite carryforward of these credits by the student to the extent that they are not transferred in the year earned to a spouse or supporting individual. Students are permitted to transfer part of the unused credits and carry forward the remainder. ITA: 118.61

¶10,345 Transfer of tuition, education, and textbook credits to spouse and parent and grandparent

The tuition fee, education, and textbook credits may be transferred to a spouse or to a parent or grandparent of the student. To qualify, the student must designate, in writing, an amount transferred to a spouse or to a parent or grandparent. The formula for calculating the amount that may be claimed as a tax credit by the spouse or by the parent or grandparent is the lesser of: ITA: 118.8, 118.81, 118.9

(a) the amount determined by the formula A – B

where A is the lesser of:

(a) $750 (i.e., 15% of $5,000), and ITA: 118.01, 118.02, 118.03

(b) the student's tuition credit and education credit for the year (excluding unused amounts carried forward).

B is the amount of the student's Part I tax payable after deducting credits for personal, age, pension, and employment, public transit passes, children's fitness, mental or physical impairment, EI and CPP, and unused tuition and education, and ITA: 118, 118.3, 118.7

(b) the amount designated by the student in writing for the transfer to a spouse or to a parent or grandparent.)

In effect, this formula allows the transfer of the excess of up to $750 of a student's tuition, education, and textbook credits over those credits required by the student to reduce federal tax to nil.

Example Problem 10-9

Debbie, who is not dependent upon any person, was enrolled as a full-time student at the University of Toronto for eight months during 2013. Debbie provides you with the following information for 2013:

Scholarship income	$12,000
Summer employment	12,000
Interest income — Canadian	1,000
Qualified tuition fees paid in 2013 (8 months)	4,500

— REQUIRED

(A) Determine the amount of Debbie's federal tuition and education credits which can be transferred to her parent.

(B) Determine the amount of Debbie's unused federal tuition and education tax credits at the end of 2013, assuming she transfers the maximum amount.

— SOLUTION

(A) Scholarship income [not taxable]	$ Nil
Employment income	12,000

Interest		1,000
Division B and taxable income		$13,000
Federal tax @ 15%		$ 1,950
Basic personal tax credit ($11,038 × 15%)		(1,656)
Canada employment credit ($1,117 × 15%)		(168)
Federal tax payable		$ 126
Tuition fee, education, and textbook tax credit:		
Tuition fee tax credit (15% of $4,500)		$ 675
Education tax credit (15% of $400 × 8)		480
Textbook tax credit (15% of $65 × 8)		78
Total tax credit		$ 1,233
Tuition fee and education tax credit transfer to parent:		
Lesser of:		
(a) $750		
(b) Student's tuition fee and education tax credit: $1,233		$ 750
Less: amount of student's Part I tax net of secs. 118, 118.02, 118.03, 118.3, 118.61, and 118.7 credits		126
Net amount available for transfer		$ 624
(B) Unused tuition, education, and textbook tax credits at December 31, 2012		Nil
Plus: 2013 tuition, education, and textbook credits	$1,233	
Less: Debbie's tax payable before deducting the current year's tuition, education, and textbook credits	(126)	$1,107
Minus: Unused tuition, education, and textbook credits deducted in 2012		(Nil)
Tuition, education, and textbook credits transferred		(624)
Unused tuition, education, and textbook tax credits at December 31, 2013		$ 483

¶10,350 Credit for interest on student loans

A student may deduct a federal tax credit of 15% (10% used for provincial tax credit) of interest on a federal or provincial student loan payable in respect of the year or in any of the five preceding taxation years. Qualifying loans are those made under the *Canada Student Loans Act* or a similar provincial statute. ITA: 118.62

¶10,360 Credit for Employment Insurance Premiums and CPP Contributions

The federal tax credit is equal to 15% (10% used for provincial tax credit) of: ITA: 118.7

(a) all amounts payable by the individual in respect of an employee's premiums for Employment Insurance;

(b) all amounts payable by the individual as an employee's contributions under the Canada (or Quebec) Pension Plan; and

(c) all amounts payable by the individual as a contribution for self-employed earnings under the Canada (or Quebec) Pension Plan.

For 2013, the Employment Insurance premium rate for the employee is 1.88% of earnings to a maximum annual earnings amount of $47,400. At this level of earnings the maximum level of premium of $891 is reached. (Employers must pay a premium of 2.63% (i.e., 1.4 times the employee payment), for a total maximum of $1,247.)

The rate of contribution to the Canada Pension Plan for 2013 is 4.95% of pensionable earnings. The maximum pensionable earnings is $51,100 with a basic exemption of $3,500. Thus, the maximum contribution is calculated as follows:

4.95% of ($51,100 – $3,500) = $2,356

For a self-employed individual, the maximum is twice the above amount or $4,712.

¶10,370 Transfer of Unused Credits to Spouse or Common-Law Partner

Certain unused tax credits may be transferred to a spouse or common-law partner. These tax credits are: ITA: 118.8

(a) the tuition, education, and textbook credits (to a maximum of $750); ITA: 118.5, 118.6

(b) the age amount; ITA: 118(2)

(c) the pension income amount; ITA: 118(3)

(d) the mental or physical impairment credit; and ITA: 118.3(1)

(e) the child amount.

The amount that may be transferred is calculated by the following formula:

A + B – C

where A is the lesser of:

- $750, and
- the spouse's tuition fee, education, and textbook tax credits;

B is the sum of the following tax credits available to the spouse:

- the age amount,
- the pension income amount,
- the mental or physical impairment credit, and
- the child amount; and

C is the amount, if any, by which

(a) the spouse's Part I tax payable after deducting:

- the basic single personal credit, ITA: 118(1)(*c*)
- unused tuition, education, and textbook credits, and ITA: 118.61
- the EI and CPP credits ITA: 118.7

exceeds

(b) the lesser of:

(i) the tuition, education, and textbook credit deductible by the spouse; and

(ii) the spouse's Part I tax payable after deducting:

- the basic personal credit,
- the adoption expense credit,
- the Canada employment credit,
- the public transit passes credit,
- the children's fitness credit,
- the impairment credit,
- the unused tuition, education, and textbook credits, and
- the EI and CPP credit.

Example Problem 10-10

Mrs. Ahmed, age 75, received the following income in 2013:

Registered pension plan payments	$ 700
Old Age Security pension	6,550
Canada Pension Plan payments	600
Interest from Canadian corporations	400
Division B income	$8,250

Mrs. Ahmed has been confined to a wheelchair for several years but is quite active and is registered as a full-time student at a post-secondary institution for eight months, paying tuition of $2,000 at the senior citizens' rate.

— REQUIRED

Calculate the amount of federal tax credit transfer available to her husband for 2013. ITA: 118.8

— SOLUTION

Transfer of credits to Mr. Ahmed in accordance with the formula:

A + B − C

(A)	Tuition, education, and textbook credits transferred			
	Lesser of: (a) dollar limit		$ 750	
	(b) tuition, education, and textbook tax credits [15% of ($2,000 + ($400 + 65) × 8)]		$ 858	
	lesser amount			$ 750
(B)	Age credit		$1,028	
	Pension credit[1]		105	
	Disability credit		1,155	2,288
				$3,038
(C)	Mrs. Ahmed's Part I tax ($1,238 = 15% of $8,250) net of the basic personal tax credit ($1,656), unused tuition, education, and textbook credits (nil), and CPP and EI credits (nil)		$ Nil	
	Minus lesser of:			
	(i) tuition, education, and textbook tax credits deductible by Mrs. Ahmed	Nil		
	(ii) Mrs. Ahmed's Part I tax ($1,238) net of the basic personal tax credit ($1,656), the disability credit ($1,155), Canada employment (nil), adoption (nil), public transit passes (nil), children's fitness (nil), the unused tuition, education, and textbook credits (nil), and CPP and EI credits (nil)	Nil		
	lesser amount		Nil	(Nil)
				$3,038

ITA: 118.81

— NOTE TO SOLUTION

(1) The Old Age Security pension and CPP payments do not qualify for the pension tax credit. The pension credit is calculated as 15% of the lesser of: ITA: 118(8)

(a) $2,000; and

(b) pension income of $700.

¶10,380 Dividend Tax Credit and Subsection 82(3) Election

¶10,385 Dividend tax credit

The federal dividend tax credit available to an individual is a non-refundable tax credit. There are two rates of dividend tax credit depending on the source of the dividends: ITA: 121

- a rate of 2/3 of the gross-up applies to dividends paid before 2014 by a CCPC from income subject to tax at the low rate applicable to active business income (ABI) and aggregate investment income (AII); ITA: 82(1)(*b*)(i)
- a rate of 13/18 of the gross-up applies to dividends paid after 2013 by a CCPC from income subject to tax at the low rate applicable to active business income and aggregate investment income; and
- a rate of 6/11 of the gross-up applies to dividends paid by ITA: 82(1)(*b*)(ii)

 (i) a public corporation resident in Canada (and any other non-CCPC resident in Canada) from income subject to tax at the general corporate tax rate, and

 (ii) a CCPC resident in Canada to the extent that its income (other than investment income) is taxed at the general corporate rate.

Since the gross-up is a fraction of the dividend, the dividend tax credit can be calculated in three different ways depending on the information available:

Source of dividend	CCPC, on income taxed at the low rate on ABI and AII before 2014	CCPC, on income taxed at the low rate on ABI and AII after 2013	Canadian-resident public corporation or other corporations on income taxed at the general rate
Dividend paid	100%	100%	100%
Gross-up	25%	18%	38%
Dividend tax credit			
Fraction of gross-up	2/3	13/18	6/11
Percentage of dividend paid	16⅔%	13%	20.7%
Percentage of grossed up dividend	13⅓%	11% (rounded)	15% (rounded)

For the purposes of this book, unless otherwise stated, where provincial tax credits are calculated for individuals, a theoretical dividend tax credit rate will be applied to the dividend gross-up as follows:

- a provincial rate of 1/3 where the 25% gross-up applies (for dividends before 2014); and
- a provincial rate of 5/18 where the 18% gross-up applies (for dividends paid after 2013); and
- a provincial rate of 5/11 where the 38% gross-up applies.

Theoretically, the combined federal and provincial dividend tax credit should equal the gross-up of 25% or 38% of the dividend. This will be explored in Chapter 12. This would imply a provincial dividend tax credit rate applied to the grossed-up dividend of:

Low-rate income — Dividends paid before 2014

- 2/3 federal + 1/3 provincial, for a total of 100% of the gross-up.

Low-rate income — Dividends paid after 2013

- 13/18 federal + 5/18 provincial, for a total of 100% of the gross-up.

High-rate income

- 6/11 federal + 5/11 provincial, for a total of 100% of the gross-up.

However, provinces, in their use of the tax-on-income (TONI) structure, may specify their own rate of dividend tax credit.

As a result of the reduction in the federal corporate income tax rates, the legislation adjusted the federal dividend gross-up and tax credit to coincide with the corporate tax rate reduction for Canadian resident public corporations or other corporations on income taxed at the general rate.

	Gross-up	Dividend tax credit
2009	45%	11/18
2010	44%	10/17
2011	41%	13/23
After 2011	38%	6/11

¶10,390 Election to transfer dividends to spouse

An election is available to deem taxable dividends from taxable Canadian corporations received by one spouse or common-law partner, who cannot use the dividend tax credit because of low income, to be received by the other spouse or common-law partner. However, this election can only be used if the married personal tax credit claimed by the higher income spouse for the dependent spouse or common-law partner is increased or created by transferring the dividend income in this way. If the election can be made, the taxpayer must include the grossed up dividends transferred from the spouse or common-law partner, but may deduct the dividend tax credit available on the dividends. ITA: 82(3)

Consider the following situations where the low-income spouse has $300 of grossed up dividends from Canadian-resident public corporations plus some other source of income.

Calculation of taxpayer's married tax credit	*Case 1*	*Case 2*	*Case 3*
Spouse's Division B income before election	$11,100	$ 8,000	$12,000
Married credit:			
Spouse base	$11,038	$11,038	$11,038
Spouse's Division B income	(11,100)	(8,000)	(12,000)
Net credit base	Nil	$ 3,038	Nil
Credit @ 15% of net credit base	Nil	$ 456	Nil
Spouse's Division B income after election	$10,800	$ 7,700	$11,700
Married credit:			
Spouse tax credit base	$11,038	$11,038	$11,038
Spouse's Division B income	(10,800)	(7,700)	(11,700)
Net credit base	$ 238	$ 3,338	Nil
Credit @ 15% of net credit base (rounded)	$ 36	$ 501	Nil

In Case 1, an election is available, since after the election, a credit for the spouse has been created. In Case 2, the spousal credit has increased from $456 to $501 by the transfer of the dividends and, hence, the election is available. In Case 3, the election is not available, since the spousal credit is not available either before or after the transfer.

¶10,400 Credits for Part-Year and Non-Residents

Generally, for the period of residence in Canada of a part-year resident, the individual can deduct specified tax credits prorated by the number of days that the individual is resident in the year divided by the number of days in the calendar year: ITA: 118.91

- basic personal amount, married amount, equivalent-to-married amount, dependant amount and caregiver amount; ITA: 118(1)
- age amount; ITA: 118(2)
- disability amount either for the taxpayer or transferred from a dependant; ITA: 118.3
- unused credits transferred from a spouse; and ITA: 118.8
- unused tuition and education amounts transferred from a child or grandchild. ITA: 118.9

All other personal amounts may fully be claimed if they relate to the period of residence. These include:

- the pension credit; ITA: 118(3)
- Canada employment credit; ITA: 118(10)
- the adoption expense credit; ITA: 118.01
- public transit passes credit; ITA: 118.02
- children's fitness credit; ITA: 118.03
- first-time home buyers' credit and disability purchase credit; ITA: 118.05
- charitable gifts; ITA: 118.1
- medical expenses; ITA: 118.2
- tuition, education, and textbook credits; ITA: 118.5, 118.6
- credit for interest on student loan; and ITA: 118.62
- EI and CPP credits. ITA: 118.7

A non-resident individual (i.e., an individual who at no time in the year is resident in Canada) may deduct tax credits for the following amounts: ITA: 118.94

- charitable donations, including Crown gifts and cultural gifts; ITA: 118.1
- impairment amount for the taxpayer, but not for a dependant; ITA: 118.3(1)
- tuition credit; and ITA: 118.5
- EI, CPP (or QPP) credits. ITA: 118.7

Credits for all other personal amounts may be deducted if all or substantially all of the individual's worldwide income for the calendar year is included on the return.

¶10,410 Ordering of Credits

Section 118.92 provides an ordering rule for computing basic federal tax payable by an individual under Part I of the Act. The tax credits discussed, all of which are above-the-line non-refundable tax credits, must be applied in the following order:

Ssec. 118(1)	— married, equivalent-to-married, child, single, dependant, and caregiver tax credits;
Ssec. 118(2)	— age credit;
Sec. 118.7	— Employment Insurance and Canada (or Quebec) Pension Plan credits;
Ssec. 118(3)	— pension credit;
Ssec. 118(10)	— Canada employment credit;
Sec. 118.01	— adoption expense credit;
Sec. 118.02	— public transit passes credit;
Sec. 118.03	— children's fitness credit;
Sec. 118.031	— child arts tax credit;
Sec. 118.04	— home renovation tax credit;

Sec. 118.05	— first-time home buyers' credit and disability home purchase credit;
Sec. 118.06	— volunteer firefighters tax credit;
Sec. 118.3	— mental or physical impairment credit (including dependant's unused credit);
Sec. 118.61	— unused tuition, education, and textbook tax credits carryforward;
Sec. 118.5	— tuition fee credit;
Sec. 118.6	— education credit;
Sec. 118.9	— transfer of tuition fee, education, and textbook credits;
Sec. 118.8	— transfer of unused spouse's credits;
Sec. 118.2	— medical expense credit;
Sec. 118.1	— charitable gifts credit;
Sec. 118.62	— credit for interest on student loan;
Sec. 121	— dividend tax credit.

Example Problem 10-11

The following list of income inclusions, deductions, losses, and tax credits has been determined correctly by a junior staff accountant prior to the preparation of the tax return for Ms. Samara Lowen.

Inclusions

Salary	$60,000
Canadian bank interest	1,200
Taxable capital gains	7,500
Taxable benefits from employment	1,780
Pension income	5,000
Taxable amount of dividends from taxable Canadian corporations	750

Deductions, Losses, and Tax Credits

Non-capital losses claimed	$2,000
Net capital losses carried forward	6,000
Basic personal and spousal tax credits	3,311
Registered pension plan contributions	1,000
Medical expenses tax credit	80
Interest expense to acquire Canadian shares	300
Moving expenses	600
Charitable donations tax credit	202
Pension tax credit	300
Canada Pension Plan contributions tax credit	353
Employment Insurance premiums tax credit	134
Dividend tax credit	100
Allowable capital losses	650
Business loss	3,080
Canada employment credit	168

— *REQUIRED*

(A) From the structural outlines and exhibits on the preceding pages, determine the income, taxable income, and basic federal tax net of non-refundable tax credits based upon the above correct information using the ordering rules in sections 3, 111.1, and 118.92. Assume federal tax before credits is $10,723 in 2013.

(B) Cross-reference each amount to the appropriate section of the Act. (Refer to Sectional List of the Act.)

— *SOLUTION*

Division B — Section 3

Par. 3(*a*)	*Subdivision a*				
	Sec. 5	Salary	$ 60,000		
	Par. 6(1)(*a*)	Taxable benefits	1,780	$ 61,780	
	Less				
	Par. 8(1)(*m*)	Registered pension plan contributions		(1,000)	
				$ 60,780	
	Subdivision b				
	Business		Nil		
	Property				
	Par. 12(1)(*c*)	Canadian bank interest	$ 1,200		
	Par. 12(1)(*j*)	Dividends (taxable amount)	750		
			$ 1,950		
	Par. 20(1)(*c*)	Interest expense	(300)	$ 1,650	
	Subdivision d				
	Ssec. 56(1)	Pension income		5,000	
				$ 67,430	
Par. 3(*b*)	*Subdivision c*				
	Sec. 38	Taxable capital gains	$ 7,500		
	Sec. 38	Allowable capital losses	(650)	6,850	
				$ 74,280	
Par. 3(*c*)	*Subdivision e*				
	Sec. 62	Moving expenses		(600)	
				$ 73,680	
Par. 3(*d*)	Sec. 9	Business loss		(3,080)	
		Division B income		$ 70,600	
Division C — Section 111.1					
	Par. 111(1)(*a*)	Non-capital losses	$ (2,000)		
	Par. 111(1)(*b*)	Net capital losses	(6,000)	(8,000)	
Taxable income				$ 62,600	

Division E — Section 118.92

Federal tax before credits			$ 10,723
Less tax credits:			
Sec. 118	Personal tax credits	$ 3,311	
Sec. 118.7	CPP tax credit	353	
Sec. 118.7	EI premium tax credit	134	
Ssec. 118(3)	Pension tax credit	300	
Ssec. 118(10)	Canada employment credit	168	
Sec. 118.2	Medical expense credit	80	
Sec. 118.1	Donation tax credit	202	
Sec. 121	Dividend tax credit	100	(4,648)
Basic federal tax			$ 6,075

¶10,420 Income Not Earned in a Province

This provision imposes a surtax of 48% on federal tax of an individual applicable proportionally to income for the year not earned in a province. A definition of the term "income earned in the year in a province" is provided. ITA: 120(1) ITA: 120(4); ITR: 2600

The purpose of this provision is to achieve a tax rate on income earned outside of Canada and taxable in Canada which approximates the total federal and provincial income tax on income earned in Canada.

¶10,430 Credit for Employment Outside Canada

Some relief is provided for an employee who is employed outside Canada on a temporary basis. Since, in most cases, the employee will not have made a clean break from Canada, he or she will still be resident in Canada for tax purposes. In order to provide a standard of living equivalent to that in Canada, employers have had to offer increased salaries or living allowances which resulted in a higher tax burden with no increase in disposable income to the employee. This section was enacted to help the competitive position of Canadian corporations in bidding for export contracts. ITA: 122.3

This section applies to employees of specified employers who perform specified duties outside of Canada for more than six consecutive months. The tax credit is based on the proportion of tax otherwise payable. The fraction is the lesser of:

(a) $80,000, prorated on a daily basis; and

(b) 80% of the employment income which can reasonably be attributed to those specified duties, to his or her total income;

reduced by:

(c) certain deductions provided in Division C.

This credit is not available where employment is by an employer that is, in essence, an "incorporated employee" (as discussed in Chapter 12).

The legislation will phase out this credit over four years beginning in 2013. The percentage applied to an employee's qualifying foreign employment income will be: ITA: 122.3(1.02)

- 60% in 2013,
- 40% in 2014,
- 20% in 2015, and
- 0% in 2016 and subsequent years.

This phase-out will not apply if the employer has committed in writing before March 29, 2012, in which case the 80% will apply for 2013 to 2015. However, even in this case, the credit will be eliminated in 2016.

¶10,440 Refundable Goods and Services Tax/Harmonized Sales Tax (GST/HST) Credit

A refundable goods and services tax/harmonized sales tax (GST/HST) credit is provided. This credit is designed to offset all or part of the GST for families and individuals with lower incomes. Application for the credit is made with the taxpayer's income tax return, but the credit is received separately in quarterly instalments. The payments based on the taxpayer's 2013 income tax return are made in July and October 2014 and in January and April 2015. Eligibility for the credit and the amount paid in each quarter reflects changes in family circumstances that occurred before the end of the preceding quarter. Thus, for example, the birth of a child during the year can increase the GSTC in the next quarter, rather than only in the next year. For 2013, the amount is the sum of: ITA: 122.5, 122.5(3) ITA: 122.5

(a) $265 for an eligible individual, other than a trust, who is, at the end of the year resident in Canada and married, a parent or over 18 years of age; ITA: 122.5(1), 122.5(2)

(b) $265 for a qualified relation (as discussed below) or for a qualified dependant (as discussed below) in respect of whom the individual is entitled to deduct an amount under equivalent-to-married status; ITA: 118(1)(*b*)

(c) $139 for each other qualified dependant of the individual; and

(d) where the individual has no qualified relation for the year:

(i) $139 if the individual has one or more qualified dependants for the year,

(ii) if the individual has no qualified dependants for the year, the lesser of:

(A) $139, and

(B) 2% of the excess, if any, of the individual's Division B income for the year over the base (i.e., $8,608 in 2013).

A qualified relation is a cohabiting spouse or common-law partner. However, the credit cannot be double counted (i.e., the individual or the spouse or common-law partner may make the claim but not both). A qualified dependant is also defined as, in essence, a person who is claimed as a dependant or a child of the individual who resides with the individual at the end of the year. Two credits cannot be claimed in respect of the same person as an eligible individual and as a qualified dependant. ITA: 122.5(1), 122.5(2), 122.6 ITA: 118

The credit is reduced by 5% of combined incomes, as set out in the definition of "adjusted income" over a $34,561 threshold for 2013. The refundability feature arises from the wording in the provision, which deems the amount of the credit to have been paid as tax like the refundable child tax credit. ITA: 122.5(1) ITA: 122.5(3)

Example Problem 10-12

Woody Carver is divorced and has custody of his two children, ages 8 and 13. Woody had net income of $40,000 for 2013.

— REQUIRED

Compute the refundable goods and services tax credit, beginning in July 2014, assuming no changes in his family situation.

— SOLUTION

Credit ($265 + $265 + $139 × 1)			$669
Add the GST/HST credit supplement for single parents			139
			$808
Deduct:	Income	$ 40,000	
	Threshold	(34,561)	
	Excess	$ 5,439	
	5% of the excess		(272)
GST/HST credit			$ 536

This credit will be paid in four instalments of $134 in July and October 2014 and January and April 2015.

¶10,450 Refundable Medical Expense Supplement

A refundable medical expense supplement (RMES) is provided for eligible individuals. An eligible individual is an individual who is resident in Canada throughout the year and ITA: 122.51, 122.51(1)

18 years of age or older at the end of the year. The individual's adjusted income for a taxation year is defined as being the total of the income of the individual and of the individual's cohabiting spouse.

The supplement is calculated as follows:

lesser of:
- (a) $1,142, and
- (b) the total of
  - (i) $^{25}/_{15}$ of the medical expense tax credit claimed by the eligible individual for the year, and — ITA: 118.2
  - (ii) 25% of the amount deductible for disability support — ITA: 64

less: 5% of the amount, if any, by which
- (a) the individual's adjusted income exceeds $25,278 for 2013.

Since this is a refundable federal tax credit, it does not affect provincial tax. However, an adjustment for the effect of provincial tax is contained in the $^{25}/_{15}$ fraction used in the above calculation.

This supplement is completely eroded by the 5% reduction, when adjusted income is $48,118 (i.e., ($1,142/0.05) + $25,278).

The supplement is deemed to be tax paid as part of the individual's tax liability for the year, like income tax withheld. Thus, it is available for refund if total tax paid or deemed paid exceeds tax payable for the year. ITA: 122.51(1)

The addition of 25% of the disability support deduction to the RMES ensures that disabled persons do not see their refundable medical expense credit reduced if they claim their cost of disability support as a deduction instead of a credit. The purpose of the RMES is to provide an incentive for Canadians with disabilities to work. The RMES is intended to offset the loss of coverage for medical and disability-related expenses when individuals move from social assistance to work.

¶10,460 Refundable Canada Child Tax Benefit

The Canada Child Tax Benefit (CCTB) is the main federal instrument for the provision of financial assistance to families with children. The CCTB has the following components: ITA: 122.6–122.64

- the base benefit, which is targeted to low and middle-income families; and
- two supplements:
  - the National Child Benefit (NCB) supplement, which provides additional assistance to low-income families, and
  - in recognition of the special needs of low and modest-income families with a disabled child, a $2,626 (for 2013) Child Disability Benefit (CDB) paid for children who meet the eligibility criteria for the disability tax credit.

The CCTB is paid monthly. The amount of the payments is based on family income and child care expenses of the base taxation year, as defined. The payments are not taxable and not subject to clawback. ITA: 122.6

An eligible individual is entitled to a CCTB calculated in respect of qualified dependants who are generally children who have not attained the age of 18 years. ITA: 122.6, 122.61(1)

The following is a table of the maximum benefits available under the CCTB.

	July 2012	July 2013
Base Benefit		
Basic amount per child	$ 1,405	$ 1,433
Additional benefit for 3rd and subsequent children	98	100
NCB Supplement		
First child	2,177	2,221
Second child	1,926	1,964
Third and subsequent child	1,832	1,869
Total CCTB Benefit		
First child	3,582	3,657
Second child	3,331	3,397
Third and subsequent child	3,335	3,302
Child Disability Benefit		
Each child	2,575	2,626
Phase-Out Thresholds		
Base benefit phase-out starts at	24,863	25,356
Supplement phase-out ends at	42,707	43,561
Disability benefit phase-out starts at	42,707	43,561

To target the increase in the NCB supplement to lower-income families, the income threshold at which the NCB supplement begins to be phased out will be adjusted.

Since tax preparation software manages the calculations, the point to remember is who qualifies for this benefit.

The child must be a "qualified dependent" which means a person, who:

1. has not attained the age of 18 years,
2. is not a person who has been claimed for the married or common-law partner credit, and
3. is not a person in respect of whom a special allowance under the *Children's Special Allowances Act* is payable.

The person receiving the benefit must be an "eligible individual" which means a person, who:

1. resides with the child,
2. is the parent of the child who primarily fulfils the responsibility for care and upbringing,
3. is resident in Canada,
4. is not an employee of a country other than Canada, and
5. is, or whose cohabiting spouse or common-law partner is, a Canadian citizen or a person who is a permanent resident, a temporary resident or a protected person. Each of these terms is defined under federal legislation.

¶10,470 Working Income Tax Benefit (WITB)

¶10,475 Overview

ITA: 122.7

For many low-income Canadians, taking a job can mean being financially worse off. To improve their incentives and lower their barriers to employment, the WITB was introduced.

The WITB provides a refundable tax credit equal to 20% of each dollar of earned income in excess of $3,000 to a maximum credit of $989 for single individuals without dependants (single individuals) and $1,797 for families (couples and single parents). Earned income for purposes of the WITB means the total amount of an individual's or family's income for the year from employment and business and is determined without reference to any losses arising or claimed in that year.

To target assistance to those with low income, the credit is reduced by 15% of net family income in excess of $11,231 for single individuals and $15,509 for families in 2013. Hence, no WITB is available when a single individual's earned income reaches $17,824 (i.e., $989/0.15 + $11,231) or a family's earned income reaches $27,489 (i.e., $1,797/0.15 + $15,509) in 2013. Net income is calculated on the same basis as is currently used for the Canada Child Tax Benefit and the GST/HST credit.

An individual is eligible for the WITB if resident in Canada throughout the year and 19 years of age at the end of the year. In addition, a single parent must be the primary caregiver to the dependent child in Canada.

Students, as defined for the education tax credit, with no dependent children, who are enrolled as full-time students for more than three months in the year are not eligible for the WITB.

Example Problem 10-13

Bill is single and working as a mechanic in a bicycle shop earning $15,000 per year. His sister, Mary, is married and she and her husband make $22,000 per year.

— *REQUIRED*

Will they qualify for the working income tax benefit?

— *SOLUTION*

	Bill	**Mary**
Income	$15,000	$22,000
Base amount	(3,000)	(3,000)
Net working income over base	$12,000	$19,000
Lesser of $989/$1,797 and 25% of above amount	$ 989	$ 1,797
Reduction (below)	(565)	(974)
WITB	$ 424	$ 823
Income	$15,000	$22,000
Threshold	(11,231)	(15,509)
Base of reduction	$ 3,769	$ 6,491
Reduction: 15% of base	$ (565)	$ (974)

Both Bill and Mary will qualify for the working income tax benefit.

¶10,480 WITB supplement for persons with disabilities

Persons with disabilities face significant barriers to their participation in the labour force. The WITB provides an additional supplement for each individual, other than a dependant, who is eligible for the disability tax credit and who has at least $1,150 of earned income and who meets the other eligibility requirements for the WITB. For each dollar in excess of $1,150, the individual is supplemented at a rate of 25% up to a maximum credit of $495. This supplement is reduced by 15% of net family income in excess of $17,827 for single individuals and $27,489 for families in 2013.

¶10,485 WITB prepayment

To maximize the effectiveness of the WITB, a prepayment mechanism was put in place. Individuals and families who are eligible for the GST/HST credit, and who are eligible for the WITB, are eligible to apply to the CRA for a prepayment of one-half of their estimated WITB.

¶10,490 Foreign Tax Credits

Since a resident of Canada is subject to tax on worldwide income, any income earned from a foreign source must be included in total income being taxed in Canada. However, the foreign income may also have been taxed in the country in which it was earned. In the absence of a tax treaty which removes the income from the tax base of either Canada or the other country, the income would be taxed twice. The Act provides tax credits deductible from tax payable in Canada for income tax paid in another country. Residents of Canada may claim a tax credit for non-business income tax paid (such as tax on investment income) in another country and a tax credit for business income tax paid in another country. Both credits are limited to a proportion of tax payable in Canada that can be considered to be attributed to the income from the foreign source. This limit is computed by formula. ITA: 126(1), 126(2) ITA: 126

For individuals, the foreign non-business tax credit is computed as the lesser of: ITA: 126(1)

(a) non-business income tax paid to a foreign country, and

(b) $\dfrac{\text{net non-business foreign income included under Division B}}{\text{total income included under Division B net of certain adjustments}} \times$ tax for the year otherwise payable under Part I

Note that part (b) attempts to estimate the Canadian tax paid on the foreign income. As a result, the credit against Canadian tax cannot exceed the estimated Canadian tax paid on the foreign income.

The definition of "non-business income tax" excludes an amount that was deductible from property income in respect of foreign taxes in excess of 15% on income from property and an amount that was deducted in respect of foreign non-business income tax paid. ITA: 20(11), 20(12), 126(7)

The denominator of the fraction, which uses total income under Division B as the base, is reduced by amounts that are attributable to specific types of income which are offset by Division C deductions and, hence, do not generate tax. These amounts include:

(a) amounts deducted as net capital losses; or ITA: 111(1)(*b*)

(b) amounts deductible in respect of:

(i) shares, ITA: 110(1)(*d*), (*d*.1), (*d*.2), or (*d*.3)

(ii) a deduction for workers' compensation or social assistance, or ITA: 110(1)(*f*)

(iii) a home relocation loan. ITA: 110(1)(*j*)

The term "tax for the year otherwise payable under this Part" is defined for the purposes of the foreign non-business income tax credit. As it applies generally to individuals, it is the tax payable under Part I of the Act before specified deductions from tax, including the deduction of the dividend tax credit and the credit for employment outside Canada. ITA: 126(7) "tax for the year otherwise payable under this Part" (*a*)

The foreign business income tax credit, also, applies to individual taxpayers and is similar in its calculation. The major difference is that any business income tax paid but not deducted is available as an "unused foreign tax credit" to be carried back three years and forward 10 years. This foreign tax credit will be dealt with in more detail, as it applies to corporations, in the next chapter. ITA: 126(7)

Where either non-business or business income taxes paid are not deductible as a credit, all or part of the excess may be eligible for a deduction from an individual's liability for surtax. ITA: 126, 180.1(1.1)

Furthermore, a non-deductible excess of non-business income tax paid may be eligible for a provincial foreign tax credit.

¶10,500 Federal Political Contribution Tax Credit

A tax credit is available for contributions to a registered federal political party, a registered association, or a candidate for election to the House of Commons. Receipts signed by the registered agent of the party or the official agent of the candidate are required to substantiate the credit claimed. The maximum credit is $650 which is reached with a contribution of $1,275 or more on the following sliding scale: ITA: 127(3)

Contribution	*Credit*
$400 or less	75% of the contribution
More than $400, but not more than $750 . . .	$300 + 50% of the contribution over $400
More than $750, but not more than $1,275	$475 + 33⅓% of the contribution over $750
More than $1,275	$650

¶10,510 Tax on Old Age Security Benefits

The Part I.2 tax results in the repayment of federal Old Age Security benefits included in computing the taxpayer's income, to the extent that the taxpayer's income is in excess of an indexed threshold ($70,954 for 2013). The repayment is computed as: ITA: 60(*w*), 180.2

the lesser of:		
(a) Old Age Security benefits		$xxx
(b) income under Division B without par. 60(*w*) deduction	$ xxx	
less	70,954	
excess, if any	$ xxx	
15% of excess, if any		$xxx

Note that the amount of this tax is deductible from income; however, offsetting the Part I.2 tax in part (b), above, through the deduction removes the potential double tax on this amount, as discussed in Chapter 9. ITA: 60(*w*)

Example Problem 10-14

Joanne, a widow, received the Old Age Security benefit of $6,550 in 2013. Her Division B income, excluding the deduction for the Part I.2 tax, is $75,000. ITA: 60(*w*)

— *REQUIRED*

Outline all of the tax implications of receiving the Old Age Security benefit in this case.

— *SOLUTION*

(a) The amount of the Old Age Security benefit received must be included in Joanne's income. ITA: 56(1)(*a*)

(b) The following repayment of the Old Age Security payment is required: ITA: 180.2

the lesser of:		
(i) Old Age Security benefit		$ 6,550
(ii) Division B income (excluding clawback deduction)	$75,000	
less	70,954	
excess, if any	$ 4,046	
15% of excess		$ 607

ITA: 60(*w*)

(c) The $607 repayment is deductible. ITA: 60(*w*)

(d) The net effect is as follows:

(i) inclusion of Old Age Security benefit	$ 6,550	
(ii) deduction of repayment	(607)	$ 5,943
(iii) cash received	$ 6,550	
(iv) repayment of Old Age Security benefit (paid special Part I.2 tax)	(607)	$ 5,943

¶10,520 Tax Reduction on Retroactive Lump-Sum Payments

When an individual receives a lump-sum payment in a year that relates to prior years, the graduated tax rate schedule, when applied to the lump sum, may result in more income tax payable in the year of receipt than in the prior years had the lump sum been spread over those previous years. The legislation provides for a reduction of tax on the following lump sums: ITA: 110.2, 120.31

- income from an office or employment or income received because of the termination of an office or employment, received under the terms of a court judgment, arbitration award or in settlement of a lawsuit;
- superannuation or pension benefits, other than non-periodic benefits;
- spouse or child support payments; and
- employment insurance and other benefits that may be prescribed by regulations.

The right to receive the lump sum must have existed in a prior year. For the tax reduction to apply, the lump sum received in the year must be at least $3,000.

The amount of income that is eligible for this special treatment is deducted in arriving at taxable income and then subject to notional tax. The notional tax is calculated as if the lump-sum payment had actually been received in the year to which it related. Interest, calculated at a prescribed rate, is added to the tax to reflect the fact that the notional tax was not actually paid in a previous year. ITA: 110.2, 120.31

This calculation will not affect any income-based benefits or deductions in those prior years.

¶10,530 Application of Rules for Computation of Tax and Credits

Example Problem 10-15

The following 2013 correct computation of taxable income for John Q. Citizen has been prepared for your analysis:

Income — Division B		
Employment income for tax purposes		$52,000
Business and property income, composed of:		
Dividends from Canadian-resident public corporations	$ 3,000	
Gross-up 38%	1,140	
Dividends — Foreign ($150 of tax withheld)	1,000	5,140
Pension income (including OAS benefit of $6,550)		15,000
Taxable capital gain		2,500
		$74,640
Less: Subdivision e deductions:		
RRSP contributions	$ 1,000	
Old Age Security benefit clawback	245	
Moving expenses	1,050	(2,295)
Division B income		$72,345
Less: net capital losses		(1,000)
Taxable income		$71,345

Additional Information

(1) John, age 67, and his wife Jill, age 64, are both resident in your province. Jill has no income and is blind.

(2) John has made the following selected payments in 2013:

Donations:	
Federal political party (registered)	$ 500
Provincial political party (registered)	400
United Appeal (registered) (made annually)	500

(3) John's employer correctly withheld the following amounts:

Employment Insurance	$ 891
Canada Pension Plan	2,356

(4) John filed his return on April 30, 2014.

— *REQUIRED*

Compute the total amount of federal taxes payable for the year.

— *SOLUTION*

Sec. 117	Federal tax on first	$43,561			$ 6,534
	Tax on balance	27,784	@ 22%		6,112
		$71,345			
	Total				$12,646
	Less: federal non-refundable tax credits:				
Ssec. 118(1)	Basic personal credit base			$11,038	
	Married credit base (with family caregiver credit)			13,078	
Ssec. 118(10)	Canada employment credit base			1,117	
Ssec. 118(2)	Age credit base(1)			1,187	
Sec. 118.7	Employment Insurance credit base			891	
	Canada Pension Plan credit base			2,356	
Ssec. 118(3)	Pension credit base			2,000	
Sec. 118.8	Transfer of spouse's impairment credit base			7,697	
				$39,364	
	15% thereof				(5,905)
					$ 6,741
Sec. 118.1	Charitable donations tax credit				
	First	$200	@ 15%	$ 30	
	Excess	$300	@ 29%	87	(117)
		$500			
Sec. 121	Federal dividend tax credit ($\frac{6}{11}$ × $1,140)				(622)
	Basic federal tax				$ 6,002
	Less: other federal tax credits:				
Sec. 126	Federal foreign tax credit(2)				
	Lesser of:				
	(a) $150				
	(b) $\frac{\$1,000}{\$72,345 - \$1,000} \times (\$6,002 + \$622) = \$80$				(93)
	Federal tax				$ 5,909

Ssec. 127(3)	Federal political donations[3]	(350)
	Net federal Part I tax payable	$ 5,559
Sec. 180.2	Old Age Security benefit clawback[4]	245
	Net federal tax payable	$ 5,804

— NOTES TO SOLUTION

(1) Age tax credit base $6,854

Less: base reduction of lesser of:

(a) Amount of credit base		$6,854
(b) Division B income	$72,345	
Less: threshold	34,562	
	$37,783 × .15 =	$5,667
Lesser amount		5,667
Net base		$1,187

(2) In this case, the foreign non-business tax credit is computed as the lesser of:

(a) the foreign non-business tax paid, and

(b) $\frac{\text{the foreign non-business income included under Division B}}{\text{Division B income less net capital losses claimed}} \times$ basic federal tax plus dividend tax credit

(3) The Act permits the deduction of a contribution to a federal registered party or person nominated as a candidate to serve in the House of Commons. The formula is: ITA: 127(3)

75% of first $400	$300
50% of next $350 ($500 – $400 in this situation)	50
33⅓% on next $525 (none in this situation)	Nil
	$350

The maximum credit is $650 on $1,275 of contributions.

(4) Lesser of:

(a) Old Age Security benefit		$6,550
(b) income under Division B (excluding clawback deduction)	$72,590	
less	70,954	
excess, if any	$ 1,636	
15% of excess		$ 245

ITA: 60(*w*)

Example Problem 10-16

Joshua's computation of taxable income for 2013 is as follows:

Income from employment	$57,500
Net income from rental properties	1,230
Public company dividend income	2,000
Gross-up 38%	760
Taxable capital gain	1,200
RRSP contribution	(4,000)
Child care expenses	(2,500)
Net income for tax purposes	56,190
Less: Net capital loss carryforward	(1,200)
Taxable income	$54,990

NOTES:

(a) Assume Joshua was resident in Canada on December 31, 2013.

(b) Assume that Joshua's taxable income was prepared correctly.

(c) Joshua is divorced and lives with his 7-year-old son, Jamie.

(d) During the year Joshua incurred the following expenses:

United Way donation (made annually)	$50
Cancer Society donation	20
Registered political party contribution	100
Transit passes (purchased monthly)	1,140
Tuition (part-time university course — 3 months)	175
Medical expenses for Jamie (dental and ophthalmic)	1,755

(e) T4 information:

Employment insurance	891
Canada Pension Plan	2,356
Tax withheld by employer	9,800

— *REQUIRED*

Compute Joshua's federal and provincial taxes payable. Assume the provincial tax rates are as set out in ¶10,130. Also assume that the provincial tax credit amounts are the same as the federal amounts; there are no over/under payments of EI and CPP.

— *SOLUTION*

Federal tax on the first	$43,561	$ 6,534
Excess	11,429 × 22%	2,514
Federal tax on taxable income	$54,990	$ 9,048
Less:		
Non-refundable tax credits (Sch. 1)		($4,583)
Dividend tax (9/11 × $760)		(415)
Basic federal tax		$ 4,168
Less: federal political tax credit		(75)
Net Federal Tax		$ 4,093
Provincial Tax (Sch. 2)		2,327

Total Tax Payable		$ 6,420
Less: tax deducted		(9,800)
Total tax refund		$ 3,380

Schedule 1: Federal non-refundable tax credits		**Tax Base**	**Federal Credit (15%)**
Basic personal credit		$11,038	$1,656
Equivalent-to-spouse credit		11,038	1,656
Child tax credit		2,234	335
Canada Pension Plan credit		2,356	353
Employment Insurance credit		891	134
Canada Employment credit		1,117	168
Public transit		1,140	171
Tuition fees		175	26
Education amount		360	54
Textbook credit		60	9
Medical expense credit			
Total medical expenses	$ 1,755		
3% × $56,190 (net income)	1,686		
Excess		69	10
Charitable donations credit		70	11
Non-refundable credits		$30,548	$4,583
Federal political tax credit		$ 100	$ 75

Schedule 2: Provincial tax calculation		
Provincial tax on the first	$43,561	$ 4,356
Excess	11,429 × 12%	1,371
Provincial tax on taxable income	$54,990	$ 5,727
Less:		
Provincial non-refundable credits	$30,548 × 10%	(3,055)
Provincial dividend tax credit ($760 × 5/11)		(345)
Provincial Tax		**$ 2,327**

¶10,540 Minimum Tax

The minimum tax addresses a government concern about the ability of some high-income individuals to take advantage of tax incentives and shelter virtually all of their income. Thus, a signal that minimum tax might apply in a particular case would be large deductions of CCA on tax shelters or large resource property deductions. ITA: 120.2, 127.5

¶10,545 Minimum amount

An individual's minimum tax is calculated by the following formula: ITA: 127.51

$$A (B - C) - D$$

where A is 15% (i.e., the appropriate percentage for the year),

B is adjusted taxable income, ITA: 127.52

C is the basic exemption ($40,000), and ITA: 127.53

D is the basic minimum tax credit. ITA: 127.531

This "minimum amount" minus a special foreign tax credit is then compared to regular Part I tax, net of all non-refundable tax credits (generally, before adding the 48% surtax for income not earned in a province). The greater amount becomes the basis of federal Part I tax for the year. The special foreign tax credit is basically equal to the greater of the foreign tax credit determined under normal rules or 15% of foreign income. ITA: 127.54(2)

Other tax credits, such as dividend tax credits and political donation credits will not be deductible from the minimum amount. In addition, even where the minimum amount is less than Part I tax, the restricted tax credits will be available only to the extent that Part I tax payable for the year does not go below the minimum amount.

¶10,550 Adjusted taxable income

The provision sets out the rules for computing adjusted taxable income, being a recalculation of taxable income using certain assumptions set out in the section. The CRA's form T691, for simplicity, starts with regular taxable income and adds back or subtracts amounts to arrive at adjusted taxable income. The amounts added back include: ITA: 127.52

- the portion of the loss (including a share of a partnership loss) from certified film or videotape properties that relates to CCA or carrying charges such as interest and financing charges;
- losses on resource properties as a result of certain incentive deductions such as Canadian exploration expense, Canadian development expense, depletion allowance, or Canadian oil and gas property expense;
- 30% of the excess of capital gains over capital losses for the year;
- ³⁄₅ of the employee stock option deductions and the other share deductions; ITA: 110(1)(*d*), 110(1)(*d*.1), 110(1)(*d*.2), 110(1)(*d*.3)
- the home relocation loan deduction; and ITA: 110(1)(*j*)
- losses of investments required to be identified under the tax shelter identification rules.

Deducted in computing adjusted taxable income are:

- the gross-up of Canadian dividends; and
- the non-deductible fraction of allowable business investment losses claimed in the year.

¶10,555 Basic exemption

In the case of an individual, other than a trust, the basic exemption is $40,000. Therefore, it is only adjusted taxable income in excess of $40,000 that is subject to minimum tax. ITA: 127.53(1)

¶10,560 Basic minimum tax credit

An individual's basic minimum tax credit is the sum of the tax credits that may be deducted in computing tax payable under Part I of the Act: ITA: 127.531

Ssec. 118(1)	— Personal credits for married status, equivalent-to-married status, child, single, dependants, and caregiver;
Ssec. 118(2)	— Age credit;

Ssec. 118(10)	— Canada employment credit;
Ssec. 118.01(2)	— Adoption expense credit;
Ssec. 118.02(2)	— Public transit pass credit;
Ssec. 118.03(2)	— Children's fitness credit;
Sec. 118.031	— Child arts credit;
Sec. 118.1	— Charitable gifts credit;
Sec. 118.2	— Medical expense credit;
Ssec. 118.3(1)	— Mental or physical impairment credit;
Sec. 118.5	— Tuition credit;
Sec. 118.6	— Education and textbook credits;
Sec. 118.61	— Unused tuition and education tax credits;
Sec. 118.62	— Credit for interest on student loan; and
Sec. 118.7	— Credit for Employment Insurance premium and CPP contribution.

¶10,565 Minimum tax carryforward

To recognize that a taxpayer who is not normally subject to minimum tax may, through unusual circumstances, be subject to minimum tax in a given year, the Act contains a carryforward provision. A taxpayer may carry forward for seven years the excess of the minimum tax over regular Part I tax for a particular year. The amount of the carryforward deductible in a subsequent year is restricted to the excess of regular Part I tax over the minimum tax in that subsequent year. As a result, in a carryforward year in which Part I tax exceeds the minimum tax, all or some part of the minimum tax paid in the previous year is recoverable as, in essence, a tax credit against Part I tax payable. ITA: 120.2

¶10,570 Impact of the minimum tax

The minimum tax directly affects only a small minority of Canadian taxpayers. The $40,000 basic exemption generally protects most non-top bracket taxpayers from minimum tax. Most top bracket taxpayers who do not invest in tax shelters are also unlikely to be affected by the minimum tax. However, it is necessary for taxpayers who could potentially be affected to do minimum tax calculations as a part of their tax planning each year. Thus, the tax adds a significant additional degree of complexity to the tax system.

Example Problem 10-17

Determine the federal tax payable in 2013 by Scoop, an unmarried taxpayer, with the following sources of income and deductions and a $400 federal political donation tax credit.

Employment income for tax purposes	$ 90,000
Interest income	15,512
Cash dividend from Canadian-resident public corporation	12,800
Gross-up on dividend @ 38%	4,864
Taxable capital gain (½ × $112,500)	56,250
RRSP contribution	(7,500)
Support of former spouse	(20,000)
Tax shelter loss due to film CCA	(25,000)
Net income for tax purposes	$126,926
QSBC share capital gains deduction	(50,000)
Taxable income	$ 76,926

Maximum Employment Insurance of $891 and CPP of $2,356 were withheld from salary.

— *SOLUTION*

Regular Part I tax				
on first	$43,561			$ 6,534
on balance of	33,365	@ 22%		7,340
	$76,926			$ 13,874
Less tax credits:				
Basic personal (15% of $11,038)			$1,656	
Employment Insurance (15% of $891)			134	
CPP (15% of $2,356)			353	
Employment (15% of $1,117)			168	
Dividend tax credit (6/11 of $4,864)			2,653	$ (4,964)
Basic federal tax under regular rules				$ 8,910(A)
Less: political donation tax credit (75% of $400)				(300)
Federal tax under regular rules				$ 8,610(B)
Adjusted taxable income:				
Taxable income				$ 76,926
Add back: 30% of capital gain				33,750
CCA loss				25,000
Less: dividend gross-up				(4,864)
Adjusted taxable income				$130,812
Less: basic exemption				(40,000)
Net				$ 90,812
Minimum tax before minimum tax credit (15% of $90,812)				$ 13,622
Less basic minimum tax credit:				
Basic personal			$1,656	
Employment Insurance premium			134	
CPP			353	
Employment			168	(2,311)
Minimum amount				$ 11,311(C)
Federal tax — greater of (B) and (C)				$ 11,311

Therefore, minimum tax is incurred in this situation.

¶10,800 REVIEW QUESTIONS

(1) Ms. Gnu, a new client of yours, has brought in her tax information and is confused. In prior years, she has had some financial difficulties and has lost money in a number of her business ventures. As a result, she has some net capital and some non-capital losses. This year, she earned some income, but she does not know how to decide which losses to apply against this income. What advice do you have for her?

(2) Evan earns over $150,000 of employment income and has come to you to talk about his investment income. He earns $10,000 of dividend income from a Canadian-resident public corporation in the year. He wants you to tell him what his marginal tax rate is on this dividend income.

(3) Phil earns over $150,000 of employment income and has come to you to talk about his investment income. He earns $10,000 of interest income in the year. He wants you to tell him what his marginal tax rate is on this interest income.

(4) Karen earns over $150,000 of employment income and has come to you to talk about her investment income. She realized a $10,000 capital gain in the year and wants you to tell her what her marginal tax rate is on this capital gain.

(5) Ms. Aarts is a painter who specializes in watercolours. In the artistic tradition, she does not make a great deal of money. In fact, she has never made over $20,000 of taxable income in any year. This year is no exception. She expects to have taxable income of $20,000 but she is also planning to donate one of her watercolours to a local charity to be used in one of their fundraising events. The value of the painting is $8,000 and her cost of the painting is $200. She has heard that there are special rules for artists making charitable donations of their work but she does not know if these rules will help her. She does not make any other donations. What is your advice?

(6) During the year Patricia had full-time employment income from employer A of $55,000 and from employer B of $50,000. Both employer A and employer B each deducted $2,356 from her salary for CPP. What impact will the CPP contributions for her employment income have on her personal tax return?

(7) ABC Contracting Inc., a taxable Canadian corporation, has a construction contract in Kuwait. Mr. Jones has been asked to move from Canada to Kuwait to help with the supervision. He will be there for a period of 15 months, after which time he will move back to Canada to take up his duties with the company. Due to the short-term nature of the work he will not move his family with him. He will move to Kuwait on January 1, 2013, and will not come back to Canada until April 1, 2014. His income for 2013 while in Kuwait will be $120,000. Comment on the tax issues in 2013.

¶10,825 MULTIPLE CHOICE QUESTIONS

Question 1

Banbury Ltd. (BL) is a Canadian-controlled private corporation (CCPC). Brad King is one of BL's employees and deals at arm's length with BL. On April 30, 2010, Brad was granted an option to purchase 1,000 BL shares at $2 per share. Brad exercised the stock option on June 30, 2011, when the market price was $5 per share. In December 2013, Brad sold the shares for $7 each. The fair market value of the shares on April 30, 2010, was $2.50.

Which one of the following amounts represents the increase in Brad's taxable income resulting from the above transactions?

(A) $3,000 in 2011 and $1,000 in 2013

(B) $2,250 in 2011 and $1,000 in 2013

(C) $2,500 in 2013

(D) $4,000 in 2013

Question 2

Bob, a widower who is 65 years old, has correctly calculated his taxable income for 2013 as follows:

Employment income under Subdivision a	$10,000
Pension income (registered pension plan)	20,000
Old Age Security and Canada Pension Plans	10,000
Dividends from Canadian-resident public corporations (grossed up)	2,760
Interest income	5,000
	$47,760

What is the maximum amount (rounded to the nearest dollar) of federal income tax credits that Bob can claim on his 2013 tax return?

(A) $2,854

(B) $2,802

(C) $3,269

(D) $3,566

Question 3

In 2013, Shabir Hassam attended McGill University on a full-time basis for eight months, paying tuition fees of $3,900 for that period. In April 2013, Shabir moved back to Toronto to stay with his family and worked as a waiter. Shabir earned $9,500 in wages and $1,500 in tips during the summer. His moving costs were $200 to Toronto in April 2013 and $500 to Montreal in September 2013. Shabir also received a $1,500 scholarship from McGill in September 2013.

What is the maximum amount of federal personal income tax credits that Shabir can transfer to a parent in respect of his university education in 2013?

(A) $585

(B) $636

(C) $750

(D) $1,143

Question 4

Kyle, who is employed by a CCPC, had the following sources of income for the year:

Salary	$ 60,000
Dividends from Canadian-resident public corporation (amount received)	20,000
Employee stock option benefit	200,000
Capital gain	200,000

The stock option benefit relates to 50,000 shares that Kyle acquired under an employee stock option plan in January 2013 when the fair market value of the shares was $10 per share. Kyle paid $6 per share for the stock, which was the fair market value of each share at the time that the employee stock options were granted to him. He sold the stock when it was worth $14 per share.

Kyle is married and his wife works full-time. Their three children attend university. Each child has transferred the $5,000 maximum amount of education, tuition, and textbook credits to Kyle.

Based on this information, what is Kyle's federal Part I tax for the year under the regular rules, ignoring the minimum tax rules?

(A) $64,599
(B) $66,540
(C) $68,744
(D) $93,599

Question 5

Based on the information in Question 4, above, what is Kyle's minimum amount of federal tax for the year under minimum tax, after deducting minimum tax credits? ITA: 127.53

(A) $52,176
(B) $49,926
(C) $43,176
(D) $34,176

¶10,850 EXERCISES

Exercise 1

ITA: 3

Paragraph 3(*a*) of the *Income Tax Act* requires that all non-capital sources of income be included. It is necessary to disclose each source of income in the computation of net income for tax purposes. Consider the following:

(a) Dividend income from a CCPC.

(b) Loss from a sole proprietorship.

(c) Cashier's income from a grocery store.

(d) Commissions earned from sales with a real estate company.

(e) Research consulting fees.

(f) Rental income earned on a single dwelling.

(g) Bonus income.

(h) Gain on the sale of land by a real estate development company.

(i) Profit from the sale of shoes earned in an incorporated company.

(j) Employment insurance income.

(k) Dividend income earned from a foreign investment.

(l) Tips earned as a hair stylist.

— *REQUIRED*

Identify the source of income for each of the above.

Exercise 2

ITA: 3, 111

The following information has been provided by your client, Ms. Campbell.

	2011	*2012*	*2013*
Capital gains (CG)	$37,500	$50,000	$11,250
Capital losses (CL) (excluding BIL)	15,000	—	22,500
Business investment loss (BIL)	—	30,000	—

Additional Information

(1) The above capital gains do not include capital gains from qualified farm property or qualified small business corporation shares.

(2) Ms. Campbell had a $7,500 net capital loss which was realized in 2009.

(3) Ms. Campbell has never had a taxable capital gain prior to 2011 and did not claim any net capital losses in 1985 to 2010.

(4) Ms. Campbell had a property loss of $7,000 in 2012 and property income of $1,000 and $2,000 for 2011 and 2013, respectively.

— *REQUIRED*

(A) Determine Ms. Campbell's income from the sources indicated for 2011 to 2013 according to the ordering rules in section 3.

(B) Determine Ms. Campbell's taxable income from the sources indicated for 2011 to 2013 according to the ordering rules in Division C after amending the returns.

Exercise 3

ITA: 3, 111

Consider the following two taxpayer situations.

Taxpayer	*A*	*B*
Gross salary	$45,000	$15,000
Interest income	2,000	
Self-employed income (assume for tax purposes)	5,000	
Loss from business		(18,000)
Charitable donations	(280)	
Income tax paid	(15,000)	(3,200)
Net cash flow	$36,720	($6,200)

— *REQUIRED*

Compute each taxpayer's net income for the year, utilizing the aggregating formula of section 3 of the *Income Tax Act*. Where necessary, compute the net capital loss or the non-capital loss.

Exercise 4

ITA: Divisions B and C

Mr. Ethan Benjamin has provided you with a list of various sources of income, losses, deductions, and credits for the purpose of determining his basic federal tax.

Inclusions:	
His share of tax profit from a partnership business	$10,000
Canadian bank interest	3,000
Retiring allowance from a former employer	20,000
Gross salary from new employer	60,000
Director's fee	5,000
Taxable capital gains	20,000
Taxable benefits from employment	3,000
Rental income from a triplex	25,000
Deductions, Losses, and Tax Credits:	
Mortgage interest on triplex	23,000
Canada Pension Plan contributions tax credit	353
Property taxes and insurance on triplex	4,500
Non-capital losses from a previous year	4,000
Allowable capital loss for this year	2,000
Education and textbook tax credits transfer from son	80
Net capital losses from a previous year	5,000
Maintenance costs for triplex	1,500
Contribution to employer's registered pension plan	4,000
Basic personal and spousal tax credits	3,312
Fees to a professional engineering society	300
Employment Insurance premiums tax credit	134
Tuition tax credit for night course on computer applications	68
Charitable gifts tax credit	550
Canada employment tax credit	168

— *REQUIRED*

(A) Determine the income, taxable income and basic federal tax based on the above correct information using the ordering rules in sections 3, 111.1, and 118.92. Assume that federal tax before credits is $19,906 in 2013.

(B) Cross-reference each amount to the appropriate section of the Act.

Exercise 5

ITA: 118, 122.6, 122.61; IT-513R

Dan, age 50, supported the following persons during 2013:

	Net income for tax purposes
Wife, Dolly, age 45	$3,000
Son, Don, age 24	3,800
Son, Dave, age 18, infirm and living with Dan and Dolly	3,200
Daughter, Doris, age 17	2,800
Son, Dan Jr., age 14	Nil
Mother, age 83, infirm and living with Dan and Dolly	7,000

Don is attending university; Dave has been unemployed most of the year; and Doris and Dan Jr. attend high school. Ages are given as of the end of 2013.

— REQUIRED

Determine Dan's total federal personal tax credits under section 118 for 2013.

Exercise 6

ITA: 118; IT-513R

Jack and Jill were married on December 1, 2013. Jill and her two children of a previous marriage moved into Jack's home. Jill's children are 14 and 16 and have no income.

Jack and Jill have the following income for tax purposes for 2013:

	Prior to the marriage	*Subsequent to the marriage*
Jack	$33,000	$3,000
Jill	9,800	800

— REQUIRED

(A) Determine the optimum personal tax credits under section 118 for both Jack and Jill for 2013.

(B) How would your answer change in 2014 if the income levels remain the same?

Exercise 7

ITA: 8(1)(*m*), 56(1)(*a*), 118(3)

Sally was employed for a little under two years at the Banff Springs Hotel as a bellhop. When Sally resigned her position, she withdrew her total contributions of $800 from her employer's pension plan. Sally's contribution to this plan for her last year was $300.

— REQUIRED

Determine the tax consequences of the above situation.

Exercise 8

ITA: 118.6, 118.8, 118.9

Sammy, who was a resident of Canada and who attended the University of Alberta on a full-time basis for eight months during 2013, has employment income for tax purposes of $5,000. He paid tuition fees of $1,800 in 2013. Withheld from his income were $94 in Employment Insurance premiums and $74 in CPP contributions.

— REQUIRED

(A) Determine the amount Sammy can transfer under section 118.8 or 118.9 to another qualified person.

(B) List the potential persons to whom Sammy can transfer his tuition and education tax credits.

Exercise 9

ITA: 118.8

Tina, age 72, has income for tax purposes from the following sources in 2013:

Pension income:		
Old Age Security pension	$6,550	
Canada Pension Plan	2,755	
Registered pension plan	350	$ 9,655
Investment income:		
Canadian bank interest		100
Total Division B income		$ 9,755

— REQUIRED

Determine the amount Tina can transfer to her husband Tom in 2013.

Exercise 10

ITA: 82(3)

Henry, a resident of your province, cannot decide whether it would be advisable to elect to include in his income, his wife's cash dividends of $900 received from Canadian-resident public corporations. This is her only income for 2013.

— REQUIRED

Determine whether Henry should elect under subsection 82(3) for 2013 assuming his federal tax rate is 29%.

Exercise 11

ITA: 126(1)

The following selected information has been taken from the 2013 tax return of Adam, who is a bachelor:

Income — Division B	$156,800
Taxable income	150,800
Basic federal tax	33,146

Included in the Division B income was foreign interest of $1,500. Withholding tax of $225 had been deducted by the foreign government. This income is not subject to an international tax agreement.

Also included in the computation of Division B income were $300 of dividends received from Canadian-resident public corporations. Included in the computation of taxable income were deductions for net capital losses carried forward of $6,000.

ITA: 111(1)(*b*)

— REQUIRED

Determine the amount of the federal foreign tax credit that can be claimed.

Exercise 12

ITA: Division E, E.1

Compute the federal tax at the top bracket, under minimum tax and regular Part I tax for 2013 on $100 of:

(A) interest;

(B) cash dividends from Canadian-resident public corporation;

(C) capital gains.

Exercise 13

ITA: 117(2), 120

Marginal tax rates, or the tax rate applicable to the next dollar of income earned, are relevant to many decisions. Jacob earns $90,000.

— *REQUIRED*

Calculate Jacob's marginal tax rate using the federal and notional provincial rates provided in this chapter.

Exercise 14

ITA: Division E, E.1

The following is a correct calculation of Betty's Division E tax payable for 2013:

Employment income				$160,000
Dividends from Canadian-resident public corporation				30,000
Gross-up @ 38%				11,400
Loss created by resource property shelter				(103,200)
Net income for tax purposes and taxable income				$ 98,200
Tax on first	$ 87,123			$ 16,118
on next	11,077	@ 26%		2,880
	$ 98,200			$ 18,998
Less tax credits:				
Basic personal (15% × $11,038)			$1,656	
Employment Insurance premiums (max.) (15% × $891)			134	
CPP contributions (max.) (15% × $2,356)			353	
Dividend tax credit ($^{6}/_{11}$ × $11,400)			6,218	
Employment (15% of $1,117)			168	(8,529)
Division E tax				$ 10,469

— *REQUIRED*

Determine if Betty is subject to minimum tax in 2013.

Exercise 15

ITA: 63, 118

Mr. and Mrs. Ataila immigrated to Canada on May 1 (not a leap year). Mr. Ataila earned $12,400 in Argentina and $72,400 as a senior geologist in Canada. Mrs. Ataila is a homemaker, and mother of three children over the age of 6. Her child care expenses totalled $4,580 for the time she spent planning her entry into the workforce.

Mr. and Mrs. Ataila have approached you for assistance with their Canadian tax returns.

— *REQUIRED*

Discuss what you believe are the areas of their returns that they are most interested in.

Exercise 16

ITA: 63, 118

Pierino's wife died last year. Her income for the year was $28,000. Pierino has a 15-year-old dependent son, James. Pierino works for the Saskatoon Transit Commission and earns $65,000 yearly. He also has a part-time farming operation on which he has a loss of $8,000. Pierino contributed $10,000 to his RRSP by transferring some shares in Public Co. Ltd. to his self-administered RRSP. The ACB of the shares was $6,000. He has $3,000 in net capital losses being carried forward.

— *REQUIRED*

Calculate Pierino's taxable income and the base amounts of his personal tax credits. Ignore any CPP and EI contributions.

¶10,875 ASSIGNMENT PROBLEMS

Problem 1

ITA: 2(2), 3, 111

Blake, a recent accounting program graduate, earned the following during the year:

Gross income from employment	$ 7,000
Provincial lottery winnings	2,500
Capital gain on ABC shares	1,200
Inheritance from grandmother	12,000
Interest income from inheritance	800

— *REQUIRED*

(a) In accordance with section 3 of the *Income Tax Act*, compute Blake's net income for tax purposes for the year.

(b) Assume that Blake has a non-capital loss carryforward from last year of $3,000. Compute his taxable income for the year.

Problem 2

ITA: 2(2), 3, 111

Jeffrey Lowe is an associate in a local law firm. He also has a number of sources of income from various investments and sideline businesses. Jeffrey has provided you with the following information for 2013:

Salary from law practice	$120,000
Business loss	(7,500)
Gross rents received from rental property	25,000
Operating expenses on rental property	(31,000)
Capital gain on sale of shares	10,000
Net interest income	9,000
Allowable capital loss (including allowable business investment loss of $6,000)	(11,000)
Contribution to RRSP	(1,000)
Share of net income from duplex rental property (owned by Jeffrey and his sister)	15,000
Net capital losses from 2007	(3,000)

— *REQUIRED*

Calculate Jeffrey's 2013 net income for tax purposes in accordance with the ordering rules in section 3 of the *Income Tax Act*.

Problem 3

ITA: Division B, C

The following tax information is extracted from Mrs. Hawkins' books and records:

Employment income (before effects of items below)	$72,000
Interest income	5,000
Capital gains (on securities)	9,900
Deductible carrying charges	1,000

The following balances are losses carried forward from December 31, 2010:

Non-capital loss arising — 2007	$24,000
— 2008	26,000
— 2011	28,000
Total non-capital losses	$78,000
Net capital loss arising in 2012	$12,000

During the latter part of 2013, Mrs. Hawkins moved from Montreal to Toronto to commence working for Leaves Co. Ltd. She received a $100,000 housing loan from Leaves Co. Ltd., which she used to help purchase a house in Toronto. Mrs. Hawkins received the interest-free loan on October 1, 2013.

Mrs. Hawkins previously worked for Les Habitants Co. Ltée (a public company). Prior to leaving Les Habitants Co. Ltée on April 15, Mrs. Hawkins exercised the stock option that she held in Les Habitants Co. Ltée. Mrs. Hawkins was able to purchase 2,000 listed common shares of Les Habitants Co. Ltée for $4 per share (the fair market value of the shares at the time the option was granted). The shares were trading at $10 per share at the time she exercised her option to purchase the shares.

Assume that the prescribed interest rate for the last quarter of 2013 is 7%.

— REQUIRED

Calculate Mrs. Hawkins' income and taxable income in 2013, in accordance with the ordering rules of Divisions B and C. Ignore any effects of the leap year.

Problem 4

ITA: 3, 111

The following information has been provided by your client, Mr. Stanley Norman:

	2011	*2012*	*2013*
Employment income	$75,000	$80,000	$ 90,000
Property income (loss)	(4,000)	3,000	(6,000)
Capital gains (CG)	144,000	—	160,000
Capital losses (CL) (excluding BIL)	18,000	22,500	80,000
Business investment loss (BIL)	36,000	54,000	—

Additional Information

(1) The above capital gains do not include capital gains from qualified farm property or qualified small business corporation shares.

(2) Mr. Norman had a $21,000 net capital loss which was realized in 2008.

(3) Mr. Norman has not had a capital gain prior to 2011 and did not claim a net capital loss in the period 1985 to 2010.

— REQUIRED

Dealing with each item line-by-line across the years, rather than one year at a time:

(A) determine Mr. Norman's income from the sources indicated for 2011 to 2013 according to the ordering rules in section 3, and

(B) determine Mr. Norman's taxable income from the sources indicated from 2011 to 2013 according to the ordering rules in Division C after amending the returns.

Problem 5

ITA: 3, 111, 111.1

The following selected tax information has been taken from the books and records of your client, Mr. Weilman.

	2012	*2013*
Employment income	$ 40,000	$ 48,000
Other business income (loss)	(14,000)	(23,000)
Property income:		

	2012	2013
Canadian interest	7,000	16,000
Rental income from real property (loss)	3,000	(4,000)
Other income — pension	7,000	7,000
Capital gains (capital losses):*		
Listed personal property	6,000	20,250
Other personal-use property	2,000	(4,000)
Other capital property	6,000	(45,000)
Other deductions:		
RRSP	1,000	3,000
Support of former spouse	7,000	7,000

* The 2013 other capital property loss includes a business investment loss of $24,000.

The following balances are losses carried forward from December 31, 2011:

Non-capital loss arising in 2009	$33,000
Net capital loss arising in 2010	25,000
Listed personal property loss arising in 2009	5,000

Mr. Weilman was not a member of a registered pension plan and, hence, his pension adjustment for the relevant years was nil. His earned income for 2011 was $33,250.

— REQUIRED

Prepare a schedule for the calculation of income and taxable income for 2012 and 2013, in accordance with the ordering rules under Divisions B and C, after applying any loss carryforward and loss carryback provisions through an amended return. (Deal with each item line-by-line across the years, rather than computing income one year at a time.)

Problem 6

ITA: 245; Division B, C

Ms. Isabelle Cardin had a tumultuous year in 2013. She broke her engagement early in the year and quit her job. She moved to a resort area to take a waitress job and to start up a fitness instruction business. She has had the following items correctly calculated and classified as either inclusions, deductions or tax credits for the purposes of determining her taxable income and federal tax.

Inclusions:

Benefit received from Employment Insurance program	$ 600
Board and lodging provided by employer during busy season of resort	8,000
Bonus from resort employer	500
Business revenue from fitness instruction fees	2,000
Gratuities as a waitress	12,100
Interest on Canada Savings Bonds	775
Rental revenue	6,000
Salary received as a waitress	12,000
Taxable capital gain	3,750
Retiring allowance from previous employer	800

Deductions, Losses, and Tax Credits:

Allowable capital loss	4,500
Capital cost allowance on fitness business equipment	1,300
Capital cost allowance on rental building	1,200
Charitable gifts tax credit	26
Child care expenses	1,800
Canada Pension Plan contributions tax credits on employment earnings	215
Medical expenses tax credit	9
Business expenses of earning fitness instruction fees	900

Expenses of objection to a tax assessment	65
Interest on funds borrowed to pay expenses of earning fitness instruction fees	75
Maintenance on rental property	1,100
Mortgage interest on rental property	2,500
Moving expenses	1,700
Non-capital losses from previous year	600
Personal tax credit	1,656
Property tax on rental property	1,000
Employment Insurance premiums tax credit	92
Union dues	100
Canada employment credit	168

— REQUIRED

(A) Determine the income, taxable income and basic federal tax based on the above correct information using the ordering rules in sections 3, 111.1, and 118.92. Assume federal tax before credits is $4,565 in 2013.

(B) Cross-reference each amount to the appropriate section of the Act.

Problem 7

ITA: 56(1)(*u*), 56(1)(*v*), 74.1(1), 110(1)(*f*), 118, 118.3, 118.6, 118.9, 122.6, 122.61

Mrs. Plant, age 47, is married and has three children: Amanda, age 24, Joan, age 17, and Courtney, age 16. Her own income for tax purposes of $60,000 includes employment income of $52,000.

Amanda has been certified as impaired by a medical doctor. Her only income is $7,000 from social assistance payments relating to her disability. She took a university course on a part-time basis for four months. Mrs. Plant paid her tuition fees of $300.

Joan attended a university on a full-time basis in another city for eight months, had employment income for tax purposes of $4,200 from a summer job while living at home and received a $2,500 scholarship. Mrs. Plant paid Joan's tuition fees of $3,000 and Joan paid her own moving costs to and from the university which were $150 each way.

Courtney, who is attending high school, had employment income for tax purposes of $2,800 from summer employment and a part-time job.

Mr. Plant, age 50, has the following sources of income:

Worker's Compensation payment	$5,000
Cash dividends from shares of Canadian-resident public corporations purchased with Mrs. Plant's savings	4,000
Bank account interest earned from reinvestment of dividend income	100

— REQUIRED

(A) Calculate the non-refundable tax credits available to Mrs. Plant for 2013. Compute Joan's taxable income to determine if any of her tuition, education, and textbook tax credits will be available to Mrs. Plant. Prepare detailed calculations supporting your claim. All ages are given as of the end of 2013.

(B) Determine whether Mrs. Plant is entitled to claim the Canada Child Tax Benefit.

Problem 8

ITA: 118(4)

Angelina and Romeo are the divorced parents of Maria, who is 10 years old. Angelina and Romeo have joint custody and Maria lives every second month with the other. Both Angelina and Romeo have claimed Maria for the eligible dependent tax credit.

— REQUIRED

Is the claim by Angelina and Romeo allowed?

Problem 9

ITA: 118, 118.2–118.9; IT-513R

Mrs. Jackson, age 66, separated from her husband on October 17, 2013. She started receiving support payments from Mr. Jackson of $2,500 per month in November 2013. All of the support payments made commencing in November 2013 are considered to be pursuant to the divorce settlement. Of the $2,500 monthly payment, $1,000 is for the support of their daughter, Rachel. (In 2013, Mr. Jackson earned a salary of $100,000 per year and also earned other investment income.) Mrs. Jackson has income of $26,200.

Their eldest daughter Rachel is 40 and infirm and lives with Mrs. Jackson since she is severely mentally handicapped. She has been certified as impaired by a medical doctor. A part-time attendant helps care for Rachel at a cost of $12,000 per year. Rachel has no income.

— *REQUIRED*

Discuss the tax credits related to her daughter Rachel that are available to Mrs. Jackson.

Problem 10

ITA: 118.2

Mr. Jennings provides you with the following medical expenses and additional information for himself and members of his family who live with him, when he asks you to prepare his 2013 tax return.

Assume that you have correctly computed the incomes under Division B for 2013 as follows:

Mr. Jennings	$55,000
Mrs. Jennings	Nil
Son, age 19	8,000
Son, age 15	2,000
Daughter, age 14	1,800

Medical expenses for 2012:

February	Prescription drugs for daughter	$ 20
May	Doctor's bill paid for son, 15	15*
June	Chiropractor's bill for the past year	1150*
July	Glasses for Mr. and Mrs. Jennings	300
		$1,485

Medical expenses to March 31, 2014:

February	Orthodontist fee for daughter		$2,550
March	Expenses relating to older son's car accident:		
	Hospital	$1,500	
	Surgery	1,000	
	Drugs	200	2,700*

Additional expenses anticipated by May 31, 2014:

(a) Additional medical bills from son's accident	$ 750*
(b) Eyeglasses for his younger son and daughter ($225 each)	450
(c) Dental bills (2/3 for Mr. & Mrs. Jennings)	375
(d) Chiropractor's bill for the past year	1,050

* Excess over provincial plan payments.

— *REQUIRED*

Discuss the tax implications of Mr. Jennings claiming the above medical expenses for each of 2013 and 2014. Assume that all income amounts for 2014 will be the same as those for 2013.

Problem 11

ITA: 82, 118, 118.8

Mr. and Mrs. Reid, ages 55 and 50, received the following income during 2013:

Mr. Reid:

Employment income (commission)	$15,000
Employment expenses	(13,000)
Investment income:	
Canadian interest	2,000
Dividends received (in Cdn. $):	
Canadian-resident public corporations	1,000
U.S. corporations (net of 15% withholding tax)	680

Mrs. Reid:

Employment income	54,000
Investment income:	
Canadian interest	1,000
Dividends received from Canadian-resident public corporations	2,000

— REQUIRED

Calculate Mrs. Reid's federal tax (ignoring the foreign tax credit) under the following situations:

(A) No election to include spousal dividends. ITA: 82(3)

(B) With an election to include spousal dividends. ITA: 82(3)

Problem 12

ITA: 118.5(1), 118.6; Income Tax Folio S1-F2-C2 — Tuition Tax Credit

Pamela is 38 years old and lives in Welland, Ontario. She commutes daily to Niagara University, in Niagara Falls, New York. She is completing a full-time Masters in Education that is 12 consecutive months in duration. Her tuition fees are the equivalent of C$20,000 per year.

— REQUIRED

(A) Advise Pamela if she can claim the tuition fees on her personal income tax return.

(B) Refer to part (a). Is Pamela eligible for the education and textbook credits?

Your answer should be supported with appropriate references to the Act.

Problem 13

ITA: 118.5; Income Tax Folio S1-F2-C2 — Tuition Tax Credit

Stuart presents to you the following information concerning tuition fees paid for 2011, 2012, and 2013.

2011	Harvard University, Masters in Business Administration, fall term	$15,000
2012	Harvard University, Masters in Business Administration, winter and fall terms	30,000
2013	Harvard University, Masters in Business Administration, winter term	15,000
	Re-read fee for failed course	300
	Make-up course at Harvard for failed course, July–August	3,000
	Income tax course at University of Toronto, fall term; the tuition fee of $500 was paid through a scholarship that Stuart received from his father's employer, Universal Exports Inc.	500
	Fitness course taken at a local secondary school in Ontario	35

— REQUIRED

Discuss the tax implications of the above tuition fee payments.

Problem 14

ITA: 117, 118, 121, 122.2, 122.5, 122.6–122.64, 180.1

Patty, a single parent of two children (ages nine and seven) works part-time as a clerk in a law office. She has provided you with the following information for 2013:

Income:	
Workers' Compensation payments	$ 9,000
Employment income (Subdivision a)	35,000
Cash dividend from Canadian-resident public corporations	480
University scholarship received	600
Expenses:	
Canada Pension Plan contributions	1,559
Employment Insurance contributions	658
Cost of subsidized day care for the children (three days a week)	2,400
University tuition paid for a three-month evening course	600

Patty receives the Workers' Compensation payment because of the accidental death of her husband two years ago. Her two minor children have no income.

Patty had $700 of tax withheld from her employment income and has paid no income tax instalments.

— REQUIRED

(A) Based on the information above, compute Patty's total federal and provincial tax for 2013 and her tax refund or balance due.

(B) Determine if Patty is eligible for the refundable goods and service tax credit and Canada Child Tax Benefit. Explain.

Problem 15

ITA: Division B, C, E

Clare and Alan, both age 70, widowers, and retired successful businesspeople, love to argue. The one fact that they agree upon is that they pay too much income tax. They both receive $6,500 of Old Age Security and $9,000 of Canada Pension Plan payments each year. Clare has $52,000 of income from a registered pension plan. Alan receives $52,000 in dividends from the active business income taxed at the low rate in his incorporated business, a CCPC, which is now managed by his son.

— REQUIRED

Determine which one of the two pays the most federal income tax for 2013. ITA: 82(3)

Problem 16

ITA: Division E, E.1

Dawn, a client of yours, generally has employment income from her company and some investment income. In early 2013, you arranged Dawn's affairs such that she would crystallize her $500,000 capital gains exemption on qualified small business corporation shares. For 2013, her income is estimated as follows:

Employment income (CPP $1,931)	$ 42,500
Interest	12,800
Dividends from Canadian-resident public corporations	20,000
Gross-up @ 38%	7,600
Taxable capital gains	250,000
Interest expense	(10,000)
RRSP contribution	(14,500)
Capital gains deduction	(250,000)
Taxable income	$ 58,400

— REQUIRED

Calculate what effect, if any, minimum tax will have on Dawn's 2013 federal tax payable.

[For more problems and solutions thereto, see the DVD accompanying this book.]

Chapter 11

Computation of Taxable Income and Tax After General Reductions for Corporations

TOPICS DISCUSSED

LEARNING GOALS

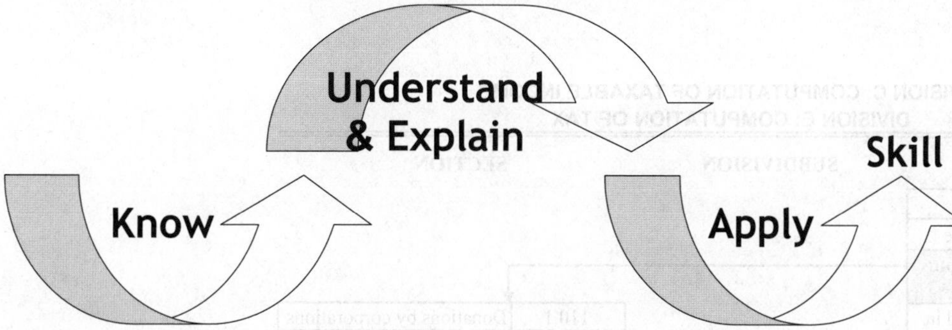

Know

By the end of this chapter you should know the key provisions used in the calculation of the taxable income and the basic tax, net of some general tax credits, for a corporation. Completing the Review Questions (¶11,800) and Multiple Choice Questions (¶11,825) is a good way to learn the technical provisions

Understand and Explain

You should understand and be able to explain:

- how to compute taxable income for a corporation;
- why most Canadian-source inter-corporate dividends are deducted in the calculation of taxable income, after having been included in Division B income for tax purposes;
- how loss carryovers are restricted — particularly, after an acquisition of control;
- how federal corporate taxes are computed with an abatement for provincial taxes; and
- how and why certain tax credits are provided to corporations to reduce basic federal tax.

Completing the Exercises (¶11,850) is a good way to deepen your understanding of the material.

Apply

You should be able to apply your knowledge and understanding of the key provisions pertaining to the calculation of:

- taxable income for a corporation to evaluate the consequences of an acquisition of control and to decide on the best strategy for dealing with losses in that situation, and
- tax for a corporation to do a basic calculation of corporate tax.

Completing the Assignment Problems (¶11,875) is an excellent way to develop your ability to apply the material in increasingly complex situations.

OVERVIEW

In the computation of the taxable income of a corporation, several deductions may be taken from the net income for tax purposes determined in Division B of Part I of the Act. Three of these, namely, charitable donations, loss carryovers and intercompany dividends, are covered in the example problem material of this chapter. The computation of tax for a corporation is made under the provisions of Part I, Division E, Subdivisions b (which applies only to corporations) and c (which applies to all taxpayers). This chapter introduces the basic computation of tax for corporations. Next, several tax credits are introduced. Then two tax credits that are available to all taxpayers, including corporations and individuals, are presented with a focus on their applicability to corporations: the foreign tax deduction and the investment tax credit.

The following chart will help to position in the Act some of the major provisions dealt with in this Chapter.

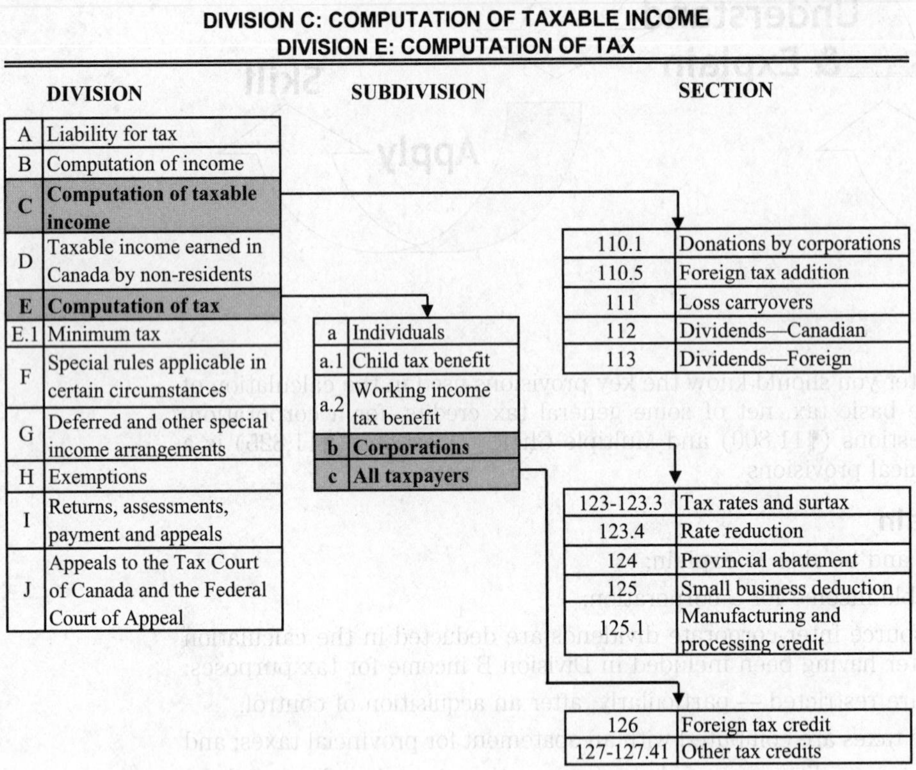

¶11,000 COMPUTATION OF TAXABLE INCOME FOR A CORPORATION

¶11,010 Overview

The aggregating formula included in section 3 of the Act applies to corporations as well as individuals. Generally, financial statements are prepared in accordance with GAAP and, therefore, the accounting income presented in the financial statements is income defined by GAAP. Canada required the adoption of International Financial Reporting Standards (IFRS) by public enterprises by 2011. As a result, the term "generally accepted accounting principles" (GAAP) for public enterprises will refer to IFRS. A private corporation may choose to use IFRS, but it is not required to do so. The alternative for a private corporation is to use Accounting Standards for Private Enterprise (ASPE).

From those financial statements, adjustments are required to reconcile accounting income to income for tax purposes. There can be many or few additions and deductions to determine the income for tax purposes. For example, accounting amortization is added to accounting income and then the allowable CCA is deducted to compute net income for tax purposes.

Computing net income for tax purposes for an incorporated business follows the same rules as computing net income for a proprietorship business. Incorporating a business does not mean that more expenses may be deducted. Sections 9 to 20 of Subdivision b apply to income or loss from a business or property. The vehicle in which the income is earned is irrelevant. A corporation, a trust, and an individual are all subject to the same basic rules.

The differences arise in Subdivisions d (Other Sources of Income) and e (Deductions in Computing Income) of the Act. For example, other sources of income, such as alimony and pension receipts, apply only to individuals. Likewise, deductions such as moving expenses and child care apply only to individuals. These amounts are considered personal rather than an expense incurred to earn business income.

The Subdivision c rules for computing taxable capital gains and allowable capital losses also apply to corporations. The only difference in the taxation of capital gains is that the capital gains deduction (section 110.6) applies to individuals only.

Recall that taxable income results from the deduction of certain amounts listed in Division C of Part I from net income for tax purposes computed under Division B of Part I. The following is the calculation of taxable income showing the different components of Division B income and the deduction of Division C deductions. ITA: 110.1, 111, 112

	Individuals	*Corporations*
Sources of Income:		
Employment	$xxx	$ — [1]
Business & property	xxx	xxx
Capital gains & losses	xxx	xxx
Other income	xxx	— [1]
Other deductions	(xxx)	— [1]
Division B Income	$xxx	$xxx
Division C Deductions	(xxx)	(xxx)
Taxable Income	$xxx	$xxx

[1] A corporation cannot earn employment income. Very few items of "other income" or "other deductions" pertain to most corporations.

Exhibit 11-1 lists the common Division C deductions and indicates which of these are available to corporations.

EXHIBIT 11-1
Selected Division C Deductions

Provisions	*Deduction*	*Individuals*	*Corporations*
Par. 110(1)(*d*), (*d*.1)	Employee stock options	X	
Par. 110(1)(*f*)	Deductions for certain social assistance payments	X	
Par. 110(1)(*j*)	Home relocation loan	X	
Par. 110.1(1)(*a*)	Charitable gifts*		X
Par. 110.1(1)(*a*.1)	Gifts of medicine		X
Par. 110.1(1)(*b*)	Gifts to Her Majesty*		X
Par. 110.1(1)(*c*)	Gifts of cultural property to institutions*		X
Par. 110.1(1)(*d*)	Ecological gifts*		X
Sec. 110.2	Lump-sum payments	X	
Sec. 110.6	Capital gains deduction	X	
Par. 111(1)(*a*)	Carryover of non-capital losses	X	X
Par. 111(1)(*b*)	Carryover of net capital losses	X	X
Par. 111(1)(*c*)	Carryover of restricted farm losses	X	X
Par. 111(1)(*d*)	Carryover of farm losses	X	X
Par. 111(1)(*e*)	Carryover of limited partnership losses	X	X
Sec. 112	Dividends from Canadian corporations		X
Sec. 113	Dividends from foreign affiliates		X

* Non-refundable tax credits available in subsection 118.1(3) for an individual.

¶11,020 Deduction of Taxable Dividends

Certain dividends received by a corporation are deductible in the calculation of its taxable income. This deduction offsets the inclusion of the dividend under Subdivision b of Division B, so that qualifying dividends have no effect on the taxable income of the corporation. The dividends that qualify for the deduction are from: ITA: 112(1)

(a) taxable Canadian corporations; ITA: 112(1)(*a*)

(b) taxable subsidiary corporations resident in Canada; ITA: 112(1)(*b*)

(c) non-resident corporations carrying on business in Canada and, hence, taxable in Canada; and ITA: 112(2)

(d) foreign affiliates which have been appropriately taxed in a foreign jurisdiction which has a treaty with Canada. ITA: 113

¶11,025 Purpose

The purpose of the deduction is to prevent the double taxation of corporate income. When dividends are paid, the source of the dividends is usually after-tax retained earnings of the payer corporation. If a recipient corporation were to pay tax on the dividends it receives, the income that gave rise to the dividends would effectively be taxed twice. A provision prevents that second imposition of tax at the level of the recipient corporation. In fact, retained earnings can, in many cases, be flowed through any number of shareholder corporations in the form of taxable dividends without attracting tax under Part I. When the retained earnings are ultimately paid as dividends to an individual shareholder, the dividend gross-up ITA: 112(1) and tax-credit mechanism will operate to reduce, at the individual taxpayer level, the potential double taxation of income generated by a corporation.

¶11,025.10 *Concept of integration of individual and corporate tax on income*

The dividend deduction for corporate shareholders is the second building block of the theory of integration. The first building block, the dividend gross-up and tax credit for individual shareholders, was previously discussed in Chapters 6 and 10. The function of the dividend deduction for a corporation is to remove some of the potential multiple taxation of dividend income as the income moves through a series or chain of corporations.

Simply stated, the integration concept, discussed in more detail in Chapter 12, requires that a tax system should be designed so that a taxpayer is indifferent (i.e., pays the same amount of tax), no matter what type of entity or person earns the income. In the context of corporations and their shareholders under a perfectly integrated tax system, the total tax burden should be identical whether the individual receives the income directly or indirectly, as a shareholder, from dividends through the corporate structure.

The Canadian income tax system is not perfectly integrated. Near perfect integration occurs numerically where the combined corporate rate of tax (federal and provincial) is equal to:

- 20% [15.3% for dividends paid after 2013, as proposed in the March 2013 federal Budget] for Canadian-controlled private corporations on their business and investment income eligible for a low rate of tax, and
- about 28% for Canadian-resident corporations on their income subject to the higher general rate of tax.

However, even at these rates there are flaws in the system. For example, the dividend tax credit should represent the underlying tax paid by the corporation. However, under our present income tax system, even when the corporation has not paid any tax due to losses, for example, shareholders still receive a dividend tax credit.

¶11,025.20 *Application of the concept of integration*

To illustrate the corporate dividend deduction aspect of integration, assume that there is a chain of three taxable Canadian corporations: A Ltd., a Canadian-resident public corporation, owns 100% of B Ltd., which in turn owns 100% of C Ltd. Also, assume that each of the corporations is taxed at a combined rate of 28%, and the individual shareholders of A Ltd. are all taxed at a combined rate of 40%; all of the after-tax income is passed up to the next level in the form of eligible dividends, i.e., eligible for the 38% gross-up and tax credit in the hands of an individual shareholder. In the absence of a corporate deduction for dividends received from another corporation the following would result.

Person	*Income*	*Tax*	*Dividend*
C Ltd.	$1,000	$280	$720
B Ltd.	720	202	518
A Ltd.	518	145	373
Shareholders of A Ltd.	515*	62**	311***
		$689	

* $373 × 1.38 (i.e., the grossed-up dividend)
** ($515 × .40) – ((.15 + .13) × $515) = $62 where .13 reflects the provincial dividend tax credit.
*** Cash received (i.e., $373 – $62).

The result of this example is that on the $1,000 of income initially earned by C Ltd., the ultimate tax burden is $689. The dividend deduction, as discussed above, eliminates the corporate tax in both B Ltd. and C Ltd. The tax burden remaining would be composed of the $280 on the income earned initially by C Ltd. and the tax of $120 on the $994 grossed-up dividend received by the individual shareholders calculated as follows:

Dividend received by shareholders of A Ltd.	$ 720
Gross-up (.38 × $720)	274
Grossed-up dividend	$ 994
Tax @ 40%	$ 398
Dividend tax credit @ (15% federal + 13% provincial) of $994	(278)
Net tax on shareholders of A Ltd.	$ 120

The total income tax is now $400 (i.e., $280 corporation + $120 shareholder) compared to $689. If the total tax (corporate and personal) is $400, integration is perfect at these rates since the tax on $1,000 of income earned by an individual in the 40% tax bracket would be $400. For perfect integration, the total of the corporate tax and the tax on the individual shareholder has to be $400, in this example. Therefore, if the corporate tax rate were higher than 28%, the net rate of tax on the individual shareholder would have to be less than 12% after the dividend tax credit.

¶11,025.30 *Conclusion*

From the above example, one can conclude that where dividend income flows through a series of corporations there will be only two incidents of income tax. Initially, the corporation that earns the business or property income will pay income tax and eventually the individual shareholder who receives the income in the form of a dividend will also pay some income tax. In the next chapter, the topic of integration will be expanded even further with different corporate rates and other factors.

¶11,030 Dividends paid from untaxed income

Over the years, the intercorporate dividend deduction has created problems which the government has attempted to rectify. For example, a corporation may pay a dividend from income that was not taxed in the payer corporation. This might occur when income for accounting purposes is higher than income for tax purposes, due to a more rapid write-off of assets for tax purposes. The utilization of carried over losses may also offset income, so that some amounts that are distributed as dividends may not be taxed fully in the corporation that pays the dividend. This is usually due to timing differences between the payment of the dividend and the offset of losses. In these cases, there is a breakdown of the assumption that underlies the intercorporate dividend deduction, namely, that the dividend deduction prevents double taxation because the income that gave rise to the dividends *was* taxed in the payer corporation. This problem is compounded when individual shareholders gross up the dividends and deduct a dividend tax credit, on the assumption that the payer corporation or a predecessor corporation paid tax on the income it distributed as dividends. The purpose and effect of the dividend gross-up and tax-credit mechanism will be discussed more fully in the next chapter.

¶11,035 "After-tax financing"

Another problem that is linked with the intercorporate dividend deduction occurs when what has become known as "after-tax financing" is undertaken. A corporation that has generated losses in the past may not find debt financing attractive. This is because the deduction for interest expense provides no immediate tax relief where the corporation does not have to pay tax currently. Instead, the interest expense deduction merely increases the corporation's non-capital losses which may be deductible in the future or may expire. Alternatively, a corporation with unused losses could issue preferred shares to another corporation, such as a financial institution, to obtain the necessary financing. The result is that the corporation that issues the preferred shares will, obviously, not receive a deduction for dividends paid on the preferred shares. However, the financing corporation, because of the intercorporate dividend deduction, will not ordinarily pay tax on the dividends it receives. Consequently, because interest income is taxable and dividends are ordinarily not, the financing corporation may be prepared to lend funds at a rate lower than the market rate of interest. Rules are designed to eliminate the benefits of after-tax financing on "term preferred shares", "short-term preferred shares" and collateralized preferred shares. ITA: 248(1) ITA: 112(2.1)–(2.9)

¶11,040 Dividends paid on shares subsequently sold for a loss

The intercorporate dividend deduction is also linked to a potential problem when dividends are received on shares held by a corporation for a short period and subsequently sold at a loss. Such dividends would ordinarily be deductible in computing taxable income, or in the case of certain dividends (e.g., capital dividends), would be tax exempt. On the other hand, the loss on the disposition of the shares would be deductible as an allowable capital loss (if the shares were held as a capital property), or as a business loss (if the shares were held as inventory). It may be argued that, to some extent, the loss on disposition may have been caused by the payment of the dividend; for example, witness the normal decline in the value of shares after the ex-dividend date.

Consequently, there are rules that, when certain conditions are present, will reduce the corporation's capital loss or inventory loss by an amount equal to the aggregate of certain types of dividends received on such shares prior to the disposition. These rules are often referred to as "stop-loss rules". The loss reductions will occur if one of the following conditions is present: ITA: 112(3), 112(3.01), 112(4)

(a) the corporation owned the shares for less than 365 continuous days immediately prior to the disposition date, or

(b) the corporation owned more than 5% of the issued shares of any class of the capital stock on which the dividends were received.

The type of dividends that will reduce such capital losses are essentially taxable dividends (deductible in computing the corporation's taxable income), and tax-exempt capital dividends received on the shares during the period of ownership. Similarly, inventory losses are reduced by deductible taxable dividends received by any taxpayer-shareholder plus non-taxable dividends received. ITA: 112(3), 112(4)

¶11,050 Charitable Donations

While individuals are provided with a non-refundable tax credit for various donations, as discussed in Chapter 10, corporations are permitted a deduction in Division C. The types of donation that provide a corporation with this deduction are the same as the types of donation that provide an individual with a tax credit. Also, a corporation's deduction for gifts is, generally, limited to 75% of the corporation's net income for tax purposes under Division B. However, the deduction is limited to 100% of the amount of a taxable capital gain in respect of gifts of appreciated capital property. As well, the deduction limit is 100% of any CCA recapture arising on the gift of depreciable capital property. ITA: 110.1(1)

Any unused donations for a given year can be carried forward five years to be deducted in a carryforward year. The total claim for donations carried forward to a year and current ITA: 110.1(2) donations made in that year cannot exceed the Division B income limit. The maximum donation need not be deducted in a given year, such that undeducted amounts are available within the carryforward period. To be deducted, a donation must be proven, if necessary, by a receipt that contains prescribed information.

¶11,060 Loss Carryovers

The rules governing the deductibility of net capital losses and non-capital losses are the same for corporations and individuals. A capital loss carryover from the current year may be carried back to a prior year in which income included capital gains and non-capital losses. The capital loss would then be offset against the capital gain, reducing the amount of non-capital losses needed to minimize taxes payable for the prior year. This increases the non-capital losses available to be carried over into the current year. The carryforward of non-capital losses, restricted farm losses, and farm losses arising in the 2006 and subsequent taxation years is 20 years. ITA: 111

The following table shows the carryover period for net and non-capital losses.

	Back	Forward
Net capital loss	3	Indefinitely
Non-capital loss for years ending after December 31, 2005	3	20

¶11,065 Non-capital loss

A non-capital loss for a particular year, as it affects a corporation (for the purposes of this text), is generally defined to include: ITA: 111(8)

Aggregate of:			
losses from business			$ xxx
losses from property			xxx
allowable business investment losses			xxx
net capital losses deducted in the year			xxx
dividends deductible under sec. 112 (and certain other dividends)			xxx
			$ xxx (E)
Less aggregate of the amounts determined under par. 3(*c*):			
income from business		$ xxx	
income from property (including dividends deductible under sec. 112)		xxx	
income from other sources [secs. 56–59]		xxx	
taxable capital gains (other than from listed personal property)	$ xxx		
taxable net gains from listed personal property	xxx		
	$ xxx		
less: allowable capital losses (other than from listed personal property) in excess of allowable business investment losses that are included in allowable capital losses	(xxx)*	xxx *	
		$ xxx	

less: other deductions [secs. 60–66]	(xxx)	$ (xxx)*(F)
		$ xxx *
Less: farm loss (included in losses from business above)		(xxx) (D)
Non-capital loss		$ xxx *

* Cannot be negative.

This definition is designed to offset the current year's losses from various sources (items (E) and (D)) against the current year's income from other sources (item (F)). Then the balance or the unabsorbed excess loss can be carried over and deducted in another year. Non-capital losses and farming and fishing losses may be carried back three taxation years and forward 20 taxation years. To carry losses back to a taxation year for which a return has been filed, the corporation need only file one form (Schedule 4) and not a full, amended tax return. ITA: 111(1)(*d*), 111(8) ITA: 111(1)(*a*), 111(1)(*d*), 111(8)

Although a 20-year carryforward period is quite long, it is possible for carried-over losses to expire. Recognize that 20 years is a very long time for a business to sustain losses with no income earned to offset those losses. Most businesses would not last that long with those losses. However, planning should be undertaken to ensure that the losses are utilized within the carryover period. Income can be increased to absorb non-capital losses by omitting optional or permissive deductions such as capital cost allowances, cumulative eligible capital amounts, scientific research and experimental development expenditures or reserves. The deduction of these amounts can be deferred to future years when there is offsetting income.

The Canada Revenue Agency (CRA) usually permits the revision of a permissive deduction for a prior year. An Information Circular indicates that a letter to the director of the taxpayer's district taxation office that outlines the requested revisions will be sufficient if other conditions set out in paragraphs 9 and 10 are met. In addition, the corporation should consider the sale of unnecessary or redundant assets to generate income which could be used to absorb losses. The CRA may also allow the substitution of one type of loss for another, as long as the year in which the substitution is made is still open to assessment (as discussed in Chapter 14). For example, a non-capital loss may have been carried back to a year in which there was a net taxable capital gain. Subsequently, an allowable capital loss may arise. The resultant net capital loss may be carried back and substituted for the non-capital loss, leaving the freed non-capital loss available for carryforward. IC 84-1, par. 11

Example Problem 11-1

The operations of Balloons Ltd. generated the following data for its December 31, 2013 taxation year:

Business losses	$(60,000)
Dividends received and deducted under sec. 112	10,000
Bond interest	5,000
Allowable business investment loss	(3,000)
Taxable capital gains	15,000
Allowable capital losses	(7,000)
	$(40,000)

In its 2012 taxation year, its first profitable year in several, Balloons Ltd. had taxable income under Division C of $40,000.

— REQUIRED

Compute the non-capital loss for Balloons Ltd. in 2013 and determine the amount of that loss that can be carried back to 2012

— *SOLUTION*

Before calculating the non-capital loss for 2013, a review of the construction of section 3 income would be useful in understanding the basic concept. The following calculation reorganizes the above information using the ordering and application rules in section 3.

Par. 3(*a*)	Income — business	Nil	
	— property: dividends	$10,000	
	interest	5,000	$15,000
Par. 3(*b*)	Net taxable capital gains:		
	Taxable capital gains	$15,000	
	Allowable capital losses	(7,000)	8,000
Par. 3(*c*)	(No Subdivision e deductions taken)		$23,000
Par. 3(*d*)	Business loss	$60,000	
	Allowable business investment loss	3,000	(63,000)
Net income from Division B			Nil

Non-capital loss arising in 2013	
Business loss	$ 60,000
Allowable business investment loss	3,000
Dividends	10,000
	$ 73,000

Less: Par. 3(*c*) income (as shown above):					
Income from property					ITA: 3(*a*)
Bond interest	$ 5,000				
Dividends (see commentary below)	10,000	$15,000			
Net taxable capital gains					ITA: 3(*b*)
Taxable capital gains	$15,000				
Allowable capital loss	(7,000)	8,000	(23,000)		
Non-capital loss for 2013			$ 50,000		

Carryback of non-capital loss to 2012:

Lesser of:

(a) Non-capital loss (as calculated above)	$ 50,000
(b) Taxable income for 2012	$ 40,000

Thus, $40,000 of the 2013 non-capital loss could be carried back to 2012 leaving $10,000 to carry forward to 2014 through 2033.

Dividend income deductible in the calculation of a corporation's taxable income (i.e., $10,000), when added to the business loss and the allowable business investment loss, has the effect of offsetting the dividend income included in the paragraph 3(*c*) income under paragraph 3(*a*). As a result, this dividend income has no effect on the amount of losses available for carryover. As previously discussed, dividends are deductible to offset the dividend income inclusion and, therefore, have no effect on the taxable income of a corporation. Therefore, a similar adjustment is necessary to the non-capital loss calculation to remove the effect of the inclusion of these dividends in property income, as shown above. If the addition of taxable dividends to the business loss had not been made, the 2012 non-capital loss available for ITA: 12(1)(*j*), 112 carryover would have been only $40,000 (i.e., $60,000 + $3,000 – $23,000), not $50,000 as shown above.

¶11,070 Treatment of allowable business investment loss

A "business investment loss" is a capital loss that arises from the disposition of shares or debt of a "small business corporation". The concept of a small business corporation (SBC) is discussed in some detail in Chapter 13. A business investment loss (BIL) must arise from either an arm's length disposition of the shares and/or debt, establishing a debt to be bad, or a bankruptcy action. ITA: 39(1)(*c*), 248(1) "small business corporation" ITA: 50(1)

An "allowable business investment loss" (ABIL) is defined as ½ of a business investment loss. Unlike an allowable capital loss, an allowable business investment loss may, in the year in which it is realized, be deducted against any source of income. Hence, the deductibility of an allowable business investment loss is less restricted than an allowable capital loss. To the extent that it cannot be absorbed against these other sources of income in the year in which it is incurred, it becomes part of the aggregate of non-capital losses to be carried over in the manner discussed above. Furthermore, any amount of allowable business investment loss that cannot be utilized within the carryover period of a non-capital loss can be added to net capital losses which can be carried forward indefinitely as discussed next. See Figure 7-2 in ¶7,720 for a flow-chart summary of these rules. ITA: 3(*d*), 38(*c*)

Example Problem 11-2

The operations of Blyth Limited generated the following data for the year ended December 31, 2013:

Business investment loss on sale of shares	$116,000
Capital gains	4,000
Other capital losses	10,000
Other Division B income	30,000

— *REQUIRED*

Compute the taxable income of the corporation for 2013 and indicate the loss carryovers available for other years.

— *SOLUTION*

Par. 3(*a*)	Other Division B income		$30,000
Par. 3(*b*)	Taxable capital gains (½ × $4,000)	$ 2,000	
	Allowable capital losses (½ × $10,000)	(5,000)	Nil
Par. 3(*c*)	Income		$30,000
Par. 3(*d*)	Allowable business investment loss deductible (max: ½ × $116,000 = $58,000)		(30,000)
	Income and taxable income		Nil
	Net capital loss available for carryover		$ 3,000[(1)]
	Non-capital loss available for carryover		$28,000[(2)]

— *NOTES TO SOLUTION*

(1) (½ × $10,000 capital loss incurred in the year) *less* ($2,000 claimed in the year as an allowable capital loss) = $3,000.

(2) (½ × $116,000 business investment loss incurred in the year) *less* ($30,000 claimed in the year as an ABIL) = $28,000.

¶11,075 Net capital losses

¶11,075.10 *Definition*

For corporations, a "net capital loss" (net CL) is, essentially, the excess of allowable capital losses, excluding losses on listed personal property and allowable business investment losses, over taxable capital gains, including taxable net gains from listed personal property. ITA: 111(8)

This is given by the following computational format:

Allowable capital losses excluding losses on listed personal property and allowable business investment losses	(A)	$xxx
Less: taxable capital gains including taxable net gains from listed personal property	(B)	(xxx)
	(A – B)	$xxx
Add: allowable business investment loss unutilized in the tenth year of its carryforward as a non-capital loss (see comment in previous section)		xxx
Net capital loss		$xxx

The exclusion of allowable capital losses on listed personal property results from the fact that listed personal property losses are carried forward and back under Division B, not Division C, as are all other allowable capital losses. (See Chapter 7 for a more complete discussion.) The term "net gain" from listed personal property refers to the amount of taxable capital gain net of the application of any listed personal property current losses and loss carryovers.

¶11,075.20 *Adjustment for years with different inclusion rates*

Net capital losses can be carried back three taxation years and forward indefinitely. However, they can only be deducted to the extent of the excess, if any, of taxable capital gains over allowable capital losses in the carryover years. Rules which determine the amount that a person may deduct in respect of net capital losses are the result of the differing inclusion rates for capital gains and capital losses discussed in Chapter 10. ITA: 111(1.1)

The historical inclusion rates are as follows:

Prior to 1988	½
1988 and 1989	⅔
1990 to February 27, 2000	¾
February 28 to October 17, 2000	⅔
After October 17, 2000	½

The purpose of the rules is to ensure that the amount of net capital losses, carried forward or carried back from a taxation year with a particular inclusion rate, is converted to the inclusion rate of the taxation year in which the net capital losses are deducted. This is done by means of a formula as illustrated below.

Assume the following facts for a corporation which has $45,000 of net capital losses (representing ¾ of a $60,000 capital loss) realized in 1997 and available for carryforward:

	2000	2001
Capital gains realized	$60,000	$10,000
Capital losses realized	(10,000)	(4,000)
Net capital gains	$50,000	$ 6,000
Inclusion rate for the year	2/3*	1/2

* After February 27, 2000 and before October 18, 2000.

The following net capital losses could be deducted under par. 111(1)(*b*):

	2000	2001
Net taxable capital gain for the year	$33,333	$ 3,000
Net capital loss deduction under par. 111(1)(*b*) per ssec. 111(1.1) as computed below	(33,333)	(3,000)
Effect on taxable income	Nil	Nil

The limit on the net capital loss deduction is given by: ITA: 111(1.1)

	2000	2001
Lesser of:		
(a) Net taxable capital gain for the year	$33,333	$ 3,000
(b) $A \times \frac{B}{C}$		
Where A = net capital loss from a loss year available for deduction in the particular year (see below)	$45,000	$ 7,500
B = inclusion rate in particular year of deduction	2/3	1/2
C = inclusion rate in loss year	3/4	3/4
$45,000 × 2/3 / 3/4	$40,000	
$7,500 × 1/2 / 3/4		$ 5,000
Net capital loss deduction (lesser amount)	$33,333	$ 3,000

ITA: 3(*b*)

Note that the denominator C in the fraction B/C, in effect, divides the net capital loss A by the inclusion rate of the loss year. Thus, when the 1997 net capital loss of $45,000, which is a 3/4 amount, is divided by 3/4, the result is $60,000, which was the full capital loss in 1997. Then, B, which is the inclusion rate for the year in which the loss is being deducted, is multiplied by the full loss, the result is 2/3 of $60,000, or $40,000, which is the net capital loss for 2000.

To deal with the carryover of these losses conceptually, it may be easier to carry full amounts of capital losses realized either back or forward against full gains in the carryover year. Then the appropriate inclusion rate could be applied to the net full gains in the carryover year. Unfortunately, as discussed below, the definition of net capital loss (i.e., the amount available for carryover) is given in terms of the fractional allowable capital losses.

The amount of net capital loss realized in 1997 and deducted in 2000 and 2001 and, hence, the amount of net capital loss available for carryforward after 2001 can be reconciled as follows:

	Capital loss (gross amount)	*Net capital loss at 1997 inclusion rate of 3/4*	*Adjustment factor B/C*	*Adjusted net capital loss deducted*
Loss realized in 1997	$60,000	$45,000		
Loss deducted in 2000 limited to net gains realized in the year	(50,000)	(37,500)	2/3 / 3/4	$33,333

Loss available in 2001	$10,000	$ 7,500		
Loss deducted in 2001 limited to net gains realized in the year	(6,000)	(4,500)	½ / ¾	$ 3,000
Loss available after 2001	$ 4,000	$ 3,000	½ / ¾	$ 2,000

¶11,080 Restrictions and ordering of deductions

A taxpayer can choose how much, if any, of its previously unclaimed carried-over losses to deduct in a particular year and in which order to deduct such losses and other Division C deductions. However, the taxpayer must deduct a loss of a particular type (that is, non-capital loss, net capital loss, restricted farm loss or farm loss) in the chronological order in which the loss was incurred. Logic would suggest that those deductions in Division C, which are more restricted in their deductibility, be claimed as soon as possible and before those deductions which are less restricted. ITA: 111(3)

There are two basic types of restriction on losses available for carryover.

(1) The first is a restriction on the type of income against which the loss carryover can be deducted. This type of restriction is often referred to as "streaming".

(2) The other is a restriction on the number of years a loss can be carried over.

For example, a net capital loss can only be applied against net taxable capital gains, but is unrestricted as to carryforward time. A non-capital loss can be applied against any source of income, but is time-restricted. A restricted farm loss is restricted both as to the type of income against which it can be applied and to time. Therefore, restricted farm losses should usually be deducted first. Between net capital losses and non-capital losses, the decision depends on whether taxable capital gains are anticipated. If there are current taxable capital gains and an examination of the corporation's balance sheet indicates no accrued or prospective capital gains, then net capital losses should probably be deducted before non-capital losses.

EXHIBIT 11-2
Summary for Carryover Rules for Division C Deductions

Type of deduction	*Type of income applied against*	*Carryover Back*	*Carryover Forward*
Dividends	Any type	*	*
Donations	Any type	0	5
Net capital losses	Net taxable capital gains	3	Indefinitely
Non-capital losses	Any type	3	20**
Restricted farm losses	Farm income	3	20**
Farm losses	Any type	3	20**

Application of Division C deductions

Consider: (1) Type of income the deduction can be applied against.
(2) Number of years available in the carryover period.
(3) The likelihood that the type of income needed will arise in the carryover period.

Generally apply most restrictive first.

* Technically, no carryover rule applies specifically to dividends, although they have an impact on the non-capital loss carryover balance.

** 20 for taxation years ending after 2005.

¶11,085 Choice to deduct net capital losses to preserve non-capital losses

Item E in the definition of non-capital loss enables taxpayers, at their option, to deduct net capital losses to preserve non-capital losses. The purpose of this choice is to correct a long-standing anomaly in the legislation which inadvertently penalized taxpayers in certain specific situations, as shown in the example below. Whether a taxpayer decides to utilize this option depends upon whether the corporation is expected to generate, in the near future, adequate business income or taxable capital gains. ITA: 111(8)

The non-capital loss can be increased by the amount of any net capital loss actually deducted for that year. The only restriction on the deduction of a net capital loss is that there is a net taxable capital gain in the year that is at least equal to the net capital loss being deducted. For example, assume that a corporation (or an individual) has a business loss of $100,000, a net taxable capital gain of $40,000 and an adjusted net capital loss of $60,000 carry forward. The tax consequences are as follows:

Par. 3(*a*): Income from business	Nil
Par. 3(*b*): Net taxable capital gain	$ 40,000
	$ 40,000
Less: Subdivision e deductions	Nil
Par. 3(*c*):	$ 40,000
Par. 3(*d*): Business loss	(100,000)
Par. 3(*f*): Division B income	Nil

If the definition of non-capital loss did not contain the addition for net capital losses deducted, a corporation could deduct $40,000 of the net capital loss of $60,000 (equal to the net taxable capital gain) but would not do so because such a deduction would have no impact upon the taxable income which would still be zero. In addition, if the $40,000 was deducted, the taxpayer would no longer have a potential use of the $40,000 net capital loss in the future when the taxpayer is in a taxable position. ITA: 3(*b*), 111(8)

The non-capital loss without the addition would be:

Par. 3(*d*): Business loss	$ 100,000
Par. 3(*c*): — see above calculation	(40,000)
Non-capital loss	$ 60,000

The result is that the net taxable capital gain has been used to offset the business loss resulting in a lower non-capital loss (i.e., $60,000 versus $100,000). The taxpayer may or may not be happy with this result depending upon the taxpayer's expected future income sources. Since net capital losses can only be applied to net taxable capital gains (i.e., $40,000) a potential net capital loss deduction has been blocked by the current business loss of $100,000.

The addition of deducted net capital losses to the non-capital loss balance provides a positive tax consequence to claiming a net capital loss deduction, even though the deduction has no impact upon the taxable income as shown below.

Division B income — see previous sec. 3 computation	Nil	
Division C — net capital loss deduction limited to par. 3(*b*) amount	$(40,000)	ITA: 111(1)(*b*)
Taxable income	Nil	

However, as a result of the deduction of net capital losses, the non-capital loss is increased by a net capital loss deducted:

Par. 3(*d*): Business loss	$100,000
Add: Net capital loss deducted in the year	40,000
	$140,000
Less: Par. 3(*c*) balance — see above	40,000
	$100,000

The result is that $40,000 of the net capital loss carryover has been deducted under Division C to offset the $40,000 of net taxable capital gain under paragraph 3(*b*). This preserves the full $100,000 of business loss to be carried over as a non-capital loss, which can be deducted from any source of income in a carryover year.

Example Problem 11-3

The following data summarize the operations of Parliamentary Fertilizers Limited, a Canadian-controlled private corporation, for the years 2010 to 2013 ended December 31.

	2010	*2011*	*2012*	*2013*
Income (loss): fertilizer business	$ 62,500	$(187,500)	$75,000	$100,000
Dividend income — taxable Cdn. corporation	37,500	62,500	12,500	—
Capital gains (losses)	25,000	(50,000)	7,500	12,000
Charitable donations made	(18,750)	(10,000)	(12,500)	(6,000)
Income (loss): other business	7,500	(20,000)	2,500	5,000
Income (loss) per financial accounting statements	$113,750	$(205,000)	$85,000	$111,000

The corporation has a net capital loss balance of $18,750 which arose in 1997.

— *REQUIRED*

Calculate the taxable income of the company for each of the years indicated, on the assumption that future other business income and taxable capital gains are uncertain, and tabulate the losses available for carryover at the end of 2013. (For the purposes of this type of problem, dealing with each item, line by line, across the years, will help keep track of carryovers more easily than dealing with income one year at a time.)

— *SOLUTION*

		2010	*2011*	*2012*	*2013*
Par. 3(*a*)	Income from business				
	— fertilizer	$ 62,500	— (1)	$75,000	$100,000
	— other	7,500	— (1)	2,500	5,000
	Income from property	37,500	$ 62,500	12,500	
		$107,500	$ 62,500	$90,000	$105,000
Par. 3(*b*)	Taxable capital gain	12,500	—	3,750	6,000
	Allowable capital loss		(2)		
Par. 3(*c*)	Total	$120,000	$ 62,500	$93,750	$111,000
Par. 3(*d*)	Loss from business				
	— fertilizer	—	(187,500)(3)	—	—
	— other	—	(20,000)		
	Income for the year(4)	$120,000	Nil(3)	$93,750	$111,000
Sec. 112	Dividends from taxable Canadian corporations	(37,500)(5)	— (6)	(12,500)(5)	—
		$ 82,500	Nil	$81,250	$111,000
Sec. 110.1	Donations made				
	— carryover	—	—	(10,000)	—
	— current	(18,750)	—	(12,500)(7)	(6,000)
		$ 63,750	Nil	$58,750	$105,000

		2010	2011	2012	2013
Par. 111(1)(*b*)	Net capital losses	(12,500)[8]	—	(3,750)[8]	(6,000)[8]
		$ 51,250	Nil	$55,000	$ 99,000
Par. 111(1)(*a*)	Non-capital losses	(51,250)[9]	—	(55,000)[9]	(99,000)[9]
	Taxable income	Nil	Nil	Nil	Nil

— NOTES TO SOLUTION

[1] Items aggregated from the various non-capital sources under paragraph 3(*a*) cannot be negative. Losses from these sources are deducted under paragraph 3(*d*).

[2] Allowable capital losses are only deductible to the extent of taxable capital gains under paragraph 3(*b*). The remainder is available for carryover to another year.

[3] Losses from the various non-capital sources and from allowable business investment losses are only deductible under paragraph 3(*d*). However, the net income amounts after the deductions in paragraph 3(*d*) cannot be negative. Note that the excess of the deductions in paragraph 3(*d*) over the aggregate income in paragraph 3(*c*) is only one component of the addition to the non-capital loss carryover balance computed below.

[4] Income for the year cannot be negative. There is no statutory order in which Division C deductions must be taken. However, the time and source restrictions of loss carryovers, as previously discussed, should be taken into account. In addition, where the income under Division B is not large enough to cover all potential Division C deductions, then the dividend deduction under section 112 should always be taken first. Dividends from taxable Canadian corporations are the only Division C deduction for corporations which do not have a carryover clause.

[5] Dividends from taxable Canadian corporations should be deducted first in case there is not enough income for any further Division C deductions. Undeducted dividends cannot be carried over.

[6] A deduction in the computation of taxable income should not be taken if it reduces the balance to a negative number, since normally negative taxable income has no meaning. The one exception to this rule is in respect of net capital losses which can be added to the non-capital loss balance if they are deducted in a particular year.

[7] The deduction of charitable donations is limited to 75% of Division B income for the year. Donations not deducted in the year they are made, can be carried forward to the next five taxation years. However, the Division B income limitation applies to the sum of donations carried forward and current donations. Since the unused donations of a particular taxation year have a time restriction of 5 years, it would be advisable to claim them prior to claiming current year donations.

[8] Deductions for net capital loss carryovers are restricted to the extent of the net taxable capital gains included in paragraph 3(*b*) for the carryover year.

Subsection 111(1.1) adjusts the 2010 net capital loss deduction by a formula which corrects for the fact that in the loss year (1997) the inclusion rate for capital gains was three-quarters, while in the year that the loss is being claimed (i.e., 2010) the inclusion rate is one-half.

Lesser of (a) amount under par. 3(*b*) in 2010	$12,500
(b) $A \times \frac{B}{C}$ = $18,750 × ½ / ¾ = ...	$12,500

where: A is the amount of the net capital loss available (i.e., $18,750) from 1997 (the loss year),

B is the ½ inclusion rate for the deduction year (i.e., 2010), and

C is the ¾ inclusion rate for the loss year (i.e., 1997).

Since the inclusion rate is the same for 2011 and 2012, no adjustment is necessary for the 2011 capital loss:

Net capital loss for 2011 (½ × $50,000)	$25,000
Loss deductible to the extent of net capital gains under par. 3(*b*):	
2012 — limited to TCG	(3,750)
	$21,250
2013 — limited to TCG	(6,000)
Remaining carryforward	$15,250

(9) "Non-capital loss" is computed for carryforward in: ITA: 111(8)

	2010	*2011*	*2012*	*2013*
Sum of:				
(a) loss from business or property	Nil	$207,500	Nil	Nil
(b) ABIL	Nil	Nil	Nil	Nil
(c) dividends deductible under sec. 112	$ 37,500	62,500	$ 12,500	Nil
(d) net capital loss deducted	12,500	Nil	3,750	$ 6,000
	$ 50,000	$270,000	$ 16,250	$ 6,000
Less:				
(e) par. 3(*c*) total	(120,000)	(62,500)	(93,750)	(111,000)
Non-capital loss for the year	Nil	$207,500	Nil	Nil
Non-capital loss carryforward balance:				
Non-capital loss carryforward to the year	Nil	Nil	$156,250	$101,250
Added in the year	Nil	$207,500	Nil	Nil
Applied	Nil	(51,250)*	(55,000)	(99,000)
Non-capital loss carryforward balance	Nil	$156,250	$101,250	$ 2,250

* Carried back to 2010.

¶11,090 Acquisition of Control of a Corporation and Its Effect on Losses

¶11,095 Conceptual overview

When control of the corporation is acquired by another person or another group of persons, a corporation's ability to carry forward or carry back non-capital losses or farm losses is severely restricted. In addition, net capital losses, losses from property and allowable business investment losses (ABILs) that are unutilized at the time of the acquisition of control may not be carried forward — they simply expire. ITA: 111(4), 111(5), 111(5.1), 111(5.2), 111(5.3)

The loss utilization restrictions become operative when control of a corporation is acquired by another person or another group of persons. The acquisition of control is considered to occur when control over the voting rights (i.e., *de jure* or legal control that exists where more than 50% of the votes necessary to elect the Board of Directors is held) of the corporation is acquired by a person or group of persons. While it is clear that control refers to voting control, some uncertainty exists as to how the CRA will interpret the phrase "group of persons" for the purposes of these rules. The CRA has indicated that it will look for evidence of a group's intention to "act in concert" to control a corporation. IT-302R3, pars. 3–6

[The March 2013 federal Budget proposes to introduce an anti-avoidance rule that will, generally, apply to acquisitions of shares after March 20, 2013. This rule will apply the acquisition of control provisions where two conditions are met:

(1) a person or group of persons acquires shares of a corporation that have more than 75% of the fair market value of all of the shares of the corporation without acquiring legal control; and

(2) it is reasonable to conclude that one of the main reasons that legal control was not acquired was to avoid the loss restriction rules imposed by an acquisition of legal control.

Where the two conditions of the proposed provision apply, the person or group is deemed to acquire control of the corporation and the restrictions on losses that result from an acquisition of legal control will apply. The effect of this proposal is to expand the concept of control, beyond legal control, for the purposes of the acquisition of control restrictions.]

Corporations are often unable to generate appropriate or sufficient income to utilize losses and, hence, are unable to recover taxes previously paid or reduce taxes payable. Consequently, such loss corporations become attractive targets for acquisition by profitable corporations which, through a variety of strategies, could shelter their income from tax by utilizing the losses of the acquired corporation. Because such strategies ultimately result in reduced tax revenues, the government, understandably, does not view such transactions with favour. As a result, over the years the government has introduced increasingly restrictive legislation to curb such transactions which are sometimes referred to as "tax-loss trading".

Two of the more common loss utilization strategies are outlined as follows:

(1) In the first, after control of the loss corporation is acquired, the operations of the income-earning acquirer corporation and the loss corporation are restructured so that income is generated in the latter corporation. For example, the assets of a profitable business or division in the income-generating corporation are transferred to the loss corporation. Usually the transfer will be accomplished by means of a tax-free rollover by moving profit-generating assets to the loss corporation. The income that is so generated is used to absorb the losses of the loss corporation. ITA: 85(1)

(2) The second strategy involves implementing intercompany transactions which produce expense deductions to the income-generating corporation while generating income for the loss corporation. Interest on loans, rental contracts, management contracts, and commission contracts are examples of such intercompany transactions.

The government has considered changes to the current approach to utilizing tax losses within corporate groups, including a more formalized system of loss transfers or some form of consolidated reporting. Consultations with the business community and the provinces, both of which are affected, did not result in agreement on an acceptable approach. The March 2013 federal Budget announced that this is not a current priority.

The current legislative restrictions which are aimed at curtailing the utilization of tax losses, are based on certain transactions and events which are deemed to occur when there has been an acquisition of control. These transactions and events, as well as other rules that comprise the restrictions, are discussed below.

¶11,100 Deemed year-end

The corporation is deemed to have a taxation year-end immediately before the time of the acquisition of control of the corporation (referred to hereinafter as the "deemed taxation year-end"). The result is that various adjustments that are normally made at a year-end, are required to be made before the acquisition of control. For example, the requirement that inventory be valued at the lower of cost or market at a taxation year-end will cause any accrued losses in inventory to be realized. This adjustment will increase the corporation's pre-acquisition non-capital losses or farm losses. As will be explained later, such pre-acquisition losses are available for carryforward, but only after certain restrictive conditions are satisfied. The advent of the deemed year-end causes other adjustments (discussed below) to increase the corporation's pre-acquisition of control non-capital losses and farm losses. ITA: 249(4) ITA: 10; ITR: 1801

As a result of the deemed year-end, the corporation is required to satisfy the normal compliance requirements of filing tax returns, reviewing unpaid amounts, determining the status of charitable donations and loss carryovers and their carryforward period, etc. ITA: 78(1), 78(4)

However, a short taxation year that may result from an acquisition of control will not advance the replacement period required to benefit from the rollovers available for an involuntary or voluntary disposition. These rollovers allow a full 24 months and 12 months after an ITA: 13(4), 44(1) involuntary and voluntary disposition, respectively, from the end of the short taxation year in which such a disposition occurs.

Unless the deemed year-end coincides with the corporation's normal year-end, the corporation may have two taxation years lasting less than 24 months in total. To illustrate this, assume that a corporation whose normal taxation year-end is December 31, experiences an acquisition of control on April 1, 2013. The corporation will have a deemed year-end of March 31, 2013. If the corporation chooses to return to its original taxation year-end of December 31, the corporation will have two taxation years ending in the 12-month period ending December 31, 2013. The first taxation year will be three months long, the second nine months long. If the corporation chose a date for its subsequent taxation years to be, say, March 31, as permitted, it would then have two taxation years lasting a total of only 15 months — namely, the deemed taxation year ending on March 31, 2013 will be 3 months long and the taxation year ending March 31, 2014 will be 12 months long. The foregoing example can be illustrated with the following diagram: ITA: 249(4), 249(4)(*d*)

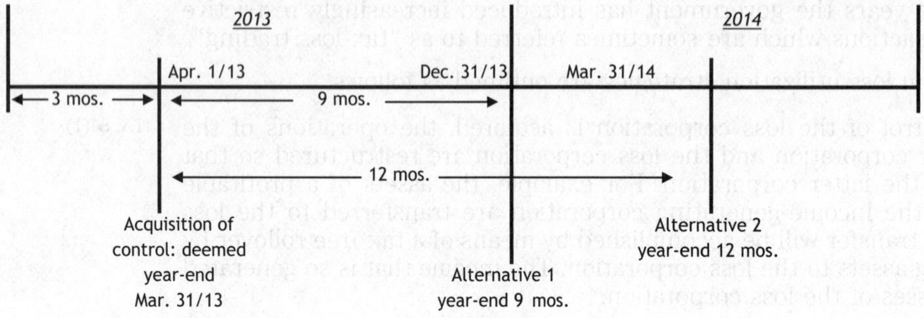

The upshot of this is that the normal 276-month (3 years back plus 20 years forward) carryover period for non-capital losses is reduced. This, in itself, represents a constraint in that the corporation has a shorter period over which to generate income to utilize the losses. A short taxation year will also cause any capital cost allowance or small business deduction (discussed in Chapter 12) to be proportionately reduced.

¶11,105 Accrued or unrealized losses on inventory

A taxpayer is required to value its inventory at the end of each taxation year. The Act requires that each item of inventory be valued at the lower of cost and market (LCM), while the Regulations permit valuation at the fair market value of the entire inventory. Either way, the result is that any accrued or unrealized inventory losses are realized in the deemed taxation year, thus, decreasing the taxpayer's income or increasing its non-capital losses or farm losses in the pre-acquisition period. ITA: 10(1) ITR: 1801

¶11,110 Accrued or unrealized losses on accounts receivable

The restrictions and their consequences that apply to accrued inventory losses are parallelled in the provisions that relate to accrued losses on accounts receivable. The largest amount that a corporation could deduct as a reserve for doubtful accounts for each separate trade receivable, must be claimed as an actual bad debt in the deemed taxation year. That is, where there has been an acquisition of control, the normal method of computing a reserve by aging the accounts and applying a fixed percentage to each age category is not permitted. Instead, each debt must be considered individually as to its collectibility and, if collection is doubtful, the debt must be written off as a bad debt. The amount deducted is deemed to be a separate debt and any amount or amounts subsequently received in respect of the separate debt must be included in income. ITA: 20(1)(*l*), 20(1)(*p*) ITA: 111(5.3) IT-442R, par. 24 ITA: 12(1)(*i*)

As is the case in accrued inventory losses, accrued losses on accounts receivable become part of time-limited non-capital or farm losses, which are deductible only if certain restrictive conditions are satisfied.

¶11,115 Accrued or unrealized losses on depreciable capital property

Accrued or unrealized losses on depreciable capital property are measured as the amount by which:

(a) the undepreciated capital cost (UCC), at the deemed year end, in a prescribed class

exceeds the aggregate of:

(b) the fair market value of all the property in the class at the deemed year end, plus

(c) any capital cost allowance (CCA) and any terminal losses deducted in that class in the deemed taxation year. ITA: 111(5.1)

The excess is deemed to be claimed as a capital cost allowance deduction from income for the deemed taxation year. Thus, the corporation's income/loss for the deemed taxation year is increased or decreased accordingly. Where there is a loss, the ultimate effect is to increase the corporation's pre-acquisition non-capital losses or farm losses. At the same time, the balance of the undepreciated capital cost is reduced by the amount of the excess. ITA: 20(1)(*a*), 111(5.1)

The restrictive aspects of the rule are, therefore, as follows:

- first, an accrued loss (i.e., unclaimed capital cost allowance) that would otherwise not be subject to any time limitation, as far as its deductibility is concerned, becomes part of a time-limited non-capital loss or farm loss;
- second, the corporation commences the first post-acquisition of control taxation year with a reduced undepreciated capital cost balance in the particular class.

¶11,120 Accrued or unrealized losses on eligible capital property

Rules that deem accrued or unrealized losses on eligible capital property to be realized apply in much the same way as the rules, discussed above, that apply to depreciable capital property. The accrued or unrealized losses on eligible capital property are measured as the amount by which: ITA: 111(5.2)

(a) the cumulative eligible capital (CEC) balance of a particular business at the deemed year-end

exceeds the aggregate of:

(b) three-quarters[1] of the fair market value, at the deemed year-end, of the eligible capital property of the business, plus

(c) any amount deducted, in respect of that business (cumulative eligible capital amount) in the deemed taxation year. ITA: 20(1)(*b*)

The consequences of these rules that apply to eligible capital property are similar to those that apply to depreciable property with respect to the time restrictions that affect non-capital losses and farm losses, as well as the impact that the adjustment has on the cumulative eligible capital balance of the corporation in the first taxation year after the acquisition of control.

¶11,125 Accrued or unrealized losses on non-depreciable capital property

Accrued or unrealized capital losses on non-depreciable capital property are deemed to have been realized at the deemed taxation year-end. The accrued losses are measured as the excess of: ITA: 111(4)(*c*), 111(4)(*d*)

(a) the adjusted cost base (ACB)

over

(b) the fair market value,

[1] The three-quarters fraction is used in order to place components (a) and (b) of the formula on a common basis, since the CEC balance is a ¾ amount, based on original cost that has been amortized.

at the deemed year-end, of each non-depreciable capital property (e.g., marketable securities, land used in the business) of the corporation. These rules result in the following:

- first, the capital losses that are so triggered, offset any capital gains produced in the deemed taxation year or increase any existing net capital losses of the corporation;
- second, the adjusted cost base of each affected capital property is reduced by the amount of the applicable excess.

Therefore, any deemed realized allowable capital losses that cannot be utilized against taxable capital gains realized in the deemed taxation year become part of the corporation's net capital losses immediately before the acquisition of control. If nothing further is done, these allowable capital losses, now embedded in the net capital loss balance, will expire. However, there are two possible remedies to this situation. First, the net capital losses can be deducted in arriving at taxable income for the deemed taxation year to the extent of net taxable capital gains in that year. As previously discussed, these deducted net capital losses will increase the non-capital loss balance. However, a further set of restrictions (discussed later in the chapter) is imposed on the utilization of non-capital losses on an acquisition of control. The second alternative is to create elective taxable capital gains to offset the deemed allowable capital losses as described in the next section.

¶11,130 Elective capital gains and recapture

¶11,130.10 *Election range*

A corporation is permitted to elect to have a deemed disposition for any depreciable or non-depreciable capital property on which capital gains or recapture have accrued. The objective of the elective provision is to permit the corporation to trigger capital gains or recapture, which is income from business, to reduce the amount of net capital losses or non-capital losses that would otherwise expire on account of the acquisition of control. Upon making the election, the corporation must also choose (i.e., designate) an amount to represent the deemed proceeds of disposition. The designated amount or deemed proceeds must be equal to the lesser of: ITA: 111(4)(*e*)

(a) the fair market value of the property; and

(b) the greater of:

(i) the adjusted cost base of the property, and

(ii) an amount designated (or chosen) by the corporation.

The effect of the above rule is that the corporation can choose proceeds of disposition (amount designated) at any point between fair market value and the adjusted cost base of the particular capital property. This rule also prevents the designated amount from being greater than the fair market value of the property. In addition, the designated amount (proceeds of disposition) cannot be less than the adjusted cost base (capital cost in respect of depreciable property). Note that the election is not available where an accrued terminal loss exists since that loss is deemed to be realized automatically. However, the above formula does allow a corporation to elect proceeds of disposition which would trigger recapture on depreciable capital property. ITA: 111(5.1)

¶11,130.20 *Partial election*

In determining the partial amount which should be designated where there are losses about to expire, the following formula should be used to trigger a taxable capital gain. This taxable capital gain should be sufficient to offset expiring losses. The elected proceeds will be: ITA: 111(4)(*e*)

the sum of:

(a) 2 (based on a ½ inclusion rate) times the sum of:

(i) any allowable capital loss arising in the deemed taxation year about to expire,

(ii) the net capital losses about to expire, and

(iii) the sum of the property losses and ABILs about to expire; and

(b) the adjusted cost bases of the properties chosen to be elected upon.

The taxable capital gain, using the above deemed proceeds of disposition, should result in the utilization of all of the losses about to expire upon the acquisition of control.

This procedure of creating only enough taxable capital gains to offset the property losses and capital losses about to expire also optimizes the step-up in the cost base of an asset elected upon as discussed below. In addition, this minimum elected amount preserves the business losses which can be utilized after the acquisition of control.

In summary, the deemed proceeds on the asset(s) chosen to be elected upon can be determined as follows:

Deemed proceeds of disposition	=	2 × ((i) + (ii) + (iii)) (as described above)	+	the ACB(s) of properties chosen to be elected upon

¶11,130.30 *Consequences of the election*

The properties and amounts elected upon must be designated in the corporation's tax return for the deemed taxation year. While a corporation will focus mainly on the capital gain implications of an election, an election made in respect of a depreciable capital property may, also, give rise to recaptured capital cost allowance which may affect the non-capital losses of the corporation. Consequently, both the capital gain and recaptured capital cost allowance implications must be carefully considered when an election is contemplated. ITA: 111(4)(*e*)

The rules also provide for a deemed reacquisition of the depreciable or non-depreciable capital properties that are elected upon. A non-depreciable capital property is deemed to be reacquired at a cost equal to the amount of the deemed proceeds of disposition. For the purpose of computing future capital gains or losses, a depreciable capital property is deemed to be reacquired at a cost equal to the amount of the deemed proceeds of disposition. On the other hand, for the purpose of determining future capital cost allowance and recapture amounts, a depreciable capital property is deemed to be reacquired at a cost equal to the amount that is the capital cost plus the realized taxable capital gain (i.e., ½ of the capital gain elected). Thus, the increase in the base for capital cost allowance is limited to the amount of the gain that has been included in income, i.e., the taxable capital gain plus recapture. ITA: 111(4)(*e*) ITA: 13(7)(*f*)

Where the deemed proceeds give rise to recapture, but no capital gain is triggered at the same time, the capital cost is deemed to be that amount immediately before the disposition (original capital cost). Capital cost allowance is deemed to have been taken equal to the excess of the original capital cost over the deemed proceeds calculated according to the formula described above. The result of this provision is to retain the original capital cost for purposes of future recapture calculations and to prevent double counting of the recapture recognized on the exercise of the election. ITA: 111(4)(*e*)(iii), 111(4)(*e*)(iv)

Example

Mentors Inc. needs to trigger enough income to offset the expiry of $10,000 of property losses just prior to an acquisition of control. Mentors Inc. has already elected and designated an amount equal to the accrued capital gain on all the other capital and depreciable assets. The only asset remaining is a depreciable one that has a capital cost of $70,000, an undepreciated capital cost of $35,000 and fair market value of $60,000.

Obviously, there is no accrued capital gain on the depreciable asset. In fact, there has been a decline in value. Capital losses are denied on depreciable assets, because a decline in value is handled through the CCA system. There is, however, potential recapture to a current maximum amount of $25,000 (i.e., $35,000 – $60,000), depending upon the designated amount or proceeds of disposition. Therefore, Mentors Inc. may attempt to designate, in this fact situation, an amount of $45,000 as the proceeds of disposition so that a desired $10,000 of recapture will be triggered. ITA: 39(1)(*b*)(i)

In this case, however, the elected amount or deemed proceeds must be equal to the lesser of:

(a) the fair market value of the asset		$60,000	
(b) the greater of:			$60,000
(i) the ACB of the asset	$70,000		
		$70,000	
(ii) the amount designated	$45,000		

As a result of the formula, the full $25,000 of recapture must be included in income, calculated as: ITA: 111(4)(*e*)

UCC		$35,000
Less: the lower of:		
(a) capital cost	$70,000	
(b) proceeds	60,000	60,000
Recapture		$25,000

Therefore, in some cases, it may not be worthwhile to elect, because all of the unrealized recapture will be triggered.

From the perspective of the Mentors Inc., the capital cost is deemed to be the original capital cost of the acquired corporation, i.e., $70,000. In addition, Mentors Inc. is deemed to have taken capital cost allowance equal to the difference between the capital cost of $70,000 and the proceeds of $60,000. The effect of these two deeming provisions is to make Mentors Inc. assume responsibility for the remaining potential recapture of $10,000. The undepreciated capital cost, on which future capital cost allowance may be computed, is now set at $60,000.

¶11,135 Allowable business investment losses and losses from property

As a general rule, non-capital losses include allowable business investment losses (ABILs) and losses from property. However, when there has been an acquisition of control of a corporation, the rules restrict the carryover of non-capital losses or farm losses to those losses which can reasonably be attributed to the carrying on of a business. As a result, unutilized allowable business investment losses and losses from property expire after the deemed taxation year and must be removed from the non-capital loss balance. Even ABILs and property losses created in years prior to the acquisition of control are removed from the non-capital loss balance. ITA: 111(5)

¶11,140 Unused charitable contributions

A corporation's unused charitable contributions cease to be deductible after the deemed year-end resulting from an acquisition of control. Furthermore, the deduction of a gift of property made after an acquisition of control is denied if the property was owned at the time of the acquisition of control and it was expected that a gift of the property would be made after the acquisition of control. The purpose of these provisions is to discourage charitable deduction trading transactions. ITA: 110.1 (1.2)

¶11,145 Deductibility of non-capital losses after an acquisition of control

¶11,145.10 *Requirement that the loss business be carried on with a reasonable expectation of profit*

Non-capital losses and farm losses carried forward to taxation years beyond the deemed taxation year are deductible only if the following conditions are satisfied: ITA: 111(5)(*a*)(i)

(i) the business that generated the losses must be carried on throughout the year in which the corporation seeks to make a deduction for non-capital losses or farm losses; and ITA: 111(1)(*a*), 111(1)(*d*)

(ii) the particular business must be carried on for profit or with a reasonable expectation of profit.

An important feature of this rule is that the legislation identifies the non-capital losses and farm losses with a particular business. Note that the word "business" is not synonymous with the word "corporation"; that is, a corporation can carry on more than one business.

With regard to the condition (ii), above, there are no guidelines in the Act dealing with the "expectation of profit" test in this context. Accordingly, there is some uncertainty as to how the CRA will apply this test. One court case on the issue is *Garage Montplaisir Ltée v. M.N.R.*, where the Court discovered that the acquisition of the loss corporation was for the purpose of eliminating a competitor, not for the purpose of earning income from the loss business. On appeal to the Federal Court–Trial Division, it was found that there was no evidence that the taxpayer had continued to carry on any significant part of the loss business "for profit or with a reasonable expectation of profit". The latter decision was affirmed by the Federal Court of Appeal. It would be advisable to develop a turnaround plan for the loss business to help establish a "reasonable expectation of profit". The checklist in Exhibit 4-3 can be consulted in the development of that plan.

92 DTC 2317 (T.C.C.)

96 DTC 6557 (F.C.T.D.)

2001 DTC 5366 (F.C.A.)

¶11,145.20 *Requirement that non-capital losses must be applied only against income from the same or similar products or services*

The principle of identifying non-capital losses and farm losses with a particular business is only the first step in determining the deductibility of these losses. As a second step in the determination, non-capital losses and farm losses that are carried forward beyond the deemed taxation year are deductible only against income generated by the particular business and by any other business substantially all of whose income is derived from the sale, leasing, rental or development of similar properties or the rendering of similar services. ITA: 111(5)(*a*)(ii); IT-302R3, par. 13

This other business is often referred to, generally, as a "similar" business, but the wording of the Act may be more restrictive in specifying "similar properties" or "similar services". The CRA's opinion of the meaning of the word "similar" in this context is interpreted as "of the same general nature or character". The determination is highly fact-dependent. IT-302R3, par. 14; IT-206R, par. 5

Note that, in addition to the more obvious horizontally integrated business, a vertically integrated business is also considered a similar business. It is not clear whether products or services from various stages of a vertically integrated business are considered to be similar for the purposes of this provision. The case of *Manac Inc. Corp. v. The Queen* presents facts to address this issue. Although the decision in this case was based on the "substantially all" condition in the provision, the court made the following comments on the vertical integration and the "similar properties" issue: "we do not see how property which loses its identity when incorporated into an end product can be described as property similar to the end product".[2] 98 DTC 6605 (F.C.A.)

In any case, only income from a business can be offset by losses that are carried over. The wording of the Act, therefore, precludes income from property, for example, from being offset by these carryover losses.

The principle of matching the losses of a particular business against income from that business or the income of similar products and services is sometimes referred to as "streaming". Because the stream of income against which the losses can be applied is limited, there is an increased possibility that losses will not be deductible in the appropriate carryover period. Hence, the principle of streaming is inherently restrictive as far as the utilization of losses is concerned.

[2] For a more liberal interpretation of a different set of facts, consider the case of *Crystal Beach Park Limited v. The Queen*, 2006 DTC 2845 (T.C.C.), in which the corporation redeveloped an amusement park property into a marina and condominium development, and utilized the park losses to offset profits from the redeveloped property. The Court concluded, at 2854, that "the business . . . was the exploitation of a recreational site".

¶11,150 Loss carryback rules

The preceding commentary focuses on the carryforward of non-capital losses and farm losses. In general, the restrictions that were described above apply with equal effect in situations where post-acquisition of control losses are carried back to a taxation year preceding the acquisition of control. Again, only income from a business can be offset by these carryover non-capital losses. ITA: 111(5)(*b*)

¶11,155 Summary and application

The effects of the restrictive legislation on loss utilization, following an acquisition of control, may be summarized as follows:

(a) net capital losses, allowable business investment losses, property losses and unused charitable contributions expire and are not carried forward beyond the deemed taxation year;

(b) accrued losses of various kinds are deemed to be realized and, thus, increase the amount of non-capital losses and farm losses of a corporation; as non-capital losses or farm losses, they are subject to time restrictions as to their deductibility; and

(c) the principle of streaming, which matches losses from a particular business against income from the particular business and a similar business, increases the likelihood that non-capital losses and farm losses will not be deductible within their carryforward periods.

Example Problem 11-4

Wonder Inc.'s tax return for its year ended December 31, 2012, showed the following balances in its loss accounts:

Type of Loss	*Balance*	*Year Incurred*
Net capital loss	$ 8,000	2009
Non-capital loss	$10,000	2010

During the period January to December 2013, Wonder Inc. earned business income of $1,000 per month, computed in accordance with the *Income Tax Act*. On April 1, 2013, an unrelated person acquired 51% of the voting shares of Wonder Inc.

— REQUIRED

Discuss the tax implications of the above information.

— SOLUTION

Legal control (greater than 50% of the voting shares) of Wonder Inc. has been acquired by an unrelated person. This has the following tax implications for Wonder Inc.: ITA: 256(7)(*a*)

(1) The taxation year of Wonder Inc. is deemed to have ended on March 31, 2013, being immediately before the acquisition of control. ITA: 249(4)(*a*)

(2) A new taxation year is deemed to begin April 1, 2013. ITA: 249(4)(*b*)

(3) Wonder Inc. can choose any date up to 53 weeks in the future as its new taxation year end. ITA: 249(4)(*d*)

(4) The net capital loss expires on March 31, 2013, and can never be deducted by Wonder Inc. after that date. ITA: 111(4)(*a*)

(5) The non-capital loss, to the extent that it is a loss from carrying on business (not a loss from a property source), can be deducted in future taxation years, provided the following tests are met:

(i) the business in which the loss was incurred is carried on at a profit or with a reasonable expectation of profit throughout the taxation year the loss is claimed, and ITA: 111(5)(*a*)(i)

(ii) the non-capital loss is deducted against income from the business that generated the non-capital loss and/or income from a business selling similar products or providing similar services. ITA: 111(5)(*a*)(ii)

Thus, Wonder Inc. will claim $3,000 of its non-capital loss to offset its taxable income (i.e., three months × $1,000) for the three-month deemed taxation year ended March 31, 2013. As to whether the remaining $7,000 will ever be deducted depends on point (5), above.

The net capital loss cannot be deducted in the deemed year ended March 31, 2013, as there are no capital gains to deduct it against. Since it expires on March 31, 2013, it will never be used.

Example Problem 11-5

On May 1, 2013, an unrelated person acquired 60% of the voting shares of Novell Inc. The values of the assets owned by Novell Inc. at May 1, 2013, were as follows:

Assets	*Cost*	*UCC/CEC*	*FMV*
Inventory	$10,000	N/A	$ 8,000
Accounts receivable	20,000	N/A	15,000
Equipment	30,000	$28,000	12,000
Marketable securities	40,000	N/A	10,000
Eligible capital property	50,000	36,000	42,000

In determining the value of the receivables, the collectibility of each debt was considered individually.

— *REQUIRED*

Which of the accrued (unrealized) losses in the above assets must be recognized by Novell Inc. in determining its income for tax purposes for the deemed year ended April 30, 2013?

— *SOLUTION*

The accrued loss in the inventory must be recognized. Inventory is valued at the lower of cost or market	$ 2,000	ITA: 10(1); ITR: 1801
The largest amount that Novell Inc. could deduct as a reserve for doubtful accounts for each trade receivable, must be claimed as a bad debt	5,000	ITA: 20(1)(*l*), 20(1)(*p*), 111(5.3)
The UCC of the equipment is reduced to $12,000. The reduction is deducted as CCA in the deemed year-end	16,000	ITA: 111(5.1)
The ACB of the marketable securities is reduced to $10,000. The reduction is deemed to be a capital loss in the deemed year-end. The allowable capital loss is $30,000 × 1/2 = $15,000 and is deductible only to the extent there are taxable capital gains in the deemed year ended April 30, 2013, or in any of the three preceding years. No such gains are evident in this case.		ITA: 111(4)(*c*), 111(4)(*d*)
The CEC for the eligible capital property is reduced to $31,500, being 3/4 × FMV ($42,000). The reduction is deducted as CECA in the deemed year-end	4,500	ITA: 111(5.2)
Total reduction to the business income of Novell Inc. for its deemed year ended April 30, 2013	$27,500	

Example Problem 11-6

Universal Ltd.'s tax return for its year ended December 31, 2013, showed the following balances in its loss accounts:

Type of Loss	*Balance*	*Year Incurred*
Net capital loss	$12,000*	1999
Non-capital loss	$10,000	2010

* In 1999 the capital gain inclusion rate was 75% so the adjusted net capital loss is $12,000 × 1/2 / 3/4 = $8,000, which is available for carry forward to 2013.

On June 1, 2013, an unrelated person acquired 75% of the voting shares of Universal Ltd. The accountant has calculated the business loss for the deemed year ended May 31, 2013, to be $25,000, including the accrued losses required to be recognized on the acquisition of control. The capital assets owned by Universal Ltd. at June 1, 2013, had the following values:

Capital Assets	*Cost*	*UCC/CEC*	*FMV*
Land	$ 40,000	N/A	$ 70,000
Building	60,000	$45,000	90,000
	$100,000		$160,000

The accountant is projecting income of $100,000 for Universal Ltd. over the next 12 months. The projected income is from the business that incurred the losses.

— *REQUIRED*

Universal Ltd. is considering making an election. Recommend the asset(s) that should be designated and the amount(s) which should be designated in the election. ITA: 111(4)(*e*)

— *SOLUTION*

Universal Ltd. should elect to recognize a taxable capital gain of $8,000 in order to utilize the $8,000 adjusted net capital loss expiring May 31, 2013. The election should be made on the land and not on the building as recapture would be incurred on the building. Such recapture would reduce the current (deemed) year's business loss and, thus, would be disadvantageous, because there would be $15,000 (i.e., $60,000 – $45,000 = $15,000 recapture) less in non-capital losses to carry forward to the next 20 years.

To trigger a $8,000 taxable capital gain on the land, proceeds of $56,000 should be designated. (Current ACB of the land ($40,000) + desired taxable capital gain grossed up to the full capital gain ($8,000 × 2) = $56,000). The resulting income under section 3 and taxable income for the year would be calculated as follows:

par. 3(*a*) income from business, property		$ Nil
par. 3(*b*) taxable capital gains ($56,000 – $40,000) × ½	$ 8,000	
allowable capital loss	0	8,000
par. 3(*c*)		$ 8,000
par. 3(*d*) loss from business	$(25,000)	
loss from property	0	(25,000)
Division B net income (technically cannot be negative)		$(17,000)
Division C deductions:		
Net capital losses (only restricted by par. 3(*b*) amount)		(8,000)
Non-capital losses		0
Non-capital loss for the deemed year ended May 31, 2013		$(25,000)

Universal has non-capital losses of $10,000 + $25,000 = $35,000 at May 31, 2013. This amount can be used to offset the prospective $100,000 of income from the business that generated the loss, if at least $35,000 of the income is actually earned. This is the same with or without the election. The advantage of the election is that the ACB of the land is bumped up to $56,000. The higher ACB of the land will reduce a future capital gain on a disposition. ITA: 111(4)(*e*)

Example Problem 11-7

Chandra Inc. is a ladies' shoe retailer with a December 31 year end. During its first fiscal year in 2011, the corporation incurred non-capital losses of $37,500 and capital losses of $4,000. On December 1, 2013, the voting shares of Chandra Inc. were sold to Maysha Ltd., a retailer of ladies' handbags, belts and costume jewellery. Maysha Ltd. is a well-established business that operates a number of profitable retail outlets.

Accounting and income tax data relating to Chandra Inc.'s operations from January 1 to November 30, 2013, were assembled for the purpose of the share-sale transaction. The data contained the following information:

(1) Loss from retail operations $12,500

(2) Long-term debt from Farrford Inc. written off (Farrford Inc., a small business corporation and manufacturer of ladies' shoes, was declared bankrupt on March 1, 2013) 12,000

(3) Values of various assets at November 30, 2013:

Assets	*Cost*	*UCC*	*FMV*
Inventory	$24,000	—	$22,000
Store fixtures and equipment	36,000	$35,000	30,000
Marketable securities	9,000	—	5,000
Land	86,000	—	126,000
Building (purchased new in 2011)	110,000	104,000	118,000

During the short year ended December 31, 2013, Chandra Inc. produced net income for tax purposes of $3,500. No other income or losses were incurred. Chandra Inc. chose to return to its December 31 year end for business reasons.

During its 2014 taxation year, the financing and marketing operations of Chandra Inc. were revamped and integrated with those of Maysha Ltd. As well, Chandra Inc.'s inventory was expanded to include merchandise carried in the Maysha Ltd. stores.

Chandra Inc.'s operations during the year ended December 31, 2014, produced the following income (losses):

Retailing operations — ladies' shoes	$ (5,000)
— handbags, belts, jewellery	12,000
Taxable capital gain on marketable securities	8,000

— *REQUIRED*

(A) Discuss the income tax implications of the acquisition of control of Chandra Inc. on December 1, 2013, ignoring all possible elections/options.

(B) Determine the income tax consequences of the acquisition of control of Chandra Inc. under the assumption that:

(i) the maximum amount of elections/options is utilized, and

(ii) the partial amount of all elections/options is utilized so that only enough income is generated to offset the losses which would otherwise expire in the acquisition of control.

For each of the above alternatives, determine the appropriate cost, undepreciated capital cost or adjusted cost base value for each of inventory, shop fixtures, marketable securities and paintings at December 1, 2013.

— *SOLUTION*

First, it is necessary to determine the losses and potential elections available at the deemed year-end as follows:

Losses from Non-Capital Sources and Potential Recapture		
Non-capital losses carried forward from 2012	$37,500	
Current-year losses from non-capital sources and ABIL:		
Retail operations	$12,500	
ABIL (Farrford Inc. loan: ½ × $12,000)	6,000	ITA: 38(1)(*c*), 39(1)(*c*), 50(1)
Inventory loss ($22,000 – $24,000)	2,000	ITA: 10(1); ITR: 1801
Deemed CCA on store fixtures ($30,000 – $35,000)	5,000	ITA: 111(5.1)
	$25,500	
Unrealized Capital Losses and Potential Capital Gains		
Potential election of recapture on building ($110,000 – $104,000)	$ 6,000	ITA: 111(4)(*e*)
Net capital losses carried forward from 2012 ($4,000 × ½)	$ 2,000	ITA: 111(1)(*b*), 111(8)

Current-year allowable capital losses:
Securities (½ × ($5,000 − $9,000)) . . . . $ 2,000 ITA: 111(5.1)

Potential election of taxable capital gain: ITA: 111(4)(*e*)
Land (½ × ($126,000 − $86,000)) $20,000

Building (½ × ($118,000 − $110,000)) . . . . $ 4,000

The preceding data can be summarized as follows:

carryforward losses	*non-capital losses*	*net capital losses*	*expiration after deemed year-end*
2012	$37,500	$2,000 →	$2,000

current deemed year-end losses	*from non-capital sources*	*allowable capital losses*	
securities		$2,000 →	$2,000
business – operations	$12,500		
– inventory	2,000		
– store fixtures	5,000		
	$19,500		
ABIL	$ 6,000 →		6,000
			$10,000

potential elections	*business income*	*taxable cap. gain*
recapture – building	$6,000	
TCG – land		$20,000
– building		4,000
		$24,000

The following statements will become evident from an understanding of how the system computes income for tax purposes and taxable income. With that understanding, the consequences of the acquisition of control can be determined from the above summary of the data.

General conclusion

(a) No election

If no election is made, there is no income to offset the current business loss of $19,500 or the non-capital loss carryforward of $37,500. Therefore the non-capital loss available to carry forward from November 30, 2013, is $57,000 (i.e., $19,500 + $37,500).

(b) Maximum election

If the maximum election is made, the $6,000 of recapture offsets or reduces the business loss, leaving $13,500 (i.e., $19,500 − $6,000) of net business loss. The $24,000 of taxable capital gain offsets the $10,000 of expiring losses, leaving $14,000 (i.e., $24,000 − $10,000) to offset the remaining $13,500 of business loss. There is still $500 (i.e., $14,000 − $13,500) of taxable capital gain which offsets some of the $37,500 non-capital loss carryforward. As a result, the non-capital loss available for carry forward from November 30, 2013, is $37,000.

(c) Partial election

If only a partial election is made to offset the $10,000 of expiring losses, the current business loss of $19,500 is not offset and, hence, is available to carry forward, along with the $37,500 of non-capital losses, from November 30, 2013 for a total of $57,000.

Specific analysis

(A) Compute the Division B income of Chandra Inc. for its taxation year deemed to end on November 30, 2013 as a result of the acquisition of control on December 1, 2013. Division B income is calculated, using the ordering rules in section 3, as follows: ITA: 249(4)

			No election
Par. 3(*a*): Income from non-capital sources (≧ 0)			Nil
Par. 3(*b*): Net taxable capital gains (≧ 0):			
Deemed taxable capital gain (elective):			
land		Nil	
building		Nil	
Accrued allowable capital loss (automatic):			
securities		$ (2,000)	Nil
Par. 3(*c*): par. 3(*a*) + par. 3(*b*)			Nil
Par. 3(*d*): Losses from non-capital sources and ABILs:			
Loss from retail operation		$(12,500)	
Deemed recapture (elective) on building		Nil	
ABIL — Farrford Inc. loan		(6,000)	
Accrued losses — Inventory (automatic)		(2,000)	
Deemed CCA — Store fixtures (automatic)		(5,000)	$(25,500)
Division B income			Nil
Optional net capital loss deducted			Nil
Non-capital loss deducted			Nil
Taxable income			Nil

Determine the relevant tax balances, at November 30, 2013, as follows:

		No election
Non-Capital Losses Available for Carryforward at Deemed Taxation Year Ended Nov. 30, 2013:		
Balance from Dec. 31, 2012		$ 37,500
Non-capital loss — Nov. 30, 2013:		
Par. 3(*d*) losses — see above	$ 25,500	
Add: net capital losses deducted	Nil	
	$ 25,500	
Less: par. 3(*c*) income — see above	Nil	25,500
		$ 63,000
Less: losses utilized at Nov. 30, 2013	Nil	
losses not utilized but expired: ABIL	$ 6,000	6,000
Available for carryforward from Nov. 30, 2013		$ 57,000
Net Capital Losses Available for Carryforward		Nil
Other Tax Balances:		
Inventory(1)		$ 22,000
Store fixtures(2) — UCC		$ 30,000
Marketable securities(3) — ACB		$ 5,000
Land(4) — ACB		$ 86,000
Building(5) — UCC		$ 104,000
ACB		$ 110,000

In the one-month taxation year ended December 31, 2013, Division B income is $3,500. This would allow a deduction of $3,500 from the non-capital loss balance carried forward from November 30, 2013, leaving a non-capital loss balance to carry forward from December 31, 2013, of $53,500 (i.e., $57,000 – $3,500). The $3,500 is deductible because the ladies' shoe retail business ("the particular business") was carried on throughout the year ending December 31, 2013, for profit. The non-capital loss is applied against income from the particular business. ITA: 111(1)(*a*)

Division B income for the full year ended December 31, 2014, is calculated, using the ordering rules in section 3, as follows:

Par. 3(*a*): Income from handbags, etc. retailing	$12,000
Par. 3(*b*): Taxable capital gains — securities	8,000
Par. 3(*c*): par. 3(*a*) + par. 3(*b*)	$20,000
Par. 3(*d*): Loss from shoes retailing	(5,000)
Division B income	$15,000

Non-capital losses available for carryforward from December 31, 2014, are computed under two possible assumptions as follows:

Assumption 1: The retailing of handbags, belts, jewellery is the sale of "similar" products.

Balance from Dec. 31, 2013 (see above)	$ 53,500
Less: Non-capital losses claimed against "streamed" income included in net income in the year	12,000(6)
Balance at Dec. 31, 2014	$ 41,500(7)

Assumption 2: The retailing of handbags, belts, jewellery is not the sale of "similar" products.

Balance from Dec. 31, 2013	$ 53,500
Less: Non-capital losses claimed against "streamed" income included in net income in the year	Nil(8)
Balance at Dec. 31, 2014	$ 53,500(9)

(B)(i) The analysis, in (A), above, of Division B income, non-capital losses available for carryforward from November 30, 2013, and the other tax balances is repeated under the assumption that all possible elections/options are utilized. The "no election" results, as determined above, are presented for comparative purposes.

		No election		Maximum election	
Par. 3(*a*):	Income from non-capital sources (≧ 0)		Nil		Nil
Par. 3(*b*):	Net taxable capital gains (≧ 0):				
	Deemed taxable capital gains (elective):				
	land	Nil		$ 20,000	
	building	Nil		4,000	
	Accrued allowable capital loss (automatic): securities	$ (2,000)	Nil	(2,000)	$ 22,000
Par. 3(*c*):	Par. 3(*a*) + par. 3(*b*)		Nil		$ 22,000
Par. 3(*d*):	Losses from non-capital sources and ABILs:				
	Loss from retail operations	$(12,500)		$(12,500)	
	Deemed recapture (elective): building	Nil		6,000	
	ABIL — Farrford Inc. loan	(6,000)		(6,000)	
	Accrued losses (automatic): inventory	(2,000)		(2,000)	
	Deemed CCA (automatic): store fixtures	(5,000)	$(25,500)	(5,000)	(19,500)
Division B income			Nil		$ 2,500
Optional net capital loss deducted			Nil		(2,000)(10)
Non-capital loss deducted			Nil		(500)
Taxable income			Nil		Nil

Determine the relevant tax balances, at November 30, 2013, as follows:

Non-Capital Losses Available for Carryforward at Deemed Taxation Year Ended Nov. 30, 2013:

	No election		Maximum election	
Balance from Dec. 31, 2012		$ 37,500		$ 37,500
Non-capital loss — Nov. 30, 2013:				
Par. 3(*d*) losses — see above	$ 25,500		$ 19,500	
Add: net capital losses deducted	Nil		2,000	
	$ 25,500		$ 21,500	

	No election		*Maximum election*	
Less: par. 3(*c*) income — see above	Nil	25,500	22,000	Nil
		$ 63,000		$ 37,500
Less: losses utilized at Nov. 30, 2013	Nil		$ 500	
losses not utilized but expired: ABIL	$ 6,000	6,000	Nil	500
Available for carryforward from Nov. 30, 2013		$ 57,000		$ 37,000
Net Capital Losses Available for Carryforward		Nil		Nil
Other Tax Balances:				
Inventory		$ 22,000		$ 22,000
Store fixtures — UCC		$ 30,000		$ 30,000
Marketable securities — ACB		$ 5,000		$ 5,000
Land — ACB		$ 86,000		$126,000[11]
Building — UCC		$104,000		$114,000[12]
— ACB		$110,000		$118,000[12]

Note how under the "no election" alternative, the non-capital loss balance is larger than in the "maximum election" alternative. However, under the latter alternative, the ACBs of the land and building and the UCC of the building are larger. Non-capital losses must be recovered by offsetting them against income in what remains of their 20-year carryforward. The ACBs of the land and building will be recovered on their sale. The UCC will be recovered through CCA at the Class 1 rate of 6% declining balance, since the building was purchased new in 2011. The better alternative depends on how optimistic the new owners are about generating enough income within the next 20 years to offset the non-capital losses. If they are optimistic, then the "no election" alternative is better, because the non-capital losses will shield income from tax more quickly than the CCA tax shield and the ACB. shield of capital gains on a disposition. Also, the 20-year carry-forward period gives the corporation a long time to become profitable. If it cannot generate profits of at least $57,000 in that time period, it may not stay in business sustaining continual losses.

(B)(ii) The amount of the partial election should be sufficient to offset the ABIL of $6,000, the allowable capital loss of $2,000 and the net capital loss of $2,000 that will expire if not used in the deemed taxation year. This requires income, therefore, of $10,000. Since creating recapture only serves to reduce the loss in paragraph 3(*d*) and a taxable capital gain is needed to offset the expiring allowable capital loss and net capital losses, a taxable capital gain of $10,000 should be created. This will require a capital gain of $20,000 (i.e., 2 × $10,000). If an election is made on the land to be deemed to have disposed of it at $106,000 (i.e., $86,000 + $20,000), a deemed taxable capital gain of $10,000 will result. None of the capital gain on the building should be elected, because, if the election is made, recapture will result, in addition to the capital gain, when an election is made for deemed proceeds above capital cost.

Under the assumption that a partial election of a capital gain of $20,000 is made on the land, the analysis, in (B)(i), above, of Division B income, non-capital losses available for carryforward from November 30, 2013 and the other tax balances is repeated. The "no election" and the "maximum election" results, as determined above, are presented for comparative purposes.

		No election		*Maximum election*		*Partial election*	
Par. 3(*a*):	Income from non-capital sources (≧ 0)		Nil		Nil		Nil
Par. 3(*b*):	Net taxable capital gains (≧ 0):						
	Deemed taxable capital gains (elective):						
	land	Nil		$ 20,000		$ 10,000	
	building	Nil		4,000		Nil	
	Accrued allowable capital loss (automatic):						
	securities	$ (2,000)	Nil	(2,000)	$22,000	(2,000)	$ 8,000

		No election		Maximum election		Partial election
Par. 3(*c*): Par. 3(*a*) + par. 3(*b*)		Nil		$22,000		$ 8,000
Par. 3(*d*): Losses from non-capital sources and ABILs:						
Loss from retail operations	$(12,500)		$(12,500)		$(12,500)	
Deemed recapture (elective): building	Nil		6,000		Nil	
ABIL — Farrford Inc. loan	(6,000)		(6,000)		(6,000)	
Accrued losses (automatic): inventory	(2,000)		(2,000)		(2,000)	
Deemed CCA (automatic): store fixtures	(5,000)	$(25,500)	(5,000)	(19,500)	(5,000)	(25,500)
Division B income		Nil		$ 2,500		Nil
Optional net capital loss deducted		Nil		(2,000)[10]		$(2,000)[10]
Non-capital loss deducted		Nil		(500)		Nil
Taxable income		Nil		Nil		Nil

Determine the relevant tax balances, at November 30, 2013, as follows:

Non-Capital Losses Available for Carryforward at Deemed Taxation Year Ended Nov. 30, 2013:

	No election		Maximum election		Partial election	
Balance from Dec. 31, 2012		$ 37,500		$ 37,500		$ 37,500
Non-capital loss — Nov. 30, 2013:						
Par. 3(*d*) losses — see above	$25,500		$19,500		$25,500	
Add: net capital losses deducted	Nil		2,000		2,000	
	$25,500		$21,500		$27,500	
Less: par. 3(*c*) income — see above	Nil	25,500	22,000	Nil	8,000	19,500[13]
		$ 63,000		$ 37,500		$ 57,000
Less: losses utilized at Nov. 30, 2013	Nil		$ 500		Nil	
losses not utilized but expired:						
ABIL	$ 6,000	6,000	Nil	500	Nil	Nil
Available for carryforward from Nov. 30, 2013		$ 57,000		$ 37,000		$ 57,000
Net Capital Losses Available for Carryforward		Nil		Nil		Nil
Other Tax Balances:						
Inventory		$ 22,000		$ 22,000		$ 22,000
Store fixtures — UCC		$ 30,000		$ 30,000		$ 30,000
Marketable securities — ACB		$ 5,000		$ 5,000		$ 5,000
Land — ACB		$ 86,000		$126,000		$106,000
Building — UCC		$104,000		$114,000		$104,000
ACB		$110,000		$118,000		$110,000

Note that the amount of non-capital losses available for carryforward of $57,000 under the "partial election" alternative is the same as the amount under the "no election" alternative. In the list of other tax balances, the only difference between the "partial election" and the "no election" alternatives is the ACB of the land which is higher for the "partial election" alternative. Therefore, the "partial election" alternative is better than the "no election" alternative.

Comparing the "maximum election" alternative with the "partial election" alternative, the amount of the non-capital losses available for carryforward under the "partial election" alternative is higher than the amount under the "maximum election" alternative, because some of the business losses of the deemed year end were offset by income elected under the maximum election option. However, the tax balances for the land and building are higher for the "maximum election" alternative. Only the increased UCC balance under the "maximum election" alternative shields income from tax immediately after the deemed year end through increased CCA. The maximum present value of the CCA shield from the increased UCC in Class 1 of $10,000 (i.e., $114,000 – $104,000) can be calculated by formula to be about $750, assuming a 20% corporate tax rate and a 10% rate of return (i.e., $C(d/(d + r))t = \$10,000 \times (.06/(.06 + .10)) \times .20 = \$750$). However, the increased non-capital loss balance is available to shield income from tax in the next 20 years. The better alternative depends on how optimistic the new owners of the corporation are in generating at least the additional $20,000 (i.e., $57,000 – $37,000) of income against which the additional non-capital losses available for carryforward can be offset in the next 20 years. Again, if they are not optimistic about turning the business profitable in the next 20 years, they may not be in business very long.

— *NOTES TO SOLUTION*

(1) The tax cost at December 1, 2013 is $22,000, being either the value based on LCM or FMV. ITA: 10(1); ITR: 1801

(2) The undepreciated capital cost balance at December 1, 2013 is $30,000, being the previous $35,000 undepreciated capital cost balance less the $5,000 excess that was deemed to be a deduction of capital cost allowance claimed in the year ending November 30, 2013. Capital cost allowance claimed for the short taxation years ended November 30, 2013, and December 31, 2013, must be prorated for the number of days in each of those taxation years. ITA: 20(1)(*a*), 111(5.1)

(3) The adjusted cost base balance at December 1, 2013, is $5,000, being the previous $9,000 adjusted cost base less the $4,000 excess which was deemed to be a capital loss in the year ending November 30, 2013.

(4) The adjusted cost base balance at December 1, 2013, remains at $86,000, since no election was made. ITA: 111(4)(*e*)

(5) The adjusted cost base at December 1, 2013, remains at $110,000 and the UCC remains at $104,000, since no election was made. ITA: 111(4)(*e*)

(6) The corporation's income for tax purposes for the year ending December 31, 2014, is $15,000 as computed by section 3. The corporation may apply the losses of the ladies' shoe retail business against the total of the corporation's *income* from that business and from the sale of similar products. The result of the aggregation is, therefore, $12,000, being nil from the ladies' shoe retail business plus $12,000 from the sale of similar products with the $8,000 taxable capital gain being excluded. Thus, the maximum deduction is $12,000. ITA: 111(5)(*a*)(ii)

(7) This amount is available for carryforward as follows:

2012 Dec. 31 non-capital loss balance:			
2012 non-capital loss		$37,500	
Less: Dec. 31, 2013 deduction	$ 3,500		
Dec. 31, 2014 deduction	12,000	15,500	$22,000
2013 Nov. 30 non-capital loss:			
Loss from retail operation		$12,500	
Deemed CCA — store fixtures		5,000	
Inventory loss		2,000	19,500
			$41,500

The 2012 loss expires on December 31, 2031, i.e., in 20 taxation years, including the deemed taxation year at November 30, 2013, and the one-month taxation year at December 31, 2013. The November 2013 loss expires on December 31, 2032, i.e., in 20 taxation years.

(8) The corporation's income for tax purposes for the year ending December 31, 2014, is $15,000. However, the corporation may make a deduction to the extent of nil under this assumption because the ladies' shoe retail business generated no income in the year and there was no income from the sale of similar products or services by the assumption made in this alternative. ITA: 111(5)(*a*)(ii)

(9) This amount is available for carryforward as follows, assuming a December 31 taxation year-end is chosen:

— $34,000 (being the 2012 loss of $37,500 – $3,500 claimed in the December 31, 2013 year) expires on December 31, 2030;

— $19,500 (see note (7)) expires on December 31, 2032, i.e., 20 taxation years.

(10) On the assumption that the optional net capital loss deduction is taken in order to increase the non-capital losses for the deemed taxation year.

(11) The adjusted cost base balance at December 1, 2013 is $126,000, being the deemed proceeds of disposition in the deemed disposition elected upon. ITA: 111(4)(*e*)

(12) The adjusted cost base balance (i.e., capital cost, in the case of depreciable property) at December 1, 2013, for future capital gains purposes, is $118,000, being deemed proceeds of disposition in the deemed disposition elected upon. The UCC $114,000 at the same date is increased by all of the recapture of $6,000, but only ½ of the capital gain of $8,000 elected as deemed proceeds on the deemed disposition, (i.e., $104,000 + $6,000 + ½ × $8,000). ITA: 13(7)(*f*), 111(4)(*e*)

(13) The addition of $19,500 to the non-capital loss balance is logical, since the $19,500 represents the loss from business sources for the deemed year-end.

Once an acquisition of control is recognized, the steps outlined in Exhibit 11-3 can be taken. An acquisition of control should be recognized, in its basic form, when shares of a corporation (or its parent corporation) are acquired by a third party that obtains control of the target corporation. While the rules apply even when a target corporation has no realized or unrealized losses at the time of the acquisition of control, the rules are designed to restrict the utilization of realized or unrealized losses where a purchaser acquires control of a loss company. The rationale is that the purchaser will not have taken the risks that generated the losses, particularly those that expire, and should not gain the benefit of the tax shields from those losses against the purchaser's income.

EXHIBIT 11-3
Acquisition of Control

Steps to Take

1. Deemed year-end on the day before

2. Determine any accrued losses and unrealized gains

- Realize "accrued" losses automatically
  - Terminal losses
  - Allowance for doubtful accounts
  - Capital losses
  - CEC losses
- Identify "accrued" gains for purposes of the election
  - Recapture
  - Capital gains

3. Determine the tax position of the company with the automatic realization of the accrued losses

- Calculate non-capital and net capital losses carried forward from previous years
- Calculate Division B income, using the ordering rules of section 3, and losses from non-capital sources and allowable capital losses for the year
- Identify expiring property losses, ABILs, and capital losses in the carryforward balances and in the deemed year
- Determine whether any losses that will survive the acquisition of control restrictions are likely to be utilized in their remaining carryover period

4. Consider election to create income

- Offset losses that will expire at the deemed year end, or
- Offset losses that may expire after the deemed year end
  - Due to carryforward period running out
  - Due to restrictions on use of carryforwards
- Avoid electing recapture that offsets losses that will survive the acquisition of control restrictions

5. Recalculate Division B and taxable incomes after the election

- Apply loss carryovers
- Determine which losses expire
  - Net capital losses
  - Non-capital losses
    - Property losses
    - ABILs
- Recalculate non-capital losses by year

6. Recalculate cost base of properties

- For purposes of
  - Capital gains
  - Recapture

7. Determine whether

- The loss business is being carried on with a reasonable expectation of profit, and
- The company is carrying on the same business or selling the same or similar products or services in order to see whether the losses being carried over can be applied against future income

8. Determine the steps needed to use up the non-capital loss carryovers with loss utilization planning tools

- Create a source of intercompany income in the loss company
- Transfer of income-producing assets
- Amalgamation
- Winding-up

The amounts computed in Steps 3 and 4 of Exhibit 11-3 can be summarized using the format shown in the solution to Example Problem 11-7 for reference in the election decision. In fact, the results of each election choice can be determined from that summary format.

¶11,160 Taxable Income of a Corporation in General

Recall that the starting point for the calculation of a corporation's taxable income is its net income for tax purpose computed under Division B. Where financial statements have been prepared using generally accepted accounting principles, it may be necessary to adjust income for financial accounting purposes to income for tax purposes as determined by Division B. This usually involves a reconciliation process, introduced in previous chapters. Generally, expenditures deducted for financial accounting purposes but not deductible for tax purposes, must be added to financial accounting income, and expenditures not deducted for financial accounting purposes but deductible for tax purposes may be deducted in the reconciliation. To perform this reconciliation in the preparation of a corporate tax return, Schedule 1 is completed. ITA: 110–112

Example Problem 11-8

FT Limited reported a net loss for financial accounting purposes of $53,000 for 2012 and a net income of $126,000 for 2013. It showed a provision for income taxes of $113,000 for 2013 only. Expenses deducted for financial accounting purposes in both years included: charitable donations of $15,000 per year, depreciation of $105,000 per year and bond discount amortization of $5,000 per year. The corporation included in financial accounting income, in both years, dividends from taxable Canadian corporations of $23,000 and dividends of $15,300 net of a 15% withholding tax from foreign corporations which were not foreign affiliates. The corporation had no capital gains in either year.

In 2012, capital cost allowance of $10,278 had been taken on a brick building purchased in 2009 (Class 1 (separate): 6%) leaving an undepreciated capital cost balance of $246,667 on January 1, 2013, the beginning of the 2013 taxation year. In addition, $44,800 in capital cost allowance had been taken on equipment leaving an undepreciated capital cost balance of $179,200 on January 1, 2013. In 2013, no additions or disposals were made to these classes of assets.

The corporation had non-capital losses of $18,000 available for carryover until 2026 and a 1999 net capital loss of $5,000 available for carryover.

— *REQUIRED*

Calculate the taxable income of the corporation for the years indicated.

— *SOLUTION*

		2012		2013	
Net income (loss) per financial statements		$(53,000)		$126,000	
Add items not deductible for tax purposes:					
Provision for income taxes(1)	—		$113,000		
Withholding tax on foreign dividends(2)	$ 2,700		2,700		
Charitable donations(3)	15,000		15,000		
Depreciation	105,000		105,000		
Amortized bond discount(4)	5,000	127,700	5,000	240,700	
Deduct items tax deductible:					
Capital cost allowances(5)		(55,078)		(50,640)	
Income for tax purposes		$ 19,622		$316,060	
Deductions in computation of taxable income:					
Inter-company dividends	$ 23,000(6)		$ 23,000		ITA: 112
Charitable donations					ITA: 110(1)(*a*)
— carried over	—		15,000(7)		
— current	Nil(7)		15,000(7)		
Non-capital loss carryover(8)	—		18,000		ITA: 111(1)(*a*)
Net capital loss carryover(9)	—	(23,000)	—	(71,000)	ITA: 111(1)(*b*)
Taxable income		Nil		$245,060	

—*NOTES TO SOLUTION*

(1) Income tax is not an expenditure made to produce income. It is an appropriation of profits after they have been earned.

(2) This is not an expenditure made to produce income for tax purposes, but an appropriation of profits after they have been earned. However, a foreign tax credit may be available in the computation of tax.

(3) Donations, normally, are not deductible in the computation of income, but are deductible in the computation of taxable income of a corporation.

(4) Bond discount amortizations are prohibited, but payments reflecting bond discounts are deductible at the earlier of redemption or maturity. ITA: 18(1)(*f*), 20(1)(*f*)

(5) Capital cost allowances for 2013 were computed as follows:

	Building Class 1: 6%	*Equipment Class 8: 20%*
2013: UCC, January 1, 2013	$246,667	$179,200
CCA for 2013 (total expense: $50,640) . . .	(14,800)	(35,840)
2014: UCC, January 1, 2014	$231,867	$143,360

(6) Even though $23,000 was deducted, only $19,622 of the dividends deducted have any effect since there is no loss carryover for dividends not deducted. Even where there is a loss from business and property, the addition to the non-capital losses of dividends deducted under section 112 is offset by the paragraph 3(*c*) income which in fact includes the dividends in question. The dividend deduction only neutralizes the paragraph 3(*c*) inclusion, as can be seen by a substitution of these numbers in the definition of non-capital loss. ITA: 111(8)

(7) The amount of charitable donations that may be deducted in a year is limited to 75% of income as computed in Division B of Part I. However, charitable donations not deducted in the current year can be carried forward five years. ITA: 110.1(1)(*a*)

(8) Non-capital losses would not be deducted in 2012, because after the dividends have been deducted, there is no income against which to absorb them in that year.

(9) Net capital loss carryovers cannot be deducted in 2012 and 2013 because there were no taxable capital gains against which to absorb them in these years. However, if there are net taxable capital gains available under paragraph 3(*b*) in the future or in the three years before 2012 (to the extent the taxable capital gains have not been offset by allowable capital losses), there is a potential increase in the non-capital losses at the taxpayer's discretion. The decision to utilize this option will depend upon which source of income will be generated first, business income or net taxable capital gains.

¶11,200 BASIC COMPUTATION OF TAX FOR ALL CORPORATIONS

¶11,210 Objectives of Provisions Affecting Taxation of Corporations

Although a corporation is regarded as a separate entity, in an economic sense the separation of a corporation and its shareholders may be artificial. However, the flexibility provided by corporations, often involving tax planning, has resulted in considerable complexity of the legislation pertaining to the taxation of corporations. This legislation appears to have three main objectives.

The first objective is the alleviation of the multiple taxation of corporate income by taxing income at the level of the corporation and, then, at the level of the shareholder on dividends received from after-tax corporate earnings. The Act attempts to integrate these two taxes primarily by way of the dividend gross-up and tax credit mechanism. If the system of integration were perfect, it would completely eliminate the double taxation of corporate income, as previously discussed at the beginning of this chapter and demonstrated in

Chapter 12. The Canadian system of integration is not perfect in this sense, but it does remove much of the effect of double taxation on investment income and some types of business income. The examination of this aspect will be continued in detail in the next chapter.

The second objective of these provisions is to prevent the avoidance of tax through the use of a corporation. In prior years, there was a considerable incentive to convert amounts that would normally be distributed to *individual* shareholders as dividends into amounts that resulted in capital gains. This was known as "dividend stripping" and many provisions were put in place to stop this practice. The incentive to convert dividends into capital gains was renewed with the introduction of the capital gains deduction which continues for shares of qualified small business corporations. Major anti-avoidance provisions are found in the Act. However, in making distributions to *corporate* shareholders, there has been an incentive to convert what might be taxed as a capital gain into a non-taxable intercorporate dividend. Hence, provisions to prevent such "capital gains stripping" have been implemented.

ITA: 55(2)

ITA: 110.6, 245, 246

The third objective of these provisions is to provide tax incentives to certain types of corporations. The small business deduction, which will be discussed in the next chapter, is probably the most important of these. The small business deduction will be shown to substantially reduce tax for a Canadian-controlled private corporation. The manufacturing and processing profits deduction will be alluded to. Investment tax credits, including the credit for scientific research expenditures, will be discussed.

¶11,212 Types of Corporations

The Canadian corporate tax system draws a distinction among types of corporations. For the purpose of this text, we need to consider three types:

- a private corporation;
- a Canadian-controlled private corporation; and
- a public corporation.

Certain tax preferences, such as the small business deduction, or tax accounts, such as the capital dividend account, apply to only certain types of corporations. Hence, the need to distinguish the types of corporations is important.

¶11,213 Private corporation

The Act defines a "private corporation" as one that is resident in Canada and not controlled by one or more public corporations (or a prescribed federal Crown corporation). A private corporation has certain tax preferences or considerations, as discussed in Chapter 12, such as a capital dividend account and a refundable dividend tax on hand account.

ITA: 89(1)

In public practice, much tax consulting work is done for private corporations, since they are more numerous than public corporations. Some types of private corporations enjoy the most favourable tax rates. Some tax credits are also more favourable for private corporations than for public corporations, such as the investment tax credit on scientific research and experimental development expenditures. Remember, private corporations include not only small and medium-sized companies; they include large-sized companies as well. There are numerous large private corporations operating in Canada — a prime example is McCain Foods, owned by the McCain family.

¶11,214 Canadian-controlled private corporation (CCPC)

A "CCPC" is defined as a private corporation that is a Canadian corporation that is not controlled, directly or indirectly, in any manner whatever, by one or more non-residents, by one or more public corporations, or by a combination of the two. Also, no class of its shares are listed on a designated stock exchange. Notice that the definition is negative. That is, there is no requirement that it be Canadian-controlled, it just cannot be controlled by non-residents or public corporations. Consequently, a Canadian private corporation that is controlled 50% by Canadian residents and 50% by non-residents is a CCPC.

ITA: 125(7)

One of the principal tax advantages of a CCPC is the small business deduction. From an individual's perspective, capital gains deduction eligibility is based on the corporation having CCPC status. Also, a CCPC and its shareholders enjoy the highest level of integration.

¶11,215 Public corporations

Public corporations are those resident in Canada and which have a class of shares listed on a "designated stock exchange" in Canada, as designated by the Minister of Finance. Public corporations do not enjoy any of the tax preferences available to private corporations. The tax system has become almost fully integrated at the public corporation level, as a result of the higher gross-up and the tax credit for eligible dividends. ITA: 89(1), 248(1), 262

¶11,216 Diagrammatic summary of types of corporations

Figure 11-1 shows the three basic types of corporations.

Figure 11-1
Types of Corporations

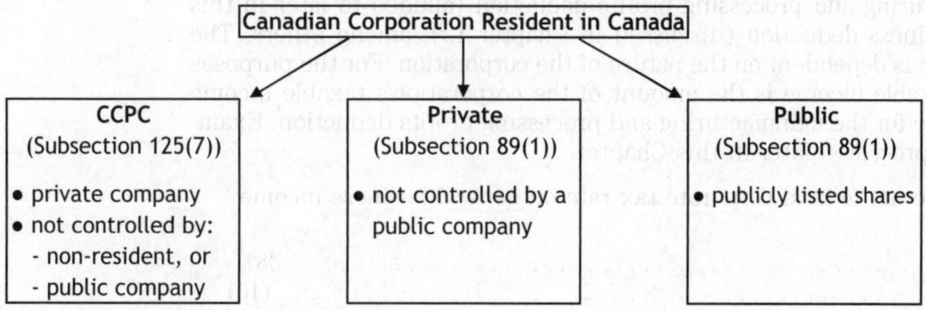

¶11,220 General Rates for Corporations

¶11,225 Overview of rates and credits

The general federal rate of tax to be paid on the taxable income of all corporations under Part I of the Act is 38%. However, the basic federal rate of 38% is subject to modification, depending on the type of corporation. The Act provides for the following adjustments to the tax rate: ITA: 123 ITA: 123.2–127

- tax rate reduction for corporations;
- 10% abatement from federal tax payable, in recognition of provincial income taxes;
- small business deduction and manufacturing and processing deduction for certain corporations;
- foreign tax credits; and
- other tax credits including political contribution tax credit, the investment tax credit, and the apprenticeship job creation tax credit.

¶11,235 Effect of provincial corporate tax rates

In addition to the federal taxes imposed, each province levies an additional income tax on a corporation's taxable income. Furthermore, the taxable income calculation may vary from province to province because of provincial taxing statutes. The provincial rate varies from province to province, but on the whole lies between 0% and 16%.

¶11,240 Effect of corporation type

As mentioned previously, the type and status of the corporation has a bearing on how its income is taxed. There are three major classifications of corporations to be concerned with. These are described in ¶11,212 to ¶11,216.

As a result of the combined federal and provincial rate and several of the modifications to that rate, the rates of tax applicable to Canadian corporations will vary from a low of about 11% to a high of about 31%, depending on the classification of the corporation and the type of income earned.

¶11,245 General rate reduction

The Act provides a corporation with a deduction from tax, computed by multiplying the corporation's "general rate reduction percentage" by its "full-rate taxable income". The "general rate reduction percentage" is 13%. The full-rate taxable income of a corporation, generally, is a corporation's taxable income that has not benefited from special rate reductions, such as the manufacturing and processing profits deduction (alluded to later in this chapter) and the small business deduction (discussed in Chapter 12), among others. The amount of the rate reduction is dependent on the nature of the corporation. For the purposes of this chapter, full-rate taxable income is the amount of the corporation's taxable income minus income, if any, eligible for the manufacturing and processing profits deduction. Examples of this calculation are presented later in this Chapter. ITA: 123.4(2) ITA: 123.4(1)

The following shows the net federal corporate tax rate on general business income:

Basic	38%
Abatement	(10)
General rate reduction	(13)
	15%

¶11,250 Abatement from Federal Tax for Income Earned in a Province

¶11,255 Purpose of the provision

A federal abatement of 10% of a corporation's taxable income earned in Canada is deducted from income tax otherwise calculated. This abatement is based on taxable income earned in a Canadian province or territory; that is, the reduction allows for the imposition of such a provincial tax. All of the provinces and the territories impose an income tax on corporations at general rates, which vary from 10% to 16%. In all but Alberta and Quebec, this tax is filed with and collected by the federal government together with the federal tax. Alberta and Quebec have their own rules for the taxation of corporations. All of these tax rates are set out in the "Current Tax Rates and Credits" section at the beginning of the CCH edition of the CANADIAN INCOME TAX ACT WITH REGULATIONS. ITA: 124(1)

Exhibit 11-4 shows a hypothetical calculation, applicable to most corporations, of effective total tax on taxable income eligible for the abatement. Note that the provincial tax is calculated separately on a tax base which may or may not equal taxable income under the federal Act depending on the particular province levying the tax. For illustrative purposes only, Exhibit 11-4 *assumes* that the tax base for income earned in a hypothetical province is equal to taxable income for federal corporate income tax. The exhibit also assumes that the provincial corporate rate of tax is 13% of the taxable income earned in that province.

EXHIBIT 11-4
Hypothetical Tax Rates Applicable to Taxable Income Eligible for Abatement

Basic federal tax rate	38%	ITA: 123(1)
Federal abatement for provincial tax	(10)	ITA: 124(1)
Net federal tax	28%	
Federal tax reduction	(13)	
Net federal tax	15%	
Provincial tax (assumed)	13	
Effective total tax	28%	

¶11,260 Applicable income tax regulations

Part IV of the Regulations provides the prescribed method to determine the taxable income earned in a province by a corporation. The term "taxable income earned in the year in a province" by a corporation is defined as being the aggregate of the taxable incomes of the corporation earned in the year in each of the provinces. The Regulations also set out the method of calculating the taxable income earned in a particular province during the year. The taxable income earned in a particular province is that taxable income which is attributable to a *permanent establishment* that the corporation has in the province. If a company has no permanent establishment in a province, it will not have earned any taxable income in that province for the purposes of the abatement. ITR: 400(1), 402

The term "permanent establishment" is defined as a fixed place of business of the corporation, including an office, a branch, a mine or oil well, a farm, a timber land, a factory, a workshop or a warehouse. Where the corporation does not have a fixed place of business, its permanent establishment is the principal place in which the corporation's business is carried out. A corporation is deemed to have a permanent establishment in a place, if the corporation carries on business through an employee or agent, established in a particular place: ITR: 400(2), 400(2)(*b*)

(a) who has general authority to contract for his or her employer or principal; or

(b) who has a stock of merchandise owned by his or her employer or principal from which he or she regularly fills orders which he or she receives.

However, the fact that a corporation has business dealings through a commission agent, broker or other independent agent, or maintains an office solely for the purchase of merchandise, does not of itself mean that the corporation has a permanent establishment. The use of substantial machinery or equipment in a particular place at any time in a taxation year constitutes a permanent establishment in that place as does the ownership of land in a province by a corporation that, otherwise, has a permanent establishment in Canada. The CRA indicates that the application of the criteria for a permanent establishment set out in the Regulations will often involve questions of fact which must be answered by the circumstances of each case. ITR: 400(2)(*d*), 400(2)(*e*), 400(2)(*f*) IT-177R2 ITR: 400(2)

¶11,265 Cases on the meaning of permanent establishment

The case of *M.N.R. v. Panther Oil and Grease Manufacturing Co. of Canada Ltd.* presents a specific fact situation. Here the taxpayer had a factory in Ontario, but maintained a sizable sales force throughout Canada under the direction of district sales managers. These sales managers were under the direction of division managers, one of whom lived in Quebec. He had an office, not listed as the company's, in his home. The division and district managers kept a small quantity of the company's goods on hand for small orders when quick delivery was requested. However, most orders were filled from Ontario. 61 DTC 1222 (Ex. Ct.)

It was held that the extensive sales organization in Quebec, itself, constituted a branch in that province and district managers constituted "agencies" of the company. It was also found that the stock of merchandise from which small orders were filled qualified as a permanent establishment.

In the case of *Enterprise Foundry (N.B.) Ltd. v. M.N.R.*, the appellant was incorporated in New Brunswick, but all of its sales were made to customers in Quebec. About 40% of its orders were filled from a stock of merchandise maintained in a public warehouse in Montreal. The taxpayer's key employee had the authority to deliver goods from the stock of merchandise and also had general authority to contract for his employer. It was held that there was a permanent establishment in Quebec. 64 DTC 660 (T.A.B.)

Example Problem 11-9

The taxpayer corporation, whose head office was in Ontario, manufactured electrical appliances which it sold exclusively to wholesalers throughout the country. The company employed a sales representative and junior salesmen in the Province of Quebec. Orders received by the sales representative, who had no authority to accept them, were forwarded to head office and, if accepted there, the goods were shipped directly to the purchaser. During the years in question, the Quebec representative maintained an office in his home at his own expense. There was no agreement with the company to set up the office, but he found it convenient to do so. The company supplied him with company stationery and literature, price sheets, catalogues, sales promotional material and inter-office memoranda. He was also supplied with substantial quantities of samples of the company's products the value of which varied from $4,700 to $11,000 to be used in demonstrations and in promoting sales. The telephone directory did not list the representative's residence as the company's place of business and there was no business sign of any type on the premises. The office was used for taking orders and for training junior salesmen.

During six months of one year, the company maintained a stock of appliances valued at about $120,000 in rented warehouse space in Montreal and filled Quebec orders from this stock. The company had no employees at that warehouse; the handling of goods there was carried out by the warehouse personnel. The company had no control over any part of the warehouse and the public had no knowledge of the company's goods being stored there.

— *REQUIRED*

Determine whether or not the company has a "permanent establishment" in the Province of Quebec by reference to Regulation 400(2).

— *SOLUTION*

[Reference: *M.N.R. v. Sunbeam Corporation (Canada) Ltd.*, 61 DTC 1053 (Ex. Ct.).]

The definition of "permanent establishment" begins with a general statement and then lists several situations which describe specific permanent establishments. Consider the potentially applicable specific provisions first. ITR: 400(2)

(1) A corporation must carry on business through an employee or agent who has general authority to contract or who has a stock of merchandise owned by the employer from which he regularly fills orders. In this case, the sales representative had no authority to accept orders. Furthermore, orders were filled from head office in Ontario. Therefore, the conditions for a permanent establishment are not met. ITR: 400(2)(*b*)

(2) Did the company meet the condition of the Regulations that refers to the use of substantial machinery and equipment? The use of the company's sample appliances for demonstration purposes was not "the use of substantial machinery or equipment" in Quebec. The provision was probably intended to refer to the use of heavy or large machinery or equipment by such persons as contractors or builders who may move such equipment from one province to another in carrying out their normal operations. ITR: 400(2)(*e*)

If none of the specific conditions in the Regulations are met, the analysis should turn to the more general definition of "permanent establishment". The following questions can be posed. ITR: 400(2)

(1) Did the company have a fixed place of business including an office, a branch or a factory? The office of the Quebec sales representative was not an office of the company. This office was maintained by the sales representative in his home for his own convenience and at his own expense. There was no business sign of any sort on the premises and the telephone directory did not list the residence as the company's place of business.

(2) Did the company have a warehouse in the Province of Quebec? The company merely used the facilities of another company's warehouse for the storing of goods. The company had no control over the warehouse. As a result, the warehouse cannot be considered a fixed place of business of the company.

On the basis of this analysis, it was held that the company did not have a permanent establishment in Quebec.

¶11,270 Taxable income earned in a province or territory

Once it is determined that a corporation has a permanent establishment in a province or territory, a portion of the company's taxable income is attributed to that jurisdiction. To determine the attribution, a formula must be used. The formula is based on the proportion of gross revenues earned through a permanent establishment in a province or territory and the proportion of salaries and wages expense paid through the same permanent establishment in that jurisdiction, relative to total gross revenues and salaries and wages expense, respectively, of the corporation. The total taxable income allocated to all provinces and territories provides the basis for the 10% abatement. The allocations to individual jurisdictions, other than Alberta and Quebec, provide the basis for provincial or territorial corporate income tax. ITR: 402

A taxpayer must first determine the gross revenue for the year which is reasonably attributable to each permanent establishment. Rules are provided for determining the permanent establishment to which gross revenue is attributable where merchandise is shipped by a corporation to its customers outside of Canada. ITR: 402(3)(*a*), 402(4)

Where the gross revenue reasonably attributable to a permanent establishment in a province has been determined, this amount will be divided by the corporation's total gross revenue for the year and the resulting fraction will be multiplied by its taxable income for the year. Certain types of investment income including interest on securities, dividends and rentals or royalties from properties not used in the main business of the corporation are excluded from gross revenue. ITR: 401, 402(5)

It will also be necessary to determine the aggregate of the salaries and wages paid in the year by the corporation to employees of a permanent establishment in each particular jurisdiction. This will then be divided by the aggregate of all salaries and wages paid in the year by the corporation and the resulting fraction will be multiplied by its taxable income for the year. ITR: 401, 402(3)(*b*)

Example Problem 11-10

Barry and the Wild Bunch Limited, with its head office in Ottawa, Ontario and other permanent establishments in the provinces of New Brunswick and Quebec, and in the United States, has taxable income of $325,000.

Assume that the corporation's gross revenue and salaries and wages are attributable to its permanent establishments as follows: ITR: 402

	Gross revenue	*Salaries and wages*
Ontario	$ 780,000	$ 130,000
New Brunswick	2,340,000	520,000
Quebec	2,600,000	585,000
United States	390,000	65,000
Total	$6,110,000	$1,300,000
Dividends not attributable	130,000	—
	$6,240,000	$1,300,000

ITR: 402(5)

— *REQUIRED*

Compute the amount of the company's taxable income attributable to each province and determine the amount of the company's abatement. ITA: 124(1)

— *SOLUTION*

The proportion of taxable income attributable to each province would be computed as follows: ITR: 402

	Gross revenue		*Salaries & wages*		
	Amount	*%*	*Amount*	*%*	*Average %*
Ontario	$ 780,000	12.8%	$ 130,000	10.0%	½ (12.8% + 10.0%) = 11.4%
New Brunswick	2,340,000	38.3	520,000	40.0	½ (38.3% + 40.0%) = 39.2%
Quebec	2,600,000	42.6	585,000	45.0	½ (42.6% + 45.0%) = 43.8%
Subtotal	$5,720,000	93.7%	$1,235,000	95.0%	½ (93.7% + 95.0%) = 94.4%
U.S.	390,000	6.3	65,000	5.0	
Total	$6,110,000	100.0%	$1,300,000	100.0%	

Allocation of taxable income to each province:

Ontario	11.4% of $325,000 =	$ 37,050
New Brunswick	39.2% of $325,000 =	127,400
Quebec	43.8% of $325,000 =	142,350
Total taxable income earned in a province or territory		$306,800

Note that the remaining $18,200 (i.e., $325,000 – $306,800) of taxable income earned in the U.S. does not have the 10% abatement applied, since it is not earned in a province or territory of Canada.

The amount deductible from the corporation tax otherwise payable would be computed as follows: ITA: 124(1)

10% of $306,800 .... $30,680

¶11,300 TAX DEDUCTIONS/CREDITS

The Act provides for the following deductions/credits, applicable to all corporations:

- Manufacturing and Processing (M&P) Profits Deduction
- Foreign Tax Deduction (Credit — FTC)
- Federal Political Tax Credit
- Investment Tax Credit (ITC)
- ITC for Apprenticeship Expenditures
- ITC for Child Care Spaces

¶11,310 Manufacturing and Processing Profits Deduction

ITA: 125.1

The Act provides a deduction from corporate tax, in essence a tax credit, for manufacturing and processing (M&P) profits taxable in Canada. The amount of this tax deduction or credit is the same as the general rate reduction on other business income taxable in Canada. As a result, there is no difference in the net federal tax rate applied to M&P profits or the rate applied to profits from other types of business, such as retailing, wholesaling, service, etc.

This deduction from tax (i.e., a tax credit) is a tax incentive to all incorporated Canadian manufacturing and processing businesses taxable in Canada. The provision operates to reduce the net rate of federal tax, after the federal abatement, on manufacturing and processing (M&P) income to 15%. In general, the reduced rate of tax applies to the lesser of the corporation's Canadian manufacturing and processing profits (a specifically defined term) and the portion of the corporation's taxable income considered to be derived from eligible manufacturing and processing activities. The base for this deduction excludes manufacturing and processing profits eligible for the small business deduction, discussed in the next chapter. Exhibit 11-5 summarizes the provisions as they would apply to a corporation that is not a Canadian-controlled private corporation. ITA: 125.1(1)(*a*) ITA: 125.1(1)

EXHIBIT 11-5
Manufacturing and Processing Profits Deduction for Public Corporations

13% (i.e., the rate equal to the general rate reduction) of lesser of:

(a) manufacturing and processing profits, and

(b) taxable income, less four times the foreign business tax deduction (computed without reference to the general rate reduction). ITA: 126(2)

Exhibit 11-6 illustrates how the manufacturing and processing profit deduction affects the calculation of effective total corporate tax introduced in Exhibit 11-4.

EXHIBIT 11-6
Hypothetical Tax Rates Applicable to Taxable Income Eligible for Provincial Manufacturing and Processing Profits Deduction

Federal tax rate	38%	ITA: 123(1)
Abatement for provincial tax	(10)	ITA: 124(1)
Net federal tax after abatement	28%	
M&P deduction	(13)	ITA: 125.1(1)(*a*)
Net federal tax	15%	
Provincial tax (assumed)*	11	
Effective total tax	26%	

* Some provinces have a reduced tax rate for M&P profits.

Note that the net federal tax at 15% is the same as that shown in Exhibit 11-4 after the general rate reduction. The only difference in rates results from a lower provincial rate where a province provides for an M&P deduction.

Apparently, the main reason for the continued existence of the M&P profits deduction legislation in the federal Act is to accommodate provinces that offer an M&P profits deduction from provincial tax based on the federal calculation of M&P profits.

¶11,320 Foreign Tax Deduction

¶11,325 Purpose and approach

Residents of Canada, including corporations, are taxable on their world income even though part of this income may have been subject to tax in a foreign country. Foreign tax deductions are designed to mitigate the effects on a Canadian individual or corporate taxpayer of double taxation on income arising from a source outside Canada. Relief is granted by ITA: 126

means of a deduction, from the Canadian tax otherwise payable, of all or part of the foreign tax.

The theory underlying this arrangement for a tax deduction is that the country where the income is earned has the first right to tax the income. If the country of the taxpayer's residence levies a higher rate of tax on the income, the taxpayer will pay tax at the higher rate, but part of that tax is paid to the country where the income was earned while the remainder will be paid to the country of the taxpayer's residence.

Since the foreign tax deduction is meant to reduce Canadian tax on foreign income that has been taxed elsewhere, there is no foreign tax deduction available on foreign income that is not taxed in Canada. If a source of income is exempt from tax in Canada, there is no Canadian tax to reduce with a foreign tax deduction. For example, certain dividends received by corporations resident in Canada from corporations, such as foreign subsidiaries, resident in another country are not taxable in Canada. Such dividends are, effectively, not taxable in Canada because, although they are included in Division B income, they are deductible in the calculation of taxable income in Division C. This provision is similar to the provision which provides a deduction for dividends received from taxable Canadian corporations. These dividends, from foreign affiliates, that are deductible in Division C are not eligible for the foreign tax credit, since any tax "that may reasonably be regarded as having been paid by the taxpayer in respect of income from a share of the capital stock of a foreign affiliate of the taxpayer" is excluded from foreign tax which is eligible for the credit. A foreign affiliate is defined, basically, as a corporation in which the taxpayer has at least 10% equity ownership.

ITA: 113

ITA: 112

ITA: 126(1)(*a*)

ITA: 95(1)

On the other hand, types of foreign income that are included in Canadian income and, hence, are eligible for a foreign tax deduction include: income from an unincorporated foreign branch, dividend income that is not eligible for deduction in the calculation of taxable income (e.g., dividends from a country with which Canada does not have a tax treaty, such as the Cayman Islands), or dividends income from a corporation which is not a foreign affiliate.

ITA: 113

The Act takes three separate approaches to the foreign tax deduction. The first two, on which this chapter will focus, apply to residents of Canada. One refers to "non-business-income tax". The other refers to "business-income tax". The third applies to non-residents of Canada referring to tax on certain capital gains on "taxable Canadian property". Where the taxpayer is eligible for a foreign tax deduction for "non-business-income tax" or on "business-income tax" paid to more than one foreign country, the taxpayer is required to compute separate deductions for each country. It should be emphasized that with few exceptions, the same rules apply to both individuals and corporations. However, the following discussion will focus on the foreign tax deduction rules as they apply to corporations.

ITA: 126(1), 126(2)–(2.2), 126(6)

¶11,330 Non-business income tax deduction

¶11,330.10 *Calculation*

Where a taxpayer has non-business income (e.g., interest income) from another country and has paid foreign income or profits taxes to the government of that country or to the government of a state, province or other political subdivision of that country, the taxpayer may take a deduction from Canadian tax equal to the lesser of:

ITA: 126(1), 126(7)

(i) the foreign non-business-income tax paid in respect of that foreign income; and

(ii) $\dfrac{\text{foreign non-business income (Div. B)}}{\text{Income (Div. B) for the year (from all sources) plus or minus certain amounts}} \times$ tax otherwise payable [ssec. 126(7)]

Note that part (ii) attempts to estimate the Canadian tax paid on the foreign income. As a result, the credit against Canadian tax cannot exceed the estimated Canadian tax paid on the foreign income.

Both the numerator and denominator of the fraction in part (ii), above, are limited to the amounts of income (excluding income from a foreign affiliate) attributable to the period in the year during which the taxpayer was resident in Canada.

The amounts to be subtracted from the Division B income of a corporation in the denominator of the fraction are:

(i) the claims for net capital losses carried over because they directly offset taxable capital gains, with the result that they are not taxed; and ITA: 111(1)(*b*)

(ii) the amount of taxable dividends received and deductible and the amount of dividends received from a foreign affiliate and deductible, because they are not taxed under Part I. ITA: 112, 113

¶11,330.20 *Definition of "tax otherwise payable"*

The term "tax otherwise payable" is defined in the Act under the heading "tax for the year otherwise payable under this Part". For purposes of the foreign non-business income tax deduction, "tax otherwise payable" is defined for corporations as federal taxes less: ITA: 126(7)

- 10% abatement
- general tax rate reduction (other than CCPC)

Note that the "tax otherwise payable" is determined before deducting the manufacturing and processing profits deduction, the foreign tax deduction, and some other deductions from tax. ITA: 123.4, 124, 125, 125.1, 126

The net result is to determine an amount of tax that would include the Canadian tax on foreign non-business income. That amount would be net of the abatement and the general rate reduction for a corporation, other than a Canadian-controlled private corporation. Note that if a Canadian resident corporation's only source of income is from a foreign non-business asset that is not real estate,[3] all of its taxable income would be considered to be earned in a province and the corporation would receive a tax abatement of 10% of its full taxable income. Therefore, the Canadian tax otherwise payable on that income, conceptually, would be after the 10% reduction. ITA: 127, 127.2–127.4

¶11,330.30 *Interpretation of terms*

The following should be noted about the term "non-business income tax paid" as it applies to a corporation: ITA: 126(1), 127(7)

(a) the foreign tax must be paid, not merely payable and the conversion of the foreign tax into its Canadian-dollar equivalent must be made at the rate of exchange prevailing at the time payment is made;

(b) the foreign tax must generally be in the nature of an income or profits tax;

(c) the term includes such income tax paid to the government of another country or to the government of a state, province or other political subdivision of that country;

(d) the term excludes "business income tax" paid in the other country; and

(e) foreign non-business income tax deducted as an expense in Division B must be excluded. Unlike a foreign "business" income deduction, described below, an unused foreign non-business income deduction cannot be carried forward. Therefore, consideration should be given to using the deduction from income for these amounts. Since a deduction from tax (i.e., a tax credit) is preferable to a deduction from income, eligibility for a foreign tax credit should be determined first, with any unused balance of foreign taxes paid being taken as a deduction. This may result in a circular calculation because of the credit's dependence on net income after the deduction. An algebraic approach may be necessary to solve this problem. ITA: 20(12)

[3] Where the non-business income-producing asset is real property, i.e., real estate, located in a foreign jurisdiction, the presence of real property would normally result in a permanent establishment in that country and, hence, the corporation would not be eligible for the federal abatement.

¶11,335 Business income tax deduction

Where a resident of Canada carries on business in a foreign country, the foreign tax deduction rules allow for a three-year carryback and a 10-year carryforward of unabsorbed foreign business income tax paid in a taxation year. Thus, foreign business income tax paid in a taxation year but not deducted may be carried over and treated as if it were paid in a carryover taxation year.

In the case of a corporation resident in Canada, it would be considered to carry on business in a foreign country if the corporation had an *unincorporated* branch in that foreign country. If the Canadian resident corporation established a subsidiary in the foreign country, the business income of the subsidiary would be taxed by the foreign country as a separate entity and no business foreign tax credit would be available to the parent. Where the corporation operates in foreign countries through unincorporated branches, a business foreign tax credit will arise.

¶11,335.10 *Calculation*

The deduction, as it applies to a corporation, is computed as the least of: ITA: 126(2)

(a) the total of the "business-income tax paid" for the year in respect of all businesses carried on through an unincorporated branch by the taxpayer in a particular country, plus any "unused foreign tax credit" from other years in respect of the same country as the taxpayer may wish to claim; ITA: 126(7) "business-income tax paid"

(b) $\frac{\text{foreign business income}}{\text{income (Div. B) for the year (from all sources) plus or minus certain amounts}^{(1)}} \times \text{tax otherwise payable}$

(c) the tax otherwise payable after deducting any non-business income tax deduction under subsection 126(1).

(1) The amounts to be added to and subtracted from Division B income are the same as those that were identified for the non-business income tax deduction.

¶11,335.20 *Definition of "tax otherwise payable"*

For the foreign business income tax deduction, the "tax otherwise payable" is defined as the federal tax before any deduction for the federal tax abatement and other corporate tax credits. Note that, if foreign business income were a Canadian resident corporation's only source of income, none of its taxable income would likely be considered to be earned in a province and the corporation would receive no tax abatement. Therefore, the Canadian tax otherwise payable on that income, conceptually, would be before the 10% abatement. ITA: 126(7); ITA: 124, 123.2; ITA: 125–127.41

The "tax otherwise payable", in this case, or used in part (c) of the calculation, above, is the same amount as that described above. ITA: 127(7)

Example Problem 11-11

You have audited the books of International Money Limited, a public corporation, and have determined that the income for tax purposes of $472,000 for the year ended December 31, 2013, has been calculated correctly. The following additional data are available:

Interest received from:	
a U.S. company (net of $3,000 tax withheld)	$17,000
a British company (net of $1,500 tax withheld)	8,500
Business income (net of $9,800 tax paid) earned from an unincorporated branch in Turkey	18,200
Donations	20,000
Dividend received from a taxable Canadian corporation	52,000
Taxable income earned in a province (computed by Reg.)	375,000

— REQUIRED

Compute the maximum foreign tax credit available to the corporation for 2013.

— SOLUTION

(a) Calculation of taxable income:

Income for tax purposes		$472,000	
Less: donations	$20,000		ITA: 110(1)(*a*)
dividends	52,000	72,000	ITA: 112
Taxable income		$400,000	

(b) Calculation of tax otherwise payable:

(i) For foreign non-business income tax credit:

Tax otherwise payable (38% of $400,000)	(A)	$152,000
Less: 10% of $375,000		37,500
Net		$114,500
Tax rate reduction @ 13% of $400,000		(52,000)
Tax otherwise payable	(B)	$ 62,500

(ii) For foreign business income tax credit:(1)

Tax otherwise payable, per (A), above		$152,000
Less: tax rate reduction		(52,000)
Tax otherwise payable	(C)	$100,000

(c) Calculation of foreign tax deduction:(2) ITA: 126(1)

(i) Foreign non-business income:

Interest from U.S. company

lesser of:

(I) tax paid $3,000

(II) $\frac{\text{income from U.S.}}{\text{income less dividends}} \times \text{tax otherwise payable (B)}$

$= \frac{\$20,000}{\$472,000 - \$52,000} \times \$62,500$ .... $2,976 → $2,976

Interest from British company

lesser of:

(I) tax paid $1,500

(II) $\frac{\text{income from Britain}}{\text{income less dividends}} \times \text{tax otherwise payable (B)}$

$= \frac{\$10,000}{\$472,000 - \$52,000} \times \$62,500$ .... $1,488 → $1,488

(ii) Foreign business income: ITA: 126(2)

least of:

(I) tax paid $9,800

(II) $\frac{\text{income from Turkey}}{\text{income less dividends}} \times \text{tax otherwise payable (C)}$

$= \frac{\$28,000}{\$472,000 - \$52,000} \times \$100,000$ .... $6,667 → $6,667

(III) tax otherwise payable (C) less non-business income tax deduction ($100,000 – ($2,976 + 1,488)) $95,536

(d) Total foreign tax deduction:

Foreign non-business income		
U.S. source	$2,976	
British source	1,488	$ 4,464
Foreign business income		6,667
Total deduction from tax		$11,131

— *NOTES TO SOLUTION*

(1) If the Canadian income tax effects on foreign investment income could be isolated, as in the case where the corporation's only source of income was foreign non-business income (other than from real property), such as interest income, it would be considered to be earned in the province of which the taxpayer is a resident and, therefore, would be eligible for the federal tax abatement. As a result, it is the tax otherwise payable (B) after the abatement on which the non-business income tax deduction is based. On the other hand, foreign business income is assumed to be earned in a permanent establishment in the foreign country and, therefore, is not eligible for the federal tax abatement. Thus, the tax otherwise payable (C) before the abatement is the relevant base for the business income tax deduction.

(2) Note how these credits against Canadian tax do not exceed foreign tax paid on the foreign income. These reductions of Canadian tax are also restricted to the estimated amount of Canadian tax paid on the foreign income.

¶11,337 Federal Political Tax Credit

The federal political tax credit rules are the same as those applied to individuals. These rules were discussed in Chapter 10. ITA: 127(3)

¶11,340 Investment Tax Credit

¶11,345 Overview

¶11,345.10 *Purpose*

The investment tax credit (ITC) was introduced in 1975 as a temporary extra incentive to stimulate new investment in Canada in certain specific business sectors and regional locations. Since that time, the original credit has been pared back to apply regionally only to the Gaspé and the Atlantic provinces for certain specific capital expenditures. However, three credits apply to all of Canada:

- scientific research and experimental development (SR&ED) expenditures,
- apprenticeship job creation tax credit, and
- child care spaces tax credit.

Conceptually, the available investment tax credit is simply calculated by applying a "specified percentage" or other limit for one of the categories described above to the capital cost of the asset acquired or the expenditure incurred. The actual amount of the ITC claimed by the taxpayer is deducted in the following taxation year from the capital cost of the asset acquired or the SR&ED pool. In addition, there is a carryover mechanism for available investment tax credits not claimed in a particular year.

The purpose of this section is to introduce, conceptually, the ramifications of this extremely important tax credit and to provide some simple examples of its application.

¶11,345.20 *Computation of investment tax credit*

One provision defines the basis for the computation of the available investment tax credit: the category of the asset or expenditure that is eligible for a credit, the "specified percentage" or the expenditure limit applicable to that category and the carryover rules. ITA: 127(9)

The cost of the capital asset to which the "specified percentage" is applied must be reduced by all government assistance (e.g., grants, subsidies, loans, etc.) and non-arm's length third-party assistance including certain specified contract payments for goods and services. ITA: 127(11.6)–(11.8), 127(16)–(21)

The amount of the *available* investment tax credit which can be applied in a year is limited only by the Part I tax remaining after the deduction of any of the other corporate tax credits. Those available ITCs that are not applied in the year of acquisition or expenditure can be carried back three taxation years and forward 20 taxation years. Because of the generous carryforward time-frame, it is reasonable that ITCs should be deducted last.

Exhibit 11-7 lists the investment tax credit rates which apply to the most common types of properties and expenditures, incurred by taxpayers other than Canadian-controlled private corporations (which are discussed in Chapter 12), which give rise to such credits. The specified percentages listed in the Exhibit vary, depending on the geographic location and nature of the property or expenditure.

All of the terms describing property will be discussed in more detail following the Exhibit.

EXHIBIT 11-7
General Rates of Investment Tax Credits[1]
[ssec. 127(9)]

	Atlantic provinces and Gaspé	*Balance of Canada*
Qualified property	10%	0%
Qualified SR&ED[2]	20	20
Apprenticeship expenditure[3]	10	10
Child care spaces[4]	25	25

[1] Rates applicable to Canadian-controlled private corporations are discussed in Chapter 12.

[2] SR&ED refers to scientific research and experimental development as discussed in Chapter 4. The 20% SR&ED investment tax credit rate is reduced to 15% for taxation years ending after 2013.

[3] Limited to $2,000 per eligible apprentice.

[4] Limited to $10,000 per eligible space.

¶11,350 Qualified property

¶11,350.10 *Time of acquisition*

"Qualified property" is property that is a prescribed building, grain elevator or machinery and equipment. Generally, a taxpayer is considered to have acquired depreciable property when title passes or when the taxpayer obtains all the incidents of title including possession, use and risk. Property is deemed not to have been acquired and, hence, not eligible for ITC until the property is "available for use", as discussed in Chapter 5.

ITR: 4600; ITA: 127(9)

ITA: 127(11.2)

¶11,350.20 *Type of property*

To be "qualified property" the property must be new property which has not been used for any purpose prior to its acquisition. It must also meet certain other conditions prescribed by a regulation which lists prescribed buildings and prescribed machinery and equipment.

ITR: 4600

¶11,350.30 *Use of the property*

To qualify for the credit, the prescribed building or machinery and equipment must be used primarily in one of a broad range of activities. There is no minimum use period and no provision for recapture of the credit in the event of a change to a non-qualifying use or the sale of the asset. Uses of qualified property include a broad range of business activities. In the case of *Mother's Pizza Parlour (London) Limited et al. v. The Queen*, the Federal Court–Trial Division (affirmed by the Federal Court of Appeal) held that buildings from which dining room, take-out and delivery service was provided were not used for processing goods for sale, but for selling finished goods, since all ingredients for the pizza, including the dough, were purchased from independent suppliers. Hence, the building was not "qualified

ITA: 127(9) "qualified property" (*c*), (*d*); 85 DTC 5271 (F.C.T.D.), aff'd 88 DTC 6397 (F.C.A.)

property" eligible for an investment tax credit at the time. In the case of a building, which is used primarily for eligible activities and partly for functions such as administration or warehousing, the entire cost would be recognized, providing the principal use of the building is an eligible activity.

¶11,350.40 *Capital cost reduction*

In the taxation year following the year in which the investment tax credit is claimed, the capital cost of the depreciable asset is reduced by the amount of the credit claimed. In situations where the asset no longer exists (i.e., the property has been disposed of), there would be an income inclusion as a substitute for the capital cost reduction of the capital asset. ITA: 12(1)(*t*), 13(7.1)(*e*)

Example Problem 11-12

In 2013, Investit Limited has acquired $100,000 of Class 8 (20%) assets eligible as "qualified property" for the 10% investment tax credit in the Gaspé area. The corporation's federal income tax rate after the abatement and the general rate reduction is 15%. Its taxable income before capital cost allowance on the eligible property is $30,000.

The corporation is not eligible for any other tax credits and paid no tax in the preceding three years.

— REQUIRED

(A) What is the maximum investment tax credit available?

(B) Compute the net federal Part I tax payable after the investment tax credit.

(C) What is the amount of the investment tax credit available for carryover?

(D) Compute the UCC balance in Class 8 at the end of the following year, assuming the new assets are the only assets in the class.

— SOLUTION

(A) The maximum investment tax credit available will be $10,000 (i.e., 10% of $100,000).

(B)

Taxable income before capital cost allowance on qualified property	$30,000
Less: capital cost allowance on qualified property: ½ × 20% of $100,000	(10,000)
Taxable income	$20,000
Net federal tax @ 15%	$ 3,000
Less: investment tax credit	(3,000)
Net federal tax payable under Part I	Nil

(C) The remaining investment tax credit of $7,000 (i.e., $10,000 – $3,000) may be carried back three and forward 20 years.

(D)

UCC in Class 8 before CCA in first year	$100,000
Less: CCA claimed in first year	(10,000)
UCC at beginning of second year	$ 90,000
Less: ITC claimed in first year	(3,000)
UCC before CCA in second year	$ 87,000
Less: CCA claimed in second year @ 20%	(17,400)
UCC balance after CCA	$ 69,600

Note that any investment tax credit for depreciable property carried over to another year and used to reduce tax in that year will reduce the undepreciated capital cost balance in the year following the year of use or the year following the purchase, whichever is later. This will occur until the remaining investment tax credit is fully utilized or expires. The undepreciated capital cost balance will not be reduced by expired investment tax credits. Under certain conditions, it may be worthwhile to deduct no capital cost allowance in order to be able to claim more investment tax credit that would otherwise expire. However, the facts of each case must be analyzed carefully.

¶11,355 Qualified scientific research expenditure

¶11,355.10 *Overview*

Scientific research and experimental development expenditures are very generously treated by Canadian tax legislation. Not only is there a potential 100% write-off of qualifying expenditures and equipment, but there is also a 20% investment tax credit available [to be reduced to 15% for expenditures made after 2013]. In addition, many of the provincial governments provide additional incentives for SR&ED expenditures. In the next chapter it will be shown that certain qualifying Canadian-controlled private corporations benefit from an even greater "specified percentage" and a potential refund for unclaimed ITCs. ITA: 37

¶11,355.20 *Qualified SR&ED expenditure*

"Qualified expenditure" is defined to include scientific research and experimental development expenditures on new property and described in the Act as current expenditures and capital expenditures. However, certain capital expenditures are not included, such as: ITA: 127(9); ITR: 2903 ITA: 37(1)(*a*), 37(1)(*b*) ITR: 2902 ITA: 37(8)(*d*)

— any capital expenditure made in respect of a building, including a leasehold interest (other than a prescribed special purpose building);

— any rental expense incurred for a building (other than a prescribed special purpose building); and

— starting in 2014, all capital expenditures made after 2013 are excluded from SR&ED deductions and investment tax credits.

¶11,355.30 *Application*

In the taxation year following the year in which an ITC deduction is made, the amount of the ITC claimed is deducted from the pool of unclaimed SR&ED expenditures. Remember that both current and capital expenditures that are eligible SR&ED expenditures are either written off in the year of the expenditure or placed in a pool of unclaimed expenditures. Therefore, for capital expenditures that are eligible SR&ED expenditures there is no capital cost from which the ITC could be deducted; hence, the deduction reduces the unclaimed SR&ED expenditure pool. Where this pool is nil, then there would be an income inclusion. ITA: 12(1)(*t*)

Example Problem 11-13

In 2013, Developit Limited incurred $100,000 of qualified scientific research and experimental development expenditures eligible for the 20% investment tax credit. The corporation's federal income tax rate after the abatement and the general rate reduction is 15%. Its taxable income before the deduction of the SR&ED expenditures under section 37 is $150,000.

The corporation is not eligible for any other tax credits and paid no tax in the preceding three years.

— *REQUIRED*

(A) What is the maximum investment tax credit available?

(B) Compute the net federal Part I tax payable after the investment tax credit.

(C) What is the amount, if any, of the investment tax credit carryover?

(D) Compute the corporation's deduction or income included in the following year if no further SR&ED expenditures are made.

— *SOLUTION*

(A) The maximum investment tax credit is:
20% of $100,000 = $20,000

(B) Taxable income before sec. 37 deduction	$150,000
Sec. 37 deduction	(100,000)
Taxable income	$ 50,000
Net tax @ 15%	$ 7,500
Investment tax credit (maximum)	(7,500)
Net federal tax payable under Part I	Nil

(C) The remaining investment tax credit of $12,500 (i.e., $20,000 – $7,500) may be carried back three years and forward 20 years. In this particular case, the corporation paid no tax in the preceding three years, so it must carry the balance of ITC forward.

(D) Sec. 37 SR&ED expenditures in 2013	$100,000
Sec. 37 SR&ED deduction in 2013	(100,000)
Balance in the pool at the beginning of 2014	Nil
Income in 2014 based on ITC claimed in 2013	7,500
Income effect in 2014	$ 7,500

ITA: 12(1)(*t*)

As the remaining ITC of $12,500 is claimed in a carryforward year, the amount claimed must be brought into income, as recapture, in the year following the year of claim.

Had there been a balance of the $100,000 that was not deducted under section 37, the balance would form a pool of SR&ED expenditures which could be deducted in a future year. Where a balance in the SR&ED pool exists, the amount claimed as ITC in a year is deducted from the balance in the SR&ED pool in the following year.

The following diagram shows the process of handling the SR&ED expenditures and ITC in this example problem.

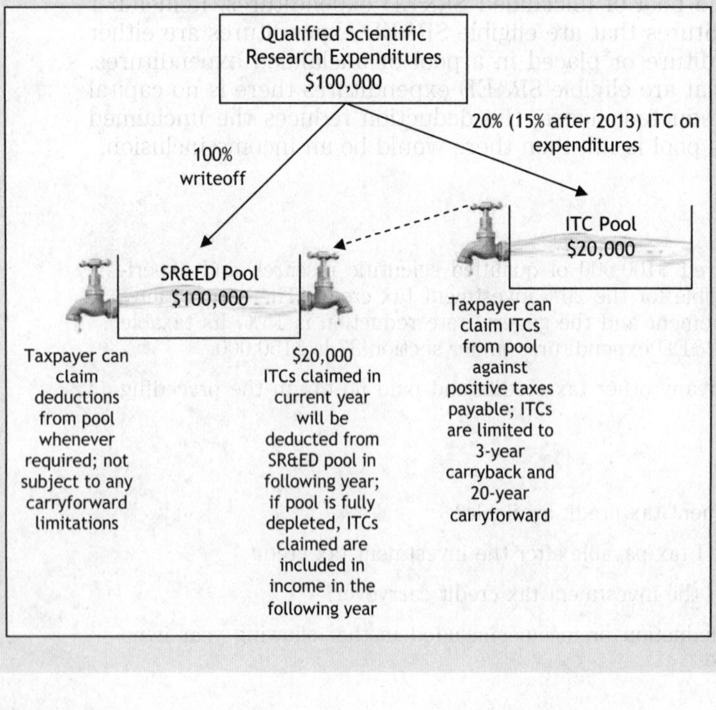

¶11,355.40 *Prescribed proxy amount*

Where business overhead expenses can be allocated to scientific research and experimental development costs, such overhead expenses will be included in the base on which the 20% (15% after 2013) investment tax credit for SR&ED expenditures is calculated. In a situation where a business is unable to allocate overhead expenses to SR&ED, the investment tax credit base would be relatively lower, resulting in a lower investment tax credit. As an alternative to allocating overhead expenses, for the purposes of computing the investment tax credit, use of a prescribed proxy amount (PPA) is permitted. The PPA is computed by a formula, provided in the Regulations, which is based on salaries paid to employees directly engaged in SR&ED in Canada. Use of the PPA method to account for overhead expenses in the calculation of the SR&ED investment tax credit must be elected annually. A more elaborate discussion of the PPA method and an example in which the calculation is demonstrated is presented in Chapter 12, where the application of the SR&ED investment tax credit to Canadian-controlled private corporations is discussed. However, it should be recognized that the PPA election is available to all taxpayers eligible for a SR&ED investment tax credit.

ITA: 127(9) "qualified expenditure" (*b*)
ITR: 2900(4), 2900(5)
ITA: 127(5)

¶11,360 ITC for Apprenticeship Expenditures

The apprenticeship expenditure ITC is provided to encourage employers to hire new apprentices in eligible trades. Employers receive a non-refundable tax credit equal to 10% of the salaries and wages paid to "eligible apprentices". "Eligible salary and wages" are defined to include the amounts paid to an eligible apprentice in respect of the first 24 months of the apprenticeship. Excluded from the definition is remuneration that is based on profits, bonuses, fringe benefits, and stock options. The maximum credit is $2,000 per apprentice per year. Unused credits may be carried back 3 years and forward 20 years to reduce federal income taxes otherwise payable.

ITA: 127(11.1)(*c*.4)
ITA: 127(9) "eligible apprentice"

Special rules apply where an apprentice works for two or more related employers to limit the credit to $2,000. In essence, one corporation in a related group must be designated as the employer of an eligible apprentice who is employed by more than one corporation in the group.

ITA: 127(11.4)

An eligible apprentice is one who is working in a qualifying trade in the first two years of his or her provincially registered apprenticeship contract with an eligible employer. The qualifying trades are prescribed in the Regulations and include the 45 trades currently included in the Red Seal trades, which allow a journey person to engage in his or her trade in any province or territory in Canada where the trade is recognized.

ITR: 7310

¶11,370 ITC for Child Care Spaces

An ITC for taxpayers, other than taxpayers in the business of providing child care services, is available to those who create child care spaces for their employees and for the surrounding community. The "child care space amount" eligible for the ITC is equal to:

ITA: 127(11.1)

the lesser of:

ITA: 127(9)

(a) $10,000, and

(b) 25% of the taxpayer's eligible expenditures in respect of the child care space.

An "eligible child care space expenditure" is defined to be an expenditure incurred for the sole purpose of the creation of a new child care space in a licensed child care facility operated for the benefit of children of the employees of the taxpayer and other children. Specifically, eligible expenditures will include:

ITA: 127(9)

- the cost of depreciable property, other than a motor vehicle or property attached to a residence of certain individuals who are owners or employees of the taxpayer's business; and
- a "specified child care start-up cost", including:
  — landscaping to create an outdoor play area for children,
  — initial fees for licensing, regulatory, and building permits,

ITA: 127(9)

— architectural fees for designing the child care facility, and

— children's educational material.

A provision recaptures the ITC claimed on an eligible expenditure if there is a disposition of the property included in an eligible expenditure or if the child care space ceases to be available within five calendar years after the creation of the space. ITA: 127(27.11), 127(27.12)

¶11,800 REVIEW QUESTIONS

(1) Mr. Clements has been trying to prepare the corporate tax returns for his company and cannot seem to get the treatment of charitable donations sorted out. He cannot find the place to put the tax credit for the donations and he is not sure what the limits are. Can you help him?

(2) If a company finds that it has non-capital loss carryovers that are going to expire in the next few years, what tax planning steps can be taken to use up some of these losses without selling the company or buying another company?

(3) Mr. Jones has just bought all of the shares of a company that has some net capital losses being carried forward as well as accrued capital losses on some of its assets. What happens to them? Is there any relief?

(4) There are two basic types of restrictions on losses available for carryover. What are these restrictions and how do they affect the application of losses?

(5) Mr. Magee bought all the shares of Profitco Ltd. on July 1 of this year, and is expecting to combine the profitable operations of Profitco with the loss operations of his current corporation. However, for Profitco's deemed year-end of June 30, he hopes to offset the six months of profitable operations with a full year of CCA in order to minimize the tax liability. Profitco's normal year-end was December 31. Comment on his plan.

(6) What are the three main objectives of tax provisions affecting the taxation of corporations?

(7) MultiCo Inc. has permanent establishments in Ontario and Alberta. The Alberta operation normally accounted for 20% of the allocation of taxable income. However, in the current year, a salesman in Ontario sold a large order to a customer in Alberta and the goods were shipped directly from Ontario. How does this special sale impact the allocation to Alberta?

(8) Since residents of Canada are taxable on their world income, why does Canada give a foreign tax credit for taxes paid to another country?

(9) In the calculation of non-business foreign tax credit the "tax otherwise payable" calculation is reduced by the 10% federal abatement. Why?

(10) Lossco Inc. has a loss from operations for the year while at the same time earning interest of $5,000 from the United States on which $750 of tax was withheld. How can Lossco treat the $750 of foreign tax paid on its tax return?

¶11,825 MULTIPLE CHOICE QUESTIONS

Question 1

Helen acquired all of the voting shares of Lossco Inc. from a non-related individual on February 1, 2013 Lossco has always had a December 31 year end since its incorporation. Which one of the following statements is TRUE?

(A) Lossco had a deemed year end February 1, 2013.

(B) Lossco may select any date, within the 53-week period commencing February 1, 2013, as its new year end.

(C) Lossco must continue to have a December 31 year end unless the CRA grants permission for a change.

(D) Lossco had a deemed year end on January 31, 2013 and is required to keep January 31 as its year end for the future.

Question 2

Jim acquired control of Smart Ltd. from an unrelated person on May 15, 2013. The following information relates to the inventory and capital assets owned by Smart Ltd. at that time.

	Cost	*FMV*
Inventory	$120,000	$100,000
Land	200,000	140,000
Building	100,000	75,000
Marketable securities	20,000	30,000

For its taxation year ended on May 14, 2013, Smart Ltd. is required to recognize a capital loss of:

(A) $85,000

(B) $80,000

(C) $60,000

(D) $50,000

Question 3

On April 1, 2013, Calm Corp purchased 72% of the voting shares of X Ltd. from an unrelated person. The tax position of the fixed assets of X Ltd. at that time is summarized below.

	Cost	*UCC*	*FMV*
Automobiles (Class 10)	$100,000	$ 42,000	$45,000
Computer equipment (Class 45)	64,000	38,000	33,000
Computer software (Class 12)	30,000	Nil	5,000
Office furniture & equipment (Class 8)	80,000	58,000	48,000

The business loss of X Ltd. for the year ended March 31, 2013, will be increased by deemed CCA of:

(A) $7,000

(B) $10,800

(C) $15,000

(D) $23,000

Question 4

For its year ended December 31, 2012, its first year end since its incorporation, Lakehead Co. (Lakehead) reported the following income (losses) for tax purposes.

Business loss (retailer of widgets)	$ (20,000)
Capital loss	(6,000)

On January 1, 2013, Pacific Co. acquired control of Lakehead from an unrelated person and transferred its profitable gadget retailing business to Lakehead. For its year ending December 31, 2013, Lakehead is expected to have the following income/losses.

Business loss (widgets)	$(3,000)
Business income (gadgets)	15,000
Taxable capital gain on sale of capital asset	6,000

Assuming widgets and gadgets are similar products, which one of the following statements is TRUE?

(A) For its year ending December 31, 2013, Lakehead will be able to deduct net capital losses of $3,000, provided the widget retailing business is carried on throughout the taxation year ended December 31, 2013 with a reasonable expectation of profit.

(B) For its year ending December 31, 2013, Lakehead will be able to deduct non-capital losses of $18,000 (maximum), provided the widget retailing business is carried on throughout the taxation year ended December 31, 2013, with a reasonable expectation of profit.

(C) For its year ending December 31, 2013, Lakehead will be able to deduct non-capital losses of $12,000 (maximum), provided the widget retailing business is carried on throughout the taxation year ended December 31, 2013, with a reasonable expectation of profit.

(D) For its year ending December 31, 2013, Lakehead will be able to deduct non-capital losses of $15,000 (maximum), provided the widget retailing business is carried on throughout the taxation year ended December 31, 2013, with a reasonable expectation of profit.

Question 5

During 2013, Curran Ltd, a public corporation, has net income for tax purposes of $600,000, including $100,000 of dividends from taxable Canadian corporations and $500,000 of retailing profits. It made $200,000 of charitable donations during the year. Income earned in a province was 90%.

What is Curran Ltd's taxable income for the year?

(A) $600,000

(B) $500,000

(C) $400,000

(D) $300,000

Question 6

Refer to the facts given in Question 5, above. What is Curran Ltd.'s federal tax payable for the year?

(A) $22,000

(B) $48,000

(C) $87,000

(D) $52,500

¶11,850 EXERCISES

Exercise 1

ITA: 110.1, 111

Generous Limited has income (loss) under Division B of $(7,350) in 2011, $22,050 in 2012, and $14,700 in 2013. During this period it made donations to registered charities of $2,625 in 2011, $4,700 in 2012, and $12,000 in 2013. It also made a donation of ecologically sensitive land valued at $19,700 to the Government of Canada in 2012. The company began operations in 2011.

— REQUIRED

Compute the corporation's taxable income for the years indicated.

Exercise 2

ITA: 110.1, 111

Determined Limited predicts, with reasonable accuracy, its income under Division B before capital cost allowances will be: $100,000 in 2011, $115,000 in 2012, and $132,250 in 2013. Capital cost allowances available are expected to be $200,000 in 2011, $170,000 in 2012, and $150,000 in 2013. It made charitable donations of $10,000 in 2007 and $11,500 in 2008, which it could not absorb before 2011.

— REQUIRED

How can the company maximize its charitable donation deduction while minimizing the taxes it pays in the period shown? (Hint: Take advantage of the loss carryover rules.)

Exercise 3

ITA: 111(8)

TPM Limited has computed the following income (loss) for the year ended December 31, 2013:

Loss from business	$(129,000)
Income from property including dividends of $10,750 received from taxable Canadian corporations	32,250
Capital gains	46,400
Capital losses	(12,000)
Business investment loss	(16,000)

The corporation has a net capital loss of $27,000 arising from 2007.

— REQUIRED

Compute the corporation's non-capital loss for the year.

Exercise 4

ITA: 111(8)

CLR Limited had a large allowable capital loss of $51,750 on one transaction during its taxation year ended December 31, 2013. In addition, the following information pertains to its situation for the year:

Income from business	$155,250
Income from property	17,000
Taxable capital gain	4,700
Allowable business investment loss (not included in above allowable capital loss)	(8,300)

— REQUIRED

Compute the corporation's net capital loss for the year.

Exercise 5

ITA: 111(1), 111(1.1)

Abigail Corporation has income from business of $55,500 and a taxable capital gain of $37,000 in 2013. It also has the following losses:

Non-capital losses (expiring beyond 2013)	$ 82,500
Net capital losses (1999)	$ 60,000

— *REQUIRED*

How much of the above losses will be available for carryforward after this year?

Exercise 6

ITA: 111(4), 111(5), 111(5.1), 111(5.2)

All of the voting shares of Lofty Limited, a manufacturer of widgets, have been acquired by Holdco Ltd., an investment holding company. At the time of the acquisition on March 10, 2013, Lofty Limited had non-capital business losses of $600,000 generated in 2012. Lofty Limited also had $30,000 of net capital losses carried forward from 1999. As well, at the time of the acquisition, it was discovered that the balance of undepreciated capital cost in its Class 8 was $70,000 while the fair market value of the assets in that class was only $40,000. The balance in its cumulative eligible capital account (being from the acquisition on August 31, 2012, of an exclusive customer list) was $50,000 while the fair market value of the customer list was $68,000. The corporation's inventory had a cost of $630,000, while its market value was $680,000. The book value of the corporation's receivables was $240,000, while its realizable value was estimated at $225,000. The corporation's only non-depreciable capital property, land, had accrued gains of $56,000 over its cost of $200,000. Lofty Limited has a December 31 year end.

The corporation had business losses of $3,000 from January 1 to March 9, 2013.

The holding company will inject added capital and augment the management of Lofty Limited in an attempt to turn Lofty's widget manufacturing business around.

— *REQUIRED*

(A) What are the tax implications of the acquisition of the shares of Lofty Limited by Holdco Ltd., assuming the maximum election under paragraph 111(4)(*e*) is made?

(B) Determine the minimum amount of elected proceeds under paragraph 111(4)(*e*) to offset expiring losses, if the accrued gains on the land were $100,000 instead of the $56,000 and Lofty Limited had an additional loss arising from property of $10,000.

Exercise 7

ITA: 3, 110.1–112

Reconsider the example problem of FT Limited in this chapter in ¶11,160. If $3,378 less capital cost allowance had been taken in 2012, all $23,000 of the inter-company dividends could have been deducted, pursuant to section 112, in 2012.

— *REQUIRED*

Recalculate the taxable income of the corporation for the years indicated after taking $7,900 less in capital cost allowance for Class 8 in 2012. Comment on whether the corporation is in a better tax position at the end of 2013 with respect to capital cost allowance and taxable income under this alternative.

Exercise 8

ITA: 110.1, 111, 112

Plego Limited, a Canadian corporation, had its net income under Division B computed as follows for the year ending December 31:

Par. 3(*a*)	Income from non-capital sources:	
	Income from business operations	$ 66,625
	Income from foreign property	7,175
	Dividends from taxable Canadian corporations	12,300
Par. 3(*b*)	Net taxable capital gains	30,750
Income under Division B		$116,850

During the year the corporation made charitable donations of $80,000. Its carryforward position from the previous year was as follows:

Charitable donations	$10,250
Non-capital losses	61,500
Net capital losses (realized in 1999)	41,000

— REQUIRED

Compute the corporation's taxable income for the current year.

Exercise 9

ITA: 126

Exporter Limited is a Canadian public company carrying on a part of its business through an unincorporated branch in Japan. Its income from that business in Japan for the current taxation year ended December 31 was 75,593,884 yen. The corporation paid income tax instalments on that income during the year of 30,237,521 yen. During the year the exchange rate was 1 yen = C$0.0108.

During its current taxation year ended December 31, Exporter's income under Division B was $2 million excluding the income from Japan. During the year, the corporation received dividends of $100,000 from taxable Canadian corporations. This amount was included in the computation of Division B income. The corporation was also able to deduct $25,000 of its net capital losses carried forward. There was no foreign investment income during the year. Taxable income earned through a permanent establishment in Canada comprises 75% of total taxable income.

— REQUIRED

Compute the corporation's foreign business tax credit for the year.

Exercise 10

ITA: 110–112, 123, 124, 125.1, 126, 127

Maxprof Limited is a Canadian public company with the following income under Division B for its taxation year ended December 31, 2013:

Wholesaling income	$1,495,000
Foreign business profits (before $36,800 in taxes paid)	115,000
Dividends from taxable Canadian corporations	517,500
Dividends from foreign investments (before $25,875 in taxes withheld)	172,500
Canadian interest income (investment income)	345,000
Income under Division B	$2,645,000

During the year the company made donations of $69,000 to registered charities and $5,750 to federal political parties. It was carrying forward non-capital losses of $127,600. It is considered to earn 86% of its taxable income in Canada, as computed by the Regulation.

— REQUIRED

Compute the federal Part I tax payable for the year.

Exercise 11

ITA: 127

Consider the following data:

Cost of qualified property eligible for investment tax credit in Nova Scotia	$900,000
Capital cost allowance class (rate)	Class 1 (6%)
Taxable income before capital cost allowance on above	$300,000
Federal tax rate after abatement and reduction	18%
Federal political contributions tax credit	$500

— REQUIRED

Compute the amount of the investment tax credit that will be deductible for the year and the net federal Part I tax payable after the investment tax credit.

Exercise 12

ITA: 110–112, 123, 125.1, 126, 127, 127.1

Reconsider the data in Exercise 10. Assume that "qualified property" for Class 10 has been purchased in the Atlantic provinces for $3.5 million in 2013. Also, assume that wholesaling income given as $1.495 million in Exercise 10 will be reduced by capital cost allowance on this new property.

— REQUIRED

Compute the maximum investment tax credit deduction for the year.

¶11,875 ASSIGNMENT PROBLEMS

Problem 1

ITA: 3, 110.1–112

The following data summarize the operations of Red Pocket Limited for the years of 2010 to 2013 ended September 30.

	2010	*2011*	*2012*	*2013*
Income (loss) from business	$54,000	$32,000	$(75,000)	$62,500
Dividend income — Taxable Canadian corporations	42,500	22,500	18,000	10,500
Taxable capital gains	11,000	2,500	5,000	9,000
Allowable capital losses	2,000	4,500	3,500	—
Allowable business investment loss	3,750	—	—	—
Charitable donations	23,000	9,000	3,000	13,000

The corporation has a net capital loss balance of $13,500 which arose in 1999.

— *REQUIRED*

Compute the taxable income for Red Pocket Limited for the years indicated and show the amounts that are available for carryforward to 2014. (Deal with each item line-by-line across the years, rather than computing income one year at a time.)

Problem 2

ITA: 111(4), 111(5), 111(5.1), 249(4)

In 2010, a chain of bakeries, called Buscat Ltd., commenced operation. The industry is highly competitive and because of Mr. Buscat's lack of marketing skills, the corporation incurred losses in the first three taxation years of operations as follows:

Taxation year end	*Non-capital losses (business)*	*Capital losses*
Dec. 31, 2010	$60,000	$12,000
Dec. 31, 2011	45,000	8,000
Dec. 31, 2012	25,000	4,000

On July 1, 2013, Mr. Buscat decided to sell 75% of his common shares to Mr. Bran, owner of Buns Plus Ltd. Mr. Bran has been in the business of supplying bread dough, pastry dough and bun bags for 10 years and has been very successful. Buns Plus Ltd. has two divisions: a bakery and a coffee shop, which it intends to transfer to Buscat Ltd.

The following income tax data relates to Buscat Limited's operations from January 1, 2013 to June 30, 2013:

(a) Business loss (before inventory valuation)	$10,000
(b) Allowable capital loss	2,000
(c) Property loss (assets sold in April)	5,500
(d) Assets at June 30, 2013:	

	Cost/ACB	*UCC*	*FMV*
Inventory	$ 85,000	—	$ 65,000
Land	155,000	—	195,000
Building (Class 1: 4%)	65,000	$45,000	75,000
Bakery equipment	100,000	86,000	70,000

During the later part of the 2013 calendar year, the bakery/coffee shop of Buns Plus Ltd. was transferred to Buscat Ltd. For the six-month period ending on December 31, 2013, Buscat Limited had net income of $90,000 from all its businesses.

The net income earned was as follows:

Buscat bakery	$(55,000)
Buns Plus bakery	130,000
Coffee shop	15,000
	$ 90,000

In the 2014 taxation year, Buscat Ltd. expects to earn $250,000, of which $65,000 will be from the original Buscat bakery business and $20,000 from the coffee shop business.

— REQUIRED

Prepare an analysis of the income tax implications of the acquisition of shares. In your analysis, consider the two election options from which an election choice is most likely to be made.

Problem 3

On November 1, 2013, Chris purchased all the issued shares of Transtek Inc. from an acquaintance, Tom. Transtek carries on a transmission repair business and has done so since its incorporation on January 1, 2012. In addition to the transmission repair business, Transtek rents out a small building it owns. Neither the transmission repair business nor the rental endeavour has been successful.

When Chris purchased Transtek, his financial projections indicated that Transtek would have significant income within two years. Chris credited Transtek's failure to Tom's brash personality and laziness. Chris, on the other hand, has a strong work ethic and has many contacts in the automotive industry to refer work to him.

The values of the capital assets owned by Transtek at the time of purchase by Chris are as follows:

	Repair shop		*Rental property*	
	Land	*Building*	*Land*	*Building*
FMV	$140,000	$230,000	$70,000	$120,000
Cost/ACB	80,000	150,000	90,000	120,000
UCC	—	147,000	—	120,000

Chris selected June 30, 2014, as the first fiscal year-end for Transtek after his purchase. The following is a schedule of Transtek's income (and losses) from its inception, January 1, 2012 through June 30, 2015.

Period	*Transmission repair business*	*Rental income (loss)*	*Capital Loss*
Jan. 1/2012–Dec. 31/2012	$ (40,000)	$(2,000)	$ (10,000)
Jan. 1/2013–Oct. 31/2013	(60,000)	(5,000)	—
Nov. 1/2013–June 30/2014	(25,000)	6,000	—
July 1/2014–June 30/2015	54,000	11,000	—

— REQUIRED

(A) Discuss the tax implications of the acquisition of Transtek Inc. on November 1, 2013, ignoring all possible elections/options.

(B) Determine the tax consequences of the acquisition of Transtek Inc. under the assumption that:

(i) the maximum amount of all elections/options is utilized; and

(ii) the partial amount of all elections/options is utilized so that only enough income is generated to offset most or all of the losses which would otherwise expire on the acquisition of control.

ITA: 111(4), 111(5), 111(5.1), 249(4)

Problem 4

ITA: 9–20, 38–55, 110.1–112

The controller of Video Madness Inc. has prepared the accounting income statement for the year ended April 30, 2013:

VIDEO MADNESS INC.
INCOME STATEMENT
FOR THE YEAR ENDED APRIL 30, 2013

Sales		$995,000
Cost of sales	$523,000	
Administrative expenses	185,000	(708,000)
Operating income		$287,000
Other income and expenses		55,000
		$342,000
Provision for income taxes		(102,000)
Net income		$240,000

Other Information

(1) Included in the calculation of "Administrative expenses":

(a) Interest on late income tax payments	$ 435
(b) Amortization (maximum capital cost allowance of $149,500)	104,900
(c) Club dues for the local Country Club	1,750
(d) Federal political contributions	2,500
(e) Donations to registered charities	22,500
(f) Property tax with respect to vacant land not being used in the course of the business	3,000
(g) Life insurance premium with respect to the president (the company is the beneficiary; not required for financing)	1,950
(2) Included in the calculation of "Other income and expenses":	
(a) Landscaping of ground around new premise	4,800
(b) Fees paid with respect to the investigation of a suitable site for the company's manufacturing plant	5,500
(c) Dividends received from taxable Canadian corporation of $42,800 and foreign corporation dividends received (not from a foreign affiliate) of C$5,500	48,300
(d) Gain from the sale of another piece of land, used in the business, sold for $200,000 in March (purchased for $73,800)	126,200
(e) Loss on sale of investments held as capital property purchased for $85,000 and sold for $75,000	10,000
(3) Loss carryforwards from 2012 are:	
(a) Non-capital losses	73,800
(b) Net capital losses (realized in 1999)	75,000

— REQUIRED

Prepare a schedule reconciling the accounting net income to income for tax purposes and taxable income. Indicate the appropriate statutory reference for your inclusions or exclusions.

Problem 5

ITA: 124; ITR: 400

The taxpayer, whose head office was in Manitoba, manufactured and sold various fans. Local sales agencies were maintained in Ontario and in Quebec. At the Ontario agency, two qualified representatives handled business under the company name. They were authorized to sign quotations. Contracts could be made, terms of payment arranged and credit given without reference to the head office in Winnipeg. The company name was displayed for public visibility, was used on calling cards, and was listed in the telephone directory. The Ontario agency, occupying one-half of a building with warehouse facilities, maintained an inventory worth about $6,000. Orders for standard-sized fans were filled from stock-in-trade. Orders for large fans were filled from the head office in Winnipeg. The Quebec agency was substantially similar to that in Ontario.

— REQUIRED

Determine whether or not the company has a "permanent establishment" in the provinces of Ontario and Quebec. In reaching a conclusion, compare this situation with the case of *M.N.R. v. Sunbeam* discussed in this chapter. 61 DTC 1063 (Ex. Ct.)

Problem 6

ITA: 123, 124, 126

Barltrop Limited is a Canadian public company involved in the software consulting business. Its controller provided you with the following information related to its 2013 taxation year ended December 31:

Income under Division B from consulting business including $100,000 earned in U.S. operations (before deducting $16,000 U.S. tax paid)	$264,000
Canadian investment royalty income	10,000
U.K. non-foreign affiliate dividend income (before $3,000 tax withheld)	20,000
Taxable dividend received from non-connected Canadian corporations	5,000
Taxable capital gains	6,000
Charitable donations	100,000
Unused foreign tax credit in respect of U.S.	3,000
Net capital losses carried forward arising in 1999	12,000

Barltrop Limited has permanent establishments in the United States, British Columbia, and Alberta. Its gross revenues and salaries and wages data have been allocated as follows:

	British Columbia	*Alberta*	*United States.*
Gross revenues	$3,000,000	$3,000,000	$4,000,000
Salaries and wages	500,000	300,000	200,000

Assume that the British Columbia and Alberta corporation tax rates are both 10%. Also, assume that taxable income for Alberta is computed on the same basis as federal taxable income.

Gross revenues exclude income from property not used in connection with the principal business operation of the corporation.

— *REQUIRED*

Compute the total tax payable by the company for the 2013 taxation year, including provincial tax. Show all calculations.

Problem 7

ITA: 12(1)(*t*), 37, 127(5)–(11); ITR: 2900

Infotech is a public company in its first year of business in the information technology industry. It operates out of a plant in Ottawa, Ontario. In 2013, it incurred $2.2 million of SR&ED which qualifies for deduction under subsection 37(1) of the Act. The breakdown of these expenses is as follows:

Current SR&ED expenditures		$1,700,000	ITA: 37(1)(*a*)
Capital SR&ED expenditures			ITA: 37(1)(*b*)
• new equipment	$300,000		
• used equipment	200,000	500,000	
Total SR&ED expenditures		$2,200,000	

Infotech's federal income tax rate after abatement is 15%. Its taxable income before deducting the $2.2 million claim under section 37 is $3.2 million.

— *REQUIRED*

(A) Compute the maximum investment tax credit available to Infotech in 2013.

(B) Compute the company's net federal Part I tax payable after the investment tax credit, assuming a maximum section 37 deduction is claimed.

(C) What is the amount, if any, of the investment tax credit carryover?

(D) Compute the company's deduction or income inclusion in the following year if no further SR&ED expenditures are made.

Problem 8

ITA: 123, 124, 125.1, 126, 127(5)

Up, Up and Away Limited is a public corporation that distributes hot air balloons in the Province of New Brunswick. For the year ended September 30, 2013, its accounting income statement was as follows:

Sales	$1,225,000
Cost of sales and other expenses including CCA	(725,000)
Operating profit	$ 500,000
Other net income	198,500
Net income before taxes	$ 698,500
Provision for taxes	(200,725)
Net income	$ 497,775

Selected Additional Information

(1) Other income includes:

Dividends from taxable Canadian corporation	$ 85,000
Canadian interest income	52,500
Foreign interest income, net of withholding taxes of $10,000	61,000

(2) Up, Up and Away Limited has a non-capital loss carryforward of $255,545.

(3) Up, Up and Away Limited purchased qualified equipment costing $250,000 which is eligible for the investment tax credit.

(4) Donations to registered charities were $9,755 (deducted from accounting income).

— *REQUIRED*

Calculate the total taxes payable for 2013 using an 11% provincial rate of tax.

Problem 9

ITA: 123, 124, 125.1, 126, 127(5)

Tecniquip Limited is a public corporation whose head office is located in Toronto, Ontario. The activities of the corporation are carried on through permanent establishments in the provinces of Ontario and Alberta, and in the United States.

The following is an allocation of selected items for the fiscal year ended December 31, 2013.

	Ontario ($ '000)	*Alberta* ($ '000)	*U.S.* ($ '000)	*Total* ($ '000)
Sales	$ 6,000	$ 400	$ 4,600	$11,000
Salaries	$ 2,540	$ 960	$ 2,360	$ 5,860

For the year ended December 31, 2013, Tecniquip Limited obtained the following results:

Income from distribution operations in Ontario	$1,000,000
Income from distribution operations in Alberta	240,000
Income from distribution operations in the United States (before C$200,000 of U.S. taxes paid)	800,000
	$2,040,000
Canadian-source interest income (investment)	12,000
Foreign-source investment income (before $3,000 in foreign tax withheld)	20,000
Taxable capital gain	10,000
Taxable dividends from taxable Canadian corporations	15,000
Net income under Division B	$2,097,000

In computing income from distribution, the corporation claimed a deduction of $150,000 under subsection 37(1) of the Act for SR&ED. One-hundred thousand dollars of the deduction related to expenditures of a current nature and $50,000 was the cost of equipment purchased during the year for use by it in scientific research and experimental development carried on in Canada. No SR&ED expenditures are expected to be made in 2014.

During the year, the corporation made charitable donations totalling $50,000 and claimed non-capital losses of $60,000 and the net capital losses carried forward from 1999 of $9,000.

— *REQUIRED*

Compute the federal Part I tax payable and provincial tax at 11.5% for Ontario and 10% for Alberta, assuming that taxable income allocated to those provinces is the appropriate provincial tax base. Show all calculations, whether or not necessary to your final answer.

[For more problems and solutions thereto, see the DVD accompanying this book.]

¶11,880 ADVISORY CASE

King Enterprises Inc.

Ian King has operated a successful office supply wholesaling business, King Enterprises Inc., for many years. Last week, he called to tell you that he is interested in putting an offer in on the shares of a company that is in some financial difficulty, Royal Forms Inc. ("Royal").

Royal is in the business of producing custom, as well as standard, forms for business use. In fact, Royal is a supplier of King Enterprises. This company has been in business for the past eight years, but has been losing money for the past six years. Last year they sold the land and building they used in their operations in a depressed real estate market, in order to get some cash. Their big problem seems to be that they are undercapitalized.

Ian sees this purchase as a real opportunity for him to pick up a company at a bargain price, turn it around to profitability and, at the same time, reduce King Enterprises' tax liability with the losses. He would like you to prepare a report for him on the tax issues before he decides whether to make an offer.

Chapter 12

Integration for Business and Investment Income of the Private Corporation

TOPICS DISCUSSED

LEARNING GOALS

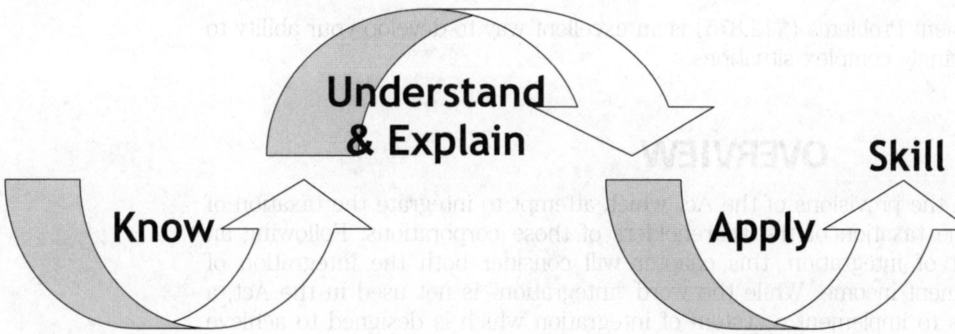

Know

By the end of this chapter you should know how the income tax system works to integrate the tax on individual shareholders with the tax on private corporations for business and investment income. Completing the Review Questions (¶12,800) and Multiple Choice Questions (¶12,825) is a good way to learn the technical provisions.

Understand and Explain

You should understand and be able to explain:

- the concept of integration;
- how the small business deduction from tax is computed and how it helps to achieve integration of business income;
- the rules for the association of corporations and why they exist;
- the base on which the additional investment tax credit for a Canadian-controlled private corporation is computed and how it is limited for scientific research and experimental development expenditures;
- what investment income of a private corporation is and how it is taxed to achieve integration; and
- the advantages and disadvantages of incorporating sources of business income and sources of investment income.

Completing the Exercises (¶12,850) is a good way to deepen your understanding of the material.

Apply

You should be able to apply your knowledge and understanding of the key provisions pertaining to:

- associated corporations, where that term is used in the legislation;
- the calculation of:

— the small business deduction,

— the additional investment tax credit for scientific research and experimental development expenditures,

— the income taxes on investment income of a private corporation, including refundable tax;

- the complete calculation of taxes payable by a private corporation with income from business and investment sources; and
- the decision to incorporate a source of income.

Completing the Assignment Problems (¶12,875) is an excellent way to develop your ability to apply the material in increasingly complex situations.

OVERVIEW

This chapter deals with the provisions of the Act which attempt to integrate the taxation of private corporations with the taxation of the shareholders of those corporations. Following an introduction to the concept of integration, this chapter will consider both the integration of business income and investment income. While the word "integration" is not used in the Act, a series of provisions attempts to implement a system of integration which is designed to achieve certain objectives.

One of the most important reductions of tax available to corporations is the small business deduction which applies to Canadian-controlled private corporations as defined in the Act. This chapter will discuss the rules for computing the small business deduction. It will also deal with the rules for computing the additional investment tax credit where a corporation is eligible for the small business deduction. Then the chapter considers the integration of investment income, including the refundable tax system. This chapter presents the remaining rules that must be followed to make a complete calculation of the tax payable by a corporation.

ITA: 125(7)

The following chart will help to position in the Act some of the major provisions dealt with in this chapter.

PART I

DIVISION E: COMPUTATION OF TAX
DIVISION F: SPECIAL RULES

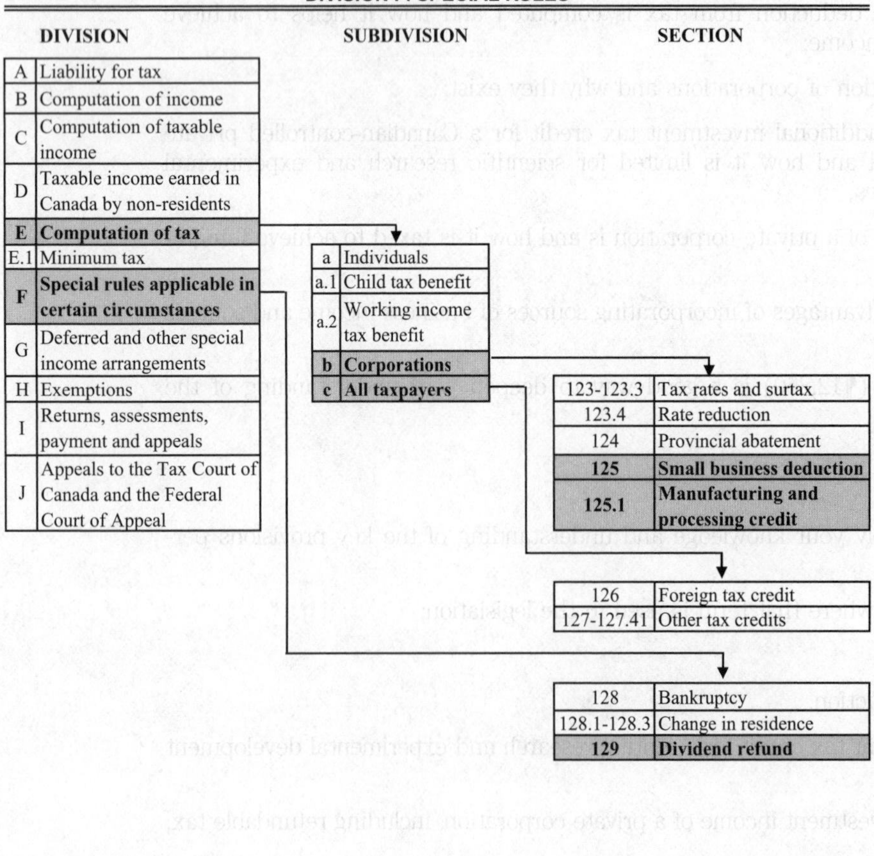

DIVISION
SUBDIVISION
SECTION
A Liability for tax
B Computation of income
C Computation of taxable income
D Taxable income earned in Canada by non-residents
E Computation of tax
E.1 Minimum tax
F Special rules applicable in certain circumstances
G Deferred and other special income arrangements
H Exemptions
I Returns, assessments, payment and appeals
J Appeals to the Tax Court of Canada and the Federal Court of Appeal
a Individuals
a.1 Child tax benefit
a.2 Working income tax benefit
b Corporations
c All taxpayers
123-123.3 Tax rates and surtax
123.4 Rate reduction
124 Provincial abatement
125 Small business deduction
125.1 Manufacturing and processing credit
126 Foreign tax credit
127-127.41 Other tax credits
128 Bankruptcy
128.1-128.3 Change in residence
129 Dividend refund

¶12,000 THE CONCEPT OF INTEGRATION

¶12,010 Issues Addressed by Integration

From a legal perspective, a corporation is an entity separate from its shareholders. In economics, however, there is no more separation between a corporation and its shareholders than between a proprietorship and its proprietor, a partnership and its partners or an investment portfolio and its owner.

As a taxpayer, a corporation is a person which is taxed separately from the natural persons (individuals) who are its shareholders. Hence, this could give rise to double taxation, with the same income being taxed, first, at the corporate level and then, again, at the individual shareholder level. Conceptually, a corporation should really be treated as a non-taxable conduit through which income flows to the individual shareholders, in the same way that a proprietorship business or a partnership business is a conduit through which income flows to the individual proprietor or partners. However, as subsequent comments in this chapter will illustrate, if only individuals and not corporations are subject to tax, problems of an economic or political nature may arise.

¶12,020 Objectives of Integration

Ideally, integration should cause the total tax paid by a corporation and its shareholders to be equal to the total tax paid by an individual who carries on the same economic activity directly and not through the corporation. By integrating the corporate and personal tax systems, the double taxation of corporate income can be avoided. This would make the tax system neutral with respect to the form of organization, used to carry on an economic activity, because there would be no tax advantage or disadvantage to one form of organization over another. Integration would also make the system equitable by ensuring that the tax imposed on income passed through a corporation to an individual is equal in amount to the tax that is imposed on the same amount and type of income earned directly by an individual. Stated differently, the total tax levied on the corporation and the individual in the former situation should be equal in amount to the tax imposed on the individual in the latter situation.

Perfect integration depends on the existence of two assumptions in the tax system. First, where the corporation itself pays tax, the shareholder should include in income and pay taxes on the full pre-tax income earned by the corporation and then receive a full credit for all of the income tax paid by the corporation. To the extent that the shareholder's tax on this income is less than the corporation's tax paid on behalf of the shareholder, the shareholder should get a refund of the difference. This approximates the approach that is taken for employment income. Salaries or wages are subject to withholding, but the employee gets full credit for all taxes withheld. If taxes withheld exceed taxes payable for the year, a refund is due.

The second assumption is that all after-tax income of the corporation should be either paid out as dividends in the year earned or taxed at the shareholder level in that year to avoid the indefinite deferral of tax. This potential deferral would occur if corporate tax rates were lower than individual tax rates. This assumption equates the position of the shareholder with the position of the proprietor, partner or owner of investments who must pay tax on income from his or her economic activity whether or not it is distributed.

¶12,030 The Major Tool for Integration in the Income Tax Act

¶12,035 The concept of integration

The mainstay of the integration system as it applies to individual shareholders of all taxable Canadian corporations is the gross-up and tax credit procedure which is illustrated in Exhibit 12-1. The gross-up is intended to add to the dividend received by the individual shareholder an amount equal to the total income tax (including provincial tax) paid by the corporation on the income that gave rise to the dividend. Thus, the grossed-up dividend is intended to represent the corporation's pre-tax income. The shareholder will pay tax on the grossed-up dividend at his or her personal rate. The combined federal and provincial tax credit is intended to give the shareholder credit for the total tax paid by the corporation on the shareholder's behalf. This procedure is intended to equalize the tax paid on the income that is flowed through the corporation to its shareholders, with the tax paid on the same income that is earned directly. The potential double taxation of corporate income is thereby avoided.

EXHIBIT 12-1
Theoretical Taxation of Dividends to Individuals That Demonstrates Perfect Integration

Facts: An individual can earns $1,000 of active business income either personally or in a corporation

Calculate

(1) A = the personal after-tax cash available, if the income is earned by an individual

		Personal
Combined federal and provincial tax rate		34%
Active business income		$1,000
Personal tax		$ 340
After-tax cash — personal	A	$ 660

(2) B = the corporate after-tax cash available for payment of a dividend, if the income is earned in a corporation owned by the individual

Corporate tax rate		**20.0%**	**15.3%**	**27.5%***
Corporate income		$1,000	$1,000	$1,000
Corporate tax, including provincial tax (theoretical rate, i.e., 20%, 15.3% and 27.5%)		200	153	275
After-tax income available for distribution as a dividend	B	$ 800	$ 847	$ 725

(3) C = the personal after-tax cash available, if the corporation distributed its after-tax income as a dividend to the individual as the shareholder

Corporate tax rate		**20.0%**	**15.3%**	**27.5%***
Individual Shareholder				
Dividend		$ 800	$ 847	$ 725
Gross-up (theoretically equal to corporate tax or 25%, 18%** and 38% of the dividend)		200	153	275
Taxable income (yjeoretically equal to pre-tax corporae income		$1,000	$1,000	$1,000
Combined personal tax — federal and provincial		$ 340	$ 340	$ 340
Combined dividend tax credit		200	153	275
Combined personal tax paid on the dividend		$ 140	$ 187	$ 65
After-tax cash available to the individual shareholder from the dividend	C	$ 660	$ 660	$ 660

Compare

A = the personal after-tax cash available, if the income is earned personally, to

C = the corporate after-tax cash available, if the income earned in a corporation and, then, the after-tax corporate retained earnings are distributed as a dividend to the individual as a shareholder

If A = C, integration is perfect

* Possible imperfections in corporate tax rate, given a fixed gross-up and a theoretical total dividend tax credit of 38%.

** [The March 2013 federal Budget proposes to reduce the 25% gross-up rare to 18% for dividends paid after 2013.]

Another way to look at perfect integration is to examine tax rates paid by the individual and the corporation. If the income is earned directly by the individual, he or she will be taxed at the assumed marginal tax rate of 34%. Under perfect integration, the corporation and shareholder will pay 34% in total, if the income is earned through a corporation. Thus, theoretically, under perfect integration, the potential deferral of shareholder tax is simply the difference between the corporate and individual rate as shown below:

Individual tax rate	34%	34%	34%
Corporate tax rate	20%	15.3%	28%
Shareholder net tax rate (potential deferral)	14%	18.7%	6%

Perfect Integration

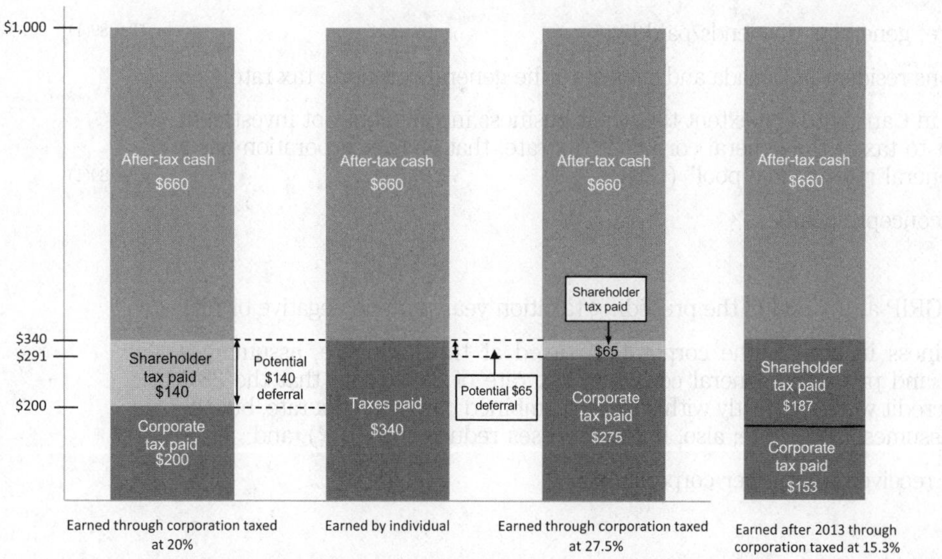

Note that the total tax paid on the income is the same in all three cases. The difference, where a corporation is used, is in the amount of the total tax paid by the corporation compared to the individual. This split is determined by the corporate tax rate. The higher the corporate tax rate, the larger is the share of the total tax paid by the corporation, but the total tax paid by the corporation and the individual shareholder is the same.

Also, the higher the corporate tax rate, the lower is the potential deferral of tax on the dividend.

[Note, also, that under the March 2013 federal Budget proposal to reduce the gross-up on low-rate corporate income, the first column would show corporate tax paid of $153 (instead of $200) and shareholder tax paid of $187 (instead of $140). The potential deferral would be $187, i.e., the tax on the dividend to the individual shareholder.]

¶12,040 Application of the concept in theory

Historically, integration has worked where the corporate tax rate was 20%. As shown in the 20% column of Exhibit 12-1, $1,000 of corporate income attracts tax of $200. The resulting $800 is paid as a dividend to an individual who then grosses this up by 25%, or $200, resulting in taxable income of $1,000, which was equal to the pre-tax corporate income. The individual then pays personal tax on the dividend at, for example, 34%, or $340, and receives a dividend tax credit equal to the underlying corporate tax of $200. The end result is that the corporation and individual together pay the same amount of tax ($340) as if the individual earned the income directly. This is an example of perfect integration.

[In recognition of the fact that the low corporate rate is now less than 20% in all provinces and territories, when the federal and provincial tax rates are combined, the March 2013 federal Budget proposes an 18% gross-up that will result in perfect integration at a combined corporate rate of 15.3%. The 25% gross-up, when applied to corporate income taxed at less than 20%, resulted in an unintended tax savings from incorporating income taxed at the low rate.]

To address issues that arose from the imperfections in the integration system where the corporate tax rate was considerably higher than 20%, a different gross-up and tax credit for "eligible dividends" paid out of the general rate income pool (GRIP) was introduced. The 27.5% column of Exhibit 12-1, assumes an underlying corporate tax rate of 27.5%. Then, the gross-up is 38% to return the personal income to the pre-tax corporate level. Again, the dividend tax credit is equal to the underlying corporate tax and gross-up to result in the shareholder being indifferent between earning the $1,000 personally or through a corporation. As the general corporate tax rate on business income has been reduced, the gross-up has been reduced to 38%.

"Eligible dividends" are, generally, dividends paid by: ITA: 89(1)

(i) public corporations resident in Canada and subject to the general corporate tax rate, and

(ii) CCPCs resident in Canada to the extent that their business income, but not investment income, is subject to tax at the general corporate tax rate; that is, the corporation has a balance in its "general rate income pool" (GRIP). ITA: 89(1)

The GRIP, in general concept, includes:

the sum of:

- the corporation's GRIP at the end of the preceding taxation year (can be negative or nil),
- the after-tax business income of the corporation taxed at the high rate, assuming a combined federal and provincial general corporate tax rate of 28% (note that the 38% gross-up and tax credit works perfectly with a 27.5% combined corporate tax rate, but the GRIP definition assumes a 28% rate; also, business losses reduce the GRIP), and
- eligible dividends received from other corporations

less:

- eligible dividends paid in the preceding taxation year.

There are also special rules:

- to allow a CCPC that receives an "eligible dividend" to pay an "eligible dividend", and
- to require a corporation that can normally pay an "eligible dividend" but has received an "ineligible dividend" to pay the "ineligible dividend" first, or be subject to a penalty.

Note that the 28% assumed corporate rate, used above, was derived from a specified "general rate factor" of 72% (i.e., .28 = 1.00 – .72). ITA: 89(1)

Under perfect integration, the corporate tax is like a withholding tax on the shareholder's income which the corporation earns on behalf of the shareholder. In a sense, it is similar to the withholding of tax on the salary or wages of an employee. Thus, the corporate tax prevents the tax on income earned by a corporation from being deferred until a dividend is paid and is then taxed in the hands of the shareholder. When the shareholder receives a dividend, the full pre-tax income earned by the corporation is reported by the shareholder, through the gross-up mechanism, just as an employee reports gross salary or wages. Then, tax is computed at the shareholder's personal rate. In the same way that taxes withheld from salary or wages are used to reduce the employee's final tax payable, so the dividend tax credit (representing the tax paid by the corporation) reduces the shareholder's tax payable on the dividend income.

¶12,045 Basis for the calculation of the dividend tax credit

A major assumption in Exhibit 12-1 is that the dividend tax credit for individuals is equal to the underlying corporate tax and the gross-up. Using the facts in Exhibit 12-1, this can be illustrated as follows: ITA: 121

Total corporate tax rate	*20%*	*15.3%*	*27.5%*
Dividend	*Non-eligible*	*Non-eligible (after 2013)*	*Eligible*
Calculation based on gross-up (per ss. 82(1))			
Dividend gross-up from Exhibit 12-1	$ 200	$ 153	$ 275
Federal dividend tax credit			
⅔ of the gross-up	$ 133		
13/18 of the gross-up		$ 110	
6/11 of the gross-up			$ 150
Provincial dividend tax credit (theoretical)			
⅓ of the gross-up	67		
5/18 of the gross-up		43	
5/11 of the gross-up			125
	$ 200	$ 153	$ 275

The federal dividend tax credit provides for the credit to be equal to two-thirds [13/18 for dividends paid after 2013] of the gross-up on taxable dividends, other than eligible dividends, from a corporation resident in Canada, and 6/11 of the gross-up on eligible dividends received. ITA: 82(1)(*b*), 121

Dividends eligible for the 25% [18% after 2013] gross-up are:

- dividends from the active business income of CCPCs that is eligible for the small business deduction
- dividends from the investment income of CCPCs

Dividends eligible for the 38% gross-up are:

- dividends from the active business income of CCPCs that is **not** eligible for the small business deduction
- dividends from Canadian public companies, and other corporations that are not CCPCs, that are resident in Canada and subject to the general corporate income tax rate

Where the combined federal and provincial corporate rate of tax is anything other than 20% [15.3% after 2013] or 27.5%, the system of integration breaks down. The imperfections in the integration system will be considered in more detail in this chapter. The chapter will also consider some tools of integration that help to bring the corporate rate of tax close to the perfect 20% [15.3% after 2013] on the first $500,000 of active business income and on all of the investment income earned by a Canadian-controlled private corporation.

¶12,100 INCOME FROM AN ACTIVE BUSINESS OF A CCPC

¶12,110 Introduction to the Small Business Deduction

The small business deduction represents a credit against the tax otherwise payable on income "from an active business carried on in Canada" and is designed only for small "Canadian-controlled private corporations" in order to assist them to retain capital to expand their businesses. Note, however, that the corporation does not have to be "small" in order to qualify for the credit.

The benefits of the small business deduction are phased out for very large Canadian-controlled private corporations. The rules that implement this phase-out are presented in the next segment of this topic.

Exhibit 12-2 illustrates how the small business deduction affects the calculation of the effective total corporate tax introduced in Exhibit 11-3.

EXHIBIT 12-2
Tax Rates Applicable to Taxable Income Eligible for Small Business Deduction

Federal tax rate	38.00%	ITA: 123(1)
Federal abatement for provincial tax	(10.00)	ITA: 124(1)
Net federal tax after federal abatement	28.00%	
Small business deduction	(17.00)	ITA: 125(1)
Total federal tax	11.00%	
Provincial tax (hypothetical) on income qualifying for small business deduction	4.00	
Effective total tax	15.00%	

Note that the effective total tax rate is below the 20% total corporate tax rate that results in perfect integration. Many provinces have a lower rate than the 4% used in the exhibit, making the effective total tax even lower. The significance of a total corporate rate under 20% will be discussed later in this chapter. [The existence of total corporate tax rates lower than 20% is the reason for the March 2013 federal Budget proposal to reduce the gross-up to 18% on dividends from income taxed at that low corporate rate.]

The hypothetical provincial tax rate of 4% used in Exhibit 12-2 above reflects an average provincial equivalent of the federal small business deduction. Remember that in Chapter 11, Exhibit 11-4 used an assumed provincial rate of 13% because most provincial basic tax rates lie between 10% and 16%. Most provinces also give an equivalent small business tax credit, resulting in an effective provincial rate ranging from 0% to 8% on the first $500,000 of active business income.

The prime qualification that a corporation must meet to get the benefit of the small business deduction is that it be, throughout the taxation year, a "Canadian-controlled private corporation" (CCPC). This term is discussed by the CRA in an Interpretation Bulletin. A CCPC is distinguished, on the basis of control, from a "private corporation". A "private corporation" is further distinguished from a "public corporation", primarily on the basis of whether any of the corporation's shares are listed on a designated Canadian or foreign stock exchange. ITA: 89(1), 125(7) IT-458R2

¶12,120 Mechanics of Calculation of Small Business Deduction

¶12,125 The basic limits

¶12,125.10 *Eligibility*

A Canadian-controlled private corporation calculates its tax liability by first applying the standard corporate rate to its total taxable income. After this basic tax amount is determined, the corporation makes various deductions (e.g., M&P profits deduction, investment tax credit, etc.) to determine the final taxes payable. One such deduction is the small business deduction.

A corporation must be a Canadian-controlled private corporation *throughout* the year to qualify for the small business deduction which is a deduction from the tax otherwise payable. For such a corporation, the deduction is calculated by the following formula: ITA: 125(1)

¶12,125.20 *The formula*

Small business deduction = 17% (i.e., the "small business deduction rate" for the year) of the least of: ITA: 125(1), 125(1.1)

(a) net Canadian active business income (i.e., income minus losses);

(b) taxable income fully taxed in Canada achieved by removing from the total taxable income, foreign-source income estimated as the sum of:

(i) foreign-source investment income, estimated as $^{100}/_{28}$ [Bill C-48, which received Royal Assent and became law on June 26, 2013] times the foreign tax credit on foreign non-business income, determined without reference to the additional refundable tax on investment income, ITA: 126(1)

(ii) foreign-source business income, estimated as the relevant factor (i.e., 4)[1] times the foreign tax credit on foreign business income, and ITA: 126(2), 248(1) definition of "relevant factor"

(iii) taxable income exempt from Part I tax by reason of an enactment of Parliament; and

(c) the business limit, i.e., $500,000 *less* any portion allocated to associated corporations (to be discussed later in this chapter). ITA: 125(2), 125(3)

¶12,125.30 *Interpretation of the formula*

Items (b)(i) and (ii) ensure that foreign income not taxed in Canada, because of a foreign tax credit, is removed from the base amount on which the small business deduction is calculated. This is necessary since Canada should not allow the small business deduction on income on which the corporation does not pay tax as a result of a foreign tax credit or base a tax credit on income that is not Canadian-source active business income.

Conceptually, the adjustment in item (b)(i), above, removes from taxable income an estimate of foreign investment income by multiplying by $^{100}/_{28}$ the tax credit which is assumed to be 28% of the foreign investment income. The 28% rate is based on an assumed corporate rate of 38% reduced by the 10% federal abatement for income earned in a province or territory. Investment income is subject to that abatement, because it is thought to be earned in a province or territory where the corporation is established, as explained in the previous chapter in the discussion of the foreign tax credit calculation.

Conceptually, the adjustment in item (b)(ii), above, removes from taxable income an estimate of foreign business income by multiplying by 4 the tax credit which is assumed to be 25% of the foreign business income. The 25% rate is intended to approximate corporate income tax rates on this type of income, i.e., 38% − 13%.

Similarly, item (b)(iii) removes from the base for the small business deduction an amount that is not subject to tax. This removal follows from the concept that an amount that is not taxed in Canada should not be in the base for a tax credit which reduces taxes payable in Canada.

¶12,130 Elimination of small business deduction for large CCPCs

Large Canadian-controlled private corporations are not fully eligible for the small business deduction. The amount of the small business deduction is phased out or "clawed back" with a formula based on the amount of taxable capital employed in Canada for the preceding taxation year. The phase-out range is taxable capital employed in Canada between $10 and $15 million. The business limit of $500,000 for purposes of the small business deduction is reduced by $1 for every $10 (i.e., ($15,000,000 − $10,000,000) ÷ $500,000) of taxable capital employed in Canada in excess of $10 million. To offset the effect of short taxation years on this reduction of a CCPC's business limit, the large corporations tax base is grossed up to reflect a full taxation year. Reductions in the business limit for short taxation years are based on a daily proration. ITA: 125(5.1), Part I.3

The above limitation also applies to a group of associated corporations. Therefore, the associated corporations' total taxable capital employed in Canada in excess of $10 million serves as the basis for the corporate group's business limit reduction.

"Taxable capital employed in Canada" is a term that is defined in the Act. ITA: 181.2

ITA: 125(5.1)

[1] The definition of "relevant factor" in subsection 248(1) provides a formula that results in a factor of 4 (i.e., 1/(.38 − .13). The .13 in the formula represents the general rate reduction [introduced in Bill C-48, which received Royal Assent and became law on June 26, 2013].

This reduction in the small business deduction is implemented through the formula:

$$A \times \frac{B}{\$11{,}250}$$

where

A is the corporation's business limit for the year, and

B is 0.225% × (D – $10 million),

where

D is the corporation's, or the associated group's, total taxable capital employed in Canada for its preceding taxation year.

While the reduction is theoretically based on taxable capital employed in Canada, the formula uses the large corporations tax, which is no longer applicable. The $11,250 in the formula represents the former Part I.3 tax rate of 0.225% on $15 million of taxable capital employed in Canada (0.225% × ($15,000,000 – $10,000,000) = $11,250). Note that when taxable capital reaches $15 million, the business limit is fully clawed back.

As shown in the following example problem, an easier way to obtain the same result is to multiply the business limit allocated to the corporation by the fraction where the numerator is the excess of taxable capital over $10 million and the denominator is $5 million, which is the range of taxable capital over which the clawback occurs.

Example Problem 12-1

Lennox Inc., a Canadian-controlled private corporation, has a fiscal year-end of December 31. Little-Big Inc. is not associated with any other corporation and all of its income is earned in Canada. The following selected tax information has been provided for 2013:

Active business income	$ 350,000
Taxable income	500,000
Taxable capital employed in Canada in 2012	13,000,000

— REQUIRED

Determine Little-Big Inc.'s small business deduction for the 2013 taxation year.

— SOLUTION

Business limit:

Before reduction . . . $ 500,000

Reduction:

$$\$500{,}000 \times \frac{.00225 \times (\$13{,}000{,}000 - \$10{,}000{,}000)}{\$11{,}250}$$

$$= \$500{,}000 \times \frac{\$3{,}000{,}000}{\$5{,}000{,}000} \quad (300{,}000)^*$$

Business limit . . . $ 200,000

Small business deduction for 2013:

17% of least of:

(a) active business income	$350,000
(b) taxable income	$500,000
(c) business limit	$200,000
Least amount	$ 200,000

17% of $200,000	$ 34,000

* The same result can be achieved by multiplying the business limit of $500,000 by the fraction that the excess of taxable capital over $10 million (i.e., $3,000,000) is of the $5 million range over which the clawback occurs. In this case, $500,000 × ($3,000,000/$5,000,000) = $300,000.

¶12,140 Definition of "Active Business"

¶12,145 The "default" definition

One of the major issues with the implementation of the small business deduction in 1972 was the lack of a statutory definition of "active business". An Interpretation Bulletin outlined the CRA's opinion of the meaning of the term, but it was often successfully challenged in the courts. A definition of "active business" was subsequently added to the legislation. IT-73R6

The current definition of the term reads as follows: ITA: 125(7)

> "active business carried on by a corporation" means any business carried on by the corporation other than a specified investment business or a personal services business and includes an adventure or concern in the nature of trade.[2]

Note how this definition is a "default" definition, since the income must be determined not to be from a specified investment business or a personal services business.

¶12,150 Specified investment business

As noted in the definition of active business income, all income from carrying on a business is considered to be active *other than* for a specified investment business or a personal services business. Consequently, income earned by a specified investment business (SIB) does not qualify for the small business deduction. The purpose of introducing the small business deduction (SBD) was to establish a special low rate of tax applicable to the income of a CCPC from an "active business carried on in Canada". The concept of specified investment business was introduced as the mechanism by which property income is excluded from enjoying the benefits of the small business deduction. This provision ensures that no incentive is provided for individuals who might incorporate in order to obtain lower tax rates by having income from property earned by a private corporation. ITA: 125(7)

A "specified investment business" (SIB), which is excluded from that definition of "active business", is defined to mean: ITA: 125(7)

- a business (other than the business of a credit union or of leasing property other than real property),
- the principal purpose of which is to derive income from property (including interest, dividends, rents and royalties),
- *unless* the corporation employs in the business throughout the year *more than* five full-time employees.

In the decision of *489599 B.C. Ltd. v. The Queen*, the Tax Court of Canada, based on strong reasoning, concluded that five full-time and two part-time employees met the condition requiring more than five full-time employees. This conclusion was not appealed by the Crown. The CRA has announced that it will follow the decision in *489599 B.C. Ltd.* 2008 DTC 4107 (T.C.C.) Doc. 2008-02991617

In paragraph (*b*) of the definition "specified investment business", the Act goes on to allow an exception where a corporation would have employed more than five full-time employees but does

[2] Note that this definition is used only for the purpose of section 125. A definition of "active business" can be found in subsection 248(1) which is to be used whenever the term is used elsewhere in the Act. The phrase, "an adventure or concern in the nature of trade", is not included in the definition of "active business" in subsection 248(1). However, the phrase is part of the definition of "business" in subsection 248(1).

not because another corporation associated with it provides the services that would otherwise have been performed by its own employees.

A specified investment business is restricted to a business which generates property income, including dividends, interest, rent (leasing) and royalties. Note that by virtue of the exception contained in the brackets in the definition, the business of leasing movable property (i.e., not real property) is an active business. The taxation of investment income, including income from a specified investment business, will be discussed later in the chapter.

Example Problem 12-2

Ava Ltd. owns an apartment building in downtown St. John's. The only employees of Ava are the two shareholders. Ava earns income from rents and has some interest income.

— *REQUIRED*

(a) Is Ava a specified investment business?

(b) Would it matter if all the apartments were on leases and not month-to-month tenancies?

(c) What if Ava had seven full-time employees?

— *SOLUTION*

(a) Yes, as Ava earns its income in the form of rents and does not have more than five full-time employees.

(b) No, that makes no difference, as the leasing income is from leasing real property.

(c) In that case, Ava would be eligible for the small business deduction. Whether the interest income would qualify for the SBD depends on whether the interest is from a "permanent" investment (no SBD) or is ancillary income (SBD applies). See ¶12,160 for a discussion of this concept.

¶12,155 Personal services business

A personal services business (PSB) is the second type of business income specified as ineligible for the small business deduction. A "personal services business" can be thought of as an incorporated employee. In such a situation, income from the personal services business does not qualify as ABI. In addition, deductions are limited to those that may be claimed in computing income. A company that would otherwise constitute a PSB is exempt if it has more than five full-time employees or when the service is provided to, and the income is received from, an associated corporation.

ITA: 125(7)

ITA: 18(1)(*p*)

A "personal services business" (PSB) is also excluded from the definition of the term "active business". A "personal services business" is defined to mean:

ITA: 125(7)

- a business of providing services where
  - (i) an individual who performs services on behalf of the corporation ("incorporated employee"), or
  - (ii) any person related to the incorporated employee

  is a specified shareholder defined to mean, in part, an owner, directly or indirectly, of 10% or more of the shares of the corporation;

ITA: 248(1) "specified shareholder"

- the incorporated employee would reasonably be regarded as an officer or employee of the entity to which services are provided;
- *unless*

(iii) the corporation employs throughout the year more than five full-time employees, or

(iv) services are provided to an associated corporation (to be discussed subsequently).

To determine whether "the incorporated employee would reasonably be regarded as an officer or employee of the entity to which services are provided", it may be necessary to perform an employee versus self-employed analysis, as presented in Chapter 3. The package of common law tests should be applied to the facts pertaining to the relationship between the incorporated employee and the entity to which services are provided. This was done in the case of *Criterion Capital Corporation v. The Queen*. Criterion was held not to be carrying on a PSB and, hence, was eligible for the small business deduction, in part, on the application of the "control" and "ownership of tools" tests. 2001 DTC 921 (T.C.C.)

Classification as a PSB is not advantageous. The category exists to discourage individuals (who would otherwise be employees of the entity to which services are provided) from incorporating, in an attempt to gain the tax advantage of the small business deduction with its low corporate rate. The only deductions allowed to a PSB are: ITA: 18(1)(*p*)

- salary/wages paid to the incorporated employee;
- cost of benefits/allowances paid to the incorporated employee;
- amounts that would have been deductible under section 8 by the employee; and
- legal expenses to collect amounts owing for services.

A corporation carrying on such a personal services business is not eligible for a small business deduction or the general rate reduction [Bill C-48, which received Royal Assent and became law on June 26, 2013] in respect of its PSB income. Furthermore, such a corporation is denied any deductions from the income of the personal services business of the corporation, other than salary, wages and other benefits provided to the individual who performed the services in respect of the personal services business. In addition, the corporation may deduct amounts, in respect of the PSB, that would have been deductible by an employee as costs incurred in selling property or negotiating contracts or legal expenses incurred in collecting amounts owing for services. As indicated in Chapter 11, the credit for employment outside Canada is not available to a corporation carrying on a PSB. ITA: 18(1)(*p*), [123.4(1), proposed]

¶12,160 Income incidental to an active business

"Income of the corporation for the year from an active business" includes any income for the year from an "active business", including any income for the year pertaining to or incident to that business; income from a property held for investment in Canada is specifically excluded. ITA: 125(7)

Ancillary income incidental to the carrying on of an active business will, therefore, be considered as income from an active business in addition to income directly from an active business. Examples of such ancillary income include interest from short-term investment of surplus cash, recaptured capital cost allowance on assets used in the active business, interest on accounts receivable and bad debt recoveries, among others. An Interpretation Bulletin indicates the CRA's interpretation of the concept of ancillary income. IT-73R6, par. 5

It is important to note that a corporation may have income from more than one source. Therefore, it is necessary to analyze the corporate income (Division B) and break it down into its components.

¶12,170 Associated Companies

¶12,175 Overview

When two or more Canadian-controlled private corporations are associated for tax purposes, the business limit of $500,000, or the reduced amount, must be allocated annually, in any manner, among the associated companies for the purpose of determining the small business deduction in each company. A number of other provisions of the Act, also, rely on the concept of association. These include the definitions of the terms "specified investment business" and "personal services business" which were introduced previously in this chapter. The concept of association is, also, used to determine certain limits and rates for the investment tax credit, as discussed later in this chapter.

ITA: 125(3), 127(10.1), 127.1

ITA: 125(7)

ITA: 125(10.1), 127.1

The deeming rule, which will be discussed subsequently in this chapter, pertaining to certain intercorporate payments, depends on association between corporations.

ITA: 129(6)

¶12,180 Related persons

The term "associated corporations" may depend on the definition of "related persons". Related persons include relationships between individuals, between individuals and corporations and between corporations.

ITA: 251, 256

¶12,180.10 *Related individuals*

The key to the definition of relationships is found in relationships between individuals who are connected by blood relationship, marriage or adoption. Exhibit 12-3 (which was introduced in Chapter 6 as Exhibit 6-2) attempts to diagram these relationships (i.e., individuals who are related to a taxpayer (i.e., "you")) schematically. On the horizontal axis, do not attempt to relate individuals at the extreme outer limits (i.e., the second bullet) to each other. They are related to "you".

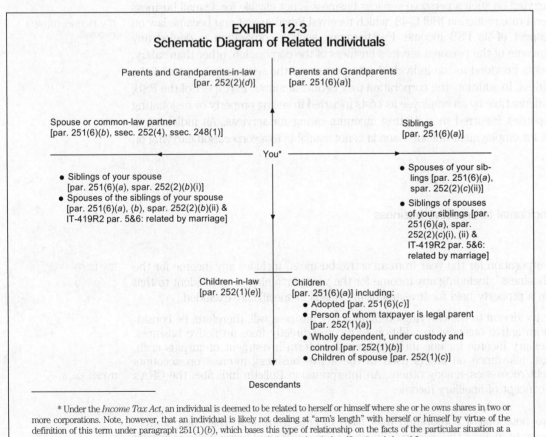

EXHIBIT 12-3
Schematic Diagram of Related Individuals

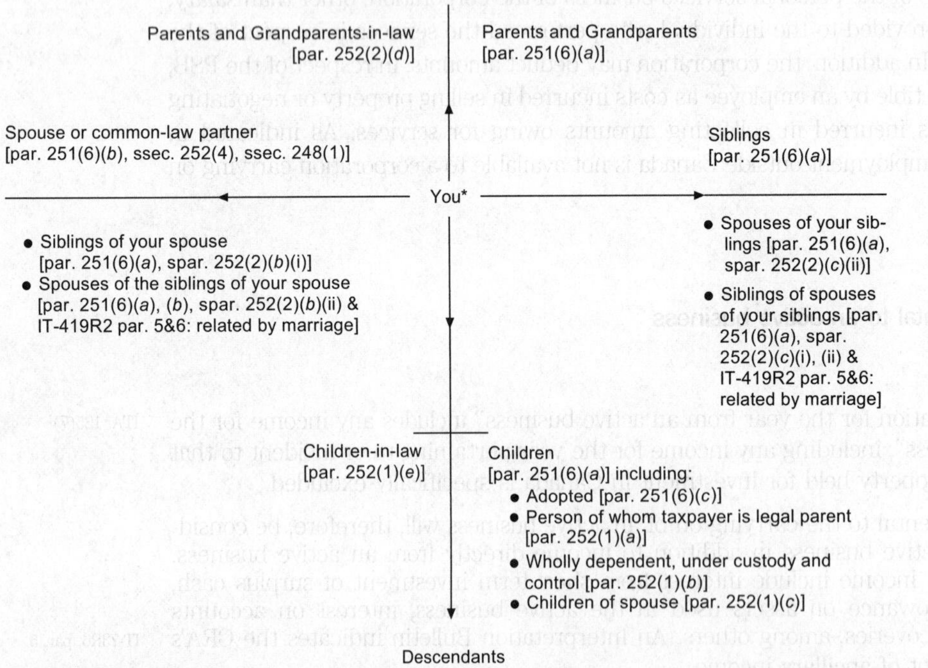

* Under the *Income Tax Act*, an individual is deemed to be related to herself or himself where she or he owns shares in two or more corporations. Note, however, that an individual is likely not dealing at "arm's length" with herself or himself by virtue of the definition of this term under paragraph 251(1)(*b*), which bases this type of relationship on the facts of the particular situation at a particular moment in time. Therefore, be careful which term is being used — "related" or "arm's length".

ITA: 251(5)(*c*), 256(1.5)

Certain individuals who would normally be regarded as related to other individuals are not considered to be related for tax purposes. These individuals, who do not appear in Exhibit 12-3, include: aunts, uncles, nieces, nephews and cousins.

Note that where the word "spouse" is used, the provision extends to a "common-law partner". This term is defined as two persons, regardless of sex, who cohabit in a conjugal relationship and have done so for a continuous period of at least 12 months. ITA: 248(1) "common-law partner"

¶12,180.20 *Relationships involving corporations*

Corporations can be related to individuals and other corporations. The key to understanding corporate relationships is the concept of control. In this context, control refers to legal (*de jure*) control which is generally understood to mean the right of control that rests in the ownership of such number of shares of the corporation as to give a majority of the voting power in the corporation. Control can either be direct or indirect. The latter, for example, could be accomplished through an intermediary corporation.

An example of indirect control would be where A, an individual, owns 80% of the voting shares of A Ltd. which in turn owns 60% of the voting shares of B Ltd.

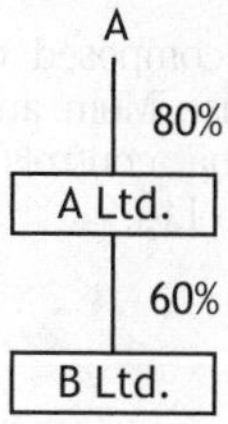

A has more than 50% of the votes of A Ltd. and in turn controls 60% of the votes of B Ltd. through his or her control of A Ltd.

The rules that govern corporate relationships are based on control by individuals or corporations, or groups of either or both. Conceptually, a person (an individual or corporation) is related to a corporation if that person controls the corporation. Similarly, if a person is a member of a related group that controls the corporation, then the person and the corporation are related. A related group is a group of persons each of whom is related to each member of the group. In addition, persons, who are themselves related to the controlling person(s), are deemed to be related to the controlled corporation. ITA: 251(2)(*b*)(i)

A relationship rule expands these concepts to include control by related and unrelated groups, and is summarized below. ITA: 251(2)(*c*), 251(4)

Two corporations are related where:

(a) both corporations are controlled by the same person(s) which could be referred to as a common group;

(b) one corporation is controlled by one person, who is related to a person or any member of a related group that controls the other corporation;

(c) one corporation is controlled by one person or a related group and that person or one member of the related group is related to each member of an unrelated group which controls the other corporation; and

(d) two corporations are controlled by unrelated groups and at least one member of one of the groups is related to each member of the other group.

Example Problem 12-3

Consider the following two groups, each of which controls a corporation with a 50/50 ownership of the shares:

Group One Ltd.	Mom and Dad
Group Two Ltd.	Child of Mom and Dad and Mom's brother

— *REQUIRED*

Determine whether Group One Ltd. and Group Two Ltd. are related.

— *SOLUTION*

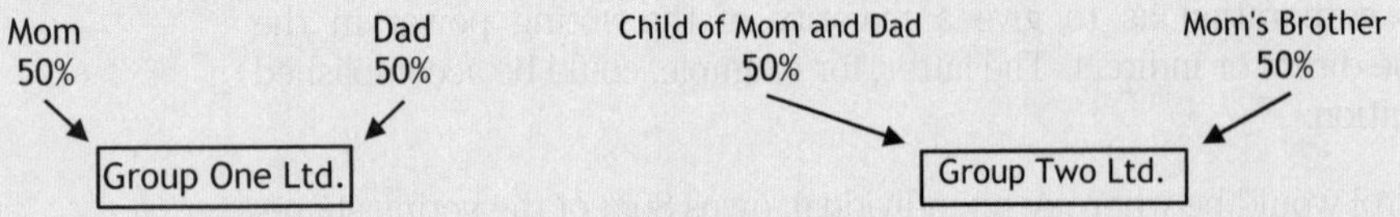

Group Two Ltd. is controlled by an unrelated group since it is composed of an uncle and a niece/nephew. Group One Ltd. is controlled by a related group, because Mom and Dad are related through marriage. In this situation, each member of the related group that controls Group One Ltd. is related to each member of the unrelated group that controls Group Two Ltd.

Therefore, the corporations are related. ITA: 251(2)(*c*)(v)

¶12,185 Basic association rules

Conceptually, two companies are associated for tax purposes, when one company controls the other, or both companies are controlled by the same person or group of persons. However, the definition of associated corporations goes on to list other conditions for association. Therefore, the definition must be consulted to properly evaluate a particular set of facts. The first two general rules each require that only one straightforward condition be met in order to apply. ITA: 256, 256(1)(*a*), 256(1)(*b*)

The last three general rules each contain three conditions, all joined by the word "and", which means that all three conditions must be satisfied for the rule to apply. ITA: 256(1)(*c*), 256(1)(*d*), 256(1)(*e*)

¶12,185.10 *Paragraph 256(1)(c)*

The three conditions that must be met for this rule to apply are:

(i) each of the corporations must be controlled, directly or indirectly in any manner whatever, by a person (which includes an individual or another corporation) (hereinafter referred to as the "control test");

(ii) the person who controls one of the corporations must be related to the person who controls the other corporation (hereinafter referred to as the "related test"); and

(iii) either of the two persons owns not less than 25% of the issued shares of any class, other than a specified class (as defined below), of the capital stock of each corporation (hereinafter referred to as the "cross-ownership test").

Shares of a "specified class" are excluded from the cross-ownership conditions. The term "specified class" is defined to mean a class of shares where: ITA: 256(1.1)

(a) the shares are neither convertible nor exchangeable;

(b) the shares are non-voting;

(c) dividends payable on the shares are fixed in amount or rate;

(d) the annual rate of dividend on the shares, expressed as a percentage of the fair market value of the consideration for which the shares were issued, does not exceed the prescribed rate of interest at the time the shares were issued; and

(e) the amount that a holder of the shares is entitled to receive on their redemption, cancellation or acquisition by the corporation (or by a person not at arm's length with the corporation) cannot exceed the fair market value of the consideration for which the shares were issued (usually, their paid-up capital) plus any unpaid dividends.

The exclusion of a specified class of shares and the 25% cross-ownership test allow a person to invest funds in a corporation controlled by a related person without subjecting his or her own corporation to the consequences of association.

Example Problem 12-4

Dad and Son (age 25) both own 100% of the common shares of their respective corporations: Dadco Ltd. and Sonco Ltd. Dad owns 100% of the preferred shares of Sonco Ltd. The preferred shares are voting, bear a dividend rate of 8%, and are redeemable at $100,000. At the time the preferred shares were issued, the prescribed rate was 10% and the fair market value was $100,000.

—REQUIRED

Determine whether Dadco Ltd. and Sonco Ltd. are associated under subsection 256(1). Substantiate your conclusions by reference to the related provisions of the Act and the conditions contained therein.

—SOLUTION

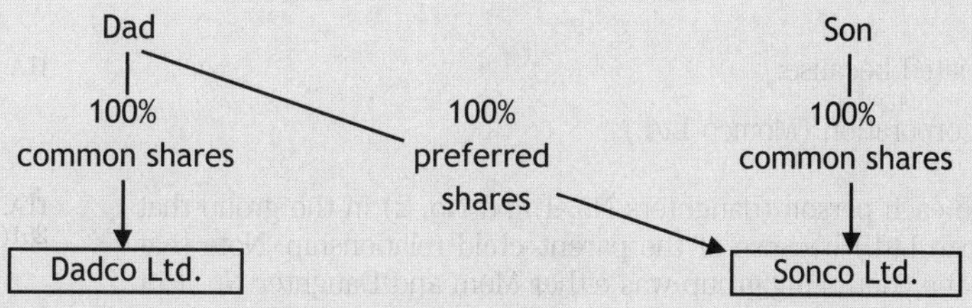

Dadco Ltd. and Sonco Ltd. are associated because: ITA: 256(1)(*c*)

(a) the corporations are controlled directly by either Dad or Son;

(b) Dad and Son are related by blood (i.e., parent–child); ITA: 251(1)(*a*), 251(6)

(c) one of the persons (Dad) owns not less than 25% of issued shares of any class of both corporations, other than specified shares (i.e., 100% of the common shares of Dadco Ltd. and 100% of the preferred shares of Sonco Ltd.); and

(d) the preferred and common shares are not specified shares since both classes have voting rights. ITA: 256(1.1)

¶12,185.20 *Paragraph 256(1)(d)*

Whereas the preceding rule applies to two corporations each controlled by a single person, this rule applies to a situation in which one corporation is controlled by a single person and the other corporation is controlled by a group of persons. The three conditions (involving a control test, a related test and a cross-ownership test) that must be met are:

(i) one of the corporations must be controlled, directly or indirectly in any manner whatever, by one person (control test);

(ii) that person must be related to each member of a group of persons (not necessarily a related group) that controls the other corporation (related test); and

(iii) that person must own not less than 25% of the issued shares of any class, other than specified shares, of the capital stock of the other corporation (cross-ownership test).

Example Problem 12-5

Mom owns 100% of the common shares of Momco Ltd. Her adult daughters, No. 1 and No. 2, each own 35% of the common shares of Sibco Ltd. Mom owns the remaining 30% of the outstanding common shares of Sibco Ltd.

— REQUIRED

Determine whether Momco Ltd. and Sibco Ltd. are associated. Substantiate your conclusions by reference to the related provisions of the Act and the conditions contained therein.

— SOLUTION

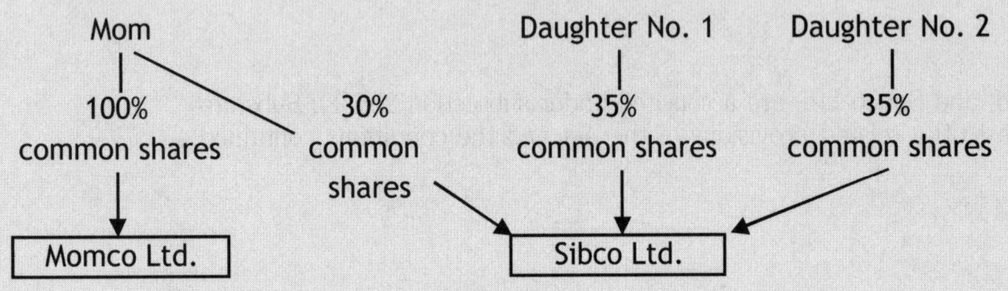

Momco Ltd. and Sibco Ltd. are associated because: ITA: 256(1)(*d*)

(a) one person (Mom) controls one corporation (Momco Ltd.);

(b) that person (Mom) was related to each person (daughters No. 1 and No. 2) in the group that controls the other corporation (Sibco Ltd.) because of the parent–child relationship. Note that the condition would also be met if the controlling group was either Mom and Daughter No. 1 or Mom and Daughter No. 2, since Mom is deemed to be related to herself as a shareholder of both corporations; ITA: 251(1)(*a*), 251(5)(*c*), 251(6)(*a*)

(c) that person (Mom) owns not less than 25% of non-specified shares in the other corporation (30% of the common shares of Sibco Ltd.); and

(d) the common shares of Sibco Ltd. are not specified shares since these shares have voting rights and no restriction on the amount of dividends.

¶12,185.30 *Paragraph 256(1)(e)*

Finally, this rule applies to two group-controlled corporations if the following three conditions (involving a control test, a related test and a cross-ownership test) are met:

(i) each of the corporations must be controlled, directly or indirectly in any manner whatever, by a related group , i.e., a group in which each member of the control group is related to each other member of that control group (control test);

(ii) each member of one of the related groups must be related to all of the members of the other related group (related test); and

(iii) one or more members of both related groups must own, either alone or together, not less than 25% of the issued shares of any class, other than a specified class, of shares of the capital stock of the other corporation (cross-ownership test).

Example Problem 12-6

Alpha and Beta, who are married, each own 50% of the common shares of AB Ltd. Their son, Alpha Jr., age 30, and his wife own 40% and 30%, respectively, of the common shares of Junior Ltd. Beta owns the other 30% of the common shares of Junior Ltd.

— REQUIRED

Determine whether AB Ltd. and Junior Ltd. are associated. Substantiate your conclusions by the related provisions of the Act and the conditions contained therein.

— SOLUTION

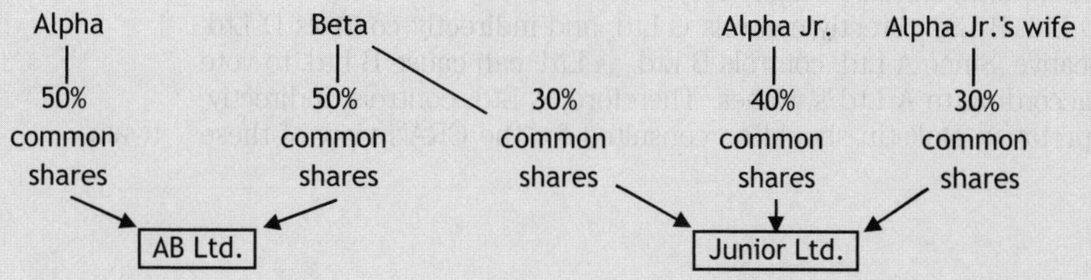

AB Ltd. and Junior Ltd. are associated because: ITA: 256(1)(*e*)

(a) each corporation (AB Ltd. and Junior Ltd.) is controlled by a related group:

- AB Ltd. is controlled by Alpha (50%) and Beta (50%) who are related by marriage; ITA: 251(1)(*a*), 251(6)(*b*)
- Junior Ltd. is controlled by any of:

  (i) Alpha Jr. (40%) and his wife (30%) who are related by marriage, ITA: 251(1)(*a*), 251(6)(*b*)

  (ii) Beta (30%) and Alpha Jr. (40%) who are related by blood, ITA: 251(1)(*a*), 251(6)(*a*)

  (iii) Beta (30%) and Alpha Jr.'s wife (30%) who are related through the extended definition of child, ITA: 252(1)(*e*)

  (iv) Alpha Jr. (40%), Alpha Jr.'s wife (30%) and Beta (30%), all of whom are related;

(b) each member of one related group (Alpha and Beta) is related to all members of the other related group. Note that in cases (ii), (iii), and (iv), above, Beta is related to herself as a shareholder of both corporations; ITA: 251(5)(*c*)

(c) one (or more) member of *both* related groups (Beta) must own not less than 25% (Beta owns 30% in Junior Ltd.) of the issued shares of any class other than specified shares of the other corporation; and

(d) common shares are not specified shares. ITA: 256(1.1)

The following is a list of the key words used in each of the paragraphs of subsection 256(1).

Par. (*a*)	controlled
Par. (*b*)	controlled, person, group of persons
Par. (*c*)	controlled, person, related, owned not less than 25%, specified class
Par. (*d*)	controlled, person, group of persons, related, owned not less than 25%, specified class
Par. (*e*)	controlled, related group, owned not less than 25%, specified class

¶12,190 Concept of control

¶12,190.10 *Legal control*

As a first approximation to the interpretation of the concept of control, the common law definition of legal or *de jure* control can be applied. Legal control means ownership of more than 50% of the voting shares or, more precisely, "ownership of such a number of shares as carries with it the right to a majority of the votes in the election of the Board of Directors".[3] Indirect control applies to the situation where there are multi-tiered corporations but is still based on legal control of more than 50% of the voting shares. For example, assume there is a chain of corporations whereby each parent corporation has 60% of all the voting shares of its subsidiary:

A Ltd. —60%→ B Ltd. —60%→ C Ltd. —60%→ D Ltd.

In each situation, the parent corporation controls its subsidiary. A Ltd. directly controls B Ltd. and indirectly controls C Ltd. and D Ltd. B Ltd. directly controls C Ltd. and indirectly controls D Ltd. Note that control is not multiplicative. Since A Ltd. controls B Ltd., A Ltd. can cause B Ltd. to vote all of B Ltd.'s shares in C Ltd. according to A Ltd.'s wishes. Therefore, A Ltd. controls, indirectly, C Ltd.[4] Furthermore, the Interpretation Bulletin should be consulted for the CRA's view of these rules.[5] [IT-64R4]

¶12,190.20 *Factual control*

A broadening of the concept of legal control may occur in fact situations to which the concept of "control in fact" applies. Using factual control to determine association further restricts the multiplication of the small business deduction by extending the circumstances under which corporations are considered to be associated. As indicated, the concept of control has been interpreted to mean legal or *de jure* control that vests in the ownership of more than 50% of the voting shares, as set out in the *Buckerfield's* case.[6] The expression "controlled, directly or indirectly in any manner whatever" when used throughout the Act, extends the concept of control to actual or *de facto* control which might exist by virtue of a person having any direct or indirect influence. The Technical Notes which accompanied the introduction of the legislation provided the following example of actual control: "where a person held 49% of the voting control of a corporation and the balance was widely dispersed among many employees of the corporation or held by persons who could reasonably be considered to act in respect of the corporation in accordance with his wishes". The Note stated further that "whether a person can be said to be in actual control of a corporation, notwithstanding that he does not legally control more than 50% of its voting shares, will depend in each case on all of the circumstances". [ITA: 256(5.1)]

¶12,195 Extended meaning of control

The concept of control is further broadened by another provision. In determining whether a corporation was controlled by a group of persons, a group means any two or more persons each of whom owned shares of the same corporation. A corporation can be considered to be controlled at the same time by several persons or groups of persons. This concept is shown in the preceding example problem dealing with paragraph 256(1)(*e*). Note how four different groups control Junior Ltd. [ITA: 256(1.2)(*a*), 256(1.2)(*b*)]

A person or group of persons will be deemed to control a corporation when the person or group owns: [ITA: 256(1.2)(*c*)]

(i) shares representing more than 50% of the fair market value of all issued and outstanding shares of the corporation, or

---

[3] Stated in the case of *Buckerfield's Limited et al. v M.N.R.*, (Ex. Ct.) 64 DTC 5301.

[4] For a case on indirect holdings resulting in control see *Vineland Quarries and Crushed Stone Ltd. v. M.N.R.*, 66 DTC 5092 (Ex. Ct.).

[5] As examples of the application of these rules to a fact situation see the cases of *Radio CFUN Limited* and *Wellport Broadcasting Limited v. M.N.R.*, 69 DTC 420 (T.A.B.); *Southside Car Market Ltd. et al. v. The Queen*, 82 DTC 6179 (F.C.T.D.); *Wynndel Logging Co. Ltd. v. M.N.R.*, 80 DTC 1125 (T.R.B.); *Roclar Leasing Ltd. et al. v. M.N.R.*, 81 DTC 544 (T.R.B.); and *B.B. Fast & Sons Distributors Ltd. v. The Queen*, 84 DTC 6554 (F.C.T.D.), affirmed by the Federal Court of Appeal (86 DTC 6106).

[6] See also the case of *The Queen v. Imperial General Properties*, 85 DTC 5500 (S.C.C.).

(ii) common shares representing more than 50% of the fair market value of all issued and outstanding common shares of the corporation.

Note how this rule ignores the voting rights of the shares and looks at the underlying value of the shares in question. For example, assume that a corporation is capitalized with $1,000,000 of non-voting retractable shares owned by Individual A and $1,000 of common shares owned by Individual B. Both A and B control the corporation — Individual B through his or her voting rights and Individual A through the preferred shares which represent more than 50% of the total fair market value of the share capital of $1,001,000.

Since the value of a share can be affected by voting rights and certain other special features, these features are to be disregarded for the purposes of determining the fair market value of a share in this context. Likewise, "term preferred shares" and shares included in a "specified class" should be disregarded for purposes of making the fair market valuation.

ITA: 256(1.2)(*g*)

ITA: 248(1)

ITA: 256(1.1), 256(1.2), 256(1.6)

¶12,200 Ownership of shares

¶12,200.10 *Look-through rules*

The association rules use both of the words "controlled" and "owned". As previously demonstrated, indirect control of a corporation can flow through a chain of corporations through *de jure* control. However, the courts have held that ownership, including indirect ownership, cannot be traced through a chain of corporations. Therefore, provisions were enacted to provide a series of indirect ownership rules which are referred to as the "look-through" rules. These rules apply where shares of a corporation are held by another corporation, a partnership or a trust. A shareholder of a corporation, a member of a partnership or a beneficiary of a trust that holds shares in a corporation would be deemed to own a number of the shares of the corporation as is proportionate to his or her economic interest in the corporation, partnership or trust that actually owns the shares.

ITA: 256(1.2)(*d*), 256(1.2)(*e*), 256(1.2)(*f*)

¶12,200.20 *Example of control and ownership through a corporation*

Consider the facts in the following diagram:

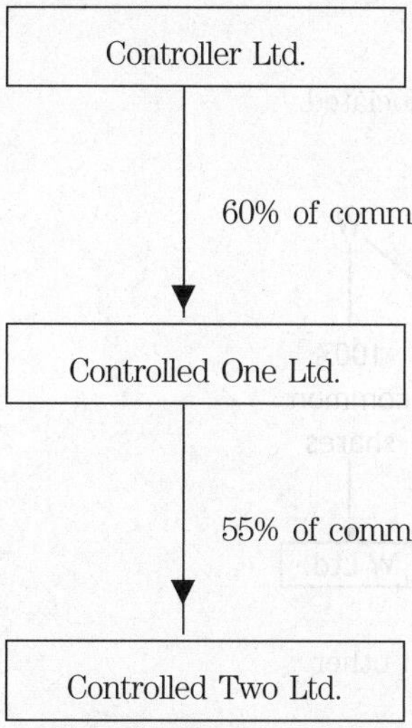

With its 60% ownership of the common shares of Controlled One Ltd., Controller Ltd. controls Controlled One Ltd. Since Controller Ltd. controls Controlled One Ltd., it can cause Controlled One Ltd. to vote the latter's 55% controlling interest in Controlled Two Ltd. in the interest of Controller Ltd. Therefore, Controller Ltd. controls Controlled Two Ltd. through Controlled One Ltd. Controller Ltd. does not own any shares directly in Controlled Two Ltd. through its ownership of shares in Controlled One Ltd. However, paragraph 256(1.2)(*d*) deems Controller Ltd. to *own* 33% (i.e., 60% of 55%) of Controlled Two Ltd.

¶12,200.30 *Shares owned by a minor*

Another such rule deems that shares of a corporation owned by a minor child are owned by each parent of the child. Even if the shares are deemed to be owned by the minor child by another provision of section 256, the shares will be deemed to be owned by each parent. However, an exception is provided if it may reasonably be considered that the child manages the business and affairs of the corporation and does so without a significant degree of influence by the parent. This exception is intended to accommodate young entrepreneurs. ITA: 256(1.3)

¶12,200.40 *Two other deeming rules*

One of these rules pertains to rights to acquire shares (e.g., options) or rights to cause a corporation to redeem shares of other shareholders. The holder of such rights is deemed to be in the same position as if the rights were exercised. The other rule deems a person to be related to himself or herself in his or her capacity as shareholder of two or more corporations. ITA: 256(1.4) ITA: 256(1.5)

¶12,205 Association with third corporation

Where two corporations, that would not otherwise be associated, are both associated with a third corporation, the two corporations are normally deemed to be associated with each other. However, relief from this deeming rule is available, for the purposes of the small business deduction only, if the third corporation is not a Canadian-controlled private corporation or if the third corporation elects not to be associated with either of the other two corporations. For this election to apply, the two corporations associated through a third corporation cannot be associated by any other rule. Note that the election is an annual one. The result of the election is that the business limit of the third corporation is deemed to be nil. ITA: 256(2) ITA: 125

Example Problem 12-7

H and W, a married couple, have incorporated their separate businesses, H Ltd. and W Ltd., both of which are CCPCs. In order to avoid duplication of administrative costs, H and W incorporated a management corporation, M Ltd., to provide support services for H Ltd. and W Ltd. H and W each own 50% of the common shares of M Ltd.

— *REQUIRED*

Determine whether H Ltd., W Ltd. and M Ltd. are associated.

— *SOLUTION*

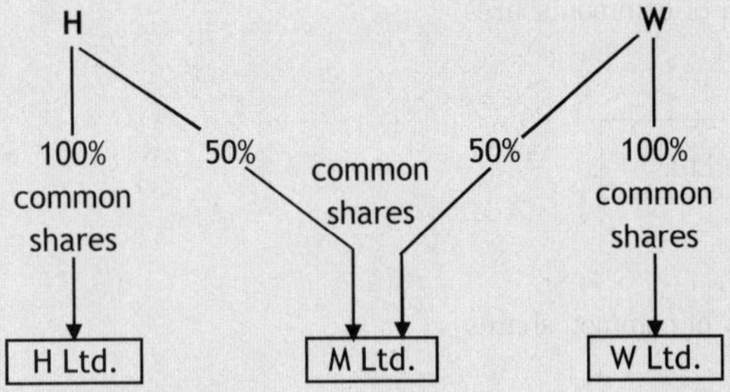

H Ltd., W Ltd. and M Ltd. are all associated with each other.

H Ltd. and M Ltd. are associated: ITA: 256(1)(*d*)

- H controls (100% of common shares) H Ltd.;
- H and W control M Ltd. (50% of common shares each);
- H is related to:

 (a) W through marriage; and ITA: 252(1)(*a*), 252(6)(*b*)

 (b) H through the deemed related rule for a shareholder; and ITA: 256(1.5)

- H owns not less than 25% of non-specified shares of the other corporation (100% of H Ltd. and 50% of M Ltd.).

W Ltd. and M Ltd. are associated also, using the same logic. ITA: 256(1)(*d*)

Therefore, H Ltd. and W Ltd. are associated through a common third corporation, M Ltd. Note that without M Ltd., H Ltd. and W Ltd. would not be associated. ITA: 256(2)

However, if M Ltd. elects, in prescribed form and on a year-by-year basis, not to be associated with either of the other two corporations, then H Ltd. and W Ltd. are deemed not to be associated for that particular year for purposes of the small business deduction. The business limit of M Ltd. is deemed to be nil for the taxation year, so that M Ltd. cannot, itself, benefit from the small business deduction. No election is needed if M Ltd. is not a Canadian-controlled private corporation.

¶12,210 Deemed association

Where one of the main reasons for the separate existence of two corporations that are otherwise not associated is tax considerations, the two corporations may be deemed to be associated. The provision also contains a reasonableness test.[7] The decisions in the *Jutan Importers* and *Leggat Leasing* cases (see footnote 7) suggested that if the taxpayer can show a valid, non-tax reason for the separate existence of a corporation, the presence of a tax reason should not result in the application of the deemed association rule. ITA: 256(2.1)

¶12,220 Corporate Partnerships

The associated corporations rules were designed to prevent the splitting of a business into numerous corporations each of which could qualify for the maximum small business deduction. Thus, corporations within an associated group must share that maximum small business deduction. To prevent the splitting of a business into numerous non-associated corporations operating as partners and each qualifying for the maximum small business deduction, further rules were designed to require that the maximum annual small business deduction limit of $500,000 be shared by corporate partners or groups of corporate partners. These rules are necessary because partnerships are not taxed as separate entities. ITA: 125(6)

Legislation limits deferral opportunities for corporations with significant interests in partnerships. Where a corporation carries on a business through a partnership that has a fiscal period ending after the corporation's taxation year, under current tax legislation, income of the partnership for the later year is included in the income of the corporation for its subsequent taxation year, thereby allowing the corporation to defer tax on its share of the partnership income. This is considered to be inequitable. The proposals will require an accrual of partnership income earned during the taxation year of a corporate partner.

¶12,230 Manufacturing and Processing Profits and the Small Business Deduction

In the previous chapter, the manufacturing and processing profits deduction was alluded to without reference to the effect of the small business deduction on the manufacturing and processing profits deduction. Essentially, there is no manufacturing and processing profits deduction on that portion of Canadian manufacturing and processing profits eligible for the small business deduction. The amount of manufacturing and processing profits deduction for a CCPC is derived conceptually as the excess of manufacturing and processing profits over the amount of income eligible for the small business deduction. Hence, income eligible for the small business deduction will not be eligible for the M&P profits deduction as well. ITA: 125.1(1)

---

[7] For examples of fact situations in which the predecessor to subsection 256(2.1) (i.e., subsection 247(2)) was at issue, see the cases of *Doris Trucking Company Limited v. M.N.R.*, 68 DTC 5204 (Ex. Ct.); *Jordans Rugs Ltd. et al. v. M.N.R.*, (Ex. Ct.) 69 DTC 5290; *Griffin Head Farms Limited v. M.N.R.*, 72 DTC 1225 (T.R.B.); *C.P. Loewen Enterprises Ltd. v. M.N.R.*, 72 DTC 6298 (F.C.T.D.); *Jutan Importers Ltd. v. M.N.R.*, 76 DTC 1289 (T.R.B.); *Leggat Leasing (Halton) Limited v. M.N.R.*, 78 DTC 1035 (T.R.B.); *Lenco Fibre Canada Corp. v. The Queen*, 79 DTC 5292 (F.C.T.D.); *Covertite Limited v. M.N.R.*, 79 DTC 136 (T.R.B.); and *Alpha Forming Corp. Ltd. et al. v. The Queen*, 83 DTC 5021 (F.C.T.D.). A more recent Tax Court of Canada case on this issue, where the decision was in favour of the taxpayer, is *LJP Sales Agency Inc. v. Her Majesty the Queen*, 2004 DTC 2007 (T.C.C.).

Exhibit 12-1 and Exhibit 12-2 are equally applicable in determining the effective total corporate tax rate for income from manufacturing and processing activity that is eligible for the small business deduction.

Example Problem 12-8

During its first taxation year (of 365 days) which ended December 31, 2013, Logic Ltd., a Canadian-controlled private corporation, reported the following incomes:

Manufacturing and processing profits	$ 80,000
Total active business income earned in Canada (including M&P)	105,000
Foreign active business income (foreign tax paid $1,125)	5,000
Taxable income	75,000
Division B income	110,000
Taxable dividends paid in the year	40,000

The corporation carries on business in Canada and is not associated with any other Canadian-controlled private corporation. All foreign tax paid is recovered as a foreign tax credit under subsection 126(2). According to the abatement allocation formula in Regulation 402, 96% of the corporation's taxable income is earned in a province in Canada.

— REQUIRED

Compute the tax payable for 2013 by the corporation under Part I of the Act, assuming a 5% provincial rate of tax.

— SOLUTION

Taxable income			$ 75,000
Basic federal tax (38% of $75,000)			$ 28,500
Federal abatement (10% of 96% of $75,000)			(7,200)
Foreign business tax credit			(1,125)
Small business deduction:			
17% of least of:			
(a) Income from active business carried on in Canada		$105,000	
(b) Taxable income	$75,000		
Less: 4 × foreign business income tax credit (see above: 4 × $1,125)	(4,500)	$ 70,500	
(c) Business limit		$500,000	
17% of $70,500			(11,985)
Manufacturing and processing profits deduction (all of this income is eligible for the small business deduction)			Nil
Federal Part I tax payable			$ 8,190
Provincial tax @ 5% of 96% of $75,000			3,600
Total tax payable			$ 11,790

¶12,235 The General Rate Reduction Revisited

The 13% general rate reduction was introduced in Chapter 11. The objective of this provision is to reduce corporate business income taxed at the full corporate tax rate. Where ITA: 123.4

the corporation is a Canadian-controlled private corporation, some of its income, like income eligible for the small business deduction, aggregate investment income (to be discussed later in this chapter), and personal services business income are not taxed at full corporate rates and, hence, is not eligible for the general rate reduction. As a result, it must be removed from taxable income and that is done by the following calculation:

Taxable income

Less: the amount of income eligible for the manufacturing and processing profits deduction

income from a personal services business

the amount of income eligible for the small business deduction

aggregate investment income

The net is the base for the 13% general rate reduction for a CCPC. That base is the business income of the corporation that is taxed at the full corporate rate.

¶12,240 Investment Tax Credit Revisited

¶12,245 Overview

The investment tax credit (ITC), as described in Chapter 11, is also available for Canadian-controlled private corporations. Refer to the diagram at the end of Example Problem 11-13 for a conceptual overview of the process of dealing with the deduction of the expenditures and the ITC. However, additional incentives are provided for CCPCs. These incentives are obtained by adhering to a strict set of limitations many of which are similar to the restrictions for the small business deduction. This section will describe the advantages and limitations imposed by the legislation.

¶12,250 The ITC rate for CCPCs

¶12,250.10 *Basic rates*

Investment tax credits are presently restricted to qualifying scientific research and experimental development (SR&ED) expenditures[8] for all jurisdictions within Canada. The one very limited exception is the credit for qualifying property expenditures for the Atlantic provinces and the Gaspé at a rate of 10% as described in Chapter 11. The basic SR&ED rate is 20%[9] for all taxpayers including individuals, trusts and corporations. This basic ITC rate of 20% has no dollar limit, except that all of the qualifying expenditures must meet the rules set out in section 37, as described in Chapter 4. ITA: 127(9)

¶12,250.20 *Additional rate of ITC for SR&ED expenditures*

An additional ITC incentive of 15% [20% after 2013] is provided where the taxpayer is a CCPC throughout the taxation year in which the expenditure is made. This additional rate results in a combined tax credit rate of 35%. However, the 15% [20% after 2013] additional credit bears additional restrictions as described below. ITA: 127(10.1)

The additional 15% credit is restricted in total to $3 million of qualifying expenditures, referred to as the SR&ED expenditure limit, but only where the preceding year's taxable income of the corporation and all associated corporations does not exceed the $500,000 small business deduction limit for the year. Where the preceding year's taxable income of the corporation and all associated corporations exceeds $500,000, the SR&ED expenditure limit of $3 million is reduced by $10 for every dollar of excess. Once the corporate group's taxable income reaches $800,000, the SR&ED expenditure limit is reduced to zero. The actual calculation of the expenditure limit in the provision is, generally, $8 million minus 10 times the greater of $500,000 and the taxable income of the associated group for the immediately preceding taxation year. The $3 million expenditure limit is further reduced if the taxable ITA: 127(10.2)

[8] Capital expenditures will be excluded from SR&ED deductions and investment tax credits for property acquired after 2013.

[9] The 20% SR&ED investment tax credit rate will be reduced to 15% for expenditures made after 2013.

capital of the corporation and any associated corporations exceeds $10 million. The expenditure limit is reduced by $3 for every $40 in taxable capital in excess of $10 million. At $50 million of taxable capital, the expenditure limit is nil.

¶12,255 Refundable investment tax credit

Since many small Canadian businesses may not be in a position to pay taxes because of a weak profit position or losses incurred, the investment tax credit is not a strong incentive to invest. Therefore, cash refunds are available to certain taxpayers, in respect of available investment tax credits which cannot be used to offset taxes payable in a particular year. The extent to which a refund is available is a function of the status of the taxpayer, the nature of the expenditure that gave rise to the credit and when the expenditure was made. Investment tax credits that are available for deduction in a taxation year and which cannot be offset against taxes payable or converted into a cash refund, are available for carryover back three taxation years and forward 20 taxation years. However, any ITC that is deducted or refunded in the year must be included in income for the following year in respect of current SR&ED expenditures or deducted from the capital cost of qualifying depreciable capital property acquisitions.

ITA: 12(1)(*t*), 13(7.1)

ITA: 127.1

ITA: 12(1)(*r*), 13(7.1)

The refundable investment tax credit rates available to a qualifying CCPC, i.e., a CCPC or an associated group with total taxable income of less than the $500,000 small business deduction limit, are:

(a) 100% cash refund of the available 35% ITC based on qualifying SR&ED current expenditures not in excess of the expenditure limit for the year;

(b) 40% cash refund of the available 35% ITC based on qualifying SR&ED capital expenditures;[10] and

(c) 40% cash refund of the available 20% [15% after 2013] ITC on qualifying SR&ED current expenditures in excess of the expenditure limit.

Note that the available ITC refers to the ITC as determined by the rules described in the previous section of this chapter.

Example Problem 12-9

Small Limited, a CCPC with a December 31 year-end, spent $4 million in current qualifying SR&ED expenditures in 2013. Small Limited is not associated with any other corporation and may be eligible for an ITC of 35%. Its taxable capital for the preceding year was $9 million.

— *REQUIRED*

Determine the amount of ITCs and refundable ITCs for 2013 on the assumption that its taxable income for the preceding year was:

(a) $500,000,

(b) $600,000, and

(c) $800,000.

— *SOLUTION*

Taxable income of preceding year (2012)	*Expenditure limit*	*Refundable ITC*	*Non-refundable ITC*
(a) $500,000	$3,000,000	$1,130,000[(1)]	$ 120,000[(2)]
(b) $600,000	2,000,000[(3)]	Nil[(4)]	1,100,000[(5)]
(c) $800,000	Nil[(6)]	Nil[(7)]	800,000[(8)]

[10] Capital expenditures will be excluded from SR&ED deductions and investment tax credits for property acquired after 2013.

— *NOTES TO SOLUTION*

(1) (35% × $3,000,000 × 100%) + (20% × $1,000,000 × 40%)

(2) 20% × $1,000,000 × 60%

(3) $8,000,000 – ($600,000 × $10)

(4) Refundable ITC is nil because taxable income in the prior year was in excess of the small business deduction limit.

(5) $2,000,000 × 35% + $2,000,000 × 20%

(6) $8,000,000 – ($800,000 × $10)

(7) Refundable ITC is nil because taxable income in the prior year was in excess of the small business deduction limit.

(8) $4,000,000 × 20%

¶12,260 Prescribed proxy amount

As indicated in Chapter 11, an elective alternative for the treatment of SR&ED overhead expenditures eligible for the investment tax credit was introduced to reduce the amount of record-keeping required. Under this annual election, referred to as a prescribed proxy amount (PPA), a prescribed amount rather than the actual overhead expenditure is eligible for ITC. Under the PPA election, the actual overhead expenditures are deductible from business income as ordinary expenditures rather than as SR&ED expenditures, which are credited to the SR&ED expenditure pool and written off as required. For a more detailed explanation of the treatment of SR&ED expenditures, see Chapter 4. The major difference in the write-off treatment of the two methods is the 20-year limited period of carryforward for ordinary business expenses, as compared to the indefinite carryover for the SR&ED expenditure pool. ITA: 37

The PPA is only used in respect of the determination of ITCs related to SR&ED expenditures, not the deduction of overhead expenditures. The statutory reference to a PPA is found in the definition of the ITC base, a qualified expenditure. The PPA itself is defined in and computed by the Regulations. ITA: 127(9) ITR: 2900(4), 2900(5)

The PPA is basically a substitute for an item-by-item accounting for and allocating of overhead expenditures *directly* attributable to SR&ED in Canada. The PPA (i.e., the amount eligible for the ITC) is 60%[11] of the salary base which is the portion of the salaries of employees directly engaged in SR&ED in Canada. The "portion", referred to above, is determined on a reasonable time allocation basis for each employee engaged in SR&ED, including direct technical management activities. For employees who spend all or substantially all (i.e., 90%) of their time on qualifying SR&ED activities, the whole amount of their salaries is included in the salary base. ITR: 2900(4)

A modification to this rule relates to "specified employees". A specified employee is one who is a specified shareholder of the corporate employer or who does not deal at arm's length with the employer-entity. A specified shareholder is defined as a person who owns, together with the shares of related persons, 10% or more of any class of shares of the corporation. The salary base for specified employees is limited to the lesser of three-quarters of their full salary and 2.5 times the year's maximum pensionable earnings for CPP purposes (i.e., $51,100 for 2013). ITA: 248(1) "specified employees", "specified shareholder" ITR: 2900(7)

Where a PPA election is used, eligible expenditures for SR&ED and the related ITC are restricted to the following non-overhead expenditures: ITA: 37

(a) wages and benefits of employees *directly* engaged in SR&ED activities;

(b) leasing expenses of equipment, other than general-purpose office equipment or furniture, used *all or substantially all* in SR&ED activities;

(c) qualifying third-party payments for subcontracted SR&ED activities;

[11] The prescribed proxy amount for SR&ED purposes will be reduced to 55% for 2014 and subsequent years.

(d) costs of materials used directly in SR&ED activities;

(e) qualified SR&ED capital expenditures used *all or substantially all* (i.e., at least 90%) in SR&ED activities but excluding general purpose office equipment or furniture — see the next topic below; and

(f) capital cost allowance on 50% of the cost of leased equipment, other than general-purpose office equipment or furniture used *primarily* (i.e., more than 50%, but less than 90% (see (b), above)), for SR&ED activities. (See the next topic heading for an expansion of this topic.)

A restriction prevents the PPA from being greater than the total amount, with some adjustments, that would otherwise be deductible as business expenses. ITR: 2900(6)

As a consequence of this election, the definition of a qualified expenditure has been expanded to include PPAs. Therefore, ITCs in respect of a PPA are treated in the same manner as all ITCs in respect of SR&ED and reduce the SR&ED expenditure pool. ITCs in respect of PPAs are also eligible for refundable investment tax credit treatment as previously discussed.

¶12,265 Capital expenditures

Under the normal SR&ED rules, a qualifying capital expenditure[12] must be intended to be used *all or substantially all* (i.e., 90%) in SR&ED activities. This rule is a particularly harsh one since equipment, which is used less than 90% for SR&ED purposes and, therefore, is *shared* with other business activities, does not qualify for an ITC unless it can meet the 90% test. ITA: 37

Therefore, ITC rules exist for equipment which is *shared* between SR&ED activities and other business activities, referred to as *shared-use-equipment*. The ITC rate on shared-use-equipment is one-half the normal rate and is earned on a usage basis over two time-periods (one-quarter for each time-period). These shared-use-equipment capital expenditures are not deductible as SR&ED, but must be deducted under the normal CCA rules. ITA: 37(1)(*b*)

The first time period starts with the initial usage of the shared-use-equipment until the end of the next taxation year which must be at least 12 months after the initial use. The second time period again begins with the initial use but ends at the second following taxation year that is at least 24 months after the initial usage. Furthermore, the equipment can only qualify for the second time period ITC if it qualified initially for the first time period ITC.

Example Problem 12-10

Mr. A owns all the common shares of ABC Limited, a Canadian-controlled private corporation. ABC Limited incurred certain costs in the development of a new process that qualifies for SR&ED expenditures treatment.

Direct material	$250,000
Direct labour	200,000
Indirect material and labour costs	150,000

Of the indirect costs, Mr. A believes that approximately 20% is applicable to the development of the new process, but the corporation's accounting system is not sophisticated enough to identify the direct overhead costs.

Included in the direct labour costs is a salary of $50,000 paid to Mr. A's daughter, a professional engineer who spent 90% of her time on SR&ED activities.

ABC Limited has not had any SR&ED expenditures in the past and had taxable income for the preceding year of $135,000. Taxable capital in the preceding taxation year was $800,000. ABC Limited is not associated with any other corporation. The corporation does not anticipate that it will have any taxable income for this taxation year.

[12] Capital expenditures will be excluded from SR&ED deductions and investment tax credits for property acquired after 2013.

— *REQUIRED*

Describe the tax treatment of the direct and indirect development costs of the new process on the assumption that the new process meets the requirements as SR&ED expenditures for the taxation year ending December 31, 2013.

— *SOLUTION*

All of the direct material and direct labour costs, for a total of $450,000, are deductible as current SR&ED expenditures since they are directly attributable to the development of the new process. Any amount of these expenses that are not deductible this year will qualify for the SR&ED expenditure pool and can be deducted in any future year. Any ITC deducted or refunded in this year or in future years is deducted from the expenditure pool. ITA: 37

In addition, all of the direct material and direct labour costs qualify for an ITC of 35% since ABC Limited's taxable income in the preceding year was under the small business deduction limit (i.e., $500,000) and the total of these direct costs was less than the expenditure limit of $3 million. Also, taxable capital was less than $10 million. The ITC would be $157,500, i.e., 35% of $450,000.

Since the indirect material and labour costs cannot be traced directly to the development of the new process, they are not deductible under section 37 but are expensed in the normal manner under section 9. An ITC can also be claimed on the indirect material and labour costs of $150,000 by electing the proxy amount method for the current taxation year. The amount of the ITC is calculated below:

Direct labour costs		$200,000
Less: Daughter's salary (a specified employee)		50,000
		$150,000
Plus: Eligible portion of the daughter's salary — Lesser[(1)] of:		
(a) 75% of $50,000	= $ 37,500	
(b) 2.5 × $51,100[(2)]	= $127,750	$ 37,500
		$187,500
Amount eligible for the proxy amount (60% [for 2013, 55% for 2014] of $187,500)		$112,500
ITC 35% thereof		$ 39,375

Note that these labour costs are used as the basis of the proxy amount for overhead. The deduction of labour expenses and other overhead expenses as business expenses is not affected by this proxy amount calculation.

Mr. A's daughter is considered to be a specified shareholder since she is *deemed* to own all of her father's shares and, therefore, owns not less than 10% of the issued shares (i.e., 100% in this situation). ITA: 248(1) "specified shareholder" (*a*)

Since ABC Limited does not expect to have any taxable income this year it can apply for a 100% cash refund of the total ITCs of $196,875 ($157,500 + $39,375). Alternatively, ABC Limited can apply these ITCs against taxes payable in the three preceding years or against future taxes in the next 20 years.

In the following taxation year, ABC Limited will have to include in income the amount of the ITC deducted or refunded of $196,875. ITA: 12(1)(*t*)

— *NOTE TO SOLUTION*

(1) Limited by Regulation for a specified employee, but cannot exceed the portion of actual salary allocated to SR&ED (i.e., 90% of $50,000 or $45,000, in this case). ITR: 2900(7)

(2) The year's maximum pensionable earnings for CPP purposes, i.e., $51,100 for 2013.

¶12,270 Incorporated Business Income and Integration

¶12,275 Corporate tax rate incentives to incorporate in general

Now that the complete system for the taxation of business income has been presented, an analysis can be done to determine whether there is a tax advantage to incorporating business income. The answer to the question is affected largely by the combined federal and provincial corporate tax rate applicable to the business income. Generally, business income not eligible for the small business deduction at the corporate level will attract higher tax costs when earned through a corporation than when earned directly by an individual even with the 38% gross-up and tax credit. Exhibit 12-4 illustrates this point, using the corporate tax rates developed in Exhibit 11-4.

EXHIBIT 12-4
Tax Impact of Incorporating Active Business Income Not Eligible for the Small Business Deduction

Facts: An individual earns $1,000 of active business income and is deciding whether to incorporate.

The company is not able to claim the small business deduction and has a combined federal and provincial tax rate of 28% including a provincial rate of 13%.

The individual pays tax at a combined federal and provincial rate of either 25% or 46%.

The dividend gross-up will be 38% and the dividend tax credit will be 6/11 federally and 5/11 provincially.

Calculate

(1) A = the personal after-tax cash available, if the amount and type of income is earned by an individual

		Personal	
Combined federal and provincial tax rate		**25%**	**46%**
Active business income		$1,000	$1,000
Personal tax		$ 250	$ 460
After-tax cash — personal	**A**	$ 750	$ 540

(2) B = the corporate after-tax cash available for payment of a dividend, if the amount and type of income is earned in a corporation owned by the individual

		Corporate
Active business income		$1,000
Corporate tax @ 28% (38% – 10% – 13% + 13%)		280
After-tax income available for distribution as a dividend	**B**	$ 720

(3) C = the personal after-tax cash available, if the corporation distributed its after-tax income as a dividend to the individual as the shareholder

		Personal	
		25%	**46%**
Dividend paid — from Calculation 2		$ 720	$ 720
Gross-up @ 38%		274	274
Taxable dividend		$ 994	$ 994
Combined federal and provincial tax		$ 249	$ 457
Combined dividend tax credit ((6/11 + 5/11) × gross-up)		(274)	(274)
Personal tax paid on the dividend		$ 25	$ 183
After-tax cash — Personal	**C**	$ 745	$ 537

Determine tax savings or cost

To determine if a tax savings or a tax cost will result from incorporation, perform the following analysis:

		Personal	
Combined federal and provincial tax rate		**25%**	**46%**
Tax savings (if C > A)	**C-A**	$ -	$ -
Tax cost (if A > C)	**A-C**	$ 5	$ 3

(1) **Compare**

A = the personal after-tax cash available, if the income is earned personally, to

C = the corporate after-tax cash available, if the income earned in a corporation and, then, the aftertax corporate retained earnings are distributed as a dividend to the individual as a shareholder

(2) **Determine** the **tax savings** from incorporation — (if C > A)

(C–A) = the amount of tax savings that will be realized if C is greater than A

Since the total corporate tax on the income and personal tax paid on the dividend when flowed through the corporation is greater than the personal tax on the original income there is not a tax savings.

(3) **Determine** the **tax cost** from incorporation — (if A > C)

(A–C) = the amount of tax cost that will be incurred if A is greater than C

Since the total corporate tax on the income and personal tax paid on the dividend when flowed through the corporation is greater than the personal tax on the original income, there is a tax cost to incorporating of $5 at the 25% personal tax rate and $3 at the 46% tax rate.

Determine tax deferral or prepayment

A tax deferral is realized by having the income earned and taxed in the corporation and then not paying a dividend but leaving the money in the company. The amount of the deferral is the personal tax on the amount of the dividend that is being deferred.

To determine the amount of the tax deferral or prepayment, perform the following analysis:

		Personal	
Combined federal and provincial tax rate		**25%**	**46%**
Deferral (if B is greater than A)	**B-A**	$ -	$180
Prepayment (if A is greater than B)	**A-B**	$ 30	$ -

(1) **Compare**

A = the personal after-tax cash available, if the income is earned personally, to

B = the corporate after-tax cash available, if the income is earned and retained by the corporation by not distributing the income immediately as a dividend

(2) **Determine** the **tax deferral** from incorporation — (if B > A)

(B–A) = the amount of tax deferred that will be realized if B is greater than A

(3) **Determine** the **tax prepayment** from incorporation — (if A > B)

(A–B) = the amount of tax prepayment that will be realized if A is greater than B

Results:

At a personal tax rate of 25% there is a $25 prepayment of tax by leaving the money in the corporation to be paid out at a later date since the corporate tax rate is higher than the personal tax rate.

However, at the 46% personal tax rate, $183 of personal tax can be deferred by leaving the money in the corporation to be paid out at a later date.

The following diagrams show the tax on the income more conceptually.

Combined Individual Federal and Provincial Tax Rate: 25%

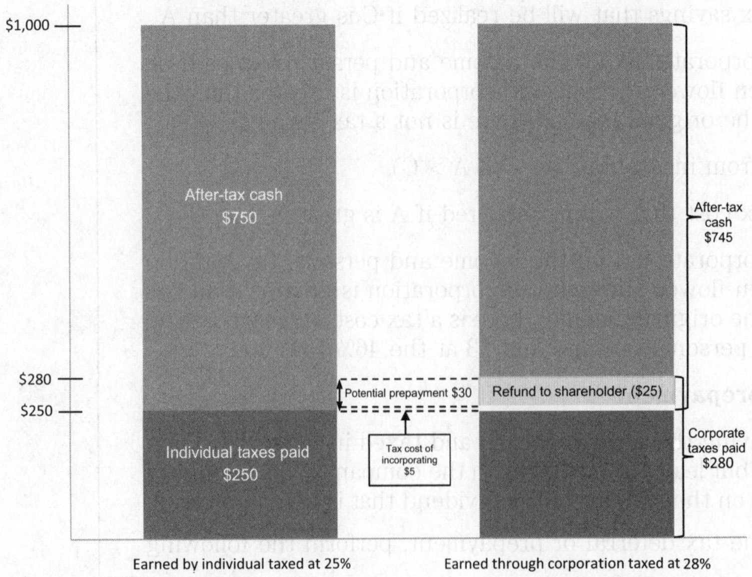

Combined Individual Federal and Provincial Tax Rate: 46%

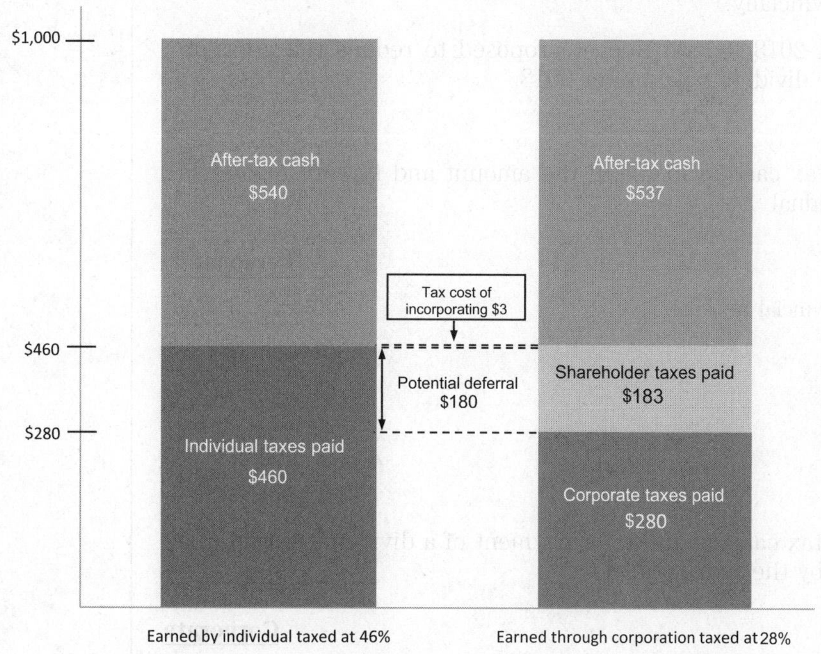

However, there may be the possibility of a tax deferral to the extent that dividends from the business income earned are not paid out immediately. This deferral possibility exists when the personal taxes which must be paid immediately on directly-earned business income exceed the corporate taxes, on the same business income. For example, in Exhibit 12-4, for the top tax bracket, the combined federal and provincial personal tax rate is 46%. Hence, item (C) is $460 and (C) – (A) in the last line of the exhibit reflects a deferral of $180. If the time value of money is considered, this deferral advantage may outweigh the added tax cost of incorporating this business income in a province with relatively high personal tax rates. Of course, there are other, non-tax reasons for incorporating such business income.

On active business income eligible for the small business deduction, a small tax saving results from the incorporation of such income compared to receiving it directly if the total corporate tax rate is lower than the theoretical 20% where integration is perfect, using the 25% gross-up and tax credit on low-rate business income. There is, however, the possibility of deferring tax on dividends ultimately distributed to the shareholders by delaying that distribution. Exhibit 12-5 illustrates these effects which result in a small tax saving using the theoretical corporate tax rates developed in Exhibit 12-2. Remember that, although most provincial corporate rates lie between 10% and 16%, the equivalent of the federal small business deduction is also given by most provinces to give an approximate effective rate of 4%.

EXHIBIT 12-5
Tax Impact of Incorporating Active Business Income Eligible for the Small Business Deduction*

Facts: An individual earns $1,000 of active business income and is deciding whether to incorporate.

The company is able to claim the small business deduction on this income and has a combined federal and provincial corporate tax rate of 16% including a provincial rate of 5%.

The individual pays tax a combined federal and provincial rate of either 25% or 46%.

The dividend gross-up will be 18% and the dividend tax credit will be 13/18 federally and 5/18 provincially.

Note: The March 21, 2013 federal Budget proposed to reduce the gross-up from 25% to 18% for dividends paid after 2013.

Calculate

(1) A = the personal after-tax cash available, if the amount and type of income is earned by an individual

		Personal	
Combined federal and provincial tax rate		**25%**	**46%**
Active business income		$1,000	$1,000
Personal tax		$ 250	$ 460
After-tax cash — personal	**A**	$ 750	$ 540

(2) B = the corporate after-tax cash available for payment of a dividend earned in a corporation owned by the individual

		Corporate
Active business income		$1,000
Corporate tax @ 16% (38% − 10% − 17% + 5%)		160
After-tax income available for distribution as a dividend	**B**	$ 840

(3) C = the personal after-tax cash available, if the corporation distributed its after-tax income as a dividend to the individual as the shareholder

		Personal	
		25%	**46%**
Dividend paid — from Calculation 2		$840	$840
Gross-up @ 18%		151	151
Taxable dividend		$991	$991
Combined federal and provincial tax		$248	$456
Combined dividend tax credit ((13/18 + 5/18) × gross-up)		151	151
Personal tax paid on the dividend		$ 97	$305
After-tax cash — Personal	**C**	$743	$535

Determine tax savings or cost

To determine if a tax savings or a tax cost will result from incorporation, perform the following analysis:

		Personal	
Combined federal and provincial tax rate		**25%**	**46%**
Tax savings (if C > A)	**C-A**	$ -	$ -
Tax cost (if A > C)	**A-C**	$ 7	$ 5

(1) **Compare**

A = the personal after-tax cash available, if the income is earned personally, to

C = the corporate after-tax cash available, if the income earned in a cotporation and, then, the after-tax corporate retained eamings are distributed as a dividend to the individual as a shareholder

(2) **Determine** the **tax savings** from incorporation — (if C > A)

(C–A) = the amount of tax savings that will be realized if C is greater than A

Since the total corporate and personal tax paid is more when flowed through the corporation than if the income is earned personally, there is not a tax savings.

(3) **Determine** the **tax cost** from incorporation — (if A > C)

(A–C) = the amount of tax cost that will be incurred if A is greater than C

Since the total corporate and personal tax paid is more when flowed through the corporation, there is a tax cost to incorporating of $7 at the 25% personal tax rate and $5 at the 46% tax rate.

Determine tax deferral or prepayment

A tax deferral is realized by having the income earned and taxed in the corporation and then not paying a dividend but leaving the money in the company. The amount of the deferral is the personal tax on the amount of the dividend that is being deferred.

To determine the amount of the tax deferral or prepayment, perform the following analysis:

		Personal	
Combined federal and provincial tax rate		**25%**	**46%**
Deferral (if B > A)	**B-A**	$ 90	$300
Prepayment (if A > B)	**A-B**	$ -	$ -

(1) **Compare**

A = the personal after-tax cash available, if the income is earned personally, to

B = the corporate after-tax cash available, if the income is earned and retained by the corporation by not distributing the income immediately as a dividend

(2) **Determine** the **tax deferral** from incorporation — (if B > A)

(B–A) = the amount of tax deferred that will be realized if B is greater than A

(3) **Determine** the **tax prepayment** from incorporation — (if A > B)

(A–B) = the amount of tax prepayment that will be realized if A is greater than B

Results:

At the 25% personal tax rate, $97 of personal tax can be deferred by leaving the money in the corporation to be paid out at a later date. At the 46% personal tax rate, $305 of personal tax can be deferred by leaving the money in the corporation.

The following diagrams show the tax on the income more conceptually.

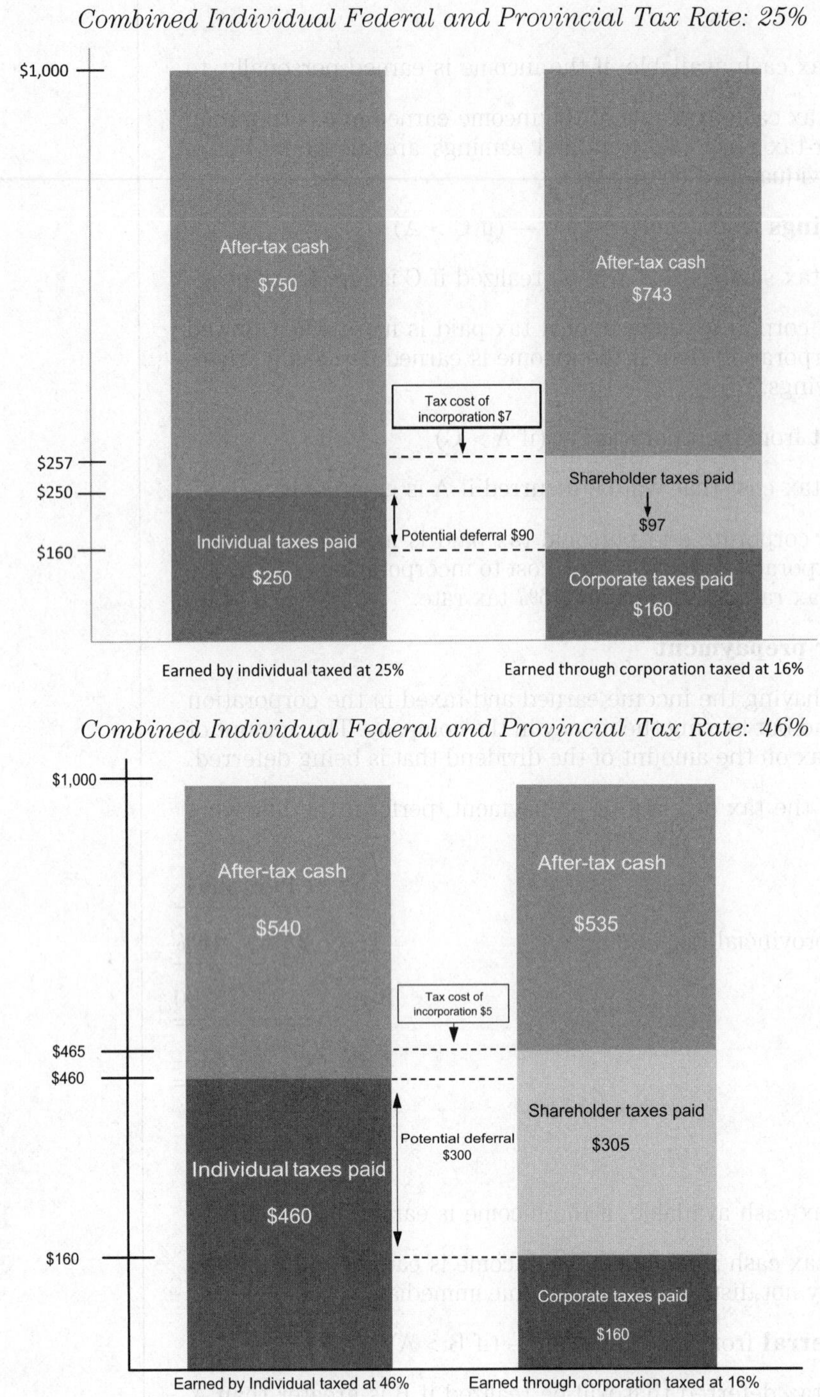

* Using 18% gross-up for dividends paid after 2013.

It will take a provincial rate of tax below 4.3% (15.3% – (38% – 10% – 17%)) to provide tax savings from the incorporation of income eligible for the small business deduction. For all higher corporate provincial income tax rates, the total corporate tax rate will be above the 15.3% [after 2013] rate necessary for perfect integration of the tax on low-rate income and, as a result, there will be a tax cost to incorporation.

[The March 2013 federal Budget proposal to reduce the gross-up to 18% of the dividend paid after 2013 from low-rate corporate income will remove most or all of the tax savings advantage from incorporating this type of income. However, a deferral advantage will continue, as intended, to encourage the retention and reinvestment of corporate earnings for growth of the corporation.]

¶12,280 Specific tax savings (cost) and deferral (prepayment) possibilities

The concept of a "tax cost" is based on the excess of the total tax liability when the income is flowed through a corporation as compared to income earned through an unincorporated business. Under the tax cost concept it is assumed that all of the after-tax cash of the corporation will be paid out in dividends. In Exhibit 12-4, the tax cost at an individual's lowest rate of tax (25%) is $5 whereas the tax cost at the highest tax rate (46%) is only $3. The difference between the two is $2 which is due largely to the difference in the tax rates of 21% (46% – 25%) times the $6 difference between the individual's unincorporated business income of $1,000 and the grossed-up dividend income of $994. Therefore, as an individual's tax increases, the tax cost of using a corporation decreases.

A tax prepayment or deferral is based on a similar concept except for the assumption that none of the corporate after-tax cash is paid out immediately but is retained in the corporation. The ultimate benefits of a deferral are twofold: the present value of the deferred tax payment and after-tax financing costs avoided by the use of its retained earnings. In Exhibit 12-4, at the lowest rate of an individual's tax (25%) there was a prepayment of taxes of $30 because of the difference between the individual's low rate (25%) and the corporate rate of 28% or 3% on the business income of $1,000. At the highest rate of individual tax (46%), there was a tax deferral of $180 (i.e., 46% – 28% = 18%; 18% × $1,000 = $180 of business income) because of the lower corporate tax rate. The higher the individual tax rate relative to the corporate tax rate, the greater the potential deferral.

¶12,285 Summary of advantages and disadvantages of incorporating active business income

From the foregoing analysis, it should be possible to draw some conclusions of both a tax and non-tax nature regarding the incorporating of business operations.

¶12,285.10 *Advantages of incorporation*

The advantages of incorporation appear to include the following:

- limited liability, although it should be recognized that to the extent creditors of an incorporated business demand personal guarantees from shareholders, limited liability is negated;
- tax savings if the combined corporate tax rate is under 20% [15.3% after 2013];
- a tax savings will result from a provincial corporate tax rate of less than 9% in 2013 [less than 4.3% after 2013];
- tax deferral at higher personal income levels on business income not eligible for the small business deduction and at all personal income levels on business income eligible for the small business deduction;
- income splitting potential in carefully planned and very restrictive situations (as discussed previously with respect to the attribution rules and tax on split income) with family members as employees or shareholders;
- estate planning advantages on the transfer of future growth in the corporation's shares to children (as discussed in a subsequent chapter);
- availability of registered pension plans, including defined benefit plans, to the owner as an employee of a corporation is not possible in the unincorporated form;
- separation of business and personal activities;
- stabilization of income of the individual through salary payments or greater flexibility in the timing of the receipt of income subject to personal tax;

- continuity of the separate legal entity;
- deferral of accrued capital gains on transfer of shares to a spouse (as discussed in a subsequent chapter);
- potentially easier access to financing;
- availability of the capital gains exemption for qualified small business corporation shares or business investment loss treatment for securities of a small business corporation; and
- availability of the deferral of capital gains on the sale of eligible small business corporation shares, if replacement shares are acquired. ITA: 44.1(1)

¶12,285.20 ***Disadvantages of incorporation***

The disadvantages of incorporating business operations appear to include:

- a tax cost if the combined corporate tax rate is over 20% [15.3% after 2013] for income eligible for the small business deduction and 27.5% for other business income;
- a prepayment of tax at lower levels of personal income on business income not eligible for the small business deduction;
- the additional legal and accounting costs of maintaining a corporation; and
- a loss of the availability of business and capital losses to offset personal income. While this disadvantage may be offset, to some extent, by the availability of allowable business investment loss treatment for shares of a small business corporation, the loss is only one-half deductible and it is deductible only on sale of the shares or bankruptcy of the corporation.

Often the tax saving, if any, or deferral will, in many cases, outweigh the disadvantages of incorporating such income, at least for rates of corporate tax in existence at less than 20% [15.3% after 2013] for income eligible for the small business deduction and 27.5% for other business income. This is particularly so where business income eligible for the small business deduction is earned through a corporation.

¶12,300 INCOME FROM INVESTMENTS OF A CCPC

¶12,310 Overview of Integration for Income from Investments of a CCPC

¶12,315 Purpose

¶12,315.10 ***Investment income***

(i) The theory

The tax system provides special rules for private corporations which are meant to eliminate some of the tax biases between income earned by an individual and income earned by a corporation. One bias arises from the potential double taxation of investment income. For the moment, think of investment income as property income (i.e., interest, rents, etc., but not dividends). Later on, a more precise definition will be given. Without special rules, investment income would be taxed once in the corporation and again at the shareholder level when dividends are paid. To eliminate this bias, the concept of a refundable tax was developed, whereby a portion of the initial corporate tax on such income is refunded when dividends are paid. The tax on investment income was intended to be reduced to an approximate rate of tax of 20%. The 25% gross-up and dividend tax credit then would allow the shareholder credit for that 20% tax paid by the company and complete integration of corporate and personal taxes would be achieved. Thus, a Canadian who transfers his or her investments to a private corporation and flows the income through the corporation, would, theoretically, retain the same amount of after-tax investment income as he or she would if the investments were held personally and had received the income from the investments directly.

When investment income is flowed through a corporation, an indefinite deferral of tax is possible if the initial corporate tax rate is relatively low and if the investment income is left in the corporation and not distributed by way of dividends to the shareholders. In contrast, an individual Canadian who holds his or her investments personally, is required to pay tax on the income as it is received or accrued. The tax system attempts to eliminate this bias by ensuring that investment income earned in a corporation is taxed initially at a high corporate rate. Then the corporate tax is partially refunded when the investment income is distributed, by way of taxable dividends, to the corporation's shareholders who then pay tax on the income at their personal rate.

The system of integration was intended to bring the effective corporate rate of tax on investment income down to 20%. This rate is the same rate that was intended to apply on up to $500,000 of active business income. As mentioned previously, at a corporate rate of 20% the objective of theoretically perfect integration is achieved. However, the specific rules applied to each type of income achieve the objective in opposite ways. On the one hand, the rules applied to active business income provide for a low initial rate of corporate tax, after the small business deduction, to allow for greater retention of income for reinvestment in the business. On the other hand, the rules applied to investment income provide for a high initial rate of corporate tax to prevent the use of a corporation as a means of deferring tax on investment income. When retained earnings are distributed as dividends, the dividend refund was intended to bring the total effective corporate tax rate on that investment income down to 20%.

The provisions which increase the dividend gross-up and tax credit on eligible dividends do not apply to investment income earned in a Canadian-controlled private corporation. As a result, for dividends from investment income, the gross-up is 25% [18% after 2013] and the federal dividend tax credit is $^{13}/_{18}$ of the gross-up.

Exhibit 12-6 shows the tax rates on which the refundable system for investment income was based theoretically to achieve perfect integration.

EXHIBIT 12-6
Theoretical Corporate Tax Rates for Perfect Integration on Investment Income Eligible for a Dividend Refund and the First $500,000 of Active Business Income of a Canadian-Controlled Private Corporation

	Investment income	*Active business income*
Federal tax rate (theoretical)	40%	40%
Abatement for provincial tax	(10)	(10)
Net federal tax	30%	30%
Small business deduction	—	(17)
Refund of tax paid on investment income on the payment of dividends	(20)	—
Net federal tax after dividend refund and small business deduction	10%	13%
Provincial tax (theoretical)	10%	7%
Effective total tax	20%	20%

(ii) The reality: Imperfection

The theoretical model in Exhibit 12-6, in reality, does not operate perfectly for a number of reasons. First, the basic federal tax rate is 38%, not 40%. Second, provincial taxes are generally greater than the theoretical model, e.g., 10% to 16% for investment income and up to 8% for the first $500,000 of active business income. [Also, the proposed 18% gross-up is designed to integrate perfectly corporate income tax at a 15.3% combined federal and provincial rate.]

Even with these imperfections, it would be possible to defer tax on investment income through the use of a corporation, because the total tax at the corporate level would be less than the top personal tax rate in most provinces. In order to remove the deferral of tax on investment income, an additional refundable tax of 6⅔% is levied. ITA: 123.3

Exhibit 12-7 shows the effective tax rate on investment income, including the additional refundable tax of 6⅔%.

EXHIBIT 12-7
Effective Tax Rate on Investment Income*

Federal tax rate	38.00%
Abatement for provincial tax	(10.00)
Net federal tax	28.00%
Additional refundable tax	6.67
Refund on the payment of dividends	(26.67)
Net federal tax after dividend refund	8.00%
Provincial tax** (hypothetical)	13.00
Effective total rate	21.00%

* Investment income includes all types of property income such as interest, royalties and rent, but does not include dividends from taxable Canadian corporations.

** A provincial corporate tax rate of 12% on investment income would result in an effective total tax rate of 20% which would result in perfect integration. However, provincial taxes vary between 10% and 16%.

Exhibit 12-8 shows a calculation of effective total tax applicable to taxable investment income of a Canadian-controlled private corporation eligible for a refund on the payment of dividends, referred to as a dividend refund, using a hypothetical provincial rate and including the 6⅔% additional refundable tax on investment income.

EXHIBIT 12-8
Comparison of Tax Rates Applicable to Investment Income Eligible for a Dividend Refund and on the First $500,000 Active Business Income of a Canadian-controlled Private Corporation

	Investment income(1)	*Active business income*(2)	
Federal tax rate	38.00%	38.00%	ITA: 123(1)(*a*)
Abatement for provincial tax	(10.00)	(10.00)	ITA: 124(1)
Net federal tax	28.00%	28.00%	
Additional refundable tax on investment income	6.67	Nil	
Small business deduction	—	(17.00)	
Refund on payment of dividends from investment income	(26.67)	—	ITA: 129(1)
Net federal tax after dividend refund	8.00%	11.00%	
Provincial tax (theoretical)	13.00(3)	4.00(4)	
Effective total tax	21.00%	15.00%	

(1) Investment income includes all types of property income except dividends from taxable Canadian corporations.

(2) This column of the table reflects the tax on the first $500,000 of active business income. Over $500,000, there is no small business deduction, but there is a 13% general rate reduction; therefore, the effective tax rate would be 28%, assuming a full hypothetical provincial tax rate of 13%.

(3) A provincial corporate tax rate of 12% on investment income would result in an effective total tax of 20%, which would allow for perfect integration. However, provincial tax rates average around 13%.

(4) Several provinces also give a small business deduction on the first $500,000 of active business income. In this example, a net 4% provincial rate after a provincial small business deduction was assumed.

Exhibit 12-8 clearly demonstrates that effective tax rates for investment income are above the 15.3% rate at which integration is perfect with the proposed 18% gross-up for dividends paid after 2013. Active business income, at or below $500,000, is taxed at a corporate rate that results in close to perfect integration. However, for a CCPC with active business income over $500,000 or investment income, there is a significant difference in the effective tax rates on these two types of income (i.e., 28% for business income versus 21% for investment income). This difference may encourage some taxpayers to attempt to recharacterize some of their active business income (over $500,000) as investment income so as to attract the investment income net rate (21%) which has no cap (like the $500,000 business limit). Remember, however, that one important downside of investment income is that the initial corporate tax rate before the dividend refund is at the high 47⅔% (i.e., 28% + 6⅔% + 13%) rate (i.e., no general rate reduction), including a 6⅔% additional refundable tax, and that dividends must be paid in order to trigger the refund of Part I tax of 26⅔%. While the corporate rate after the refund is low at 21% (i.e., 47⅔% – 26.67%), the shareholders receive a dividend which is taxable to complete the integration process.

Remember too that the higher 38% dividend gross-up and tax credit apply to business income taxed at the high rate. On high-rate income the theoretical rate for integration is 27.5%. As a result, the discrepancy is not as great, and the incentive to recharacterize high-rate business income as investment income is greatly reduced.

¶12,315.20 *Portfolio dividends*

Another bias arises because intercorporate dividends are deductible in order to arrive at taxable income and, therefore, not subject to tax under Part I of the Act. By placing dividend-yielding investments in a corporation, an individual, particularly one in a high tax bracket, could defer tax on dividend income indefinitely. A 33⅓% Part IV refundable tax that certain corporations pay on such dividends is intended to eliminate this bias. ITA: 186

If it were not for the Part IV tax on what are referred to as "portfolio dividends", it would be extremely attractive for an individual to make portfolio investments in dividend-producing shares through an investment holding corporation. No tax would be paid under Part I on the dividends received by the holding corporation. By contrast, an individual who owned the portfolio investments directly, would pay tax under Part I at his or her personal rate on any dividends received. Thus, the Part IV tax of 33⅓% levied on the recipient corporation is an initial tax roughly equivalent to the tax that would be paid by the individual in the top federal tax bracket receiving a dividend from a taxable Canadian corporation. The Part IV tax is fully refundable when the recipient corporation itself pays a dividend to its shareholders. Thus, after the refund, the corporation is effectively not taxed on the dividend that it received from another corporation and passed on to its shareholders. This preserves the integration system by preventing double taxation of the income that gave rise to the original dividend from the originating corporation to the holding corporation.

¶12,316 Capital Dividend Account

The purpose of the capital dividend account is to complete integration of corporate and personal income tax on capital gains and similar receipts. When an individual realizes a capital gain of, say, $400, the individual pays income tax on ½ of the capital gain or $200. The other $200 is not taxed. When a private corporation realizes the same capital gain of $400, the private corporation is taxed (including additional refundable tax and net of any dividend refund) on $200. The other ½ or $200 is added to the private corporation's capital dividend account, to be distributed tax free to the corporation's shareholders. This is done to ensure that the integration concept applies to capital gains.

¶12,317 Components of the account

This account begins to accumulate amounts only for private corporations. For most private corporations, the period covered would be from the date of incorporation, but this cannot be earlier than January 1, 1972.

¶12,317.10 *The components in concept*

Conceptually, for the purposes of this chapter, this account includes five basic components:

(a) the portion of net capital gains (i.e., capital gains in excess of capital losses) not recognized in computing income for tax purposes, that is, the non-taxable portion of net capital gains, *plus*

(b) capital dividends received from another corporation, *plus*

(c) the portion of net gain not recognized in the cumulative eligible capital account, that is, the non-taxable portion of the economic gain (now ½ of the excess of proceeds over actual original cost) on the disposition of eligible capital property, *plus*

(d) proceeds arising on death from certain life insurance policies received by the corporation net of the cost basis of the policies, *minus*

(e) capital dividends paid.

¶12,317.20 *The major components technically*

The balance of this account is computed for the entire period (refer to the next session for a discussion of "the period") as the sum of the following abridged amounts described here in simplified terms:

(a) *the untaxed portion of net capital gains which is computed as:*

(i) generally, the excess, if any, of all capital gains (net of capital losses), ITA: 89(1) par. (*a*) of definition

minus:

(ii) taxable capital gains (net of allowable capital losses) included in income at the appropriate inclusion rate on a disposition during the period;[13]

(b) *capital dividends received:* capital dividends received from another corporation; ITA: 83(2), 89(1) par. (*b*) of definition

(c) *the untaxed portion of gains on eligible capital property:* for taxation years ending after October 17, 2000, the addition to the capital dividend account, at the end of a taxation year in which a disposition occurs, is equal to ½ of the "economic gain" on the disposition of eligible capital property. The "economic gain" is considered to be, conceptually, the excess, if any, of the full proceeds for eligible capital property disposed over the full cost of all eligible capital property reflected in the CEC account balance. This amount should be equal to the taxed portion of the economic gain. Refer to Chapter 5 for the details of the cumulative eligible capital amount. There may be other adjustments that are not addressed in this book. ITA: 89(1) par. (*c*.2) of definition

(d) *untaxed insurance proceeds:* proceeds received, or in certain circumstances deemed to be received, as a result of death, from certain life insurance policies by the corporation in a period since it last became a private corporation, as a beneficiary of a policy, minus the adjusted cost basis of the policy; ITA: 89(1) par. (*d*) of definition

minus (from the aggregate of the above four items)

(e) capital dividends paid or payable by the corporation. ITA: 89(1)

Note that, technically, this account does not continue a balance from one year to the next with one year's opening balance being the previous year's closing balance. Each subparagraph accumulates from the beginning of "the period" to the particular time that a calculation of the balance in the account is being made. In this respect, notice that all subparagraphs except (b) require the inclusion of "the amount, *if any*, by which" the aggregate of one item exceeds another item. Thus, it is not possible to have a negative amount for these subparagraphs at a particular point in time. However, at a subsequent point in time the aggregate for one of these subparagraphs may be positive after offsetting aggregate losses or expenditures at that particular time.

[13] Inclusion rates have changed over the years as follows: ½ for gains and losses realized before 1988, ⅔ for gains and losses realized in 1988 and 1989, ¾ for gains and losses realized from 1990 to February 27, 2000, ⅔ for gains and losses realized from February 28, 2000 to October 17, 2000 and ½ thereafter.

¶12,318 "The period"

As indicated previously, the specific wording of the definition of the "capital dividend account" must be read very carefully (not just the above summary) when actually doing the capital dividend account calculation. The major confusion relates to the various time periods referred to. The first time period is described in clause (*a*)(i)(A) of the definition and is referred to as "the period", as introduced above. Since only private corporations can have a capital dividend account, this concept is important when corporations can change their characteristics (e.g., a private corporation becomes a public corporation upon the listing of its shares or acquisition of control by a public corporation or a public corporation becomes a private corporation under prescribed conditions). For private corporations, which were incorporated prior to 1972, this time period starts "on the first day of the first taxation year commencing after the corporation last became a private corporation", or January 1, 1972, the day upon which the tax legislation made a distinction between public and private corporations, if that date is later. Note that the subparagraphs dealing with the disposition of eligible capital property and life insurance proceeds received, also use the term "the period" to refer to this time condition. Hence, the balance date for the cumulative eligible capital account "at the commencement of the period" would be January 1, 1972 for corporations incorporated prior to 1972 and, as a result, would have a nil balance at that time. Similarly, private corporations incorporated after 1971 would have a nil balance in the cumulative eligible capital account on the first day they became private corporations. However, for public corporations which become private corporations, there may very well be a balance in the cumulative eligible capital account on this first day.

ITA: 89(1)

ITA: 89(1) "private corporation", "public corporation"

¶12,319 Example of disposition of eligible capital property

Facts: A Canadian-controlled private corporation with a fiscal year end of December 31, had the following transactions.

Cost of eligible capital property on November 30, 2011	$12,000
Proceeds of disposition on January 15, 2013	20,000
Economic gain on disposition	8,000

As of January 1, 2011 the corporation had no balance in its CEC pool.

Application of the law:

CEC Account	
ECE × ¾ [$12,000 × ¾]	$ 9,000
CECA — 2011 [7%]	(630)
Balance December 31, 2011	$ 8,370
CECA — 2012 [7%]	(586)
Balance December 31, 2012	$ 7,784
ECA × ¾ [$20,000 × ¾]	(15,000)
Negative balance	$ (7,216)
Previous CECA	1,216
Final balance	$ (6,000)
Income inclusion on December 31, 2013	
Recapture of previous CECA	$ 1,216
⅔ × final balance ($6,000)	4,000
Income*	$ 5,216
Capital dividend account at December 31, 2013	
⅔ × final balance ($6,000)	$ 4,000

ITA: 14(1)

* The total of:

(a) the lesser of:

(i) negative balance $7,216; and		
(ii) total CECA claimed ($630 + $586) $1,216		
the lesser is		$ 1,216
(b) ⅔ × [$7,216 – $1,216]		4,000
Income		$ 5,216

Remember, for eligible capital property, the addition to the capital dividend account does not take place at the time of the transaction (January 15), but at the year end of the corporation (December 31).

Conceptually, this is equal to 50% of the economic gain on the eligible capital property i.e., 50% × [$20,000 – $12,000].

Example Problem 12-11

Surplus Accumulation Ltd. provides you with the following information:

Dispositions during the fiscal year ended December 31, 2013.

	Cost	*Selling costs*	*Proceeds*
Land	$20,000	$ 1,500	$35,000
Equipment	5,000	100	500
Securities	3,000	200	2,000

Capital dividends received in "the period"	$10,000	ITA: 83(2)
Capital dividends paid in "the period"	5,000	

In 2003, the corporation purchased goodwill for $6,000 and has deducted CECA of $2,325 to the present. In 2013, it sold an indefinite-life franchise for $19,000.

— *REQUIRED*

Compute the balance in the corporation's capital dividend account as at December 31, 2013.

— *SOLUTION*

Capital dividend account:

Untaxed fraction of net capital gains or losses:				ITA: 89(1) par. (*a*) of definition
Land				
P of D		$ 35,000		
ACB	$20,000			
Selling costs	1,500	21,500		
Capital gain		$ 13,500		
½(1) thereof			$ 6,750	
Equipment				
(No capital loss on depreciable property)			Nil	
Securities				
P of D		$ 2,000		
ACB	$ 3,000			
Selling costs	200	3,200		
Capital loss		$ (1,200)		
½ thereof			(600)	
Excess			$ 6,150	
Capital dividends received			10,000	ITA: 89(1) par. (*b*) of definition
Untaxed fraction of gain on eligible capital property				ITA: 89(1) par. (*c*.2) of definition
CEC balance ($6,000 × ¾(2) – $2,325)		$ 2,175		

Proceeds × 3/4 ($19,000 × 3/4)	(14,250)	
Negative balance	$(12,075)	
Recaptured CECA (income)	2,325	
	$ (9,750)	
Income (2/3[(3)] × $9,750 + $2,325)	$ 8,825	
Addition to capital dividend account (2/3[(3)] × $9,750)		$ 6,500
		$22,650
Less: capital dividends paid		(5,000)
Balance — December 31, 2013		$17,650

ITA: 83(2)

The following alternative format may be useful to keep track of the transactions, particularly when they occur in different years.

Capital dividend account

Year	*Asset*	*Untaxed fraction of net cap. gains*	*Capital dividend received*	*Untaxed fraction of net gain on ECP*	*Untaxed life ins. proceeds*	*Capital dividend paid*	*Balance*
2003	Goodwill			(3,000)[(4)]			
2013	Land	$6,750					
	Equipment	Nil					
	Securities	(600)					
	Franchise			$ 9,500[(4)]			
	Capital dividend received		$10,000				
	Capital dividend paid					($5,000)	
		$6,150	$10,000	$ 6,500		$(5,000)	$17,650

— NOTES TO SOLUTION

(1) The one-half rate represents the current untaxed portion of the capital gain which is computed in the definition of capital dividend account as the full capital gain minus the taxable capital gain at the 1/2 inclusion rate. ITA: 89(1) par. (*a*) of definition

(2) On the purchase of goodwill in 2003, 3/4 of the cost would have been added to the CEC balance.

(3) Because the CEC pool uses the 3/4 inclusion rate, the fraction used here (2/3) brings the result to 1/2 (3/4 × 2/3 = 1/2). This can be conceptually equated to the capital gains calculation by taking one-half of the economic gain into income and the other half into the capital dividend account. For example, $19,000 of proceeds − $6,000 cost = $13,000 gain.

(4) Neither the amount in respect of the cost of goodwill (in effect, 1/2 × $6,000 = $3,000) nor the amount in respect of the proceeds of disposition for the franchise (in effect, 1/2 × $19,000 = $9,500) affects the capital dividend account balance until the end of the year of the disposition, in this case, of the franchise.

¶12,320 Conceptual illustration of integration

Exhibit 12-9 illustrates conceptually how investment income, such as interest income, capital gains and portfolio dividends are integrated through a private corporation that qualifies for refundable tax treatment. Recall that one of the objectives of the integration system is to ensure that income from investments, which flows through a qualifying private corporation to its shareholders, bears the same total tax burden (at the combined corporate and individual level) that would be borne on that income if it were earned directly by an individual. For simplicity of illustration, and to demonstrate total integration, the corporate tax is assumed to be 40% plus the additional refundable tax of 6⅔% and the dividend tax credit, including the provincial tax effect, is assumed to be equal to a theoretical 18% (after 2013) gross-up, except for portfolio dividends from Canadian-resident public corporations eligible for the 38% gross-up. Remember that CCPCs that receive "eligible dividends" can flow those dividends out to the shareholders as dividends eligible for the 38% gross-up. The combined federal and provincial tax rates for individuals is assumed to be 34% for this illustration, although *any individual's combined federal and provincial marginal tax rate* could have been used to show perfect integration. Under these assumptions, this objective of integration is met perfectly.

EXHIBIT 12-9
Conceptual Illustration of Integration (or Tax Impact of Incorporating Investment Income)

Facts: An individual earns $1,000 of each of interest income, capital gains, and portfolio dividends and is deciding whether or not to incorporate.

	Investment Income	Dividends
Corporate tax		
Part I combined federal (28%) & provincial (12%)	40%	
Additional refundable tax	6⅔%	
Part IV tax rate		33⅓%
Dividend refund	26⅔%	33⅓%

	Investment Income	Flow through of low-rate dividends	Flow through of eligible dividends
Dividend gross-up	18%	18%	38%
Dividend tax credit — federal (fraction of gross-up)	13/18	13/18	6/11
Dividend tax credit — provincial (fraction of gross-up)	5/18	5/18	5/11

The individual will pay tax at a combined federal and provincial rate of 34%.

[Note: The March 21, 2013 federal Budget proposed to reduce the gross-up from 25% to 18% for dividends paid after 2013.]

Calculate

(1) A = the personal after-tax cash available, if the alnount and type of income is earned by an individual

		Personal				
			Capital Gain		Dividend	
		Interest	Taxable	Non-taxable	18% Gross-up	38% Gross-up
Income		$1,000	$1,000	$1,000	$1,000	$1,000
Gross-up					180	380
Taxable income		$1,000	$1,000	$1,000	$1,180	$1,380
Tax @ 34%		$ 340	$ 340		$ 401	$ 469
Dividend tax credit					180	380
Total personal tax		$ 340	$ 340	$ -	$ 221	$ 89
After-tax cash — personal	A	$ 660	$ 660	$1,000	$ 779	$ 911

The non-taxable portion of the capital gain can be distributed by the corporation as a capital dividend and received tax-free by the shareholder (discussed in a subsequent chapter).

(2) B = the corporate tax that would be paid, if the amount and type of income is earned in a corporation owned by the individual

		Corporate				
			Capital Gain		Portfolio Dividends	
		Interest	Taxable	Non-taxable	18% Gross-up	38% Gross-up
Income		$1,000	$1,000	$1,000	$1,000	$1,000
Division C deduction					1,000	1,000
Taxable income		$1,000	$1,000	$1,000	$ -	$ -
Part I Tax @ 40%		$ 400	$ 400			
Part IV Tax @ 33 1/3%					$ 333	$ 333
Additional refundable tax @ 6⅔%		67	67			
Total tax - initially before refund		467	467		333	333
Corporate after-tax cash available before dividend refund	B	$ 533	$ 533		$ 667	$ 667
Dividend refund @ 26⅔%		267	267			
Dividend refund @ 33⅓%					333	333
Net corporate tax		$ 200	$ 200		$ 0	$ 0
Cash available for dividends		$ 800	$ 800		$1,000	$1,000

(3) C = the personal after-tax cash available, if the corporation distributed its after-tax income as a dividend to the individual as the shareholder

		Personal				
			Capital Gain		Portfolio Dividends	
		Interest	Taxable	Non-taxable	18% Gross-up	38% Gross-up
Dividend paid — from Calculation 2		$ 800	$ 800	$1,000	$1,000	$1,000
Gross-up @ 18%/38%		144	144		180	380 st]
Taxable income		$ 944	$ 944	$1,000	$1,180	$1,380
Combined federal and provincial personal tax @ 34%		$ 321	$ 321		$ 401	$ 469
Dividend tax credit		144	144		180	380
Net personal tax		$ 177	$ 177	$ -	$ 221	$ 89
After-tax cash — personal	C	$ 623	$ 623	$1,000	$ 779	$ 911

Notice that the dividend gross-up no longer brings taxable income back up to $1,000 for interest and taxable capital gains. This imperfection will cause the tax cost shown in the next step.

Determine tax savings or cost

To determine if a tax savings or a tax cost will result from incorporation, perform the following analysis:

		Personal				
			Capital Gain		Portfolio Dividends	
		Interest	Taxable	Non-taxable	18% Gross-up	38% Gross-up
Tax savings (if C > A)	C–A	$ -	$ -		$ -	$ -
Tax cost (if A > C)	A–C	$ 37	$ 37		$ -	$ -

(1) **Compare**

A = the personal after-tax cash available, if the income is earned personally, to

C = the corporate after-tax cash available, if the income eamed in a corporation and, then, the after-tax corporate retained earnings are distributed as a dividend to the individual as a shareholder

(2) **Determine** the **tax savings** from incorporation — (if C > A)

(C–A) = the amount of tax savings that will be realized if C is greater than A

Interest and Taxable Capital Gains

Since the total corporate and personal tax paid is more when flowed through the corporation than if the income is earned personally, there is not a tax savings.

Portfolio Dividends

Since the total corporate and personal tax paid when flowed through the corporation is equal to the personal tax paid if the income is earned personally, there is not a tax savings.

(3) **Determine** the **tax cost** from incorporation — (if A > C)

(A–C) = the amount of tax cost that will be incurred if A is greater than C

Interest and Taxable Capital Gains

Since the total corporate and personal tax paid is more when flowed through the corporation than if the income is earned personally, there is a tax cost of $37.

Portfolio Dividends

Since the total corporate and personal tax paid when flowed through the corporation is equal to the personal tax paid if the income is earned personally, there is not a tax cost.

Determine tax deferral or prepayment

A tax deferral is realized by having the income earned and taxed in the corporation and then not paying a dividend but leaving the money in the company. The amount of the deferral is the personal tax on the amount of the dividend.

To determine the amount of the tax deferral or prepayment, perform the following analysis:

		Personal				
			Capital Gain		Portfolio Dividends	
		Interest	Taxable	Non-taxable	18% Gross-up	38% Gross-up
Deferral (if B > A)	B-A	$ -	$ -		$ -	$ -
Prepayment (if A > B)	A-B	$ 127	$ 127		$ 112	$ 244

(1) **Compare**

A = the personal after-tax cash available, if the income is earned personally, to

B = the corporate after-tax cash available, if the income is earned and retained by the corporation by not distributing the income immediately as a dividend

(2) **Determine** the **tax deferral** from incorporation — (if B > A)

(B–A) = the amount of tax deferred that will be realized if B is greater than A

(3) **Determine** the **tax prepayment** from incorporation — (if A > B)

(A–B) = the amount of tax prepayment that will be realized if A is greater than B

Results:

For all types of investment income, at a personal tax rate of 34%, there is a prepayment of tax by leaving the money in the corporation to be paid out at a later date since the dividend refund to the corporation from paying the dividend is higher than the personal tax paid on the dividend.

For example, for the interest and taxable capital gain, if the dividend is paid, the individual shareholder will pay tax of $177 but the corporation will receive a dividend refund of $267 giving the advantage to paying the dividend and not deferring it.

The following diagrams show the tax on the income more conceptually.

$1,000 Interest Income

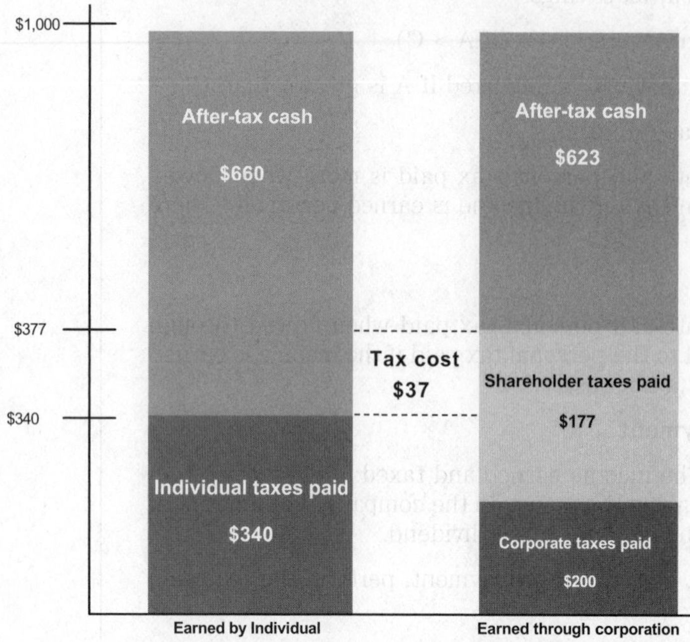

Note: No deferral by using corporation because of ART and subsequent refund on payment of dividend.

$2,000 Capital Gain

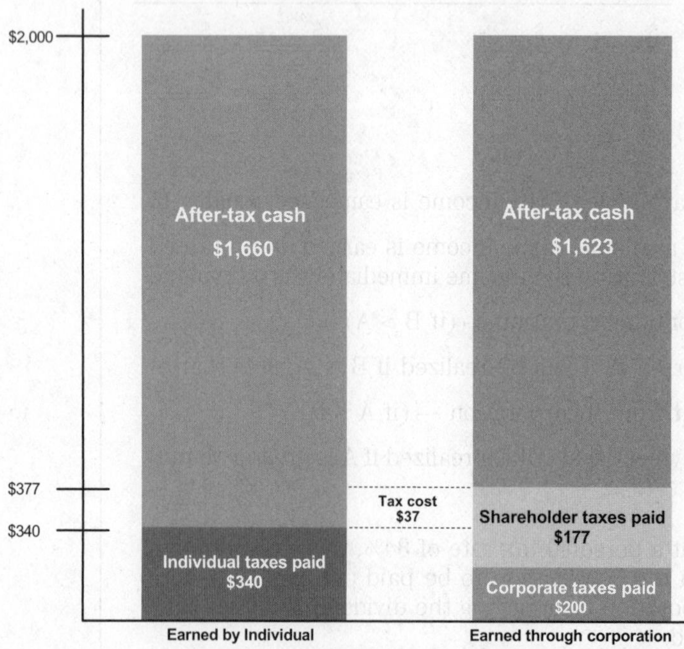

Note: No deferral by using corporation because of ART and subsequent refund on payment of dividend.

$1,000 Portfolio Dividend
18% Gross-Up

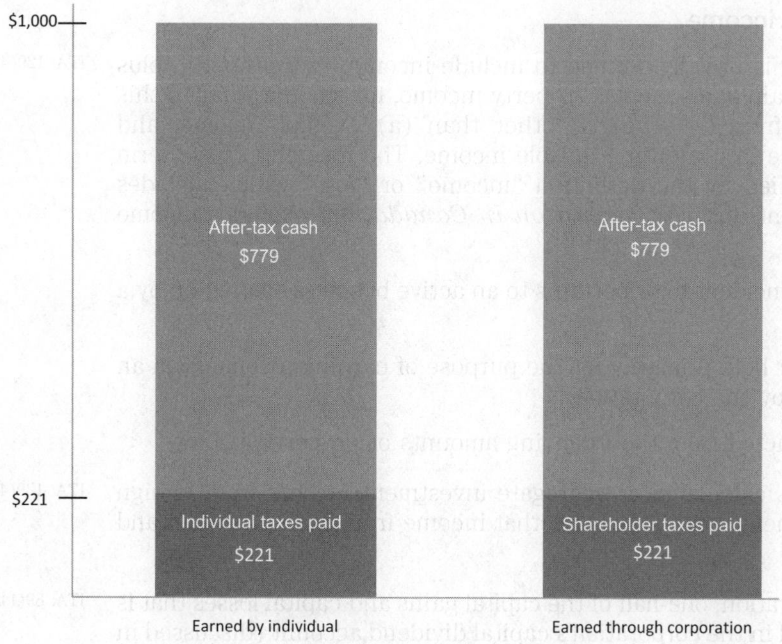

Note: No deferral by using corporation because of Part IV tax and subsequent refund on payment of dividend.

$1,000 Portfolio Dividend
38% Gross-Up

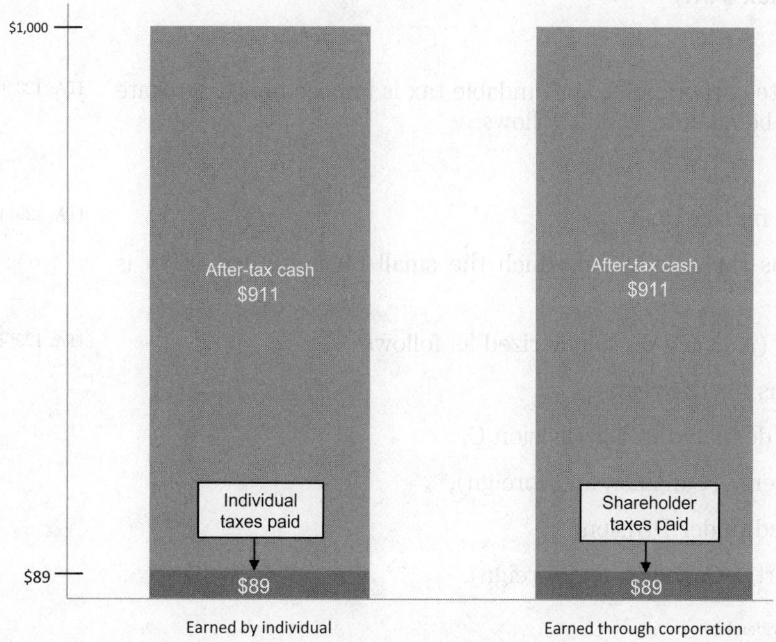

Note: No deferral by using corporation because of Part IV tax and subsequent refund on payment of dividend.

¶12,330 Special Refundable Taxes in Respect of Income from Investments of a CCPC

¶12,335 Aggregate investment income

Aggregate investment income is broadly defined to include income from property, plus net taxable capital gains, less certain adjustments. Property income, for the purposes of this definition, includes net income from all property, other than (a) exempt income, and (b) dividends which are deductible in computing taxable income. The meaning of the term "income from property" is amplified by the definition "income" or "loss" which includes income from a specified investment business *carried on in Canada*, but excludes income from the following sources: ITA: 129(4)

(a) from any property that is incident to or pertains to an active business carried on by a corporation, or

(b) from any property used or held primarily for the purpose of earning income from an active business carried on by the corporation.

Net losses from property are deducted from the foregoing amounts of property income.

Foreign investment income is calculated as aggregate investment income from foreign sources. Hence, aggregate investment income includes that income from both Canadian and foreign sources. ITA: 129(4)

As part of the system of integration, one-half of the capital gains and capital losses that is not included in income, is included in the corporation's capital dividend account (discussed in a subsequent chapter). The Act permits the corporation to pay a dividend out of the capital dividend account. The capital dividend is received free of tax by the shareholder. This completes the full integration of capital gains through a private corporation or Canadian-controlled private corporation and, with respect to the tax-free portion of the capital gains, places the shareholder in the same position as if he or she received the gain directly. ITA: 89(1) ITA: 83(2)

¶12,340 Additional refundable tax (ART)

¶12,340.10 *Basic rules*

For Canadian-controlled private corporations, a refundable tax is imposed on "aggregate investment income". This tax can be summarized as follows: ITA: 123.3

6⅔% × the lesser of:

(a) aggregate investment income, and ITA: 129(4)

(b) taxable income minus the amount on which the small business deduction is based.

Aggregate investment income (AII) can be summarized as follows: ITA: 129(4)

- Net taxable capital gains for the year,
- Less: net capital losses deducted under Division C,
- Plus: income from property (Canadian and foreign),*
- Less: dividends deducted under Division C,
- Less: losses from property (Canadian and foreign).

* Includes interest, royalties, rents and dividends.

¶12,340.20 *Avoiding the potential circular calculation with ART*

The calculation of the ART has been complicated by the fact that a number of the components of the corporate tax calculation are interrelated. For example:

- the small business deduction must be calculated in order to complete the ART;
- the foreign tax credit (FTC) calculations are needed to calculate the small business deduction; and
- the "tax for the year otherwise payable under this Part", which normally would include the ART, is needed to calculate the FTCs. ITA: 126(7)

As a result, there could have been a circular calculation if the following provisions were not introduced:

- the "tax for the year otherwise payable under this Part" for the business FTC excludes ART; and ITA: 126(7)
- the small business deduction calculation that grosses up the non-business FTC ($^{100}/_{28}$ × non-business FTC) must be calculated on the assumption that the non-business FTC calculation does not include the ART. ITA: 125(1)(*b*)(i)

To minimize confusion, Exhibit 12-10 sets out the steps that should be taken when calculating the ART when foreign tax credits are involved. Of course, where computer tax software is being used, this circularity issue does not have to be addressed, as it does in a manual calculation.

EXHIBIT 12-10
Steps To Be Taken to Calculate ART When FTCs are Involved

(1) Calculate the non-business FTC excluding ART from the "tax for the year otherwise payable under this Part" [spar. 125(1)(*b*)(i), ssec. 126(1)].

Non-business foreign tax credit (NBFTC)

Lesser of:

(a) Amount paid

(b) $\dfrac{\text{Foreign non-business income}}{\text{Div. B} - (\text{Divs.} + \text{Net CL})} \times$ [tax after abatement and general tax rate reduction]

(2) Calculate the business FTC (by definition, this excludes ART from "tax for the year otherwise payable under this Part" [ssec. 126(2)].

Business foreign tax credit (BFTC)

Least of:

(a) Amount paid and unused amounts

(b) $\dfrac{\text{Foreign business income}}{\text{Div. B} - (\text{Divs.} + \text{Net CL})} \times$ [tax before abatement – general tax rate reduction]

(c) Tax otherwise payable – non-business FTC

(3) Calculate the small business deduction using the above numbers.

Small business deduction

17% of least of:

(a) Active business income (Canadian-source)

(b) Taxable income

Less: $^{100}/_{28}$ non-business foreign tax credit (as calculated above)
4 × business foreign tax credit (as calculated above)

(c) Business limit

(4) Calculate the ART.

ART

6⅔% of lesser of:

(a)	Aggregate investment income
(b)	Taxable income – small business deduction

(5) Recalculate the final non-business FTC and include ART in the "tax for the year otherwise payable under this Part".

Final non-business foreign tax credit

Lesser of:

(a) Amount paid

(b) $\frac{\text{Foreign non-business income}}{\text{Div. B} - (\text{Divs.} + \text{Net CL})}$ × [tax after abatement and general tax rate reduction + ART]

(6) Recalculate the business FTC with the final non-business FTC (normally, no change will result).

Final business foreign tax credit

Least of:

(a) Amount paid and unused amounts

(b) $\frac{\text{Foreign business income}}{\text{Div. B} - (\text{Divs.} + \text{Net CL})}$ × [tax before abatement – general tax rate reduction]

(c) Tax otherwise payable – non-business FTC

¶12,345 "Refundable dividend tax on hand" (RDTOH)

¶12,345.10 *The concept*

"Refundable dividend tax on hand" (RDTOH) may be viewed as an account which accumulates all of the tax paid by a private company on its portfolio dividend income (i.e., Part IV tax at 33⅓%) and a portion of the Part I tax paid by a Canadian-controlled private corporation on other investment income. The principal components of the account are as follows:

- the refundable portion of Part I tax (including the ART) that is paid on investment income; ITA: 129(3)(*a*)
- the amount of Part IV tax that is paid on taxable dividends (the Part IV tax is discussed in more detail below); and ITA: 129(3)(*b*), 186
- the RDTOH balance at the end of the previous year, less "dividend refunds" (explained below) of the previous year that arise when the corporation pays taxable dividends. ITA: 129(3)(*c*), 129(3)(*d*)

The taxes that are accumulated in the RDTOH account are refundable to the company at the rate of $1 of refund for every $3 of taxable dividends paid. These refunds are commonly referred to as "dividend refunds", which reduce the balance in the RDTOH account. ITA: 129(1)(*a*)(i) ITA: 129(3)(*d*)

The following diagram illustrates these rules conceptually:

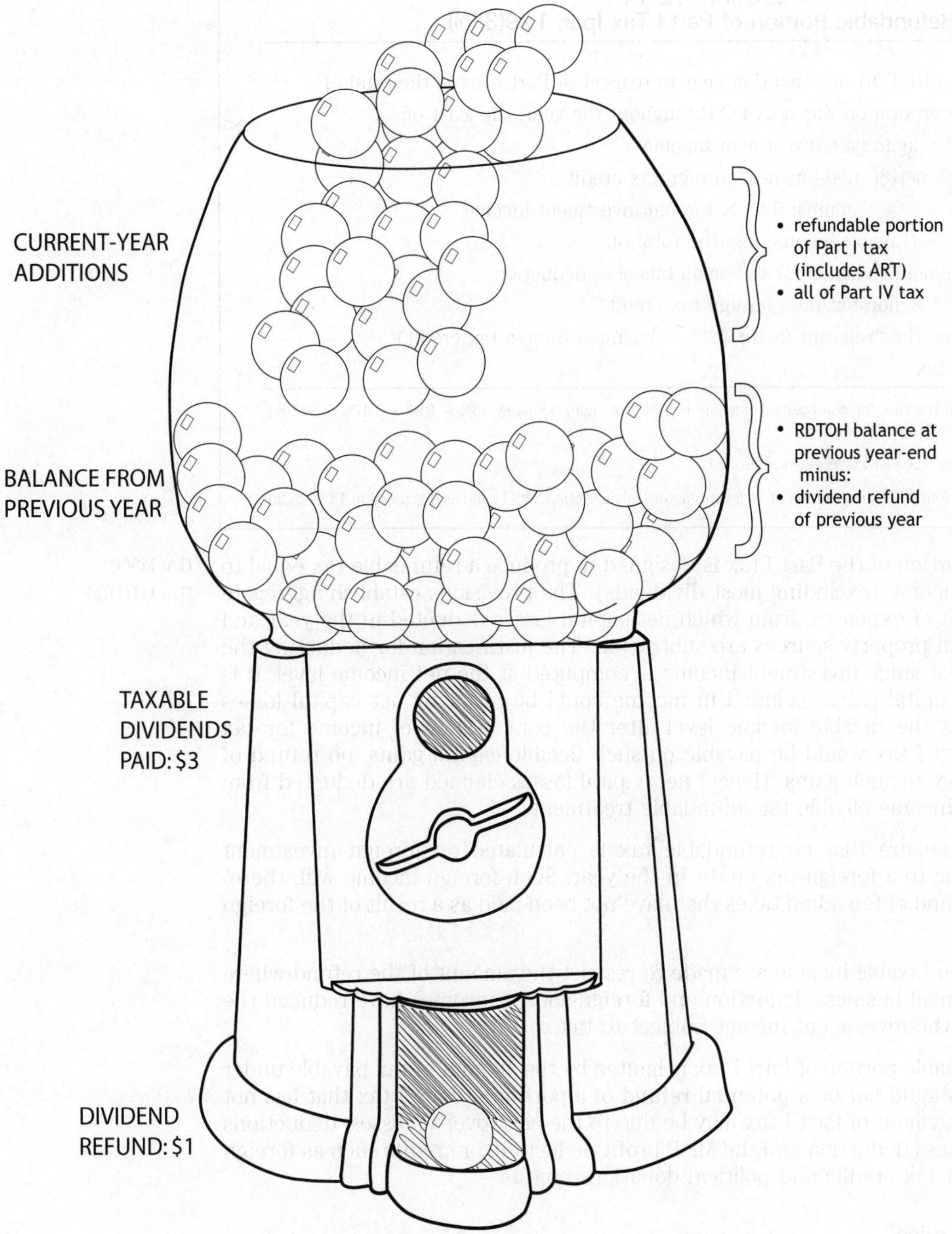

¶12,345.20 *Interpretation of the law*

RDTOH is illustrated, in part, in Exhibit 12-11. The basic purpose of the calculation is to aggregate the two types of refundable taxes (i.e., refundable portion of Part I tax for investment income (shown in the Exhibit) and Part IV tax for portfolio dividends), net of the amount of refundable taxes actually received. ITA: 129(3)

EXHIBIT 12-11
Refundable Portion of Part I Tax [par. 129(3)(*a*)]

The amount added to RDTOH in a taxation year in respect of Part I tax is the total of:

(a) where the corporation was a CCPC throughout the year, the least of:

(i) $26\frac{2}{3}\% \times$ aggregate investment income
less the net of: non-business foreign tax credit
minus: $9\frac{1}{3}$* $\times$ foreign investment income

(ii) $26\frac{2}{3}\% \times$ (taxable income less the total of:

- the amount eligible for the small business deduction
- $\frac{100}{35}$** $\times$ non-business foreign tax credit
- 4 (i.e., the "relevant factor")*** $\times$ business foreign tax credit)

(iii) Part I tax

* The notional federal tax rate for non-business income is 36% (i.e., approximately 38% - 10% + 6.67% = 34.7%). $9\frac{1}{3}\%$ is the notional 36% rate less $26\frac{2}{3}\%$.

** Based on a 35% rate (i.e., 34.7% as above, rounded).

*** 4 = 1/(.38-.13), as found in the definition of "relevant factor" in subsection 248(1) and as discussed in ¶12,125.20.

The refundable portion of the Part I tax is designed to produce a refundable tax equal to $26\frac{2}{3}\%$ of investment income (excluding most dividends). The provisions establish aggregate investment income, net of expenses, from which net capital losses deducted in the year and losses for the year from property sources are subtracted. The justification for deducting the net capital losses is that since investment income is computed at the net income level, it is possible that taxable capital gains included in income could be offset by net capital losses which are deducted at the taxable income level after the computation of income for tax purposes. Since no Part I tax would be payable on such taxable capital gains, no refund of unpaid tax should apply to such gains. Hence, net capital losses claimed are deducted from aggregate investment income eligible for refundable treatment. ITA: 129(4) ITA: 111(1)(*b*)

The calculations ensure that no refundable tax is calculated on foreign investment income which gives rise to a foreign tax credit in the year. Such foreign income will, therefore, not result in a refund of Canadian taxes that have not been paid as a result of the foreign tax credit.

The adjustments to taxable income are made to restrict the amount of the refund where other items (i.e., the small business deduction and foreign-source income) have reduced the taxable income below the investment income subject to tax.

Finally, the refundable portion of Part I tax is limited by the amount of tax payable under Part I, because there should not be a potential refund of a portion of Part I tax that has not been paid. Such non-payment of Part I tax may be due to the carryover of losses, deductions such as the small business deduction and the M&P profit deduction, or credits such as foreign tax credits, investment tax credits and political donations credits.

¶12,350 "Deeming rules"

What are known in practice as "deeming rules" are provided as an anti-avoidance provision that converts what would be property income (e.g., rent and interest) into active business income. However, this deeming provision only applies in situations where the income was derived from an associated corporation that had deducted the same amount in determining its active business income. ITA: 129(6)

Were it not for these deeming rules, it would be possible for a corporation that was approaching the $500,000 business limit for its small business deduction, for example, to transfer certain of its assets to an associated corporation which would rent the assets back to the original corporation. The rental expense incurred by the original corporation would be deductible, thereby reducing its active business income and preventing income in excess of $500,000 from being taxed at full corporate rates. The rental income to the associated corporation would be considered income from property or income from a specified investment business and would, therefore, be eligible for refundable treatment. However, as a result of the deeming rules, the amounts received are deemed to be active business income of the recipient.

As a result, the combined active business income of the original corporation and of the associated corporation, which receives the rent deemed to be active business income is the same as it would have been if the new corporation had not been set up; that is, the fact that the two corporations must share the $500,000 business limit has no effect on the total active business income of the group. Thus, any active business income in excess of $500,000 within the associated group will be taxed at full corporate rates as it would have been without the associated corporation. These deeming rules are summarized in Exhibit 12-12.

EXHIBIT 12-12
"Deeming Rules" [ssec. 129(6)]

Conditions	(1) Amount that would be income of the recipient corporation from property. (2) Amount deductible in computing income from an active business of an *associated* payer corporation.
Effect	(1) Amount not included in income from property. (2) Amount deemed to be income of the recipient from an active business [spar. 129(6)(*b*)(i)].
Application of small business deduction	Eligible for the small business deduction to the extent that the associated group of corporations has not exceeded the $500,000 business limit [ssec. 125(1)].

As indicated previously, the incentive to recharacterize business income, that would be taxed at the high corporate rate, as investment income is greatly reduced with the higher 38% gross-up and tax credit on eligible dividends. However, combined federal and provincial corporate tax rates may exist that make the imperfection of the taxation of high-rate business income a greater tax cost than the imperfection of the taxation of investment income. As a result, the incentive to recharacterize income in this context may continue.

¶12,355 Part IV tax on portfolio and other dividends

Normally, when a private corporation (or a "subject corporation", which is discussed below) receives a taxable dividend from another Canadian company (or an exempt dividend from a foreign affiliate), the dividend is deductible, in Division C, in computing taxable income. However, a 33⅓% tax must be paid on some of these dividends. A calculation of the Part IV tax is made in the T2 corporate tax return to meet the filing requirements for this tax. Late-filed payments of this tax are subject to interest at the prescribed rate. This special Part IV tax is fully refundable to the corporation when the dividend income is passed on to its shareholders as previously discussed.

ITA: 186(1)(*a*)
ITA: 187(1), 187(2)
ITA: 129(1)(*b*)

Part IV tax is a temporary, i.e., fully refundable, tax of 33⅓% levied on "assessable dividends" received by a "private corporation" or a "subject corporation" with an exception for dividends received from "connected corporations". Terms are discussed below. The objective of this tax is to discourage the use of a corporation to hold dividend-paying shares to defer tax to be paid by an individual shareholder on those dividends.

¶12,355.10 *Assessable dividends*

Dividends subject to Part IV tax have often been referred to as "portfolio dividends" even though the Act does not use this term. The term "assessable dividend" is defined to include dividends that are deductible under Division C. ITA: 186(3)

¶12,355.20 *Private corporation*

A private corporation is a corporation that is resident in Canada and that is neither a public corporation nor controlled by a public corporation. ITA: 89(1)

¶12,355.30 *Subject corporation*

A "subject corporation" is a corporation resident in Canada (other than a private corporation). A subject corporation is controlled (in the common law sense of ownership of shares with more than 50% of the votes), whether because of a beneficial interest in one or more trusts or otherwise, by or for the benefit of an individual or related group of individuals. An example is a Canadian public corporation that is controlled in the manner described above. This part of the Part IV tax provision was directed to investment holding corporations which were, essentially, private corporations, but which could otherwise avoid Part IV tax by listing a class of their shares on a prescribed exchange to meet the definition of a public corporation. The result of being a "subject corporation" is to be treated as a private corporation with respect to Part IV tax and its refund only (i.e., the refundable Part I tax provisions do not apply). Rules provide for a subject corporation to keep track of its RDTOH. ITA: 186(3) ITA: 186(5)

¶12,355.40 *Connected corporation*

A corporation is connected with another corporation where: ITA: 186(4)

(a) the corporation is controlled by the other corporation (where control represents ownership of more than 50% of the voting shares by any combination of the other corporation and persons with whom it does not deal at arm's length); or

(b) the corporation's shares are held by the other corporation and these shares represent more than 10% of the voting shares and more than 10% of the fair market value of all the issued shares in the corporation.

The definition of control is expanded for the purposes of the concept of connected corporation. The provision requires that in determining "control", shares owned by non-arm's length persons must be included in that determination. For example, this provision allows avoidance of the Part IV tax where the share ownership is split in lots of 10% among family members. ITA: 186(2)

This concept of a "connected corporation" is illustrated in Exhibit 12-13.

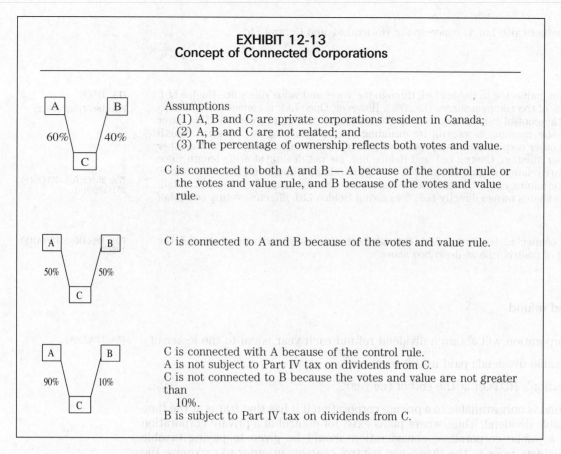

EXHIBIT 12-13
Concept of Connected Corporations

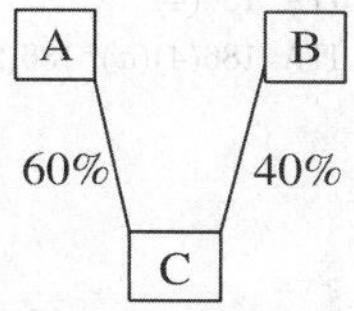

Assumptions
(1) A, B and C are private corporations resident in Canada;
(2) A, B and C are not related; and
(3) The percentage of ownership reflects both votes and value.

C is connected to both A and B — A because of the control rule or the votes and value rule, and B because of the votes and value rule.

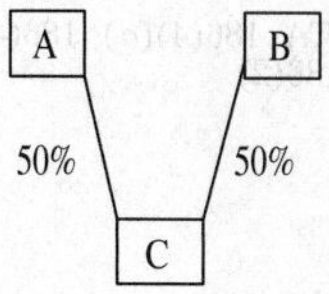

C is connected to A and B because of the votes and value rule.

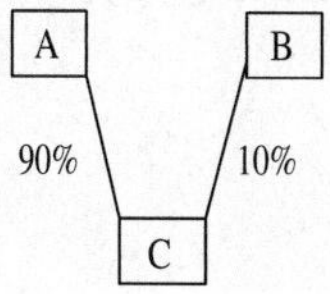

C is connected with A because of the control rule.
A is not subject to Part IV tax on dividends from C.
C is not connected to B because the votes and value are not greater than
10%.
B is subject to Part IV tax on dividends from C.

Note that the "connected" concept flows from C to A and B. Therefore, C may be connected to A and B, but A and B are not connected to C.

Example Problem 12-12

Mr. and Ms. Cheng hold common shares in two private corporations resident in Canada, as shown in the chart below. These corporations in turn hold common shares in another private corporation, Opco Ltd. The balance of the common shares are held by unrelated individuals. Assume that the share-ownership percentage also reflects their underlying value.

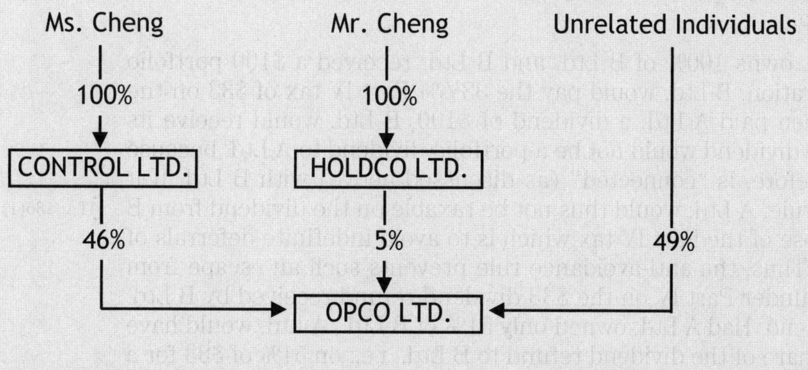

— REQUIRED

Determine whether Opco Ltd. is connected to Holdco Ltd. and Control Ltd.

— SOLUTION

Opco Ltd. is not connected to Holdco Ltd. through the votes and value rule since Holdco Ltd. holds less than 10% of the common shares (i.e., 5%). However, Opco Ltd. is connected to Holdco Ltd. by virtue of the control rule as modified by the extended meaning of control. This latter provision extends the meaning of control by including shares belonging to non-arm's length persons, including other corporations and persons who do not deal at arm's length with the other corporations. In this situation, Control Ltd. and Holdco Ltd. are not dealing at arm's length since both corporations are related because Mr. and Ms. Cheng are related through marriage. Therefore, for purposes of determining control, Holdco Ltd. is deemed to own the shares held by Control Ltd. (i.e., 46%) plus the shares owned directly (i.e., 5%) giving Holdco Ltd. effective voting control of Opco Ltd.

ITA: 186(4)
ITA: 186(4)(*a*), 186(2)
ITA: 251(2)(*a*), 251(2)(*b*), 251(2)(*c*)(ii)

Opco Ltd. is connected to Control Ltd. through both the votes and value rule and the extended meaning of control rule as described above.

ITA: 186(4)(*a*), 186(4)(*b*), 186(2)

¶12,360 Dividend refund

The private corporation will obtain a dividend refund each year equal to the lesser of

ITA: 129(1)(*a*)

(a) ⅓ of all taxable dividends paid in the year, and

(b) the corporation's RDTOH at the end of the year.

A dividend refund is only available to a private corporation if it has that status at the time that it pays the taxable dividend. Thus, where plans exist for control of a private corporation to be acquired by a public corporation, consideration should be given to paying taxable dividends to shareholders prior to the time when control changes in order to maximize the dividend refund to the corporation.

¶12,365 Anti-avoidance rule

The Part IV tax is generally not payable on dividends received from companies with which the private corporation (or a "subject corporation") is "connected", i.e., where the recipient corporation has more than merely a portfolio interest in the shares of the payer corporation. However, where a connected private corporation has been entitled to a refund of tax in the year, the receiving corporation will pay a refundable Part IV tax. The amount of the tax represents its share of any tax refunded to the payer corporation as a result of the dividend. This prevents corporations in a connected group from escaping the Part IV tax by the payment of dividends from a corporation in the group, receiving portfolio dividends, to another corporation in the group.

ITA: 186(1)(*b*)

For example, assume A Ltd. owns 100% of B Ltd. and B Ltd. received a \$100 portfolio dividend from some other corporation. B Ltd. would pay the 33⅓% Part IV tax of \$33 on the dividend it received. If B Ltd. then paid A Ltd. a dividend of \$100, B Ltd. would receive its dividend refund of \$33. The \$100 dividend would not be a portfolio dividend to A Ltd. because A Ltd. controls B Ltd. and, therefore, is "connected" (as discussed above) with B Ltd. If it were not for this anti-avoidance rule, A Ltd. would thus not be taxable on the dividend from B Ltd. This would defeat the purpose of the Part IV tax which is to avoid indefinite deferrals of tax on dividends of this nature. Thus, the anti-avoidance rule prevents such an escape from the Part IV tax by taxing A Ltd. under Part IV on the \$33 dividend refund received by B Ltd. on the payment of the \$100 dividend. Had A Ltd. owned only 51% of B Ltd., A Ltd. would have paid the Part IV tax only on its share of the dividend refund to B Ltd., i.e., on 51% of \$33 for a tax of \$16.83. Thus, A Ltd. pays Part IV tax on its proportionate share of the B Ltd. dividend refund triggered by the dividend paid by B Ltd.

ITA: 186(1)(*b*)

¶12,370 Summary of conditions for Part IV tax

Exhibit 12-14 summarizes the conditions under which the Part IV tax is paid on dividends received based on the percentage ownership of a recipient corporation in a payer corporation.

EXHIBIT 12-14
Liability for Part IV Tax

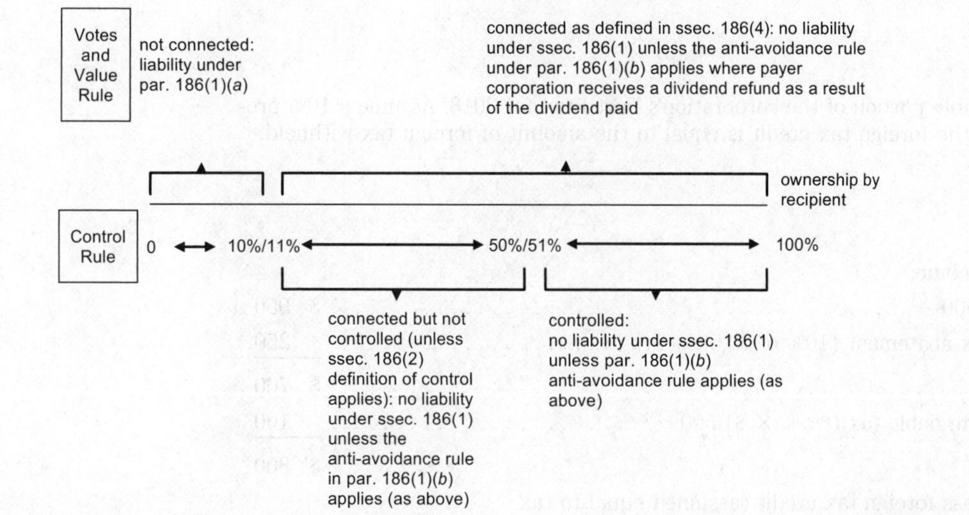

¶12,375 Application of non-capital losses

The recipient private corporation may *choose* to reduce the amount subject to the Part IV tax by applying otherwise available non-capital losses of the year or of a carryover year. These losses *cannot* be deducted subsequently from other income under Division C. Either the non-capital losses can be deducted, in effect, from dividend income subject to Part IV tax or they can be deducted in the calculation of taxable income subject to Part I tax. The same non-capital losses *cannot* be deducted under both provisions. It is, therefore, usually preferable to use the losses against income taxed at normal corporate rates, under Part I if that is possible, since the tax savings are usually greater and the Part IV tax otherwise payable is potentially refundable to the corporation. ITA: 186(1)(*c*), 186(1)(*d*)

¶12,380 Actual Application of the Scheme

The following two examples demonstrate the interaction of Part I tax and the refundable taxes. The first example problem deals with Canadian investment income and active business income. The second example adds the element of portfolio dividends subject to Part IV tax and then demonstrates the interaction of the two refundable taxes on RDTOH and the dividend refund.

Example Problem 12-13

Murphy Corporation Limited, a Canadian-controlled private corporation with a December 31, 2013 year end, has made the following calculation of its taxable income.

Canadian investment income	$1,000
U.S. investment income ($150 withheld at source)	1,000
Canadian active business income	1,000
	$3,000
Donations	500
Taxable income	$2,500

— *REQUIRED*

Compute the refundable portion of the corporation's Part I tax for 2013. Assume a 10% provincial tax rate and that the foreign tax credit is equal to the amount of foreign tax withheld.

— *SOLUTION*

Part I tax on taxable income:				
Tax @ 38% on $2,500				$ 950
Deduct: Federal tax abatement (10% of $2,500)				250
Net amount				$ 700
Add: Additional refundable tax ($6\frac{2}{3}\%$ × $1,500[(1)])				100
				$ 800
Deduct: Non-business foreign tax credit (assumed equal to tax paid)			$ 150	
Small business deduction (17% of $1,000)			170	
Tax reduction[(2)]			Nil	320
Total federal tax under Part I				$ 480
Provincial tax @ 10% of $2,500				250
Total tax				$ 730
Refundable portion of Part I tax:				
Least of:				
(a) $26\frac{2}{3}\%$ × aggregate investment income (AII) ($26\frac{2}{3}\%$ × $2,000)		$ 533		
Less: non-business foreign tax credit	$ 150			
minus: $9\frac{1}{3}\%$ × foreign investment income ($9\frac{1}{3}\%$ × $1,000)	(93)	(57)		$476
(b) Taxable income	$ 2,500			
Less: Amount eligible for the SBD	(1,000)			
$^{100}/_{35}$ × non-business FTC	(429)			
4 × business FTC	—			
$26\frac{2}{3}\%$ ×	$ 1,071	=		$286
(c) Part I tax				$480
Least amount				$289

— *NOTES TO SOLUTION*

(1) 6⅔% × lesser of:

Aggregate investment income (AII)	$2,000
Taxable income (TI) – income eligible for SBD ($2,500 – $1,000)	$1,500

(2) There is no tax reduction in this case since all active business income is eligible for the small business deduction and any other income of this CCPC is aggregate investment income.

Example Problem 12-14

VTL Limited is a Canadian-controlled private corporation with its first fiscal year ended December 31, 2013. The following data resulted in the indicated computation of taxable income and Part I tax payable:

Taxable dividends paid during the year		$ 30,000	
Active business income (assume equal to income eligible for the small business deduction)		$148,560	
Investment income:			
Taxable capital gains less allowable capital losses	$ 3,000		
Net income from property:			
Canadian-source rental income	2,000		
Foreign-source (before foreign tax of $375) interest income	2,500		
Total Canadian and foreign investment income		7,500	
Dividends (eligible for deduction under sec. 112 from non-connected Canadian-resident public corporations)		13,000	
Total net income		$169,060	
Deduct: dividends		13,000	ITA: 112
net capital losses		700	
Taxable income		$155,360	
Part I tax on taxable income:			
Tax @ 38% on $155,360		$ 59,037	
Deduct: Federal tax abatement (10% of $155,360)		15,536	
Net amount		$ 43,501	
Add: Additional refundable tax (6⅔% × $6,800*)		453	
		$ 43,954	
Deduct: Non-business foreign tax credit (assumed equal to tax paid)	$ 375		
Small business deduction (17% of $148,560)	25,255		
Tax reduction**	Nil	25,630	
Total federal tax under Part I		$ 18,324	
Provincial tax (assumed) @ 10% of $155,360		15,536	
Total tax		$ 33,860	

*6⅔% × lesser of:

(a) AII ($3,000 + $2,000 + $2,500 – $700) = $6,800

(b) TI – SBD amount ($155,360 – $148,560) = $6,800

**There is no tax reduction in this case, since all active business income is eligible for the small business deduction and any other income of this CCPC is aggregate investment income.

— REQUIRED

Compute the refundable dividend tax on hand at the end of the 2013 taxation year and the dividend refund for the 2013 taxation year.

— SOLUTION

Part IV tax on taxable dividends received:			
Taxable dividends subject to Part IV tax			$13,000
Part IV tax payable: $33\frac{1}{3}\%$ of $13,000			$ 4,333(1)
Refundable dividend tax on hand:			
Refundable portion of Part I tax:			
Least of:			
(a) $26\frac{2}{3}\%$ × aggregate investment income (AII) ($26\frac{2}{3}\%$ × $6,800)		$ 1,813	
Less: non-business foreign tax credit	$ 375		
minus: $9\frac{1}{3}\%$ × foreign investment income ($9\frac{1}{3}\%$ × $2,500)	(233)	(142)	$ 1,671
(b) Taxable income		$ 155,360	
Less: Amount eligible for SBD		(148,560)	
$^{100}/_{35}$ × non-business FTC ($375)		(1,071)	
4 × business FTC		—	
$26\frac{2}{3}\%$ ×		$ 5,729 =	$ 1,528
(c) Part I tax			$18,324
Refundable portion of Part I tax			$ 1,528
Part IV tax payable			4,333
Refundable dividend tax on hand			$ 5,861
Dividend refund:			
Taxable dividends paid: $30,000 × $\frac{1}{3}$		$ 10,000(F)	
Refundable dividend tax on hand at year end		$ 5,861(G)	
Dividend refund: lesser of (F) and (G)			$ 5,861
Summary of taxes payable:			
Part I tax (including assumed provincial tax)			$33,860
Part IV tax			4,333
			$38,193
Less: dividend refund			5,861
Net taxes payable			$32,332

— NOTE TO SOLUTION

(1) Had any of the dividends deductible under section 112 been received from a connected corporation, such dividends would not have been subject to the Part IV tax, unless those dividends gave rise to a dividend refund to the connected corporation.

¶12,390 Summary of advantages and disadvantages of incorporating investment income eligible for refundable tax

¶12,390.10 *Advantages*

The advantages of incorporating investment income eligible for refundable tax would appear to include the following:

- a tax deferral if the shareholder's combined marginal tax rate is greater than the theoretical combined corporate rate of 46⅔%;
- a negligible absolute tax saving as a result of the operation of the dividend tax credit in some provinces and a small tax saving where the combined federal and provincial corporate tax rate is less than the theoretical 46⅔%;
- a tax savings will result from a provincial corporate tax rate of less than 12% in 2013 [7.3% after 2013];
- greater flexibility in the timing of the receipt of income subject to personal tax;
- estate planning advantages on the transfer of property and the transfer of future growth to children (as discussed in a subsequent chapter);
- possible family income splitting in carefully planned and very restrictive situations (to be discussed subsequently with respect to the corporate attribution rules) through family members as shareholders and, perhaps, employees; and
- possible avoidance of foreign estate taxes by placing foreign property in a Canadian corporation.

¶12,390.20 *Disadvantages*

On the other hand the disadvantages of incorporating investment income would appear to include the following:

- a prepayment (as opposed to a deferral) of tax if the shareholder's combined marginal tax rate is less than the corporate tax rate plus the additional refundable tax;
- an additional tax cost if the combined federal and provincial corporate tax rate is ever raised to a rate in excess of the theoretical 46⅔%;
- an additional cost of maintaining a corporation in the form of administrative, accounting and legal costs; and
- a loss of the availability to the individual of investment and capital losses.

Given the relatively small tax savings resulting from the incorporation of investment income in many cases, these disadvantages may outweigh the advantages. However, the beneficial effects of estate planning and income splitting must be analyzed.

¶12,400 Imperfections and Policy Choices in the Integration System for Income of a CCPC

As discussed and illustrated, perfect integration results where corporate income, taxed at the corporate level and then at the individual shareholder level on dividends attracts the same total tax as the same income in the hands of an individual. Given the gross-up and dividend tax credit system, the major tool of integration, specified by the Act, perfect integration arises from:

(1) a combined federal and provincial corporate tax rate of:

(a) 27.5% on business income producing dividends eligible for the 38% gross-up (i.e., eligible dividends), or

(b) 15.3% [after 2013] on business income that has benefited from the small business deduction and investment income that has benefited from the refundable tax system eligible for the 18% gross-up [after 2013]; and

(2) a combined federal and provincial dividend tax credit equal to the gross-up.

¶12,405 Imperfections

¶12,405.10 *The high corporate rate on business income*

Imperfections from the combined federal and provincial corporate tax rate not being the perfect 27.5% or 15.3% result because of variations in the provincial corporate rates of tax. For a combined federal and provincial corporate rate of tax of 27.5% to exist, the provincial component of that corporate tax rate must be 12.5% (i.e., 38% – 10% – 13% + **12.5%** = 27.5%). In fact, provincial corporate rates on this type of income range from 10% to 16%. Where the combined corporate rate is less than 27.5%, due to a provincial rate of less than 12.5%, a tax savings imperfection will result from incorporation, relative to earning the income in an unincorporated form, like a proprietorship or a partnership. On the other hand, where the combined corporate rate is greater than 27.5%, due to a provincial rate of greater than 12.5%, a tax cost imperfection will result from incorporation relative to an individual earning the same income directly in an unincorporated form.

¶12,405.20 *The low corporate rate on business income*

At the low combined federal and provincial corporate rate of 15.3%, the provincial component of the tax rate has to be 4.3% (i.e., 38% – 10% – 17% + **4.3%** = 15.3%) on income eligible for the small business deduction. In fact, provincial rates of tax on income eligible for the small business deduction range from 0 to 8%. Where the provincial corporate rates are lower than the perfect rate of 4.3%, a tax savings results, and where the provincial corporate rates are higher, a tax cost results from incorporation.

¶12,405.30 *The low corporate rate on investment income*

On investment income eligible for refundable tax, the provincial corporate rate of tax has to be 7.3% (i.e., 38% – 10% + 6.67% – 26.67% + **7.3%** = 15.3%). The actual provincial rates on this type of income range from 10% to 16%. Where the provincial corporate rates are lower than the perfect rate of 7.3%, a tax savings results, and where the provincial corporate rates are higher, a tax cost results from incorporation.

¶12,405.40 *The Part IV tax on dividend income*

On dividend income subject to Part IV tax, there is no provincial tax and the Part IV tax is fully refundable when this income is paid out as a dividend to the shareholders. There is no tax savings or cost on this type of income earned through a corporation.

¶12,405.50 *The dividend tax credit*

Perfect integration requires a dividend tax credit that is equal to the gross-up. The federal component of the dividend tax credit for dividends subject to the 38% gross-up is $6/11$ of the gross-up. That means that the provincial component of the dividend tax credit has to be equal to $5/11$ of the gross-up. If the provincial tax credit rate is less than $5/11$ of the gross-up, then the total dividend tax credit will be less than the gross-up and there will be a tax cost to distributing after-tax corporate income as dividends with the result that there would be a tax advantage to paying salary. Of course, if the provincial dividend tax credit is higher than $5/11$ of the gross-up, then there will be a tax advantage to paying dividends.

The federal component of the dividend tax credit for dividends paid after 2013 subject to the proposed 18% dividend tax credit is $13/18$ of the gross-up. To be perfect, the provincial component has to be $5/18$ of the 18% gross-up. A provincial tax credit rate of less than the perfect $5/18$ of the gross-up results in a tax cost to paying a dividend relative to paying a salary or bonus, whereas a provincial tax credit rate of more than 5/18 of the gross-up results in a tax savings from paying dividends rather than a salary or bonus.

¶12,410 A deferral of tax as a government policy choice

A corporation can be used to defer tax on income earned by a corporation compared to the same income earned directly by an individual, if the combined federal and provincial corporate tax rate is less than the combined federal and provincial personal tax rate on that income. In this case of a lower corporate tax rate compared with the personal tax rate, the deferral that results is a deferral of tax on the dividend paid out of after-tax corporate income to an individual shareholder, until the time that the dividend is paid.

The availability of this deferral is not an imperfection in the system, but a government policy choice for corporate tax rates. The government may wish to maintain lower corporate tax rates on, say, business income, for international competition purposes. One way of achieving this is to introduce a general rate reduction on that income. The government may wish to provide more internally generated funds for reinvestment in the corporate business to allow that business to grow. One way of achieving this is to provide a small business deduction. Of course, the lower the corporate rate, the more deferral is possible, if the income is retained in the corporation and not paid out as dividends to attract tax in the hands of the individual shareholder.

If the government's objective was to eliminate a tax deferral altogether, it could implement a system of taxing all corporate income at the same tax rate as an individual would pay on the same income, whether it is distributed as a dividend or not. That is the way income from an unincorporated entity, like a proprietorship or a partnership is taxed. In the unincorporated form, income is taxed in the hands of the owners, whether or not they withdraw it. In this system, there would be no deferral, but the benefits of a lower corporate tax rate would not be available.

The opposite of a deferral effect is a prepayment of tax through an initial corporate rate that is higher than personal tax rates. This occurs by design for investment income, because there is no economic advantage to the government from encouraging the formation of corporations to generate investment income, compared to generating business income. Therefore, the system applicable to investment income of a CCPC has been designed to tax the corporation, initially, at a corporate rate that is, generally, higher than the top personal tax rate. This has necessitated the additional refundable tax and, of course, no eligibility for the general rate reduction. That results in a combined initial federal and provincial corporate tax rate of 46⅔% (i.e., 38% – 10% + 6⅔% + 12%), using a hypothetical provincial corporate rate of 12%. At this total corporate rate, there is virtually no deferral advantage from incorporating a source of investment income. However, at that high corporate rate, there is a considerable tax cost to incorporating that type of income which is only eligible for the 18% [after 2013] gross-up and tax credit. That is why the system allows for a refund of some of the corporate tax at the high rate to bring the corporate rate, after the dividend refund, closer to the corporate rate necessary for perfect integration where the tax cost is substantially reduced. The corporation receives the dividend refund when it pays a taxable dividend, so there is no deferral possibility at that time. In fact, at the time that the corporation receives the refund to lower its effective tax rate, the individual pays the tax on the dividend.

¶12,415 Analyzing the decision to incorporate

The decision to incorporate a particular type of income, from a tax perspective, can be based on the opportunity to save tax or to defer tax or both. The following steps should be taken to properly analyze this decision.

- **Calculate**

(1) the personal after-tax cash available, if the amount and type of income is earned by an individual;

(2) the corporate after-tax cash available for payment of a dividend, if the amount and type of income is earned in a corporation owned by the individual; and

(3) the personal after-tax cash available, if the corporation distributed its after-tax income as a dividend to the individual as the shareholder.

- **Determine tax savings or cost**

To determine if a tax savings or a tax cost will result from incorporation, perform the following analysis:

(1) Compare

— the personal after-tax cash available, if the income is earned personally, to

— the personal after-tax cash available, if the income is earned in a corporation and, then, the after-tax corporate retained earnings is distributed as a dividend to the individual as a shareholder.

(2) Determine the tax savings

— if the individual, as a shareholder, has more personal after-tax cash, when the income is flowed through the corporation, then this is the amount of tax savings that will be realized.

(3) Determine the tax cost

— if the individual, as a shareholder, has less personal after-tax cash, when the income is flowed through the corporation, then this is the amount of tax cost that will be incurred.

- **Determine tax deferral or prepayment**

To determine if a tax deferral or a tax prepayment will result from incorporation, perform the following analysis:

(1) Compare

— the personal after-tax cash available, if the income is earned personally, to

— the corporate after-tax cash available, if the income is earned and retained in the corporation by not distributing the income immediately as a dividend.

(2) Determine the tax deferral

— if the corporation has more corporate after-tax cash than the individual has in personal after-tax cash, then this is the amount of tax deferral that will result.

(3) Determine the tax prepayment

— if the individual has more personal after-tax cash than the corporation has in corporate after-tax cash, then this is the amount of prepayment of tax that will result.

¶12,500 COMPREHENSIVE SUMMARY OF TYPES OF CORPORATE INCOME AND FEDERAL CORPORATE INCOME TAX RATES

Exhibit 12-15 presents a comprehensive summary of types of corporate income that can be earned by a Canadian corporation and the federal marginal income tax rates applicable to each type of income.

EXHIBIT 12-15
Summary of Corporate Income Types and Federal Marginal Tax Rates

	ABI			*Investment*		*Cdn.dividends*	
	Cdn.	*For'n.*	*PSB*	*Cdn.*	*For'n.*	*Conn.*	*Port.*
Business & property:							
Business	X						
Interest, rent				X	X		
Foreign branch		X					
Dividends						X	X
Employment			X				
Taxable capital gains				X	X		
Net Income for Tax							
	%	%	%	%	%	%	%
Federal Part I tax rates:							
Basic	38.00	38.00	38.00	38.00	38.00		
Abatement	(10.00)		(10.00)	(10.00)	(10.00)		
	28.00	38.00	28.00	28.00	28.00		
Eligible for:							
SBD	17.00						
M&P > SBD	13.00						
RDTOH				26.67	26.67	33.33	33.33
FTC		Yes			Yes		
General rate reduction	13.00	13.00	13.00*				
Additional refundable tax				6.67	6.67		
Part IV tax:							
3 × dividend refund						33.33	
Portfolio dividend							33.33

* Nil for taxation years that begin after October 31, 2011 [per October 31, 2011 draft legislation].

Corporate marginal income tax rates are summarized in the following table. In the calculation of income tax for a corporation, these marginal rates are not applied to the various sources of income separately. However, these marginal rates may be helpful in planning analyses. The table also indicates the opportunity to save and to defer tax at the corporate rates shown.

Corporate Marginal Income Tax Rates
(Provincial Rates Hypothetical)

	Fully Taxed Income	*M&P*	*ABI ≤$500K SBD Eligible*	*Investment*
	%	%	%	%
Basic federal rate	38.0	38.0	38.0	38.0
Abatement (Canadian-source income)	(10.0)	(10.0)	(10.0)	(10.0)
Net	28.0	28.0	28.0	28.0
General rate reduction	(13.0)*			
M&P deduction		(13.0)		
Small business deduction			(17.0)	
Additional refundable tax				6.7
Net	15.0	15.0	11.0	34.7
Provincial (hypothetical)	13.0	11.0	4.0	13.0

Subtotal	28.0	26.0	15.0	47.7
Dividend refund				(26.7)
Total	28.0	26.0	15.0	21.0
Tax savings potential	No	Yes**	Yes***	No
Tax-deferral potential	Yes****	Yes****	Yes	No

* The general rate reduction does not apply to PSB income. The result is a 41% total corporate tax rate, with a significant tax cost and a tax deferral only in the top personal tax bracket.

** Very minor.

*** Very minor with the 18% gross-up for dividends paid after 2013.

**** Only in top two federal personal tax brackets.

Example Problem 12-15

James Fish Distributors Inc. (JFDI) is a Canadian-controlled private corporation located in Burnaby, British Columbia. The company's income for tax purposes for its December 31, 2013 taxation year end was calculated correctly as follows:

Distributing income	$ 145,000
Wholesaling income	195,000
Maintenance service contract loss	(65,000)
Patent income(1)	45,000
Rental income(2)	35,000
Taxable capital gains net of losses(3)	55,000
Recapture of CCA(3)	15,000
Interest income on outstanding account receivable on wholesaling income	10,000
Interest income from loan to wholly owned subsidiary(4)	20,000
Interest income from a sinking fund trust for replacement of a building	50,000
Foreign business income (gross amount — $Cdn.)(5)	40,000
Foreign non-business income (gross amount — $Cdn.)(6)	25,000
Dividends from CCPCs (non-connected)	12,500
Dividends from the wholly owned subsidiary which received a $1,500 dividend refund as a result of paying this dividend	17,500
Profit on sale of excess land(7)	90,000
Net income for tax purposes — Division B	$ 690,000

(1) The patent income has been determined to be property income.

(2) The rental income was derived from leasing the entire space on a 5-year lease in an unused warehouse in a small town in the northern part of the province.

(3) The net taxable capital gain and the recapture concerned the disposition of certain specialized maintenance service equipment.

(4) The funds were used to buy equipment for its active business.

(5) Foreign income tax in the amount of $10,000 ($Cdn.) was paid on the foreign business income.

(6) Withholding tax on the non-business income was $4,000 ($Cdn.).

(7) The land had been held for approximately 5 years. It was purchased with the intent of realizing a profit on sale.

Additional Information:

(1) JFDI made the following selected payments during the year:

Political donations	$ 7,500
Charitable donations	22,500
Dividends paid on July 15, 2013	37,500

(2) The balances in the tax accounts on January 1, 2013 were:

Charitable donation carryforward	$ 2,500
Unused business foreign tax credit	3,500
Non-capital losses	42,500
Net capital losses (arising in 1999)	13,500
RDTOH balance	Nil

(3) Taxable income earned in British Columbia, which is the only Canadian jurisdiction in which JFDI operates, is approximately 85% of the total.

(4) The business limit is allocated to JFDI to offset its Canadian-source ABI.

— REQUIRED

(A) Calculate the federal tax and provincial tax at an assumed net rate of 10% on federal taxable income payable by the company for 2013.

(B) Compute the refundable dividend tax on hand balance as at December 31, 2013, and compute the dividend refund for 2013.

— SOLUTION

Analysis of Division B Income

	ABI			*Investment*		*Dividend*		
Source	*Cdn.*	*For'n.*	*PSB*	*Cdn.*	*For'n.*	*Conn.*	*Port.*	*Total*
Distributing	$145,000							$145,000
Wholesaling	195,000							195,000
Maintenance service	(65,000)							(65,000)
Patent				$ 45,000				45,000
Rental				35,000				35,000
Net taxable capital gains				55,000				55,000
Recapture	15,000							15,000
Interest — A/R	10,000							10,000
loan	20,000(1)							20,000
sinking fund				50,000				50,000
Foreign		$40,000			$25,000			65,000
Dividend						$17,500	$12,500	30,000
Profit	90,000							90,000
Division B income	$410,000	$40,000	Nil	$185,000	$25,000	$17,500	$12,500	$690,000

(A) *Tax Payable*

Division B income		$ 690,000
Division C deductions:		
Charitable donations ($22,500 + $2,500) — max. 75% of $690,000	$25,000	
Dividends from taxable Canadian corporations ($17,500 + $12,500)	30,000	
Non-capital losses	42,500	
Net capital losses ($13,500 × ½ / ¾)	9,000	(106,500)
Taxable income		$ 583,500
Tax @38% of $583,500		$ 221,730
Deduct: Federal abatement (10% of 85% (given) of $583,500)		49,598
Net amount		$ 172,132
Add: Additional refundable tax (Schedule 1)		11,567
		$ 183,699
Deduct: Non-business foreign tax credit (Schedule 2)	$ 4,000	
Business foreign tax credit (Schedule 3)	13,500	
Small business deduction (Schedule 4)	69,700	
Tax reduction (Schedule 5)	Nil	
Federal political contributions tax credit — max.	650	(87,850)
Part I tax payable		$ 95,849
Provincial tax @ 10% of 85% of $583,500		49,598
Part IV tax payable ((33⅓% of $12,500) + $1,500)		5,667
Total tax		151,114
Less: dividend refund		(12,500)
Net tax		$ 138,614

Schedule 1: Additional refundable tax

6⅔% of lesser of:

(a) AII ($185,000 + $25,000 + $17,500 + $12,500 – $9,000 – $30,000)	$ 201,000
(b) Taxable income – SBD amount[(2)] ($583,500 – $410,000)	$ 173,500

6⅔% of $173,500 = $11,567

Schedule 2: Non-business foreign tax credit

Lesser of:

(a) Amount paid .... $ 4,000

(b) $\dfrac{\text{Foreign non-business income}}{\text{Div. B} - (\text{Divs.} + \text{Net CL})} \times$ [tax after abatement + ART]

$\dfrac{\$25{,}000}{\$690{,}000 - (\$30{,}000 + \$9{,}000)} \times \$183{,}699$ .... $ 7,054

Lesser amount = $4,000

Schedule 3: Business foreign tax credit

Least of:

(a) Amount paid + unused amount ($10,000 + $3,500) .... $ 13,500

(b) $\dfrac{\text{Foreign business income}}{\text{Div. B} - (\text{Divs.} + \text{Net CL})} \times$ [tax before abatement − general rate reduction]

$\dfrac{\$40{,}000}{\$690{,}000 - (\$30{,}000 + \$9{,}000)} \times (\$221{,}730 - \text{Nil})$ .... $ 13,624

(c) Tax otherwise payable − non-business FTC:
($221,730 − Nil) − $4,000 = ... $217,730

Least amount = $13,500

Schedule 4: Small business deduction

17% of least of:

(a) Active business income (Canadian-source)			$410,000
(b) Taxable income		$583,500	
Less: $^{100}/_{28}$ × NBFTC ($^{100}/_{28}$ × $4,000) . . .	$14,286		
4 × BFTC (4 × $13,500)	54,000	68,286	$515,214
(c) Business limit (allocated to equal ABI, above)			$410,000

17% of $410,000 = $69,700

Schedule 5: General tax reductions

Taxable income		$583,500
Less: income eligible for the small business deduction	$410,000	
AII	201,000	(611,000)
Net		$ Nil
13% of Nil		$ Nil

(B) *Refundable Portion of Part I Tax*

Least of:

(a) 26⅔% of AII (26⅔% of $201,000).................		$ 53,600	
Less: non-business foreign tax credit	$ 4,000		
minus: 9⅓% of foreign investment income (9⅓% of $25,000)	2,333	1,667	$ 51,933

(b) Taxable income		$583,500	
Less: Amount eligible for SBD	$410,000		
$^{100}/_{35}$ × NBFTC ($^{100}/_{35}$ × $4,000)	11,429		
4 × BFTC (4 × $13,500)	54,000	475,429	
26⅔% of		$108,071	$ 28,819
(c) Part I tax			$ 95,849

Least amount = $28,819

RDTOH

Balance, January 1, 2013	Nil
Add: Refundable portion of Part I tax	$ 28,819
Part IV tax	5,667
Balance, December 31, 2013	$ 34,486

Dividend refund

Lesser of:

(a) Taxable dividends paid × ⅓ ($37,500/3)	$ 12,500
(b) RDTOH balance, December 31, 2013	$ 34,846

Lesser amount = $12,500

— NOTE TO SOLUTION

(1) The interest on the loan to the subsidiary is deemed to be active business income. JFDI and the subsidiary are associated. The interest is ordinarily income from property, but is deducted from the ABI of the associated payer. ITA: 129(6)

(2) Initially, the SBD amount is assumed to be $410,000, since Canadian-source ABI is $410,000 and taxable income (before adjustment for foreign tax credits) is $583,500. This assumption, which is verified later in Schedule 4, allows for a calculation of ART.

¶12,800 REVIEW QUESTIONS

(1) Explain the purpose behind the concept of integration.

(2) It has been said that "ideal integration depends on the existence of two factors in the tax system". Briefly explain what they are.

(3) The dividend gross-up and tax credit has been described as the major tool of integration in the Act. Give a brief explanation of how it works in theory.

(4) What is the purpose of the small business deduction?

(5) On July 15th of this year, Mr. Smith bought all the shares of a company which was the Canadian subsidiary of a U.S. parent. There are no losses or ITCs being carried forward by the company. What advice would you have for Mr. Smith with regard to his choice of year-end for the acquired corporation?

(6) Give an example of when paragraph 125(1)(*b*) will give a lower limit for the small business deduction than paragraph 125(1)(*a*).

(7) What is the purpose of subparagraphs 125(1)(*b*)(i) and (ii)? Explain the overall concept and why they use the fractions they do in each of them.

(8) List some tax and non-tax advantages of incorporation.

(9) List some tax and non-tax disadvantages of incorporation.

(10) Mr. Mould has just started up a manufacturing operation to supply parts to the auto industry. Given his need for start-up capital, he is happy that his tax rate is reduced by both the small business deduction of 17% and the M&P profits deduction of 13%. Comment.

(11) Are there any tax rules that prevent an individual from deferring tax on portfolio dividends by flowing them through a corporation?

(12) What are five tools that are used in the tax laws to integrate the taxation of investment income earned through a corporation?

(13) Theoretically, what does the 25% [18% after 2013] or 38% gross-up on dividends from taxable Canadian corporations represent?

(14) Theoretically, what does the dividend tax credit represent?

(15) Explain how integration theoretically works if a $1,000 capital gain is realized in a CCPC.

(16) Mr. Orville owns all the shares of Holdco which in turn owns all of the shares of Opco, a CCPC carrying on an active business in Canada. In recent years, Opco has done very well and its income is well in excess of the business limit. Last year Mr. Orville paid a dividend of $150,000 from Opco to Holdco. However, since he needed the cash in Opco to expand, he loaned the money back to Opco and charged 10% interest. The interest charged to Opco amounted to $15,000 in the year. How will this interest income be taxed in Holdco?

(17) A number of years ago a reorganization was undertaken so that now A Ltd. owns voting preferred shares in B Ltd. These preferred shares have only 7% of the votes and are now only worth 7% of the value. The other shares of B Ltd. are owned by the son of the only shareholder of A Ltd. Are A Ltd. and B Ltd. connected?

(18) Under paragraphs 186(1)(*c*) and (*d*), the recipient private corporation may choose to reduce the amount subject to the Part IV tax by applying otherwise available non-capital losses of the year or of a carryover year. Either the non-capital losses can be deducted from dividend income subject to Part IV tax or they can be deducted in the calculation of taxable income subject to Part I tax. What factors should be considered in deciding which option to choose?

¶12,825 MULTIPLE CHOICE QUESTIONS

Question 1

Concept Corp, a CCPC, correctly calculated its taxable income for its year ended December 31, 2013 as follows:

Income from retailing business carried on in Canada	$ 120,000
Loss from retailing business carried on in United States	(20,000)
Interest income from long-term bonds	30,000
Taxable capital gain from sale of a capital asset	5,000
Net income	$ 135,000
Non-capital losses	(3,000)
Taxable income	$ 132,000

Concept Corp and X Ltd. are associated corporations. X Ltd. claimed a 17% small business deduction on $385,000 for 2013. The taxable capital of Concept Corp and X Ltd. is significantly less than $10 million. Which one of the following amounts is the maximum 17% small business deduction for Concept Corp for 2013?

(A) $17,000

(B) $19,550

(C) $20,400

(D) $22,440

Question 2

M Ltd. provides management advisory services to ACC Ltd. and is not involved in any other business. Mr. Mud is the sole shareholder and only employee of M Ltd. Mr. Mud and his son each own 50% of the issued shares of ACC Ltd. Which one of the following statements is TRUE?

(A) If Mr. Mud would reasonably be regarded as an employee of ACC Ltd., but for the existence of M Ltd., then M Ltd. is carrying on a "personal services business".

(B) M Ltd. is carrying on a "personal services business", unless it employs in the business more than five full-time employees throughout the year, which it does not.

(C) M Ltd. is carrying on a "specified investment business".

(D) M Ltd. is carrying on an "active business".

Question 3

B Ltd. is a Canadian-controlled private corporation which distributes plastic bottles. The following information relates to its year ended December 31, 2013.

Active business income earned in Canada	$495,000
Net income, Division B	520,000
Taxable income	520,000

B Ltd. is not associated with any other corporation. B Ltd. did not earn any foreign business income nor any investment income. B Ltd.'s taxable capital is well below $10 million. Which of the following amounts is the maximum general rate reduction for the December 31, 2013 year:

(A) $2,600

(B) $3,250

(C) $53,411

(D) $67,600

Question 4

A Ltd., a private corporation, received dividends from B Ltd. and C Ltd. during its year ended December 31, 2013.

	B Ltd.	*C Ltd.*
Amount of dividend received by A Ltd.	$120,000	$120,000
Percentage of shares owned by A Ltd. (votes and value)	70%	8%
Dividend refund received by the payer of the dividend	$ 40,000	$400,000

A Ltd. and C Ltd. are not related. All three are taxable Canadian corporations. Which one of the following amounts is the Part IV tax payable by A Ltd.?

(A) $60,000

(B) $64,000

(C) $68,000

(D) $80,000

Question 5

Joanne owns 55% of the common shares of J Co. and Doug (her spouse) owns 55% of the common shares of D Co. Which of the following would *not* make J Co. and D Co. associated?

(A) If Joanne owned 25% of the common shares of D Co.

(B) If Doug owned 25% of the common shares of J Co.

(C) If a trust for their twin two-year-old daughters controls T Co. and no special elections were made.

(D) If J Co. and D Co. each owned 40% of the shares of R Co., a corporation carrying on a retailing business.

Question 6

In which of the following situations are X Ltd. and Y Ltd. NOT associated?

(A) Rod owns 10% of voting shares of X Ltd. and 50% of the voting shares Y Ltd. and Patrick owns 60% of the voting shares of X Ltd. and 10% of the voting shares of Y Ltd. Rod and Patrick are not related.

(B) The adult son of the controlling shareholder of X Ltd. controls Y Ltd. and owns 25% of the voting shares of X Ltd.

(C) A mother controls Company X. Her two adult daughters each own 30% of the voting shares of Y Ltd. Her adult son owns 25% of the voting shares of Y Ltd.

(D) A brother and sister each own 30% of the voting shares of Sibco Inc. A mother and father each own 20% of the shares. The mother and father each own 50% of the voting shares of Parentco Inc.

¶12,850 EXERCISES

Exercise 1

ITA: 125(7)

The taxpayer company carried on the business on a comparatively small scale of lending money on mortgages. The company was operated by two individuals who also owned and managed a number of other companies. All the companies operated out of the same office premises and used more or less the same office staff and equipment. The taxpayer company had no full-time employees. It was listed in the telephone directory but did no direct advertising. No attempt was made to keep track of the amount of time spent by the office staff on the work of each company and no specific charge was made for office space, use of telephones and equipment or staff.

The company made loans to potential borrowers referred to it by independent agents. Its clientele came mainly from those who found it difficult to obtain loans through the normal commercial channels. The agents had a general idea of the sort of loans which might be acceptable, but because those were relatively high-risk loans, the company had to examine them very carefully. Occasionally, an outside appraisal was made, but normally someone from the company would visit the property to examine it. Often considerable negotiations as to terms were involved. Post-dated cheques for five years would be obtained from borrowers and turned over to the bank as collateral for the company's line of credit.

For the year in question, the company held three mortgages involving $11,084. The sale of a small property, interest and other income resulted in total income of $4,609. Net income before taxes was shown as $3,479. The mortgages outstanding and net income of the company increased continuously from the year in question to the present time. During the year in question, the company's line of credit at the bank was estimated at $7,500 to $15,000, but it is now $25,000.

— REQUIRED

From the facts provided in the case, determine the type of business that is carried on by the company under the current legislation.

Exercise 2

ITA: 251

(A) By reference to provisions of the *Income Tax Act*, determine which of the following individuals or groups of individuals are not at arm's length with Alpha Corporation Limited:

(i) Mr. Beta, who owns 25% of the shares of Alpha and is not related to any other shareholders.

(ii) Mr. Beta and his brother, who together own 55% of the shares of Alpha and they are not related to any other shareholder.

(iii) Mr. Delta, who has an option to purchase all of the shares held by Mr. Beta and his brother anytime during the next three years.

(iv) Mr. Epsilon, who has an option to purchase all of the shares held by Mr. Beta and his brother from their estates within five years of their death.

(B) By reference to provisions of the *Income Tax Act*, determine under which of the following conditions Tau Corporation Limited and Lambda Corporation Limited do not deal with each other at arm's length:

(i) Tau is controlled by two brothers, A and B, and Lambda is controlled by A.

(ii) Three unrelated individuals together control Tau and one of these individuals controls Lambda.

(iii) Tau is related to Sigma Corporation Limited and Sigma is related to Lambda.

Exercise 3

ITA: 251, 256

Consider each of the following unrelated cases:

(A) Ava owns 55% of the shares of Jay-one Ltd. and 70% of the shares of Jay-two Ltd. Jay-one Ltd. owns 60% of the shares of Jay-three Ltd. The remaining shares in all three corporations are owned by persons unrelated to Ava.

(B) Abigail owns 30% of the common shares of Benco Ltd. and all of the shares of Rayco Ltd. The other 70% of the common shares of Benco Ltd. are owned by Abigail's cousin. However, Abigail's mother owns all of the voting preferred shares of Benco Ltd. and has sufficient votes to elect more than 50% of the Board of Directors of Benco Ltd.

(C) Adam owns 100% of the shares of Adamco Ltd. and 25% of the shares of Kidco Ltd. His daughter and son-in-law each own 20% of the shares of Kidco Ltd. and the remainder of the shares are owned by persons unrelated to all three.

(D) Sister One and Sister Two each own 50% of Sisco Ltd. and 25% of Cousco Ltd. Each sister has a daughter over the age of 18 who owns 25% of Cousco Ltd.

— *REQUIRED*

In each unrelated case, determine whether the corporations named are associated. Substantiate your answer by reference to specific provisions of subsection 256(1).

Exercise 4

ITA: 125(1), 256(1), 256(2.1)

Alpha and Beta are two sisters living in Halifax. While Alpha controls Taxit Ltd., Beta owns 25% of the shares of the corporation. Beta also owns 100% of the shares of Sibling Ltd. The active business income for Taxit during the current taxation year was $465,000 and for Sibling was $560,000. The taxation years for both corporations end December 31.

— *REQUIRED*

How much should each company claim as a small business deduction on their active business income for the taxation year?

Exercise 5

ITA: 251, 252, 256

The common shares of Chutzpah Enterprises Limited were owned by the three Chutzpah brothers as follows:

Aleph Chutzpah	40%
Bett Chutzpah	40%
Gimmel Chutzpah	20%

The common shares of Schlock Sales Limited were owned by the following:

Bett Chutzpah	45%
Dallied Chutzpah	45%
Unrelated person	10%

Aleph Chutzpah is married to Dallied Chutzpah.

— *REQUIRED*

Determine whether the two corporations are associated. Substantiate your answer by reference to specific provisions of subsection 256(1).

Exercise 6

ITA: 123–126

The following data pertains to Moosonee Company Limited, a Canadian-controlled private corporation for its fiscal year ended December 31, 2013:

Canadian-source business income	$110,000
Foreign investment income ($1,050 in tax withheld)	7,000
Income under Division B	117,000
Taxable income all of which is earned in Canada	79,700

— *REQUIRED*

Compute the federal Part I tax payable plus provincial tax at a 5% rate for 2013 if all of the business income is considered to be active. Assume that the foreign non-business tax credit is equal to the foreign tax paid through withholding.

Exercise 7

ITA: 186

Ex Ltd., a Canadian-controlled private corporation, received a taxable dividend of $90,000 from its Canadian subsidiary Little Ex Ltd. The subsidiary had paid a total dividend of $120,000 and had received a dividend refund of $18,000.

— *REQUIRED*

Compute the Part IV tax payable by Ex Ltd.

Exercise 8

ITA: 123–127, 129, 186

Why Limited is a Canadian-controlled private corporation operating solely in Newfoundland and Labrador. For its taxation year ended December 31, 2013, the company reported the following income under Division B:

Active business income	$ 85,000
Taxable capital gain	37,500
Canadian-source interest income	45,000
Taxable portfolio dividends from Canadian-resident public corporations	18,750
Income under Division B	$186,250

The corporation is carrying forward the following amounts:

Non-capital losses	$ 37,500
Net capital losses (arising in 1999)	68,750

The balance in the refundable dividend tax on hand account at December 31, 2012 was nil. On November 30, 2013, the company paid $112,500 in taxable dividends to its shareholders all of whom are individuals. The taxable portfolio dividends of $18,750 were received on November 1, 2013.

— *REQUIRED*

(A) Compute the federal Part I tax and provincial tax at an 8% rate payable by the company for 2013.

(B) Compute the refundable dividend tax on hand balance as at December 31, 2013 and compute the dividend refund for 2013.

Exercise 9

ITA: 123–127, 129, 186

Ay Ltd. is a Canadian-controlled private corporation with a December 31, 2013 fiscal year end. The company operates primarily in Alberta, but has a very small business operation in the United States where 5% of its total taxable income as calculated by Regulation 402(3) is generated. Taxable income for the year is calculated as follows:

Canadian-source business income		$ 90,000
Dividends from CCPCs:		
Non-connected corporations		30,000
Wholly owned corporation which received a dividend refund of $4,000 as a result of paying the dividend		20,000
Canadian-source investment income		50,000
Foreign-source non-business income (foreign tax credit will be $4,000)		30,000
Foreign-source business income (foreign tax credit will be $1,000)		20,000
Canadian-source taxable capital gains		20,000
Income under Division B		$260,000
Less: donations	$ 40,000	
taxable dividends from CCPCs	50,000	
non-capital losses	20,000	
net capital losses	20,000	130,000
Taxable income		$130,000

The refundable dividend tax on hand account had a nil balance at the end of the previous year. No dividends were paid in the preceding year. Dividends of $70,000 had been paid during the year to the only shareholder, an associated corporation which has only income from investments.

— *REQUIRED*

(A) Compute the federal Part I tax and provincial tax at a 7% rate (using federal taxable income as the tax base) payable by the company for the 2013 taxation year.

(B) Compute the refundable dividend tax on hand balance at the end of the year and the dividend refund for the taxation year.

Exercise 10

ITA: 125, 129, 186, 256(1)

Sunlight Limited is owned 50% by H Ltd. and 50% by W Ltd. The two holding companies are 100% owned by Mr. Bennett and Mrs. Bennett, respectively. Sunlight Limited derives all of its income from active business carried on in Canada. It rents facilities from H Ltd. to which it pays $120,000 in annual rent, deducting this amount as a business expense. Sunlight also pays dividends to the two holding companies which is the only other income of those corporations.

— *REQUIRED*

(A) What is the nature of the rental income to H Ltd.?

(B) Is there a Part IV tax liability for the two holding companies on the dividends received from Sunlight Limited?

Exercise 11

ITA: 125, 129, 256

Janna Management Limited owns a building most of which it rents to Rayna Consulting Services Limited which carries on an active business. Janna and Rayna each own 50% of both corporations. Janna Management Limited also provides managerial, administrative and maintenance services to the unincorporated professional practice of Dr. Adam. The result of these transactions is that Janna Management Limited receives 60% of its income from rent and 40% from providing services and has available an excess business limit for the purposes of the small business deduction.

— *REQUIRED*

Determine the nature of its income and the deductions from tax available to Janna Management Limited.

Exercise 12

ITA: Part I, IV

Dana Toews lives in a province with a 15.5% corporate tax rate and owns an investment portfolio that generated the following Canadian-source income during the year:

Interest	$ 7,000
Portfolio dividends from CCPCs	15,000
Capital gains	6,000

Her cash needs require that $15,000 of the corporation's after-tax profits be distributed as a dividend. The corporation will retain and reinvest the remainder. She already has taxable income of $20,000 from other sources. She has federal personal tax credits of $1,800 and provincial tax credits of $1,200.

— *REQUIRED*

Compare the total tax on the income from the portfolio with the total tax if a corporation owned the securities. Use the 18% gross-up applicable to dividends paid after 2013.

Exercise 13

ITA: 123.3, 126, 129(1), 129(6), 256

Johnson & Co Ltd. holds all the issued shares in Johnson & Co (USA) Inc. Two years ago, the Canadian corporation advanced $100,000 in the form of a loan to the U.S. corporation. The U.S. corporation pays Johnson & Co interest at the rate of 5%. This 5% is comparable to the cost of borrowing at a U.S. bank, but is less than the prescribed interest rate under the Canadian Act. Assume that rate is 7%. (Ignore any subsection 17(1) considerations.)

— *REQUIRED*

Explain the tax obligations of the Canadian corporation relative to this 5% interest.

¶12,875 ASSIGNMENT PROBLEMS

Problem 1

ITA: 125(7)

The taxpayer company, a private corporation, owned and operated a small shopping centre from which it received rental income. There were seven separate tenants, only one of them being what is sometimes referred to as a "Triple A" tenant, namely, a Canadian bank. The corporation, through its principal officer, negotiated all the leases, took care of all the complaints from the tenants and arranged for the maintenance of the shopping centre. It required some activity by the company almost daily. The rental income of the company was mainly for use of the property, but also, to a much lesser extent, for services and other things supplied by the company such as heat, repairs, etc.

— REQUIRED

From the facts provided in the case, determine the type of income that the corporation derives from the business that it carries on under the current legislation.

Problem 2

ITA: 256

Consider each of the following unrelated cases, involving the ownership of the common shares of Canadian-controlled private corporations, for taxation years of all corporations ending on December 31:

(A) Leah Ltd. owns 55% of the shares of Elaine Ltd.

(B) Ms. Miriam owns 51% of the shares of Abigail Ltd. and 60% of the shares of Ethan Ltd.

(C) Ms. Irene and Mr. Mordechai each own 50% of the shares of Clare Ltd. In addition, they each own 50% of the shares of Philip Ltd. Ms. Irene and Mr. Mordechai are not related.

(D) Mrs. Lyn owns 60% of the shares of Jay Ltd. and Mrs. Sarah owns the other 40%. Mrs. Lyn and Mrs. Sarah each own 50% of the shares of Alex Ltd. Mrs. Lyn and Mrs. Sarah are not related.

(E) Janna Ltd., Rayna Ltd. and Adam Ltd. each own ⅓ of the shares of Stan Ltd. Janna Ltd. and Rayna Ltd. each own 50% of the shares of Jonathan Ltd.

(F) Ms. Ruth owns all of the shares of Rick Ltd. Ms. Ruth owns 25% of the shares of Daniel Ltd. and Ms. Ruth's daughter, Elana, who is over 18 years old owns the other 75%.

(G) Mr. Joshua owns 100% of the shares of Gord Ltd. and Ms. Dahlia owns 100% of the shares of Rosalyn Ltd. Mr. Joshua and Ms. Dahlia each own 30% of the shares of Rebecca Ltd. The other 40% of the shares of Rebecca Ltd. are owned by Eden, who is not related to any of the others. Mr. Joshua is the brother of Ms. Dahlia's husband.

(H) Mrs. Yael owns 60% of the shares of Benjamin Ltd. and 30% of the shares of Livi Ltd. Another 25% of the shares of Livi Ltd. are owned by Benjamin Ltd. and the remaining 45% of the shares of Livi Ltd. are owned by Joy, who is not related to any of the others.

(I) Ms. Daniella owns 60% of the shares of Elizabeth Ltd. and 25% of the shares of Ava Ltd. Ms. Samara, who is not related to Ms. Daniella, owns the other 75% of the shares of Ava Ltd. Ms. Daniella holds an option to buy all of the shares owned by Ms. Samara at any time in the next 10 years.

(J) Mr. and Mrs. Jonathan each own 50% of Isabelle Ltd. Mr. Jonathan and his two brothers and one sister each own 25% of Maya Ltd.

— REQUIRED

In each of the above *unrelated* cases determine whether the corporations are associated. Substantiate your answer by reference to the specific conditions in the provisions of section 256, and consider all possible alternatives.

Problem 3

ITA: 256

Consider each of the following unrelated cases, involving the ownership of shares of Canadian-controlled private corporations. Assume all of the issued shares are common shares unless specifically stated otherwise.

(A) Rachel and Monica, friends, each own 50% of the issued shares of A Ltd. In addition, Rachel owns 80% and Monica owns 20% of the issued shares of B Ltd.

(B) Charlie and Claudia are siblings. Charlie owns 80% of A Ltd. which in turn owns 40% of B Ltd. Claudia owns 60% of B Ltd.

(C) Bob, Bill, and Bert are three brothers who share equally the income of a professional partnership. The partnership owns 100% of the shares of A Ltd. Bert owns 100% of the shares of B Ltd.

(D) Anne and Barbara are sisters. They each own 100% of their respective corporations, A Ltd. and B Ltd. A Ltd. and B Ltd. each own 40% of the shares of C Ltd.

(E) Valerie, Brandon, and Claire are strangers. They each own ⅓ of the shares of A Ltd. Brandon owns 40% of the shares of B Ltd. The remaining 60% are owned by Claire. Claire also owns 100% of the shares of C Ltd.

(F) Valerie and her two nieces each own 25% of the shares of A Ltd. Valerie's husband, Dilon, and his nephew each own 50% of the shares of B Ltd. Dilon also owns the remaining 25% of the shares of A Ltd.

(G) Father owns 100% of the shares of F Ltd. His son, Sean, age 17, owns 100% of the common shares of S Ltd. F Ltd. owns 30% of the issued preferred shares of S Ltd. The preferred shares have the following characteristics:

- non-voting,
- dividend rate fixed at 6%,
- redeemable at $1,000 per share, and
- issue price $1,000 per share.

The prescribed rate of interest was 8% at the time the preferred shares were issued.

— REQUIRED

Determine which of the corporations are associated and substantiate your answer by reference to specific provisions of the Act.

Problem 4

ITA: 256

Both corporations in this case were incorporated for the purpose of buying and selling anti-freeze products. Warren Packaging Limited sold its product ("Dual Duty") to wholesalers who serviced and supplied garages and service stations ultimately for the consumers. Its sole shareholder and president was Mr. Warren. Bradford-Penn Oil Inc. sold its product ("Viceroy") to retailers who sold it on a cash and carry basis to its clients. Mr. Warren's wife was the sole shareholder and president of the latter company.

In essence, both companies were directed by the same person in the same premises. They both had the same year-end. The product came in bulk from the same supplier and was packed in smaller quantities with the different brand names.

Management of the companies felt that it was too risky to have the same company distribute the anti-freeze product to both the wholesalers and the retailers. There was only one supplier of bulk anti-freeze available to the two corporations and that supplier marketed its own brand and, as a result, was also in competition with Warren Packaging and Bradford-Penn Oil. Maintaining the source of supply at a competitive price made the business risky.

Management also felt that it was necessary to have two companies with two different brand names to cover the wholesale market and the retail market. Experience had shown that if the same brand were supplied to both the wholesalers and the retailers, one or the other of the markets would be lost. Even if the same company name appeared on the package of the two different brands, it would be difficult to maintain both markets because of price differentials from the different outlets to the ultimate consumers.

In his testimony, Mr. Warren testified that he did not remember his counsellor discussing taxation with him when he decided to separately incorporate the two companies. He also testified that he had given a personal guarantee to the bank to obtain a loan for Warren Packaging Limited and he felt it was necessary to have a limited liability in that corporation. He believed that limited liability was accomplished by his wife's sole ownership of the shares of Bradford-Penn Oil Inc.

— REQUIRED

(A) Would subsection 256(5.1) apply in this case and, if so, what would be the effect of that application?

(B) Assuming that subsection 256(5.1) does not apply, determine whether Warren Packaging Limited and Bradford-Penn Oil Inc. are associated. Provide reasons for your determination by reference to the legislation and to the facts of the case.

Problem 5

ITA: 123–126

The accountant, Ryan Mailling, of Double-D Retailing Ltd. (DRL), a Canadian-controlled private corporation, has requested your assistance with respect to the calculation of the company's Part I tax payable.

Ryan has provided you with the following information.

(1) DRL is not associated with any other corporation.

(2) For DRL's December 31 taxation year-end, the corporation correctly reported:

Active business income	$320,000
Investment income	
Canadian	5,000
Foreign	12,000
Charitable donations	9,000
Net capital loss deducted	2,000
Non-capital loss deducted	10,000
Taxable income	316,000

(3) Withholding tax on the foreign investment income was $1,800.

(4) Taxable capital employed in Canada in 2012 was $11.9 million.

— REQUIRED

Calculate the federal Part I tax payable for the taxation year ended December 31, 2013. Assume that the foreign non-business tax credit is equal to the foreign tax paid through withholding. Show all calculations whether or not relevant to the final answer.

Problem 6

ITA: 37, 127(5)–(11), 127.1

Natalia, a resident of Canada, owns 100% of the shares of New Age Limited (NAL). NAL carries on scientific research and experimental development (SR&ED) activities with respect to finding the ingredients for a cream which will reduce fat and tone muscles when massaged into the skin.

During its fiscal year ended December 31, 2013, NAL incurred the following costs related to its SR&ED activities:

Salaries for research technicians and assistants	$600,000
Materials consumed	200,000
Supplies consumed	40,000
Small equipment purchased for the laboratory	80,000
A special machine purchased to mix the ingredients in a temperature controlled environment	100,000

The machine and the lab equipment will have no value when the research project is completed.

Additional overhead costs were incurred in 2013 because of the SR&ED project. The accounting system was not sophisticated enough to properly allocate these expenses. Overhead expenses for the year totalled $500,000.

NAL paid Natalia a bonus of $40,000 in 2013 in addition to her salary of $80,000. Natalia spent 25% of her time on the SR&ED project in 2013.

NAL does not expect to have any taxable income for 2013. It had taxable income of $100,000 in 2012. Its taxable capital does not exceed $10 million. It is not associated with any other corporation.

— *REQUIRED*

(A) Which of the above costs incurred by NAL in 2013 qualify for deduction under subsection 37(1) as qualifying SR&ED expenditures?

(B) Determine the amount of ITCs and refundable ITCs for 2013.

Problem 7

ITA: 110.1–112, 123–126, 127(3)

Neville Ltd. is a Canadian-controlled private corporation which was incorporated in 1997 with a December 31 year end. In 2013, Neville Ltd. earned net income of $250,000 before taxes for accounting purposes. Included in the calculation of that amount were the following items:

Canadian active business income	$159,000
Dividends from taxable Canadian subsidiary corporations	8,000
Other Canadian investment income:	
— rental income	$ 4,000
— interest income	15,000
— royalty income	1,000
— taxable capital gain	9,000
U.S. interest income ($2,000 withheld)	15,000
U.S. business income ($20,000 tax paid)	96,000
Income under Division B	$307,000
Donations to registered charities	$ 60,000
The company also has the following balances at January 1, 2013:	
1999 Net capital loss	$ 15,000
Charitable donations carried forward from 2012	10,000

The company retails its products in Canada and the United States. Its total proportion of taxable income earned in Canada, as per Regulation 402, is 75%. Assume that the provincial tax rates on taxable income are 12% and that Neville Ltd.'s foreign tax credits are equal to the U.S. tax withheld on the income.

Neville Ltd.'s 100% owned subsidiary has used $350,000 of the business limit for the small business deduction in 2013. Together, Neville Ltd. and its subsidiary have $8 million of taxable capital in Canada.

— *REQUIRED*

Compute the federal Part I tax and provincial tax payable by Neville Ltd. for 2013. Show *all* calculations.

Problem 8

ITA: 123–127, 129, 186

The following selected information has been taken from the records of Sharp Ltd., a Canadian-controlled private corporation, for its fiscal year ended December 31, 2013.

(1) Income for tax purposes:

Active business income (retailing)	$100,000
Foreign business income (retailing)	60,000
Canadian bond interest	20,000
Foreign bond interest	10,000
Taxable dividends received from taxable Canadian corporations	40,000
Taxable capital gains	30,000
Net income under Division B	$260,000

(2) Division C deductions claimed:

Donations	(2,000)
Net capital losses	(5,000)
Non-capital losses	(13,000)
Taxable dividends received from taxable Canadian corporations	(40,000)

(3) Taxable income $200,000

(4) Part I tax payable is $19,817 including additional refundable tax of $3,667. In computing Part I tax, the following deductions were made:

Small business deduction	$17,000
Foreign non-business tax deduction	1,500
Foreign business tax deduction	18,000

(5) Summary of taxable dividends received from taxable Canadian corporations:

Date received	*Payer*	*% of voting shares owned*	*Amount of dividend received*	*Dividend refund received by payer corp.*
Aug. 1, 2012	A Ltd.	6%	$20,000	$30,000
Oct. 1, 2012	B Ltd.	80%	20,000	5,000
			$40,000	

(6) Summary of dividends paid by Sharp Ltd.:

Type of dividend	*Amount*	*Date declared*	*Date paid*
Taxable dividend	$60,000	July 15, 2013	Aug. 15, 2013
Tax-free ssec. 83(2) dividend	20,000	Oct. 15, 2013	Nov. 15, 2013
Taxable dividend	24,000	Dec. 15, 2013	Jan. 15, 2014

(7) The refundable dividend tax on hand balance at December 31, 2012 was $12,000. The dividend refund for 2012 was $4,000.

— *REQUIRED*

(A) Compute the dividend refund for 2013.

(B) What would change if Sharp Ltd. was a private corporation, and not a CCPC? Explain.

Problem 9

ITA: 123–127; 129, 186

Multi Enterprises Ltd. is a Canadian-controlled private corporation whose fiscal period coincides with the calendar year. For the year 2013, the company's taxable income was calculated as follows:

Income from distributing net of CCA		$191,000
Dividends from taxable corporations:		
(a) connected corporation, dividend payment triggering a dividend refund of $2,750 to the wholly owned subsidiary		11,000
(b) non-connected corporation (portfolio dividends)		20,000
Taxable capital gain	$29,000	
Allowable capital losses	12,000	17,000

Royalties		9,000
Recapture of CCA on disposal of sales equipment		4,000
Income from rental of an apartment building (no full-time employees and tenants provide virtually all of their own services)		14,000
Foreign non-business income (i.e., interest income) (foreign tax credit of $3,450 equal to foreign tax withheld)		23,000
Foreign business income (foreign tax credit of $1,800 equal to foreign tax paid)		6,000
Interest charged on accounts receivable		5,000
Net income for tax purposes		$300,000
Less: net capital losses carried over	$ 7,000	
non-capital losses carried over	10,000	
donations	26,000	
dividends from taxable Canadian corporations	31,000	74,000
Taxable income		$226,000

At December 31, 2012, there was a nil balance in the refundable dividend tax on hand account. The company paid $72,000 in dividends during 2013 to individual shareholders.

It has been agreed that $200,000 of the business limit for small business deduction will be claimed by the parent, Multi Enterprises Ltd., leaving the remainder for the subsidiary.

The company has a permanent establishment in New Brunswick and in the United States. Its gross revenue, net of dividends and net of rentals, and its salaries and wages are attributed to its permanent establishments as follows:

	Gross revenue	*Salaries & wages*
New Brunswick	$1,776,000	$238,000
United States	220,000	16,000
Totals	$1,996,000	$254,000

In the United States a salesman worked out of his home in which he kept a small stock of merchandise from which he filled orders.

During the year the company made eligible child care space expenditures in the amount of $32,000 for use in its New Brunswick distributing facilities. Capital cost allowance for the year has been adjusted for these expenditures.

— *REQUIRED*

(A) Compute the federal Part I tax and assumed provincial tax at a 5% rate on federal taxable income payable by the company for 2013. Show in detail the calculation of all deductions in the computation, using a separate schedule for each special deduction. In calculating the small business deduction list all ineligible items of income, if any, and indicate the amount of the business limit available for the subsidiary.

(B) Compute the refundable dividend tax on hand balance as at December 31, 2013, showing, in detail, your calculations and compute the dividend refund for 2013.

Problem 10

ITA: 110.1–112, 123–127

The controller of Tek Enterprises Ltd. provided the Accountant with the following information.

Tek Enterprises Ltd.
Income
For the fiscal year ended December 31, 2013

Canadian wholesaling income		$251,500
Canadian retail business income		50,000
Foreign retail business income (before foreign tax paid of $15,000)		40,000
Taxable capital gains		4,500
Interest income:		
Canadian long-term bonds	$20,000	
Interest on accounts receivable outstanding for more than 30 days in the Canadian retail business	5,000	25,000
Dividend income:		
From taxable Canadian corporations	$ 9,000	
From foreign corporations (before foreign tax of $1,800) (Tek Enterprises Ltd. owns less than 5% of the shares)	12,000	21,000
Net income		$392,000

Notes:

(1) Tek Enterprises Limited is a CCPC. It is not associated with any corporations. It paid federal Part I tax of $35,000 in 2013.

(2) The following items were deducted in the computation of Canadian wholesaling income above:

SR&ED expenditures (current in nature)	$50,000
Federal political contributions	1,000

(3) The taxable capital gain was calculated as follows:

	Marketable securities	*Equipment*	*Total*
Proceeds	$15,000	$ 200	$15,200
Cost	3,000	3,200	6,200
Gain (Loss)	$12,000	$ (3,000)	$ 9,000
			× ½
			$ 4,500

(4) The corporation has net capital losses (incurred in 1999) of $13,000. It has unused foreign business tax credits (from 2012) of $100.

(5) Taxable capital employed in Canada in 2012 was $10.3 million.

The Accountant assigned a junior staff member to calculate the federal Part I tax payable for Tek Enterprises Ltd. The following is his calculation.

Net income		$392,000
Dividends		(21,000)
Donations		(75,000)
Net capital losses		(13,000)
Taxable income		$283,000
Basic federal tax (40% × $283,000)		$113,200
Abatement: Taxable income	$283,000	
Foreign business income	(40,000)	
	$243,000 × 10%	24,300
		$137,500

Foreign tax credit:

Lesser of: (a) Foreign tax paid ($15,000 + $1,800) = $16,800

(b) $\frac{\text{Foreign income } \$52{,}000}{\$283{,}000 + \$21{,}000 + \$13{,}000} \times \$137{,}500 = \$22{,}555$ (16,800)

Small business deduction:

17% × the least of: (a) Active business income:

Wholesaling business	$251,500	
Cdn. retail business	50,000	
Foreign retail business	40,000	
	$341,500	
(b) $283,000 – 4 × $16,800 =	$215,800	
(c) Business limit:	$500,000	(36,686)
Political contribution tax credit		(650)
General rate reduction (13% × $283,000)		(28,300)
Federal Part I tax payable		$ 55,064

—REQUIRED

Write a memo in point-form explaining to the junior staff member the errors in his calculation. Do not redo the calculations. Only describe his incorrect procedures in arriving at Part I tax so that the calculation may be redone correctly.

Problem 11

ITA: 123–127, 129, 186

Rob's Shameless Self-Promotion Sales (RSS-PS) Inc. is a Canadian-controlled private corporation located in London, Ontario. For its fiscal year ended December 31, 2013, the corporation had correctly calculated its income for tax purposes under Division B as follows:

Canadian source:	
Consulting income	$160,000
Advertising agency loss	(30,000)
Rental income from warehouse fully rented on a five-year lease	20,000
Retailing income	75,000
Interest on outstanding accounts receivable in retailing business	25,000
Recapture of CCA from sale of fixtures used in retailing business	25,000
Interest income from five-year bonds	75,000
Taxable capital gain	70,000
Dividends from non-connected taxable Canadian corporations	12,000

Foreign sources:	
Interest earned on Bermuda bank account (no withholding tax)	20,000
U.S. business income (foreign tax credit of $6,000 equal to foreign tax paid)	23,000
Division B net income for tax purposes	$475,000

Additional information:

RSS-PS Inc. made the following selected payments during the year:

Scientific research and experimental development (current expenses and new equipment)	$100,000
Charitable donations	14,000
Taxable dividends	120,000

The balances in the tax accounts on December 31, 2012 were:

Charitable donations from 2010	$ 1,000
Non-capital losses from 2009	56,000
Net capital losses from 1999	18,000
Refundable dividend tax on hand	20,000
Dividend refund for 2012	9,000

Taxable income earned in Canada is considered to be 90% of the total earned by RSS-PS Inc. RSS-PS Inc. allocated $370,000 of its $500,000 business limit to other associated corporations. The only scientific research and experimental development expenditures of the associated group were made by RSS-PS Inc.

— REQUIRED

(A) Compute the federal Part I tax and provincial tax at a 11.5% rate on federal taxable income for the 2013 taxation year.

(B) Compute the dividend refund for 2013 and the amount of any RDTOH to be carried forward.

Problem 12

ITA: 125, 129, 186, 256

Carl owns 100% of the issued shares of Compunet. He incorporated Compunet earlier this year to provide computer consulting services to Vitamins Inc., a retailer of energy-producing vitamins. Prior to the incorporation of Compunet, Carl headed the computer service division of Vitamins Inc. One hundred per cent of the issued shares of Vitamins Inc. are owned by Carl's cousin, Vince.

Carl's daughter, Sulee, received a degree in computer science from the University of Toronto in April and has been employed by Compunet as a computer consultant since then. Sulee and Carl work well together. They are the only employees of Compunet.

Compunet owns a warehouse. One-half of the warehouse is rented to Vitamins Inc. and the remainder is rented to Mindblasters, a wholly owned subsidiary of Compunet. Mindblasters is a successful retailer of computer games.

During the current year, Compunet received taxable dividends from Mindblasters and paid taxable dividends to Carl.

— REQUIRED

Determine the type(s) of income being earned by Compunet, the rate of tax for each type and any refunds available.

Problem 13

ITA: 125, 129, 256

Lemon Ltd. provides management services for Toys-4-U Limited (Toys), a retailer of educational toys, and for certain other corporations described below. Les Lemon is the sole shareholder and only employee of Lemon Ltd. Prior to this year, Les had been employed by Toys as vice-president of financial and administrative services.

Les owns all of the common shares of Rental Ltd. (Rental), which is in the business of renting commercial properties. Rental has no employees, except for Les, and subcontracts all maintenance and administrative services. Rental's income for tax purposes can be broken down as follows:

Lemon Ltd.	10%
Cheap Leasing Ltd. (see below)	25%
Arm's length parties	65%
	100%

Les is also involved with Cheap Leasing Limited (Cheap), which is in the business of leasing educational equipment. The ownership of the common shares of Cheap is as follow:

Les Lemon	25 shares
Lucy Lemon, Les' wife	20 shares
Lemon Ltd.	30 shares
Larry Lemon, Les' uncle	10 shares
Arm's length parties	15 shares

Cheap derives approximately 80% of its income from the educational equipment leasing business. The balance of its income is interest from a loan to Toys. Cheap has four employees in addition to Les.

All of the above corporations are Canadian-controlled private corporations and have December 31 year-ends.

— REQUIRED

Identify the various sources of income for the above corporations indicating the reasoning behind your conclusions. Also indicate the *federal* tax rate and any refundable taxes applicable to each income source.

Problem 14

ITA: Part I, IV

Mr. Humphries, a resident of a province with a 40% effective federal and provincial corporate tax rate (before the additional refundable tax), has just won a lottery prize of $750,000. He is considering the following investment of these funds: $200,000 of bonds yielding 8% and $550,000 of common shares of Growth Unlimited Limited (a CCPC earning active business income less than the business limit), which pay a dividend to yield 5%. Having taken a course in security analysis, Mr. Humphries can predict with great confidence that he will realize a 10.5% capital gain on the shares within the year. Mr. Humphries currently has taxable income of $30,000. He has federal personal tax credits of $2,100, and provincial personal tax credits of $1,400.

— REQUIRED

Advise Mr. Humphries on whether he should use an investment corporation with a permanent establishment in the province of which he is a resident to hold the securities he proposes to purchase. Include in your analysis the realization of the predicted capital gain. Use 2013 personal tax rates and the 18% dividend gross-up proposed for dividends paid after 2013. Also, consider any non-quantitative factors that may be relevant to the decision.

Problem 15

ITA: 123–125, 129, 186

You recently met Susan Taylor at a cocktail party. As a result of your conversation with her, Susan has come to you for tax advice. She wants to know how her income will be taxed. She also wants to know whether she should incorporate and earn the same types of income through a corporation called High Income Limited. She would be the sole shareholder and only employee of that corporation. Susan has received various types of income in 2013. These incomes are as follows:

- Interest income from GIC — $5,000
- Dividend income from a publicly traded corporation — $10,000
- Capital gains from selling public company shares — $20,000
- Susan owns 40% of all the issued and outstanding common shares of Stage Lighting Limited (Stage). Her best friend, Mary, who lives in Ontario, owns the rest of the common shares. The company is in the business of manufacturing customized lighting products. She received $20,000

in dividends (for which Stage *did not* receive any dividend refund) from Stage this year. All income earned by Stage is eligible for the small business deduction.

Susan would like to understand whether she should incorporate a holding company to earn the four different types of income mentioned above.

Susan runs a small fashion store selling high-end handmade scarves. The business is operated as a sole proprietorship. Active operations started four years ago and the business started to make sizable profit last year. The estimated taxable retail income in 2013 is $200,000. Susan would like to know whether she should incorporate this business.

Additional Information and Assumptions

Assume that the effective combined federal and provincial corporate tax rates for 2013 on the following types of income are:

- Active business income (ABI) (eligible for the small business deduction)

38% – 10% – 17% + 5% (net provincial)	16%

- Specified investment business income

38% – 10% + $6\frac{2}{3}$% + 14% (provincial) – initially	$48\frac{2}{3}$%
$48\frac{2}{3}$% – $26\frac{2}{3}$% – ultimately when dividends paid	22%

- Capital gains

Taxed portion is taxed as income from a SIB above	
Non-taxed portion	0%

The non-taxed portion of the capital gain is added to the capital dividend account. Dividends can be paid out of the balance of this account with no tax cost to the recipient shareholder.

Assume that, if the ABI increases to the point where it exceeds $500,000 (small business deduction), then the effective federal rate on the ABI in excess of the small business limit will be

- Combined federal and provincial rate:

38% – 10% – 13% (general rate reduction) + 14 (provincial)	29%

Assume that the effective combined federal and provincial personal tax rates for 2012 are:

- The effective combined federal and provincial personal tax rate:

Top marginal rates 29% (federal) + 17% (provincial)	46%

- Effective combined federal and provincial tax rate for dividends from:

Low Rate Income Pool [for dividends paid after 2013]	36.3%
General Rate Income Pool	25.5%

— REQUIRED

Please draft a memo analyzing the tax implications of the above situation. Your memo should address and conclude on the following issues:

(A) Based on the theory and a conceptual understanding of incorporation, determine whether Susan can save and/or defer income tax by incorporating a holding company to earn interest income, dividend income from a public company, capital gains from selling public company shares, and dividend income from Stage Lighting Limited. [Use the 18% gross-up for dividends paid after 2013.]

(B) Based on the theory and a conceptual understanding of incorporation, determine whether Susan can save and/or defer income tax through incorporation of her fashion business.

(C) Discuss some of the general (i.e., not specific to Susan) quantitative and qualitative pros and cons of incorporation.

[For more problems and solutions thereto, see the DVD accompanying this book.]

¶12,880 ADVISORY CASE

Waterloo Group

Mickey and Nicki Waterloo are husband and wife entrepreneurs. Most of the time, when they start a business, they will do so with another person, in order to let that person handle the day-to-day business matters and, also, to provide a potential buyer at some point in the future. Usually this other person will have a shareholding in the operating company, but Mickey and/or Nicki will maintain control. It is, also, usual for each company to have a shareholder agreement with a buy/sell provision that calls for a corporate repurchase on death, disability, bankruptcy, or retirement. Maximizing the use of the small business deduction is also a goal.

At this time, Mickey and Nicki have the following interests, which are all held through a holding company (Holdco) owned 100% by Mickey.

(1) Holdco owns 20% of a company called Sales Co. Inc. The other 80% is owned by Joe Shea, who runs the company. In order to finance the operations, Holdco has invested $100,000 in non-voting preference shares with a redemption value of $100,000 and a dividend rate of 8%.

(2) Holdco and Fred Smith have shared ownership of two companies. Holdco owns 90% of Retail One Inc. and 10% of Retail Two Inc., while Fred owns the other 10% of Retail One Inc. and 90% of Retail Two Inc.

Mickey and Nicki share ownership in two companies. Mickey owns 40% of Ours Inc., Nicki owns 100% of Mine Inc., and Mine Inc. own 60% of Ours Inc. Both Mickey and Nicki are actively involved in these businesses.

On the advice of their lawyer, they set up a discretionary trust for their two children, Dick, who is 12 years old, and Jane, who is 10 years old. This trust borrowed money from the bank (with personal guarantees from Mickey and Nicki) and bought treasury shares from a newly incorporated company, Kids Are Fun Inc. This company sells games through a retail store. It was capitalized with a loan from Nicki.

Advise Mickey and Nicki of the tax implications of the share ownerships outlined above on the small business deduction.

Chapter 13

Planning the Use of a Corporation and Shareholder-Manager Remuneration

TOPICS DISCUSSED

LEARNING GOALS

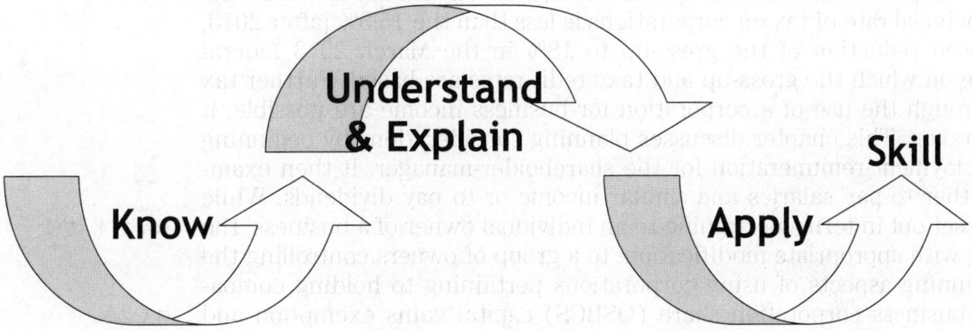

Know

By the end of this chapter, you should know the basic provisions of the *Income Tax Act* that relate to the compensation of a corporation's owner-manager and that relate to the general anti-avoidance rule. Completing the Review Questions (¶13,800) and Multiple Choice Questions (¶13,825) is a good way to learn the technical provisions.

Understand and Explain

You should understand and be able to explain:

- the more common elements in the remuneration of a shareholder-manager, including salary, bonus, dividend, and loan and the considerations needed to make a choice;
- the salary versus dividend trade-off, including the amount of dividends that can be distributed tax free;
- the reasons for the use of a holding corporation, the benefits of the capital gains deduction, and rules that inhibit family income splitting through a corporation; and
- why the general anti-avoidance rule exists and how it has been interpreted and used.

Completing the Exercises (¶13,850) is a good way to deepen your understanding of the material.

Apply

You should be able to apply your knowledge and understanding of the key elements of compensation to:

- choose the optimal compensation components to minimize remuneration costs in a particular owner-manager situation;
- maintain the eligibility of shares for the capital gains exemption;
- avoid the adverse income tax effects of using a corporation to split family income; and
- generally determine whether the general anti-avoidance rule might apply in a particular planning situation.

Completing the Assignment Problems (¶13,875) is an excellent way to develop your ability to apply the material in increasingly complex situations.

OVERVIEW

The previous chapter demonstrated that the integration system, when applied to business income earned by a corporation, can result in tax savings in certain cases where the combined federal and provincial rate of tax on corporations is less than the 15.3% [after 2013, as a result of the proposed reduction of the gross-up to 18% in the March 2013 federal Budget] or the 27.5% rate on which the gross-up and tax credit rates are based. Further tax savings and flexibility through the use of a corporation for business income are possible, if proper planning is undertaken. This chapter discusses planning considerations by beginning with the planning of employment remuneration for the shareholder-manager. It then examines the question of whether to pay salaries and similar income or to pay dividends. While much of the discussion is set out in terms pertaining to an individual owner of a business, the principles can be applied, with appropriate modification, to a group of owners controlling the business. Some other planning aspects of using corporations pertaining to holding companies, the qualified small business corporation share (QSBCS) capital gains exemption and attribution are discussed next. The final section of the chapter discuss the general anti-avoidance rule (GAAR) of the *Income Tax Act*, which may limit more aggressive planning and, hence, must be considered.

ITA: 74.4, 110.6

ITA: 245

For the purposes of computing the total income tax of an individual, the following table will be used in this chapter. Provincial rates of tax used in their table are hypothetical. Actual provincial rates vary. In addition, provincial tax brackets may vary, due to the use of a provincial Consumer Price Index and the impact of provincial surtaxes. Provinces may also establish a different number of tax brackets.

Combined Federal and Hypothetical Provincial Tax Rates

		Federal		*Provincial*		*Total*	
Taxable Income		*Tax on lower limit*	*Tax rate on excess*	*Tax on lower limit*	*Tax rate on excess*	*Tax on lower limit*	*Tax rate on excess*
—	$ 43,561	—	15%	—	10%	—	25%
$ 43,562	87,123	$ 6,534	22%	$ 4,356	12%	$10,890	34%
87,124	135,054	16,118	26%	9,583	15%	25,701	41%
135,055	and over	28,580	29%	16,773	17%	45,353	46%

¶13,000 EMPLOYMENT REMUNERATION

¶13,010 Considerations in Choosing Elements of Shareholder-Manager Remuneration

¶13,015 Cash needs

The prime consideration in deciding on remuneration for the shareholder-manager is his or her cash requirements, both immediately and in the future on retirement. The objective of the decision is to find the optimum method of providing the shareholder-manager with the necessary cash, while at the same time leaving the corporation with maximum cash for reinvestment. This process might involve paying out more than necessary in salaries and bonuses, as long as this is reasonable. The purpose of such payments would be to be taxable at the corporate level only on income eligible for the small business deduction or to qualify for Canada Pension Plan, registered retirement savings plan, deferred profit sharing plan or registered pension plan contributions. Any after-tax salary paid to the shareholder-manager in excess of his or her cash requirements can be loaned back to the corporation for reinvestment.

¶13,020 Individual's tax bracket

Also important to the remuneration decision are the other sources of income that the shareholder-manager may have. If he or she is already in a high tax bracket, it might be wise to freeze salaries and bonuses to take advantage of a tax deferral on the income left in the corporation, even though the ultimate total tax may be higher. The time value of money may make the saving now greater than the added cost at some time in the future.

For example, consider the case of a corporation taxable at a net 15% rate, including provincial tax on its active business income eligible for the small business deduction and at a net 28% rate on its business income not eligible for the small business deduction. This corporation faces the choice of whether to pay a bonus of $1,000 now or a dividend of $1,000 at some time in the future. Exhibit 13-1 shows the comparative calculation that might be made assuming that the individual tax rate (federal plus provincial) is approximately 46%. The "dividend later" column is broken down into two options. Column A shows the results if the dividend gross-up and tax credit is 18% [as proposed in the March 2013 federal Budget for dividends paid after 2013] on dividends from the low rate income pool (LRIP). Column B assumes that active business income not eligible for the small business deduction would qualify for the enhanced gross-up and credit of 38% on eligible dividends from the general rate income pool (GRIP).

EXHIBIT 13-1
Comparison of $1,000 Paid as a Bonus Now or as a Dividend in the Future

	Bonus now	*Dividend later*	
		LRIP	GRIP
		A	B
Corporation			
Corporate income	$1,000	$ 1,000	$1,000
Bonus	1,000	—	—
Corporate taxable income	Nil	$ 1,000	$1,000
Corporate tax @ 15%/28% (rounded)	—	(150)	(280)
Funds available for dividend	Nil	$ 850	$ 720

	Bonus now	Dividend later	
Shareholder			
Income	$1,000	$ 850	$ 720
Dividend gross-up 18%/38%	—	153	274
Taxable income	$1,000	$ 1,003	$ 994
Combined federal and provincial tax @ 46% (rounded)	$ 460	$ 461	$ 457
Dividend tax credit @ 18%/38% of actual dividend (combined federal and provincial effect)	—	(153)	(274)
Net tax	$ 460	$ 308	$ 183
Cash available	$ 540	$ 542	$ 537
Tax deferral ($460 – $150) and ($460 – $280)		$310	$180
Tax savings (cost) ($460 – ($150 + $308)) and ($460 – ($280 + $183))		$ 2	$ (3)

¶13,025 Eighteen per cent dividend gross-up and credit [proposed]

Where the gross-up is 18% for non-eligible dividends out of the LRIP, there is a tax deferral of $310 (i.e., $460 – $150) because the initial tax on the corporation for the dividend alternative is $150, while the tax on the individual for the bonus alternative is $460. However, when the dividend is paid, personal tax of only $308 must be paid on the dividend. Thus, paying a dividend in the future will result in a lower tax now by $310 and an overall tax savings later of $2 when personal tax is paid on the dividend. The tax on the dividend, at $308, is the tax deferred until the dividend is paid.

¶13,030 Thirty-eight per cent dividend gross-up and credit

Column B (GRIP) in Exhibit 13-1 shows the effect of the 38% gross-up on eligible dividends, i.e., dividends paid from active business income not eligible for the small business deduction. In this case, the tax deferral of $180 is lower than in Column A (LRIP); the corporate tax on the income of $1,000 is still lower than the personal tax on the bonus of $1,000. However, the tax cost on the payment of a dividend is $3, compared with the savings of $2 on the LRIP dividend. If the tax cost of the GRIP dividend had been much greater than $3, it might be interesting to determine the number of years that the income must be left in the corporation for the deferral to offset the cost. This can be calculated by a formula developed for that purpose.[1]

---

[1] The number of years that the dividend must be deferred for the tax deferral advantage to exceed the tax cost can be determined using the following analysis involving the time value of money. Assume that the pre-tax time value of money is 7% for both the owner-manager and the corporation. This is reasonable if the owner-manager can reinvest a bonus in the corporation by lending the after-tax bonus amount to the corporation at a pre-tax 7% interest rate. A $1,000 bonus will attract tax at an assumed 46% rate in the hands of the owner-manager who can reinvest the $540 (i.e., $1,000 (1 – .46)) at a pre-tax 7% rate or an after-tax rate of 3.8% (i.e., 7% (1 – .46)) for n years. Income earned by the corporation on the reinvested bonus will be offset by the tax deductible interest paid by the corporation on the loan from the owner-manager.

On the other hand, if the corporation does not pay the bonus, it will pay tax at the assumed 28% total rate, leaving it with $720 (i.e., $1,000 (1 – .28)) after tax. That $720 can be reinvested by the corporation in its business at a pre-tax 7% or an after-tax 5% (i.e., 7% (1 – .28)) for n years. However, in n years, the accumulated amount will be paid as a dividend and taxed at a net combined federal and provincial rate, after the dividend gross-up and tax credit in the top bracket, of about 25.5% after the 38% gross-up.

Generally, the lower the discount rate used, the higher is the breakeven number of years, n. Also, the higher the corporate tax rate used, the higher is the breakeven number of years. This analysis assumes a constant time value of money and constant personal and corporate tax rates over the period.

Solving the following equation for n:

$$\$1{,}000\,(1 - .46)(1 + .07\,(1 - .46))^n = \$1{,}000\,(1 - .28)(1 + .07\,(1 - .28))^n(1 - .255)$$

$$n \approx \text{about 2 months, i.e., a negligible period.}$$

The formula can be generalized as follows:

$$\$1{,}000\,(1 - t_p)(1 + r\,(1 - t_p))^n = \$1{,}000\,(1 - t_c)(1 + r\,(1 - t_c))^n(1 - t_{pd}).$$

The number of years, n, can be solved using logarithms.

¶13,035 Availability of tax deferral

A tax deferral of this nature will be possible wherever the initial corporate rate of tax is less than the individual's personal rate of tax. In cases of lower corporate tax rates, it has been shown with the analysis above that a tax deferral is possible without additional tax on the ultimate dividend. Therefore, the deferral advantage is much greater for a corporation eligible for the small business deduction. Of course, to obtain the deferral, earnings must be retained in the corporation, rather than being paid as dividends.

¶13,040 Avoid exceeding the business limit for the small business deduction

As shown in the previous chapter, the availability of the small business deduction is essential to certain tax deferrals and possible savings on business income. Thus, the remuneration policy should be designed to maintain corporate income below the business limit of $500,000 to prevent Canadian business income from being taxed at full corporate rates and, hence, to incur a tax cost when integration is not perfect.[2] Yet, such a policy must recognize that added salary or bonuses necessary to its implementation, taxed at a high personal rate of a shareholder-manager, may have adverse tax consequences not considered in the above breakeven analysis. Salary may increase a payroll tax such as the health levy, used in several provinces to finance health care.

The payment of interest or dividends is favoured, if it is desirable to reduce the cumulative net investment loss (CNIL) account, as will be discussed later in this chapter, to preserve access to the QSBCS capital gains deduction. Note that interest paid on shareholder debt has the same effect as salary in reducing corporate income to the business limit of $500,000 and attracts the same tax as salary in the hands of the individual. However, interest income reduces the cumulative net investment loss and salary does not.

Other considerations would include the company's need for funds to be used in the business, as indicated above. They would also include the effects of the remuneration decision on the value of the company's shares which may be important if a sale of the business is contemplated. Finally, changes in tax rates and tax law in general must be monitored constantly in terms of their effect on the remuneration decision.

¶13,050 Salaries, Bonuses, and Other Payments to the Shareholder-Manager

¶13,055 General guidelines

A primary guideline to follow is to ensure that various basic deductions and personal tax credits available to employees and individuals, in general, are fully utilized by the payment of salaries and bonuses or other similar amounts of employment income. These basic deductions and credits would include items listed in section 8 of the Act and Division C and personal tax credits listed in Division E.

As already indicated, another guideline would involve the payment of salaries and bonuses, perhaps to reduce active business income to as low a level approaching the business limit of $500,000 business limit, as would be considered reasonable to avoid a tax cost, if only slightly, on income taxed at a corporate rate in excess of 27.5%. This can also be accomplished by having a shareholder, who cannot be paid a salary, hold some of his or her investment in the corporation in the form of debt such that the corporation can make interest payments which will reduce corporate income. Again, payments of this nature, which are not needed immediately by the shareholder, can be loaned back to the corporation. When needed, the funds can then be withdrawn as a repayment of debt with no further tax consequences.

[2] Even with the 38% gross-up and tax credit, there may be some tax cost if combined federal and provincial corporate tax rates exceed 27.5%. If the deferral advantage cannot be achieved, because corporate earnings are to be distributed immediately, to meet owner-manager needs, the payment of salary or bonuses down to the $500,000 small business deduction limit may be better than the payment of dividends.

¶13,060 Salaries and bonuses

In order to be deductible by the corporation, salaries and bonuses paid, must be reasonable in the circumstances. There are no concrete guidelines as to what is meant by the word "reasonable". Where the employee is at arm's length with the corporation, generally any salary and/or bonus would qualify as "reasonable". However, this is not the case in the situation of a controlling shareholder-manager. In such a case, the value of his or her services may be assessed. The Canada Revenue Agency (CRA) could look at what executives in other corporations are being paid. The gross revenue and profitability of the corporation are probably the major factors to consider when justifying a large salary or bonus to a key person.[3] ITA: 67

On the other hand, there may be no incentive for the CRA to use section 67 to challenge the amount of salary paid to a controlling shareholder-manager. While the salary may be deductible to the corporation, it is included in the income of the recipient shareholder-manager. At high salary levels, the tax on the income in the hands of the shareholder-manager will generally be higher than the tax saving from the deduction of salary by the corporation.

In the case of *Totem Disposal Co. Ltd. v. M.N.R.*, the Tax Review Board held that the company's policy of limiting its net income to below the small business deduction limit by the accrual of management salary was for the purpose of tax reduction and not for the purpose of gaining or producing income. Therefore, the accrued salary expense was not allowed. This decision would not necessarily preclude the actual payment, as opposed to accrual, of a reasonable salary or bonus to achieve the same objective. In contrast to the *Totem Disposal* case, the Tax Court of Canada, in rejecting the argument that accruals were not made to produce income, set out the following criteria[4] for deductibility: 81 DTC 493 (T.R.B.)

- reasonableness of the bonus in relation to profit and services rendered;
- payment for real and identifiable service;
- some justification for expecting a bonus over regular salary (e.g., a company policy);
- reasonableness of the time between determining profit and establishing the bonus; and
- a legal obligation to pay the accrued bonus.

Where a director's resolution authorizing payment of management bonuses contained uncertainties regarding the actual payment, the Tax Court of Canada, in *Samuel F. Investments Limited v. M.N.R.*, held that the liability was contingent in nature and, therefore, not deductible. 88 DTC 1106 (T.C.C.)

The CRA's position on the issue of reasonableness of salaries or bonuses is that the reasonableness of salaries or bonuses paid to employee-shareholders is to be determined based on the facts of the case. However, they will generally not challenge the reasonableness of salaries or bonuses to shareholder-managers if profits are usually distributed by way of bonuses to the shareholder-managers or the company has a policy of paying bonuses to compensate them for their special knowledge or skills.[5]

¶13,065 Accrued bonuses and other amounts

¶13,065.10 *Unpaid remuneration*

Where an amount in respect of employee remuneration (including salaries, wages, pension benefits, and retiring allowances) is unpaid 180 days after the end of the employer's fiscal period, the amount is deductible only in the employer's fiscal period in which the amount is actually paid. (By administrative practice, the CRA allows payment on the 180th day, despite the clarity of the legislation on this point.) Thus, the accrual method is ITA: 78(4) IT-109R2, par. 10

[3] For a case on the issue of the reasonableness of bonuses, see *La Compagnie Ideal Body Inc. v. The Queen*, 89 DTC 5450 (F.C.T.D.). See also "Shareholder/Manager Remuneration" in *Income Tax Technical News* No. 22, Canada Customs and Revenue Agency, January 11, 2002.

[4] These criteria were quoted in the case of *Earlscourt Sheet Metal Mechanical Limited v. M.N.R.*, 88 DTC 1029 (T.C.C.).

[5] Question 42 of the "CRA Round Table" in the *1981 Conference Report* of the Canadian Tax Foundation.

denied to the employer on amounts unpaid after the 179-day period. Note that a shareholder-manager has far greater flexibility when the corporation's fiscal year ends during the last 179 days of the calendar year. Since a bonus can be paid at any time during the following 179 days from the year-end of the accrual, income can be triggered in the current calendar year by a payment to the owner-manager. Alternatively, income can be deferred to the following year by an accrual in the fiscal period and a payment in the following year, if this is more beneficial. Of course, the benefit from deferring the payment of the bonus to the employee is reduced considerably by the requirement by the employer to withhold tax at the time of paying the bonus. With a fiscal year-end in the first half of the calendar year, the accrued bonus must be paid in the same calendar year, as it is accrued, thereby reducing the deferral flexibility.

¶13,065.20 *Non-arm's length accruals other than remuneration*

Where an amount, other than remuneration, is deductible by a taxpayer, like a corporation, and owed to a non-arm's length person, like a majority shareholder, another limited accrual rule applies to the unpaid amount. As an example of the application of these rules, consider a situation where *property* owned by a majority shareholder personally is transferred to a corporation in return for certain income payments, such as, a royalty payment. The royalties can be accrued by the corporation as an expense in one year and paid up to two years after the taxation year of the corporation in which the amount was accrued. This gives the company an immediate expense deduction, but the shareholder, if using the cash basis, has no income until the amount is paid. The amount must be paid prior to the end of the second taxation year after the year in which it is expensed where the shareholder is not at arm's length with the corporation. If it is not paid by the end of the second taxation year following the year of accrual, the amount must be added back to the income of the corporation in the third taxation year of the corporation following the year of accrual. This could result in double taxation, unless the shareholder forgives the amount payable, because on ultimate payment the corporation would not get a deduction, while the shareholder would have to report the income. On the forgiveness of a debt of this nature, the forgiven amount would be included in income. However, if section 78 applies, the amount payable is considered "an excluded obligation" and the debt forgiveness rules will not apply.

ITA: 78(1)
ITA: 78(1)(*a*)
ITA: 80(1)

To avoid this problem, the corporation and the shareholder-manager must file an agreement on or before the date on which the corporation must file its tax return for the third taxation year following the year of accrual. This agreement deems the amount to have been paid by the corporation and received by the shareholder-manager on the first day of the third taxation year following the year of accrual. In addition, the amount deducted is deemed to have been lent back to the corporation by the shareholder-manager.

ITA: 78(1)(*b*)

¶13,065.30 *Example of non-arm's length accrual effects*

For example, assume a corporation's year-end is June 30. Royalties accrued on June 30, 2011 must be paid by June 30, 2013 or added back to the corporation's income for the year ended June 30, 2014 unless an agreement is filed on or before December 31, 2014. In that case, the royalties are deemed to have been received by the non-arm's length shareholder-manager and loaned back to the corporation on July 1, 2013. The effect of the agreement is to put the shareholder in the same position as he or she would have been had the royalties actually been paid. When the corporation ultimately repays the loan resulting from the unpaid royalties, there are no further tax consequences because the royalties were already taxed on their deemed receipt under the agreement.

ITA: 78(1)(*b*)

The agreement can be filed late, that is, after the filing deadline. However, if the agreement is filed late, 25% of the unpaid amount is added back in the third year to the corporation's income. This will not affect the treatment of the full unpaid amount. Thus, in the above example, 25% of the unpaid amount would be added back to the corporation's income in the 2014 taxation year, but under the agreement the entire amount of unpaid royalties would be deemed to have been paid by the corporation and received by the shareholder-manager and to have been loaned back on July 1, 2013. When the corporation ultimately pays back the loan, there will be no further tax consequences. The corporation will

ITA: 78(3)
ITA: 78(1)(*a*)

have deducted the entire amount of royalties in its 2011 taxation year, but will have added back 25% in its 2014 taxation year. Thus, the 25% amount will, in effect, not have been deducted, thereby creating a penalty for a late-filed agreement.

The foregoing non-arm's length accrual rules and their effects, which apply if the accrual is not actually paid within two years, can be diagrammed as follows, assuming a $10,000 royalty accrual:

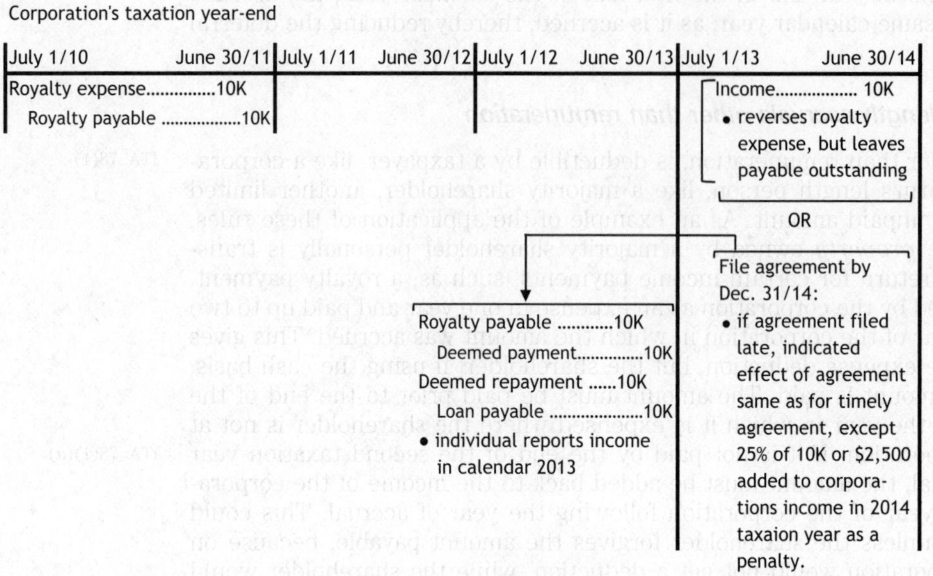

¶13,065.40 *Genuine, not contingent liability*

There are other potential problems with the accrual of amounts. In order to be deductible in the year accrued, there must be a legal obligation to pay the amount. If the legal obligation is not established, then a deduction would be allowed only in the year of payment and not in the year of accrual. Thus, the liability should be established by recording the amount in the minutes of the directors' meeting prior to the year-end and by attempting to establish, in the case of a bonus, some formula for computing the bonus representing objective standards. The payment should not be made contingent on some event which might take place after the year-end. Having established a real liability in this manner, if the amount is not paid on time and if the election is not filed, the shareholder may decide to forgive the amount so that the corporation need not pay it, subject to the double taxation previously mentioned.

An Interpretation Bulletin suggests that if an unpaid amount does not constitute a genuine liability, no deduction will be allowed. The Interpretation Bulletin states that "for genuine liability to exist, there must be an enforceable claim by the creditor with a reasonable expectation that the debt will in fact be paid by the debtor." ITA: 18(1)(*e*); IT-109R2, par. 15(e)

¶13,070 Shareholder Benefits and Loans

¶13,075 Shareholder benefits

There are provisions that are designed to prevent the distribution of part of the accumulated surplus of a corporation (other than by way of taxable dividends) to shareholders while the corporation is a going concern. There are exceptions to the broad application of these rules for particular situations that are dealt with elsewhere in the Act, notably in the provision dealing with the taxation of dividends and options. In all other cases, the Act requires an amount to be included in income, but the amount is not deemed to be a dividend and, therefore, is not eligible for the dividend tax credit. This provision was applied in the case of *No. 403 v. M.N.R.*, in which a controlling shareholder purchased a house from his company at $38,000 when it had been purchased a year earlier by the company for $45,000. The $7,000 benefit to the shareholder was included in his income from property. In this situation, the corporation will be considered to have received proceeds equal to its fair market value at the time of the sale to the shareholder. If this sale triggers any income, it must be included by the corporation. In this particular case, if the corporation's cost was $45,000, there would have been no income with proceeds of $45,000.

ITA: 15(1)

57 DTC 120 (T.A.B.)

ITA: 69(4)

Where a loan to a shareholder is forgiven by a corporation, that is, the shareholder is not required to repay all or some part of the principal amount of the loan, a rule provides that the amount of the principal forgiven must be included in the shareholder's income.

ITA: 15(1.2)

ITA: 15(1)

Benefits conferred on shareholders must be included in their income just as employment benefits conferred on employees must be included in employment income. Many of the related subsections in section 15, applicable to shareholders, provide a treatment similar to section 6, applicable to employees, as shown in Exhibit 13-2.

ITA: 15(1); 6(1)(*a*)

EXHIBIT 13-2
Selected Shareholder and Employee Benefits

	Shareholder subsection 15(1) and	*Employee paragraph 6(1)(a) and/or*
Automobile	Subsection 15(5)*	Paragraphs 6(1)(*e*), (*k*) and subsection 6(2)
Interest on loans ...	Subsections 15(9) and 80.4(2)	Subsections 6(9) and 80.4(1)
Forgiveness of loans	Subsection 15(1.2)	Subsection 6(15)

* Refers to subparagraph 6(1)(*e*)(i) and subsections 6(1.1) and (2).

The question often arises, when dealing with a shareholder-manager, as to which provision is applicable — section 6 dealing with employees or section 15 dealing with shareholders. The capacity (often referred to by the Latin word *qua*) in which the person is operating and which, in turn, depends upon the specifics of the particular relationship, will determine which provision will apply. A good rule of thumb is that a person operates in his or her capacity as shareholder (that is, *qua* shareholder) if he or she receives a benefit which he or she would not have received if he or she was an ordinary employee.[6]

The word "benefit" is another of those key words that is undefined and yet sprinkled liberally throughout the Act. The standard test to determine whether a benefit has been conferred on a shareholder is the "*bona fide* transaction" test as set out in *M.N.R. v. Pillsbury Holdings Ltd.* The court made the distinction between a *bona fide* transaction and transactions that are devices and arrangements for conferring benefits or advantages on a shareholder. A *bona fide* transaction might occur where a shareholder deals with the corporation in the same manner or capacity as a customer (i.e., *qua* customer) or as a

64 DTC 5184 (Ex. Ct.)

[6] For a more detailed discussion of this topic see Robert E. Beam and Stanley N. Laiken, "The 'Capacity' Issue in Corporate Transactions with Shareholders", Personal Tax Planning Feature (1992), Vol. 40, No. 2, *Canadian Tax Journal*, pp. 412–439.

supplier (i.e., *qua* supplier). Further comments on the concept of a benefit are made in ¶3,125 of Chapter 3.

Once it has been established that a benefit has been conferred, then the next step is to determine its value, if any. In *Youngman v. The Queen*, the Federal Court of Appeal determined that the value of a benefit of a house provided to its shareholders was not based on the equivalent rental fair market value, but instead was based on the value of the house itself. 90 DTC 6322 (F.C.A.)

Example Problem 13-1

Smart Manufacturing Ltd. built a 21-room house for its principal shareholder-officer on a country property owned by him. The company expensed the costs as promotion expenses on the basis that he would use the property to entertain distributors of the company's products to ensure continuing outlets for the company's products.

— REQUIRED

Consider the tax consequences to the individual and the company in this case.

— SOLUTION

The value of the house plus the HST, if any, on that value must be included in the income of the shareholder since it represents a benefit conferred on the shareholder. Since the company does not own the property on which the house was built and it has expensed the cost on its books, it appears clear that the shareholder has received a taxable benefit. ITA: 15(1)

The company would ordinarily be allowed to deduct an expenditure made or incurred to produce income. In this case, the house would be a capital asset subject to the capital cost allowance system to the extent that some part of the house was used for business purposes. However, if the house is considered to be a lodge, in any way, the Act would prohibit the corporation from deducting any expense or outlay considered for the use or maintenance of that property. ITA: 18(1)(*l*)(i)

Example Problem 13-2

Mr. Edwards owns all of the outstanding shares of Edwards Inc., a large property management company, which manages over 20 large apartment buildings. One spring Mr. Edwards had the repair crew spend five days at his cottage making extensive repairs to the building. The value of these repairs was $8,500 (including HST). Because of his busy schedule, Mr. Edwards apparently forgot to tell his controller to send him a bill for the work done.

— REQUIRED

If the CRA were to discover this transaction during their audit, how would they reassess?

— SOLUTION

The CRA would begin by assessing Mr. Edwards a shareholder benefit in the amount of $8,500, since funds of the corporation were directed to the benefit of a shareholder. This amount would be treated as income from property in the calendar year that the repairs were made. ITA: 15(1)

The company, Edwards Inc., would probably also be reassessed to deny the deduction for the cost to the company of the repairs on the basis that the expenses were not incurred to earn income since no billing was ever sent, or on the basis that the expense was a personal or living expense. ITA: 18(1)(*a*), 18(1)(*h*)

As a result, there is double taxation. Mr. Edwards includes an amount in income for which the company does not receive a deduction.

¶13,080 Shareholder loans or indebtedness

¶13,080.10 *Principal*

Normally, when funds are borrowed, the principal amount of the debt, that is, the amount borrowed, is not considered to be income and the amount of the debt repaid is not deductible. Incurring and repaying the debt is a capital transaction. However, in the case of a shareholder, particularly a significant shareholder who can influence the decisions of the corporation, it would be easy to escape tax on the distribution of corporate surplus, if it were not for the shareholder loan. In the absence of these rules, a shareholder could borrow funds from the corporation, instead of receiving taxable salary, interest or dividends from the corporation, and never repay these funds. However, certain circumstances are recognized as exceptions.

ITA: 15(2)
ITA: 15(2.2)–(2.6)

Loans and other forms of indebtedness to shareholders (other than corporate shareholders) or to persons not at arm's length with the shareholder (i.e., connected with a shareholder) are required to be included in income of the borrower for the year in which the loan was made. In the case of *The Queen v. Silden*, the Federal Court of Appeal confirmed that subsection 15(2) must be applied where a loan is made to a shareholder. The capacity in which the individual receives the loan, i.e., as a shareholder or as an employee, is not relevant to the application of that rule, but maybe relevant for certain specific exceptions. Related persons, discussed in a previous chapter, do not deal with each other at arm's length.

ITA: 15(2.1)
93 DTC 5362 (F.C.A.)
ITA: 251, 252

¶13,080.20 *Exceptions*

There are two general exceptions to the application of the shareholder loan inclusion rule. The first excepts indebtedness between non-resident persons. The second excepts debt that arises in the ordinary course of the lender's business, as long as *bona fide* arrangements are made at the time the loan is made for repayment within a reasonable time. This exception protects a borrower who happens to be a shareholder of, for example, a bank at which he or she borrowed.

ITA: 15(2.2)
ITA: 15(2.3)

Another provision allows specific exceptions for four types of loans, for which the principal amount can be excluded from a shareholder's income if received:

ITA: 15(2.4)

(a) a loan made by the corporation to a shareholder who is, also, an employee, but not a specified employee (defined, very generally, as an employee who, together with non-arm's length persons, owns at least 10% of the shares of any class of a corporation or who does not deal at arm's length with the corporation); or

ITA: 248(1) "specified employee"

(b) a loan made by the corporation to a shareholder who is, also, an employee to assist him or her to acquire:

(i) a home for his or her own occupation (even if the loan is made to the employee's spouse), ITA: 15(2.4)(*b*)

(ii) previously unissued, fully paid shares of the corporation purchased directly from the corporation, or ITA: 15(2.4)(*c*)

(iii) a motor vehicle (as defined) to be used in the performance of his or her duties of employment. ITA: 15(2.4)(*d*), 248(1)

For the principal amount of the loan to be excluded, there are two additional conditions. The first condition requires that the loan arise because of the employee's employment (often referred to, using the Latin, *qua* employee) and not because of his or her shareholdings (*qua* shareholder). The second condition requires that *bona fide* arrangements be made at the time of the loan for repayment within a reasonable period of time. An Interpretation Bulletin suggests that normal commercial practice is used as the basis for *bona fide* arrangements. For example, a 25-year amortization period would be appropriate for a housing loan and the security of a mortgage on the property should be taken for large loans.

ITA: 15(2.4)(*e*)
ITA: 15(2.4)(*f*)
IT-119R4, par. 12

Thus, for the shareholder loan inclusion rule, the recipient of the loan must be a shareholder. Note that all four of these exceptions require that the recipient also be an employee. Therefore, to exclude the principal amount of the loan under all four of the exceptions, the recipient must be an employee. An employee-capacity condition is imposed on these exceptions, which results in exclusion of the principal, if the other conditions are met. That is, the loan must be received by the employee in his or her capacity as an employee, in addition to meeting the other conditions, for the loan to be excluded. ITA: 15(2) ITA: 15(4.2) ITA: 15(2.4)(*e*)

A loan or indebtedness that is repaid within one year of the end of the taxation year of the lender in which it was made or incurred is excluded if the repayment is not part of a series of loans and repayments. If a loan is outstanding over two successive taxation years of the lender, the loan must be included in the income of the shareholder for the year in which the loan was made. ITA: 15(2.6)

¶13,080.30 *Deduction of repayment*

Where an amount has been included in income for a preceding year, the taxpayer is permitted to deduct any repayment of the loan or indebtedness from his or her income in the year of repayment provided the repayment was not part of a series of loans and repayments. While the CRA states in an Interpretation Bulletin that whether a repayment is part of such a series is a question of fact, it also states that a shareholder's loan account with several loan and repayment transactions will give rise to a series unless there is clear evidence otherwise. ITA: 15(2), 20(1)(*j*) IT-119R4, par. 29

The CRA also states in the same Interpretation Bulletin that, notwithstanding that there is a series of loans and repayments, they will administratively allow a deduction for a decrease in the loan account, unless the decrease is temporary. A numerical example of the application of the CRA's policy on how the net decrease should be calculated is provided, based on a FIFO allocation of repayments of the loan balance. However, the calculation of both the inclusion in income and the deduction are based on administrative practice only. However, since this is a particularly tricky area in practice, the Bulletin should be studied carefully. ITA: 20(1)(*j*) IT-119R4, par. 36

The CRA's practice is to consider that dividends, salaries or bonuses paid or credited to the shareholder loan account (i.e., amounts owing to the shareholder by the corporation) to repay the balance at the end of the previous year are not part of a "series of loans or other transactions and repayments" for purposes of these two provisions. *Income Tax Technical News*, No. 3, dated January 30, 1995 and the Interpretation Bulletin, indicate that the Agency has based its position on two Tax Court of Canada cases.[7] IT-119R4, par. 29

Note that not all charges to a shareholder loan account are necessarily *bona fide* loans. Some charges might be construed as salary, dividends or an appropriation. Therefore, it is necessary to properly document loans. If the corporation incurs interest charges, it should in turn charge interest to the shareholder or some of the interest it pays may be disallowed as not for the purpose of earning income. This applies even if the loan falls under the exception rules discussed above. [Draft legislation on interest deductibility, released on December 20, 1991, but not introduced into Parliament, addressed the issue of deducting interest paid to a third party to provide funds for employee and shareholder loans. A proposal would permit the deduction of reasonable interest paid by an employer on funds borrowed to make a loan to an employee or a prospective employee. Similarly, another proposal would allow the deduction of interest paid by a corporation on funds borrowed to make a loan to a shareholder. However, the deduction in this case is limited to the amount of the shareholder's imputed interest benefit discussed below.] An Interpretation Bulletin comments on the deductibility of interest on borrowed money used to make interest-free loans to employees and shareholders. The CRA's position is similar to that proposed in the 1991 draft legislation for loans to employees. However, the CRA makes the statement that "interest on money borrowed to make interest-free loans to individuals in their capacity as shareholders would not generally qualify." ITA: 20(1)(*c*)(v) [proposed] ITA: 20(1)(*c*)(vi) [proposed] ITA: 80.4 IT-533, par. 26

[7] *Joel Attis v. M.N.R.*, 92 DTC 1128, and *Uphill Holdings Ltd. et al. v. M.N.R.*, 93 DTC 148.

Example Problem 13-3

Sally owns all the outstanding shares of Sally Inc. On July 15, 2012, Sally Inc. loans Bob, Sally's brother, $10,000 to buy a sailboat. Sally Inc. has a December 31 year end. On January 1, 2014, the loan is still outstanding.

— *REQUIRED*

What are the income tax consequences to Bob?

— *SOLUTION*

In this case, Bob received a loan from Sally Inc. and Bob is connected to his sister Sally, the shareholder, because they are related. Since the loan was not repaid before January 1, 2014, Bob will have to take the principal amount of the loan, $10,000, into income in the year the loan was received which was 2012. The following timeline of the facts and consequences may be helpful.

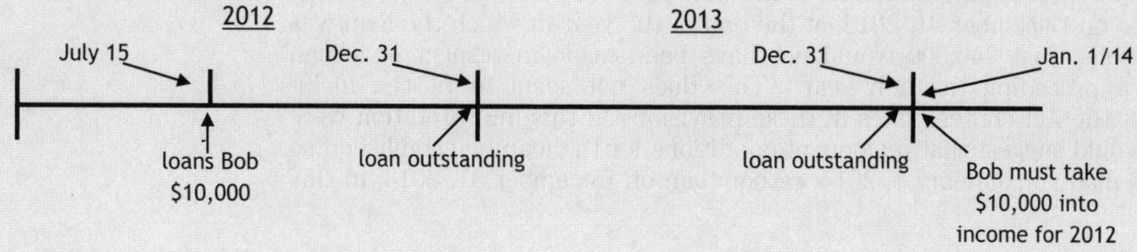

Example Problem 13-4

Ms. Alpha owns 100% of the shares of Xenon Ltd., which carries on a retailing business and has a December 31 year end. At the beginning of January 2013, Xenon Ltd. loaned Ms. Alpha $200,000 for personal purposes that would not result in an exclusion of the principal amount of the loan, by virtue of subsection 15(2.4). Under the terms of the loan, the principal was to be repaid in five equal annual instalments, commencing December 31, 2013.

— *REQUIRED*

If repayments are made on schedule, how much of the principal amount of the loan must be included in Ms. Alpha's income for 2013?

— *SOLUTION*

This particular fact situation does not seem to have been resolved in case law or in published commentary by practitioners or the CRA. Neither the CRA's Interpretation Bulletin IT-119R4 nor any published technical interpretation document addresses this fact pattern. The following discusses some possible interpretations.

ITA: 15(2), (2.6), 20(1)(*j*); IT-119R4

One interpretation that is not supported in common law but reflects unpublished administrative practice has been offered by the CRA.[8] Using this approach would include in 2013 income the $120,000 (i.e., $200,000 – ($40,000 + $40,000)) that is outstanding after the one-year repayment period. This interpretation would allow any repayments within that period to be excluded from the taxpayer's income in the year that the loan is received. Repayments of the loan made after December 31, 2014 would be deducted in the year in would be deducted in the year in which they were made. While the CRA did not offer support in the law for its administrative position, it may be possible to interpret subsection 15(2.6) with an emphasis on the word "indebtedness". A part of a loan might be considered to be an indebtedness, which if repaid within the one-year period, as specified, could be excluded from income.

[8] Corporate Finance Section, Income Tax Rulings directorate, Legislative Policy and Regulatory branch, unpublished Document No. 2012-044252, August 12, 2012.

Another perspective on the provisions in question is based on a conservative interpretation. The basic rule on the inclusion of shareholder debt requires that the "*amount* of the loan" be included in income in the year that the loan is received. Focusing on the use of the word "loan", this inclusion rule "does not apply to *a loan* . . . repaid within one year after the end of the taxation year of the lender . . . in which *the loan* was made". The use of the words "a loan" and "the loan" might be interpreted to mean that the exclusion of the loan from income will only arise if the full amount of the loan is repaid within the one-year period. ITA: 15(2) ITA: 15(2.6)

This interpretation might be supported by the use of slightly different wording in the provision that allows for a deduction of "*such part* of any loan . . . repaid by the taxpayer in the year . . . as was included in computing the taxpayer's income for a preceding taxation year". The use of the words "such part" in the deduction provision but not in the exclusion provision might suggest that the exclusion only applies in the case of a repayment of the full amount of the loan within the one-year period because the "such part" wording could have been used in the exclusion provision but was not. ITA: 20(1)(*j*)

This conservative interpretation would result in the inclusion of the full $200,000 amount of the loan in this case since it was not fully repaid within the one-year period. Then, repayments of the loan could be deducted as those repayments were made. The problem with this interpretation is that the repayment made on December 31, 2013, at the end of the year in which the loan was made, may not be deductible. That $40,000 would not have been made in respect of a loan included "in income for a preceding taxation year". This does not seem to fit the inclusion/deduction scheme that the Act contemplates in these provisions. If this interpretation were to prevail, then planning would suggest that repayment conditions for the loan be established so that the first repayment is made on January 1, 2014, rather than on December 31, 2013, in this type of loan situation.

As an intermediate position, it may be possible to consider the amount of the loan in 2013 to be $160,000, that is, net of the repayment made in 2013. Then, any subsequent repayment would be deducted in the year that it is made.

While the fact situation presented is realistic, there is no definitive answer to the question that can be found in common law or published administrative practice at this time. Since the apparent CRA administrative practice is favourable and can possibly be supported, in this case, it should be used with caution, because it is not necessarily supported in law.

¶13,080.40 *Imputed interest benefit*

Where the principal amount of the loan is not included in income because it meets one of the exclusion conditions discussed above, a provision dealing with imputed interest on loans may apply. The Act requires any person who received a loan or otherwise incurred a debt by virtue of: ITA: 80.4

- an individual's employment or intended employment (as discussed in Chapter 3),
- shareholdings in a corporation, or
- a shareholding of a person who does not deal at arm's length with a shareholder,

to include in his or her income an amount in respect of interest on low-interest or interest-free loans. The *qua* or capacity issue is very relevant for purposes of the imputed interest benefit rules. It is always a question of fact whether a person will receive a benefit under this section by virtue of his or her employment or by virtue of his or her shareholdings. ITA: 6(9), 15(9)

An interest benefit is imputed by one rule as a consequence of a previous, a current or an intended office or employment. Another rule imputes an interest benefit by virtue of the taxpayer's shareholdings in the lending corporation or a related corporation. A taxpayer may fall into either category, depending on the facts under which the loan was granted. Therefore, a decision will have to be made as to the source of this benefit based on the facts of the situation. ITA: 80.4(1) ITA: 80.4(2)

By virtue of employment

If the loan is a "home purchase loan" or a "home relocation loan", the definitions of which are applicable only to loans by virtue of employment, the imputed interest benefit is calculated for each quarter[9] as the lesser of: ITA: 80.4(4), 80.4(7)(*a*), 248(1)

(a) the prescribed rate in effect at the time the loan was received; and

(b) the prescribed rate (changed on a quarterly basis) in effect during that quarter.

However, a new loan will be deemed to have been received every five years on longer-term home purchase or relocation loans. This deemed disposition will have the effect of changing the rate of imputed interest at least every five years. Finally, the interest benefit is the amount of imputed interest in excess of the interest actually paid in the year or within 30 days after the end of the taxation year on the loan. ITA: 80.4(6)

Note that a home relocation loan is eligible for a deduction of the imputed interest benefit on the first $25,000 of the loan under certain specific rules in Division C, which was explained more fully in Chapter 10. ITA: 110(1)(*j*)

By virtue of shareholdings

An interest benefit is imputed to a person who receives a loan by virtue of shareholdings rather than as a consequence of employment. The recipient of the loan may include a shareholder or a person not at arm's length with a shareholder of a corporation who receives a loan from, or incurs a debt to, the corporation or a related corporation. Since the special provisions for a home purchase loan or a home relocation loan refer only to a loan received by virtue of an office or employment, these provisions cannot apply where the loan is received by virtue of shareholdings. In this case, the individual must include in income the amount by which interest on the loan computed at the prescribed rate tied to the treasury bill rate exceeds the interest actually paid in the year or within 30 days after the end of the taxation year on such a loan. ITA: 80.4(2) ITA: 80.4(4) ITR: 4300(7)

Two additional exceptions to the application of the imputed interest rules are provided. First, a benefit will not arise where the rate of interest payable is equal to or greater than the rate of interest that would have been agreed upon in an arm's length transaction at the time the obligation was incurred. Second, where the principal amount of the loan has already been included in the income of a person, the loan is exempt from imputed interest, whether the loan is received by virtue of employment or shareholdings. ITA: 80.4(3) ITA: 80.4(3)(*a*) ITA: 80.4(3)(*b*)

Receiving a loan by virtue of shareholding and receiving a deemed interest benefit is not as common as receiving a loan by virtue of employment and receiving a deemed interest benefit. This is the case since receiving a loan by virtue of shareholding may result in the loan principal being included in income. However if an individual receives a loan by virtue of shareholding and repays it within the time period required to avoid including the principal in income, then there will be a deemed interest benefit by virtue of shareholdings included in income.

The Act deems the interest benefit to be interest paid or payable in the year pursuant to a legal obligation for purposes of interest deduction provisions, as long as the conditions of these two interest deduction provisions are met. Thus, an offsetting deduction may be available for interest deemed to have been paid, depending on the use of the borrowed funds. ITA: 80.5 ITA: 8(1)(*j*), 20(1)(*c*)

¶13,080.50 *Application of shareholder loan rules*

Exhibit 13-3 provides a flow chart of the shareholder loan rules in sections 15 and 80.4 and the consequences of their application.

[9] The quarter-by-quarter method is used by the CRA for the "lesser of" calculation and may result in a slightly smaller income inclusion than the traditional annual calculation.

EXHIBIT 13-3
Shareholder Loans
Section 15 and Section 80.4

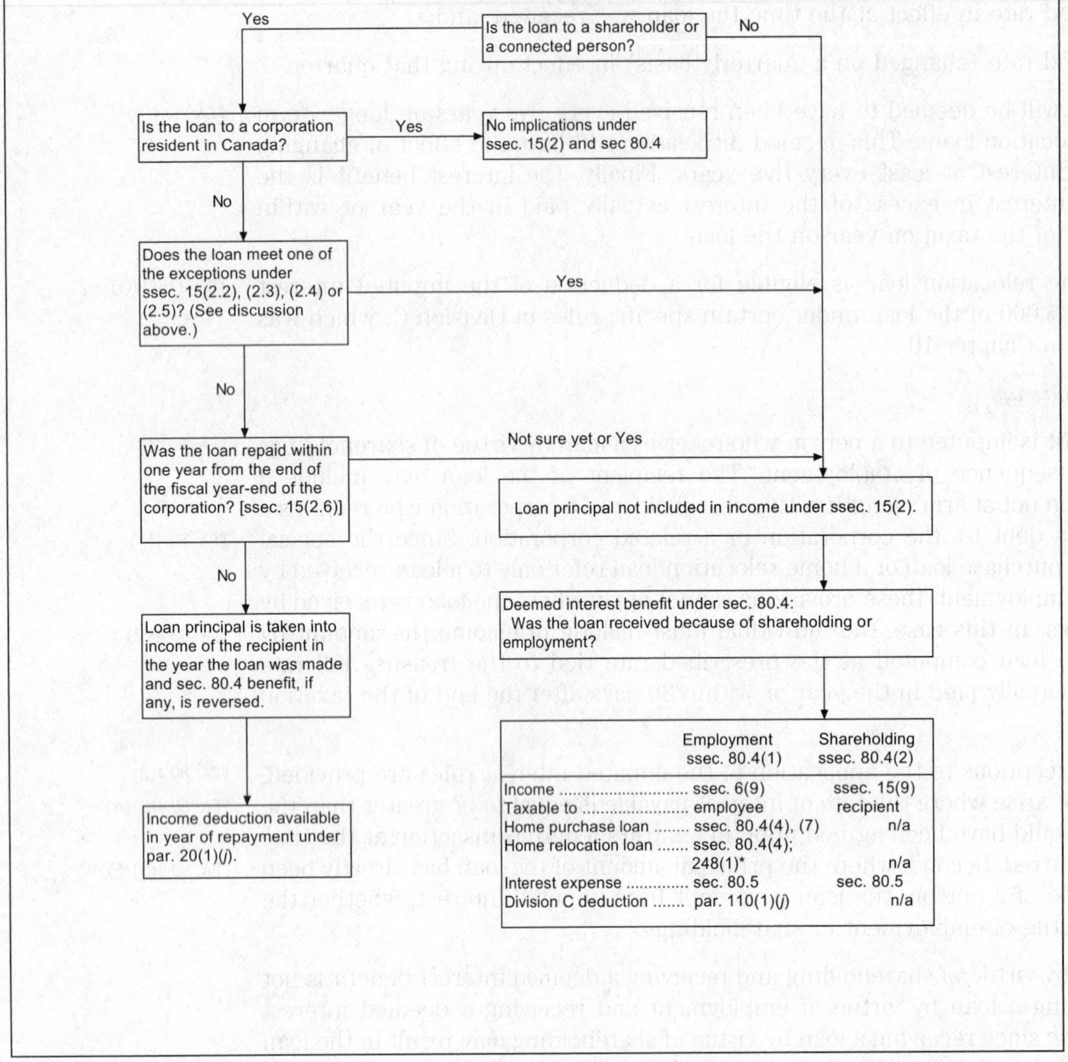
Is the loan to a shareholder or a connected person?
Yes
No
Is the loan to a corporation resident in Canada?
Yes
No implications under ssec. 15(2) and sec 80.4
No
Does the loan meet one of the exceptions under ssec. 15(2.2), (2.3), (2.4) or (2.5)? (See discussion above.)
Yes
No
Was the loan repaid within one year from the end of the fiscal year-end of the corporation? [ssec. 15(2.6)]
Not sure yet or Yes
Loan principal not included in income under ssec. 15(2).
No
Loan principal is taken into income of the recipient in the year the loan was made and sec. 80.4 benefit, if any, is reversed.
Deemed interest benefit under sec. 80.4: Was the loan received because of shareholding or employment?
Income deduction available in year of repayment under par. 20(1)(j).
Employment ssec. 80.4(1)
Shareholding ssec. 80.4(2)
Income .... ssec. 6(9) ssec. 15(9)
Taxable to .... employee recipient
Home purchase loan .... ssec. 80.4(4), (7) n/a
Home relocation loan .... ssec. 80.4(4); 248(1)* n/a
Interest expense .... sec. 80.5 sec. 80.5
Division C deduction .... par. 110(1)(j) n/a

Example Problem 13-5

Mr. Potter owns all the outstanding shares of Run for Your Life Limited, a health and fitness club. He is the company president. On July 1, 2013 the company made a loan to Mr. Potter of $19,500 which he used to acquire an automobile at fair market value. All of the other six employees of the corporation are eligible to receive this type of loan on the same terms and four have, in fact, taken advantage of the opportunity. He requires the automobile to carry out his business duties for the company. (He drives behind members of the club in case of an emergency while they are jogging.) The loan is repayable in two equal annual instalments starting July 2014 without interest.

— *REQUIRED*

(A) Does Mr. Potter receive a taxable benefit in 2013? Substantiate your answer. (Ignore the effects of the leap year.)

(B) Can the company's income position be affected either positively or negatively by this loan? Again, substantiate your answer.

Assume a prescribed rate of 4% throughout the relevant period in this problem. For a table of actual prescribed rates set out in Regulation 4301(1), see Chapter 14, or the table of Prescribed Quarterly Interest Rates in the Tables of Rates and Credits section in the preface materials of the CCH Edition of the CANADIAN INCOME TAX ACT WITH REGULATIONS.

— *SOLUTION*

(A) The general rule applies to Mr. Potter since he is a shareholder, but an exception rule permits the loan described to be exempted from inclusion in income because: ITA: 15(2), 15(2.4)

(i) the loan was to assist a shareholder/employee to purchase a motor vehicle to be used by him in the performance of the duties of his office; ITA: 15(2.4)(*d*)

(ii) the loan was received because of his employment and not because of his shareholdings, since all employees were eligible for this type of loan and four have received one; ITA: 15(2.4)(*e*)

(iii) *bona fide* repayment arrangements were made; and

(iv) repayment was scheduled within a reasonable time. ITA: 15(2.4)(*f*)

However, the fact that this was an interest-free loan results in the application of the interest benefit rule. Since Mr. Potter is probably acting in his capacity as an employee, he will be deemed to have received a benefit equal to the unpaid interest on the loan calculated at the prescribed rate in effect during the period in the year that the loan was outstanding. The prescribed rate, for this purpose, is given as 4% for all relevant quarters. Therefore, the amount of the benefit would be calculated as follows: ITA: 80.4(1)

4% of $19,500 × 92/365 =	$ 196.60
4% of 19,500 × 92/365 =	196.60
	$ 393.20

The $393.20 will be considered interest paid on a car loan for purposes of determining Mr. Potter's deduction of interest paid from employment income. This will allow him to deduct the business-use portion of the interest deemed to have been paid within the limits for the deduction of interest. ITA: 80.5, 8(1)(*j*) ITA: 67.2

(B) From the company's position, the foregone interest on the loan is not an allowable deduction. In fact, if the loan had been for more than the fair market value of the car and the car was bought from the company, interest income could be imputed to the company. However, there is no need to charge interest in a *bona fide* loan and no interest will be imputed in a fair market value transaction. ITA: 16(1)

If the company borrowed the funds which it loaned to Mr. Potter, it would be able to deduct the interest it paid provided it was part of reasonable total remuneration to Mr. Potter as an employee. IT-533, par. 26

¶13,090 Other Planning Considerations for Shareholder-Manager Remuneration

¶13,095 Income splitting

It is possible to pay a spouse or other family members a tax-deductible salary. Of course, the salary must be reasonable in the circumstances and based on the value of the actual services performed for the business, as discussed previously. Such payments will split the income of a business so that it is subject to tax at lower personal tax rates. The trade-off for this benefit is the possible loss of a marital status tax credit for the spouse.

Unlike the case of remunerating a controlling shareholder-manager with salary, there may be an incentive for the CRA to challenge, on the basis of reasonableness, the deduction of the amount of salary paid to relatives, because they may be in a lower tax bracket than the corporation after the payment of salary. The case of *Gabco Limited v. M.N.R.* presents an interesting situation of this nature. Late in 1962, Jules, the president of a construction company, hired Robert, his brother aged 19, with the intention of making him the number two man. Robert immediately became an energetic and innovative driving force in the company ITA: 67 68 DTC 5210 (Ex. Ct.)

and, according to his brother Jules, gave better service than anyone in the company, including the superintendent who was Robert's immediate superior. The company deducted the following sums from its income as expenses for Robert's remuneration: $20,371 for three months in 1962 consisting of $851 in salary and $19,520 in bonus and $35,673 in 1963 consisting of $5,280 in salary and $30,393 in bonus. These bonuses were paid in accordance with the company's practice of paying its permanent employees mainly by way of a yearly bonus proportionate to each employee's shareholdings which were based on service.

The CRA took the position that only $1,800 in 1962 and $7,200 in 1963 was a reasonable deduction for remuneration in the circumstances. This position was based on Robert's youth, his record of academic failures and the fact that his earnings for the three months in 1962 were greater than the superintendent's salary for that year. An expert appearing for the company testified that Robert was, in fact, the number two man in the company and that, as such, he would normally receive 70% of the most senior man's salary. Jules' salary was $48,000 in 1962 and $57,000 in 1963.

The company's position was upheld on the basis that Robert's remuneration was reasonable in the circumstances. The question to be answered was: would a reasonable business person have paid the remuneration in the circumstances? It was found that the bonus arrangement was a legitimate way of remunerating the company employees. Having regard to Robert's contemplated status in the company, which was subsequently fulfilled, and to the legitimate consideration of future benefits to be derived from his employment, the court found that his remuneration for the three-month period in 1962 was not unreasonable but in proportion to the value of his services to the company. The court also found, on the basis of the evidence that 70% of the most senior person's salary was a normal salary for his second in command, that Robert's remuneration for 1963 was reasonable.

¶13,100 Fringe benefits

¶13,100.10 *Contributions to RPP*

The remuneration package for a shareholder-manager may include a number of fringe benefits such as private health insurance and group sickness or accident insurance, among others. It might include retirement benefits from an employer's contribution to a registered pension plan. Since only employees are eligible, the owner of an unincorporated business, who is not considered to be an employee, cannot participate in such a pension plan. However, a personal contribution to a registered retirement savings plan could still be made. There are criteria which must be met by a registered pension plan for a shareholder-manager. IT-470R ITA: 147.1

¶13,100.20 *Payment of premiums for life and/or disability insurance*

Sometimes the life and disability insurance coverage provided in the group insurance package is not adequate to meet the needs of the shareholder-manager. If the company were to pay for additional life insurance premiums on an individual policy owned by the shareholder-manager (in his or her capacity as a shareholder), then the full premium would be a shareholder benefit. Similarly, if the company were to pay the premiums on a disability insurance policy owned by the shareholder-manager, and if the benefit was received in his or her capacity as shareholder, then the full amount of the premium would be a shareholder benefit. ITA: 15(1)

¶13,100.30 *Retiring allowance*

A retiring allowance could also be paid by the company which would receive a tax deduction. The tax on that income could be deferred by the shareholder-manager by rolling the allowance into a registered retirement savings plan or a registered pension plan. Note, however, that the Act will restrict the amount that can be rolled in this manner. A limit, for years of service prior to 1989, of $3,500 will apply for each year that the taxpayer was not a member of a registered pension plan, or was a member of a plan whose benefits for those years did not vest, and $2,000 for each year that the taxpayer was a member of such a plan whose benefits did vest. For years of service after 1988 and before 1996, there is a single limit ITA: 60(j.1) of $2,000 for each year of service. Therefore, no amount in respect of years of service after 1995 can be rolled into an RRSP.

¶13,100.40 *Company car*

Finally, a company car can be provided as a fringe benefit. Exhibit 13-4 presents an example which shows the possible advantage of the company providing a car subject to the standby charge in comparison with the individual providing himself or herself with the same car. The decision in this comparison will depend on the specific facts of each case. However, the calculation at the bottom of Exhibit 13-4 would suggest a benefit to a company car when the actual cost of the personal use of the company car exceeds the amount of the benefit that must be added to the shareholder-manager's employment income for the particular car in question. It should be noted that if the car is used primarily for personal purposes as a perquisite, there may be a reduction in the standby charge, but the decision in this case will not change. Note that the example neutralizes the company's position by assuming that lease costs and operating costs would be added to the salary of the shareholder-manager where he or she assumed these expenses. Exhibit 13-4 is a relatively simple example. The analysis can be much more complex (e.g., luxury cars with a cost or lease payments over $30,000 or $800, respectively).

EXHIBIT 13-4
Company Car as a Fringe Benefit

Assumptions:

Annual car lease cost (added to salary if leased by shareholder-manager), including HST (13%)	$ 6,000
Annual operating costs of car (added to salary if leased by shareholder-manager)	$ 2,880
Shareholder-manager has taxable income before car benefit of:	
if car leased by company	$154,000
if car leased personally ($154,000 + $6,000 + $2,880)	$162,880
Business use of car (4,800/24,000 km)	20%

Company Leases Car		*Shareholder-Manager Leases Car Personally*	
Benefit from use of car:		Incremental taxable income	$ 8,880
— value of operating costs of personal use [par. 6(1)(*k*)] (27¢ × 19,200 km)	5,184	Less: deduction for business use of car (20% of ($2,880 + $6,000))	(1,776)
			$ 7,104
— standby charge* [par. 6(1)(*e*)] (⅔ × $6,000)	4,000	HST rebate (13/113 × $1,776)	$ 204
	$ 9,184	Tax @ 46% on income	$ 3,268
Tax @ 46%	$ 4,225	Tax @ 46% on HST rebate	$ 94
		Net tax ($3,268 − $204 + $94)	$ 3,158

Difference: $1,067

Conclusion: If considering only net cash in shareholder-manager's hands he or she would choose to lease the car personally.

Reason: Cost of personal use of car ($8,880 –$1,776) + HST rebate included in the year of receipt ($204)	$7,308
Less: benefit added to income under ssec. 6(1) ($5,184 + $4,000)	9,184
Net income difference	$1,876
Tax on net saving @ 46%	$ 863
HST rebate received	204
Total cash difference	$1,067

Note that present value considerations on the rebate which is received and taxed in the following year have been ignored, although the tax on the rebate inclusion is considered by the inclusion of the rebate in income. Also, ignored is the effect of the input tax credit (ITC) received by the corporation if it incurs the annual lease and operating costs. If the corporation pays additional salary equal to its net costs for these items after ITC and, hence, if the shareholder-manager must pay the HST from other sources, it can be shown that the shareholder-manager's after-tax retention is reduced by the after-tax equivalent of the HST costs.

* Since business travel does not comprise the primary (usually more than 50%) purpose of the distance travelled, the reduction factor in subsection 6(2) does not apply (i.e., A/B = 1 in the formula). Lease costs in this calculation include HST @ 13%.

¶13,200 SALARY VERSUS DIVIDENDS

¶13,210 The Basic Trade-Off

On the one hand, salaries which are deductible by the corporation are subjected to personal tax. On the other hand, dividends which are not deductible by the corporation must be generated from income that is subjected to corporate tax; in turn, such dividends are subjected to personal tax which is reduced by the dividend tax credit.

Exhibit 12-1 demonstrated that integration of personal and corporate income tax works perfectly if the combined corporate tax rate is 15.3% where the proposed 18% gross-up applies for dividends paid after 2013 and about 27.5% where the 38% gross-up applies. Since the federal tax rate on income eligible for the small business deduction is 11%, a provincial corporate tax rate of 4.3% (15.3% – 11%) on this type of income would provide perfect integration. If the provincial tax rate is less than 4.3% then there is an advantage from incorporating income eligible for the small business deduction and receiving dividends, since the dividend tax credit claimed on the personal tax return will be greater than the underlying corporate tax. If the provincial corporate tax rate is higher than 4.3%, then there will be a disadvantage from incorporating this type of income, since the dividend tax credit will be less than the underlying corporate tax. In this case, salary, and not dividends, will generally be preferred. Since the federal tax rate on business income subject to the higher corporate tax rate is 15%, the breakeven provincial corporate tax rate on that income must be 12.5% (27.5% – 15%).

Further, salaries can reduce income to maintain corporate income at or below the $500,000 business limit for the small business deduction, whereas dividends will not. On the other hand, dividends reduce the cumulative net investment loss balance, to help preserve access to the capital gains deduction and may generate a dividend refund, but salaries do not.

¶13,220 Approximate Amounts of Taxable Dividends That Can Be Distributed Tax-Free

Exhibit 13-5 demonstrates that it is possible to distribute a considerable amount of dividends which will be received tax-free by the shareholder, if he or she has no other sources of income. This fact might be advantageous in family income splitting where various members of a family hold different classes of shares. However, in the case of *Champ v. The Queen*, the court rejected such an arrangement where the two classes of common shares were identical, but dividends were only paid on one class. The court treated the two share classes as one and assigned a proportional share of the dividends to each class. The basis for this decision was the corporate common law rule that dividends must be shared *pro rata*. 83 DTC 5029 (F.C.T.D.)

The case of *The Queen v. McClurg*, presents a different set of facts resolved in favour of the taxpayer because the Articles of Incorporation allowed the "sprinkling" of dividends among various classes of shares at the discretion of the directors. However, it must be remembered that in order for the company to pay the dividends indicated it must generate income which will be subjected to corporate taxes. 91 DTC 5001 (S.C.C.)

Dividends distributed out of low-rate income (small business deduction) are subject to the proposed 18% gross-up for dividends paid after 2013, while dividends distributed out of high-rate active business income are subject to the 38% gross-up. Exhibit 13-5 shows the possibility of receiving a significant dividend without any personal tax.

EXHIBIT 13-5
Approximate Amounts of Taxable Dividends That Can Be Distributed Tax-Free in 2014

	LRIP 18% Gross-up	*GRIP 38% Gross-up*
Taxable dividend[(1), (2)]	$22,609	$ 67,919
Gross-up (18%/38%)	4,070	25,809
Taxable income	$26,679	$ 93,728
Federal and provincial tax	$ 6,670	$ 28,409
Less: assumed personal tax credits	(2,600)	(2,600)
dividend tax credit	(4,070)	(25,809)
Total tax[(3)]	$ —	$ —
Net cash retained	$22,609	$ 67,919

NOTES: (1) Amounts will change with indexing of tax brackets. The increase in dividends will be approximately equal to the increase in the indexing factor for the year.

(2) None of these amounts will be affected by the minimum tax.

(3) In this exhibit, federal and provincial tax and credits were combined. In reality, the federal and provincial calculations are done separately. As a result, federal credits can exceed federal tax, but federal tax cannot be negative, since the tax credits are non-refundable. Therefore, the dividend would be calculated to arrive at a basic federal tax of nil. As a result, some provincial tax would be paid, but the provincial tax rate is lower than the federal tax rate.

¶13,230 Distribution Out of Income Taxed at Small Business Rate

Exhibit 13-6 shows the tax saving resulting from the payment of a dividend rather than salary from income eligible for the small business deduction in a province with a 4% corporate tax rate. Generally, dividends from the active business income of a CCPC taxed at the low rate are preferred to salary at all personal rates when total corporate rates are less than 15.3% (after 2013). This is because the dividend tax credit is larger than the tax paid by the corporation, resulting in what is known as "over integration" which produces a tax savings from the use of a corporation. Corporate rates will be less than 15.3% where a corporation is eligible for the federal small business deduction and where the provincial corporate tax rate is about 4.3% or less.

However, there is a range which will vary annually with indexing within which a combination of salaries and dividends will provide the lowest tax cost. Below the lower limit of the range, which is approximately equal to the level of the individual's total personal credit base (i.e., the level of income at which tax is offset by personal tax credits), salaries alone result in the lowest tax cost because they are deductible by the corporation and in the hands of the individual are offset by personal credits and, therefore, not taxable. For example, a salary of $11,038 (for 2013) will be fully deductible by the corporation, and the individual can offset his or her taxes payable using just the basic personal amount. Above the upper limit of the range, dividends alone result in the lowest tax cost. The latter case is demonstrated in Exhibit 13-7 using a $120,000 level of pre-tax corporate income. In that case, the payment of the salary is not fully integrated, because it is deductible by the corporation at a relatively low tax rate, assumed to be 15%, and taxable to the individual at a relatively high rate, including provincial tax, at a 46% rate. On the other hand, the dividend benefits from "over-integration" because the total corporate rate of tax is less than 15.3%.

An appropriate range can be computed for situations where the corporate income accrues to a single owner-manager or for more than one owner-manager. When corporate tax rates total 15.3% or more on income eligible for the small business deduction, salaries alone will result in the lowest tax cost.

EXHIBIT 13-6
Income Eligible for Small Business Deduction

		Individual	
		Combined federal and provincial tax bracket	
		25% (up to $43,561)	*46% (over $135,054)*
Tax on $1,000 of salary	(A)	$ 250	$460
Tax on $1,000 corporate income distributed as a dividend after corporate tax:			
Corporate tax @ 15% (i.e., 38% − 10% − 17% + 4% (assumed prov.))	(B)	$ 150	$150
Combined federal and provincial personal tax* on remainder distributed as a dividend (tax on $1,000 − $150 = $850 dividend)		$ 98	$308
	(C)	$ 248	$458
Tax saving on dividend alternative (A) − (C)		$ 2	$ 2
Tax deferred while funds left in corporation (A) − (B)		$ 100	$310

* Includes the effect of the combined federal and provincial rates on the grossed-up dividend and dividend tax credit — e.g., at the lower personal rate: [25% × (1.18 × $850) − 18/18 (0.18 × $850)] and at the higher personal rate: [46% × (1.18 × $850) − 18/18 × (0.18 × $850)].

EXHIBIT 13-7
Salary Versus Dividends

A. Data

Company earns $120,000 of active business income eligible for small business deduction.

Shareholder has no other income and has federal personal tax credits of $2,100 and provincial personal tax credits of $1,400 that are allowable for both regular Part I tax and minimum tax.

B. Comparison

	Salary	*Dividend*
Pre-tax corporate income	$ 120,000	$ 120,000
Salary	(120,000)	—
Taxable income of corporation	—	$ 120,000
Combined federal and provincial corporate tax @ 15% (i.e., 38% − 10% − 17% + 4%)	—	(18,000)
Available for payment of dividend	—	$ 102,000
Combined federal and provincial personal tax on salary or dividend	$ 35,681	$ 17,468*
Add: corporate tax	—	18,000
Total tax paid	$ 35,681	$ 35,468
Difference	$ 213	
Savings as a percentage of $120,000	0.18%	
Savings as a percentage of tax on salary	0.6%	

* Federal minimum tax would not apply to the dividend, as shown by the following calculation of federal tax:
Greater of:

(a) regular basic federal tax (only) under Part I on dividend of $102,000	$ 11,499	$11,499
(b) minimum tax [15% of ($102,000 − $40,000) − $2,100]	$ 7,200	

Example Problem 13-6

Ethan Corporation Limited, a Canadian-controlled private corporation carrying on business in a province with a 4% corporate tax rate on its income (i.e., a total corporate tax rate of 15%), has earned $36,000 in its taxation year ended December 31 before a salary has been paid to the shareholder-manager. The shareholder-manager has federal personal tax credits of $2,500 and provincial personal tax credits of $1,613 and no income from other sources.

— *REQUIRED*

(A) If the full $36,000 is to be distributed either by way of salary or dividends, which should be chosen? Use the 18% gross-up for dividends paid after 2013.

(B) Is there a combination of salary and dividends that is better?

— *SOLUTION*

		Part A		Part B
Corporation:		*Salary*	*Dividend*	*Combination*
Income before salary	(I)	$36,000	$36,000	$36,000
Salary		(36,000)	—	(9,655)
Taxable income		Nil	$36,000	$26,345
Corporate tax @ 15% (i.e., 38% – 10% – 17% + 4%)	(II)	Nil	(5,400)	(3,952)
Available for dividend		Nil	$30,600	$22,393
Shareholder:				
Income from salary and/or dividend*		$36,000	$30,600	$32,048
Gross-up @ 18%		—	5,508	4,031
Taxable income		$36,000	$36,108	$36,079
Federal tax		$ 5,400	$ 5,416	$ 5,412
Personal tax credits		(2,500)	(2,500)	(2,500)
Dividend tax credit @ 13/18 of gross-up		—	(3,978)	(2,912)
Basic federal tax (B.F.T.)**		$ 2,900	Nil	Nil
Provincial tax		3,600	3,611	3,608
Provincial personal tax credits		(1,613)	(1,613)	(1,613)
Provincial dividend tax credit @ 5/18 of gross-up		Nil	(1,530)	(1,120)
Total tax**	(III)	$ 4,887	$ 468	$ 875
Cash retained (I – (II + III))		$31,113	$30,132	$31,173

* A dividend of these amounts would not be affected by the minimum tax.

** Cannot be negative.

Note that in Part A, when the dividend is paid, there is an excess of $1,062 in federal non-refundable dividend tax credit and personal tax credits that cannot be used to offset tax on other income. Suppose salary were increased by $100. At the corporate level the following would occur since all of the income is distributed:

Increase in salary expense	$ 100
Decrease in corporate tax ($100 × .15)	(15)
Decrease in amount available for dividend	$ 85

At the shareholder-manager level the following would occur since all of the income is distributed:

Increase in salary	$ 100.00
Decrease in dividend	(85.00)
Decrease in gross-up	(15.30)
Decrease in taxable income	$ (0.30)
Decrease in federal tax @ 15% of $0.30	$ (0.05)
Decrease in federal dividend tax credit (13/18 × .18 × $85)	11.05
Increase in basic federal tax	$ 11.00

Thus, every $100 increase in salary within the 15% federal marginal tax bracket will result in an increase in federal tax of $11 where all the income is distributed. To eliminate $1,062 (i.e., $5,416 – 2,500 – 3,978) in excess federal dividend tax credit with additional salary, a salary of $9,655 (i.e., $1,062/.11) should be paid.

Note that this mix of salary and dividend in Part B is better than the all-salary alternative by $60 (i.e., $31,173 – $31,113). Note also that a tax saving of $60 is the difference between the tax of $3,952 at the corporate level plus $875 at the provincial personal level resulting from a salary of only $9,655 and the tax of $4,887 at the shareholder level resulting from a salary of $36,000. Thus, where the all-dividend remuneration is not taxed in the hands of the shareholder-manager due to excess federal dividend tax credit, it is better to pay a combination of some dividends and some salary to reduce the tax at the corporate level and offset any excess federal dividend tax credit at the shareholder level.

Note that the difference between the cash retained of $30,132 from the all-dividend alternative of Part A and the cash retained of $31,173 from the combination alternative of Part B is $1,041. This is exactly the difference in corporate tax plus provincial personal tax paid between the two alternatives (i.e., $5,400 + $468 – ($3,952 + $875) = $1,041).

Note that a salary was found to bring basic federal tax to nil since the federal tax rate is higher than the provincial rate.

Example Problem 13-7

Bryan Hill owns all of the issued shares of Hill & Associates Inc., a consulting firm he started five years ago. Bryan's only source of income is from the corporation and he has federal personal, non-refundable tax credits of $2,500 and provincial tax credits of $1,700. The corporation has a tax rate of 15% on its income eligible for the small business deduction.

— REQUIRED

Determine the best combination of salary and/or dividend that Bryan should take in order to minimize the total corporate and personal tax for the year, assuming that the corporation earned net income of $100,000 before owner compensation and income tax. Bryan needs a pre-tax amount of $36,000 in cash to meet his personal expenses. Use the 18% gross-up for dividends paid after 2013.

— SOLUTION

		Salary	*Dividend*	*Combination*(1)
Corporation				
Income before salary	(I)	$100,000	$100,000	$100,000
Salary		(36,000)	—	(7,845)
Taxable income		$ 64,000	$100,000	$ 92,155
Corporate tax @ 15% (i.e., 38% – 10% – 17% + 4%)	(II)	(9,600)	(15,000)	(13,823)
Available for dividend		$ 54,400	$ 85,000	$ 78,332
Paid as dividend		—	(36,000)	(28,155)
Retained by corporation		$ 54,400	$ 49,000	$ 50,177
Shareholder				
Income from salary		$ 36,000	—	$ 7,845

Income from dividend	—	$ 36,000	28,155
Gross-up @ 18%	—	6,480	5,068
Taxable income	$ 36,000	$ 42,480	$ 41,068
Federal tax	$ 5,400	$ 6,372	$ 6,160
Personal tax credits	(2,500)	(2,500)	(2,500)
Dividend tax credit (13/18 gross-up)	—	(4,680)	(3,660)
Basic federal tax	$ 2,900	Nil	Nil
Provincial tax	3,600	4,248	4,107
Provincial personal tax credits	(1,700)	(1,700)	(1,700)
Provincial dividend tax credit (5/18 of gross-up)	Nil	(1,800)	(1,408)
Total tax (III)	$ 4,800	$ 748	$ 999
Net cash retained initially (I – (II + III))	$ 85,600	$ 84,252	$ 85,178
Ultimate tax on dividend(2)	(19,747)	(17,787)	(18,214)
Net retained ultimately after tax	$ 65,853	$ 66,465	$ 66,964

This situation shows that it would be best to pay a combination of salary and dividends since it results in $499 (i.e., $66,964 – $66,465) of additional after-tax cash. This result is largely due to the fact that the combined federal and provincial corporate tax rate at 15% is only slightly less than 15.3%.

— NOTES TO SOLUTION

(1) Note that, when the remuneration is paid as a dividend, there is an excess of $808 in federal non-refundable dividend tax credit and personal tax credits that cannot be used to offset tax on other income.

In this case, the marginal analysis to use up the excess tax credits is a little different, because only part of the corporate income is being distributed. Suppose salary were increased by $100. At the corporate level, the following would occur:

Increase in salary expense	$ 100.00
Decrease in corporate tax ($100 × .15)	(15.00)
Decrease in amount available for dividend	$ 85.00

This only affects the amount retained by the corporation. At the shareholder-manager level, the following would occur when $100 of dividend is traded for $100 of salary:

Increase in salary	$ 100.00
Decrease in dividend	(100.00)
Decrease in gross-up	(18.00)
Decrease in taxable income	$ (18.00)
Decrease in federal tax @ 15% of $18	$ (2.70)
Decrease in federal dividend tax credit (13/18 × .18 × $100)	13.00
Increase in basic federal tax	$ 10.30

Thus, every $100 increase in salary within the 15% personal federal marginal tax bracket will result in an increase in tax of $10.30. To eliminate $808 in excess federal dividend tax credit with additional salary, a salary of $7,845 (i.e., $808/.103) should be paid as part of the combination of salary and dividends of $28,155 to total the pre-tax $36,000 in cash needed.

(2) When the amount retained by the corporation is paid out as a dividend, it will attract personal tax at that time. The combined federal and provincial tax can be estimated at a top rate of 36.3% (i.e., (.46 × 1.18) – .18) of the cash dividend paid. If the shareholder is in a lower tax bracket at the time that the dividend is paid, the effective tax rate on the dividend will be lower. When this amount is deducted from the net cash retained initially, the ultimate net after-tax retention is computed. Of course, the tax on the dividend paid from corporate retention has not been reduced by the time value of money, which depends on when the dividend is ultimately paid.

¶13,240 Distributions Out of Income Not Eligible for the Small Business Deduction

To this point the analysis has focused on the question of salaries versus dividends as remuneration from income eligible for the small business deduction. Exhibit 13-8 presents the comparison for income *not* eligible for the small business deduction. Note that salaries will generally be preferable. However, where income is taxed at the high corporate business income rate, the dividend alternative produces a tax deferral advantage for individuals in the higher tax brackets. Recognize that the amount of tax deferred can be reinvested in the corporation to, perhaps, make up the added tax cost. Thus, the added tax cost of not paying a salary may be offset by the deferral advantage of dividends if there is no immediate need for the funds. In making this comparison, it is important to consider the amount of this deferral advantage and the length of time the added tax can be deferred by delaying the payment of dividends.

Exhibit 13-8 uses the 38% dividend gross-up and related tax credit on dividends paid out of high tax rate active business income. In this case, we are assuming that the income under consideration is above the small business deduction business limit of $500,000 and is, therefore, eligible for this new treatment.

Under the 25% tax column, the personal tax on the dividend is actually negative. This is as a result of the fact that the dividend tax credit is greater than the tax on the gross-up and, therefore, available to offset tax on other income.

The result is that the tax cost on the dividend alternative is not significant, and the tax deferral at the 46% personal tax rate can provide an advantage to leaving the money in the corporation and paying a dividend at a later date.

EXHIBIT 13-8
Canadian Business Income Not Eligible for Small Business Deduction

		Individual	
		Combined federal and provincial tax bracket	
		25% (up to $43,561)	*46% (over $135,054)*
Tax on $1,000 of salary	(A)	$ 250	$460
Tax on $1,000 corporate income distributed as a dividend after corporate tax:			
Corporate tax @ 28% (i.e., 38% − 10% − 13% + 13%) .	(B)	$ 280	$280
Personal tax* on remainder distributed as a dividend (tax on $1,000 − $280 = $720)		(25)	183
	(C)	$ 255	$463
Tax cost on dividend alternative (C) − (A)		$ 5	$ 3
Tax deferral (prepayment) while funds left in corporation (A) − (B)		$ (30)	$180

* Includes the effect of the combined federal and provincial rates on the grossed-up dividend and dividend tax credit — e.g., at the lower personal rate, [25% × (Dividend × 1.38)] − (0.38 × Dividend) = −0.035 × Dividend, and at the higher personal rate, [46% × (Dividend × 1.38)] − (0.38 × Dividend) = 0.2548 × Dividend.

The following table summarizes the results of Exhibit 13-6 and Exhibit 13-8.

Summary of Tax Savings/Cost and Deferrals for $1,000 Paid as Salary or Dividend

	Individual	
	Combined federal and provincial tax bracket	
	25% (up to $43,561)	*46% (over $135,054)*
Income Eligible for Small Business deduction		
Tax savings/(cost) on dividend alternative . . .	$ 2	$ 2
Tax deferred while funds left in corporation	$100	$310
Canadian Business Income Not Eligible for Small Business Deduction		
Tax saving/(cost) on dividend alternative . . .	$ (5)	$ (3)
Tax deferred/(prepayment) while funds left in corporation	$(30)	$180

¶13,250 Summary of the Salary Versus Dividends Issue

Once the decision to incorporate has been made, the key issue becomes how to compensate the owner-manager. Should the compensation be in the form of salary/bonus or in the form of dividends or a combination of both? Exhibit 13-9 outlines the steps that should be taken in the analysis of that decision.

EXHIBIT 13-9
Steps to Take in the Analysis of the Salary or Dividend Decision

Calculate:

1. The corporate tax that would be paid, based on the type of income that is earned in a corporation owned by the individual if all or some remuneration is distributed as a salary or as a dividend.
2. The personal tax that would be paid by the individual, if the corporation paid some or all of its after-tax income out as a dividend to the individual as the shareholder.
3. The personal tax that would be paid by the individual if the corporation paid some or all of its after-tax income out as a salary/bonus to the individual as the employee.

If the all-dividend option results in excess non-refundable federal tax credits, consider a combination of salary and dividends to eliminate the excess federal credits.

Determine tax savings or cost

Determine if a savings occurs from using one option compared to the other. A savings occurs when overall tax is reduced by choosing to take money out of the corporation either through salary/bonus and/or dividends.

1. Compare
   — The total of personal and corporate tax paid when the specified salary/bonus is paid to the individual
   to
   — The total of personal and corporate tax paid when the specified salary/bonus is left in the corporation to be taxed and the after-tax cash is paid as a dividend to the individual.
2. A savings is realized by paying a dividend if the individual has more after-tax personal cash when the income is flowed through the corporation and paid as a dividend compared to paying a salary/bonus.
3. A savings is realized by paying a salary/bonus if the opposite is true.

Determine tax deferral or prepayment

Determine if a deferral occurs from using one option compared to the other. A deferral occurs when after-tax money is left in the corporation and not paid out.

1. Compare
   — The total of personal tax paid when the specified salary/bonus is received by the individual
   to
   — The corporate tax paid when the specified salary/bonus is left in the corporation to be taxed and not paid as a dividend to the individual.
2. A "deferral" is realized if the tax on the salary/bonus is greater than the tax in the corporation.
3. A "prepayment" is realized if the tax on the salary/bonus is less than the tax in the corporation.

The factors affecting a decision on whether to remunerate the shareholder-manager of a corporation by salary or by dividends include the following:

- the corporate tax rate, including both federal and provincial components, applicable to the type of income of the corporation;
- the personal tax rate, including both federal and provincial components with surtaxes, applicable to the shareholder as a result of income other than that from the business;
- whether the dividends are eligible for the 38% dividend gross-up and tax credit;
- the amount of the shareholder's personal tax credits and deductions; and
- the shareholder's participation in the Canada Pension Plan, registered pension plans and registered retirement savings plans which require income in the nature of salary rather than dividends.

The number of variables involved in a specific set of circumstances make it necessary to do a set of calculations similar to those presented in this chapter to determine the best mix of salaries and/or dividends in the particular case.

The ranking found in these computations will not be the same in all circumstances. At much lower levels of pre-tax corporate income the payment of dividends will be better. At much higher levels of pre-tax corporate income the payment of salary may be better. Generally, an optimal mixture of salary and dividends can be found where the total corporate tax rate is less than 15.3% as is the case, for example, where income is eligible for the small business deduction and a provincial corporate tax rate is about 4% or less.

Where the corporate rate is above 15.3%, it may be preferable to distribute all of the owner-manager's remuneration in the form of salary, unless the dividend is eligible for the 38% dividend gross-up and tax credit and dividends are expected to be deferred.

Recognize that if no salary is paid, the owner-manager does not have income that will qualify him or her to make deductible Canada Pension Plan or registered retirement savings plan contributions. Each of these provides for an initial tax deduction, the sheltering of income and the deferral of the ultimate payment of tax until the receipt of benefits. Similar benefits can be achieved when funds are left in the corporation after dividends have been paid to provide the shareholder-manager with the same disposable income as a required amount of salary.

¶13,300 OTHER PLANNING ASPECTS OF USING CORPORATIONS

¶13,310 Use of Holding Companies

¶13,315 An extension of integration

Inserting a holding company between a shareholder and another company requires an extension of the concept of integration, discussed in the previous chapter, to allow income ultimately to flow through the holding company to the shareholder to be taxed in his or her hands. To put this into effect, dividends must not be taxed at the corporate shareholder's level. This occurs under Part I since intercorporate dividends between Canadian companies are deductible under Division C leaving the taxable income of the recipient unaffected. However, there is the possibility of a tax under Part IV of the Act on such dividends received by a private corporation. This tax is refundable when the recipient corporation pays a taxable dividend to its shareholders such that the recipient corporation itself is not ultimately taxable on the dividends that pass through to the individual shareholder.

¶13,320 Compensation

Where there are two or more owner-managers of an operating company, the use of holding companies may give more flexibility in the salary–dividend mix decision. Where there is only one corporation, the payment of dividends must be done, under corporate law, *pro rata* according to the shareholdings. Therefore, one shareholder-manager cannot normally receive all dividends and the other shareholder-manager cannot receive all salary. By inserting a management-holding company between each of the shareholders and an operating company, the operating company can pay only dividends to the holding companies. Then each holding corporation can determine what dividends are appropriate for its shareholder(s).

For example, assume Jim and Bob each own 50% of Jimbo Inc. and each have different cash flow needs. Bob is nearing retirement and wants to defer his income while Jim has a young family and needs cash. If dividends are paid, then both Jim and Bob will receive the dividends *pro rata* even if Bob does not want them. They will each then be liable for personal income tax on these dividends. In this case, each of Jim and Bob could set up holding companies to own their shares of Jimbo Inc. as follows:

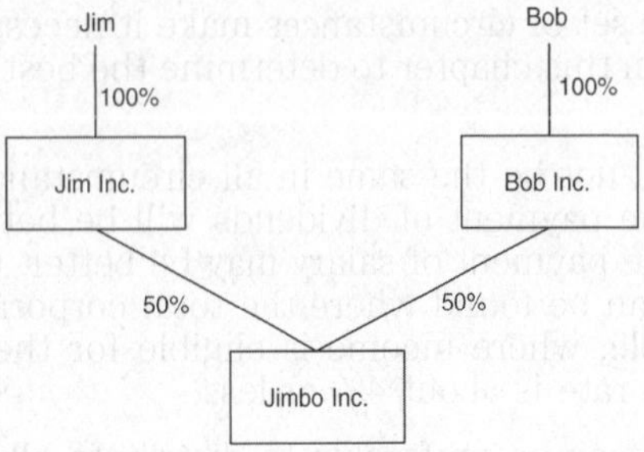

As dividends are paid from Jimbo Inc. they will be received by the holding companies without either Part I or Part IV tax. Bob can then defer his personal tax liability by leaving his dividends in Bob Inc. while Jim could take the cash he needs by paying a dividend to himself from Jim Inc.

¶13,325 Deferral of tax on dividends

The use of a holding company may be advisable in the situation of a non-controlling shareholder-employee of an operating company that is paying out more taxable dividends than necessary for the shareholder-employee's immediate needs. In such a case, the shareholder could transfer his or her shares in the operating company to a holding company which he or she controls. If the holding company owned more than 10% of the total voting shares and more than 10% of the fair market value of all the issued shares in the operating company, the two corporations are connected. The dividends then could be received by the holding company without attracting the Part IV tax as long as the holding company and the operating company which had no investment income or portfolio dividends were connected.

A much smaller deferral of tax (if any) is possible on dividends from non-connected corporations on which Part IV tax is payable. The Part IV tax is levied at a 33⅓% rate. Therefore, there will only be a deferral benefit when the personal combined rate of federal and provincial tax plus surtaxes exceeds 33⅓%.

¶13,330 Implementing an estate freeze

Another reason for the use of a holding company to own shares of an operating company would be to effect a planning device known as an estate freeze. To give a very simple example, the owner of an operating company may wish to freeze or stop the growth in his or her interest in the operating company to avoid further capital gains on these shares which would ultimately be triggered at his or her death. The owner could arrange to transfer his or her common shares in the operating company to a holding company in which the common shares were owned by the next generation in the family, the children. The owner could take back in return, perhaps, preferred shares with voting rights in the holding company. These preferred shares would not grow in value, but could pay a sufficient dividend to meet his or her personal needs and would maintain control over the operating company through the voting privileges. Dividends paid on the common shares of the operating company would flow to the holding company free of Part IV tax as long as the operating company had no investment income or portfolio dividends to trigger a dividend refund while the two companies were connected.

¶13,340 Qualified Small Business Corporation Share (QSBCS)

The corporate entity referred to as a "small business corporation" (SBC) is widely used throughout the Act. For example, the term is used in connection with a small business development bond and a business investment loss and an exemption from the effects of the corporate attribution rules. Dispositions of the shares of small business corporations may qualify for the capital gains deduction. ITA: 15.1, 39(1)(*c*), 74.4

A capital gains deduction to a maximum of $375,000 [$400,000 in 2014 and indexed thereafter, as proposed in the March 2013 federal Budget] of taxable capital gains net of any portion of the capital gains deduction of previously claimed is available. This amount is the equivalent of a gross capital gain of $750,000 [$800,000 in 2014]. ITA: 110.6(2.1)

Since there is also an equivalent deduction for qualified farm and fishing property, these two are integrated to ensure that the maximum deduction with respect to all properties combined does not exceed $375,000 [$400,000 in 2014]. ITA: 110.6(4)

¶13,345 Small business corporation (SBC)

A small business corporation (SBC) is defined as a Canadian-controlled private corporation of which all or substantially all of the assets, on a fair market value basis, are used principally in an active business, carried on primarily in Canada by the corporation or a related corporation. The reference to a related corporation means that assets leased or loaned to a related corporation also qualify. Alternatively, the assets meeting the "all or substantially all" test may be shares or debt in an SBC that is a connected corporation, or a combination of assets in direct use and securities of a connected corporation. ITA: 248(1) ITA: 186(4)

The CRA's interpretation of the phrase "all or substantially all", as stated in about 10 different Interpretation Bulletins, is that it means at least 90%. However, in the case of *Wood v. M.N.R.*, on another issue, but in respect of the phrase "all or substantially all", the Tax Court of Canada concluded that the CRA "might be hard pressed to refuse a claim where the percentage was 89%, maybe even 85% or 80% or lower". The court concluded that the "term 'substantially all' does not lend itself to a simple mathematical formula" like at least 90%. The court preferred the meaning given by "small unrelated amounts" reducing the total to arrive at substantially all. The word "primarily", while not defined in the Act, is generally considered to mean more than 50%. Elsewhere, the CRA states that the word "principal" is not defined in the Act but it is considered that the words "chief" and "main" are synonymous to it. While a principal or main use may be less than 50% if the use is the most of many uses, the CRA has generally interpreted the word to mean more than 50%. Exhibit 13-10 presents the definition of a small business corporation in point form. IT-151R5, par. 31 87 DTC 312 (T.C.C.) IT-73R6, par. 12

EXHIBIT 13-10
Small Business Corporation (SBC)
[ssec. 248(1)]

A Small Business Corporation is a corporation which was at any particular time:

— a Canadian-controlled private corporation, and

— all or substantially all (90% test) of the fair market value of assets (including unrecorded assets but excluding liabilities) were

(a) used principally in an active business carried on primarily (>50%) in Canada by

- the particular corporation, or
- a corporation related [sec. 251] to the particular corporation; or

(b) shares or debt

- of a SBC that was connected [ssec. 186(4)] with the particular corporation; or

(c) a combination of (a) and (b).

Example Problem 13-8

Maya lives in Toronto and owns 100% of Maya's Ltd. The corporation was incorporated 10 years ago, in Ontario, to operate a retail clothing establishment in Toronto. The following is the recent balance sheet for the corporation.

Maya's Ltd.
BALANCE SHEET
as at December 31, 2013

Assets	
Current	
Cash	$ 2,500
Marketable securities	200,000
Accounts receivable (net of reserve)	95,000
Inventory	270,000
Prepaid expenses	2,000
Total (equal to fair market value)	$ 569,500
Fixed	
Land, at cost (FMV: $225,000)	150,000
Building, at net book value (FMV: $350,000)	160,000
Equipment, at net book value (FMV: $100,000)	120,500
	$1,000,000
Liabilities	
Current	
Accounts payable	$ 265,000
Income taxes payable	5,000
Due to shareholder	80,000
	$ 350,000
Mortgage payable	275,000
	$ 625,000

Shareholder's Equity	
Share capital	1,000
Retained earnings	374,000
	$1,000,000

The goodwill of the business has been valued at $250,000.

— *REQUIRED*

Determine whether Maya's Ltd. is a small business corporation, assuming that the marketable securities were held:

(A) as a short-term investment of surplus cash at the low-point of the corporation's inventory cycle, and

(B) as a long-term investment to produce investment income.

— *SOLUTION*

In this case the critical condition in the definition of a small business corporation is the 90% test. It must be determined whether all or substantially all of the fair market value of the assets, including unrecorded goodwill, was used principally in an active business carried on primarily in Canada by Maya's Ltd. Retailing is an active business and it is being carried on exclusively in Canada in this case.

(A) If the marketable securities are held for use in the business, as would be the case if they represented a short-term investment of cash surplus, pending the build-up of inventory, then it can be concluded that all of the fair market value of the assets is used principally in an active business carried on primarily in Canada. Therefore, the company meets the 90% test and is a small business corporation.

(B) If the marketable securities are not considered to be used in the active business of retailing, then their relative value must be determined as follows:

	Fair market value	%
Cash	$ 2,500	0.17
Marketable securities	200,000	13.38
Accounts receivable	95,000	6.36
Inventory	270,000	18.07
Prepaid expenses	2,000	0.13
Land	225,000	15.06
Building	350,000	23.42
Equipment	100,000	6.69
Goodwill	250,000	16.72
Total	$1,494,500	100.00%

Since the marketable securities comprise more than 10% of the fair market value of the assets, the 90% test in the definition of a small business corporation is not met. (Note that the legislation does not quantify the term "all or substantially all". The courts may not interpret this term as meaning at least 90% as used administratively by the CRA.) Note that the definition of a small business corporation applies at a particular point in time. Therefore, if some of the marketable securities can be removed from the corporation: either sold with the proceeds used to pay off liabilities or invested in assets used in the active retailing business, the 90% test can be met after the removal or reinvestment. Thus, the corporation can be "purified" to meet the 90% test. It is not enough to convert the marketable securities into cash, if the cash is not used in an active business carried on by the corporation.

¶13,350 Basic QSBCS rules applied to a single corporation

This analysis will attempt to break down the provision into several easy-to-understand components. The first application will be to a single corporation. Next, the rules will be applied to a parent and subsidiary relationship. Application beyond two corporations becomes too complex for an introductory tax course and really requires the assistance of a tax specialist.

The term "qualified small business corporation share" of an individual is defined as follows: ITA: 110.6(1)

(a) a share of the capital stock of a corporation that is a small business corporation (SBC) at the time of disposition (i.e., the determination time) and is owned by the individual, by the individual's spouse or by a partnership related, as specifically defined for this purpose, to the individual (related party) (for determining whether a person or partnership is related to an individual); ITA: 110.6(14)(*d*)

(b) the share was not owned by anyone, other than the individual or a person (including a personal trust) or partnership related to the individual throughout the 24-month period preceding the disposition (without exception to the 24-month period in the case of a deemed disposition caused by death);

(c) the share was, throughout that part of the 24-month period ending immediately before the disposition that the share was owned by the individual or a person or partnership related to the individual:

(i) a share of a corporation that was a Canadian-controlled private corporation, and

(ii) more than 50% of the fair market value of the corporation's assets were used principally in an active business carried on primarily in Canada by the corporation or a related corporation.

Each of the above three parts of the definition can be considered as tests which will be referred to, respectively, as:

(a) the SBC Test,

(b) the Holding Period Test, and

(c) the Basic Asset Test (50% Test).

Exhibit 13-11 presents the foregoing tests in point form for ease of reference.

EXHIBIT 13-11
Qualified Small Business Corporation Share (QSBCS)
[ssec. 110.6(1)]

Basic Tests

A Qualified Small Business Corporation Share is:

— at any time (i.e., determination time)

- typically at time of disposition or deemed disposition;

— a share that meets the following tests:

(a) SBC Test

— an SBC at determination time

— owned by:

- the individual,
- the individual's spouse, or
- a partnership related to the individual [par. 110.6(14)(*d*)];

(b) Holding Period Test

— throughout the 24 months preceding the determination time

— owned by no one other than

- the individual, or
- a person or partnership related to the individual [pars. 110.6(14)(*c*), (*d*), (*e*), (*f*)] (i.e., related party);

(c) Basic Asset Test (50% Test)

— throughout that part of the 24 months preceding the determination time while owned by the individual or related party

- share of a CCPC for which more than 50% of the fair market value of its assets were used principally in an active business carried on primarily in Canada by the corporation or by a related corporation.

Graphically, the timing factor in each of the three tests could be depicted as follows:

		Determination time
(a) SBC Test		I
(b) Holding Period Test	I← 24 months	→I
(c) Basic Asset Test	I← 24 months	→I

Note that the SBC Test and the Basic Asset Test are calculated similarly, but the SBC Test is determined at a particular point in time, while the Basic Asset Test is determined over a period of 24 months.

Example Problem 13-9

Reconsider the facts of the previous example problem. Assume that the problem raised by the marketable securities has been resolved by removing the marketable securities from the corporation. Also, assume that the relative proportion of assets held at December 31, 2013 has not changed in the last five years.

— *REQUIRED*

Determine whether the shares are eligible for the capital gains exemption, assuming:

(A) the shares were acquired on incorporation 20 years ago, and

(B) the shares were acquired from the brother of Maya in blocks of 200 shares annually for the last five years.

— *SOLUTION*

At the time of their disposition or deemed disposition, to qualify for the capital gains exemption, the shares must meet three tests. The difference between parts (A) and (B) of the Required will be seen in the application of the second test.

(1) SBC Test

The shares must be of an SBC at the time of the disposition or deemed disposition. In this case, steps have been taken to make the corporation an SBC, if it did not already qualify as such, as discussed in the previous example problem.

(2) Holding Period Test

Throughout the 24 months preceding the disposition, the shares cannot be owned by anyone other than Maya or a related party (i.e., Maya's brother).

(A) This test is met, because the shares were held for the preceding two years by Maya.

(B) Where the shares have been acquired from the related individual (i.e., Maya's brother) even within the previous 24-month period, the test is still met. If the individual from whom the shares were acquired was not related, then the shares would have to be held by the present shareholder for the full 24 months. Since the holding period test is applied to each share, a series of dispositions can be staged as the shares meet the 24-month test on a first-in, first-out basis as permitted. ITA: 110.6(14)(*a*)

(3) Basic Asset Test (50% Test)

This test requires that throughout the 24 months preceding a disposition or deemed disposition, while the shares were held by a particular individual (i.e., Maya) or related party (i.e., Maya's brother), the shares were of a Canadian-controlled private corporation in which more than 50% of the fair market value of the assets were used principally in an active business carried on primarily in Canada by the corporation or by a related corporation. Since no other corporation is involved in this situation, the other parts of the test pertaining to a connected corporation do not apply. In this case, even with a 13.38% investment in marketable securities which may not be considered to have been used in the active business of the corporation, the 50% asset test is still met throughout the 24 months preceding a contemplated disposition or deemed disposition at this time, since the proportion of marketable securities has been stable throughout those 24 months. Remember that, even though the securities have been disposed of to meet the SBC test, they were still assets of the corporation during the 24 months preceding the disposition.

¶13,355 Modification of the asset test (stacking rule)

Even where there are a number of connected corporations, the basic rules as described above must be applied, including the 50% basic asset test in the definition paraphrased above. If the particular corporation to be sold (i.e., a parent corporation) can meet the 50% basic active business asset test with its own active business assets, its shares will meet the asset test. ITA: 110.6(1) "qualified small business corporation share" (*c*)(i)

However, where the active business assets of the parent corporation are 50% or less, then the parent corporation may still qualify by including shares and indebtedness of corporations connected with it. However, the rules are further modified to ensure that one of the two levels of corporations (i.e., parent or connected subsidiaries) meets an all or substantially all test (90%) while the other level of corporations meets a "primarily" test (50%) of the aggregate of active business assets and debts or shares of a connected CCPC. ITA: 110.6(1) "qualified small business corporation share" (*d*)

Recall, from the discussion of the Part IV tax in Chapter 12, that a connected corporation is a defined term. A corporation is connected with another corporation where: ITA: 186(4)

(a) the other corporation controls the corporation, or ITA: 186(2), 186(7)

(b) the other corporation holds more that 10% of the vote and fair market value in shares of the corporation.

Thus, if the parent meets the 90% test throughout the 24-month period before the disposition with a combination of its own active business assets and shares and debt of a connected corporation, the connected subsidiary need only meet the 50% test on its assets. Alternatively, if the parent does not meet the 90% test throughout the 24-month period before the disposition, the connected subsidiary must meet the 90% test. Thus, the 50% test must be met by both corporations at all times in the 24-month period before the disposition. Furthermore, if the parent does not meet the 90% test throughout the 24-month period before the disposition, then the connected subsidiary must meet the 90% test to have its securities considered as assets of the parent company which help the parent company to meet the 50% test. This modification of the 50% test is presented in Exhibit 13-12 in point form.

Another way of stating the conclusions on the application of these tests is as follows. Where more than 50% of the assets of a particular corporation are active business assets, the Basic Asset Test (50% Test) discussed in the previous segment is met and the type of assets held by connected corporations in the chain below the particular corporation is not relevant. The modified test need not apply. It is only when the 50% Asset Test is not met by the given corporation with its own active business assets that the 90% Modified Asset Test must be used. Where the modification applies in a two-corporation chain, the given corporation and the other connected corporation below it in the chain must meet the 50% Asset Test with their own active business assets in combination with the shares and debt of connected corporations and one of the parent or the connected corporation must meet the 90% test.

EXHIBIT 13-12
Qualified Small Business Corporation Share (QSBCS)
[ssec. 110.6(1)]
Modification of the Basic Asset Test (50% Test)

— Modification of the 50% Basic Asset Test where:

- there is a corporation (subsidiary) connected [ssec. 186(4)] to a particular corporation (parent); the subsidiary must be connected, but not necessarily a SBC,
- the particular corporation (parent) does not meet the 50% Test (on its own active business assets (i.e., excluding the shares and debt of a connected corporation)).

[*Exhibit 13-12 — continued*]

— Conclusion on modification of Asset Test:

- throughout the 24 months ending at the determination time,
  - — both the parent and the connected corporation must each meet the 50% Test with a combination of their own active business assets and shares and debt of a connected corporation;
  - — one of either the parent or the connected corporation must meet the 90% Test with a combination of its own active business assets and shares and debt of a connected corporation.

— Therefore,

- conceptually, the test is
  - — 90/50 for parent/connected, or
  - — 50/90 for parent/connected.

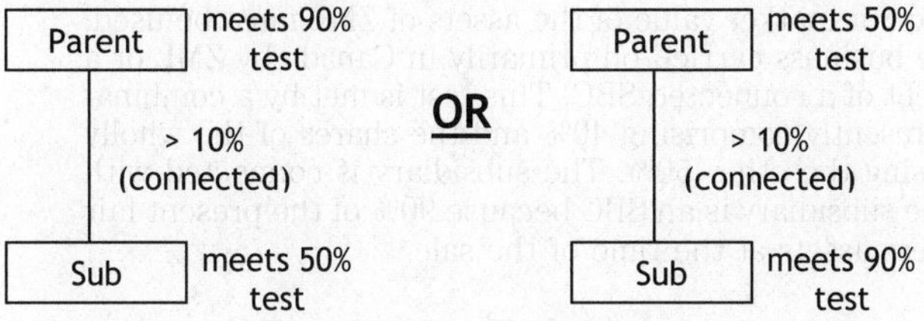

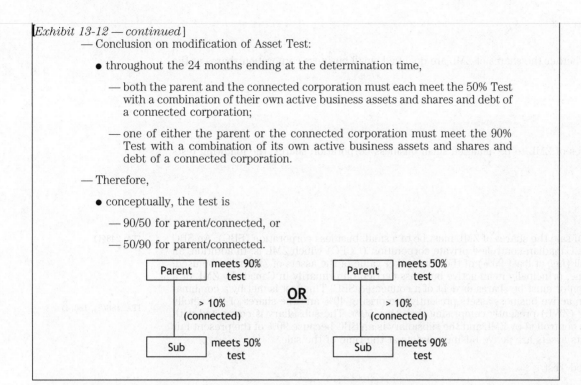

If a holding company owns more than one connected subsidiary corporation, then the modified asset test applies as follows.

1. If the holding company meets the 90% test with a combination of its own active business assets and shares or debt of a connected corporation that meets the 50% test, the modified asset test is passed.
2. If the holding company meets the 50% test with a combination of its own active business assets and shares or debt of a connected corporation that meets the 90% test, the modified asset test is passed.

Example Problem 13-10

Zeto, a resident of Canada, has owned 100% of the shares of Zeto's Manufacturing Limited (ZML), a Canadian-controlled private corporation, since its incorporation 20 years ago. The corporation carries on a manufacturing business in Canada. He is presently considering the sale of his shares. The fair market value of the assets of ZML is comprised as follows:

	FMV at present	%	*FMV throughout past 24 months*	%
Active business assets	$200,000	40	$160,000	40
Shares of 100%-owned subsidiary	250,000	50	120,000	30
Investments	50,000	10	120,000	30
	$500,000	100	$400,000	100

The subsidiary, Zeto Wholesale Ltd. (ZWL), was incorporated by ZML 15 years ago to carry on a wholesaling business in Canada. The fair market value of its assets consists of the following:

	FMV at present	%	*FMV throughout past 24 months*	%
Active business assets	$270,000	90	$157,500	90
Investments	30,000	10	17,500	10
	$300,000	100	$175,000	100

— *REQUIRED*

Determine whether the shares of ZML are qualified small business corporation shares at the present time.

— *SOLUTION*

For the shares of ZML to be qualified small business corporation shares, the following tests must be met:

(1) SBC Test

At the time of sale the shares of ZML must be of a small business corporation (SBC). An SBC is defined to be a Canadian-controlled private corporation (CCPC) which ZML is. In addition, all or substantially all (i.e., at least 90%) of the fair market value of the assets of ZML must be used, at the present time, principally in an active business carried on primarily in Canada by ZML or a related corporation or must be shares or debt of a connected SBC. This test is met by a combination of ZML's own active business assets presently comprising 40% and the shares of the wholly owned subsidiary (ZWL) presently comprising the other 50%. The subsidiary is connected with ZML because it is controlled by ZML and the subsidiary is an SBC because 90% of the present fair market value of its assets are active business assets at the time of the sale. ITA: 248(1) ITA: 186(2), 186(4)

(2) Holding Period Test

Throughout the 24 months preceding the present time, the shares cannot have been owned by anyone other than Zeto or a related party. This test is met because only Zeto owned the shares since 1985.

(3) Basic Asset Test (50% Test)

Throughout the 24 months preceding the present time, the shares must be of a CCPC with more than 50% of the fair market value of its assets used principally in an active business carried on primarily in Canada. However, ZML does not meet the 50% Test based on its active business assets alone. Therefore, the Modified Asset Test must be applied.

(4) Modified Asset Test

This test requires, first, that both corporations, ZML and ZWL, must hold more than 50% of their assets in a combination of active business assets and shares or debt of a connected corporation throughout the 24 months preceding the present time. This condition is met by ZML with its 40% active business assets in combination with its 30% in shares of the subsidiary. The subsidiary meets the test with its 90% active business assets. Then, one of the corporations must meet the 90% test with a combination of its active business assets and shares or debt of a connected corporation throughout the preceding 24 months. This condition is met by the subsidiary with its active business assets.

Since all of the relevant tests have been met, the shares of ZML are qualified small business corporation shares.

¶13,360 Capital Gains Deduction

The 1985 Budget introduced a lifetime cumulative deduction for net taxable capital gains (net TCGs) for individuals (other than trusts) resident in Canada. The 1992 federal Budget restricted the deduction on gains from most real property disposed of after February 1992 (referred to as non-qualifying property) and the 1994 federal Budget completely eliminated the deduction for dispositions of all property after February 22, 1994, except for shares of qualifying small business corporations (QSBC) and qualified farm property.

¶13,365 Overview

The current capital gains deduction applies to individuals (other than trusts) who are resident in Canada throughout the year. There is, however, a deeming provision which extends the definition of a resident, for purposes of this section only, to include individuals who were resident at any time in the year and who were resident in Canada throughout either the preceding or the following taxation year. This rule allows an individual who has either ended or commenced residence in Canada during a particular year to qualify for the deduction on a disposition. ITA: 110.6(5)

The deduction applies to net taxable capital gains (the excess of taxable capital gains (TCGs) over allowable capital losses (ACLs)) on QSBC shares and qualified farm and fishing property. Also eligible for the deduction are capital gains reserves on dispositions of farm and fishing property or QSBC shares.

The maximum fractional capital gains deduction for qualified small business corporation shares and/or qualified farm and fishing property is $375,000 (i.e., ½ × $750,000). Note that in this text the term "exemption" is used to refer to the full amount of a capital gain and the term "deduction" is used to refer to the fractional amount of the capital gain that gives rise to the actual deduction from taxable income of an individual.

¶13,370 Computation of deduction

The amount of the deduction is discretionary and is limited by cumulative taxable capital gains net of allowable capital losses, that is, net taxable capital gains exposed to tax over an individual's lifetime, to the extent of the maximum permissible deduction. The limit on the QSBC capital gains deduction in a particular year is set at the least of three amounts.

(a) Unused lifetime deduction — This restriction limits the deduction to $375,000 [$400,000 in 2014] (½ × $750,000 [$800,000 in 2014]) *minus* all previously claimed capital gains deductions adjusted to the appropriate inclusion rate for the year in which the limit is being computed.[10] ITA: 110.6(2.1)(*a*)

(b) Annual gains limit — This amount is the lesser of the net taxable capital gains (net TCG) for the particular year and the amount of the net TCG that would be determined only taking into account dispositions of QSBC shares and qualified farm property after 1984, *minus* ITA: 3(*b*), 110.6(1)

(i) net capital losses of other years deducted in the current year, and

(ii) the allowable business investment losses (ABILs) realized during the year whether or not they are claimed. ITA: 3(*d*)

[10] The following table shows the factor to use to convert a capital gains deduction claimed in a prior year to the inclusion rate in use after October 17, 2000:

Year capital gain deduction claimed	*Inclusion rate in that year*	*Factor to convert to post–Oct. 17, 2000 period*
1985–1987	½	no adjustments
1988–1989	⅔	½ / ⅔ = ¾
1990–Feb. 27, 2000	¾	½ / ¾ = ⅔
Feb. 28, 2000–Oct. 17, 2000	⅔	½ / ⅔ = ¾
After Oct. 17, 2000	½	

(c) Cumulative gains limit — This amount aggregates, without an adjustment for changing inclusion rates, *all the components* of the "annual gains limit for all years" *minus* two additional amounts: ITA: 110.6(1)

(i) the capital gains deductions claimed in preceding years, without an adjustment for changing inclusion rates, and

(ii) the cumulative net investment loss (CNIL) — a limitation which is defined below.

This description of the computation is relatively conceptual, rather than technical. However, it is complicated by the allowable business investment loss (ABIL) rules and the cumulative net investment loss (CNIL).

¶13,375 Allowable business investment losses

As previously discussed in Chapter 7, allowable business investment losses are deductible from all sources of income. The definition of a business investment loss includes capital losses arising from the disposition of shares and debts of a small business corporation (SBC). Reference should be made to the material on allowable business investment losses in Chapter 7. In particular, Figure 7-2 should be reviewed for details on the treatment of a business investment loss. ITA: 3(*d*), 39(1)(*c*), 248(1)

¶13,380 Cumulative net investment loss (CNIL)

As previously indicated, there is a further restriction to the "cumulative gains limit" which reduces the potential availability of the capital gains deduction. This reduction is basically the excess of property expenses over property income. The purpose of this restriction is to remove the perceived double benefit of capital gains offset by a capital gains deduction and non-capital sources of income offset by excess investment expenses at the same time.

The cumulative net investment loss (CNIL) is defined as the excess of investment expenses (a defined term) over investment income (another defined term) aggregated for all years after 1987. ITA: 110.6(1)

"Investment expense" which, generally, relates to expenses incurred to earn investment income is defined as the sum of:

(a) all property expenses, including interest (either actually incurred or deemed to have been paid by section 80.5) and carrying charges, deducted by the taxpayer in computing property income, with certain resource property exceptions;

(b) certain specific expenses, including interest and carrying charges, deducted from the income of a partnership of which the taxpayer is a specified member (basically defined as a limited partner or a member who is not actively engaged in the business or a similar business on a regular, continuous, and substantial basis);

(c)(i) losses incurred in the year from a partnership of which the taxpayer is a specified member, and

(ii) limited partnership loss carryovers deducted in the year; ITA: 111(1)(*e*)

(d) ½ of certain resource and exploration expenses incurred and flowed through by a corporation or incurred by a partnership of which the taxpayer is a specified member;

(e) losses from all property and, specifically, rental properties (i.e., business losses from rental properties) and capital cost allowance for a certified production deducted by the taxpayer or a partnership of which he or she was an *ordinary* member; and

(f) net capital losses carried over and deducted against certain net taxable capital gains of the carryover year that were not eligible for the capital gains deduction.

"Investment income" is defined as the sum of: ITA: 110.6(1)

(a) income from all property, including recaptured capital cost allowance that was considered to be income from property and not from a business;

(b) income from a partnership of which the taxpayer is a specified member;

(c) ½ of certain recovered exploration and development expenses;

(d) income (including recapture) from rental property of the taxpayer or partnership of which he or she was an ordinary member;

(e) the interest element of certain annuities included in income; and ITA: 56(1)(*d*), 56(1)(*d*.1), 60(*a*)

(f) net taxable capital gains on certain property not eligible for the capital gains deduction.

¶13,385 Other related provisions

At this stage, there are several other provisions related to the capital gains deduction worth noting.

- An individual must file a tax return if a taxable capital gain was realized or a disposition of capital property has occurred in the taxation year. ITA: 150(1)

- An individual who is resident in Canada for only part of a taxation year is deemed to be a resident throughout the entire year if he or she is resident in Canada throughout the immediately preceding or the following taxation year. ITA: 110.6(5)

- A capital gains deduction in respect of a particular transaction is denied forever where the capital gain was not reported on a filed tax return or where the tax return is not filed within a one-year grace period and where the Minister can prove the taxpayer knowingly or under circumstances amounting to gross negligence did not report the gain. ITA: 110.6(6)

- A number of anti-avoidance provisions prevent abuses of the capital gains deduction. ITA: 110.6(7)–(12)

- An individual may elect to use the capital gains deduction in respect of qualified small business corporation shares when the corporation becomes a public corporation because its shares are listed on a designated stock exchange in Canada. ITA: 48.1

Example Problem 13-11

Lenny disposed of some shares of Underground Airways Limited, a QSBC, in January 2013 and realized a taxable capital gain of $305,000. In addition, he received $13,750 in interest and incurred a net rental loss of $2,500.

Also in 2013, Lenny realized a business investment loss (before any adjustment) of $50,000. ITA: 39(9)

Prior to 2013, Lenny received cumulative interest income of $6,875 and grossed-up taxable dividends of $1,563. He also incurred a cumulative net rental loss of $12,500 and carrying charges of $12,188. In 1999, Lenny realized taxable capital gains of $25,000 on QSBCS which he fully offset with the capital gains deduction. Lenny had no previous capital transactions.

— REQUIRED

Compute Lenny's capital gains deduction for 2013 supported by all the necessary calculations. ITA: 110.6(2.1)

— SOLUTION

(A) Unused lifetime deduction in 2013:			
Lifetime cumulative deduction limit [$400,000 in 2014]			$375,000
Less: prior years' deductions:			
Capital gains deduction claimed in 1999		$25,000	
Less: adjustment to 2013 inclusion rate		8,333	16,667
Unused lifetime capital gains deduction available for 2013			$358,333
(B) Annual gains limit for 2013:			
Net TCGs for 2013(1)			$288,333
Minus:			
Net CLs deducted in 2013		Nil	
ABILs realized in 2013(1)		$ 8,333	8,333
Annual gains limit for 2013			$280,000
(C) Cumulative gains limit for 2013:(2)			
Cumulative net TCGs ($25,000 + $288,333)			$313,333
Minus:			
Cumulative net capital losses deducted		Nil	
Cumulative ABILs realized		$ 8,333	
Cumulative CGs deductions		25,000	
Cumulative net investment loss:			
Investment expenses:			
Cumulative interest expenses and carrying charges	$12,188		
Cumulative net rental losses ($2,500 + $12,500)	15,000		
	$27,188		
Investment income:			
Cumulative investment income ($6,875 + $1,563 + $13,750)	(22,188)	$ 5,000	$ 38,333
Cumulative gains limit for 2013			$275,000
(D) Least of (A), (B), (C)			$275,000

— NOTES TO SOLUTION

(1) Allowable business investment loss (ABIL):

BIL before reduction			$ 50,000	ITA: 39(9)
Disallowed portion — Lesser of:				
(a) BIL		$50,000		
(b) Adjustment factor × cumulative CG deductions of previous years (4/3 × $25,000)	$33,333			
Minus: Cumulative disallowed BIL of prior years	Nil	$33,333		
Lesser of (a) and (b)			(33,333)	
BIL after adjustment			$ 16,667	
ABIL (1/2 × $16,667)			$ 8,333	

Allowable capital loss (ACL):	
Disallowed portion of BIL	$ 33,333
ACL (½ × $33,333)	$ 16,667
Net TCG for 2013:	
TCG	$305,000
Less: ACL	16,667
Net TCG	$288,333

(2) The components of the cumulative gains limit are not adjusted for inclusion rate changes over the period of accumulation.

¶13,390 Attribution Through a Corporation

Since the attribution rules for spouses and minors have been extended to apply to loans affecting such individuals, corporations have become the obvious vehicle to attempt income splitting among family members. Consider the situation where the low-income spouse incorporates a company using a nominal amount of his or her own funds. The high-income spouse then loans to the corporation a large amount of money through a non-interest bearing note. Income earned on these loans and subsequently paid out in the form of dividends is not caught by the attribution rules since these provisions deal with individuals and trusts only. Hence, the Act contains a series of rules to attribute back to the transferor income in the form of a deemed interest receipt on property transferred or loaned to a corporation.

ITA: 74.1(1), 74.1(2)

ITA: 74.4

These rules only apply during the period in which there were "designated persons" who benefit from the transfer or loan to a corporation and the corporation was not a small business corporation (SBC) as discussed above in relation to qualified small business corporation shares. A designated person is the transferor's spouse or a minor who is either not at arm's length with the transferor or who is a niece or nephew of that individual. The designated person must also be a specified shareholder defined, generally, as a person who owns at least 10% of the shares of any class of the corporation. Note that a small business corporation is one that, by definition, would generate mostly active business income which, if earned on a direct transfer or loan of funds, would not be subject to attribution. Also, note how designated persons are the same individuals to whom direct transfers or loans would be subject to income attribution. If the corporation, with designated persons as shareholders, ceased to be a small business corporation at some point during the year, the imputed interest benefit would be prorated for the part of the year that the corporation was not an SBC.

ITA: 248(1) "designated persons"

ITA: 74.5(5), 251

ITA: 248(1) "specified shareholder"

¶13,395 Imputed interest

The corporate attribution rule applies where one of the main purposes of the transfer or loan may reasonably be considered to be to reduce the income of the transferor and to benefit a designated person. If this rule applies, the transferor is deemed to receive, as *interest*, the following amount:

ITA: 74.4(2)

- interest imputed on the outstanding amount of the loan or transferred property at the basic prescribed rates in effect during the year, for the period when the corporation was not an SBC and designated persons were specified shareholders

ITA: 74.4(3); ITR: 4301(*c*)

less the sum of:

- interest received by the transferor in respect of the loan or transfer,
- all grossed-up taxable dividends received by the transferor on shares received as consideration for the loan or transfer of property, and

- dividends that are received by the designated person and that can reasonably be considered to be part of the benefit sought to be conferred then the amount included in the designated person's "split income". ITA: 120.4

The term "outstanding amount", which is the base for the deemed interest receipt, is defined to be the fair market value of property "transferred or loaned" to the corporation in excess of the fair market value of consideration, other than "excluded consideration", *received* from the corporation in return. The term "excluded consideration" is defined to mean debt, shares of the corporation or rights to receive debt or shares of the corporation. Note that excluded consideration does *not* reduce the base for computing the deemed interest receipt because only consideration *other than* excluded consideration reduces the outstanding amount. Consideration that reduces the outstanding amount would include, for example, cash. While debt or shares received from the corporation do not reduce the outstanding amount, interest and the grossed-up amount of taxable dividends paid to the transferor on the debt or shares received reduce the deemed interest receipt to the transferor, as shown by the above computational formula. ITA: 74.4(3) ITA: 74.4(1)

Note how the reduction of the deemed interest income is as a result of the payment by the corporation of actual income that would attract tax in the hands of the transferor or lender and, therefore, would reduce the benefits of income splitting. It should also be noted that the deemed interest income included in the individual's income is not allowed as a deduction to the corporation.

Example Problem 13-12

Fresser and Klutz are spouses. Fresser operates a construction company, Fresser Inc., which uses all of its assets (fair market value of $1.2 million) in its active business carried on in Calgary. Klutz received an inheritance of $100,000 which he invested in Fresser Inc. 4% preference shares on January 1, 2011. Fresser Inc. immediately used this cash to pay down a bank loan. On January 1, 2012, Fresser Inc. ceased operations and liquidated its assets leaving $200,000 of cash in the company until January 31, 2013, when the 4% preference shares were redeemed for $100,000. In each of 2011 and 2012, dividends of $4,000 were paid on the preference shares.

— REQUIRED

Determine the amount attributed to Klutz over the three years, assuming that the prescribed interest rate is a constant 3% and that dividends were paid from the low-rate income pool.

— SOLUTION

2011: The rule would not attribute any amount to Klutz since Fresser Inc. was a "small business corporation" throughout the taxation year of Klutz. Klutz's income would include only the $4,000 of dividends paid on the preference shares. ITA: 74.4(2)

2012: Fresser Inc. was not a small business corporation throughout 2010; therefore, the rule applies as follows: ITA: 74.4(2)

Interest imputed at 3% on the outstanding amount ($100,000 × 3%)	$3,000
Less: 1.18 × dividends received ($4,000 × 1.18)	(4,720)
Interest received	Nil
Amount deemed to be received by Klutz as interest	Nil

Klutz will report the $4,000 of dividends ($4,720 grossed up) received from the company.

2013: Fresser Inc. was not a small business corporation during that portion of the year when the shares were outstanding; therefore, the rule applies as follows: ITA: 74.4(2)

Interest imputed at 3% on the outstanding amount ($100,000 × 3% × 30/365)	$ 247
Less: 1.18 × of dividends received	Nil
Interest received	Nil
Amount deemed to be received by Klutz as interest	$ 247

Remember that there is a purpose test. It may be possible to argue that, since the purpose of the loan was to finance an active business, these attribution rules do not apply. On the other hand, it may be argued that since the money was used in the business for such a short period (13 months) that "one of the main purposes of the transfer" must have been to reduce the income of Klutz and benefit Fresser. ITA: 74.4(2)

¶13,400 Income-Splitting Tax ("Kiddie Tax")

A special income tax computed at the top marginal rate is levied on specified income of an individual under 18 years of age at the end of a calendar year. This income-splitting tax was discussed in Chapter 6, as an alternative to the income attribution rules, for income of a minor from business sources that is not subject to the attribution rules. ITA: 120.4

The tax is levied, generally, on the following types of income:

- taxable dividends, taxable capital gains, and other shareholder benefits derived from unlisted shares of any corporation, received either directly or indirectly through a trust or partnership; and
- income, including taxable capital gains, from a trust or partnership which derives income from the business of providing property or services to a business carried on by a relative of the minor or a corporation in which the relative is a specified shareholder.

The tax on split income extends to taxable capital gains that are included in the income of a minor and that are from a disposition of shares to a non-arm's length person if taxable dividends on such shares would have been subject to the tax on split income. An amount equal to two times these taxable capital gains will be deemed to be dividends, but not eligible dividends, and subject to kiddie tax at the top marginal rate. Since capital gains are considered to accrue from reinvested retained earnings, it would otherwise be possible to avoid the tax on split income in a non-arm's length situation by retaining income rather than paying it out as a dividend. ITA: 120.4(4), (5)

Income subject to this income-splitting tax is deductible from the Part I income of the minor, so that it is not taxed twice in the hands of the minor. Similarly, income such as the dividend income, subject to the income-splitting tax, is not subject to attribution and, therefore, not taxed additionally in the hands of the transferor of the dividend-paying shares. The only tax credits permitted in computing the income-splitting tax are the dividend tax credit and the foreign tax credit. If a parent was active in the business from which the income subject to the income-splitting tax was derived, then the parent is jointly liable for the income-splitting tax payable by the minor. ITA: 20(1)(*ww*)

The income-splitting tax is not applicable to: ITA: 120.4(1) "excluded amount"

- minors who have no parent who is resident in Canada at any time in the year;
- income from property and taxable capital gains from the disposition of property inherited by a minor from a parent; and
- income from property and taxable capital gains from the disposition of property inherited by a minor from anyone else if, during the year in which the minor receives the income, the minor is:

- in full-time attendance at a post-secondary educational institution, or
- eligible for the disability tax credit.

To the extent that income is subject to the "kiddie tax", that same income is not subject to the regular attribution rules. In addition, if taxable dividends are subject to kiddie tax, then they may reduce the deemed interest penalty calculated for corporate attribution purposes. ITA: 56(5), 74.4(2)(*g*), 74.5(13)

¶13,500 GENERAL ANTI-AVOIDANCE RULE UNDER THE INCOME TAX ACT

¶13,510 The Statutory Provision

¶13,515 Purpose

The technical notes released on June 30, 1988 to explain this provision when it was first introduced made the following statement: ITA: 245

> New section 245 of the Act is a general anti-avoidance rule which is intended to prevent abusive tax avoidance transactions or arrangements but at the same time is not intended to interfere with legitimate commercial and family transactions. Consequently, the new rule seeks to distinguish between legitimate tax planning and abusive tax avoidance and to establish a reasonable balance between the protection of the tax base and the need for certainty for taxpayers in planning their affairs.

The main statement of the general anti-avoidance rule (GAAR), or provision, in essence, provides that the tax benefit that results from an avoidance transaction is denied. In order to determine the amount of the tax benefit that is denied, the provision indicates that the tax consequences of the transaction to a person will be determined as is reasonable in the circumstances. ITA: 245(2)

¶13,520 Defined terms

The term "avoidance transaction" is defined as any transaction that by itself or as part of a series of transactions (i.e., a "step transaction") results in a tax benefit, unless the transaction can reasonably be considered to have a *bona fide* purpose other than obtaining the tax benefit. The technical notes indicate that "the vast majority of business, family or investment transactions will not be affected by proposed (as it was then) section 245 since they will have *bona fide* non-tax purposes". The notes go on to state that "a transaction will not be considered to be an avoidance transaction because, incidentally, it results in a tax benefit or because tax considerations were significant, but not the primary purpose for carrying out the transaction". On the other hand, the notes indicate that: ITA: 245(3)

> Ordinarily, transitory arrangements would not be considered to have been carried out primarily for *bona fide* purposes other than the obtaining of a tax benefit. Such transitory arrangements might include an issue of shares that are immediately redeemed or the establishment of an entity, such as a corporation or a partnership, followed within a short period by its elimination.

The term "tax benefit" is defined to mean "a reduction, avoidance or deferral of tax or other amount payable under this Act or an increase in a refund of tax or other amount under this Act". According to the technical notes, "the references to 'other amount payable under this Act' and 'other amount under this Act' are intended to cover interest, penalties, the remittance of source deductions, and other amounts that do not constitute tax". The term "tax consequences" is, also, defined and is necessary, as indicated previously, to determine the amount of the benefit that will be denied. The actual determination of the tax consequences is provided by a rule which sets out some of the methods by which a benefit will be denied. ITA: 245(1) ITA: 245(5)

¶13,525 Limitation

A limitation on the application of the GAAR is provided. In the overview commentary on the GAAR, the technical notes make the following statement: ITA: 245(4)

> Transactions that comply with the object and spirit of other provisions of the Act read as a whole will not be affected by the application of this general anti-avoidance rule. For example, a transaction that qualifies for a tax-free rollover under an explicit provision of the Act, and that is carried out in accordance not only with the letter of that provision but also with the spirit of the Act read as a whole, will not be subject to new section 245. However, where the transaction is part of a series of transactions designed to avoid tax and results in a misuse or abuse of the provision that allows a tax-free rollover, the rule may apply. If, for example, a taxpayer, for the purposes of converting an income gain on a sale of property into a capital gain, transfers the property, on a rollover basis to a shell corporation in exchange for shares in a situation where new section 54.2 of the Act does not apply and subsequently sells the shares, the new section could be expected to apply.
>
> The new rule applies as a provision of last resort after the application of the other provisions of the Act, including specific anti-avoidance measures.

¶13,530 Examples in the technical notes

The commentary in the technical notes states that "the application of new subsection 245 [*sic*] must be determined by reference to the facts in a particular case in the context of the scheme of the Act". The notes then provide the following three examples of planning that would not be affected by the GAAR. ITA: 245(4)

> . . . the attribution provisions of the Act set out detailed rules that seek to prevent a taxpayer from transferring property by way of a gift and thereby transferring income to a spouse or minor children. A review of the scheme of these provisions indicates that income splitting is only of concern in transfers of property involving spouses or children under 18 years of age. The attribution rules are not intended to apply to other transfers of property such as gifts to adult children. This can be discerned from a review of the scheme of the Act, its relevant provisions and permissible extrinsic aids. Thus, a straightforward gift from a parent to his adult child will not be within the scope of section 245 either because it is made primarily for non-tax purposes or because it may reasonably be regarded as not being an abuse of the provisions of the Act. If, however, the gift is made so that the adult child acquires an investment and, through a series of transactions, disposes of it and subsequently transfers the proceeds, including any income therefrom, to the parent, proposed section 245 should apply where the purpose of the transaction is the reduction, avoidance or deferral of tax. (Note that subsection 56(4.1) deals with this type of avoidance where a *loan* is made to a related person.)
>
> As another example, "estate freezing" transactions whereby a taxpayer transfers future growth in the value of assets to his children or grandchildren will not ordinarily be avoidance transactions to which the proposed rules would apply despite the fact that they may result in a deferral, avoidance or reduction of tax. Apart from the fact that many of these transactions may be considered to be primarily motivated by non-tax considerations, it would be reasonable to consider that such transactions do not ordinarily result in a misuse or abuse given the scheme of the Act and the recent enactment of subsection 74.4(4) of the Act to accommodate estate freezes. (See also IC 88-2, paragraph 10.)
>
> Another example involves the transfer of income or deductions within a related group of corporations. There are a number of provisions in the Act that limit the claim by a taxpayer of losses, deductions and credits incurred or earned by unrelated taxpayers, particularly corporations. The loss limitation rules contained in subsections 111(4) to (5.2) of the Act that apply on a change of control of a corporation represent an important example. These rules are generally restricted to the claiming of losses, deductions and other amounts by unrelated parties. There are explicit exceptions intended to apply with respect to transactions that would allow losses, deductions or credits earned by one corporation to be claimed by related Canadian corporations. In fact, the scheme of the Act as a whole, and the expressed object and spirit of the corporate loss limitation rules, clearly permit such transactions between related corporations where these transactions are otherwise legally effective and comply with the letter and spirit of these exceptions. Therefore, even if these transactions may appear to be primarily tax-motivated, they ordinarily do not fall within the scope of section 245 since they usually do not result in a misuse or abuse. (See also IC 88-2, paragraph 8.)

¶13,535 Administration and application

Finally, it should be noted that the Act provides rules that pertain to the administration of the legislation in the GAAR. ITA: 245(6)–(8)

On October 21, 1988, the CRA issued an Information Circular which was intended to provide guidance on the application of the GAAR. It contains over 20 fact situations which are interpreted by the CRA in the context of the application of the GAAR. IC 88-2

The GAAR applies, not only to a misuse or abuse of the provisions of the *Income Tax Act*, but also to the provisions of the *Income Tax Regulations*, the *Income Tax Application Rules*, or a tax treaty.

A paper,[11] which resulted from a panel discussion held at the 1989 Annual Conference of the Canadian Tax Foundation, presented a "GAAR Decision Tree" to outline the logic that can be used to determine whether the GAAR would apply. Exhibit 13-13 attempts to diagram the logic used.

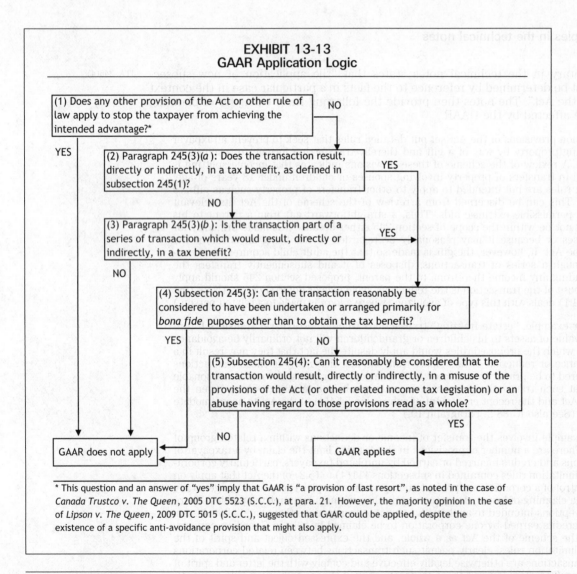

EXHIBIT 13-13
GAAR Application Logic

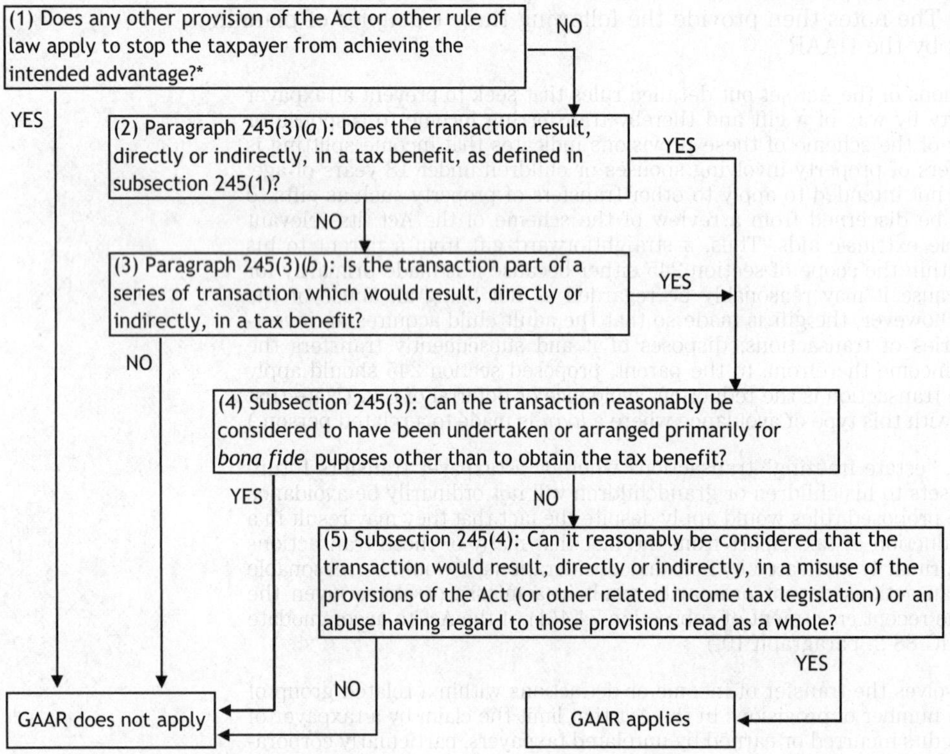
(1) Does any other provision of the Act or other rule of law apply to stop the taxpayer from achieving the intended advantage?*
NO
YES
(2) Paragraph 245(3)(a): Does the transaction result, directly or indirectly, in a tax benefit, as defined in subsection 245(1)?
YES
NO
(3) Paragraph 245(3)(b): Is the transaction part of a series of transaction which would result, directly or indirectly, in a tax benefit?
YES
NO
(4) Subsection 245(3): Can the transaction reasonably be considered to have been undertaken or arranged primarily for bona fide puposes other than to obtain the tax benefit?
YES
NO
(5) Subsection 245(4): Can it reasonably be considered that the transaction would result, directly or indirectly, in a misuse of the provisions of the Act (or other related income tax legislation) or an abuse having regard to those provisions read as a whole?
YES
NO
GAAR does not apply
GAAR applies

* This question and an answer of "yes" imply that GAAR is "a provision of last resort", as noted in the case of *Canada Trustco v. The Queen*, 2005 DTC 5523 (S.C.C.), at para. 21. However, the majority opinion in the case of *Lipson v. The Queen*, 2009 DTC 5015 (S.C.C.), suggested that GAAR could be applied, despite the existence of a specific anti-avoidance provision that might also apply.

[11] Robert D. Brown, Robert Couzin, Cy M. Fien, William R. Lawlor and William J. Strain, "GAAR and Tax Practice: More Questions than Answers", *1989 Conference Report: Report of the Proceedings of the Forty-First Tax Conference*, Canadian Tax Foundation, Toronto, 1989, pp. 11:3-4.

¶13,540 Federal Court of Appeal — OSFC Holdings Ltd.

¶13,545 The findings

The appeal by the taxpayer in *OSFC Holdings Ltd. v. The Queen* was the first decision of the Federal Court of Appeal on the GAAR.[12] After a thorough analysis of the GAAR, the court dismissed the taxpayer's appeal. It held that a series of transactions resulted in a tax benefit. The court upheld the finding of the Tax Court that the primary purpose of the transaction was to obtain a tax benefit. It also found that the transactions in question violated a clear and unambiguous general policy of the Act and, hence, concluded that the avoidance transaction resulted in an abuse of the provisions of the Act read as a whole. In June 2002, the Supreme Court of Canada refused to grant OSFC Holdings Ltd. leave to appeal. 2001 DTC 5471 (F.C.A.)

¶13,550 Application of OSFC case analytical framework

The analytical framework used in the *OSFC* case was applied in the Crown's appeal in *The Queen v. Canadian Pacific Limited*. First, the court concluded that there was a tax benefit. The court, then, upheld the Tax Court finding that the primary purpose of the transaction in question was not to minimize tax. Although the latter finding was sufficient to dismiss the Crown's appeal, the court considered the argument that there had been an abuse of the provisions of the Act read as a whole on the basis that the transaction in question contravened a policy of the Act. This argument was rejected. The court concluded that the conditions for the GAAR did not apply to the facts of this case.[13] 2002 DTC 6742 (F.C.A.)

The three-step analytical framework developed by the Federal Court of Appeal in the *OSFC* case was applied in the case of *The Queen v. Imperial Oil Limited*. The following summary of the three steps is quoted from the *Imperial Oil* case, in the indicated paragraphs. 2004 DTC 6044 (F.C.A.)

1. First, a court must determine if there is a "tax benefit", as defined. If there is not, GAAR will not apply and the inquiry ends [par. 34]. ITA: 245(3)
2. If there is a "tax benefit", a court must take the second step and determine whether there is an "avoidance transaction", as defined. If there is no "avoidance transaction", GAAR will not apply and, again, the inquiry ends [par. 34]. ITA: 245(3)
3. If the transaction confers a "tax benefit" and constitutes an "avoidance transaction", a court must take the third step and determine whether the transaction is a "misuse" or an "abuse". This inquiry involves taking two smaller steps [par. 35]. ITA: 245(4)

   (a) First, a court must determine "if it may reasonably be considered that the transaction would not result directly or indirectly in a misuse"[14] of the provisions of the Act. To determine if there has been a misuse, a court must identify the object, or underlying policy or policies, of the relevant provision or provisions of the Act, and decide if the avoidance transaction is contrary to those objectives or policies. If it is, the transaction constitutes a misuse and GAAR applies [par. 36].

   One must infer from the statutory language the policy, if any, on which the relevant provisions of the Act are unambiguously based. This exercise in statutory interpretation must be undertaken with the assistance of such extrinsic aids as: judicial statements, Hansard, ministerial or departmental statements, explanatory notes, bulletins, circulars, texts, periodicals and others [par. 49].

   (b) However, if there is no misuse, the second smaller step must be taken. This requires a court to decide if the transaction is an abuse, having regard to the provisions of the Act, other than those dealing with GAAR, when read as a whole.

[12] An extensive commentary on this case by Thomas B. Akin appears in *Tax Topics*, Number 1546, CCH Canadian Limited, October 25, 2001, pp. 5-8.

[13] The Crown's appeals were also dismissed in the cases of *The Queen v. Produits Forestiers Donohue Inc.*, 2002 DTC 7512 (F.C.A.), and *The Queen v. Jabin Investments Ltd.*, 2003 DTC 5027 (F.C.A.). In both of these cases the OSFC framework was applied in the analysis of the applicability of the GAAR. In the latter case, the "clear and unambiguous" threshold for policy was clarified.

[14] In 2004, the wording of this part of the provision was changed to remove the word "not" and, in effect, to change the test to a positive test for the application of the GAAR.

The question is whether the transaction contravenes any policy or policies underlying the provisions of the Act as a whole. If it does, the transaction may constitute an abuse for the purpose of GAAR [par. 37].

While the Act does not expressly provide that the policy must be "clear and unambiguous", this is implicit in the language of the GAAR, which permits the exemption for a tax avoidance scheme where "it may reasonably be considered that the transaction would not result directly or indirectly in a misuse of the provisions of this Act or an abuse having regard to the provisions of this Act . . . read as a whole [based on former wording of the provision]." [par. 39] ITA: 245(4)

Thus, if the scheme may reasonably be considered not to result directly or indirectly in a misuse or an abuse, GAAR does not apply: in effect, the taxpayer is given the benefit of any doubt. Consequently, for GAAR to apply it must be clear that the provisions of the Act are being misused or the Act as a whole is being abused. It is not enough that a court might reasonably consider them to be misused or abused [par. 40].

¶13,560 Supreme Court of Canada — Canada Trustco and Mathew et al.

On October 19, 2005, the Supreme Court of Canada (S.C.C.) released two decisions on the GAAR, *Canada Trustco Mortgage Co.* and *Mathew et al.* (sub nom. *Kaulius*). 2005 DTC 5523 (S.C.C.); 2005 DTC 5538 (S.C.C.)

¶13,565 The transactions

In the *Canada Trustco* case, the taxpayer had purchased trailers and then leased them back to the vendor. A major purpose for this transaction was to allow Canada Trustco to claim CCA on these trailers while the arrangements were structured so the taxpayer had little or no financial risk. While there are special rules in the Act to counter this type of transaction, trailers were exempt from them. The CRA reassessed under the GAAR to deny the CCA claimed. The Supreme Court of Canada decision held in favour of the taxpayer, dismissing the Crown's appeal. 2005 DTC 5523 (S.C.C.)

In the *Mathew* case, Standard Trust, an insolvent trust company, transferred a loan portfolio, with accrued losses of $52 million, to a partnership that had arm's length partners. The losses were then realized and allocated to these arm's length partners. The CRA reassessed under the GAAR to deny the losses claimed. The Supreme Court of Canada held in favour of the Crown, dismissing the taxpayer's appeal. 2005 DTC 5538 (S.C.C.)

¶13,570 Application of the OSFC tests and interpretations

In both cases, the Court applied the three tests set out in *OSFC Holdings* with the following results.

Test 1: There was a tax benefit.

Test 2: There was an avoidance transaction.

Test 3: The issue before the Court was whether there was a misuse of the provisions of the Act or an abuse of those provisions read as a whole.

The Supreme Court stated, at paragraph 66 of the *Canada Trustco* case, 2005 DTC 5523 (S.C.C.)

[t]he approach to s. 245 of the *Income Tax Act* may be summarized as follows.

1. Three requirements must be established to permit application of the GAAR:

(1) A tax benefit resulting from a transaction or part of a series of transactions (s. 245(1) and (2));

(2) that the transaction is an avoidance transaction in the sense that it cannot be said to have been reasonably undertaken or arranged primarily for a *bona fide* purpose other than to obtain a tax benefit; and

(3) that there was abusive tax avoidance in the sense that it cannot be reasonably concluded that a tax benefit would be consistent with the object, spirit or purpose of the provisions relied upon by the taxpayer.

2. The burden is on the taxpayer to refute (1) and (2), and on the Minister to establish (3).
3. If the existence of abusive tax avoidance is unclear, the benefit of the doubt goes to the taxpayer.
4. The courts proceed by conducting a unified textual [words used], contextual [context of provision] and purposive [purpose of analysis] analysis of the provisions giving rise to the tax benefit in order to determine why they were put in place and why the benefit was conferred. The goal is to arrive at a purposive interpretation that is harmonious with the provisions of the Act that confer the tax benefit, read in the context of the whole Act.
5. Whether the transactions were motivated by any economic, commercial, family or other non-tax purpose may form part of the factual context that the courts may consider in the analysis of abusive tax avoidance allegations under s. 245(4). However, any finding in this respect would form only one part of the underlying facts of a case, and would be insufficient by itself to establish abusive tax avoidance. The central issue is the proper interpretation of the relevant provisions in light of their context and purpose.
6. Abusive tax avoidance may be found where the relationships and transactions as expressed in the relevant documentation lack a proper basis relative to the object, spirit or purpose of the provisions that are purported to confer the tax benefit, or where they are wholly dissimilar to the relationships or transactions that are contemplated by the provisions.
7. Where the Tax Court judge has proceeded on a proper construction of the provisions of the *Income Tax Act* and on findings supported by the evidence, appellate tribunals should not interfere, absent a palpable and overriding error.

The following are some of the other comments made in the *Canada Trustco* case that might shed some light on the third requirement for the application of the GAAR.

> [36] The third requirement for application of the GAAR is that the avoidance transaction giving rise to a tax benefit be abusive. The mere existence of an avoidance transaction is not enough to permit the GAAR to be applied. . . .
>
> [39] . . . Parliament could not have intended this two-step approach, which on its face raises the impossible question of how one can abuse the Act as a whole without misusing any of its provisions. We agree with the Tax Court judge, in the present case [2003 DTC 587], at para. 90, that "[i]n effect, the analysis of the misuse of the provisions and the analysis of the abuse having regard to the provisions of the Act read as a whole are inseparable." . . .
>
> [40] There is but one principle of interpretation: to determine the intent of the legislator having regard to the text, its context, and other indicators of legislative purpose. The policy analysis proposed as a second step by the Federal Court of Appeal in *OSFC* is properly incorporated into a unified, textual, contextual, and purposive approach to interpreting the specific provisions that give rise to the tax benefit.
>
> [41] The courts cannot search for an overriding policy of the Act that is not based on a unified, textual, contextual and purposive interpretation of the specific provisions in issue. First, such a search is incompatible with the roles of reviewing judges. The *Income Tax Act* is a compendium of highly detailed and often complex provisions. To send the courts on the search for some overarching policy and then to use such a policy to override the wording of the provisions of the *Income Tax Act* would inappropriately place the formulation of taxation policy in the hands of the judiciary, requiring judges to perform a task to which they are unaccustomed and for which they are not equipped. Did Parliament intend judges to formulate taxation policies that are not grounded in the provisions of the Act and to apply them to override the specific provisions of the Act? Notwithstanding the interpretative challenges that the GAAR presents, we cannot find a basis for concluding that such a marked departure from judicial and interpretative norms was Parliament's intent.
>
> [42] Second, to search for an overriding policy of the *Income Tax Act* that is not anchored in a textual, contextual and purposive interpretation of the specific provisions that are relied upon for the tax benefit would run counter to the overall policy of Parliament that tax law be certain, predictable and fair, so that taxpayers can intelligently order their affairs. Although Parliament's general purpose in enacting the GAAR was to preserve legitimate tax

minimization schemes while prohibiting abusive tax avoidance, Parliament must also be taken to seek consistency, predictability and fairness in tax law. These three latter purposes would be frustrated if the Minister and/or the courts overrode the provisions of the *Income Tax Act* without any basis in a textual, contextual and purposive interpretation of those provisions.

[43] For these reasons we conclude, as did the Tax Court judge, that the determinations of "misuse" and "abuse" under s. 245(4) are not separate inquiries. Section 245(4) requires a single, unified approach to the textual, contextual and purposive interpretation of the specific provisions of the *Income Tax Act* that are relied upon by the taxpayer in order to determine whether there was abusive tax avoidance.

. . .

[45] . . . An abuse may also result from an arrangement that circumvents the application of certain provisions, such as specific anti-avoidance rules, in a manner that frustrates or defeats the object, spirit or purpose of those provisions. By contrast, abuse is not established where it is reasonable to conclude that an avoidance transaction under s. 245(3) was within the object, spirit or purpose of the provisions that confer the tax benefit.

. . .

[52] In general, Parliament confers tax benefits under the *Income Tax Act* to promote purposes related to specific activities. For example, tax benefits associated with business losses, CCA and RRSPs, are conferred for reasons intrinsic to the activities involved. Unless the Minister can establish that the avoidance transaction frustrates or defeats the purpose for which the tax benefit was intended to be conferred, it is not abusive.

¶13,580 The Saga Continues — Decisions Since Canada Trustco

The following two cases have been decided by the Supreme Court since *Canada Trustco*.

¶13,585 Earl Lipson and Jordan B. Lipson (2006 DTC 2687 (T.C.C.)/2007 DTC 5172 (F.C.A.)/2009 DTC 5015 (S.C.C.))

This is a case about the conversion of interest expense from being non-deductible to being deductible. Earl and his wife, Jordanna, agreed to purchase a home for $750,000. A few months later, on closing, Jordanna borrowed $560,000 from the bank to buy shares of a family company from Earl. Earl agreed to repay the loan the next day. Jordanna and Earl then borrowed an additional $560,000 from the bank, secured by a mortgage on their new home, to pay off the original loan to buy the shares. By not electing under subsection 73(1) on the sale of shares from Earl to Jordanna, there was no gain on this transaction and the attribution rules would then cause any dividend income and interest expense to be reported in Earl's return. The judge concluded that there was a "tax benefit" and that it could not be said "to have been reasonably undertaken or arranged primarily for a *bona fide* purpose other than to obtain a tax benefit", as required by the Act. 2006 DTC 2687 (T.C.C.)

As a result, the third test of misuse or abuse was the determining factor. On this issue, at the Tax Court of Canada, the judge found, at paragraphs 31 and 32,

> This case is, in my view, an obvious example of abusive tax avoidance. Whatever commercial or other non-tax purpose, if any, is served by transferring Earl's shares to Jordanna, it is subservient to the objective of making the interest on the purchase of the house deductible by Earl.
>
> In this case I am not looking to any "overarching policy" that supersedes the specific provisions of the ITA. I am simply looking at the obvious purpose of the various provisions that are relied on and have concluded that those purposes have been subverted and those sections turned on their heads. I mentioned above that section 245 must itself be subjected to a textual, contextual and purposive analysis. If there ever was a case at which section 245 was aimed, it is this one.

The Federal Court of Appeal confirmed the decision of the Tax Court of Canada in the *Lipson* case. The Supreme Court of Canada also held that the GAAR applied. It was a majority decision of four judges with two dissenting opinions given by three judges. It was the use of 2007 DTC 5172 (F.C.A.), 2009 DTC 5015 (S.C.C.)

the attribution rules and not the interest deductibility rules that resulted in the conclusion that the GAAR applied in this particular case.

¶13,586 Copthorne Holdings Ltd. v. The Queen, 2012 DTC 5007 (S.C.C.)

In a unanimous decision by a full panel of nine judges, the Supreme Court of Canada applied the GAAR to a series of transactions involving a form of amalgamation that resulted in the preservation of paid-up capital (PUC) that was paid to a non-resident shareholder as a tax-free return of capital, thereby avoiding withholding tax on a dividend. An avoidance transaction was held by the Court to exist; it was further held that the transaction defeated the purpose of a provision of the Act and was, therefore, abusive.

In its decision, the Court addressed the three questions that it had set out in *Canada Trustco* to be decided in a GAAR analysis:

(1) Was there a tax benefit?

(2) Was the transaction giving rise to the tax benefit an avoidance transaction?

(3) Was the avoidance transaction giving rise to the tax benefit abusive?

In its analysis of the third question, the Court made the following comments of a general nature, at the indicated paragraphs:

> [65] The most difficult issue in this case is whether the avoidance transaction was an abuse or misuse of the Act. The terms abuse or misuse might be viewed as implying moral opprobrium regarding the actions of a taxpayer to minimize tax liability utilizing the provisions of the *Income Tax Act* in a creative way. That would be inappropriate. Taxpayers are entitled to select courses of action or enter into transactions that will minimize their tax liability (see *Duke of Westminster*).
>
> [66] The GAAR is a legal mechanism whereby Parliament has conferred on the court the unusual duty of going behind the words of the legislation to determine the object, spirit or purpose of the provision or provisions relied upon by the taxpayer. While the taxpayer's transactions will be in strict compliance with the text of the relevant provisions relied upon, they may not necessarily be in accord with their object, spirit or purpose. In such cases, the GAAR may be invoked by the Minister. The GAAR does create some uncertainty for taxpayers. Courts, however, must remember that s. 245 was enacted "as a provision of last resort" ([*Canada*] *Trustco*, at para. 21).
>
> [67] A court must be mindful that a decision supporting a GAAR assessment in a particular case may have implications for innumerable "everyday" transactions of taxpayers. A decision affecting PUC is a good example. There are undoubtedly hundreds, and perhaps thousands of share transactions each year in which the PUC of a certain class of shares may be a relevant consideration. Because of the potential to affect so many transactions, the court must approach a GAAR decision cautiously. It is necessary to remember that "Parliament must . . . be taken to seek consistency, predictability and fairness in tax law" ([*Canada*] *Trustco*, at para. 42). As this Court stated in *Trustco*:
>
> > Parliament intends taxpayers to take full advantage of the provisions of the *Income Tax Act* that confer tax benefits. Indeed, achieving the various policies that the *Income Tax Act* seeks to promote is dependent on taxpayers doing so. [para. 31]
>
> [68] For this reason, "the GAAR can only be applied to deny a tax benefit when the abusive nature of the transaction is clear" ([*Canada*] *Trustco*, at para. 50). The court's role must therefore be to conduct an objective, thorough and step-by-step analysis and explain the reasons for its conclusion.
>
> [69] In order to determine whether a transaction is an abuse or misuse of the Act, a court must first determine the "object, spirit or purpose of the provisions . . . that are relied on for the tax benefit, having regard to the scheme of the Act, the relevant provisions and permissible extrinsic aids" ([*Canada*] *Trustco*, at para. 55). The object, spirit or purpose of the provisions has been referred to as the "legislative rationale that underlies specific or interrelated provisions of the Act" (V. Krishna, *The Fundamentals of Income Tax Law* (2009), at p. 818).
>
> [70] The object, spirit or purpose can be identified by applying the same interpretive approach employed by this Court in all questions of statutory interpretation — a "unified

textual, contextual and purposive approach" ([*Canada*] *Trustco*, at para. 47; *Lipson v. Canada*, [2009 DTC 5015] 2009 SCC 1, [2009] 1 S.C.R. 3, at para. 26). While the approach is the same as in all statutory interpretation, the analysis seeks to determine a different aspect of the statute than in other cases. In a traditional statutory interpretation approach the court applies the textual, contextual and purposive analysis to determine what the words of the statute mean. In a GAAR analysis the textual, contextual and purposive analysis is employed to determine the object, spirit or purpose of a provision. Here the meaning of the words of the statute may be clear enough. The search is for the rationale that underlies the words that may not be captured by the bare meaning of the words themselves. However, determining the rationale of the relevant provisions of the Act should not be conflated with a value judgment of what is right or wrong nor with theories about what tax law ought to be or ought to do.

[71] Second, a court must consider whether the transaction falls within or frustrates the identified purpose ([*Canada*] *Trustco*, at para. 44). As earlier stated, while an avoidance transaction may operate alone to produce a tax benefit, it may also operate as part of a series of transactions that results in the tax benefit. While the focus must be on the transaction, where it is part of a series, it must be viewed in the context of the series to enable the court to determine whether abusive tax avoidance has occurred. In such a case, whether a transaction is abusive will only become apparent when it is considered in the context of the series of which it is a part and the overall result that is achieved (*Lipson*, at para. 34, *per* LeBel J.).

[72] The analysis will then lead to a finding of abusive tax avoidance: (1) where the transaction achieves an outcome the statutory provision was intended to prevent; (2) where the transaction defeats the underlying rationale of the provision; or (3) where the transaction circumvents the provision in a manner that frustrates or defeats its object, spirit or purpose ([*Canada*] *Trustco*, at para. 45; *Lipson*, at para. 40). These considerations are not independent of one another and may overlap. At this stage, the Minister must clearly demonstrate that the transaction is an abuse of the Act, and the benefit of the doubt is given to the taxpayer.

[73] When applying this test, there is no distinction between an "abuse" and a "misuse". Instead, there is a single unified approach ([*Canada*] *Trustco*, at para. 43 . . .

¶13,600 Proposals To Require Information Reporting of Tax Avoidance Transactions

As a result of a proposal in the March 4, 2010 federal Budget, draft legislation was introduced on August 27, 2010 to implement a reporting regime requiring taxpayers to report aggressive tax avoidance transactions. These rules had not been enacted at the time of writing and are not intended to replace the GAAR.

The objective of the proposed reporting regime is to help the CRA to identify potentially abusive transactions and their participants. The determination of whether a transaction or series of transactions must be reported will be based on the existence of specified "hallmarks" of aggressive tax planning. These hallmarks are thought to reflect certain situations that are present in tax avoidance transactions of interest. Identification of these transactions through the reporting requirements may lead to a challenge under existing law such as the GAAR.

Under these proposals, a "reportable transaction" is defined as a transaction that is classified as an "avoidance transaction" under the GAAR or a transaction that is part of a series of transactions that includes an avoidance transaction if, at any time, two of the following three hallmarks come into existence in respect of the transaction or series:

(1) a promoter or tax adviser in respect of the transaction is entitled to fees that are to any extent

- based on the amount of the tax benefit from the transaction,
- contingent upon the obtaining of a tax benefit from the transaction, or
- attributable to the number of taxpayers who participate in the transaction or who have been provided access to advice given by the promoter or adviser regarding the tax consequences from the transaction;

(2) a promoter or tax adviser in respect of the transaction requires "confidential protection" with respect to the transaction. In this respect, a "confidential protection" is defined as any limitation on disclosure to any other person, including the CRA, that is placed by a promoter or tax adviser on the taxpayer, or on a person who entered into the transaction for the benefit of the taxpayer, in respect of the details or structure of the avoidance transaction that give rise to any tax benefit;

(3) the taxpayer or the person who entered into the transaction for the benefit of the taxpayer obtains "contractual protection" in respect of the transaction (otherwise than as a result of a fee described in the first hallmark).

A penalty for failure to report will be imposed.

¶13,800 REVIEW QUESTIONS

(1) Mr. Smith owns a small manufacturing company that has suddenly become very profitable. This year his accountant has told him to declare a bonus to himself of approximately $150,000 in order to reduce his corporate income to the business limit. His dilemma is that he also needs the money in his business in order to finance expansion. What should he do?

(2) Mr. Jones owns a distributing company that is earning well over $500,000 each year. He has been declaring a bonus to himself each year but is now rethinking this strategy. What items should he consider when deciding whether to pay the bonus or leave the money in the company? Assume that the provincial corporate income tax rate is 13% on their income in excess of the small business deduction limit.

(3) What is the range of fiscal year-ends that might be chosen to allow the owner of a company to declare a bonus and be taxed on it personally in either of two calendar years?

(4) What are the five criteria for the deductibility of bonus accruals as decided in the *Totem Disposal* case?

(5) Mr. Chow is the sole shareholder of Chocobar Inc. His wife's brother has just come to him and asked to borrow some money in order to start up his professional accounting practice. Mr. Chow has decided to have Chocobar Inc. lend his wife's brother $20,000 on October 31, 2013, with interest only for the first two years and then principal payments of $10,000 per year starting in the third year. The fiscal year-end of the company is December 31. Discuss the tax implications of the loan.

(6) Ms. Jones is the President and sole shareholder of a construction company. She has two vice-presidents who are not related to her. As part of their compensation package she has agreed that all employees of the company are entitled to an interest-free loan from the company of up to $25,000. Ms. Jones herself has taken her $25,000 loan and bought a boat. Comment.

(7) If your province of residence were to declare a tax holiday for all CCPCs, what impact would this have on compensation for your owner-manager clients?

(8) How much personal tax will a single individual pay on $30,000 of dividend income if that is his or her only source of income and his or her only non-refundable tax credit is his or her personal credit. Assume the gross-up of 18% applies.

(9) Ms. Simpson owned 10% of the shares of a small business corporation that went out of business. Six months after it ceased business she sold her shares to an arm's length person, Mr. X, for $1. When she went to claim a loss on her investment she did not know how much she could write off. In order to have the loss treated as an ABIL, the company needed to be a small business corporation at the time of sale and at that time it did not have any assets used in an active business. She has not used any of her capital gains exemption before. Can you clarify this situation for her?

(10) What does the phrase "all or substantially all" mean?

(11) A corporation that has had 40% of its assets invested in term deposits for the last two years, and the balance in active business assets, qualifies as a "small business corporation" but not a "qualified small business corporation". Do you agree or disagree? Explain.

(12) Mr. Smith incorporated his company 20 years ago for $100 of share capital. It has prospered since then and it now has some excess capital. He has decided to have his wife set up an investment holding company and his company will lend her company $100,000 of cash for her to invest and thereby split income. Will the attribution rules apply?

¶13,825 MULTIPLE CHOICE QUESTIONS

Question 1

Stan owns 100% of the shares of S Ltd. which has a December 31 year end. He is also an employee of S Ltd. On January 1, 2013, S Ltd. loaned Stan $200,000 interest-free to assist him in purchasing a new home. Stan signed a promissory note for the loan. Under the terms of the note, the loan is to be repaid in five equal annual instalments commencing January 1, 2014. Such a loan is not available to other employees. Which *one* of the following statements is *true* under current tax administrative practice?

(A) Stan will have $200,000 included in his income in 2013.

(B) Stan will have $160,000 included in his income in 2013.

(C) An imputed interest benefit will be calculated for 2013 using a rate not in excess of the rate in effect at January 1, 2013, as the loan was used to purchase a home.

(D) The portion of the loan not repaid by December 31, 2014, will be included in Stan's income in 2015.

Question 2

In 2013, S Ltd., which has a December 31 year end, made the following loans to shareholders. All of the shareholders are resident in Canada and are not related to S Ltd. This was the first time that these shareholders had received a loan or had become indebted to S. Ltd. Since S Ltd. was not in the business of lending money, it was very careful, in each case, to ensure that *bona fide* arrangements were made at the time the loan was made for repayment of the loan within a reasonable time. Taking all this into consideration, which one of the following loan principal amounts will be included in the borrower's income in 2013?

(A) A loan to Mrs. A, a vice-president and 20% shareholder. The loan was made to assist Mrs. A in the purchase of newly issued shares of S Ltd. The loan was made on April 1, 2013, and repaid on April 1, 2014. No other employees have received similar loans.

(B) A loan made to B Ltd., a corporation which is a 20% shareholder of S Ltd. The loan was used to help B Ltd. repurchase some of its shares for cancellation and pay off a bank loan.

(C) A loan to Mrs. C, a vice-president and 20% shareholder. The loan was made to assist Mrs. C in the purchase of a home. The loan was made on April 1, 2013, and will be repaid on April 1, 2015. No other employees have received similar loans.

(D) A loan to Mr. D, an S Ltd. vice-president and 5% shareholder. Mr. D deals at arm's length with S Ltd. The loan was made to assist Mr. D in the purchase of a home computer for employment use. Five other employees of the company currently work at home and have received similar loans. None of the other employees are shareholders. Mr. D's loan was made on April 1, 2013, and will be repaid on April 1, 2015.

Question 3

In computing the net income on the financial statement of Fortelli Inc. for its year ended December 31, 2013, bonuses of $300,000 were accrued. On August 15, 2014, $100,000 of the bonus was paid to the owner-manager, and the remaining $200,000 of bonuses were paid to the sales staff on August 31, 2014. Which one of the following statements is *true*?

(A) If the $100,000 bonus, due to a related party, was not paid by December 31, 2015, it would be included in Fortelli Inc.'s income in the year 2016.

(B) The $100,000 bonus is not deductible in 2013, but the $200,000 bonus is deductible.

(C) An election is available to deem the bonus paid and loaned back to the corporation. This election can be used if the bonuses are not going to be paid by the appropriate deadline.

(D) The $300,000 bonus is not deductible in 2013.

Question 4

The Act contains a general anti-avoidance provision often referred to as the GAAR. Which one of the following statements concerning the GAAR is *false*?

(A) The tax benefit that results from an avoidance transaction will be denied.

(B) When the GAAR is applied, a penalty will be assessed, in addition to the tax owing plus interest.

(C) An avoidance transaction is any transaction that results in a tax benefit, unless the transaction can reasonably be considered to have a *bona fide* purpose other than obtaining the tax benefit.

(D) The GAAR applies to transactions that result in a misuse or abuse of the Act read as a whole.

Question 5

The general anti-avoidance provision, GAAR, is most likely to apply to which *one* of the following transactions?

(A) As part of an estate freeze, Bill had a trust for his adult children acquire 80% of the common shares of B Ltd. Until then, Bill had owned all the shares of B Ltd., a successful grocery retail outlet. Each year B Ltd. pays dividends to the trust which are paid to the children. The dividends are received by the children tax-free due to the dividend tax credit, since, as university students, they have no other income.

(B) Sam transferred his unincorporated pizza business, on tax-deferred basis, to a corporation, for the sole purpose of reducing tax by claiming the small business deduction.

(C) Paul gave his son a gift of $10,000 and the son invested it in dividend-paying shares. His son does not pay tax on the dividend income as he is a 19-year-old student with little other income. Paul will celebrate his 65th birthday two years after his son graduates. It is anticipated that Paul will receive a birthday gift of $10,000 from his son at that time.

(D) Mary owns all the shares of M Ltd., a CCPC which carries on an active business. For M Ltd.'s taxation year ended June 30, 2012, Mary accrued herself a bonus of $700,000 which reduced M Ltd.'s taxable income to $300,000.

Question 6

Mrs. Boehmer owns all the Class A common shares of a corporation which has an investment portfolio worth $500,000. The corporation has no other assets and has a December 31 year-end. On January 1 of the current year, Mr. Boehmer (Mrs. Boehmer's husband) subscribed for $1 million of Class B shares of the corporation and paid for them in cash. The purpose of this transaction was to income-split with his wife. The corporation earned $10,000 during the year (assume 2014) and paid a $10,000 cash dividend to Mrs. Boehmer. Assuming the prescribed rate is 3% throughout the year, what is the minimum amount of income that Mr. Boehmer must report in the year in respect of his investment in the corporation?

(A) $10,000

(B) $11,800

(C) $15,000

(D) $30,000

Question 7

Ms. Prentice owns P Ltd., a Canadian-controlled private corporation with assets worth $4 million and liabilities amounting to $1 million. Sixty per cent of its assets are used in an active business carried on in Canada by the corporation and 20% are used in an active business carried on in Canada by a corporation controlled by Ms. Prentice's brother. The remaining assets (non-active business assets) earn investment income. Which of the following is the minimum amount of non-active business assets that P Co must sell in order for its shares to qualify as shares of a small business corporation? Assume that the after-tax proceeds on the sale will be used to pay off some of the corporation's liabilities.

(A) None

(B) $400,000

(C) $444,445

(D) $1,333,333

¶13,850 EXERCISES

Exercise 1

ITA: 78

Slipit Ltd. declared a bonus payable of $10,000 to Mr. Schneider, its president and majority shareholder, on September 30, 2013, its fiscal year end. If the bonus is paid it will be subject to withholding tax in the amount of $3,500.

— *REQUIRED*

(A) If the corporation is to get a deduction with no future consequences for the bonus payable, by what date must the bonus be paid?

(B) What are the consequences of not paying the bonus by this date?

(C) Assume that, instead of a bonus, the amount owing to Mr. Schneider is rent, properly included on the cash basis, on the only rental property he owns and rents to the corporation:

(i) If the corporation is to get a deduction with no future consequences for the rent payable, by what date must the rent be paid?

(ii) What are the consequences of not paying the rent by this date?

(iii) How can these consequences be avoided without paying the rent?

Exercise 2

ITA: 15(2), 80.4

Mr. Nesbitt relocated his private business, Leverage-Lovers Limited, to Alberta from Ontario at the end of May 2013. As a result of the move, the corporation made the following loans on June 1, 2013 to Mr. Nesbitt, the president and majority shareholder:

(a) a $75,000 loan at 2% interest per year with a five-year term but amortized over a 25-year period to purchase a house in the new location;

(b) a $5,000 loan at 5% interest per year with no definite term to buy furniture for the new house; and

(c) a $10,000 loan with no interest but with a five-year term to buy previously unissued, fully paid shares from the corporation.

The corporation uses the calendar year as its fiscal year and by the end of 2014 the loans described were still outstanding. Any interest required to be paid on the loans at the indicated rates was paid in 2013. Assume that the prescribed rates applicable to shareholder loans during 2013 were: 1st quarter, 4%; 2nd quarter, 3%; 3rd quarter, 4%; and 4th quarter, 4%. Ignore the effects of the leap year, if applicable.

— *REQUIRED*

Discuss the tax consequences in 2013 of the loan described, if Mr. Nesbitt received the loans:

(A) by virtue of his employment;

(B) by virtue of his shareholdings.

Exercise 3

ITA: 15(2), 20(1)(*j*)

Mr. Sims is a shareholder of Wonder Ltd. which has a December 31 year-end. Consider the following transactions in his shareholder loan account:

Date	*Loan (repayment)*	*Balance*
Dec. 31/Year 1	—	Nil
Jan. 31/Year 2	$ 20,000	$ 20,000
Apr. 30/Year 2	25,000	45,000
June 30/Year 3	(15,000)	30,000
Sept. 30/Year 3	(17,000)	13,000
Mar. 31/Year 4	(12,000)	1,000
Nov. 30/Year 4	10,000	11,000
May 31/Year 5	(11,000)	Nil
Nov. 30/Year 5	23,000	23,000
July 31/Year 6	(14,000)	9.000
Dec. 31/Year 6	—	9,000

— REQUIRED

(A) If it is assumed that these transactions result in the conclusion that there is a series of loans and repayments, compute the principal amounts that must be included or the repayments that may be deducted for each of the years indicated according to the guidelines in IT-119R4.

(B) If there has not been a series of loans and repayments, how would the amounts differ from the above? How would you argue there was no series of loans and repayments?

Exercise 4

ITA: 15(2), 80.4; ITR: 4300

Colton Marlach is a major shareholder and senior executive of Burlon Ltd. He was required to use a car about 60% for the duties of his employment. On April 1, under a plan available to the five other senior executives of the corporation, he was granted a loan of $35,000 at a rate of interest of 3% *per annum* and agreed to annual payments on the anniversary day of $7,000 for principal and monthly payments of interest at the end of each month. During the year, he faithfully made the monthly interest payments for seven months but neglected to make the interest payments for the last two months of the year.

— REQUIRED

What are the income tax consequences to the taxpayer? Assume that the prescribed rates were as follows:

first quarter	5%	third quarter	5%
second quarter	4%	fourth quarter	6%

Ignore the effects of the leap year, if applicable.

Exercise 5

ITA: 6(1)

Consider the data provided in Exhibit 13-4 in ¶13,100.

— REQUIRED

Analyze the situation if the business use of the car is 20,000 out of 30,000 km.

Exercise 6

ITA: 82(1), 117, 121, 123–125

Payton Hewitt is the sole shareholder and employee of Conduit Corporation Ltd. which operates a processing business in a province with a 4% corporate rate (i.e., a total corporate rate of 15%) on its income. The corporation has income of $20,000 before salaries and corporate taxes which is eligible for the small business deduction. Mr. Hewitt has no other income and has federal tax credits of $2,000 and provincial tax credits of $1,290. He requires all of the income generated by the business. Use the 18% gross-up for dividends paid after 2013.

— REQUIRED

Consider the following three remuneration alternatives:

(A) all salary,

(B) all dividends, and

(C) $10,000 in salary and the remainder in dividends.

Compare the net cash to Mr. Hewitt for these alternatives ignoring employment income deductions available to an employee. Can the best of these alternatives be improved upon?

Exercise 7

ITA: 82(1), 117, 121, 123–125

Aaron Storey is a sole proprietor generating $80,000 in income before taxes from a processing business operating in a province with a 4% corporate rate (i.e., a total corporate rate of 15%). He requires $25,000 before taxes for living expenses and has federal personal tax credits of $2,100 and provincial tax credits of $1,400. He has no other source of income or deductions (except as assumed for (B)(iii), below). The business has a December 31 taxation year-end.

— REQUIRED

(A) Compute the tax that would be paid if he continues to operate the business as an unincorporated proprietorship.

(B) Compare your answer in (A) with the total tax that would be paid if he incorporates the business and remunerates himself by the following alternative methods:

(i) $25,000 in salary;

(ii) $25,000 in dividends; and

(iii) $4,630 in salary and $20,370 in dividends. (Assume that the excess federal tax credits resulting from this case can be used against tax on other income.)

Ignore deductions available to employees. Use the 18% gross-up for dividends paid after 2013.

Exercise 8

ITA: 248(1)

Consider each of the following independent proportions of assets at fair market value. Assume the assets are owned by a Canadian-controlled private corporation. Active business assets refer to assets used principally in an active business carried on primarily in Canada.

	A	*B*	*C*	*D*
Active business assets	85%	50%	—	40%
Marketable securities	15	—	20%	20
Shares of a connected small business corporation	—	50	80	40
	100%	100%	100%	100%

— REQUIRED

Determine whether each of the above proportions meets the test of a small business corporation as defined in the Act.

Exercise 9

ITA: 110.6

Bobby Mills has provided you with the following information:

	2012	*2013*	*2014*
Taxable capital gains on sale of qualified small business corporation shares	$75,000	—	$300,000
Business investment loss (before ssec. 39(9) adjustment)	—	—	160,000
Interest income	—	$ 600	1,200
Grossed-up taxable dividends	—	140	—
Net rental income (loss)	—	(1,100)	(220)
Carrying charges	—	1,075	—

The 2012 taxable capital gain was fully offset by a capital gains deduction in that year.

— *REQUIRED*

Determine Bobby's capital gains deduction for 2014 supported by all the necessary calculations. Assume that there were no other capital transactions before 2012.

Exercise 10

ITA: 74.4

Mrs. Albert owns all of the outstanding common shares of a corporation, Prince Albert Inc., which operates a small retail store in Saskatoon. Her husband owns the building with a fair market value of $200,000, in which the store is located. He is planning to transfer it to Prince Albert Inc. in exchange for $60,000 of cash, a 5% demand note for $20,000 and preference shares for $120,000. The fair market value of the business assets (which are all of the assets excluding cash used to pay for the building) in the company immediately before the transfer is $600,000. Of the total space in the building, 20% is used in the retail business. The net rental income that Mr. Albert earned in the previous year was $20,000.

— *REQUIRED*

Determine the tax consequences, if any, to Mr. Albert for 2013, assuming the prescribed interest rate is a constant 4% and that the sale took place on January 1, 2013. The corporation's year-end is September 30. Dividends of $2,000 were paid on the preference shares in 2013. ITR: 4301(*c*)

Exercise 11

ITA: 245

Gangster Production Ltd., a Canadian-controlled private corporation, paid its shareholder-manager, Herb, a salary of $250,000 which reduced the corporation's income to $499,500 for the taxation year. The amount of the salary is considered to be reasonable.

— *REQUIRED*

Determine whether the general anti-avoidance rule (GAAR) would apply in this situation.

Exercise 12

Over the past two years, your client, a lawyer in sole practice, has developed several software packages for the preparation of legal contracts. At a recent small-business seminar, your client learned that she could pay her spouse and children a salary. By doing so, your client's total tax paid as a family unit would drop substantially.

— *REQUIRED*

If tax is avoided, how would the general anti-avoidance rule affect the transactions?

¶13,875 ASSIGNMENT PROBLEMS

Problem 1

ITA: 15(1), 18(1)

Mia Gibbons is a vice-president of Pump You Up Ltd., a private corporation she started and currently owns with three of her university colleagues. Mia has recently signed a lease for an upscale downtown condominium which she intends to move into next month. It has been agreed that Pump You Up Ltd. will pay the $2,000 monthly rental for the condominium.

— *REQUIRED*

Discuss the income tax consequences of this arrangement to Mia and to Pump You Up Ltd.

Problem 2

Kristie owns 35% of Big City Developments Inc. (BCD), which has a December 31 year end. She is also an employee of the company. On March 31, Year 1, she purchased her shares of BCD from treasury for $150,000. BCD lent her all the funds for the share purchase at an interest rate of 4%. She is required to repay the loan at the rate of $25,000 each January 1.

On May 15, Year 1, BCD loaned Kristie $75,000 to purchase a new motor home and boat. Since she is a significant shareholder, she was not required to repay any of the loan in Year 1 or Year 2. At the end of Year 3, Kristie repaid $25,000 of the loan.

— *REQUIRED*

Calculate the income tax implications to Kristie as a result of receiving these loans for Years 1, 2, and 3. Assume the prescribed rate of interest for shareholder loans was 6% throughout all the years. (Ignore the effects of a leap year, if applicable.)

Problem 3

ITA: 15(2), 20(1)(*j*), 20(1)(*q*), 67, 78, 80.4, 80.5, 147, 147.2

As the auditor for Skies Limited, a Canadian-controlled private corporation, you have discovered in your 2013 year-end audit several items that require further consideration. Mr. Scott is an 80% shareholder and president of the company which has a December 31 fiscal year-end.

The following items were expensed during the year:

Salary for Mr. Scott (assume equal to employment compensation)	$90,000
Royalty payable to Mr. Scott on material prepared for the corporation	54,000
Contribution to registered pension plan (money purchase plan) for Mr. Scott whose employee contributions are being matched by the corporation	3,000

The royalty was the only item not paid during the fiscal year. In fact, it was still unpaid at the time of the audit and Mr. Scott indicated to you that it could not be paid until sometime in 2014 when he anticipated that the company would have sufficient cash.

The records showed that the corporation had made several loans to Mr. Scott or to his son, age 30, who owns the other 20% of the shares of the corporation and is, also, an employee of the corporation. Each of the following was evidenced by a separate promissory note, duly signed and approved by the Board of Directors:

(a) a $180,000 non-interest bearing loan, dated August 1, 2013, repayable in $18,000 annual instalments, to permit Mr. Scott's son to purchase previously unissued, fully paid shares from the corporation at their fair market value;

(b) a $270,000 3% loan, dated June 1, 2013, repayable over 15 years in equal instalments of principal payable on the anniversary date, but with interest payable monthly, to enable Mr. Scott to purchase a new home, a few blocks from his old home; and

(c) a $24,000 4% loan, dated October 1, 2013, with no principal repayment arrangements, but with interest paid quarterly, to permit Mr. Scott to purchase a car to be used in his employment with the corporation.

Mr. Scott had repaid $4,800 of the car loan on May 31, 2014 and expressed the intention to repay $4,800 annually for four more years.

Any interest required to be paid on the loans at the indicated rates was paid in 2013. Assume the prescribed rates for 2013 were 4% for the first and second quarters, and 5% for the third and fourth quarters.

— *REQUIRED*

(A) Discuss the deductibility of expenses contained in the foregoing information (excluding the shareholder loans).

(B) Discuss the tax implications of the shareholder loans if Mr. Scott and his son received the loans by virtue of being:

(i) shareholders,

(ii) employees.

Support your answer with specific calculations where appropriate and provide reasons for your conclusions.

Problem 4

ITA: 15(2), 15(2.3), 15(2.4), 15(2.6), 20(1)(*j*), 80.4; ITR: 4300(7)

In 2013, Sunshine Publishing Ltd., a book publishing company with a fiscal year end on December 31, made a loan of $100,000 to Stuart Sunshine, the president and majority shareholder. Both Stuart and Sunshine Publishing Limited are Canadian residents.

This is the first loan that Stuart ever received from the company, and it helped him finance the purchase of a new home which was built just outside Toronto, 10 kilometres farther from the corporate headquarters than Stuart's previous home. The loan was made on May 1, 2013, and a mortgage agreement was signed on that date. This agreement requires that the $100,000 owing be repaid over five years in equal instalments of $20,000 on each anniversary date, starting on May 1, 2015, without interest. Early prepayments of principal are allowed.

Assume that the prescribed rates applicable to taxable benefits are: 3% for the first quarter of 2013, 4% for the second quarter, 5% for the third quarter, 4% for the fourth quarter and 3% for all of 2014. (Ignore the effects of a leap year, if applicable.)

— *REQUIRED*

(A) It is now December 2013 and Stuart has asked you to advise him on the tax consequences of the loan. It is not a company policy to make housing loans to employees and no other loans have been made to employees on similar conditions. What are the income tax consequences of this loan to Stuart in 2013 and 2014?

(B) If it was a company policy to make such loans to employees and other loans had been made to employees on similar terms and conditions, how would this change your answer to Part (A)?

(C) Assume the following facts: it was a company policy to make such loans to employees; other loans had been made to employees on similar terms and conditions; Stuart was a 9.5% shareholder rather than a majority shareholder; he was not related to any shareholders of the company; and the loan was to buy a rental property rather than a home. How would this change your answer to Part (B)?

Problem 5

ITA: 82(1), 117, 121, 123–125

Nancy Ball presently operates a retailing proprietorship with a December 31, year-end and makes $150,000 of net income for tax purposes annually. She is thinking of incorporating her business and has asked for your advice. She lives in a province where the provincial corporate tax rate is 5% of this type of federal taxable income. She has $2,100 of federal personal tax credits, $1,400 of provincial personal tax credits, and no other income.

— *REQUIRED*

(A) Estimate the personal taxes that Nancy would pay currently on $150,000 of business income compared with the amount of corporate and personal taxes that would be paid if she incorporated her business and only took out a salary of $50,000? Ignore all payroll taxes (e.g., Canada Pension Plan premiums) when making your estimates.

(B) Based on your calculations in (A), estimate the amount of personal tax that Nancy defers by keeping the remaining after-tax retained earnings in her company this year? [Hint: compute the additional personal tax that she would pay on a dividend equal to the corporation's after-tax retained earnings.] Use the 18% gross-up for dividends paid after 2013.

Problem 6

ITA: 82(1), 117, 121, 123–125

Mrs. Edwards presently operates a retailing proprietorship with a December 31 fiscal year end. She expects net income for tax purposes of $210,000 from the business. Since the business currently requires considerable amounts of working capital, she can only afford to withdraw $50,000 annually to meet her family's needs.

She lives in a province where the provincial corporate tax rate is 4% of federal taxable income. She is married and has two children (ages 18 and 19) who will start university soon. Her husband, who looks after their home, has no income and no interest in the business.

Mrs. Edwards has federal personal credits of $2,400, provincial personal tax credits of $1,600 and has no other income. She is contemplating the incorporation of her business. If she does so, she has been advised that if she makes all withdrawals from the business in the form of $50,000 salary, she will end up with enough after-tax to meet her family's needs. Although she is not considering it at present, she expects to pay dividends at a time when her other taxable income is at about the same level as it is currently.

— *REQUIRED*

(A) Compare the total tax that Mrs. Edwards would pay in 2013 on the $210,000 earned personally with the total tax that would be paid if she incorporated her business and only took out a salary of $50,000. Ignore any Canada Pension Plan premiums payable on the income.

(B) How much personal tax does Mrs. Edwards defer each year by keeping the remaining after-tax retained earnings in her company? [Hint: compute the additional personal tax that she would pay on a dividend equal to the corporation's after-tax retained earnings.]

(C) Compare the total income tax incurred by using a corporation to earn income with the personal tax incurred when the income is earned directly by Mrs. Edwards. Consider the corporate tax plus the personal tax on the salary and the dividend paid out of after-tax retained earnings. What is the absolute income tax cost or savings for Mrs. Edwards if she incorporates? Use the 18% gross-up for dividends paid after 2013.

(D) Assuming Mrs. Edwards chooses the incorporated form of business, what additional tax savings could be achieved by income splitting with her family members?

Problem 7

ITA: 82(1), 117, 121, 123-125.1

Iris Kroneman approaches you with the following information:

(a) She resides in a province with a 3% corporate tax rate (i.e., a total tax rate of 14%) where she owns and operates an incorporated business which generates income in the amount of $125,000 before taxes.

(b) She has federal personal tax credits of $2,100 and provincial personal tax credits of $1,400 including, among others, the marital status tax credit.

(c) She requires $65,000 before taxes for living expenses each year.

(d) She wants to maximize her Canada Pension Plan contributions each year. The CPP calculations are as follows:

Pensionable earnings (salary)	$51,100
Basic exemption	(3,500)
Maximum contributory earnings	$47,600
Employee rate	4.95%
Maximum contribution	$ 2,356

(e) She wants to make the maximum RRSP contribution based on the earned income you determine she should have. Assume that her earned income for 2012 is the same as for 2013.

— *REQUIRED*

Determine the tax consequences of the salary/dividend combination for Ms. Kroneman that will achieve her goals. Use the 18% gross-up for dividends paid after 2013.

Problem 8

ITA: 110.6

Karen owns all the common shares of K Ltd. which was incorporated in 1998 to hold her 85% interest in Cyber Corp. Cyber Corp. distributes computer equipment and games to retail stores in southern Ontario. Both corporations are CCPCs. The following is a balance sheet prepared as at December 31, 2013.

Cyber Corp.
Balance Sheet
as at December 31, 2013

Assets	
Cash	$ 4,500
Marketable securities (FMV $700,000)	300,000
Accounts receivable (FMV $780,000)	800,000
Inventory (FMV $920,000)	920,000
Prepaid expenses (FMV $1,000)	1,000
Fixed assets (FMV $150,000)	140,000
	$2,165,500
Liabilities & Shareholders' Equity	
Accounts payable and accrued liabilities	$ 600,000
Loans payable	400,000
Future income taxes	100,000
Share capital	1,000
Retained earnings	1,064,500
	$2,165,500

The relative values of Cyber Corp.'s assets have remained stable over the past three years. The marketable securities comprise Cyber Corp.'s investment portfolio which is not held as part of the corporation's business activities. The estimated value of the goodwill of the business is $200,000.

K Ltd. was recently offered $1,450,000 for the 85% interest in Cyber Corp. However, Karen has talked the prospective purchaser into buying the shares of K Ltd. instead of the shares of Cyber Corp., as she understands that by selling the shares of K Ltd. she is able to receive a tax-free $750,000 capital gain.

K Ltd. has term deposits of $100,000 in addition to the shares of Cyber Corp.

— *REQUIRED*

(A) Advise Karen as to whether the shares of K Ltd. are qualified small business corporation (QSBC) shares.

(B) If the shares of K Ltd. are not QSBC shares, then suggest a method for purifying K Ltd. and indicate the tax consequences of your recommendations.

Problem 9

ITA: 110.6

Rogo Dan owns all of the common shares of Julie Inc. which in turn owns all of the shares of two other companies, Opco Inc. and RE Inc. Opco Inc. carries on an active business in Sudbury. RE Inc. owns real estate, of which 100% is used by Opco Inc. in its business. All three corporations are CCPCs. The following are further details:

Julie Inc. assets:	
Shares of Opco Inc. at FMV	$850,000
Shares of RE Inc. at FMV	800,000
Portfolio investments at FMV	75,000
Opco Inc. assets and liabilities:	
Active business assets at FMV	$900,000
Term deposits	50,000
Liabilities	100,000
RE Inc. assets and liabilities:	
Land and building at FMV	$800,000
Portfolio investments at FMV	200,000
Mortgage	200,000

The proportion of assets in each of the companies has been constant over the past three years. Rogo has owned the shares of Julie Inc. for the past five years.

— *REQUIRED*

(A) Determine whether Julie Inc. meets each of the three tests necessary for its shares to be qualifying small business corporation shares.

(B) If the shares of Julie Inc. are not QSBC shares, then suggest ways of purifying Julie Inc. and indicate the tax consequences of your recommendations.

Problem 10

ITA: 110.6

Phil Zamboni realized taxable capital gains of $12,000 in 1999. This gain was offset by a capital gains deduction of $12,000 in that year.

In 2011, Zamboni received interest income of $825 and grossed-up taxable dividends of $200. He also incurred a net rental loss of $15,000 and carrying charges totalling $1,475 in 2011.

In 2012, Zamboni earned investment income of $200. He had a rental loss that year in the amount of $13,000 and carrying charges of $2,000. He also realized a business investment loss of $20,000 in December 2012.

In 2013, Zamboni sold the shares of Maps Unlimited Ltd., a qualified small business corporation, for a capital gain of $185,000 and he realized a capital loss of $21,000 on the sale of public company shares. He also received $1,650 in interest and incurred a net rental loss of $1,000 in 2013.

Zamboni had no other previous capital transactions, investment income, or investment expenses.

— *REQUIRED*

Compute Zamboni's capital gains deduction for 2013 supported by all the necessary calculations.

Problem 11

ITA: 74.4

Bob Smith incorporated Smith Inc. 20 years ago and owns all of the shares himself. Smith Inc. is a "small business corporation" which carries on an active business in Victoria, B.C. Thirteen years ago, Bob felt that he would like to involve his wife Betty in the share ownership and, on the advice of his accountant, Holdco Inc. was incorporated with Bob and Betty each owning 50 common shares which they bought for $1 each with their own funds. Bob then transferred his common shares of Smith Inc., which were worth $600,000, to Holdco Inc. on a tax-free basis. As consideration for the transfer, Bob received 6% non-cumulative preference shares with a fair market value of $600,000.

On July 1, 2013, Smith Inc. sold some property that was used in the active business for net proceeds of $150,000. This amount was then paid as a dividend from Smith Inc. to Holdco Inc. on the same day. Bob and Betty plan to have the corporation invest this amount and use it as capital for their retirement. After the sale of the property and the payment of the dividend to Holdco Inc., Smith Inc. has a fair market value of $800,000 and is still a "small business corporation". Bob received $6,000 in dividends on his preferred shares of Holdco Inc.

— *REQUIRED*

Determine the tax consequences of the 2013 transactions as they relate to the corporate attribution rules. Assume that the prescribed rate for 2013 was 4%. ITR: 4301(*c*)

Problem 12

ITA: 245

Consider each of the following independent fact situations.

(1) Adam Aref has contributed the maximum amount to an RRSP on the first business day of each year in respect of the previous year and shortly thereafter has withdrawn the funds.

(2) Bill Sheridan loaned his wife $1,000,000 five years ago through a non-interest bearing promissory note. His wife invested the funds in GICs and earned $80,000 of interest income which was properly attributed to him, except for any compound interest. Bill gave his wife another cash amount to cover the income tax on the compound interest.

(3) Wells Ltd. is owned 100% by Mrs. Hogart. Stieb Ltd. is owned by Mrs. Hogart's husband and minor children. Wells Ltd. made an interest-free loan out of its taxable surplus to Stieb Ltd. such that the corporate attribution rule does not apply. Stieb Ltd. used the proceeds of the loan to earn property income.

(4) Traub has $200,000 of investments and a mortgage on his personal home for a similar amount. Traub sold the investments, paid off the mortgage, and reborrowed to acquire the investments.

(5) Andy made a loan to his adult child's corporation, Vancouver Hockey Puck Ltd., in order to avoid attribution, since the corporation used the funds to earn property income.

— REQUIRED

Discuss whether the general anti-avoidance rule (GAAR) applies to the above situations.

Problem 13

ITA: 245; IC 88-2

Consider each of the following independent fact situations:

(1) An individual transfers his or her unincorporated business to a corporation primarily to obtain the benefit of the small business deduction.

(2) An individual provides services to a corporation with which he or she does not deal at arm's length. The company does not pay a salary to the individual because payment of a salary would increase the amount of a loss that the company will incur in the year.

(3) A taxable Canadian corporation, which is profitable, has a wholly owned taxable Canadian corporation that is sustaining losses and needs additional capital to carry on its business. The subsidiary could borrow the monies from its bank but the subsidiary could not obtain any tax saving in the current year by deducting the interest expense. Therefore, the parent corporation borrows the money from its bank and subscribes for additional common shares of the subsidiary and reduces its net income by deducting the interest from its business.

(4) Profitco and Lossco are taxable Canadian corporations. Lossco is a wholly owned subsidiary of Profitco. Lossco has non-capital losses that would be deductible if Lossco had income. In order to generate income in Lossco from which its non-capital losses may be deducted, Profitco borrows from its bank and uses the monies to subscribe for common shares of Lossco. Lossco lends these monies to Profitco at a commercial rate of interest. Profitco repays the bank. The amount of share subscription is not in excess of the amount of monies that Lossco could reasonably be expected to be able to borrow for use in its business on the basis solely of its credit from an arm's length lender.

(5) Each of two private corporations owns less than 10% of the common shares of a payer corporation that is to pay a substantial taxable dividend. The payer corporation will not be entitled to a dividend refund on the payment of the dividend. None of the corporations is related to any of the others. The private corporations form a corporation, Newco, transfer their shares of the payer corporation to Newco in exchange for common shares of Newco, and elect under subsection 85(1) (assume that this is done correctly to avoid tax on the transfer) in respect of the transfer. Following the transfer of the payer corporation's shares to Newco, Newco will be connected with the payer corporation. The payer corporation pays the dividend to Newco, free of Part IV tax. Newco pays the same amount to the private corporations as a dividend, free of Part IV tax. The primary purpose of the transfer of the shares is to avoid the Part IV tax which would be payable if the dividend were received directly by the private corporations.

(6) The owner of land inventory has agreed to sell the property to an arm's length purchaser. The purchaser wants to buy the property for cash, but the owner does not want to have the profits recognized in the year of sale. The owner sells the land inventory to an intermediary company deferring receipt of the proceeds of disposition of the land for several years after the date of sale. In this way, a reserve can be claimed under paragraph 20(1)(*n*). The intermediary sells the land to the third party for cash. The owner receives interest from the intermediary in respect of the monies received by the intermediary from the third party.

— REQUIRED

Discuss whether the part of the general anti-avoidance rule (GAAR) that asks the question "can it reasonably be considered that the transaction would not result, directly or indirectly, in a misuse of the provisions of the Act or an abuse having regard to the provisions of the Act read as a whole" applies to the above situations.

[For more problems and solutions thereto, see the DVD accompanying this book.]

¶13,880 ADVISORY CASES

Case 1: Aurora Collectibles

Herb Smith, the tax partner, has just talked to you about one of his clients, John Barwell. John has owned his retail store, Aurora Collectibles, for the past four years. Despite a recession, he has been able to do very well with the store by offering customers decorating advice along with the antiques and other unusual items that he sells. Last year, his store earned net income of $125,000.

When he first started the business, he set it up as a proprietorship and financed it with a loan of $100,000 from his wife, Alison, and a $75,000 bank operating loan. Currently, both of the loans remain unpaid, since both John and Alison enjoy a lifestyle that uses up all of their cash flow. Both John and Alison agree that they are going to improve their spending habits. They want John to pay off the bank operating loan from the business earnings. Once this is done, any excess cash will be used by John to invest in some property that they will eventually move the store into.

Herb wants you to identify the tax issues and tell him what analysis you propose to do to help John and Alison. He doesn't want you to get into the numbers yet.

Case 2: Charles Wong

Charles Wong, the vice-president of Arctic Oil Corporation, loves to minimize his income taxes. He spends much of his time hiring tax professionals to seek loopholes in the *Income Tax Act*. One loophole that he discovered was as follows.

Since Arctic Oil Corporation is in a loss position this year, he has found a way to defer much of his employment income to the next year. It won't cost the firm any money at all and his corporation is even willing to loan him funds (interest free) to live on.

Arrangements like this lead to legislation of rules for "salary deferral arrangements" and provisions for the taxation of benefits received as low-interest loans. However, the business-purpose and the substance-over-form concepts were enacted in the general anti-avoidance rule to place a broad restriction on taxpayer behaviour. Charles is having less and less success in his pursuit of loopholes in the tax system.

You have realized that Charles needs to have a better understanding of the difference between tax minimization and effective tax planning. Charles may have to change his objective of tax minimization. In your opinion, a better understanding of the concept of substance over form may help him to avoid being caught under the general anti-avoidance rule. As his tax adviser, help Charles to understand this by explaining:

- the difference between tax minimization and effective tax planning;
- why he should change his tax minimization objective; and
- how he can avoid the application of the GAAR.

Chapter 14

Rights and Obligations Under the Income Tax Act

TOPICS DISCUSSED

LEARNING GOALS

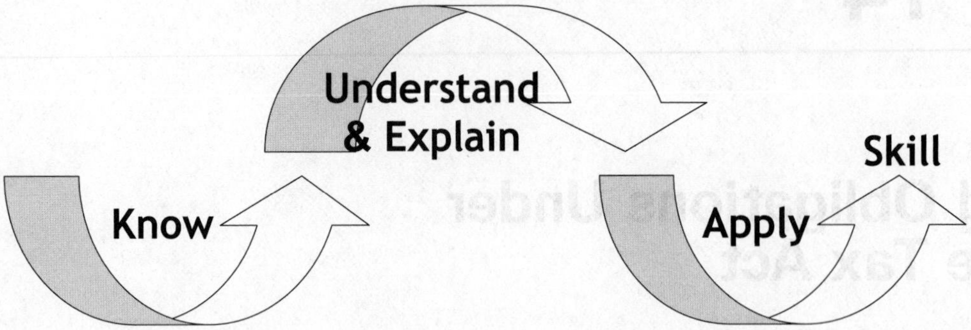

Know

By the end of this chapter you should know the basic provisions of the *Income Tax Act* and the *Excise Tax Act* that relate to the taxpayer compliance rules, the powers of the Canada Revenue Agency (CRA), and a taxpayer's rights and requirements on appeals. Completing the Review Questions (¶14,800) and Multiple Choice Questions (¶14,825) is a good way to learn the technical provisions.

Understand and Explain

You should understand and be able to explain:

- The requirements for taxpayers of income tax and registrants for GST/HST to make payments, file returns, and, possibly, incur penalties and interest, if the taxpayer does not comply with the legislation on an accurate and timely basis;
- The powers and obligations of the CRA to assess and reassess a taxpayer's or registrant's filings;
- The rights of taxpayers and registrants to appeal within deadlines; and
- The compliance rules applicable to employers, other payers of tax, and representatives of deceased taxpayers.

Completing the Exercises (¶14,850) is a good way to deepen your understanding of the material.

Apply

You should be able to apply your knowledge and understanding of the key elements of compliance pertaining to payment of tax and filing returns and appeals to achieve a client's goals of minimizing interest and penalties in the early stages of the process. Completing the Assignment Problems (¶14,875) is an excellent way to develop your ability to apply the material in increasingly complex situations.

OVERVIEW

Canadian income tax is based on the self-assessment system. The obligation of calculating taxable income and taxes payable and of paying taxes owing is that of the taxpayer and not the CRA. The *Income Tax Act* enumerates these obligations and also specifies the rights and powers of the CRA to enforce the system. Finally, taxpayers are given the right to appeal any actions taken by the CRA.

In the interest of efficiency and enforcement, the Act shifts some of the obligations from the taxpayer to other persons. These include employers and persons paying interest, dividends, and other payments to non-residents. The obligations of these persons to report payments and/or withhold tax and remit it to the CRA will also be discussed.

Under the *Excise Tax Act*, containing the legislation pertaining to the goods and services tax/harmonized sales tax (GST/HST), registrants are agents of the Crown and are responsible to collect tax on their taxable supplies. In addition, registrants are responsible to remit the net tax to the Receiver General and to meet certain reporting requirements.

The following chart outlines the major provisions of Part I, Division I of the *Income Tax Act*, pertaining to returns, assessments, payments and appeals discussed in this chapter.

PART I — DIVISION I
RETURNS, ASSESSMENTS, PAYMENT AND APPEALS

DIVISION

A	Liability for tax
B	Computation of income
C	Computation of taxable income
D	Taxable income earned in Canada by non-residents
E	Computation of tax
E.1	Minimum tax
F	Special rules applicable in certain circumstances
G	Deferred and other special income arrangements
H	Exemptions
I	**Returns, assessments, payment and appeals**
J	Appeals to the Tax Court of Canada and the Federal Court of Appeal

SUBDIVISION

SECTION

150	Returns
150.1	Electronic filing
151	Estimate of tax
152	Assessment
153-160.4	Payment of tax
161	Interest
161.1-161.2	Offset of refund interest and arrears interest
161.3-161.4	Small amounts owing
162-163.1	Penalties
163.2	Misrepresentation of a tax matter by a third party (civil penalty)
164	Refunds
165	Objections to assessments
166-167	General
168	Revocation of registration of certain organizations and associations

¶14,000 OBLIGATIONS OF THE TAXPAYER UNDER THE INCOME TAX ACT

¶14,010 Returns, Penalties, and Criminal Offences

¶14,015 Returns

¶14,015.10 *Filing deadlines*

The Act requires taxpayers to file returns in prescribed form and containing prescribed information, and specifies the date by which the returns must be filed as follows:

(a) Corporations — within six months after the end of the taxation year. ITA: 150(1)(*a*)

(b) Individuals — on or before April 30 of the next year, unless an individual or the individual's cohabiting spouse carried on a business in the year, in which case the filing deadline is June 15 of the following year. ITA: 150(1)(*d*)

(c) Deceased individuals — where an individual has died after October of a particular year and before the filing date for that year (April 30th or June 15th, as discussed above), the return for the particular year of the deceased must be filed by the legal representative by the later of:

(i) six months after the date of death, and

(ii) the usual filing date (i.e., April 30th or June 15th) following the particular year. ITA: 150(1)(*b*)

Where the death has occurred outside of these time limits, the normal filing dates as discussed in (b), above, apply.

The objective of these rules is to provide the legal representative of the deceased a minimum of six months after the date of death within which to file a return. These rules are discussed in more detail later in this chapter.

(d) Trusts or estates — within 90 days after the end of the taxation year. ITA: 150(1)(*c*)

The following summarizes the filing deadlines:

Income tax return	Filing date	
Corporations	6 months	ITA: 150(1)(*a*)
Individuals	April 30 or June 15	ITA: 150(1)(*d*)
Deceased individuals	Later of 6 months after death and the normal due date	ITA: 150(1)(*b*)
Trusts	90 days	ITA: 150(1)(*c*)

¶14,015.20 *Requirements to file a return*

Note that corporations that are resident in Canada or carry on business in Canada must file for each taxation year, but individuals are only required to file if one of the following applies:

(a) a balance of tax is owing for the year; ITA: 150(1.1)(*b*)(i)

(b) a capital property has been disposed of in the year; ITA: 150(1.1)(*b*)(ii)

(c) a non-resident individual has a taxable capital gain (e.g., claimed a capital gains reserve in the previous year); ITA: 150(1.1)(*b*)(iii)

(d) the individual's Home Buyer Plan (HBP) balance or Lifelong Learning Plan (LLP) is a positive amount; or ITA: 146.01(1), 146.02(1), 150(1.1)(*b*)(iv)

(e) a return is demanded by the Minister. ITA: 150(2)

Of course, individuals entitled to a refund due to over-withholding or refundable tax credits should file in any case. Low-income taxpayers should file to receive income-based benefits such as the GST/HST credit, the Canada Child Tax Benefit (CCTB) and the Guaranteed Income Supplement (GIS). If they do not file a tax return, they are not eligible to receive these amounts.

¶14,015.30 *Electronic and other filing options*

Individuals can file their personal returns electronically. The CRA encourages this by not mailing return forms to individual taxpayers who have used software to prepare their previous returns. The primary benefit of the electronic filing program for taxpayers is that processing of a tax refund can be much faster. The primary benefit to the CRA is the elimination of data inputting errors on their computer system. ITA: 150.1

Taxpayers who electronically file their tax return are not required to submit any receipts or other supporting documentation. The CRA, however, has the right to request supporting documentation, which, in fact, may delay the processing of the return.

Taxpayers are eligible to NETFILE their personal return if specified conditions are met.

While there are some exceptions, corporations that have annual gross revenues in excess of $1 million in a taxation year are required to file their income tax returns electronically. There are penalties for non-compliance. ITA: 150.1(2.1), 162(7.2)

¶14,018 Functional currency tax reporting

Under specified conditions, Canadian-resident corporations are allowed to report their Canadian tax results in their elected functional currency, other than the Canadian dollar. An election into the foreign functional currency for tax reporting removes the need to convert financial results into Canadian dollars. This is a benefit to corporate taxpayers that maintain their books and records for financial reporting purposes in a foreign currency. In these cases, the taxpayers would otherwise have to translate their financial results to Canadian dollars only to compute their Canadian tax liabilities. Opting for functional currency tax reporting in Canada reduces the distortions that may arise under conditions of currency volatility when foreign currency results have to be translated into Canadian dollars. For the purposes of the functional currency election, a "qualifying currency" is limited to the currency of the United States, the European Monetary Union, the United Kingdom, Australia, and a currency prescribed by regulation. ITA: 261

¶14,020 Penalties

¶14,020.10 *Failure to file return*

The Act provides penalties for failure to file a tax return as and when required. The penalty is 5% of the tax unpaid at the date on which the return was due to be filed. In addition, a further penalty of 1% of the unpaid tax is levied for each complete month that the return was late, for up to 12 months. ITA: 150(1) ITA: 162(1)(*a*) ITA: 162(1)(*b*)

A higher penalty is imposed for a taxpayer who has already been assessed a penalty for failure to file a return in any of the three preceding years. This penalty equals 10% of unpaid tax plus 2% per month, for up to 20 months. ITA: 162(2)

¶14,020.20 *Failure to report an amount of income*

A penalty of 10% of the income that a taxpayer has failed to report is imposed if there had been a previous failure to report in the preceding three years. However, no penalty will apply where the more severe penalty for false statements or omission (below) has been applied or where the previous failure was more than three years ago. ITA: 163(1) ITA: 163(2)

¶14,020.30 *False statements or omission*

Where taxpayers knowingly or under circumstances amounting to gross negligence under-report income, the Act imposes a penalty equal to the greater of $100 and 50% of the difference in tax liability. This provision is invoked frequently in cases involving omission of income on returns. The term "gross negligence" has been interpreted to include errors which amount to little more than careless omissions, if the taxpayer knew or should have known that the amount was omitted.[1] This provision would not be applied to amounts excluded because of an honest dispute as to their taxability. ITA: 163(2)

¶14,020.40 *Interplay of penalty provisions*

The interplay between the penalties for failure to report and for false statements or omission should be noted. On the first failure to report income, the first penalty would not apply, so the CRA could impose the penalty for false statements or omissions. On a repeated failure to report income within the three years specified, the CRA may have a choice between the failure to report penalty, which is based on 10% of income, and the false statement or omission penalty, which is based on 50% of tax. For example, if no tax is payable on unreported income, due to the availability of loss carryovers, the penalty for failure to report could be used to yield 10% of the unreported income. ITA: 163(1), 163(2) ITA: 163(1) ITA: 163(2) ITA: 163(1) ITA: 163(2) ITA: 163(1)

¶14,020.50 *Penalty for late or deficient instalments*

The Act imposes a penalty of 50% of the interest, charged on late or underpaid instalment payments, in excess of the greater of $1,000 or 25% of the interest calculated as if no instalments had been paid. This section applies if *any* instalment for the year is late or deficient, as discussed later in this chapter. ITA: 161, 163.1

¶14,020.60 *Civil penalties for misrepresentation of a third party*

The Act imposes civil penalties for misrepresentations by third parties in respect of another person's tax matters. The penalty is directed to tax professionals, appraisers and valuators and promoters of tax shelters and other tax minimization schemes. Two penalties are imposed. ITA: 163.2

The first penalty, referred to as the planner's penalty, is a penalty that is imposed when the third-party person makes or furnishes, or participates in the making of, or causes another person to make or furnish, a statement that the person knows, or would reasonably be expected to know but for circumstances amounting to "culpable conduct" (as defined in the ITA: 163.2(2) ITA: 163.2(1)

[1] See *Cowan v. M.N.R.*, 69 DTC 553 (T.A.B.), and *Nesbitt v. The Queen*, 96 DTC 6588 (F.C.A.), for cases in this area.

provision) is a false statement or omission that may be used by another person for tax purposes.

The penalty is one of two amounts. The first amount applies where a "false statement" (as defined in the provision) is made in the course of a "planning activity" or a "valuation activity" (as defined). The penalty is the greater of $1,000 and the total of the person's "gross entitlement" (as defined) in respect of the planning activity and the valuation activity calculated at the time at which the notice of assessment of the penalty is sent to the person. The second amount is $1,000, which applies in any other case of a false statement in a situation that falls outside of the definition of a "planning activity" or a "valuation activity" or, perhaps, in which there is no gross entitlement. ITA: 163.2(3) ITA: 163.2(1) ITA: 163.2(1) ITA: 163.2(1)

The second penalty, referred to as the preparer's penalty, is a penalty imposed on a third-party person who makes, or participates in, assents to or acquiesces in the making of a false statement or omission statement to, or by or on behalf of, another person.

The statement must be established as one that the person knows, or would be reasonably expected to know but for circumstances amounting to "culpable conduct", is a false statement or omission that may be used for tax purposes by or on behalf of the other person. The penalty is the greater of two amounts. The minimum amount is $1,000. The maximum amount is, generally, 50% of the amount of tax sought to be avoided, or the amount of excess refund sought to be obtained, but the upper limit is $100,000 plus the fee charged by the preparer. Additional discussion and clarification of the CRA's position on third party civil penalties, with examples, is contained in an Information Circular. ITA: 163.2(4), 163.2(5) IC 01-1

The following flow chart may be helpful in applying these civil penalties.

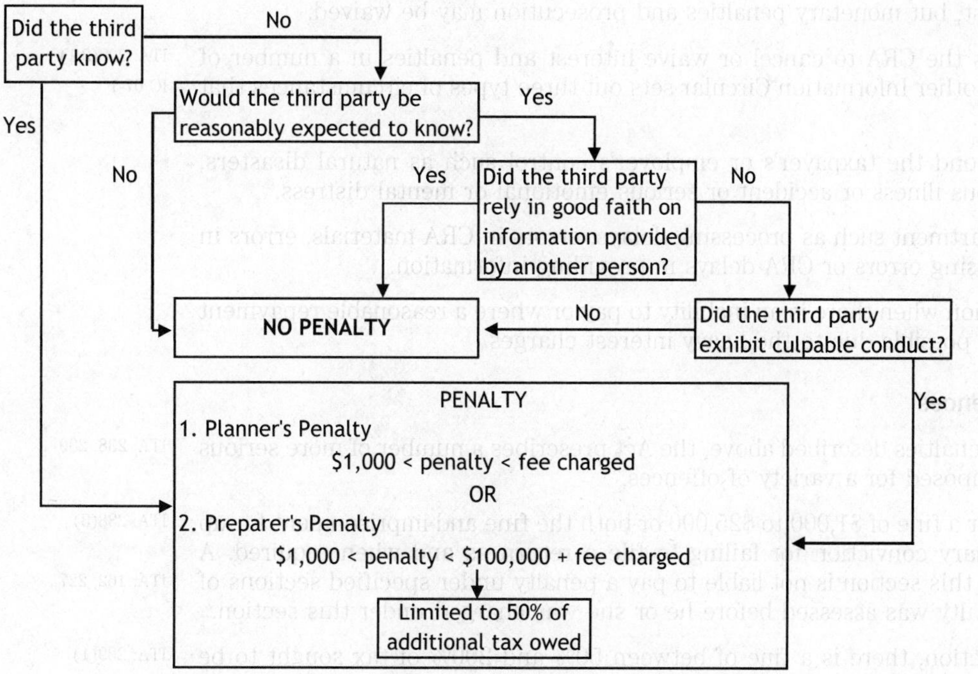

¶14,020.70 *Summary of penalties*

The following table summarizes the above penalties.

Offence	Penalty	
Late-filed tax return	Balance of tax owing × 5% + 1% for each complete month late: Maximum = 17%	ITA: 162(1)
Late-filed tax return — repeat offender	Balance of tax owing × 10% + 2% for each complete month late: Maximum = 50%	ITA: 162(2)
Failure to report income — repeat offender	Income not reported × 10%	ITA: 162(1), 162(2)
Under-reporting income — knowingly or gross negligence	Minimum = $100 Maximum = increased tax liability × 50%	ITA: 162(1), 162(2)
Late or deficient instalments	[Interest charged–greater of (a) $1,000 and (b) 25% of interest that would have been charged if no instalments were made] × 50%	ITA: 163.1
Third party civil penalty Planner's penalty	Minimum = $1,000 Maximum = Fee charged for the planning	ITA: 163.2(2), 163.2(3)
Third party civil penalty Preparer's penalty	Minimum = $1,000 Maximum = $100,000 + Fee charged Limited to 50% × tax on unreported income	ITA: 163.2(4), 163.2(5)

¶14,020.80 *CRA power to waive or cancel interest and penalties*

The CRA has the legislative authority to waive or cancel penalties, if the taxpayer makes a voluntary disclosure. The CRA's voluntary disclosure program is outlined in an Information Circular. Where a taxpayer makes voluntary disclosures to correct inaccurate or incomplete information or to disclose previously unreported information, the taxpayer will have to pay taxes owing plus interest, but monetary penalties and prosecution may be waived. ITA: 220(3.1) IC 00-1R2

The Act also allows the CRA to cancel or waive interest and penalties in a number of other circumstances. Another Information Circular sets out three types of circumstances that would warrant a waiver. ITA: 230(3.1) IC 07-1

1. Circumstances beyond the taxpayer's or employer's control such as natural disasters, postal strikes, serious illness or accident or serious emotional or mental distress.
2. Actions of the Department such as processing delays, errors in CRA materials, errors in CRA advice, processing errors or CRA delays in providing information.
3. To facilitate collection when there is an inability to pay or where a reasonable repayment arrangement is not possible due to the heavy interest charges.

¶14,025 Criminal offences

In addition to the penalties described above, the Act prescribes a number of more serious penalties that can be imposed for a variety of offences. ITA: 238, 239

A person is liable for a fine of $1,000 to $25,000 or both the fine and imprisonment for up to 12 months on summary conviction for failing to file a return as and when required. A person convicted under this section is not liable to pay a penalty under specified sections of the Act unless that penalty was assessed before he or she was charged under this section. ITA: 238(3) ITA: 162, 227

On summary conviction, there is a fine of between 50% and 200% of tax sought to be evaded or both the fine and imprisonment for up to two years for: ITA: 239(1)

(a) making a false statement in a return;

(b) destroying books and records;

(c) falsifying books and records;

(d) wilfully attempting to evade compliance with the Act; and

(e) conspiring to commit any of the above four offences.

If the foregoing five offences are prosecuted by indictment at the election of the Attorney General of Canada, as indicated in the case of *The Queen v. Smythe*, a conviction can result in a fine of 100% to 200% of the tax sought to be evaded and imprisonment for up to five years. Again, a person convicted under this section is not liable for the penalty under specified sections of the Act for the same attempt to evade tax unless that penalty was assessed before charges were laid under this section.

ITA: 239(2), 239(3)
70 DTC 6382 (Ont. S.C.)
ITA: 162, 163, 163.2

¶14,030 Payments and Interest

The following is a summary of the payment deadlines.

ITA: 248(1)

Taxpayers	Balance-due day
Individuals	April 30
Corporations	2 months after year-end
CCPC claiming Small Business Deduction with taxable income under the business limit in the previous year	3 months after year-end
Trusts	Due date for trust return

¶14,035 Individuals

¶14,035.10 *Instalment threshold*

Individuals whose primary sources of income are wages and salary generally do not have to pay instalments because their employers are remitting withholding tax on a monthly basis. However, not all of a taxpayer's income may be subject to withholding in a year. If the difference between the total tax liability (federal and provincial for all provinces, except Quebec) in the current year and one of the two preceding years exceeds the amount of tax withheld at source by the instalment threshold, then, quarterly instalments must be paid. That threshold is $3,000 ($1,800 if resident in Quebec). For example, if the total tax liability on income not subject to withholding (that is, net tax owing) for an individual living in a province other than Quebec is $2,900 in 2011, $3,100 in 2012, and $3,300 in 2013, then quarterly instalments must be paid in 2013. In this case, the net tax owing in 2013, the current year, and in 2012, one of the two preceding years, exceeds the $3,000 threshold.

ITA: 156, 156.1(1)

¶14,035.20 *Instalment amounts and timetable*

These instalments must be paid by the 15th day of each calendar quarter (i.e., the 15th day of March, June, September, and December), with the balance of tax due the following April 30. Each instalment is computed as the least of:

(a) one-quarter of the estimated tax payable for the current year;

(b) one-quarter of the instalment base (defined for this purpose in a regulation, in essence, as tax payable excluding the effect of certain tax credits) for the immediately preceding year; and

ITR: 5300

(c) one-quarter of the instalment base for the second preceding year for the March and June instalments, and one-half of the instalment base for the preceding taxation year net of the March and June payments for the September and December instalments.

Individuals are informed by the CRA with respect to the exact amount of their instalment requirement under option (c) described previously. For example, in respect of 2013, the March and June instalments are based on one-quarter of the 2011 instalment base. The

September and December instalments are equal to 50% of the excess of the individual's 2012 instalment base over 50% of the 2011 instalment base. Instalments can continue to be based on the estimated liability for the year but will be subject to interest penalties on understated amounts where an estimate is too low, as discussed below.

¶14,035.30 *Interest on deficient or late instalments*

The Act charges interest on deficient and late instalments from the day the instalment should have been made to the day the final payment of tax is due (e.g., April 30 for individuals). An instalment interest offset is available on prepaid or overpaid instalments. However, this credit offset can only be applied against instalment interest owing; it is not refundable and may not be applied against any other debts. Interest is calculated from the date the final payment is due until the amount is paid. Interest charges on deficient instalments can be avoided by computing instalments on a preceding year's instalment base as in options (b) or (c) outlined in ¶14,035.20, above, even if the current year's income is likely to be higher. Interest on deficient instalments may be cancelled if the interest does not exceed $25 for a taxation year. ITA: 161(2) ITA: 161(2.2) ITA: 161(1) ITA: 161(4.01) ITA: 161.3

The prescribed interest rate is set quarterly in relation to the average interest rate on 90-day treasury bills during the first month of the preceding quarter. Exhibit 14-1 lists the recent prescribed rates under Part XLIII of the Regulations.

EXHIBIT 14-1

Prescribed Interest Rates Under Part XLIII of Regulations

Year	*Quarter*	*Employee or shareholder loans*	CRA refunds* *Non-corp.*	CRA refunds* *Corp.*	*Unpaid tax and instalments*
2011	1	1	3	1	5
	2	1	3	1	5
	3	1	3	1	5
	4	1	3	1	5
2012	1	1	3	1	5
	2	1	3	1	5
	3	1	3	1	5
	4	1	3	1	5
2013	1	1	3	1	5
	2	1	3	1	5
	3	1	3	1	5

* The interest rate paid by the CRA to corporations is the basic prescribed rate (i.e., without the additional 2%).

The lowest prescribed rate applies to imputed interest benefit calculations on employee or shareholder loans. The basic prescribed rate is increased by two percentage points for the purpose of calculating interest on amounts, such as refunds, owed by the CRA to a non-corporate taxpayer. The rate applicable to late and deficient instalments and tax payments is increased by four percentage points. Also, subject to the highest rate of interest are unpaid employee source deductions and other amounts withheld at source. ITR: 4301

Interest paid on unpaid tax and instalments, arrears interest, is not deductible for tax purposes. However, interest received must be included in income. Refund interest accruing over a period can offset any arrears interest that accrues over the same period, to which the refund interest relates. Hence, only the excess refund interest is taxed to the individual. ITA: 18(1)(*t*) ITA: 161.1

The rate of interest paid on refunds is calculated at the basic rate described above plus two percentage points for taxpayers other than corporations, e.g., individuals or trusts. ITA: 161(2.2)

Refund interest for corporations is at the basic rate. However, contra-interest, as an interest offset on overpayments of tax, contains the additional four percentage points indicated for deficient payments.

Note that all interest is compounded daily, based on the quarterly prescribed rates. ITA: 248(11)

Example Problem 14-1

Joe is self-employed. According to the CRA Instalment Remittance form, his 2012 instalments due were $1,000 for March 15 and June 15 and $1,500 for September 15 and December 15. Due to a cash flow problem, he did not pay any instalments until September 15, 2012 when he wrote a cheque to the Receiver General for the full $5,000. On April 30, 2013, he paid the remaining balance of the tax owing. The prescribed rate, for this purpose, for 2012 is 5%, and for the first and second quarters of 2013, the assumed prescribed interest rate is 6%.

— *REQUIRED*

Calculate the interest and penalty Joe will be charged on his deficient instalments. Assume that Joe pays the interest owing on April 30, 2013. Ignore the effects of the leap year.

— *SOLUTION*

Date	*Amt. owing to CRA: opening balance*(1)	*Instalment due*	*Amt. paid*	*Amt. owing to CRA: closing balance*
Mar. 15/12	—	$1,000	—	$1,000.00
Mar. 31/12	$1,002.19	—	—	1,002.19
June 15/12	1,019.02	1,000	—	2,019.02
June 30/12	2,025.67	—	—	2,025.67
Sept. 15/12	2,060.14	1,500	$5,000.00	(1,439.86)
Dec. 15/12	(1,468.86)	1,500	—	31.14
Dec. 31/12	31.14	—	—	31.24
Apr. 30/13	31.86	—	31.86	—
		$5,000	$5,031.86	

Total interest charged = $5,031.86 − $5,000 = $31.86

Penalty is nil, since $31.86 is less than $1,000. ITA: 163.1

— *NOTE TO SOLUTION*

(1) Calculation of opening balances above:

Mar. 15–Mar. 31/12 (16 days): $\$1,000.00 \times (1 + \frac{.05}{365})^{16} = \$1,002.19$

Mar. 31–June 15/12 (76 days): $\$1,002.19 \times (1 + \frac{.05}{365})^{76} = \$1,019.02$

June 15–June 30/12 (15 days): $\$2,019.02 \times (1 + \frac{.05}{365})^{15} = \$2,025.67$

June 30–Sept. 15/12 (77 days): $\$2,025.67 \times (1 + \frac{.05}{365})^{77} = \$2,060.14$

Sept. 15–Dec. 15/12 (91 days): $\$1,439.86 \times (1 + \frac{.05}{365})^{91} = \$1,468.86$

Dec. 15–Dec. 31/12 (16 days): $\$31.14 \times (1 + \frac{.05}{365})^{16} = \$\ \ 31.24$

Jan. 1/–Apr. 30/13 (120 days): $\$31.24 \times (1 + \frac{.06}{365})^{120} = \$\ \ 31.86$

¶14,040 Corporations

¶14,040.10 *Instalment threshold and interest considerations*

Corporations must make instalment payments of their tax with the number of instalments dependent on the type of the corporation. A private corporation is permitted to reduce its monthly instalments by 1/12 of the corporation's dividend refund on the payment of dividends for the year. A corporation is not required to make instalments if taxes payable for the current or preceding year do not exceed $3,000. Corporate instalments will only be considered to have been received on time if received by the due date, i.e., postmarks will not suffice. ITA: 157(1), 157(3); ITA: 157(2.1); ITA: 248(7)

The offsetting of interest on corporate tax overpayments and underpayments is permitted. This is different from the contra interest mechanism previously discussed. The provision is aimed at situations most commonly encountered by corporations with complex tax matters, where multiple taxation years may be reassessed concurrently to reallocate income and expenses from one taxation year to another. The provision allows a corporation to avoid paying non-deductible arrears interest for a period for which refund interest is being calculated in the corporation's favour. A written application will be required for the interest offset mechanism to be implemented. ITA: 161.1; ITA: 161(2.2); ITA: 161.1(2)

¶14,040.20 *Quarterly instalments for eligible Canadian-controlled private corporations (small CCPCs)*

Only an eligible CCPC may pay quarterly instalments, which are due on the last day of each quarter of the CCPC's taxation year. A CCPC will be considered to be an eligible CCPC if: ITA: 157(1.1)

(a) the corporation has, together with any associated corporation, in either the current or the previous taxation year:

(i) taxable income not exceeding $500,000 (i.e., the small business deduction limit), and ITA: 157(1.2)(*a*), 157(1.3)

(ii) taxable capital employed in Canada for the taxation year not exceeding $10,000,000; ITA: 157(1.2)(*b*), 157(1.4)

(b) a small business deduction was claimed in computing the corporation's income tax payable for either the current or the previous taxation year; and ITA: 157(1.2)(*c*)

(c) the corporation has a "perfect compliance history", as outlined below, at the time that the quarterly instalment is due. ITA: 157(1.2)(*d*)

A corporation will be considered to have a "perfect compliance history" at the time that a quarterly instalment is due if, throughout the 12-month period before that time, it has no compliance irregularities pertaining to remittance of tax and filing of returns under the *Income Tax Act* or the GST/HST portion of the *Excise Tax Act*. ITA: 157(1.2)(*d*)

Eligible CCPCs will be permitted three options to determine the amount of their quarterly instalments, computed as follows: ITA: 157(1.1)(*a*)

(a) four instalments equal to 1/4 of the estimated tax payable for the current taxation year; ITA: 157(1.1)(*a*)(i)

(b) four instalments equal to 1/4 of the tax payable for the previous taxation year; or ITA: 157(1.1)(*a*)(ii)

(c)(i) a first instalment equal to 1/4 of the tax payable for the second preceding year, and ITA: 157(1.1)(*a*)(iii)

(ii) three instalments equal to 1/3 of the amount by which the tax payable for the previous taxation year exceeds the first instalment paid for the current year.

This pattern of three options parallels that for quarterly instalments paid by individuals, as outlined above, and for monthly instalments paid by corporations that are not eligible for quarterly instalments, to be discussed next. The only difference is in the third option, which varies with the deadline and base instalments for instalments.

Interest and penalty provisions that are applicable to other corporations are discussed in the following section.

Example Problem 14-2

Abigail Ltd. is a small CCPC eligible to make quarterly instalments of its corporate income taxes. The corporation has a December 31 year-end. Ava, the owner-manager, has estimated that the corporation's tax liability for the 2013 taxation year will be $50,000. Your files indicate that the 2013 tax liability was assessed at $45,000 and the 2011 tax liability was assessed at $40,000.

— *REQUIRED*

What are the options available to Abigail Ltd. to calculate quarterly income tax instalments?

— *SOLUTION*

An eligible CCPC may pay its quarterly instalments on the last day of each quarter in its taxation year. In this case, with a December 31 year-end, the instalments are due on March 31, June 30, September 30, and December 31. The three options are computed as follows: ITA: 157(1.1)

(a)	$\frac{1}{4}$ × $50,000 (estimated tax liability for 2013)	$ 12,500
(b)	$\frac{1}{4}$ × $45,000 (actual tax liability for 2012)	$ 11,250
(c)	$\frac{1}{4}$ × $40,000 (actual tax liability for 2011), payable on March 31, 2013	$ 10,000
	$\frac{1}{3}$ × ($45,000 – $10,000), payable on June 30, September 30, and December 31, 2013	$ 11,667

¶14,040.30 *Monthly instalments for other corporations*

Corporations that are not eligible small CCPCs must make monthly instalment payments of their tax at the end of each month. The corporation must compute the instalments on one, usually the least, of the following bases:

i. $\frac{1}{12}$ of the estimated tax liability calculated at current rates on the estimated taxable income for the current year;

ii. $\frac{1}{12}$ of the instalment base (defined, in essence, as tax payable for the company) for the immediately preceding taxation year; or

iii. $\frac{1}{12}$ of the instalment based (defined as above) for the second preceding taxation year for the first two months, then for the next ten months $\frac{1}{10}$ of the quantity computed as the instalment base (defined as above) for the immediately preceding taxation year minus the amount paid in instalments for the first two months.

The basics of the calculation of monthly instalments, along with the liability of all corporations for interest and penalties, are illustrated by the following problem.

Example Problem 14-3

No Flab Enterprises Limited is an incorporated company involved in the sale of muscle building and physical fitness equipment. For the fiscal year ended March 31, 2010, the company generated taxes payable of $1.86 million. In fiscal 2011, taxes payable were $1.9 million.

Mr. Fiennes, president and controlling shareholder of the company, planned a reduced sales effort on his part for the fiscal year ended March 31, 2012. As a result, he estimated the company's taxes payable at $1.524 million for the year and paid 12 equal monthly instalments based on this amount. By March 2012, Mr. Fiennes had tabulated the profits and knew that the company's taxes payable would be $2.154 million.

Since Mr. Fiennes had reinvested all of the profits for fiscal 2012, he did not have the cash to pay the additional $630,000 in tax, so he paid nothing further. He filed the corporation's tax return on December 31, 2012, and, in order to avoid showing the further taxes payable, he did not report income for the corporation's 2012 fiscal year, thereby reducing taxes for the year by the

$630,000. He reasoned that he would declare this income in the following year and pay the taxes on that income then.

Furthermore, instead of using the corporate tax return form readily available at his local District Tax Services Office, he filed his corporation's return on some accounting paper. As a result of filing in this way, however, his return did not contain all of the information required to be filed by the corporation.

In May 2013, the corporation's file was randomly selected for a full-scale audit during which discussions with Mr. Fiennes revealed the omitted taxable income. He argued with the tax auditor that the added taxable income resulted from his forgetting to record the sales of 123,000 units in September 2012. He was forcefully requested to pay the added tax by June 30, 2013 which he planned to do by that date. In addition to the added tax and interest, the tax auditor decided to assess the corporation for appropriate penalties, in this case, based on the evidence on hand. These were included in the notice of assessment requiring payment by June 30, 2013.

— *REQUIRED*

(A) Set out the basis on which the interest that the corporation must pay on June 30, 2013 would be computed, assuming it was not eligible for the small business deduction. ITA: 125

(B) Indicate which penalties would be imposed.

— *SOLUTION*

(A) Interest

As indicated above, the corporation must compute the instalments on one, usually the least, of the following bases: ITA: 157(1)

(i) 1/12 of the estimated tax liability calculated at current rates on the estimated taxable income for the current year (estimated to be $1.524 million in taxes payable for the year in this case);

(ii) 1/12 of the instalment base (defined, in essence, as tax payable for this company) for the immediately preceding taxation year (amounting to $1.9 million for the year in this case); or ITR: 5301

(iii) 1/12 of the instalment base (defined as above) for the second preceding taxation year (amounting to $1.86 million for the year in this case) for the first two months, then for the next 10 months 1/10 of the quantity computed as the instalment base (defined as above) for the immediately preceding taxation year minus the amount paid in instalments for the first two months.

Whichever base is used for installments, the difference between the estimate of the tax payable at the end of the fiscal period and the instalments paid must be paid two months after the end of the taxation year. However, for Canadian-controlled private corporations eligible for the small business deduction in the current or preceding year and with taxable income for an associated group of corporations under the small business deduction limit of $500,000 in the preceding year, the balance of tax is not due until three months after the end of the taxation year. Prudent financial management would suggest that a corporation use the base which allows it to pay the lowest amount in monthly instalments, while avoiding interest on a deficiency of installments. In periods of rising income, this will generally be the third alternative. ITA: 125

The monthly instalments of corporate tax and other amounts payable by corporations will be deemed for the rules relating to interest and penalties to have been remitted only when received by the Receiver General or his or her representative, not on the date of mailing. ITA: 248(7)

Interest paid on a deficiency of instalments of a corporation is limited to interest on the difference between the amount of instalments actually paid and an amount based on the least of: ITA: 161(4.1) ITA: 157(1)

(a) the tax payable for the year (in this case $2.154 million);

(b) the instalment base for the immediately preceding taxation year (in this case $1.9 million); and

(c) the instalment base for the second preceding taxation year (in this case $1.86 million) and the immediately preceding taxation year (in this case $1.9 million).

The deficiency of instalments in this case could be set out as follows (000s omitted from chart):

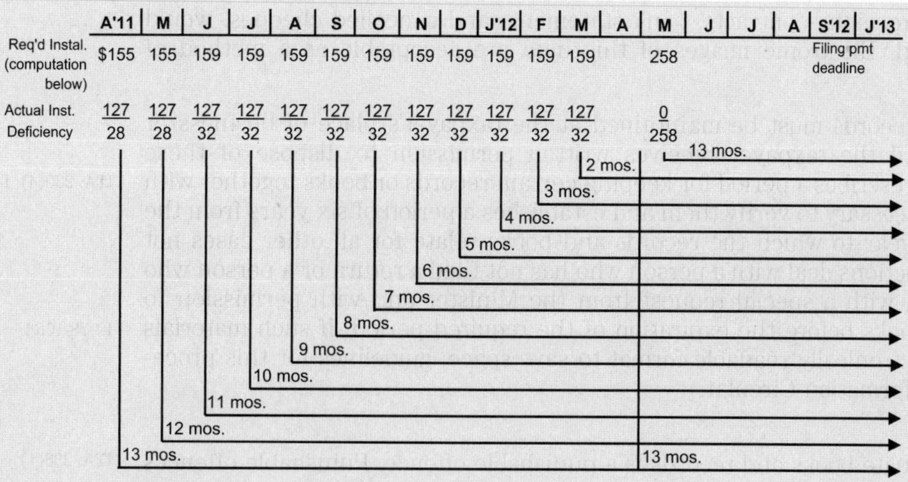

The required instalments are computed as follows:

(a) first two months: $\frac{1}{12}$ × $1,860,000 = $155,000

(b) next 10 months: $\frac{1}{10}$ × [$1,900,000– (2 × 155,000)] = $159,000

(c) final instalment: $2,154,000 – [(10 × $159,000) + (2 × $155,000)] = $254,000

Interest is imposed at prescribed rates on underpaid instalments. This interest runs from the time when the instalment payment was due to either the date of payment or the date when the remainder of tax payable should be paid, whichever is earlier, and is compounded daily. Interest is imposed on the tax *and interest* owing on May 31, 2012 from the date the remainder of tax payable and interest payable is due until it is paid on June 30, 2013. ITA: 161(2); ITR: 4301 ITA: 157(1)(*b*) ITA: 161(1)

(B) Penalties

A penalty is provided for failure to file the corporate tax return on September 30, 2012. The penalty is 5% of the tax unpaid at the date on which the return was due for filing. In this case, since the return was not filed on time in the prescribed form, the penalty would be 5% of the $630,000 in unpaid taxes or $31,500. In addition, the provision levies a further penalty of 1% of the unpaid tax per complete month that the return was past due for up to 12 months. In this case, the penalty would be 1% of the unpaid taxes of $630,000 for three months or $18,900. ITA: 162(1)(*a*) ITA: 162(1)(*b*)

The Act imposes a penalty of $100 for failing to provide the required information on a prescribed form. ITA: 162(5)

The requirement for a corporation to file electronically applies to taxation years that end after 2012. The penalty for failing to file a return of income in the appropriate manner applies for returns to be filed in 2013 and thereafter. ITA: 150.1(2.1), 162(7.2)

Where information is provided resulting in lower tax than that under proper information, the penalty is the greater of $100 and 50% of the difference in tax liability. In this case, the penalty would be 50% of the $630,000 in reduced taxes or $315,000. ITA: 163(2)

Interest is charged on unpaid penalties, calculated from the date the tax return was due. ITA: 161(11), 162, 163

The Act imposes a penalty of 50% of the excess interest, if any, (after any interest offsets) charged on deficient instalments of tax minus the greater of $1,000 or 25% of the interest if no instalments had been paid. ITA: 161, 163.1

¶14,050 Books and Records

Taxpayers are required to keep adequate books and records. This requirement is for all persons carrying on a business and persons required to pay or collect taxes, among others. While the word "adequate" is not defined or illustrated, the records (including inventory documentation) must be sufficient to support a determination of income subject to tax or of amounts to be remitted. In an Information Circular, the CRA implies that basic transaction ITA: 230 IC 78-10R4 data, including invoices, receipts, contracts, bank statements and cancelled cheques, would be the minimum required. Electronic images of this data are acceptable as a method of keeping records.

All such books and records must be maintained at the taxpayer's place of business or residence in Canada until the taxpayer receives written permission to dispose of these materials. A set of rules prescribes a period for keeping certain records or books together with accounts and vouchers necessary to verify them and establishes a period of six years from the end of the last taxation year to which the records and books relate for all other cases not prescribed. Further subsections deal with a person who has not filed a return or a person who has a case under appeal, with a special request from the Minister and with permission to dispose of records and books before the expiration of the required period. If such materials are maintained in an electronically readable format to save space, guidelines for this procedure are set out in an Information Circular. ITA: 230(4); ITR: 5800 IC 78-10R4

Failure to keep adequate books and records is a punishable offence. Punishable offences will be discussed later in this chapter. ITA: 238(1)

¶14,100 POWERS AND OBLIGATIONS OF THE CRA

While the Department of Finance formulates tax policy, the CRA controls, regulates, manages and supervises the income tax system. The duties of the Minister of National Revenue and the employees of his or her agency are set out in the Act. The Commissioner of the Canada Revenue Agency, the CRA's chief executive officer, is empowered to exercise all the powers and perform all of the duties of the Minister under the Act. ITA: 220

¶14,110 Assessments and Reassessments

Having made a quick check of the return in the initial assessment process for verifying the basic information and calculations, the CRA can do a detailed review of the return, subject to the time restrictions, where applicable. The CRA may assess tax, interest and penalties and, furthermore, it may reassess or make additional assessments in the following situations: ITA: 152(4)

(a) at any time, if the taxpayer or person filing the return has made any misrepresentation that is attributable to neglect, carelessness or wilful default or has committed any fraud in filing the return or in supplying any information under the Act;

(b) within the normal reassessment period, which is defined to be four years from the date of mailing a notice of assessment for all corporations, other than Canadian-controlled private corporations, and three years from the date of mailing of a notice of assessment for Canadian-controlled private corporations and all other taxpayers; ITA: 152(3.1)

(c) within three years of the expiration of the normal reassessment period, if the taxpayer was reassessed or was eligible to be reassessed. This allows the CRA to reassess, for example, for both a given year and any of the previous years to which a loss may have been carried back; ITA: 152(6)

(d) at any time, if the taxpayer has filed, within the normal assessment period, a waiver of the statutory assessment period. A waiver might be used where the taxpayer wishes to be able to re-open a return for a year in which there was a very complex problem that is expected to take longer than the normal assessment period to sort out. The ability to reassess is *limited* to the matter(s) specified in the waiver, and the waiver can be revoked upon six months' notice.

The normal reassessment period can be summarized as follows.

Taxpayers	Normal reassessment period
Individuals	three years
Trusts	three years
CCPCs	three years
Corporations other than CCPCs	four years

The Act gives the Minister the discretion to reassess beyond "the normal reassessment period" where an application has been made by an individual or a testamentary trust for a reduction of taxes, interest and penalties. Taxpayers might make such an application where they inadvertently forget to claim a deduction or tax credit. However, it should be remembered that the provision gives the Minister the discretion to either reject or accept the application. In addition, the Minister also has the discretion to waive any assessed interest and penalties. There is a 10-year limit on a reassessment and a waiver in these circumstances. ITA: 152(4.2) ITA: 220(3.1) ITA: 152(4.2), 220(3.1)

The Minister is permitted to reassess beyond "the normal reassessment period" in situations where a reassessment within "the normal reassessment period" affects the tax liability for a year which is outside "the normal reassessment period". However, a reassessment of this type is permitted only to the extent that it relates to the change in a particular balance of a taxpayer for a particular year. For example, if the amount of a net capital loss is redetermined by a subsequent assessment within "the normal reassessment period" but impacts on the carryback or carryforward of taxation periods outside of "the normal reassessment period", then the Minister has the authority to reassess those statute-barred taxation years. Obviously, this provision can work either in favour of or to the disadvantage of the taxpayer. ITA: 152(4.3), 152(4.4)

Where fraud or misrepresentation is alleged through the issue of a reassessment after the normal assessment period, the onus is on the CRA to prove it if the taxpayer appeals the assessment. However, having proved it, the onus shifts to the taxpayer to show that the assessment of tax resulting from the fraud or misrepresentation is incorrect. In tax matters, the taxpayer always has the burden of proving that an assessment is incorrect, since it is assumed that under our self-assessment system the taxpayer has all of the basic data under his or her own control.[2]

In the case of *M.N.R. v. Taylor*, it was established that the standard of proof need only be that of the "balance of probabilities" used in civil cases rather than the more rigorous standard of "beyond reasonable doubt" used in criminal proceedings. 61 DTC 1139 (Ex. Ct.)

It should also be noted that misrepresentation has been interpreted to include "innocent" misrepresentation, that is, a false statement made in the honest belief that it is true, but under the current wording of the Act it may be more restricted in concept. Finally, it should be noted that where the Minister reassesses beyond the normal reassessment period, the reassessment may only be made in respect of an amount which the taxpayer failed to include in the situation under consideration either for fraud or misrepresentation or for the waiver of the normal reassessment period. ITA: 152(4.01), 152(5)

Example Problem 14-4

Mr. Don Godfather filed a personal tax return on April 30, 2013 declaring income of $2,500 for the year ended December 31, 2012. As a result of an investigation, the CRA determined that, at December 31, 2011, Mr. Godfather had total assets estimated at $125,000 and total liabilities estimated at $90,000. At December 31, 2012, the taxpayer had total assets estimated at $140,000 and total liabilities estimated at $102,500. It was also determined by the CRA that a sum of $15,500 represented personal or living expenses of the taxpayer and it was further established that the taxpayer won $1,000 from playing poker with friends during the course of the year.

[2] This onus of proof was affirmed in the case of *Violi v. M.N.R.*, 80 DTC 1191 (T.R.B.).

— *REQUIRED*

(A) What legal right given by the Act does the CRA have to dispute Mr. Godfather's signed declaration of income?

(B) What will the CRA argue is the income of Mr. Godfather for 2012?

(C) What are the possible arguments available to him to substantiate a lower income figure?

— *SOLUTION* [*See Philippe Tremblay v. M.N.R.*, 54 DTC 132 (T.A.B.).][3]

(A) The Minister of National Revenue is not bound by a return of information supplied by or on behalf of a taxpayer, and may, notwithstanding such a return of information, assess the taxpayer. It is under this provision that the Minister of National Revenue, where he or she is dissatisfied with a return, makes what are known as arbitrary assessments, in which he or she assesses the income which he or she believes the taxpayer to have had. ITA: 152(7)

(B) The most common method used is the "net worth" method which involves ascertaining the taxpayer's net worth at the beginning and end of the period. The income for the period is arrived at by adding the increase in net worth to his estimated non-deductible expenditures and deducting non-taxable receipts such as gifts. In the problem at hand, the following estimate of income might be made:

(i)	net worth ('11)	= assets ('11) – liabilities ('11)
		= $125,000 – $90,000
		= $35,000
(ii)	net worth ('12)	= assets ('12) – liabilities ('12)
		= $140,000 – $102,500
		= $37,500
(iii)	increase in net worth	= $37,500 – $35,000 = $2,500
(iv)	income	= increase in net worth + personal or living expenses – windfalls
		= $2,500 + $15,500 – $1,000
		= $17,000

(C) The onus is on the taxpayer to show that this assessment is incorrect. The taxpayer might, therefore, argue using appropriate evidence that:

(i) net worth ('11) was actually higher than estimated because assets ('11) were higher or liabilities ('11) were lower;

(ii) net worth ('12) was actually lower than estimated because assets ('12) were lower (e.g., they belonged to a spouse) or liabilities ('12) were higher;

(iii) personal or living expenses were actually lower than estimated; or

(iv) windfalls (e.g., inheritance, gambling winnings) were actually higher.

¶14,120 Refunds and Interest

The Act also requires the Minister to determine the amount of any refund owing to a taxpayer as a result of overpayment of tax. The Minister *may* pay the refund upon assessment but *must* pay it upon application in writing by the taxpayer within the normal reassessment period. However, the Minister is given the authority to make refunds of tax paid beyond "the normal reassessment period". There is a 10-year limit on such refunds. As a practical matter, refund cheques are generally mailed out with notices of assessment. If the taxpayer has other tax liabilities, the Minister may apply the refund to that liability. ITA: 152 ITA: 164 ITA: 164(1.5)

[3] For other cases involving the use of arbitrary assessments, see *George v. M.N.R.*, 64 DTC 516 (T.A.B.), and *Courtois v. The Queen*, 79 DTC 506 (T.R.B.), and 80 DTC 6175 (F.C.T.D.).

Interest, compounded daily at the prescribed rate shown in Exhibit 14-1, is paid in most cases on overpayments of tax from the latest of: ITA: 164(3)

(a) the day the overpayment arose;

(b) for individuals, 30 days after the balance-due day for the year, which is April 30 of the following year;

(c) for corporations, 120 days after the end of the taxation year; and

(d) where the return was filed after the filing-due date, 30 days after the date the return was filed for individuals, and the day the return was filed for corporations.

Where a refund arose from a loss carryback or other provision that changed the tax payable in a previous year, no interest is payable for the period prior to the filing of the tax return for the subsequent year in which the loss was established. Similar rules are provided for other carryback provisions in the Act. The effect of the loss carryback is also ignored in computing interest charged on deficient instalments in that carryback year. ITA: 164(5) ITA: 164(5.1) ITA: 161(7)

Note that any refund interest received is taxable as interest income in the year received.

¶14,200 RIGHTS OF THE TAXPAYER

¶14,210 Objections and Appeals

A taxpayer may discover that the CRA disagrees with his or her calculation of tax payable either when a CRA auditor questions particular items (more usual for large corporations which routinely undergo an audit every few years) or when a notice of assessment or reassessment is received. If matters cannot be resolved favourably through informal negotiation, the next step is to file a notice of objection. All taxpayers, except individuals, must file a notice of objection within 90 days of the mailing of the notice of assessment. The due date for the notice of objection for individuals and testamentary trusts is the later of: ITA: 165(1)(*b*)

(a) one year after the filing-due date of the taxpayer for the year; and

(b) 90 days after the day of mailing of the notice of assessment.

The "filing-due date" is defined to be the day on or before which the taxpayer's return for the year is required to be filed, and is: ITA: 248(1) "filing-due date"

(a) for a trust, 90 days after the end of the year;

(b) for a deceased individual who died after October of one year or before June 16 of the next year, the later of six months after the day of death and the date the return would otherwise be required to be filed; and

(c) in any other case, April 30 of the following year or June 15 of the following year where an individual or a cohabiting spouse carried on a business in the year.

Deadlines for the filing of a Notice of Objection are summarized as follows.

Taxpayers	Notice of objection due date
Individuals & testamentary trusts	Later of – Mailing date on the Notice + 90 days – Tax return filing-due date + 1 year
Other taxpayers	Mailing date on the Notice + 90 days

Even if the dispute appears headed for a favourable resolution, taxpayers often file a notice of objection as protection if the 90-day period is about to expire. Limits are placed upon the right to object to assessments and determinations in respect of court decisions and specified provisions. ITA: 165(1.1), 165(1.2)

A notice of objection can be delivered or mailed to the Chief of Appeals in a Tax Services Office or Taxation Centre of the CRA. The objection may be submitted on Form T400A. The use of this form is not mandatory. The only requirement is that the notice must contain the facts and reasons for the appeal. The notice of objection is limited for individuals and trusts to assessments under Part I of the Act, individual surtax and tax on Old Age Security benefits. ITA: 165(2) ITA: 165(2.1)

¶14,220 Amended Returns

The Act does not provide general procedures for filing an amended tax return, other than:

- situations relating to reassessments where options granted by a taxpayer are exercised in a subsequent year; ITA: 49(4)
- a situation which requires the Minister to amend a return if a loss or tax credit is being carried back to that year; and ITA: 152(6)
- situations relating to amendments made by a legal representative of a deceased taxpayer. ITA: 164(6)

With respect to the carryback of a loss, it should be noted that the Minister is only required to do so if the prescribed form (e.g., the T1A for individuals or T2A for corporations) or an amended return is filed by the date the tax return for the year the loss is incurred is required to be filed.

To amend other items, if the 90-day period for filing a Notice of Objection has not expired, the return may be amended by filing the Notice of Objection. Otherwise, the CRA's administrative policy is that a return may only be amended if the taxpayer makes a written request for a refund within three years of the end of the year in question and: IC 75-7R3

(a) the CRA is satisfied that the previous assessment was wrong;

(b) the reassessment can be made within the normal reassessment period or the taxpayer has filed a waiver;

(c) the requested decrease in taxable income assessed is not based solely on a permissive deduction such as an increased claim for capital cost allowance where the taxpayer originally claimed less than the allowable amount; and

(d) application for a refund is not based solely on a successful appeal to the courts by another taxpayer.

Often, a previous assessment was not wrong but the taxpayer wishes to amend the discretionary deductions he or she claimed (or failed to claim) in a previous year. For example, a company in a loss position may choose not to claim capital cost allowance in the loss year because unclaimed capital cost allowance can be carried forward indefinitely whereas non-capital losses expire in seven years. Two years later, the company may find itself profitable, and may wish to claim the capital cost allowance for the previous year to increase the loss carryforward.

The CRA allows such amendments to change discretionary deductions where the amendment would not alter taxes payable for that year. Where a loss is increased by claiming additional capital cost allowance, no increase in taxes payable could, of course, result. IC 84-1

¶14,300 OBLIGATIONS OF PAYERS AND OTHER PERSONS

¶14,310 Employers

Every person paying salary, wages, or other remuneration or any of the other amounts listed in section 153 is required to withhold prescribed amounts from the payments and remit them to the Receiver General. Where the average monthly remittances, including CPP and EI premiums, in the second preceding calendar year are between $15,000 and $50,000, tax ITR: 108(1.1) withheld from remuneration paid in the first 15 days of a month is due on the 25th of that month, and from remuneration paid in the balance of the month on the 10th of the following month. Where the average monthly remittances in any particular month exceed $50,000, employers are required to remit up to four times a month.

A regulation relaxes these rules on an elective basis as follows: ITR: 108(1.11)

(a) employers with average monthly remittances in the preceding calendar year of less than $15,000 are required to remit on the 15th of the month following payment; and

(b) employers with average monthly remittances between $15,000 and $50,000 for the preceding calendar year (and over $50,000 in the second preceding year) are allowed to remit on the 25th and 10th days as described above.

Small employers with average monthly withholding amounts of less than $1,000 for the second preceding calendar year and no compliance irregularities in the preceding 12 months are allowed to remit quarterly. Remittances for each quarter are due April 15, July 15, October 15 and the following January 15. ITR: 108(1)

The employee completes a TD1 form listing personal credits and certain other deductible amounts, and the withholding amount is based on gross salary less these amounts. The amounts of withholding on both periodic and lump-sum payments are prescribed. The employee can elect to increase the amount withheld if he or she so chooses. ITR: 100–200

In addition, the Act provides for a reduction in the amount withheld if the amount required to be withheld would cause "undue hardship". The CRA district offices will generally approve applications by employees for reduced withholding if a *pro forma* tax return indicates that a substantial refund will be forthcoming due to substantiated deductions such as RRSP contributions or support payments. ITA: 153(1.1)

The payer is also required to file information returns as prescribed. Employers, for example, must complete forms T4 Summary and T4 Supplementary by the last day in February, and send two copies of the T4 Supplementary to the employee. ITR: 205

Every person paying a fee, commission or other amount to a non-resident in respect of services rendered in Canada is required to withhold 15%. Non-residents exempt from paying Canadian tax by virtue of the Act or a tax treaty can apply for a waiver of this requirement. ITR: 105

While paragraph 153(1)(*a*) requires an employer to withhold on payments of "salary, wages, or other remuneration", stock option benefits appear to escape this withholding requirement because the employer does not "pay" this form of remuneration. As a result, the provision in subsection 153(1.01) is required to consider a stock option benefit to have been remuneration paid as a bonus. This makes the stock option benefit subject to withholding. ITA: 153(1)(*a*), (1.01)

Any person required to withhold by section 153 who fails to withhold tax is liable for a penalty of 10% of the tax that should have been withheld, together with interest. A second or further occurrence of failure to withhold under section 153 will result in a penalty of 20% of the tax that should have been withheld. Withholding taxes will only be considered to have been received on time if received by the due date, i.e., postmarks will not suffice. Any person who withheld tax but failed to remit it is required to pay, in addition to the tax withheld, a penalty of 10% of the amount that should have been remitted. Once again, the penalty doubles to 20% of the tax withheld for second-time offenders. If a taxpayer had tax withheld at source and the withholder did not remit the amount, the CRA cannot require the taxpayer to pay the amount. See, for example, *Lalonde v. M.N.R.*, in which the employee was paid in cash and the employer neither remitted the tax nor provided a T4 or other documentation that tax had been withheld. ITA: 227(8) ITA: 248(7) ITA: 227(9) 82 DTC 1772 (T.R.B.)

Example Problem 14-5

The *Toronto Gazette* employs a number of foreign correspondents who are often required to report from war zones. On September 30, 2013, "Ace" Johnson, a veteran reporter, is killed while reporting from Iraq. The *Gazette* decides to continue his monthly salary of $4,000 to his widow for the balance of 2013.

— *REQUIRED*

What are the obligations of the *Gazette* in terms of withholding tax under the Act?

— *SOLUTION*

The payer is required to withhold tax on a death benefit, which is defined as an amount received "upon or after the death of an employee in recognition of the employee's service". The amount of withholding for periodic payments of remuneration is prescribed. Remuneration is defined as including a death benefit. However, the definition of death benefit excludes the lesser of $10,000 or the amount received as the death benefit. Thus, withholding would only be required on the amount received in excess of $10,000 (i.e., $2,000 = ($4,000 × 3) – $10,000, in this case).

ITA: 153(1)(*d*), 248(1) "death benefit"; ITR: 102(1)

ITR: 101

The Regulations are silent on how the withholding should be spread, e.g., over all the payments or only once the total amount paid exceeds $10,000. If the widow has no other source of income for the year, the tax on the $2,000 would be less than her personal tax credits for the year and she could file a TD1 so that no withholding would be required. Otherwise, the CRA has suggested that the lump-sum withholding rate in Regulation 103(4) ($^{103}/_{152}$ of 10% in Ontario on amounts less than $5,000) would be satisfactory.

¶14,320 Obligations of Other Payers, Trustees, etc.

¶14,322 Liability of directors

Where a corporation has failed to:

ITA: 227.1

- deduct or withhold certain amounts under the Act,
- remit such amounts, or
- pay certain amounts of tax for a taxation year,

the directors of the corporation at the time that the corporation was required to deduct, withhold, remit, or pay are jointly and severally liable together with the corporation to pay the amount and any interest or penalties relating to it. Note that the liability of the director does not include the corporation's ordinary liability for Part I tax. Joint and several liability means that each director is liable for the amount of the liability, although the liability can be shared among directors. This liability is limited to situations in which the corporation is being dissolved or the corporation has made an assignment in bankruptcy.

A director is not liable for a failure of the corporation, where the director exercised the degree of care, diligence, and skill to prevent the failure that a reasonably prudent person would have exercised in comparable circumstances. Any proceedings to recover an amount from a director must be commenced within two years after the director ceased to be a director.

¶14,324 Taxpayer's legal representative

Before making a distribution of a taxpayer's property, the taxpayer's representative, with possession or control of the property, must obtain a clearance certificate from the CRA. The certificate certifies that all amounts owed or expected to be owed by the taxpayer have been paid or secured in a manner acceptable to the CRA. If the taxpayer's legal representative fails to obtain a clearance certificate, the legal representative is personally liable for the payment of the amounts owed by the taxpayer to the extent of the value of the property distributed. A trustee in bankruptcy is excluded from the application of this provision.

ITA: 159(2), (3)

¶14,325 Payments to residents of Canada

The Act allows the Governor in Council to make any regulations requiring "any class of person to make information returns respecting any class of information required in connection with assessment under the Act". The provisions also require any such person to supply copies of the information to the person whose income is being reported. The Minister is allowed to demand a prescribed information return, and penalties for failure to make such returns are prescribed. In addition, the offences on which penalties are imposed apply to failure to make information returns, or giving false information on such returns.

ITA: 221(1)(*d*)

ITA: 162(7), 233

ITA: 238, 239

Regulations prescribe which persons are required to make information returns, and other information such as filing dates. In addition to employers, these regulations affect payers of interest, dividends and royalties and persons making payments to non-residents. Other persons required to make information returns include trustees of RRSPs and other deferred income plans. Unless otherwise indicated, such returns are due the last day of February (e.g., the T5 Summary and Supplementary in respect of dividends and interest).

ITR: 200–235

Promoters of tax shelters are required to file an information return in prescribed form containing information on the persons who acquired interests and the amount paid for each interest. There are also filing requirements for partnerships, and securities dealers handling sales of shares, commodities, etc., with penalties for failure to file, as discussed earlier.

ITA: 237.1

ITR: 229, 230

¶14,330 Payments to non-residents

The Act specifies the payments on which tax must be withheld by Canadians remitting amounts to non-residents. The rate of withholding specified is 25%, but this is often reduced or eliminated by the applicable tax treaty. Such payers are also required to file information returns (e.g., NR4 Summary and Supplementary). Some forms of interest payments are subject to withholding tax. However, all arm's length payments of interest to non-residents are exempted from this withholding tax. Also exempted are interest payments to non-arm's length U.S. residents under the treaty between Canada and the United States.

ITA: 212

IC 76-12R6

ITA: 212(1)(*b*)

Non-residents receiving rent from real property in Canada or a timber royalty in Canada can elect to file a Canadian income tax return reporting the net rental or royalty income, rather than paying the flat withholding tax (under Part XIII) on the gross rents or royalties. There are no personal credits permitted on such returns, but the graduated tax rates do apply to individuals. A return must be filed within two years from the end of the year in which the rent or royalty was paid and is in addition to any other returns that may be required under Part I. While withholdings must still be made by the non-resident's agent on the gross rent or royalty, the election allows for a refund of excess Part XIII tax withheld, where Part I tax on the net rental or royalty income is lower.

ITA: 216

ITA: 216

ITA: 215(3)

If, in addition to the general election, the non-resident files an election on form NR6 with the CRA, committing to file a Canadian return relating to the rents or royalties, an agent for the non-resident can withhold tax on the basis of net (instead of gross) income. However, the same withholding rate applies. In this case, the tax return must be filed within six months from the end of the year that the rents or royalties are paid.

ITA: 216, 216(4)

Failure to withhold, remit, or file information returns results in the same penalties imposed on persons making payments to residents in Canada.

¶14,335 Foreign reporting requirements

The Act imposes reporting requirements on Canadian corporations with respect to transactions with non-arm's length non-residents to be filed within six months from the end of the year.

ITA: 233.1

Canadian taxpayers and partnerships are required to report certain information relating to foreign investments.

The Act requires a person who transfers or loans property to certain foreign trusts to file information returns. Certain resident taxpayers and partnerships are required to file information returns relating to foreign property held, if the cost of such property exceeds $100,000. Resident taxpayers and partnerships are required to file information returns with respect to foreign affiliates Certain Canadian entities that own a beneficial interest in a non-resident trust and are not required to file an information return for transfers or loans to a foreign trust are required to file an information return in each year they receive a distribution from or become indebted to the trust. ITA: 233.2 ITA: 233.3 ITA: 233.4 ITA: 233.2, 233.5

There are penalties for failure to file such returns and for providing false statement or omissions in these information returns. ITA: 162(7)–(10.1), 163

Example Problem 14-6

Reconsider the previous example problem.

— *REQUIRED*

If the death benefit had been paid to a resident of the U.K. instead of Canada, what would the withholding tax requirement have been?

— *SOLUTION*

A 25% withholding tax is imposed on a death benefit as defined by the Act, i.e., the amount in excess of $10,000. The Canada–U.K. Tax Convention is silent on the issue of death benefits and, thus, the 25% rate would still apply. ITA: 212(1)(*j*)

¶14,340 Deceased Taxpayers

A number of special rules apply to tax returns and payment of tax for deceased taxpayers. Note that rules governing the deemed disposition of the deceased's capital property are covered in Chapter 7, ¶7,500.

¶14,345 Tax returns

There are two provisions which govern the filing of deceased taxpayers' tax returns. Where the individual has died after October of a year and on or before the usual filing due date for the year (i.e., April 30 or June 15 of the following year), the individual's legal representative has six months or until the day the return would otherwise have to be filed, whichever is later, to file the return. Where the taxpayer has died outside of this time period, the normal filing deadline of April 30 (or June 15 where the deceased individual or his or her spouse carried on business in the year) is imposed. The key to understanding how these two provisions interact is to identify the particular tax return year to which these rules apply. ITA: 150(1)(*b*) ITA: 150(1)(*d*)

¶14,345.10 *Prior taxation year*

Where the taxpayer has died in the period from January 1 to the usual filing due date for the prior year, the legal representative of the taxpayer has six months after the date of death to file a tax return for the immediately preceding year and pay the balance of tax. For example, for a taxpayer who died on March 1, 2012 without filing his or her 2011 tax return, the return and balance would be due September 1, 2012. ITA: 150(1)(*b*)

¶14,345.20 *Terminal return*

The legal representative of the taxpayer must also file a final or terminal return for the period in the year to the date of death (e.g., January 1 to March 1 in the above example). The deadline for the terminal return and the payment of any balance owing depends on the date of death. For those persons who have died between January 1 and October 31, the terminal return is due April 30 or June 15 of the following year. For those persons who have died between November 1 and December 15, the terminal return is due 6 months from the date of death, or in the case of an individual who carried on business in the year, June 15, and for deaths between December 16 and December 31, six months from the date of death. Therefore, in the example of a death on March 1, 2013, the terminal return for 2013 is due April 30 or June 15, 2014. No instalments are required in respect of a terminal return.

Amounts in respect of periodic payments, such as interest, rent, salary, etc., must be accrued on a daily basis to the date of death and reported on the terminal return. ITA: 70(1)

The full year's personal tax credits may be claimed, although the taxpayer was alive for only part of the year. The reserves that may be claimed on a terminal return are limited. ITA: 72

¶14,350 Rights or things

The legal representative of the taxpayer is allowed to report the income from "rights or things" of the deceased on a separate tax return. The return is due on the date that is the later of one year after death and 90 days after assessment of any return for the year of death. This alternative return is generally advantageous, since personal tax credits equal to those claimed in the terminal return may be claimed on the rights or things return as well as on the terminal return, in addition to the benefit of lower marginal tax brackets on both returns. ITA: 70(2) ITA: 118(1), 118(2), 118.93

Rights or things are amounts which are receivable at the date of death but have not been received such as:

- matured, uncashed bond coupons;
- declared, unpaid dividends;
- farm crops; and
- declared, unpaid bonus or commissions (unless ordinarily paid periodically), vacation pay or CPP, if pertaining to pay periods *completed* before date of death.
- lump-sum payments out of a pension plan.

Alternatively, the legal representative can assign, under the directions of a will, the income from "rights or things" to a particular beneficiary or beneficiaries. However, the income must be distributed to the beneficiary prior to the expiry of the deadline for the rights or things election as described above. This alternative would be advantageous where the beneficiary would be taxed at a lower rate as compared to the rights or things election for a separate return of the deceased. ITA: 70(3) ITA: 70(2)

The CRA states that where there is genuine doubt about whether the income is a periodic payment or a right or thing, its treatment is generally resolved in favour of the taxpayer. IT-212R3, par. 3

Rights or things do not include accrued periodic amounts taxable in the terminal return. With the provision of acceptable security, tax owing on a rights or things return may be paid in up to 10 annual instalments. Of course, interest will be charged until the balance owing is paid in full. ITA: 70(1), 159(5) ITA: 70(2)

¶14,355 Other return

One other return may be used to report income of the deceased taxpayer.

Beneficiaries of a trust report their trust income based on the income earned by the trust in the trust year that ends in the taxation year of the beneficiary. Also, a testamentary trust can have a year-end other than December 31 as long as the first year-end chosen is not more than 12 months from the death of the individual who created the trust. As a result, an individual beneficiary of the trust who dies after the trust year-end will have to report not only the income from the trust (12 months), but also any further income earned by the trust after the trust year-end and before the date of death that is payable to the deceased individual. For example, assume that a testamentary trust had a year-end of March 31, 2013, and that the sole beneficiary died on July 31, 2013. On the final return, the deceased would report the 12 months of income from the trust year that ended March 31, plus the four months of income earned by the trust from March 31 to July 31. To alleviate this burden, the Act allows ITA: 104(23) ITA: 104(23)(*d*) the representative of the deceased to file a separate return that includes the "stub period" income, being that income earned by the trust from March 31 to July 31.

In this case, personal tax credits equal to those claimed in the terminal return may be claimed in the separate return. ITA: 118(1), 118(2), 118.93

This return is due on the date that is the later of six months after the date of death and April 30 or June 15 of the year following the year of death.

¶14,360 Personal tax credits

As previously noted, the personal tax credits can be claimed on all of the three tax returns. This includes the basic personal credit, the married or equivalent-to-married credit, the infirm dependant credit and the age credit. The marital status tax credit must be reduced by the income of the surviving spouse for the full year of death in excess of the threshold for that credit. For the remainder of the credits, the claim on the terminal return and the elective returns, combined, cannot exceed the credits that could have been claimed on the terminal return, if no elective returns were filed. Some credits can only be claimed on the return on which the related income is reported (e.g., pension credit, CPP and EI credits). Note that the credit for the transfer of unused credits for a spouse can only be deducted in the terminal return according to CRA administrative practice.

ITA: 118(1), 118(2)

IT-513R, Appendix A — Terminology: "Income"

ITA: 118.93

ITA: 118.8; IT-350R3, par. 11

¶14,365 Summary of filing deadlines

The following summarizes the returns and respective filing deadlines for deceased individuals:

Income Tax Return	*Filing date*
Prior taxation year	Later of six months after the date of death and April 30 or June 15 of the year following the year for which the return is being filed (i.e., the usual filing deadline for that year).
Terminal or final return	Later of six months after death and April 30 or June 15 of the year following the year of death (i.e., the usual filing deadline for the year of death).
Rights or things return	Later of one year after death and 90 days after assessment of any return for the year of death.
Trust beneficiary's return	Later of six months after the date of death and April 30 or June 15 of the year following the year of death (i.e., the usual filing deadline for the year of death).

¶14,400 OBLIGATIONS OF THE REGISTRANT UNDER THE EXCISE TAX ACT

¶14,410 Collection and Remittance of Tax

A registrant who makes a taxable supply in Canada is required, as an agent of the Crown, to collect any tax payable by the recipient in respect of the supply. ETA: 221(1)

Any GST/HST collected by a person is deemed to be held in trust for the Crown until it is remitted. Input tax credits that may be claimed by the person may be deducted from the amount held in trust when the GST/HST return for the period is filed. ETA: 222(1) ETA: 222(2)

¶14,420 Disclosure of Tax

Registrants are required to provide certain information regarding the GST/HST content of taxable supplies made by them. Registrants may either: ETA: 223(1)

(a) indicate on the invoice or receipt issued, or on the written agreement entered into, the consideration paid or payable and the amount of GST/HST payable in respect of that supply; or

(b) indicate on the documentation that the amount paid or payable by the recipient includes the GST/HST payable in respect of that supply.

The Disclosure of Tax (GST/HST) Regulations (P.C. 1990-2747) prescribe a third method of fulfilling the disclosure requirements. Where a registrant includes GST/HST in the price but does not indicate on the invoice or receipt the amount of GST/HST payable, or that GST/HST is included in the price, the registrant must provide a clearly visible notice at the place of supply (the business establishment) that GST/HST is included in the price of purchases. As with the second disclosure method noted above, the purchaser is able to compute the GST/HST content in purchases of taxable supplies by multiplying the tax-included price by $^{5}/_{105}$ (or the applicable HST factor for HST purposes).

The ETA requires that a registrant to provide, if requested by another registrant receiving a supply from that registrant, particulars of the transaction that may be necessary to substantiate an input tax credit claim. ETA: 223(2)

¶14,430 Returns and Reporting Periods

Registrants are required to file returns for each reporting period by the dates specified. The net tax for a reporting period must generally be remitted by the date on which the return is filed, as discussed in the next section. The reporting period of a registrant may be either the fiscal month, quarter or year. If a registrant's reporting period is the fiscal month, a return must be filed for each month. If the fiscal quarter is used as the reporting period, a return must be filed for each quarter. If the fiscal year is used as the reporting period, only one return must be filed for the year, although quarterly instalments must be filed, as discussed below. Conditions for these options are discussed below. ETA: 238(1)

The "fiscal year" of a person is defined as either the person's taxation year, or the period elected to be the person's fiscal year. "Taxation year" is defined in the same subsection as the person's taxation year for purposes of the *Income Tax Act*. Where the taxation year of a person is not the calendar year, the person may elect to have fiscal years that are calendar years, effective on the first day of any calendar year. "Fiscal month" and "fiscal quarter" are determined in accordance with the ETA. ETA: 123(1) ETA: 244(1) ETA: 243(1), 243(2)

In general, larger businesses that are registered for GST/HST purposes are required to adopt monthly reporting periods, and thus must file GST/HST returns on a monthly basis. A registrant's reporting period is automatically the fiscal month if the registrant's yearly revenues from taxable (including zero-rated) supplies exceeds $6 million. Revenue in these circumstances is determined by reference to the registrant's threshold amount for the fiscal year and the fiscal quarter. The threshold amount for a fiscal year and fiscal quarter refers to taxable (including zero-rated) supplies made during the preceding fiscal year or preceding fiscal quarters ending in the current year. Thus, monthly returns are required where revenue is greater than $6 million in the preceding fiscal year or in the previous quarters ending in the current fiscal year. ETA: 245(2)

Quarterly and annual reporting periods are available for smaller businesses, depending on the level of sales. Quarterly reporting is required where revenue is $6 million or less in the preceding fiscal year and in the preceding quarters ending in the current fiscal year. An election for quarterly reporting is also available in certain circumstances. An election to file on a yearly basis rather than quarterly is available where revenue in the preceding year does not exceed $1.5 million. New registrants who qualify for annual reporting based on this threshold are automatically entitled to file on an annual basis (i.e., the election is not required). ETA: 245(2) ETA: 247(1) ETA: 248

The above reporting period requirements are summarized by the following.

GST/HST Returns — Reporting periods & remittances

Annual taxable sales and revenues	Reporting period	Optional reporting periods
$1,500,000 or less	Annual	Monthly, quarterly
$1,500,001 – $6,000,000	Quarterly	Monthly
$6,000,001 or more	Monthly	Nil

Returns for monthly and quarterly filers must be filed within one month following the end of the registrant's reporting period. Persons filing on an annual basis are required to file their annual return within three months following the end of their reporting period.

Any registrant can opt to file on a monthly basis if desired. For example, exporters may wish to file on a monthly basis in order to obtain GST/HST refunds on a more frequent basis (since exports are zero-rated). However, once a registrant has decided on the frequency of filing its GST/HST return, it must proceed on that basis for the entire fiscal year. ETA: 246(1)

A registrant can apply to the Minister of National Revenue to have one or more reporting periods designated for the purpose of not having to file returns. Reporting periods eligible for designation are essentially those in which the total of the GST/HST collected (received) or collectible (receivable) for the period (plus any other amounts that are remittable for the period) does not exceed $1,000. Input tax credits or other allowable deductions are ignored for purposes of this calculation. If more than one period is to be designated, the $1,000 threshold is determined in a cumulative basis. ETA: 238.1

Returns are generally filed on a legal-entity basis. However, where a corporation has divisions with separate accounting systems, an election can be made to file on a divisional basis. In these cases, the divisions must be identifiable by virtue of their activities or locations, and separate records must be maintained. ETA: 239(1)

¶14,440 Remittance of Tax

In filing a return for a period, registrants are required to calculate "the net tax" for the period and to remit that tax. Where the net tax for a reporting period is a negative amount, a refund may be claimed. Net tax is determined by adding the total amount of GST/HST that was collected (received) or became collectible (receivable) during the period plus any amount that is required to be added for that period, and then subtracting the total amount of input tax credits claimed for the period and any amount that may be deducted for the period. For example, assume $50,000 of GST/HST has been collected, $10,000 is collectible but not yet collected, and another $5,000 must be added because a bad debt that was previously written off and deducted from net tax is recovered. Further, an input tax credit of $45,000 may be claimed and $6,000 may be deducted to reflect a refund made to a purchaser of excess GST/HST that was previously collected. The net tax in this example is calculated as [($50,000 + $10,000 + $5,000) – ($45,000 + $6,000)] = $14,000. Where net tax is owed for a reporting period, that amount must be remitted to the Receiver General by the date on which the return is due. ETA: 228(1), 228(2) ETA: 228(3) ETA: 225(1)

In determining net tax, where an amount was previously included in calculating the amount of GST/HST that was collected or collectible for a period, it must not be included in a return for a subsequent period. Similarly, where an amount was previously claimed as an input tax credit, it may not be claimed again in a later period. These two subsections are intended to prevent double-counting. ETA: 225(2) ETA: 225(3)

There is a four-year time limit on claiming input tax credits. For most registrants, an input tax credit is not available unless it is claimed in a return filed within four years from the time the return in which the claim could have originally been made was required to be filed. For example, if a registrant who files GST/HST returns on a monthly basis purchased goods to ETA: 225(4) be used in commercial activities on February 1, 2011, an input tax credit could have been claimed in a return filed for that period (i.e., for the month of February), which is due March 31, 2011. If the input tax credit was not claimed at that time, the registrant has until March 31, 2015 to claim the credit before entitlement to the credit would be lost.

Large registrants, i.e., those with more than $6 million in annual taxable supplies, face a two-year limit for carrying input tax credits. An input tax credit for a particular reporting period is not available to these registrants unless it is claimed in a return filed for a reporting period that ends within two years after the period in which the ITC could have first been claimed.

Where annual reporting has been elected, quarterly instalments of tax are required. The instalments are payable to the Receiver General within one month after the end of each fiscal quarter. The amount of each instalment is equal to one-quarter of the registrant's previous year's net tax. Where the instalment base for a reporting period is less than $3,000, the instalment base for that period is deemed to be nil. ETA: 237, 248

Under the instalment base formula, a registrant is able to base instalments for the current year on an estimate of the net tax for the year, on a similar basis to income tax instalments. This is advantageous for registrants who anticipate that less tax will be payable in the current year than had been payable in the preceding year.

¶14,450 Books and Records

Registrants are required to maintain documentation to support input tax credits, as prescribed by regulation. These requirements, which are contained in the *Input Tax Credit (GST/HST) Information Regulations* (P.C. 1990-2755), are not restricted in terms of form or physical characteristics. Supporting documentation may include invoices, receipts, credit card receipts, debit notes, books or ledgers of account, written contracts or agreements, computer records, and other validly issued or signed documents. ETA: 169(4)

Depending on the value of the purchase, the information requirements vary. The relevant information and thresholds at which requirements change are summarized below.

(1) Purchases under $30:

- the vendor's name or trading name,
- sufficient information to identify when the GST/HST was paid or became payable, and
- the total consideration paid or payable for the supply.

(2) Purchases of $30 or more and less than $150:

- the above, plus
- the vendor's GST/HST registration number, and
- the total amount of GST/HST charged on the supply or, if prices are on a tax-included basis, a statement to this effect (however, if one document is used in respect of both taxable and exempt supplies, the tax status of each supply must be indicated).

(3) Purchases of $150 or more:

- the above, plus
- the purchaser's name or trading name,
- sufficient information to ascertain the terms of sale (e.g., cash or credit sale), and
- a description sufficient to identify the supply.

To a large extent, documents already being used to support expense deductions under the *Income Tax Act* may be used to support input tax credit claims. The retention period is also generally six years. Supporting documentation is not required for items such as a reasonable *per diem* reimbursements, or other cases where the Minister is satisfied that sufficient records are otherwise available. ETA: 169(5)

Registrants are required to issue an appropriate document containing the requisite information if requested by a purchaser who is also a registrant. ETA: 223(2)

Similar to the requirements under the *Income Tax Act*, adequate books and records must be kept. The following persons are required to maintain records and books of account for the CRA's audit purposes: ETA: 286(1)

- persons who carry on business or engage in a commercial activity in Canada;
- persons who are required to file a GST/HST return; or
- persons who make an application for a refund or rebate.

The records must be adequate to determine the amount of the person's liability under the ETA or the amount of any refund or rebate to which the person is entitled. The records must be kept in either English or French at the person's place of business in Canada, unless otherwise permitted by the Minister. As under the *Income Tax Act*, the retention period is generally six years. Chapter 15.2 of the GST/HST Memoranda Series sets out the CRA's administrative policy in respect of computerized records.

¶14,500 POWERS AND OBLIGATIONS OF THE CRA IN RESPECT OF THE EXCISE TAX ACT

While the Department of Finance has the responsibility for tax policy, the CRA is responsible for the administration and enforcement of the ETA. The duties of the Minister of National Revenue and his or her employees are set out in section 275 of the ETA. The Commissioner, the CRA's chief executive officer, is empowered to exercise all the powers and perform all of the duties of the Minister under the ETA. On imported goods, the GST/HST is administered and enforced by the Canada Border Services Agency (CBSA).

¶14,510 Assessments and Reassessments

The CRA is given broad powers to assess persons for tax remittable or payable, and for interest and penalties. Reassessments and additional assessments may also be made. The CRA may also assess or reassess rebate applications. Assessments must be made within the following time limits: ETA: 296(1) ETA: 297(1) ETA: 298

(a) at any time, if the person has committed fraud or made any misrepresentation that is attributable to the person's neglect, carelessness or wilful default;

(b) within four years after the later of the day on which the return for a period was filed or the day on which it was required to be filed; or

(c) at any time if the person has filed a waiver.

The Minister of National Revenue has authority, on an *ex parte* application to the court, to obtain judicial authorization to assess and take action to recover an amount determined by the Minister to be remittable by a registrant at the time the application is heard. This gives the Minister the power to take action to recover tax before the normal due date for the registrant's remittance. Where the court is satisfied that any delay in issuing the assessment would jeopardize the collection of GST/HST and consequently grants the authorization, the CRA will be permitted to issue the assessment and take immediate collection action. ETA: 322.1

¶14,520 Refunds and Interest

If the net tax for a reporting period is a negative amount, a refund may be claimed in the return for that period. The Minister is required to pay the refund with all due dispatch. Interest on unpaid refunds begins accruing 30 days after the tax return claiming the particular refund has been filed, provided that all required returns have been filed up to that time. Interest is payable at the prescribed rate.[4] In assessing net tax, the Minister is required to apply the amount of any net tax overpayment against any GST/HST liability of the person for any other reporting period and refund that part of the overpayment that was not so applied. ETA: 228(3) ETA: 229(1) ETA: 229(1), 229(2), 229(3) ETA: 296(3)

Interest at the same prescribed rate used for late or deficient remittances and instalments is paid on overpayments of net tax 30 days from the later of:

(a) the day on which the return for the period was filed; and

(b) the day on which the return was required to be filed.

Interest on rebate claims is payable, provided that a rebate application has been filed; interest accrues from the 30th or 60th day after filing, depending on the nature of the rebate. ETA: 297

Interest is compounded daily.[5] Any refund interest received is taxable under the *Income Tax Act* as interest income in the year received.

¶14,600 RIGHTS OF THE REGISTRANT

¶14,610 Objections and Appeals

Where a person is unable to resolve a dispute with the CRA after receiving a notice of assessment, a notice of objection may be filed within 90 days of the mailing of the notice of assessment. As noted earlier in this chapter, taxpayers often file a notice of objection as protection if the 90-day period is about to expire, even if a favourable resolution appears likely. ETA: 301(1.1)

If, in response to the notice of objection, the Minister confirms the assessment or reassesses, the person may appeal to the Tax Court of Canada. The appeal must be made within 90 days after notice is sent that the Minister has confirmed the assessment or has reassessed. ETA: 302

As described earlier in this chapter, a person seeking to appeal to the Tax Court of Canada may choose to have the appeal heard under the more formal general procedure or under the informal procedure. The various time limits described earlier also apply to appeals that relate to GST/HST.

A decision of the Tax Court of Canada may be appealed to the Federal Court of Appeal and from there, possibly to the Supreme Court of Canada.

¶14,620 Amended Returns and GST/HST Adjustments

The legislation does not contain any provisions regarding amendments to previously filed GST/HST returns. The CRA's administrative guidelines regarding such adjustments are set out in Policy Paper P-149R. Registrants are advised to contact their local district office, in

[4] Subsection 229(2) provides that a net tax refund will not be paid to a person at any time until the person files all returns, of which the Minister of National Revenue has knowledge, that the person is required to file up to that time under the ETA (both GST/HST and non-GST/HST portions), the *Air Travellers Security Charge Act*, the *Excise Act, 2001*, and the *Income Tax Act*. Bill C-60 (2013), *Economic Action Plan 2013 Act*, No. 1 proposes to add new subsection 229(2.1), which provides that a net tax refund is not required to be paid to a registrant unless the Minister is satisfied that all information relating to the identification, contact information, and business description of the registrant that was required to be given on the application for registration has been provided and is accurate.

[5] The calculation of interest rates is as follows:

- on amounts payable to the Minister, the 90-day treasury bill rate, adjusted quarterly, rounded up to the nearest whole percentage, plus four percentage points, and
- on amounts payable by the Minister, the 90-day treasury bill rate, adjusted quarterly, rounded up to the nearest whole percentage, plus two percentage points.

writing, to request adjustments to previously filed GST/HST returns. Amounts included on previously filed GST/HST returns may be adjusted, except where a registrant is attempting to increase the amount of input tax credits or other credit adjustments without a corresponding increase in GST/HST liability for the same reporting period.

In certain circumstances, administrative flexibility may be exercised. For example, in the case of an annual filer who would be required to wait over 12 months in order to claim a missed input tax credit, the registrant may amend the originally submitted GST return through a request for an assessment or a reassessment of the previously filed return. Resource availability and the circumstances surrounding the registrant's request will be taken into account by the CRA in deciding whether to assess or reassess the previously filed return. Flexibility may also be exercised in situations of financial hardship where delaying a net tax refund by not making an adjustment for a missed input tax credit would have a severe negative impact on the registrant's business.

The legislation outlines the procedure for refunding GST/HST to purchasers in certain circumstances. The ETA permits an adjustment, refund or credit of the GST/HST in two situations. First, where an excess amount of GST/HST has been charged or collected, and secondly, where consideration for a supply is reduced after the GST/HST has been charged or collected and the supplier adjusts, refunds or credits the GST/HST charged on the original consideration. Any such adjustment, refund or credit must be made within two years after the end of the supplier's reporting period in which the tax was collected or charged, or within four years in the case of a price reduction. To document the tax adjustment, the supplier may issue a credit note or the recipient may issue a debit note. ETA: 232

¶14,700 SIMPLIFIED METHOD AND QUICK METHOD

Special simplified accounting methods have been introduced to help small businesses minimize paperwork and to reduce accounting and bookkeeping costs. These simplified accounting procedures are the Quick Method and the Simplified Method. The rules for these methods are authorized in the ETA and are contained in the *Streamlined Accounting (GST/HST) Regulations* (P.C. 1990-2748). ETA: 227(1)

The simplified method is available to small businesses with annual taxable supplies of $500,000 or less and taxable purchases (excluding zero-rated purchases) of $2 million or less (based on the preceding fiscal year). These businesses are permitted to calculate their input tax credits by simply multiplying the total amount of their GST/HST-taxable purchases (including GST/HST, provincial sales taxes and gratuities) by a factor of $^5/_{105}$ (or the applicable HST factor for HST purposes). This factor also applies in the case of reimbursements for taxable expenses incurred by employees and partners.

The quick method is available to small businesses with annual taxable supplies of $200,000 or less, with some exceptions (e.g., accountants, lawyers, financial consultants). Under the quick method the amount of GST/HST to remit is calculated as a percentage of taxable supplies for the period, including GST/HST, but not provincial sales tax.

¶14,800 REVIEW QUESTIONS

(1) In each of the following situations indicate whether the answer is true or false and give a reference to the Act.

(a) The taxable income of Unco Inc., a corporation resident in Canada, was nil for the year. As a result, it did not have to file a corporate tax return.

(b) Mr. Austen sold his shares in a qualified small business corporation and realized a $200,000 capital gain. The full amount of the gain was eligible for the capital gains exemption leaving his taxable income at nil. He does have to file a tax return for the year.

(c) Instalments for individuals are due on the 30th of March, June, September, and December.

(2) Mr. Smith paid his first instalment on time but was unable to pay his second one on time. He paid both the second and the third instalments on September 15. Is there any way he can avoid the interest that was charged to him for the late payment on the second instalment?

(3) Bearings Inc. has been quite profitable, but this year the corporation realized a business loss that it is going to carry back to the third preceding year. They are also hoping to collect interest from the date they filed the return for that third preceding year. What do you think?

(4) Ms. Taylor received a Notice of Reassessment from the CRA to disallow certain expenses that she had claimed. She contacted her accountant who sent a letter to the CRA outlining the basis for the deduction. Both Ms. Taylor and her accountant feel that the deduction will be allowed. Should she also file a Notice of Objection?

(5) Murray Corp. has had a bad year. The corporation lost money for the first time in its history and some of its key employees have left. Because of all this confusion Murray Corp. was late in getting its financial records in shape and it did not file its corporate tax returns until seven months after the end of the year. Murray Corp. still needs the cash so it is waiting anxiously for the tax refund from the loss being carried back to the third preceding year. Do you think Murray Corp. will be disappointed?

(6) Describe the different tax returns that can be filed for a deceased individual.

¶14,825 MULTIPLE CHOICE QUESTIONS

Question 1

Jane filed her tax return for the 2012 taxation year on September 15, 2013. She enclosed with the return a cheque for $10,000, the balance of tax owing. Neither Jane nor her husband carried on business in 2012. Jane will be assessed a late filing penalty of:

(A) $500

(B) $900

(C) $950

(D) $1,000

Question 2

A Canadian-controlled private corporation received a notice of assessment for its taxation year ended December 31, 2012. The date of mailing on the notice of assessment was August 15, 2013. The normal reassessment period for the corporation's 2012 taxation year ends:

(A) December 31, 2015

(B) August 15, 2016

(C) December 31, 2016

(D) August 15, 2017

Question 3

Darol disagrees with the notice of assessment he received for his 2012 tax return. The date of mailing on the notice of assessment was October 16, 2013. The tax return was filed on June 15, 2013 as Darol carried on a business in 2012. The notice of objection must be filed by:

(A) December 31, 2013

(B) January 14, 2014

(C) April 30, 2014

(D) June 15, 2014

Question 4

Bill was a lawyer with a very successful law practice. He died March 31, 2013. Which *one* of the following is the due date for his 2012 tax return?

(A) April 30, 2013

(B) June 15, 2013

(C) June 30, 2013

(D) September 30, 2013

Question 5

The controller of X Ltd., a Canadian-controlled private corporation, estimates that the company's taxes payable for its year ended December 31, 2013, will be $200,000. Taxes payable for each of the previous three years was as follows:

2010 — $212,000

2011 — $180,000

2012 — $140,000 (taxable income was $600,000)

What is the minimum monthly instalment that X Ltd., which is not an eligible small CCPC, must pay in the 2013 taxation year and the due date for the final balance of tax?

(A) The minimum monthly instalment is $11,667 and the due date for the final balance of tax is February 28, 2014.

(B) The minimum monthly instalment is $16,667 and the due date for the final balance of tax is February 28, 2014.

(C) The minimum monthly instalment is $16,667 and the due date for the final balance of tax is March 31, 2014.

(D) The minimum monthly instalment is $15,000 and the due date for the final balance of tax is February 28, 2014.

Question 6

Ms. Jones is a retired partner in a law firm and has taxable income of $70,000 each year from the partnership, her RRIF and her investments. She expects to pay $25,000 in tax in respect of 2013. She paid $16,400 in tax in respect of 2012 and $15,300 in respect of 2011. No tax is withheld on any of this income.

Which of the following is the minimum amount that Ms. Jones should pay for her 2013 quarterly income tax instalments, in order to avoid any unnecessary interest costs?

(A) 4 payments of $6,250

(B) 2 payments of $4,100 and 2 payments of $6,250

(C) 2 payments of $3,825 and 2 payments of $4,100

(D) 2 payments of $3,825 and 2 payments of $4,375

¶14,850 EXERCISES

Exercise 1

ITA: 150(1)

When must the tax returns for the following be filed: (a) a corporation, (b) a deceased person (terminal return only), (c) a trust, and (d) an individual?

Exercise 2

ITA: 152(4)

An individual filed her 2012 tax return on April 30, 2013. The CRA responded with a notice of assessment mailed on May 27, 2013. If the CRA wishes to make an additional assessment of tax for 2012, by what date must it issue a notice of reassessment?

Exercise 3

ITA: 153(1)

List five payments from which the payer must withhold tax.

Exercise 4

Give two examples of a windfall that would reduce an estimate of income in a net worth assessment.

Exercise 5

ITA: 156(1)

In 2014, Mr. Owens projects his income to be $40,000 consisting of employment income of $25,000 and income from a small business, operated as a sideline, of $15,000. He expects that his tax liability will be $6,000 on the business income. During 2012 and 2013 he paid $3,000 and $4,000, respectively, in tax on the business income. Is he required to make instalments for 2014? If so, how much must he pay in instalments during 2014 so that he does not incur interest and when must each instalment be paid?

Exercise 6

ITA: 157(1)

A corporation that is not an eligible small CCPC uses the calendar year for its taxation year. In 2012, it paid tax of $158,400. By the end of March 2014, it had computed its tax for 2013 at $237,600. It estimates that it will have to pay $356,400 in tax for 2014. Is the corporation required to make instalments for 2014 If so, how much must it pay in instalments during 2014 and when must each be paid?

Exercise 7

ITA: 165, 169

Rachel, a new client, requested some assistance with her personal income tax assessment. The CRA is claiming that her car expenses are not deductible because they were incurred to earn employment income. Rachel argues that the expenses were incurred to earn commission income in accordance with her employment contract and the *Income Tax Act.*

— REQUIRED

Outline the legal rights that Rachel has with respect to her assessment and the steps she should undertake with the CRA.

Exercise 8

ITA: 150(1), 162(1), 238(1)

X, Y, and Z filed their tax returns on May 5, 2013, for the 2012 year. X and Y are employees and Z is a proprietorship business owner. X determined that he owed $4,700 in tax on that date and enclosed a cheque for the $4,700; Y computed a refund of $2,000; and Z included a cheque for $3,500 relating to his balance of tax. What penalties and offences might each be liable for?

Exercise 9

ITA: 152(4), 163, 220(3.1); IC 00-1R

Mr. DeHaan has approached you, on July 12, 2014, for some advice considering a reassessment notice for the 2009 year which he has received. Mr. DeHaan has misplaced the reassessment notice but assures you that it was dated June 15, 2013. In your conversation with Mr. DeHaan, he reveals that he has had considerable difficulty with the CRA in the past, and has had to pay penalties under the Act. Mr. DeHaan is positive that he has complied with the law in this situation and wishes to dispute the assessment. ITA: 162, 163

— REQUIRED

(A) Determine what additional information you require from Mr. DeHaan before discussing the relative merits of the particular disputed items.

(B) Assuming you accept the engagement, what steps would you immediately take?

(C) Explain to Mr. DeHaan the penalty under section 163.

Exercise 10

ITA: 163(2), 163.2

Mr. Turner visited his accountant Ms. Blackford, on March 31, 2013, to discuss the tax consequences of a large dividend received on January 10, 2013. Mr. Turner owns 30% of the shares of Dot.com Ltd. which paid the dividend.

Ms. Blackford explained that if he had transferred his shares of Dot.com Ltd. to a holding corporation on December 31, 2013, he could have deferred tax on the dividend until they were paid out of the holding corporation.

Ms. Blackford indicated that the documentation with respect to the transfer of the shares to the holding corporation and the payment of the dividend to the holding corporation can be back-dated to achieve the result desired.

— REQUIRED

What are the tax consequences of back-dating the documentation with respect to the transfer of the securities?

Exercise 11

ITA: 161, 164

Compare the calculation and tax treatment of interest paid on amounts owing to the CRA and interest paid on refunds by the CRA.

Exercise 12

ITA: 163.2; IC 01-1

You have been engaged by Sid Fisher, a self-employed new client, to prepare an income statement and his tax return. Sid has instructed you to prepare these based on a figure for his total revenue and a list of his business expenditures, which he has provided to you. Based on your quick review of these data, you concluded that the expenditures were consistent with Sid's type of business and the amounts appeared to be reasonable. You prepared the income tax return, showing $100,000 of total revenue and $70,000 of expenses.

Subsequently, Sid's return was selected for audit. The CRA determined that many of the expenses deducted in the return could not be substantiated by adequate records. The CRA concluded that some of these expenditures may not have been made. The CRA, also, discovered that only 65% of the actual revenues of the business had been reported.

— REQUIRED

Determine whether you are at risk of being assessed under the civil penalties provisions of the Act. ITA: 163.2

Exercise 13

ITA: 165(1), 169, 172, 180

Outline briefly the full appeal procedure indicating the time allowed between steps in the procedure.

Exercise 14

ITA: 216, 220(3)

A non-resident individual owns a rental property in Canada and has paid non-resident withholding tax on the gross rental revenue since 2008. He has heard that he may be able to recover some of this withholding tax if he files Canadian income tax returns for those years. What would you advise him?

Exercise 15

ITA: 161

Mr. Steve Parrott's only source of income is from his dry cleaning business. In March and June of 2012, he paid instalments of $2,000 each in respect of his 2012 taxes. By September, he realized things were not going well and he would likely have a loss for the year. He, therefore, paid no further instalments.

On June 15, 2013, Steve filed his 2012 tax return claiming a loss and a refund of his $4,000 instalments. He also filed a T1A carrying the loss back to 2011. He expects a tax refund of $5,000 from the carryback.

— *REQUIRED*

What interest can Steve expect to receive on his tax refunds?

Exercise 16

ITA: 70, 104, 111

Sam Elder died on September 10, 2013. Discuss how the following are to be reported:

(A) $200, accrued but unpaid, interest on his bank account.

(B) $100 dividend declared on September 15, 2013 and paid on September 30 (the previous dividend was paid on March 30).

(C) CPP of $600 for August 2013, received on September 3 and $200 for the period September 1 to 10, received on October 4.

(D) Charitable donations for the period January 1 to September 10, 2013.

(E) Capital losses incurred in 2012 of $4,000, of which no amount was deducted in 2012.

(F) Income of $900 from a trust established on his wife's death, of which Sam was a beneficiary, for the year ended May 31, 2013.

(G) $50,000 in life insurance payable on Sam's death.

Exercise 17

ITA: 70, 150

After the 2012 personal tax season, the brother (Mr. Kaye) of one of your clients (Ms. Kaye) contacted you with respect to his sister. He indicated that his sister had passed away on May 2, 2013, at the age of 50.

Mr. Kaye indicated that his sister had the following income from January 1 to May 2, 2013:

(a) Salary — $22,000, of which $2,000 was vacation pay that had not been paid at the time of her death.

(b) Bond interest payable of $950 which had not been received at the time of death.

(c) Interest in her savings/chequing account of $150.

(d) Interest of $140 on a 60-day GIC which matured on May 15, 2013.

(e) Grossed-up dividend income of $250 on 100 Flying High shares, payable on April 30, 2013, but had not been paid at the time of her death.

(f) The fair market value of Flying High shares on May 2, 2013, was $25/share. These shares had been purchased for $10/share in 2006.

(g) Her RRSP had a value of $34,000 at the date of her death. In February 2013, Ms. Kaye made an RRSP contribution, in respect of 2013, of $9,000. Her earned income for 2012 was $80,000.

— *REQUIRED*

Discuss the tax implications and filing requirements as a consequence of Ms. Kaye's death.

¶14,875 ASSIGNMENT PROBLEMS

Problem 1

ITA: 156, 156.1, 161, 163.1

Bert Logan's daughter Amanda is an accounting student. After a brief review of Bert's previous tax returns she advised him that he would likely have to begin making income tax instalments for 2014; however, she was uncertain about how these instalments were to be calculated and the consequences of making inadequate instalments. Amanda called one of the tax specialists at her employer firm, First and Partners, for assistance.

Amanda provided the following information:

(a) 2012 actual tax liability was $8,750;

(b) 2013 actual tax liability was $7,640; and

(c) 2014 estimated tax liability is $5,520.

— *REQUIRED*

You are the tax specialist. Write a memo, in point form, for partner review explaining the options available to calculate instalment payments for Bert Logan and the consequences if incorrect instalments are made.

Problem 2

ITA: 157, 162, 163, 163.1

Ruffle Limited, a public company, specializes in the games business. For their fiscal year ended October 31, 2011, the company's tax liability was $54,024. Due to the success of the board game, Run About, the company's bottom line has increased significantly, resulting in a tax liability of $69,036 for the fiscal period ended October 31, 2012.

Ruffle Limited's climb to success came to a halt in the next fiscal year. Due to increased competition, profits are expected to decline significantly and the controller of Ruffle Limited estimates the tax payable for the fiscal period ending October 31, 2013 to be $45,000.

In addition, the controller informed you that, due to cash flow problems, the actual instalments for June, July, and August 2013 were $1,050 less than the amount required. The controller also indicated that in order to compensate for this shortfall an instalment payment of $4,500 was made in October 2013 and that the remaining outstanding balance would be included in the December remittance.

— *REQUIRED*

The controller has asked you, his tax accountant, to provide him with the following information:

(A) The required instalments for the 2013 taxation year.

(B) Assuming that the estimated tax of $45,000 for 2013 is correct, what payment should be made on December 31, 2013 to stop further interest charges?

Assume that the prescribed interest rates on the deficient instalments are:

- last quarter of 2012: 9%
- first quarter of 2013: 8%
- second and third quarters of 2014: 7%
- last quarter of 2015: 8%.

Problem 3

ITA: 161, 162, 163.1; IC 00-1R

On September 1, 2013, you started in your new position as manager of taxation for Malic Corporation, a large public company with a December 31 year-end. On the second day into the job, Maureen Smythe, the VP Finance, comes into your office with a folder entitled "Outstanding Items". She tells you that the folder was found in the bottom drawer of your desk when the office was cleaned up after the previous manager of taxation left. She is concerned about the following items found in the file:

(a) A letter from the CRA, paper-clipped to the corporation's notice of assessment for the 2007 taxation year (dated September 30, 2008), is a reassessment, dated April 30, 2013, and states that the corporation has been assessed additional tax for the 2007 taxation year in the amount of $722,500.

(b) A memo to the tax files from the previous manager stating that for the 2012 taxation year minimum instalments were made for January to October, no instalment was made in November, and an instalment of $1.45 million was made in December.

(c) A partially completed tax return for the 2012 taxation year indicating taxes payable of $10.76 million. The return had not been filed.

Ms. Smythe leaves the file with you and asks you to do the following.

— REQUIRED

(A) Determine the validity of the CRA letters and the threat of seizure.

(B) Determine if the corporation owes any additional tax and/or penalty with respect to the 2012 taxation year and, if so, the amount of the tax and/or penalty. Previous tax returns indicate the tax liabilities for the 2009 to 2011 taxation years were $7.5 million, $5.4 million, and $9.2 million, respectively. Ignore the effects of the leap year, if applicable.

The prescribed interest rate required by Regulation 4301, to be used for the purpose of computing imputed interest on employee and shareholder loans, is 1% for all of 2012 and assume 1% for all of 2013. Assume also that for the purposes of the section 163.1 penalty the amount of interest which would have been payable if no instalments were paid is $350,000.

Problem 4

ITA: 163.2; IC 01-1

Bill, an accountant, lives in an exclusive neighbourhood where house prices are in excess of $1,000,000. He has recently become friendly with a new neighbour and in March the neighbour hired Bill to prepare his personal tax return. The neighbour gave Bill a T4 reporting $60,000 of income. Thinking that the income was on the low side, Bill asked if this was all the income he had and the neighbour replied that it was. Bill did not ask any further questions but prepared the tax return. When the neighbour's tax return was audited by the CRA, it was discovered that he had in excess of $300,000 in income for the year.

— REQUIRED

Advise Bill as to whether he is at risk of being assessed under the civil penalty provisions in the Act. ITA: 163.2

Problem 5

ITA: 212(1), 215(3), 215(6), 216(1); IC 77-16R4

After several years of visiting Florida, Mr. Singh moved from Toronto to Florida on December 31, 2012, and became a non-resident of Canada. Mr. Singh decided to rent his house in Canada for the next few years. Mr. Singh has arranged with a relocation agency, Gone-Today-Here-Tomorrow, to collect the rent, pay all expenses and remit the balance to him quarterly. During 2013, the house was rented for $1,950 for January to June, and $2,150 for July to December. Expenses amounted to $1,550 per month.

— REQUIRED

Discuss withholding tax and other tax implications concerning Mr. Singh's rental property.

Problem 6

ITA: 153

A Canadian university hires a well-known American lecturer to lecture on American history. The work will take approximately six weeks and she is to be paid $20,000.

— REQUIRED

Is there any requirement to withhold Canadian tax on the $20,000?

Problem 7

ITA: 153, 162(1), 162(2), 212(1)(*d*), 233.3; ITR: 108(1.11); IC 77-16R4

On January 10, 2013, you started your new job as controller for Bordessa Corporation, a Canadian-controlled private corporation with a December 31 year-end. On your first day, the president and owner-manager of the company has asked you to follow up on some personal and corporate tax concerns that he has.

(1) The company is the exclusive Canadian manufacturer and distributor of menswear designed by a famous U.S. designer and pays the designer a royalty equal to 10% of sales each quarter. Royalty payments are due one month after each quarter end (i.e., on April 30, July 31, October 31, and January 31). The company's financial statements show a 2012 royalty expense of $60,000. The financial statements also show the amount of royalties payable at the company's December 31, 2012 year-end to be $20,000 (the comparable number for December 31, 2011 is $10,000). According to the company's 2012 cheque register, however, only $45,000 has been paid to the menswear designer and only $5,000

has been paid to the CRA. The president wants to know how much the company should remit when it makes its January 31, 2013 payment to make up for unpaid royalties and withholding taxes it owes in respect of 2012.

(2) The company accrued a $100,000 bonus payable to the President on its financial statements. This bonus was declared by way of a director's resolution at the company's Board of Directors' last 2012 meeting. The president understands that his bonus must be paid within 180 days after the year-end in order for it to be deductible in 2012 and you have verified that this is correct. This is the first time the company has accrued such a bonus and the president wants to know the deadline for the remittance of payroll deductions on the bonus. You do a quick review of payroll remittances for 2012 and 2011 and find that they amounted to about $120,000 in each year. ITA: 78(3)

(3) The president tells you that he filed his 2011, 2010, and 2009 tax returns yesterday (January 9, 2013) after receiving a demand to file these returns in December 2012. He is expecting a net refund of $5,490 (see the schedule below). He wants to know whether he will be assessed any penalties for late filing and what the amount of the penalties will be. He tells you that his wife is a self-employed medical doctor.

	Balance due (Refund $)
2009	(20,500)
2010	10,000
2011	5,010
Net refund expected	(5,490)

(4) During 2012, the president of the company inherited U.S. stock from a distant relative who lived in the U.S. The value of the stock at the date of the relative's death was C$120,000. The president has asked you if he has to report this on his 2012 tax return. The stock is held in safekeeping at a stockbroker's office in Toronto.

— REQUIRED

Report your findings to the president.

Problem 8

ITA: 60, 70, 118.93; IT-210R2, IT-212R3, IT-326R3

In early March, you were preparing your client list with respect to the personal tax return preparation season. When you came across Mr. Ricky's name you realized that Mrs. Ricky had called you regarding her husband's death. Mr. Ricky had passed away March 1, 2013, at age 62.

Mr. Ricky owned and operated a Canadian-controlled private corporation, Shining Ltd., involved in reconditioning cars. Mr. Ricky's 100 shares had an adjusted cost base and paid-up capital of $55,000. The fair market value of the shares at the date of death was $750,000. Seventy-five per cent of the shares were left to his wife and the rest of the shares were left to his 25-year-old son.

Mr. Ricky earned $15,000 per month in salary. A non-periodic bonus of $35,000 had been declared on February 15, 2013, but had not yet been paid at the time of his death. His accumulated vacation pay of $10,000 and his February salary was due on the last day of the month, but was paid on March 10, 2013.

In addition to his shares, Mr. Ricky owned bonds which earned $5,500 of interest income in 2012 and accrued $917 of interest in 2013 to the date of his death. He owned another bond on which there was $500 in uncashed bond interest due on January 4, 2013, the anniversary date of that bond. Further, Mr. Ricky had owned two rental properties. Net rental income after capital cost allowance from January 1, 2012 to December 31, 2012 was $45,000 and net rental income before capital allowance was $4,000 for each of the months of January and February 2013.

Other Information:

(1) All assets of Shining Ltd. have been used in the active business of the corporation.

(2) The shares of Shining Ltd. have been owned by Mr. Ricky since 1996.

(3) Mr. Ricky had earned income in 2011 and 2012 of $95,000. He contributed to his RRSP the maximum amount allowed as a deduction in 2012. His RRSP was worth $295,000 at the time of his death. Mrs. Ricky is the designated beneficiary of his RRSP.

(4) Mr. Ricky had a savings/chequing account which earned $2,500 interest in 2012 and $150 during January and February 2013.

(5) Mr. Ricky had utilized $350,000 of his capital gains exemption.

(6) All of Mr. Ricky's other assets have been left to his wife, except for the two rental properties which are bequeathed to his 20-year-old daughter.

(7) The rental properties had a fair market value of $100,000 each. Both properties had the following details:

	Unit #1	*Unit #2*
Capital cost	$72,000	$83,000
UCC	50,000	52,000

— *REQUIRED*

Prepare a letter, in draft form for partner review, to Mrs. Ricky explaining the tax implications and the filing requirements in respect of Mr. Ricky's death. Calculate taxable income for 2013.

Problem 9

ETA: 169(4), 169(5), 223; 225(1)–(4), 228(1)–(3), 237(1), 238(1), 238.1, 239(1), 243, 244(1), 245(2), 246(1), 248, 286(1)

Mr. E. Evans has decided to open a small car detailing company. The individual at the name registration office suggested that Mr. Evans walk down to the CRA office and pick up the information package with respect to tax filing, etc.

Mr. Evans had anticipated that the package of information obtained at the CRA office would include information on the harmonized sales tax (HST). Unfortunately, this information was not included in the package obtained. Mr. Evans approached his son, Sam, who is an accountant, to explain the obligations of a registrant under the *Excise Tax Act*.

— *REQUIRED*

As Sam, provide the appropriate explanations.

[For more problems and solutions thereto, see the DVD accompanying this book.]

Appendix I

International Taxation in Canada

TOPICS DISCUSSED

LEARNING GOALS

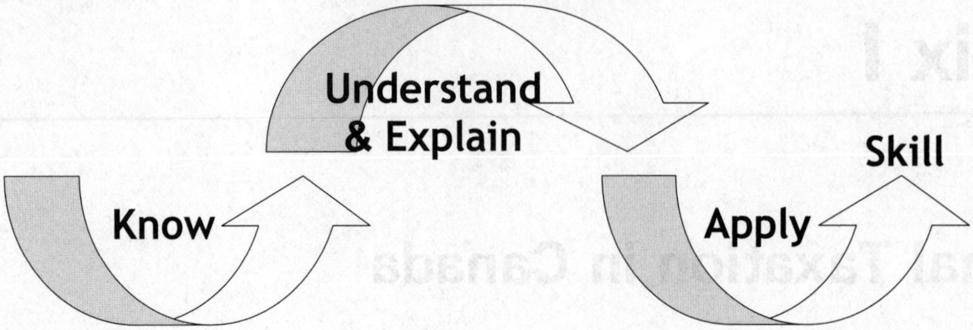

Know

By the end of this chapter you should know the basics of Canadian taxation of non-residents, Canadian tax law applicable to cross-border transactions, and Canadian taxation of residents with foreign investments. Completing the Review Questions (¶19,800) and Multiple Choice Questions (¶19,825) is a good way to learn the technical provisions.

Understand and Explain

You should have a basic understanding and be able to explain:

- The taxation of non-residents with Canadian investments or business dealings.
- The tax treatment of cross-border transactions between Canadian residents and foreign persons.
- The taxation of Canadian residents earning income from foreign investments.
- The basic application of tax treaties.

Completing the Exercises (¶19,850) is a good way to deepen your understanding of the material.

Apply

You should be able to apply your knowledge and understanding of the key provisions in the Act applicable to non-residents, cross-border transactions, and foreign income earned by Canadian residents to determine:

- Tax compliance requirements for a non-resident with Canadian investments or business dealings.
- The application and impact of a tax treaty on the taxation of various sources of income earned by non-residents in Canada.
- The Canadian taxation of cross-border loans and transactions.
- The Canadian taxation of foreign investment by Canadian residents.

Completing the Assignment Problems (¶19,875) is an excellent way to develop your ability to apply the material in increasingly complex situations.

OVERVIEW

No study of taxation in Canada is complete without at least an overview of international tax matters from a Canadian perspective. Canadians hold a significant amount of foreign investments and, conversely, foreign investors hold a significant amount of Canadian investments. In addition to direct and indirect investments, there are tax consequences flowing from cross-border employment and business activities. Business has become more global, and knowing the essence of the approaches to international taxation is a necessity. This area is highly complex and some practitioners choose to focus solely in this area. This chapter provides an essential overview of how international taxpayers, both Canadian and foreign, and their related transactions are taxed in Canada. An overview is all that can be accomplished due to the sheer magnitude and details of international taxation issues.

¶19,000 LIABILITY FOR CANADIAN TAX

¶19,010 Residents

The concept of residency is discussed in detail in Chapter 2. Residency is the basis under which Canada has jurisdiction to tax income. Citizenship is irrelevant. Persons who are residents of Canada for the entire year are taxed in Canada on their worldwide income for the year. Foreign tax credits for foreign taxes paid on foreign-source income may be available in computing Canadian income taxes payable. ITA: 2(1) ITA: 126

¶19,020 Non-Residents

Canadian-source income earned by non-residents is subject to tax in Canada under either Part I or Part XIII of the *Income Tax Act* (the Act). Part I tax generally applies to Canadian income sources considered to be active in nature. Part XIII tax generally applies to passive sources of income, such as investment income, and applies lower tax rates. Where there is greater attachment to location, activities, or properties owned by the non-resident in Canada, the tax liability and filing requirements are more extensive under Part I of the Act. ITA: 2(3); IT-420R3

For non-residents, Canada has jurisdiction to tax income and gains considered to be from a Canadian source. Canadian-source income and gains in general terms include amounts attributable to business or employment activities in Canada and amounts attributable to the disposition of business or real properties located in Canada. The Act provides that where a person who is not a resident for a taxation year, but ITA: 2(3); IT-420R3

(a) was employed in Canada;

(b) carried on a business in Canada; or

(c) disposed of a taxable Canadian property,

at any time in the year or a previous year, shall pay tax on their taxable income earned in Canada for the year determined in accordance with Division D of the Act.

Canadian-source income also includes income from passive sources such as dividends or interest paid from Canadian residents to non-resident investors. Canada retains jurisdiction to tax such income amounts through withholding tax provisions in Part XIII, "Tax on Income from Canada of Non-Resident Persons". The main rule provides that: ITA: 212(1)

> Every non-resident person shall pay an income tax of 25% on every amount that a person resident in Canada pays or credits, or is deemed by Part I to pay or credit, to the non-resident person as, on account or in lieu of payment of, or in satisfaction of, the various forms of passive income as listed.

Taxing income earned in Canada by a non-resident raises the possibility of double taxation, as that income might also be taxable in the country with residence jurisdiction, where the non-resident lives. To eliminate, or to avoid as much double taxation as possible, Canada has bilateral tax treaties with other countries. These treaties (sometimes called conventions), in conjunction with a country's domestic law, generally resolve this problem by including provisions on double taxation and effectively take precedence over certain taxing provisions of the *Income Tax Act*. The provisions usually stipulate that the Canadian tax paid by the non-resident can be claimed in the taxpayer's country of residence as a foreign tax credit. However, not all countries have signed tax agreements with Canada and the possibility of double taxation must not be ignored by non-residents.

¶19,100 NON-RESIDENTS

¶19,110 Income Earned in Canada by Non-Residents

A non-resident's income and gains from Canadian sources (with the exception of Canadian-source income subject to withholding tax under Part XIII) are included in the computation of net income and taxable income for Canadian tax purposes as determined under Division D of the Act. Where there is a tax convention between Canada and the non-resident's country of residence, the tax convention may impact the sourcing of the income. Canadian-source income under Canadian domestic tax law may be exempt from Canadian taxation under the treaty. A deduction is available in computing taxable income for income taxable under Canadian domestic law but exempt under the treaty. ITA: 110(1)(*f*)

The normal filing due dates for Canadian corporations and individuals apply for non-residents. Non-resident individuals, similar to Canadian residents, do not need to file if tax is not payable under Part I of the Act, unless the non-resident has disposed of taxable Canadian property (except for dispositions of excluded property, which includes certain property exempt from tax under a treaty). ITA: 116(6) ITA: 150(1.1), (5)

Canadian-source income subject to withholding tax under Part XIII is not included in income of a non-resident in Division D and, therefore, is not included on a Canadian tax return.

¶19,115 Employment income

The determination of a non-resident's Canadian employment income is the same as if the person were resident in Canada. The portion of income from an office or employment related to duties performed in Canada is required to be included in Division D income. Income includes employment benefits and deductions for employment expenses can be claimed. The determination of a non-resident individual's status as an employee or an independent contractor (i.e., carrying on business in Canada) is a question of fact and is examined using the tests described in Chapter 3.[1] Where a non-resident is employed in Canada, deductions at source must be withheld from his or her salary as if the individual were a Canadian resident. Whether the employer is a Canadian resident has no impact on this obligation of withholding deductions at source. This requirement ensures that the non-resident pays income taxes in Canada that, at a minimum, is the amount withheld from salary and wages. When the non-resident files a Canadian personal tax return for the year, the withholdings will be applied against taxes payable. Many treaties exempt employment income from taxation where amounts are small or the non-resident is present in Canada for a short period of time (see ¶19,310). ITA: 115(1) ITA: 5–8 ITA: 153(1) ITR: 101, 102

¶19,120 Business income

The computation of a non-resident's Canadian income from a business is substantially the same as if he or she were resident in Canada. The major question surrounding business income is whether the person is "carrying on business in Canada". Understanding that term is easier if you contrast it with "carrying on business with Canada". ITA: 9–20

Carrying on business in Canada is deemed to include producing, growing, mining, creating, manufacturing, fabricating, improving, packing, preserving, or constructing anything in Canada. Also included is the solicitation of orders or offering anything for sale in Canada through an agent or servant or disposing of Canadian resource property, timber resource property, or real or immovable property (other than capital property) situated in Canada. Most of Canada's current tax treaties override Canadian domestic law and provide that business profits are taxable only where they are attributable to a permanent establishment located in Canada. ITA: 253

[1] This issue was discussed in the case *Wolf v. The Queen*, 2002 DTC 6853 (F.C.A.).

The definition of "permanent establishment" in the Canada–U.S. Tax Convention includes a fixed place of business in Canada, including a place of management, office, branch, factory, or workshop. It includes a building site or construction or installation project if it lasts more than 12 months. It includes a person acting on behalf of the non-resident, if such person has, and habitually exercises in Canada, an authority to conclude contracts in Canada in the name of the non-resident. A permanent establishment is deemed not to include a fixed place of business used solely for, or a person engaged solely in, Cda-U.S. TT: Art. V, par. 1, 2 Cda–U.S. TT: Art. V, par. 3, 5

- the use of facilities for storage, display, or delivery of goods of the non-resident, Cda-U.S. TT: Art. V, par. 6
- the maintenance of goods belonging to the non-resident for the purpose of storage, display, delivery, or for the purpose of processing by another person,
- the purchase of goods or collection of information for the non-resident, or
- advertising, the supply of information, scientific research, or similar activities with a preparatory or auxiliary character for the non-resident.

Services of an enterprise can be deemed to be performed through a permanent establishment where services are provided in the state for 183 days or more in a 12-month period. Cda–U.S. TT: Art. V, par. 9

Example Problem 19-1

A U.S. corporation, Tellco Inc., employs three sales employees who live and work in Canada. The sales employees work from home offices. Tellco Inc. does not have an office or other facility in Canada. The employees are paid a monthly salary and quarterly commissions based on sales volume. The employees solicit sales from Canadian customers. The customers order products directly from the U.S. company online or by phone. Goods are shipped directly from the U.S. warehouse to Canadian customers.

— REQUIRED

(a) Is Tellco Inc. carrying on business in Canada?

(b) Does Tellco Inc. have a permanent establishment in Canada?

(c) Does Tellco Inc. have a withholding requirement for Canadian employees?

— SOLUTION

(a) Tellco is offering product for sale in Canada through a servant (employee) and would be considered to be carrying on business in Canada under domestic law. ITA: 253

(b) Tellco would be deemed to have a permanent establishment in Canada, if the employees negotiate and habitually conclude contracts in Tellco's name. As long as the sales contracts are concluded in the U.S., Tellco would not have a permanent establishment in Canada. The Convention overrides Canadian domestic law. Cda-U.S. TT: Art. V, par. 5

(c) Source deductions are required for payments of salary, wages, or other remuneration. Remuneration includes commissions paid to an officer or employee. Tellco must withhold and remit prescribed amounts to the Receiver General for the Canadian employees. Assuming that the employees are residents of Canada, Canadian personal tax returns will be filed and the withholdings will reduce the taxes payable on the returns. ITA: 153(1) ITR: 100(1) ITR: 101, 102

¶19,123 Regulation 105 withholding requirements

Every person paying a fee, commission, or other amount to a non-resident in respect of services rendered in Canada (other than remuneration) is required to withhold and remit a 15% tax. A non-resident carrying on a business that involves providing services in Canada will be impacted by Regulation 105 because the customer will withhold 15% of the fees to be paid to the non-resident to remit to CRA. A waiver application can be filed by the non-resident with the CRA to claim a treaty exemption where the non-resident will not be liable for tax on the payments because the non-resident does not have a permanent establishment in Canada. Where a waiver is not requested or accepted by the CRA, the non-resident can obtain a refund of any excess of the tax withheld over any taxes payable on the income from carrying ITR: 105(1); IC 75-6R2 on business included in the Canadian tax return. Regulation 105 ensures the protection of Canada's tax base by placing the tax liability with the Canadian resident payer at the time the payment for services is made. It is easier for the CRA to collect tax from a Canadian resident. Regulation 105 also ensures that a minimum tax of 15% is collected with respect to such income.

¶19,125 Branch tax

A branch tax is imposed on non-resident corporations carrying on business in Canada through a branch, i.e., not a separate entity incorporated in Canada. This tax is charged in addition to any Part I tax and is computed as 25% (unless reduced by a tax treaty) of after-tax Canadian-source income, after a number of technical adjustments such as an allowance for investment in property in Canada. The branch tax is intended to put the branch in the same position as a Canadian subsidiary which must withhold tax on dividends paid to the foreign parent. The branch tax, in essence, is paid on Canadian-source income of the branch that is not retained and reinvested in Canada, just as a withholding tax is levied on dividends which represent income that is not retained and reinvested in Canada.

ITA: 219
ITR: 808
IT-137R3

This tax is subject to overriding provisions within an income tax treaty. For example, the branch tax rate under the Canada–U.S. Tax Treaty is 5%. The Treaty also exempts the first C$500,000 of branch profits not reinvested in the state from branch tax. Treaties generally exempt non-resident corporations from Canadian tax, including branch tax, unless there is a permanent establishment in Canada.

Cda-U.S. TT: Art. X, par. 6

Example Problem 19-2

International Links Inc. is a telecommunications company incorporated in the United States with a December 31 year end. It began operating one small pilot project office in Toronto in fiscal 2012 in addition to its 52 U.S. offices. The corporation is not resident in Canada; however, the Canadian office is considered a permanent establishment under the Canada–U.S. Tax Treaty. The corporation's taxable income from Canadian operations was $280,000 in 2013. It received $60,000 in dividends from investments in Canadian-controlled private corporations and realized a $20,000 capital gain on land used in the Canadian business. The corporation has $50,000 of qualified investment property in Canada. At the end of fiscal 2012, it had $20,000 of qualified investment property.

— REQUIRED

Compute the corporation's branch tax liability for 2013 on the assumption that the Ontario provincial corporate tax rate is 11.5%. (Ignore surtaxes.)

— SOLUTION

5%(1) of:		
Taxable income earned in Canada	$280,000	ITA: 219(1)(*a*)
Add: Amounts deducted under par. 115(1)(*e*)	60,000	ITA: 219(1)(*b*)
Taxable capital gain from a disposition of taxable Canadian property that is property used in a Canadian business	10,000(2)	ITA: 219(1)(*d*), 219(1.1)
Amount claimed in previous year as investment allowance	20,000	ITA: 219(1)(*g*)
Deduct: Tax payable under Part I	(42,000)(3)	ITA: 219(1)(*h*)
Tax payable to a province	(32,200)(4)	ITA: 219(1)(*h*)
Allowance in respect of qualified investment property in Canada	(50,000)(5)	ITA: 219(1)(*j*)
	$245,800	
Branch tax (5% × $245,800)	$ 12,290(6)	

— *NOTES TO SOLUTION*

(1) The Canada–U.S. Tax Treaty limits the rate of branch tax to 5%.

(2) The taxable capital gain on the disposition of land used in the business is not an excluded gain under subsection 219(1.1) because the property is used in a business carried on in Canada. The adjustment results in branch tax applying to the full capital gain on the disposition of the property.

(3) \$280,000 × (38% – 10% – 13%). This tax rate is the basic federal rate net of the federal abatement and the general rate reduction.

(4) \$280,000 × 11.5%. This tax rate reflects a provincial rate of tax on Canadian business income.

(5) Regulation 808(2) lists the specific components of qualified investment property in Canada. Reference to this regulation will be necessary when determining qualified investment property.

(6) Depending on the level of business profits associated with the branch in 2012, the branch tax could be eliminated under Article X of the Canada–U.S. Tax Convention.

¶19,130 Disposing of taxable Canadian property

Non-residents who dispose of taxable Canadian property are liable for Canadian tax on taxable capital gains less allowable capital losses related to that property.

The definition of taxable Canadian property includes: ITA: 248(1)

- real or immovable property situated in Canada;
- property used or held in, eligible capital property in respect of, or inventory of a business carried on in Canada (with certain exceptions for property used in a life insurance business, and ships and aircraft used principally in international traffic);
- a share of a corporation (other than a mutual fund corporation) that is not listed on a designated stock exchange, an interest in a partnership, or a capital interest in a trust if at any time during the 60 months immediately preceding the disposition, more than 50% of the fair market value of the shares or interest was derived from real or immovable property situated in Canada; and
- a share of a corporation listed on a designated stock exchange (a mutual fund corporation or a unit in a mutual fund trust), if, at any time during the 60 months immediately preceding the disposition, the non-resident and non-arm's length persons owned 25% or more of the issued shares of the capital stock of the corporation (or trust units) and more than 50% of the fair market value of the shares (or unit) was derived from real or immovable property situated in Canada.

Effectively, taxable Canadian property includes properties used in a business operating in Canada or properties tied to real properties located in Canada. The definition coordinates Canada's domestic tax law with many of its tax treaties.

For some provisions in the Act, the definition is extended to include:

- Canadian resource properties; and
- timber resource properties.

¶19,130.10 *Section 116 certificates*

To ensure that non-residents comply with their obligations to report dispositions of taxable Canadian property and that the taxes are paid, the *Income Tax Act* imposes a withholding tax at the time of disposition.

A non-resident who plans to dispose of taxable Canadian property (other than depreciable property or excluded property[2]) may file a notice with the Minister at any time prior to the disposition, or within 10 days of the disposition, indicating the name and address of the proposed purchaser, a description of the property, the estimated sale price, and the ACB of the property. Where the non-resident vendor does not obtain a certificate of compliance, a "failure to comply" penalty will be assessed.

ITA: 116(1), 116(3)
Form T2062; IC 72-17R6
ITA: 162(7)

The non-resident must include with the notice a tax payment of 25% of the capital gain on the property. The non-resident can provide acceptable security in lieu of the withholding tax. Once the tax is paid, or the security provided, the non-resident is provided with a certificate to that effect. If the actual proceeds are more than the estimated proceeds, the purchaser must withhold an amount equal to 25% of the excess of the total purchase price of the property over the limit indicated on the certificate. Without a certificate, 25% of the full purchase price must be remitted by the purchaser.

ITA: 116(2)
ITA: 116(5)

The rules put the onus on the purchaser, who is usually a resident of Canada, to ensure that the tax owing on the disposition of taxable Canadian property is collected by the Canadian government.

Similar requirements apply to dispositions or proposed dispositions of depreciable and eligible capital property (other than excluded property) that is taxable Canadian property, real property inventory, Canadian resource property, and timber resource property. The non-resident must include a tax payment of 25% of the capital gain plus estimated tax on recaptured CCA or CECA, with the notice filed with the Minister, or furnish acceptable security to receive a certificate of compliance. If the actual proceeds are more than the estimated proceeds, the purchaser must withhold an amount equal to 50% of the excess of the purchase price of the property over the limit indicated on the certificate. Without a certificate, 50% of the purchase price must be remitted by the purchaser. Again, the onus is on the purchaser to pay the tax if the vendor does not obtain a certificate.

ITA: 116(5.2)
Form T2062A

The purchaser must remit any amount required to be withheld within 30 days after the end of the month in which the property was acquired. The purchaser is personally liable for the withheld tax and is entitled to recover the tax by deducting it from any amount due the vendor, or by other means.

ITA: 116(5), (5.3)

A disposition of taxable Canadian property is exempt from the withholding requirements if the property is at the time of its disposition a treaty-protected property. This exemption increases the level of accountability of the purchaser to avoid liability for withholdings. A purchaser of property from a non-resident vendor need not withhold if:

ITA: 116(5.01), (6)

(a) the purchaser concludes after reasonable inquiry that the vendor is a resident of a country that has a tax treaty with Canada; ITA: 116(5), (5.3)

(b) the property is treaty-protected (gains/income arising on disposition are exempt from tax under treaty); and

(c) the purchaser sends a notice to the Minister within 30 days of the date of acquisition. ITA: 116(5.02)

Example Problem 19-3

Joe Solder is a resident of the United States and owns 25% of the shares of a Canadian-controlled private corporation with operations in Waterloo. The value of the shares is $150,000. He was issued the shares for $300 on incorporation in 1994. Joe's brother, Samuel, owns 75% of the shares of the company. Samuel lives and works in Waterloo. Samuel has offered to purchase Joe's shares at fair market value on April 1, 2013.

— REQUIRED

Part A — Assuming the shares are not treaty protected:

(a) If the date is January 15, 2013, what compliance requirements should be met by Joe?

[2] Excluded property includes inventory (other than real property inventory) of a business carried on in Canada, listed shares of a corporation, and treaty-exempt property.

(b) If the date is April 20, 2013 and the transaction has already occurred, what compliance requirements should be met by Joe and Samuel?

Part B — Answer the above assuming the shares are treaty protected.

— *SOLUTION*

Part A — Not treaty-protected under Article XIII

Taxable Canadian property includes unlisted shares of a corporation resident in Canada if, at any time during the 60 months immediately preceding the disposition, more than 50% of the fair market value of the shares was derived from real or immovable property situated in Canada. Under the Canada–U.S. Tax Convention, Article XIII, gains on the disposition of shares of a Canadian resident corporation are subject to tax in Canada if the value of the shares is derived principally from real property situated in Canada. Part A assumes that the gain on the shares is not exempt from tax because they meet the definition of real property situated in Canada under Article XIII.

(a) Anytime before the disposition, or not later than 10 days after the disposition, Joe may complete Form T2062, "Request by a Non-Resident of Canada for a Certificate of Compliance Related to the Disposition of Taxable Canadian Property", to report the disposition and pay 25% of the gain, i.e., 25% of ($150,000 – $300) or provide acceptable security. The Minister will provide a certificate of compliance. If Form T2062 is not filed, a "failure to comply" penalty will be assessed under subsection 162(7).

(b) If Form T2062 is not completed within the above-noted time frame or the purchase price exceeds the limit fixed in a certificate requested before the disposition, Samuel will become liable for 25% of the cost of the shares, i.e., 25% of $150,000 (or 25% of $150,000 less the limit fixed in the certificate). He must remit the amount to the Receiver General by May 30, 2013. Samuel can deduct or withhold the amount from any amount paid or credited to Joe or otherwise recover the amount paid.

Joe must file a personal Canadian tax return to report the gain from the disposition of taxable Canadian property by April 30, 2014. His taxes payable will be reduced by any tax paid to the Minister with Form T2062.

Part B — Treaty-protected under Article XIII

Part B assumes that, although the shares meet the definition of taxable Canadian property, the gain is exempt because the shares are not real property situated in Canada under Article XIII.

The non-resident vendor is not required to complete form T2062 for the disposition. The purchaser must file a notice with the Minister including the date of the transaction, the amount paid, the name and address of the non-resident, and identifying the Canada–U.S. Tax Convention as the treaty providing protection within 30 days of the acquisition (i.e., May 1, 2012) or become liable for 25% of the purchase price. Joe will not need to file a personal Canadian tax return as long as there is no Part I tax payable for the year, and he does not owe tax for a prior tax year. ITA: 116(5.02) ITA: 150(1.1), (5)

The certificate and withholding tax requirement applies to property that is transferred by way of a gift, or to a non-arm's length person for consideration that is less than full value. In these cases, the proceeds are based on fair market value. The certificate and withholding tax requirements do not apply to property transferred because of a non-resident's death. Although the certificate requirement does not apply, the deceased non-resident may be liable for Canadian tax because of a deemed disposition of taxable Canadian property at the time of death. ITA: 116(5.1) ITA: 70

¶19,140 Deductions and Credits Allowed a Non-Resident

Certain deductions in determining the non-resident's taxable income for Canadian tax purposes are allowed. Specifically, the non-resident can deduct: employment losses, business losses, business investment losses, loss carryovers under section 111, stock option benefits, amounts exempt from tax under a tax convention, and other types of compensation that are not taxable in Canada. For corporations, the deductions for dividends received by a corporation in determining taxable income and charitable gifts are available. ITA: 115(1) ITA: 110(1)(*f*)

Where all or substantially all (which is 90% or more) of the non-resident person's income for the year is included in computing the non-resident person's taxable income earned in ITA: 115(1)(*f*)

Canada for the year, such of the other deductions permitted for the purpose of computing taxable income (i.e., other Division C deductions) may be deducted as may reasonably be considered wholly applicable.

¶19,145 Tax credits available to non-residents

The following non-refundable tax credits may be claimed by all non-residents, irrespective of the type and amount of their Canadian-source income, if they satisfy the conditions of eligibility. ITA: 118.94

- Charitable gifts ITA: 118.1
- Mental or physical impairment tax credit ITA: 118.3(1)
- Tuition tax credit ITA: 118.5, 118.81
- EI and CPP/QPP tax credits ITA: 118.7
- Student loan interest ITA: 118.62

The following credits may be claimed by those non-residents whose Canadian-source income represents at least 90% of their worldwide income. The non-resident may be required to furnish the CRA with evidence to establish that is the case.

- Basic personal, married (or common-law partner), equivalent-to-married, caregiver, and dependant tax credits ITA: 118(1)
- Age credit ITA: 118(2)
- Pension income credit ITA: 118(3)
- Canada Employment credit ITA: 118(10)
- Adoption expense tax credit ITA: 118.01
- Public transit pass tax credit ITA: 118.02
- Children's fitness and arts tax credits ITA: 118.03
- First-time home buyers' credit and disability home purchase credit ITA: 118.05
- Medical expense credit ITA: 118.2(1)
- Disability credit for dependant ITA: 118.3(2)
- Education and textbook credits ITA: 118.6
- Credits transferable from spouse/child/grandchild ITA: 118.8, 118.9

¶19,150 Provincial/Territorial Income Tax Obligation

A non-resident will typically be liable to pay provincial or territorial income tax in addition to federal income tax on income earned in a province. The rates of tax vary from province to province (and territory). For these purposes, income earned in a province is the aggregate of the taxpayer's income from an office or employment that is reasonably attributable to the duties performed by him in the province and the taxpayer's income for the year from carrying on business earned in the province. Provincial tax is payable on these amounts and the additional tax would not apply. If a non-resident's income subject to federal tax is not considered income earned in a province, an additional tax of 48% of the federal tax otherwise payable is added in respect of that income. Note that a non-resident's taxable capital gains from the disposition of taxable Canadian property will not be considered earned in a province, and, therefore, will be subject to the additional federal tax. The additional federal tax has the effect of making the non-resident's tax on a gain approximately the same as would apply to a resident who has to pay provincial income tax (that is, combined federal plus provincial tax). ITR: 2602(1) ITA: 120(1)

¶19,160 Withholding Taxes on Canadian-Source Income — Part XIII Tax

While non-residents are liable for Canadian income taxes under Part I, subsection 2(3) on income from employment, carrying on business in Canada, and any gain on dispositions of taxable Canadian property, this is not the only possible taxation of a non-resident's Canadian-source income.

Part XIII of the Act, requires a resident who pays or credits certain amounts (such as interest, dividends, royalties, and pensions) to a non-resident to withhold 25% for Canadian tax. Part XIII tax should not be confused with Part I tax. These are two separate taxing provisions. If a non-resident pays Part XIII tax on a particular source of income, then the non-resident does not have to pay Part I tax on that same source, and *vice versa*. No tax return is required to be filed by the non-resident for income subject to Part XIII tax. ITA: 212; IC 76-12R6, IC 77-16R4

Common income types subject to Part XIII withholding tax are as follows:

(a) Management fees; ITA: 212(1)(*a*)

(b) Interest paid or payable to a non-arm's length person (that is not fully exempt interest) and participating debt interest; ITA: 212(1)(*b*), 212(3)

(c) Estate or trust income; ITA: 212(1)(*c*)

(d) Rents and royalties; ITA: 212(1)(*d*)

(e) Pension benefits; ITA: 212(1)(*h*)

(f) Registered retirement savings plan and registered retirement income fund payments; ITA: 212(1)(*l*), 212(1)(*q*)

(g) Deferred profit sharing plan payments; ITA: 212(1)(*m*)

(h) Annuity payments; and ITA: 212(1)(*o*)

(i) Taxable dividends and capital dividends. ITA: 212(2)

An exclusive list can be found in the Act. Many provisions in the section include exemptions for certain types of payments within the above categories. A thorough review of this provision and related provisions may be required to determine applicability of the withholding tax. ITA: 212

Generally, the payer is responsible for withholding and remitting the Part XIII tax to the CRA. If the payer does not withhold or remit, he or she may be held liable for the tax not withheld, plus interest and penalties. ITA: 215(6)

The payer resident is required to file an NR4 return (similar to a T4/T4A return) with the CRA. The non-resident then uses this NR4 information slip to report the income in their country of residence and claim any foreign tax credit that the foreign country might grant under its tax system.

Example Problem 19-4

Janet Smith is about to emigrate from Canada. She has $50,000 in her RRSP.

— *REQUIRED*

What are her alternatives in connection with this RRSP?

— *SOLUTION*

Janet could collapse the RRSP prior to leaving Canada. In this case, the RRSP would be included as income in her final Canadian tax return and taxed at her marginal rate. Alternatively, she could collapse the RRSP after having left Canada. In that case, there would be a 25% withholding tax. The income may be subject to tax in the foreign jurisdiction and a foreign tax credit received for the Canadian withholding tax. She should choose the approach that produces the lesser tax. ITA: 212(1)(*l*)

The 25% withholding rate in Part XIII can be reduced pursuant to a treaty between Canada and the country of the income recipient. It is the payer's responsibility to withhold at the appropriate rate. A new form (NR301), "Declaration of Benefits under a Tax Treaty for a Non-resident Taxpayer", has been developed by the CRA to help non-residents establish and assure payers of eligibility for treaty rate reductions.

¶19,165 Rental income alternative — Section 216 elections

The Part XIII 25% withholding tax on rental income may be punitive, as it applies to the gross rental income when the non-resident might have mortgage payments, property taxes, maintenance, and other types of expenses that are funded by the rental income. To address this, the non-resident is provided with an option to report net rental income subject to the regular Part I tax rates to recoup all or a portion of the Part XIII tax. ITA: 216; IT-393R2

The non-resident may elect to file a Canadian income tax return and report the rental income and expenses. The expenses allowed in this optional tax return are the same as those allowed against rental income of a resident, including capital cost allowance on the property. This return is optional on an annual basis, and must be filed within two years after the end of the applicable taxation year in which the income was earned, showing only rental income from property in Canada. Where the alternative is chosen, income taxes are payable based on the net rental income. This election does not relieve the Canadian payer from the obligation to withhold the Part XIII tax; however, the 25% withholding tax is considered an instalment on account against those taxes payable, and any excess is refundable. This tax return is separate from any other income tax return the non-resident may otherwise be required to file. No deductions in computing taxable income or any tax credits may be claimed in completing the tax return. Tax is computed using the rates in effect for the year that are applicable to the type of non-resident person filing the return. For example, graduated rates would apply for non-resident individuals. Corporate tax rates would apply for non-resident corporations. ITA: 216(1); Form T1159

While the alternative to file a tax return provides the non-resident with an opportunity to reduce his or her Canadian tax liability, it does not assist with the cash-flow difficulties that the 25% withholding tax requirement might impose. For this reason, the non-resident is given yet another alternative for Canadian rental income. ITA: 216(4)

The non-resident may file an undertaking with the CRA, that the elective tax return will be filed within six months of the end of the taxation year. The undertaking must be filed no later than January 1 of each year or the date on which the first rental payment is made. The undertaking allows the non-resident's Canadian agent, to elect to pay the 25% withholding tax on net rental income (before CCA). Filing this elective tax return allows the non-resident to declare net rental income, after deducting CCA and again receive a refund of any excess Part XIII tax. Form NR6

Example Problem 19-5

Jack Lajoha is a resident of Spain, but has a rental property in Canada. The gross rents are $1,500 monthly, and are collected by Jack's agent, Tom Kelly. From the rental income, Tom pays his rental agent's fee, the mortgage, property taxes, and maintenance totalling $14,400. Available CCA on the property will be $5,000 for 2013. On average there is about $300 a month net cash available.

— REQUIRED

How does Jack Lajoha account for this rental income in Canada?

— SOLUTION

Tom Kelly is required to deduct 25% of the gross monthly rental income and remit it to the CRA as withholding tax. The withholding tax of $375 exceeds, on average, the net cash available. Jack will have to send Tom about $75 a month to meet the cash-flow requirements.

Jack may, if he so chooses, file a Canadian tax return (Form T1159) within two years, and receive a refund of the withholding tax over the actual tax required by that return as follows:

Estimated rental income for 2013:		
Gross rentals		$ 18,000
Expenses before CCA	$14,400	
CCA (maximum allowed)	3,600	(18,000)
Net rentals		$ —
If an election is made under subsection 216(1)		
Net income and taxable income		$ —
Part I tax		$ —
Less: Income tax deducted (25% × $18,000)		4,500
Refund		$ 4,500

Another alternative would be for Jack to provide an undertaking by January 1, 2013 (Form NR6) to file a tax return within six months of the end of the taxation year. This would allow Tom to elect to remit the withholding tax of $900, based on 25% of the $300 available monthly. Jack would then receive a refund of the amount ($900) on filing the tax return. Jack should file the income tax return under Part I no later than June 30 following the end of the taxation year.

Where the undertaking is given, it is the non-resident's Canadian agent or representative who elects to remit the withholding tax based on the lesser "amount available". If the non-resident does not file the required tax return or does not pay any additional tax required on filing the tax return, the Canadian agent/representative will be liable to pay the difference between the amount actually remitted and 25% of the gross rents. ITA: 216(4)

When a non-resident disposes of real property in Canada and CCA was claimed in prior years on a tax return under Part I, a tax return must be filed, and any recapture of CCA resulting from the disposition is included in income. ITA: 216(5)

Note that Part XIII withholding tax only applies to rental income that is not considered to be income from carrying on a business in Canada. The determination of whether rental income is business or property income is a question of fact tied to the level of services provided by the landlord. Where rental income is income from carrying on business in Canada, the net rental income is taxed under Part I. A certificate request confirming that Part XIII does not apply should be received from the Minister. ITR: 805; IT-434R; ITA: 2(3), 115(1); ITR: 805.1

¶19,170 Canadian benefits alternative — Section 217 election

Non-residents receiving the following types of income (referred to as "Canadian benefits") are provided with another alternative to the 25% withholding tax requirement: ITA: 217

- pension benefits;
- death benefits (and others under section 56);
- retiring allowances;
- supplementary unemployment benefits (SUB plans);
- RRSP benefits;
- DPSP benefits; or
- RRIF benefits.

The non-resident is able to file a Canadian income tax return within six months of the taxation year-end and elect that section 217 apply. This should only be done where the tax liability, as calculated under Part I in that return, is less than the 25% Part XIII withholding tax (or the reduced rate under the applicable treaty). Unlike the alternative rental income return under section 216, this section 217 return is not separate from any other return the ITA: 217(2) non-resident is required to file (employment income, business income, disposition of taxable Canadian property).

The tax rate applicable to an individual who makes a section 217 election is determined using the greater of the individual's taxable income in Canada or his or her worldwide income. This is calculated through an inclusion of worldwide income in taxable income and the deduction, in computing tax payable, of the estimated tax attributable to the foreign income. The deduction is summarized by the following formula: ITA: 217(3), 217(6)

$$\text{tax payable under Part I} \times \frac{\text{worldwide income} - \text{Canadian-source income}}{\text{worldwide income}}$$

Therefore a small amount of Canadian-source pension income could result in a higher tax liability under a 217 election than under the withholding tax provisions depending on the level of foreign income of the non-resident.

Where the ratio of the Canadian-source income is 90% or more of worldwide income, personal tax credits are allowed on the same basis as if the taxpayer were a resident of Canada. Where the ratio is less than 90%, personal tax credits are allowed at the *lesser of* 15% of: ITA: 217(4) ITA: 217(5)

- the personal tax credits; and
- the Canadian benefits being reported under section 217.

¶19,200 PART-YEAR RESIDENTS

¶19,210 Income, Deductions, and Credits

Persons who are residents of Canada for only a part of the year are subject to specific rules. A person may be a Canadian resident for only part of the year under two situations: ITA: 114

- when a Canadian resident leaves the country at some point in the year to take up permanent residence in another country (emigration); and
- when a resident of another country leaves that country at some point in the year to become a permanent Canadian resident (immigration).

For income tax purposes, this person is considered a resident of Canada only during the time of permanent residence. The Canadian tax liability, under Part I, is based on worldwide income during the period in the year a person was resident in Canada, and on Canadian-source income for the period when the person was non-resident. ITA: 2(1) ITA: 2(3)

A part-year resident does not include an individual deemed a resident as a sojourner. Such an individual is deemed resident throughout the year. ITA: 250(1)(*a*)

When calculating *net* income in Canada for a part-year resident, certain deductions, such as RRSP contributions and spousal and child support payments made during the period of residency in Canada, are allowed under the normal rules. Qualifying child care expenses for the period of residency in Canada are also allowed under the normal rules.

The deductions generally allowed in calculating *taxable* income for a part-year resident are the employee stock option deduction and loss carryforwards. The capital gains deduction (CGD) can be deducted by part-year residents only if they were resident throughout either the preceding or the immediately following taxation year. ITA: 114(*b*) ITA: 110.6(5); IT-262R2

The income tax rates used to compute the tax payable under Part I by a part-year resident are the same as those for all other Canadian residents. The tax credits allowed to reduce income tax payable are more limited in comparison to those for a person residing in Canada all year.

In the year of immigration or emigration, some of the personal tax credits of the taxpayer are prorated based on the number of days that the individual is resident in Canada. The following credits are prorated: ITA: 118.91

- basic personal tax credit, married or common-law status, equivalent-to-spouse credit, child credit, caregiver credit, and dependant credit; ITA: 118(1)
- age amount; ITA: 118(2)
- disability (mental or physical impairment) for self or transferred from dependant; ITA: 118.3
- unused credits transferred from a spouse or common-law partner; and ITA: 118.8
- unused tuition and education amounts transferred from a child or grandchild. ITA: 118.9

The personal tax credits that are not prorated and that can be claimed in full for the period in which the individual is resident in Canada are the credits for:

- pension income amount; ITA: 118(3)
- Canada employment; ITA: 118(10)
- adoption expenses; ITA: 118.01
- public transit passes; ITA: 118.02
- children's fitness; ITA: 118.03
- children's arts; ITA: 118.031
- charitable gifts; ITA: 118.1
- medical expenses; ITA: 118.2
- tuition, education, and post-secondary textbooks; ITA: 118.5, 118.6, 118.6(2.1)
- student loan interest; and ITA: 118.62
- EI and CPP/QPP withheld during the period the individual was resident in Canada. ITA: 118.7

Example Problem 19-6

Aaron Levy immigrated to Canada during 2013, arriving on August 15. Aaron had earned a salary in Israel of C$35,000 before coming to Canada. On arriving in Canada, he went to work for the City of Winnipeg, where he earned $15,000 in employment income. He also attended the University of Winnipeg on a part-time basis for four months and his tuition fees were $900.

— REQUIRED

Aaron asks you to help him with his Canadian income taxes.

— SOLUTION

Income for Canadian tax purposes:			
Israeli salary	$ 0	(not taxable, earned before resident)	
Canadian salary	15,000		
	$15,000		
Federal and provincial tax (15% + 10% = 25%)	$ 3,750		
Personal tax credits (federal + provincial): 25% of the total of:			
Basic	$ 4,204	($11,038 × 139/365 days)	ITA: 118(1)
Tuition	900	(tuition paid)	ITA: 118.5
Education and textbook	560	(part-time, $140 × 4)	ITA: 118.6
Employment credit	1,117		ITA: 118(10)
CPP	569	(4.95% of ($15,000 – $3,500) = $569)	ITA: 118.7

EI	282	(1.88% of $15,000 = $282)
	$ 7,632	
Credits	$ 1,908	

Aaron would owe tax of $1,842 for 2013.

¶19,220 Deemed Acquisition on Entering Canada

Taxpayers taking up Canadian residence are deemed to have disposed of each of the properties that they owned before entering Canada, and to have reacquired the properties at their then fair market value. This rule applies to most types of property and not just to capital property, although capital property is the most common application. Consequently, for future dispositions, the gain or loss accrued on property owned before entering Canada will not be considered for Canadian income tax purposes. The deemed acquisition amount becomes the cost base for Canadian tax purposes. ITA: 128.1(1)(*b*), (*c*)

This rule ensures that immigrants are only subject to Canadian tax on gains made after becoming residents.

Example Problem 19-7

When Aaron Levy immigrated to Canada, he owned 5,000 shares of a public company listed on the New York Stock Exchange. His original purchase price was US$18 a share, and the fair market value of the shares when he entered Canada was US$24 a share. The exchange rate was at par.

— *REQUIRED*

What is his adjusted cost base ("ACB") for tax purposes? If Aaron sold the shares in 2013 for $32 per share, what amount would be included in his Division B income for tax purposes? Assume that the exchange rate at the date of sale was also at par.

— *SOLUTION*

Aaron is deemed to have acquired the shares at US$24, or US$120,000 in total. The exchange rate applicable at the time of entry in Canada is used to convert the U.S. dollars to Canadian dollars. Aaron's ACB upon entering Canada is $120,000. ITA: 128.1(1)(*c*)

On the disposition of the shares, Aaron would include a taxable capital gain in Division B income of:

Proceeds of disposition ($32 × 5,000)	$ 160,000
Adjusted cost base ($24 × 5,000)	(120,000)
Capital gain	$ 40,000
Taxable capital gain	$ 20,000

The deemed disposition/acquisition rule does not apply to the following properties held by an individual: ITA: 128.1(1)(*b*)

- taxable Canadian property (see definition in ¶19,130);
- inventory of a business carried on in Canada;
- eligible capital property of a business carried on in Canada;
- "excluded rights or interests", which include rights under most pension and deferred income plans including salary deferral arrangements, registered pension plans, retirement compensation arrangements, registered retirement savings plans, rights to ITA: 128.1(10)

receive benefits under the *Canada Pension Plan* and the *Old Age Security Act*, and employee stock options.

These properties are exempt from the deemed disposition/acquisition rule and the tax cost is not increased when taking up residence. These properties are exempt from the rules because income and gains attributed to ownership of these properties are Canadian sources regardless of the owner's residency status.

¶19,230 Deemed Disposition on Leaving Canada

When a taxpayer gives up his or her Canadian residence, the taxpayer is deemed to have disposed of all his or her property at its then fair market value. This rule applies, with certain exceptions, to both capital and non-capital property. By deeming a disposition, Canada is assured that taxes are paid on any income/gains accrued on the property while the taxpayer was a resident of Canada. Depending on the nature of the property, this deemed disposition may result in a taxable capital gain, allowable capital loss, capital cost allowance recapture, terminal loss, or business income or loss. The tax on this deemed disposition is commonly referred to as "departure tax". ITA: 128.1(4); Form T1243

Because of the potential tax consequences for an individual leaving Canada, it is very important to establish the date on which he or she becomes a non-resident. This is generally the latest of the dates on which:

- the individual leaves Canada;

Income Tax Folio S5-F1-C1 — Determining an Individual's Residence Status

- the spouse and/or dependants, if any, leave Canada; or
- the individual becomes a resident of another country.

Example Problem 19-8

Carol Ann Thomas emigrated from Canada this year. At the time she left, she owned 500 shares of XYZ Ltd., a listed company on a designated Canadian stock exchange. The fair market value of the shares at that time was $20. Her ACB was $8 per share.

— *REQUIRED*

What would Carol Ann report on her Canadian tax return for the year of departure?

— *SOLUTION*

Deemed proceeds ($20 × 500)	$10,000
ACB ($8 × 500)	4,000
Capital gain	$ 6,000
Taxable capital gain	$ 3,000

Properties of an individual exempt from the deemed disposition rule are:

(i) real property situated in Canada, Canadian resource properties, or timber resource properties; ITA: 128.1(4)(*b*)

(ii) property (including capital property, eligible capital property, and inventory) of a business carried on in Canada by the taxpayer through a permanent establishment in Canada at the time of emigration;

(iii) "excluded rights or interests", which include rights under most pension and deferred income plans, including salary deferral arrangements, registered pension plans, retirement compensation arrangements, registered retirement savings plans, ITA: 128.1(10) rights to receive benefits under the *Canada Pension Plan* and the *Old Age Security Act*, and employee stock options;

(iv) certain properties if the individual was a short-term resident (resident in Canada for 60 months or less during the 10-year period preceding the cessation of Canadian residence); and

(v) property where the taxpayer elects to unwind the deemed disposition from a previous departure upon returning to Canada. ITA: 128.1(6)

Again, properties exempt from the deemed disposition are generally properties for which future gains and income attributed to ownership of the property are Canadian-source and continue to be taxed in Canada.

An individual can elect that the deemed disposition at fair market value apply to properties described in (i) or (ii), above. An emigrant may file this election to use a loss on such properties against gains arising because of the deemed disposition. Losses realized because of the election may only offset the increase in the taxpayer's income from the deemed disposition and cannot be used against other sources of income. ITA: 128.1(4)(*d*) Form T2061A

Each property subject to the deemed disposition rule is deemed to have been reacquired by the individual at its fair market value. 128.1(4)(*c*)

As these rules may result in a large tax burden because there is no actual disposition and no cash generated on the deemed disposition, tax relief is also included in the legislation. Individuals ceasing to be resident can elect to post security with the CRA for the purpose of deferring the payment of the tax that results from the deemed disposition rule. The election must be made and the security provided on or before the balance due date for the year in which emigration takes place. Where the election is made, the payment of the tax can be deferred without interest until the properties are actually sold. Security is not required for tax calculated on the first $100,000 of capital gains (i.e., $50,000 of taxable income) using the highest tax bracket rate. ITA: 220(4.5), (4.51) Form T1244

In addition, individuals who cease to be resident in Canada and own property that has a total fair market value of greater than $25,000 at the time of their departure are required to file a form to list such property. Personal-use property that has a fair market value of less than $10,000 will be excluded from this requirement. Form T1161

¶19,300 IMPACT OF CANADA–FOREIGN COUNTRY TAX TREATIES

Canada has entered into bilateral tax conventions or agreements with more than 80 countries for the purpose of avoiding double taxation, preventing tax evasion, facilitating and encouraging business transactions between the countries, determining the distribution of tax revenues to the governments of the contracting countries, and exchanging tax-related information. Canada is a party to the Vienna Convention on the Law of Treaties and, as a result, is required to abide by its provisions under international law. Generally, tax conventions avoid double taxation in two ways: by determining each jurisdiction's right to tax or not to tax a particular type of income, and by requiring the contracting countries to grant tax credits for income tax paid on such income to the other country.

To prevent tax evasion, most of Canada's tax treaties contain an article pertaining to the exchange of information between the contracting countries. The Canada–U.S. Tax Convention goes further in this area than any other existing treaty. Canada and the United States have agreed to provide comprehensive assistance to each other in the enforcement of their respective tax laws.

The terms of any tax convention or agreement are given the force of law in Canada by virtue of legislation passed by the Parliament of Canada to implement them. The implementing statutes establish that in the event of inconsistency between the terms of Canadian income tax law and the terms of the agreement or convention, the terms of the agreement are to prevail.

The Income Tax Conventions Interpretation Act (ITCIA) defines terms and provides clarification for concepts used in income tax conventions with other countries signed by Canada. Some of the provisions in the ITCIA can override a treaty.

Tax treaties are not documents possessing the same degree of intricacy that, for example, characterizes the *Income Tax Act*. In interpreting the terms of legislation implementing a tax convention, it may not be proper to apply the strict rules of interpretation that normally apply to taxing statutes. The *OECD Model Tax Convention on Income and Capital* (OECD Model) and the *United Nations Model Double Taxation Convention Between Developed and Developing Nations* (UN Model) have been used by the Canadian government to develop Canada's tax treaties. The commentary of the provisions of the OECD Model is widely used and accepted as a guide to interpretation of most treaties worldwide. The Canadian courts have identified the OECD Model as an important interpretation tool. In the *Crown Forest Industries Ltd. v. Canada* case, the OECD Model and commentary was considered more than a supplementary source of interpretation and was of "high persuasive value". 95 DTC 5389 (S.C.C.), at 5398

The tax systems of provincial governments are not bound by tax treaties. Provincial legislation must be reviewed to determine whether treaties or specific articles of the treaties are recognized for provincial tax purposes.

¶19,310 Application of the treaties

The Canadian taxation of non-residents as covered in this text, has used the domestic law of Canada — the *Income Tax Act* — as its basis. In reality, this income is subject to the treatment provided by the applicable Canadian tax treaty, if any, with the country in which the non-resident resides. In other words, the tax convention has priority over the contracting countries' tax legislation. Where there is a conflict between the Act and the treaty, generally the treaty provision prevails.

The tax conventions between Canada and other countries are relevant for Canadian residents and for non-residents. Canadian residents need to refer to treaties to determine the taxation of their foreign sources of income and relief available from double taxation. Non-residents need to determine the taxation of their Canadian sources of income and relief available from double taxation. For example, if a Canadian corporation expands its business by establishing a branch in another country, the analysis of the relevant tax convention will be important to determine whether the income from the foreign operation will be taxed in the foreign country. If it will, the analysis will also be important to ensure that relief from double taxation is available. Furthermore, the opening of a branch in another country could imply the transfer of some employees to the other country. These employees, in certain circumstances, will become non-residents of Canada. The convention will be important with respect to determining how their Canadian-source income, if any, will be taxed.

It is well recognized that tax conventions do not levy income taxes but limit the tax otherwise assessed by the contracting countries. The following citation is found in the analysis by the Supreme Court of Canada in the tax case, *The Queen v. Melford Developments Inc.*: "It is well to remind ourselves in analysing these statutes and the subtended tax Agreement that the international Agreement does not itself levy taxes but simply authorizes the contracting parties, within the terms of the Agreement, to do so". 82 DTC 6281 (S.C.C.), at 6285.

When dealing with international transactions, the practice requirement is to first examine the *Income Tax Act* to determine whether an income item is taxable. If it is established to be taxable under the Act, then the appropriate tax convention should be consulted to determine in which country it is taxable and at what tax rate.

The Canada–U.S. Tax Convention contains articles commonly used in Canada's tax treaties. The application of selected articles from the Convention is highlighted as follows:

Article I — Personal Scope: The treaty is only applicable to residents of one or both countries.

Article IV — Residence: Residents of one or both countries. This article defines the meaning of the term "resident of a Contracting State" for the purpose of Article I. The article also includes what is commonly referred to as a tiebreaker rule. It determines the residency status of a person where the person is a resident of both Canada and the United States under each country's respective domestic law.

Article V — Permanent Establishment: This article is used in conjunction with Article VII. (See discussion at ¶19,120.)

Article VII — Business Profits: Business profits of a resident of one country are only taxed in the country of residence unless the business is carried on through a permanent establishment in the other country. Business profits attributable to the permanent establishment are taxed in the other country. This provision can override Canada's jurisdiction to tax income from carrying on business in accordance with subsection 2(3) of the Act where a U.S. resident is carrying on business but does not have a permanent establishment in Canada.

Article IX — Related Persons: The treaty partners are authorized to adjust the amount of "income, loss or tax payable" for arrangements between a person in one state and a related person in another if the arrangements "differ from those that would be made between unrelated persons". Time frames for adjustments are provided. This article is consistent with the transfer pricing provisions in the Act. ITA: 247

Article X — Dividends: The 25% withholding tax rate under the Act is limited to 5% if the beneficial owner is a company owning "at least 10% of the voting stock of the company paying the dividends" and 15% in all other cases. The article also limits branch tax to 5% and exempts the first $500,000 of cumulative income from branch tax. ITA: 212

Article XI — Interest: Withholding tax under the Act is eliminated on cross-border interest payments between Canada and the United States. There is also guidance on the sourcing of interest payments in specific circumstances. [For interest paid between unrelated persons, the full exemption applied starting January 1, 2010. For 2008 and 2009, the rate was reduced to 7% and 4%, respectively.] ITA: 212

Article XIII — Gains: Capital gains of U.S. residents on Canadian property are exempt from Canadian tax unless the property is (a) real property situated in Canada, or (b) a share in a Canadian resident corporation or an interest in a partnership or trust, the value of which is derived principally from real property in Canada. Capital gains of Canadian residents on U.S. property are exempt from U.S. tax unless the property is real property situated in the U.S. or a "real property interest" as defined in section 897(c) of the *Internal Revenue Code*, which includes shares of a U.S. corporation meeting an asset-ratio test.

Article XV — Dependent Personal Services: Wages and other employment remuneration earned by a resident of one country for services performed in the other are not taxable in the other country if

- the remuneration is $10,000 or less (in the currency of the other country), or
- the person is present in the other country for 183 days or less in any 12-month period commencing or ending in the year and the remuneration was not paid by or on behalf of a person resident in the other country or borne by a permanent establishment in the other country.

Article XXVI — Mutual Agreement Procedure: Competent authority procedures and notification time limits are outlined for resolving cases with a result that is not in accordance with provisions of the treaty (e.g., double taxation).

The Canada–U.S. Tax Convention includes a technical explanation for each article and is a useful interpretation tool for applying the convention. It reflects understandings reached during the negotiation of the treaty on the meaning of provisions used in the articles. It is important to recognize that these technical explanations are not legally binding. For other Canadian tax treaties, no technical explanation is provided and reference to the OECD model and UN model commentaries, or case law is necessary for interpretation purposes.

A reference table in the front of CCH's CANADIAN INCOME TAX ACT WITH REGULATIONS summarizes in table format the withholding tax requirements under the various Canada–foreign country treaties. A quick glance at that table reveals that the 25% withholding rate required under the Act is often reduced under a treaty. ITA: 212

¶19,400 CROSS-BORDER TRANSACTIONS AND LOANS

¶19,410 Transfer Pricing

The phrase "transfer pricing" refers to the pricing used by a Canadian taxpayer for transactions with a related non-resident person. Transactions can involve goods, services, and/or intangibles. Transfer pricing legislation is designed to ensure that transfer prices between related persons are set at arm's length prices. Without legislation, it would be easy for taxpayers to arrange transfer prices in a manner that would allocate profits to lower tax jurisdictions. ITA: 247; IC 87-2R

In the Canadian *Income Tax Act*, transfer price is defined as, "a price, a rental, a royalty, a premium or other payment for, or for the use, production or reproduction of, property or as consideration for services (including services provided as an employee and the insurance or reinsurance of risks) as part of the transaction". A "transfer pricing adjustment" (either income or capital) will result where a taxpayer and a non-arm's length non-resident participate in a transaction: ITA: 247(1)

(a) where the terms and conditions differ from those that would apply in an arm's length transaction, or

(b) that would not have been entered into by arm's length persons and the purpose was to obtain a tax benefit.

The "transfer pricing adjustment" is whatever is required in terms of adjusting the price used for the transaction or, in the case of (b), above, changing the nature of the transaction to what would have occurred between arm's length persons.

The OECD Transfer Pricing Guidelines recommend a number of transfer pricing methodologies to be used to determine an arm's length price. The traditional transaction methods (TTMs) include the comparable uncontrolled price (CUP) method, the resale price method (commonly used for distributors) and the cost plus method (commonly used for contract manufacturers and service providers). The transactional profit methods (TPMs) include the profit split method and transactional net margin method. The CRA has expressed preference for the use of TTMs over TPMs and view there to be a natural hierarchy in methods with the CUP method being most reliable.

Where an adjustment is made, a penalty is assessable. The penalty is calculated as 10% of the transfer pricing adjustment. The penalty does not apply if the taxpayer made reasonable efforts to determine and use arm's length prices for the transaction. A taxpayer is deemed to have made reasonable efforts if contemporaneous documentation was prepared and includes the information specified in the Act. The documentation must have been prepared by the person's tax filing due date for the year and must be provided within three months of a written request from CRA. The penalty also does not apply if the transfer pricing adjustment is less than the lesser of 10% of the taxpayer's gross revenue for the year and $5 million. ITA: 247(3) ITA: 247(4)

Example Problem 19-9

A Canadian importer (Canco) purchases goods from an arm's length U.S. supplier at a price of C$30/unit. The Canadian company's gross annual revenue is $6 million. The Canadian importer incorporates a subsidiary (BCo) in a low tax jurisdiction. The U.S. supplier begins to sell the goods to BCo at the C$30/unit price. The Canadian importer purchases the goods from the subsidiary at a price of C$40/unit. The goods are shipped directly to the Canadian importer's customers.

— *REQUIRED*

(a) Will a transfer pricing adjustment apply to Canco?

(b) Will a penalty apply to Canco?

— *SOLUTION*

(a) Canco and BCo are related persons. The terms of the transactions between Canco and BCo do not appear to be at arm's length. The CRA is likely to adjust the cost of sales of Canco to an amount that reflects an arm's length price and increase taxable income of the Canadian company. The arm's length price is likely the C$30/unit, unless Canco can prove that a comparable uncontrolled price is at a higher amount, i.e., Canco can purchase the same product from an arm's length supplier at the higher price.

(b) A penalty will apply if the transfer pricing adjustment is greater than $600,000 (10% of $6,000,000) unless Canco can produce contemporaneous documentation supporting the pricing used within three months of a written request from the CRA.

Where a Canadian company has overpaid for goods, services, or intangibles purchased from a non-arm's length non-resident, the overpayment will be deemed to be a dividend immediately before the end of the tax year of the adjustment. An overpayment to a controlled foreign affiliate as defined in section 17 will not be subject to Part XIII tax. ITA: 247(12), 212(2); TPM-02

Where the non-resident person pays an amount to the corporation with the concurrence of the Minister, the dividend can be reduced by the amount the Minister considers appropriate. Penalties will not apply for failed withholding tax. Interest applies to the Part XIII tax from the time of the deemed dividend to the time of repayment and/or the withholding tax is paid. ITA: 214(13) ITA: 227(8.5)

¶19,420 Corporate Debt Owed to a Non-Resident — Inbound Loans

¶19,425 Thin capitalization

Interest on loans used to earn income from business or property is deductible in computing taxable income of a Canadian corporation. The tax deductibility of interest creates preference for financing Canadian operations through debt rather than equity, particularly where tax rates are lower in the lending jurisdiction. ITA: 20(1)(*c*)

The "thin capitalization rules" are a set of rules designed to prevent non-resident shareholders, either alone or together with related persons, who hold significant equity positions (25% or more of votes or fair market value) in a Canadian corporation from removing profits of that corporation by way of tax deductible interest payments instead of through dividends. ITA: 18(4); IT-59R3

The deduction for interest paid or payable by a corporation resident in Canada in computing its business or property income is restricted if debt relative to equity is too high. The restriction is imposed if outstanding debts to specified non-resident shareholders or persons related to them exceed the shareholders' equity of the corporation by a ratio of more than 1.5 to one for taxation years ending after March 28, 2012. For taxation years beginning after 2000, the required debt-to-equity ratio to avoid non-deductible interest was two to one.

The otherwise-deductible interest that is disallowed as a deduction is determined by the following formula:

$$A \times \frac{(B - (1.5 \times C))}{B}$$

A — Interest otherwise deductible, (paid or payable) in the year, on outstanding debts to specified non-residents.

B — The average of the greatest amount of the corporation's outstanding debts to specified non-residents for each month in the year.

C — The sum of the corporation's beginning retained earnings for the year, the average of the non-resident's share of beginning contributed surplus for each month ending in the year, and the average of beginning paid-up capital of the non-resident's shares for each month ending in the year.

Example Problem 19-10

Canada Corp. is owned 100% by specified non-residents. The existing equity in the corporation (beginning retained earnings, the monthly average of beginning contributed surplus by specified non-residents, and the monthly average of beginning paid-up capital of the specified non-residents' shares) is $200,000. Interest paid in the year on a $1 million debt (average of the greatest amount of debt for each month) due to the specified non-resident shareholders was $125,000 for 2013.

— *REQUIRED*

What is the impact, if any, of the thin capitalization rule on the corporation's 2013 Division B income calculation?

— *SOLUTION*

The maximum interest deduction allowed by Canada Corp. on the debt owing to specified non-residents is limited by the formula provided by subsection 18(4). The denied deductible interest is $87,500, as calculated:

$$\$125{,}000 \text{ interest} \times (\$1{,}000{,}000 - 1.5\ (\$200{,}000))\ /\ \$1{,}000{,}000 = \$87{,}500$$

Therefore, Canada Corp, can deduct $50,000 of interest for the year ($125,000 interest paid – $75,000 non-deductible interest in computing Division B income).

Note that even short-term increases in debt owing to specified non-residents or related non-residents could result in or increase the non-deductible portion of interest because of the averages used in the formula. Where a thin capitalization problem becomes evident midway through a taxation year, steps can be taken to repay debt, infuse capital, or convert debt to capital to reduce the non-deductible interest.

Subsection 18(4) also applies to debts owed by partnerships of which a Canadian resident corporation is a member. Disallowed interest under the thin capitalization rules is deemed to have been paid as a dividend by the corporation at the end of the tax year for the purposes of Part XIII tax. Penalties for failure to withhold will not apply. ITA: 214(16), (17)

¶19,427 Upstream Loans

Proposed amendments released on August 19, 2011, with revisions in an October 24, 2012 Bill, introduce upstream loan provisions to the ITA. The upstream loan rules are designed to prevent the avoidance of a Canadian income inclusion and related tax that would arise on dividends paid from hybrid and taxable surplus of foreign affiliates through structuring the flow of cash through loans instead of dividend payments. The rules apply where a person who meets the definition of a specified debtor receives a loan from a foreign affiliate of a taxpayer resident in Canada. The loan amount defined as the "specified amount" is included in the income of the taxpayer in the year the loan is received by the specified debtor. ITA: 90(6), (15)

A specified debtor is defined to include the taxpayer and a person who is non-arm's length with the taxpayer. It also includes partnerships of which the taxpayer or non-arm's length persons are members. A specified debtor cannot include a controlled foreign affiliate of the taxpayer. ITA: 90(15)

The result is that the provisions will apply where a foreign affiliate of a Canadian corporation makes a loan directly to the Canadian corporation, and also where the foreign affiliate makes a loan to any person non-arm's length with the Canadian corporation as long as the person is not a controlled foreign affiliate of the Canadian corporation. The specified amount included in the income of each Canadian taxpayer with an interest in the foreign affiliate providing the loan is determined based on its surplus entitlement percentage in the foreign affiliate. Where there is only one class of share of the foreign affiliate, the surplus entitlement percentage is the Canadian company's equity interest in the foreign entity. ITA: 90(15); ITR: 5905(13)

The loan is only included in the income of the Canadian taxpayer if it is not repaid within two years of the date the loan was made and did not arise in the ordinary course of business of the creditor where *bona fide* arrangements for repayment within a reasonable time were ITA: 90(8) made at the time of the loan. Therefore, short-term loans by foreign affiliates are not caught by the rules.

Where there is an income inclusion, an offsetting deduction can be made based on the exempt, hybrid, and taxable surplus balances of the foreign affiliate and represents that amount that would have been deductible under Division C if the loan had been paid as a dividend to the Canadian taxpayer. The deductible amount is treated as a reserve and included in income the next year so that there is an annual inclusion/deduction for the period the loan is outstanding. The reserve is intended to allow taxpayers to make loans instead of paying dividends where there is no intention to achieve a Canadian tax benefit. ITA: 90(9), 113(1) ITA 90(12)

When repayments of the loan included in the income of the Canadian taxpayer are made, a deduction is available to each Canadian resident in proportion to the specified amount that was originally included in the income relative to the full amount of the loan. The reserve deduction is not allowed for the portion of the specified amount repaid. ITA: 90(13)

¶19,430 Corporate Debt Owed by a Non-Resident — Outbound Loans

¶19,435 Cross-border shareholder loans/balances

ITA: 90(6), (15)

In a domestic context, the shareholder loan provisions (per ¶13,080) of the ITA prevent Canadian shareholders of closely held corporations from removing funds from the corporation tax-free through loans instead of through the receipt of dividends taxable under Part I of the Act. The shareholder loan provisions also apply in a cross-border context to prevent a Canadian corporation from loaning funds to a related non-resident instead of paying a dividend that would be subject to withholding tax under Part XIII. The shareholder loan provisions will result in the loan being deemed to be a dividend for purposes of Part XIII withholding tax. ITA: 15(2), 214(3)(*a*)

A loan from a Canadian corporation to a non-resident shareholder or non-resident person[3] related to a shareholder will be deemed to have been paid to the non-resident as a dividend if the balance is not repaid within one year of the end of the year in which the loan was made. Withholding tax will apply to the dividend at the reduced rate (if any) under the applicable treaty. The dividend is deemed to have been paid at the time the loan was made. Administratively, the CRA will calculate the interest on the Part XIII tax from the 15th day of the first month following the taxation year of the loan. A refund of the withholding tax may be received upon written application to the CRA within two years after the calendar year in which a repayment of the loan balance is made. ITA: 15(2.6) ITA: 227(6.1)

Where a loan is repaid within one year of the end of the taxation year in which the loan is made, the loan balance will not be deemed to be a dividend. However, if the interest rate charged on the loan for the period outstanding is less than the prescribed interest rate, an interest benefit computed at the prescribed rate less interest paid on the loan (by 30 days of the end of the applicable taxation year) will be deemed to be a dividend paid to the non-resident and will be subject to Part XIII tax. Similarly, if a refund of Part XIII tax applicable to the loan balance is received because the loan balance was repaid, an interest benefit (if any) will be computed on the loan balance for the period the loan was outstanding. Part XIII tax will apply to the interest benefit deemed to be a dividend. ITA: 15(9), 80.4(2), 214(3)(*a*) ITA: 227(6.1)

Example Problem 19-11

Canco, a Canadian subsidiary of a U.S. parent company (USCo.) loans excess cash to USCo. in its December 31, 2012 taxation year end and does not charge interest.

— *REQUIRED*

Does subsection 15(2) apply to the loan transaction?

— *SOLUTION*

The loan to USCo., a non-resident shareholder, will be deemed a dividend unless the amount is repaid by USCo. by December 31, 2013. Withholding tax is owing by Canco on the deemed ITA: 15(2), 214(3)(*a*), 227(6.1)

[3] Other than a foreign affiliate of the corporation (or of a Canadian resident who is non-arm's length with the corporation).

dividend plus interest computed from January 15, 2013. If USCo. repays the loan balance in the future, it can apply no later than two years after the end of the calendar year of the repayment to receive a refund of the withholding tax.

If the balance is repaid and Part XIII tax refunded, an interest benefit, equal to the prescribed rate applied to the loan for the period it was outstanding, will be deemed to be a dividend subject to Part XIII tax.

The provisions discourage Canadian companies from distributing profits through loans to related non-residents to avoid the Part XIII implications instead of paying dividends.

¶19,440 Low-interest cross-border loans/balances

In addition to potential Part XIII tax implications, loans from Canadian residents to non-residents can also result in a deemed interest income inclusion for the Canadian company. ITA: 17(1)

To prevent Canadian corporations from avoiding Canadian income taxes by providing capital to non-residents at low or no interest, the Act requires a minimum amount of interest (deemed interest) income to be recognized. This provision only applies to debt that has been outstanding for more than one year.

Where the Canadian resident corporation's income inclusion related to the amount owing from the non-resident (including any amount included in income that is received or receivable from a trust and foreign accrual property income attributed to the amount owing) is less than a reasonable rate of interest on the balance, the Canadian corporation is required to report interest income equal to the prescribed rate, less the amount already included in income. Whether interest is computed at a reasonable rate is a question of fact, and has to be measured in market terms after giving consideration to the risk inherent in the loan (i.e., quality of any security or lack thereof).

Example Problem 19-12

Harold Chui is the sole shareholder of CCPC Ltd. and of USCO Inc. CCPC Ltd. has advanced USCO Inc. $100,000 to assist in financing its relatively new operations in Port Huron, Michigan. USCO Inc. does not pay any interest to CCPC Ltd. on this indebtedness, which has been outstanding for more than a year.

— REQUIRED

Is this loan of any consequence to CCPC Ltd.'s Canadian taxes?

— SOLUTION

Yes, CCPC Ltd. is required to report deemed interest on the $100,000 at the prescribed rate. Assuming a prescribed rate of 2%, CCPC Ltd. will have to report deemed interest income of $2,000 annually. Note that USCO Inc. does not have to be related to CCPC Ltd. for subsection 17(1) to apply. ITA: 17(1)

The deemed interest rules do not apply to a loan by a Canadian resident corporation to:

(1) a controlled foreign affiliate if the loan is used for the purpose of earning active business income; ITA: 17(8)

(2) a loan to an unrelated person arising from the sale of goods or services under arm's length terms or conditions; or ITA: 17(9)

(3) a loan if Part XIII withholding tax has been paid on the amount as is the case where the shareholder loan provisions discussed in ¶19,435 apply. Where a refund of the Part XIII withholding tax is applied for and received when the loan balance is repaid, the deemed interest rules will apply during the period the loan balance was outstanding. ITA: 17(7) ITA: 227(6.1) ITA: 17(1)

An anti-avoidance provision prevents the Canadian resident corporation from circumventing the income inclusion resulting from the deemed interest rules by making an indirect loan to a non-resident.[4] The provision applies where a loan or transfer of property (or ITA: 17(2) ITA: 17(1)

[4] Similar anti-avoidance provisions apply for loans through and to partnerships and through trusts.

anticipated loan or transfer of property)[5] by a Canadian resident corporation results in an amount owing between non-residents. In such a case, the non-resident receiving the loan is deemed to owe the amount to the Canadian resident corporation for purposes of determining the income inclusion under the deemed interest rules. The anti-avoidance rule does not apply where:

(1) both non-residents are controlled foreign affiliates of the corporation resident in Canada; or ITA: 17(3)

(2) the non-residents are not related and the terms or conditions of the loan between them are arm's length. For purposes of this exception, a controlled foreign affiliate is controlled by Canadian residents. ITA: 17(15)

Example Problem 19-13

CCPC Ltd., per Example Problem 19-12, attempts to circumvent the income inclusion under the deemed interest rules by investing the $100,000 in share capital of another corporation, Bermuda Inc., owned by Harold Chui, instead of making a direct loan to USCO Inc. Bermuda Inc. loans the funds interest-free to USCO Inc. The loan is outstanding for more than a year. ITA: 17(1)

— REQUIRED

What are the income tax consequences of this plan? Assume a prescribed interest rate of 2%.

— SOLUTION

The investment in shares of Bermuda Inc. would be considered a non-exempt transfer of property by CCPC Ltd. The anti-avoidance provision would deem USCO Inc. to owe the $100,000 to CCPC Ltd. CCPC Ltd. would report interest income of $2,000. USCO Inc. would not be a controlled foreign affiliate of CCPC Ltd., and USCO Inc. and Bermuda Inc. are related persons so neither of the exceptions would apply. ITA: 17(2) ITA: 17(3)

¶19,450 Foreign Affiliate Dumping

In the March 2012 federal Budget, foreign affiliate dumping provisions were added to the ITA to address erosion of the Canadian tax base through investment by Canadian subsidiaries of foreign-based multinational groups in foreign affiliates. The erosion of the tax base arises due to interest deductions in Canada on funds borrowed by the Canadian entity to invest in a foreign affiliate and/or through the ability to extract corporate surplus from Canada free of dividend withholding tax. The provisions apply to transactions that occur after March 28, 2012. ITA: 212.3

The provisions apply where a Canadian-resident corporation (CRIC) controlled by a non-resident corporation invests in a foreign affiliate of the CRIC. The CRIC is deemed to have paid a dividend to the foreign parent equal to the fair market value of any property transferred or obligation assumed/incurred related to the investment. Also, in computing the paid-up capital of the shares of the CRIC, there is a deduction for any increase in the PUC of the CRIC's shares that relate to the investment. ITA: 212.3(2)

The provisions will not apply where the CRIC demonstrates that ITA: 212.3(16)

(1) The business activities of the foreign affiliate are more closely connected to the business activities of the CRIC than the business activities of a foreign non-arm's length corporation.

(2) Officers of the CRIC who are residents and work principally in Canada (or in a country in which a CFA of the CRIC carries on business activities) exercised the principal decision-making authority in respect to making the investment.

(3) The officers of the CRIC will have and exercise the ongoing principal decision-making authority in respect of the investment, the majority of the officers will be resident and work principally in Canada or in a country in which a connected affiliate is resident, and the

[5] Other than an exempt loan or transfer defined in subsection 17(15).

performance evaluation and compensation of the officers will be based on the results of the foreign affiliate more so than will be for officers of a non-resident corporation.

The exception does not apply where the investment is a preferred share investment in the foreign affiliate. ITA: 212.3(19)

An investment in the foreign affiliate can include: ITA 212.3(10), (18)

(1) A direct or indirect (if certain conditions are met) acquisition of shares of the foreign affiliate. The acquisition of shares in a related party transaction is excepted.

(2) A contribution of capital or benefit conferred.

(3) A transaction resulting in an amount owing to the CRIC other than an amount arising in the ordinary course of business of the CRIC and repaid within 180 days.

(4) A non-arm's length acquisition of a debt obligation of the foreign affiliate.

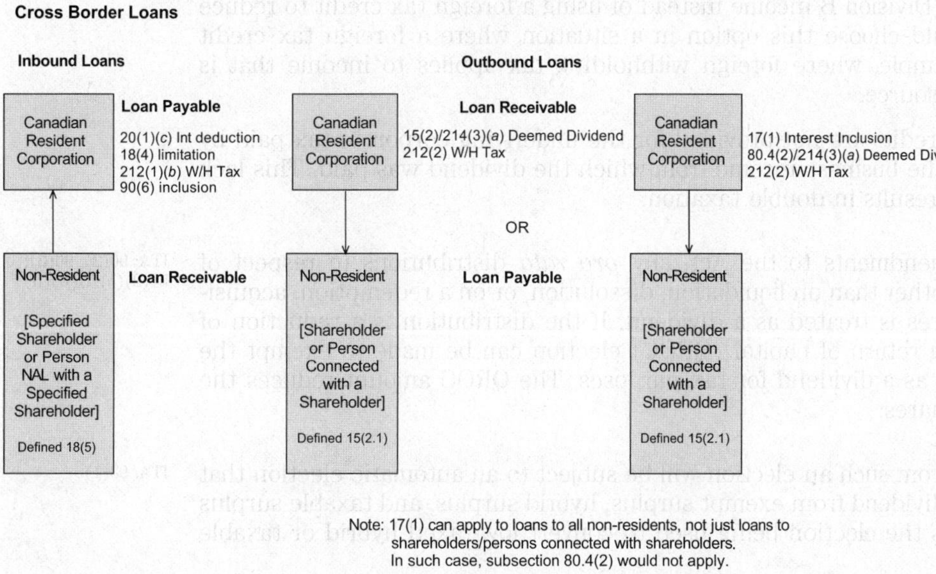

¶19,500 TAXATION OF CANADIAN RESIDENTS WITH FOREIGN INVESTMENTS

The Canadian tax treatment of investment by a Canadian resident in a foreign country depends on the nature of the investment. The tax treatment of investment in active business in a foreign jurisdiction differs from the tax treatment of investment in passive activities.

¶19,510 Active Business Income Earned in a Foreign Jurisdiction

¶19,515 Unincorporated foreign branch operations

Canadian residents are taxable on worldwide income. Consequently, a Canadian resident earning business income in a foreign jurisdiction through an unincorporated branch includes the income in Canadian taxable income computed under Part I of the *Income Tax Act*. If the income is also subject to tax in the foreign jurisdiction after considering the applicable tax treaty, if any, a foreign tax credit (business income tax deduction, described at ¶11,335) can be used to reduce the Canadian Part I tax liability. Any unused tax deduction can be carried back three years and carried forward ten years. ITA: 126(2)

¶19,520 Individuals receiving dividends from foreign corporations

A Canadian resident individual earning business income in a foreign jurisdiction through an incorporated entity will not pay tax on the income as it is earned. When dividends are paid from the foreign entity, the dividend is included in income. A foreign tax credit (non-business income tax deduction, described at ¶10,490) can be used to reduce Canadian Part I tax for the foreign tax withheld from the dividend and remitted to the foreign taxing authority. Only tax withheld at a rate of 15% or less can be used to reduce Part I tax. An individual may deduct any withholding tax in excess of 15% against income from property in computing Division B income. The inability to claim a full foreign tax credit for withholding taxes above 15% reflects the Canadian government's unwillingness to relinquish tax jurisdiction for withholding tax rates higher than 15% to a foreign country. This can result in double taxation. Canada's tax treaty with the United States addresses this issue of double taxation by resourcing property income to allow a credit in the United States for Canadian tax paid on the income in excess of 15%.

ITA: 12(1)(*k*), 90(1)

ITA: 126(1)

ITA: 20(11), 126(7)

Article XXIV Canada–U.S. Convention, par. 5

Alternatively, the individual has the option to claim a deduction for all of the tax withheld on a dividend in computing Division B income instead of using a foreign tax credit to reduce Part I tax. A taxpayer would choose this option in a situation where a foreign tax credit cannot be claimed, for example, where foreign withholding tax applies to income that is considered to be Canadian-source.

ITA: 20(12), 126(7)

Note that foreign tax credits are not provided for the underlying corporate tax paid by the foreign corporation on the business income from which the dividend was paid. This lack of cross-border integration results in double taxation.

In August 19, 2011 amendments to the Act, any *pro rata* distributions in respect of shares of a foreign affiliate other than on liquidation, dissolution, or on a redemption, acquisition, or cancellation of shares is treated as a dividend. If the distribution is a reduction of paid-up capital, a qualifying return of capital (QROC) election can be made to exempt the distribution from treatment as a dividend for tax purposes. The QROC amount reduces the adjusted cost base of the shares.

ITA: 90(2), 90(3), 53(2)(*b*)(i)(B)(II)

A capital gain arising from such an election will be subject to an automatic election that treats the capital gain as a dividend from exempt surplus, hybrid surplus, and taxable surplus in that order. This prevents the election being used to convert low-taxed hybrid or taxable surplus to a capital gain.

ITA: 93(1)

¶19,525 Corporations receiving dividends from non-foreign affiliates

A Canadian resident corporation earning business income in a foreign jurisdiction through an incorporated entity, again, will not pay tax on the income as it is earned. When dividends are paid from the foreign entity to the Canadian corporation, the tax treatment of the dividend depends on whether the dividend is received from a foreign affiliate of the Canadian corporation. A foreign affiliate is a non-resident corporation in which a Canadian resident owns not less than 1% of the shares and not less than 10% of the shares with related persons. If the foreign entity is not a foreign affiliate of the Canadian corporation, the dividend will be included in income and a full foreign tax credit for the foreign tax withheld can be claimed. Again, no credit is provided for the underlying corporate tax paid to the foreign jurisdiction on the business income earned by the corporation from which the dividend was paid, resulting in double taxation. The corporation has the option to claim a deduction for the tax withheld against income from business or property in computing Division B income instead of using a foreign tax credit to reduce Part I tax.

ITA: 95(1)

ITA: 12(1)(*k*), 90(1), 126(1)

ITA: 20(12), 126(7)

Example Problem 19-14

Jane Snow received $20,000 in dividend income in 2013 from a 5% investment she owns in her boyfriend's company in Tanzania. Withholding tax of 25% applied to the dividend. Jane also earned Canadian employment income of $60,000 in 2013.

— *REQUIRED*

(a) Compute the tax liability Jane paid on her 2013 income.

(b) What option exists regarding the tax treatment of the withholding tax?

(c) What would change if the share investment had been held by Jane's Canadian corporation?

— *SOLUTION*

(a)

Employment income	$ 60,000
Property income	$ 20,000
Subsection 20(11) deduction (withholding tax in excess of 15% of dividend)	$ (2,000)
Taxable income	$ 78,000
Federal tax:	
15% of $43,561	$ 6,534
22% of $34,439	$ 7,577
	$ 14,111
Tax credits:	
Personal (15% of $11,038)	$ (1,656)
Employment (15% of $1,117)	$ (168)
CPP (15% of $2,356)	$ (353)
EI (15% of $891)	$ (134)
Part I tax payable	$ 11,800
Foreign tax credit	$ (3,000)
Federal tax payable	$ 8,800

Foreign tax credit calculation:

Lesser of

(a) Non-business income tax paid to a foreign country = $3,000 ($20,000 × 15% limit)

(b) $\frac{\text{Net non-business foreign income included under Division B}}{\text{Total income included under Division B}} \times$ tax otherwise payable under Part I

$\frac{\$20,000}{\$78,000} \times \$11,911 = \$3,054$

(b) Jane could claim a deduction for the full amount of the withholding tax of $5,000 under subsection 20(12). However, this alternative would only make sense where a full foreign tax credit was not available, i.e., she would save tax of only $660 (22% of 3,000) through a deduction compared to $3,000 available as a foreign tax credit.

(c) If the dividend was received by a Canadian corporation, the dividend would be included in the computation of Division B income. A Division C deduction would not be available because the dividend is from a corporation that is not a foreign affiliate of the Canadian corporation. Taxable income would be subject to a federal corporate tax rate of 21.67% (38% – 10% – 13% + 6⅔%). A foreign tax credit would be available under subsection 126(1) of: ITA: 12(1)(*k*)

Lesser of:

(a) Non-business income tax paid to a foreign country = $5,000

(b) $\frac{\text{Net non-business foreign income included under Division B}}{\text{Income included under Division B}} \times$ tax otherwise payable under Part I

$\frac{\$20,000}{\$20,000} \times \$4,333 = \$4,333$

Assuming a provincial tax rate of 11.5%, the remaining withholding tax ($5,000 – $4,333), i.e., $667, could be claimed as a foreign tax credit against provincial tax.

¶19,530 Corporations receiving dividends from foreign affiliates

If the corporation paying the dividend is a foreign affiliate of the Canadian resident corporation, the tax treatment of the dividend depends on whether the dividend is paid out of exempt surplus, taxable surplus, or pre-acquisition surplus as defined by Regulation. The dividend will be included in income and offsetting Division C deductions will be claimed depending on the classification of the income from which the dividend is determined to have been paid. ITR: 5907(1); ITA: 12(1)(*k*), 90(1), 113(1)

Exempt surplus dividends are fully deductible under Division C. The exemption for dividends paid from exempt surplus results in the income being taxed at foreign country rates. Canada has relinquished its jurisdiction to tax this type of income. Exempt surplus includes active business income earned in countries with which Canada has a tax convention or a comprehensive tax information exchange agreement (TIEA), i.e., designated treaty countries, as well as capital gains on the disposition of property used or held by the foreign affiliate principally for the purpose of gaining or producing income from an active business carried on by it in a designated treaty country. Exempt surplus also includes 50% of capital gains (representing the non-taxable portion of the gains) on other properties (for example, properties used or held principally to gain or produce active business income but not in a designated treaty country, and shares of foreign affiliates). Thus, dividends paid from the non-taxable portion of gains are not taxed in Canada. This treatment is consistent with the tax treatment of the non-taxable portion of gains realized on the disposition of properties held directly by Canadian residents. ITA: 113(1); ITR: 5907(1) ITR: 5907(1) "exempt earnings"; ITA: 95(1) "excluded property"

The Division C deduction for dividends paid from taxable surplus relates to both the underlying tax paid by the foreign entity on the earnings from which the dividend was paid and the foreign withholding tax paid on the dividend. Instead of providing a credit against Part I tax for these amounts, the deduction converts the underlying tax and withholding tax using the "relevant tax factor" to an equivalent deduction against income. The end result is that the dividend is taxed at Canadian rates and double taxation is prevented through a deduction for the underlying tax and withholding tax paid to the foreign jurisdiction. Taxable surplus earned by a foreign affiliate includes active business income earned by the entity in a country with which Canada does not have a tax convention or TIEA and foreign accrual property income (FAPI). Taxable surplus also includes 50% of capital gains (representing the taxable portion of the gains) on properties not used or held principally to gain or produce active business income in a designated treaty country and on the disposition of shares of foreign affiliates. Note that if the foreign affiliate is a controlled foreign affiliate, the taxable portion of gains on the disposition of shares of foreign affiliates may also be FAPI and taxed annually. ITA: 95(1) ITA: 113(1)(*b*), 113(1)(*c*) ITR: 5907(1);

Where a foreign corporation has both exempt and taxable surplus balances, dividends are considered to be first paid from exempt surplus, then taxable surplus, and finally from pre-acquisition surplus. Pre-acquisition surplus dividends represent a return of investment and are fully deductible and thus non-taxable. Pre-acquisition surplus dividends are deducted from the adjusted cost base of shares of a foreign affiliate. If the dividend exceeds the adjusted cost base, a capital gain results. ITR: 5901(1) ITA: 113(1)(*d*) ITA: 40(3)

A Canadian-resident corporation earning a dividend from a foreign affiliate cannot claim a foreign tax credit for the foreign withholding tax on the dividend. ITA: 126(1)

Thus, active business income earned by a corporation in a foreign jurisdiction is exempt from tax in the Canadian shareholder corporation in the case of business income earned in treaty and TIEA countries. Canadian tax on active business income earned in non-treaty, non-TIEA countries is deferred until dividends are paid. One exception applies where before March 19, 2007, Canada either began negotiations for a comprehensive TIEA or sought by written invitation to enter into negotiations for a comprehensive TIEA in the country in which a controlled foreign affiliate (CFA) resides. In such case, the income of the CFA will be treated as FAPI. ITA: 95(1) "non-qualifying country", "non-qualifying business"

Example Problem 19-15

Canco, a Canadian resident corporation, holds a 50% common share interest in two foreign subsidiaries. Both subsidiaries were incorporated in 2000. Canco was issued the shares at the time of incorporation. Subsidiary A is located in the United States and is a furniture manufacturer earning 100% business income. Subsidiary B is located in Guatemala and produces textiles used by Subsidiary A. In its December 31, 2013 taxation year end, Subsidiary A paid a dividend of C$60,000 to Canco. Subsidiary A withheld tax at 5% from the dividend. Subsidiary A pays tax at a rate of 18% on its earnings. In the same year, Subsidiary B paid a dividend of C$50,000 to Canco. Subsidiary B withheld tax at 10% from the dividend. Subsidiary B pays tax at a rate of 5% on its earnings. Subsidiary B had a taxable surplus balance of C$500,000 on December 31, 2012.

— REQUIRED

How will the dividends be treated for tax purposes by Canco? Assume that only active business income has been earned by both subsidiaries since incorporation and both subsidiaries have been profitable each year since incorporation. Unrelated, non-resident persons own the other 50% of shares of each company.

— SOLUTION

Subsidiary A and Subsidiary B are foreign affiliates of Canco because Canco owns not less than 10% of the shares of each company. The dividends received by Canco will be included in income. Dividends from Subsidiary A will be considered to have been paid from exempt surplus because the dividend is paid from active business income earned in a country with which Canada has a tax convention. The dividend will be fully deductible. A foreign tax credit will not be available for the 5% withholding tax paid to the U.S. government. ITA: 90(1), 113(1)(*a*)

Dividends from Subsidiary B will be considered to have been paid from taxable surplus because the dividend is paid from active business income earned in a country with which Canada does not have a tax convention or TIEA. The deduction for the underlying tax will be computed as follows:

The "underlying foreign tax" related to the taxable surplus balance is $26,316 computed as $500,000/.95 – $500,000 = $26,316.[1] ITR: 5907

The "underlying foreign tax applicable" to the $100,000 dividend paid by Subsidiary B from taxable surplus is: ITR: 5907

$26,316 × $100,000/$500,000 = $5,263

The foreign tax applicable to the $50,000 dividend received by Canco is:

$5,263 × $50,000/$100,000 = $2,632 ITR: 5900(d)

The Division C deduction for the underlying tax paid by Subsidiary B on the taxable surplus from which the $50,000 dividend is paid is computed as the lesser of: ITA: 113(1)(*b*)

i) $2,632 × (1/(38% – 13%) – 1) = $7,896, and

ii) $50,000

The Division C deduction for the withholding tax paid by Subsidiary B on the $50,000 dividend is the lesser of: ITA: 113(1)(*c*)

i) $50,000 × 10% × (1/(38% – 13%)) = $20,000 (withholding tax × the relevant tax factor)

ii) $50,000 – $7,896 = $42,104 (taxable surplus dividend less: par. 113(1)(*b*) deduction)

Overall Canco will pay tax on the following:

Dividends	$ 110,000
Par. 113(1)(*a*)	$ (60,000)
Par. 113(1)(*b*) deduction for underlying tax	$ (7,896)
Par. 113(1)(*c*) deduction for withholding tax	$ (20,000)
	$ 22,104
Tax at 25%	$ 5,526

Note that the result is the same as if the income earned by Subsidiary B from which the dividend was paid was taxed at Canadian rates and a foreign tax credit was provided for the underlying tax paid on that income and withholding taxes paid on the dividend as follows:

Income of Subsidiary B before tax ($50,000/.95)	$ 52,632
Tax at Canadian rate (25%)	$ 13,158
Foreign tax credit for underlying tax ($52,632 × 5%)	$ (2,632)
Foreign tax credit for withholding tax	$ (5,000)
Net tax payable	$ 5,526

— *NOTE TO SOLUTION*

(1) The taxable surplus balance of $500,000 is net of the underlying foreign tax paid on the company's earnings.

¶19,530.10 *Hybrid surplus*

In the August 19, 2011 amendments to the Act, a new surplus account was created to include gains on the disposition of foreign affiliates. As a result, exempt surplus will no longer include 50% of the gain (the non-taxable portion) from the disposition of shares of a foreign affiliate. Taxable surplus will no longer include 50% of the gain (the taxable portion) from the disposition of shares of a foreign affiliate, except to the extent the taxable portion of the capital gain is included in FAPI. When a foreign corporation has exempt surplus, hybrid surplus, and taxable surplus, dividends are considered to be first paid from exempt surplus, then hybrid surplus, then taxable surplus, and finally from pre-acquisition surplus. As a result, it will no longer be possible to distribute only the exempt portion of the gain on the disposition of the shares of a foreign affiliate and defer the taxable portion of the gain, as both components will be distributed together. Hybrid surplus results for dispositions to only a designated person or partnership after August 19, 2011 and for 2012. After 2012 any other disposition of a foreign affiliate results in a hybrid surplus. A designated person is a person who is non-arm's length with the taxpayer or a partnership a member of which is a designated person.

In November 21, 2012 amendments to the Act, taxpayers can elect to have dividends paid from pre-acquisition surplus instead of following the above-noted ordering rules. ITR: 5901(2)(*b*)

A capital gain arising from such an election will be subject to an automatic election which treats the capital gain as a dividend from exempt surplus, hybrid surplus, and taxable surplus in that order. This prevents the election being used to convert low-taxed hybrid or taxable surplus to a capital gain. ITA: 40(3), 93(1)

Main Components of Surplus Balances

Exempt Surplus (Pre August 19, 2011 Amendments)	Taxable Surplus (Pre August 19, 2011 Amendments)	Hybrid Surplus (Post August 19, 2011 Amendments)
Active business income in a designated treaty country. (treaty or TEIA)	Active business income in a non-treaty/non-TEIA country.	
Capital gains on dispositions of property used in an active business carried on in a designated treaty country.	Taxable capital gains on dispositions of property used in an active business carried on in a non-treaty/non-TEIA country.	
Non-taxable portion of capital gains on dispositions of shares of foreign affiliates.	Taxable capital gains on dispositions of shares of foreign affiliates that are excluded property.	Capital gains on dispositions of shares of foreign affiliates that are excluded property.
Non-taxable portion of capital gains on dispositions of all other properties.	FAPI (including taxable capital gains on dispositions of shares of foreign affiliate that are not excluded property)	
	Taxable capital gains on dispositions of all other properties (not included in exempt surplus)	

Excluded property includes property of the foreign affiliate that is used or held principally for the purpose of gaining or producing income from an active business carried on by it and shares of the capital stock of another foreign affiliate of the taxpayer where all or substantially all of the fair market value of the property of the foreign affiliate is attributable to property that is excluded property. ITA: 95(1) "excluded property"

Taxation of Canadian Residents with Foreign Investments

Active Business Income Earned in the Foreign Country

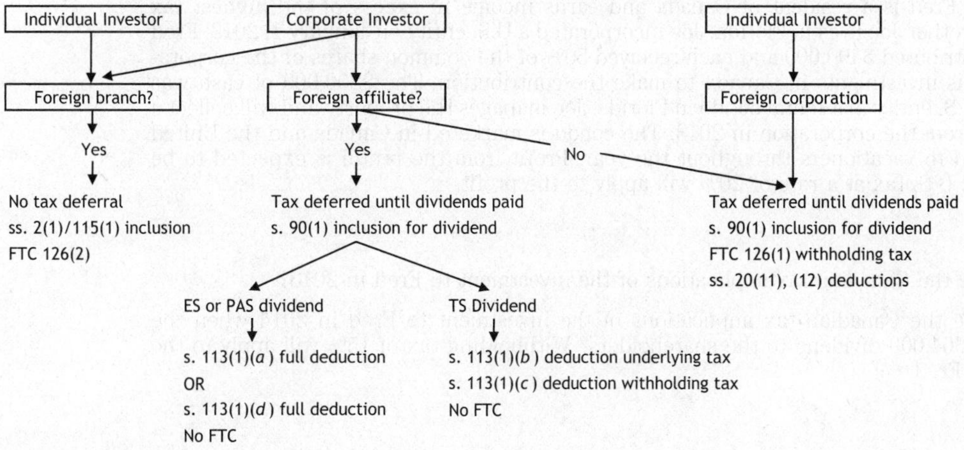

ES = Exempt surplus
TS = Taxable surplus
PAS = Pre-acquisition surplus
FTC = Foreign tax credit

¶19,540 Passive Income Earned in a Foreign Jurisdiction

¶19,545 Controlled foreign affiliates (CFAs)

Where a Canadian resident individual or corporation holds an interest in a CFA, the participating percentage of the FAPI income earned by the CFA must be included in the Canadian resident's Division B income each year and is subject to Part I tax. FAPI income, in general terms, represents passive investment income earned by the CFA. It also includes active business income earned by a CFA in countries with which Canada does not have a treaty or TIEA and prior to March 19, 2007 was negotiating, or sought to negotiate, a TIEA. The FAPI rules prevent the deferral of tax on passive investment income earned in a controlled foreign entity. A deduction is available for the underlying foreign tax paid by the foreign entity on the FAPI. The income inclusion, net of the deduction, is added to the adjusted cost base of the share investment to prevent double taxation on the disposition of the shares of the CFA.

ITA: 95(1)

ITA: 91(1)

ITA: 95(1) "non-qualifying country", "non-qualifying business"

ITA: 91(4)

ITA: 92(1)

Effectively, when the FAPI is fully paid to the investor as a dividend, the previous FAPI inclusions/deductions related to the investment are reversed to eliminate double taxation. When a dividend is paid by the CFA out of FAPI, the dividend is included in income. An offsetting deduction limited to the amount of the dividend income inclusion is available for the amount of previous FAPI inclusions (net of the deductions for underlying tax). If the investor is an individual, a foreign tax credit is provided for the foreign withholding tax on the dividend. If the investor is a corporation, the taxable surplus dividend deduction precedes the FAPI deduction and a foreign tax credit is not available.

ITA: 12(1)(*k*), 90(1)

ITA: 91(5)

ITA: 126(1)

ITA: 91(5), 113(1)(*b*), 113(1)(*c*)

A CFA is a foreign affiliate of the Canadian resident that is controlled by

ITA: 95(1)

(1) the Canadian resident alone;

(2) the Canadian resident and persons (foreign or Canadian) who are related to the Canadian resident;

(3) the Canadian resident and up to four Canadian residents (relevant Canadian shareholders) not related to the Canadian resident taxpayer; or

(4) the Canadian resident, relevant Canadian shareholders, and persons (foreign or Canadian) related to relevant Canadian shareholders.

Example Problem 19-16

Up until the end of 2012, Fred Murphy held stock and mutual fund investments in an investment account with a Canadian bank. In 2012, he earned $32,000 in interest and dividends on the investments. Fred is a resident of Canada and earns income in excess of the highest tax bracket. Fred's brother Joe lives in Florida. Joe incorporated a U.S. entity on January 1, 2013. Fred and Joe each contributed $400,000 and each received 50% of the common shares of the corporation. Fred sold his investments in Canada to make the contribution. The $800,000 of cash was invested by the U.S. entity in a rental condo in Florida. Joe manages the property and will collect a $100,000 salary from the corporation in 2013. The condo is marketed in Canada and the United States and rented to vacationers throughout the year. Profit from the rental is expected to be $80,000 for 2013. U.S. tax at a rate of 20% will apply to the profit.

— *REQUIRED*

(a) What are the Canadian tax implications of the investment to Fred in 2013?

(b) What are the Canadian tax implications of the investment to Fred in 2014 when the company pays a $64,000 dividend to the shareholders? Withholding tax of 15% will apply to the dividend paid to Fred.

— *SOLUTION*

(a) For 2013, the income earned by the corporation will meet the definition of FAPI. FAPI includes income from property. Income from property includes income from an investment business. An investment business is a business, the principal purpose of which is to derive income from property including rents. The U.S. entity does not employ more than five full-time employees.

ITA: 95(1)

The U.S. corporation will be a foreign affiliate of Fred because Fred will own not less than 1% of the shares of the corporation and not less than 10% of the shares with related persons. The U.S. corporation is a controlled foreign affiliate because the corporation is a foreign affiliate of Fred that is controlled by Fred and Joe, who is non-arm's length with Fred. As a result, Fred must include 50% of the FAPI in his income for each year. His income inclusion for 2013, will be as follows: ITA: 95(1)

Income Inclusion for FAPI 50% of $80,000	$ 40,000	ITA: 91(1)
Deduction for underlying tax		ITA: 91(4)
Lesser of:		
(i) Foreign accrual tax (20% of $40,000) × RTF = $8,000 × 2.2 = $17,600		
(ii) FAPI inclusion $40,000	$ (17,600)	
2013 Net Inclusion	$ 22,400	

$22,400 will be added to the adjusted cost base (ACB) of the shares held by Fred.

Note that, at the highest personal tax rate of 46%, Fred would pay $10,304 of tax on the net income inclusion. This amount is approximately equal to the personal tax that Fred would pay on his share of the $80,000 of profit of the corporation at the highest personal rate less a foreign tax credit for $8,000 of underlying tax paid by the corporation on Fred's share of income, i.e., 46% × $40,000 – $8,000 = $10,400. [The $96 difference is because a relevant tax factor of 2.2 converts the underlying tax to an equivalent Canadian tax using a tax rate of 45.45%.]

(b) Fred will receive a dividend of $32,000, which will be included in income. He will receive a deduction to reverse the 2013 income inclusion as follows: ITA: 90(1)

Lesser of:

(i) Dividend from a CFA = $32,000

ITA: 91(5)

(ii) Net amounts added to the ACB of the share before the dividend was received = $22,400

The ACB of Fred's shares will be reduced by $22,400 back to the original balance. He will also receive a foreign tax credit for the $4,800 of withholding tax paid on the dividend.

Note that once the income of the corporation is paid as a dividend, the FAPI inclusion is reversed. Overall, the same amount of income has been taxed as though a dividend were paid in the year the income was earned but spread over two years. The rental income, i.e., passive investment income, earned by the foreign corporation and not paid out as dividends until a later year, is taxed in the year earned, i.e., a tax deferral is not possible.

Taxation of Canadian Residents with Foreign Investments

Passive Income Earned in the Foreign Country

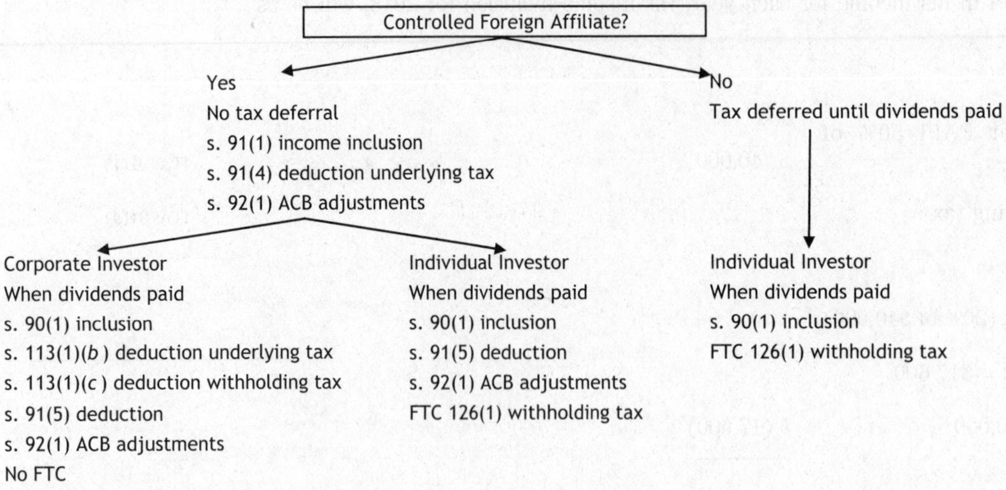

FAPI is taxable surplus for the purpose of subsection 113(1) deductions. ITR: 5907 "taxable earnings"

¶19,600 INFORMATION REPORTING

In the mid-1990s, the Canadian government became concerned with the likelihood of Canadian residents owning foreign property and (presumably) not reporting any income on those properties. A system of information reporting was proposed, but this system eventually became a simple "check-the-box" approach. At the top of page 2 of the annual T1 income tax return, a "yes" or "no" answer is required to the question "At any time in (year 'x') did you hold foreign property with a total cost of more than C$100,000?".

Where the question is answered affirmatively, a form must be filed with the tax return (or partnership information return). The form requires reporting of the types of property, the cost of the property, and where the property is located. It is the cost of the property that is determinative of the filing requirement. The current value of the property is not relevant. Additionally, and importantly, some foreign property holdings are not included. The two most common exclusions are property held in the course of carrying on an active business and personal-use property (such as a vacation home). Excluded property is not included in the base $100,000 requirement, so for many Canadian tax filers, the reporting is not a requirement. [The 2013 federal Budget proposes to extend the normal reassessment period by three years if the taxpayer has failed to file form T1135 when required or has failed to report the information required on the form and failed to report income from the foreign property required to be reported.] ITA: 233.3; Form T1135

The form is not the only information return required with respect to foreign properties. Other forms are detailed in the following table.

Other Foreign Property Information Returns Required under the *Income Tax Act*

T106	Non-arm's length transactions with non-residents
T1141	Transfers or loans to a non-resident trust
T1134A	Non-controlled foreign affiliates
T1134B	Controlled foreign affiliates
T1142	Distributions from and indebtedness to a non-resident trust

Failure to file an information return can result in a penalty of $500 a month (24-month maximum). ITA: 162(2.1)

¶19,800 REVIEW QUESTIONS

(1) Describe two objectives that international tax treaties strive to achieve.

(2) Distinguish between a part-year resident and a non-resident.

(3) Briefly explain the intention behind the "transfer pricing" legislation.

(4) Briefly explain the "thin capitalization rules" and what they are designed to prevent.

(5) Is a non-resident who owns shares in a Canadian corporation taxable on the disposition of those shares? Does the purchaser have a withholding requirement?

(6) Can a part-year resident claim the full amount of personal tax credits in the year of arrival/departure?

(7) How would you calculate the gain on the disposition of a rental property that an immigrant to Canada owned for five years prior to coming to Canada and is disposing after his or her move.

(8) When is a non-resident employer required to withhold and remit Canadian tax from an employee's employment income?

(9) What withholding tax rate applies to dividends from a Canadian corporation to a shareholder resident in the United States?

(10) When is it best for a non-resident to make a section 217 election for Canadian RRSP benefits received?

(11) Would a non-interest-bearing loan by a Canadian corporation to its non-resident parent company result in a Canadian tax liability?

(12) What is the purpose of deeming that an immigrant has disposed of and reacquired all of his or her capital property on entering Canada?

(13) Under what circumstances might a non-resident be entitled to the same or similar total personal tax credits that are allowed to a resident?

(14) When and how much of a foreign tax credit can be claimed by a Canadian resident for withholding taxes paid to a foreign jurisdiction on dividend income?

(15) What is the purpose of the FAPI rules related to foreign passive income?

(16) How would you describe exempt surplus and its treatment for Canadian tax purposes?

¶19,825 MULTIPLE CHOICE QUESTIONS

Question 1

Jari Kitsopolous is a resident of Greece. Last year, he disposed of real estate located in Saskatchewan for a gain. Jari will pay Canadian income taxes at which of the following rates?

(A) Federal tax based on the tax rate schedule plus Saskatchewan taxes.

(B) Federal tax based on the tax rate schedule plus an additional federal tax.

(C) Withholding tax only at 25%.

(D) Withholding tax only at 33⅓%.

Question 2

Prior to immigrating to Canada, Mai Kim had money on deposit in a Canadian bank and earned $1,000 interest. After taking up Canadian residence, she immediately used that deposit towards a down payment on a home. Which of the following is the correct tax treatment of the $1,000 interest earned in the year of immigration?

(A) She pays a 25% non-resident tax and the interest is excluded from the Canadian tax return for the period of residency.

(B) She does not pay any Canadian tax in relation to the interest.

(C) The income is included in her Canadian tax return for the period of residency, but she receives a foreign tax credit for any taxes paid in her previous country of residence.

(D) The income is included in her Canadian tax return for the period of residency based on a proration calculated as the number of days resident divided by 365 days.

Question 3

Antonio Sperilli immigrated to Canada from Brazil last year, but continues to be a partner in a Brazilian business. What is the correct tax treatment of any income earned from the partnership?

(A) It is subject to tax only in Brazil.

(B) It is included in Antonio's Canadian income tax return, but any Brazilian taxes are deductible from the partnership income.

(C) It is included in Antonio's Canadian income tax return, but a foreign tax credit may be claimed in Antonio's Brazilian tax return for any Canadian income taxes paid.

(D) It is included in Antonio's Canadian income tax return, and a foreign tax credit may be claimed for any Brazilian taxes paid.

Question 4

Betty Albright emigrated from Canada to the United States last year. At the time that she gave up her Canadian residence, she held an RRSP with a fair market value of $100,000. Which of the following statements is true?

(A) The RRSP is taxable Canadian property and Betty will have to file a Canadian non-resident tax return when she disposes of the RRSP.

(B) There is a deemed disposition of the RRSP at fair market value on emigration.

(C) There will be a withholding tax at the time Betty terminates the RRSP and has it paid to her.

(D) Non-resident withholding tax should be paid, at 25%, from the income earned in the RRSP after emigration.

Question 5

Maxwell Rock Ltd. is a Canadian incorporated entity with a December 31 year-end. The corporation has a gravel pit operation owned and operated in Collingwood, Ontario. The company expanded operations into the United States this year through a 100% acquisition of a U.S. incorporated company with gravel pits operating in Michigan. The U.S. corporation also has a mining operation in Paraguay. In the U.S. corporation's first taxation year-end since acquisition, the U.S. company earned C$100,000 of business income from its Michigan operation and C$200,000 of business income in Paraguay. At the end of its tax year, the U.S. company paid a dividend to Maxwell Rock Ltd. of C$150,000. Which of the following statements is true?

(A) Maxwell will include the C$150,000 dividend in taxable income for the year in which the dividend was received. A foreign tax credit can be claimed for the withholding tax paid to the U.S. government on the dividend.

(B) Maxwell will include the C$150,000 dividend in Division B income for the year in which the dividend was received. An offsetting deduction of C$100,000 will be available for the portion of the dividend paid from exempt surplus.

(C) Maxwell will include the C$150,000 dividend in Division B income for the year in which the dividend was received. An offsetting deduction will be available in computing taxable income for C$150,000 because the dividend was from exempt surplus.

(D) Maxwell will include the C$150,000 dividend in Division B income for the year in which the dividend was received. A deduction will be available in computing taxable income for the underlying tax paid by the U.S. company on the business income earned in the United States and Paraguay.

Question 6

Bob Smith is a Canadian resident and owns a condominium in Arizona that he and his family use during their winter holidays. The property is left vacant the rest of the year. What is Bob's filing obligations regarding this property?

(A) Bob is required to file Form T1135 reporting foreign property ownership.

(B) Bob is exempt from filing a Form T1135 as the property is personal-use property.

(C) Bob is required to file a Form T1135 only if the property has a cost of over $100,000.

(D) Bob needs to file a U.S. Form 1040NR (non-resident income tax return) and declare the ownership of the property to the U.S. Internal Revenue Service.

Question 7

Jane Alison, a resident of Canada, sold $100,000 of her Canadian mutual funds and invested the funds in common shares of a newly incorporated U.S. corporation. Jane's friend, Tori, also a Canadian resident, invested $500,000, and a third friend, a U.S. resident, invested $400,000 in common shares of the corporation. The $1 million was invested in fixed income securities with future plans to invest in U.S. stock markets. Which statement is correct regarding the interest income on the investments?

(A) It will not be taxed in Canada until dividends are paid to the shareholders. A foreign tax credit will be available for the U.S. withholding tax.

(B) It will not be taxed in Canada until dividends are paid to the shareholders. An offsetting deduction will be available under Division C because the dividend will be paid from taxable surplus.

(C) It will not be taxed in Canada until dividends are paid to the shareholders. An offsetting deduction will be available under Division C because the dividend will be paid from exempt surplus.

(D) It will be included in income of the Canadian shareholders because the company is a controlled foreign affiliate.

¶19,850 EXERCISES

Exercise 1

Alan Croupier is moving to Venezuela on August 1. In anticipation of this move, he has sold all of his assets except for 1,000 common shares in Tell Canada (a TSX listed company). The shares have a value of $40,000 and his adjusted cost base is $28,000. What is Alan's tax position on these shares should they remain unsold at the time of his departure?

— REQUIRED

Are there any alternatives available to Alan in respect to the Tell Canada shares in the year of departure?

Exercise 2

A non-resident is liable for Canadian taxes where they are employed in Canada, carry on business in Canada, or dispose of taxable Canadian property. In most countries, the non-resident will also be subject to tax in his or her country of residence on this same income. Tax treaties will alleviate the double taxation burden by allowing for foreign tax credits.

— REQUIRED

As the income will be taxed in two countries, does the taxpayer claim a foreign tax credit in both countries? If not, in which country is a foreign tax credit claimed?

Exercise 3

Sam-son Industries Inc. is a small American company located in Minneapolis, Minnesota. Sam-son sells various items by mail-order, mostly advertising trinkets such as pens, telephone diaries, post-it notes, and similar items, to Canadian businesses. Last year was the first year the company did this and profits on its Canadian sales amounted to $76,000. The company did not have sales representatives enter Canada during the year. The principals of Sam-son are worried about their liability for Canadian income tax and have come to you for advice.

— REQUIRED

Advise Sam-son on their Canadian tax liability. Include an explanation of your rationale.

Exercise 4

Johnson & Co Ltd., a Canadian-controlled private corporation, holds all the issued shares in Johnson & Co (USA) Inc. Two years ago, the Canadian corporation advanced $100,000 in the form of a loan to the U.S. corporation. The U.S. corporation pays Johnson & Co interest at the rate of 1%. This 1% is comparable to the cost of borrowing at a U.S. bank, but is less than the prescribed interest rate under the Canadian Act. Assume that rate is 2%.

— REQUIRED

Describe the tax obligations of the Canadian corporation relative to this 1% interest.

Exercise 5

Mary Jane is a Canadian citizen and has been living and working in Singapore for the past 11 years. Mary Jane moved back to Canada on October 13, 2012 and incurred $8,000 in moving expenses. Mary Jane paid her own moving expenses and did not receive a reimbursement from her new employer. She earned $25,000 in employment income from October 13 to December 31, 2012.

— REQUIRED

Advise Mary Jane if she is entitled to claim her moving expenses.

Exercise 6

Canco is a Canadian incorporated manufacturer and wholly owned subsidiary of a U.S. incorporated company. In 2011, Canco invested C$500,000 of excess cash in a newly incorporated Dutch company (Dutchco) and received an 80% common share interest in the entity. The U.S. parent invested C$125,000 for the remaining 20% interest. All except C$200,000 was used to acquire a distribution business. The distribution business will distribute products manufactured in Canada and the United States to European customers. For its December 31, 2013 year end, Dutchco earned C$30,000 from the distribution business and C$12,000 in interest on a money market account holding the C$200,000 of excess cash. For its December 31, 2013 year end, Dutchco earned C$50,000 from the distribution business and C$12,000 in interest. The company paid a C$50,000 dividend to its shareholders in February 2013. Dutchco paid corporate tax of 20% on its income each year. Withholding tax of 5% applied to the dividend paid to Canco.

— *REQUIRED*

Determine the Canadian tax consequences of the investment in Dutchco and the dividend received in 2013.

Exercise 7

Mr. and Ms. Doe are citizens and residents of China. They purchased a condominium in their names in Waterloo, Ontario, for their son, Joe. Joe moved to Waterloo in August 2013 to attend university and rented two rooms to his friends, Sam and Harry, who are both Canadian residents. Joe will live in Canada for at least four years while attending school. Sam and Harry each pay rent of $400 per month to Joe, who deposits the funds into his parents' Canadian bank account. Joe pays the mortgage, utilities, and property taxes for the property from this account. His parents will occasionally withdraw excess funds from the account.

— *REQUIRED*

(A) Discuss the Canadian tax implications associated with the rental of the property and any options available to the non-residents.

(B) What will happen if the condominium is sold in the future?

(C) Would it have been better for Joe's parents to give or lend Joe funds to purchase the condominium in his name?

¶19,875 ASSIGNMENT PROBLEMS

Problem 1

Andrew English has agreed to play professional soccer with the Toronto Metros of the Canadian Soccer League starting March 1, 2014. Andrew lives in England and will live in Canada temporarily for the five months of the soccer season. His three-year contract calls for an annual salary of $55,000. At the time of signing this contract in England in the fall of 2013, the Metros gave Andrew a signing bonus of $25,000. Andrew's agent was paid $5,000 to represent him in negotiating the contract. Andrew will earn C$100,000 playing soccer in England during the other seven months.

— REQUIRED

Determine Andrew's Canadian income tax obligations. What deductions/credits may he claim against Canadian income?

Problem 2

Kresna Dubchuk lives in Kenya and is in the process of selling her Canadian real property, situated in New Brunswick, which has been rented to various tenants over the last 10 years. The selling price of the property is $100,000 and her ACB is $35,000. She will incur $6,500 in real estate commissions and $500 in legal fees in connection with the sale.

A few days after complying with the requirements concerning the proposed disposition of the property, Kresna receives a copy of a proposed assessment from the CRA from the agent collecting the rent on her behalf in Canada. The assessment is for income taxes, plus penalties and interest.

— REQUIRED

(A) Describe and detail Kresna's Canadian tax obligations arising on the sale of this property.

(B) What is the probable cause of the proposed assessment? Can you offer Kresna and her agent any professional assistance with regard to the proposed assessment? If so, detail what you might advise her.

Problem 3

A corporation resident in the United States (USCO) recently expanded its sales activities in Canada. Up until two years ago, the company had been selling small amounts of product directly to Canadian customers. The Canadian sales resulted from U.S. tradeshows, industry magazines, and the company's website. USCO did not have a sales force in Canada or a direct advertising program. Starting last year, USCO hired three sales employees to work from an office rented by USCO in Toronto. The company uses an independent wholesaler and bonded warehouse in Mississauga to keep a supply of its products on hand. Shipping instructions are faxed to the warehouse. Invoicing is done in Dallas and payments are remitted to the U.S. head office. All purchase orders are subject to approval and acceptance by USCO's home office.

The Canadian balance sheet and income statement for USCO's second year of operations ending December 31 was as follows:

Balance Sheet (000s)

Assets		Liabilities/Equity	
Cash (Cdn currency)	$ 50	Accounts payable	$ 400
Accounts receivable	150	Bank loan (used to purchase fixed assets)	150
Inventory	400	Tax liability	104
Fixed assets (UCC)	200	Home office account	146
Total assets	**$800**	**Total liabilities/equity**	**$800**

Income Statement (000s)		
Sales		$ 500
Expenses		
Sales expenses	$ 120	
Office expenses	30	
Advertising	90	
Total expenses		240
Pre-tax profit		260
Tax provision		104
After tax profit		**$ 156**

For its first year of operations ending December 31, the Canadian operations incurred a taxable loss of $4,000 and had an investment allowance, as defined in the Regulations, of $2,000. ITR: 808

The aggregate FMV of the assets is $820,000 (Cash — $50,000, A/R — $150,000, Inventory — $410,000, Fixed Assets — $210,000). The $50,000 cash balance was the lowest balance outstanding for the year.

Assume an Ontario income tax rate of 12%.

— *REQUIRED*

(A) How will USCO be taxed under Canadian domestic tax law?

(B) Without considering the Canada–U.S. Tax Convention, calculate USCO's total federal and provincial Canadian tax liability under Parts I and XIV of the Act. Assume that pre-tax profit represents taxable income.

(C) Would USCO be considered to have a permanent establishment under paragraphs 1, 2, or 5 of Article V of the Canada–U.S. Tax Convention? How does paragraph 6, Article X of the Canada–U.S. Tax Convention impact the Canadian tax return for the company? Perform calculations to reflect the impact.

Problem 4

Sally Juarez is retired and lives in Mexico, but virtually all of her investment assets, and her income, are Canadian. In 2013, Sally realized the following income (all Canadian except as identified):

Dividends on shares in Canadian Public Co Ltd.	$ 5,000
Interest on deposit in bank	8,000
Gain on sale of raw land (assume business income)	60,000
Gain on sale of Public Co Ltd. shares	15,000
Gain on sale of real estate	30,000
Share of income from business partnership	7,000
Mexican pension income	20,000

Sally has paid $7,500 in Canadian withholding tax on the property gains.

— *REQUIRED*

Without considering the implications of the Canada–Mexico Tax Convention, calculate Sally's taxable income earned in Canada and tax owing (refund). Identify any other Canadian tax requirements. Assume any business income was earned in a province where the personal tax rates are the hypothetical rates shown in ¶10,130 of Chapter 10. Ignore any CPP/QPP implications.

Problem 5

Cal Murphy is emigrating from Canada to take up residence in Jakarta, Indonesia. At the time of his departure, Cal will have the following Canadian assets:

	FMV	Cost
Principal residence	$250,000	$135,000
RRSP	75,000	N/A
20% interest in CCPC (active)	45,000	1,000
GIC at TrustCo	15,000	15,000

Cal has been impressed by the capital appreciation he has made on his residence, so he intends to keep it and rent it out for $1,500 monthly. He intends to sell it at some future opportune time but believes this will be many years from now. The expected expenses for the mortgage, taxes, repairs, insurance, and sundry for the house are expected to be about $1,200 a month. Cal's brother, Joseph, will be collecting the rents for him and depositing them to Cal's Canadian bank. This money will be kept at the bank in a savings account in case of any unanticipated expenses.

His 20% shareholding in the CCPC is not easily liquidated, and so he is retaining it, for now, to earn about $5,000 in annual dividend income. He is anxious to dispose of the shares, but has not yet found a prospective purchaser, despite a fairly exhaustive attempt to do so. The $45,000 fair market value was determined by a chartered business valuator.

Cal is not at all sure what to do with the RRSP. He can liquidate it either before or after his planned departure date. Cal intends to renew the GIC when it matures as he is uncertain as to the Indonesian banking system, and won't transfer the money to an Indonesian bank until he's done some research.

Cal and his wife separated last year, and Cal has custody of their only child, who will be moving to Indonesia with Cal. Cal receives $500 in monthly child support and Mrs. Murphy will continue to pay the support to Cal in Indonesia.

Cal has engaged you to advise him of his current (year of departure) and any future Canadian tax obligations.

— REQUIRED

Identify and advise Cal of his current and future Canadian tax position. Ignore the Canada–Indonesia Tax Convention in your analysis. Include any options or alternatives he may have available and any planning advice you think appropriate.

Problem 6

Samsystems Inc. (SI) is a Canadian-controlled private corporation and a leading edge developer and manufacturer of furniture components with subsidiaries worldwide. You are the tax manager for SI. The controller of the corporation is very concerned that the corporation's intercompany transactions do not meet the transfer pricing requirements of the Act. In a recent meeting, the controller provided you with the following information concerning the company's transactions with foreign corporations. ITA: 247

Transactions with Samsystems Netherlands Inc. (SNI)

SI sells metal drawer slides to its newly acquired, wholly owned subsidiary and Netherlands resident, SNI. SNI was acquired by SI in July and has two divisions: a manufacturing division that manufactures ergonomically designed furniture components, and a distribution division that distributes curtain rod products purchased from Thailand and now drawer slides purchased from SI, as well. All products purchased by the distribution division are sold to arm's length European distributors.

Until the purchase of SNI, SI was selling drawer slides directly to European distributors for all European sales. Now all European sales are through SNI. Over the next two years, SNI plans to replace the use of distributors in the European market and sell SI's slides directly to original equipment manufacturers. SNI does not own any trademarks related to the sale of SI products. SNI is responsible for collection of receivables from European distributors. However, SI is responsible for all warranty costs associated with the sale of its products by SNI. All patents for Canadian-manufactured products are owned by SI.

For Canadian sales, SI sells drawer slides to arm's length distributors in Canada. All international sales of the slides are sold by subsidiaries of SI (including SNI) in various countries.

A subsidiary of SI, U.S. resident Samsystems United States Inc. (SUSI) (see below), manufactures a similar drawer slide to SI's. These slides are sold by the U.S. company to arm's length distributors in the U.S. market.

For its taxation year ending December 31, SNI's distributor division earned a gross margin of 30% and an operating profit of 5% of sales for its sales of SI product. For sales of curtain rods, the division earned a gross margin percentage of 35% and an operating profit of 8% of sales.

Transactions with SUSI

SUSI was acquired by SI through a share purchase in July. For several years prior to the acquisition, SUSI had purchased ergonomic furniture components from SI for distribution to original equipment manufacturers in the U.S. After the acquisition of SUSI, SI continued to sell these products to the company. SUSI does not own any trademarks for the sale of SI's product and does not distribute products for any other entity. SI sells its ergonomic products in Canada through arm's length Canadian distribution companies.

— REQUIRED

Advise the controller on the possible transfer pricing methodologies that could be applied to the above transactions under section 247. Indicate why discarded methodologies would not be appropriate. Describe how you would apply these methodologies and indicate what additional information you will need from the client to help you determine the appropriate methodology.

Problem 7

Ergold Ltd. is a Canadian subsidiary of a Swedish company. The company is a distributor of automated milking machines to dairy farmers in Canada. Its sole supplier is the Swedish parent company. The current transfer pricing policy between Ergold Ltd. and its parent company has resulted in losses in Canada for its years of operation since incorporation as follows:

Year Ended December 31	Taxable Loss	Gross Revenue
2011	$ 200,000	$ 3,000,000
2012	$ 400,000	$ 6,500,000
2013	$ 850,000	$ 9,500,000

The company does not appear to have any internal or external uncontrolled comparable transactions that would allow you to apply a traditional transaction method. In discussions with some of your colleagues in your Toronto office transfer pricing group, you have discovered that recent transfer pricing studies have concluded, using the transactional net margin method, that similar distributors operating in Canada earn an operating margin percentage of 5% of sales. You mention this to the controller. He indicates that he does not believe that there is much of a concern as he has heard that because of the company's small size there would not be any penalties applicable if the CRA were to audit. Ergold's effective tax rate is approximately 26.5%.

— REQUIRED

How would you respond to the controller? How can you convince the controller that he should consider having your firm prepare a transfer pricing report to provide it with documentation to support its transfer pricing?

Problem 8

Witmold Ltd., a subsidiary of a U.S. corporation, received a high-rate loan from the U.S. parent company of $6 million on December 2, 2012 to purchase manufacturing equipment. The company started making loan payments of $72,500 per month on January 2, 2013. On July 15, due to a problem collecting from its major customer, the company borrowed an additional $600,000 from the U.S. parent. This loan was a 2% loan and was repaid 14 days after receipt when the customer paid the accounts receivable.

Because of the above problem, the company did not make its August to October payments on the loan but began making payments again in November. Witmold Ltd. plans to catch up and make its August to October payments sometime in 2014. The total interest expense booked to the financial statements for 2013 was $458,808 for both loans.

In November 2013, Witmold's controller realized that, due to thin capitalization restrictions, the interest deduction on the loan for tax purposes would be limited. As a result, on November 30, 2013, $500,000 of the loan balance was converted to paid-up capital of the common shares held by the U.S. parent company. There were no other share capital transactions during the year. Witmold's comparative balance sheet for its December 31, 2013 taxation year was as follows:

	2013	2012
Assets		
Cash	$ 250,000	$ 6,200,000
A/R	300,000	500,000
Inventory	1,200,000	800,000
Fixed assets	6,600,000	400,000
Total assets	**$ 8,350,000**	**$ 7,900,000**
Liabilities		
Accounts payable	$ 450,000	$ 300,000
Loan to parent	5,345,300	6,039,452
Equity		
Retained earnings	1,754,700	1,260,548
Common stock	800,000	300,000
Total liabilities & equity	**$ 8,350,000**	**$ 7,900,000**

The details of the loan balance after each payment for 2013 was as follows:

Date	Loan Balance
02-Dec-12	$6,000,000
02-Jan-13	5,966,952
02-Feb-13	5,933,687
02-Mar-13	5,900,203
02-Apr-13	5,866,499
02-May-13	5,832,573
02-Jun-13	5,798,424
02-Jul-13	5,764,051
02-Aug-13	5,801,951
02-Sep-13	5,840,101
02-Oct-13	5,878,502
02-Nov-13	5,844,655
30-Nov-13	5,380,524
02-Dec-13	5,310,382
02-Jan-14	5,272,800

— REQUIRED

Compute the amount of interest that the company will be able to deduct for tax purposes for its December 31, 2013 taxation year end.

Problem 9

Ronal Canada Ltd. is a Canadian subsidiary of Ronal Inc., a U.S. multinational public corporation. You are the tax manager responsible for reviewing the corporate tax return and tax provision for the Canadian company for its December 31, 2012 taxation year end. During your review, you ask for a detailed summary of the intercompany receivable balance of $6.5 million on the company's financial statements. The controller has provided you with the following information:

Receivable from Ronal Argentina Ltd.	$4,100,000
Receivable from Ronal Germany Ltd.	540,000
Receivable from Ronal Switzerland Ltd.	1,860,000
Total intercompany receivable	$6,500,000

The receivable from Ronal Argentina Ltd. relates to a 1% loan made by Ronal Canada Ltd. to Ronal Argentina Ltd. October 1, 2010. The loan was repaid in January 2014. Ronal Argentina Ltd. is a wholly owned subsidiary of Ronal Inc.

The receivable from Ronal Germany Ltd. is a trade receivable related to the sale of goods by Ronal Canada Ltd. to Ronal Germany Ltd. in November 2013. Ronal Germany Ltd. usually pays its trade payable within 90 days of receiving an invoice. Ronal Canada Ltd. sells goods to related companies under the same terms as sales to its regular customers. Ronal Germany Ltd. is a wholly owned subsidiary of Ronal Inc.

The receivable from Ronal Switzerland Ltd. relates to a sale of a piece of equipment to Ronal Switzerland Ltd. December 1, 2012 to be used in its ongoing manufacturing operations in Zurich. Ronal Switzerland is not required to pay interest on the payable to Ronal Canada Ltd. Ronal Switzerland Ltd. is a wholly owned subsidiary of Ronal Canada Ltd.

The controller indicated that, on January 15, 2012, Ronal Canada Ltd. had used excess cash of $5 million to invest in common shares of a subsidiary of Ronal Inc., Ronal Luxembourg Ltd. Ronal Luxembourg used the funds to make a non-interest-bearing loan to Ronal Germany Ltd. on that same day.

— *REQUIRED*

(a) Does subsection 15(2) and/or subsection 80.4(2) apply to the receivable from Ronal Argentina? If so, how will this impact Ronal Canada Ltd.'s tax provision? Consider the application of subsection 227(6.1) in your response.

(b) Does subsection 17(1) apply to the receivable from Ronal Argentina? If so, how will this impact Ronal Ltd.'s tax provision?

(c) Does subsection 15(2) and/or subsection 80.4(2) apply to the receivable from Ronal Germany Ltd.? Does subsection 17(1) apply to this loan? If so, how will this impact Ronal Ltd.'s tax provision?

(d) Does subsection 15(2) and/or subsection 80.4(2) apply to the receivable from Ronal Switzerland Ltd.? Does subsection 17(1) apply to this loan? If so, how will this impact Ronal Ltd.'s tax provision?

(e) Does subsection 17(1) apply to the investment in Ronal Luxembourg? If so, what advice could you provide to the client?

Problem 10

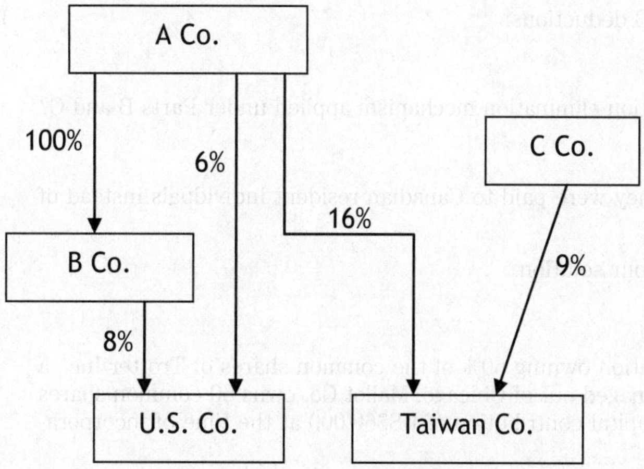

A Co., B Co., and C Co. are Canadian resident corporations. C Co. is not related to either A Co. or B Co. B Co.'s share capital consists of 1,000 common shares. The companies have a December 31 year end.

A Co. and B Co. received dividends of C$36,000 and C$48,000, respectively, out of a total dividend of C$600,000 paid by U.S. Co. on December 31, 2013. U.S. Co.'s taxation year end is October 31.

U.S. Co. was incorporated in the United States in 2011, issuing 100 common shares to its shareholders. The share structure of the corporation has not changed since incorporation. The company is operated and managed from the U.S. The company's only business is the manufacturing of auto parts supplied to various customers, including A Co. U.S. Co. earned net income from its operations of C$900,000 from the time of incorporation up to its October 31, 2013 taxation year end. U.S. Co. paid U.S. federal and state tax of C$180,000 on those earnings. U.S. Co. has not paid any dividends and has not incurred capital gains or losses in previous years. The company does not own shares in any other company.

Taiwan Co. is a cut-and-sew sweatshop. For its first taxation year ending December 31, 2013, the company earned C$500,000 net income from its operations. On this net income, the company paid a 20% tax to the government of Taiwan. The company does not own shares in any other company and did not incur any capital gains or losses in the year.

Taiwan Co. paid a dividend to shareholders of C$222,000 on January 31, 2014; this is the first dividend payment made by the company. A Co. and C Co. received dividends of C$35,520 and C$19,980, respectively. A dividend withholding tax of 3% applied to the dividends.

— REQUIRED

Part A

Determine whether the corporation paying the dividend is a foreign affiliate of the Canadian company receiving the dividend. ITA: 95(1)

Part B

Depending on your response in Part A, determine whether a Division C deduction is available to the Canadian corporation in respect of the dividend. If not, how will the dividend be treated for tax purposes? ITA: 113(1) ITA: 126(1)

Part C

If a Division C deduction is available, follow these steps to calculate the deduction:

(1) Compute the relevant surplus balances for the company showing all components. ITR: 5907

(2) Compute the portion of the full amount of the dividend (whole dividend) paid out of each surplus balance. ITR: 5901

(3) Compute the portion of the dividend received by the Canadian shareholder out of each surplus balance. ITR: 5900

(4) If needed, compute the foreign tax applicable to the portion of the dividend received by the Canadian shareholder out of taxable surplus. (Refer to the definition of "underlying foreign tax"). ITR: 5900(1)(*d*) ITR: 5907

(5) Calculate the subsection Division C deductions. ITA: 113(1)

Part D

What is the rationale for the double taxation elimination mechanism applied under Parts B and C?

Part E

How would the dividends be treated if they were paid to Canadian resident individuals instead of corporations?

Ignore foreign exchange differences in your solution.

Problem 11

Mallot Co. is a Canadian-resident corporation owning 60% of the common shares of Trotter Inc., a U.S.-incorporated company operating and managed out of Chicago. Mallot Co. owns 60 common shares of the company that were issued to it for a capital contribution of US$60,000 at the time of incorporation.

The other 40% of Trotter Inc. is owned by Mr. Tellus, a Canadian resident. Trotter Inc. has been operating a medical supplies business since its incorporation on January 1, 2007 and has an October 31 year end. Mr. Tellus owns 40 common shares of the company that were issued to him for a capital contribution of US$40,000.

You are filing the December 31, 2012 tax return for Mallot Co. and have been provided with the following information:

(1) Trotter Inc. had earnings (losses) from its active business operations in the United States and related tax liabilities (refunds) since incorporation as follows:

Taxation Year End	Earnings (Loss) (US$)	Tax Paid (Refunded) (US$)
October 31, 2008	$200,000	$50,000
October 31, 2009	$100,000	$25,000
October 31, 2010	$100,000	$25,000
October 31, 2011	($200,000)	($50,000)
October 31, 2012	$50,000	$12,500

(2) In the October 31, 2009 taxation year end, Trotter Inc. sold some equipment used in its operations incurring a capital gain of US$100,000 on which it paid a tax of US$20,000. It also paid a dividend of US$100,000 to shareholders that year.

(3) On October 31, 2010, Trotter Inc. received a dividend for US$200,000 from a wholly owned subsidiary, BVI, located in the British Virgin Islands. BVI has a December 31 year end and was acquired in an arm's length transaction in 2010 for US$50,000. You have been told that the dividend represented all of BVI's active business income for 2010 and that no underlying income tax on the income and no withholding tax on the dividend was paid to the British Virgin Island's government. U.S. domestic tax of US$50,000 was paid by Trotter Inc. on the dividend.

(4) On September 1, 2012, Trotter Inc. disposed of 100% of its shares in BVI to the controlling Canadian shareholder of Mallot Inc. and incurred a capital gain on the sale of US$150,000 on which it paid tax of US$15,000. You have been told that all of the assets of BVI were used in its active business operations. BVI earned active business income of US$50,000 in 2011 and US$50,000 to the date of disposition in 2012.

Assume that the Canadian dollar is on par with the US dollar.

(1) Compute the surplus balances for Trotter Inc. as of December 31, 2012.

(2) Compute the surplus balances for Trotter Inc. as of December 31, 2012 taking into account the November 21, 2012 proposed amendments to the foreign affiliate rules.

Problem 12

Ragyun Co. (Ragyun) is incorporated and operates in Hungary. The structure of the corporation is as follows:

All unrelated Canadian residents:

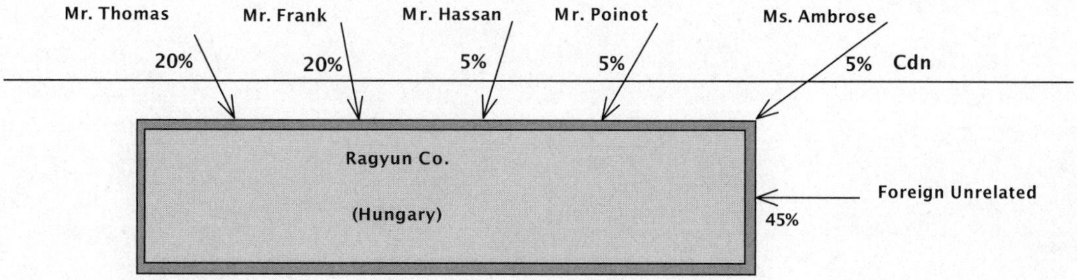

Ragyun was formed on January 1, 2013 and has an October 31 year end. The company was formed to hold a patented technology that the Canadian shareholders developed in Canada and transferred to the corporation at the time of incorporation. The technology was valued at $55,000 at the time of transfer. The foreign unrelated shareholders contributed cash of $45,000 at the time of incorporation for common shares. The company holds the patented technology, a small amount of cash, and investment properties.

Ragyun's income for 2013 included a $20,000 gain on the sale of shares in another foreign entity, Maya Inc. Ragyun owned 1% of the shares of Maya Inc. as a speculative investment. Also included in income was a $10,000 gain on the sale of shares of Tech Inc., a corporation that Ragyun owned in

Hungary. Tech Inc. is an engineering firm (whose activities and assets relate only to the engineering business) that provided services to Ragyun in the final development phase of the technology. Because of a dispute with the firm, Ragyun sold the 60% share interest to another shareholder of Tech Inc. Ragyun's income also included $5,000 of dividend and interest income from investments in mutual funds, and $25,000 in royalties from licensing the technology to unrelated foreign corporations.

Ragyun has two employees. One is responsible for administration and accounting for the company, and the other is responsible for marketing and arranging licence agreements.

Ragyun paid tax of $7,200 on its income to the Hungarian taxing authorities for the 2013 taxation year-end. On January 31, 2014, Ragyun paid a dividend of $52,800 to its shareholders. A 15% withholding tax applied to dividends paid to the Canadian shareholders.

— REQUIRED

Part A

Is Ragyun a foreign affiliate or controlled foreign affiliate (CFA) of Ms. Ambrose?

Part B

Is Ragyun a foreign affiliate or controlled foreign affiliate (CFA) of Mr. Frank?

Part C

Calculate foreign accrual property income (FAPI) for Ragyun for 2013. Calculate the impact of the FAPI on Mr. Frank's taxable income for 2013 and the adjusted cost base of his shares.

Part D

How will the January 31, 2014 dividend affect Mr. Frank's taxable income for 2014 and the adjusted cost base of his shares?

Part E

How will the January 31, 2014 dividend affect Ms. Ambrose's taxable income for 2013?

Part F

How would your response to C and D above change if Mr. Frank were Frank Corporation, a Canadian resident corporation with a December 31 year end?

[For more problems and solutions thereto, see the DVD accompanying this book.]

Appendix II

Individual Tax Facts

TOPICS DISCUSSED

¶20,100 Personal Income Tax Rate Components — 2013 (including surtaxes)

This table is prepared from information available as of June 10, 2013.

		Basic Tax Rates	Basic Tax Brackets	Surtax
Federal[1]		15.00%	$0	
		22.00%	$43,561	
		26.00%	$87,123	
		29.00%	$135,054	
Provincial or Territorial	Alberta	10.00%	$0	No surtax
	British Columbia	5.06%	$0	
		7.70%	$37,568	
		10.50%	$75,138	
		12.29%	$86,268	
		14.70%	$104,754	
	Manitoba	10.80%	$0	
		12.75%	$31,000	
		17.40%	$67,000	
	New Brunswick	9.39%	$0	
		13.46%	$38,954	
		14.46%	$77,908	
		16.07%	$126,662	
	Newfoundland and Labrador	7.70%	$0	
		12.50%	$33,748	
		13.30%	$67,496	
	Northwest Territories	5.90%	$0	
		8.60%	$39,453	
		12.20%	$78,908	
		14.05%	$128,286	
	Nova Scotia	8.79%	$0	
		14.95%	$29,590	
		16.67%	$59,180	
		17.50%	$93,000	
		21.00%	$150,000	
	Nunavut	4.00%	$0	
		7.00%	$41,535	
		9.00%	$83,071	
		11.50%	$135,054	
	Ontario	5.05%	$0	20% of tax above $4,289 + 36% of tax above $5,489
		9.15%	$39,723	
		11.16%	$79,448	
		13.16%	$509,000	
	Prince Edward Island	9.80%	$0	10% of tax above $12,500
		13.80%	$31,984	
		16.70%	$63,969	
	Quebec[1]	16.00%	$0	No surtax
		20.00%	$41,095	
		24.00%	$82,190	
		25.75%	$100,000	
	Saskatchewan	11.00%	$0	
		13.00%	$42,906	
		15.00%	$122,589	
	Yukon	7.04%	$0	5% of tax above $6,000
		9.68%	$43,561	
		11.44%	$87,123	
		12.76%	$135,054	
Non-residents[2]		7.20%	$0	No surtax
		10.56%	$43,561	
		12.48%	$87,123	
		13.92%	$135,054	

Notes:

1. In Quebec, federal tax is reduced by 16.5% for Quebec's abatement of basic federal tax.
2. Instead of provincial or territorial tax, non-residents pay an additional 48% of basic federal tax on income taxable in Canada that is not earned in a province or territory. Non-residents are subject to provincial or territorial rates (in this table) on employment income earned, and business income connected with a permanent establishment, in the respective province or territory. Different rates may apply to non-residents in other circumstances.

¶20,200 Personal Tax Credits — 2013

This table is prepared from information available as of June 10, 2013.

The two tables below contain information concerning select non-refundable personal tax credits. The first table contains the federal and provincial/territorial rates used in the calculation of personal tax credits. The second table shows the value of the credits. Provinces and territories use their own prescribed amounts to determine their personal tax credits.

		Personal tax credit rates (See table below for some limitations)													
		Federal	**Alt.**	**B.C.**	**Man.**	**N.B.**	**Nfld. & Lab.**	**N.W.T.**	**N.S.**	**Nun.**	**Ont.**	**P.E.I.**	**Que.**[1]	**Sask.**	**Yukon**
General factor[2] / **Charitable donations**[4]	First $200	15%	10%	5.06%	10.8%	9.39%	7.7%	5.9%	8.79%	4%	5.05%	9.8%	20%	11%	7.04%
	Amount over $200	29%	21%	14.7%	17.4%	17.95%	13.3%	14.05%	21%	11.5%	11.16%	16.7%	24%	15%	12.76%
Dividend tax credit[3] (on grossed-up amount)	Eligible	15.02%	10%	10%	8%	12%	11%	11.5%	8.85%	5.51%	6.4%	10.5%	11.9%	11%	15.08%
	Non-eligible	13.33%	3.5%	3.4%	1.75%	5.3%	5%	6%	7.7%	4%	4.5%	2.9%	8%	4%	4.51%

		Federal Amounts	Maximum value (before surtaxes) of credits that are based on prescribed amounts													
			Federal[6]	**Alt.**	**B.C.**	**Man.**	**N.B.**	**Nfld. & Lab.**	**N.W.T.**	**N.S.**	**Nun.**	**Ont.**	**P.E.I.**	**Que.**[1]	**Sask.**	**Yukon**
Basic					$520		$882	$651				$483	$755	$2,239[1]		
Spouse		$11,038[5]	$1,656[5]	$1,759	$448	$959	$748	$532	$799	$745	$498	$411	$642	N/A	$1,677	$777[5]
Equivalent to spouse													$617			
Age 65		$6,854	$1,028	$490	$224	$403	$430	$415	$391	$364	$374	$236	$369	$482[1]	$511[7]	$483
Disability	Basic	$7,697	$1,155	$1,357	$374	$667	$714	$439	$648	$645	$498	$391	$675	$509		$542
	Under 18 supplement	$4,490	$674							$303			$394			$316
Infirm dependant (18 or over)		$6,530[5]	$980[5]	$1,018	$218	$389	$416	$207	$265	$246	$180	$228	$240	N/A[1]	$988	$460[5]
Caregiver		$4,490[5]	$674[5]	$1,019						$431						$316[5]
Pension income		$2,000	$300	$136	$51	$108	$94	$77	$59	$103	$80	$67	$98	$428[1]	$110	$141
Child		$2,234[5]	$335[5]	N/A				N/A[8]	N/A	N/A[9]		N/A	N/A[9]	N/A	$636	$157[5]
Adoption		$11,669	$1,750	$1,203	$590	$1,080	N/A	$878	N/A			$590	N/A	N/A[1]	N/A	$821
Children's fitness		$500	$75	N/A	$25	$54[10]	N/A			$44	N/A	N/A[11]	N/A	N/A[1]	N/A[12]	$35[13]
Children's arts										N/A						
Canada Pension Plan (CPP)		$2,356	$353	$236	$119	$254	$221	$181	$139	$207	$94	$119	$231	N/A	$259	$166
Quebec Pension Plan (QPP)		$2,428	$364	N/A										N/A[1]	N/A	
Employment Insurance (EI)	not in Quebec	$891	$134	$89	$45	$96	$84	$69	$53	$78	$36	$45	$87	N/A	$98	$63
	in Quebec	$720[1]	$108	N/A										N/A[1]	N/A	
Canada Employment		$1,117	$168	N/A												$79
Education (per month)	Full-time	$400	$60	$68	$10	$43	$38	$15	$24	$18	$16	$26	$39	$413[1]	$44	$28
	Part-time	$120	$18	$21	$3	$13	$11	$5	$7	$5	$5	$8	$12	N/A	$13	$8
Textbook (per month)	Full-time	$65	$10	N/A							$3	N/A				$5
	Part-time	$20	$3								$1					$1
												× 1.2 or × 1.56	*× 1.1*			*× 1.05*

Factors at bottom of table increase value of credits to reflect surtaxes.[14]

Notes:

1. See below for Quebec's special credits and rules.
2. The general factor, multiplied by the federal (or provincial/territorial) amount, yields the value of the federal (or provincial/territorial) credit.
3. Eligible dividends are designated as such by the payor. They are grossed up by 38% and include dividends paid by:
   - public corporations or other corporations that are not Canadian-controlled private corporations (CCPCs), that are resident in Canada and are subject to the federal general corporate income tax rate (i.e., 15% in 2013); or
   - CCPCs, to the extent that the CCPC's income is:
     - not investment income (other than eligible dividends from public corporations); and
     - subject to the federal general corporate income tax rate (i.e., the income is active business income not subject to the federal small business rate).

   Non-eligible dividends are grossed up by 25% and include dividends paid out of either income eligible for the federal small business rate or a CCPC's investment income (other than eligible dividends received from public corporations).
4. The 2013 federal budget introduces a temporary First-time Donor's Super Credit (FDSC) that can be claimed by first-time donors only once in a taxation year after 2012 and before 2018. The FDSC is an additional 25% tax credit (on top of claiming the Charitable Donations Tax Credit) on up to $1,000 of donations made after March 20, 2013.
5. Caregivers of dependants with a mental or physical infirmity can claim the Family Caregiver Tax Credit. This credit, which is valued at $306 (i.e., $2,040 x 15%), is already included in the infirm dependant (18 or over) tax credit, or increases the spouse/equivalent to spouse, caregiver or child tax credit. Only one Family Caregiver Tax Credit can be claimed for each infirm dependant. The Yukon has paralleled this credit, with an increase of up to $151 (i.e., $2,040 x 7.04% x 1.05).
6. In Quebec, federal values are reduced by 16.5%.
7. In Saskatchewan, an additional credit of $135 is available to individuals who are 65 or older, regardless of their income.
8. In Newfoundland and Labrador, parents can claim a non-refundable tax credit amount equal to the child care expenses that are deductible from their income.
9. A non-refundable tax credit for children under six is available in Nova Scotia (up to $105 per year), in Nunavut ($48 per year) and Prince Edward Island (up to $129 per year).
10. In Manitoba, individuals up to age 24 can claim the fitness credit. The credit can be up to $108 for an individual with a disability. The arts credit provides up to $54 for a child under 17 (up to $108 for a child under 19 with a disability).
11. In Ontario, a refundable tax credit provides up to $54 for a child under 17 (up to $107 for a child under 19 with a disability) for fitness and certain non-fitness activities.
12. In Saskatchewan, a refundable tax credit provides up to $150 per child under 19, for cultural, recreational and sports activity fees.
13. In the Yukon, a tax credit for children's arts can be claimed, starting 2012.
14. For taxpayers affected by provincial/territorial surtaxes, the value of the credits shown will be higher by the factors indicated. For example, for a taxpayer in Ontario's top bracket, the $483 shown for the basic Ontario credit would be worth $753 (i.e., $483 × 1.56).

Quebec's Special Credits and Rules — 2013

The following special rules apply to Quebec's non-refundable tax credits:

- the minimum basic personal credit, the Quebec Pension Plan (QPP), Employment Insurance (EI), Health Services Fund and Quebec Parental Insurance Plan (QPIP) credits are combined into a single basic personal credit equal to $11,195;
- employees, employers and the self-employed must contribute to the QPIP, from which maternity, adoption and parental leave benefits are paid. As a result, federal EI premiums are lower for Quebec employees than for other employees ($720 instead of $891). A federal credit is available to individuals for QPIP premiums;
- an adult student can transfer the unused portion of the basic personal credit to a parent, but if this transfer is made, the other dependant (18 or over) credit of $601 cannot be claimed for that student;
- most non-refundable credits, such as the basic personal credit and the age credit, can be transferred to a spouse, if not used by the taxpayer;
- the age, pension and living alone credits are reduced if net family income exceeds $32,480;
- a person that lives alone or with a dependant can claim a credit of $262;
- a person that qualifies for the living alone credit and lives with an eligible student is eligible for an additional $325 credit;
- the maximum education credit of $413 per term (maximum two terms per year) can be claimed by a supporting Quebec parent (but is not transferable) for a child under 18 who attends post-secondary school full-time (part-time for infirm dependants);
- a student can transfer the unused portion of the tuition and examination tax credits to a parent or grandparent; and
- the medical expense credit is based on the amount by which qualifying expenses exceed 3% of net family income (see below for details on the refundable medical expense credit).

Select Quebec refundable tax credits are listed in the table below.

	Details
Adoption	50% of eligible adoption expenses (maximum credit of $10,000)
Child care	26% to 75% of qualifying child care expenses (limits apply)
Youth activities[1]	Maximum credit is $20 for children aged five to under 17; $40 for children with a disability aged five to under 19; available to families with incomes of $130,000 or less
Caregivers[2, 3]	Maximum credit of $775 plus supplement of $509, which is reduced if the dependant's income exceeds $22,620
Respite expenses for informal caregivers	30% of eligible respite expenses paid for the care of a person who resides with the caregiver and has a significant disability; maximum credit of $1,560 is reduced if family income exceeds $54,790
Informal caregivers	Maximum credit of $500 for each care recipient can be allocated to a volunteer who provides home respite to informal caregivers of the care recipient
Home support for seniors[4]	31% of eligible expenses; maximum credit of $6,045 for independent seniors (reduced if family income exceeds $54,790) and $7,905 for dependent seniors, aged 70 and over; expenses eligible for this credit will not qualify for the medical expense credit
Medical	25% of medical expenses eligible for the non-refundable credit and 25% of amount deducted for impairment support products and services; maximum credit of $1,130 is reduced if family income exceeds $21,870

Notes:

1. Quebec's November 20, 2012 budget introduces a tax credit for youth activities, starting 2013. The credit will increase, in stages, from 2014 to 2017, to up to $100 per child aged five to under 17, and up to $200 per child with a disability aged five to under 19.
2. The caregivers credit consists of separate credits for:
   - informal caregivers who house, in the strict sense of the term, an eligible relative;
   - informal caregivers who cohabit with an eligible relative unable to live alone; and
   - certain informal caregivers caring for an elderly spouse (credit is not affected by the spouse's income).
3. For the caregivers credit, the maximum credit will gradually increase from $775 in 2013 to $1,000 in 2016 (indexed thereafter).
4. For the home support for seniors credit, the tax credit rate and maximum credits will gradually increase from 31% (maximum credit of $6,045 for independent seniors and $7,905 for dependent seniors) in 2013, to 35% (maximum credit of $6,825 for independent seniors and $8,925 for dependent seniors) in 2017.

Personal Tax Credits: Federal Limitations and Other Information

This table presents additional information related to federal credits. Other restrictions may also apply. The provinces/territories may have comparable thresholds and rules.

	Limitations	To whom the credit may be transferred	Carry-forward
Tuition	Credit available only if at least $100 is paid in fees to an institution	Spouse, parent or grandparent (Maximum combined tuition, education and textbook credits transferable is $750)	Indefinite
Education	Credit is $60/month for full-time students and certain disabled part-time students; $18/month for other part-time students		
Textbook	Credit is $10/month for full-time students and certain disabled part-time students; $3/month for other part-time students		
Medical	Credit is based on amount by which qualifying medical expenses exceed the lesser of $2,152 and 3% of net income (generally, expenses for any twelve-month period ending in the year can be claimed)	Either spouse may claim	
CPP/QPP and EI	For employees, maximum credit is $487 (in Quebec, $472); self-employed persons deduct 50% of CPP/QPP premiums paid for their own coverage (maximum deduction of $2,356; in Quebec $2,428) and claim a credit for the non-deductible half of premiums paid (maximum credit $353; in Quebec $364); self-employed persons do not pay EI premiums	N/A	
Canada Employment	Credit is based on employment income		
Transit pass	Public transit passes (monthly or longer) and certain weekly and electronic payment cards for travel are eligible	Spouse or parent	
Student loan interest	Interest must be paid on qualifying student loans	N/A	5 years
Charitable donations	Eligible donations are limited to 75% of net income	Either spouse may claim	
Spousal and equivalent to spouse	Reduced by any net income of the spouse or qualifying dependant	N/A	
Infirm dependant	Reduced if dependant's income exceeds $6,548		
Caregiver	For providers of in-home care for an adult relative (reduced if relative's income exceeds $15,334)		
Age	Reduced if income exceeds $34,562	Spouse	
Pension	Credit is not available for CPP, QPP, Old Age Security or Guaranteed Income Supplement payments		
Child	Credit available for each child under 18		
Adoption	Must be claimed in the year the adoption period ends		
Children's fitness	Maximum credit is $75 for children under 17; $150 for children under 19 who qualify for the disability tax credit	Either parent may claim	
Children's arts			
Disability — Basic	For individuals with severe and prolonged impairment	Spouse, parent, grandparent, child, grandchild, sibling, aunt, uncle, niece or nephew	
Disability — Under 18 supplement	Reduced if child care expenses and attendant care expenses (claimed as a medical expense for child) exceed $2,630		

¶20,300 Filing Deadline and Payment of Taxes for Individuals

Both federal and Quebec returns must be **filed by April 30** (June 15 for self-employed individuals and the individual's spouse or common-law partner) following each calendar year. Employed individuals have taxes withheld at source. Individuals who have other sources of income resulting in federal tax payable in excess of $3,000 ($1,800 if a Quebec resident) in either of the two preceding years must remit instalments on a quarterly basis due on the 15th of March, June, September, and December.

There are three bases for making current year quarterly instalments:

1. Divide the preceding year's tax and CPP (or QPP) due by four.
2. First two instalments based on the second preceding year's tax and CPP (or QPP) divided by four, and the second two instalments at the balance required to bring the total instalment payments for the year to the same as #1.
3. Estimated current year liability divided by four.

Alternatively, the CRA will inform taxpayers of the quarterly instalment due. Failure to receive this advice from the CRA does not exempt the taxpayer from interest charges for failing to make sufficient instalments.

¶20,400 Canadian-Controlled Private Corporation (CCPC) Income Tax Rates (for December 31, 2013 Year End) (%)

This table is prepared from information available as of June 10, 2013.

	Active business income of CCPCs[1] up to $500,000[2]		Investment income[3]	
Federal rate (before deductions)		**28**		**28**
Small business deduction[2]		(17)		n/a
Refundable investment tax		n/a		6.67
Federal rate		**11** ↓		**34.67** ↓
	Provincial/ Territorial	**Combined**	Provincial/ Territorial	**Combined**
Alberta[4]	3	**14**	10	**44.67**
British Columbia[5]	2.5	**13.5**	10.75	**45.42**
Manitoba[6]	Nil* or 12*	**11* or 23***	12	**46.67**
New Brunswick[7]	4.5	**15.5**	11.01	**45.67****
Newfoundland and Labrador[8]	4 **H**	**15**	14 **H**	**48.67**
Northwest Territories[9]	4	**15**	11.5	**46.17**
Nova Scotia[10]	3.5* **H** or 16*	**14.5* or 27***	16	**50.67**
Nunavut[11]	4	**15**	12	**46.67**
Ontario[12, 13]	4.5 **H**	**15.5**	11.5 **H**	**46.17**
Prince Edward Island[14]	3.64 **H**	**14.64**	16 **H**	**50.67**
Quebec[15]	8 **H**	**19**	11.9 **H**	**46.57**
Saskatchewan[16]	2	**13**	12	**46.67**
Yukon[17] M&P	2.5	**13.5**	n/a	
Yukon[17] Non-M&P	4	**15**	15	**49.67**

H = Tax holidays are available to certain corporations in the provinces indicated.

* The lower rate applies to active business income of CCPCs up to $400,000. The higher rate applies to active business income of CCPCs from $400,000 to $500,000.

** Although 34.67% (federal) + 11.01% (New Brunswick) = 45.68%, the exact rate is 45.6749%.

Notes:

1. See the table, **General and M&P Corporate Income Tax Rates**, for the rates that apply to CCPCs on active business income above $500,000.

   The federal small business threshold increased from $400,000 to $500,000 on January 1, 2009. The $500,000 threshold also applies in:
   - New Brunswick, Newfoundland and Labrador, Northwest Territories, Nunavut, Ontario (see footnote 13 below), Prince Edward Island and Saskatchewan;
   - Quebec, after March 19, 2009 (see footnote 15 below);
   - Alberta, after March 31, 2009 (see footnote 4 below);
   - British Columbia, after December 31, 2009 (see footnote 5); and
   - the Yukon, after December 31, 2010 (see footnote 17).

   Manitoba and Nova Scotia have not harmonized with this increase.
2. See footnote 4 to the table, **Federal Corporate Tax Rates**, for:
   - recent changes to the federal small business threshold; and
   - a description of the federal small business deduction clawback and threshold.

   The clawback also applies for the purposes of the provincial/territorial small business deductions in the territories and all provinces except Ontario. Ontario had a clawback before July 1, 2010, as outlined in footnote 13, below.
3. Rates on investment income are 19.67% higher than the general rates for 2013 (see the table, **General and M&P Corporate Income Tax Rates**), because:
   - CCPC investment income does not benefit from the 13% federal general rate reduction; and
   - the rates on investment income include a 6⅔% tax that is refundable when the CCPC pays taxable dividends.

   Generally, 26⅔% of a CCPC's aggregate investment income is added to its refundable dividend tax on hand (RDTOH). This amount is refundable at a rate of $1 for every $3 of taxable dividends paid by the CCPC.

CCPC Income Tax Rates — 2013 (continued)

4. Recent Alberta changes are shown in the following table:

	Alberta changes effective after December 31, 2008		
	From	To	Effective
CCPC rate on over-integrated income*	3%	9.7%	January 1, 2009
Threshold up to which CCPC rate applies	$460,000	$500,000	April 1, 2009

* Commencing January 1, 2009, an "over-integration tax payable" effectively increases Alberta's tax rate by 6.7% from 3% to 9.7% on income that is eligible for the Alberta CCPC small business deduction (SBD), but exceeds the federal SBD threshold. In general, this 6.7% tax applies only when this income is distributed as eligible dividends. However, because the federal SBD threshold increased from $400,000 to $500,000 on January 1, 2009, this tax in effect no longer applies.

5. Recent British Columbia changes are shown in the following table:

	British Columbia changes effective after December 31, 2008		
	From	To	Effective
Threshold up to which CCPC rate applies	$400,000	$500,000	January 1, 2010

6. Recent and planned Manitoba changes are shown in the following table:

	Manitoba changes effective after December 31, 2008		
	From	To	Effective
CCPC rate	2%	1%	January 1, 2009
	1%	0%	December 1, 2010
Threshold up to which CCPC rate applies	$400,000	$425,000	January 1, 2014

7. Recent New Brunswick changes are shown in the following table:

	New Brunswick changes effective after December 31, 2008		
	From	To	Effective
CCPC rate	5%	4.5%*	January 1, 2012
Threshold up to which CCPC rate applies	$400,000	$500,000	January 1, 2009

* New Brunswick's 2013 budget states that "it is [the] government's intention to suspend further reductions in the small business income tax rate" (the 2011 budget had indicated that the small business tax rate would decrease from 5% to 2.5% over four years).

8. Recent Newfoundland and Labrador changes are shown in the following table:

	Newfoundland and Labrador changes effective after December 31, 2008		
	From	To	Effective
CCPC rate	5%	4%	Taxation years beginning after March 31, 2010
Threshold up to which CCPC rate applies	$400,000	$500,000	January 1, 2009

9. Recent Northwest Territories changes are shown in the following table:

	Northwest Territories changes effective after December 31, 2008		
	From	To	Effective
Threshold up to which CCPC rate applies	$400,000	$500,000	January 1, 2009

10. Recent and planned Nova Scotia changes are shown in the following table:

	Nova Scotia changes effective after December 31, 2008		
	From	To	Effective
CCPC rate	5%	4.5%	January 1, 2011
	4.5%	4%	January 1, 2012
	4%	3.5%	January 1, 2013
	3.5%	3%	January 1, 2014
Threshold up to which CCPC rate applies	$400,000	$350,000	January 1, 2014

11. Recent Nunavut changes are shown in the following table:

	Nunavut changes effective after December 31, 2008		
	From	To	Effective
Threshold up to which CCPC rate applies	$400,000	$500,000	January 1, 2009

CCPC Income Tax Rates — 2013 (continued)

12. Corporations subject to Ontario income tax may also be liable for corporate minimum tax (CMT) based on adjusted book income. The minimum tax is payable only to the extent that it exceeds the regular Ontario income tax liability. For rates and thresholds, see the table, **General and M&P Corporate Income Tax Rates** (footnote 7).
13. Recent Ontario changes are shown in the following table:

	Ontario changes effective after December 31, 2008		
	From	**To**	**Effective**
CCPC rate	5.5%	4.5%	July 1, 2010

Recent changes related to Ontario's CCPC clawback are shown below:

Ontario CCPC clawback* effective after December 31, 2008				
Lower threshold	**Upper threshold**	**Addition to rate (between thresholds) due to clawback** Non-M&P	M&P	**Effective**
$500,000	$1,500,000	4.25%	3.25%	Before July 1, 2010
n/a	n/a	0%	0%	July 1, 2010

* Before July 1, 2010, a surtax clawed back the benefit of Ontario's small business deduction when taxable income of associated corporations exceeded $500,000. The benefit was eliminated completely once taxable income, on an associated basis, reached $1,500,000. The addition to the rate, due to the clawback, increased the rate that would otherwise apply.

14. Recent Prince Edward Island changes are shown in the following table:

	Prince Edward Island changes effective after December 31, 2008		
	From	**To**	**Effective**
CCPC rate	3.2%	2.1%	April 1, 2009
	2.1%	1%	April 1, 2010
	1%	4.5%	April 1, 2013
Threshold up to which CCPC rate applies	$400,000	$500,000	January 1, 2009

15. Recent Quebec changes are shown in the following table:

	Quebec changes effective after December 31, 2008		
	From	**To**	**Effective**
Threshold up to which CCPC rate applies	$400,000	$500,000	March 20, 2009

16. Recent Saskatchewan changes are shown in the following table:

	Saskatchewan changes effective after December 31, 2008		
	From	**To**	**Effective**
CCPC rate	4.5%	2%	July 1, 2011

17. Recent Yukon changes are shown in the following table:

	Yukon changes effective after December 31, 2008		
	From	**To**	**Effective**
Threshold up to which CCPC rate applies	$400,000	$500,000	January 1, 2011

¶20,500 Corporate Income Tax Rates by Province/Territory — 2013 (%)

This table is prepared from information available as of June 10, 2013.

All rate changes must be pro-rated for taxation years that straddle the effective date. Use the rate changes to determine rates for taxation years ending on December 31, 2009 or later.

Tax holidays may reduce or eliminate provincial tax.

In addition to income tax:

- before 2013, some provinces imposed general capital tax on corporations that had a permanent establishment there, the last being Nova Scotia, which eliminated its general capital tax on July 1, 2012 (see **Capital Tax Rates and Exemptions for 2013**); and
- financial institutions may also be subject to Part VI Financial Institution Capital Tax (see **Other Federal Corporate Tax Rates for 2013**) and provincial capital taxes (see **Capital Tax Rates and Exemptions for 2013**).

General and M&P Corporate Income Tax Rates

(for December 31, 2013 year end) (%)

The percentages shown in the table below reflect the combined federal and provincial/territorial corporate rates (general and manufacturing and processing (M&P)) for a 12-month taxation year ended December 31, 2013, on income allocated to provinces or territories. For Canadian-controlled private corporations (CCPCs), this table does not apply to:

- the first $500,000 ($400,000 in Manitoba and Nova Scotia) of active business income; and
- investment income.

For more CCPC rates, see the table, **Canadian-Controlled Private Corporation (CCPC) Income Tax Rates**.

		General and Manufacturing & Processing (M&P)	
Basic federal rate			**38**
Provincial abatement			(10)
Federal rate (before deductions)			**28**
General rate reduction[2] or M&P deduction[2]			(13)[1]
Federal rate			**15**[1] ↓
		Provincial/Territorial	**Combined**
Alberta		10	**25**
British Columbia[3]		10.75	**25.75**
Manitoba[4]		12	**27**
New Brunswick[5]		11.01	**26.01**
Newfoundland and Labrador	General	14 **H**	**29**
	M&P	5 **H**	**20**
Northwest Territories		11.5	**26.5**
Nova Scotia		16	**31**
Nunavut		12	**27**
Ontario[6, 7]	General	11.5 **H**	**26.5**
	M&P	10 **H**	**25**
Prince Edward Island		16 **H**	**31**
Quebec[8]		11.9 **H**	**26.9**
Saskatchewan[9]	General	12	**27**
	M&P	10[10]	**25**
Yukon	General	15	**30**
	M&P	2.5	**17.5**

H = Tax holidays are available to certain corporations in the provinces indicated.

Notes:

1. Footnote 3 to the table, **Federal Corporate Tax Rates** indicates when the general rate reduction and M&P deduction do not apply.
2. For recent changes to the general rate reduction and M&P deduction, see footnote 2 to the table, **Federal Corporate Tax Rates**.
3. Recent British Columbia changes are shown in the following table:

	British Columbia changes effective after December 31, 2008		
	From	**To**	**Effective**
General and M&P	11%	10.5%	January 1, 2010
	10.5%	10%	January 1, 2011
	10%	11%*	April 1, 2013*

* British Columbia's 2013 budget accelerates the rate increase to 11% by one year (the 2012 budget had announced that the increase would occur on April 1, 2014, and would be triggered only if the province's fiscal situation worsens).

Corporate Income Tax Rates by Province/Territory — 2013 (%) (continued)

4. Recent Manitoba changes are shown in the following table:

	Manitoba changes effective after December 31, 2008		
	From	To	Effective
General and M&P	13%	12%*	July 1, 2009

* Manitoba's general and M&P rate was scheduled to drop from 12% to 11% at a date to be determined, subject to balanced budget requirements; however, this is no longer being considered by the province.

5. Recent and planned New Brunswick changes are shown in the following table:

	New Brunswick changes effective after December 31, 2008		
	From	To	Effective
General and M&P	13%	12%	July 1, 2009
	12%	11%	July 1, 2010
	11%	10%*	July 1, 2011
	10%	12%	July 1, 2013

* New Brunswick repealed the legislated corporate income tax rate of 8% that was to apply on July 1, 2012.

6. Recent Ontario changes are shown in the following table:

	Ontario changes effective after December 31, 2008		
	From	To	Effective
General	14%	12%	July 1, 2010
	12%	11.5%*	July 1, 2011
M&P	12%	10%	July 1, 2010

* Ontario's 2012 budget froze the general income tax rate at 11.5%, until the province returns to a balanced budget (scheduled for 2017-18). The rate was to drop to 11% on July 1, 2012, and to 10% on July 1, 2013.

7. Corporations subject to Ontario income tax may also be liable for corporate minimum tax (CMT) based on adjusted book income. The minimum tax is payable only to the extent that it exceeds the regular Ontario income tax liability. Recent Ontario CMT changes are shown in the following table:

		Ontario changes effective after December 31, 2008		
		From	To	Effective
Corporate Minimum Tax (CMT) rate		4%	2.7%	July 1, 2010
Thresholds for CMT to apply*	Total assets	> $5 million	≥ $50 million	Taxation years ending after June 30, 2010
		or	and	
	Annual gross revenues	> $10 million	≥ $100 million	

* Thresholds apply on an associated basis.

8. Recent Quebec changes are shown in the following table:

	Quebec changes effective after December 31, 2008		
	From	To	Effective
General and M&P	11.4%*	11.9%	January 1, 2009

* For financial institutions (other than insurance corporations) and oil refining companies, the rate is 11.9% and the combined rate is 31.4% for December 31, 2008 year ends. However, deposit insurance corporations are not financial institutions and were subject to a rate of 5.75%, which increased to 11.9% on June 23, 2009.

9. Planned Saskatchewan changes are shown in the following table:

	Saskatchewan changes effective after December 31, 2008		
	From	To	Effective
General	12%	10%*	To be determined*

* Saskatchewan's 2013 budget defers the province's general corporate income tax rate decrease to 10% (from 12%) until it is "affordable and sustainable, within a balanced budget." The province is no longer committed to reducing the rate by 2015 as had been announced in its 2012 throne speech.

10. The general rate (12% in 2013) is the maximum Saskatchewan rate. A rebate of up to the difference between the general rate and 10% (2% in 2013) of manufacturing profits allocated to Saskatchewan is available.

¶20,600 Filing Deadlines and Payments of Taxes for Corporations

Both the federal and any provincial returns must be **filed within six months** after each taxation year end. The balance of any taxes due must be paid within two months of the year end (three months for Canadian-controlled private corporations). Instalments may be based on any of the following:

- 1/12 of estimated taxes payable,
- 1/12 of the preceding year's tax liability,
- 1/12 of the second preceding year's tax liability for the first two months and 1/10 of the immediately preceding year's tax liability less the first two months.

Provincial income and capital tax returns must be filed with respective Provincial Treasury or Finance Departments. Each province has its own filing requirements.

Late or deficient instalments are subject to interest at the prescribed rate plus a penalty equal to ½ times the interest amount charged for the year in excess of the greater of:

(a) $1,000, or

(b) 25% of the instalment interest.

¶20,700 Alphabetical List of Assets — Capital Cost Allowance Classes and Rates

The following table sets out the current capital cost allowance rates. This table is for use only as a quick reference guide for the capital cost allowance classes and rates for certain types of assets. See Part XI and Schedules II, III, IV, V, and VI of the *Income Tax Regulations* for detailed rules relating to capital cost allowance.

Item	Rate	Class
Access roads and trails for the protection of standing timber	30%	10
Air conditioning equipment (other than window units) — same rate as building[1]		
Aircraft[16]	25%	9
furniture and fittings	25%	9
hangars[1]	10%	6
Airplane runways[16]	8%	17
Amusement park components (including fences, bridges, canals, stalls, tractors, etc.)	15%	37
land improvements[39]	15%	37
Apparel, used for earning rental income[1,26]	100%	12
Asphalt surface, storage yard[16]	8%	17
Assets, tangible capital[1,2]	20%	8
used primarily in manufacturing or processing[10,15]		29, 39, 40, 43
Automobiles[1]	30%	10
acquired after June 17, 1987 in excess of prescribed amount (Reg. 7307(1))[1,7]	30%	10.1
for lease or rental[22]	40%	16
Automotive equipment[1]	30%	10
designed for and used in amusement parks	15%	37
Bar code scanners — see Cash registers		
Billboards		
acquired before 1988	35%	11
acquired after 1987[10]	20%	8
Biogas production equipment[35]	50%	43.2
Boats — see Vessels		
Boilers		
heating use — same rate as building		
used primarily in manufacturing or processing[10,15]		29, 39, 43
Books of lending libraries[26]	100%	12
Breakwaters		
wooden	10%	6
other	5%	3
Bridges[1]	4%	1
Buildings[1]		
addition or alteration — same class as buildings[13]		
amusement park stalls	15%	37
brick, stone, cement, etc., acquired before 1988	5%	3
brick, stone, cement, etc., acquired after 1987	4%	1
component parts — generally same class as building (see individual items)		
farm ensilage storage	20%	8
foundation excavation — same rate as building		
frame, log, stucco on frame, galvanized iron or corrugated metal[25]	10%	6
kiln, tank, vat used in manufacturing or processing	20%	8
manufacturing or processing[43]	4%	1
mining (except refineries and office buildings not at mine)	30%	10
multiple-unit residential[7,18]		
non-residential[43]	4%	1
portable camp	30%	10
rental property[7]		
storage of fresh fruits and vegetables	20%	8
Buses	30%	10
Cable TV converters and descramblers		
acquired before Mar. 5, 2010	30%	10
acquired after Mar. 4, 2010	40%	30
Cables — telephone, telegraph or data communication		
acquired before Feb. 23, 2005	5%	3
acquired after Feb. 22, 2005	12%	42
fibre optic	12%	42
Calculator	20%	8
Canals[1]	4%	1
Canoes	15%	7
Capital tangible assets[1,2]	20%	8
used primarily in manufacturing or processing[10,15]		29, 39, 40, 43
Cash registers	20%	8
electronic, to record multiple sales taxes acquired after Aug. 8, 1989 and before 1993	100%	12
Catalyst[21]	5%	26
Cattle	nil	—
Chinaware[26]	100%	12
Cold storage structures	20%	8
Computer hardware and systems software		
acquired before Mar. 23, 2004[30]	30%	10
acquired after Mar. 22, 2004 and before Mar. 19, 2007[44]	45%	45
acquired after Mar. 18, 2007[44]	55%	50
acquired after Jan 27, 2009 and before Feb. 2011[26,44]	100%	52
Computer software[10,16,24,30]	100%	12
Concessions, for a limited period[26]		14
Condominiums — same rate as buildings		

Capital Cost Allowance Classes and Rates (continued)

Item	Rate	Class
Contractors' movable equipment, heavy	30%	10
acquired before 1988[5]	50%	22
acquired after 1987[5,10]	30%	38
Conversion cost — see Vessels		
Copyrights, for a limited period[26]		14
Costume and accessories for earning rental income[1,26]	100%	12
Culverts[1,10]	4%	1
Cutlery[26]	100%	12
Cutting part of a machine[1,27]	100%	12
Dams[1]	4%	1
Data communication equipment — wire and cable		
acquired before Feb. 23, 2005	5%	3
acquired after Feb. 22, 2005	12%	42
Data communication switching equipment[16]	8%	17
Dental instruments (costing less than $500; $200 limit if acquired before May 2, 2006)[1,26,29]	100%	12
Deuterium enriched water[21]	5%	26
Dies[1,27]	100%	12
Digital video disk — See DVD		
Display fixtures (window)	20%	8
Distribution equipment for heat, electrical energy, or water[4]		
acquired before 1988	6%	2
acquired after 1987	4%	1
for water or steam, acquired after Feb. 27, 2000	8%	17
for electrical energy, acquired after Feb. 22, 2005[34]	8%	47
Docks[1]	5%	3
Drive-in theatre property	30%	10
DVD, for rental[23,26]	100%	12
Electrical advertising signs[10,16]	20%	8
Electrical generating and distributing equipment[6,10]		
acquired before 1988[4]	6%	2
acquired after 1987	4%	1
acquired after Feb. 27, 2000 for generation[10]	8%	17
acquired after Feb. 22, 2005 for transmission or distribution[34]	8%	47
combustion turbines acquired after Feb. 22, 2005[34]	15%	48
energy efficient generating equipment[19,34,35]	50%, 30%, 50%	34, 43.1, 43.2
portable or maximum load 15 kw	20%	8
Electric wiring — same rate as building		
Electronic communications equipment including fax machines and telephone equipment[10]	20%	8
Electronic data processing equipment[1,15,16,30]		
used primarily in manufacturing or processing[15]		10, 29, 40
Electronic data processing equipment — data network infrastructure and systems software		

Item	Rate	Class
acquired before Mar. 23, 2004[10]	20%	8
acquired after Mar. 22, 2004	30%	46
Electronic data processing equipment — general purpose and systems software		
acquired before Mar. 23, 2004[10]	30%	10
acquired after Mar. 22, 2004 and before Mar. 19, 2007[44]	45%	45
acquired after Mar. 18, 2007[44]	55%	50
acquired after Jan 27, 2009 and before Feb. 2011[26,44]	100%	52
Elevators — same rate as building		
Equipment (see specific types)		
if not specifically mentioned[2]	20%	8
manufacturing or processing[10,15]		29, 39, 40, 43
Escalators — same rate as building		
Farming and fishing assets[38]		
Fences[1]	10%	6
Fibre optic cable	12%	42
Films, motion pictures[16]	30%	10
Canadian production[7,36]	30%	10
certified production[36]	100%	12
certified production acquired after 1987 and before March 1996[7,36]	30%	10
television commercials	100%	12
Franchises, for a limited period[26]		14
Furniture (not otherwise listed)[15]	20%	8
Gas manufacturing and distributing equipment, plants and pipelines[4,8]		
acquired before 1988[10]	6%	2
acquired after 1987	4%	1
distribution pipelines acquired after Mar. 18, 2007[33]	6%	51
liquefied natural gas facilities acquired after Mar. 18, 2007[34]	8%	47
transmission pipelines acquired after Feb. 22, 2005[10,33]	8%	49
Gas well equipment		
acquired after 1987	25%	41
acquired before 1988	30%	10
Generating equipment and plant of producer or distributor of electrical energy[4,6]		
acquired before 1988	6%	2
acquired after 1987	4%	1
acquired after Feb. 27, 2000	8%	17
energy efficient[34,35]	30%, 50%	43.1, 43.2
wave and tidal energy equipment[34,35]	30%, 50%	43.1, 43.2
Glass tableware[1,26]	100%	12
Grain drying machinery[11]	20%	8
Grain storage facilities — see buildings[11]		

Capital Cost Allowance Classes and Rates (continued)

Item	Rate	Class
Greenhouses [1]	10%	6
rigid frame with plastic cover	20%	8
Hangars [1]	10%	6
Harness equipment [1]	30%	10
Heat production and recovery equipment [19,34,35]	50%, 30%, 50%	34, 43.1, 43.2
Heating equipment		
distribution plant, acquired before 1988	6%	2
distribution plant, acquired after 1987	4%	1
general — same rate as building		
solar or energy efficient, acquired before Feb. 22, 1994 [19,34]	50%	34
solar or energy efficient, acquired after Feb. 21, 1994 [19,34,35]	30%, 50%	43.1, 43.2
Heavy water [21]	5%	26
Herbs	nil	—
Horses	nil	—
Instruments, dental or medical costing less than $500 [1,26,29]	100%	12
Jetties [16]	5%	3
wood	10%	6
Jigs [1,27]	100%	12
Kitchen utensils costing less than $500 [1,26,29]	100%	12
Land	nil	
deemed depreciable [7]	nil	36
Lasts [1,27]	100%	12
Leasehold interest		13
Lending library books [1,26]	100%	12
Licences, for a limited period [26]		14
Lighting fixture — same rate as building		
Linen [1,26]	100%	12
Logging mechanical equipment [3]	30%	10
Machinery and equipment		
additional capital cost allowance on grain elevators [11]	14%	8
not specifically listed [2]	20%	8
used primarily in manufacturing or processing [10,15]		29, 39, 40, 43
Marine railways	15%	7
Medical instruments costing less than $500 [1,26,29]	100%	12
Mining equipment	30%	10
Mining equipment, acquired after Feb. 25, 1992 for processing foreign ore in Canada	30%	43
Mining equipment, new or expanded mines [7,14]		
acquired before 1988	30%	28
acquired after 1987	25%	41
oil sands property acquired after March 18, 2007	25%	41.1
Moles [1,16]	5%	3
Motion picture drive-in theatres	30%	10
Motion picture films — see Films		
Moulds [1,27]	100%	12
Multiple-unit residential buildings [7,18]	5%, 10%	31, 32
Office equipment [30]	20%	8
Offshore drilling platforms		
acquired before 1988	30%	10
acquired after 1987	25%	41
Offshore drilling vessels [7,16,17]		
acquired before 1988	15%	7
acquired after 1987	25%	41
Oil pipelines		
acquired before 1988 [8,10]	6%	2
acquired after 1987	4%	1
acquired after Feb. 22, 2005 — transmission [33]	8%	49
Oil sands — see Mining equipment, new or expanded mines		
Oil storage tanks [1,15]	10%	6
used primarily in manufacturing or processing [15]		29, 39, 43
Oil well equipment [1]		
acquired before 1988	30%	10
acquired after 1987 [14]	25%	41
Overburden removal cost, designated [1,26]	100%	12
Parking area [16]	8%	17
Passenger vehicles — see Automobiles		
Patents [20]		14
	25%	44
Patterns [1,27]	100%	12
Photocopy machines [10,15,30]	20%	8
Pinball machines — see Video games		
Pipelines		
acquired before 1988 [8,10]	6%	2
acquired after 1987	4%	1
acquired after February 22, 2005 and used for transmission of oil and natural gas [33]	8%	49
acquired after March 18, 2007 for distribution of natural gas [33]	6%	51
acquired after Feb. 25, 2008 for transmission of carbon dioxide	8%	49
Plumbing — same rate as building		
Pollution control equipment [12]		
air, certified, acquired before 1999	50%	27
water, certified, acquired before 1999	50%	24
not specifically listed — Class 1, 2, 6, 8, or 43 depending on type of asset		
Portable construction camp buildings	30%	10
Portable electrical generating equipment [16]	20%	8
Portable equipment used for temporary rentals	30%	10
Power operated movable equipment [5,15]		
acquired before 1988	50%	22

Capital Cost Allowance Classes and Rates (continued)

Item	Rate	Class
acquired after 1987	30%	38
Power plants — see Electrical power plants		
Production equipment of distributor of heat (including structures)		
acquired before 1988[4]	6%	2
acquired after 1987	4%	1
acquired after Feb. 27, 2000	8%	17
Pumping and compression equipment		
Gas and oil acquired before Feb. 23, 2005	20%	8
Gas and oil acquired after Feb. 22, 2005[10,33]	15%	7
Carbon dioxide acquired after Feb. 25, 2008[33]	15%	7
Radar equipment[16]	20%	8
Radio communication equipment (excluding satellites)[16]	20%	8
Radium	nil	—
Railway car and rail suspension devices[1,7,16,31]		
acquired before Feb. 28, 2000[31]	7%	35
acquired after Feb. 27, 2000[31]	15%	7
Railway locomotive (excluding automotive railway car)[16]		
acquired after May 25, 1976[16,31]	10%	6
acquired after February 27, 2000[31]	15%	7
acquired after February 25, 2008[31]	30%	10
Railway, marine	15%	7
Railway track or grading[1,7,31]	4%	1
Railway traffic control or signalling equipment[1,7,16,31]	4%	1
Rapid transit car[40]	20%	8
Refrigeration equipment	20%	8
Renewable energy generation equipment[6,19,34,35]		
acquired after February 21, 1994	30%	43.1
acquired after Feb. 22, 2005 and before 2020[35]	50%	43.2
Rental property[7]		
Roads[1,16]	8%	17
acquired in relation to a mine	25%	41
forestry (may be depreciated with timber limit)[3]		
oil and gas mining temporary access[41]		
Roller rink floors	30%	10
Rowboats	15%	7
Satellites[7]		
acquired before 1988	40%	30
acquired after 1987	30%	10
Scanners, bar codes, acquired after Aug. 8, 1989 and before 1993	100%	12
Scows	15%	7
Shaping part of a machine[1,27]	100%	12
Ships, including ships under construction[17]	15%	7
Shrubs	nil	—
Sidewalks[16]	8%	17
Sleighs[1]	30%	10

Item	Rate	Class
Solar heating equipment[19]		
acquired before Feb. 22, 1994[34]	50%	34
acquired after Feb. 21, 1994[34,35]	30%	43.1
acquired after Feb. 22, 2005 and before 2020[34,35]	50%	43.2
Spacecraft (telecommunication)[7]		
acquired before 1988	40%	30
acquired after 1987	30%	10
Spare parts for an aircraft[16]	25%	9
Sprinkler systems — same rate as building		
Stable equipment[1]	30%	10
Storage area[16]	8%	17
Storage tanks, oil or water[1]	10%	6
direct manufacturing use[15]		29, 39, 43
Subway or tunnel[1,16]	4%	1
Systems software — general purpose electronic data processing equipment[1,16,44]		
acquired before Mar. 23, 2004[10]	30%	10
acquired after Mar. 22, 2004 and before Mar. 19 2007[44]	45%	45
acquired after Mar. 18, 2007[44]	55%	50
acquired after Jan 27, 2009 and before Feb. 2011[26,44]	100%	52
primary manufacturing purpose, acquired after March 18, 2007 and before January 28, 2009[15,44]		10, 29, 40
Tableware, glass[1,26]	100%	12
Tangible capital assets[1,2]	20%	8
Tank cars, railway[1,7,16]	7%	35
Tanks, oil and water storage[1]	10%	6
used primarily in manufacturing or processing[15]		29, 39, 43
Taxicabs[16]	40%	16
Telecommunication spacecraft[7]		
acquired before 1988	40%	30
acquired after 1987	30%	10
Telegraph and telephone equipment, wires and cables[16]		
acquired before Feb. 23, 2005[1,16]	5%	3
new and acquired after Feb. 22, 2005	12%	42
poles and masts[1,16]	5%	3
fibre optic cable	12%	42
Telephone or telegraph communication non-electronic switching equipment[16]	8%	17
Telephone system (purchased)[30]	20%	8
Television aerial[16]	20%	8
Television commercials	100%	12
Television set-top boxes		
Cable acquired before March 5, 2010	30%	10
Cable acquired after March 4, 2010	40%	30
Satellite acquired before March 5, 2010	20%	8

Capital Cost Allowance Classes and Rates (continued)

Item	Rate	Class
Satellite acquired after March 4, 2010	40%	30
Timber cutting and removing equipment[3]		10, 15
Timber limits — see Sched. VI of the Income Tax Regulations[3,7]		
Timber resource property[3]	15%	33
Tools costing less than $500[1,26,29]	100%	12
Tractors[1]	30%	10
for hauling freight[28]	40%	16
Trailers[1,37]	30%	10
Tramways[4,9]	6%	4
Trees	nil	—
Trestles[1]	5%	3
Trolley bus	30%	10
Trolley bus system[4]	6%	4
Trucks, automotive[1]	30%	10
for hauling freight[28]	40%	16
Tunnel[1,16]	4%	1
Uniforms[1,26]	100%	12
Vessels[7,17]	15%	7
furniture, fittings and spare engines[17]	15%	7
offshore drilling after 1987[32]	25%	41
Video cassettes, video laser disks and DVDs[23,26]	100%	12
Video games (coin operated) acquired after Feb. 15, 1984	40%	16
Video tapes[1,16]	30%	10
television commercial	100%	12

Item	Rate	Class
Wagons[1]	30%	10
Water pipelines		
acquired before 1988[10]	6%	2
acquired after 1987	4%	1
Water pollution control equipment — see Pollution control equipment		
Water storage tanks[1]	10%	6
primary manufacturing purpose[15]		
Water distribution plant and equipment[4]		
acquired before 1988	6%	2
acquired after 1987	4%	1
Well equipment, oil or gas (for use above ground)		
acquired after 1987	25%	41
acquired before 1988	30%	10
oil sands property acquired after Mar. 18, 2007	25%	41.1
Wharves[1]	5%	3
wooden[1]	10%	6
Wind energy conversion system[19]		
acquired before Feb. 22, 1994	50%	34
acquired after Feb. 21, 1994[34,35]	30%	43.1
acquired after Feb. 22, 2005 and before 2020[34,35]	50%	43.2
Windmills[1,42]	5%	3
Wiring, electric — same rate as building		

Notes:

1 Unless included in another class of assets subject to a different rate.

2 Not applicable to land, animals, herbs, trees, shrubs or similar growing things, gas wells, mines, oil wells, radium, rights of way, timber limits, tramway track or certain vessels.

3 See IT-481 and IT-501 regarding timber limits, timber resource property, and logging assets. Class 15 assets are not subject to the half-year rule.

4 Except property included in Class 10, 13, 14, 26 or 28. For distributors of gas, not including a property acquired to produce or distribute gas normally distributed in portable containers, to process natural gas before its delivery to a gas distribution system and to produce oxygen or nitrogen. See also under Gas manufacturing and distribution equipment, plants and pipelines; and Pipelines.

5 Power-operated and designed for the purpose of excavating, moving, placing or compacting earth, rock, concrete or asphalt.

6 Electrical generating equipment may be allocated to one of the following different classes: Class 1, if large and acquired by a producer; Class 2, if acquired before 1988; Class 8, if small; Class 9, if acquired before May 26, 1976 and not owned by a producer; or Class 17, if new and acquired after February 27, 2000 (with certain exclusions). Energy-efficient equipment may be in Class 34, if acquired before February 22, 1994; Class 43.1, if acquired after February 21, 1994; or Class 43.2 if acquired after February 22, 2005 and before 2020, and certain requirements are met (see note 35). Only a detailed reading of the classes can determine the appropriate one; see Schedule II of the Income Tax Regulations. If used in manufacturing or processing, see note 15.

7 Separate classes may be required for each asset, including: certain rental properties costing $50,000 or more; automobiles in Class 10.1; certain vessels, including Canadian vessels and offshore drilling vessels; and Class 28, 41 or 41.1 property relating to a particular mine or group of mines. See Regulation 1101 for the provisions regarding separate classes.

8 Unless, in the case of a pipeline for oil or natural gas, the Minister is satisfied that the main source of supply for the business is likely to be exhausted within 15 years; such pipelines, not being specifically listed, fall under the general rate of 20% (Class 8).

9 Tramway tracks: 100% on cessation of tramcar operation.

10 Separate class elections may be available for certain assets or groups of assets, including: non-residential buildings in Class 1; certain electronic equipment in Class 8; transmission pipelines in Class 49; and equipment relating to transmission pipelines in Class 7. See Regulation 1101 for the provisions regarding separate classes.

11 A grain elevator or addition to a grain elevator situated in "Eastern Canada", acquired after April 1, 1972 and before August 1, 1974, is entitled to an additional allowance equal to the lesser of: 22% (Class 3), 20% (Class 6), or 14% (Class 8) of the lesser of $15,000 and the capital cost; or the undepreciated capital cost at the end of the taxation year before the allowance. New grain drying equipment for a farm acquired after July 31, 1968 and before January 1, 1970 or after April 1, 1972 but before August 1, 1974 may be depreciated at the rate equal to the lesser of 14% of the capital cost or $15,000.

12 Certified pollution control equipment in Class 24 or 27 is depreciated 25/50/25 over three years for additions made before 1999. If not certified, the equipment may be Class 8, 39 or 43 if used primarily in manufacturing, or Class 1, 3 or 6, depending on its nature.

13 An addition or alteration to a building originally placed in Class 3, 6 or 20, but which would no longer be in that class under current rules, may be added to the old class within certain dollar and transitional rule limitations. See IT-79R3 and Regulation 1102(19).

14 Qualifying assets are included in a special class for each mine. The full amount of undepreciated capital cost up to the amount of income from a mine may be claimed on property for new or expanded mines. This additional allowance is being phased out for oil sands property acquired after March 18, 2007. See paragraphs 1100(1)(*w*) to (*ya.1*) of the Income Tax Regulations.

Capital Cost Allowance Classes and Rates (continued)

[15] Specified property used primarily in manufacturing or processing may be allocated to one of the following classes: Class 29 (25%/50%/25% straight line), if acquired after March 18, 2007 and before 2016; Class 43 (30%), if acquired after February 25, 1992 and before March 19, 2007 or after 2013; and Class 39 if acquired after 1987 and before February 26, 1992. (Class 40 applied for certain property acquired in 1988 or 1989.). See note 44 for general-purpose electronic data processing equipment and system software used primarily in manufacturing or processing (Class 29 if acquired after March 18, 2007 and before January 28, 2009). The description of the specified property varies depending on the date it is acquired and the class. See the descriptions of the classes in Schedule II of the Income Tax Regulations.

[16] Acquired after May 25, 1976. Property of this type acquired before May 26, 1976 may be in a different class. See Schedule II of the Income Tax Regulations.

[17] Accelerated capital cost allowances of 331/3% are provided on certain prescribed vessels and conversion costs (generally, Canadian vessels and furniture and fittings attached thereto). See Regulations 1100(1)*(va)* and 1101(2a).

[18] Multiple-unit residential buildings acquired after June 17, 1987 are Class 1(4%). Such buildings acquired before June 18, 1987 that would otherwise be included in Class 3 or 6 and in respect of which a certificate is issued by the Canada Mortgage and Housing Corporation are Class 31 (5%). Such buildings acquired before 1980 that would otherwise be in Class 6 are Class 32 (10%).

[19] Such property acquired after May 25, 1976 and before February 21, 1994 is Class 34. Such assets acquired after this date are eligible for CCA at 30% in Class 43.1. Certain Class 43.1 assets acquired after February 22, 2005 and before 2020 may be eligible for a CCA rate of 50% in Class 43.2. See Regulation 1102(16.1) that would allow a taxpayer to elect Class 29 treatment for property acquired after March 18, 2007 and before 2016 that would otherwise be in Class 43.1 or Class 43.2 and is used in manufacturing or processing.

[20] Patents for a limited or unlimited period acquired after April 26, 1993 are in Class 44 (25%). Patents for a limited period acquired before April 27, 1993 are in Class 14, written off on a straight-line basis over the the life of the patent, but a taxpayer can elect out of Class 44 into Class 14 for limited period patents acquired after April 26, 1993.

[21] The heavy water must be acquired after May 22, 1979. Prior to May 23, 1979, a catalyst was depreciable at 1%.

[22] Automobiles acquired after November 12, 1981 for lease or rental other than to any one person for more than 30 days in a 12-month period.

[23] Items must be acquired for the purpose of renting to any one person for no more than 7 days in any 30-day period.

[24] Computer software in Class 12 is subject to the half-year rule. Systems software is in Class 10, 29, 45, 50, or 52, depending on the date acquired. See note 44.

[25] Building must be used in farming or fishing business, or be unsupported below the ground, or have been acquired before 1979.

[26] The half-year rule does not apply to this item. It may be written off in full in the first year claimed.

[27] The half-year rule applies to assets of this description acquired after December 31, 1987. Prior acquisitions could be written off at 100% in the first year claimed.

[28] Trucks or tractors acquired after December 6, 1991 that have a gross vehicle weight rating in excess of 11,788 kg.

[29] Tools, kitchen utensils, and medical and dental instruments costing more than the $500 limit are Class 8. The limit was $200 for tools, kitchen utensils, and medical and dental instruments acquired before May 2, 2006. Portable tools acquired to earn short-term rental income are Class 10 (30%).

[30] May be eligible for a separate class. Up to $50,000 of computer expenditures (hardware and software combined) may be eligible for 100% deduction in year of acquisition if acquired by a small or medium-sized business in the period January 1, 1998 to October 31, 1999 to deal with year 2000 problems.

[31] Railway equipment may be subject to additional allowances over and above the class rate. Railway locomotives, railway cars and railway suspension devices acquired after February 27, 2000, (other than property included in paragraph *(y)* of Class 10) are eligible for Class 7 (15%) rather than a combined rate of 10% or 13% (7% + additional allowance of 3% or 6%) previously available for Class 35 assets. Leased assets are included in Class 7 (15%) only if the lessor elects specified leasing property treatment. Railway locomotives acquired after February 25, 2008 and not used previously by any taxpayer for any purpose are Class 10*(y)* (30%)

[32] After November 7, 2001, Class 41 for offshore drilling vessels is not available if the Minister of Industry has agreed to a structured financing facility. In such a case, the maximum CCA rate applicable to the vessel and its attachments will be 15% under Class 7 (see Regulation 1101(2c)).

[33] Class 49 applies to new transmission pipelines. Taxpayers may elect in the year the pipelines are acquired, to place them in a separate CCA class. The rate for new natural gas distribution pipelines acquired after March 18, 2007 changed from Class 1 (4%) to Class 51 (6%). Eligible assets will include control and monitoring devices, valves, metering and regulating equipment and other equipment ancillary to a distribution pipeline, but not buildings or other structures. See Class 7 for pumping and compression equipment used to move product along a transmission pipeline.

[34] Specified energy property rules may apply. See Regulations 1100(24) to (29).

[35] Class 43.2 (50%) applies to certain assets in Class 43.1 (30%) if they are acquired after February 22, 2005 and before 2020. Co-generation equipment described in paragraphs *(a)* to *(c)* of Class 43.1 will be eligible for Class 43.2 if the equipment has a heat rate attributable to fossil fuel not exceeding 4,750 BTU (Class 43.1 allows up to 6,000 BTU). Paragraph *(d)* of Class 43.1 sets out various other types of renewable energy assets that are eligible for Class 43.2, including active solar equipment, geothermal equipment, photovoltaic equipment, ground source heat pump systems, wind energy conversion systems, equipment used to collect landfill gas and digester gas, equipment used to generate heat energy from eligible waste fuel, and equipment used to produce and store biogas. Budget 2013 proposes expanding Class 43.2 applicability to include additional biogas production equipment and all cleaning and upgrading equipment that can be used to transform biogas into biomenthane.

[36] Additional allowance and separate class treatment available in certain circumstances. For 1995 and subsequent taxation years, the accelerated CCA incentive for Canadian-owned film or video productions was replaced by a Canadian Film or Video Production Tax Credit under section 125.4 of the *Income Tax Act*. For taxation years ending after October 1997, other film or video productions may qualify for the Film or Video Production Services Tax Credit in section 125.5 of the *Income Tax Act*.

[37] Includes trailers designed for use on both highways and railway tracks.

[38] A straight-line method may be used for assets acquired before 1972 and used in a farming or fishing business.

[39] This item excludes landscaping costs deductible under paragraph 20(1)*(aa)* of the Act.

[40] Used for public transportation within a metropolitan area and not part of a railway system.

[41] Temporary access roads in the oil and gas mining sectors may qualify as Canadian exploration or development expenses.

[42] Not to be confused with wind energy conversion systems included in Class 43.1 or 43.2.

[43] Additional allowances are available for buildings in Class 1 acquired after May 18, 2007 (including new buildings which are under construction on March 19, 2007) that are used at least 90% (measured by square footage) for manufacturing or processing in Canada or for other non-residential purposes at the end of the year. The additional allowances are 6% for such a building used for manufacturing or processing and 2% for other non-residential buildings. In each case, the building is required to be placed in a separate class in order to claim the additional allowance.

[44] Class 52 (100%) applies to certain general-purpose electronic data processing equipment and systems software for that equipment, acquired after January 27, 2009 and before February 2011 (i.e., situated in Canada and not previously used). Property that is general-purpose electronic data processing equipment and systems software for that equipment is included in Class 29 if acquired after March 18, 2007 and before January 28, 2009 and used primarily in manufacturing or processing. Property that is general-purpose electronic data processing equipment and systems software for that equipment acquired after March 18, 2007, that is not in Class 29 or Class 52, is Class 50 (55%). Such property acquired after March 22, 2004 and before March 19, 2007 is Class 45 (45%). Class 52 assets are not subject to the half-year rule.

Appendix III

Withholding Tax

RATES OF WITHHOLDING TAX UNDER INCOME TAX AGREEMENTS SIGNED BY CANADA

The chart on the following pages is intended for use only as a quick reference guide for the rates of withholding tax for selected types of payments under the income tax agreements Canada has signed with various countries. The rates listed in the chart are the maximum rates that Canada and the other country may withhold for the type of payment noted. Many of the treaties have unique exceptions and qualifications on withholding tax which cannot be listed in a chart such as this. Therefore, the specific treaty should be consulted when determining whether or not there is a tax liability exigible on a payment.

Rates of Withholding Tax Under Income Tax Agreements Signed by Canada

Countries	*Date*	*Interest*	*Dividends — % of Ownership*	*Regular Dividends*	*Royalties*	*Pension and Annuity*	*From Estate or Trust*
Algeria	1999	15%[3]	15%	15%	15%, royalties for use of computer software and patents exempt.	15%[9,14,16]	—
Argentina	1993	12.5%[3]	10%[5]	15%	15% generally 3%, 5%, 10% for specific items	15%[9,14,16]	—
Armenia	2004	10%[3]	5%[5]for investment >US $100,000.	15%	10%	pen. 15%[9,14,16]	15%
Australia......	1980[2]	10%	5%[4,6]	15%	10%	15%[10,17]	15% (Can)
Austria	1976[2]	10%[3]	5%[4,6]	15%	10%[8]	[9,11]	15% (Can)
Azerbaijan	2004	10%[3]	10%[4]	15%	5% on computer software, patents, industrial, commercial or scientific experience royalties; 10% on other royalties	—	15%
Bangladesh....	1982	15%[3]	15%	15%	10%	15%[9]	—
Barbados	1980	15%[3]	15%	15%	10%[7]	15%[9,14,16]	15% (Can)
Belgium	2002	10%[3]	5%[4]	15%	10%[8]	[9,11] [13] for certain pensions	15%
Brazil	1984	15%[3] 10% Brazil in certain circumstances	15%[4]	[11]	15% 25% on trademarks	[15,] [9] unless over $4,000	—
Bulgaria	1999	10%[3]	10%[4,6]	15%	10%[7]	pen. 15% ann. 10%[9]	15% (Can)
Cameroon	1982	15% (Can) 20% (Cam)	15% (Can) 20% (Cam)	15% (Can) 20% (Cam)	15% (Can) 20% (Cam)	[11]	—
Chile.........	1998	15%	10%[5]	15%	15%	pen.[13,] ann. 15%[9]	15% (Can)
China	1986	10%[3]	10%[4]	15%	10%	[11]	—
Colombia	2008	10%[3]	5%[4]	15%	10%	15%[9,14,16]	15% (Can)
Croatia	1997	10%	5%[4,5,6]	15%	10%	pen. 15%[15,] ann. 10%[9]	15%
Cyprus	1984	15%[3]	15%	15%	10%[7]	15%[9] [13,] for certain pensions[15,16]	15%
Czech Republic	2001	10%[3]	5%[4]	15%	10%	15%[9]	15%
Denmark	1997	10%[3]	5%[5](if owned by a company)	15%	10%[8]	[9,13]	15%

Countries	*Date*	*Interest*	*Dividends — % of Ownership*	*Regular Dividends*	*Royalties*	*Pension and Annuity*	*From Estate or Trust*
			10% if paid by Cdn. NRO invest. corp.				
Dominican Republic	1976	18%[3]	18%	18%	18%[7]	18%[9, 16]	18%
Ecuador	2001	10%[3]	5%[5]	15%	10% on use of industrial, commercial, or scientific equipment; 15% on other	pen. 15%[14, 16, 15,] ann. 15%[9]	15%
Egypt	1983	15%[3]	15%	15% (20% if paid to an individual resident in Canada)	15%	[11]	15%
Estonia	1995	10%[3]	5%[5, 6]	15%	10%	15%[16,] ann. 10%[9]	15%
Finland	2006	10%[3]	5%[4]	15%	10%[8]	pen. 20%[14,] ann. 15%[9]	15%
France	1975[2]	10%[3]	5%[4] 10% if paid by Cdn. NRO invest. corp.	15%	10%[8]	pen.[13, 14,] ann.[9, 11]	15%
Gabon	2002	10%[3]	15%	15%	10%	pen.[11,] ann.[11]	—
Germany	2001	10%[3]	5%[4]	15%	10%[8]	pen.[11,] ann.[9, 11]	—
Greece	2009	10%[3]	5%[5]	15%	10%[7]	15%[9, 14, 15, 16]	15%
Guyana	1985	15% (Can)[3,] 25% (Guy)[3]	15%	15%	10%	[9, 11, 14]	—
Hong Kong (PRC)	2012[1]	10%[3]	5%[4]	15%	10%	pen.[11]	—
Hungary	1992[2]	10%[3]	5%[5] 10% if paid by Cdn. NRO invest. corp.	15%	10%[7]	pen. 15%[14, 16,] ann. 10%[9]	15%
Iceland	1997	10%[3]	5%[4, 6]	15%	10%[8]	pen. 15%[14, 16,] ann. 15%[9]	15%
India	1996	15%[3]	15%[4]	25%	10% 15% 20%	[13]	15%
Indonesia	1979[2]	10%[3]	10%[5]	15%	10%	15%[9, 14]	—
Ireland	2003	10%[3]	5%[4, 6]	15%	10%[8]	pen. 15%[14, 16] ann. 15%	15%
Israel	1975	15%[3]	15%	15%	15%[7]	15%[9, 14, 17]	15%
Italy	2002	10%[3]	5%[4, 6]	15%	5%[7,] on computer software, patents, industrial, commercial or scientific experience royalties, 10% on other royalties[7]	pen. 15%[14, 15, 16]	15%
Ivory Coast ...	1983	15%[3]	15% 18% on certain divs. from Ivory Coast	15% 18% on certain divs. from Ivory Coast	10%	15%	—
Jamaica	1978	15%[3]	15% 22.5% (Jam)[4]	15%	10%	pen.[11, 14, 16,] ann. 15%[9]	15% (Can)
Japan	1986[2]	10%[3]	5%[5]	15%	10%	[11]	—
Jordan	1999	10%[3]	10%[4, 6]	15%	10%	[13]	—

Countries	*Date*	*Interest*	*Dividends — % of Ownership*	*Regular Dividends*	*Royalties*	*Pension and Annuity*	*From Estate or Trust*
Kazakhstan . . .	1996	10%[3]	5%[4,6]	15%	10%	pen. 15%[9,13] for certain pensions	—
Kenya	1983	15%[3]	15%[4]	25%	15%	15%	—
Korea	2006	10%[3]	5%[5]	15%	10%	pen. 15%[9,16] ann. 10%	—
Kuwait	2002	10%[3]	5%[4,5,6]	15%	10%	15%	—
Kyrgyzstan	1998	15%[3]	15%	15%	10%[8]	15%[9,14,16]	15%
Latvia	1995	10%[3]	5%[5,6]	15%	10%	pen. 15%[16], ann. 10%[9]	15%
Lebanon	1998[1]	10%[3]	5%[4,6]	15%	5% on cultural, computer software, industrial, commercial or scientific "know-how" royalties, 10% on other royalties	pen. 15%[9,14]	—
Lithuania	1996	10%[3]	5%[5,6]	15%	10%	pen. 15%[16], ann. 10%[9]	15%
Luxembourg . . .	1999	10%[3]	5%[4](if owned by a company) 10% if paid by Cdn. NRO invest. corp.	15%	10%[8]	[9,11,14,13] for certain pensions	15%
Malaysia	1976	15%[3]	15%	15%	15% certain royalties excluded	15%[14,16]	15% (Can)
Malta	1986	15%[3]	15% (Can) not to exceed tax on profits (Malta)	15% (Can) not to exceed tax on profits (Malta)	10%[7]	15%[9,14,16]	15%
Mexico	2006	10%[3]	5%[4]	15%	10%[7]	pen. 15%[9,14,16] ann. 15%	15%
Moldova	2002	10%[3]	5%[5]	15%	10%	15%[14]	15%
Mongolia	2002	10%[3]	5%[4]	15%	5% on cultural, computer software, patent, industrial, commercial or scientific experience royalties, 10% on other royalties	pen. 15%[14,16], ann. 15%[9]	15%
Morocco	1975	15%[3]	15%	15%	10% 5% on cultural royalties	[11]	—
Namibia	2010[1]	10%[3]	5%[5]	15%	10%[7]	pen.[12]	15%
Netherlands . . .	1986[2]	10%[3]	5%[4,5](if owned by a company) 10% if paid by Cdn. NRO invest. corp.	15%	10%[8]	15%[9]	15% (Can)
New Zealand	1980	15%	15%	15%	15%	15%[15,16]	15% (Can)
New Zealand	2012[1]	10%[3]	5%[4]	15%	5% on cultural, computer software, industrial, commercial or scientific info; 10% on other royalties	pen. 15%[14,16], ann. 15%[9]	15% (Can)
Nigeria	1992	12.5%[3]	12.5%[4]	15%	12.5%	[14,11]	—
Norway	2002	10%[3]	5%[4,6]	15%	10%[8]	15[9,14]	15%

Countries	*Date*	*Interest*	*Dividends — % of Ownership*	*Regular Dividends*	*Royalties*	*Pension and Annuity*	*From Estate or Trust*
Oman	2004	10%[3]	5%[4]	15%	10%[8]	pen. 15%[14,16,] ann. 15%[9]	15%
Pakistan	1976	15% (Can)[3,] 25% (Pak)[3]	15% (Can) 15% (Pak)[5]	15% (Can) 20% (Pak)	15% (Can)[7,] 20% (Pak)[7]copyright, trademark equipment, films 15% (Pak) technical know-how	[13] Canada may withhold 15% on alimony	15% (Can)
Papua New Guinea	1987	10%[3]	15% (Can) 25% (PNG)	15% (Can) 25% (PNG)	10%	15%[10,14,16]	—
Peru	2001	15%	10%[4]	15%	15%	15%[9,14]	15%
Philippines	1976	15%[3]	15% (Can) 15% (Phil)[4]	15% (Can) 25% (Phil)	10% (Can) 25% (Phil)	[13]	—
Poland	1987	15%[3]	15%	15%	10%[7]	15%[9,14,16]	15%
Poland	2012[1]	10%[3]	5%[4]	15%	5% on cultural, industrial, commercial, or scientific info; 10% on other royalties	pen. 15%[14,16,] ann. 15%[9]	15%
Portugal	1999	10%[3]	10%[5,6]	15%	10%	15%[9,14,16]	15%
Romania	2004	10%[3]	5%[4]	15%	10% 5% on cultural, software, industrial, commercial, scientific info.	pen. 15%	—
Russia	1995	10%[3]	10%[4]	15%	10%[8]	[13]	—
Senegal	2001	15% (Can)[3,] 20% (Sen)[3,] 16% (Sen)[3]	15% (Can) 16% (Sen)	15% (Can) 16% (Sen)	15%	15%[9,14]	15%
Serbia	2012[1]	10%[3]	5%[5]	15%	10%	pen. 15%	15%
Singapore	1976	15%[3]	15% 0% (Sing) depending on domestic law	15% 0% (Sing) depending on domestic law	15%	[13] Canada may withhold 15% on alimony	15% (Can)
Slovak Republic	2001	10%[3]	5%[4]	15%	10%[7]	pen. 15%[14,16] ann. 15%	15%
Slovenia	2000	10%[3]	5% (Can)[4,6,] 5% (Slo)[5]	15%	10%	pen. 15%[16,](Can) (Slo)[13,] ann. 10%[9]	15%
South Africa	1995	10%[3]	5%[4,6]	15%	10% 6% on cultural, software, industrial, commercial, scientific info.	[11]	15%
Spain	1976	15%[3]	15%	15%	10%[7]	15%[9,14,16]	—
Sri Lanka	1982	15%[3]	15%	15%	10%[7]	15%[9,14,16]	15% (Can)
Sweden	1996	10%[3]	5%[5] 10% if paid by Cdn. NRO invest corp.	15%	10%[8]	[9,14,11]	15% (Can)
Switzerland	1997[2]	10%[3]	5%[4]	15%	10%[8]	15%[9,14]	—
Tanzania	1995	15%[3]	20%[5]	25%	20%	15%[9,14,16] (Can)	—

Countries	*Date*	*Interest*	*Dividends — % of Ownership*	*Regular Dividends*	*Royalties*	*Pension and Annuity*	*From Estate or Trust*
Thailand......	1984	15% (Can) 10% (Thai) if to fin. instit. 25% (Thai) otherwise[3]	15% (Can) 15% (Thai) in certain cases 20%[5] (Thai)	15% (Can) taxed under laws of Thailand	15% 5% on cultural	[13]	15% (Can)
Trinidad and Tobago.......	1995	10%[3]	5%[4,6]	15%	10%[7]	pen. 15%[9,14]	—
Tunisia.......	1982	15%[3]	15%	15%	20%[7] on patents, trademarks, films, videos, industrial, commercial, scientific or harbour equip.; 15% on other	[11]	15%
Turkey.......	2009	15%[3]	15%[4]	20%	10%	15%[9,14,15,16]	—
Ukraine......	1996	10%[3]	5%[5,6]	15%	10% computer software exempt	[13]	15%
United Arab Emirates......	2002	10%[3]	5%[4] 10% if paid by Cdn. NRO invest. corp.	15%	10%[8]	[11]	15%
United Kingdom.....	1978[2]	10%[3]	5%[4]	15%	10%[8]	pen.[12], ann. 10%[9]	15% (Can)
U.S.A.........	1980[2]	0%[3,18]	5%[4]	15%	10%[8]	15%[9,14]	15%
Uzbekistan....	1999	10%[3]	5%[4]	15%	5% on cultural, computer software, industrial, commercial or scientific "know-how" royalties, 10% on other royalties	[13]	—
Venezuela.....	2001	10%[3]	10%[5]	15%	5% on cultural, computer software, industrial, commercial or scientific experience royalties, 10% on other royalties	[11,14]	—
Socialist Republic of Vietnam......	1997	10%[3]	5% (if 70% controlled by corporate owner) 10% (if 25%–69% controlled by corporate owner)	15%	10%	pen. 15% ann.[9,11]	15%
Zambia.......	1984	15%[3]	15%	15%	15%	15%[14]	15% (Can)
Zimbabwe....	1992	15%[3]	10%[5]	15% (Can) 20% (Zim)	10%	15%[9,14,16]	15% (Can)

Notes:

[1] Not yet ratified.

[2] Revised by subsequent Protocol.

[3] No withholding tax under the treaty on certain types of interest. After 2007, the Canadian *Income Tax Act* exempts interest payments to non-residents from withholding tax, except for certain interest paid or payable to a non-arms length person or participating debt interest. See paragraph 212(1)(*b*).

[4] If recipient owns at least 10% of voting stock or has 10% of voting power of stock on which dividends are paid (see specific treaty).

[5] If recipient owns at least 15% to 25% of capital or voting power of stock on which dividends are paid (see specific treaty for level of ownership specified).

[6] Does not apply to dividends from a non-resident-owned investment corporation resident in Canada.

[7] Cultural royalties are exempt from withholding tax. These include copyright royalties for production or reproduction of literary, dramatic, musical or artistic work. They usually do not include royalties on films or videotapes.

[8] Cultural royalties, computer software, industrial, commercial or scientific "know-how" royalties are exempt.

[9] Alimony and child support taxed only in the country of person receiving the payment.

[10] Alimony and child support taxed only in the paying country.

[11] May be taxed in source country — No treaty rate.

[12] Exempt from tax in source country.

[13] Taxed only in source country.

[14] Certain pensions exempt from tax in both countries.

[15] Tax withheld only if payment over a certain amount.

[16] For pensions, tax withheld is not to exceed the amount that would be payable if the recipient were resident in the source country.

[17] For pensions and annuities, tax withheld is not to exceed the amount that would be payable if the recipient were resident in the source country.

[18] Under the Canada–U.S. Treaty, the Fifth Protocol provides that withholding tax on interest will be completely eliminated for interest paid or credited after December 31, 2009. The maximum rate for withholding on interest paid or credited between January 1, 2008 and December 31, 2008 is 7%, and 4% on interest paid or credited between January 1, 2009 and December 31, 2009.

Topical Index

Please note that the numerical references following index entries are to paragraph numbers (¶) used in the text, not page numbers of the book.